Customer Support Information

Plunkett's Sports Industry Almanac 2010

Please register your book immediately...

if you did not purchase it directly from Plunkett Research, Ltd. This will enable us to fulfill your replacement request if you have a damaged product, or your requests for assistance. Also it will enable us to notify you of future editions, so that you may purchase them from the source of your choice.

If you are an actual, original purchaser but did not receive a FREE CD-ROM version with your book...*

you may request it by returning this form.

____ YES, please register me as a purchaser of the book.
I did not buy it directly from Plunkett Research, Ltd.

____ YES, please send me a free CD-ROM version of the book.
I am an actual purchaser, but I did not receive one with my book. (Proof of purchase may be required.)

Customer Name ______________________________

Title ______________________________

Organization ______________________________

Address ______________________________

City ______________ State ________ Zip ____________

Country (if other than USA) ______________________________

Phone ______________ Fax ______________

E-mail ______________________________

Mail or Fax to: **Plunkett Research, Ltd.**

Attn: FREE CD-ROM and/or Registration
P.O. Drawer 541737, Houston, TX 77254-1737 USA
713.932.0000 · Fax 713.932.7080 · www.plunkettresearch.com

* Purchasers of used books are not eligible to register. Use of CD-ROMs is subject to the terms of their end user license agreements.

PLUNKETT'S SPORTS INDUSTRY ALMANAC 2010

The Only Comprehensive Guide to the Sports Industry

Jack W. Plunkett

Published by:
Plunkett Research, Ltd., Houston, Texas
www.plunkettresearch.com

PLUNKETT'S SPORTS INDUSTRY ALMANAC 2010

Editor and Publisher:
Jack W. Plunkett

Executive Editor and Database Manager:
Martha Burgher Plunkett

Senior Editors and Researchers:
Brandon Brison
Addie K. FryeWeaver
Christie Manck
John Peterson

Editors, Researchers and Assistants:
Kalonji Bobb
Elizabeth Braddock
Michelle Dotter
Michael Esterheld
Austin Hansell
Kathi Mestousis
Lindsey Meyn
Andrew Olsen
Jana Sharooni
Jill Steinberg
Kyle Wark
Suzanne Zarosky

E-Commerce Managers:
Mark Cassells
Emily Hurley
Lynne Zarosky

Information Technology Manager:
Wenping Guo

Cover Design:
Kim Paxson, Just Graphics
Junction, TX

Special Thanks to:
ESPN
Forbes Magazine
NFL Players Association
Major League Baseball Association
Sporting Goods Manufacturing Association International (SGMA)
U.S. Bureau of Labor Statistics
U.S. Department of Commerce
U.S. International Trade Administration

Plunkett Research, Ltd.
P. O. Drawer 541737, Houston, Texas 77254, USA
Phone: 713.932.0000 Fax: 713.932.7080
www.plunkettresearch.com

Published by:
Plunkett Research, Ltd.
P.O. Drawer 541737
Houston, Texas 77254-1737

Phone: 713.932.0000
Fax: 713.932.7080
Internet: www.plunkettresearch.com

ISBN13 # 978-1-59392-145-3

Disclaimer of liability for use and results of use:

The editors and publishers assume no responsibility for your own success in making an investment or business decision, in seeking or keeping any job, in succeeding at any firm or in obtaining any amount or type of benefits or wages. Your own results and the job stability or financial stability of any company depend on influences outside of our control. All risks are assumed by the reader. Investigate any potential employer or business relationship carefully and carefully verify past and present finances, present business conditions and the level of compensation and benefits currently paid. Each company's details are taken from sources deemed reliable; however, their accuracy is not guaranteed. The editors and publishers assume no liability, beyond the actual payment received from a reader, for any direct, indirect, incidental or consequential, special or exemplary damages, and they do not guarantee, warrant nor make any representation regarding the use of this material. Trademarks or tradenames are used without symbols and only in a descriptive sense, and this use is not authorized by, associated with or sponsored by the trademarks' owners. Ranks and ratings are presented as an introductory and general glance at corporations, based on our research and our knowledge of businesses and the industries in which they operate. The reader should use caution.

PLUNKETT'S SPORTS INDUSTRY ALMANAC 2010

CONTENTS

Continued on next page

Continued from previous page

A Short Sports Industry Glossary

10-K: An annual report filed by publicly held companies. It provides a comprehensive overview of the company's business and its finances. By law, it must contain specific information and follow a given form, the "Annual Report on Form 10-K." The U.S. Securities and Exchange Commission requires that it be filed within 90 days after fiscal year end. However, these reports are often filed late due to extenuating circumstances. Variations of a 10-K are often filed to indicate amendments and changes. Most publicly held companies also publish an "annual report" that is not on Form 10-K. These annual reports are more informal and are frequently used by a company to enhance its image with customers, investors and industry peers.

Above the Line (ATL) Marketing: Traditional advertising through large media outlets, such as newspapers, radio and television. See "Below the Line (BTL) Marketing."

Adams Division: Part of the Wales Conference in the National Hockey League prior to the 1994 reorganization. Now called the Northeastern Division of the Eastern Conference.

Advertising: Within the media industry, a paid publication in a mass media outlet such as a newspaper, magazine or television.

Affiliate: A broadcast radio or television station that is an "affiliate" of a national network, such as NBC or CBS, contracts with the national network, which provides programming to the affiliate for all or part of each day. In return, the affiliate provides the network with an agreed-upon number of minutes of advertising time, which the network then resells to advertisers.

AFL: Arena Football League. See www.arenafootball.com.

AHL: American Hockey League. See www.theahl.com.

All-Star Game: An exhibition game featuring a sport's star players, usually elected by the fans.

AM: See "Amplitude Modulation (AM)."

Amplitude Modulation (AM): Radio broadcasts in the range of 535 kHz to 1705 kHz.

American Football Conference (AFC): One of two football conferences in the National Football League. The AFC is divided into four divisions: AFC East, AFC West, AFC North and AFC South. The winner of the AFC playoff plays against the winner of the NFC playoff in the Super Bowl.

American Football Conference (South): One of four divisions that make up the American Football Conference. The division includes the Indianapolis Colts, Jacksonville Jaguars, Houston Texans and Tennessee Titans.

American Football Conference East (AFC East): One of four divisions that make up the American Football Conference. The division includes the New England Patriots, New York Jets, Buffalo Bills and Miami Dolphins.

American Football Conference North (AFC North): One of four divisions that make up the American Football Conference. The division includes the Pittsburgh Steelers, Baltimore Ravens, Cincinnati Bengals and Cleveland Browns.

American Football League West: One of four divisions that make up the American Football Conference. The division includes the San Diego Chargers, Denver Broncos, Kansas City Chiefs and Oakland Raiders.

American League: One of two leagues in Major League Baseball. The American League is divided into three divisions: East, West and Central. The winner of the National League playoff plays the winner of the American League playoff in the World Series. See www.mlb.com.

American League Central: One of the three divisions of the American League. The division includes the Chicago White Sox, Minnesota Twins, Detroit Tigers, Cleveland Indians and Kansas City Royals.

American League East: One of the three divisions of the American League. The division includes the Baltimore Orioles, Boston Red Sox, Toronto Blue Jays, New York Yankees and Tampa Bay Devil Rays.

American League West: One of the three divisions of the American League. The division includes the Los Angeles Angels, Texas Rangers, Oakland Athletics and Seattle Mariners.

American Research Bureau (ARB): One of several national firms that conduct audience research. ARB is the founder of Arbitron ratings.

America's Cup: A major international yacht race.

Area of Dominant Influence (ADI): A market area established by Arbitron that places cities and/or parts of counties into groupings that are reached by the same local radio or television stations. It is similar to Nielsen's "Designated Market Area." For example, advertising on radio stations in Boston will reach listeners far outside of Boston within the surrounding ADI.

Astroturf: An artificial grass used on many professional sports fields.

Atlantic Coast Conference: An NCAA (National College Athletic Association) Division I-A sports conference including Virginia Tech, Florida State, Miami, Virginia, North Carolina, Clemson, Georgia Tech, Maryland, North Carolina State, Wake Forrest and Duke.

Audience: Total number of households or individuals that can be reached by a vehicle. See "Vehicle."

Below the Line (BTL) Marketing: Nonstandard (and generally less expensive) advertising and marketing efforts, such as direct mailing, sales promotion and public relations activities.

Big 10 Conference: An NCAA (National College Athletic Association) Division I-A sports conference that includes Iowa, Michigan, Wisconsin, Northwestern, Ohio State, Purdue, Michigan State, Minnesota, Penn State, Illinois and Indiana.

Big 12 Conference: An NCAA (National College Athletic Association) Division I-A sports conference including Baylor, Colorado, Iowa State, Kansas, Kansas State, Missouri, Nebraska, Oklahoma, Oklahoma State, Texas, Texas A&M and Texas Tech.

Big East Conference: An NCAA (National College Athletic Association) Division I-A sports conference that includes Boston College, Pittsburgh, West Virginia, Syracuse, Connecticut, Rutgers and Temple.

Bowl Game (College Football): An exhibition game played in college football after the end of the regular season. Examples include the Rose Bowl and the Orange Bowl. The BCS (Bowl Championship Series) bowl is played by the two top ranked teams to determine the national championship.

Brand: A combination of several identifying factors, such as name, logo and color scheme, that separates a product, group of products or a company from competing products or companies.

Brand Development Index (BDI): A measure of how the brand sales in a particular market compare to the number of people in that market, as a portion of the national totals.

Brand Equity/Capital: The level of influence a brand has in swaying a customer to buy a product purely based on the brand.

Brand Extension: Putting an old brand on a new kind of product, e.g., Body Glove branded cell phone covers.

Branding: A marketing strategy that places a focus on the brand name of a product, service or firm in order to increase the brand's market share, increase sales, establish credibility, improve satisfaction, raise the profile of the firm and increase profits.

BRIC: An acronym representing Brazil, Russia, India and China. The economies of these four countries are seen as some of the fastest growing in the world. A 2003 report by investment bank Goldman Sachs is often credited for popularizing the term; the report suggested that by 2050, BRIC economies will likely outshine those countries which are currently the richest in the world.

Broadcast: Electronic transmission of media by radio or television; generally refers to wireless methods.

Cable TV: A television system consisting of a local television station that is equipped with an antenna or satellite dish. The antenna or dish receives signals from distant, central network stations and retransmits those signals via TV cable to the local subscriber.

CAFTA-DR: See "Central American-Dominican Republic Free Trade Agreement (CAFTA-DR)."

Call Letters: Letters that identify a station, e.g., KTRU. Call letters are established by the Federal Communications Commission. Each broadcast station has unique letters. The letters may denote whether the station is in the eastern or western U.S.

Captive Offshoring: Used to describe a company-owned offshore operation. For example, Microsoft owns and operates significant captive offshore research and development centers in China and elsewhere that are offshore from Microsoft's U.S. home base. Also see "Offshoring."

Central American-Dominican Republic Free Trade Agreement (CAFTA-DR): A trade agreement signed into law in 2005 that aimed to open up the Central American and Dominican Republic markets to American goods. Member nations include Guatemala, Nicaragua, Costa Rica, El Salvador, Honduras and the Dominican Republic. Before the law was signed, products from those countries could enter the U.S. almost tariff-free, while American goods heading into those countries faced stiff tariffs. The goal of this agreement was to create U.S. jobs while at the same time offering the non-U.S. member citizens a chance for a better quality of life through access to U.S.-made goods.

CFL: Canadian Football League. See www.cfl.ca.

Chain Break: A pause in program broadcasting used to identify the television or radio station, and to air additional advertisements.

Champions League: In UEFA European football (soccer), the Champions League consists of 32 teams that have won qualifying rounds.

CIS: See "Commonwealth of Independent States (CIS)."

Commissioner (Sports): The chief executive of a sports league.

Commonwealth of Independent States (CIS): An organization consisting of 11 former members of the Soviet Union: Russia, Ukraine, Armenia, Moldova, Georgia, Belarus, Kazakhstan, Uzbekistan, Azerbaijan, Kyrgyzstan and Tajikistan. It was created in 1991. Turkmenistan recently left the Commonwealth as a permanent member, but remained as an associate member. The Commonwealth seeks to coordinate a variety of economic and social policies, including taxation, pricing, customs and economic regulation, as well as to promote the free movement of capital, goods, services and labor.

CONCACAF: The Confederation Norte-Centroamericana y Del Caribe de Footbal. CONCACAF is the regional organization of North American and Central American soccer under which World Cup qualifying matches are played.

Conference USA: An NCAA (National College Athletic Association) Division I-A sports conference that includes Louisville, Memphis, Alabama Birmingham, Cincinnati, Southern Mississippi, Texas Christian University, Tulane, South Florida, Houston, Army and East Carolina.

Conferences: Groups of teams in professional or college football, typically based on geographical regions.

Consumer Price Index (CPI): A measure of the average change in consumer prices over time in a fixed market basket of goods and services, such as food, clothing and housing. The CPI is calculated by the U.S. Federal Government and is considered to be one measure of inflation.

Customer Relationship Management (CRM): Refers to the automation, via sophisticated software, of business processes involving existing and prospective customers. CRM may cover aspects such as sales (contact management and contact history), marketing (campaign management and telemarketing) and customer service (call center history and field service history). Well known providers of CRM software include Salesforce, which delivers via a Software as a Service model (see "Software as a Service (Saas)"), Microsoft and Siebel, which as been acquired by Oracle.

Demographic Segmentation: Dividing a given population into ethnic and cultural groups in order to target different groups with tailored advertisements.

Demographics: The breakdown of the population into statistical categories such as age, income, education and sex.

Draft (NFL Draft): The annual, league-wide system by which teams in the National Football League (NFL) select players who are ready to leave college teams and enter the realm of professional football. The system is designed so that the teams with the worst records in the previous year have preference in making selections.

E-Commerce: The use of online, Internet-based sales methods. The phrase is used to describe both business-to-consumer and business-to-business sales.

Enterprise Resource Planning (ERP): An integrated information system that helps manage all aspects of a business, including accounting, ordering and human resources, typically across all locations of a major corporation or organization. ERP is considered to be a critical tool for management of large organizations. Suppliers of ERP tools include SAP and Oracle.

ERP: See "Enterprise Resource Planning (ERP)."

EU: See "European Union (EU)."

EU Competence: The jurisdiction in which the EU can take legal action.

European Community (EC): See "European Union (EU)."

European Cup: The championship series for European football (soccer). See "UEFA."

European Union (EU): A consolidation of European countries (member states) functioning as one body to facilitate trade. Previously known as the European Community (EC), the EU expanded to include much of Eastern Europe in 2004, raising the total number of member states to 25. In 2002, the EU launched a unified currency, the Euro. See europa.eu.int.

Expansion Team: A new team added to a sports league.

Facilities Management: The management of a company's physical buildings and/or information systems on an outsourced basis.

Fantasy Team: A standardized, Internet-based system that allows individuals who have subscribed to a fantasy league through one of several providers to draft a team of players. An individual's team competes against those of friends or strangers in customizable leagues. Each team accumulates statistics during the season that are reflected in overall standings, eventually leading to a league champion.

Farm Team: In baseball, a minor league team that is owned by a major league team. The farm team is used to develop new talent.

FC: Football Club.

Federal Communications Commission (FCC): The U.S. Government agency that regulates broadcast television and radio, as well as satellite transmission, telephony and all uses of radio spectrum.

FIFA: Federation International de Football Association. FIFA is the worldwide governing body of soccer and sponsors the World Cup tournament every four years. See www.fifa.com. Note, in Europe and elsewhere, soccer is referred to as "football."

Final Four: The last four teams in the NCAA (National College Athletic Association) basketball tournament.

FM: See "Frequency Modulation (FM)."

Frequency Modulation (FM): Radio broadcasts in the range of 88 MHz to 108 MHz.

Franchise (Sports): A team; the legal arrangement that establishes ownership of a team.

Franchise Player: A star player around which a franchise is built.

Free Agent: A player whose contract with his most recent team has expired, allowing him to sign a new contract with any team that makes him an offer.

GDP: See "Gross Domestic Product (GDP)."

Globalization: The increased mobility of goods, services, labor, technology and capital throughout the world. Although globalization is not a new development, its pace has increased with the advent of new technologies, especially in the areas of telecommunications, finance and shipping.

Gross Domestic Product (GDP): The total value of a nation's output, income and expenditures produced with a nation's physical borders.

Gross National Product (GNP): A country's total output of goods and services from all forms of economic activity measured at market prices for one calendar year. It differs from Gross Domestic Product (GDP) in that GNP includes income from investments made in foreign nations.

Gross Rating Points (GRPs): Measures the audience share of a television program's audience delivery. GRPs are the sum of individual ratings for all programs in a particular time slot. See "Ratings/Ratings Points/Ratings Share."

Heisman Trophy: An award presented annually by the Downtown Athletic Club of New York to the best college football player in the United States.

Image Advertising: Advocating a product based on its affiliation with a particular type of person or activity rather than the properties of the product itself, such as promoting a soda by claiming that basketball players drink it.

Indianapolis 500 (Indy 500): A popular 500-mile car race, first held in 1911, held annually at the Indianapolis Motor Speedway in Speedway, Indiana.

Initial Public Offering (IPO): A company's first effort to sell its stock to investors (the public). Investors in an up-trending market eagerly seek stocks offered in many IPOs because the stocks of newly public companies that seem to have great promise may appreciate very rapidly in price, reaping great profits for those who were able to get the stock at the first offering. In the United States, IPOs are regulated by the SEC (U.S. Securities Exchange Commission) and by the state-level regulatory agencies of the states in which the IPO shares are offered.

Insourcing: A unique and increasingly popular business method. It is similar to "outsourcing," in that it is a continuing business service or process provided to a company by an outside organization. The intent is to enable the client company to focus on its core strengths, while hiring outside firms to provide other needs such as warehouse, call center or human resources management. However, with insourcing, the services provider moves into or near the client company's facility and sets up shop. For example, ARAMARK has a business unit that will set up and manage an employee cafeteria within a client company's facility. (Occasionally, the term "insourcing" has also been used to describe the creation of jobs in America by foreign firms.) Also see "Third-Party Logistics (3PL)."

IOC: International Olympic Committee. See www.olympic.org.

Kentucky Derby (Horse Racing): A 1.25 mile horse race held at the Churchill Downs racetrack in Louisville, Kentucky. Winning the Kentucky Derby is the first step in attaining the Triple Crown.

LAC: An acronym for Latin America and the Caribbean.

LDCs: See "Least Developed Countries (LDCs)."

Least Developed Countries (LDCs): Nations determined by the U.N. Economic and Social Council to be the poorest and weakest members of the international community. There are currently 50 LDCs, of which 34 are in Africa, 15 are in Asia Pacific and the remaining one (Haiti) is in Latin America. The top 10 on the LDC list, in descending order from top to 10th, are Afghanistan, Angola, Bangladesh, Benin, Bhutan, Burkina Faso, Burundi, Cambodia, Cape Verde and the Central African Republic. Sixteen of the LDCs are also Landlocked Least Developed Countries (LLDCs) which present them with additional difficulties often due to the high cost of transporting trade goods. Eleven of the LDCs are Small Island Developing States (SIDS), which are often at risk of extreme weather phenomenon (hurricanes, typhoons, Tsunami); have fragile ecosystems; are often dependent on foreign energy sources; can have high disease rates for HIV/AIDS and malaria; and can have poor market access and trade terms.

Licensed Brands: Brands for which the licensor (owner of a well-known name) enters a contractual arrangement with a licensee (a retailer or a third party). The licensee either manufactures or contracts with a manufacturer to produce the licensed product and pays a royalty to the licensor. Many fashion designers license their names, such as Ralph Lauren.

Lifestyle Merchandising: Development of merchandise lines based on consumer living patterns.

Location-Based Entertainment: The use of entertainment themes and attractions to draw consumers to specific locations, such as shopping malls, casinos and restaurants.

Logo/Logotype: The simple mark or picture most often used to indicate a brand (e.g., the stylized GE that represents General Electric or the multicolored flag that represents Microsoft Windows).

LPGA: Ladies Professional Golf Association. See www.lpga.com.

Market Segmentation: The division of a consumer market into specific groups of buyers based on demographic factors.

Marketing: Includes all planning and management activities and expenses associated with the promotion of a product or service. Marketing can encompass advertising, customer surveys, public relations and many other disciplines. Marketing is distinct from selling, which is the process of sell-through to the end user.

Mass Media: Refers to all media that disseminate information throughout the world, including television, radio, film, print, photography and electronic media.

Media: Used loosely to refer to the entire communications system of reporters, editors, producers, print publications, broadcast programs, magazines and online publications.

Media Outlet: A broadcast or publication that brings news and features to the public through a distribution channel.

Medium: Any form of communication on a large scale, seen as a possible avenue for advertising. Different media types include television, radio, the Internet, newspapers and magazines.

Merchandising: Any marketing method utilized to foster sales growth.

Mid-American Conference: An NCAA (National College Athletic Association) Division I-A sports conference that is divided into two divisions, East and West. The Eastern Division includes Miami (Ohio), Akron, Marshall, Kent St., Ohio, Buffalo and Central Florida. The Western Division includes Toledo, Northern Illinois, Bowling Green, Eastern Michigan, Central Michigan, Ball State and Western Michigan.

MLB: Major League Baseball. See www.mlb.com.

MLS: Major League Soccer. See www.mlsnet.com.

Mountain West Conference: An NCAA (National College Athletic Association) Division I-A sports conference that includes Utah, New Mexico, Brigham Young, Wyoming, Air Force, Colorado State, San Diego State and Nevada Las Vegas.

MVP: Most Valuable Player.

NAFTA: See "North American Free Trade Agreement (NAFTA)."

National Basketball Association Eastern Conference: One of two conferences in the National Basketball Association. The winner of the Eastern Conference playoff plays the winner of the Western Conference playoff in the NBA Championship. The Eastern Conference is divided into three divisions: Atlantic, Central and Southeast.

National Basketball Association Western Conference: One of two conferences in the National Basketball Association. The winner of the Eastern Conference playoff plays the winner of the Western Conference playoff in the NBA Championship. The Western Conference has three divisions Northwest, Pacific and Southwest.

National Collegiate Athletic Association (NCAA): A voluntary association of over 1,200 colleges and universities in the U.S. whose role is to establish standards and protect the integrity of amateurism for student-athletes. See www2.ncaa.org.

National Football Conference (NFC): One of two football conferences in the National Football League. The NFC is divided into four divisions: NFC East, NFC West, NFC North and NFC South. The winner of the American Football Conference playoff plays the winner of the National Football Conference playoff in the Super Bowl.

National Football Conference East (NFC East): One of four divisions that make up the National Football Conference. The division consists of the Philadelphia Eagles, New York Giants, Dallas Cowboys and Washington Redskins.

National Football Conference North: One of four divisions that make up the National Football Conference. The division includes the Chicago Bears, Detroit Lions, Green Bay Packers and Minnesota Vikings.

National Football Conference South (NFC South): One of four divisions that make up the National Football Conference. The division includes the Atlanta Falcons, Carolina Panthers, New Orleans Saints and Tampa Bay Buccaneers.

National Football Conference West (NFC West): One of four divisions that make up the National Football Conference. The division consists of the Seattle Seahawks, St. Louis Rams, Arizona Cardinals and San Francisco 49ers.

National Invitational Tournament (NIT): A college basketball tournament in which teams that are not selected for the NCAA (National Collegiate Athletic Association) tournament may be invited to play.

National League: One of two leagues in Major League Baseball. The National League is divided into three divisions: East, West and Central. The winner of the National League playoff plays the winner of the American League playoff in the World Series. See www.mlb.com.

National League Central: One of the three divisions of the National League. The division includes the St. Louis Cardinals, Milwaukee Brewers, Chicago Cubs, Houston Astros, Pittsburgh Pirates and Cincinnati Reds.

National League East: One of the three divisions of the National League. The division includes the Florida Marlins, Atlanta Braves, Washington Nationals, New York Mets and Philadelphia Phillies.

National League West: One of the three divisions of the National League. The division includes the Los Angeles Dodgers, Arizona Diamondbacks, San Francisco Giants, San Diego Padres and Colorado Rockies.

NBA: National Basketball Association. See www.nba.com.

NBA Finals: The post-season playoffs in the National Basketball Association.
NCAA: See "National Collegiate Athletic Association (NCAA)."

Newspaper Syndicate: A firm selling features, photos, columns, comic strips or other special material for publication in a large number of newspapers. For example, a typical fee charged by a syndicate to a daily newspaper for a popular comic strip is $10 per day. Generally, the syndicate splits the fee with the author.

NFL: National Football League. See www.nfl.com.

NHL: National Hockey League. See www.nhl.com.

Nielsen Ratings: Ratings created by ACNielsen, a company engaged in television audience ratings and other market research.

Nielsen Station Index (NSI): An index that rates individual television stations.

Nielsen Television Index (NTI): An index that rates national television network programming.

North American Free Trade Agreement (NAFTA): A trade agreement signed in December 1992 by U.S. President George H. W. Bush, Canadian Prime Minister Brian Mulroney and Mexican President Carlos Salinas de Gortari. The agreement eliminates tariffs on most goods originating in and traveling between the three member countries. It was approved by the legislatures of the three countries and had entered into force by January 1994. When it was created, NAFTA formed one of the largest free-trade areas of its kind in the world.

OECD: See "Organisation for Economic Co-operation and Development (OECD)."

Offshoring: The rapidly growing tendency among U.S., Japanese and Western European firms to send knowledge-based and manufacturing work overseas. The intent is to take advantage of lower wages and operating costs in such nations as China, India, Hungary and Russia. The choice of a nation for offshore work may be influenced by such factors as language and education of the local workforce, transportation systems or natural resources. For example, China and India are graduating high numbers of skilled engineers and scientists from their universities. Also, some nations are noted for large numbers of workers skilled in the English language, such as the Philippines and India. Also see "Captive Offshoring" and "Outsourcing."

Organisation for Economic Co-operation and Development (OECD): A group of 30 countries that are strongly committed to the market economy and democracy. Some of the OECD members include Japan, the U.S., Spain, Germany, Australia, Korea, the U.K., Canada and Mexico. Although not members, Chile, Estonia, Israel, Russia and Slovenia are invited to member talks; and Brazil, China, India, Indonesia and South Africa have enhanced engagement policies with the OECD. The Organisation provides statistics, as well as social and economic data; and researches social changes, including patterns in evolving fiscal policy, agriculture, technology, trade, the environment and other areas. It publishes over 250 titles annually; publishes a corporate magazine, the OECD Observer; has radio and TV studios; and has centers in Tokyo, Washington, D.C., Berlin and Mexico City that distributed the Organisation's work and organizes events.

Outsourcing: The hiring of an outside company to perform a task otherwise performed internally by the company, generally with the goal of lowering costs and/or streamlining work flow. Outsourcing contracts are generally several years in length. Companies that hire outsourced services providers often prefer to focus on their core strengths while sending more routine tasks outside for others to perform. Typical outsourced services include the running of human resources departments, telephone call centers and computer departments. When outsourcing is performed overseas, it may be referred to as offshoring. Also see "Offshoring."

Pacific 10 Conference: An NCAA (National Collegiate Athletic Association) Division I-A sports conference that includes Southern California, California, Arizona State, Oregon State, UCLA, Oregon, Washington State, Stanford, Arizona and Washington.

Pay-Per-View (PPV): A service that enables television subscribers, including cable and satellite viewers, to order and view events or movies on an individual basis. PPV programming may include sporting events.

PGA: Professional Golfers Association. See www.pga.com. Also see "LPGA."

PPP: See "Purchasing Power Parity (PPP)."

Purchasing Power Parity (PPP): Currency conversion rates that attempt to reflect the actual purchasing power of a currency in its home market, as opposed to examining price levels and comparing an exchange rate. PPPs are always given in the national currency units per U.S. dollar.

Ratings/Rating Points/Ratings Share: The rating of a medium is its audience size expressed as a percentage of the measured market, where one rating point is equivalent to 1% of the base. Ratings are often referred to as "percent coverage." A television show with a 22% share has 22 points, or 22% of the total TV audience within its market.

Red Shirt: A designation given to a college athlete who did not play in any games during a particular year due to injury or coach's choice; such a player is permitted to practice with the team during that season and is granted an additional year of eligibility.

Return on Investment (ROI): A measure of a company's profitability, expressed in percentage as net profit (after taxes) divided by total dollar investment.

Rookie: An athlete in his or her first year of a sport.

Saas: See Software as a Service (Saas)."

Satellite Broadcasting: The use of Earth-orbiting satellites to transmit, over a wide area, TV, radio, telephony, video and other data in digitized format.

Share: In broadcasting, the percentage of television households tuned into a particular program or category of programming. The higher the share, the larger the amount that can be charged for advertising on the program.

Software as a Service (SaaS): Refers to the practice of providing users with software applications that are hosted on remote servers and accessed via the Internet. Excellent examples include the CRM

(Customer Relationship Management) software provided in SaaS format by Salesforce. An earlier technology that operated in a similar, but less sophisticated, manner was called ASP or Application Service Provider.

South Eastern Conference (SEC): An NCAA (National Collegiate Athletic Association) Division I-A sports conference that is divided into two divisions, East and West. The Eastern Conference includes Tennessee, Georgia, Florida, South Carolina, Kentucky and Vanderbilt. The Western Conference includes Auburn, Louisiana State, Alabama, Arkansas, Mississippi and Mississippi State.

Special Olympics: An international organization dedicated to empowering individuals with intellectual disabilities to become physically fit, productive and respected members of society through sports training and competition. Special Olympics offers children and adults with intellectual disabilities year-round training and competition in 26 Olympic-type summer and winter sports. There is no charge to participate in Special Olympics. See www.specialolympics.org.

Specialty Publication: A trade or professional magazine that is industry- or audience-specific (e.g., Shopping Center World magazine).

Subsidiary, Wholly-Owned: A company that is wholly controlled by another company through stock ownership.

Sun Belt Conference: An NCAA (National Collegiate Athletic Association) Division I-A sports conference that includes North Texas, Troy, New Mexico State, Louisiana-Monroe, Middle Tennessee, Arkansas State, Louisiana-Lafayette, Utah State and Idaho.

Super Bowl: The U.S. national championship game of the National Football League (NFL).

Superstation: A local television station with a signal that is retransmitted via satellite to distant cable systems that cannot be reached by over-the-air signals.

Supply Chain: The complete set of suppliers of goods and services required for a company to operate its business. For example, a manufacturer's supply chain may include providers of raw materials, components, custom-made parts and packaging materials.

Syndicated: A report, story, television program, radio program or graphic that is sold to multiple media outlets simultaneously. For example, popular newspaper columns are commonly syndicated to various newspapers throughout the United States, but only one newspaper per market is allowed to participate.

System (Cable): A facility that provides cable television service in a given geographic area, consisting of one or more headends.

Third-Party Logistics (3PL): A specialist firm in logistics, which may provide a variety of transportation, warehousing and logistics-related services to buyers or sellers. These tasks were previously performed in-house by the customer. When 3PL services are provided within the client's own facilities, it can also be referred to as insourcing.

Time Shifting: Services that allow viewers to digitally record television programs for playback at a later, more convenient time. Such services include video-on-demand (VOD) and personal TV services. Time shifting will eventually make up a significant portion of all television viewing.

Triple Crown: Horse racing's greatest prize. To win the Triple Crown, the horse must first win the Kentucky Derby, then the Preakness Stakes and, finally, the Belmont Stakes.

U.S. Open (Golf): First played in 1895 and is considered to be the premier golf tournament in the U.S.

UEFA: The governing body of European football (soccer). See www.uefa.com.

UEFA Cup: In European football (soccer), a competition for the runners up and the cup winners from each nation, along with other selected teams.

UHF: See "Ultra High Frequency (UHF)."

Ultra High Frequency (UHF): The frequency band ranging from 300 MHz to 3,000 MHz, which includes TV channels 14 through 83.

USCF: United States Cycling Federation. See www.usacycling.org.

USGA: United States Golf Association. See www.usga.org.

USL: United Soccer Leagues. See www.uslsoccer.com.

USOC: United States Olympic Committee. See www.usoc.org.

USTA: United States Tennis Association. See www.usta.com.

Value Added Tax (VAT): A tax that imposes a levy on businesses at every stage of manufacturing based on the value it adds to a product. Each business in the supply chain pays its own VAT and is subsequently repaid by the next link down the chain; hence, a VAT is ultimately paid by the consumer, being the last link in the supply chain, making it comparable to a sales tax. Generally, VAT only applies to goods bought for consumption within a given country; export goods are exempt from VAT, and purchasers from other countries taking goods back home may apply for a VAT refund.

Vehicle: Any particular publication or broadcasting channel that carries advertisements.

Very High Frequency (VHF): The frequency band ranging from 30 MHz to 300 MHz, which includes TV channels 2 through 13 and FM radio.

VHF: See "Very High Frequency (VHF)."

Western Athletic Conference: An NCAA (National Collegiate Athletic Association) Division I-A sports conference that includes Boise State, UTEP, Fresno State, Louisiana Tech, Hawaii, Nevada, Tulsa, SMU, Rice and San Jose State.

Wild Card: A U.S. football team that makes the NFL (National Football League) playoffs by having one of the two best records among non-division winners in its conference.

WNBA: Women's National Basketball Association. See www.wnba.com.

World Cup: The worldwide soccer championship tournament sponsored by FIFA (the Federation International de Football Association).

World Series: The championship series for Major League Baseball (MLB).

World Trade Organization (WTO): One of the only globally active international organizations dealing with the trade rules between nations. Its goal is to assist the free flow of trade goods, ensuring a smooth, predictable supply of goods to help raise the quality of life of member citizens. Members form consensus decisions that are then ratified by their respective parliaments. The WTO's conflict resolution process generally emphasizes interpreting existing commitments and agreements, and discovers how to ensure trade policies to conform to those agreements, with the ultimate aim of avoiding military or political conflict.

WTO: See "World Trade Organization (WTO)."

INTRODUCTION

PLUNKETT'S SPORTS INDUSTRY ALMANAC, the fifth edition of our guide to the sports and recreation field, is designed as a general source for researchers of all types.

The data and areas of interest covered are intentionally broad, ranging from the various types of businesses involved in sports and recreation, to the teams and leagues that make up professional sports of all types, to an in-depth look at the major firms (which we call "THE SPORTS 350") within the many segments that make up the sports industry.

This reference book is designed to be a general source for researchers. It is especially intended to assist with market research, strategic planning, employment searches, contact or prospect list creation (be sure to see the export capabilities of the accompanying CD-ROM that is available to book and eBook buyers) and financial research, and as a data resource for executives and students of all types.

PLUNKETT'S SPORTS INDUSTRY ALMANAC takes a rounded approach for the general reader and presents a complete overview of the sports and recreation field (see "How To Use This Book").

THE SPORTS 350 is our unique grouping of the biggest, most successful corporations in all segments of the sports, leisure and recreation industry. Tens of thousands of pieces of information, gathered from a wide variety of sources, have been researched and are presented in a unique form that can be easily understood. This section includes thorough indexes to THE SPORTS 350, by geography, industry, sales, brand names, subsidiary names and many other topics. (See Chapter 4.)

Especially helpful is the way in which PLUNKETT'S SPORTS INDUSTRY ALMANAC enables readers who have no business background to readily compare the financial records and growth plans of sports companies and major industry groups. You'll see the mid-term financial record of each firm, along with the impact of earnings, sales and strategic plans on each company's potential to fuel growth, to serve new markets and to provide investment and employment opportunities.

No other source provides this book's easy-to-understand comparisons of growth, expenditures, technologies, corporations and many other items of great importance to people of all types who may be studying this, one of the fastest growing industry sectors in the world today.

By scanning the data groups and the unique indexes, you can find the best information to fit your personal research needs. The major companies in sports and recreation are profiled and then ranked using several different groups of specific criteria. Which firms are the biggest employers? Which companies earn the most profits? These things and much more are easy to find.

In addition to individual company profiles, a thorough analysis of trends in sports, leisure and recreation sectors is provided. This book's job is to help you sort through easy-to-understand summaries of today's trends in a quick and effective manner.

Whatever your purpose for researching the sports field, you'll find this book to be a valuable guide. Nonetheless, as is true with all resources, this volume has limitations that the reader should be aware of:

- Financial data and other corporate information can change quickly. A book of this type can be no more current than the data that was available as of the time of editing. Consequently, the financial picture, management and ownership of the firm(s) you are studying may have changed since the date of this book. For example, this almanac includes the most up-to-date sales figures and profits available to the editors as of mid-2009. That means that we have typically used corporate financial data as of late-2008.

- Corporate mergers, acquisitions and downsizing are occurring at a very rapid rate. Such events may have created significant change, subsequent to the publishing of this book, within a company you are studying.

- Some of the companies in THE SPORTS 350 are so large in scope and in variety of business endeavors conducted within a parent organization, that we have been unable to completely list all subsidiaries, affiliations, divisions and activities within a firm's corporate structure.

- This volume is intended to be a general guide to a vast industry. That means that researchers should look to this book for an overview and, when conducting in-depth research, should contact the specific corporations or industry associations in question for the very latest changes and data. Where possible, we have listed contact names, toll-free telephone numbers and Internet sites for the companies, government agencies and industry associations involved so that the reader may get further details without unnecessary delay.

- Tables of industry data and statistics used in this book include the latest numbers available at the time of printing, generally through 2008. In a few cases, the only complete data available was for earlier years.

- We have used exhaustive efforts to locate and fairly present accurate and complete data. However, when using this book or any other source for business and industry information, the reader should use caution and diligence by conducting further research where it seems appropriate. We wish you success in your endeavors, and we trust that your experience with this book will be both satisfactory and productive.

Jack W. Plunkett
Houston, Texas
June 2009

HOW TO USE THIS BOOK

The two primary sections of this book are devoted first to the sports industry as a whole and then to the "Individual Data Listings" for THE SPORTS 350. If time permits, you should begin your research in the front chapters of this book. Also, you will find lengthy indexes in Chapter 4 and in the back of the book.

THE SPORTS INDUSTRY

Glossary: A short list of sports industry terms.

Chapter 1: Major Trends Affecting the Sports Industry. This chapter presents an encapsulated view of the major trends that are creating rapid changes in the sports, leisure and recreation industry today.

Chapter 2: Sports Industry Statistics. This chapter presents in-depth statistics including an industry overview.

Chapter 3: Important Sports Industry Contacts – Addresses, Telephone Numbers and Internet Sites. This chapter covers contacts for important government agencies, industry organizations and trade groups. Included are numerous important Internet sites.

THE SPORTS 350

Chapter 4: THE SPORTS 350: Who They Are and How They Were Chosen. The companies compared in this book (the actual count is 361) were carefully selected from the sports industry, largely in the United States. 55 of the firms are based outside the U.S. For a complete description, see THE SPORTS 350 indexes in this chapter.

Individual Data Listings:

Look at one of the companies in THE SPORTS 350's Individual Data Listings. You'll find the following information fields:

Company Name:

The company profiles are in alphabetical order by company name. If you don't find the company you are seeking, it may be a subsidiary or division of one of the firms covered in this book. Try looking it up in the Index by Subsidiaries, Brand Names and Selected Affiliations in the back of the book.

Ranks:

Industry Group Code: An NAIC code used to group companies within like segments. (See Chapter 4 for a list of codes.)

Ranks Within This Company's Industry Group: Ranks, within this firm's segment only, for annual sales and annual profits, with 1 being the highest rank.

Business Activities:
A grid arranged into six major industry categories and several sub-categories. A "Y" indicates that the firm operates within the sub-category. A complete Index by Industry is included in the beginning of Chapter 4.

Types of Business:
A listing of the primary types of business specialties conducted by the firm.

Brands/Divisions/Affiliations:
Major brand names, operating divisions or subsidiaries of the firm, as well as major corporate affiliations—such as another firm that owns a significant portion of the company's stock. A complete Index by Subsidiaries, Brand Names and Selected Affiliations is in the back of the book.

Contacts:
The names and titles up to 27 top officers of the company are listed, including human resources contacts.

Address:
The firm's full headquarters address, the headquarters telephone, plus toll-free and fax numbers where available. Also provided is the World Wide Web site address.

Financials:
Annual Sales (2008 or the latest fiscal year available to the editors, plus up to four previous years): These are stated in thousands of dollars (add three zeros if you want the full number). This figure represents consolidated worldwide sales from all operations. 2008 figures may be estimates or may be for only part of the year—partial year figures are appropriately footnoted.

Annual Profits (2008 or the latest fiscal year available to the editors, plus up to four previous years): These are stated in thousands of dollars (add three zeros if you want the full number). This figure represents consolidated, after-tax net profit from all operations. 2008 figures may be estimates or may be for only part of the year—partial year figures are appropriately footnoted.

Stock Ticker, International Exchange, Parent Company: When available, the unique stock market symbol used to identify this firm's common stock for trading and tracking purposes is indicated. Where appropriate, this field may contain "private" or "subsidiary" rather than a ticker symbol. If the firm is a publicly-held company headquartered outside of the U.S., its international ticker and exchange are given. If the firm is a subsidiary, its parent company is listed.

Total Number of Employees: The approximate total number of employees, worldwide, as of the end of 2008 (or the latest data available to the editors).

Apparent Salaries/Benefits:
(The following descriptions generally apply to U.S. employers only.)

A "Y" in appropriate fields indicates "Yes."

Due to wide variations in the manner in which corporations report benefits to the U.S. Government's regulatory bodies, not all plans will have been uncovered or correctly evaluated during our effort to research this data. Also, the availability to employees of such plans will vary according to the qualifications that employees must meet to become eligible. For example, some benefit plans may be available only to salaried workers—others only to employees who work more than 1,000 hours yearly. Benefits that are available to employees of the main or parent company may not be available to employees of the subsidiaries. In addition, employers frequently alter the nature and terms of plans offered.

NOTE: Generally, employees covered by wealth-building benefit plans do not *fully* own ("vest in") funds contributed on their behalf by the employer until as many as five years of service with that employer have passed. All pension plans are voluntary—that is, employers are not obligated to offer pensions.

Pension Plan: The firm offers a pension plan to qualified employees. In this case, in order for a "Y" to appear, the editors believe that the employer offers a defined benefit or cash balance pension plan (see discussions below).The type and generosity of these plans vary widely from firm to firm. Caution: Some employers refer to plans as "pension" or "retirement" plans when they are actually 401(k) savings plans that require a contribution by the employee.

- Defined Benefit Pension Plans: Pension plans that do not require a contribution from the employee are infrequently offered. However, a few companies, particularly larger employers in high-profit-margin industries, offer defined benefit pension plans where the employee is guaranteed to receive a set pension benefit upon retirement. The amount of the benefit is determined by the years of service with the company and the employee's salary during the later years of employment. The longer a person works for the employer, the higher the retirement benefit. These defined benefit plans are funded entirely by the employer. The benefits, up to a reasonable limit, are guaranteed by the Federal

Government's Pension Benefit Guaranty Corporation. These plans are not portable—if you leave the company, you cannot transfer your benefits into a different plan. Instead, upon retirement you will receive the benefits that vested during your service with the company. If your employer offers a pension plan, it must give you a summary plan description within 90 days of the date you join the plan. You can also request a summary annual report of the plan, and once every 12 months you may request an individual benefit statement accounting of your interest in the plan.

- Defined Contribution Plans: These are quite different. They do not guarantee a certain amount of pension benefit. Instead, they set out circumstances under which the employer will make a contribution to a plan on your behalf. The most common example is the 401(k) savings plan. Pension benefits are not guaranteed under these plans.
- Cash Balance Pension Plans: These plans were recently invented. These are hybrid plans—part defined benefit and part defined contribution. Many employers have converted their older defined benefit plans into cash balance plans. The employer makes deposits (or credits a given amount of money) on the employee's behalf, usually based on a percentage of pay. Employee accounts grow based on a predetermined interest benchmark, such as the interest rate on Treasury Bonds. There are some advantages to these plans, particularly for younger workers: a) The benefits, up to a reasonable limit, are guaranteed by the Pension Benefit Guaranty Corporation. b) Benefits are portable—they can be moved to another plan when the employee changes companies. c) Younger workers and those who spend a shorter number of years with an employer may receive higher benefits than they would under a traditional defined benefit plan.

ESOP Stock Plan (Employees' Stock Ownership Plan): This type of plan is in wide use. Typically, the plan borrows money from a bank and uses those funds to purchase a large block of the corporation's stock. The corporation makes contributions to the plan over a period of time, and the stock purchase loan is eventually paid off. The value of the plan grows significantly as long as the market price of the stock holds up. Qualified employees are allocated a share of the plan based on their length of service and their level of salary. Under federal regulations, participants in ESOPs are allowed to diversify their account holdings in set percentages that rise as the employee ages and gains years of service with the company. In this manner, not all of the employee's assets are tied up in the employer's stock.

Savings Plan, 401(k): Under this type of plan, employees make a tax-deferred deposit into an account. In the best plans, the company makes annual matching donations to the employees' accounts, typically in some proportion to deposits made by the employees themselves. A good plan will match one-half of employee deposits of up to 6% of wages. For example, an employee earning $30,000 yearly might deposit $1,800 (6%) into the plan. The company will match one-half of the employee's deposit, or $900. The plan grows on a tax-deferred basis, similar to an IRA. A very generous plan will match 100% of employee deposits. However, some plans do not call for the employer to make a matching deposit at all. Other plans call for a matching contribution to be made at the discretion of the firm's board of directors. Actual terms of these plans vary widely from firm to firm. Generally, these savings plans allow employees to deposit as much as 15% of salary into the plan on a tax-deferred basis. However, the portion that the company uses to calculate its matching deposit is generally limited to a maximum of 6%. Employees should take care to diversify the holdings in their 401(k) accounts, and most people should seek professional guidance or investment management for their accounts.

Stock Purchase Plan: Qualified employees may purchase the company's common stock at a price below its market value under a specific plan. Typically, the employee is limited to investing a small percentage of wages in this plan. The discount may range from 5 to 15%. Some of these plans allow for deposits to be made through regular monthly payroll deductions. However, new accounting rules for corporations, along with other factors, are leading many companies to curtail these plans—dropping the discount allowed, cutting the maximum yearly stock purchase or otherwise making the plans less generous or appealing.

Profit Sharing: Qualified employees are awarded an annual amount equal to some portion of a company's profits. In a very generous plan, the pool of money awarded to employees would be 15% of profits. Typically, this money is deposited into a long-term retirement account. Caution: Some employers refer to plans as "profit sharing" when they are actually 401(k) savings plans. True profit sharing plans are rarely offered.

Highest Executive Salary: The highest executive salary paid, typically a 2008 amount (or the latest year available to the editors) and typically paid to the Chief Executive Officer.

Highest Executive Bonus: The apparent bonus, if any, paid to the above person.

Second Highest Executive Salary: The next-highest executive salary paid, typically a 2008 amount (or the latest year available to the editors) and typically paid to the President or Chief Operating Officer.

Second Highest Executive Bonus: The apparent bonus, if any, paid to the above person.

Other Thoughts:

Apparent Women Officers or Directors: It is difficult to obtain this information on an exact basis, and employers generally do not disclose the data in a public way. However, we have indicated what our best efforts reveal to be the apparent number of women who either are in the posts of corporate officers or sit on the board of directors. There is a wide variance from company to company.

Hot Spot for Advancement for Women/Minorities: A "Y" in appropriate fields indicates "Yes." These are firms that appear either to have posted a substantial number of women and/or minorities to high posts or that appear to have a good record of going out of their way to recruit, train, promote and retain women or minorities. (See the Index of Hot Spots For Women and Minorities in the back of the book.) This information may change frequently and can be difficult to obtain and verify. Consequently, the reader should use caution and conduct further investigation where appropriate.

Growth Plans/ Special Features:

Listed here are observations regarding the firm's strategy, hiring plans, plans for growth and product development, along with general information regarding a company's business and prospects.

Locations:

A "Y" in the appropriate field indicates "Yes." Primary locations outside of the headquarters, categorized by regions of the United States and by international locations. A complete index by locations is also in the front of this chapter.

Chapter 1

MAJOR TRENDS IN THE SPORTS INDUSTRY

1) Introduction to the Sports Industry

The sports business means many different things to different people. This is a truly global industry, and sports stir up deep passion within spectators and players alike in countries around the world. To one person, sports are a venue for gambling; to another, they are a mode of personal recreation and fitness, be it skiing, cycling, running or playing tennis. To business people, sports provide a lucrative and continually growing marketplace worthy of immense investments. To athletes, sports may lead to high levels of personal achievement, and to professionals sports can bring fame and fortune. To facilities developers and local governments, sports are a way to build revenue from tourists and local fans. Sports are deeply ingrained in education, from elementary through university levels. Perhaps we can't state with confidence that sports enrich the lives of all of us, but they certainly entertain a huge swath of the world's population. In addition to economic impact, the largest single effect that sports create is that of gripping entertainment: hundreds of millions of fans around the globe follow sports daily, whether via radio, television, printed publications, online or in person, as spectators or participants.

Sports are big business. Combined, the "Big 4" leagues in America, the National Football League (NFL), National Basketball Association (NBA), the National Hockey League (NHL) and Major League Baseball (MLB) leagues bring in about $17 billion in annual revenue, but that's just the tip of the iceberg. U.S. sporting equipment sales at retail sporting goods stores are roughly $41 billion yearly, according to U.S. government figures. A reasonable estimate of the total U.S. sports market would be $400 to $425 billion yearly. However, the sports industry is so complex, including ticket sales, licensed products, sports video games, collectibles, sporting goods, sports-related advertising, endorsement income, stadium naming fees and facilities income; that it's difficult to put an all-encompassing figure on annual revenue. When researching numbers in the sports industry, be prepared for apparent contradictions. For example, the NFL receives more than eight times as much money each year for TV and cable broadcast rights as MLB, despite the fact that MLB teams play about 10 times more games yearly than NFL teams.

When the astonishing variety of sports-related sectors are considered, a significant portion of the workforce in developed nations such as the U.S., U.K., Australia and Japan rely on the sports industry for their livelihoods. Official U.S. Bureau of Labor Statistics figures as of May 2008 found that there were 13,960 professional American athletes plus 175,720 coaches and scouts, along with 12,970 umpires, referees and officials. Meanwhile, as of 2008, 510,300 Americans work in fitness centers (up from 508,300 a year earlier), 36,900 work in snow skiing facilities (up from 36,500), 76,600 work in bowling centers (down from 77,900) and 351,500 work at country clubs or golf courses (down from 353,000). In total, approximately 1.5 million Americans work directly in amusement, gambling and recreation sectors. Another 50,200 work in wholesale trade of sporting goods, and 244,600 work in retail sporting goods stores.

While it may not seem like it to the casual observer, the sports sector is constantly evolving in terms of personal tastes, popular games and technologies. For example, the decades-old Indy 500 has been eclipsed by NASCAR in many ways. In fact, the personality and popularity of a top athlete can have a tremendous impact on the current popularity of a particular sport—seven-time Tour de France winner Lance Armstrong being a superb example with his extremely positive impact on cycling.

Numbers published in an annual study by the Sporting Goods Manufacturers Association (SGMA) are particularly informative about changes in individual sports, exercise and recreation in America. For example, tennis is making a comeback (up 43% from 2000-2007). The fact that tennis is among the least costly sports in which one can participate, combined with the fact one can usually get to a tennis court without a long, gasoline-guzzling drive in an automobile, could easily push tennis to new popularity in today's tepid economy and high gas prices.

Which brings up the entire problem of gasoline prices in recreation and sports: clearly, expensive gasoline significantly dampens the popularity of motor boats, RVs and anything else that has a large engine. If gasoline prices rise to $3 or more in the U.S., sales of motorized recreation equipment are going to plummet, except in cases where that equipment is known for high energy efficiency. Sailing anyone?

Meanwhile, the number of people playing golf in America has been dropping. In other categories, SGMA reports that some of the highest increases in participation for 2000-2008 were in the activities of running/jogging, table tennis, lacrosse, spinning, pilates and paintball.

Then there's the fact that large audiences have been watching high-stakes poker tournaments on television recently. Does that qualify as sports broadcasting? It's certainly a game. Moreover, thanks to the Internet, fantasy sports teams and online betting on sports events are soaring.

One of the strongest, long-term growth trends in all of the recreation business is in fitness-related activities. In the U.S. alone, health clubs boast 40 million members, and another 25 million Americans use exercise machines in their homes. America's 78 million baby boomers, with time and money on their hands plus a growing concern about their quality of life, will boost this sector further. Among the fastest growing activities of all, according to SGMA, are exercise categories like spinning classes (advanced stationary bicycles), Pilates, use of treadmills and use of the elliptical motion trainer.

Finally, evolving technologies and fashions have an immense impact on sales of sporting goods within specific sectors. Sporting goods makers are constantly trying to create reasons for consumers to buy new equipment. Golf ball and club makers adopt new technologies with great success. Snow ski and board makers use new technologies as soon as they become available. Additionally, ski gear manufacturers introduce new fashions, new colors and new styles yearly in an effort to get consumers to buy new or buy up, regardless of whether significant new technologies are involved.

Meanwhile, the media used to deliver sports and sports related information is evolving quickly. Sports coverage is one of the most widely viewed categories online. At the same time, digital TV recording devices (DVRs), such as TiVo, are enabling fans to watch events according to their own schedules. Finally, the rapid emergence of sports news and events video delivered via state-of-the-art cell phone screens is having a major impact. Watch for continued rapid change throughout the sports industry, as consumers' tastes and manufacturers' product lines evolve.

The global recession had a significant effect on sports and recreation in 2008 and into mid 2009. Professional teams have encountered difficulty selling tickets and revenues for manufacturers of sports and recreation equipment dropped. Gambling revenues plummeted. Consumers are still keenly interested in their favorite sports and recreation, but they are reducing their expenses, and they are cutting back on luxury and discretionary purchases in particular. Since ticket prices for professional sports have become extremely expensive, sales are suffering. Golf courses are suffering revenue declines, and a few have closed while many have delayed refurbishing projects. Travel and tourism related to sports have declined. On the highest end, purchases of the most expensive sports and recreation items like boats and RVs have declined significantly. At least one major sports team fell seriously behind on its debt. Even the NFL laid off 150 employees at the end of 2008. For the mid term, the sports industry will face significant challenges in controlling expenses while pricing products and services in a manner that will maintain their appeal to worried consumers.

The biggest opportunities in the sports industry today lie in providing exciting, high-value opportunities for sports fans, such as high-tech recreational gear at reasonable prices; spectator sports ticket packages that represent better value; high-value family recreation items that can be used at home or near the home; exercise/fitness services and programs that will appeal to aging baby boomers; and equipment and apparel that represents high value and exciting design. Consumers still want to play, but they want to do so at a more reasonable cost.

2) NFL: The Biggest Money in U.S. Sports

According to *Forbes* magazine, the most valuable professional franchises among football, basketball, baseball and hockey are National Football League (NFL) teams, which have an average value of $1.04 billion as of late 2008. The NFL commands by far the greatest revenue, plays in the largest and most expensive stadiums and amasses more viewers in the United States than any other sport. This is all the more remarkable in light of the fact that the NFL plays far fewer games per season than does MLB (Major League Baseball) or the NBA (National Basketball Association).

Average Ticket Prices in 2008

NFL	$72.20
NBA	$48.83
NHL	$48.72
MLB	$25.40

Source: ESPN

The most valuable franchise in the NFL and in all of U.S. sports is the Dallas Cowboys, owned by Jerral ("Jerry") Jones. Valued at $1.6 billion, it overtook the Washington Redskins as the most valuable team in 2007, according to *Forbes*. The Redskins were valued in second place at $1.53billion, followed by the New England Patriots at $1.32 billion and the New York Giants at $1.17 billion. The Cowboys are number one in this category (if not on the playing field) due to the promise of their enormous new stadium, a potentially lucrative stadium naming rights deal that has yet to be announced, savvy broadcasting and advertising agreements, and a hometown full of loyal and wealthy ticket holders.

The team will move to a new, $1.1 billion state of the art facility for the 2009 season. The new structure will have 80,000 seats (compared to the old

Texas Stadium's 65,595 seats) and some 300 luxury suites which will were hoped to lease for as much as $350,000 per season. *Forbes* estimated that the Cowboys' operating income could top $100 million when the new stadium opens.

The Cowboys may reap further millions if they are able to sell a stadium naming rights deal in which a corporate sponsor will pledge a large amount of money over several years. For example, FedEx Stadium, home to the Redskins, affords the franchise $207 million from FedEx over 27 years for naming rights, which averages to around $7.6 million per year. That average is beaten only by Reliant Stadium, home of the Houston Texans, which brings in $10 million per year in naming rights; and Phillips Arena, home of the Atlanta Hawks and Thrashers, which costs a mere $9.3 million per year for naming rights.

Naming rights for the new Cowboys stadium were still available as of mid-2009. Sales of naming rights have plummeted due to the global economic crisis. The stadium was planned and funded during the economic boom preceding the financial crisis of 2008-2009, making the timing of the opening unfortunate, to say the least. In today's economic climate, corporations, especially banks which have received billions in taxpayer-funded relief, are unwilling or unable to make multimillion dollar expenditures. The Cowboys organization may have a lengthy wait for a naming rights buyer.

Until recently, player salaries for the Cowboys, as for all NFL teams, were officially capped at 65% of the team's revenue. Although top players earn millions, owners' costs were somewhat protected by the salary cap. Player bonuses, on the other hand, are prorated over the life of a contract.

NFL owners agreed to increase the salary cap from $116 million per franchise in 2008 to $128 million in 2009. The cap is part of a collective bargaining agreement between the Players Association and the NFL, which is a key element in keeping NFL teams competitive. In 2008, NFL owners voted to opt out of the collective bargaining agreement, making it possible for the salary cap to be abandoned as of 2010 if a new agreement is not reached.

The NFL maintains the greatest control over labor costs compared with other professional sports leagues. Player salaries have grown about 9% yearly on average since 1990, while growth in other leagues such as the NHL, NBA and MLB average yearly growth over the same period is between 12% and 16%. The minimum NFL team salary in 2009 was $107.7 million, according to FoxSports.com.

The business model established in the NFL stipulates partial revenue sharing among teams and a player free-agency system in addition to the salary cap. For the entire NFL, broadcast rights, licensed merchandise and certain other revenue streams are shared evenly among the teams. This includes sharing a recent four-year extension of an exclusive deal with DirecTV to air the Sunday Ticket game package worth $4 billion. The result is a league of 32 teams which, regardless of each team's individual value and record, all have a chance to hire top players and to win. Each team is able to recruit and pay competitive talent so that fans never know from game to game, season to season which team will win the Super Bowl.

The system is not foolproof. Teams share revenues generated by television fees, national sponsorship and licensing contracts. However, local revenue from stadium luxury suites and local sponsorships is not shared, and teams are facing tough times as more fans choose to stay home during the economic recession, draining ticket and concession revenue.

The NFL is actively seeking new revenue through several ventures. One is NFL On Location, a unit which offers fans the chance to purchase travel packages to major games such as the Super Bowl and the Pro Bowl. A typical Super Bowl four-day ticket package includes tickets to the game, hotel rooms, parking spots at the stadium, stadium tours and access to hospitality sites. Several trip options are available for each event and prices for Super Bowl XLIV in 2010 range between $2,799 and $5,199 without air fare. Prices have dropped significantly since 2009 because of the global economic crisis. Hotel room prices have been slashed, marketing efforts have greatly increased to lure shrinking numbers of fans who can spend thousands on entertainment.

Another potential revenue generator is the NFL's attempt to drum up interest in foreign markets. In China, for example, the league began introducing flag football programs for children in five cities in 2003. In 2007, Chinese state TV channels began airing weekly NFL games. The league's International Division has six priority markets: Mexico and Canada in the near term; the U.K. and Germany in the mid-term; and China and Japan in the long term. In October 2007, the first regular season NFL game was played in London when the Miami Dolphins host the New York Giants at Wembley Stadium. This was followed in 2008 by a game in the same venue between the New Orleans Saints and the San Diego Chargers.

SPOTLIGHT: If You Build It They Will Come?

Sports stadiums have historically been built using large amounts of local taxpayer dollars, voted in by fans willing to bear part of the burden for hosting a professional team. This trend is fading as voters in Florida and Missouri nixed bills supporting new stadium projects in 2005. In 2006, the San Diego Chargers abandoned a $450 million stadium proposal which asked voters for 60 city acres free of charge, due to lack of voter confidence. Other projects are finding some funds from municipal support, but must look for the rest of the money elsewhere. In some cases, funds come from a slice of sales taxes on tourist activities. For example, the relatively new Reliant Stadium, home of the Houston Texans football team, is supported by an additional 2% tax on city hotels and a 5% tax on car rentals.

Funding can be raised by selling seat licenses to season ticket holders in addition to multi-million dollar naming rights. The $1.3 billion, 82,500-seat Meadowlands stadium for the New York Jets and the New York Giants (both teams will share the facility) is being funded in part by one-time only seat licenses to season ticket holders. The teams are expected to raise between $100 million and $125 million from these sales. The NFL's G-3 loan program which provides construction loans at low interest rates will pony up $300 million to be repaid over 15 years. The new Meadowlands stadium is planned to open in time for the 2009 season.

Yet another twist to stadium finance is packaging a stadium within a larger complex that also includes offices, retail and commercial space. San Diego's PetCo Park incorporates a renovated 95 year-old office building, a condominium tower and a sandy "beach" play area in its 26-block ballpark redevelopment area.

All of these projects are facing difficult times selling seats due to the economic downturn. Where plans once called for selling luxury boxes and premium seats for cash, teams are now offering season ticket financing, shorter contract commitments on suites and redesigning luxury suites to serve as party rooms available on a per-game basis.

3) Revenue Sharing Boosts Major League Baseball

Gross revenue for MLB in 2008 reached $6.5 billion, up from 2007's $6 billion, according to MLB.com. Average team worth rose also to $482 million, up 2.1% from 2006. Despite these figures, MLB, along with other professional sports, is facing daunting challenges in 2009 due to the global economic recession. Total attendance for MLB games in 2008 was 78.6 million, down slightly from 2007's 79.5 million, and further declines are expected.

Teams are responding by lowering season ticket prices and offering incentives such as free additional seats to existing season ticket holders. According to Team Marketing Report, 10 of the league's 30 teams have reduced their ticket prices. In April 2009, the New York Yankees cut premium seat prices in half, while the San Diego Padres cut their average season ticket prices by 27%. Despite these efforts, season ticket sales were falling. The league-wide rate of retaining season ticket holders fell from about 85% in 2008 to approximately 75% in 2009.

Success both on the field and off for particular teams is spread across the entire league thanks to a revenue-sharing system by which all 30 teams in baseball must abide. Teams with revenue above the league average must make payments (worth the difference between the team's actual revenue and the league average) that are split among teams with revenue lower than the average figure. In 2008, the New York Yankees topped the revenues list, followed by the New York Mets and the Boston Red Sox. As a result, poorer teams such as the Oakland Athletics, Minnesota Twins and Florida Marlins have increased their operating incomes, earning more than $20 million each, according to *Forbes* magazine.

Revenue sharing is an attempt to even the playing field between franchises. Otherwise, wealthy teams with the capital to pay big salaries (such as the Yankees and the Red Sox) could easily dominate the league, winning year after year by forming very expensive dynasties. The idea is that with shared revenue, less wealthy teams have the wherewithal to attract (and pay top salaries to) leading players. The goal is to achieve parity, making almost any team capable of winning the World Series and therefore bringing more excitement to the game.

Since 2002, when the current revenue-sharing standards were put into place, less wealthy teams have made appearances in the annual World Series championship and have even won it. In both 1999 and 2000, the Yankees won the World Series and had the highest aggregate team payroll (ranked number one in the league). In 2002, the Anaheim Angels won, with a number 15 payroll rank. Even more telling, the 2003 champion team was the Florida Marlins with a payroll rank of 25. Most recently, 2006 World Series champs St. Louis Cardinals ranked 6th in salaries, beating the Detroit Tigers who ranked 9th (up from 15th in 2005). The win by the 2007 World Series Champions, the Boston Red Sox, as the third most valuable team according to *Forbes* rankings, opened the door for revenue sharing opponents, who argue that revenue shared with poorer teams is not spent on player salaries and does not necessarily promote parity. 2008's World Series appearance by the Tampa Bay Rays supports the parity concept, despite the fact that they lost the championship to the Philadelphia Phillies.

Big changes are taking place on many teams as owners are scaling back on player costs such as salaries, bonuses and benefits. Since the 2003 season, player costs have fallen to 56% of revenue from 66%, according to *Forbes.* As a result, operating incomes are rising, averaging more than $16 million per team in 2007 and 2008. The recession of 2008-2009 impacted the league; however, the average franchise value of $482 million is skewed by the wealthy New York Yankees and the New York Mets, both of which have new ballparks opening this year. Only eight teams have values higher than the league average, while 10 teams suffered decreases in value from 2007 to 2008.

SPOTLIGHT: MLB.com

Major League Baseball's web site, www.mlb.com, which is owned and operated by Major League Baseball Advanced Media (BAM), was the first to master streaming online technology that allows it to broadcast live games on its site. In 2008, the site aired more than 12,000 streamed events through the year. In the first weeks of the 2009 season, MLB.com averaged 9.4 million visitors per day. More than 1.5 million subscribers have signed up since the site's launch in 2003, which includes all out-of-market games, priced at $79.95 to $119.95 per season. In addition, BAM sells $80 million in MLB merchandise such as hats, jerseys and signed balls.

Moreover, the site operates a network of mobile sites enabling fans to access the latest baseball news and video streams. Fans have downloaded more than 1.1 million MLB.com and club icons to their BlackBerry smartphones for one-click access, and the MLB.com At Bat 2009 application for iPhones and iPod touch units remains a top selling sports application available from Apple. BAM began with an initial $80 million investment by all 30 MLB clubs. Thanks to its rapid success, the media company paid each club a dividend of $3 million in 2007.

4) NBA Lacks Revenue Sharing/NBA China Progresses

Unlike the NFL and MLB, the National Basketball Association (NBA) has no revenue sharing. The result is a league of haves and have-nots which is largely determined by the size of the market each team represents. On the high end is the New York Knicks with a 2008 value of $613 million (according to *Forbes*), up 1% from the previous year, and revenues of $208 million. The Knicks are followed by the Los Angeles Lakers, worth $584 million (up 4% from 2007) and earning $191 million in 2008 revenues. On the low end, the Milwaukee Bucks were worth $278 million in 2008 (an increase of 5% over the previous year) with revenues of $94 million. Of the NBA's 30 franchises, eight lost value from 2007 to 2008, the worst being the New Jersey Nets' drop of 13% to $295 million.

The exception to the market size rule is the San Antonio Spurs. Although San Antonio is the NBA's third-smallest market, the Spurs have won four NBA titles, including the 2007 win over the Cleveland Cavaliers, and the team is worth $415 million (a 3% jump over the previous year). Not only do the Spurs have a superb record on the court, the franchise makes money thanks to its luxurious $175 million AT&T Center arena in downtown San Antonio.

Overall ticket sales in the 2008-2009 season were even with the previous season at 8,500 seats sold per game on average. However, analysts expect sales for the 2009-2010 season to drop based on falling renewal rates. According to the SportsBusiness Journal, the NBA's average renewal rate fell from 80% to 84%. Most teams are responding to the decreasing market by either freezing ticket prices or lowering them. As of early 2009, the NBA reported that 19 teams were expected to freeze prices while seven had announced plans to cut prices.

Revenue sharing in the NBA is beginning to become a reality, thanks to a League-sponsored study by consultants McKinsey & Co. in 2003 of each team's operations. Based on the results of that study, a portion of the "luxury tax" proceeds collected from teams that exceed a payroll tax threshold of $61.7 million were distributed to poorer teams for the first time in 2006. NBA Commissioner David Stern expects the McKinsey analysis to the basis of any revenue sharing the League may instigate in the future.

A noteworthy marketing initiative is the availability of games (both from the current season and past seasons) for download from www.nba.com. First available in May 2007, single games are offered at $3 each and come free of commercials or timeouts and feature League announcers. An entire series is also available for $13 and all playoff games for $80. An NBA League Pass program is also available to cable and satellite TV subscribers for $179 per season. Digitizing and logging of all the games at NBA.com is expected by 2015.

SPOTLIGHT: NBA Basketball Comes to China

The NBA is looking overseas for expansion, specifically in China, where an estimated 300 million people play basketball, according to the Chinese Basketball Association. The NBA has been actively recruiting in China for years (Houston Rockets center Yao Ming is an example), but in an ambitious move, the Association established a new league there after the conclusion of the 2008 Summer Olympics. NBA China is endorsed by all 30 North American teams, and has $253 million in financial backing from ESPN (a division of The Walt Disney Company), Bank of China Group Investment, Legend Holdings Limited, Li Ka Shing Foundation and China Merchants Investments. Collectively, this group owns 11% of the new enterprise. While ticket sales slow in the U.S. due to the recession, sales in China are reported to be rising from 30%-40% per year.

NBA China is working closely with the Chinese Basketball Association, making use of its players and coaches as well as facilities. The NBA has a stake in an arena in Beijing built for the Olympics. In addition, the Association has relationships with 51 Chinese telecasters. In late 2008, global sports and entertainment firm AEG Worldwide and NBA China formed a joint venture to build NBA-style arenas in cities throughout China.

5) NHL Ticket Sales Slow

Until recently, hockey teams in Canada and the U.S. were riding high. Canadian teams especially were flourishing because of a surging Canadian dollar. Team values soared, most especially the Toronto Maple Leafs, worth $448 million in 2008 (per *Forbes* magazine) with a growth of 9% over 2007; the Montreal Canadiens, worth $334 million in 2008 with an 18% growth over 2007; and the Vancouver Canucks, worth $236 million in 2008 with a growth of 12% over 2007. As for U.S. teams, the New York Rangers' value grew by 12% in 2008 to reach $411 million.

The average NHL team as of late 2008 was worth $219.5 million, up from $200 million in 2007. Operating incomes averaged $4.72 million in 2008, compared to $3.2 million in 2007. Revenue sharing in the NHL is active, with predominantly Canadian teams ponying up the lion's share. Six teams (Vancouver Canucks, Edmonton Oilers, Calgary Flames, Toronto Maple Leafs, Ottawa Senators and Montreal Canadiens) contributed $41 million to lesser teams, most of which are in the southern U.S. This is a typical pattern in the NHL, and, not surprisingly, the Canadian NHL owners are frustrated with the system, and also with an increasing salary cap that forces teams to carry a minimum payroll of $40.7 million. Some owners charge that underperforming franchises intentionally keep their revenues under the sharing threshold so as not to contribute.

The outlook for the 2009-2010 season is flat at best. Teams are looking for ways to cut their budgets, 50% of which come from ticket revenue, which is expected to slow. One NHL team has already cut its budget by $1 million through staff attrition and lowering overhead expenditures. Teams also began marketing renewal packages for the 2009-2010 season by the end of February 2009.

The NHL attracts the smallest fraction of television audiences when compared to other sports such as football, baseball and basketball (games aired on NBC garnered a 1.0 rating from Nielsen Co. compared to ratings as high as 29.6 for *Monday Night Football*). The league is attempting to reach a younger audience through an online service called GameCenter Live. The service, which launched in 2008, affords subscribers the ability to watch almost any NHL game live on its web site. The service is available for $169 for the entire season

The League expanded recently with the creation of the Minnesota Wild. Despite relatively low player salaries, the new team ranks an impressive 11th out of 30 with a 2008 value of $217 million and won the Northwest Division Championship in the 2007-2008 season.

6) NASCAR Revenues Face Challenges/Best Teams Require Massive Investment

NASCAR (the National Association for Stock Car Auto Racing) is a family-run business that was founded in 1948. The founder, "Big Bill" France, wisely saw the demand for a car racing circuit in the Southern states. His son turned the business into a giant that is now run by his grandson. NASCAR has built sweeping popularity among racing fans far outside the South. Races are now held in cities like Miami, Chicago and Los Angeles.

However, the global economic crisis of 2008-2009 is squeezing team sponsorships and keeping fans at home when they used to buy race tickets. Four of the 24 NASCAR Sprint Cup Series teams suspended operations in 2008, and to date, six team owners have been forced to raise cash by selling team stakes to investors. Costs of running a team are staggering. It takes as much as $10 million to hire a winning driver for one year and $25 million to keep a car on the track. Major sponsors such as Domino's Pizza, Coors Light and Eastman Kodak have withdrawn from NASCAR, sending owners scrambling for funding. Richard Petty, a seven-time champion, sold his team in 2008 to Boston Ventures, which has since sold the Petty name to a team owned by George Gillett.

The exception in the NASCAR downturn is Hendrick Motorsports, a team owned by Rick Hendrick III, which leads the sport in value at $335 million (up 13% from 2007) according to *Forbes*. Hendrick has signed top drivers (Jeff Gordon, Dale Earnhardt, Jr. and Jimmie Johnson all drive for Hendrick and lead the sport in earnings at $32 million, $31 million and $23 million respectively); invested $20 million since 2006 in driver training grounds and machine shops; and expanded its sponsorship deal with Pepsi. Industry analysts estimate the team's 2008 operating profit was $21.3 million.

Meanwhile, NASCAR is facing soaring costs. According to *Forbes* magazine, team budgets have grown by double-digits since the 1990s and 20% of the most valuable teams lost money in 2008. Average attendance in 2008 fell for the third year in a row to 118,000, down from 2007's 130,000.

Despite these problems, the majority of NASCAR teams managed to earn substantial profits in 2008. The average team in 2008 enjoyed $7.5 million in profits, down from 2007's $12.3 million, according to *Forbes*. Average NASCAR team worth is $119 million, down from $120 million in 2007, and average revenue was $80 million, compared to 2007's $84 million.

NASCAR's deals with television networks have been extremely lucrative, further boosting total revenue. The circuit's television audience was one of the largest among all sports, second only to pro football. The association signed a $4.48 billion, eight year deal with ABC, ESPN, Fox and TNT in 2007. However, ratings have been sliding, falling 21% since their peak in 2005. Nielsen estimates report that ad spending for NASCAR's premier Sprint Cup circuit fell 16% in 2008 to $351 million.

7) Lucrative Television Rights Bring in Big Bucks

Television rights to NFL games are big business. After 35 years of airing *Monday Night Football*, ABC lost the weekly slot beginning with the 2006 season to cable sports company ESPN, although the program ultimately remains under its original corporate umbrella since both ABC and ESPN are owned by the Walt Disney Company. Disney is paying dearly for the privilege, since the price tag for the next eight years of the program is a hefty $1.1 billion per year, approximately double what ABC had been paying.

According to the *Sports Business Journal*, current network deals to air NFL games have been extended through 2013 for two networks as of May 2009. Fox's deal before the extension was an annual average of about $712.5 million for the Sunday afternoon NFC league package through 2011, while CBS had agreed to pay an annual average of about $622.5 million for the Sunday afternoon AFC package (NFC teams tend to be in larger markets with larger numbers of fans, hence the difference in fees). Under the new extension, which runs through the 2013 season, CBS will broadcast the 2013 SuperBowl in New Orleans, Louisiana, and Fox will broadcast the SuperBowl in 2014. Prices for the extended broadcast rights should rise between 3% and 5%. The extension benefits both networks, which have insured broadcast rights through 2014 in an uncertain economy for relatively small hikes in fees. In the 2008-2009 season, Fox averaged a 10.5 rating and 17 million viewers for its regular season games, while CBS averaged a 10.0 rating and 16.2 million viewers.

Another element in the extension deal is the agreement by both CBS and Fox to allow the NFL Network's cable Sunday Ticket Red Zone channel to air live game "look-ins" during Sunday afternoon games when teams are in scoring position. With network permission granted, the NFL was free to hammer out a long-disputed deal with Comcast for including the NFL Network in the same tier of digital subscription service that offers MLB games. The package is called Digital Classic and has about 10 million subscribers. In order to accomplish this, the NFL slashed its 70-center per subscriber license fee to between 40 and 45 cents to seal the deal.

Meanwhile, DirecTV's $3.5 billion, five-year rights through 2010 for the NFL Sunday Ticket package were also extended through 2014 for about $1 billion per year. This is a 43% increase on an annual basis from the roughly $700 million per year that the satellite company was paying. The package affords satellite subscribers the ability to see every NFL game on Sundays.

NBC's rights still extend through 2011, and amount to $3.6 billion for the total four-year deal. ESPN is currently in a $4.8 billion, eight-year agreement through 2013 for rights to games other than *Monday Night Football.* ESPN is limited by the fact that it reaches only 84% of the homes to which ABC broadcasts. ESPN charges the highest rates of any national cable network at $2.86 per subscriber according to Kagan Research. That revenue, plus advertising sales, enables the network to afford the steep price it paid for the *Monday Night* games.

Overall, television revenue alone for the NFL for 2008 was about $4 billion per year according to Nielsen estimates. This was more than was spent in 2004 for television rights for NBA, MLB, NASCAR, PGA, NCAA tournament basketball and the Summer Olympics combined.

Meanwhile, prime time U.S. broadcast rights for Major League Baseball (MLB) are locked up by Fox which negotiated a seven year, $1.75 billion deal starting with the 2007 post-season. This is significantly les than its previous $2.5 billion, six-year contract because Fox gave up the American and National League Divisional Series games to other networks as well as American League and National League championship series games in alternating years. MLB also has an eight-year, $2.37 billion contract with ESPN through 2013 and a smaller agreement for limited games with Turner Broadcasting.

The National Basketball Association (NBA) wound up a $2.4 billion, six-year deal with ABC and ESPN at the end of the 2007-2008 season in addition to a Turner Broadcasting contract for $2.2 billion ending at the same time. A new, eight-year, $7.5 billion deal with ABC, ESPN and Turner began in the 2008-2009 season. The NBA also broadcasts games to approximately 15 million homes through NBA TV.

8) World Soccer Faces Trouble Due to Lack of Parity/MLS Holds Its Own

As in American baseball, global soccer players have reaped rewards from owners with deep pockets who are willing to write astronomical contracts for top talents. For example, Barcelona's Ronaldinho earns $13 million per year (plus an estimated $24 million in endorsements for Nike, Pepsi and others), while David Beckham, formerly of Real Madrid, signed a deal with the Los Angeles Galaxy that could be worth as much as $250 million over five years, including bonuses and endorsements. *Forbes* reported that his 2007 base salary of $5.5 million was more than doubled by his percentage of the team's ticket, merchandise and sponsorship revenue; with another estimated $40 million in endorsements.

Unlike strictly-governed U.S. sports leagues such as MLB and the NBA, there is no revenue sharing in soccer. There is a wide gulf between the haves and have-nots, and it appears to be widening each year. While European soccer (in Europe the game is referred to as "football") generates approximately $12 billion annually in revenue, roughly 400 first division teams throughout the region are fighting for a piece of it. Only those elite qualifiers for the two main championship tournaments at the end of the season, the UEFA Champions League and the UEFA Cup, have the opportunity to score when it comes to revenue and profits. According to global accounting firm Deloitte Touche Tohmatsu, teams making it to these championships can add more than $50 million to their annual revenue.

Wealthy teams such as Spain's Real Madrid, England's Manchester United and Italy's AC Milan not only have the capital to pay star players multi-million-dollar salaries, they have the cash and the clout to form lucrative alliances with Adidas-Salomon, Nike and other apparel manufacturers. Manchester United, for example, has a $520-million agreement with Nike that empowers the apparel maker to handle all of the team's merchandising on a global basis.

Poorer teams haven't the wherewithal to strike such deals, and they gamble seriously by trying to play the top-salary game. A losing season means revenue losses in the millions due to lower ticket sales and lost television revenue, as well as the very real possibility of sliding from first league status into the second league, even while a poorly performing player continues to be paid big bucks.

Savvy team owners are well aware of the challenges before them and are taking steps to safeguard their investments. Player contracts are beginning to include clauses relating compensation to performance. Owners are also increasing stadium seating and adding luxury boxes to attract higher ticket prices, as well as recruiting young, international talent as opposed to established (and therefore expensive) players. Young players can work together over time to build a cohesive team, while players from foreign countries such as China open marketing opportunities on a global scale. For example, Sun Jihai plays for Manchester City and Dong Fangzhuo plays for Manchester United, attracting hundreds of millions of Chinese viewers of televised games. Broadband users in China viewed Britain's Premier League and Europe's 2008 championship thanks to a $200 million, three-year contract with NOW Broadband TV (a unit of Hong Kong telecom company PCCW). Chinese fans now make up 20% of soccer's global audience, according to *Forbes*. The U.K.'s top league, the Premiership, signed a three-year, $50 million deal in 2007 with Guangdong Provincial Television's WinTV. Watch for these changes to take root and strengthen European soccer over the mid-term.

In the U.S., Major League Soccer (MLS), although it has nowhere near the financial eminence and prestige of world soccer, is enjoying a modest success. Investors have pumped more than $1 billion into MLS since 2004. Energy drink maker Red Bull spent $100 million to buy New York's MetroStars and promptly changed the team name eponymously to the Red Bulls. In 2005, Adidas-Salomon announced plans to invest $150 in the league through 2015. In addition, Soccer United Marketing, a commercial soccer promotion company holding promotion rights for the MLS and for other leagues, sold the U.S. broadcast rights for the next two World Cups for $400 million. Following record ticket sales in 2007 of $33.74 million, average attendance figures fell in 2008 by 1.8% to 16,459 per game, according to the *SportsBusiness Journal*. However, despite the global economic recession, season ticket renewals for 2009 were reported to be keeping pace with 2008.

9) NCAA Sports Are Big Business

The National Collegiate Athletic Association (NCAA) football teams command staggering revenues. Of the top ten for the year ended 2006, Ohio State University led the pack with $104.7 million, followed by $97.8 million for the University of Texas and $92.7 million for the University of Virginia. Revenue producing sports are football and, as a distant second, men's basketball. In addition to ticket revenues and booster and alumni club dues, many schools attract multimillion dollar endowments and donations from alumni and other supporters. For example, T. Boone Pickens, an alumnus of Oklahoma State University, donated $165 million to his alma mater's athletic department in 2006 (followed by a $100 million donation in 2008 to endow major faculty chairs and professorships).

These huge budgets fund top salaries for winning coaches as well as state of the art facilities. Urban Meyer, coach of the 2006 NCAA National Champion Florida Gators, was hired at a salary of $2 million in 2004. After winning the championship, his salary was raised to $3.25 million per year. As for facilities, the *Chronicle of Higher Education* reports that from 2002 to 2007, schools in the U.S.' top six athletic conferences raised upwards of $3.9 billion for stadium expansions and renovations, new practice facilities and training centers. One example is the University of Michigan's $226 million stadium renovation to be completed in 2010.

Amid concerns about big money in college sports, an investigation by the U.S. Senate Finance Committee in 2007 concluded that college gifts earmarked for sports accounted for an average of 14.7% of all gifts to colleges in 1998 and rose to 26% in 2003. In effect, funding for football and men's' basketball endows another 18 sports played on the college level.

The NCAA includes more than 1,000 members, each categorized into one of three divisions. Division I teams, for example, are required to sponsor at least seven sports for men and seven for women (or six for men and eight for women). Several other regulations and requirements must be met at various Division levels. Sports involved range from bowling and fencing to field hockey, golf, gymnastics, wrestling and more. The NCAA itself, operating on behalf of its member universities, had a 2008-2009 budget calling for revenues totaling $661 million. About 90% of that revenue is generated by television and marketing rights fees, with the balance generated by the annual championships, investments and membership fees. From that revenue, about 95% was budgeted to be distributed to member colleges or spent on event services for those colleges.

10) Golf Tournaments Face Sponsorship Challenge

The Professional Golfers' Association (PGA) conducts more than 50 tournaments each year, which, up until the global economic crisis of 2008-2009, easily attracted corporate sponsors anxious to reach the highly prized demographics of typical PGA Tour fans. Generally males between the ages of 40 and 65, ticket holders to these events have above-average incomes and are prime targets for corporate marketing departments. However, major tournament sponsors in the past have often been automotive manufacturers, banks and other financial institutions that have drastically cut advertising and sponsorships. Some of these potential sponsors have recently accepted emergency funding from the U.S. government. Those that no longer have the funds for sponsorships have been dropping out and those that do are vulnerable to critical comments about frivolous spending.

A title sponsorship, that is, the highest level of sponsorship that affords the sponsor's name on the tournament (e.g., Shell Houston Open, Travelers Championship, Buick Open) goes for about $6 million. The USGA, which operates the U.S. Open and another 12 tournaments each year, also offers major sponsorships.

In addition to PGA and USGA Tour events, opportunities for sponsors include the Champions Tour, which showcases players ages 50 and over; the LPGA, the association for female professional golfers; and the Nationwide Tour, which is a tournament circuit for young, up-and-coming players.

Hefty sponsor fees (up to $8.5 million for a title sponsorship of a PGA Champions Tour event) are split between prize money and a host of expenses including signage, tournament apparel and hospitality. When it comes to golf tournaments, hospitality is the operative word. Hospitality tents are erected all around tournament courses in which clients and top employees of participating corporations are wined and dined throughout the tournaments. Tournament activities for sponsor guests vary from a day of professional-amateur play, in which wealthy aficionados can buy a round partnered with a pro, through up-close viewing of three days of play, usually ending on a Sunday when the winner takes the third and final round. Corporate sponsors, whether title sponsors or those on lower levels, line up to pay for the privilege of association with golf.

A number of tournaments across the U.S. have already lost their major sponsors, or will do so when current commitments expire. The Memorial Tournament, for example, has a contract with Morgan Stanley that expires in 2010; and for the 2009 tournament in June, all client entertainment associated with the event was cancelled. The U.S. Bank Championship will lose U.S. Bank's title sponsorship after 2009; and the Buick Open's contract with GM runs out after 2010.

Amateur play in the U.S. is stagnating. Although an estimated 3 million people pick up the game of golf each year, about the same number quit. Also, the total number of rounds played in the U.S. declined in 2002 and 2003 and has remained at that lower level since then. All told, about 26 million people play the sport (down from 30 million in 2000, according to the Golf Foundation and SGMA), which generates in the neighborhood of $60 billion per year in revenues.

Golf course construction has ground to a halt. The National Golf Foundation reports that the number of new courses in the U.S. opened in 2008 (80 in all) was the smallest in 20 years. Meanwhile, almost 100 courses were scheduled to close in 2008.

The PGA is hoping to boost those numbers with its Play Golf America program, which includes free lessons and links on its web site to a network of courses, and facilities that cater to new players; and the First Tee program, which hosts under-privileged kids from urban environments.

11) Fantasy Sports Post Growth, Creating $500 Million in Revenue Online

Leagues of fantasy sports in which players off the field choose professional players to be on pretend ("fantasy") teams have taken off in a big way. Players contribute to a winning pot and then follow their chosen players on-field statistics throughout the season. At the end of the season, the fantasy team with the best statistics wins the pot. The practice began in the early 1980s among baseball fans and has expanded to a wide variety of sports, both professional and amateur. Annual global revenues have reached $500 million, according to Ipfos, a market research firm. Today, of course, fantasy teams are conducted over the Internet.

Players early on paid a fee to fantasy "operators," but many leagues now allow play free of charge. Revenues come from the sale of draft guides, expert analysis and advertising. Operators typically pay licensing fees of 5% to 10% of revenues for the rights to professional players' names and statistics. The largest of the operating companies pay as much as $1.5 million per year for these rights.

For Major League Baseball alone, 10.8 million fantasy players participate, subscribing to any of a dozen fantasy sports magazines, approximately 200 web sites (some free and some fee-based) and hundreds of amateur blogs. The Fantasy Sports Trade Association estimates that betting sums, magazine sales and stat-service subscriptions amount to about $468 per player per year, or about a $5 billion total industry.

12) Equipment Manufacturers Scramble to Offer the Latest High-Tech Advantages

Major strides have been made in sports equipment technology, especially in golf. Equipment manufacturers such as Callaway Golf, Wilson Golf and Titleist spend millions of dollars on developing new, cutting-edge clubs, balls and accessories that offer hope to those who want to increase distance and precision while lowering handicaps. In a depressed economy, manufacturers are hoping to lure customers by developing game-changing new equipment.

The real news in golf equipment is the emergence of high-tech tools ranging from gauges that can plot a golfer's distance from the hole using GPS, to room-size simulators that can recreate course conditions from famous courses around the world. The SkyCaddie by SkyHawke Technologies is a GPS that measures distance coordinates for 23,000 courses around the world. Prices start at $259.95 and range up to $399.95 for a deluxe model. The Vector Pro Launch Monitor System by Accusport is a $2,995 gadget that uses infrared light and twin cameras to measure ball spin and speed and video swing analysis. On the super luxury end, the Indoor Resort by TruGolf is a simulator with a tee area and a high resolution video screen and software that can double as a home theater. Available in home and commercial models, the simulator runs between $35,000 and $45,000 and offers realistic simulation of play on courses such as Northern California's Pebble Beach and Scotland's St. Andrews. The MX Motion Capture System by Vicon Motion Systems (formed by the merger of Vicon Motion Systems and Peak Performance, Inc.) can be used to analyze a golfer's swing. The system utilizes dozens of sensors attached to a golfer's body to minutely analyze every move. The price for this system runs between $50,000 and $150,000.

Until recently, most sales of golf equipment occurred in pro shops on golf courses. There was little competition and prices remained high. However, with the growing availability of golf equipment in discount stores and the advent of golf superstores located in malls and strip centers, golfers are taking their equipment business off the links. Of course, the Internet is providing even more competition, not only for new equipment, but also for used equipment on auction sites such as eBay. The National Golf Foundation reports that non-course retailers take in 80% of the dollars spent on equipment.

Retailers such as Golfsmith, the largest chain of specialty golf stores in the U.S., are trying to make the best of a difficult economy with a combination of competitive pricing and a highly knowledgeable staff. Owned by Golfsmith International Holdings, the stores' sales in 2008 were $378.8 million, down from $388.2 million in 2007. The outlets offer in-store putting greens and computerized swing analysis.

SPOTLIGHT: TopGolf

Owned and operated by World Golf Systems, a British firm that developed and licensed an innovative golf ball tracking technology system called the I.D. Ball System, TopGolf (www.topgolf.com) is a practice range concept that takes driving practice to a whole new level. There are six TopGolf Game Centers (three in the U.K. and three in the U.S.), which offer driving bays from which up to five players tee off, aiming for targets that range in distance from 20 to 240 yards. Balls are equipped with microchips that broadcast exact positions, earning players points depending upon where their balls land. Each bay is equipped with a flat screen monitor that tracks points, food and bar service, plus there are pros available for lessons, pro shops with equipment and attire for sale and miniature golf courses for children.

The centers attract not only hard core golfers, but people young and old who are looking for entertainment as well as companies who bring their staffs for team building exercises. Each TopGolf facility costs between $5 and $7 million to build, and generates revenues through sales of games (20 balls vary in price between $3 and $6), food and beverage sales, retail sales, mini golf, events and lessons. In addition, the firm owns and operates 70 TopPutt locations throughout the U.K. where players can use the I.D. Ball System to play a putting game.

In Hockey, heated blade technology made by a company called Thermablade is helping players move more quickly on the ice. The Canadian firm has patented the placement of small "smart" batteries and electronics in a skate's blade holder which heats the blade to five degrees above freezing. The ice beneath the blade melts slightly, forming a sheet of water that has far less resistance than ice. Thermablade says that the blade reduces gliding resistance by up to 55% and starting resistance up to

75%. The company hoped its technology would be adopted by the NHL, but the league's general managers voted down the use of the skates in late 2008.

Soccer may be impacted by the creation of Adidas' Intelligent Ball, which uses a small, walnut-sized transmitter suspended inside the ball. When the ball crosses the goal line (which has been wired beneath the playing field), the referee is alerted by a signal sent to his watch that confirms the goal. The technology was developed by Cairos Goal Line Technology, and has been tested in play at the FIFA Club World Cup in Japan.

13) Lacrosse May Be the Fastest-Growing Team Sport in America

Until recently, few sports fans were familiar with lacrosse, although it is a game that originated hundreds of years ago among native North American tribes. It is considered by experts to be North America's oldest sport. For the most part, lacrosse was long thought of as a tough but popular team game played only at better eastern colleges and prep schools such as Princeton and Kent School. Today, however, lacrosse is sweeping the U.S., with thousands of amateur and school teams for youngsters, men and women as well as fledgling pro teams. It is a big NCAA college sport. In fact, ticket sales for the 2008 NCAA lacrosse tournament broke all previous records, reaching more than 48,970.

Lacrosse is played on a large, rectangular field between two teams. Rules vary, depending on whether men, women or youths are playing, but the rules are all similar. Players wield a long stick (the "crosse") that has a small pouch on its end capable of catching the game's ball. The idea is to control the ball and get it past the opposing team's goalie, into the goal. Men play in teams of 10. The field is about 110 yards long by 60 yards wide. The ball is about eight inches in circumference and weighs five ounces. Lacrosse is fast and fun to watch. It can be a very physical game. While men's lacrosse is a contact sport, officially sanctioned women's games do not allow contact. For men, body checking is permitted if the opponent has the ball or is within five yards of a loose ball. All body contact must occur from the front or side, above the waist and below the shoulders, and with both hands on the stick. An opponent's crosse may also be stick checked if it is within five yards of a loose ball or ball in the air.

US Lacrosse, with more than 300,000 members as of early 2009, is the governing body of American amateurs in this sport (www.lacrosse.org). One of its goals is to promote safety. The organization reports that lacrosse participation in the U.S. rose 9.1% in 2008 from the previous year, with 524,230 players who were members of organized teams, including youth levels through professionals. Youth participation saw the largest rise, up 9.8% to 265,214 players; while high school players rose in number by 8.3% to 218,823. Post-collegiate play also rose by 9.3%. Large numbers of lacrosse players are below 14 years of age, playing in organized clubs. The size of teams ranges from 20 to 40 members.

An additional, non-contact version of the game is called InterCrosse. This sport is played throughout the U.S. and in many other nations. It is officially governed by the Federation Internationale d'InterCrosse (www.intercrosse.tk), based in Quebec, Canada. InterCrosse is especially popular at elementary and junior high schools because of its safety aspects.

On the professional level, Major League Lacrosse (www.majorleaguelacrosse.com) had six teams as of mid-2009, in areas including Denver, Boston, Long Island, Toronto, Chicago and Washington. Also, the National Lacrosse League (www.nll.com) is a 12-team league with expansion plans. It plays indoors.

Lacrosse offers exciting potential for corporate sponsors and expansion team owners, as well as equipment and apparel makers. The largest factor holding the sport back at present may be a lack of experienced coaches. The situation is analogous to the explosive growth in amateur soccer among students a few years ago. Don't be surprised to find lacrosse terms, such as crosse or stalling, becoming household words over the long term.

14) Sports Agents Become Indispensable/Sports Marketing Booms in China

Sports agency, as we know it today, is largely defined by the efforts of the late superagent Mark McCormack, founder of IMG Worldwide, Inc. (formerly International Management Group). World-class athletes can earn millions by excelling in their sports, but they can also multiply their incomes significantly by endorsing products, participating in special events and speaking to groups. Golf superstar Tiger Woods (an IMG client) is the world's highest-paid athlete, earning more than $110 million in 2008. Over the course of his career, he has earned more than $97.9 million playing golf alone and by 2010 is expected to be the first athlete to surpass $1 billion in earnings including endorsements.

Sports agents make this possible by serving athletes in an ever-increasing number of ways. From contract negotiation to endorsement deals to special event planning to investment planning to personal handling, agents have become indispensable to top athletes in every sport.

McCormack's career as an agent started with a 1960 handshake deal with famed professional golfer Arnold Palmer. He was the first to arrange endorsements, signing Palmer as a spokesperson for everything from golf clubs to motor oil. McCormack planned and executed golf tournaments, selling rounds of golf played with Palmer to executives around the world for hefty fees. The golfer is still a highly paid inspirational speaker. Today, long after Palmer's official retirement, he still earns $20 million a year from deals struck by IMG.

From golf, McCormack's IMG branched out into 10 other sports, modeling and the arts. The firm's television division produces 11,000 hours of multi-genre programming per year, which generates approximately one-half of the company's revenue. On any given day, eight to nine IMG-run sporting, entertainment or arts events take place around the world.

Other powerhouse sports agency firms include Octagon Worldwide, which promotes football star John Elway and Olympic swimmer Michael Phelps; BDA Sports Management, which represents basketball greats Steve Nash and Yao Ming; and William Morris Endeavor Entertainment's sports marketing segment (the William Morris Agency and Endeavor merged in 2009), which serves tennis star Serena Williams. With commissions ranging from 3% to 5%, sports agencies have significant earning power. In fact, IMG was acquired by private equity firm Forstmann Little & Co. in 2004 for about $750 million. Since then, IMG has acquired the Collegiate Licensing Company, CSI Sports, Quintus and the BSI Speedway, among others. In 2008, the company signed a deal with Chinese national TV broadcaster CCTV to launch a joint venture aimed at increasing commercialization of sports in China.

Outside the U.S., China is a hotbed of opportunity for sports marketing largely due to the 2008 Summer Olympics in Beijing. China's growing middle class were exposed to talented athletes from around the world. These athletes and their agents are looking for ways to tap the growing Chinese market. Sports marketing consulting firm Zou Marketing estimates that the sports marketing and sponsorship industry has grown from $1 billion per year in 1994 to $15 billion in 2008. While Yao Ming, a native of China, has long been a familiar face in Chinese ads and at personal appearances, athletes including Serena Williams and Kobe Bryant are making deals to do the same.

15) New Platforms Revolutionize Electronic Games

Electronic games are an immense global business. Global revenues in 2007 for the video game industry (including hardware and software) reached $41.9 billion, according to PriceWaterhouseCoopers. The firm expected worldwide revenues to escalate to $68.3 billion by 2012, although that projection may be tempered by the global economic crisis of 2008-2009. The big news is the release of ever-more-complex game machine technology. While Wii is the technical standout due to its remarkable virtual motion reality, all of today's advanced machines not only combine games with MP3 and DVD players, but offers full Internet access and interactive TV as well. Game players can find online opponents, check e-mail, shop online and download music and video entertainment with a single system. The future of games lies in one word: online.

Sony's Play Station 2, released in the fall of 2001, was the first unit to play DVDs and audio CDs while offering top-of-the-line high-tech gaming. By mid-2007, Play Station 2 had sold 115 million units worldwide, and the company dropped its retail price from $179 to $129, thereby extending the sales life of the unit.

Microsoft was hoping to break Sony's dominance in the market with its Xbox, which was released in November 2001 (with a $500-million marketing budget). Xbox is a major step in the company's attempt to revolutionize the home in the same way that PCs revolutionized the office. The unit is a combination of some of the functions of a high-end PC, complete with high-speed Internet port and a powerful graphics chip; a video game console; and ultimately a headset that will allow players to talk to other players down the street or in another country via the Internet.

Xbox Live, Microsoft's online gaming subscription service, was launched in November 2003 and had 20 million members by early 2009, and Microsoft had sold an astonishing 30 million Xbox game player units. It provides gamers with the ability to play against each other using the Internet and is becoming a key component to the video gaming experience. Xbox Live's popularity places the software giant in contention for the first time with top-rated Sony, long the number-one video game company in the world.

More news in the Sony-versus-Microsoft video game war was Sony's release of the PlayStation Portable, or PSP. Launched in late 2004 in Japan, and in mid-2005 in the U.S., the PSP was Sony's first hand-held portable game player. It boasts cutting-edge graphics and the ability to play MP3 music files as well as movies on a 4.3-inch-wide screen. Users can also access the Internet via built-in Wi-Fi connectivity and web browser.

Sony's PlayStation 3 (PS3) went on sale with great fanfare in November 2006. By the end of February 2009, Sony had sold 21 million units worldwide, well behind the cheaper Nintendo Wii and Microsoft Xbox. Priced starting at $399 and up (depending on the size of the hard drive), PS3 includes a high-definition DVD player using the Sony standard called Blu-ray. This was a bold move since, in 2006, the entertainment industry was still undecided as to which DVD technology would be embraced by the buying public, and stand-alone Blu-ray players had starting price tag of about $400 and went up to $2,000 for high-end models. Sony was actually taking a loss on the DVD player included in PS3 in order to market the new technology and soften the blow for movie watchers who would have to buy high-definition versions of their favorite DVDs. The gamble paid off since Blu-ray has become the high-definition format of choice. However, sales for PS3 began slowing in 2009 due the global recession and Sony's high price point.

The debut of Microsoft's $4-billion baby, the Xbox 360, was a major milestone in video gaming. Released for sale at midnight, November 22, 2005, Xbox 360 is a completely redesigned game console, which, not surprisingly, continues to focus on games as part of Microsoft's complete home entertainment concept. In addition to the game console, the high-end model has a wireless controller, cables for TV connection, a DVD player, a removable hard drive, a headset and a complimentary pass to Xbox Live. The console includes ports for attaching digital cameras, portable MP3 music players (including Apple's iPod) or Microsoft's Windows Media Center PC. The software giant hopes that sales of its new game systems will spur further sales of its other home products.

The Xbox 360, with its three-core 3.2-gigahertz custom chip from IBM, has been a big hit so far, with about 3 million units selling in the first 90 days alone. Hundreds of thousands of would-be Xbox owners were forced to place their names on waiting lists as initial supplies sold out immediately. The Xbox 360 Elite model features a massive 120GB hard drive. In September 2008, Microsoft sharply cut its Xbox 360 prices to court the mass market. Prices now range from $199 for the least expensive model, to $399 for the Xbox 360 Elite.

Nintendo, the third key player in video game sets, has been outdoing its rivals in many ways. Its hand-held game player Nintendo DS (first released in 2004) was the best selling game machine in the U.S. at the end of 2007. Meanwhile, in a vigorous attempt to hold on to its top spot and to compete with Sony's PSP, Nintendo launched a super small player in 2005, the Game Boy Micro. Starting at $89.99, it is barely four inches wide and two inches tall. It has a leg up over other portable devices because it is compatible with more than 700 games designed for earlier Game Boy models.

Nintendo released its revolutionary game system, Nintendo Wii (pronounced "we"), in 2006, which has been a smashing success. Equipped with a state-of-the-art wireless controller and priced at $249, the system offers gamers new, sensory-enhanced playing. The controller communicates with sensors mounted near a television that respond to the player's hand and arm movements. A fishing game, for example, causes the controller to "tug" on the player's hand when a fish is hooked, and the player can then "jerk" on the controller like a fishing pole to reel the catch in. The new technology works with long-time game favorites including *Pokémon*, *Mario Bros.* and *The Legend of Zelda*. As of early 2009, Nintendo had sold more than 50 million Wii units.

Not surprisingly, because of its lengthy history of dominating certain software segments, Microsoft maintains complete control over the licensing of its Xbox consoles and the games that can be played on it. Conversely, Sony allows almost any game developer to design games that can be run on Play Station 2 and on PS3 as well. This allows online interaction between Sony players without subscribing to an additional service such as Xbox Live.

As for online games, that is, games played via the Internet, they have become one of the largest and fastest-growing sectors of the worldwide entertainment business. In the U.S., online video games generate $1 billion per year, according to NPD Group. Each month, more than 11 million U.S. players subscribe to online games.

Gaming has presented new ways of making money. Multi-player games (known as massively multiplayer online games or MMOGs) have sparked a new market in which players broker deals to buy and sell game currency, point-building online items and even winning players' online personas, which are called avatars. Many games, such as Sony Online Entertainment's EverQuest or Vivendi subsidiary Blizzard Entertainment's phenomenally popular World of Warcraft are designed so that players must conquer a large number of challenges to win points and proceed to higher levels. Game masters reach the pinnacle by performing all tasks, which can number as many as 60 or 70. Gamers looking to cash in on the booming popularity of these games (World of Warcraft had 11.5 million subscribers worldwide as of early 2009) are finding ways to buy and sell virtual assets for real currency.

Second Life, a 3-D "virtual world" may not be a game exactly, but it is the leader in a category that utilizes game-like features such as avatars. Second Life is a world-like online platform where "members" create personalities, open businesses, create buildings and interact with each other—even to the point of getting married in a virtual, fantasy sort of way.

For a time, winning player avatars and other assets were traded on eBay (the auction site has since ceased to allow these kinds of items on its site), and numerous private buying and selling sites have sprung up, such as IGE (www.ige.com) to handle the demand. Some game companies are setting up real money trade (RMT) services of their own. In July of 2005, Sony created Station Exchange, which hosted $540,000 in RMTs in its first three months, charging a 10% commission on each transaction. The site is operated under Sony subsidiary Sony Online Entertainment LLC.

The potential for this new market is huge. IGE estimates that by 2009 the marketplace for virtual assets will reach $7 billion. The practice raises some sticky questions, however, about the true ownership of cyber-assets. Some game companies maintain that all currency, points, avatars and other assets are their property and not that of its players. Others disagree. As greater and greater sums are being made from virtual asset brokerage, the question becomes more important. Is a game company liable to its players for their cyber-assets should it discontinue the game or alter its rules? It is also possible that in the U.S., the Internal Revenue Service will begin taxing profits made selling these assets.

When most people think of video game enthusiasts, they picture kids and young men playing violent, action-packed titles such as *Counter-Strike* and *EverQuest*. However, 82.5 million people in the U.S. play "simple" online games such as checkers, mah jong and bridge, vastly larger than the number of people who play sophisticated titles. It's a market that earns $450 million per year for game companies, largely through advertising. Less than 2% of the players of these kinds of games pay to subscribe.

The average "simple" online player is female and between the ages of 35 and 54. Game playing is as much a social activity as a solitary pursuit, as many players connect online with opponents both known and unknown. Xfire (www.xfire.com), an advertiser-supported web site that tracks friends, browses servers, posts game statistics and provides instant messaging, is cashing in on the play-with-friends trend. It debuted in January 2004 with $5 million in venture funding and was acquired by Viacom in 2006. In mid-2008, the site surpassed 10.2 million registered users.

Simple games such as hearts and pool not only attract more users, they are much cheaper and easier to produce. A major shoot 'em up action game can require dozens of computer coders and designers as well as budgets of between $5 million and $15 million. Simple games, such as Yahoo!'s hit pool game, take one developer and about $100,000 to put together. A typical Friday afternoon finds upwards of 36,000 people playing pool on Yahoo!'s gaming site.

Microsoft is capitalizing on the popularity of its video games as a way to gain a strong position in the entertainment industry. The firm's online gaming site, Zone.MSN.com, is extremely successful. However, it is facing tough competition from firms such as Electronic Arts, Yahoo! and Sony, who are all looking for the next smash (read simple) online game.

The incredibly popular iPhone, having sold more than 20 million units by mid-2009, is also fueling the market for electronic games. Analysts at comScore released a study in May 2009 that found that 12 of the 25 most popular applications downloaded for use on iPhones are games. Among the most popular are Tap Tap Revenge, Touch Hockey: FS5, Pac-Man, iBowl, Labyrinth, Mazefinger and Cube Runner.

16) Bowling Looms Large/The Least Expensive Sports and Recreation Activities Draw the Most Participants

Here's another set of facts you might find surprising: Research conducted by American Sports Data, Inc., titled "Superstudy of Sports Participation" and using data as of the end of 2007, ranked bowling number one in America in terms of the total number of annual participants, followed by treadmill exercise, tent camping, stretching, fitness walking and freshwater fishing (not including fly fishing).

According to the U.S. Bowling Congress (USBC), 67 million American aged six and older bowled at least once during 2008. Participants aged seven and up who bowled more than once numbered 43.5 million, according to the National Sporting Goods Association. Participation is growing especially among teenagers. The USBC reports that there were 51,744 bowlers of high-school age in the 2007-2008 season, up 17% from the previous season. Meanwhile, 200 colleges offer bowling as a varsity or club sport as of 2009.

It's interesting to note that bowling historically thrives during economic downturns. In the years between 1933 and the beginning of World War II in 1941, the number of bowlers increased from 148,000 to 874,000. The sport also saw increased participation during the recession of the late 1980s.

The rest of the activities in the top 10 on this list include day hiking, running/jogging, billiards/pool and basketball, in that order. It is instructive to note that these top 10 activities can all be extremely inexpensive to participate in. This is an important point, since professional spectator sports ticket prices have reached the stratosphere and the soft economy of 2008-2009 is squeezing household budgets.

An annual study most recently released in March 2009 by SGMA, the Sporting Goods Manufacturers Association, also found inexpensive sports to be among the most popular by number of core participants. This respected study estimated that 76.3 million Americans walk for fitness regularly, 28.1 million use a treadmill, 27.6 million do stretching, 26.9 million use hand weights, 23.4 million use weight machines, 23.4 million do running or jogging and 22.5 million use dumbbells, each with a "core" frequency of 50+ days per year per activity. This study also found that the top growth sport for overall participation from 2000-2008 was bowling, and that the top three activities by overall participation were bowling, billiards and golf.

17) Aging Baby Boomers Will Cause Significant Changes in the Leisure Sector, Including Sports and Activity-Based Travel

The term "baby boomer" generally refers to someone born in the U.S. or Western Europe from 1946 to 1964. The term evolved to describe the children of soldiers and war industry workers who were involved in World War II. When those veterans and workers returned to civilian life, they started or added to families in large numbers. As a result, the baby boom generation is one of the largest demographic segments in the U.S., at 78 million people. Some baby boomers have already started reaching early retirement age. In 2006, the first of the boomers reached 60, a common early retirement age. In 2011, millions will begin turning traditional retirement age (65), resulting in extremely rapid growth in the senior portion of the population. The baby boom segment will have distinct requirements that should be considered by businesses that want to succeed in evolving markets. A major consideration will be the fact that many boomers will attempt to reap the health benefits of exercise for the first time in years, if not for the first time in their lives. Aerobic activity will become vital to those who want to maintain healthy lifestyles, but activities and equipment must be adapted to aging bodies. For example, leaders in the bicycle marketplace are introducing a growing number of models that enable older riders to sit more upright, while leaning over less. Bicycle seats and suspension that are kinder to older bodies will sell well.

Firms that design and make equipment for high-impact or repetitive-motion sports will be striving to create equipment that is easier on older joints and muscles. For example, golf clubs or tennis rackets that have bigger sweet spots or provide more power with less effort in the stroke are logical products for this market.

Lower-impact sports and exercise will gain in favor. Swimming, power walking and day hiking should all have bright futures, as should the firms that manufacture equipment for these activities. Exercise and gym equipment makers will do well to make lines of equipment adapted to, or specifically for, older users. For example, instruction labels on gym equipment will need to have larger font sizes so that the type will be easy for older eyes to read. Softer, more ergonomic grips on weights and other gym equipment make sense. Activities that are easy for older people to enter for the first time will prosper in this market. Pilates and yoga, when taught in a manner suitable for stiffer, older bodies, could continue to boom.

Travel and tours centered on sports and recreation activities will continue to do well, especially where at least some venues are tailored to appeal to older participants. The exploding number of affluent, retired consumers will be looking for healthy activities and recreation on their travels. Tours that combine cycling, hiking, walking and other activities of moderate intensity make sense in this market, and demand will grow sharply. Tours that combine hiking or cycling with luxury accommodations or unique lodging in pristine remote settings (including the rapidly growing trend of ecotourism) will find large numbers of customers. Sporting goods manufacturers would do well to provide sponsorships and test equipment to tour operators and should seek ways to offer seminars and sports instruction that fit neatly with the growing activity-based tour business. They will do especially well to target the 60+ age segment with marketing, products and services tailored to that group.

Members of the baby boom generation aren't the only seniors in the market for sports, recreation, fitness and travel. As of July 2008, Americans older than the baby boom set numbered more than 40 million, including 11.4 million who were 80 years of age or more (92 thousand of them were 100 or older).

18) Athletic Footwear Draws Big Names from Athletes to Designers

Athletic shoes have long been sporting the names and endorsements of famous professional athletes, particularly basketball legend Michael Jordan. Nike's line of Air Jordan shoes has been the top selling shoe brand of all time. Other athletes in the Nike stable are Kobe Bryant, Dwayne Wade, LeBron James and Carmelo Anthony. Adidas-Salomon AG offers shoes from Tracy McGrady and Kevin Garnett. This trend to sell a shoe under an athlete's name is called "marquee footwear."

A new twist to marquee footwear is that which sports a famous designer's name instead of an athlete's. Stella McCartney, a high-fashion designer and daughter of former Beatle Paul McCartney, began collaborating with Adidas in 2005 for hip athletic shoes and clothing. Another designer/athletic shoe partnership is that between traditional shoe maker Cole Haan which was acquired by Nike. The combination resulted in a line of comfortable street shoes called Cole Haan Nike Air.

All is not golden in the land of big name shoes, however, since consumers are balking at high prices (especially since the advent of the global economic crisis). Most marquee athletic shoes in 2007 ran in the $125 to $175 range, but prices have dropped. In 2009 for example, Nike Zoom LeBron V men's basketball shoes retailed for $79.99 at Foot Locker stores.

There are cheaper, more fashionable alternatives on the market which are attracting teen consumers especially. One big leader in the trend toward chic athletic footwear is Germany-based Puma. Puma, which experienced dismal sales in the 1980s while Nike leaped to the top of the market, is enjoying a renaissance. Puma's 2008 revenues topped $3.3 billion, up from $3.1 billion in 2007. What helped to turn the company around was a focus on fashion, aided by designers such as Germany's Jil Sander and American supermodel-turned-yoga guru Christy Turlington. Although Puma's sales figures are still dwarfed by heavy hitters like Nike and Reebok, it is growing at a significant rate.

Nike, which garnered more than $18.6 billion in sales in fiscal 2008 (14% above its 2007 revenues), overhauled its computerized supply systems to increase efficiency and focused on international markets for soccer and fashion shoes and apparel. (Nike gets more than one-half of its revenues from markets outside the U.S.) Nike's marketing budget is legendary. Basketball great LeBron James signed a $90 million Nike endorsement contract in 2003, while still a high school senior. More recent contracts include a 2007 deal with NBA star Kevin Durant for $60 million over seven years. Golf phenomenon Tiger Woods is said to have earned $100 million from Nike over five years for his endorsements.

19) The Vast Majority of Shoes Sold in the U.S. Are Now Made in China

U.S. retail stores specializing in shoes sold $23.2 billion in goods during 2008, per U.S. Census Bureau reports. This was down from $27.1 billion during 2007. According to the American Apparel & Footwear Association (www.apparelandfootwear.org, Americans purchase more than 2.2 billion pairs of shoes yearly. More than 98% of those shoes are imported, and China is the largest supplier by far. Major Chinese shoe manufacturers include Yue Yuen Industrial Holdings Ltd. (which had about $4.9 billion in 2008 sales), Li Ning Co. Ltd. ($977 million in 2008 sales) and Belle International Holdings Ltd. ($1.6 billion in 2007 sales). While a handful of manufacturers, such as Allen-Edmonds (a high-end maker of men's shoes with about $100 million in annual sales), are able to maintain factories in the U.S., domestic manufacturing is all but dead.

Another exception is New Balance. This maker of high-end running and athletic shoes operates six factories in the U.S. While New Balance gets much of its inventory from overseas factories, the firm has taken an interesting position with its manufacturing philosophy. The only large American maker of athletic shoes, New Balance still has plants in the U.S., while its major competitors, such as Nike and Reebok, get most or all of their shoes from Asia.

20) Exercise Apparel Sales Fall Slightly

While most apparel sales are suffering percentage drops in the double digits for 2008 from 2007 figures, sales of exercise apparel, especially apparel for women, appear to be weathering the economic crisis much better. Wholesale sports apparel sales fell by just 2.2% in 2008 to $28.9 billion from 2007's record $29.5 billion, according to the Sporting Goods Manufacturers Association (SGMA). Designers and manufacturers such as Stella McCartney, Juicy Couture and Norma Kamali are promoting sports apparel, and big sports names such as Nike and Adidas are courting sales with an ever-increasing variety of styles that go from gym to nightclub.

While Americans (as well as residents of many other countries from Mexico to China) have been putting on weight, they have also developed a keen interest in sports apparel and workout gear to wear at the gym and in other leisure activities. This is one of the fastest-growing product categories in the apparel and shoe sector. Over 40 million Americans have some sort of gym membership, and they need appropriate clothing to wear while they workout.

Retailers such as Sports Authority, Inc. and Dick's Sporting Goods, Inc. are also promoting women's merchandise. They are expanding their lines of women's apparel and devoting more floor space to it.

Nike, Inc. and Apple Computer, Inc. sell a wireless system that allows a sensor inserted into specially designed Nike shoes (as well as other kinds of apparel including t-shirts, shorts and running pants) to transmit performance data wirelessly to Apple's iPod nano digital music player. Data recorded includes distance, pace, time and calories burned. The data can be downloaded to a computer using Apple's iTunes software and permanently stored on nikeplus.com. The system can be used by runners outdoors, and by people using cardio equipment indoors. Compatible cardio machines such as treadmills, elliptical machines and stationary bikes made by firms such as LifeFitness, Precor and Cybex have ports to which iPods can be connected to record pace, time and distance. In addition, iTunes is featuring upbeat music for workouts, favorite playlists from famous athletes and even real-time voice feedback during exercise. The sensor and transmitter, dubbed the Nike+iPod Sport Kit, goes for about $29 (plus the cost of the shoes or other apparel and the iPod nano). Adidas has attempted to provide similar sensor technology. Its latest effort is a partnership with Samsung called miCoach in which a sensor attached to Adidas running shoes links to the Samsung F110 music-mobile phone and a heart rate monitor as well as an online workout journal. The Adidas-Samsung system retails for about $600 for all components.

21) Nanotechnology Has a Growing Role in Sports Equipment

Nanotechnology will grow in importance in the sports industry as the strength and lightweight advantages of carbon nanotubes are utilized for such items as baseball bats, tennis rackets and golf clubs. In addition, nanotech-based fabrics will be incorporated to a growing extent in sports apparel for added strength, stain resistance, moisture wicking or other benefits.

Carbon nanotubes are molecules of pure carbon atoms joined together to form tubes one-billionth of a meter in diameter. Properly used, nanotubes offer amazing strength. A nanotube can be more than 20 times stronger than steel. Easton-Bell Sports, Inc., of Van Nuys, California, is using nanotube technology in new sports products. Easton-Bell, a firm that specializes in the manufacture of high-performance sports equipment, has introduced nanotube-based bicycle components and baseball bats. For example, Easton-Bell's MonkeyLite handlebar offers high strength, minimal weight and high resistance to material fatigue—all qualities that are greatly valued by bicycle enthusiasts.

Nanotechnology is impacting golf equipment as well. Nanostructures are being embedded in golf balls to help decrease airborne drag or increase strength and resiliency, making the balls shoot off the club head with more velocity. A Buffalo, New York-based NanoDymanics is selling a ball with these kinds of structures, as is Wilson Sports. In addition, golf club shafts such as the AccuFLEX Evolution brand use nano composite technology to decrease weight while increasing fiber density. The result is shafts that are stronger, more durable and provide better performance.

Products enhanced with nanotechnology sell at the upper end of the price scale, making them appropriate for the introduction of costly new technologies. However, over the long term, nanotechnology-based products will lessen in price to reach wider numbers of consumers. An excellent example is the growing use of nano-fibers with stain- and wrinkle-resistant qualities, which are already available in inexpensive lines of mass-market clothing.

22) High-Tech, Nanotech and Smart Fabrics Proliferate

With the advent of Rayon in the 1920s, high-tech fabrics were born. Rayon, introduced by DuPont as a "continuous filament viscose fiber," was then and is now durable and silky-soft, and it costs much less than organic fabrics made of silk. Today's high-tech fabrics are either treated with chemicals, polymers or combinations thereof, or specially engineered for durability, stain-proofing, wrinkle-resistance or weather protection. In addition to these wonders, scientists are producing smart fabrics, which are engineered on a molecular level for wearability advantages as well as an astounding array of potential protective and clinical abilities. Through the use of special fabrics capable of conducting data flow, telecommunications and computing abilities may also be enabled in apparel.

The abilities of high-tech materials to keep athletes dry and comfortable have sparked a $9-billion market for high-performance outdoor apparel. An excellent example of the power of this industry niche is the wildly successful Gore-Tex fabric produced by W.L. Gore & Associates, Inc. The fabric is a fluoropolymer, a manufactured fiber that forms a barrier to wind and water but still allows air to pass through it. Body heat and moisture can evaporate through Gore-Tex even while it protects from wind, rain, sleet or snow. It's used in everything from jackets to shoes to backpacks, and it generates impressive sales since apparel treated with Gore-Tex often costs three times as much as non-treated pieces. W.L. Gore's annual revenues are about $2.4 billion, and it employs more than 8,500 people.

A surprising material found in some apparel is silver. Long known to fight bacteria and odors, silver has been used historically to store foodstuffs. However, many manufacturers are finding new ways to use the metal. In 2006, Samsung Electronics launched a washer that utilizes silver ions to sanitize laundry without using hot water. Today, Adidas, Brooks Sports, Victoria's Secret and Polartec are using a silver-coated nylon fiber called X-Static (which is produced by Noble Biomaterials, Inc.). The fibers, which are used in shirts, pants, caps and socks, protect against odor and promote thermal regulation, since silver is a natural energy conductor. A company called NanoHorizons, Inc., www.nanohorizons.com, is furthering the cause of silver for use in apparel by developing an engineering process that disperses silver pellets uniformly through the materials used for textile applications. The process, which is marketed under the SmartSilver brand, prolongs the silver's presence in fabric even through repeated washings.

Yet another high-tech sports apparel example is Textronics, Inc.'s (www.textronicsinc.com) use of electro textiles. The fabric has circuitry, sensors and functional component woven in that render the material capable of enabling electronic devices such as cell phones of music players, providing heat for the wearer or sensing external changes such as shifts in temperature. Textronics makes a sports bra under the NuMetrex brand which senses the wearer's heart rate and communicates that data to a wrist monitor. Retailing for about $99 (including a combination wrist monitor/watch), the bras free female athletes from wearing separate heart rate monitor straps and sensors.

Swimwear maker Speedo International launched its LZR Racer suit in 2008. The $550 LZR Racer is a seamless suit made of fabric tested in NASA wind tunnels for its ability to reduce surface friction. In addition, the suit has panels that cover the torso, gluteal and upper hamstring muscles that reduce muscle and skin vibration. The result is staggering number of new world records set by swimmers wearing the new suits. Speedo has been inundated with orders, despite the suit's high price tag. NCAA swim teams are spending as much as $20,000 for a season's supply. Rival manufacturers are producing their own versions of the suit, including Tyr's Racer Light, which retails for $320 and BlueSeventy's Nero, which retails for $395.

Manufacturers are hoping to take high-tech fabrics indoors by applying new technology to fabrics used in suits, sweaters, ties and more. They believe that consumers will buy into clothing that can't be crushed when packed and is stain-proof as well as waterproof. Retailers such as Eddie Bauer are already stocking casual cotton pants made of nanotextiles—materials constructed at the molecular level of particles so tiny that moisture cannot penetrate them.

Another nanotech company, Schoeller Textil of Switzerland, produces a nanofinish called NanoSphere which repels liquids without affecting the feel and drape of the underlying fabric. Clothing manufacturers such as Beyond of Eugene, Oregon and Contourwear of Alameda, California use NanoSphere to coat everything from pants to jackets. The coating is also used for a line of luggage under the Victorinox brand, made by a division of TRG Group.

The future for high-tech fabrics and smart fabrics in the near term sounds to many like something out of science fiction. Nonetheless, specialized fabrics will be sensitive to a wide variety of external substances, including harmful toxins or chemical agents. The U.S. military has already incorporated patches worn on uniform cuffs that change color when harmful agents are detected in the surrounding air. Scientists at MIT have created smart fabrics that filter or shield wearers from radiation by combining synthetic fibers with an optical device called a dielectric mirror.

The possibilities are fascinating. Want to wear a favorite shirt in a different color? Smart fabrics made of winged fibers that change how special dyes reflect light can do the job. Engineers at the Australian Commonwealth Scientific and Research Organization (CSIRO) have even developed a t-shirt that can be played like a guitar (arm movements are beamed to a computer which generates sound, making "air guitar" players audible for the first time). What remains to be seen is how consumers respond to these innovations and how much they will be willing to pay for them.

Chapter 2

SPORTS INDUSTRY STATISTICS

Contents:

Sports Industry Overview

	Amount	Units	Year/Season	Source
Estimated Size of the Entire Sports Industry, U.S.	410.6	Bil. US$	2009	PRE
Annual Company Spending for Sports Advertising, U.S.	30	Bil. US$	2009	PRE
Major League Baseball (MLB)				
MLB League Revenue	6.2	Bil. US$	2009	PRE
Overall Operating Income	501	Mil. US$	2008	Forbes
Number of MLB Teams	30	Teams	2009	MLB
Average MLB Game Attendance (162 Game Season)	32,516	Spectators	2008	ESPN
Average MLB Team Value	482	Mil. US$	2008	Forbes
National Football League (NFL)				
NFL League Revenue	6.0	Bil. US$	2009	PRE
Overall Operating Income	790	Mil. US$	2008	Forbes
Number of NFL Teams	32	Teams	2009	NFL
Average NFL Game Attendance (16 Game Season)	68,034	Spectators	2008	ESPN
Average NFL Team Value	1.0	Bil. US$	2008	Forbes
National Basketball Association				
NBA League Revenue (Basketball Related Income)	3.2	Bil. US$	2008/09	PRE
Overall Operating Income	318	Mil. US$	2007/08	Forbes
Total Value of Media Contracts	7.4	Bil. US$	2008/09-15/16	Forbes
Number of NBA Teams	30	Teams	2008/09	NBA
Average NBA Game Attendance (82 Game Season)	17,497	Spectators	2007/08	ESPN
Average NBA Team Value	379	Mil. US$	2007/08	Forbes
National Hockey League				
NHL League Revenue	2.4	Bil. US$	2008/09	PRE
Overall Operating Income	141	Mil. US$	2007/08	Forbes
Number of NHL Teams	30	Teams	2008/09	NHL
Average NHL Game Attendance (82 Game Season)	17,476	Spectators	2008/09	ESPN
Average NHL Team Value	220	Mil. US$	2007/08	Forbes
Sporting Equipment Sales				
Revenues, U.S. Sporting Goods Manufacturers.*	66.3	Bil. US$	2008	SGMA
Retail Sporting Equipment Sales	42	Bil. US$	2009	PRE
Other Sports Industry Revenue				
Other Spectator Sports Leagues	3.3	Bil. US$	2009	PRE
Horse Racing	8	Bil. US$	2009	PRE
Golf Courses	19.5	Bil. US$	2009	PRE
Fitness & Recreational Centers	20	Bil. US$	2009	PRE
Other Amusement & Recreation	19	Bil. US$	2009	PRE
Other Revenues Associated With U.S. Sports Industry**	165	Bil. US$	2009	PRE

PRE = Plunkett Research estimate; SGMA = Sporting Goods Manufacturing Association.

* Includes sporting goods equipment, sports apparel, fitness equipment, recreational transport equipment and athletic footwear.
** All other revenues, including peripheral revenue such as sports-related publishing, facility construction, food service, licensing, sponsorships, travel, gambling, etc., estimated at 38.95% of all sports revenue.

Source: Plunkett Research, Ltd.

www.plunkettresearch.com

Selected U.S. Sports Industry Revenues: 2000-2007

(In Millions of US$; Latest Year Available)

NAICS Code	Kind of business	2007	2006	2005	2004	2003	2002	2001	2000
Selected sports industry revenues for employer firms									
7112	Spectator sports	28,757	26,531	24,402	23,659	22,445	22,313	20,392	19,339
711211	Sports teams and clubs	17,418	15,742	14,067	14,115	13,257	13,025	11,461	10,739
711212	Racetracks	7,877	7,584	7,358	7,022	6,582	6,702	6,473	6,349
711219	Other spectator sports	3,462	3,205	2,977	2,522	2,606	2,586	2,458	2,251
7113	Promoters of performing arts, sports, and similar events	18,830	17,187	14,338	13,571	12,872	12,168	10,993	10,098
7114	Agents & managers for artists, athletes, entertainers & other public figures	4,633	4,089	3,909	3,819	3,604	3,602	3,381	3,184
7139	Other amusement & recreation industries	57,103	54,559	51,795	49,814	47,611	46,674	44,012	42,833
71391	Golf courses and country clubs	19,279	19,082	18,533	17,880	16,987	17,533	16,862	16,692
71392	Skiing facilities	2,414	2,234	2,049	1,980	1,839	1,801	1,635	1,551
71393	Marinas	4,187	4,018	3,663	3,393	3,382	3,352	3,389	3,379
71394	Fitness & recreational sports centers	19,507	18,519	17,620	16,839	16,130	14,987	13,542	12,543
71395	Bowling centers	3,738	3,347	3,427	3,505	3,293	3,075	2,882	2,762
71399	All other amusement & recreation industries	7,978	7,359	6,503	6,217	5,980	5,926	5,702	5,906

NAICS Code	Kind of business	2007/06	2006/05	2005/04	2004/03	2003/02	2002/01	2001/00
Percent change in revenue for selected sports industries' employer firms								
7112	Spectator sports	8.4	8.7	3.1	5.4	0.6	9.4	5.4
711211	Sports teams and clubs	10.6	11.9	-0.3	6.5	1.8	13.6	6.7
711212	Racetracks	3.9	3.1	4.8	6.7	-1.8	3.5	2.0
711219	Other spectator sports	8.0	7.7	18.0	-3.2	0.8	5.2	9.2
7113	Promoters of performing arts, sports, and similar events	9.6	19.9	5.7	5.4	5.8	10.7	8.9
7114	Agents & managers for artists, athletes, entertainers & other public figures	13.3	4.6	2.4	6.0	0.1	6.5	6.2
7139	Other amusement & recreation industries	4.7	5.3	4.0	4.6	2.0	6.0	2.8
71391	Golf courses and country clubs	1.0	3.0	3.7	5.3	-3.1	4.0	1.0
71392	Skiing facilities	8.1	9.0	3.5	7.7	2.1	10.2	5.4
71393	Marinas	4.2	9.7	8.0	0.3	0.9	-1.1	0.3
71394	Fitness & recreational sports centers	5.3	5.1	4.6	4.4	7.6	10.7	8.0
71395	Bowling centers	11.7	-2.3	-2.2	6.4	7.1	6.7	4.3
71399	All other amusement & recreation industries	8.4	13.2	4.6	4.0	0.9	3.9	-3.5

Notes: Estimates are based on data from the 2007 Service Annual Survey and administrative data. Estimates for 2006 and prior years have been revised to reflect historical corrections to individual responses. Dollar volume estimates are published in millions of dollars; consequently, results may not be additive. Estimates have been adjusted using results of the 2002 Economic Census. Estimates cover taxable and tax-exempt firms and are not adjusted for price changes. The introduction and appendixes give information on confidentiality protection, sampling error, nonsampling error, sample design, and definitions. Links to this information on the Internet may be found at <www.census.gov/svsd/www/cv.html>.

Source: U.S. Census Bureau
Plunkett Research, Ltd.
www.plunkettresearch.com

Sports Industry Expenses & Sources of Revenue, U.S.: 2004-2007

(In Millions of US$; Latest Year Available)

NAICS Code	Sources of Revenue for Taxable Employer Firms	2007	2006	2005	2004	% Chg.: 2007/06
711211	**Sports Teams and Clubs**					
Total revenue		17,418	15,742	14,067	14,115	10.6
Admissions revenue		6,494	5,826	5,132	5,227	11.5
All other revenue		10,924	9,916	8,935	8,888	10.2
711212	**Racetracks**					
Total revenue		7,877	7,584	7,358	7,022	3.9
Admissions revenue		1,310	1,140	1,116	1,098	14.9
All other revenue		6,567	6,444	6,242	5,924	1.9
711219	**Other Spectator Sports**					
Total revenue		3,462	3,205	2,977	2,522	8.0
Admissions revenue		435	407	431	396	6.9
All other revenue		3,027	2,798	2,546	2,126	8.2
NAICS Code	**Expenses for Employer Firms**	**2007**	**2006**	**2005**	**2004**	**% Chg.: 2007/06**
Percent change in revenue for selected sports industries' employer firms						
7112	Spectator sports	27,790	25,836	23,943	24,059	7.6
711211	Sports teams and clubs	18,807	17,869	15,773	15,905	5.2
711212	Racetracks	5,718	5,042	5,313	5,639	13.4
711219	Other spectator sports	3,264	2,925	2,857	2,515	11.6
7113	Promoters of performing arts, sports, and similar events	15,240	14,425	12,361	11,686	5.6
7114	Agents & managers for artists, athletes, entertainers & other public figures	3,516	3,097	2,995	3,197	13.5
7139	Other amusement & recreation industries	49,748	47,990	46,425	44,338	3.7
71391	Golf courses and country clubs	18,227	18,175	17,650	16,757	0.3
71392	Skiing facilities	1,718	1,649	1,568	1,525	4.2
71393	Marinas	2,591	2,557	2,404	2,330	1.3
71394	Fitness & recreational sports centers	17,674	16,872	16,895	15,893	4.8
71395	Bowling centers	3,043	2,747	2,593	2,637	10.8
71399	All other amusement & recreation industries	6,494	5,991	5,315	5,197	8.4

Notes: Estimates are based on data from the 2007 Service Annual Survey and administrative data. Estimates for 2006 and prior years have been revised to reflect historical corrections to individual responses. Dollar volume estimates are published in millions of dollars; consequently, results may not be additive. Estimates have been adjusted using results of the 2002 Economic Census. Estimates cover taxable and tax-exempt firms and are not adjusted for price changes. The introduction and appendixes give information on confidentiality protection, sampling error, nonsampling error, sample design, and definitions. Links to this information on the Internet may be found at <www.census.gov/svsd/www/cv.html>.

Source: U.S. Census Bureau

Plunkett Research, Ltd.

www.plunkettresearch.com

U.S. Spectator Sports, Performing Arts & Related Industries, Breakdown of Expenses: 2004-2007

(In Millions of US$; Latest Year Available)

Expenses	2007	2006	2005	2004	% Chg.: 07/06
Total Operating Expenses	**69,853**	**63,323**	**58,264**	**57,417**	**10.3**
Personnel costs	32,822	31,014	27,427	27,165	5.8
Gross annual payroll	28,445	27,262	24,040	23,927	4.3
Employer's cost for fringe benefits	3,486	2,960	2,738	2,581	17.8
Health insurance	1,080	NA	NA	NA	NA
Pension plans	953	NA	NA	NA	NA
Defined benefit pension plans	624	NA	NA	NA	NA
Defined contribution plans	329	NA	NA	NA	NA
Other	1,453	NA	NA	NA	NA
Temporary staff & leased employee expense	891	793	650	657	12.4
Expensed materials, parts & supplies (not for resale)	1,853	1,736	1,640	1,571	6.7
Expensed equipment	208	201	204	193	3.5
Expensed purchase of other materials, parts & supplies	1,645	1,535	1,436	1,377	7.2
Expensed purchased services	5,898	5,416	5,478	5,267	8.9
Expensed purchases of software	96	90	114	106	6.7
Purchased electricity and fuels (except motor fuels)	660	616	542	516	7.1
Purchased electricity	521	NA	NA	NA	NA
Purchased fuels (except motor fuels)	139	NA	NA	NA	NA
Lease & rental payments	2,608	2,214	2,257	2,159	17.8
for machinery, equipment & other tangible items	707	NA	NA	NA	NA
for land, buildings, structures, etc.	1,901	NA	NA	NA	NA
Purchased repair & maintenance	554	599	S	S	-7.5
to machinery & equipment	285	NA	NA	NA	NA
to buildings, structures & offices	269	NA	NA	NA	NA
Purchased advertising & promotional services	1,981	1,897	1,770	1,714	4.4
Other operating expenses	29,282	25,156	23,719	23,415	16.4
Depreciation & amortization charges	2,937	2,631	2,624	2,661	11.6
Governmental taxes & license fees	758	883	879	814	-14.2
All other operating expenses	25,587	21,642	20,216	19,940	18.2

Notes: Estimates are based on data from the 2007 Service Annual Survey and administrative data. Estimates for 2006 and prior years have been revised to reflect historical corrections to individual responses. Dollar volume estimates are published in millions of dollars; consequently, results may not be additive. Estimates have been adjusted using results of the 2002 Economic Census. Estimates cover taxable and tax-exempt firms and are not adjusted for price changes. The introduction and appendixes give information on confidentiality protection, sampling error, nonsampling error, sample design, and definitions. Links to this information on the Internet may be found at <www.census.gov/svsd/www/cv.html>.

S = Estimate does not meet publication standards because of high sampling variability (coefficient of variation is greater than 30%) or poor response quality (total quantity response rate is less than 50%). Unpublished estimates derived from this table by subtraction are subject to these same limitations and should not be attributed to the U.S. Census Bureau. For a description of publication standards and the total quantity response rate, see http://www.census.gov/quality/S20-0_v1.0_Data_Release.pdf.

Source: U.S. Census Bureau
Plunkett Research, Ltd.
www.plunkettresearch.com

Estimated Annual Sporting Goods Stores Retail Sales, Inventories & Purchases: 1999-2007

(In Millions of US$; Latest Year Available)

Annual Retail Sales: SGHBMS* (NAICS 451)

1999	2000	2001	2002	2003	2004	2005	2006	2007
72,764	76,112	77,138	76,988	77,335	80,061	81,822	84,492	86,906

Annual Retail Sales: Sporting Goods Stores (NAICS 45111)

1999	2000	2001	2002	2003	2004	2005	2006	2007
23,826	25,436	26,286	26,347	27,168	28,853	30,881	34,141	36,281

End-of-Year Retail Inventories: SGHBMS* (NAICS 451)

1999	2000	2001	2002	2003	2004	2005	2006	2007
18,519	19,935	19,607	19,297	19,520	20,530	20,592	21,317	22,501

Annual Purchases: SGHBMS* (NAICS 451)

1999	2000	2001	2002	2003	2004	2005	2006	2007
46,191	48,165	47,150	47,394	47,473	48,819	49,849	51,822	52,934

Gross Margin: SGHBMS* (NAICS 451)

1999	2000	2001	2002	2003	2004	2005	2006	2007
27,834	29,363	29,660	29,284	30,085	32,252	32,035	33,395	35,156

Gross Margin as a Percentage of Sales: SGHBMS* (NAICS 451)

1999	2000	2001	2002	2003	2004	2005	2006	2007
38.3	38.6	38.5	38.0	38.9	40.3	39.2	39.5	40.5

Per Capita Retail Sales: SGHBMS* (NAICS 451) *(In US$)*

1999	2000	2001	2002	2003	2004	2005	2006	2007
267	270	271	268	266	273	277	283	288

End-of-Year Accounts Receivable: SGHBMS* (NAICS 451)

Total			Open-end			Closed-End		
2005	2006	2007	2005	2006	2007	2005	2006	2007
1,062	1,110	1,308	602.0	620.0	751.0	S	S	S

Note: Estimates are based on data from the Monthly Retail Trade Survey, Annual Retail Trade Survey and administrative records. They have been adjusted using results of the 2002 Economic Census. Retail total and other subsector totals may include data for kinds of business not shown. Estimates have not been adjusted for price changes. Additional information on confidentiality protection, sampling error, nonsampling error, sample design, and definitions can be found on the Internet at www.census.gov/svsd/www/artstbl.html.

* SGHBMS = Sporting goods, hobby, book and music stores.

S = Estimate does not meet publication standards because of high sampling variability (coefficient of variation is greater than 30%) or poor response quality (total quantity response rate is less than 50%). Unpublished estimates derived from this table by subtraction are subject to these same limitations and should not be attributed to the U.S. Census Bureau. For a description of publication standards and the total quantity response rate, see http://www.census.gov/quality/S20-0_v1.0_Data_Release.pdf.

Source: U.S. Census Bureau
Plunkett Research, Ltd.
www.plunkettresearch.com

Exports of Sporting & Athletic Equipment, U.S.: 2001-2008

(In Thousands of US$; Latest Year Available)

Country	2001	2002	2003	2004	2005	2006	2007	2008	% Chg.: '07-'08
Canada	368,639	369,313	368,036	368,924	357,767	374,941	390,787	437,814	12.0%
United Kingdom	271,138	256,885	248,996	278,109	278,897	258,371	280,832	257,237	-8.4%
Japan	378,749	286,279	260,710	254,248	252,897	271,653	246,353	247,854	0.6%
Korea	58,259	60,287	62,051	58,172	85,546	104,385	133,189	125,337	-5.9%
Australia	65,586	65,414	71,912	88,587	97,037	97,802	101,694	104,270	2.5%
Netherlands	35,796	47,109	60,353	74,722	91,299	102,972	99,785	103,452	3.7%
Mexico	97,327	81,520	85,627	72,375	80,933	86,427	78,357	69,051	-11.9%
Hong Kong	53,358	61,504	68,819	63,923	75,148	69,345	58,572	59,419	1.4%
Germany	71,183	67,204	63,180	68,499	53,439	54,330	57,565	59,260	2.9%
Singapore	31,371	30,762	30,134	30,341	32,897	39,965	34,830	40,174	15.3%
Belgium	16,241	18,522	22,792	23,181	18,390	21,743	24,176	36,928	52.7%
China	13,524	12,179	19,850	31,054	26,685	28,901	34,694	34,765	0.2%
France	42,358	36,662	35,787	46,191	43,682	51,250	46,140	30,558	-33.8%
South Africa	14,957	11,724	14,613	20,565	29,363	28,671	33,975	30,087	-11.4%
Sweden	21,293	21,973	20,562	29,699	24,948	24,953	26,278	26,116	-0.6%
Russia	8,963	13,801	11,434	15,500	16,531	18,653	19,601	23,989	22.4%
Thailand	8,981	10,552	11,010	10,988	17,014	14,389	14,643	20,883	42.6%
United Arab Emirates	10,517	13,554	11,927	15,484	13,315	13,941	17,127	20,766	21.2%
Saudi Arabia	9,502	9,478	9,176	10,046	11,973	14,582	15,690	20,679	31.8%
Italy	25,851	20,031	20,351	20,383	20,884	22,097	17,496	19,112	9.2%
Subtotal :	1,603,590	1,494,752	1,497,321	1,580,988	1,628,644	1,699,373	1,731,782	1,767,751	2.1%
All Other:	259,424	213,384	232,961	283,552	296,217	326,102	354,486	389,513	9.9%
Total	**1,863,015**	**1,708,136**	**1,730,283**	**1,864,540**	**1,924,861**	**2,025,475**	**2,086,268**	**2,157,263**	**3.4%**

Note: Data have been compiled from tariff and trade data from the U.S. Department of Commerce and the U.S. International Trade Commission.

Source: U.S. International Trade Administration
Plunkett Research, Ltd.
www.plunkettresearch.com

Imports of Sporting & Athletic Equipment, U.S.: 2001-2008

(In Thousands of US$; Latest Year Available)

Country	2001	2002	2003	2004	2005	2006	2007	2008	% Chg.: '07-'08
China	1,973,157	2,379,111	2,699,688	3,135,848	3,499,449	4,033,723	4,287,072	4,304,776	0.4%
Taiwan	465,792	437,285	410,084	412,179	424,491	430,590	421,391	432,613	2.7%
Canada	366,278	342,074	349,952	311,689	276,326	290,151	274,250	230,114	-16.1%
Mexico	204,976	191,538	202,526	190,505	172,211	183,681	195,006	178,561	-8.4%
Thailand	171,349	162,251	177,659	163,988	136,393	147,257	133,184	148,142	11.2%
Japan	144,756	133,865	118,179	124,308	130,926	133,426	119,227	116,184	-2.6%
Indonesia	72,442	70,427	64,662	63,480	72,574	90,213	116,175	87,317	-24.8%
Korea	129,533	97,320	83,104	87,951	77,922	79,190	77,408	61,889	-20.0%
Vietnam	175	10,539	16,826	14,874	21,303	33,062	49,502	61,227	23.7%
Italy	84,632	72,102	67,180	57,275	53,210	66,772	61,789	56,218	-9.0%
Philippines	53,048	55,618	54,530	45,290	57,306	56,319	62,521	54,423	-13.0%
Austria	55,100	57,461	61,142	62,004	47,435	49,769	48,622	46,723	-3.9%
Pakistan	42,612	42,038	37,886	37,000	37,375	42,482	38,528	41,136	6.8%
Germany	46,478	46,466	52,225	45,031	41,479	40,691	42,908	40,441	-5.7%
France	72,296	63,747	67,117	65,076	54,801	45,897	45,674	38,039	-16.7%
Hong Kong	37,565	36,831	51,923	55,016	38,809	39,497	57,198	37,979	-33.6%
Malaysia	37,394	33,639	30,789	39,874	37,907	33,390	37,686	36,599	-2.9%
Czech Republic	6,409	4,093	9,600	27,552	25,954	23,785	32,869	34,502	5.0%
India	11,301	11,640	12,766	13,674	15,600	17,614	18,650	21,572	15.7%
Estonia	4,998	7,575	9,014	14,276	14,626	15,364	17,246	19,730	14.4%
Subtotal :	4,002,984	4,277,643	4,598,812	4,984,464	5,250,326	5,860,666	4,239,900	4,536,023	7.0%
All Other:	196,755	189,531	189,288	214,935	204,675	218,678	162,281	164,380	1.3%
Total	**4,199,739**	**4,467,174**	**4,788,101**	**5,199,398**	**5,455,002**	**6,079,344**	**4,402,181**	**4,700,402**	**6.8%**

Note: Data have been compiled from tariff and trade data from the U.S. Department of Commerce and the U.S. International Trade Commission.

Source: U.S. International Trade Administration
Plunkett Research, Ltd.
www.plunkettresearch.com

Overview of the Media Contracts of the Four Big Sports

National Football League (NFL)

Network TV	CBS: Sun. afternoon AFC games, $3.73 billion, 2006-11, Super Bowl in '07
	FOX: Sun. afternoon NFC games, $4.27 billion, 2006-11, Super Bowl in '08
	NBC: Sunday night games, $3.6 billion, 2006-11, Super Bowl in '09 and '12
Cable TV	ESPN: Monday Night Football, $8.8 billion, 2006-13
Satellite TV	DirecTV: Out-of-market games, $3.5 billion, 2006-2010
Terrestrial Radio	Westwood One: $30 million, 2009-2010; Sports USA Radio Network
Satellite Radio	Sirius: $220 million, 2004-10
Video Games	EA: Exclusive deal, > $350 million[1], 2009-2012
Internet	NFL.com (formerly operated by ESPN and later CBS, now run by NFL).

Major League Baseball (MLB)

Network TV	FOX: $3 billion (w/ TBS), 2007-13, Saturday afternoon games (exclusive), All-Star Game, alternate League Championship Series, World Series	
Cable TV	ESPN: $2.4 billion, 2006-2013, Mon. & Wed. night, Sun. night (exclusive)	TBS: $3 billion (w/ FOX), 2007-13, tiebreaker games, Division Series, alt. League Championship Series
	iNDemand: Out-of-market games & Baseball channel, 2007-13[1]	
Satellite TV	DirecTV: Out-of-market games & Baseball channel, < $700 million[2], 2007-2013	
Terrestrial Radio	ESPN Radio: ~$66 million, 2005-2010, Nat'l broadcast rights, Sunday Night Baseball, playoffs, World Series (exclusive). Teams also have their own regional networks.	
Satellite Radio	XM: $650 million, 2005-15	
Video Games	Take-Two: $150 million, 2006-2012[3]	
Internet	MLB Advanced Media: Out-of-market games (MLBtv)	

National Basketball Association (NBA)

Network TV	ABC: (w/ESPN): ~$3.5 bil., 2008/09-2015/16, 15 season & 5 playoff games, NBA Finals
Cable TV	ESPN: (w/ABC): ~$3.5 bil., 2008/09-2015/16, 75 season games, some playoffs & NBA Draft
	TNT: ~$3.5 bil., 2008/09-2015/16, 52 season games & some playoffs
Satellite TV	DirecTV: Out-of-market games (exclusive), starting 2009/10[1]
Terrestrial Radio	ESPN Radio: 2008/09-2015/16[1]
Satellite Radio	Sirius: Exclusive contract, 24/7 NBA Radio[1]
Video Games	Electronic Arts, Take-Two, Sony Computer Entertainment America, Midway Games & Atari
Internet	NBA TV: 96 regular season games & 9 playoff games

National Hockey League (NHL)

Network TV	NBC: Revenue-sharing agreement	**Canada**: CBC
Cable TV	Versus: 3 years, 2009-2011, $120 mil.	**Canada**: TSN
Satellite TV	DirecTV & Dish: Out-of-market games (non-exclusive)	
Terrestrial Radio	Non-exclusive	
Satellite Radio	Sirius & XM: Non-exclusive deals, revenue-sharing agreements	
Video Games	EA, Sony, Take-Two	

[1] No dollar amount disclosed.
[2] The deal had originally been for exclusive out-of-market broadcast rights at $700 million. The contract was restructured when MLB was forced to offer the same package on cable.
[3] Third-party rights only. Microsoft, Sony and Nintendo may make games for their platforms.

Source: Plunkett Research Ltd.

www.plunkettresearch.com

Sports Industry Employment by Business Type, U.S.: 2003-2008

(Annual Estimates in Thousands of Employed Workers; Not Seasonally Adjusted)

NAICS Code[1]	Industry Sector	2003	2004	2005	2006	2007	2008
Leisure & Hospitality							
711	Performing arts & spectator sports*	371.7	367.5	376.3	398.5	405.0	406.3
7112	Spectator sports	123.9	120.3	123.3	130.8	131.1	128.8
711211	Sports teams & clubs	56.9	55.7	57.5	64.5	63.8	63.5
711212	Racetracks	45.1	41.3	41.9	42.3	43.0	39.9
711219	Other spectator sports	21.9	23.3	23.9	24.0	24.4	25.3
7113 7114	Arts & sports promoters & agents & managers for public figures	86.9	89.6	93.4	100.7	106.9	109.4
7139	Other amusement & recreation industries	1,043.4	1,069.1	1,094.6	1,115.1	1,138.2	1,136.8
71391	Golf courses & country clubs	308.7	323.3	345.7	344.6	353.0	351.5
71392	Skiing facilities	35.2	34.0	31.5	34.2	36.5	36.9
71393	Marinas	28.4	30.5	30.5	31.6	34.3	32.0
71394	Fitness & recreational sports centers	472.8	483.9	493.5	504.2	508.3	510.3
71395	Bowling centers	75.7	76.3	76.0	76.8	77.9	76.6
71399	All other amusement & recreation industries	122.5	121.2	117.4	123.8	128.3	129.6
Wholesale Trade							
42391	Sporting goods	47.8	48.1	47.8	49.0	50.2	48.1
Retail Trade							
45111	Sporting goods stores	204.0	209.5	218.2	232.3	244.6	250.3

Occupation Code	May 2008 Data	# Employed[2]	Median Hourly	Mean Hourly	Mean Annual[3]	Mean RSE[4]
13-1011	Agents & Business Managers of Artists, Performers & Athletes	12,110	30.26	39.21	$81,550	4.0%
27-2021	Athletes & Sports Competitors	13,960	[5]	[5]	$79,460	5.5%
27-2022	Coaches & Scouts	175,720	[5]	[5]	$35,580	1.0%
27-2023	Umpires, Referees & Other Sports Officials	12,970	[5]	[5]	$28,330	2.0%

[1] For a full description of the NAICS codes used in this table, see www.census.gov/epcd/www/naics.html.
[2] Estimates for detailed occupations do not sum to the totals because the totals include occupations not shown separately. Estimates do not include self-employed workers.
[3] Annual wages have been calculated by multiplying the hourly mean wage by a "year-round, full-time" hours figure of 2,080 hours; for those occupations where there is not an hourly mean wage published, the annual wage has been directly calculated from the reported survey data.
[4] The relative standard error (RSE) is a measure of the reliability of a survey statistic. The smaller the relative standard error, the more precise the estimate.
[5] Wages for some occupations that do not generally work year-round or full time are reported either as hourly wages or annual salaries depending on how they are typically paid.

Source: U.S. Bureau of Labor Statistics
Plunkett Research, Ltd.
www.plunkettresearch.com

Chapter 3

IMPORTANT SPORTS INDUSTRY CONTACTS

Addresses, Telephone Numbers and Internet Sites

Contents:

I. Advertising/Marketing Industry Associations

National Sports Marketing Network (NSMN)
Phone: 212-227-1300
E-mail Address:
jenkarpf@sportsmarketingnetwork.com
Web Address: www.sportsmarketingnetwork.com
The National Sports Marketing Network (NSMN) seeks to serve as the national organizing body for networking opportunities, education and industry discussion for the sports business industry. Chapters are located in major cities including Atlanta, Boston, Chicago, Denver, Los Angeles, New York City, Philadelphia, San Francisco and Washington, DC.

Sport Marketing Association (SMA)
University of Memphis
204B Fieldhouse
Memphis, TN 38152 US
Fax: 901-678-5014
E-mail Address:
office@sportmarketingassociation.com
Web Address: www.sportmarketingassociation.com
The Sport Marketing Association (SMA) is a professional association for sport marketing practitioners and academics. The SMA, whose

business operations are housed at the University of Memphis Bureau of Sport & Leisure Commerce, seeks to develop beneficial relationships between sport marketing professionals and academicians and expand the field's body of knowledge.

Sports Marketing Association-Villanova
Attn: Marketing and Promotions
800 Lancaster Ave.
Villanova, PA 19805 US
Phone: 610-519-6594
E-mail Address: *l.anderson@villanova.edu*
Web Address: villanova.cstv.com/ot/promos/spec-rel/nova-sma.html
The Sports Marketing Association-Villanova is a foundation of undergraduate students who interact with and learn from the Villanova University Athletics Department. The purpose of this association is to provide support for the Athletics Department and learn and experience various aspects of the department as a whole.

II. Automobile Racing Associations

Fédération Internationale de l'Automobile (FIA)
8 Place de la Concorde
Paris, 75008 France
Phone: 33-1-43-12-4455
Fax: 33-1-43-12-4466
Web Address: www.fia.com
The Fédération Internationale de l'Automobile (FIA) is the governing body for world motor sport and the federation of one of the world's leading motoring organizations. Founded in 1904, with headquarters in Paris, the FIA is a nonprofit association. It brings together 219 national motoring and sporting organizations from 130 countries on five continents. Its member clubs represent over 100 million motorists and their families.

Singapore Motor Sports Association
20 Maxwell Rd.
10-18 Maxwell House
069113 Singapore
Phone: 65-6227-7889
Fax: 65-6227-0911
E-mail Address: *smsa@pacific.net.sg*
Web Address: www.smsa.org.sg
The Singapore Motor Sports Association is a nonproft organization representing and promoting the motor sports and racing in Singapore.

III. Broadcasting, Cable, Radio & TV Associations

American Sportscasters Association (ASA)
225 Broadway , Ste. 2030
New York, NY 10007 US
Phone: 212-227-8080
Fax: 212-571-0556
E-mail Address:
info@americansportscastersonline.com
Web Address: www.americansportscasters.com
The American Sportscasters Association (ASA) is a professional organization for the promotion and support of sports broadcasters. The ASA is also a resource for those interested in becoming sportscasters.

IV. Careers-First Time Jobs/New Grads

Black Collegian Online (The)
140 Carondelet St.
New Orleans, LA 70130 US
Phone: 504-523-0154
Web Address: www.black-collegian.com
The Black Collegian Online features listings for job and internship opportunities, as well as other tools for students of color; it is the web site of The Black Collegian Magazine, published by IMDiversity, Inc. The site includes a list of the top 100 minority corporate employers and an assessment of job opportunities.

Collegegrad.com, Inc.
234 E. College Ave., Ste. 200
State College, PA 16801 US
Phone: 262-375-6700
Toll Free: 1-800-991-4642
Web Address: www.collegegrad.com
Collegegrad.com, Inc. offers in-depth resources for college students and recent grads seeking entry-level jobs.

Job Web
Nat'l Association of Colleges & Employers (NACE)
62 Highland Ave.
Bethlehem, PA 18017-9085 US
Phone: 610-868-1421
Fax: 610-868-0208
Toll Free: 800-544-5272
E-mail Address: *editors@jobweb.com*
Web Address: www.jobweb.com

Job Web, owned and sponsored by National Association of Colleges and Employers (NACE), displays job openings and employer descriptions. The site also offers a database of career fairs, searchable by state or keyword, with contact information.

MBAjobs.net
Fax: 413-556-8849
E-mail Address: *contact@mbajobs.net*
Web Address: www.mbajobs.net
MBAjobs.net is a unique international service for MBA students and graduates, employers, recruiters and business schools. The MBAjobs.net service is provided by WebInfoCo.

MonsterTRAK
11845 W. Olympic Blvd., Ste. 500
Los Angeles, CA 90064 US
Toll Free: 800-999-8725
E-mail Address: *trakstudent@monster.com*
Web Address: www.monstertrak.monster.com
MonsterTRAK features links to hundreds of university and college career centers across the U.S. with entry-level job listings categorized by industry. Major companies can also utilize MonsterTRAK.

National Association of Colleges and Employers (NACE)
62 Highland Ave.
Bethlehem, PA 18017-9085 US
Phone: 610-868-1421
Fax: 610-868-0208
Toll Free: 800-544-5272
E-mail Address: *mcollins@naceweb.org*
Web Address: www.naceweb.org
The National Association of Colleges and Employers (NACE) is a premier U.S. organization representing college placement offices and corporate recruiters who focus on hiring new grads.

V. Careers-General Job Listings

Career Exposure, Inc.
805 S. W. Broadway, Ste. 2250
Portland, OR 97205 US
Phone: 503-221-7779
Fax: 503-221-7780
E-mail Address: *lisam@mackenzie-marketing.com*
Web Address: www.careerexposure.com
Career Exposure, Inc. is an online career center and job placement service, with resources for employers, recruiters and job seekers.

CareerBuilder, Inc.
200 N. LaSalle St., Ste. 1100
Chicago, IL 60601 US
Phone: 773-527-3600
Toll Free: 800-638-4212
Web Address: www.careerbuilder.com
CareerBuilder, Inc. focuses on the needs of companies and also provides a database of job openings. The site has 1.5 million jobs posted by 300,000 employers, and receives an average 23 million unique visitors monthly. The company also operates online career centers for 150 newspapers, 1,000 partners and other online portals such as America Online. Resumes are sent directly to the company, and applicants can set up a special e-mail account for job-seeking purposes. CareerBuilder is primarily a joint venture between three newspaper giants: The McClatchy Company (which recently acquired former partner Knight Ridder), Gannett Co., Inc. and Tribune Company. In 2007, Microsoft acquired a minority interest in CareerBuilder, allowing the site to ally itself with MSN.

CareerOneStop
Toll Free: 877-348-0502
E-mail Address: *info@careeronestop.org*
Web Address: www.careeronestop.org
CareerOneStop is operated by the employment commissions of various state agencies. It contains job listings in both the private sector and in government. CareerOneStop is sponsored by the U.S. Department of Labor. It includes a wide variety of useful career resources and workforce information.

JobCentral
DirectEmployers Association, Inc.
9002 N. Purdue Rd., Quad III, Ste. 100
Indianapolis, IN 46268 US
Phone: 317-874-9000
Fax: 317-874-9100
Toll Free: 866-268-6206
E-mail Address: *info@jobcentral.com*
Web Address: www.jobcentral.com
JobCentral, operated by the nonprofit DirectEmployers Association, Inc., links users directly to hundreds of thousands of job opportunities posted on the sites of participating employers, thus bypassing the usual job search sites. This saves employers money and allows job seekers to access many more job opportunities.

LaborMarketInfo
Employment Dev. Dept., Labor Market Info. Div.

800 Capitol Mall, MIC 83
Sacramento, CA 95814 US
Phone: 916-262-2162
Fax: 916-262-2352
Toll Free: 800-480-3287
Web Address: www.labormarketinfo.edd.ca.gov
LaborMarketInfo, formerly the California Cooperative Occupational Information System, is geared to providing job seekers and employers a wide range of resources, namely the ability to find, access and use labor market information and services. It provides demographical statistics for employment on both a local and regional level, as well as career searching tools for California residents. The web site is sponsored by California's Employment Development Office.

Recruiters Online Network
947 Essex Ln.
Medina, OH 44256 US
Phone: 888-364-4667
Fax: 888-237-8686
E-mail Address: *info@recruitersonline.com*
Web Address: www.recruitersonline.com
The Recruiters Online Network provides job postings from thousands of recruiters, Careers Online Magazine, a resume database, as well as other career resources.

True Careers, Inc.
Web Address: www.truecareers.com
True Careers, Inc. offers job listings and provides an array of career resources. The company also offers a search of over 2 million scholarships. It is partnered with CareerBuilder.com, which powers its career information and resume posting functions.

USAJOBS
U.S. Office of Personnel Management
1900 E St. NW
Washington, DC 20415 US
Phone: 202-606-1800
Web Address: usajobs.opm.gov
USAJOBS, a program of the U.S. Office of Personnel Management, is the official job site for the U.S. Federal Government. It provides a comprehensive list of U.S. government jobs, allowing users to search for employment by location; agency; type of work, using the Federal Government's numerical identification code, the General Schedule (GS) Series; or by senior executive positions. It also has a special veterans' employment section; an information center, offering resume and interview tips and other useful information such as hiring trends and a glossary of Federal terms; and allows users to create a profile and post a resume.

Wall Street Journal - CareerJournal
Wall Street Journal
200 Liberty St.
New York, NY 10281 US
Phone: 212-416-2000
Toll Free: 800-568-7625
E-mail Address: *onelinejournal@wsj.com*
Web Address: www.online.wsj.com/careers
The Wall Street Journal's CareerJournal, an executive career site, features a job database with thousands of available positions; career news and employment related articles; and advice regarding resume writing, interviews, networking, office life and job hunting.

Yahoo! HotJobs
45 W. 18th St., 6th Fl.
New York, NY 10011 US
Phone: 646-351-5300
Web Address: www.hotjobs.yahoo.com
Yahoo! HotJobs, designed for experienced professionals, employers and job seekers, is a Yahoo-owned site that provides company profiles, a resume posting service and a resume workshop. The site allows posters to block resumes from being viewed by certain companies and provides a notification service of new jobs.

VI. Careers-Job Reference Tools

NewsVoyager
Newspaper Assoc. of America
4401 Wilson Blvd., Ste. 900
Arlington, VA 22203-1867 US
Phone: 571-366-1000
Fax: 571-366-1195
E-mail Address: *sally.clarke@naa.org*
Web Address: www.newsvoyager.com
NewsVoyager, a service of the Newspaper Association of America (NAA), links individuals to local, national and international newspapers. Job seekers can search through thousands of classified sections.

Vault.com, Inc.
75 Varick St., 8th Fl.
New York, NY 10013 US
Phone: 212-366-4212
E-mail Address: *feedback@staff.vault.com*
Web Address: www.vault.com

Vault.com, Inc. is a comprehensive career web site for employers and employees, with job postings and valuable information on a wide variety of industries. Vault gears many of its features toward MBAs. The site has been recognized by Forbes and Fortune Magazines.

VII. Careers-Sports

Jobs in Sports
2038 N. Clark St., Ste. 107
Chicago, IL 60614-4713 US
E-mail Address: *comments@jobsinsports.com*
Web Address: www.jobsinsports.com
Jobs in Sports is an employment web site that provides job listings in areas including sports marketing, sports media, sales, health and fitness, computers and administration, as well as other job resources.

National Sports Employment News
Web Address: www.sportsemploymentnews.com
National Sports Employment News is an employment agency for the sports industry.

SportManagementClub.com
P.O. Box 18012
Cleveland Heights, OH 44118-0012 US
E-mail Address: *info@sportmanagementclub.com*
Web Address: www.sportmanagementclub.com
SportManagementClub.com provides access to sports jobs information, an internship database, sports career tips and other information and services for sports career seekers.

Sports Careers
2990 E. Northern Ave., Ste. B101
Phoenix, AZ 85028 US
Phone: 602-485-5555
Fax: 480-467-0196
E-mail Address: *info@sportscareers.com*
Web Address: www.sportscareers.com
Sports Careers offers a range of services to help individuals and employers in the sports industry, including job listings, a resume bank, industry contacts and salary information.

Sports Job Board
E-mail Address: *info@sportsjobboard.com*
Web Address: www.sportsjobboard.com
The Sports Job Board is an employment website for the sports industry.

SportsCastingJobs.com
Phone: 303-623-5565
E-mail Address: *comments@sportscastingjobs.com*
Web Address: www.sportscastingjobs.com
SportsCastingJobs.com is an online employment site for sportscasters. The site was created by veteran sportscaster Dave Benz in 1999.

Women Sports Jobs
Women's Sport Services, LLC
P.O. Box 11
Huntington Beach, CA 92648 US
Phone: 714-848-1201
Fax: 714-848-5111
E-mail Address: *Feedback@WSServices.com*
Web Address: www.womensportsjobs.com
Women Sports Jobs is an employment web site specializing in jobs for women in the sports industry. The site is offered by Women's Sport Services, LLC.

Work in Sports, LLC
7335 E. Acoma Dr., Ste. 200
Scottsdale, AZ 85260 US
Phone: 480-905-7221
Fax: 480-905-7231
E-mail Address: *info@workinsports.com*
Web Address: www.workinsports.com
Work in Sports, LLC is an online employment resource for the sports industry that posts hundreds of jobs on its web site.

VIII. Corporate Information Resources

bizjournals.com
120 W. Morehead St., Ste. 400
Charlotte, NC 28202 US
Web Address: www.bizjournals.com
Bizjournals.com is the online media division of American City Business Journals, the publisher of dozens of leading city business journals nationwide. It provides access to research into the latest news regarding companies small and large.

Business Wire
44 Montgomery St., 39th Fl.
San Francisco, CA 94104 US
Phone: 415-986-4422
Fax: 415-788-5335
Toll Free: 800-227-0845
Web Address: www.businesswire.com
Business Wire offers news releases, industry- and company-specific news, top headlines, conference calls, IPOs on the Internet, media services and access

to tradeshownews.com and BW Connect On-line through its informative and continuously updated web site.

Edgar Online, Inc.
50 Washington St., 11th Fl.
Norwalk, CT 06854 US
Phone: 203-852-5666
Fax: 203-852-5667
Toll Free: 800-416-6651
Web Address: www.edgar-online.com
Edgar Online, Inc. is a gateway and search tool for viewing corporate documents, such as annual reports on Form 10-K, filed with the U.S. Securities and Exchange Commission.

PR Newswire Association LLC
810 7th Ave., 32nd Fl.
New York, NY 10019 US
Phone: 201-360-6700
Toll Free: 800-832-5522
E-mail Address: *information@prnewswire.com*
Web Address: www.prnewswire.com
PR Newswire Association LLC provides comprehensive communications services for public relations and investor relations professionals ranging from information distribution and market intelligence to the creation of online multimedia content and investor relations web sites. Users can also view recent corporate press releases. The Association is owned by United Business Media plc.

IX. Economic Data & Research

Eurostat
Phone: 32-2-299-9696
Toll Free: 80-0-6789-1011
Web Address: www.epp.eurostat.ec.europa.eu
Eurostat is the European Union's service that publishes a wide variety of comprehensive statistics on European industries, populations, trade, agriculture, technology, environment and other matters.

STAT-USA/Internet
STAT-USA, HCHB, U.S. Dept. of Commerce
Rm. 4885
Washington, DC 20230 US
Phone: 202-482-1986
Fax: 202-482-2164
Toll Free: 800-782-8872
E-mail Address: *statmail@esa.doc.gov*
Web Address: www.stat-usa.gov
STAT-USA/Internet offers daily economic news, statistical releases and databases relating to export and trade, as well as the domestic economy. It is provided by STAT-USA, which is an agency in the Economics & Statistics Administration of the U.S. Department of Commerce. The site mainly consists of two main databases, the State of the Nation (SOTN), which focuses on the current state of the U.S. economy; and the Global Business Opportunities (GLOBUS) & the National Trade Data Bank (NTDB), which deals with U.S. export opportunities, global political/socio-economic conditions and other world economic issues.

X. Entertainment & Amusement Associations

Information Display and Entertainment Association (IDEA)
2001 E. Lohman Ave., Ste. 110-165
Las Cruces, NM 88001-3116 US
Phone: 575-405-1666
Fax: 575-524-4813
Toll Free: 888-832-4332
E-mail Address: *info@ideaontheweb.org*
Web Address: www.ideaontheweb.org
The Information Display and Entertainment Association (IDEA) is a worldwide association of electronic display system and scoreboard operators.

International Association of Assembly Managers (IAAM)
635 Fritz Dr., Ste. 100
Coppell, TX 75019-4442 US
Phone: 972-906-7441
Fax: 972-906-7418
E-mail Address: *mike.meyers@iaam.org*
Web Address: www.iaam.org
The International Association of Assembly Managers (IAAM) is an international trade organization representing managers and suppliers of public assembly facilities, such as arenas, amphitheaters, auditoriums, convention centers/exhibit halls, performing arts venues, stadiums and university complexes.

International Ticketing Association (INTIX)
330 W. 38th St., Ste. 605
New York, NY 10018 US
Phone: 212-629-4036
Fax: 212-629-8532
E-mail Address: *info@intix.org*
Web Address: www.intix.org

International Ticketing Association (INTIX) is a nonprofit professional and trade organization for the admission services industry, representing professionals in the performing arts, theater, entertainment, professional sports and college and university athletics.

National Association of Ticket Brokers (NATB)
1300 I (Eye) St. NW, Ste. 400 E
Washington, D.C. 20005 US
Phone: 202-625-0600
Fax: 202-338-6340
E-mail Address: *gadler@ralaw.com*
Web Address: www.natb.org
The National Association of Ticket Brokers (NATB) is a nonprofit trade organization representing the ticket broker industry. The association promotes consumer protection and the education of the public concerning the ticket brokers industry.

XI. Fitness

President's Council on Physical Fitness and Sports (PCPFS)
200 Independence Ave. SW, PCPFS Dept. W.
Rm. 738-H
Washington, DC 20201-0004 US
Phone: 202-690-9000
Fax: 202-690-5211
E-mail Address: *fitness@hhs.gov*
Web Address: www.fitness.gov
The President's Council on Physical Fitness and Sports (PCPFS) offers information about exercise for people of all ages and it works to promote physical activity and sports.

Society of Chinese Scholars on Exercise Physiology and Fitness (SCSEPF)
Hong Kong Baptist University
Rm. NAB210, David C. Lam Bldg., Shaw Campus
Kowloon Tong, Hong Kong China
Phone: (852) 3411 5758
Fax: (852) 3411 5756
E-mail Address: *enquiry@scsepf.org*
Web Address: www.scsepf.org/home.htm
The Society of Chinese Scholars on Exercise Physiology and Fitness (SCSEPF) is a nonprofit professional organization committed exclusively to the advancement and improvement of exercise physiology and fitness.

XII. Government Agencies-Singapore

Singapore Government Online (SINGOV)
140 Hill St.
MICA Bldg., 5th Fl.
179369 Singapore
E-mail Address: *singov_webmaster@mica.gov.sg*
Web Address: www.gov.sg
Singapore Government Online (SINGOV) is the default homepage for the Singapore Government and is a portal for governmenal information. The website lists governmental agencies, news, information, policies and inititives.

XIII. Health Care Business & Professional Associations

American Academy of Kinesiology and Physical Education (AAKPE)
c/o Human Kinetics
P.O. Box 5076
Champaign, IL 61820-2200 US
Phone: 217-351-5076
Fax: 217-351-2674
Toll Free: 800-747-4457
E-mail Address: *kims@aakpe.org*
Web Address: www.aakpe.org
The American Academy of Kinesiology and Physical Education (AAKPE) promotes research of human movement and physical activity. AAKPE's members transmit knowledge about human movement and physical activity through yearly meetings and publications.

American Alliance for Health, Physical Education, Recreation & Dance (AAHPERD)
1900 Association Dr.
Reston, VA 20191-1598 US
Phone: 703-476-3400
Toll Free: 800-213-7193
Web Address: www.aahperd.org
The American Alliance for Health, Physical Education, Recreation & Dance (AAHPERD) is an organization of professionals who support and assist those involved in physical education, fitness, leisure, dance, health promotion and education. AAHPERD includes the National Association for Sport & Physical Education (NASPE) and the National Association for Girls & Women in Sport (NAGWS), as well as other national and district associations.

American College of Sports Medicine (ACSM)
401 W. Michigan St.
Indianapolis, IN 46202-3233 US
Phone: 317-637-9200
Fax: 317-634-7817
E-mail Address: *publicinfo@acsm.org*
Web Address: www.acsm.org
The American College of Sports Medicine (ACSM) promotes and integrates research, education and applications of sports medicine and exercise science to maintain and enhance quality of life. ACSM has more than 20,000 international, national and regional chapter members.

American Medical Society for Sports Medicine (AMSSM)
11639 Earnshaw
Overland Park, KS 66210 US
Phone: 913-327-1415
Fax: 913-327-1491
E-mail Address: *office@amssm.org*
Web Address: www.newamssm.org
The mission of the American Medical Society for Sports Medicine, Inc. (AMSSM) is to offer a forum that fosters a collegial relationship among dedicated, competent primary care sports medicine physicians as they seek to improve their individual expertise and raise the general level of the sports medicine practice.

American Orthopedic Society for Sports Medicine (AOSSM)
6300 N. River Rd., Ste. 500
Rosemont, IL 60018 US
Phone: 847-292-4900
Fax: 847-292-4905
E-mail Address: *aossm@aossm.org*
Web Address: www.sportsmed.org
American Orthopedic Society for Sports Medicine (AOSSM) is a trade association for orthopedic doctors and sports medicine practitioners. The AOSSM works to improve the identification, prevention, treatment and rehabilitation of sports injuries.

Association for Applied Sport Psychology (AASP)
2810 Crossroads Dr., Ste. 3800
Madison, WI 53718 US
Phone: 608-443-2475
Fax: 608-443-2474, 608-443-2478
Web Address: appliedsportpsych.org
The Association for Applied Sport Psychology (AASP) provides information about applied sports psychology to coaches, athletes, students, parents, certified consultants and AASP members.

North American Society for the Psychology of Sport and Physical Activity (NASPSPA)
P.O. Box 5076
Champaign, IL 61825-5076 Canada
Phone: 306-966-1079
Fax: 217-351-1549
Toll Free: 800-747-4457
E-mail Address: *info@hkusa.com.*
Web Address: www.naspspa.org
The North American Society for the Psychology of Sport and Physical Activity (NASPSPA) is an association of scholars from the behavioral sciences and related professions that seeks to advance the scientific study of human behavior in sport and physical activity.

XIV. Industry Research/Market Research

Forrester Research
400 Technology Sq.
Cambridge, MA 02139 US
Phone: 617-613-6000
Fax: 617-613-5200
Toll Free: 866-367-7378
Web Address: www.forrester.com
Forrester Research identifies and analyzes emerging trends in technology and their impact on business. Among the firm's specialties are the financial services, retail, health care, entertainment, automotive and information technology industries.

Marketresearch.com
11200 Rockville Pike, Ste. 504
Rockville, MD 20852 US
Phone: 240-747-3000
Fax: 240-747-3004
Toll Free: 800-298-5699
E-mail Address:
customerservice@marketresearch.com
Web Address: www.marketresearch.com
Marketresearch.com is a leading broker for professional market research and industry analysis. Users are able to search the company's database of research publications including data on global industries, companies, products and trends.

Plunkett Research, Ltd.
P.O. Drawer 541737
Houston, TX 77254-1737 US
Phone: 713-932-0000

Fax: 713-932-7080
E-mail Address:
customersupport@plunkettresearch.com
Web Address: www.plunkettresearch.com
Plunkett Research, Ltd. is a leading provider of market research, industry trends analysis and business statistics. Since 1985, it has served clients worldwide, including corporations, universities, libraries, consultants and government agencies. At the firm's web site, visitors can view product information and pricing and access a great deal of basic market information on industries such as financial services, infotech, e-commerce, health care and biotech.

XV. MBA Resources

MBA Depot
Phone: 512-499-8728
Web Address: www.mbadepot.com
MBA Depot is an online community for MBA professionals.

XVI. Motorcycle Industry Associations (MIC)

Singapore Motor Cycle Trade Association (SMCTA)
40 Sam Leong Rd.
207930 Singapore
Phone: 65-6297-1991
Fax: 65-6297-1313
E-mail Address: *smcta@singnet.com.sg*
Web Address: www.smcta.org.sg
Singapore Motor Cycle Trade Association (SMCTA) represents the motorcycle trade and related industries in Singapore.

XVII. Real Estate Industry Associations

International Facility Management Association (IFMA)
1 E. Greenway Plz., Ste. 1100
Houston, TX 77046-0194 US
Phone: 713-623-4362
Fax: 713-623-6124
E-mail Address: *ifma@ifma.org*
Web Address: www.ifma.org
The International Facility Management Association (IFMA) is a trade association of facilities managers. IFMA certifies facility managers, provides educational programs, conducts research, recognizes facility management degree and certificate programs and produces World Workplace, a facility management-related conference and exposition.

XVIII. Restaurant Industry Associations

National Association of Concessionaires (NAC)
35 E. Wacker Dr., Ste. 1816
Chicago, IL 60601 US
Phone: 312-236-3858
Fax: 312-236-7809
E-mail Address: *info@NAConline.org*
Web Address: www.naconline.org
The National Association of Concessionaires (NAC) is the trade association for owners and operators of businesses in the recreation and leisure-time food and beverage concessions industry.

XIX. Spa Industry Associations

International Spa Association (ISPA)
2365 Harrodsburg Rd., Ste. A325
Lexington, KY 40504 US
Phone: 859-226-4326
Fax: 859-226-4445
Toll Free: 888-651-4772
E-mail Address: *ispa@ispastaff.com*
Web Address: www.experienceispa.com
The International Spa Association (ISPA) is recognized worldwide as one of the leading professional organizations and voices of the spa industry. It provides educational and networking opportunities, promotes the value of the spa experience and speaks as the authoritative voice to foster professionalism and growth. ISPA represents more than 3,000 health and wellness facilities and providers in 75 countries.

XX. Sporting Goods Industry Associations

Canadian Sporting Goods Association (CSGA)
300 rue du Saint-Sacrement, Ste. 420
Montreal, QC H2Y 1X4 Canada
Phone: 514-393-1132
Fax: 514-393-9513
Toll Free: 888-393-3002
E-mail Address: *csga@csga.ca*
Web Address: www.csga.ca
The Canadian Sporting Goods Association (CSGA) represents the sporting goods industry in Canada.

National Ski and Snowboard Retailer Association (NSSRA)
1601 Feehanville Dr., Ste. 300
Mt. Prospect, IL 60056-6035 US
Phone: 847-391-9825
Fax: 847-391-9827
E-mail Address: *info@nssra.com*
Web Address: www.nssra.com
The National Ski and Snowboard Retailer Association (NSSRA) provides ski and snowboard retailers across the U.S. with information and services. NSSRA also represents ski shops at the meetings of the American Society for Testing and Materials (ASTM) committee on snow skiing.

National Sporting Goods Association (NSGA)
1601 Feehanville Dr., Ste. 300
Mt. Prospect, IL 60056 US
Phone: 847-296-6742
Fax: 847-391-9827
Toll Free: 800-815-5422
E-mail Address: *info@nsga.org*
Web Address: www.nsga.org
The National Sporting Goods Association (NSGA) is a sporting goods trade association, designed to help its members profit in a competitive marketplace.

Sporting Goods Manufacturers Association (SGMA)
1150 17th St. NW, Ste. 850
Washington, DC 20036 US
Phone: 202-775-1762
Fax: 202-296-7462
E-mail Address: *info@sgma.com*
Web Address: www.sgma.com
The Sporting Goods Manufacturers Association (SGMA) is a trade organization representing manufacturers of sporting goods equipment.

World Federation of the Sporting Goods Industry (WFSGI)
Maison du Sport Int'l, 54 Ave. De Rhodanie
3rd Fl., Bldg. C
Lausanne, 1007 Switzerland
Phone: 41-21-612-61-61
Fax: 41-21-612-61-69
E-mail Address: *info@wfsgi.org*
Web Address: www.wfsgi.org
The World Federation of the Sporting Goods Industry (WFSGI) is a global, nonprofit, independent association of sporting goods industry suppliers, national sporting goods organizations and other industry-related businesses.

XXI. Sports Associations

Amateur Athletic Union (AAU)
P.O. Box 22409
Lake Buena Vista, FL 32830 US
Phone: 407-934-7200
Fax: 407-934-7242
Toll Free: 800-228-4872
E-mail Address: *anita@aausports.org*
Web Address: aausports.org
The Amateur Athletic Union (AAU) is a nonprofit, volunteer sports organization dedicated to the promotion and development of amateur sports and physical fitness programs.

American Baseball Coaches Association (ABCA)
108 S. University Ave., Ste. 3
Mt. Pleasant, MI 48858-2327 US
Phone: 989-775-3300
Fax: 989-775-3600
E-mail Address: *abca@abca.org*
Web Address: www.abca.org
The American Baseball Coaches Association (ABCA) is a trade organization serving 6,200 baseball coaches from 23 countries. ABCA works with many of the governing bodies represented by its coaches, including the National Collegiate Athletic Association, the National Association of Intercollegiate Athletics, the National Junior College Athletic Association and the National Federation of State High School Associations.

American Football Coaches Association (AFCA)
100 Legends Ln.
Waco, TX 76706 US
Phone: 254-754-9000
Fax: 254-754-7373
E-mail Address: *info@afca.com*
Web Address: www.afca.com
The American Football Coaches Association (AFCA) is the primary professional association representing all levels of football and the football coaching profession. The organization's 10,000 members include more than 90% of head coaches from 700-plus schools which sponsor football on the college level.

American Hockey Coaches Association (AHCA)
7 Concord St.
Joe Bertagna, Exec. Dir.
Gloucester, MA 01930 US
Phone: 781-245-4177
Fax: 718-245-2492

E-mail Address: *jbertagna@hockeyeastonline.com*
Web Address: www.ahcahockey.com
The American Hockey Coaches Association (AHCA) is a trade organization that represents professional, junior, high school and youth coaches. AHCA also represents referees, administrators, sales representatives, journalists and fans.

American Volleyball Coaches Association (AVCA)
2365 Harrodsburg Rd., Ste. A325
Lexington, KY 40504 US
Phone: 859-226-4315
Fax: 859-226-4338
Toll Free: 866-544-2822
E-mail Address: *will.engle@avca.org*
Web Address: www.avca.org
The American Volleyball Coaches Association (AVCA) provides professional volleyball coaches with educational programs, recognition opportunities and a forum for information exchange.

American Youth Soccer Organization (AYSO)
12501 S. Isis Ave.
Hawthorne, CA 90250 US
Fax: 310-643-5310
Toll Free: 800-872-2976
Web Address: www.soccer.org
The American Youth Soccer Organization (AYSO) is a nonprofit organization engaged in developing and delivering youth soccer programs across the U.S.

Association of Professional Ball Players of America (APBPA)
1820 W. Orangewood Ave., Ste. 206
Orange, CA 92868 US
Phone: 714-935-9993
Fax: 714-935-0431
E-mail Address: *ballplayersassn@aol.com*
Web Address: www.apbpa.org
The Association of Professional Ball Players of America (APBPA) provides financial assistance to both major and minor league professional baseball players, coaches, umpires, scouts and clubhouse men in need.

Canadian Football League Players' Association (CFLPA)
603 Argus Rd., Ste. 207
Oakville, ON L6J 6G6 Canada
Phone: 905-844-7852
Fax: 905-844-5127
Toll Free: 800-616-6865
E-mail Address: *admin@cflpa.com*
Web Address: www.cflpa.com
The Canadian Football League Players' Association (CFLPA) is the union for football players in the Canadian Football League (CFL).

Chinese Olympic Committee (COC)
8 Tiyuguan Rd.
Chongwen District
Beijing, 100763 China
Phone: (010)87182635
Fax: (010)87182686
E-mail Address: *shike@olympic.cn*
Web Address: en.olympic.cn
The Chinese Olympic Committee (COC) is a nonprofit organization representing China in international Olympic sports.

Hong Kong Schools Sports Federation (HKSSF)
1/F, 7 Carmel Village St., Rm. 203
Kowloon, China
Phone: (852) 2711 9182
Fax: (852) 2761 9808
E-mail Address: *hkssf@hkssf.org.hk*
Web Address: www.hkolympic.org
Hong Kong Schools Sports Federation (HKSSF) represents the primary and secondary schools' sports and student athletes focusing on the quality training required for them to achieve higher performance in the All China Secondary School Students Games, inter-city and other international competitions.

Hong Kong Sports Institute
2 On Chun St.
Ma On Shan
Sha Tin, N.T. Hong Kong
Phone: (852) 2681 6888
Fax: (852) 2695 4555
E-mail Address: *trisha@hksi.org.hk*
Web Address: www.hksi.org.hk
Hong Kong Sports Institute works closely with the national sports associations and other bodies in the identification of talents for elite sports training, as well as provide assistance in sectors of the community in order to develop and delivery elite sports training programs and services.

Indian Olympic Association
Olympic Bhawan
B-29 Qutab Institutional Area
New Delhi, 110 016 India
Phone: 91-11-2685-2480
Fax: 91-11-2685-2386
E-mail Address: *ioa@nde.vsnl.net.in*

Web Address: www.olympic.ind.in
The Indian Olympic Association website provides contact information regarding national sports federations, state associations and other recognized sports federations in India. In addition, included is a games result and gallery section.

International Olympic Committee (IOC)
Chateau de Vindy
Lausanne, 1007 Switzerland
Phone: 41-21-621-65-11
Fax: 41-21-621-65-16
Web Address: www.olympic.org
The International Olympic Committee (IOC) is the governing body for the Olympic Games.

Major League Baseball Players Alumni Association (MLBPAA)
MLB Advanced Media, L.P.
75 9th Ave.
New York, NY 10011 US
Phone: 212-485-3788
Fax: 212-485-8111
E-mail Address: *stacey@mlbpaa.com*
Web Address:
mlb.mlb.com/mlb/features/alumni/index.jsp
The Major League Baseball Players Alumni Association (MLBPAA) is a nonprofit organization composed of both current and former major and minor league players, umpires, managers and coaches, as well as baseball fans. It promotes the game of baseball and raises money for charity.

Major League Baseball Players Association (MLBPA)
12 E. 49th St.
24th Fl.
New York, NY 10017 US
Phone: 212-826-0808
Fax: 212-752-4378
E-mail Address: *feedback@mlbpa.org*
Web Address: mlbplayers.mlb.com/pa/index.jsp
The Major League Baseball Players Association (MLBPA), founded in 1968, is the union for professional baseball players.

National Association of Basketball Coaches (NABC)
1111 Main St., Ste. 1000
Kansas City, MO 64105-2136 US
Phone: 816-878-6222
Fax: 816-878-6223
E-mail Address: *ricknabc@gmail.com*
Web Address: nabc.cstv.com
The National Association of Basketball Coaches (NABC) is a professional organization representing college basketball coaches.

National Athletic Trainers' Association (NATA)
2952 Stemmons Fwy., Ste. 200
Dallas, TX 75247 US
Phone: 214-637-6282
Fax: 214-637-2206
E-mail Address: *info@nata.org*
Web Address: www.nata.org
The National Athletic Trainers' Association (NATA) is a trade association for athletic trainers and those who support the athletic training profession.

National Basketball Players Association (NBPA)
310 Lenox Ave.
New York, NY 10027 US
Phone: 212-655-0880
Fax: 212-655-0881
E-mail Address: *info@nbpa.com*
Web Address: www.nbpa.com
The National Basketball Players Association (NBPA) is the union for professional basketball players.

National Collegiate Athletic Association (NCAA)
700 W. Washington St.
P.O. Box 6222
Indianapolis, IN 46206-6222 US
Phone: 317-917-6222
Fax: 317-917-6888
E-mail Address: *pmr@ncaa.org*
Web Address: www.ncaa.org
The National Collegiate Athletic Association (NCAA) is a collegiate sports organization serving the needs of its college, university and conference members.

National Field Hockey Coaches Association (NFHCA)
11921 Meadow Ridge Ter.
Glen Allen, VA 23059 US
Phone: 804-364-8700
Fax: 804-364-5467
E-mail Address:
NFHCAexecutivedirector@nfhca.org
Web Address: www.nfhca.org
The National Field Hockey Coaches Association (NFHCA) is a nonprofit advocacy organization serving field hockey coaches across the U.S.

National Football League Coaches Association (NFLCA)
Phone: 202-463-2200
Toll Free: 800-372-2000
Web Address: www.nflcoaches.com
The National Football League Coaches Association (NFLCA) is the union for National Football League coaches.

National Football League Players Association (NFLPA)
1133 20th St. NW
Washington, DC 20036 US
Fax: 202-756-9312
Toll Free: 800-372-2000
E-mail Address: *carl.francis@nflplayers.com*
Web Address: www.nflplayers.com
The National Football League Players Association (NFLPA) is the union for professional football players in the National Football League (NFL).

National Golf Coaches Association (NGCA)
5905 NW 54th Cir.
Coral Springs, FL 33067 US
Fax: 800-381-0769
Toll Free: 800-381-0769
E-mail Address: *roger@ngca.com*
Web Address: www.ngca.com
The National Golf Coaches Association (NGCA) is a professional organization for coaches in women's golf. The association has more than 400 coaches from Division I, II, III and NAIA collegiate programs.

National Golf Foundation (NGF)
1150 S. U.S. Hwy. 1, Ste. 401
Jupiter, FL 33477 US
Phone: 561-744-6006
Fax: 561-744-6107
Toll Free: 888-275-4643
E-mail Address: *general@ngf.org*
Web Address: www.ngf.org
The National Golf Foundation (NGF) provides golf business research, information and consulting services to companies and organizations world-wide, including its 6,000 member companies.

National Hockey League (NHL) Alumni
170 Atwell Dr., Ste. 650
Toronto, ON M9W 5Z5 Canada
Phone: 416-798-2586
Fax: 416-798-2582
E-mail Address: *info@nhlalumni.net*
Web Address: www.nhlalumni.net
The National Hockey League (NHL) Alumni is an organization for former National Hockey League players.

National Hockey League Players Association (NHLPA)
20 Bay St., Ste. 1700
Toronto, ON M5J 2N8 Canada
Fax: 416-313-2301
Web Address: www.nhlpa.com
The National Hockey League Players Association (NHLPA) is the union for hockey players in the National Hockey League (NHL).

National Thoroughbred Racing Association (NTRA)
2525 Harrodsburg Rd.
Lexington, KY 40504 US
Phone: 859-245-6872
Toll Free: 800-792-6872
E-mail Address: *ntra@ntra.com*
Web Address: www.ntra.com
The National Thoroughbred Racing Association (NTRA) is the governing body of thoroughbred racing in the U.S.

Professional Hockey Players' Association (PHPA)
1 St. Paul St., Ste. 701
St. Catharines, ON L2R 7L2 Canada
Phone: 905-682-4800
Fax: 905-682-4822
Web Address: www.phpa.com
The Professional Hockey Players' Association (PHPA) is the union for professional hockey players in the American Hockey League (AHL) and the Elite Competition Hockey League (ECHL).

Professional Lacrosse Players' Association (PLPA)
E-mail Address: *comments@plpa.com*
Web Address: www.plpa.com
The Professional Lacrosse Players' Association (PLPA) is a union for professional lacrosse players in North America.

Special Olympics
1133 19th St. NW
Washington, DC 20036 US
Phone: 202-628-3630
Fax: 202-824-0200
E-mail Address: *info@specialolympics.org*
Web Address: www.specialolympics.org

The Special Olympics is an international organization dedicated to athletes who have intellectual disabilities.

United States National Soccer Team Players Association (USNSTPA)
Washington, D.C.
Web Address: www.usnstpa.com
The United States National Soccer Team Players Association (USNSTPA) is the labor organization for current members of the United States Men's National Team, as well as a membership organization for alumni members of the National Team.

United States Olympic Committee (USOC)
1 Olympic Plz.
Colorado Springs, CO 80909 US
Phone: 719-632-5551
E-mail Address: *media@usoc.org*
Web Address: www.olympic-usa.org
The United States Olympic Committee is a federally chartered nonprofit corporation which preserves Olympic ideals and supports Olympic and Paralympic athletes.

Women's Basketball Coaches Association (WBCA)
4646 Lawrenceville Hwy.
Lilburn, GA 30047 US
Phone: 770-279-8027
Fax: 770-279-8473
E-mail Address: *wbca@wbca.org*
Web Address: www.wbca.org
The Women's Basketball Coaches Association (WBCA) promotes women's basketball by providing a network for coaches of professional and amateur women's basketball teams, including those of college and high school level teams.

XXII. Sports Industry Associations

All-China Sports Federation
8 Tiyuguan Rd., Chongwen District
4th Fl., Main Bldg.
Beijing, 100061 China
Phone: 86-10-67158866
Fax: 86-10-67158822
Web Address: www.sport.org.cn
The All-China Sports Federation promotes sports in China and international fitness.

Association of Luxury Suite Directors (ALSD)
135 Merchant St., Ste. 145
Cincinnati, OH 45246 US
Phone: 513-674-0555
Fax: 513-674-0577
E-mail Address: *feedback@alsd.com*
Web Address: www.alsd.com
The Association of Luxury Suite Directors (ALSD) serves and represents businesses in the premium seating industry, especially those offering seating for stadiums and arenas.

Association of Professional Sports Agents (APSA)
Federation House
NAC
Stoneleigh Park, Warwickshire CV8 2RF UK
Phone: 44-24-76-414999
Fax: 44-24-76-414990
E-mail Address: *kate@sportsandplay.com*
Web Address: www.apsa.org.uk
The Association of Professional Sports Agents (APSA) provides sports agents in the United Kingdom with advocacy, information, education and discounts.

Black Coaches & Administrators (BCA)
201 S. Capitol Ave.,
Pan American Plz., Ste. 495
Indianapolis, IN 46225 US
Phone: 317-829-5600
Fax: 317-829-5601
Toll Free: 877-789-1222
Web Address: www.bcasports.org
Black Coaches & Administrators (BCA) is a nonprofit organization whose primary purpose is to foster the development of ethnic minorities at all levels of sports on a national and international basis.

Black Entertainment & Sports Lawyers Association (BESLA)
Rev. Phyllicia M. Hatton
P.O. Box 441485
Fort Washington, MD 20749-1485 US
Phone: 301-248-1818
Fax: 301-248-0700
E-mail Address: *BESLAmailbox@aol.com*
Web Address: www.besla.org
The Black Entertainment & Sports Lawyers Association (BESLA) is an international nonprofit organization of lawyers and other sports industry and entertainment executives, providing its members networking and continuing education programs. BESLA also offers internship opportunities and scholarships for law students.

Black Sports Agents Association (BSAA)
9255 Sunset Blvd., Ste. 1120
Beverly Hills, CA 90069 US
Phone: 310-858-6565
Fax: 310-858-1520
E-mail Address: *info@sportsagentsassociation.com*
Web Address: www.blacksportsagents.com
The Black Sports Agents Association (BSAA) was founded by the Reverend Jesse Jackson in 1996 to develop the involvement, image and cohesiveness of African Americans in the sports industry.

Black Women in Sport Foundation (BWSF)
4300 Monument Ave.
Philadelphia, PA 19131-1690 US
Phone: 215-877-1925 ext. 320
Fax: 215-877-1942
E-mail Address: *info@blackwomeninsport.org*
Web Address: www.blackwomeninsport.org
The Black Women in Sport Foundation (BWSF) is a nonprofit organization dedicated to facilitating the involvement of black women in U.S. sports as well as around the world through grassroots sports outreach programs for young black women and girls.

College Athletic Business Management Association (CABMA)
Cleveland, OH US
Phone: 440-892-4000
E-mail Address: *pmanak@nacda.com*
Web Address: nacda.cstv.com/cabma/nacda-cabma.html
The College Athletic Business Management Association (CABMA) is an organization for those involved in athletics administration, offering educational and networking opportunities. CABMA is a member of the National Association of Collegiate Directors of Athletics (NACDA).

General Administration of Sport of China
Stadium Rd., Chongwen
Beijing, 100763 China
Phone: 010-87182008
E-mail Address: *webmaster@sport.gov.cn*
Web Address: www.sport.gov.cn
The General Administration of Sport of China is the national sports development and general administrative association of the Chinese government.

North American Society for Sport History (NASSH)
NASSH Secretary-Treasurer
P.O. Box 1026
Lemont, PA 16851-1026 US
E-mail Address: *secretary-treasurer@nassh.org*
Web Address: www.nassh.org
The North American Society for Sport History (NASSH) is a nonprofit organization engaged in the study, research and writing of the history of sport.

North American Society for Sport Management (NASSM)
NASSM Business Office, West Gym 014
Slippery Rock University
Slippery Rock, PA 16057 US
Phone: 724-738-4812
Fax: 724-738-4858
E-mail Address: *nassm@sru.edu*
Web Address: www.nassm.com
The North American Society for Sport Management (NASSM) supports professionals working in the sport, leisure and recreation fields by encouraging study, research, scholarly writing and professional development in the area of sport management.

North American Society for the Sociology of Sport (NASSS)
E-mail Address: *crking@wsu.edu*
Web Address: www.nasss.org
The North American Society for the Sociology of Sport (NASSS) is a nonprofit organization that promotes the sociological study of play, games and sport.

Singapore Sports Council (SSC)
230 Stadium Blvd.
397799 Singapore
Phone: 65-6345-7111
Fax: 65-6440-9205
Web Address: www.ssc.gov.sg
The Singapore Sports Council (SSC) is committed to promoting Singapore as a regional sports hub. SSC is a statutory board under the Ministry of Community Development, Youth and Sports of Singapore. The site contains a directory of national sports associations, a list programs, links to sports medicine and training sites and the sports museum.

Sport & Recreation Law Association (SRLA)
1845 Fairmont
Wichita State University
Wichita, KS 67260 US
Phone: 316-978-3340
Fax: 316-978-5451
E-mail Address: *lori.miller@wichita.edu*

Web Address: www.srlaweb.org
The Sport & Recreation Law Association (SRLA) is a nonprofit corporation dedicated to the study and dissemination of information regarding legal aspects of sport and recreation.

Sports Lawyers Association (SLA)
12100 Sunset Hills Rd., Ste. 130
Reston, VA 20190 US
Phone: 703-437-4377
Fax: 703-435-4390
E-mail Address: *info@sportslaw.org*
Web Address: www.sportslaw.org
The Sports Lawyers Association (SLA) is an international, nonprofit, professional organization whose purpose is to understand and advance the practice of sports law. SLA has over 1,000 members including law educators, practicing lawyers, law students and other professionals with an interest in professional and amateur sports law.

Sports Turf Managers Association (STMA)
805 New Hampshire, Ste. E
Lawrence, KS 66044 US
Fax: 800-366-0391
Toll Free: 800-323-3875
Web Address: www.stma.org
The Sports Turf Managers Association (STMA) provides a network of knowledge sharing and idea exchange between sports turf professionals.

Stadium Managers Association (SMA)
525 SW 5th St., Ste. A
Des Moines, IA 50309-4501 US
Phone: 515-282-8192
Fax: 515-282-9117
E-mail Address: *sma@assoc-mgmt.com*
Web Address: www.stadiummanagers.org
The Stadium Managers Association (SMA) is a trade organization that promotes the interest of stadium management professionals.

Women in Sports and Events (WISE)
244 5th Ave., Ste. 2087
New York, NY 10001 US
Phone: 212-726-8282
E-mail Address: *info@wiseworks.org*
Web Address: www.womeninsportsandevents.com
Women in Sports and Events (WISE) is a professional networking organization for women in the sports and sports-related events industries.

Women In Sports Careers Foundation (WISC)
Phone: 714-848-1201
E-mail Address: *info@wiscnetwork.com*
Web Address: www.wiscfoundation.org
Women In Sports Careers Foundation (WISC) serves the business and career networking needs of women involved in sports related professions.

XXIII. Sports Industry Resources

American Bar Association (ABA) Forum on the Entertainment & Sports Industries
321 N. Clark St.
Chicago, IL 60654-7598 US
Phone: 312-988-5000
Toll Free: 800-285-2221
E-mail Address: *askaba@abanet.org*
Web Address:
www.abanet.org/forums/entsports/home.html
The American Bar Association (ABA) Forum on the Entertainment & Sports Industries, formed in 1977, seeks to educate attorneys in the transactional and legal principles of sports and entertainment law. The forum's quarterly newsletter is directed toward lawyers practicing entertainment, sports, arts and intellectual property law.

ESPN, Inc.
ESPN Plz.
Bristol, CT 06010 US
Phone: 860-766-2000
Fax: 860-766-2213
Toll Free: 888-549-3776
E-mail Address: *espnpr@espn.com*
Web Address: espn.com
ESPN, Inc. is a recognized leader in sports entertainment and information. Launched in 1979, the company has several television channels, a magazine and Internet sites that provide complete coverage of professional sports. The firm is 80% owned by ABC, Inc., which is in turn an indirect subsidiary of The Walt Disney Company.

FoxSports.com
FOXSports on MSN & Fox Sports Interactive Television
1440 S. Sepulveda Dr.
Los Angeles, CA 90025 US
Phone: 212-556-2573
Fax: 212-354-6902
E-mail Address: *lou.d'ermilio@fox.com*
Web Address: msn.foxsports.com

FoxSports.com is a leader in sports broadcasting. The site is owned and operated by Fox Sports Interactive Media (FSIM), which is itself a subsidiary of News Corp.

NFLPlayer.com
NFL Players Association
1133 20th St. NW
Washington, DC 20036 US
Phone: 202-496-2860
Web Address: www.nflplayers.com
NFLPlayer.com is the NFL Players Association's sports marketing company.

Professional Business & Financial Network (PBFN)
315 14th St. NW, Ste. 2000
Atlanta, GA 30318 US
Toll Free: 877-723-6674
E-mail Address: *office@pbfn.org*
Web Address: www.pbfn.org
The Professional Business & Financial Network (PBFN) is an Internet-based organization that provides both active and retired athletes with better access to business opportunities.

Sportal-Sports Portal-Gov. of India
Dr. Rajendra Prasad Rd.
Rm. 504 B, Shastri Bhawan
New Delhi, 110 001 India
Phone: 91-11-23384152
Fax: 91-11-23384152
E-mail Address: *isrinivas@nic.in*
Web Address: www.sportal.nic.in
Sportal is the Ministry of Youth Affairs & Sports portal website for the Government of India. The site includes a glossary, calendar, and links to information, authorities and organizations relating to professional, amateur and youth sports in India.

Sportcal Global Communications Limited
Rowan Ct., 56 High St.
Wimbledon Village
London, SW19 5EE UK
Phone: 44-0-20-8944-8786
Fax: 44-0-20-8944-8740
E-mail Address: *mike.laflin@sportcal.com*
Web Address: www.sportcal.co.uk
Sportcal Global Communications Limited provides information on global sporting events as well as information about broadcasting rights and sponsorships.

Sporting News
120 W. Morehead St., Ste. 200
Charlotte, NC 28202 US
Web Address: www.sportingnews.com
Sporting News, a business name of American City Business Journals, Inc., is a leading sports magazine that covers professional football, baseball and hockey, as well as NASCAR and NCAA football and basketball.

Sports Business Journal
120 W. Morehead St., Ste. 310
Charlotte, NC 28202 US
Phone: 704-973-1410
Fax: 704-973-1401
Toll Free: 800-829-9839
E-mail Address: *rweiss@sportsbusinessjournal.com*
Web Address: www.sportsbusinessjournal.com
Sports Business Journal is a comprehensive weekly magazine for the sports industry, covering teams, players, marketing, labor and facilities.

Sports City
U.K.
Phone: +44 (0) 1733 201011
E-mail Address: *info@sports-city.org*
Web Address:
Sports City Ltd hosts a website for those involved in major sports events worldwide; organizing committees, international federations, sports bodies, event professionals, providers & suppliers, etc. The site includes news, job listings, directories and links to sporting events.

Sports Illustrated (SI)
1271 Ave. of the Americas
Prod. Office, 32nd Fl.
New York, NY 10020-1339 US
Phone: 212-522-1212
Fax: 212-522-0475
Toll Free: 800-528-5000
E-mail Address: *andrew_judelson@timeinc.com*
Web Address: sportsillustrated.cnn.com
Sports Illustrated (SI), a Time Warner company, is a leading U.S. sports publications company anchored by the Sports Illustrated magazine.

Sports Illustrated for Kids
Time, Inc.
1271 Ave. of the Americas
New York, NY 10020 US
Phone: 212-522-2084
Toll Free: 888-806-4833

E-mail Address: *sikids_inbox@sikids.com*
Web Address: www.sikids.com
Sports Illustrated for Kids, a Time Warner company, offers a magazine and website devoted to kids who are interested in sports.

Sports Links Central.com
E-mail Address: *info@sportslinkscentral.com*
Web Address: www.sportslinkscentral.com
Sports Links Central.com, a fully-owned subsidiary of Falcon Crusader Enterprises, LLC, is a comprehensive sports web directory. The site covers all aspects of the sports industry, with links to leagues and teams, federations, travel sites, sports business sites, sports education and sports facilities sites.

Sports Network (The) (TSN)
2200 Byberry Rd., Ste. 200
Hatboro, PA 19040 US
Phone: 215-441-8444
Fax: 215-441-5767
E-mail Address: *kzajac@sportsnetwork.com*
Web Address: www.sportsnetwork.com
The Sports Network (TSN) is a sports news web site that also distributes content to other media outlets. The network relies on satellite and online transmission to distribute data such as sports scores, statistics, news, injury and weather reports.

Statistics in Sports (SIS)
American Statistical Association
732 N. Alexandria St.
Alexandria, VA 22314-1943 US
Phone: 703-684-1221
Fax: 703-684-2037
Toll Free: 888-231-3473
E-mail Address: *asainfo@amstat.org*
Web Address: www.amstat.org/sections/sis
Statistics in Sports (SIS), a section of the American Statistical Association, provides links to statistical data on professional and amateur sports as well as academic departments, conferences and employers.

Team Marketing Report
645 Landwehr Rd.
Northbrook, IL 60062 US
Phone: 847-509-1010
Fax: 847-509-9781
E-mail Address: *jgreenberg@teammarketing.com*
Web Address: www.teammarketing.com
Team Marketing Report provides market research on the sports industry.

USA Today Sports
USA TODAY
7950 Jones Branch Dr.
McLean, VA 22108-0605 US
Toll Free: 800-872-0001
Web Address: www.usatoday.com/sports/front.htm
USA Today Sports provides news and information about the sports industry.

Yahoo! Sports
Yahoo! Inc.
701 1st Ave.
Sunnyvale, CA 94089 US
Phone: 408-349-3300
Fax: 408-349-3301
Web Address: sports.yahoo.com
Yahoo! Sports, a service of Yahoo! Inc., provides news and information for the sports industry.

XXIV. Sports Leagues

American Hockey League (AHL)
1 Monarch Pl., Ste. 2400
Springfield, MA 01144 US
Phone: 413-781-2030
Fax: 413-733-4767
E-mail Address: *info@theahl.com*
Web Address: www.theahl.com
The American Hockey League (AHL) is a professional ice hockey league which serves as the main developmental circuit for the National Hockey League (NHL).

Arena Football League (AFL)
105 Madison Ave., 9th Fl.
New York, NY 10016 US
Phone: 212-252-8100
Fax: 212-252-8030
Web Address: www.arenafootball.com
The Arena Football League (AFL) is the professional arena football organizing body.

Arena Football League Players Association (AFLPA)
2021 L St. NW, AFLPA Comm. Dept., Ste. 300
Washington, DC 20036 US
Phone: 202-463-2200
Fax: 202-857-1008
Toll Free: 800-372-2000
E-mail Address: *aflplayers@nflplayers.com*
Web Address: www.aflplayers.org

The Arena Football League Players Association (AFLPA) is the union for professional arena football players.

Asian Football Confederation (AFC)
57000 Kuala Lumpur
AFC House, Jalan 1/155B, Bukit Jalil
Malaysia
Phone: 603-8994-3388
Fax: 603-8994-2689
E-mail Address: *media@the-afc.com*
Web Address: www.the-afc.com
The Asian Football Confederation (AFC) is the governing body of football in Asia, including Australia but excluding Isreal and Cyprus. The AFC hosts the Asian Cup every four years. The AFC is divided into four regions: ASEAN Football Federation, East Asian Football Federation, West Asian Football Federation and the Central and South Asian Football Federation.

Canadian Football League (CFL)
50 Wellington St. E., 3rd Fl.
Toronto, ON M5E 1C8 Canada
Phone: 416-322-9650
Fax: 416-322-9651
Web Address: www.cfl.ca
The Canadian Football League (CFL) is the organizing body for professional football in Canada.

Central Hockey League (CHL)
1600 N. Desert Dr.
Tempe, AZ 85281 US
Phone: 480-949-8600
Fax: 480-949-8616
E-mail Address:
administration@centralhockeyleague.com
Web Address: www.centralhockeyleague.com
The Central Hockey League (CHL), owned by Global Entertainment Corporation, is a professional hockey league that was founded in 1992.

Continental Basketball Association (CBA)
195 Washington Ave.
Albany, NY 12210 US
Phone: 518-694-0100
Fax: 518-694-0101
E-mail Address: *info@cbahoopsonline.com*
Web Address: www.cbahoopsonline.com
The Continental Basketball Association (CBA) is a professional basketball league that develops talent for the National Basketball Association (NBA).

ECHL
116 Village Blvd., Ste. 304
Princeton, NJ 08540 US
Phone: 609-452-0770
Fax: 609-452-7147
E-mail Address: *JCarnefix@echl.com*
Web Address: www.echl.com
ECHL (formerly East Coast Hockey League) is a nationwide developmental league for the American Hockey League (AHL) and the National Hockey League (NHL).

Federation International de Football Association (FIFA)
FIFA-Strasse 20
P.O. Box 8044
Zurich, Switzerland
Phone: 41-43-222-7777
Fax: 41-43-222-7878
Web Address: www.fifa.com
The Federation International de Football Association (FIFA) is the governing body for professional soccer worldwide. The association, based in Zurich, is governed by Swiss law and has over 280 employees from over 30 nations.

Federation Internationale d'InterCrosse (FIIC)
4545 av. Pierre-de-Coubertin
C.P. 1000 Succursale M
Montreal, QC H1V 3R2 Canada
E-mail Address: *secretary@inter-crosse.com*
Web Address: www.intercrosse.tk
The Federation Internationale d'InterCrosse (FIIC) promotes and mediates rule changes for the sport of InterCrosse. InterCrosse is a non-contact version of the game lacrosse. This sport is played throughout the U.S. and Canada, as well as many other nations, and is especially popular at elementary and junior high schools because of its safety aspects.

Football Association of Singapore (FAS)
100 Tyrwhitt Rd.
01-02 Jalan Besar Stadium
207542 Singapore
Phone: 65-6348-3477
Fax: 65-6348-6477
Web Address: www.sleague.com
The Football Association of Singapore (FAS) promotes the sport of football and football professionals. FAS provides support to regional football clubs and youth development programs in Singapore.

Indy Racing League (IRL)
4565 W. 16th St.
Indianapolis, IN 46222 US
Phone: 317-492-6526
Web Address: www.indycar.com
Indy Racing League, LLC (IRL) is a subsidiary of Hulman and Co., the owner of the Indianapolis Motor Speedway complex. The Indianapolis 500 is the circuit's premier event.

International Boxing Federation & United States Boxing Association (IBF/USBA)
516 Main St., 2nd Fl.
East Orange, NJ 07018 US
Phone: 973-414-0300
Fax: 973-414-0307
Web Address: www.ibf-usba-boxing.com
The International Boxing Federation & United States Boxing Association (IBF/USBA) is one of many professional boxing organizations which sanctions world championship boxing bouts.

International Professional Rodeo Association (IPRA)
2304 Exchange
Oklahoma City, OK 73108 US
Phone: 405-235-6540
Fax: 405-235-6577
E-mail Address: *info@iprarodeo.com*
Web Address: www.iprarodeo.com
The International Professional Rodeo Association (IPRA) is the premier professional rodeo association.

Ladies Professional Golf Association (LPGA)
100 International Golf Dr.
Daytona Beach, FL 32124-1092 US
Phone: 386-274-6200
Fax: 386-274-1099
E-mail Address: *feedback@lpga.com*
Web Address: www.lpga.com
The Ladies Professional Golf Association (LPGA) is the governing organization for women's professional golf.

Little League International Baseball and Softball
539 U.S. Rte. 15 Hwy
P.O. Box 3485
Williamsport, PA 17701-0485 US
Phone: 570-326-1921
Fax: 570-326-1074
E-mail Address: *LVanauken@littleleague.org*
Web Address: www.littleleague.org
Little League International Baseball and Softball is an nonprofit organization that supervises and assists those who participate in Little League Baseball and Softball across the globe.

Major Indoor Soccer League (MISL)
1175 Post Rd. E.
Westport, CT 06880 US
Phone: 203-222-4900
Fax: 203-221-7300
Toll Free: 866-647-5638
E-mail Address: *info@misl.net*
Web Address: www.misl.net
The Major Indoor Soccer League (MISL) is the professional league for indoor soccer.

Major League Baseball (MLB)
MLB Advanced Media, L.P.
75 9th Ave., 5th Fl.
New York, NY 10011 US
Phone: 512-434-1542
Toll Free: 866-800-1275
Web Address: www.mlb.com
Major League Baseball (MLB) is the governing body for professional baseball in the United States.

Major League Lacrosse (MLL)
Brighton Landing E., 20 Guest St., Ste. 125
Boston, MA 02135 US
Phone: 617-746-9980
Fax: 617-746-9988
E-mail Address: *info@majorleaguelacrosse.com*
Web Address: www.majorleaguelacrosse.com
Major League Lacrosse (MLL) was founded in 2001 as a single entity ownership which showcases professional outdoor lacrosse.

Major League Soccer (MLS)
420 5th Ave., 7th Fl.
New York, NY 10018 US
Phone: 212-450-1200
Fax: 212-450-1300
Toll Free: 877-557-3774
E-mail Address: *feedback@mlsnet.com*
Web Address: www.mlsnet.com
Major League Soccer (MLS) is the organizing body for professional soccer in the U.S. MLS was founded in 1996 after the U.S. hosted the World Cup in 1994.

National Association for Stock Car Auto Racing (NASCAR)
P.O. Box 2875
Daytona Beach, FL 32120 US

Phone: 386-253-0611
E-mail Address: *fanfeedback@NASCAR.COM*
Web Address: www.nascar.com
The National Association for Stock Car Auto Racing (NASCAR) is the organizing body for professional stock car racing.

National Association of Professional Baseball Leagues (NAPBL)
201 Bayshore Dr. SE
St. Petersburg, FL 33701 US
Phone: 727-822-6937
Fax: 727-821-5819
Toll Free: 866-644-2687
E-mail Address:
webmaster@minorleaguebaseball.com
Web Address: web.minorleaguebaseball.com
The National Association of Professional Baseball Leagues (NAPBL), better known as Minor League Baseball (MiLB), is the organizing body for U.S. minor league baseball. It was founded in 1901.

National Basketball Association (NBA)
645 5th Ave.
New York, NY 10022 US
E-mail Address: *FanRelations@NBA.com*
Web Address: www.nba.com
The National Basketball Association (NBA) is the premier professional basketball league in the U.S.

National Basketball Development League (NBDL)
477 Madison Ave., 3rd Fl.
New York, NY 10022 US
Phone: 864-248-1108
E-mail Address: *kpartridge@nba.com*
Web Address: www.nba.com/dleague
The National Basketball Development League (NBDL) is the development league for the NBA.

National Football League (NFL)
280 Park Ave.
New York, NY 10017 US
Web Address: www.nfl.com
The National Football League (NFL) is the organizing body for professional football in the U.S.

National Hockey League (NHL)
1185 Ave. of the Americas, 15th Fl.
New York, NY 10036 US
Phone: 217-789-2000
Fax: 212-789-2020
Web Address: www.nhl.com
The National Hockey League (NHL) is the organizing body of professional hockey.

National Lacrosse League (NLL)
9 E. 45th St., 5th Fl.
New York, NY 10017 US
Phone: 212-764-1390
Fax: 917-510-9890
E-mail Address: *comments@nll.com*
Web Address: www.nll.com
The National Lacrosse League (NLL) is the organizing body for professional lacrosse in North America.

Professional Bowlers Association (PBA)
719 2nd Ave., Ste. 701
Seattle, WA 98104 US
Phone: 206-332-9688
Fax: 206-654-6030
Web Address: www.pba.com
The Professional Bowlers Association (PBA) is the governing body of the professional bowling circuit.

Professional Bull Riders, Inc. (PBR)
101 W. Riverwalk
Pueblo, CO 81003 US
Phone: 719-242-2800
Fax: 719-242-2855
E-mail Address: *admin@pbrnow.com*
Web Address: www.pbrnow.com
The Professional Bull Riders, Inc. (PBR) is the governing body of professional bull riding.

Professional Golfers Association (PGA)
100 Ave. of the Champions
Palm Beach Gardens, FL 33418 US
Phone: 561-624-8400
Fax: 531-624-8429
E-mail Address: *webmaster@pga.com*
Web Address: www.pga.com
The Professional Golfers Association (PGA) is the organizing body for professional golf in the U.S.

The Union of European Football Associations
Route de Genève 46
Case postale
Nyon 2, CH-1260 Switzerland
Phone: 41-(0)-848-00-2727
Fax: 41-(0)-848-01-2727
E-mail Address: *info@uefa.com*
Web Address: www.uefa.com

The Union of European Football Associations (UEFA) hosts the World Cup and is the governing body of European football.

U.S. Lacrosse
113 W. University Pkwy.
Baltimore, MD 21210 US
Phone: 410-235-6882
Fax: 410-366-6735
E-mail Address: *info@uslacrosse.org*
Web Address: www.uslacrosse.org
U.S. Lacrosse, with over 250,000 members, is the governing body of amateurs in this sport.

U.S. Soccer Federation
1801 S. Prairie Ave.
Chicago, IL 60616 US
Phone: 312-808-1300
Fax: 312-808-1301
Web Address: www.ussoccer.com
The U.S. Soccer Federation is the governing body of soccer in the U.S.

United European Football Association (UEFA)
Route de Geneve 46
Case postale
Nyon 2, CH-1260 Switzerland
Phone: 41-848-00-2727
Fax: 41-848-01-2727
E-mail Address: *info@uefa.com*
Web Address: www.uefa.com
The United European Football Association (UEFA) is the organizing body for professional soccer in Europe.

United Soccer Leagues (USL)
14497 N. Dale Mabry Hwy., Ste. 201
Tampa, FL 33618 US
Phone: 813-963-3909
Fax: 813-963-3807
E-mail Address: *gerald.barnhart@uslsoccer.com*
Web Address: www.uslsoccer.com
The United Soccer Leagues (USL) is North America's minor soccer league.

United States Figure Skating Association (USFSA)
20 First St.
Colorado Springs, CO 80906 US
Phone: 719-635-5200
Fax: 719-635-9548
E-mail Address: *info@usfigureskating.org*
Web Address: www.usfsa.org
The United States Figure Skating Association (USFSA) is the governing body of figure skating in the U.S.

United States Golf Association (USGA)
P.O. Box 708
Far Hills, NJ 07931 US
Phone: 908-234-2300
Fax: 908-234-9687
E-mail Address: *usga@usga.org*
Web Address: www.usga.org
The United States Golf Association (USGA) is the governing body of golf in the U.S. and Mexico. It is a nonprofit organization run by golfers.

United States Tennis Association (USTA)
70 W. Oak Ln.
White Plains, NY 10604 US
Phone: 914-696-7000
E-mail Address: *sylvan@usta.com*
Web Address: www.usta.com
The United States Tennis Association (USTA) is the governing body of tennis in the United States.

USA Cycling
1 Olympic Plz.
Colorado Springs, CO 80909 US
Phone: 719-866-4581
Fax: 719-866-4628
E-mail Address: *alee@usacycling.org*
Web Address: www.usacycling.org
USA Cycling is the official cycling organization responsible for selecting and training cyclists to represent the United States in international competitions. USA Cycling does business as the United States Cycling Federation (USCF), National Off-Road Bicycle Association (NORBA), United States Professional Racing Organization (USPRO), the National Collegiate Cycling Association (NCCA) and the BMX Association.

USA Gymnastics
201 S. Capitol Ave., Pan Am Plz., Ste. 300
Indianapolis, IN 46225 US
Phone: 317-237-5050
Fax: 317-237-5069
Toll Free: 800-345-4719
E-mail Address: *rebound@usa-gymnastics.org*
Web Address: www.usa-gymnastics.org
USA Gymnastics is the governing body for gymnastics in the U.S.

USA Hockey, Inc.
1775 Bob Johnson Dr.
Colorado Springs, CO 80906-4090 US
Phone: 719-576-8724
Fax: 719-538-1160
E-mail Address: *usah@usahockey.org*
Web Address: www.usahockey.com
USA Hockey, Inc. is the governing body of hockey in the U.S.

USA Track & Field (USATF)
132 E. Washington St., Ste. 800
Indianapolis, IN 46204 US
Phone: 317-261-0500
Fax: 317-261-0481
E-mail Address: *Jill.Geer@usatf.org*
Web Address: www.usatf.org
USA Track & Field (USATF) is the governing body for track and field in the U.S.

Women's National Basketball Association (WNBA)
Olympic Tower
645 5th Ave.
New York, NY 10022 US
Phone: 212-688-9622
Fax: 212-750-9622
Web Address: www.wnba.com
The Women's National Basketball Association (WNBA) is the professional basketball league for women.

Women's Professional Soccer
1000 Brannan St., Ste. 401
San Francisco, CA 94103 US
Phone: 415-553-4467
Fax: 415-553-4459
Web Address: www.womensprosoccer.com
WPS (Women's Professional Soccer) is a North American sports league. It was formed in September 2007 as the result of the efforts of the Women's Soccer Initiative, Inc. WPS consists of seven teams across the United States.

Women's Tennis Association (WTA)
1 Progress Plz., Ste. 1500
St. Petersburg, FL 33701 US
Phone: 727-895-5000
Fax: 727-894-1982
Web Address: www.sonyericssonwtatour.com
The Women's Tennis Association (WTA) is the governing body of the professional women's tennis tour. The organization's web site is owned by WTA Tour, Inc., which does business as Sony Ericson WTA Tour.

World Boxing Association (WBA)
Centro Comercial Ciudad Turmero, Local 21
Piso 2, Calle Petión c/c Urdaneta
Turmero, Aragua 2115 Venezuela
Phone: 0244-633-15-84
Fax: 0244-663-31-77
E-mail Address: *wbaven@wbaonline.com*
Web Address: www.wbaonline.com
The World Boxing Association (WBA) is one of three professional boxing associations.

World Boxing Council (WBC)
Cuzco 872
Colonia Lindavista
Mexico City, 07300 Mexico
Phone: 52-55-5119-5276
E-mail Address: *info@wbcboxing.com*
Web Address: www.wbcboxing.com
The World Boxing Council (WBC) is one of three professional boxing associations.

XXV. U.S. Government Agencies

Bureau of Economic Analysis (BEA)
1441 L St. NW
Washington, DC 20230 US
Phone: 202-606-9900
E-mail Address: *customerservice@bea.gov*
Web Address: www.bea.gov
The Bureau of Economic Analysis (BEA), an agency of the U.S. Department of Commerce, is the nation's economic accountant, preparing estimates that illuminate key national, international and regional aspects of the U.S. economy.

Bureau of Labor Statistics (BLS)
2 Massachusetts Ave. NE
Washington, DC 20212-0001 US
Phone: 202-691-5200
Web Address: stats.bls.gov
The Bureau of Labor Statistics (BLS) is the principal fact-finding agency for the Federal Government in the field of labor economics and statistics. It is an independent national statistical agency that collects, processes, analyzes and disseminates statistical data to the American public, U.S. Congress, other federal agencies, state and local governments, business and labor. The BLS also serves as a statistical resource to the Department of Labor.

Government Printing Office (GPO)
732 N. Capitol St. NW
Washington, DC 20401 US
Phone: 202-512-0000
Fax: 202-512-2104
Toll Free: 866.512.1800
E-mail Address: *contactcenter@gpo.gov*
Web Address: www.gpo.gov
The U.S. Government Printing Office (GPO) is the primary information source concerning the activities of Federal agencies. GPO gathers, catalogues, produces, provides, authenticates and preserves published information.

U.S. Census Bureau
4600 Silver Hill Rd.
Washington, DC 20233-8800 US
Phone: 301-763-4636
Fax: 301-457-3670
Toll Free: 800-923-8282
E-mail Address: *pio@census.gov*
Web Address: www.census.gov
The U.S. Census Bureau is the official collector of data about the people and economy of the U.S. Founded in 1790, it provides official social, demographic and economic information.

U.S. Department of Commerce (DOC)
1401 Constitution Ave. NW
Washington, DC 20230 US
Phone: 202-482-2000
E-mail Address: *cgutierrez@doc.gov*
Web Address: www.doc.gov
The U.S. Department of Commerce (DOC) regulates trade and provides valuable economic analysis of the economy.

U.S. Department of Labor (DOL)
Frances Perkins Bldg.
200 Constitution Ave. NW
Washington, DC 20210 US
Toll Free: 866-487-2365
Web Address: www.dol.gov
The U.S. Department of Labor (DOL) is the government agency responsible for labor regulations. This site provides tools to help citizens find out whether companies are complying with family and medical-leave requirements.

U.S. Securities and Exchange Commission (SEC)
100 F St. NE
Washington, DC 20549 US
Phone: 202-551-6000
Toll Free: 888-732-6585
E-mail Address: *publicinfo@sec.gov*
Web Address: www.sec.gov
The U.S. Securities and Exchange Commission (SEC) is a nonpartisan, quasi-judicial regulatory agency responsible for administering federal securities laws. These laws are designed to protect investors in securities markets and ensure that they have access to disclosure of all material information concerning publicly traded securities. Visitors to the web site can access the EDGAR database of corporate financial and business information.

XXVI. Writers, Photographers & Editors Associations

Associated Press Sports Editors (APSE)
633 Mountain Side Dr.
Allen, TX 75002 US
Phone: 804-741-1565
E-mail Address: *cgrimes@dallasnews.com*
Web Address: www.apse.dallasnews.com
Associated Press Sports Editors (APSE) is a trade organization for professional sports reporters, editors, copy editors and designers.

Association for Women in Sports Media (AWSM)
3899 N. Front St.
Harrisburg, PA 17110 US
Phone: 717-703-3086
E-mail Address: *president@awsmonline.org*
Web Address: www.awsmonline.org
The Association for Women in Sports Media (AWSM) is a global organization of over 400 women and men employed in sports writing, editing, broadcast and production, public relations and sports information.

Football Writers Association of America (FWAA)
18652 Vista del Sol
Dallas, TX 75287 US
Phone: 972-713-6198
E-mail Address: *tigerfwaa@aol.com*
Web Address: www.footballwriters.com
The Football Writers Association of America (FWAA) consists of North American journalists, broadcasters and publishers who cover college football. The FWAA also includes executives in all areas that involve the game.

National Collegiate Baseball Writers Association (NCBWA)
5201 N. O'Connor Blvd., Ste. 300

Irving, TX 75039 US
Phone: 214-774-1351
E-mail Address: *rdanderson@c-usa.org*
Web Address: www.sportswriters.net/ncbwa
The National Collegiate Baseball Writers Association (NCBWA) consists of writers, broadcasters and publicists of college baseball in the U.S.

United States Basketball Writers Association (USBWA)
1818 Chouteau Ave.
St. Louis, MO 63103 US
Phone: 314-421-0339
E-mail Address: *mitch@mvc.org*
Web Address: www.sportswriters.net/usbwa
The United States Basketball Writers Association (USBWA) is an organization representing writers who follow college and high school basketball in the U.S.

Chapter 4

THE SPORTS 350: WHO THEY ARE AND HOW THEY WERE CHOSEN

Includes Indexes by Company Name, Industry & Location, And a Complete Table of Sales, Profits and Ranks

The companies, organizations, leagues and teams chosen to be listed in PLUNKETT'S SPORTS INDUSTRY ALMANAC comprise a unique list. THE SPORTS 350 (the actual count is 361 organizations) were chosen specifically for their dominance in the many facets of the sports, leisure and recreation industry in which they operate. Complete information about each organization can be found in the "Individual Profiles," beginning at the end of this chapter. These profiles are in alphabetical order by organization name.

THE SPORTS 350 teams, leagues and companies are from all parts of the United States, Asia, Canada, Europe and beyond. Essentially, THE SPORTS 350 includes organizations that are deeply involved in the services, teams, leagues and associations that keep the entire industry forging ahead. To be included in our list, the organizations had to meet the following criteria:

1) Generally, these are organizations based in the U.S., however, the headquarters of 55 are located in other nations.
2) Prominence, or a significant presence, in sports, recreation and supporting fields. (See the following Industry Codes section for a complete list of types of manufacturers, businesses, teams and leagues that are covered).
3) The organizations in THE SPORTS 350 do not have to be exclusively in the sports and recreation industry.
4) Sufficient data and vital statistics must have been available to the editors of this book, either directly from the organization being written about or from outside sources deemed reliable and accurate by the editors. A small number of organizations that we would like to have included are not listed because of a lack of sufficient, objective data.

INDEXES TO THE SPORTS 350, AS FOUND IN THIS CHAPTER AND IN THE BACK OF THE BOOK:

INDUSTRY LIST, WITH CODES

This book refers to the following list of unique industry codes, based on the 1997 NAIC code system (NAIC is used by many analysts as a replacement for older SIC codes because NAIC is more specific to today's industry sectors). Companies profiled in this book are given a primary NAIC code, reflecting the main line of business of each firm.

Apparel

Apparel & Shoe Manufacturing

315000 Apparel Manufacturing-General
315000A Apparel Manufacturing-Athletic Clothes
316219 Shoe Manufacturing-Athletic Shoes & Misc. Shoes, Incl. Children's

Entertainment

Toys, Sporting Goods & Miscellaneous Manufacturing

339920 Sporting & Athletic Goods, Manufacturing

Publishing

511120 Magazines Publishing

Broadcasting

513111 Radio Broadcasting
513111A Radio Broadcasting via Satellite
513120 Television Broadcasting
513210 Cable TV Networks
513220 Cable & Satellite TV & Data Service

Entertainment Events & Sports

711211 Stadiums/Sports Teams
711211A Professional Baseball Teams
711211B Professional Basketball Teams
711211C Professional Football Teams
711211D Professional Soccer Teams
711211E Professional Women's Basketball
711211F Professional Hockey
711211G Professional Automobile Racing
711212 Racetracks (Motorsports), Automobile Racing Leagues
711310 Entertainment Events
813990 Sports Leagues & Associations

Gambling & Recreation

713210 Casinos/Horse Racing, Gambling
713910 Golf Courses & Country Clubs
713920 Snow Skiing Facilities
713940 Fitness Centers/Health Clubs
713950 Bowling Facilities

Hotels & Accommodations

721120 Casino Resorts

Food & Restaurants

Food Service

722110 Restaurants
722310 Food Service Contractors

InfoTech

Computers & Electronics Manufacturing

334111 Computer Hardware, Manufacturing

Software

511208 Computer Software, Games & Entertainment

Manufacturing

Food Products Manufacturing

311330 Chocolate & Confectionery Manufacturing

Beverage & Tobacco Manufacturing

312140 Beverages--Distilleries

Retailing

Boat and Accessories Dealers

441222 Boat & Accessories Dealers

Apparel & Accessories Stores

448120 Apparel Stores, Women's

Sporting Goods, Hobbies, Books & Music Stores

451110 Sporting Goods Stores
451110E Sporting Goods Stores-Online
451120 Toys/Hobbies/Games Stores

Miscellaneous Retailers

453220 Gift/Sundry Stores

Nonstore Retailers

454110A Direct Selling, Including Mail Order & Misc. Online
454110B TV Shopping

Services

Consulting & Professional Services

541800 Marketing Agencies & Related Services

Management

551110 Management of Companies & Enterprises

	Performing Arts, Spectator Sports and Related Industries
711410	Agents, Performers, Models, Athletes

INDEX OF RANKINGS WITHIN INDUSTRY GROUPS

Company	Industry Code	2008 Sales (U.S. $ thousands)	Sales Rank	2008 Profits (U.S. $ thousands)	Profits Rank
Agents, Performers, Models, Athletes					
BDA SPORTS MANAGEMENT	711410				
IMG WORLDWIDE INC	711410				
NEWPORT SPORTS MANAGEMENT	711410				
OCTAGON WORLDWIDE	711410				
WILLIAM MORRIS ENDEAVOR ENTERTAINMENT LLC	711410				
Apparel Manufacturing & Design-General					
JARDEN CORP	315000	5,383,300	2	-58,900	2
KELLWOOD CO	315000				
VF CORP	315000	7,642,600	1	602,748	1
Apparel Manufacturing-Athletic Clothes					
BILLABONG INTERNATIONAL	315000A	948,700	3	123,470	1
COLUMBIA SPORTSWEAR CO	315000A	1,317,835	2	95,047	2
DELTA APPAREL INC	315000A	322,034	5	-508	5
EVERLAST WORLDWIDE INC	315000A				
FILA USA INC	315000A				
LULULEMON ATHLETICA INC	315000A	269,942	7	30,843	4
PATAGONIA	315000A	300,000	6		
QUIKSILVER INC	315000A	2,264,636	1	-226,265	6
RUSSELL CORP	315000A				
UNDER ARMOUR INC	315000A	725,244	4	38,229	3
VARSITY BRANDS INC	315000A				
WARNACO SWIMWEAR INC	315000A				
Apparel Stores, Women's					
EVERYTHING BUT WATER INC	448120				
Beverages--Distilleries					
FORTUNE BRANDS INC	312140	7,608,900	1	317,100	1
Boat & Accessories Dealers					
MARINEMAX INC	441222	885,407	1	-134,277	2
WEST MARINE INC	441222	631,258	2	-38,800	1
Bowling Facilities					
AMF BOWLING WORLDWIDE	713950				
BOWL AMERICA INC	713950	30,104	1	3,535	1
Cable TV Networks					
ESPN INC	513210				
FOX BROADCASTING CO	513210				
FOX SPORTS NET INC	513210				
TURNER BROADCASTING SYSTEM	513210				
VIACOM INC	513210	14,625,000	2	1,251,000	2
WALT DISNEY COMPANY	513210	37,843,000	1	4,427,000	1
Cable & Satellite TV & Data Service					
BRITISH SKY BROADCASTING GROUP PLC	513220	6,840,050	6	1,000,040	3
CABLEVISION SYSTEMS CORP	513220	7,230,116	5	-227,576	4
COMCAST CORP	513220	34,256,000	2	2,547,000	2

Company	Industry Code	2008 Sales (U.S. $ thousands)	Sales Rank	2008 Profits (U.S. $ thousands)	Profits Rank
COX COMMUNICATIONS INC	513220	8,500,000	4		
ROGERS COMMUNICATIONS	513220	10,330,500	3	3,700,210	1
TIME WARNER INC	513220	46,984,000	1	-13,402,000	5
Casino Resorts					
PINNACLE ENTERTAINMENT INC	721120	1,044,684	1	-322,597	1
Casinos/Horse Racing, Gambling					
CHURCHILL DOWNS INC	713210	430,566	2	28,549	1
DOVER DOWNS GAMING & ENTERTAINMENT INC	713210	239,132	3	19,511	2
MAGNA ENTERTAINMENT CORP	713210				
PENN NATIONAL GAMING INC	713210	2,423,053	1	-153,323	3
Chocolate & Confectionery Manufacturing					
TOPPS COMPANY INC	311330				
Computer Hardware, Manufacturing					
NINTENDO CO LTD	334111	16,724,230	1	2,573,426	1
Computer Software, Electronic Games & Entertainment					
ELECTRONIC ARTS INC	511208	3,665,000	1	-454,000	3
MIDWAY GAMES INC	511208	219,556	2	-190,974	2
NTN BUZZTIME INC	511208	27,496	3	-6,466	1
Direct Selling, Including Mail Order & Misc. Online					
SPORT SUPPLY GROUP INC	454110A	251,394	2	9,733	1
TICKETMASTER ENTERTAINMENT INC	454110A	1,454,525	1	-1,005,499	2
Facilities Support Services					
GLOBAL SPECTRUM LP	561210				
SMG MANAGEMENT	561210				
Fitness Centers/Health Clubs					
24 HOUR FITNESS USA	713940				
BALLY TOTAL FITNESS HOLDING CORPORATION	713940				
CURVES INTERNATIONAL INC	713940				
GOLD'S GYM INTERNATIONAL	713940				
HEALTH FITNESS CORP	713940	77,676	3	2,722	2
LA FITNESS INTERNATIONAL	713940				
LIFE TIME FITNESS INC	713940	769,621	1	71,821	1
LITTLE GYM INTERNATIONAL	713940				
SNAP FITNESS	713940				
TOWN SPORTS INTERNATIONAL HOLDINGS INC	713940	506,709	2	2,337	3
Food Service Contractors					
ARAMARK CORPORATION	722310	13,470,200	1	39,500	1
CENTERPLATE	722310				
Gift/Sundry Stores					
DELAWARE NORTH COMPANIES	453220				
Golf Courses & Country Clubs					
ACCORDIA GOLF CO LTD	713910	817,230	2	101,030	1
AMERICAN GOLF CORP	713910				
CLUBCORP INC	713910	1,000,000	1		

Company	Industry Code	2008 Sales (U.S. $ thousands)	Sales Rank	2008 Profits (U.S. $ thousands)	Profits Rank
Magazines, Publishing					
SPORTS ILLUSTRATED	511120				
Management of Companies & Enterprises					
HICKS SPORTS GROUP HOLDINGS	551110				
ILITCH HOLDINGS INC	551110	2,000,000	1		
KROENKE SPORTS ENTERPRISES LLC	551110				
MAPLE LEAF SPORTS & ENTERTAINMENT LTD	551110				
PALACE SPORTS & ENTERTAINMENT INC	551110				
VULCAN INC	551110				
Marketing Agencies & Related Services					
SOCCER UNITED MARKETING	541800				
WASSERMAN MEDIA GROUP	541800				
Professional Automobile Racing					
DALE EARNHARDT INC	711211G	86,000	4	5,000	5
EVERNHAM MOTORSPORTS	711211G				
HENDRICK MOTORSPORTS	711211G	179,000	1	21,300	1
JOE GIBBS RACING	711211G	116,000	3	11,700	3
PENSKE RACING	711211G	85,000	5	8,600	4
PETTY ENTERPRISES	711211G	37,000	6	2,900	6
ROUSH FENWAY RACING	711211G	173,000	2	21,300	2
Professional Baseball Teams					
ARIZONA DIAMONDBACKS	711211A	177,000	18	3,900	26
ATLANTA BRAVES	711211A	186,000	13	4,700	25
BALTIMORE ORIOLES LP	711211A	174,000	20	27,200	6
BOSTON RED SOX	711211A	269,000	2	25,700	9
CHICAGO CUBS	711211A	239,000	5	29,700	4
CHICAGO WHITE SOX	711211A	196,000	8	13,800	21
CINCINNATI REDS	711211A	171,000	24	17,000	17
CLEVELAND INDIANS	711211A	181,000	16	19,500	14
COLORADO ROCKIES	711211A	178,000	17	24,500	10
DETROIT TIGERS	711211A	186,000	14	-26,300	30
FLORIDA MARLINS	711211A	139,000	30	43,700	2
HOUSTON ASTROS	711211A	194,000	11	17,000	16
KANSAS CITY ROYALS	711211A	143,000	29	9,000	24
LOS ANGELES ANGELS OF ANAHEIM	711211A	212,000	7	10,300	23
LOS ANGELES DODGERS	711211A	241,000	4	16,500	18
MILWAUKEE BREWERS	711211A	173,000	22	11,800	22
MINNESOTA TWINS	711211A	158,000	27	26,800	7
NEW YORK METS	711211A	261,000	3	23,500	11
NEW YORK YANKEES	711211A	375,000	1	-3,700	29
OAKLAND ATHLETICS	711211A	160,000	25	26,200	8
PHILADELPHIA PHILLIES	711211A	216,000	6	16,300	19
PITTSBURGH PIRATES	711211A	144,000	28	15,900	20
SAN DIEGO PADRES	711211A	174,000	21	22,900	12
SAN FRANCISCO GIANTS	711211A	196,000	9	22,400	13
SEATTLE MARINERS	711211A	189,000	12	3,800	27
ST LOUIS CARDINALS	711211A	195,000	10	66,000	1

Company	Industry Code	2008 Sales (U.S. $ thousands)	Sales Rank	2008 Profits (U.S. $ thousands)	Profits Rank
TAMPA BAY RAYS	711211A	160,000	26	29,400	5
TEXAS RANGERS	711211A	176,000	19	17,400	15
TORONTO BLUE JAYS	711211A	172,000	23	3,000	28
WASHINGTON NATIONALS	711211A	184,000	15	42,600	3
Professional Basketball Teams					
ATLANTA HAWKS	711211B	102,000	20	6,700	16
BOSTON CELTICS	711211B	149,000	8	20,100	8
CHARLOTTE BOBCATS	711211B	95,000	26	-4,900	25
CHICAGO BULLS	711211B	165,000	3	55,400	1
CLEVELAND CAVALIERS	711211B	159,000	5	13,100	12
DALLAS MAVERICKS	711211B	153,000	7	-13,600	29
DENVER NUGGETS	711211B	112,000	18	-26,300	30
DETROIT PISTONS	711211B	160,000	4	40,400	3
GOLDEN STATE WARRIORS	711211B	112,000	19	14,200	11
HOUSTON ROCKETS	711211B	156,000	6	31,200	4
INDIANA PACERS	711211B	101,000	21	-6,500	27
LOS ANGELES CLIPPERS	711211B	99,000	24	10,700	13
LOS ANGELES LAKERS	711211B	191,000	2	47,900	2
MEMPHIS GRIZZLIES	711211B	95,000	27	-3,200	24
MIAMI HEAT	711211B	131,000	12	-1,100	23
MILWAUKEE BUCKS	711211B	94,000	29	5,400	18
MINNESOTA TIMBERWOLVES	711211B	100,000	22	-5,700	26
NEW JERSEY NETS	711211B	98,000	25	-900	22
NEW ORLEANS HORNETS	711211B	95,000	28	3,200	19
NEW YORK KNICKERBOCKERS	711211B	208,000	1	29,600	5
OKLAHOMA CITY THUNDER	711211B	82,000	30	-9,400	28
ORLANDO MAGIC	711211B	100,000	23	6,200	17
PHILADELPHIA 76ERS	711211B	116,000	16	300	20
PHOENIX SUNS	711211B	148,000	9	28,900	6
PORTLAND TRAILBLAZERS	711211B	114,000	17	-900	21
SACRAMENTO KINGS	711211B	117,000	15	7,000	15
SAN ANTONIO SPURS	711211B	138,000	10	19,000	9
TORONTO RAPTORS	711211B	138,000	11	27,700	7
UTAH JAZZ	711211B	119,000	13	8,800	14
WASHINGTON WIZARDS	711211B	118,000	14	14,900	10
Professional Football Teams					
ARIZONA CARDINALS	711211C	203,000	30	19,700	21
ATLANTA FALCONS	711211C	203,000	29	30,900	9
BALTIMORE RAVENS	711211C	226,000	7	23,000	16
BUFFALO BILLS	711211C	206,000	22	12,400	28
CAROLINA PANTHERS	711211C	221,000	11	22,300	17
CHICAGO BEARS	711211C	226,000	9	33,700	7
CINCINNATI BENGALS	711211C	205,000	24	22,000	18
CLEVELAND BROWNS	711211C	220,000	12	19,300	22
DALLAS COWBOYS	711211C	269,000	3	30,600	10
DENVER BRONCOS	711211C	226,000	8	18,800	25
DETROIT LIONS	711211C	204,000	27	-3,100	32
GREEN BAY PACKERS	711211C	218,000	13	21,900	19

Company	Industry Code	2008 Sales (U.S. $ thousands)	Sales Rank	2008 Profits (U.S. $ thousands)	Profits Rank
HOUSTON TEXANS	711211C	239,000	4	43,900	2
INDIANAPOLIS COLTS	711211C	203,000	28	16,100	26
JACKSONVILLE JAGUARS	711211C	204,000	26	27,600	11
KANSAS CITY CHIEFS	711211C	214,000	17	11,900	29
MIAMI DOLPHINS	711211C	232,000	6	36,100	6
MINNESOTA VIKINGS	711211C	195,000	32	18,900	24
NEW ENGLAND PATRIOTS	711211C	282,000	2	39,200	5
NEW ORLEANS SAINTS	711211C	213,000	20	21,500	20
NEW YORK GIANTS	711211C	214,000	18	41,200	3
NEW YORK JETS	711211C	213,000	19	25,900	14
OAKLAND RAIDERS	711211C	205,000	25	27,000	12
PHILADELPHIA EAGLES	711211C	237,000	5	33,500	8
PITTSBURGH STEELERS	711211C	216,000	14	14,400	27
SAN DIEGO CHARGERS	711211C	207,000	21	19,000	23
SAN FRANCISCO 49ERS	711211C	201,000	31	4,100	31
SEATTLE SEAHAWKS	711211C	215,000	16	8,900	30
ST LOUIS RAMS	711211C	206,000	23	26,400	13
TAMPA BAY BUCCANEERS	711211C	224,000	10	39,300	4
TENNESSEE TITANS	711211C	216,000	15	24,500	15
WASHINGTON REDSKINS	711211C	327,000	1	58,100	1
Professional Hockey					
ANAHEIM DUCKS	711211F	90,000	15	1,000	17
ATLANTA THRASHERS	711211F	70,000	27	-6,100	22
BOSTON BRUINS	711211F	97,000	9	-3,000	21
BUFFALO SABRES	711211F	76,000	21	-8,900	27
CALGARY FLAMES	711211F	97,000	10	7,400	8
CAROLINA HURRICANES	711211F	75,000	22	-11,500	30
CHICAGO BLACKHAWKS	711211F	79,000	20	1,400	14
COLORADO AVALANCHE	711211F	91,000	13	2,300	12
COLUMBUS BLUE JACKETS	711211F	71,000	26	-7,100	24
DALLAS STARS	711211F	105,000	6	14,200	5
DETROIT RED WINGS	711211F	110,000	4	13,400	6
EDMONTON OILERS HOCKEY CLUB	711211F	85,000	17	11,800	7
FLORIDA PANTHERS	711211F	74,000	23	-9,400	28
LOS ANGELES KINGS	711211F	91,000	14	1,200	15
MINNESOTA WILD	711211F	94,000	12	700	18
MONTREAL CANADIENS	711211F	139,000	2	39,600	2
NASHVILLE PREDATORS	711211F	70,000	28	-1,300	19
NEW JERSEY DEVILS	711211F	97,000	8	1,900	13
NEW YORK ISLANDERS	711211F	64,000	30	-8,800	26
NEW YORK RANGERS	711211F	137,000	3	30,700	3
OTTAWA SENATORS	711211F	96,000	11	4,700	10
PHILADELPHIA FLYERS	711211F	102,000	7	-1,800	20
PHOENIX COYOTES	711211F	68,000	29	-9,700	29
PITTSBURGH PENGUINS	711211F	87,000	16	5,100	9
SAN JOSE SHARKS	711211F	85,000	18	2,400	11
ST LOUIS BLUES	711211F	73,000	25	-8,600	25
TAMPA BAY LIGHTNING	711211F	84,000	19	1,200	16

Company	Industry Code	2008 Sales (U.S. $ thousands)	Sales Rank	2008 Profits (U.S. $ thousands)	Profits Rank
TORONTO FC	711211F				
TORONTO MAPLE LEAFS	711211F	160,000	1	66,400	1
VANCOUVER CANUCKS	711211F	107,000	5	19,200	4
WASHINGTON CAPITALS	711211F	73,000	24	-6,900	23
Professional Soccer Teams					
ARSENAL FOOTBALL CLUB	711211D	330,000	4	58,000	3
ASTON VILLA FOOTBALL CLUB	711211D	150,000	9	1,000	6
BIRMINGHAM CITY FOOTBALL CLUB	711211D				
BLACKBURN ROVERS FOOTBALL CLUB	711211D				
BOLTON WANDERERS FOOTBALL CLUB	711211D				
CHARLTON ATHLETICS	711211D				
CHELSEA FOOTBALL CLUB	711211D	424,000	2	-13,000	7
CHICAGO FIRE	711211D				
CLUB DEPORTIVO CHIVAS USA	711211D				
COLORADO RAPIDS	711211D				
COLUMBUS CREW	711211D				
CRYSTAL PALACE FOOTBALL CLUB	711211D				
DC UNITED	711211D				
EVERTON FOOTBALL CLUB	711211D	151,000	8	14,000	5
FC DALLAS	711211D				
FULHAM FOOTBALL CLUB	711211D				
HOUSTON DYNAMO	711211D				
KANSAS CITY WIZARDS	711211D				
LIVERPOOL FOOTBALL CLUB	711211D	332,000	3	50,000	4
LOS ANGELES GALAXY	711211D				
MANCHESTER CITY FOOTBALL CLUB	711211D	164,000	7	-16,000	9
MANCHESTER UNITED FOOTBALL CLUB	711211D	512,000	1	160,000	1
MIDDLESBROUGH FOOTBALL CLUB	711211D				
NEW ENGLAND REVOLUTION	711211D				
NEW YORK RED BULLS	711211D				
NEWCASTLE UNITED FOOTBALL CLUB	711211D	198,000	6	-13,000	8
NORWICH CITY FOOTBALL CLUB	711211D				
PORTSMOUTH FOOTBALL CLUB	711211D				
REAL SALT LAKE	711211D				
SAN JOSE EARTHQUAKES	711211D				
SEATTLE SOUNDERS FC	711211D				
SOUTHAMPTON FOOTBALL CLUB	711211D				
TOTTENHAM HOTSPUR FOOTBALL CLUB	711211D	228,000	5	70,000	2
WEST BROMWICH ALBION FOOTBALL CLUB	711211D				
Professional Women's Basketball					
ATLANTA DREAM	711211E				
CONNECTICUT SUN	711211E				
DETROIT SHOCK	711211E				
INDIANA FEVER	711211E				
LOS ANGELES SPARKS	711211E				
MINNESOTA LYNX	711211E				
NEW YORK LIBERTY	711211E				
PHOENIX MERCURY	711211E				

Company	Industry Code	2008 Sales (U.S. $ thousands)	Sales Rank	2008 Profits (U.S. $ thousands)	Profits Rank
SACRAMENTO MONARCHS	711211E				
SAN ANTONIO SILVER STARS	711211E				
SEATTLE STORM	711211E				
WASHINGTON MYSTICS	711211E				
Racetracks (Motorsports), Automobile Racing Leagues					
DOVER MOTORSPORTS INC	711212	84,279	3	-5,679	3
INDY RACING LEAGUE LLC	711212				
INTERNATIONAL SPEEDWAY	711212	787,254	1	134,595	1
NASCAR	711212				
SPEEDWAY MOTORSPORTS	711212	610,993	2	80,040	2
Radio Broadcasting					
CLEAR CHANNEL COMMUNICATIONS INC	513111	6,688,683	1	-4,005,473	1
Radio Broadcasting via Satellite					
SIRIUS XM RADIO INC	513111A	1,663,992	1	-5,313,288	1
Restaurants					
LEVY RESTAURANTS	722110				
Shoe Manufacturing-Athletic Shoes & Misc. Shoes, Incl. Children's					
ADIDAS AG	316219	14,575,800	2	869,230	2
AND 1	316219				
ASICS CORP	316219	2,261,700	4	131,000	4
CONVERSE INC	316219				
K-SWISS INC	316219	340,160	6	20,885	5
NEW BALANCE ATHLETIC SHOE	316219	1,500,000	5		
NIKE INC	316219	18,627,000	1	1,883,400	1
PUMA AG RUDOLF DASSLER SPORT	316219	3,333,260	3	317,420	3
REEBOK INTERNATIONAL LTD	316219				
Snow Skiing Facilities					
BOOTH CREEK SKI HOLDINGS	713920				
BOYNE USA RESORTS	713920				
CRESTED BUTTE MOUNTAIN RESORT INC	713920				
INTRAWEST CORPORATION	713920				
SNOWDANCE INC	713920				
VAIL RESORTS INC	713920	1,152,156	1	102,927	1
WINTER SPORTS INC	713920				
Sporting & Athletic Goods, Manufacturing					
ADAMS GOLF INC	339920	91,451	7	-1,459	4
AMER SPORTS CORPORATION	339920	2,198,350	2	47,470	2
BRUNSWICK CORP	339920	4,708,700	1	-788,100	7
CALLAWAY GOLF COMPANY	339920	1,117,204	3	66,176	1
CAMELBAK	339920				
CANNONDALE BICYCLE CORP	339920				
COLEMAN COMPANY INC	339920				
EASTON-BELL SPORTS INC	339920	775,539	4	13,413	3
FRANKLIN SPORTS INC	339920				
GIANT MANUFACTURING CO	339920				
HEAD NV	339920	474,830	5	-13,720	5
HILLERICH & BRADSBY CO	339920				
HUFFY BICYCLE CO	339920				

Company	Industry Code	2008 Sales (U.S. $ thousands)	Sales Rank	2008 Profits (U.S. $ thousands)	Profits Rank
JOHNSON OUTDOORS INC	339920	420,789	6	-71,034	6
KING PAR CORPORATION	339920				
MAJESTIC ATHLETIC	339920				
NORTH FACE INC	339920				
PACIFIC CYCLE LLC	339920				
PRINCE SPORTS INC	339920				
RAWLINGS SPORTING GOODS	339920				
REEBOK CCM HOCKEY	339920				
SKIS ROSSIGNOL SA	339920				
SPECIALIZED BICYCLE COMPONENTS INC	339920				
TECNICA SPA	339920				
TREK BICYCLE CORPORATION	339920				
WILSON SPORTING GOODS CO	339920				
Sporting Goods Stores					
ACADEMY SPORTS & OUTDOORS LTD	451110	2,000,000	3		
BASS PRO SHOPS INC	451110				
BIG 5 SPORTING GOODS CORPORATION	451110	864,650	5	13,904	5
CABELA'S INC	451110	2,552,721	2	76,404	2
DICK'S SPORTING GOODS INC	451110	3,888,422	1	155,036	1
EASTERN MOUNTAIN SPORTS	451110				
HIBBETT SPORTS INC	451110	520,720	6	30,329	3
ORVIS COMPANY	451110				
RECREATIONAL EQUIPMENT INC (REI)	451110	1,434,569	4	14,465	4
SPORT CHALET INC	451110	402,534	7	-3,362	6
SPORTS AUTHORITY INC	451110				
SPORTSMAN'S GUIDE INC	451110				
Sporting Goods Stores-Online					
GOLF GALAXY INC	451110E				
GOLFSMITH INTERNATIONAL HOLDINGS INC	451110E	378,772	1	-516	1
Sports Leagues & Associations					
AMERICAN HOCKEY LEAGUE	813990				
ARENA FOOTBALL LEAGUE LLC	813990				
ASSOCIATION OF TENNIS PROFESSIONALS	813990				
CANADIAN FOOTBALL LEAGUE	813990				
CENTRAL HOCKEY LEAGUE	813990				
CONTINENTAL BASKETBALL ASSOCIATION	813990				
ECHL (EAST COAST HOCKEY LEAGUE)	813990				
FIFA (FEDERATION INTERNATIONALE DE FOOTBALL ASSOCIATION)	813990	902,497	1	183,655	1
INTERNATIONAL BOXING FEDERATION	813990				
INTERNATIONAL OLYMPIC COMMITTEE (IOC)	813990				
LADIES PROFESSIONAL GOLF ASSOCIATION (LPGA)	813990				
MAJOR LEAGUE BASEBALL (MLB)	813990				
MAJOR LEAGUE SOCCER (MLS)	813990				
MINOR LEAGUE BASEBALL	813990				
NATIONAL BASKETBALL ASSOCIATION (NBA)	813990				
NATIONAL FOOTBALL LEAGUE (NFL)	813990				

Company	Industry Code	2008 Sales (U.S. $ thousands)	Sales Rank	2008 Profits (U.S. $ thousands)	Profits Rank
NATIONAL HOCKEY LEAGUE (NHL)	813990				
NATIONAL THOROUGHBRED RACING ASSOCIATION	813990				
NBA DEVELOPMENT LEAGUE	813990				
PROFESSIONAL BOWLERS ASSOCIATION	813990				
PROFESSIONAL BULL RIDERS	813990				
PROFESSIONAL GOLFERS ASSOCIATION OF AMERICA (PGA)	813990				
UNION OF EUROPEAN FOOTBALL ASSOCIATIONS	813990				
UNITED SOCCER LEAGUES	813990				
UNITED STATES CYCLING FEDERATION (USCF)	813990				
UNITED STATES GOLF ASSOCIATION (USGA)	813990	155,814	2		
UNITED STATES OLYMPIC COMMITTEE (USOC)	813990				
UNITED STATES TENNIS ASSOCIATION (USTA)	813990				
US FIGURE SKATING	813990				
US SOCCER FEDERATION	813990				
USA BASKETBALL	813990				
USA GYMNASTICS	813990				
USA HOCKEY	813990	26,806	3		
USA SWIMMING	813990				
USA TRACK & FIELD INC	813990				
WOMENS NATIONAL BASKETBALL ASSOCIATION (WNBA)	813990				
WOMENS TENNIS ASSOCIATION (WTA)	813990				
WORLD BOXING ASSOCIATION	813990				
WORLD BOXING COUNCIL	813990				
Stadiums/Sports Teams					
ANSCHUTZ ENTERTAINMENT GROUP	711211				
Television Broadcasting					
ABC INC	513120	16,116,000	2		
CBS CORP	513120	13,950,400	3	-12,158,700	2
NBC UNIVERSAL	513210	16,969,000	1	3,131,000	1
Toys/Hobbies/Games Stores					
MOTORSPORTS AUTHENTICS	451120				

ALPHABETICAL INDEX

ELECTRONIC ARTS INC
ESPN INC
EVERLAST WORLDWIDE INC
EVERNHAM MOTORSPORTS
EVERTON FOOTBALL CLUB
EVERYTHING BUT WATER INC
FC DALLAS
FIFA (FEDERATION INTERNATIONALE DE FOOTBALL ASSOCIATION)
FILA USA INC
FLORIDA MARLINS
FLORIDA PANTHERS
FORTUNE BRANDS INC
FOX BROADCASTING COMPANY
FOX SPORTS NET INC
FRANKLIN SPORTS INC
FULHAM FOOTBALL CLUB
GIANT MANUFACTURING CO LTD
GLOBAL SPECTRUM LP
GOLDEN STATE WARRIORS
GOLD'S GYM INTERNATIONAL
GOLF GALAXY INC
GOLFSMITH INTERNATIONAL HOLDINGS INC
GREEN BAY PACKERS
HEAD NV
HEALTH FITNESS CORP
HENDRICK MOTORSPORTS
HIBBETT SPORTS INC
HICKS SPORTS GROUP HOLDINGS
HILLERICH & BRADSBY CO
HOUSTON ASTROS
HOUSTON DYNAMO
HOUSTON ROCKETS
HOUSTON TEXANS
HUFFY BICYCLE CO
ILITCH HOLDINGS INC
IMG WORLDWIDE INC
INDIANA FEVER
INDIANA PACERS
INDIANAPOLIS COLTS
INDY RACING LEAGUE LLC
INTERNATIONAL BOXING FEDERATION
INTERNATIONAL OLYMPIC COMMITTEE (IOC)
INTERNATIONAL SPEEDWAY CORP
INTRAWEST CORPORATION
JACKSONVILLE JAGUARS
JARDEN CORP
JOE GIBBS RACING
JOHNSON OUTDOORS INC
KANSAS CITY CHIEFS
KANSAS CITY ROYALS
KANSAS CITY WIZARDS
KELLWOOD CO
KING PAR CORPORATION
KROENKE SPORTS ENTERPRISES LLC
K-SWISS INC
LA FITNESS INTERNATIONAL LLC
LADIES PROFESSIONAL GOLF ASSOCIATION (LPGA)
LEVY RESTAURANTS
LIFE TIME FITNESS INC
LITTLE GYM INTERNATIONAL INC (THE)
LIVERPOOL FOOTBALL CLUB
LOS ANGELES ANGELS OF ANAHEIM
LOS ANGELES CLIPPERS
LOS ANGELES DODGERS
LOS ANGELES GALAXY
LOS ANGELES KINGS
LOS ANGELES LAKERS
LOS ANGELES SPARKS
LULULEMON ATHLETICA INC
MAGNA ENTERTAINMENT CORP
MAJESTIC ATHLETIC
MAJOR LEAGUE BASEBALL (MLB)
MAJOR LEAGUE SOCCER (MLS)
MANCHESTER CITY FOOTBALL CLUB
MANCHESTER UNITED FOOTBALL CLUB
MAPLE LEAF SPORTS & ENTERTAINMENT LTD
MARINEMAX INC
MEMPHIS GRIZZLIES
MIAMI DOLPHINS
MIAMI HEAT
MIDDLESBROUGH FOOTBALL CLUB
MIDWAY GAMES INC
MILWAUKEE BREWERS
MILWAUKEE BUCKS
MINNESOTA LYNX
MINNESOTA TIMBERWOLVES
MINNESOTA TWINS
MINNESOTA VIKINGS
MINNESOTA WILD
MINOR LEAGUE BASEBALL
MONTREAL CANADIENS
MOTORSPORTS AUTHENTICS INC
NASCAR
NASHVILLE PREDATORS
NATIONAL BASKETBALL ASSOCIATION (NBA)
NATIONAL FOOTBALL LEAGUE (NFL)
NATIONAL HOCKEY LEAGUE (NHL)
NATIONAL THOROUGHBRED RACING ASSOCIATION
NBA DEVELOPMENT LEAGUE
NBC UNIVERSAL
NEW BALANCE ATHLETIC SHOE INC
NEW ENGLAND PATRIOTS
NEW ENGLAND REVOLUTION
NEW JERSEY DEVILS
NEW JERSEY NETS
NEW ORLEANS HORNETS
NEW ORLEANS SAINTS
NEW YORK GIANTS
NEW YORK ISLANDERS
NEW YORK JETS
NEW YORK KNICKERBOCKERS
NEW YORK LIBERTY

NEW YORK METS
NEW YORK RANGERS
NEW YORK RED BULLS
NEW YORK YANKEES
NEWCASTLE UNITED FOOTBALL CLUB
NEWPORT SPORTS MANAGEMENT
NIKE INC
NINTENDO CO LTD
NORTH FACE INC (THE)
NORWICH CITY FOOTBALL CLUB
NTN BUZZTIME INC
OAKLAND ATHLETICS
OAKLAND RAIDERS
OCTAGON WORLDWIDE
OKLAHOMA CITY THUNDER
ORLANDO MAGIC
ORVIS COMPANY (THE)
OTTAWA SENATORS
PACIFIC CYCLE LLC
PALACE SPORTS & ENTERTAINMENT INC
PATAGONIA
PENN NATIONAL GAMING INC
PENSKE RACING
PETTY ENTERPRISES
PHILADELPHIA 76ERS
PHILADELPHIA EAGLES
PHILADELPHIA FLYERS
PHILADELPHIA PHILLIES
PHOENIX COYOTES
PHOENIX MERCURY
PHOENIX SUNS
PINNACLE ENTERTAINMENT INC
PITTSBURGH PENGUINS
PITTSBURGH PIRATES
PITTSBURGH STEELERS
PORTLAND TRAILBLAZERS
PORTSMOUTH FOOTBALL CLUB
PRINCE SPORTS INC
PROFESSIONAL BOWLERS ASSOCIATION
PROFESSIONAL BULL RIDERS INC
PROFESSIONAL GOLFERS ASSOCIATION OF AMERICA (PGA)
PUMA AG RUDOLF DASSLER SPORT
QUIKSILVER INC
RAWLINGS SPORTING GOODS COMPANY INC
REAL SALT LAKE
RECREATIONAL EQUIPMENT INC (REI)
REEBOK CCM HOCKEY
REEBOK INTERNATIONAL LTD
ROGERS COMMUNICATIONS INC
ROUSH FENWAY RACING
RUSSELL CORP
SACRAMENTO KINGS
SACRAMENTO MONARCHS
SAN ANTONIO SILVER STARS
SAN ANTONIO SPURS
SAN DIEGO CHARGERS
SAN DIEGO PADRES
SAN FRANCISCO 49ERS
SAN FRANCISCO GIANTS
SAN JOSE EARTHQUAKES
SAN JOSE SHARKS
SEATTLE MARINERS
SEATTLE SEAHAWKS
SEATTLE SOUNDERS FC
SEATTLE STORM
SIRIUS XM RADIO INC
SKIS ROSSIGNOL SA
SMG MANAGEMENT
SNAP FITNESS
SNOWDANCE INC
SOCCER UNITED MARKETING
SOUTHAMPTON FOOTBALL CLUB
SPECIALIZED BICYCLE COMPONENTS INC
SPEEDWAY MOTORSPORTS INC
SPORT CHALET INC
SPORT SUPPLY GROUP INC
SPORTS AUTHORITY INC (THE)
SPORTS ILLUSTRATED
SPORTSMAN'S GUIDE INC (THE)
ST LOUIS BLUES
ST LOUIS CARDINALS
ST LOUIS RAMS
TAMPA BAY BUCCANEERS
TAMPA BAY LIGHTNING
TAMPA BAY RAYS
TECNICA SPA
TENNESSEE TITANS
TEXAS RANGERS
TICKETMASTER ENTERTAINMENT INC
TIME WARNER INC
TOPPS COMPANY INC (THE)
TORONTO BLUE JAYS
TORONTO FC
TORONTO MAPLE LEAFS
TORONTO RAPTORS
TOTTENHAM HOTSPUR FOOTBALL CLUB
TOWN SPORTS INTERNATIONAL HOLDINGS INC
TREK BICYCLE CORPORATION
TURNER BROADCASTING SYSTEM
UNDER ARMOUR INC
UNION OF EUROPEAN FOOTBALL ASSOCIATIONS
UNITED SOCCER LEAGUES
UNITED STATES CYCLING FEDERATION (USCF)
UNITED STATES GOLF ASSOCIATION (USGA)
UNITED STATES OLYMPIC COMMITTEE (USOC)
UNITED STATES TENNIS ASSOCIATION (USTA)
US FIGURE SKATING
US SOCCER FEDERATION
USA BASKETBALL
USA GYMNASTICS
USA HOCKEY
USA SWIMMING
USA TRACK & FIELD INC
UTAH JAZZ
VAIL RESORTS INC

INDEX OF U.S. HEADQUARTERS LOCATION BY STATE

To help you locate companies geographically, the city and state of the headquarters of each company are in the following index.

SAN FRANCISCO 49ERS; Santa Clara
SAN FRANCISCO GIANTS; San Francisco
SAN JOSE EARTHQUAKES; Santa Clara
SAN JOSE SHARKS; San Jose
SPECIALIZED BICYCLE COMPONENTS INC; Morgan Hill
SPORT CHALET INC; La Canada
TICKETMASTER ENTERTAINMENT INC; West Hollywood
WALT DISNEY COMPANY (THE); Burbank
WARNACO SWIMWEAR INC; Los Angeles
WASSERMAN MEDIA GROUP LLC; Los Angeles
WEST MARINE INC; Watsonville
WILLIAM MORRIS ENDEAVOR ENTERTAINMENT LLC; Beverly Hills

COLORADO
COLORADO AVALANCHE; Denver
COLORADO RAPIDS; Commerce City
COLORADO ROCKIES; Denver
CRESTED BUTTE MOUNTAIN RESORT INC; Mt. Crested Butte
DENVER BRONCOS; Englewood
DENVER NUGGETS; Denver
KROENKE SPORTS ENTERPRISES LLC; Denver
PROFESSIONAL BULL RIDERS INC; Pueblo
SPORTS AUTHORITY INC (THE); Englewood
UNITED STATES CYCLING FEDERATION (USCF); Colorado Springs
UNITED STATES OLYMPIC COMMITTEE (USOC); Colorado Springs
US FIGURE SKATING; Colorado Springs
USA BASKETBALL; Colorado Springs
USA HOCKEY; Colorado Springs
USA SWIMMING; Colorado Springs
VAIL RESORTS INC; Broomfield

CONNECTICUT
CANNONDALE BICYCLE CORPORATION; Bethel
CENTERPLATE; Stamford
CONNECTICUT SUN; Uncasville
ESPN INC; Bristol
OCTAGON WORLDWIDE; Norwalk

DELAWARE
DOVER DOWNS GAMING & ENTERTAINMENT INC; Dover
DOVER MOTORSPORTS INC; Dover

DISTRICT OF COLUMBIA
DC UNITED; Washington
WASHINGTON MYSTICS; Washington
WASHINGTON NATIONALS; Washington
WASHINGTON WIZARDS; Washington

FLORIDA
EVERYTHING BUT WATER INC; Orlando
FLORIDA MARLINS; Miami
FLORIDA PANTHERS; Sunrise
INTERNATIONAL SPEEDWAY CORP; Daytona Beach
JACKSONVILLE JAGUARS; Jacksonville
LADIES PROFESSIONAL GOLF ASSOCIATION (LPGA); Daytona Beach
MARINEMAX INC; Clearwater
MIAMI DOLPHINS; Davie
MIAMI HEAT; Miami
MINOR LEAGUE BASEBALL; St. Petersburg
NASCAR; Daytona Beach
ORLANDO MAGIC; Orlando
PROFESSIONAL GOLFERS ASSOCIATION OF AMERICA (PGA); Palm Beach Gardens
TAMPA BAY BUCCANEERS; Tampa
TAMPA BAY LIGHTNING; Tampa
TAMPA BAY RAYS; St. Petersburg
UNITED SOCCER LEAGUES; Tampa
WOMENS TENNIS ASSOCIATION (WTA); St. Petersburg

GEORGIA
ATLANTA BRAVES; Atlanta
ATLANTA DREAM; Atlanta
ATLANTA FALCONS; Flowery Branch
ATLANTA HAWKS; Atlanta
ATLANTA THRASHERS; Atlanta
COX COMMUNICATIONS INC; Atlanta
DELTA APPAREL INC; Duluth
RUSSELL CORP; Atlanta
TURNER BROADCASTING SYSTEM; Atlanta

ILLINOIS
BALLY TOTAL FITNESS HOLDING CORPORATION; Chicago
BRUNSWICK CORP; Lake Forest
CHICAGO BEARS; Lake Forrest
CHICAGO BLACKHAWKS; Chicago
CHICAGO BULLS; Chicago
CHICAGO CUBS; Chicago
CHICAGO FIRE; Bridgeview
CHICAGO WHITE SOX; Chicago
FORTUNE BRANDS INC; Deerfield
LEVY RESTAURANTS; Chicago
MIDWAY GAMES INC; Chicago
US SOCCER FEDERATION; Chicago
WILSON SPORTING GOODS CO; Chicago

INDIANA
INDIANA FEVER; Indianapolis
INDIANA PACERS; Indianapolis
INDIANAPOLIS COLTS; Indianapolis
INDY RACING LEAGUE LLC; Indianapolis
USA GYMNASTICS; Indianapolis
USA TRACK & FIELD INC; Indianapolis

KANSAS
COLEMAN COMPANY INC (THE); Wichita

KANSAS CITY WIZARDS; Leawood

KENTUCKY
CHURCHILL DOWNS INC; Louisville
HILLERICH & BRADSBY CO; Louisville
NATIONAL THOROUGHBRED RACING ASSOCIATION; Lexington

LOUISIANA
NEW ORLEANS HORNETS; New Orleans
NEW ORLEANS SAINTS; Metairie

MARYLAND
BALTIMORE ORIOLES LP; Baltimore
BALTIMORE RAVENS; Baltimore
FILA USA INC; Sparks
UNDER ARMOUR INC; Baltimore

MASSACHUSETTS
AMERICAN HOCKEY LEAGUE; Springfield
BOSTON BRUINS; Boston
BOSTON CELTICS; Boston
BOSTON RED SOX; Boston
CONVERSE INC; North Andover
FRANKLIN SPORTS INC; Stoughton
NEW BALANCE ATHLETIC SHOE INC; Boston
NEW ENGLAND PATRIOTS; Foxborough
NEW ENGLAND REVOLUTION; Foxborough
REEBOK INTERNATIONAL LTD; Canton

MICHIGAN
BOYNE USA RESORTS; Boyne Falls
DETROIT LIONS; Allen Park
DETROIT PISTONS; Auburn Hills
DETROIT RED WINGS; Detroit
DETROIT SHOCK; Auburn Hills
DETROIT TIGERS; Detroit
ILITCH HOLDINGS INC; Detroit
KING PAR CORPORATION; Flushing
PALACE SPORTS & ENTERTAINMENT INC; Auburn Hills

MINNESOTA
GOLF GALAXY INC; Eden Prairie
HEALTH FITNESS CORP; Minneapolis
LIFE TIME FITNESS INC; Chanhassen
MINNESOTA LYNX; Minneapolis
MINNESOTA TIMBERWOLVES; Minneapolis
MINNESOTA TWINS; Minneapolis
MINNESOTA VIKINGS; Eden Prairie
MINNESOTA WILD; St. Paul
SNAP FITNESS; Chanhassen
SPORTSMAN'S GUIDE INC (THE); St. Paul

MISSOURI
BASS PRO SHOPS INC; Springfield
KANSAS CITY CHIEFS; Kansas City
KANSAS CITY ROYALS; Kansas City
KELLWOOD CO; Chesterfield
RAWLINGS SPORTING GOODS COMPANY INC; St. Louis
ST LOUIS BLUES; St. Louis
ST LOUIS CARDINALS; St. Louis
ST LOUIS RAMS; St. Louis

MONTANA
WINTER SPORTS INC; Whitefish

NEBRASKA
CABELA'S INC; Sidney

NEVADA
PINNACLE ENTERTAINMENT INC; Las Vegas

NEW HAMPSHIRE
EASTERN MOUNTAIN SPORTS; Peterborough

NEW JERSEY
ECHL (EAST COAST HOCKEY LEAGUE); Princeton
INTERNATIONAL BOXING FEDERATION; East Orange
NEW JERSEY DEVILS; East Rutherford
NEW JERSEY NETS; East Rutherford
NEW YORK GIANTS; East Rutherford
NEW YORK JETS; Florham Park
NEW YORK RED BULLS; Secaucus
PRINCE SPORTS INC; Bordentown
UNITED STATES GOLF ASSOCIATION (USGA); Far Hills

NEW YORK
ABC INC; New York
ARENA FOOTBALL LEAGUE LLC; New York
BUFFALO BILLS; Orchard Park
BUFFALO SABRES; Buffalo
CABLEVISION SYSTEMS CORP; Bethpage
CBS CORP; New York
CONTINENTAL BASKETBALL ASSOCIATION; Albany
DELAWARE NORTH COMPANIES INC; Buffalo
EVERLAST WORLDWIDE INC; New York
JARDEN CORP; Rye
MAJOR LEAGUE BASEBALL (MLB); New York
MAJOR LEAGUE SOCCER (MLS); New York
NATIONAL BASKETBALL ASSOCIATION (NBA); New York
NATIONAL FOOTBALL LEAGUE (NFL); New York
NATIONAL HOCKEY LEAGUE (NHL); New York
NBA DEVELOPMENT LEAGUE; New York
NBC UNIVERSAL; New York
NEW YORK ISLANDERS; Plainview
NEW YORK KNICKERBOCKERS; New York
NEW YORK LIBERTY; New York
NEW YORK METS; Flushing

NEW YORK RANGERS; New York
NEW YORK YANKEES; Bronx
SIRIUS XM RADIO INC; New York
SOCCER UNITED MARKETING; New York
SPORTS ILLUSTRATED; New York
TIME WARNER INC; New York
TOPPS COMPANY INC (THE); New York
TOWN SPORTS INTERNATIONAL HOLDINGS INC; New York
UNITED STATES TENNIS ASSOCIATION (USTA); White Plains
VIACOM INC; New York
WOMENS NATIONAL BASKETBALL ASSOCIATION (WNBA); New York

NORTH CAROLINA

CAROLINA HURRICANES; Raleigh
CAROLINA PANTHERS; Charlotte
CHARLOTTE BOBCATS; Charlotte
DALE EARNHARDT INC; Mooresville
EVERNHAM MOTORSPORTS; Statesville
HENDRICK MOTORSPORTS; Charlotte
JOE GIBBS RACING; Huntersville
MOTORSPORTS AUTHENTICS INC; Concord
PENSKE RACING; Mooresville
PETTY ENTERPRISES; Statesville
ROUSH FENWAY RACING; Concord
SPEEDWAY MOTORSPORTS INC; Concord
VF CORP; Greensboro

OHIO

CINCINNATI BENGALS; Cincinnati
CINCINNATI REDS; Cincinnati
CLEVELAND BROWNS; Berea
CLEVELAND CAVALIERS; Cleveland
CLEVELAND INDIANS; Cleveland
COLUMBUS BLUE JACKETS; Columbus
COLUMBUS CREW; Columbus
HUFFY BICYCLE CO; Centerville
IMG WORLDWIDE INC; Cleveland

OKLAHOMA

OKLAHOMA CITY THUNDER; Oklahoma City

OREGON

COLUMBIA SPORTSWEAR CO; Portland
NIKE INC; Beaverton
PORTLAND TRAILBLAZERS; Portland

PENNSYLVANIA

ARAMARK CORPORATION; Philadelphia
COMCAST CORP; Philadelphia
DICK'S SPORTING GOODS INC; Pittsburgh
GLOBAL SPECTRUM LP; Philadelphia
MAJESTIC ATHLETIC; Easton
PENN NATIONAL GAMING INC; Wyomissing
PHILADELPHIA 76ERS; Philadelphia
PHILADELPHIA EAGLES; Philadelphia
PHILADELPHIA FLYERS; Philadelphia
PHILADELPHIA PHILLIES; Philadelphia
PITTSBURGH PENGUINS; Pittsburgh
PITTSBURGH PIRATES; Pittsburgh
PITTSBURGH STEELERS; Pittsburgh
SMG MANAGEMENT; W. Conshohocken

TENNESSEE

MEMPHIS GRIZZLIES; Memphis
NASHVILLE PREDATORS; Nashville
TENNESSEE TITANS; Nashville
VARSITY BRANDS INC; Memphis

TEXAS

ACADEMY SPORTS & OUTDOORS LTD; Katy
ADAMS GOLF INC; Plano
CLEAR CHANNEL COMMUNICATIONS INC; San Antonio
CLUBCORP INC; Dallas
CURVES INTERNATIONAL INC; Waco
DALLAS COWBOYS; Irving
DALLAS MAVERICKS; Dallas
DALLAS STARS; Frisco
FC DALLAS; Frisco
GOLD'S GYM INTERNATIONAL; Irving
GOLFSMITH INTERNATIONAL HOLDINGS INC; Austin
HICKS SPORTS GROUP HOLDINGS; Arlington
HOUSTON ASTROS; Houston
HOUSTON DYNAMO; Houston
HOUSTON ROCKETS; Houston
HOUSTON TEXANS; Houston
SAN ANTONIO SILVER STARS; San Antonio
SAN ANTONIO SPURS; San Antonio
SPORT SUPPLY GROUP INC; Farmers Branch
TEXAS RANGERS; Arlington

UTAH

REAL SALT LAKE; Salt Lake City
UTAH JAZZ; Salt Lake City

VERMONT

SNOWDANCE INC; Brownsville
ORVIS COMPANY (THE); Sunderland

VIRGINIA

AMF BOWLING WORLDWIDE INC; Mechanicsville
BOWL AMERICA INC; Alexandria
WASHINGTON CAPITALS; Arlington
WASHINGTON REDSKINS; Ashburn

WASHINGTON

PROFESSIONAL BOWLERS ASSOCIATION; Seattle
RECREATIONAL EQUIPMENT INC (REI); Kent
SEATTLE MARINERS; Seattle
SEATTLE SEAHAWKS; Renton
SEATTLE SOUNDERS FC; Renton

WISCONSIN

INDEX OF NON-U.S. HEADQUARTERS LOCATION BY COUNTRY

AUSTRALIA

CANADA

FINLAND

FRANCE

GERMANY

ITALY

JAPAN

MEXICO

PANAMA

SWITZERLAND

INDEX BY REGIONS OF THE U.S. WHERE THE FIRMS HAVE LOCATIONS

INTRAWEST CORPORATION
JOHNSON OUTDOORS INC
KELLWOOD CO
KROENKE SPORTS ENTERPRISES LLC
K-SWISS INC
LA FITNESS INTERNATIONAL LLC
LEVY RESTAURANTS
LIFE TIME FITNESS INC
LITTLE GYM INTERNATIONAL INC (THE)
LOS ANGELES ANGELS OF ANAHEIM
LOS ANGELES CLIPPERS
LOS ANGELES DODGERS
LOS ANGELES GALAXY
LOS ANGELES KINGS
LOS ANGELES LAKERS
LOS ANGELES SPARKS
LULULEMON ATHLETICA INC
MAGNA ENTERTAINMENT CORP
MARINEMAX INC
MIDWAY GAMES INC
MOTORSPORTS AUTHENTICS INC
NASCAR
NATIONAL BASKETBALL ASSOCIATION (NBA)
NATIONAL HOCKEY LEAGUE (NHL)
NBC UNIVERSAL
NIKE INC
NINTENDO CO LTD
NORTH FACE INC (THE)
NTN BUZZTIME INC
OAKLAND ATHLETICS
OAKLAND RAIDERS
OCTAGON WORLDWIDE
OKLAHOMA CITY THUNDER
ORVIS COMPANY (THE)
PATAGONIA
PENN NATIONAL GAMING INC
PINNACLE ENTERTAINMENT INC
PORTLAND TRAILBLAZERS
PROFESSIONAL BOWLERS ASSOCIATION
PROFESSIONAL BULL RIDERS INC
PROFESSIONAL GOLFERS ASSOCIATION OF AMERICA (PGA)
QUIKSILVER INC
RAWLINGS SPORTING GOODS COMPANY INC
REAL SALT LAKE
RECREATIONAL EQUIPMENT INC (REI)
REEBOK INTERNATIONAL LTD
RUSSELL CORP
SACRAMENTO KINGS
SACRAMENTO MONARCHS
SAN DIEGO CHARGERS
SAN DIEGO PADRES
SAN FRANCISCO 49ERS
SAN FRANCISCO GIANTS
SAN JOSE EARTHQUAKES
SAN JOSE SHARKS
SEATTLE MARINERS
SEATTLE SEAHAWKS
SEATTLE SOUNDERS FC
SEATTLE STORM
SKIS ROSSIGNOL SA
SMG MANAGEMENT
SNAP FITNESS
SPECIALIZED BICYCLE COMPONENTS INC
SPEEDWAY MOTORSPORTS INC
SPORT CHALET INC
SPORTS AUTHORITY INC (THE)
SPORTS ILLUSTRATED
TICKETMASTER ENTERTAINMENT INC
TIME WARNER INC
TOPPS COMPANY INC (THE)
UNDER ARMOUR INC
UNITED STATES CYCLING FEDERATION (USCF)
UNITED STATES OLYMPIC COMMITTEE (USOC)
UNITED STATES TENNIS ASSOCIATION (USTA)
US FIGURE SKATING
US SOCCER FEDERATION
USA BASKETBALL
USA HOCKEY
USA SWIMMING
USA TRACK & FIELD INC
UTAH JAZZ
VAIL RESORTS INC
VF CORP
VIACOM INC
VULCAN INC
WALT DISNEY COMPANY (THE)
WARNACO SWIMWEAR INC
WASSERMAN MEDIA GROUP LLC
WEST MARINE INC
WILLIAM MORRIS ENDEAVOR ENTERTAINMENT LLC
WINTER SPORTS INC

SOUTHWEST

24 HOUR FITNESS USA
ABC INC
ACADEMY SPORTS & OUTDOORS LTD
ADAMS GOLF INC
AMERICAN GOLF CORP
AMF BOWLING WORLDWIDE INC
AND 1
ANSCHUTZ ENTERTAINMENT GROUP
ARAMARK CORPORATION
ARIZONA CARDINALS
ARIZONA DIAMONDBACKS
BALLY TOTAL FITNESS HOLDING CORPORATION
BASS PRO SHOPS INC
BIG 5 SPORTING GOODS CORPORATION
BRUNSWICK CORP
CABELA'S INC
CBS CORP
CENTERPLATE
CENTRAL HOCKEY LEAGUE
CLEAR CHANNEL COMMUNICATIONS INC
CLUBCORP INC

COLEMAN COMPANY INC (THE)
COMCAST CORP
COX COMMUNICATIONS INC
CURVES INTERNATIONAL INC
DALLAS COWBOYS
DALLAS MAVERICKS
DALLAS STARS
DELAWARE NORTH COMPANIES INC
DICK'S SPORTING GOODS INC
ELECTRONIC ARTS INC
EVERYTHING BUT WATER INC
FC DALLAS
FOX SPORTS NET INC
GOLD'S GYM INTERNATIONAL
GOLF GALAXY INC
GOLFSMITH INTERNATIONAL HOLDINGS INC
HEAD NV
HEALTH FITNESS CORP
HIBBETT SPORTS INC
HICKS SPORTS GROUP HOLDINGS
HOUSTON ASTROS
HOUSTON DYNAMO
HOUSTON ROCKETS
HOUSTON TEXANS
INTERNATIONAL SPEEDWAY CORP
INTRAWEST CORPORATION
LA FITNESS INTERNATIONAL LLC
LEVY RESTAURANTS
LIFE TIME FITNESS INC
LITTLE GYM INTERNATIONAL INC (THE)
LULULEMON ATHLETICA INC
MAGNA ENTERTAINMENT CORP
MARINEMAX INC
MIDWAY GAMES INC
MOTORSPORTS AUTHENTICS INC
NASCAR
NATIONAL HOCKEY LEAGUE (NHL)
NIKE INC
NTN BUZZTIME INC
ORVIS COMPANY (THE)
PATAGONIA
PENN NATIONAL GAMING INC
PHOENIX COYOTES
PHOENIX MERCURY
PHOENIX SUNS
PROFESSIONAL GOLFERS ASSOCIATION OF AMERICA (PGA)
RECREATIONAL EQUIPMENT INC (REI)
REEBOK INTERNATIONAL LTD
SAN ANTONIO SILVER STARS
SAN ANTONIO SPURS
SMG MANAGEMENT
SNAP FITNESS
SPEEDWAY MOTORSPORTS INC
SPORT CHALET INC
SPORT SUPPLY GROUP INC
SPORTS AUTHORITY INC (THE)
SPORTS ILLUSTRATED
TEXAS RANGERS
TICKETMASTER ENTERTAINMENT INC
TIME WARNER INC
UNITED STATES TENNIS ASSOCIATION (USTA)
US SOCCER FEDERATION
VAIL RESORTS INC
VF CORP
WALT DISNEY COMPANY (THE)
WEST MARINE INC

MIDWEST

24 HOUR FITNESS USA
ABC INC
ACADEMY SPORTS & OUTDOORS LTD
AMER SPORTS CORPORATION
AMERICAN GOLF CORP
AMF BOWLING WORLDWIDE INC
AND 1
ANSCHUTZ ENTERTAINMENT GROUP
ARAMARK CORPORATION
ARENA FOOTBALL LEAGUE LLC
ASSOCIATION OF TENNIS PROFESSIONALS
BALLY TOTAL FITNESS HOLDING CORPORATION
BASS PRO SHOPS INC
BDA SPORTS MANAGEMENT
BOYNE USA RESORTS
BRUNSWICK CORP
CABELA'S INC
CBS CORP
CENTERPLATE
CHICAGO BEARS
CHICAGO BLACKHAWKS
CHICAGO BULLS
CHICAGO CUBS
CHICAGO FIRE
CHICAGO WHITE SOX
CHURCHILL DOWNS INC
CINCINNATI BENGALS
CINCINNATI REDS
CLEAR CHANNEL COMMUNICATIONS INC
CLEVELAND BROWNS
CLEVELAND CAVALIERS
CLEVELAND INDIANS
CLUBCORP INC
COLEMAN COMPANY INC (THE)
COLUMBUS BLUE JACKETS
COLUMBUS CREW
COMCAST CORP
COX COMMUNICATIONS INC
CURVES INTERNATIONAL INC
DELAWARE NORTH COMPANIES INC
DELTA APPAREL INC
DETROIT LIONS
DETROIT PISTONS
DETROIT RED WINGS
DETROIT SHOCK
DETROIT TIGERS
DICK'S SPORTING GOODS INC

DOVER MOTORSPORTS INC
ELECTRONIC ARTS INC
EVERYTHING BUT WATER INC
FORTUNE BRANDS INC
FOX SPORTS NET INC
GOLD'S GYM INTERNATIONAL
GOLF GALAXY INC
GOLFSMITH INTERNATIONAL HOLDINGS INC
GREEN BAY PACKERS
HEALTH FITNESS CORP
HIBBETT SPORTS INC
HILLERICH & BRADSBY CO
HUFFY BICYCLE CO
ILITCH HOLDINGS INC
IMG WORLDWIDE INC
INDIANA FEVER
INDIANA PACERS
INDIANAPOLIS COLTS
INDY RACING LEAGUE LLC
INTERNATIONAL SPEEDWAY CORP
JOHNSON OUTDOORS INC
KANSAS CITY CHIEFS
KANSAS CITY ROYALS
KANSAS CITY WIZARDS
KELLWOOD CO
KING PAR CORPORATION
LA FITNESS INTERNATIONAL LLC
LEVY RESTAURANTS
LIFE TIME FITNESS INC
LITTLE GYM INTERNATIONAL INC (THE)
LULULEMON ATHLETICA INC
MAGNA ENTERTAINMENT CORP
MARINEMAX INC
MIDWAY GAMES INC
MILWAUKEE BREWERS
MILWAUKEE BUCKS
MINNESOTA LYNX
MINNESOTA TIMBERWOLVES
MINNESOTA TWINS
MINNESOTA VIKINGS
MINNESOTA WILD
MOTORSPORTS AUTHENTICS INC
NASCAR
NATIONAL HOCKEY LEAGUE (NHL)
NATIONAL THOROUGHBRED RACING ASSOCIATION
NBC UNIVERSAL
NEWPORT SPORTS MANAGEMENT
NIKE INC
NORTH FACE INC (THE)
ORVIS COMPANY (THE)
PACIFIC CYCLE LLC
PALACE SPORTS & ENTERTAINMENT INC
PATAGONIA
PENN NATIONAL GAMING INC
PINNACLE ENTERTAINMENT INC
PROFESSIONAL GOLFERS ASSOCIATION OF AMERICA (PGA)
RAWLINGS SPORTING GOODS COMPANY INC
RECREATIONAL EQUIPMENT INC (REI)
REEBOK INTERNATIONAL LTD
ROUSH FENWAY RACING
RUSSELL CORP
SMG MANAGEMENT
SNAP FITNESS
SPECIALIZED BICYCLE COMPONENTS INC
SPORTS AUTHORITY INC (THE)
SPORTS ILLUSTRATED
SPORTSMAN'S GUIDE INC (THE)
ST LOUIS BLUES
ST LOUIS CARDINALS
ST LOUIS RAMS
TICKETMASTER ENTERTAINMENT INC
TIME WARNER INC
TREK BICYCLE CORPORATION
UNITED STATES OLYMPIC COMMITTEE (USOC)
UNITED STATES TENNIS ASSOCIATION (USTA)
US SOCCER FEDERATION
USA GYMNASTICS
USA TRACK & FIELD INC
VF CORP
VIACOM INC
WALT DISNEY COMPANY (THE)
WEST MARINE INC
WILSON SPORTING GOODS CO

SOUTHEAST

24 HOUR FITNESS USA
ABC INC
ACADEMY SPORTS & OUTDOORS LTD
AMERICAN GOLF CORP
AMF BOWLING WORLDWIDE INC
AND 1
ANSCHUTZ ENTERTAINMENT GROUP
ARAMARK CORPORATION
ASSOCIATION OF TENNIS PROFESSIONALS
ATLANTA BRAVES
ATLANTA DREAM
ATLANTA FALCONS
ATLANTA HAWKS
ATLANTA THRASHERS
BALLY TOTAL FITNESS HOLDING CORPORATION
BASS PRO SHOPS INC
BOSTON RED SOX
BOWL AMERICA INC
BOYNE USA RESORTS
BRUNSWICK CORP
CBS CORP
CENTERPLATE
CHURCHILL DOWNS INC
CINCINNATI REDS
CLEAR CHANNEL COMMUNICATIONS INC
CLUBCORP INC
COLEMAN COMPANY INC (THE)
COMCAST CORP
COX COMMUNICATIONS INC

CURVES INTERNATIONAL INC
DELAWARE NORTH COMPANIES INC
DELTA APPAREL INC
DICK'S SPORTING GOODS INC
DOVER MOTORSPORTS INC
ELECTRONIC ARTS INC
EVERYTHING BUT WATER INC
FLORIDA MARLINS
FLORIDA PANTHERS
FOX SPORTS NET INC
GLOBAL SPECTRUM LP
GOLD'S GYM INTERNATIONAL
GOLF GALAXY INC
GOLFSMITH INTERNATIONAL HOLDINGS INC
HEALTH FITNESS CORP
HIBBETT SPORTS INC
IMG WORLDWIDE INC
INTERNATIONAL SPEEDWAY CORP
INTRAWEST CORPORATION
JACKSONVILLE JAGUARS
JOHNSON OUTDOORS INC
KELLWOOD CO
LA FITNESS INTERNATIONAL LLC
LADIES PROFESSIONAL GOLF ASSOCIATION (LPGA)
LEVY RESTAURANTS
LIFE TIME FITNESS INC
LITTLE GYM INTERNATIONAL INC (THE)
LULULEMON ATHLETICA INC
MAGNA ENTERTAINMENT CORP
MARINEMAX INC
MEMPHIS GRIZZLIES
MIAMI DOLPHINS
MIAMI HEAT
MINOR LEAGUE BASEBALL
MOTORSPORTS AUTHENTICS INC
NASCAR
NASHVILLE PREDATORS
NATIONAL BASKETBALL ASSOCIATION (NBA)
NATIONAL HOCKEY LEAGUE (NHL)
NEW ORLEANS HORNETS
NEW ORLEANS SAINTS
NIKE INC
NTN BUZZTIME INC
OCTAGON WORLDWIDE
ORLANDO MAGIC
ORVIS COMPANY (THE)
PATAGONIA
PENN NATIONAL GAMING INC
PINNACLE ENTERTAINMENT INC
PROFESSIONAL GOLFERS ASSOCIATION OF AMERICA (PGA)
RAWLINGS SPORTING GOODS COMPANY INC
RECREATIONAL EQUIPMENT INC (REI)
REEBOK INTERNATIONAL LTD
RUSSELL CORP
SMG MANAGEMENT
SNAP FITNESS
SPEEDWAY MOTORSPORTS INC
SPORT SUPPLY GROUP INC
SPORTS AUTHORITY INC (THE)
SPORTS ILLUSTRATED
TAMPA BAY BUCCANEERS
TAMPA BAY LIGHTNING
TAMPA BAY RAYS
TENNESSEE TITANS
TICKETMASTER ENTERTAINMENT INC
TIME WARNER INC
TURNER BROADCASTING SYSTEM
UNITED SOCCER LEAGUES
UNITED STATES OLYMPIC COMMITTEE (USOC)
UNITED STATES TENNIS ASSOCIATION (USTA)
US SOCCER FEDERATION
VARSITY BRANDS INC
VF CORP
WALT DISNEY COMPANY (THE)
WEST MARINE INC
WILLIAM MORRIS ENDEAVOR ENTERTAINMENT LLC
WOMENS TENNIS ASSOCIATION (WTA)

NORTHEAST
ABC INC
ADIDAS AG
AMER SPORTS CORPORATION
AMERICAN GOLF CORP
AMERICAN HOCKEY LEAGUE
AMF BOWLING WORLDWIDE INC
AND 1
ANSCHUTZ ENTERTAINMENT GROUP
ARAMARK CORPORATION
ARENA FOOTBALL LEAGUE LLC
BALLY TOTAL FITNESS HOLDING CORPORATION
BALTIMORE ORIOLES LP
BALTIMORE RAVENS
BASS PRO SHOPS INC
BDA SPORTS MANAGEMENT
BOOTH CREEK SKI HOLDINGS INC
BOSTON BRUINS
BOSTON CELTICS
BOSTON RED SOX
BOWL AMERICA INC
BRUNSWICK CORP
BUFFALO BILLS
BUFFALO SABRES
CABELA'S INC
CABLEVISION SYSTEMS CORP
CANNONDALE BICYCLE CORPORATION
CAROLINA HURRICANES
CAROLINA PANTHERS
CBS CORP
CENTERPLATE
CHARLOTTE BOBCATS
CLEAR CHANNEL COMMUNICATIONS INC
CLUBCORP INC
COLEMAN COMPANY INC (THE)

COMCAST CORP
CONNECTICUT SUN
CONTINENTAL BASKETBALL ASSOCIATION
CONVERSE INC
COX COMMUNICATIONS INC
CURVES INTERNATIONAL INC
DALE EARNHARDT INC
DC UNITED
DELAWARE NORTH COMPANIES INC
DELTA APPAREL INC
DICK'S SPORTING GOODS INC
DOVER DOWNS GAMING & ENTERTAINMENT INC
DOVER MOTORSPORTS INC
EASTERN MOUNTAIN SPORTS
ECHL (EAST COAST HOCKEY LEAGUE)
ELECTRONIC ARTS INC
ESPN INC
EVERLAST WORLDWIDE INC
EVERNHAM MOTORSPORTS
EVERYTHING BUT WATER INC
FILA USA INC
FOX SPORTS NET INC
FRANKLIN SPORTS INC
GLOBAL SPECTRUM LP
GOLD'S GYM INTERNATIONAL
GOLF GALAXY INC
GOLFSMITH INTERNATIONAL HOLDINGS INC
HEAD NV
HEALTH FITNESS CORP
HENDRICK MOTORSPORTS
HIBBETT SPORTS INC
IMG WORLDWIDE INC
INTERNATIONAL BOXING FEDERATION
INTERNATIONAL SPEEDWAY CORP
INTRAWEST CORPORATION
JARDEN CORP
JOE GIBBS RACING
JOHNSON OUTDOORS INC
KELLWOOD CO
LA FITNESS INTERNATIONAL LLC
LEVY RESTAURANTS
LIFE TIME FITNESS INC
LITTLE GYM INTERNATIONAL INC (THE)
LULULEMON ATHLETICA INC
MAGNA ENTERTAINMENT CORP
MAJESTIC ATHLETIC
MAJOR LEAGUE BASEBALL (MLB)
MAJOR LEAGUE SOCCER (MLS)
MARINEMAX INC
MOTORSPORTS AUTHENTICS INC
NASCAR
NATIONAL BASKETBALL ASSOCIATION (NBA)
NATIONAL FOOTBALL LEAGUE (NFL)
NATIONAL HOCKEY LEAGUE (NHL)
NATIONAL THOROUGHBRED RACING ASSOCIATION
NBA DEVELOPMENT LEAGUE
NBC UNIVERSAL
NEW BALANCE ATHLETIC SHOE INC
NEW ENGLAND PATRIOTS
NEW ENGLAND REVOLUTION
NEW JERSEY DEVILS
NEW JERSEY NETS
NEW YORK GIANTS
NEW YORK ISLANDERS
NEW YORK JETS
NEW YORK KNICKERBOCKERS
NEW YORK LIBERTY
NEW YORK METS
NEW YORK RANGERS
NEW YORK RED BULLS
NEW YORK YANKEES
NIKE INC
NORTH FACE INC (THE)
OCTAGON WORLDWIDE
ORVIS COMPANY (THE)
PATAGONIA
PENN NATIONAL GAMING INC
PENSKE RACING
PETTY ENTERPRISES
PHILADELPHIA 76ERS
PHILADELPHIA EAGLES
PHILADELPHIA FLYERS
PHILADELPHIA PHILLIES
PINNACLE ENTERTAINMENT INC
PITTSBURGH PENGUINS
PITTSBURGH PIRATES
PITTSBURGH STEELERS
PRINCE SPORTS INC
PROFESSIONAL GOLFERS ASSOCIATION OF AMERICA (PGA)
PUMA AG RUDOLF DASSLER SPORT
RAWLINGS SPORTING GOODS COMPANY INC
RECREATIONAL EQUIPMENT INC (REI)
REEBOK CCM HOCKEY
REEBOK INTERNATIONAL LTD
ROUSH FENWAY RACING
RUSSELL CORP
SIRIUS XM RADIO INC
SMG MANAGEMENT
SNAP FITNESS
SNOWDANCE INC
SOCCER UNITED MARKETING
SPECIALIZED BICYCLE COMPONENTS INC
SPEEDWAY MOTORSPORTS INC
SPORTS AUTHORITY INC (THE)
SPORTS ILLUSTRATED
TECNICA SPA
TICKETMASTER ENTERTAINMENT INC
TIME WARNER INC
TOPPS COMPANY INC (THE)
TOWN SPORTS INTERNATIONAL HOLDINGS INC
TURNER BROADCASTING SYSTEM
UNDER ARMOUR INC
UNITED STATES GOLF ASSOCIATION (USGA)
UNITED STATES OLYMPIC COMMITTEE (USOC)

INDEX OF FIRMS WITH INTERNATIONAL OPERATIONS

FORTUNE BRANDS INC
FULHAM FOOTBALL CLUB
GIANT MANUFACTURING CO LTD
GLOBAL SPECTRUM LP
GOLD'S GYM INTERNATIONAL
GOLFSMITH INTERNATIONAL HOLDINGS INC
HEAD NV
HEALTH FITNESS CORP
HILLERICH & BRADSBY CO
HOUSTON ASTROS
IMG WORLDWIDE INC
INTERNATIONAL OLYMPIC COMMITTEE (IOC)
INTRAWEST CORPORATION
JARDEN CORP
JOHNSON OUTDOORS INC
KANSAS CITY ROYALS
KELLWOOD CO
K-SWISS INC
LA FITNESS INTERNATIONAL LLC
LEVY RESTAURANTS
LITTLE GYM INTERNATIONAL INC (THE)
LIVERPOOL FOOTBALL CLUB
LOS ANGELES ANGELS OF ANAHEIM
LOS ANGELES DODGERS
LULULEMON ATHLETICA INC
MAGNA ENTERTAINMENT CORP
MAJESTIC ATHLETIC
MAJOR LEAGUE BASEBALL (MLB)
MANCHESTER CITY FOOTBALL CLUB
MANCHESTER UNITED FOOTBALL CLUB
MAPLE LEAF SPORTS & ENTERTAINMENT LTD
MIDDLESBROUGH FOOTBALL CLUB
MIDWAY GAMES INC
MILWAUKEE BREWERS
MINNESOTA TWINS
MINOR LEAGUE BASEBALL
MONTREAL CANADIENS
MOTORSPORTS AUTHENTICS INC
NASCAR
NATIONAL BASKETBALL ASSOCIATION (NBA)
NATIONAL HOCKEY LEAGUE (NHL)
NBC UNIVERSAL
NEW BALANCE ATHLETIC SHOE INC
NEW YORK YANKEES
NEWCASTLE UNITED FOOTBALL CLUB
NEWPORT SPORTS MANAGEMENT
NIKE INC
NINTENDO CO LTD
NORTH FACE INC (THE)
NORWICH CITY FOOTBALL CLUB
NTN BUZZTIME INC
OAKLAND ATHLETICS
OCTAGON WORLDWIDE
ORVIS COMPANY (THE)
OTTAWA SENATORS
PATAGONIA
PENN NATIONAL GAMING INC
PINNACLE ENTERTAINMENT INC
PORTSMOUTH FOOTBALL CLUB
PROFESSIONAL BULL RIDERS INC
PUMA AG RUDOLF DASSLER SPORT
QUIKSILVER INC
REEBOK CCM HOCKEY
REEBOK INTERNATIONAL LTD
ROGERS COMMUNICATIONS INC
RUSSELL CORP
SKIS ROSSIGNOL SA
SMG MANAGEMENT
SNAP FITNESS
SOUTHAMPTON FOOTBALL CLUB
SPORTS AUTHORITY INC (THE)
SPORTS ILLUSTRATED
TECNICA SPA
TICKETMASTER ENTERTAINMENT INC
TIME WARNER INC
TOPPS COMPANY INC (THE)
TORONTO BLUE JAYS
TORONTO FC
TORONTO MAPLE LEAFS
TORONTO RAPTORS
TOTTENHAM HOTSPUR FOOTBALL CLUB
TOWN SPORTS INTERNATIONAL HOLDINGS INC
TREK BICYCLE CORPORATION
UNDER ARMOUR INC
UNION OF EUROPEAN FOOTBALL ASSOCIATIONS
UNITED STATES TENNIS ASSOCIATION (USTA)
VANCOUVER CANUCKS
VF CORP
VIACOM INC
WALT DISNEY COMPANY (THE)
WASSERMAN MEDIA GROUP LLC
WEST BROMWICH ALBION FOOTBALL CLUB
WEST MARINE INC
WILLIAM MORRIS ENDEAVOR ENTERTAINMENT LLC
WILSON SPORTING GOODS CO
WOMENS TENNIS ASSOCIATION (WTA)
WORLD BOXING ASSOCIATION
WORLD BOXING COUNCIL

Individual Profiles On Each Of THE SPORTS 350

24 HOUR FITNESS USA

www.24hourfitness.com

Industry Group Code: 713940 **Ranks within this company's industry group:** Sales: Profits:

Sports:		Services:		Media:		Sales:		Facilities:		Other:	
Leagues/Associations:		Food & Beverage:		TV:		Marketing:		Stadiums:		Gambling:	
Teams:		Agents:		Radio:		Ads:		Fitness Clubs:	Y	Apparel:	
Nonprofits:		Other:		Internet:		Tickets:		Golf Courses:		Equipment:	
Other:				Print:		Retail:		Ski Resorts:		Shoes:	
				Software:		Other:		Other:		Other:	

TYPES OF BUSINESS:

Fitness Centers
Online Nutrition Information
Day Spa

BRANDS/DIVISIONS/AFFILIATES:

Forstmann Little & Company
California Fitness
24 Hour Fitness Active
24 Hour Fitness Sports
24 Hour Fitness Super-Sport
24 Hour Fitness Ultra-Sport
Re:fresh
Fit:perks

CONTACTS:

Note: Officers with more than one job title may be intentionally listed here more than once.

Carl C. Liebert III, CEO
Jeff Boyer, CFO/Exec. VP
Tony Wells, Chief Mktg. Officer
Michelle Crosby, Chief Talent Officer
Mark S. Mastrov, Chmn.

Phone: 925-543-3100	**Fax:** 925-543-3200
Toll-Free: 800-432-6348	
Address: 12647 Alcosta Blvd., 5th Fl., San Ramon, CA 94583 US	

GROWTH PLANS/SPECIAL FEATURES:

24 Hour Fitness USA is one of the world's largest privately owned and operated fitness center chains. The firm, owned by private equity company Forstmann Little and Co., has more than 3 million members and over 425 clubs across the globe. The company operates several types of clubs, including the 24 Hour Fitness Active club, Fitness EXPRESS, the Sports club, the Super-Sport club and the Ultra-Sport club. The 24 Hour Fitness Active clubs are approximately 25,000 square feet and may include free weights, cardio equipment, group exercise, personal training, locker rooms, sauna, steam room and a children' play area. 24 Hour Fitness EXPRESS clubs are anywhere from 6,000 to 10,000 square feet and offer only limited strength and cardio equipment and some exercise classes. The company's Sports clubs range from 35,000 to 50,000 square feet and include all of the Active clubs' amenities as well as basketball courts and pools. The Super-Sport clubs, generally over 50,000 square feet, have all of the Sports club offerings as well as tanning beds and massage therapy. The Ultra-Sport clubs are generally over 100,000 square feet and may also include a volleyball court, racquetball, squash, rock climbing, an indoor running track and executive locker rooms. The company has international locations in China, Malaysia, Singapore, Hong Kong and Taiwan, all under the name California Fitness. Re:fresh is the company's free-standing day spa located in San Francisco. The Fit:perks program offers discounts and benefits to all 24 Hour Fitness members. The company was the exclusive official fitness center of the U.S. Olympic Team through the 2008 Olympic Games in Beijing, and has extended its Olympic sponsorship to 2012.

24 Hour Fitness sponsors several charitable events and organizations, including the American Cancer Society, the Magic Johnson Foundation, the Lance Armstrong Foundation and the Andre Agassi Charitable Foundation.

FINANCIALS:

Sales and profits are in thousands of dollars—add 000 to get the full amount. 2008 Note: Financial information for 2008 was not available for all companies at press time.

2008 Sales: $	2008 Profits: $	**U.S. Stock Ticker: Private**
2007 Sales: $243,800	2007 Profits: $	**Int'l Ticker:** Int'l Exchange:
2006 Sales: $	2006 Profits: $	Employees: 10,000
2005 Sales: $	2005 Profits: $	Fiscal Year Ends: 12/31
2004 Sales: $	2004 Profits: $	Parent Company: FORSTMANN LITTLE & CO

SALARIES/BENEFITS:

Pension Plan:	ESOP Stock Plan:	Profit Sharing:	Top Exec. Salary: $	Bonus: $
Savings Plan:	Stock Purch. Plan:		Second Exec. Salary: $	Bonus: $

OTHER THOUGHTS:

Apparent Women Officers or Directors:
Hot Spot for Advancement for Women/Minorities:

LOCATIONS: ("Y" = Yes)

West:	Southwest:	Midwest:	Southeast:	Northeast:	International:
Y	Y	Y	Y		Y

ABC INC

abc.go.com

Industry Group Code: 513120 **Ranks within this company's industry group:** Sales: 2 Profits:

Sports:		Services:		Media:		Sales:		Facilities:		Other:	
Leagues/Associations:		Food & Beverage:		TV:	Y	Marketing:		Stadiums:		Gambling:	
Teams:		Agents:		Radio:		Ads:		Fitness Clubs:		Apparel:	
Nonprofits:		Other:		Internet:		Tickets:		Golf Courses:		Equipment:	
Other:				Print:		Retail:		Ski Resorts:		Shoes:	
				Software:		Other:		Other:		Other:	

TYPES OF BUSINESS:

Broadcast TV
Cable Networks
Television Production
Online Television

BRANDS/DIVISIONS/AFFILIATES:

Walt Disney Company (The)
Touchstone Television
Buena Vista Television
ABC Television Networks
Lost
Desperate Housewives
Ugly Betty
Grey's Anatomy

CONTACTS:

Note: Officers with more than one job title may be intentionally listed here more than once.

Anne M. Sweeney, Pres., Disney-ABC Television Group
James L. Hedges, CFO/Exec. VP-ABC Television Network & Studios
Jeffrey S. Rosen, Sr. VP-Human Resources

Phone: 212-456-7777 **Fax:** 212-456-1424
Toll-Free:
Address: 77 W. 66th St., 3rd Fl., New York, NY 10023 US

GROWTH PLANS/SPECIAL FEATURES:

ABC, Inc., a subsidiary of The Walt Disney Co., operates the ABC Television Network. The network includes 10 owned stations that supplement roughly 231 affiliated stations operating under long-term agreements, reaching 99% of all U.S. households. The ABC Television Network broadcasts programs in the following day portions: early morning, daytime, primetime, late night, news, children and sports. The network produces its own programs or acquires broadcast rights from other third-party producers, as well as production entities that are owned by the firm, and rights holders for network programming and pays varying amounts of compensation to affiliated stations for broadcasting the programs and commercial announcements included therein. It derives substantially all of its revenues from the sale to advertisers of time in network programs for commercial announcements. The ability to sell time for commercial announcements and the rates received are primarily dependent on the size and nature of the audience that the network can deliver to the advertiser as well as overall advertiser demand for time on network broadcasts. ABC produces many of the programs it broadcasts through its Touchstone Television subsidiary. In addition, the Buena Vista Television unit syndicates and distributes Disney products (both films and television shows) for broadcast. The company's Monday Night Football program is a long-standing leader in the prime-time lineup and the network also carries the NBA finals. ABC's web site makes full-length episodes of its most popular shows (Lost; Grey's Anatomy; Desperate Housewives; Ugly Betty; Six Degrees; and Daybreak) available on the Internet for a small fee.

FINANCIALS:

Sales and profits are in thousands of dollars—add 000 to get the full amount. 2008 Note: Financial information for 2008 was not available for all companies at press time.

2008 Sales: $16,116,000
2007 Sales: $15,104,000
2006 Sales: $14,638,000
2005 Sales: $13,207,000
2004 Sales: $11,780,000

2008 Profits: $
2007 Profits: $
2006 Profits: $
2005 Profits: $
2004 Profits: $

U.S. Stock Ticker: Subsidiary
Int'l Ticker: Int'l Exchange:
Employees:
Fiscal Year Ends: 9/30
Parent Company: WALT DISNEY COMPANY (THE)

SALARIES/BENEFITS:

Pension Plan: ESOP Stock Plan: Profit Sharing: Top Exec. Salary: $ Bonus: $
Savings Plan: Stock Purch. Plan: Second Exec. Salary: $ Bonus: $

OTHER THOUGHTS:

Apparent Women Officers or Directors: 1
Hot Spot for Advancement for Women/Minorities:

LOCATIONS: ("Y" = Yes)

West:	Southwest:	Midwest:	Southeast:	Northeast:	International:
Y	Y	Y	Y	Y	

Note: Financial information, benefits and other data can change quickly and may vary from those stated here.

ACADEMY SPORTS & OUTDOORS LTD

www.academy.com

Industry Group Code: 451110 **Ranks within this company's industry group:** Sales: 3 Profits:

Sports:		Services:		Media:		Sales:		Facilities:		Other:	
Leagues/Associations:		Food & Beverage:		TV:		Marketing:		Stadiums:		Gambling:	
Teams:		Agents:		Radio:		Ads:		Fitness Clubs:		Apparel:	Y
Nonprofits:		Other:		Internet:		Tickets:		Golf Courses:		Equipment:	Y
Other:				Print:		Retail:	Y	Ski Resorts:		Shoes:	Y
				Software:		Other:		Other:		Other:	

TYPES OF BUSINESS:

Sporting Goods Stores
Apparel
Footwear
Outdoor Sports Gear
Hunting Licenses

BRANDS/DIVISIONS/AFFILIATES:

CONTACTS:

Note: Officers with more than one job title may be intentionally listed here more than once.

David Gochman, CEO
Rodney Faldyn, Pres.
Rodney Faldyn, CFO
Robert Frennea, Exec. VP/Mgr.-Gen. Merch.
Michelle McKinney, Exec. VP-Corp. Dev.
David Gochman, Chmn.

Phone: 281-646-5200 **Fax:** 281-646-5000
Toll-Free: 888-922-2336
Address: 1800 N. Mason Rd., Katy, TX 77449 US

GROWTH PLANS/SPECIAL FEATURES:

Academy Sports & Outdoors, Ltd. is one of the largest sporting goods retailers in the U.S. The company operates over 112 stores throughout 11 states including Alabama, Arkansas, Florida, Georgia, Louisiana, Mississippi, Missouri, Oklahoma, South Carolina; Tennessee and Texas. Additionally, the firm plans to further expand its business by opening stores in the southern and southeastern U.S. in the near future. Academy Sports offers a broad selection of sporting equipment, apparel and footwear. The stores, which range in size from 50,000 to 80,000 square feet, are laid out in a racetrack format with athletic, casual and seasonal apparel on the inside and camping, hunting, fishing, marine, golf, fitness, team sports and footwear products on the outside. Academy Sports has experienced steady sales growth over the past decade at an average of 17% a year. The company supplies its stores through a 1 million square foot distribution center out of Katy, Texas. The center utilizes radio frequency devices (RFD), automated inventory and replenishment systems and a state-of-the-art warehouse management system to smoothly operate its large processing and inventory space.

The company offers its employees a 401(k) plan; medical, dental and vision insurance; life insurance; short- and long-term disability benefits; tuition reimbursement; merchandise discounts; bereavement leave; continuing education benefits; and business travel accident insurance.

FINANCIALS:

Sales and profits are in thousands of dollars—add 000 to get the full amount. 2008 Note: Financial information for 2008 was not available for all companies at press time.

2008 Sales: $2,000,000	2008 Profits: $	**U.S. Stock Ticker: Private**
2007 Sales: $2,060,000	2007 Profits: $	**Int'l Ticker:** Int'l Exchange:
2006 Sales: $1,840,000	2006 Profits: $	Employees: 5,243
2005 Sales: $1,215,100	2005 Profits: $65,000	Fiscal Year Ends: 1/31
2004 Sales: $1,059,000	2004 Profits: $	Parent Company:

SALARIES/BENEFITS:

Pension Plan:	ESOP Stock Plan:	Profit Sharing:	Top Exec. Salary: $	Bonus: $
Savings Plan: Y	Stock Purch. Plan:		Second Exec. Salary: $	Bonus: $

OTHER THOUGHTS:

Apparent Women Officers or Directors: 1
Hot Spot for Advancement for Women/Minorities:

LOCATIONS: ("Y" = Yes)

West:	Southwest:	Midwest:	Southeast:	Northeast:	International:
	Y	Y	Y		

ACCORDIA GOLF CO LTD

www.accordiagolf.com

Industry Group Code: 713910 **Ranks within this company's industry group:** Sales: 2 Profits: 1

Sports:		Services:		Media:		Sales:		Facilities:		Other:	
Leagues/Associations:		Food & Beverage:	Y	TV:		Marketing:		Stadiums:		Gambling:	
Teams:		Agents:		Radio:		Ads:		Fitness Clubs:		Apparel:	
Nonprofits:		Other:		Internet:		Tickets:		Golf Courses:	Y	Equipment:	Y
Other:				Print:		Retail:	Y	Ski Resorts:		Shoes:	
				Software:		Other:		Other:		Other:	

TYPES OF BUSINESS:

Golf Course Operations
Golf Equipment Sales

BRANDS/DIVISIONS/AFFILIATES:

Sunclassic Golf
Sports Shinko Co., Ltd.
Accordia Golf Asset Holding 21 Co., Ltd.
Accordia Garden Co, Ltd.
Odawara Golf Club
I.G.A. Country Club
Iga Golf Club

CONTACTS: *Note: Officers with more than one job title may be intentionally listed here more than once.*

Michihiro Chikubu, CEO
Michihiro Chikubu, Pres.
Kenichi Ito, Dir.-General Affairs & Human Resources
Kenichi Ito, Chief Dir.-Bus. Dev.
Yuji Iwasaki, Exec. Officer-Investor Rel.
Kenichi Ohta, Chief Dir.-Finance
Ryusuke Kamata, VP/Mgr.-Special Assignment Office
Hirotsugu Taniguchi, Dir.-Training Field Business & Prod. Bus.
Takashi Shinno, Chief Dir.-Course Mgmt.

Phone: 81-3-6688-1507 **Fax:** 81-3-6688-1509
Toll-Free:
Address: 2-15-1-Shibuya, Shibuya-ku, Tokyo, 150-0002 Japan

GROWTH PLANS/SPECIAL FEATURES:

Accordia Golf Co., Ltd. is principally engaged in the business of golf course operations in Japan. The firm's guiding strategy is 'It's a new game,' reflecting their intention to foster golf as a fun, casual sport available to everyone. Accordia operates in two primary divisions, cinsisting of the acquisition, renovation and maintenance of golf courses and the sale of golf goods. The company manages 123 golf courses, of which it owns 104. Accordia's golf courses are furnished with restaurant capacities, which the company outsources from a third party. Additionally, the firm offers golf membership services such as golf equipment repair, membership-only golf competitions, early morning playing times, newsletter publishing, call center operations for golf course reservations and the operation of web sites for female golf players. In February 2008, the company agreed to acquire Accordia Golf Asset Holding 21 Co., Ltd., from Tokai Kaihatsu Co., Ltd. In April 2008, another of Accordia's subsidiaries, Accordia Garden Co., Ltd., agreed to acquire Sunclassic Golf, a driving range business operated by Unitec Co., Ltd. In October 2008, the firm acquired a Japan-based company engaged in the operation of golf courses in Tokyo.

FINANCIALS: **Sales and profits are in thousands of dollars—add 000 to get the full amount. 2008 Note: Financial information for 2008 was not available for all companies at press time.**

2008 Sales: $817,230	2008 Profits: $101,030	**U.S. Stock Ticker:**
2007 Sales: $724,400	2007 Profits: $110,400	**Int'l Ticker: 2131** Int'l Exchange: Tokyo-TSE
2006 Sales: $455,520	2006 Profits: $45,550	Employees:
2005 Sales: $	2005 Profits: $	Fiscal Year Ends:
2004 Sales: $	2004 Profits: $	Parent Company:

SALARIES/BENEFITS:

Pension Plan:	ESOP Stock Plan:	Profit Sharing:	Top Exec. Salary: $	Bonus: $
Savings Plan:	Stock Purch. Plan:		Second Exec. Salary: $	Bonus: $

OTHER THOUGHTS:

Apparent Women Officers or Directors:
Hot Spot for Advancement for Women/Minorities:

LOCATIONS: ("Y" = Yes)

West:	Southwest:	Midwest:	Southeast:	Northeast:	International:
					Y

ADAMS GOLF INC

www.adamsgolf.com

Industry Group Code: 339920 **Ranks within this company's industry group:** Sales: 7 Profits: 4

Sports:		Services:		Media:		Sales:		Facilities:		Other:	
Leagues/Associations:		Food & Beverage:		TV:		Marketing:		Stadiums:		Gambling:	
Teams:		Agents:		Radio:		Ads:		Fitness Clubs:		Apparel:	
Nonprofits:		Other:		Internet:		Tickets:		Golf Courses:		Equipment:	Y
Other:				Print:		Retail:		Ski Resorts:		Shoes:	
				Software:		Other:		Other:		Other:	

TYPES OF BUSINESS:

Golf Club Manufacturing

BRANDS/DIVISIONS/AFFILIATES:

Speedline
Speedline Draw
Idea Pro Gold
Idea Tech
Puglielli Wedge
DIXX BLU

GROWTH PLANS/SPECIAL FEATURES:

Adams Golf, Inc. designs, manufactures, and distributes golf clubs. The firm's product line includes drivers, woods and irons. The driver and wood line includes the Speedline and Speedline Draw models; and the Insight Tech a4OS, Insight Tech a4, Insight XTD a3OS, Insight XTD a3 and Insight XTD Pro. The iron line includes Idea Pro Black, Idea Tech a4OS, Idea Tech a4, Idea Pro Gold, Idea a3OS, Idea a3 and Idea Pro, as well as the Idea a3OS set and the Tight Lies Set. The company also offers a hybrid line, which includes the Idea Tech a4OS, Idea Tech a4, Idea a3OS, Idea a3, Idea Pro and Idea Pro Gold. Finally, the firm offers a shortrange line, which includes Tom Watson Wedges in two finishes, Puglielli Wedge, a3OS chipper and the DIXX BLU putter. Adams Golf also has a women's line of its clubs, and provides various accessories for the golfer.

CONTACTS: *Note: Officers with more than one job title may be intentionally listed here more than once.*

Oliver G. (Chip) Brewer III, CEO
Oliver G. (Chip) Brewer III, Pres.
Eric T. Logan, CFO/Sr. VP
B.H. (Barney) Adams, Chmn.

Phone: 972-673-9000	**Fax:**
Toll-Free:	
Address: 2801 East Plano Pkwy, Plano, TX 75074 US	

FINANCIALS: Sales and profits are in thousands of dollars—add 000 to get the full amount. 2008 Note: Financial information for 2008 was not available for all companies at press time.

2008 Sales: $91,451	2008 Profits: $-1,459	**U.S. Stock Ticker: ADGF**
2007 Sales: $94,604	2007 Profits: $9,401	**Int'l Ticker:** Int'l Exchange:
2006 Sales: $76,030	2006 Profits: $9,000	Employees: 144
2005 Sales: $	2005 Profits: $	Fiscal Year Ends:
2004 Sales: $	2004 Profits: $	Parent Company:

SALARIES/BENEFITS:

Pension Plan:	ESOP Stock Plan:	Profit Sharing:	Top Exec. Salary: $425,000	Bonus: $1,544,000
Savings Plan:	Stock Purch. Plan:		Second Exec. Salary: $215,000	Bonus: $50,000

OTHER THOUGHTS:

Apparent Women Officers or Directors:
Hot Spot for Advancement for Women/Minorities:

LOCATIONS: ("Y" = Yes)

West:	Southwest:	Midwest:	Southeast:	Northeast:	International:
	Y				

ADIDAS AG

www.adidas.com

Industry Group Code: 316219 **Ranks within this company's industry group:** Sales: 2 Profits: 2

Sports:		Services:		Media:		Sales:		Facilities:		Other:	
Leagues/Associations:		Food & Beverage:		TV:		Marketing:		Stadiums:		Gambling:	
Teams:		Agents:		Radio:		Ads:		Fitness Clubs:		Apparel:	Y
Nonprofits:		Other:		Internet:		Tickets:		Golf Courses:		Equipment:	Y
Other:				Print:		Retail:		Ski Resorts:		Shoes:	Y
				Software:		Other:		Other:		Other:	

TYPES OF BUSINESS:

Athletic Shoes
Golf Equipment & Accessories
Street & Sports Apparel
Personal Care Products
Eyewear
Watches

BRANDS/DIVISIONS/AFFILIATES:

adidas Sport Performance
adidas Sport Heritage
adidas Sport Style
TaylorMade-adidas Golf
Reebok International Ltd
Maxfli
Reebok CCM Hockey
Ashworth Inc

CONTACTS: *Note: Officers with more than one job title may be intentionally listed here more than once.*

Herbert Hainer, CEO
Robin Stalker, CFO
Glenn Bennett, Exec. VP-Global Oper.
Robin Stalker, Dir.-Finance
Erich Stamminger, CEO/Pres., Adidas Brand
Herbert Hainer, Chmn.
Patrik Nilsson, Pres., Adidas North America

Phone: 49-9132-84-0 **Fax:** 49-9132-84-2241
Toll-Free:
Address: Adi-Dassler-Strasse 1-2, Herzogenaurach, 91074 Germany

GROWTH PLANS/SPECIAL FEATURES:

Adidas AG, is an athletic apparel manufacturer and one of the world's largest makers of sporting goods. The company operates more than 80 international subsidiaries and markets products under three primary brands: adidas; Reebok; and TaylorMade-adidas Golf. The adidas brand develops and markets products in three divisions: the Sport Performance Division focuses on footwear and apparel for sports such as running, basketball and soccer; the Sport Heritage Division develops and markets footwear and apparel that is fashion oriented; and the Sport Style division designs and markets products with a combination of style and performance. The company's Reebok brand develops sports apparel, footwear and athletic equipment for a variety of sports. Its divisions include Reebok, a global brand that creates and markets sports and lifestyle products in sports, fitness and women's categories; Reebok-CCM Hockey, the world's largest designer, manufacturer and marketer of hockey equipment and related apparel under two of the world's most recognized hockey brand names, Rbk Hockey and CCM; and Rockport, which designs and markets dress, dress casual, casual and outdoor footwear in addition to apparel and accessories. The firm's TaylorMade-adidas golf brand develops and markets a variety of products for the golf industry including TaylorMade drivers, Maxfli balls, Rossa putters and adidas Golf footwear. In addition to these primary offerings, the company has expanded its product line to include adidas Body, a line of fragrances and personal care products; adidas eyewear, which includes sunglasses designed for a variety of sports; and adidas watches. The firm is the official uniform and apparel provider for the National Basketball Association (NBA), Women's National Basketball Association (WNBA) and the NBA Development League. In July 2008, Adidas opened a flagship store in Beijing, expanding its Chinese presence. In November 2008, the company's TaylorMade-adidas Golf Company subsidiary acquired Ashworth, Inc.

FINANCIALS: **Sales and profits are in thousands of dollars—add 000 to get the full amount. 2008 Note: Financial information for 2008 was not available for all companies at press time.**

2008 Sales: $14,575,800	2008 Profits: $869,230	**U.S. Stock Ticker: ADDYY**
2007 Sales: $13,901,000	2007 Profits: $749,110	**Int'l Ticker: ADS** Int'l Exchange: Frankfurt-Euronext
2006 Sales: $13,481,000	2006 Profits: $654,700	Employees: 26,376
2005 Sales: $7,917,940	2005 Profits: $465,300	Fiscal Year Ends: 12/31
2004 Sales: $6,992,000	2004 Profits: $383,000	Parent Company:

SALARIES/BENEFITS:

Pension Plan:	ESOP Stock Plan:	Profit Sharing:	Top Exec. Salary: $	Bonus: $
Savings Plan:	Stock Purch. Plan:		Second Exec. Salary: $	Bonus: $

OTHER THOUGHTS:

Apparent Women Officers or Directors: 2
Hot Spot for Advancement for Women/Minorities: Y

LOCATIONS: ("Y" = Yes)

West:	Southwest:	Midwest:	Southeast:	Northeast:	International:
Y				Y	Y

AMER SPORTS CORPORATION

www.amersports.com

Industry Group Code: 339920 **Ranks within this company's industry group:** Sales: 2 Profits: 2

Sports:		Services:		Media:		Sales:		Facilities:		Other:	
Leagues/Associations:		Food & Beverage:		TV:		Marketing:		Stadiums:		Gambling:	
Teams:		Agents:		Radio:		Ads:		Fitness Clubs:		Apparel:	Y
Nonprofits:		Other:		Internet:		Tickets:		Golf Courses:		Equipment:	Y
Other:				Print:		Retail:		Ski Resorts:		Shoes:	Y
				Software:		Other:		Other:		Other:	Y

TYPES OF BUSINESS:

Sports Equipment
Winter Sports Equipment
Golf Equipment
Fitness Training Equipment
Sports Instruments
Racquet Sports Equipment
Team Sports Equipment
Cycling Components

BRANDS/DIVISIONS/AFFILIATES:

Atomic Austria GmbH
Salomon
Mavic
Suunto Oy
Wilson Sporting Goods Co
Precor
Arc'teryx

CONTACTS: *Note: Officers with more than one job title may be intentionally listed here more than once.*

Roger Talermo, CEO
Roger Talermo, Pres.
Pekka Paalanne, CFO/Exec. VP
Thomas Ehrnrooth, Sr. VP-Sales & Channel Mgmt.
Terhi Heikkinen, Sr. VP-Human Resources
Vincent Wauters, Sr. VP-IT
Kristiina Huttunen, VP-Legal Affairs
Tommy Ilmoni, VP-Corp. Comm.
Tommy Ilmoni, VP-Investor Rel.
Kai Tihila, VP-Finance & Control
Ilkka Brotherus, Vice Chmn.
Chris Considine, Pres., Wilson Sporting Goods Co.
Juha Pinomaa, Pres., Suunto Oy
Paul Byrne, Pres., Precor
Anssi Vanjoki, Chmn.
Michael Schineis, Pres., Atomic Austria GmbH
Vincent Wauters, Sr. VP-Supply Chain

Phone: 358-9-725-7800	**Fax:** 358-9-7257-8401
Toll-Free:	
Address: Makelankatu 91, Helsinki, FI-00610 Finland	

GROWTH PLANS/SPECIAL FEATURES:

Amer Sports Corporation is one of the world's largest sports equipment manufacturers. Amer divides its activities into three geographic areas: the Americas, which generated 43% of 2008 sales; EMEA, 46%; and Asia Pacific, including Japan and Australia, 11%. The company's products are also divided into three primary business segments: Winter and Outdoor, which generated 55% of 2008 sales; Ball Sports, 31%; and Fitness, 14%. The winter and outdoor segment divides into four main product areas: winter sports equipment; apparel and footwear; cycling; and sports instruments. This segment manufactures products under brands that include Atomic, Salomon, Arc'teryx, Mavic and Suunto. Atomic Austria GmbH produces skiing and snowboarding products, including those under sub-brands such as DYNAMIC and OXYGEN. Salomon products include skiing, snowboarding, hiking, trail running and climbing gear such as skis, snowboards, clothing, footwear and bags. Canada-based Arc'teryx focuses exclusively on outdoor equipment, especially clothing, climbing harnesses and packs. Mavic manufactures cycling products for mountain biking, road cycling and track racing, including wheels, rims and accessories. Finally, Suunto products cover everything from diving instruments and compasses to wrist-top computers, GPS PODs and forestry equipment. The ball sports segment offers a variety of products under the Wilson brand. It has three product areas: racquet sports, team sports and golf. Specific products include balls, bats, gloves, accessories and apparel for baseball, basketball, American football and volleyball; racquets, balls, footwear and accessories for tennis, squash, racquetball and badminton; and golf clubs, balls and accessories. Lastly, the fitness segment produces fitness equipment under the Precor brand. Precor offers technically advanced products for the commercial and home markets, including elliptical fitness cross trainers, treadmills, stationary cycles and strength-training equipment. The company devotes extensive effort toward research and development and has introduced nanotech innovations into certain product lines, notably racquets and skis.

FINANCIALS: **Sales and profits are in thousands of dollars—add 000 to get the full amount. 2008 Note: Financial information for 2008 was not available for all companies at press time.**

2008 Sales: $2,198,350	2008 Profits: $47,470	**U.S. Stock Ticker: AGPDY.PK**
2007 Sales: $2,306,410	2007 Profits: $25,830	**Int'l Ticker: AMEAS** Int'l Exchange: Helsinki-Euronext
2006 Sales: $2,796,600	2006 Profits: $109,700	Employees: 4,968
2005 Sales: $2,127,400	2005 Profits: $117,300	Fiscal Year Ends: 8/31
2004 Sales: $1,308,800	2004 Profits: $86,670	Parent Company:

SALARIES/BENEFITS:

Pension Plan:	ESOP Stock Plan:	Profit Sharing:	Top Exec. Salary: $	Bonus: $
Savings Plan:	Stock Purch. Plan:		Second Exec. Salary: $	Bonus: $

OTHER THOUGHTS:

Apparent Women Officers or Directors: 2
Hot Spot for Advancement for Women/Minorities:

LOCATIONS: ("Y" = Yes)

West:	Southwest:	Midwest:	Southeast:	Northeast:	International:
Y		Y		Y	Y

Note: Financial information, benefits and other data can change quickly and may vary from those stated here.

AMERICAN GOLF CORP

www.americangolf.com

Industry Group Code: 713910 **Ranks within this company's industry group:** Sales: Profits:

Sports:		Services:		Media:		Sales:		Facilities:		Other:	
Leagues/Associations:		Food & Beverage:		TV:		Marketing:		Stadiums:		Gambling:	
Teams:		Agents:		Radio:		Ads:		Fitness Clubs:		Apparel:	
Nonprofits:		Other:		Internet:		Tickets:		Golf Courses:	Y	Equipment:	
Other:				Print:		Retail:		Ski Resorts:		Shoes:	
				Software:		Other:		Other:		Other:	

TYPES OF BUSINESS:

Golf Courses
Resorts
Golf Promotion
Real Estate

BRANDS/DIVISIONS/AFFILIATES:

American Golf Foundation
Platinum Club

CONTACTS:

Note: Officers with more than one job title may be intentionally listed here more than once.

Paul Major, CEO
Keith Brown, COO/Sr. VP
Paul Major, Pres.
Mike Moecker, CFO/Sr. VP
Jim Allison, Sr. VP-Mktg. & Sales
Joe Stegman, VP-Human Resources
Kimberly Wong, General Counsel/Sec./Sr. VP
Craig Kniffen, Sr. VP-Maintenance

Phone: 310-664-4000	**Fax:** 310-664-4386
Toll-Free:	
Address: 2951 28th St., Santa Monica, CA 90405 US	

GROWTH PLANS/SPECIAL FEATURES:

American Golf Corporation is a premier manager of golf courses and resorts, owning and operating more than 110 private, resort and daily fee golf courses in the U.S. The company also sells real estate connected with its golf resorts and communities. Its ownerships are combined with a stated philosophy of developing the quality of life within these communities. American Golf's portfolio includes courses in 18 states, with its largest holdings in Arizona and California. The firm offers regional golfers clubs throughout the country that offer discount green fees, early twilight access and merchandise discounts. The company also offers the Platinum Club, which enables members to golf at participating American Golf private clubs and public courses all over the country for only a cart fee. Membership also allows golfers to reserve tee times up to 60 days in advance, and bring guests to private clubs for the prevailing guest rate. American Golf established the American Golf Foundation, a nonprofit organization devoted to promoting golf. The foundation utilizes a team of volunteer ambassadors to conduct fundraising activities, participate in community outreach programs, educate guests on proper golf course etiquette, rules and safety and help make the game of golf accessible to people of all ages and backgrounds.

FINANCIALS:

Sales and profits are in thousands of dollars—add 000 to get the full amount. 2008 Note: Financial information for 2008 was not available for all companies at press time.

2008 Sales: $	2008 Profits: $	**U.S. Stock Ticker: Private**
2007 Sales: $	2007 Profits: $	**Int'l Ticker:** Int'l Exchange:
2006 Sales: $	2006 Profits: $	Employees: 10,000
2005 Sales: $	2005 Profits: $	Fiscal Year Ends: 12/31
2004 Sales: $	2004 Profits: $	Parent Company:

SALARIES/BENEFITS:

Pension Plan:	ESOP Stock Plan:	Profit Sharing:	Top Exec. Salary: $	Bonus: $
Savings Plan:	Stock Purch. Plan:		Second Exec. Salary: $	Bonus: $

OTHER THOUGHTS:

Apparent Women Officers or Directors: 1
Hot Spot for Advancement for Women/Minorities:

LOCATIONS: ("Y" = Yes)

West:	Southwest:	Midwest:	Southeast:	Northeast:	International:
Y	Y	Y	Y	Y	

AMERICAN HOCKEY LEAGUE

www.theahl.com

Industry Group Code: 813990 **Ranks within this company's industry group:** Sales: Profits:

Sports:		Services:		Media:		Sales:		Facilities:		Other:	
Leagues/Associations:	Y	Food & Beverage:		TV:		Marketing:		Stadiums:		Gambling:	
Teams:		Agents:		Radio:		Ads:		Fitness Clubs:		Apparel:	
Nonprofits:		Other:		Internet:		Tickets:		Golf Courses:		Equipment:	
Other:				Print:		Retail:	Y	Ski Resorts:		Shoes:	
				Software:		Other:		Other:		Other:	

TYPES OF BUSINESS:

Hockey League
AHL Team Merchandising

BRANDS/DIVISIONS/AFFILIATES:

Albany River Rats
Grand Rapids Griffins
Iowa Chops
Lowell Devils
Philadelphia Phantoms
Providence Bruins
Chicago Wolves

CONTACTS: *Note: Officers with more than one job title may be intentionally listed here more than once.*

Dave Andrews, CEO
Dave Andrews, Pres.
Chris Nikolis, Exec. VP-Mktg.
Drew Griffin, Dir.-Admin.
Jim Mill, Exec. VP-Hockey Oper.
Chris Nikolis, Exec. VP-Bus. Dev.
Jason Chaimovitch, VP-Comm.
Drew Griffin, Dir.-Finance
Sean Lavoine, VP-Licensing & Corp. Sales
Bill Scott, Mgr.-Hockey Oper.
Ashley Grindle, Coordinator-Mktg. Svcs.
Anna Marie Travaglini, Coordinator-Mktg. Svcs.

Phone: 413-781-2030 **Fax:** 413-733-4767
Toll-Free:
Address: 1 Monarch Pl., Ste. 2400, Springfield, MA 01144 US

GROWTH PLANS/SPECIAL FEATURES:

American Hockey League, Inc. (AHL) is a minor league sports organization with 29 teams based in Canada and the U.S. It is generally considered the top-tier minor league hockey organization. The league's teams are divided into four divisions of roughly seven teams each, with the exception of one division that currently has eight teams. These divisions include the Atlantic division, East division, West division (with eight teams) and North division. At end of the regular season each year, which runs from October through April, the top AHL team from each division competes for the Calder Cup. The Calder Cup, played annually since 1937, has been won by approximately 27 members of the Hockey Hall of Fame prior to the start of their major league careers, including Johnny Bower, Terry Sawchuk, Emile Francis, Gerry Cheevers, Al Arbour, Andy Bathgate, Larry Robinson, Doug Harvey and Patrick Roy. The league is the major affiliation league for the National Hockey League (NHL), and all AHL teams are required to have an affiliation agreement with at least one NHL team. For example, the AHL Albany River Rats is a feeder team for the NHL Carolina Hurricanes; the Grand Rapids Griffins for the NHL Detroit Red Wings; the Iowa Chops for the NHL Anaheim Ducks; the Lowell Devils for the NHL New Jersey Devils; the Philadelphia Phantoms for the NHL Philadelphia Flyers; and the Providence Bruins for the NHL Boston Bruins. Many teams of the ECHL (the former East Coast Hockey League) and the Central Hockey League are also affiliated with AHL teams and act as feeders to the AHL. In 2008, the Calder Cup went to the Chicago Wolves, adding that team to the list of eight who claimed the Cup more than once.

FINANCIALS: **Sales and profits are in thousands of dollars—add 000 to get the full amount. 2008 Note: Financial information for 2008 was not available for all companies at press time.**

2008 Sales: $	2008 Profits: $	**U.S. Stock Ticker: Private**
2007 Sales: $	2007 Profits: $	**Int'l Ticker:** Int'l Exchange:
2006 Sales: $	2006 Profits: $	Employees: 12
2005 Sales: $	2005 Profits: $	Fiscal Year Ends: 6/30
2004 Sales: $	2004 Profits: $	Parent Company:

SALARIES/BENEFITS:

Pension Plan:	ESOP Stock Plan:	Profit Sharing:	Top Exec. Salary: $	Bonus: $
Savings Plan:	Stock Purch. Plan:		Second Exec. Salary: $	Bonus: $

OTHER THOUGHTS:

Apparent Women Officers or Directors: 3
Hot Spot for Advancement for Women/Minorities: Y

LOCATIONS: ("Y" = Yes)

West:	Southwest:	Midwest:	Southeast:	Northeast:	International:
				Y	

AMF BOWLING WORLDWIDE INC

www.amf.com

Industry Group Code: 713950 **Ranks within this company's industry group:** Sales: Profits:

Sports:		Services:		Media:		Sales:		Facilities:		Other:	
Leagues/Associations:		Food & Beverage:	Y	TV:		Marketing:		Stadiums:		Gambling:	
Teams:		Agents:		Radio:		Ads:		Fitness Clubs:		Apparel:	
Nonprofits:		Other:		Internet:		Tickets:		Golf Courses:		Equipment:	Y
Other:				Print:		Retail:		Ski Resorts:		Shoes:	
				Software:		Other:		Other:	Y	Other:	

TYPES OF BUSINESS:

Bowling Equipment
Bowling Centers
Billiards Tables
Bowling Software

BRANDS/DIVISIONS/AFFILIATES:

QubicaAMF
Highway 66
300 Centers
Code Hennessy & Simmons, LLC
QubicaAMF Worldwide
Skiller
300 Grill
Thunder Bowl

CONTACTS: *Note: Officers with more than one job title may be intentionally listed here more than once.*

Frederick R. Hipp, CEO
Frederick R. Hipp, Pres.
William McDonnell, CFO/VP
Merrell C. Wreden, VP-Mktg.
Anthony J. Ponsiglione, VP-Human Resources
J. Simon Shearer, Sr. VP-Facilities & Design
Joseph F. Scarnaty, VP-Food & Beverage

Phone: 804-730-4000 **Fax:** 804-559-6276
Toll-Free: 800-342-5263
Address: 7313 Bell Creek Rd., Mechanicsville, VA 23111 US

GROWTH PLANS/SPECIAL FEATURES:

AMF Bowling Worldwide, Inc., owned by private investment firm Code Hennessy & Simmons, LLC, is one of the largest owners and operators of commercial bowling centers in the U.S., with 348 bowling centers nationwide and 13 internationally. The company has operations in Japan, Mexico, the United Kingdom and France. AMF operates through three business segments: products, bowling centers and Holdings. The product segment includes its joint venture QubicaAMF. Through QubicaAMF, the company is one of the world's leading manufacturers of bowling center equipment, such as automatic pinspotters, scoring equipment, bowling center furniture, bowling pins, high-performance lanes, ball returns and spare parts, as well as bowling products such as shoes, shirts, balls and ball bags. The firm's bowling centers feature billiards, darts, video games, glow in the dark miniature golf and Xtreme Bowling with music and lights. In addition, the 300 brand includes fully stocked bars, lane side service and restaurants (called 300 Grill). The new upscale centers, called 300 Centers, are located in Austin, Atlanta, Dallas, San Jose, Long Island and New York City. AMF owns 50% of QubicaAMF Worldwide, a joint venture with Italian manufacturer Qubica Worldwide. QubicaAMF manufactures bowling and amusement products. In February 2008, the company announced the launch of new concept centers under the brand name Avenue E, featuring a first class bar and casual dining restaurant. The firm expects to open six to eight locations over the next two years, the first two in Surprise, Arizona and the metro Phoenix area.

The company offers its employees benefits including flexible spending accounts, incentive programs, a 401(k) plan, tuition assistance, scholarships and education programs, and employee discounts on bowling, food and bowling products. AMF sponsors the Dick Weber Scholarship League, which awards $350,000 worth of scholarship funds to young bowlers annually.

FINANCIALS: **Sales and profits are in thousands of dollars—add 000 to get the full amount. 2008 Note: Financial information for 2008 was not available for all companies at press time.**

2008 Sales: $	2008 Profits: $	**U.S. Stock Ticker: Private**
2007 Sales: $	2007 Profits: $	**Int'l Ticker:** Int'l Exchange:
2006 Sales: $499,149	2006 Profits: $-15,885	Employees: 9,362
2005 Sales: $569,578	2005 Profits: $-10,698	Fiscal Year Ends: 6/30
2004 Sales: $678,800	2004 Profits: $-66,800	Parent Company:

SALARIES/BENEFITS:

Pension Plan:	ESOP Stock Plan:	Profit Sharing:	Top Exec. Salary: $600,000	Bonus: $
Savings Plan: Y	Stock Purch. Plan:		Second Exec. Salary: $288,555	Bonus: $28,800

OTHER THOUGHTS:

Apparent Women Officers or Directors:
Hot Spot for Advancement for Women/Minorities:

LOCATIONS: ("Y" = Yes)

West:	Southwest:	Midwest:	Southeast:	Northeast:	International:
Y	Y	Y	Y	Y	Y

ANAHEIM DUCKS

ducks.nhl.com

Industry Group Code: 711211F **Ranks within this company's industry group:** Sales: 15 Profits: 17

Sports:		Services:		Media:		Sales:		Facilities:		Other:	
Leagues/Associations:		Food & Beverage:		TV:		Marketing:		Stadiums:	Y	Gambling:	
Teams:	Y	Agents:		Radio:		Ads:		Fitness Clubs:		Apparel:	
Nonprofits:		Other:		Internet:		Tickets:	Y	Golf Courses:		Equipment:	
Other:				Print:		Retail:	Y	Ski Resorts:		Shoes:	
				Software:		Other:		Other:		Other:	

TYPES OF BUSINESS:

Professional Hockey Team

BRANDS/DIVISIONS/AFFILIATES:

Anaheim Arena Management, LLC
Arrowhead Pond
DuckCasts
Ducks Mobile
Hockey 101
Wild Wingers Kids Club
Anaheim Ducks Foundation

CONTACTS: *Note: Officers with more than one job title may be intentionally listed here more than once.*

Michael Schulman, CEO
Tim Ryan, COO/Exec. VP
Bob Wagner, Sr. VP/Chief Mktg. Officer
Kim Kutcher, VP-Human Resources
Mike Wing, Mgr.-IT
David McNab, Sr. VP-Hockey Oper.
Wendy Yamagishi, Dir.-Community Rel. & Public Affairs
Doug Heller, VP-Finance
Randy Carlyle, Head Coach
Bob Murray, Exec. VP/General Mgr.
Aaron Teats, Dir.-Broadcasting
Wendy Grover, Dir.-Corp. Partnerships

Phone: 714-704-2700 **Fax:** 714-704-2754
Toll-Free: 877-945-3946
Address: 2695 E. Katella Ave., Anaheim, CA 92806 US

GROWTH PLANS/SPECIAL FEATURES:

The Anaheim Ducks, formerly the Mighty Ducks of Anaheim, are a professional hockey team in the National Hockey League (NHL). The team was founded in 1993 by The Walt Disney Company and named after the Disney film, The Mighty Ducks. The team made its first playoff appearance in 1997, losing to the Detroit Red Wings in the semifinals. The Ducks also had a strong run on the ice during the 2002-03 season. The team defeated defending Stanley Cup champions the Detroit Red Wings, beat the Dallas Stars in the quarterfinals and defeated the Minnesota Wild in the conference finals. The Ducks lost to the New Jersey Devils in the Stanley Cup Finals, one game away from winning the league championship. Four years later, in the 2006-2007 season, the Ducks made it all the way, beating the Ottawa Senators in the finals to win the Stanley Cup, becoming the first California team ever to do so. In 2005, Disney sold the Ducks to Henry Samueli, the co-founder and former chairman of Broadcom Corporation. Samueli also owns Anaheim Arena Management LLC, which operates Honda Center (the former Arrowhead Pond), the Ducks' home arena. The team's web site features Ducks TV, a web cast that provides game highlights and locker room interviews; DuckCasts, or podcasts; the Ducks Mobile service, which lets mobile phones and other wireless devices access news, features and scores; and Hockey 101, allowing fans to submit questions to be answered live during game intermissions. Forbes recently estimated the team's value at $202 million. The team's average home attendance in the 2008-09 season was approximately 17,000 fans per game.

FINANCIALS: **Sales and profits are in thousands of dollars—add 000 to get the full amount. 2008 Note: Financial information for 2008 was not available for all companies at press time.**

2008 Sales: $90,000
2007 Sales: $89,000
2006 Sales: $75,000
2005 Sales: $
2004 Sales: $54,000

2008 Profits: $1,000
2007 Profits: $6,600
2006 Profits: $- 200
2005 Profits: $
2004 Profits: $

U.S. Stock Ticker: Subsidiary
Int'l Ticker: Int'l Exchange:
Employees:
Fiscal Year Ends: 9/30
Parent Company: ANAHEIM DUCKS HOCKEY CLUB LLC

SALARIES/BENEFITS:

Pension Plan:	ESOP Stock Plan:	Profit Sharing:	Top Exec. Salary: $	Bonus: $
Savings Plan:	Stock Purch. Plan:		Second Exec. Salary: $	Bonus: $

OTHER THOUGHTS:

Apparent Women Officers or Directors: 3
Hot Spot for Advancement for Women/Minorities: Y

LOCATIONS: ("Y" = Yes)

West:	Southwest:	Midwest:	Southeast:	Northeast:	International:
Y					

AND 1

www.and1.com

Industry Group Code: 316219 **Ranks within this company's industry group:** Sales: Profits:

Sports:		Services:		Media:		Sales:		Facilities:		Other:	
Leagues/Associations:		Food & Beverage:		TV:		Marketing:		Stadiums:		Gambling:	
Teams:		Agents:		Radio:		Ads:		Fitness Clubs:		Apparel:	Y
Nonprofits:		Other:		Internet:		Tickets:		Golf Courses:		Equipment:	Y
Other:	Y			Print:		Retail:	Y	Ski Resorts:		Shoes:	Y
				Software:		Other:		Other:		Other:	

TYPES OF BUSINESS:

Basketball Apparel
Street Basketball Tournaments
Magazine Publishing

BRANDS/DIVISIONS/AFFILIATES:

AND 1 Mix Tape Tours
AND 1: The Player's Quarterly
American Sporting Goods
AND 1 Streetball
AND 1 TV

CONTACTS: *Note: Officers with more than one job title may be intentionally listed here more than once.*

Bart Houlihan, Pres.

Phone:	**Fax:**
Toll-Free: 866-866-1232	
Address: 101 Enterprise, Ste. 100, Aliso Viejo, CA 92656 US	

GROWTH PLANS/SPECIAL FEATURES:

AND 1 is a basketball apparel company whose strategy is to focus on hip-hop and non-professional basketball culture. The name AND 1 refers to the free throw that is taken after someone is fouled while scoring a basket. The company presents itself through a trash-talking street basketball attitude with slogans like 'Call 911, I'm on fire' gracing its t-shirts. AND 1 got started in 1993 with footwear and other basketball attire. It utilizes as its logo a faceless, raceless basketball player known as The Player. The firm offers a complete line of basketball gear including performance shoes, t-shirts, shorts, pants, team uniforms, licensed collegiate apparel and accessories. The gear is sold in over 125 countries and territories, and it is carried in stores such as Champs, FootAction and Foot Locker. The company has gained considerable fame in recent years with its AND1 Mix Tape Tours, street basketball tournaments where style is emphasized over substance. The Mix Tape Tours basketball team includes a group of 10 young men who promote the And 1 brand through the Mix Tape Tours and AND 1 TV, a series of clips from previously released mixtapes which stream on the company's web site. The tours have been televised on ESPN with DVDs and VHS tapes of the events available as well. AND 1 also publishes a street basketball mini-magazine called AND 1: The Player's Quarterly. Over 20% of NBA players wear AND 1 apparel, including Damien Wilkins, Bobby Jackson and Rafer Alston. AND1 is owned by American Sporting Goods, manufacturer of athletic shoes and golf equipment. The company also sells AND1 Streetball, a streetball video game designed to capture the hip-hop culture surrounding non-professional basketball.

FINANCIALS: **Sales and profits are in thousands of dollars—add 000 to get the full amount. 2008 Note: Financial information for 2008 was not available for all companies at press time.**

2008 Sales: $	2008 Profits: $	**U.S. Stock Ticker: Private**
2007 Sales: $	2007 Profits: $	**Int'l Ticker:** Int'l Exchange:
2006 Sales: $	2006 Profits: $	Employees:
2005 Sales: $	2005 Profits: $	Fiscal Year Ends: 12/31
2004 Sales: $	2004 Profits: $	Parent Company:

SALARIES/BENEFITS:

Pension Plan:	ESOP Stock Plan:	Profit Sharing:	Top Exec. Salary: $	Bonus: $
Savings Plan: Y	Stock Purch. Plan:		Second Exec. Salary: $	Bonus: $

OTHER THOUGHTS:

Apparent Women Officers or Directors:
Hot Spot for Advancement for Women/Minorities:

LOCATIONS: ("Y" = Yes)

West:	Southwest:	Midwest:	Southeast:	Northeast:	International:
Y	Y	Y	Y	Y	Y

ANSCHUTZ ENTERTAINMENT GROUP

www.aegworldwide.com

Industry Group Code: 711211 **Ranks within this company's industry group:** Sales: Profits:

Sports:		Services:		Media:		Sales:		Facilities:		Other:	
Leagues/Associations:		Food & Beverage:		TV:		Marketing:		Stadiums:	Y	Gambling:	
Teams:	Y	Agents:		Radio:		Ads:		Fitness Clubs:		Apparel:	
Nonprofits:		Other:		Internet:		Tickets:		Golf Courses:		Equipment:	
Other:				Print:		Retail:		Ski Resorts:		Shoes:	
				Software:		Other:		Other:		Other:	

TYPES OF BUSINESS:

Stadiums & Sports Teams
Sports Team Franchises
Sports Facilities Management & Development
Entertainment Complexes
Entertainment Investments
Concerts & Live Entertainment Events
Filmed Entertainment
Marketing & Consulting Services

BRANDS/DIVISIONS/AFFILIATES:

Anschutz Company (The)
STAPLES Center
Regal Entertainment Group
Golden Boy Promotions
O2 (The)
Houston Dynamo
Los Angeles Kings
Los Angeles Galaxy

CONTACTS: *Note: Officers with more than one job title may be intentionally listed here more than once.*

Timothy J. Leiweke, CEO
Dan Beckerman, COO/Exec. VP
Timothy J. Leiweke, Pres.
Dan Beckerman, CFO/Exec. VP
Ted Fikre, Chief Legal & Dev. Officer
Todd Goldstein, Pres., AEG Global Partnerships
Philip Anschutz, Chmn./CEO-The Anschutz Company
David Weil, CEO-Anschutz Film Group
Eric Stevens, Pres., AEG, Events & Media

Phone: 213-763-7700	**Fax:** 303-298-8881
Toll-Free:	
Address: 1100 S. Flower St., Los Angeles, CA 90015 US	

GROWTH PLANS/SPECIAL FEATURES:

Anschutz Entertainment Group, Inc. (AEG), a subsidiary of Anschutz Corporation, is a leading sports and entertainment investment, development and management company. The firm owns the STAPLES Center, Toyota Sports Center, Toyota Park, NOKIA Theatre Times Square, The Forum and the Nokia Theater at Grand Prairie. Furthermore, the company cooperated with Home Depot to build the Home Depot National Training Center in California, an official U.S. Olympic training site. The firm recently designed The O2, a 28 acre development located in London which includes a 20,000 seat arena. AEG also controls a number of domestic sports franchises, including the Los Angeles Kings, Los Angeles Riptide, Chicago Fire, Reading Royals, Houston Dynamo and the Manchester Monarchs. The firm's subsidiary AEG Marketing is a sponsorship, consulting and sales company. AEG Creative is a full service marketing and advertising agency. Parent firm Anschutz Corporation is an investment company that also has a 79% stake in the Regal Entertainment Group as well as having vested interests in film and television production companies Crusader Entertainment and Walden Media. AEG Live is a leading global concert promotion and touring companies comprised of stand-alone affiliate divisions, including AEG Live Events, AEG-TV and national entertainment promotion and touring divisions AEG LIVE Tours & Special Events, Concerts West, Goldenvoice, The Messina Group and AEG Exhibitions. In July 2008, AEG Live announced the formation of a partnership between the firm and ThemeSTAR, a global producer and presenter of family entertainment. The newly formed venture, AEG ThemeSTAR, will widen the range of product offerings from stage shows to arenas and other multi-faceted events that have broad global appeal, as well as targeted opportunities appealing to regional interests and languages. In May 2008, the firm agreed to acquire shares of Golden Boy Promotions, a boxing promotions company affiliated with Oscar De La Hoya.

FINANCIALS: **Sales and profits are in thousands of dollars—add 000 to get the full amount. 2008 Note: Financial information for 2008 was not available for all companies at press time.**

2008 Sales: $	2008 Profits: $	**U.S. Stock Ticker: Subsidiary**
2007 Sales: $	2007 Profits: $	**Int'l Ticker:** Int'l Exchange:
2006 Sales: $	2006 Profits: $	Employees:
2005 Sales: $	2005 Profits: $	Fiscal Year Ends: 12/31
2004 Sales: $	2004 Profits: $	Parent Company: ANSCHUTZ COMPANY (THE)

SALARIES/BENEFITS:

Pension Plan:	ESOP Stock Plan:	Profit Sharing:	Top Exec. Salary: $	Bonus: $
Savings Plan:	Stock Purch. Plan:		Second Exec. Salary: $	Bonus: $

OTHER THOUGHTS:

Apparent Women Officers or Directors:
Hot Spot for Advancement for Women/Minorities:

LOCATIONS: ("Y" = Yes)

West:	Southwest:	Midwest:	Southeast:	Northeast:	International:
Y	Y	Y	Y	Y	Y

ARAMARK CORPORATION

www.aramark.com

Industry Group Code: 722310 **Ranks within this company's industry group:** Sales: 1 Profits: 1

Sports:		Services:		Media:		Sales:		Facilities:		Other:	
Leagues/Associations:		Food & Beverage:	Y	TV:		Marketing:		Stadiums:		Gambling:	
Teams:		Agents:		Radio:		Ads:		Fitness Clubs:		Apparel:	
Nonprofits:		Other:		Internet:		Tickets:		Golf Courses:		Equipment:	
Other:				Print:		Retail:		Ski Resorts:		Shoes:	
				Software:		Other:		Other:		Other:	

TYPES OF BUSINESS:

Food Service Contractor
Facilities Management
Uniforms & Career Apparel Rental
Parks & Resorts Concessions & Facilities
Health Care Support Services
Apparel Manufacturing
Clinical Equipment Maintenance

BRANDS/DIVISIONS/AFFILIATES:

Galls
GS Capital Partners
CCMP Capital Advisors
J.P. Morgan Partners
Thomas H. Lee Partners
Warburg Pincus LLC

CONTACTS: *Note: Officers with more than one job title may be intentionally listed here more than once.*

Joseph Neubauer, CEO
L. Frederick (Fred) Sutherland, CFO/Exec. VP
Lynn B. McKee, Exec. VP-Human Resources
Bart J. Colli, General Counsel/Sec./Exec. VP
Debbie Albert, External Comm.
Joseph (Joe) Munnelly, Chief Acct. Officer/Controller/Sr. VP
Andrew C. Kerin, Exec. VP/Pres., North America Food & Support Svcs.
Thomas J. Vozzo, Exec. VP/Pres., ARAMARK Uniform & Career Apparel
Robert W. Wilson, Pres., ARAMARK Refreshment Svcs.
Ira Cohn, Pres., Bus. & Industry Group
Joseph Neubauer, Chmn.
Ravi K. Saligram, Exec. VP/Pres., ARAMARK Int'l

Phone: 215-238-3000 **Fax:** 215-238-3333
Toll-Free: 800-272-6275
Address: ARAMARK Tower, 1101 Market St., Philadelphia, PA 19107-2988 US

GROWTH PLANS/SPECIAL FEATURES:

ARAMARK Corporation is a leading in the food, hospitality and facilities services company, serving business, educational, healthcare and governmental institutions as well as sports, recreational and entertainment facilities. Serving clients in 22 countries, ARAMARK has three operating segments: North America Food and Support Services, which generated 66% of 2008 sales; International Food and Support Services, 21%; and Uniform and Career Apparel, 13%. Operating in the U.S. and Canada, the North America Food and Support Services segment provides food and facility services to business and industrial clients, 80 professional and college sports teams, 36 convention and civic centers, 15 state and national parks, over 1,200 healthcare and senior living facilities, 600 correctional facilities and 1,000 colleges, universities, school districts and private schools. The International Food Service and Support Services segment serves the same types of clients as the North America segment, and operates in 20 foreign countries, with its largest operations in the U.K., Germany, Chile, Ireland, Spain and Belgium. Food services provided by these segments include dining halls, on-site restaurants, convenience stores, concessions stands, banquet halls, catering and executive dining rooms. ARAMARK's facilities management services include laundry, housekeeping, facilities maintenance, plant operations, landscaping, transportation, clinical equipment maintenance, grounds keeping, custodial services and construction management. The Uniform and Career Apparel segment provides both rental and direct marketing services to customers in the manufacturing, transportation, construction, restaurant, hotel, public safety and health care industries, including gear and clothing for emergency response and law enforcement under the Galls brand. The firm operates a fabric cutting plant in Georgia and sewing plants in Puerto Rico and Mexico. ARAMARK is owned by an investor group led by Chairman and CEO Joseph Neubauer and investment funds managed by GS Capital Partners, CCMP Capital Advisors and J.P. Morgan Partners, Thomas H. Lee Partners and Warburg Pincus LLC.

FINANCIALS: **Sales and profits are in thousands of dollars—add 000 to get the full amount. 2008 Note: Financial information for 2008 was not available for all companies at press time.**

2008 Sales: $13,470,200	2008 Profits: $39,500	**U.S. Stock Ticker: Private**
2007 Sales: $12,384,300	2007 Profits: $30,900	**Int'l Ticker:** Int'l Exchange:
2006 Sales: $11,621,173	2006 Profits: $261,098	Employees: 260,000
2005 Sales: $10,963,360	2005 Profits: $288,475	Fiscal Year Ends: 9/30
2004 Sales: $10,192,200	2004 Profits: $263,100	Parent Company:

SALARIES/BENEFITS:

Pension Plan: Y	ESOP Stock Plan:	Profit Sharing:	Top Exec. Salary: $1,250,000	Bonus: $2,100,000
Savings Plan:	Stock Purch. Plan:		Second Exec. Salary: $680,577	Bonus: $500,000

OTHER THOUGHTS:

Apparent Women Officers or Directors: 1
Hot Spot for Advancement for Women/Minorities:

LOCATIONS: ("Y" = Yes)

West:	Southwest:	Midwest:	Southeast:	Northeast:	International:
Y	Y	Y	Y	Y	Y

ARENA FOOTBALL LEAGUE LLC

www.arenafootball.com

Industry Group Code: 813990 **Ranks within this company's industry group:** Sales: Profits:

Sports:		Services:		Media:		Sales:		Facilities:		Other:	
Leagues/Associations:	Y	Food & Beverage:		TV:		Marketing:	Y	Stadiums:		Gambling:	
Teams:		Agents:		Radio:		Ads:	Y	Fitness Clubs:		Apparel:	
Nonprofits:		Other:		Internet:		Tickets:	Y	Golf Courses:		Equipment:	
Other:				Print:		Retail:		Ski Resorts:		Shoes:	
				Software:		Other:		Other:		Other:	

TYPES OF BUSINESS:

Indoor Football League

BRANDS/DIVISIONS/AFFILIATES:

Gridiron Enterprises
AF2
ArenaBowl
Philadelphia Soul
San Jose SaberCats
AFL
Arena Football League Players Association (AFLPA)

CONTACTS:

Note: Officers with more than one job title may be intentionally listed here more than once.

Ed Policy, Acting Commissioner
Joseph Vrankin, COO
Richard Berthelsen, Acting Exec. Dir.
Chris McCloskey, Exec. VP-Corp. Comm.

Phone: 212-252-8100	**Fax:** 212-252-8030
Toll-Free:	
Address: 105 Madison Ave., 9th Fl., New York, NY 10016 US	

GROWTH PLANS/SPECIAL FEATURES:

Arena Football League, LLC (AFL) was founded by Gridiron Enterprises in 1987 and holds a U.S. patent for a unique football game system and method of play. AFL games are similar to NFL football but are designed to be played in indoor stadiums. Additional differences in the AFL include the size of its fields, which are 50 yards long and 85 feet wide; only eight players (who play both offense and defense) are allowed on the field; and punting is forbidden. The league consists of 16 teams nationwide. The AF2 minor league, which has 25 teams, was also conceived by Gridiron to further expand arena football. The AFL regular season contains 16 games and runs from late January to June; AF2 plays from April to July. Teams that win playoff games advance to compete in ArenaBowl, the league's championship game. NBC and Fox Sports Network provide television coverage of AFL games. Gridiron continues its efforts to expand the sport on a worldwide scale, organizing games in Canada, Mexico, Europe, Australia and East Asia. In addition to ticket sales, the firm derives revenue from marketing and advertising. Certain AFL players, such as Kurt Warner, have progressed to starring NFL careers. Numerous teams have entered and left the various division rosters in the league's 20-year history, with the newest addition being Utah Blaze (2006). In 2008, ArenaBowl XXII was held in New Orleans, Louisiana; in the game, the Philadelphia Soul beat the San Jose SaberCats 59-56. In December 2008, the AFL decided to cancel the 2009 playing season, due to economic conditions, to restructure its operations in cooperation with the Arena Football League Players Association (AFLPA). In March 2009, the two groups agreed to amendments to their labor deal; the AFL hopes to resume play in 2010.

FINANCIALS:

Sales and profits are in thousands of dollars—add 000 to get the full amount. 2008 Note: Financial information for 2008 was not available for all companies at press time.

2008 Sales: $	2008 Profits: $	**U.S. Stock Ticker: Private**
2007 Sales: $	2007 Profits: $	**Int'l Ticker:** Int'l Exchange:
2006 Sales: $	2006 Profits: $	Employees:
2005 Sales: $	2005 Profits: $	Fiscal Year Ends:
2004 Sales: $	2004 Profits: $	Parent Company:

SALARIES/BENEFITS:

Pension Plan:	ESOP Stock Plan:	Profit Sharing:	Top Exec. Salary: $	Bonus: $
Savings Plan:	Stock Purch. Plan:		Second Exec. Salary: $	Bonus: $

OTHER THOUGHTS:

Apparent Women Officers or Directors:
Hot Spot for Advancement for Women/Minorities:

LOCATIONS: ("Y" = Yes)

West:	Southwest:	Midwest:	Southeast:	Northeast:	International:
		Y		Y	

ARIZONA CARDINALS

www.azcardinals.com

Industry Group Code: 711211C **Ranks within this company's industry group:** Sales: 30 Profits: 21

Sports:		Services:		Media:		Sales:		Facilities:		Other:	
Leagues/Associations:		Food & Beverage:		TV:		Marketing:		Stadiums:	Y	Gambling:	
Teams:	Y	Agents:		Radio:		Ads:		Fitness Clubs:		Apparel:	
Nonprofits:		Other:		Internet:		Tickets:	Y	Golf Courses:		Equipment:	
Other:				Print:		Retail:	Y	Ski Resorts:		Shoes:	
				Software:		Other:		Other:		Other:	

TYPES OF BUSINESS:

Professional Football Team
Ticket Sales
Arizona Cardinals Merchandise

BRANDS/DIVISIONS/AFFILIATES:

Morgan Athletic Club
Racine Cardinals
Chicago Cardinals
St. Louis Cardinals
Phoenix Cardinals
University of Phoenix Stadium

CONTACTS: *Note: Officers with more than one job title may be intentionally listed here more than once.*

Ron Minegar, COO/Exec. VP
Michael J. Bidwill, Pres.
Adrian Bracy, CFO/Treas.
Karen Sisley, Human Resources Coordinator/Payroll
Mark Feller, VP-Tech.
Rod Graves, VP-Football Oper.
Steve Ryan, Sr. Dir.-Bus. Dev.
Kate Brandt, Web Site Coordinator
Mark Dalton, VP-Media Rel.
Ken Whisenhunt, Head Coach
William V. Bidwill, Jr., VP
Pat Tankersley, Dir.-Cardinals Charities
Tom Reed, Head Trainer
William V. Bidwill, Chmn.

Phone: 602-379-0101	**Fax:** 602-379-1819
Toll-Free: 800-999-1402	
Address: 8701 S. Hardy Dr., Tempe, AZ 85284 US	

GROWTH PLANS/SPECIAL FEATURES:

The Arizona Cardinals is a professional football team playing in the National Football League (NFL) and based in Glendale, Arizona. The franchise, founded in 1898, has the distinction of being the oldest continuously run professional team in the U.S., having won its first NFL championship in 1925. Originally named the Morgan Athletic Club and located in Chicago, the franchise has evolved through several incarnations including the Normals, the Racine Cardinals, the Chicago Cardinals, the St. Louis Cardinals and the Phoenix Cardinals before moving to play in the Sun Devil Stadium on the Arizona State University campus in Tempe, Arizona. Over the course of its history, the team has contributed more than a dozen players to the Pro Football Hall of Fame, including Charles Bidwill, Guy Chamberlin, Jimmy Conzelman, John (Paddy) Driscoll, Walt Kiesling, Earl (Curly) Lambeau, Dick (Night Train) Lane, Ollie Matson, Ernie Nevers, Jackie Smith, Jim Thorpe, Charley Trippi, Larry Wilson and Dan Dierdorf. The team is owned by William V. Bidwill. The Cardinals currently play in University of Phoenix Stadium, which opened in August 2006. Designed in part by Peter Eisenman, it is considered something of an architectural icon for the Southwest region and cost approximately $455 million to construct. The stadium is owned by the Arizona Sports and Tourism Authority, and it holds approximately 73,000 spectators at capacity. In 2008, the stadium hosted Super Bowl XLII. After a number of years with mixed results, the Cardinals' 2008-2009 season saw the team make it all the way to Super Bowl XLIII in February 2009, where they were defeated by the Pittsburgh Steelers 27-23. Forbes Magazine recently valued the Cardinals at $914 million. The team's average home game attendance in 2008 was roughly 64,100.

FINANCIALS: **Sales and profits are in thousands of dollars—add 000 to get the full amount. 2008 Note: Financial information for 2008 was not available for all companies at press time.**

2008 Sales: $203,000	2008 Profits: $19,700	**U.S. Stock Ticker: Private**
2007 Sales: $189,000	2007 Profits: $4,600	**Int'l Ticker:** Int'l Exchange:
2006 Sales: $158,000	2006 Profits: $16,600	Employees:
2005 Sales: $153,000	2005 Profits: $	Fiscal Year Ends: 1/31
2004 Sales: $131,000	2004 Profits: $	Parent Company:

SALARIES/BENEFITS:

Pension Plan:	ESOP Stock Plan:	Profit Sharing:	Top Exec. Salary: $	Bonus: $
Savings Plan:	Stock Purch. Plan:		Second Exec. Salary: $	Bonus: $

OTHER THOUGHTS:

Apparent Women Officers or Directors: 6
Hot Spot for Advancement for Women/Minorities: Y

LOCATIONS: ("Y" = Yes)

West:	Southwest:	Midwest:	Southeast:	Northeast:	International:
	Y				

ARIZONA DIAMONDBACKS

arizona.diamondbacks.mlb.com

Industry Group Code: 711211A **Ranks within this company's industry group:** Sales: 18 Profits: 26

Sports:		Services:		Media:		Sales:		Facilities:		Other:	
Leagues/Associations:		Food & Beverage:	Y	TV:		Marketing:		Stadiums:	Y	Gambling:	
Teams:	Y	Agents:		Radio:		Ads:	Y	Fitness Clubs:		Apparel:	Y
Nonprofits:		Other:		Internet:		Tickets:	Y	Golf Courses:		Equipment:	
Other:				Print:		Retail:		Ski Resorts:		Shoes:	
				Software:		Other:		Other:		Other:	

TYPES OF BUSINESS:

Professional Baseball Team
Team Merchandise
Stadium Operation

BRANDS/DIVISIONS/AFFILIATES:

Chase Field
Tucson Sidewinders
Mobile BayBears
Visalia Oaks
South Bend Silver Hawks
Yakima Bears
Missoula Osprey

CONTACTS: *Note: Officers with more than one job title may be intentionally listed here more than once.*

Derrick Hall, CEO
Derrick Hall, Pres.
Tom Harris, CFO/Exec. VP
Karina Bohn, Sr. Dir.-Mktg.
Crystal DaShiell, Mgr.-Employment
Richard Ashe, Dir.-Info. Svcs.
Jim White, Dir.-Eng.
Sandra Cox, Office Mgr.
Nona Lee, General Counsel/VP
Tom Garfinkel, Exec. VP-Bus. Oper.
Cullen Maxey, VP-Corp. Partnerships
Manuel Sanchez, Network Mgr.-Info. Systems
Dianne Aguilar, Sr. VP-Comm. Affairs & Ticket Oper.
Craig Bradley, VP-Finance
Josh Byrnes, Sr. VP/General Mgr.
Peter Woodfork, Asst. Gen. Mgr.
A.J. Hinch, Dir.-Player Dev.
Jerry Dipoto, Dir.-Player Personnel
Ken Kendrick, Managing General Partner

Phone: 602-462-6500	**Fax:** 602-462-6599
Toll-Free:	
Address: 401 E. Jefferson St., Phoenix, AZ 85004 US	

GROWTH PLANS/SPECIAL FEATURES:

The Arizona Diamondbacks joined Major League Baseball (MLB) in 1998 as a National League expansion team. In just four years the Diamondbacks (D-Backs) won the World Series, the quickest of any expansion team ever. Baseball was brought to Arizona by Jerry Colangelo, the general manager and minority owner of the Phoenix Suns, with strong support from baseball owners and MLB Commissioner Bud Selig. The team's venue, Chase Field (originally Bank One Ballpark), is the second-highest MLB ballpark in the U.S., next to Coors Field in Denver, Colorado. The stadium seats more than 49,000 and incorporates a massive air-conditioning system and retractable roof. The up-to-date seating arrangements provide optimal sight lines and a separate pavilion contains a swimming pool, hot tub and fountains. The park drew as many as 3.6 million fans in its inaugural season, but has since fallen to closer to 2 million. Part of this was due to a dismal 2004 season, when the team went 51-111, though attendance numbers had already fallen greatly by then. That summer, Jerry Colangelo sold his controlling interest in the team to a group of equal investors including Jeff Moorad, who became CEO. Colangelo left the team more than $150 million in debt through the payment of deferred contracts to the expensive veterans who helped the D-Backs win the 2001 World Series. In 2005, the team again tried to sign expensive free agents in order to build a contender, but after another losing season they hired Josh Byrnes as their general manager. Byrnes has changed the direction of the team, giving full time jobs to young players and either trading away veteran players or allowing them to sign elsewhere. Forbes recently estimated the team's value to be approximately $390 million. The team's average home attendance in the 2008 season was nearly 31,000.

FINANCIALS: Sales and profits are in thousands of dollars—add 000 to get the full amount. 2008 Note: Financial information for 2008 was not available for all companies at press time.

2008 Sales: $177,000	2008 Profits: $3,900	**U.S. Stock Ticker: Private**
2007 Sales: $327,000	2007 Profits: $-47,300	**Int'l Ticker:** Int'l Exchange:
2006 Sales: $154,000	2006 Profits: $6,400	Employees:
2005 Sales: $145,000	2005 Profits: $	Fiscal Year Ends: 10/31
2004 Sales: $	2004 Profits: $	Parent Company:

SALARIES/BENEFITS:

Pension Plan:	ESOP Stock Plan:	Profit Sharing:	Top Exec. Salary: $	Bonus: $
Savings Plan:	Stock Purch. Plan:		Second Exec. Salary: $	Bonus: $

OTHER THOUGHTS:

Apparent Women Officers or Directors: 8
Hot Spot for Advancement for Women/Minorities: Y

LOCATIONS: ("Y" = Yes)

West:	Southwest:	Midwest:	Southeast:	Northeast:	International:
	Y				

ARSENAL FOOTBALL CLUB

www.arsenal.com

Industry Group Code: 711211D **Ranks within this company's industry group:** Sales: 4 Profits: 3

Sports:		Services:		Media:		Sales:		Facilities:		Other:	
Leagues/Associations:		Food & Beverage:		TV:		Marketing:		Stadiums:	Y	Gambling:	
Teams:	Y	Agents:		Radio:		Ads:		Fitness Clubs:		Apparel:	
Nonprofits:		Other:		Internet:		Tickets:	Y	Golf Courses:		Equipment:	
Other:				Print:		Retail:		Ski Resorts:		Shoes:	
				Software:		Other:		Other:		Other:	

TYPES OF BUSINESS:

Soccer League

BRANDS/DIVISIONS/AFFILIATES:

Arsenal Holdings plc
Arsenal Ladies
Junior Gunners
Emirates Stadium

CONTACTS: *Note: Officers with more than one job title may be intentionally listed here more than once.*

Ivan Gazidis, CEO
Arsene Wenger, Mgr.
Pat Rice, Asst. Mgr.
Boro Primorac, Coach-First Team
Vic Akers, Mgr.-Arsenal Ladies
Peter Hill-Wood, Chmn.

Phone: 44-20-7704-4170 **Fax:** 44-20-7704-4171
Toll-Free:
Address: Highbury House, 75 Drayton Park, London, N5 1BU UK

GROWTH PLANS/SPECIAL FEATURES:

Arsenal Football Club is a professional English football (soccer) club based in Holloway, North London. The team plays in the Premier League, and it is one of the most successful clubs in English soccer. The club manages the Arsenal Ladies, Junior Gunners and the Arsenal men's soccer teams in London, England. Arsenal was originally started by the workers at the Woolwich Arsenal Armament Factory, which gave the team its name. The Arsenal men's team has won 13 league championships since its inception, including the 2001-02 and 2003-04 seasons. It has also won 10 FA Cups (England's national title), most recently in 2005. The Arsenal Ladies, a semi-professional women's soccer team, has won 10 National Premier League titles, most recently in 2007-08; 10 National League Cups, most recently in 2008-09; the UEFA Women's Cup once; and nine Women's FA Cups, most recently in 2007-08. The Junior Gunners, the group's youth men's team, has won the FA Premier Youth League Championship once; has been an FA National Academy Play-Off Final Winner twice; and has won the FA Youth Cup six times, most recently in 2001. Arsenal's parent company, Arsenal Holdings plc, operates as a non-quoted public limited company, but it is not traded on a public exchange; rather, its shares are traded infrequently on PLUS, a specialist market. The club is valued at roughly $1.2 billion, making it one of the most valuable sports franchises in the world. Arsenal plays at Emirates Stadium in Holloway, which was opened in 2006. During the 2007-08 season, the men's team average game attendance was approximately 60,700.

FINANCIALS: **Sales and profits are in thousands of dollars—add 000 to get the full amount. 2008 Note: Financial information for 2008 was not available for all companies at press time.**

2008 Sales: $330,000	2008 Profits: $58,000	**U.S. Stock Ticker: Subsidiary**
2007 Sales: $307,000	2007 Profits: $54,000	**Int'l Ticker:** Int'l Exchange:
2006 Sales: $246,000	2006 Profits: $20,000	Employees:
2005 Sales: $207,000	2005 Profits: $15,100	Fiscal Year Ends: 5/31
2004 Sales: $211,000	2004 Profits: $15,000	Parent Company: ARSENAL HOLDINGS PLC

SALARIES/BENEFITS:

Pension Plan:	ESOP Stock Plan:	Profit Sharing:	Top Exec. Salary: $	Bonus: $
Savings Plan:	Stock Purch. Plan:		Second Exec. Salary: $	Bonus: $

OTHER THOUGHTS:

Apparent Women Officers or Directors:
Hot Spot for Advancement for Women/Minorities:

LOCATIONS: ("Y" = Yes)

West:	Southwest:	Midwest:	Southeast:	Northeast:	International:
					Y

ASICS CORP

www.asics.com

Industry Group Code: 316219 **Ranks within this company's industry group:** Sales: 4 Profits: 4

Sports:		Services:		Media:		Sales:		Facilities:		Other:	
Leagues/Associations:		Food & Beverage:		TV:		Marketing:		Stadiums:		Gambling:	
Teams:		Agents:		Radio:		Ads:		Fitness Clubs:		Apparel:	Y
Nonprofits:		Other:		Internet:		Tickets:		Golf Courses:		Equipment:	
Other:				Print:		Retail:		Ski Resorts:		Shoes:	Y
				Software:		Other:		Other:		Other:	

TYPES OF BUSINESS:

Athletic Footwear
Sporting Goods
Apparel
Uniforms

BRANDS/DIVISIONS/AFFILIATES:

ASICS America Corp.
ASICS Tiger Do Brasil, Ltda.
Agence Quebec Plus
Jiang Su ASICS Co., Ltd.
ASICS Oceania Pty., Ltd.
Onitsuka Tiger
Impact Guide Systems
Asics Gel

CONTACTS: *Note: Officers with more than one job title may be intentionally listed here more than once.*

Kiyomi Wada, Representative Dir.
Motoi Oyama, Pres./Representative Dir.
Ryomi Tamesada, Sr. Managing Dir.
Kiyomi Wada, Chmn.

Phone: 81-78-303-2231 **Fax:** 81-78-303-2241
Toll-Free:
Address: 7-1-1, Minatojima-Nakamachi, Chuo-ku, Kobe, 650-8555 Japan

GROWTH PLANS/SPECIAL FEATURES:

ASICS Corp., based in Japan, is a manufacturer of sporting goods. The firm products include footwear, sportswear and uniforms for a variety of sports including basketball, volleyball, track and field, wrestling and running. ASICS also makes accessories such as hats, sports bags and protective gear, as well as sports apparel. Fashion-oriented items are sold through the brand name Onitsuka Tiger. Products are sold through specialty running stores, sporting good stores, department stores and online. The company markets its shoes based on several technologies such as the Impact Guide Systems (I.G.S.) designed to produce a more natural heel-to-toe movement and Gel technology for more in-shoe cushioning. Asics operates through group company offices in the U.S., Brazil, Japan, Australia, China, Korea, Taiwan, the Netherlands, Germany, France, the U.K., Italy, Spain, Norway, Denmark, Sweden, South Africa, Israel and the U.A.E., and works through distributors in numerous other countries. The firm also operates several subsidiaries, including ASICS America Corp. (North America) and ASICS Tiger Do Brasil, Ltda. A research and development center based in Kobe, Japan develops and tests new material and construction technologies. In October 2008, the company opened its first European flagship store in London.

FINANCIALS: **Sales and profits are in thousands of dollars—add 000 to get the full amount. 2008 Note: Financial information for 2008 was not available for all companies at press time.**

2008 Sales: $2,261,700	2008 Profits: $131,000	**U.S. Stock Ticker:**
2007 Sales: $1,847,900	2007 Profits: $131,800	**Int'l Ticker: 7936** Int'l Exchange: Tokyo-TSE
2006 Sales: $1,624,800	2006 Profits: $131,200	Employees: 3,708
2005 Sales: $1,393,500	2005 Profits: $66,600	Fiscal Year Ends: 3/31
2004 Sales: $1,330,000	2004 Profits: $43,800	Parent Company:

SALARIES/BENEFITS:

Pension Plan:	ESOP Stock Plan:	Profit Sharing:	Top Exec. Salary: $	Bonus: $
Savings Plan:	Stock Purch. Plan:		Second Exec. Salary: $	Bonus: $

OTHER THOUGHTS:

Apparent Women Officers or Directors:
Hot Spot for Advancement for Women/Minorities:

LOCATIONS: ("Y" = Yes)

West:	Southwest:	Midwest:	Southeast:	Northeast:	International:
Y					Y

ASSOCIATION OF TENNIS PROFESSIONALS

www.atptennis.com

Industry Group Code: 813990 **Ranks within this company's industry group:** Sales: Profits:

Sports:		Services:		Media:		Sales:		Facilities:		Other:	
Leagues/Associations:	Y	Food & Beverage:		TV:		Marketing:		Stadiums:		Gambling:	
Teams:		Agents:		Radio:		Ads:		Fitness Clubs:		Apparel:	
Nonprofits:		Other:		Internet:		Tickets:		Golf Courses:		Equipment:	
Other:				Print:		Retail:		Ski Resorts:		Shoes:	
				Software:		Other:		Other:		Other:	

TYPES OF BUSINESS:

Tennis Association

BRANDS/DIVISIONS/AFFILIATES:

ATP Properties

CONTACTS:

Note: Officers with more than one job title may be intentionally listed here more than once.

Flip Galloway, COO
Adam Helfant, Pres.
Phil Anderton, Chief Mktg. Officer
Richard Davies, CEO-ATP Properties
Mark Young, CEO-Americas
Adam Helfant, Exec. Chmn.
Brad Drewett, CEO-Int'l Group

Phone: 44-20-7381-7890	Fax: 44-20-7381-7895
Toll-Free:	
Address: Palliser House, Palliser Rd., London, W14 9EB UK	

GROWTH PLANS/SPECIAL FEATURES:

The Association of Tennis Professionals (ATP) is the governing body for men's professional tennis worldwide. ATP organizes and oversees approximately 63 tournaments in 30 countries, including singles and doubles matches. The association also maintains the South African Airways sponsored ATP rankings for singles players and the Stanford ATP Doubles Race. All players contend for titles in the ATP Masters Series and other ATP tournaments. Each season, the top eight singles players and doubles teams make the cut to play in the Tennis Masters Cup which is scheduled for November 2009 in London, U.K. Subsidiary ATP Properties, also based in the U.K., is responsible for the marketing and sales of all ATP commercial rights. ATP is affiliated with the Sony Ericsson WTA Tour, the International Tennis Hall of Fame, the International Tennis Federation, the U.S. Open Series and the BlackRock Tour of Champions. Collectively, these organizations work together to promote the sport of tennis around the world. In April 2008, ATP joined with Enel, a major European energy company, as a partner in a three year agreement that stipulates Enel's sponsorship of eight men's tournaments, including the official sponsorship of the ATP World Tour Finals in London starting in 2009.

FINANCIALS:

Sales and profits are in thousands of dollars—add 000 to get the full amount. 2008 Note: Financial information for 2008 was not available for all companies at press time.

2008 Sales: $	2008 Profits: $	**U.S. Stock Ticker: Private**
2007 Sales: $	2007 Profits: $	**Int'l Ticker:** Int'l Exchange:
2006 Sales: $	2006 Profits: $	Employees:
2005 Sales: $	2005 Profits: $	Fiscal Year Ends:
2004 Sales: $	2004 Profits: $	Parent Company:

SALARIES/BENEFITS:

Pension Plan:	ESOP Stock Plan:	Profit Sharing:	Top Exec. Salary: $	Bonus: $
Savings Plan:	Stock Purch. Plan:		Second Exec. Salary: $	Bonus: $

OTHER THOUGHTS:

Apparent Women Officers or Directors:
Hot Spot for Advancement for Women/Minorities:

LOCATIONS: ("Y" = Yes)

West:	Southwest:	Midwest:	Southeast:	Northeast:	International:
		Y	Y		Y

ASTON VILLA FOOTBALL CLUB

www.avfc.premiumtv.co.uk

Industry Group Code: 711211D **Ranks within this company's industry group:** Sales: 9 Profits: 6

Sports:		Services:		Media:		Sales:		Facilities:		Other:	
Leagues/Associations:		Food & Beverage:		TV:		Marketing:	Y	Stadiums:	Y	Gambling:	
Teams:	Y	Agents:		Radio:		Ads:	Y	Fitness Clubs:		Apparel:	
Nonprofits:		Other:		Internet:	Y	Tickets:	Y	Golf Courses:		Equipment:	
Other:				Print:		Retail:	Y	Ski Resorts:		Shoes:	
				Software:		Other:		Other:		Other:	

TYPES OF BUSINESS:

Professional Soccer Team
Ticket Sales
Merchandise

BRANDS/DIVISIONS/AFFILIATES:

Aston Villa Hospitality & Events (AVHE)
Villa Vitality
Villa in Harmony
Villan Learning Zone
Villa Direct

CONTACTS:

Note: Officers with more than one job title may be intentionally listed here more than once.

Robin Russell, CFO
Russell Jones, Head-Mktg.
Lisa Trotter, Head-Human Resources
Richard Hollingsworth, Mgr.-IT
John Greenfield, Mgr.-Merch.
John Handley, Mgr.-Oper. & Safety
Steve Tudgay, Head-Media Oper.
Martin O'Neill, Team Mgr.
Steve Walford, Coach-First Team
John Robertson, Coach-First Team
Nicola Keye, Head-Consumer Sales
Randolph Lerner, Chmn.

Phone: 44-121-327-2299 **Fax:** 44-121-322-2107
Toll-Free:
Address: Villa Park, Trinity Rd., Birmingham, B6 6HE UK

GROWTH PLANS/SPECIAL FEATURES:

Aston Villa Football Club, nicknamed the Claret and Blue after its colors and also known as the Villans, is an English Premier League soccer (football) team based in Aston, Birmingham. Founded in 1874, the team plays at Villa Park and has won the First Division Championship seven times, placing sixth overall in the Premier League in the 2007-08 season. Aston Villa is owned by U.S. billionaire Randy Lerner, who also owns the Cleveland Browns National Football League (NFL) team, and purchased the club in 2006 through his company, Reform Acquisitions Limited, for approximately $119 million. The club web site has news specific to the club and to soccer; video clips of match highlights; e-mail news alert services; season passes and single match ticket sales; a link to the official club shop, astonvilladirect.com, which sells club apparel, soccer footwear and equipment; and a link to Aston Villa Hospitality and Events (AVHE), which manages corporate relations for the stadium, Villa Park. Club revenue comes in large part from ticket sales at Villa Park; sales of replicas of current and retro player jerseys and other merchandise; and also from advertising sales. Additional revenue comes from club publications, including Villa News and Record; Claret and Blue; and Yearbook, which profiles the club's members. Notable corporate partners and sponsors include Nike; Seat U.K.; Carlsberg Beer; MBNA Europe; Coca-Cola; and Nivea for Men. Aston Villa currently holds its training sessions at its own grounds in Warwickshire. The club has been granted permission to expand the North Stand of Villa Park in time for the 2012 Summer Olympics in London. The firm's Community Department runs soccer schools and clinics; educates children about the benefits of a healthy lifestyle; and provides coaching to children with special needs.

FINANCIALS:

Sales and profits are in thousands of dollars—add 000 to get the full amount. 2008 Note: Financial information for 2008 was not available for all companies at press time.

2008 Sales: $150,000
2007 Sales: $106,000
2006 Sales: $91,000
2005 Sales: $94,000
2004 Sales: $103,000

2008 Profits: $1,000
2007 Profits: $-40,000
2006 Profits: $-21,000
2005 Profits: $
2004 Profits: $

U.S. Stock Ticker: Subsidiary
Int'l Ticker: Int'l Exchange:
Employees:
Fiscal Year Ends: 5/31
Parent Company: REFORM ACQUISITIONS LIMITED

SALARIES/BENEFITS:

Pension Plan:	ESOP Stock Plan:	Profit Sharing:	Top Exec. Salary: $	Bonus: $
Savings Plan:	Stock Purch. Plan:		Second Exec. Salary: $	Bonus: $

OTHER THOUGHTS:

Apparent Women Officers or Directors: 4
Hot Spot for Advancement for Women/Minorities: Y

LOCATIONS: ("Y" = Yes)

West:	Southwest:	Midwest:	Southeast:	Northeast:	International:
					Y

Note: Financial information, benefits and other data can change quickly and may vary from those stated here.

ATLANTA BRAVES

atlanta.braves.mlb.com

Industry Group Code: 711211A **Ranks within this company's industry group:** Sales: 13 Profits: 25

Sports:		Services:		Media:		Sales:		Facilities:		Other:	
Leagues/Associations:		Food & Beverage:		TV:		Marketing:		Stadiums:	Y	Gambling:	
Teams:	Y	Agents:		Radio:		Ads:		Fitness Clubs:		Apparel:	
Nonprofits:		Other:		Internet:		Tickets:	Y	Golf Courses:		Equipment:	
Other:				Print:		Retail:	Y	Ski Resorts:		Shoes:	
				Software:		Other:		Other:		Other:	

TYPES OF BUSINESS:

Professional Baseball Team

BRANDS/DIVISIONS/AFFILIATES:

Liberty Media Group
Atlanta National League Baseball Club, Inc.
Richmond Braves
Mississippi Braves
Myrtle Beach Pelicans
Rome Braves
Danville Braves

CONTACTS: *Note: Officers with more than one job title may be intentionally listed here more than once.*

Terry McGuirk, CEO
John Schuerholz, Pres.
Derek Schiller, Exec. VP-Mktg. & Sales
Lara Juras, Dir.-Human Resources
Sherry Millette, Dir.-IT
Robert A. Hope, Dir.-Merch.
Greg Heller, General Counsel/Sr. VP
Mike Plant, Exec. VP-Bus. Oper.
Ericka Newsome, Dir.-Comm. Affairs & Braves Foundation
Chip Moore, Sr. VP/Controller
Frank Wren, Exec. VP/Gen. Mgr.
Jim Allen, Sr. Dir.-Corp. Sales
Ed Newman, Dir.-Ticket Oper.
Beth Marshall, Dir.-Public Rel.
Terry McGuirk, Chmn.

Phone: 404-522-7630 **Fax:** 404-614-7391
Toll-Free:
Address: 755 Hank Aaron Dr., SW, Atlanta, GA 30315 US

GROWTH PLANS/SPECIAL FEATURES:

The Atlanta Braves, owned and operated by Atlanta National League Baseball Club, Inc., is one of the oldest teams in professional baseball. The team began as the Boston Red Stockings in 1871, became the Braves in 1912, moved to Milwaukee during the 1950s and finally relocated to Atlanta in 1966. The team has played its home games at the 45,000-seat Turner Field since 1997. A storied franchise, the Braves have won three World Series Championships, 17 pennants, 16 division titles and made over 20 post-season appearances since 1877. Time Warner subsidiary Turner Broadcasting bought the team from its former owner, media mogul Ted Turner, who owned the team throughout the 1990s when it was the most successful franchise in Major League Baseball (MLB). The Braves' glory days in the 1990s were propelled through the all-star playing of Tom Glavine, John Smoltz, Greg Maddux, David Justice and Fred McGriff. The team won its division an unprecedented 14 times in a row from 1991 to 2005, losing in 2006 to the New York Mets. In 2007, Time Warner sold the team for $1 billion to Liberty Media Group. The team's manager, Bobby Cox, has managed the Braves since 1990 and is currently the longest tenured manager in Major League Baseball. Minor league affiliates of the Braves include the Mississippi, Rome, Gwinnett and Danville Braves, as well as the Myrtle Beach Pelicans. The team has contributed a number of players to the National Baseball Hall of Fame, including Hank Aaron, Eddie Mathews, Warren Spahn and Phil Niekro. The team ended its 2008 season with 72 wins and 90 losses, failing to make the playoffs. According to a recent Forbes estimate, the team is worth approximately $446 million. The team's average home attendance in the 2008 season was over 31,200 fans per game.

FINANCIALS: **Sales and profits are in thousands of dollars—add 000 to get the full amount. 2008 Note: Financial information for 2008 was not available for all companies at press time.**

2008 Sales: $186,000	2008 Profits: $4,700	**U.S. Stock Ticker: Subsidiary**
2007 Sales: $199,000	2007 Profits: $28,100	**Int'l Ticker:** Int'l Exchange:
2006 Sales: $183,000	2006 Profits: $14,800	Employees:
2005 Sales: $172,000	2005 Profits: $	Fiscal Year Ends: 12/31
2004 Sales: $	2004 Profits: $	Parent Company: LIBERTY MEDIA CORP

SALARIES/BENEFITS:

Pension Plan:	ESOP Stock Plan:	Profit Sharing:	Top Exec. Salary: $	Bonus: $
Savings Plan:	Stock Purch. Plan:		Second Exec. Salary: $	Bonus: $

OTHER THOUGHTS:

Apparent Women Officers or Directors: 30
Hot Spot for Advancement for Women/Minorities: Y

LOCATIONS: ("Y" = Yes)

West:	Southwest:	Midwest:	Southeast:	Northeast:	International:
			Y		

Note: Financial information, benefits and other data can change quickly and may vary from those stated here.

ATLANTA DREAM

www.wnba.com/dream

Industry Group Code: 711211E **Ranks within this company's industry group:** Sales: Profits:

Sports:		Services:		Media:		Sales:		Facilities:		Other:	
Leagues/Associations:		Food & Beverage:		TV:		Marketing:		Stadiums:		Gambling:	
Teams:	Y	Agents:		Radio:		Ads:		Fitness Clubs:		Apparel:	
Nonprofits:	Y	Other:		Internet:		Tickets:	Y	Golf Courses:		Equipment:	
Other:				Print:		Retail:	Y	Ski Resorts:		Shoes:	
				Software:		Other:		Other:		Other:	

TYPES OF BUSINESS:

Women's National Basketball Association Team

BRANDS/DIVISIONS/AFFILIATES:

CONTACTS:

Note: Officers with more than one job title may be intentionally listed here more than once.

Bill Bolen, COO
Bill Bolen, Pres.
Paige Blankenship, VP-Mktg. & Bus. Dev.
Danielle Donehew, Exec. VP-Oper.
Dave Biggar, Exec. Dir.-Bus. Dev.
Tonya Alleyne, VP-Media Rel.
Danielle Donehew, Exec. VP-Finance
Ron Terwilliger, Owner
Marynell Meadors, Gen. Mgr./Head Coach
Allison Fillmore, VP-Ticket Sales & Service

Phone: 404-604-2626	**Fax:** 404-954-6666
Toll-Free:	
Address: 83 Walton St. NW, Ste. 500, Atlanta, GA 30303 US	

GROWTH PLANS/SPECIAL FEATURES:

The Atlanta Dream is a women's basketball team and a member of the Women's National Basketball Association (WNBA). Established in late 2007, the Dream plays in the WNBA Eastern Conference, along with the Chicago Sky, the Connecticut Sun, the Detroit Shock, Indiana Fever, New York Liberty and the Washington Mystics. The team in owned by Atlanta-area businessman and real estate developer J. Ronald Terwilliger, making it one of the minority of WNBA teams owned and operated independently of the National Basketball Association (NBA). The franchise chose for its first coach Marynell Meadors, whose WNBA experience includes work with the Charlotte Sting (during the WNBA's inaugural 1997 year), Miami Sol and Washington Mystics, in addition to more than 30 years spent coaching at the collegiate level. The Dream franchise has its home court in the $213.5 million Phillips Arena. The Arena, completed in 1999, also serves as home for the Atlanta Hawks NBA team and the Atlanta Thrashers National Hockey League (NHL) team. It holds approximately 19,445 spectators for basketball, and is owned by Atlanta Spirit LLC, the same company that owns the Hawks and Thrashers. The franchise conducts charitable work in the Atlanta area through its Dream Foundation, which has sponsored programs such as free basketball clinics and a mentoring program for middle school girls. The Atlanta Dream played its opening season in 2008, losing its first 17 games in a row and eventually finishing the season with four wins and 30 losses. In late 2008 and early 2009, the team made several trades and signed a number of new players in hopes of improving their record for the 2009 season.

FINANCIALS:

Sales and profits are in thousands of dollars—add 000 to get the full amount. 2008 Note: Financial information for 2008 was not available for all companies at press time.

2008 Sales: $	2008 Profits: $	**U.S. Stock Ticker: Private**
2007 Sales: $	2007 Profits: $	**Int'l Ticker:** Int'l Exchange:
2006 Sales: $	2006 Profits: $	Employees:
2005 Sales: $	2005 Profits: $	Fiscal Year Ends: 6/30
2004 Sales: $	2004 Profits: $	Parent Company:

SALARIES/BENEFITS:

Pension Plan:	ESOP Stock Plan:	Profit Sharing:	Top Exec. Salary: $	Bonus: $
Savings Plan:	Stock Purch. Plan:		Second Exec. Salary: $	Bonus: $

OTHER THOUGHTS:

Apparent Women Officers or Directors: 19
Hot Spot for Advancement for Women/Minorities: Y

LOCATIONS: ("Y" = Yes)

West:	Southwest:	Midwest:	Southeast:	Northeast:	International:
			Y		

ATLANTA FALCONS

www.atlantafalcons.com

Industry Group Code: 711211C **Ranks within this company's industry group:** Sales: 29 Profits: 9

Sports:		Services:		Media:		Sales:		Facilities:		Other:	
Leagues/Associations:		Food & Beverage:		TV:		Marketing:		Stadiums:		Gambling:	
Teams:	Y	Agents:		Radio:		Ads:		Fitness Clubs:		Apparel:	Y
Nonprofits:		Other:		Internet:		Tickets:	Y	Golf Courses:		Equipment:	
Other:				Print:		Retail:	Y	Ski Resorts:		Shoes:	
				Software:		Other:		Other:		Other:	

TYPES OF BUSINESS:

Professional Football Team
Ticket Sales
Atlanta Falcons Merchandise

BRANDS/DIVISIONS/AFFILIATES:

Atlanta Falcons Youth Foundation

CONTACTS:

Note: Officers with more than one job title may be intentionally listed here more than once.

Arthur M. Blank, CEO/Owner
Rich McKay, Pres.
Greg Beadles, CFO/VP
Jim Smith, VP-Mktg.
Karen Walters, Dir.-Human Resources
Danny Branch, VP-IT
Nick Polk, Dir.-Football Admin.
Reggie Roberts, VP-Football Comm.
Rob Geoffroy, Controller
Mike Smith, Head Coach
Dave Cohen, VP-Sales
Thomas Dimitroff, General Mgr.
Kendyl Moss, Dir.-Community Rel.
Arthur M. Blank, Chmn.

Phone: 770-965-3115	**Fax:** 770-965-2766
Toll-Free:	
Address: 4400 Falcon Pkwy., Flowery Branch, GA 30542 US	

GROWTH PLANS/SPECIAL FEATURES:

The Atlanta Falcons, owned and operated by Atlanta Falcons Football Club, LLC, is a professional football team based in Atlanta, Georgia. The team is a member of the National Football Conference in the National Football League (NFL). The team began in 1965, and entered its first playoff series in 1978. The Falcons team has won its division three times, in 1980, 1998 and 2004; and it has won its conference once, in 1998. The team's home stadium is the 71,250-seat Georgia Dome, the largest cable-supported domed stadium in the world, which is owned by the state of Georgia and managed by Georgia World Congress Center. The stadium's facilities include a new luxury club, private suites and lounges. The team operates a retail store for Falcons merchandise at its headquarters as well as an online store through its web site. The Falcons field a 30-member cheerleading squad, as well as Freddy Falcon, the team mascot. The team is currently owned by Arthur M. Blank, a co-founder of Home Depot. The organization conducts philanthropy through the Atlanta Falcons Youth Foundation, first established in 1985. The Foundation focuses on a variety of needs, with a particular focus on children's health and fitness, and awards more than $16 million in grants to nonprofits throughout Georgia. The team has seen two of its former players enter the Pro Football Hall of Fame over the course of its history, Eric Dickerson and Tommy McDonald. The 2008 season, in which the Falcons won 11 out of 16 regular season games, saw the team qualify for the Wild Card Playoffs for the first time since 2004, only to lose to the Arizona Cardinals 24-30. Forbes Magazine recently valued the team at $872 million. The team's average home game attendance in 2008 was roughly 64,100.

FINANCIALS:

Sales and profits are in thousands of dollars—add 000 to get the full amount. 2008 Note: Financial information for 2008 was not available for all companies at press time.

2008 Sales: $203,000	2008 Profits: $30,900	**U.S. Stock Ticker: Private**
2007 Sales: $185,000	2007 Profits: $-3,400	**Int'l Ticker:** Int'l Exchange:
2006 Sales: $170,000	2006 Profits: $6,600	Employees:
2005 Sales: $168,000	2005 Profits: $	Fiscal Year Ends: 2/28
2004 Sales: $	2004 Profits: $	Parent Company: ATLANTA FALCONS FOOTBALL CLUB LLC

SALARIES/BENEFITS:

Pension Plan:	ESOP Stock Plan:	Profit Sharing:	Top Exec. Salary: $	Bonus: $
Savings Plan:	Stock Purch. Plan:		Second Exec. Salary: $	Bonus: $

OTHER THOUGHTS:

Apparent Women Officers or Directors: 26
Hot Spot for Advancement for Women/Minorities: Y

LOCATIONS: ("Y" = Yes)

West:	Southwest:	Midwest:	Southeast:	Northeast:	International:
			Y		

Note: Financial information, benefits and other data can change quickly and may vary from those stated here.

ATLANTA HAWKS

www.nba.com/hawks

Industry Group Code: 711211B **Ranks within this company's industry group:** Sales: 20 Profits: 16

Sports:		Services:		Media:		Sales:		Facilities:		Other:	
Leagues/Associations:		Food & Beverage:		TV:		Marketing:		Stadiums:		Gambling:	
Teams:	Y	Agents:		Radio:		Ads:		Fitness Clubs:		Apparel:	
Nonprofits:		Other:		Internet:		Tickets:		Golf Courses:		Equipment:	
Other:				Print:		Retail:		Ski Resorts:		Shoes:	
				Software:		Other:		Other:		Other:	

TYPES OF BUSINESS:

Professional Basketball Team
Ticket Sales
Atlanta Hawks Merchandise

BRANDS/DIVISIONS/AFFILIATES:

Atlanta Spirit, LLC
Phillips Arena
Arena Operations, LLC
A-Town Dancers
Crowd Control
Hawks Spirit Squad
Atlanta Hawks Foundation
SkyHawk & the Sky Squad

CONTACTS: *Note: Officers with more than one job title may be intentionally listed here more than once.*

Bernard J. Mullin, CEO
Bernard J. Mullin, Pres.
Bill Duffy, CFO/Exec. VP
Lou DePaoli, Chief Mktg. Officer/Exec. VP
Ginni Siler, VP-Human Resources
Charles Gore, Dir.-IT
T. Scott Wilkinson, Chief Legal Officer/VP
Chris Grant, VP-Basketball Oper./Asst. Gen. Mgr.
David Lee, VP-Bus. Dev.
Tom Hughes, Sr. VP-Comm.
Phil Ebinger, VP-Finance
Billy Knight, Exec. VP/Gen. Mgr.
Bob Williams, Pres., Phillips Arena
Tracy White, Sr. VP-Broadcast & Corp. Partnerships
Brendan Donohue, VP-Ticket Sales & Service

Phone: 404-827-3800 **Fax:** 404-827-4229
Toll-Free:
Address: Centennial Tower, 101 Marietta St. NW, Ste. 1900, Atlanta, GA 30303 US

GROWTH PLANS/SPECIAL FEATURES:

The Atlanta Hawks franchise, playing in the National Basketball Association (NBA), was originally formed in 1946 in Illinois and Iowa as the Tri-Cities Blackhawks and has since moved to both Milwaukee, Wisconsin and St. Louis Missouri before finding its final home in Atlanta, Georgia in 1968. The Hawks franchise and its home arena are both owned by a private investment group called Atlanta Spirit, LLC. The Hawks' home stadium, Philips Arena, is managed by Arena Operations, LLC and boasts an 18,729 seating capacity, 92 private suites, nine party/rental suites and 1,866 club seats. Featured performances during game nights include the A-Town Dancers; Crowd Control; Harry the Hawk; SkyHawk and the Sky Squad; and the Hawks Spirit Squad. The Atlanta Hawks Foundation was established in order to encourage Georgian children to develop a commitment to physical fitness and recreation. Educational program sponsorships include Fast Break for Reading, the Atlanta Hawks Student Achievers Program and the Atlanta Hawks Press Pass Program. The team also hosts the Atlanta Hawks Summer Camp and the Jr. Hawks league. Former basketball legends of the Hawks include Bill Russell, Bob Pettit and Pistol Pete Maravich. Although the team was highly competitive throughout the 1980s and 1990s with small forward, Dominique Wilkins, the Hawks have not made the playoffs since the 1998-99 season. Forbes recently estimated the team to be worth approximately $306 million. In the 2008-09 season, the team's home attendance average was roughly 16,700 per game.

FINANCIALS: **Sales and profits are in thousands of dollars—add 000 to get the full amount. 2008 Note: Financial information for 2008 was not available for all companies at press time.**

2008 Sales: $102,000 — 2008 Profits: $6,700
2007 Sales: $95,000 — 2007 Profits: $9,700
2006 Sales: $92,000 — 2006 Profits: $12,900
2005 Sales: $87,000 — 2005 Profits: $
2004 Sales: $ — 2004 Profits: $

U.S. Stock Ticker: Private
Int'l Ticker: Int'l Exchange:
Employees:
Fiscal Year Ends: 6/30
Parent Company: ATLANTA SPIRIT LLC

SALARIES/BENEFITS:

Pension Plan: ESOP Stock Plan: Profit Sharing: Top Exec. Salary: $ Bonus: $
Savings Plan: Stock Purch. Plan: Second Exec. Salary: $ Bonus: $

OTHER THOUGHTS:

Apparent Women Officers or Directors: 6
Hot Spot for Advancement for Women/Minorities: Y

LOCATIONS: ("Y" = Yes)

West:	Southwest:	Midwest:	Southeast:	Northeast:	International:
			Y		

ATLANTA THRASHERS

www.atlantathrashers.com

Industry Group Code: 711211F **Ranks within this company's industry group:** Sales: 27 Profits: 22

Sports:		Services:		Media:		Sales:		Facilities:		Other:	
Leagues/Associations:		Food & Beverage:		TV:		Marketing:		Stadiums:	Y	Gambling:	
Teams:	Y	Agents:		Radio:		Ads:		Fitness Clubs:		Apparel:	
Nonprofits:	Y	Other:		Internet:		Tickets:	Y	Golf Courses:		Equipment:	
Other:				Print:		Retail:		Ski Resorts:		Shoes:	
				Software:		Other:		Other:		Other:	

TYPES OF BUSINESS:

Professional Hockey Team

BRANDS/DIVISIONS/AFFILIATES:

Atlanta Spirit, LLC
Atlanta Thrashers Foundation
Pond Hockey With a Purpose
Phillips Arena
Blueland Blog
Kids Club
Blueland Times
Thrashers School Assembly Program

CONTACTS:

Note: Officers with more than one job title may be intentionally listed here more than once.

Phil Ebinger, CFO/VP
Tracy White, Sr. VP-Mktg. & Sales
Tony Donato, Dir.-Human Resources
Charles Gore, Sr. Dir.-IT
Scott Wilkinson, Chief Legal Officer/VP
David Lee, VP-Bus. Dev.
Rob Koch, Sr. Dir.-Public Rel.
Michelle Walker, Controller/Sr. Dir.-Acct.
John Anderson, Head Coach
Bob Williams, Pres., Philips Arena
Don Waddell, Exec. VP/Gen. Mgr.
Larry Simmons, VP/Assistant Gen. Mgr.

Phone: 404-827-3300 **Fax:** 404-878-3765
Toll-Free: 866-715-1500
Address: 101 Marietta St. NW, Ste. 1900, Atlanta, GA 30303 US

GROWTH PLANS/SPECIAL FEATURES:

The Atlanta Thrashers franchise is a National Hockey League (NHL) professional hockey team based in Atlanta, Georgia. Beginning as an expansion franchise in June 1997, the team is one of the newest in the NHL. The team plays in the Southeast Division of the NHL's Eastern Conference. Atlanta Spirit, LLC owns the Thrashers, as well as the Atlanta Hawks basketball team. Atlanta Spirit purchased the franchise from Turner Broadcasting System, Inc. in 2004. The team's home venue is Phillips Arena (also owned by Atlanta Spirit). The arena, managed by Arena Operations, LLC, features 19,445 seats for basketball, 18,545 for hockey and 21,000 for concerts. It also contains an additional 92 private suites, nine party/rental suites, 23 food outlets, 12 retail outlets, four restaurants and 1,866 club seats. Notable past players of the Thrashers include Dan Snyder and Wayne Gretzky. The team also operates a children's charity, the Atlanta Thrashers Foundation. Additionally, the team participates in a number of community outreach programs, including Pond Hockey With a Purpose, a program designed to let children practice new drills and techniques. Fans can interact online with the Blueland Blog, message boards and the online newsletter Blueland Times. The club partners with Applebees to offer a Kids Club, facilitates Scores for Schools with Atlanta Public Schools, as well as the Thrashers School Assembly program with Philips. In January 2008, the NHL All-Star Game was played for the first time in Philips Arena. Forbes recently estimated the team's value to be $158 million. In the 2008-09 season, the team's average home attendance was approximately 14,600.

FINANCIALS:

Sales and profits are in thousands of dollars—add 000 to get the full amount. 2008 Note: Financial information for 2008 was not available for all companies at press time.

2008 Sales: $70,000	2008 Profits: $-6,100	**U.S. Stock Ticker: Subsidiary**
2007 Sales: $67,000	2007 Profits: $-6,500	**Int'l Ticker:** Int'l Exchange:
2006 Sales: $64,000	2006 Profits: $-5,400	Employees:
2005 Sales: $	2005 Profits: $	Fiscal Year Ends: 12/31
2004 Sales: $59,000	2004 Profits: $	Parent Company: ATLANTA SPIRIT LLC

SALARIES/BENEFITS:

Pension Plan:	ESOP Stock Plan:	Profit Sharing:	Top Exec. Salary: $	Bonus: $
Savings Plan:	Stock Purch. Plan:		Second Exec. Salary: $	Bonus: $

OTHER THOUGHTS:

Apparent Women Officers or Directors: 5
Hot Spot for Advancement for Women/Minorities: Y

LOCATIONS: ("Y" = Yes)

West:	Southwest:	Midwest:	Southeast:	Northeast:	International:
			Y		

BALLY TOTAL FITNESS HOLDING CORPORATION

www.ballyfitness.com

Industry Group Code: 713940 **Ranks within this company's industry group:** Sales: Profits:

Sports:		Services:		Media:		Sales:		Facilities:		Other:	
Leagues/Associations:		Food & Beverage:		TV:		Marketing:		Stadiums:		Gambling:	
Teams:		Agents:		Radio:		Ads:		Fitness Clubs:	Y	Apparel:	
Nonprofits:		Other:		Internet:		Tickets:		Golf Courses:		Equipment:	
Other:				Print:		Retail:		Ski Resorts:		Shoes:	
				Software:		Other:		Other:		Other:	

TYPES OF BUSINESS:

Fitness Clubs
Nutritional Supplements
Personal Training Services
Fitness Classes
Fitness Equipment
Martial Arts Training

BRANDS/DIVISIONS/AFFILIATES:

Bally Sports Clubs
Build Your Own Membership (BYOM)
Bally Total Martial Arts

CONTACTS: *Note: Officers with more than one job title may be intentionally listed here more than once.*

Michael Sheenan, CEO
William G. Fanelli, CFO
William G. Fanelli, Sr. VP-Corp. Dev.
William G. Fanelli, Sr. VP-Finance
Don R. Kornstein, Interim Chmn.

Phone: 773-380-3000 **Fax:** 773-693-2982
Toll-Free: 800-515-2582
Address: 8700 W. Bryn Mawr Ave. 2nd Fl., Chicago, IL 60631 US

GROWTH PLANS/SPECIAL FEATURES:

Bally Total Fitness Holding Corp. is one of North America's largest commercial operators of fitness centers. The firm operates nearly 300 fitness centers in 29 states. The firm's clubs are concentrated in major metropolitan areas through the U.S., but are also located in the Caribbean, Mexico, South Korea and China. The majority of the centers use the Bally Total Fitness or Bally Sports Clubs brands. Bally provides state-of-the-art gyms featuring a broad selection of cardiovascular, conditioning and strength equipment, with extensive aerobic and group training programs. Many locations also include pools, racquet courts and other athletic facilities. Bally targets customers aged 18-54 with mid-level income. The firm offers various membership options and payment plans (such as the Build Your Own Membership program), ranging from single-club memberships to premium plans, which provide access to all centers nationwide. Other products and services include personal training and private-label nutritional products, such as meal replacement shakes and drinks, energy and snack bars and multi-vitamins sold in retail outlets. Bally's licensed portable exercise equipment is also sold in retail outlets. The firm's martial arts program includes on-on-one instruction with master teachers and opened its fourth franchise in Seoul, South Korea. In 2007 the firm filed for bankruptcy and its stock was delisted. In December 2008, Bally filed for bankruptcy a second time since its emergence in late 2007.

Employees are offered medical, dental and vision insurance; a 401(k) plan and health club membership.

FINANCIALS:

Sales and profits are in thousands of dollars—add 000 to get the full amount. 2008 Note: Financial information for 2008 was not available for all companies at press time.

2008 Sales: $	2008 Profits: $	**U.S. Stock Ticker: Private**
2007 Sales: $	2007 Profits: $	**Int'l Ticker:** Int'l Exchange:
2006 Sales: $1,059,051	2006 Profits: $43,067	Employees: 8,800
2005 Sales: $1,071,033	2005 Profits: $-9,614	Fiscal Year Ends: 12/31
2004 Sales: $1,047,988	2004 Profits: $-30,256	Parent Company:

SALARIES/BENEFITS:

Pension Plan:	ESOP Stock Plan:	Profit Sharing:	Top Exec. Salary: $575,000	Bonus: $900,000
Savings Plan: Y	Stock Purch. Plan:		Second Exec. Salary: $350,000	Bonus: $225,000

OTHER THOUGHTS:

Apparent Women Officers or Directors:
Hot Spot for Advancement for Women/Minorities:

LOCATIONS: ("Y" = Yes)

West:	Southwest:	Midwest:	Southeast:	Northeast:	International:
Y	Y	Y	Y	Y	Y

BALTIMORE ORIOLES LP

www.orioles.com

Industry Group Code: 711211A **Ranks within this company's industry group:** Sales: 20 Profits: 6

Sports:		Services:		Media:		Sales:		Facilities:		Other:	
Leagues/Associations:		Food & Beverage:		TV:		Marketing:		Stadiums:	Y	Gambling:	
Teams:	Y	Agents:		Radio:		Ads:		Fitness Clubs:		Apparel:	Y
Nonprofits:		Other:		Internet:		Tickets:	Y	Golf Courses:		Equipment:	
Other:				Print:		Retail:		Ski Resorts:		Shoes:	
				Software:		Other:		Other:		Other:	

TYPES OF BUSINESS:

Professional Baseball Team
Stadium Operation
Team Merchandise

BRANDS/DIVISIONS/AFFILIATES:

Oriole Park at Camden Yards
Norfolk Tides
Bowie Baysox
Frederick Keys
Delmarva Shorebirds
Aberdeen IronBirds
Bluefield Orioles
OriolesREACH

CONTACTS: *Note: Officers with more than one job title may be intentionally listed here more than once.*

Peter Angelos, CEO
Andy MacPhail, COO/Pres., Baseball Oper.
Robert Ames, CFO/VP
Mike Flanagan, Exec. VP-Baseball Oper.
Tom Clancy, Vice Chmn.-Community Projects & Public Affairs
Dave Trembley, Mgr.
John Stockstill, Asst. Gen. Mgr./Dir.-Professional Scouting
Dave Jauss, Bench Coach
Terry Crowley, Hitting Coach
Peter Angelos, Chmn.

Phone: 410-685-9800 **Fax:** 410-547-6277
Toll-Free: 888-848-2473
Address: 333 W. Camden St., Baltimore, MD 21201 US

GROWTH PLANS/SPECIAL FEATURES:

The Baltimore Orioles LP is a Major League Baseball (MLB) team. The franchise moved from St. Louis to Baltimore in 1954 after a string of poor seasons, and took the name Orioles, which had been used in the area since the 19th century. The Orioles held a spot at the top from the mid-1960s to the mid-1980s. In all, the franchise has won three World Series, seven pennants and eight division titles. Cal Ripken Jr., the team's best-known player, broke Lou Gehrig's record for consecutive games played and spent his entire career with the Orioles. Since 1993, the team has been owned by local lawyer Peter Angelos, who is also the team's chairman and CEO. Angelos takes a very active role with the team, often intervening in trade discussions and overruling the decisions of the general manager. He was also the only owner to vote against the relocation of the Montreal Expos to Washington, D.C. in 2005. Whatever Angelos' effect, the Orioles have not been to the postseason since 1997. The team has played its games in Oriole Park at Camden Yards since 1992. The ballpark, which seats over 48,000 and has features inspired by turn-of-the-century ballparks including Fenway Park and Wrigley Field, was the first of a new wave of retro-style stadiums and helped increase attendance at Orioles games. However, due to poor performance, attendance has fallen from 3.7 million annually in 1997 to 1.95 million in 2008, which was 24rd in MLB and well below the league average. According to a recent Forbes estimate, the team is worth approximately $400 million. The team's average home attendance in the 2008 season was over 25,000 fans per game.

FINANCIALS: **Sales and profits are in thousands of dollars—add 000 to get the full amount. 2008 Note: Financial information for 2008 was not available for all companies at press time.**

2008 Sales: $174,000	2008 Profits: $27,200	**U.S. Stock Ticker: Private**
2007 Sales: $166,000	2007 Profits: $7,700	**Int'l Ticker:** Int'l Exchange:
2006 Sales: $158,000	2006 Profits: $17,100	Employees:
2005 Sales: $156,000	2005 Profits: $	Fiscal Year Ends: 6/30
2004 Sales: $	2004 Profits: $	Parent Company:

SALARIES/BENEFITS:

Pension Plan:	ESOP Stock Plan:	Profit Sharing:	Top Exec. Salary: $	Bonus: $
Savings Plan:	Stock Purch. Plan:		Second Exec. Salary: $	Bonus: $

OTHER THOUGHTS:

Apparent Women Officers or Directors:
Hot Spot for Advancement for Women/Minorities:

LOCATIONS: ("Y" = Yes)

West:	Southwest:	Midwest:	Southeast:	Northeast:	International:
				Y	Y

BALTIMORE RAVENS

www.baltimoreravens.com

Industry Group Code: 711211C **Ranks within this company's industry group:** Sales: 7 Profits: 16

Sports:		Services:		Media:		Sales:		Facilities:		Other:	
Leagues/Associations:		Food & Beverage:		TV:		Marketing:		Stadiums:		Gambling:	
Teams:	Y	Agents:		Radio:		Ads:		Fitness Clubs:		Apparel:	
Nonprofits:		Other:		Internet:		Tickets:	Y	Golf Courses:		Equipment:	
Other:				Print:		Retail:	Y	Ski Resorts:		Shoes:	
				Software:		Other:		Other:		Other:	

TYPES OF BUSINESS:

Professional Football Team
Ticket Sales

BRANDS/DIVISIONS/AFFILIATES:

M & T Bank Stadium
Baltimore Ravens Limited Partnership

CONTACTS: *Note: Officers with more than one job title may be intentionally listed here more than once.*

Richard W. Cass, Pres.
Jeff Goering, CFO/VP
Gabrielle Valdez Dow, VP-Mktg.
Elizabeth Jackson, Dir.-Human Resources
Bill Jankowski, VP-IT
Bob Eller, VP-Oper.
Mark Burdett, Sr. Dir.-Media Sales & Bus. Dev.
Kevin Byrne, Sr. VP-Public & Comm. Rel.
Jim Coller, Controller/VP
John Harbaugh, Head Coach
Stephen J. Bisciotti, Owner
Ozzie Newsome, Exec. VP/Gen. Mgr.
Arthur B. Modell, Minority Owner

Phone: 410-547-8100 **Fax:** 410-654-6239
Toll-Free:
Address: 1101 Russell St., Baltimore, MD 21230 US

GROWTH PLANS/SPECIAL FEATURES:

The Baltimore Ravens, owned and operated by the Baltimore Ravens Limited Partnership, are a professional football team in the National Football League (NFL) based in Baltimore, Maryland. The team was formed when the Cleveland Browns moved to Baltimore for the 1996 season. Preceded by the Baltimore Colts, who left the city for Indianapolis in the mid-1980s, Baltimore's new NFL franchise was named the Ravens after the Baltimore Sun received a record number of calls in support of the name, which is a tribute to the best-known poem of Baltimore's best known literary figure, Edgar Allan Poe. Although in practice the team has incorporated elements from both its previous life as the Browns and from its Baltimore predecessors, it was technically considered a new expansion franchise when it began play in 1996. Many of the Ravens' non-game operations take place at the team's 200,000-square-foot training facility in Owings Mills, a suburb north of Baltimore. The facility's field house, covering 90,000 square feet of space, features a strength-training area and a full-size training field; three outdoor fields; a kitchen and cafeteria; housing; executive offices; and meeting rooms. The team plays its home games in downtown Baltimore in the M & T Bank Stadium, which is owned by the Maryland Stadium Authority. The Ravens are owned in the majority by local businessman Stephen Bisciotti. Art Modell, former owner of the Browns and Ravens, retains a 1% share in the team. The Ravens have won one Championship, Super Bowl XXXV, in 2001. In the 2009, the team lost the AFC Championship game to the Pittsburgh Steelers, making it one win short of going to Super Bowl XLIII. Forbes Magazine recently valued the team at $1.06 billion. The team's average home game attendance in the 2008 season was 71,269.

FINANCIALS: **Sales and profits are in thousands of dollars—add 000 to get the full amount. 2008 Note: Financial information for 2008 was not available for all companies at press time.**

2008 Sales: $226,000
2007 Sales: $205,000
2006 Sales: $201,000
2005 Sales: $192,000
2004 Sales: $172,000

2008 Profits: $23,000
2007 Profits: $1,000
2006 Profits: $27,800
2005 Profits: $
2004 Profits: $

U.S. Stock Ticker: Subsidiary
Int'l Ticker: Int'l Exchange:
Employees:
Fiscal Year Ends: 1/31
Parent Company: BALTIMORE RAVENS LIMITED PARTNERSHIP

SALARIES/BENEFITS:

Pension Plan:	ESOP Stock Plan:	Profit Sharing:	Top Exec. Salary: $	Bonus: $
Savings Plan:	Stock Purch. Plan:		Second Exec. Salary: $	Bonus: $

OTHER THOUGHTS:

Apparent Women Officers or Directors: 2
Hot Spot for Advancement for Women/Minorities: Y

LOCATIONS: ("Y" = Yes)

West:	Southwest:	Midwest:	Southeast:	Northeast:	International:
				Y	

BASS PRO SHOPS INC

www.basspro.com

Industry Group Code: 451110 **Ranks within this company's industry group:** Sales: Profits:

Sports:		Services:		Media:		Sales:		Facilities:		Other:	
Leagues/Associations:		Food & Beverage:		TV:	Y	Marketing:		Stadiums:		Gambling:	
Teams:		Agents:		Radio:		Ads:		Fitness Clubs:		Apparel:	Y
Nonprofits:		Other:		Internet:		Tickets:		Golf Courses:		Equipment:	Y
Other:				Print:		Retail:	Y	Ski Resorts:		Shoes:	Y
				Software:		Other:		Other:	Y	Other:	

TYPES OF BUSINESS:

Sporting Goods, Retail
Sport Boats
Hunting & Fishing Equipment
Catalog & Online Sales
Outdoor Apparel
Resort Operations
Television Production

BRANDS/DIVISIONS/AFFILIATES:

Outdoor World
RedHead
Offshore Angler
White River Fly Shops
Tracker Marine
American Rod & Gun
Big Cedar Lodge
Dogwood Canyon

CONTACTS: *Note: Officers with more than one job title may be intentionally listed here more than once.*

James Hagale, COO
James Hagale, Pres.
Toni Miller, CFO/VP
Katie A. Mitchell, Specialist-Comm.
Martin G. MacDonald, Dir.-Public Rel. & Conservation
Jenna M. Kendall, Coordinator-Media Info.
John L. Morris, Chmn.

Phone: 417-873-5000 **Fax:** 417-873-5060
Toll-Free: 800-227-7776
Address: 2500 E. Kearney St., Springfield, MO 65898 US

GROWTH PLANS/SPECIAL FEATURES:

Bass Pro Shops, Inc. is a leader in sporting goods retail. The company markets its products through 49 sports superstores across the United States and Canada, a mail-order catalog and through Internet sites. The firm is dedicated to providing outdoor recreational products, including specialty apparel, and also aims to model and inspire environmental conservation among its customers. The sporting goods superstores operate under the Bass Pro Shop and Outdoor World brand names and range from 100,000 to 600,000 square feet. Products include boats and campers, as well as myriads of fishing, hunting, camping, automobile and marine supplies. Many of these stores sport a variety of unique features and attractions to draw more customers, including restaurants, snack bars, archery ranges, indoor fish tanks, waterfalls and video arcades. In addition to its stores, the company sells goods over the Internet and through more than 34 million mail-order catalogs under the Bass Pro Shops, RedHead, Offshore Angler and White River Fly Shops brand names. On the wholesale side, the firm owns and operates Tracker Marine, a leader in sport boat manufacturing, and American Rod & Gun, one of the largest wholesale hunting and fishing distributors in the country. In addition to offering a variety of hunting and fishing trips and contests, the Bass Pro runs Big Cedar Lodge, an outdoors-themed vacation spot in Missouri, located near the company's own nature park, Dogwood Canyon; and produces two weekly television programs on The Outdoor Channel.

FINANCIALS: Sales and profits are in thousands of dollars—add 000 to get the full amount. 2008 Note: Financial information for 2008 was not available for all companies at press time.

2008 Sales: $	2008 Profits: $	**U.S. Stock Ticker: Private**
2007 Sales: $3,000,000	2007 Profits: $	**Int'l Ticker:** Int'l Exchange:
2006 Sales: $2,660,000	2006 Profits: $	Employees: 15,000
2005 Sales: $1,915,000	2005 Profits: $	Fiscal Year Ends: 12/31
2004 Sales: $2,050,000	2004 Profits: $	Parent Company:

SALARIES/BENEFITS:

Pension Plan:	ESOP Stock Plan:	Profit Sharing:	Top Exec. Salary: $	Bonus: $
Savings Plan:	Stock Purch. Plan:		Second Exec. Salary: $	Bonus: $

OTHER THOUGHTS:

Apparent Women Officers or Directors: 3
Hot Spot for Advancement for Women/Minorities: Y

LOCATIONS: ("Y" = Yes)

West:	Southwest:	Midwest:	Southeast:	Northeast:	International:
Y	Y	Y	Y	Y	Y

BDA SPORTS MANAGEMENT

www.bdasports.com

Industry Group Code: 711410 **Ranks within this company's industry group:** Sales: Profits:

Sports:		**Services:**		**Media:**		**Sales:**		**Facilities:**		**Other:**	
Leagues/Associations:		Food & Beverage:		TV:		Marketing:	Y	Stadiums:		Gambling:	
Teams:		Agents:	Y	Radio:		Ads:		Fitness Clubs:		Apparel:	
Nonprofits:		Other:	Y	Internet:		Tickets:		Golf Courses:		Equipment:	
Other:				Print:		Retail:		Ski Resorts:		Shoes:	
				Software:		Other:		Other:		Other:	

TYPES OF BUSINESS:

Sports Management
Media Relations
Financial Services
Marketing Services
Business Services

BRANDS/DIVISIONS/AFFILIATES:

CONTACTS:

Note: Officers with more than one job title may be intentionally listed here more than once.

Bill A. Duffy, CEO
Billy Kuenzinger, COO
Bill Sanders, Chief Mktg. Officer
Billy Kuenzinger, General Counsel
Julie Neumann, Dir.-Oper.
Ilana Nunn, Dir.-Public Rel.
Julie Neumann, Dir.-Finance
Calvin Andrews, Sr. VP
Kevin Bradbury, VP-Player Rel.
Ugo Udezue, Dir.-African Basketball Player Rel.
Quique Villalobos, Dir.-Western European Basketball
Bill A. Duffy, Chmn.
Rade Filipovich, VP-BDA Int'l

Phone: 925-279-1040 **Fax:** 925-279-1060
Toll-Free:
Address: 700 Ygnacio Valley Rd., Ste. 330, Walnut Creek, CA 94596 US

GROWTH PLANS/SPECIAL FEATURES:

BDA Sports Management is a global, full-service management group offering services to professional basketball players. The company has represented over 100 professional players in the NBA and overseas and reports that it has negotiated over $500 million in contracts worldwide. BDA employs a staff of experts in many fields and maintains partnerships with companies in the entertainment, financial, legal and health fields. The company offers a wide range of services intended to assist and enhance all stages and aspects of its clients' careers: business services including contract negotiation, career management, investment planning, tax services, global management and post-career guidance; marketing services including endorsement negotiation, sponsor relations, media relations and fan relations; and personal services such as helping players pursue education, balancing their professional and personal lives and create nonprofit foundations. BDA coaches its clients in media relations and on-camera performance, assists them in pursuing motion picture and television projects and designs specialized nutrition plans customized to each athlete's blood chemistry. BDA also provides its services to athletes in Europe and Africa, identifying promising players, directing basketball events and assisting athletes' transitions to new countries. The company has helped such well-known players as Carmelo Anthony, Speedy Claxton, Yao Ming, Steve Nash, Travis Outlaw and Jay Williams within the U.S., as well as Robert Conley, Andrew Betts, Yiannis Bouroussis and Tyrone Ellis internationally. Current clients include Andris Biedrins, Daequan Cook, Chuck Hayes, Al Thornton, Goran Dragic and Jeff Foster.

FINANCIALS:

Sales and profits are in thousands of dollars—add 000 to get the full amount. 2008 Note: Financial information for 2008 was not available for all companies at press time.

2008 Sales: $	2008 Profits: $	**U.S. Stock Ticker: Private**
2007 Sales: $	2007 Profits: $	**Int'l Ticker:** Int'l Exchange:
2006 Sales: $	2006 Profits: $	Employees:
2005 Sales: $	2005 Profits: $	Fiscal Year Ends:
2004 Sales: $	2004 Profits: $	Parent Company:

SALARIES/BENEFITS:

Pension Plan:	ESOP Stock Plan:	Profit Sharing:	Top Exec. Salary: $	Bonus: $
Savings Plan:	Stock Purch. Plan:		Second Exec. Salary: $	Bonus: $

OTHER THOUGHTS:

Apparent Women Officers or Directors: 5
Hot Spot for Advancement for Women/Minorities: Y

LOCATIONS: ("Y" = Yes)

West:	Southwest:	Midwest:	Southeast:	Northeast:	International:
Y		Y		Y	Y

BIG 5 SPORTING GOODS CORPORATION www.big5sportinggoods.com

Industry Group Code: 451110 **Ranks within this company's industry group:** Sales: 5 Profits: 5

Sports:		Services:		Media:		Sales:		Facilities:		Other:	
Leagues/Associations:		Food & Beverage:		TV:		Marketing:		Stadiums:		Gambling:	
Teams:		Agents:		Radio:		Ads:		Fitness Clubs:		Apparel:	Y
Nonprofits:		Other:		Internet:		Tickets:		Golf Courses:		Equipment:	Y
Other:				Print:		Retail:	Y	Ski Resorts:		Shoes:	Y
				Software:		Other:		Other:		Other:	

TYPES OF BUSINESS:

Sporting Goods Stores

BRANDS/DIVISIONS/AFFILIATES:

Big 5 Corp.
Big 5 Services Corp.

CONTACTS:

Note: Officers with more than one job title may be intentionally listed here more than once.

Steven G. Miller, CEO
Steven G. Miller, Pres.
Barry Emerson, CFO
Jeffrey Fraley, Sr. VP-Human Resources
Gary Meade, General Counsel/Sr. VP/Corp. Sec.
Richard Johnson, Sr. VP-Store Oper.
Barry Emerson, Sr. VP/Treas.
Steven G. Miller, Chmn.
Thomas Schlauch, Sr. VP-Buying

Phone: 310-536-0611 **Fax:** 310-297-7585
Toll-Free:
Address: 2525 E. El Segundo Blvd., El Segundo, CA 90245 US

GROWTH PLANS/SPECIAL FEATURES:

Big 5 Sporting Goods Corporation is one of the leading sporting goods retailers in the U.S., with 373 locations in 11 western and southwestern states. The company offers more than 25,000 sports products in its stores, including athletic shoes; apparel and accessories for team sports; fitness equipment; camping, hunting and fishing gear; tennis and golf equipment; winter sports gear; and in-line skates. Stores offer leading brands such as Nike, Reebok, Adidas, New Balance, Wilson, Spalding and Columbia. Big 5 was founded in 1955 and sold primarily army surplus items until 1963, when the company switched to sporting goods. The company practices a systematic method of expansion, opening an average of 19 stores annually, about 68% of which are outside of California. Stores average 11,000 square feet, which is significantly smaller than the average superstore format, allowing stores to cater to smaller markets. Locations, normally freestanding or part of a multi-store shopping center, are chosen in collaboration with local real estate companies, mostly in markets close to those in which the company already has a presence. Big 5 recently completed construction of a new 953,000-square-foot distribution center in Riverside, California, and has moved all of its distribution operations to this facility. The company maintains a fleet of 39 leased and two owned tractor-trailers, and also uses contract carriers. In 2007, the firm opened 23 new stores, six of which were in California.

FINANCIALS:

Sales and profits are in thousands of dollars—add 000 to get the full amount. 2008 Note: Financial information for 2008 was not available for all companies at press time.

2008 Sales: $864,650	2008 Profits: $13,904	**U.S. Stock Ticker: BGFV**
2007 Sales: $898,292	2007 Profits: $28,091	**Int'l Ticker:** Int'l Exchange:
2006 Sales: $876,805	2006 Profits: $30,835	Employees: 8,900
2005 Sales: $813,978	2005 Profits: $27,539	Fiscal Year Ends: 12/31
2004 Sales: $782,215	2004 Profits: $33,519	Parent Company:

SALARIES/BENEFITS:

Pension Plan:	ESOP Stock Plan:	Profit Sharing:	Top Exec. Salary: $457,615	Bonus: $500,000
Savings Plan: Y	Stock Purch. Plan:		Second Exec. Salary: $310,961	Bonus: $175,000

OTHER THOUGHTS:

Apparent Women Officers or Directors: 2
Hot Spot for Advancement for Women/Minorities: Y

LOCATIONS: ("Y" = Yes)

West:	Southwest:	Midwest:	Southeast:	Northeast:	International:
Y	Y				

BILLABONG INTERNATIONAL LTD

www.billabongcorporate.com

Industry Group Code: 315000A **Ranks within this company's industry group:** Sales: 3 Profits: 1

Sports:		Services:		Media:		Sales:		Facilities:		Other:	
Leagues/Associations:		Food & Beverage:		TV:		Marketing:		Stadiums:		Gambling:	
Teams:		Agents:		Radio:		Ads:		Fitness Clubs:		Apparel:	Y
Nonprofits:		Other:		Internet:		Tickets:		Golf Courses:		Equipment:	Y
Other:	Y			Print:		Retail:	Y	Ski Resorts:		Shoes:	Y
				Software:		Other:		Other:		Other:	

TYPES OF BUSINESS:

Surfing, Skateboarding & Snowboarding Apparel
Surfboards, Skateboards & Paraphernalia
Retail Sales
Surfwear Apparel
Surfing Accessories

BRANDS/DIVISIONS/AFFILIATES:

Honolua
Kustom
Element
Von Zipper
Amazon (surf retailer)
Quiet Flight
DaKine Hawaii Inc
Sector 9

CONTACTS: *Note: Officers with more than one job title may be intentionally listed here more than once.*

Derek O'Neill, CEO
Craig White, CFO
Maria A. Manning, Corp. Sec.
Peter Casey, Gen. Mgr.-Oper.
Paul Naude, Gen. Mgr./Exec. Dir.-Billabong USA
Shannan North, Gen. Mgr.-Billabong Australia
Johnny Schillereff, Pres., Element Skateboards, Inc.
Ted Kunkel, Chmn.
Franco Fogliato, Gen. Mgr.-Billabong Europe

Phone: 61-75-589-9899 **Fax:** 61-75-589-9654
Toll-Free:
Address: 1 Billabong Pl., Burleigh Heads, QLD 4220 Australia

GROWTH PLANS/SPECIAL FEATURES:

Billabong International, Ltd. manufactures surfing, skateboarding and snowboarding apparel and accessories under the Billabong, Honolua, Kustom, Element (skateboards and apparel) and Von Zipper (sunglasses and goggles) brand names. Billabong was begun in 1973 when two surfing devotees, Gordon and Rena Merchant, began producing surfing supplies which were formerly completely unavailable to surfers, including a leg rope and board shorts. The firm began exporting products internationally in the 1980s, and now retails its products in more than 100 countries and approximately 10,000 stores across the globe. These venues include the company's wholly-owned stores in Australia, New Zealand, North America, Europe, Japan and Brazil (accounting for the majority of revenues), as well as licensed surf and extreme sports dealers worldwide. Products include a wide variety of board shorts, basic tees, slim fit tees, polos, wovens, fleece, walkshorts, pants, surf tees, wetsuits, rashvests, eyewear, bags and accessories. Billabong is committed to sponsoring junior athlete development, and also sponsors professional contests held on the Gold Coast of Australia and the Jeffreys Bau in South Africa. In June 2008, the firm acquired Quiet Flight, a U.S. retailer operating 13 stores in New York. In July 2008, the company acquired Sector 9, a skateboard brand based in Southern California. In August 2008, Billabong acquired DaKine Hawaii, Inc., a designer and manufacturer of surf, skate, snow and windsurf products.

FINANCIALS: **Sales and profits are in thousands of dollars—add 000 to get the full amount. 2008 Note: Financial information for 2008 was not available for all companies at press time.**

2008 Sales: $948,700
2007 Sales: $861,910
2006 Sales: $925,000
2005 Sales: $381,300
2004 Sales: $468,900

2008 Profits: $123,470
2007 Profits: $117,400
2006 Profits: $131,300
2005 Profits: $112,700
2004 Profits: $60,000

U.S. Stock Ticker: BLLAF
Int'l Ticker: BBG Int'l Exchange: Sydney-ASX
Employees: 1,750
Fiscal Year Ends: 6/30
Parent Company:

SALARIES/BENEFITS:

Pension Plan: ESOP Stock Plan: Profit Sharing: Top Exec. Salary: $920,000 Bonus: $816,000
Savings Plan: Stock Purch. Plan: Second Exec. Salary: $831,000 Bonus: $847,000

OTHER THOUGHTS:

Apparent Women Officers or Directors: 2
Hot Spot for Advancement for Women/Minorities: Y

LOCATIONS: ("Y" = Yes)

West:	Southwest:	Midwest:	Southeast:	Northeast:	International:
Y					Y

BIRMINGHAM CITY FOOTBALL CLUB

www.bcfc.com

Industry Group Code: 711211D **Ranks within this company's industry group:** Sales: Profits:

Sports:		Services:		Media:		Sales:		Facilities:		Other:	
Leagues/Associations:		Food & Beverage:		TV:		Marketing:		Stadiums:	Y	Gambling:	
Teams:	Y	Agents:		Radio:		Ads:		Fitness Clubs:		Apparel:	
Nonprofits:		Other:		Internet:		Tickets:	Y	Golf Courses:		Equipment:	
Other:				Print:		Retail:	Y	Ski Resorts:		Shoes:	
				Software:		Other:	Y	Other:		Other:	

TYPES OF BUSINESS:

Soccer Team
Ticket Sales
Team Merchandise

BRANDS/DIVISIONS/AFFILIATES:

St. Andrew's Stadium
F&C Investments
Professional Football Against Hunger
Birmingham FC
Blues

CONTACTS:

Note: Officers with more than one job title may be intentionally listed here more than once.

Karren Brady, Managing Dir.
David Sullivan, Co-Pres.
Adrian Wright, Head-Corp. Sales
Benjamin Rosenblatt, Sports Scientist
Julia Shelton, Football Sec.
Andy Maxey, Head-Media Rel.
Roger Bannister, Dir.-Finance
Ralph Gold, Co-Pres.
David Gold, Co-Pres.
Alex McLeish, Team Mgr.
Wendy Monks, Head-Ticketing
David Gold, Chmn.

Phone: 844--557-1875	**Fax:**
Toll-Free:	
Address: St. Andrew's Rd., Birmingham, B9 4RL UK	

GROWTH PLANS/SPECIAL FEATURES:

Birmingham City Football Club (Birmingham FC/Blues) is an English Premiership soccer team. Originally founded in 1875 as the Small Heath Alliance, the team did not sport its current name until after World War II. Birmingham FC plays in St. Andrew's Stadium, where it has done so since 1906 (with the exception of the World War II years, when the team was forced to temporarily play its home games at Villa Park). St. Andrew's record attendance is 66,844, which was reached during a 1939 game between the Blues and Everton. The team has won several division titles and Football League Championships, and has been competed in the F.A. Cup finals. Some of Birmingham FC's greatest all-time players include Joe Bradford, Jeff Hall, Trevor Francis, World Cup winner Alberto Tarantini, Alex Govan, Greg Downs and Jeff Kenna. In 1989, the team was slumped in division three for the first time in its history. Trevor Francis took over the team as manager in the mid-1990s and brought the club back to the Premiership in the year 2000. Steve Bruce then took over from Francis in 2002 and led the team to a 10th place finish in the 2004 Premiership, the club's highest finish in 30 years. Birmingham FC is a member of Europe's Professional Football Against Hunger campaign and other community outreach programs. The team's principal partner is F&C Investments; major club partners include Foster's, Subway, visitbirmingham.com and Aspen Cooling, Ltd. The club's revenue comes in largely through ticket sales, merchandise sales and broadcasting rights. In recent years, manager Steve Bruce resigned his position and was replaced by Alex McLeish. In January 2009, the team signed Lee Boyer on loan for the duration of the season. In February 2009, Birmingham FC signed formerly retired player Stephen Carr to a one-month contract.

FINANCIALS:

Sales and profits are in thousands of dollars—add 000 to get the full amount. 2008 Note: Financial information for 2008 was not available for all companies at press time.

2008 Sales: $	2008 Profits: $	**U.S. Stock Ticker: Private**
2007 Sales: $25,000	2007 Profits: $	**Int'l Ticker:** Int'l Exchange:
2006 Sales: $	2006 Profits: $	Employees: 134
2005 Sales: $	2005 Profits: $	Fiscal Year Ends:
2004 Sales: $	2004 Profits: $	Parent Company:

SALARIES/BENEFITS:

Pension Plan:	ESOP Stock Plan:	Profit Sharing:	Top Exec. Salary: $	Bonus: $
Savings Plan:	Stock Purch. Plan:		Second Exec. Salary: $	Bonus: $

OTHER THOUGHTS:

Apparent Women Officers or Directors: 7
Hot Spot for Advancement for Women/Minorities: Y

LOCATIONS: ("Y" = Yes)

West:	Southwest:	Midwest:	Southeast:	Northeast:	International:
					Y

BLACKBURN ROVERS FOOTBALL CLUB www.rovers.premiumtv.co.uk

Industry Group Code: 711211D **Ranks within this company's industry group:** Sales: Profits:

Sports:		Services:		Media:		Sales:		Facilities:		Other:	
Leagues/Associations:		Food & Beverage:		TV:		Marketing:		Stadiums:	Y	Gambling:	
Teams:	Y	Agents:		Radio:		Ads:		Fitness Clubs:		Apparel:	
Nonprofits:		Other:		Internet:		Tickets:	Y	Golf Courses:		Equipment:	
Other:				Print:		Retail:	Y	Ski Resorts:		Shoes:	
				Software:		Other:		Other:		Other:	

TYPES OF BUSINESS:

Soccer Team
Ticket Sales
Team Merchandise

BRANDS/DIVISIONS/AFFILIATES:

Ewood Park

CONTACTS:

Note: Officers with more than one job title may be intentionally listed here more than once.

Tom Finn, Managing Dir.
K. C. Lee, Pres.
Simon Williams, Head-Mktg. & Sales
Martin Goodman, Sec.
Martin Goodman, Dir.-Finance
Sam Allardyce, Team Mgr.
John Newsham, Mgr.-Stadium
Ken Beamish, Mgr.-Commercial
Karl Robinson, Coach
John Williams, Chmn.

Phone: 871-702-1875	**Fax:** 125-467-1042
Toll-Free:	
Address: Ewood Park, Blackburn, Lancashire BB2 4JF UK	

GROWTH PLANS/SPECIAL FEATURES:

Blackburn Rovers Football Club is an English Premiership soccer team based in the town of Blackburn, Lancashire. The club won the Premiership title back in 1994 with the help of star striker Alan Shearer, but slipped down into the first division in the late nineties after the 1996 trade of Shearer. The team has since rebounded to play in the Premiership and secure its first League Cup victory in 2002 under the managerial leadership of Graeme Souness. Mark Hughes took over as manager in 2004 through 2008 (in which he was replaced by Sam Allardyce), with the team finishing at 15 by the end of the 2005 season. The team earns revenue by selling tickets for its home games at Ewood Park. The stadium also plays host to the Rovers' strong performing women's club, which plays in the Women's Premier League North, as well as an under-18 Academy team. From the team web site, fans can purchase and gain access to web TV and live radio feeds. Club sponsors include Kappa, HAS and Bet24.

FINANCIALS:

Sales and profits are in thousands of dollars—add 000 to get the full amount. 2008 Note: Financial information for 2008 was not available for all companies at press time.

2008 Sales: $	2008 Profits: $	**U.S. Stock Ticker: Private**
2007 Sales: $	2007 Profits: $	**Int'l Ticker:** Int'l Exchange:
2006 Sales: $	2006 Profits: $	Employees:
2005 Sales: $	2005 Profits: $	Fiscal Year Ends:
2004 Sales: $	2004 Profits: $	Parent Company:

SALARIES/BENEFITS:

Pension Plan:	ESOP Stock Plan:	Profit Sharing:	Top Exec. Salary: $	Bonus: $
Savings Plan:	Stock Purch. Plan:		Second Exec. Salary: $	Bonus: $

OTHER THOUGHTS:

Apparent Women Officers or Directors: 2
Hot Spot for Advancement for Women/Minorities:

LOCATIONS: ("Y" = Yes)

West:	Southwest:	Midwest:	Southeast:	Northeast:	International:
					Y

Note: Financial information, benefits and other data can change quickly and may vary from those stated here.

BOLTON WANDERERS FOOTBALL CLUB www.bwfc.premiumtv.co.uk

Industry Group Code: 711211D **Ranks within this company's industry group:** Sales: Profits:

Sports:		Services:		Media:		Sales:		Facilities:		Other:	
Leagues/Associations:		Food & Beverage:		TV:		Marketing:		Stadiums:	Y	Gambling:	
Teams:	Y	Agents:		Radio:		Ads:		Fitness Clubs:		Apparel:	
Nonprofits:		Other:	Y	Internet:		Tickets:	Y	Golf Courses:		Equipment:	
Other:				Print:		Retail:		Ski Resorts:		Shoes:	
				Software:		Other:		Other:		Other:	

TYPES OF BUSINESS:

Soccer Team
Ticket Sales

BRANDS/DIVISIONS/AFFILIATES:

Burden Leisure plc
Reebok Stadium

CONTACTS:

Note: Officers with more than one job title may be intentionally listed here more than once.

Allan Duckworth, CEO
Nat Lofthouse, Pres.
Adrian Blackburn, Mgr.-Corp. Sales
Daniel Reuben, Mgr.-Comm.
Paula Mulligan, Dir.-Finance
Gary Megson, Team Mgr.
Gareth Moores, Dir.-Commercial
Steve Wigley, Head Coach
Phil Garside, Chmn.

Phone: 44-1204-673-673 **Fax:** 44-1204-673-773
Toll-Free:
Address: Reebok Stadium, Burnden Way, Bolton, Greater Manchester BL6 6JW UK

GROWTH PLANS/SPECIAL FEATURES:

The Bolton Wanderers Football Club, an English Premiership soccer team, is owned and operated by parent company Burden Leisure plc, which is predominately owned by Eddie Davies. The team can trace its history back to 1874 and is one of the oldest franchises in the league. Over 80% of Burden's revenue comes in through the soccer team's activities. The club is officially sponsored by Reebok, which provides the club with its jerseys and the name for its stadium. Reebok Stadium is a tubular steel construction that can seat 28,000 fans and has the facilities to host corporate events. The stadium has a fully integrated hotel, the DeVere Whites Hotel, with 125 rooms. The stadium was built in 1997 after the team had spent about a hundred years at its old park, Burden Park. The Wanderers also have women's team that got under way in 1999 and currently plays games at Moss Park. As part of its community involvement initiative, the club offers in-term coaching, after-school courses, holiday courses, match day experience and sponsored events. The club offers WebTV and Live Radio accessible from its web site for around $8 per month. Fans get video match highlights, exclusive interviews, live radio commentaries and other match details.

FINANCIALS:

Sales and profits are in thousands of dollars—add 000 to get the full amount. 2008 Note: Financial information for 2008 was not available for all companies at press time.

2008 Sales: $ 2008 Profits: $
2007 Sales: $ 2007 Profits: $
2006 Sales: $ 2006 Profits: $
2005 Sales: $ 2005 Profits: $
2004 Sales: $ 2004 Profits: $

U.S. Stock Ticker: Subsidiary
Int'l Ticker: Int'l Exchange:
Employees:
Fiscal Year Ends: 6/30
Parent Company: BURDEN LEISURE PLC

SALARIES/BENEFITS:

Pension Plan: ESOP Stock Plan: Profit Sharing: Top Exec. Salary: $ Bonus: $
Savings Plan: Stock Purch. Plan: Second Exec. Salary: $ Bonus: $

OTHER THOUGHTS:

Apparent Women Officers or Directors: 1
Hot Spot for Advancement for Women/Minorities:

LOCATIONS: ("Y" = Yes)

West:	Southwest:	Midwest:	Southeast:	Northeast:	International:
					Y

BOOTH CREEK SKI HOLDINGS INC

www.boothcreek.com

Industry Group Code: 713920 **Ranks within this company's industry group:** Sales: Profits:

Sports:		Services:		Media:		Sales:		Facilities:		Other:	
Leagues/Associations:		Food & Beverage:		TV:		Marketing:		Stadiums:		Gambling:	
Teams:		Agents:		Radio:		Ads:		Fitness Clubs:		Apparel:	
Nonprofits:		Other:		Internet:		Tickets:	Y	Golf Courses:	Y	Equipment:	
Other:				Print:		Retail:	Y	Ski Resorts:	Y	Shoes:	
				Software:		Other:		Other:		Other:	

TYPES OF BUSINESS:

Ski Resorts
Golf Courses
Event Hosting
Summer Recreation

BRANDS/DIVISIONS/AFFILIATES:

Northstar-at-Tahoe
Sierra-at-Tahoe
Cranmore Mountain Resort
Waterville Valley
Booth Creek Resorts
Vertical Plus program

CONTACTS:

Note: Officers with more than one job title may be intentionally listed here more than once.

Christopher P. Ryman, COO
Christopher P. Ryman, Pres.
Elizabeth J. Cole, CFO/Exec. VP
Julie Maurer, VP-Mktg. & Sales
Laura Moriarty, VP-Human Resources
Jim Mandel, Legal Affairs, Real Estate & Commercial Properties
Heath Nielsen, VP-Oper. & Commercial Properties
Tim Beck, Exec. VP-Planning
Monty Waugh, VP-Finance & Acct.
Mark St. J. Petrozzi, VP-Risk Mgmt.
Evan Dahl, VP-Bus. Planning
Chris Gunnerson, VP-Action Sports Brands

Phone: 530-550-7112 **Fax:** 530-550-9455
Toll-Free:
Address: 11025 Pioneer Trail, Ste. G100, Truckee, CA 96161 US

GROWTH PLANS/SPECIAL FEATURES:

Booth Creek Ski Holdings, Inc., operating as Booth Creek Resorts, is one of the largest ski resort operators in North America, with over 2 million visitors per year. The company's four resorts are located in California, New Hampshire and Washington, and are each within 200 miles of major skiing markets such as Boston, Seattle and the San Francisco Bay Area. Booth Creek's resorts feature thousands of acres of skiable terrain, hundreds of trails and about 50 lifts, including 12 express speed lifts and two express quad chairs. The firm's resorts are Northstar-at-Tahoe, Sierra-at-Tahoe, Waterville Valley and Cranmore Mountain Resort. These resorts provide a full range of services, such as equipment rentals, skiing lessons and restaurants. In addition to alpine skiing and snowboarding, Booth Creek's resorts offer opportunities for cross-country skiing, tubing, snowmobiling, snowshoeing and snowbiking. In the summer months, several Booth Creek properties are open for events and activities including golf, mountain biking, fly fishing, horseback riding, ATV tours and hiking and also have event facilities. At its California resorts, the company offers the Vertical Plus program. Through this program, frequent skiers and snowboarders can track the number of vertical feet that they ski via a personal wristband, which is scanned at participating lifts. These guests also receive discounts and gain access to special lift lines. Booth Creek is extensively developing the Northstar-at-Tahoe mountain, adding new ski lifts, parking, 60 new acres on which to ski and new snowmaking capabilities. Additional Northstar-at-Tahoe developments include the building of a Ritz-Carlton five star hotel and the Village at Northstar ski-in/ski-out community. The company maintains corporate partnerships with Mountain Dew, American Express, Coleman Natural and Gatorade.

Booth Creek's various resorts offer their employees skiing privileges; guest vouchers; free lessons; gift shop and equipment rental discounts; ride sharing programs; housing assistance; and employee assistance.

FINANCIALS:

Sales and profits are in thousands of dollars—add 000 to get the full amount. 2008 Note: Financial information for 2008 was not available for all companies at press time.

2008 Sales: $	2008 Profits: $	**U.S. Stock Ticker: Private**
2007 Sales: $	2007 Profits: $	**Int'l Ticker:** Int'l Exchange:
2006 Sales: $	2006 Profits: $	Employees: 4,109
2005 Sales: $	2005 Profits: $	Fiscal Year Ends: 10/31
2004 Sales: $115,400	2004 Profits: $-1,800	Parent Company:

SALARIES/BENEFITS:

Pension Plan:	ESOP Stock Plan:	Profit Sharing:	Top Exec. Salary: $335,000	Bonus: $175,000
Savings Plan:	Stock Purch. Plan:		Second Exec. Salary: $275,000	Bonus: $175,000

OTHER THOUGHTS:

Apparent Women Officers or Directors: 3
Hot Spot for Advancement for Women/Minorities: Y

LOCATIONS: ("Y" = Yes)

West:	Southwest:	Midwest:	Southeast:	Northeast:	International:
Y				Y	

Note: Financial information, benefits and other data can change quickly and may vary from those stated here.

BOSTON BRUINS

www.bostonbruins.com

Industry Group Code: 711211F **Ranks within this company's industry group:** Sales: 9 Profits: 21

Sports:		Services:		Media:		Sales:		Facilities:		Other:	
Leagues/Associations:		Food & Beverage:		TV:		Marketing:		Stadiums:		Gambling:	
Teams:	Y	Agents:		Radio:		Ads:		Fitness Clubs:		Apparel:	
Nonprofits:	Y	Other:		Internet:		Tickets:	Y	Golf Courses:		Equipment:	
Other:				Print:		Retail:	Y	Ski Resorts:		Shoes:	
				Software:		Other:		Other:		Other:	

TYPES OF BUSINESS:

Professional Hockey Team
Ticket Sales
Boston Bruins Merchandise

BRANDS/DIVISIONS/AFFILIATES:

Boston Professional Hockey Association, Inc.
TD Banknorth Garden Stadium
Providence Bruins
Delaware North Companies
Bruins Golf Tournament

CONTACTS: *Note: Officers with more than one job title may be intentionally listed here more than once.*

Jeremy M. Jacobs, CEO
Amy Latimer, Sr. VP-Sales & Mktg.
Daniel J. Zimmer, VP-Bus. Oper.
Jim Bednarek, VP-Finance
Peter Chiarelli, Gen. Mgr.
Jim Benning, Assistant Gen. Mgr.
Claude Julien, Head Coach
Bob Essensa, Goaltending Coach
Jeremy M. Jacobs, Chmn.

Phone: 617-624-1900 **Fax:** 617-523-7184
Toll-Free:
Address: 100 Legends Way, Boston, MA 02114 US

GROWTH PLANS/SPECIAL FEATURES:

The Boston Bruins, formed in 1924, is the third-oldest surviving National Hockey League (NHL) franchise. The team is based in Boston, Massachusetts and owned by the Boston Professional Hockey Association, Inc. The team plays at the TD Banknorth Garden Stadium, a 19,600-seat arena featuring 104 executive suites, 2,400 club seats and complete 360-degree LED technology. The stadium is also home to the NBA's Boston Celtics. The Bruins' primary minor league affiliate is the Providence Bruins from Providence, Rhode Island. The Boston Bruins reached the Stanley Cup playoffs every year from 1968 to 1996, a record setting 28 years, and has made 17 trips to the Stanley Cup finals, winning five championship titles, the last one in 1972. The Bruins again made it to the playoffs in 2002 and 2004. Over its long history, the team has enrolled such well-known players as Edward Shore, Lionel Hitchman, Robert Orr and Cameron Neely. The team operates the Boston Bruins Foundation, which is designed to fund charitable organizations that provide assistance to children in the Boston area. Foundation fundraisers include the sale of wristbands and the Bruins Golf Tournament played in August. Guests can plan birthday parties during Bruins games, which include discounted tickets and an autographed puck as well as a happy birthday message on the video scoreboard. The Bruins made it to 2007-08 playoffs but lost to the Canadians after seven games in the first round. In the 2008-09 season, the team won the NHL Northeast Division and NHL Eastern Conference titles subsequently qualified for the 2009 Stanley Cup playoffs. Forbes recently estimated the team's value at $263 million. The Bruins saw an average attendance of roughly 17,000 fans per home game.

FINANCIALS: **Sales and profits are in thousands of dollars—add 000 to get the full amount. 2008 Note: Financial information for 2008 was not available for all companies at press time.**

2008 Sales: $97,000	2008 Profits: $-3,000	**U.S. Stock Ticker: Subsidiary**
2007 Sales: $87,000	2007 Profits: $- 600	**Int'l Ticker:** Int'l Exchange:
2006 Sales: $86,000	2006 Profits: $4,800	Employees:
2005 Sales: $	2005 Profits: $	Fiscal Year Ends: 6/30
2004 Sales: $95,000	2004 Profits: $	Parent Company: DELAWARE NORTH COMPANIES

SALARIES/BENEFITS:

Pension Plan:	ESOP Stock Plan:	Profit Sharing:	Top Exec. Salary: $	Bonus: $
Savings Plan:	Stock Purch. Plan:		Second Exec. Salary: $	Bonus: $

OTHER THOUGHTS:

Apparent Women Officers or Directors: 1
Hot Spot for Advancement for Women/Minorities:

LOCATIONS: ("Y" = Yes)

West:	Southwest:	Midwest:	Southeast:	Northeast:	International:
				Y	

BOSTON CELTICS

www.nba.com/celtics

Industry Group Code: 711211B **Ranks within this company's industry group:** Sales: 8 Profits: 8

Sports:		Services:		Media:		Sales:		Facilities:		Other:	
Leagues/Associations:		Food & Beverage:		TV:		Marketing:		Stadiums:		Gambling:	
Teams:	Y	Agents:		Radio:		Ads:		Fitness Clubs:		Apparel:	Y
Nonprofits:		Other:		Internet:		Tickets:	Y	Golf Courses:		Equipment:	
Other:				Print:		Retail:	Y	Ski Resorts:		Shoes:	
				Software:		Other:		Other:		Other:	

TYPES OF BUSINESS:

Professional Basketball Team
Ticket Sales
Merchandise

BRANDS/DIVISIONS/AFFILIATES:

Boston Basketball Partners, LLC
Boston Celtics Shamrock Foundation
Red Auerbach Youth Foundation
Kid Zone

CONTACTS: *Note: Officers with more than one job title may be intentionally listed here more than once.*

Wyc Grousbeck, CEO
Rick Gotham, Pres.
Bill Reissfelder, CFO/Sr. VP
Barbara Reed, Dir.-Human Resources
Jay Wessel, Sr. Dir.-Tech.
Patrick Lynch, Mgr.-Oper.
Sean Barror, VP-Bus. Dev.
Peter Stringer, Mgr.-Internet Oper.
Jeffrey Twiss, VP-Media & Alumni Rel.
Barbara Reed, Dir.-Investor Svcs.
Tim Rath, Controller
Danny Ainge, Exec. Dir.-Basketball Oper.
Doc Rivers, Head Coach
Shawn Sullivan, Dir.-Game Oper. & Special Events

Phone: 617-854-8000	**Fax:** 617-367-4286
Toll-Free:	
Address: 226 Causeway St., 4th Fl., Boston, MA 02114-4714 US	

GROWTH PLANS/SPECIAL FEATURES:

The Boston Celtics, owned and operated by Boston Basketball Partners LLC, is a professional basketball team playing in the National Basketball Association (NBA) based in Boston, Massachusetts. The team is a charter member of the Basketball Association of America, which evolved into the NBA, and the team's green colors and winking leprechaun have been recognized symbols for over 50 years. The Celtics have won 16 championships including a record eight in a row from 1959-66. Great players like Bill Russell, Tommy Heinsohn, Red Auerbach, Bob Cousy, Jon Havlicek, Kevin McHale, Robert Parish and the legendary Larry Bird have played for the Celtics. The team has a strong interest in the community, creating initiatives like the Boston Celtics Shamrock Foundation, the Red Auerbach Youth Foundation and Kid Zone (with Dunkin' Donuts) to assist children in need. Celtics partners include Miller, Pepsi, Dunkin' Donuts, Bentley, Reebok, McDonalds, New England Baptist Hospital and southwest.com. The team is owned by Wycliffe Grousbeck, who led an investment group in the purchase of the team for $360 million. The Celtics play their games at TD Banknorth Garden, which holds 18,624 spectators, and is owned by Delaware North Companies, one of the world's largest foodservice, retail, and hospitalities industries company. Forbes recently estimated the team to be worth approximately $447 million. In the 2008-09 season, the team's home attendance average was roughly 18,600 per game.

FINANCIALS: **Sales and profits are in thousands of dollars—add 000 to get the full amount. 2008 Note: Financial information for 2008 was not available for all companies at press time.**

2008 Sales: $149,000	2008 Profits: $20,100	**U.S. Stock Ticker: Subsidiary**
2007 Sales: $117,000	2007 Profits: $18,300	**Int'l Ticker:** Int'l Exchange:
2006 Sales: $111,000	2006 Profits: $15,700	Employees:
2005 Sales: $110,000	2005 Profits: $	Fiscal Year Ends: 6/30
2004 Sales: $104,000	2004 Profits: $	Parent Company: BOSTON BASKETBALL PARTNERS LLC

SALARIES/BENEFITS:

Pension Plan:	ESOP Stock Plan:	Profit Sharing:	Top Exec. Salary: $	Bonus: $
Savings Plan:	Stock Purch. Plan:		Second Exec. Salary: $	Bonus: $

OTHER THOUGHTS:

Apparent Women Officers or Directors: 1
Hot Spot for Advancement for Women/Minorities: Y

LOCATIONS: ("Y" = Yes)

West:	Southwest:	Midwest:	Southeast:	Northeast:	International:
				Y	

BOSTON RED SOX

boston.redsox.mlb.com

Industry Group Code: 711211A **Ranks within this company's industry group:** Sales: 2 Profits: 9

Sports:		Services:		Media:		Sales:		Facilities:		Other:	
Leagues/Associations:		Food & Beverage:		TV:	Y	Marketing:	Y	Stadiums:	Y	Gambling:	
Teams:	Y	Agents:		Radio:		Ads:	Y	Fitness Clubs:		Apparel:	Y
Nonprofits:	Y	Other:		Internet:		Tickets:	Y	Golf Courses:		Equipment:	
Other:				Print:		Retail:	Y	Ski Resorts:		Shoes:	
				Software:		Other:		Other:		Other:	

TYPES OF BUSINESS:

Professional Baseball Team
Ticket Sales
Boston Red Sox Merchandise

BRANDS/DIVISIONS/AFFILIATES:

New England Sports Network
Fenway Park
Red Sox Foundation
Fenway Sports Group
Red Sox Destinations
Roush Fenway Racing

CONTACTS: *Note: Officers with more than one job title may be intentionally listed here more than once.*

Larry Lucchino, CEO
Mike Dee, COO
Larry Lucchino, Pres.
Steve Fitch, CFO
Sam Kennedy, Exec. VP/Chief Sales & Mktg. Officer
Mary Sprong, VP-Human Resources
Steve Conley, Dir.-IT
Mary Sprong, VP-Admin.
Maureen Cannon, Special Counsel
Theo Epstein, Exec. VP-Baseball Oper./Gen. Mgr.
Janet Marie Smith, Sr. VP-Planning & Dev.
Susan Goodenow, VP-Public Affairs
Ryan Oremus, Dir.-Finance
Jonathan Gilula, Sr. VP-Bus. Affairs
Mike Hazen, Dir.-Player Dev.
Pam Ganley, Dir.-Media Rel.
Meg Vaillancourt, Sr. VP/Exec. Dir.-Red Sox Foundation
Thomas C. Werner, Chmn.
Craig Shipley, VP-Int'l Scouting

Phone: 617-267-9440 **Fax:** 617-375-0944
Toll-Free:
Address: 4 Yawkey Way, Boston, MA 02215-3496 US

GROWTH PLANS/SPECIAL FEATURES:

The Boston Red Sox are an organization in Major League Baseball (MLB). Formerly the Boston Somersets and later the Pilgrims, the team became known as the Red Sox in 1912. One of the most recognizable and loved teams in the world, the Red Sox are especially well-known for their rivalry with the New York Yankees, which was exacerbated by the trade of Babe Ruth to New York in 1920. Many other legends have played for the Red Sox, including Ted Williams, Wade Boggs, Roger Clemens, Manny Ramirez and Pedro Martinez. In 2002 the team was sold to New England Sports Ventures LLC, a group owned by Tom Werner and former Marlins owner John Henry. At the end of the 2002 season new team president and CEO Larry Lucchino hired Theo Epstein to be the team's general manager. The Red Sox play in Fenway Park, which opened in 1912 and is the oldest major league ballpark still in operation. The team has sold out almost every game since 2003, although with just over 36,000 seats plus standing room, the stadium is one of the smallest on the circuit. The franchise won the World Series in 2004 for the first time since 1918, and then won the Series again in 2007. When not on national TV, the team's games are exclusively broadcast on NESN, the New England Sports Network, also owned by New England Sports Ventures LLC. New England Sports Ventures also owns Fenway Sports Group (FSG), a sales and marketing firm that sells advertisements and sponsorships for Boston College, MLB Advanced Media and others. FSG sells Red Sox Destinations, spring training and away-game travel packages for fans. The firm also owns a 50% stake in Roush Racing, a NASCAR team. Forbes recently estimated the value of the Red Sox at $833 million.

FINANCIALS: Sales and profits are in thousands of dollars—add 000 to get the full amount. 2008 Note: Financial information for 2008 was not available for all companies at press time.

2008 Sales: $269,000	2008 Profits: $25,700	**U.S. Stock Ticker: Private**
2007 Sales: $263,000	2007 Profits: $-19,100	**Int'l Ticker:** Int'l Exchange:
2006 Sales: $234,000	2006 Profits: $19,500	Employees:
2005 Sales: $206,000	2005 Profits: $	Fiscal Year Ends: 12/31
2004 Sales: $220,000	2004 Profits: $	Parent Company: NEW ENGLAND SPORTS VENTURES LLC

SALARIES/BENEFITS:

Pension Plan:	ESOP Stock Plan:	Profit Sharing:	Top Exec. Salary: $	Bonus: $
Savings Plan:	Stock Purch. Plan:		Second Exec. Salary: $	Bonus: $

OTHER THOUGHTS:

Apparent Women Officers or Directors: 6
Hot Spot for Advancement for Women/Minorities: Y

LOCATIONS: ("Y" = Yes)

West:	Southwest:	Midwest:	Southeast:	Northeast:	International:
			Y	Y	Y

Note: Financial information, benefits and other data can change quickly and may vary from those stated here.

BOWL AMERICA INC

www.bowl-america.com

Industry Group Code: 713950 **Ranks within this company's industry group:** Sales: 1 Profits: 1

Sports:		Services:		Media:		Sales:		Facilities:		Other:	
Leagues/Associations:		Food & Beverage:	Y	TV:		Marketing:		Stadiums:		Gambling:	
Teams:		Agents:		Radio:		Ads:		Fitness Clubs:		Apparel:	Y
Nonprofits:		Other:		Internet:		Tickets:		Golf Courses:		Equipment:	Y
Other:				Print:		Retail:	Y	Ski Resorts:		Shoes:	Y
				Software:		Other:		Other:	Y	Other:	

TYPES OF BUSINESS:

Bowling Centers
Retail Bowling Equipment
Online Sales

BRANDS/DIVISIONS/AFFILIATES:

Cosmic Bowling
Rolling Bowling
Rolling Rewards

CONTACTS:

Note: Officers with more than one job title may be intentionally listed here more than once.

Leslie H. Goldberg, CEO
Leslie H. Goldberg, Pres.
Cheryl A. Dragoo, CFO/Controller
A. Joseph Levy, Corp. Sec./Sr. VP
Ruth E. Macklin, Treas./Sr. VP
Irvin Clark, Gen. Mgr./Sr. VP

Phone: 703-941-6300	**Fax:** 703-256-2430
Toll-Free:	
Address: 6446 Edsall Rd., Alexandria, VA 22312 US	

GROWTH PLANS/SPECIAL FEATURES:

Bowl America, Inc., more than 50% owned by its CEO and his sister, operates 19 bowling centers with a total of 756 lanes in Washington, D.C.; Baltimore, Maryland; Richmond, Virginia; Jacksonville, Florida; and Orlando, Florida. The company's bowling centers are fully air-conditioned with facilities for food and beverage service, game rooms, shoe rental, rental lockers and playroom facilities. Most of its locations are equipped for Cosmic Bowling, a glow-in-the-dark bowling game and laser-light show. Bowl America sells bowling equipment, accessories and apparel at all its bowling centers. The stores carry major brands including Brunswick, Ebonite, Hammer, KR, Storm and Track. Bowl America purchases the majority of its equipment from Brunswick Corporation. Merchandise sales, including food and beverages, generate approximately 29% of its revenue, with the remaining 71% generated by fees for bowling and related services. The firm's Rolling Bowling program uses 45-foot trailers outfitted with bowling lanes and pin-setting machines to introduce elementary school students to the sport; over 30,000 children take part in the program each year. In addition, Bowl America offers students a free game for each A grade received on a final report card as an incentive for academic achievement through its Rolling Rewards program. The company's facilities are capable of hosting bowling parties ranging from 10-300 participants, with customized catering and event packages for a variety of gatherings such as corporate entertainment, holiday and birthday parties, bar/bat mitzvahs, wedding receptions, office parties and club meetings.

FINANCIALS:

Sales and profits are in thousands of dollars—add 000 to get the full amount. 2008 Note: Financial information for 2008 was not available for all companies at press time.

2008 Sales: $30,104	2008 Profits: $3,535	**U.S. Stock Ticker: BWLA**
2007 Sales: $31,974	2007 Profits: $4,189	**Int'l Ticker:** Int'l Exchange:
2006 Sales: $30,320	2006 Profits: $3,639	Employees: 700
2005 Sales: $28,607	2005 Profits: $3,849	Fiscal Year Ends: 6/30
2004 Sales: $28,433	2004 Profits: $4,701	Parent Company:

SALARIES/BENEFITS:

Pension Plan:	ESOP Stock Plan: Y	Profit Sharing: Y	Top Exec. Salary: $183,323	Bonus: $
Savings Plan:	Stock Purch. Plan:		Second Exec. Salary: $142,585	Bonus: $68,539

OTHER THOUGHTS:

Apparent Women Officers or Directors: 2
Hot Spot for Advancement for Women/Minorities: Y

LOCATIONS: ("Y" = Yes)

West:	Southwest:	Midwest:	Southeast:	Northeast:	International:
			Y	Y	

BOYNE USA RESORTS

www.boyne.com

Industry Group Code: 713920 **Ranks within this company's industry group:** Sales: Profits:

Sports:		Services:		Media:		Sales:		Facilities:		Other:	
Leagues/Associations:		Food & Beverage:	Y	TV:		Marketing:		Stadiums:		Gambling:	
Teams:		Agents:		Radio:		Ads:		Fitness Clubs:	Y	Apparel:	
Nonprofits:		Other:		Internet:		Tickets:		Golf Courses:	Y	Equipment:	
Other:	Y			Print:		Retail:	Y	Ski Resorts:	Y	Shoes:	
				Software:		Other:		Other:	Y	Other:	

TYPES OF BUSINESS:

Ski Resorts
Golf Courses
Real Estate Development
Retail Operations
Indoor Waterpark
Spas
Restaurants

BRANDS/DIVISIONS/AFFILIATES:

Big Sky Resort
Brighton Resort
Crystal Mountain
Cypress Mountain
Boyne Mountain
Boyne Highlands
Ski Lifts, Inc.
Loon Mountain Recreation Corp.

CONTACTS: *Note: Officers with more than one job title may be intentionally listed here more than once.*

Stephen Kircher, Pres.
Stephen Kircher, Pres., Eastern Oper.
Erin Ernst, Mgr.-Public Rel.
Ed Dembek, Controller

Phone: 231-549-6000 **Fax:** 231-549-6094
Toll-Free:
Address: 1 Boyne Mountain Rd., Boyne Falls, MI 49713 US

GROWTH PLANS/SPECIAL FEATURES:

Boyne USA Resorts, one of America's largest privately owned resort companies, owns and operates ski and golf resorts located in the Western and Midwestern U.S. The company's resorts include Big Sky Resort, Montana; Brighton, Utah; Crystal Mountain, Washington; Cypress Mountain, British Columbia; and Bay Harbor, Boyne Highlands and Boyne Mountain in Michigan. Boyne also operates the Gatlinburg Sky Lift in Gatlinburg, Tennessee, a scenic, year-round chairlift offering views of Great Smoky Mountain National Park. The resorts in Montana and Michigan run golf courses during the summer, as do Michigan's Country Club of Boyne, Crooked Tree Golf Club and the Inn at Bay Harbor. The company operates most of its resorts year-round, with winter snow sports and golf complemented by other activities, such as tennis, swimming, fly fishing, mountain biking, hiking, kayaking and water parks. Boyne Resorts also feature a number of restaurants and spas. Through subsidiary Boyne Realty, Boyne also markets and sells condominiums, cottages, homes and acreage on its own resort property, including locations Boyne Highlands Harbor Springs, Bay Harbor Petoskey, Boyne Mountain, Boyne City and Big Sky Resorts. The company has retail operations under the name Boyne Country Sports and offers online ski, golf and travel shopping. Boyne's web site allows customers to book lodging, purchase gift cards, arrange tee times and purchase apparel from Boyne Country Sports. In 2008, the firm purchased the equity interests in Loon Mountain Recreation Corp. and Ski Lifts, Inc. of Booth Creek Ski Holdings, Inc. In December 2008, the company opened a new Doppelmayr quad chairlift at the Boyne Mountain Resort of Boyne Falls, Michigan.

Boyne offers its employees partial tuition reimbursement and discounts on meals, skiing, golfing and pro shop purchases.

FINANCIALS: **Sales and profits are in thousands of dollars—add 000 to get the full amount. 2008 Note: Financial information for 2008 was not available for all companies at press time.**

2008 Sales: $	2008 Profits: $	**U.S. Stock Ticker: Private**
2007 Sales: $	2007 Profits: $	**Int'l Ticker:** Int'l Exchange:
2006 Sales: $	2006 Profits: $	Employees:
2005 Sales: $	2005 Profits: $	Fiscal Year Ends: 12/31
2004 Sales: $	2004 Profits: $	Parent Company:

SALARIES/BENEFITS:

Pension Plan:	ESOP Stock Plan:	Profit Sharing:	Top Exec. Salary: $	Bonus: $
Savings Plan: Y	Stock Purch. Plan:		Second Exec. Salary: $	Bonus: $

OTHER THOUGHTS:

Apparent Women Officers or Directors: 1
Hot Spot for Advancement for Women/Minorities:

LOCATIONS: ("Y" = Yes)

West:	Southwest:	Midwest:	Southeast:	Northeast:	International:
Y		Y	Y		Y

Note: Financial information, benefits and other data can change quickly and may vary from those stated here.

BRITISH SKY BROADCASTING GROUP PLC

www.sky.com

Industry Group Code: 513220 **Ranks within this company's industry group:** Sales: 6 Profits: 3

Sports:		Services:		Media:		Sales:		Facilities:		Other:	
Leagues/Associations:		Food & Beverage:		TV:	Y	Marketing:		Stadiums:		Gambling:	
Teams:		Agents:		Radio:		Ads:		Fitness Clubs:		Apparel:	
Nonprofits:		Other:		Internet:		Tickets:		Golf Courses:		Equipment:	
Other:				Print:		Retail:		Ski Resorts:		Shoes:	
				Software:		Other:		Other:		Other:	

TYPES OF BUSINESS:

Satellite TV Broadcasting
Digital TV
Broadcast TV
Mobile Phone TV
Interactive Television
Broadband Service
HD TV

BRANDS/DIVISIONS/AFFILIATES:

Sky One
Sky Travel
Sky News
Sky Sports
Sky Movies
Sky Broadband
Sky Active
News Corp

CONTACTS: *Note: Officers with more than one job title may be intentionally listed here more than once.*

Jeremy Darroch, CEO
Mike Darcey, COO
Andrew Griffith, CFO
Andy Brent, Group Dir.-Brand Mktg.
Deborah Baker, Dir.-People
Didier Lebrat, CTO
James Conyers, General Counsel
Alun Webber, Group Dir.-Strategic Project Delivery
Matthew Anderson, Group Dir.-Comm.
Vic Wakeling, Managing Dir.-Sky Sports & Sky News
Jeff Hughes, Exec. VP
Brian Sullivan, Managing Dir.-Customer Group
Sophie T. Laing, Managing Dir.-Entertainment
James Murdoch, Chmn.

Phone: 44-20-7705-3000 **Fax:** 44-20-7705-3453
Toll-Free:
Address: Grant Way, Isleworth, Middlesex TW7 5QD UK

GROWTH PLANS/SPECIAL FEATURES:

British Sky Broadcasting plc (BSkyB) is a leading U.K. pay television service. It distributes entertainment, news and sports programming to more than 9 million subscribers through cable and satellite. The firm offers over 140 channels and operates 28 on its own, including Sky One, Sky Travel, Sky News, Sky Sports and Sky Movies. Sky High Definition TV offers 19 HD channels. BSkyB owns the broadcast rights to England's professional soccer league and domestic cricket matches, as well as certain other sports events in the U.K. and Ireland, including rugby, motorsports, golf and boxing. In addition, the firm is marketing a digital video recorder called Sky+, offering 40 hours of recording time. BSkyB has also developed an interactive television network, called Sky Active, allowing viewers to interact through contests, quizzes, voting events, or shopping, all through an electronic fixture connected to the television set and a modem. Sky Travel is an entertainment and travel retail business incorporating a channel and a website. Sky Player is a PC-application that provides access to a range of on-demand programs and live channels including Sky Sports, Sky One and Sky Movies programming. Sky Anytime on Mobile is a mobile phone application that provides access to Sky Sports, Sky News, Sky One and Sky Movies mobile content. Sky Bet, Sky Poker and Sky Vegas offer a range of interactive betting and gambling services. In March 2007, the group launched Sky Anytime on TV, an on-demand service that provides access to selected programs that are added to the service overnight with approximately 30 hours of content available at any one time. The company offers broadband service to many of its customers via Sky Broadband. News Corporation owns a 39% controlling interest in BSkyB.

FINANCIALS: **Sales and profits are in thousands of dollars—add 000 to get the full amount. 2008 Note: Financial information for 2008 was not available for all companies at press time.**

2008 Sales: $6,840,050	2008 Profits: $1,000,040	**U.S. Stock Ticker: BSY**
2007 Sales: $9,119,749	2007 Profits: $959,868	**Int'l Ticker: BSY** Int'l Exchange: London-LSE
2006 Sales: $7,534,012	2006 Profits: $1,000,781	Employees: 15,000
2005 Sales: $7,426,752	2005 Profits: $1,041,370	Fiscal Year Ends: 6/30
2004 Sales: $6,607,900	2004 Profits: $784,400	Parent Company:

SALARIES/BENEFITS:

Pension Plan:	ESOP Stock Plan:	Profit Sharing:	Top Exec. Salary: $1,884,285	Bonus: $3,768,570
Savings Plan: Y	Stock Purch. Plan:		Second Exec. Salary: $1,041,315	Bonus: $1,666,105

OTHER THOUGHTS:

Apparent Women Officers or Directors: 4
Hot Spot for Advancement for Women/Minorities: Y

LOCATIONS: ("Y" = Yes)

West:	Southwest:	Midwest:	Southeast:	Northeast:	International:
					Y

BRUNSWICK CORP

www.brunswick.com

Industry Group Code: 339920 **Ranks within this company's industry group:** Sales: 1 Profits: 7

Sports:		Services:		Media:		Sales:		Facilities:		Other:	
Leagues/Associations:		Food & Beverage:		TV:		Marketing:		Stadiums:		Gambling:	
Teams:		Agents:		Radio:		Ads:		Fitness Clubs:		Apparel:	
Nonprofits:		Other:		Internet:		Tickets:		Golf Courses:		Equipment:	Y
Other:				Print:		Retail:	Y	Ski Resorts:		Shoes:	Y
				Software:		Other:		Other:	Y	Other:	Y

TYPES OF BUSINESS:

Outdoor & Indoor Recreational Equipment
Boats & Marine Engines
Fitness Equipment
Bowling & Billiards Equipment
Marine Electronics
Pool, Air Hockey & Foosball Tables
Entertainment Centers

BRANDS/DIVISIONS/AFFILIATES:

Brunswick Boat Group
Mercury Marine Group
Life Fitness
Brunswick Bowling & Billiards
Mercury MerCruiser
Mariner

CONTACTS: *Note: Officers with more than one job title may be intentionally listed here more than once.*

Dustan E. McCoy, CEO
Peter B. Hamilton, CFO/Sr. VP
B. Russell Lockridge, Chief Human Resources Officer/VP
Lloyd C. Chatfield, II, General Counsel/Corp. Sec./VP
Bruce J. Byots, VP-Corp. Rel.
Bruce J. Byots, VP-Investor Rel.
Alan L. Lowe, Controller/VP
John E. Stransky, VP/Pres., Life Fitness Div.
Andrew E. Graves, VP/Pres., U.S. Marine & Outboard Boats
Mark D. Schwabero, VP/Pres., Mercury Marine
Warren N. Hardie, VP/Pres., Brunswick Bowling & Billiards
Dustan E. McCoy, Chmn.
John C. Pfeifer, VP/Pres., EMEA, Brunswick Marine

Phone: 847-735-4700	**Fax:** 847-735-4765
Toll-Free:	
Address: 1 N. Field Ct., Lake Forest, IL 60045-4811 US	

GROWTH PLANS/SPECIAL FEATURES:

Brunswick Corp. is a manufacturer and marketer of recreational boats, boat engines, marine accessories, fitness equipment, bowling equipment and billiards equipment. Brunswick operates through four segments: the boat segment, which consists of the Brunswick Boat Group (BBG); the marine engine segment, which consists of the Mercury Marine Group (MMG); the fitness segment, which consists of its Life Fitness division (LF); and the bowling and billiards segment, which consists of the Brunswick Bowling & Billiards division (BBB). BBG manufactures and markets fiberglass pleasure boats; luxury sport-fishing convertibles and motor-yachts; high-performance boats; offshore fishing boats; and aluminum fishing, pontoon and deck boats. MMG manufactures and markets sterndrive propulsion systems, inboard engines, outboard engines and water jet propulsion systems under the Mercury, Mercury MerCruiser, Mariner and other brands. LF designs, manufactures and markets treadmills, total body cross-trainers, stair climbers, stationary exercise bicycles and strength-training equipment. BBB designs, manufactures and markets bowling balls, bowling pins, bowling lanes, automatic pinsetters, ball returns, furniture units and scoring and center management systems. BBB additionally offers bowling shoes, bags and accessories through licensing arrangements, and designs and markets a line of consumer and commercial billiards tables, Air Hockey table games and foosball tables. It also operates 104 bowling centers throughout the U.S., Canada and Europe, including 46 Brunswick Zones, which are modernized, family-oriented bowling centers that offer amenities such as laser tag and expanded game rooms. During 2008, BBB exited a joint venture that operated 14 additional bowling centers in Japan. In March 2008, Brunswick sold its Baja boat business to Fountain Powerboat Industries. In October 2008, the firm announced plans to close four boat manufacturing facilities during 2009 in an effort to resize the company.

Brunswick offers its employees tuition reimbursement, an employee assistance program, flexible spending accounts and medical, dental, prescription, vision, disability and life insurance.

FINANCIALS: **Sales and profits are in thousands of dollars—add 000 to get the full amount. 2008 Note: Financial information for 2008 was not available for all companies at press time.**

2008 Sales: $4,708,700	2008 Profits: $-788,100	**U.S. Stock Ticker: BC**
2007 Sales: $5,671,200	2007 Profits: $111,600	**Int'l Ticker:** Int'l Exchange:
2006 Sales: $5,665,000	2006 Profits: $133,900	Employees: 19,760
2005 Sales: $5,606,900	2005 Profits: $385,400	Fiscal Year Ends: 12/31
2004 Sales: $5,058,100	2004 Profits: $269,800	Parent Company:

SALARIES/BENEFITS:

Pension Plan:	ESOP Stock Plan:	Profit Sharing: Y	Top Exec. Salary: $876,077	Bonus: $483,600
Savings Plan: Y	Stock Purch. Plan: Y		Second Exec. Salary: $612,662	Bonus: $281,800

OTHER THOUGHTS:

Apparent Women Officers or Directors: 3
Hot Spot for Advancement for Women/Minorities: Y

LOCATIONS: ("Y" = Yes)

West:	Southwest:	Midwest:	Southeast:	Northeast:	International:
Y	Y	Y	Y	Y	Y

BUFFALO BILLS

www.buffalobills.com

Industry Group Code: 711211C **Ranks within this company's industry group:** Sales: 22 Profits: 28

Sports:		Services:		Media:		Sales:		Facilities:		Other:	
Leagues/Associations:		Food & Beverage:	Y	TV:		Marketing:		Stadiums:		Gambling:	
Teams:	Y	Agents:		Radio:		Ads:		Fitness Clubs:		Apparel:	Y
Nonprofits:		Other:		Internet:		Tickets:	Y	Golf Courses:		Equipment:	
Other:				Print:		Retail:	Y	Ski Resorts:		Shoes:	
				Software:		Other:		Other:		Other:	

TYPES OF BUSINESS:

Professional Football Team

BRANDS/DIVISIONS/AFFILIATES:

Ralph Wilson Stadium
Buffalo Bills, Inc.

CONTACTS: *Note: Officers with more than one job title may be intentionally listed here more than once.*

Russ Brandon, COO
Ralph C. Wilson, Jr., Pres.
Jeffrey C. Littmann, CFO/Treas.
Marc Honan, Sr. VP-Mktg.
Elisabeth Malstrom, Mgr.-Human Resources
Daniel Evans, Exec. Dir.-IT
Tim Kehoe, Dir.-Merch.
Jim Overdorf, Sr. VP-Football Admin.
David Wheat, Sr. VP-Bus. Oper.
Mary Owen, VP-Planning
Scott Berchtold, VP-Comm.
Frank Wojnicki, Controller
Dick Jauron, Head Coach
Andrew Cappuccino, Team Physician
John Frandina, VP-Stadium Oper.
Russ Brandon, Gen. Mgr.
Ralph C. Wilson, Jr., Chmn.

Phone: 716-648-1800	**Fax:** 716-649-6446
Toll-Free:	
Address: 1 Bills Dr., Orchard Park, NY 14127 US	

GROWTH PLANS/SPECIAL FEATURES:

The Buffalo Bills, owned and operated by Buffalo Bills, Inc., are a National Football League (NFL) team that plays in the eastern division of the American Football Conference (AFC). The team is based in Orchard Park, New York, and it plays its games at Ralph Wilson Stadium, which is named after the Detroit businessman whose family has owned the team since its inception in 1960. The stadium is owned by Erie County, New York. The Bills were a charter member of the American Football League (AFL), and won the AFL championship in both 1964 and 1965. The team entered the NFL when the AFL was absorbed in the league merger of 1970. From 1991 to 1994, the team reached the Super Bowl yearly (the only NFL team ever to do so) only to lose the championship game each time. The Bills hold the biggest comeback in NFL history, in 1993: down 35-3 in the third quarter, they came back to beat the Houston Oilers 41-38. The team's Hall of Fame players include O.J. Simpson, Bruce Smith and Jim Kelly. Buffalo Bills sponsors include Verizon Wireless, Visa, Pepsi, Toyota and Gatorade. In 2008, the franchise announced a multi-year contract with Gulf Oil, as well as an extension of their partnership with GEICO. Also in 2008, the team released many players, including Peerless Price, Anthony Thomas, Teyo Johnson, Courtney Anderson and Chris Denman; Buffalo also signed several players, including Spencer Johnson, Dustin Fox, Robert Felton and Demetrius Bell. From January to March 2009, the Bills signed 16 players, including C.J. Hawthorne, Marcus Smith, Ryan Fitzpatrick, Geoff Hangartner and Corey McIntyre. Forbes Magazine recently valued the team at $885 million. The team's average home game attendance in the 2008 season was 71,405.

FINANCIALS: **Sales and profits are in thousands of dollars—add 000 to get the full amount. 2008 Note: Financial information for 2008 was not available for all companies at press time.**

2008 Sales: $206,000	2008 Profits: $12,400	**U.S. Stock Ticker: Subsidiary**
2007 Sales: $189,000	2007 Profits: $34,600	**Int'l Ticker:** Int'l Exchange:
2006 Sales: $176,000	2006 Profits: $31,200	Employees:
2005 Sales: $173,000	2005 Profits: $	Fiscal Year Ends: 12/31
2004 Sales: $	2004 Profits: $	Parent Company: BUFFALO BILLS INC

SALARIES/BENEFITS:

Pension Plan:	ESOP Stock Plan:	Profit Sharing:	Top Exec. Salary: $	Bonus: $
Savings Plan:	Stock Purch. Plan:		Second Exec. Salary: $	Bonus: $

OTHER THOUGHTS:

Apparent Women Officers or Directors: 7
Hot Spot for Advancement for Women/Minorities: Y

LOCATIONS: ("Y" = Yes)

West:	Southwest:	Midwest:	Southeast:	Northeast:	International:
				Y	

BUFFALO SABRES

sabres.nhl.com

Industry Group Code: 711211F **Ranks within this company's industry group:** Sales: 21 Profits: 27

Sports:		Services:		Media:		Sales:		Facilities:		Other:	
Leagues/Associations:		Food & Beverage:		TV:		Marketing:	Y	Stadiums:	Y	Gambling:	
Teams:	Y	Agents:		Radio:		Ads:		Fitness Clubs:		Apparel:	Y
Nonprofits:		Other:		Internet:		Tickets:	Y	Golf Courses:		Equipment:	Y
Other:				Print:		Retail:	Y	Ski Resorts:		Shoes:	
				Software:		Other:		Other:		Other:	

TYPES OF BUSINESS:

Professional Hockey Team

BRANDS/DIVISIONS/AFFILIATES:

HSBC Arena
Portland Pirates

CONTACTS:

Note: Officers with more than one job title may be intentionally listed here more than once.

Larry Quinn, Managing Partner
Daniel DiPofi, COO
Rob Kopacz, Dir.-Mktg.
Birgid Haensel, Mgr.-Human Resources & Payroll
Mike Kaminska, Dir.-Merch.
Barry Becker, Chief Engineer-HSBC Arena
Chuck LaMattina, Dir.-Admin.
Dave Zygaj, Dir.-Legal Affairs & Human Resources
Stan Makowski, Jr., Dir.-Arena Oper.
John Livsey, VP-Bus. Dev. & Sales
Scott Miner, Mgr.-Web Site
Mike Gilbert, Dir.-Public Rel.
Chuck LaMattina, Dir.-Finance
B. Thomas Golisano, Owner
Darcy Regier, Gen. Mgr.
Lindy Ruff, Head Coach

Phone: 716-855-4100 **Fax:** 716-855-4122
Toll-Free: 888-223-6000
Address: HSBC Arena, 1 Seymour H. Knox III Plz., Buffalo, NY 14203-3096 US

GROWTH PLANS/SPECIAL FEATURES:

The Buffalo Sabres are a National Hockey League (NHL) team based in Buffalo, New York. Founded in 1969, the team quickly rose to prominence behind its line of Rick Martin, Hall of Famer Gilbert Perreault and Rene Robert, together known as the French Connection, finishing the 1974-75 season with a 49-16-15 record, which is still the best-ever season numbers in the franchise's history. Despite the fact that the Sabres had only been in the league for five years, the team went on to its first appearance in the Stanley Cup Finals that season, losing to the Philadelphia Flyers. One of the most notable events of the team's early history came in 1976 when the Sabres played the Soviet Wings in an exhibition game, with Cold War tension running high, defeating the Wings 12-6 in what then ranked as the worst ever loss by a Soviet team in international competition. The Sabres rosters have included such greats as Dominick Hasek (who won four consecutive Vezina trophies and two consecutive Hart Trophies, becoming the only goaltender to do so), Pat LaFontaine, Miroslav Satan, Donald Audette and Rob Ray, who holds the team's record for penalty minutes. The team is currently owned by three-time New York gubernatorial candidate B. Thomas Golisano and his firm, Hockey Western New York Hockey, LLC (HWNY). HWNY also owns HSBC Arena, the Sabres' home stadium, which seats over 18,600 spectators and also houses 80 suites, five clubs and a 5,000-square-foot team merchandising store. In June 2008, the team chose a new American Hockey League (AHL) affiliate team, the Portland Pirates of Maine, after a 29-year affiliate relationship with the Rochester Americans. Average home attendance in the 2008-09 season was 18,531. Forbes recently estimated the team's value to be $169 million.

FINANCIALS:

Sales and profits are in thousands of dollars—add 000 to get the full amount. 2008 Note: Financial information for 2008 was not available for all companies at press time.

2008 Sales: $76,000	2008 Profits: $-8,900
2007 Sales: $74,000	2007 Profits: $-4,900
2006 Sales: $70,000	2006 Profits: $4,600
2005 Sales: $	2005 Profits: $
2004 Sales: $51,000	2004 Profits: $

U.S. Stock Ticker: Subsidiary
Int'l Ticker: Int'l Exchange:
Employees:
Fiscal Year Ends: 8/31
Parent Company: HOCKEY WESTERN NEW YORK HOCKEY LLC

SALARIES/BENEFITS:

Pension Plan:	ESOP Stock Plan:	Profit Sharing:	Top Exec. Salary: $	Bonus: $
Savings Plan:	Stock Purch. Plan:		Second Exec. Salary: $	Bonus: $

OTHER THOUGHTS:

Apparent Women Officers or Directors: 23
Hot Spot for Advancement for Women/Minorities: Y

LOCATIONS: ("Y" = Yes)

West:	Southwest:	Midwest:	Southeast:	Northeast:	International:
				Y	

CABELA'S INC

www.cabelas.com

Industry Group Code: 451110 **Ranks within this company's industry group:** Sales: 2 Profits: 2

Sports:		Services:		Media:		Sales:		Facilities:		Other:	
Leagues/Associations:		Food & Beverage:		TV:		Marketing:		Stadiums:		Gambling:	
Teams:		Agents:		Radio:		Ads:		Fitness Clubs:		Apparel:	Y
Nonprofits:		Other:		Internet:		Tickets:		Golf Courses:		Equipment:	Y
Other:				Print:		Retail:	Y	Ski Resorts:		Shoes:	
				Software:		Other:		Other:		Other:	

TYPES OF BUSINESS:

Sporting Goods Stores
Hunting & Fishing Supplies
Antique & Collectible Furniture
Outdoor Apparel
Catalog & Online Sales
Credit Cards

BRANDS/DIVISIONS/AFFILIATES:

World's Foremost Bank
Cabela's Club
SIR Warehouse Sports Store
Bargain Cave
Dunn's
VanDyke's
Wild Wings
Club Visa Signature

CONTACTS: *Note: Officers with more than one job title may be intentionally listed here more than once.*

Dennis Highby, CEO
Dennis Highby, Pres.
Ralph W. Castner, CFO/VP
Patrick A. Snyder, Sr. VP-Mktg.
Charles Baldwin, Chief Human Resources Officer/VP
Patrick A. Snyder, Sr. VP-Merch. & Retail Oper.
Brian J. Linneman, Sr. VP-Oper.
Joe Arterburn, Media Contact
Chris Gay, Investor Rel. Contact
Ralph W. Castner, Chmn.-World's Foremost Bank
James W. Cabela, Vice Chmn.
Joseph M. Friebe, CEO/VP-World's Foremost Bank
Richard N. Cabela, Chmn.
Brian J. Linneman, Sr. VP-Global Supply Chain

Phone: 308-254-5505	**Fax:** 308-254-4800
Toll-Free:	
Address: 1 Cabela Dr., Sidney, NE 69160 US	

GROWTH PLANS/SPECIAL FEATURES:

Cabela's, Inc. is a leading outdoor and hunting supply store, which mails over 140 million catalogs yearly to all 50 states and to more than 170 countries. Through its web site, mail-order catalogs and retail stores, the company supplies hunting, marine, automobile, ATV, fishing, camping equipment and clothing. Cabela's also has a line of brand-name casual clothing and hunting and outdoors gear in a variety of camouflage and safety patterns. The company had 28 retail stores as of late 2008, in states such as Arizona, Idaho, Nebraska, Minnesota, Wisconsin, Michigan, Pennsylvania, West Virginia, South Dakota, Kansas, Utah, Washington, Nevada and Texas and one store in Canada. The stores, which are considered tourist attractions, receive as many as 6 million visitors per year. They are designed to communicate an outdoor lifestyle environment characterized by the outdoor feel of the lighting, wood or tile flooring, cedar wood beams, open ceilings and lodge-style atmosphere. The large-format stores contain a mountain and pond with museum-quality taxidermy and native game fish; gun libraries featuring high-quality firearms; archery training systems; virtual shooting arcades; museums or educational centers; and restaurants and banquet and meeting facilities. Additionally, the firm owns the World's Foremost Bank, a wholly-owned subsidiary managing store-branded Visa credit cards. The company also owns Canadian outdoors equipment retailer S.I.R. Warehouse Sports Store. In late 2008, the firm announced a reduction of its workforce by 10%. In January 2009, World's Foremost Bank introduced the Club Visa Signature card which allows cardholders a minimum annual spending amount of $25,000 and the opportunity to earn free Cabela's merchandise.

Employees are offered health and dental insurance; a 401(k) plan; and product discounts.

FINANCIALS: **Sales and profits are in thousands of dollars—add 000 to get the full amount. 2008 Note: Financial information for 2008 was not available for all companies at press time.**

2008 Sales: $2,552,721	2008 Profits: $76,404	**U.S. Stock Ticker: CAB**
2007 Sales: $2,349,599	2007 Profits: $87,879	**Int'l Ticker:** Int'l Exchange:
2006 Sales: $2,063,524	2006 Profits: $85,785	Employees: 14,700
2005 Sales: $1,799,661	2005 Profits: $72,569	Fiscal Year Ends: 12/31
2004 Sales: $1,555,974	2004 Profits: $64,996	Parent Company:

SALARIES/BENEFITS:

Pension Plan:	ESOP Stock Plan:	Profit Sharing:	Top Exec. Salary: $691,320	Bonus: $999,550
Savings Plan: Y	Stock Purch. Plan:		Second Exec. Salary: $436,061	Bonus: $300,425

OTHER THOUGHTS:

Apparent Women Officers or Directors:
Hot Spot for Advancement for Women/Minorities:

LOCATIONS: ("Y" = Yes)

West:	Southwest:	Midwest:	Southeast:	Northeast:	International:
Y	Y	Y		Y	Y

CABLEVISION SYSTEMS CORP

www.cablevision.com

Industry Group Code: 513220 **Ranks within this company's industry group:** Sales: 5 Profits: 4

Sports:		Services:		Media:		Sales:		Facilities:		Other:	
Leagues/Associations:		Food & Beverage:		TV:	Y	Marketing:		Stadiums:	Y	Gambling:	
Teams:	Y	Agents:		Radio:		Ads:		Fitness Clubs:		Apparel:	
Nonprofits:		Other:		Internet:	Y	Tickets:		Golf Courses:		Equipment:	
Other:				Print:		Retail:		Ski Resorts:		Shoes:	
				Software:		Other:		Other:	Y	Other:	Y

TYPES OF BUSINESS:

Cable Television Service
Professional Sports Teams
Television Programming
Communications Services
Sports & Music Venues
Voice Over Internet Protocol
High-Speed Internet

BRANDS/DIVISIONS/AFFILIATES:

Rainbow Media Holdings LLC
Lightpath, Inc.
New York Rangers
New York Knickerbockers
Hartford Wolf Pack
MSG Entertainment
Madison Square Garden
Newsday Media Group

CONTACTS: *Note: Officers with more than one job title may be intentionally listed here more than once.*

James L. Dolan, CEO
Tom Rutledge, COO
James L. Dolan, Pres.
Michael Huseby, CFO/Exec. VP
Wilt Hildenbrand, Sr. Advisor-Tech.
Wilt Hildenbrand, Sr. Advisor-Eng.
Jonathan D. Schwartz, General Counsel/Exec. VP
John Bickman, Pres., Cable & Comm.
Patricia Armstrong, Sr. VP-Investor Rel.
Joshua Sapan, Pres./CEO-Rainbow Media Holdings LLC
James L. Dolan, Chmn.-MSG
Hank J. Ratner, Vice Chmn.
Gregg Seibert, Exec. VP
Charles F. Dolan, Chmn.

Phone: 516-803-2300 **Fax:** 516-803-3134
Toll-Free:
Address: 1111 Stewart Ave., Bethpage, NY 11714 US

GROWTH PLANS/SPECIAL FEATURES:

Cablevision Systems Corp. operates solely through cable operator subsidiary CSC Holdings. CSC has investments in cable programming networks, entertainment businesses and telecommunications companies. It serves about 4.7 million basic video subscribers in and around the New York City metropolitan area. Through wholly-owned subsidiary Rainbow Media Holdings, LLC, the company owns interests in and manages numerous national and regional programming networks, the Madison Square Garden sports and entertainment businesses and cable television advertising sales companies. Through wholly-owned subsidiary Lightpath, Inc., the firm provides telephone services and high-speed Internet access to the business market. CSC operates in four segments: telecommunications services, Rainbow, Madison Square Garden and Newsday. The telecommunications services segment includes the cable television business, including its video, high-speed data and voice over Internet protocol (VoIP) and the operations of the telephone and high-speed data services provided by Lightpath. The Rainbow segment consists principally of interests in national programming services (AMC, WE tv, IFC, fuse and VOOM) and regional news programming businesses held by Rainbow Media Holdings. The division also includes a local advertising sales representation business. The Madison Square Garden segment owns and operates the Madison Square Garden Arena and the adjoining WaMu Theater at Madison Square Garden; the New York Knickerbockers professional basketball team; the New York Rangers professional hockey team; the New York Liberty professional women's basketball team; the Hartford Wolf Pack professional hockey team; the regional sports programming networks Madison Square Garden Network and Fox Sports Net New York; and MSG Entertainment. The Newsday segment includes the Newsday daily newspaper, amNew York, Star Community Publishing Group, and online web sites including Newsday.com and explore LI.com. In May 2008, Cablevision purchased the Sundance Channel, a cable network founded by Robert Redford, for about $500 million. In July 2008, the company acquired 97% of Newsday Media Group.

FINANCIALS: **Sales and profits are in thousands of dollars—add 000 to get the full amount. 2008 Note: Financial information for 2008 was not available for all companies at press time.**

2008 Sales: $7,230,116
2007 Sales: $6,484,481
2006 Sales: $5,828,493
2005 Sales: $5,082,045
2004 Sales: $4,750,037

2008 Profits: $-227,576
2007 Profits: $218,456
2006 Profits: $-126,465
2005 Profits: $89,320
2004 Profits: $-676,092

U.S. Stock Ticker: CVC
Int'l Ticker: Int'l Exchange:
Employees: 22,935
Fiscal Year Ends: 12/31
Parent Company:

SALARIES/BENEFITS:

Pension Plan: ESOP Stock Plan: Profit Sharing: Top Exec. Salary: $1,800,000 Bonus: $6,567,600
Savings Plan: Y Stock Purch. Plan: Second Exec. Salary: $1,600,000 Bonus: $5,582,800

OTHER THOUGHTS:

Apparent Women Officers or Directors: 4
Hot Spot for Advancement for Women/Minorities: Y

LOCATIONS: ("Y" = Yes)

West:	Southwest:	Midwest:	Southeast:	Northeast:	International:
				Y	

Note: Financial information, benefits and other data can change quickly and may vary from those stated here.

CALGARY FLAMES

www.calgaryflames.com

Industry Group Code: 711211F **Ranks within this company's industry group:** Sales: 10 Profits: 8

Sports:		Services:		Media:		Sales:		Facilities:		Other:	
Leagues/Associations:		Food & Beverage:		TV:		Marketing:		Stadiums:	Y	Gambling:	
Teams:	Y	Agents:		Radio:		Ads:		Fitness Clubs:		Apparel:	
Nonprofits:		Other:		Internet:		Tickets:	Y	Golf Courses:		Equipment:	
Other:				Print:		Retail:	Y	Ski Resorts:		Shoes:	
				Software:		Other:		Other:		Other:	

TYPES OF BUSINESS:

Major League Hockey Team
Ticket Sales
Team Merchandise

BRANDS/DIVISIONS/AFFILIATES:

Calgary Flames Limited Partnership
Atlanta Flames
Pengrowth Saddledome

CONTACTS:

Note: Officers with more than one job title may be intentionally listed here more than once.

Ken King, CEO
Ken King, Pres.
Michael Holditch, CFO/VP-Hockey Admin.
Peter Hanlon, VP-Comm.
Darryl Sutter, Gen. Mgr.
Mike Keenan, Head Coach
Tod Button, Dir.-Scouting
Mike Burke, Dir.-Hockey Admin.
N. Murray Edwards, Chmn.

Phone: 403-777-2177 **Fax:** 403-777-2171
Toll-Free:
Address: Pengrowth Saddledome, 555 Saddledome Rise SE, Calgary, AB T2G 3BG Canada

GROWTH PLANS/SPECIAL FEATURES:

The Calgary Flames are an NHL (National Hockey League) club owned and operated by Calgary Flames Limited Partnership (CFLP), which has eight total co-owners, including Harley N. Hotchkiss and N. Murray Edwards. The team is based in Calgary, Alberta and plays at the Pengrowth Saddledome, which is jointly controlled by the members of CFLP. The team plays in the Northwest Division of the Western Conference, along with the Vancouver Canucks, Minnesota Wild, Edmonton Oilers and Colorado Avalanche. The franchise was started in Atlanta, Georgia in 1972 as the Atlanta Flames. The team became the Calgary Flames when it moved to Canada in 1980 and has made three Stanley Cup appearances since then. Lanny McDonald, a Hockey Hall of Fame member, played forward and was the team captain that led the Flames to their only Stanley Cup victory, in 1989. The franchise has won two Presidents Trophies, for first overall in 1988 and 1989; three Clarence Campbell Conference titles in 1986, 1989 and 2004; three Smythe division playoff championships in 1988, 1989 and 1990; and two Pacific division titles in 1994 and 1995. In addition, the club has one of the best game attendance rates in the NHL. A recent Forbes list valued the team at roughly $203 million. In the 2008-09 season, the team saw an average home attendance of approximately 19,300 fans.

FINANCIALS:

Sales and profits are in thousands of dollars—add 000 to get the full amount. 2008 Note: Financial information for 2008 was not available for all companies at press time.

2008 Sales: $97,000
2007 Sales: $77,000
2006 Sales: $68,000
2005 Sales: $
2004 Sales: $70,000

2008 Profits: $7,400
2007 Profits: $- 700
2006 Profits: $2,300
2005 Profits: $
2004 Profits: $

U.S. Stock Ticker: Subsidiary
Int'l Ticker: Int'l Exchange:
Employees:
Fiscal Year Ends: 6/30
Parent Company: CALGARY FLAMES LIMITED PARTNERSHIP

SALARIES/BENEFITS:

Pension Plan: ESOP Stock Plan: Profit Sharing: Top Exec. Salary: $ Bonus: $
Savings Plan: Stock Purch. Plan: Second Exec. Salary: $ Bonus: $

OTHER THOUGHTS:

Apparent Women Officers or Directors: 1
Hot Spot for Advancement for Women/Minorities:

LOCATIONS: ("Y" = Yes)

West:	Southwest:	Midwest:	Southeast:	Northeast:	International:
					Y

CALLAWAY GOLF COMPANY

www.callawaygolf.com

Industry Group Code: 339920 **Ranks within this company's industry group:** Sales: 3 Profits: 1

Sports:		Services:		Media:		Sales:		Facilities:		Other:	
Leagues/Associations:		Food & Beverage:		TV:		Marketing:		Stadiums:		Gambling:	
Teams:		Agents:		Radio:		Ads:		Fitness Clubs:		Apparel:	Y
Nonprofits:		Other:		Internet:		Tickets:		Golf Courses:		Equipment:	Y
Other:				Print:		Retail:		Ski Resorts:		Shoes:	Y
				Software:		Other:		Other:		Other:	Y

TYPES OF BUSINESS:

Golf Equipment
Custom Club Fitting

BRANDS/DIVISIONS/AFFILIATES:

CallawayGolfPreOwned.com
Big Bertha
Top-Flite Golf Company
Callaway Golf Sales Company
Callaway Golf Interactive, Inc.
Callaway Golf Europe, Ltd.
Odyssey
uPlay LLC

CONTACTS: *Note: Officers with more than one job title may be intentionally listed here more than once.*

George Fellows, CEO
George Fellows, Pres.
Bradley J. Holiday, CFO/Sr. Exec. VP
Steven C. McCracken, Chief Admin. Officer/Sr. Exec. VP
Steven C. McCracken, Corp. Sec.
David A. Laverty, Sr. VP-Oper.
Ronald S. Beard, Chmn.
Thomas T. Yang, Sr. VP-Int'l

Phone: 760-931-1711 **Fax:** 760-930-5015
Toll-Free: 800-588-9836
Address: 2180 Rutherford Rd., Carlsbad, CA 92008 US

GROWTH PLANS/SPECIAL FEATURES:

Callaway Golf Company, together with its subsidiaries, designs, manufactures and sells high-quality golf clubs (drivers, fairway woods, hybrids, irons, wedges and putters) and golf balls. The company also sells golf accessories such as golf bags, golf gloves, golf footwear, golf and lifestyle apparel, golf headwear, eyewear, golf towels and golf umbrellas. Callaway generally sells its products to golf retailers, sporting goods retailers and mass merchants, directly and through its wholly-owned subsidiaries. The firm also sells products to third-party distributors. Callaway sells used golf products through callawaygolfpreowned.com. Callaway's products are sold throughout the U.S. and in over 100 countries around the world, with the U.S. accounting for approximately 50% of 2008 sales. Subsidiaries of the company include Callaway Golf Sales Company, Callaway Golf Ball Operations, Inc. (formerly The Top-Flite Golf Company), Callaway Golf Interactive, Inc., Callaway Golf Europe Ltd., Callaway Golf Korea Ltd., Callaway Golf Canada Ltd., Callaway Golf South Pacific Pty Ltd., and Callaway Golf (Shanghai) Trading Company, Ltd. Its popular brand names include Ben Hogan, Big Bertha and Odyssey. Callaway sponsors a wide range of golfing professionals to play with Callaway custom fitted clubs. In 2008, drivers and fairway woods together generated 24% of the firm's sales; irons, 28%; golf balls, 20%; accessories and other, 19%; and putters, 9.0%. In 2008, the Tour i Series of golf balls won eight of the 11 tournaments played on the LGPA tour. In May 2008, the firm announced the closing of its golf ball manufacturing facility in Gloversville, New York. In December 2008, Callaway acquired uPlay LLC, a developer of consumer electronic devices, including distance measuring equipment for use on golf courses.

Callaway offers employee benefits that include medical, dental and vision insurance; life and disability insurance; flexible spending accounts; product discounts; adoption assistance; tuition reimbursement; and educational scholarships.

FINANCIALS: **Sales and profits are in thousands of dollars—add 000 to get the full amount. 2008 Note: Financial information for 2008 was not available for all companies at press time.**

2008 Sales: $1,117,204	2008 Profits: $66,176	**U.S. Stock Ticker: ELY**
2007 Sales: $1,124,591	2007 Profits: $54,587	**Int'l Ticker:** Int'l Exchange:
2006 Sales: $1,017,907	2006 Profits: $23,290	Employees: 2,700
2005 Sales: $998,093	2005 Profits: $13,284	Fiscal Year Ends: 12/31
2004 Sales: $934,564	2004 Profits: $-10,103	Parent Company:

SALARIES/BENEFITS:

Pension Plan:	ESOP Stock Plan:	Profit Sharing:	Top Exec. Salary: $923,654	Bonus: $311,231
Savings Plan: Y	Stock Purch. Plan: Y		Second Exec. Salary: $550,000	Bonus: $102,850

OTHER THOUGHTS:

Apparent Women Officers or Directors:
Hot Spot for Advancement for Women/Minorities:

LOCATIONS: ("Y" = Yes)

West:	Southwest:	Midwest:	Southeast:	Northeast:	International:
Y					Y

Note: Financial information, benefits and other data can change quickly and may vary from those stated here.

CAMELBAK

www.camelbak.com

Industry Group Code: 339920 **Ranks within this company's industry group:** Sales: Profits:

Sports:		Services:		Media:		Sales:		Facilities:		Other:	
Leagues/Associations:		Food & Beverage:		TV:		Marketing:		Stadiums:		Gambling:	
Teams:		Agents:		Radio:		Ads:		Fitness Clubs:		Apparel:	
Nonprofits:		Other:		Internet:		Tickets:		Golf Courses:		Equipment:	Y
Other:				Print:		Retail:		Ski Resorts:		Shoes:	
				Software:		Other:		Other:		Other:	

TYPES OF BUSINESS:

Hydration Products
Outdoor Sports Backpacks
Military & Law Enforcement Equipment

BRANDS/DIVISIONS/AFFILIATES:

Hands-Free Hydration
M.U.L.E.
H.A.W.G.
Goblin
Cloudwalker
Alpine Explorer
Rim Runner
Chem Bio Reservoir

CONTACTS:

Note: Officers with more than one job title may be intentionally listed here more than once.

Sally McCoy, CEO
Sally McCoy, Pres.
Joe Brunetti, CFO
Dan Miller, Chmn.

Phone: 707-792-9700 **Fax:** 707-665-9231
Toll-Free: 800-767-8725
Address: 2000 S. McDowell Blvd., Petaluma, CA 94954 US

GROWTH PLANS/SPECIAL FEATURES:

CamelBak, a private company, manufactures, designs and distributes specialized hydration equipment and other gear, including gloves, tactical packs and electrolyte tablets. Originally designed for bicycle racers, its Hands-Free Hydration products are water containers worn as backpacks, with over-the-shoulder drinking tubes that enable athletes to drink water without using their hands. Scientific studies by the American College of Sports Medicine have indicated that athletes drink more fluids and perform better when using a CamelBak. The company's products are used in a wide variety of sports and professions. CamelBak offers many products that combine a hydration device with a backpack or other equipment, and many outdoor clothing and gear manufacturers design their products to be compatible with CamelBak's systems. Many of the firm's systems offer special features designed for a particular activity, such as insulated tubes and mouthpieces for winter sports or camouflaged exteriors for hunting. CamelBak also offers a line of spill-proof water bottles. In recent years, the company has seen greatly increasing demand for its products from military and law enforcement sectors. In response, CamelBak has introduced products with features such as accommodations for concealed weapons, antenna ports, low infrared reflectivity for concealment purposes, built-in microfilters and drinking tubes compatible with chem/bio protection equipment such as gas masks. Its new Chem Bio Reservoir is designed to resist contamination by chemical or biological agents.

FINANCIALS:

Sales and profits are in thousands of dollars—add 000 to get the full amount. 2008 Note: Financial information for 2008 was not available for all companies at press time.

2008 Sales: $	2008 Profits: $	**U.S. Stock Ticker: Private**
2007 Sales: $	2007 Profits: $	**Int'l Ticker:** Int'l Exchange:
2006 Sales: $	2006 Profits: $	Employees:
2005 Sales: $	2005 Profits: $	Fiscal Year Ends: 12/31
2004 Sales: $	2004 Profits: $	Parent Company:

SALARIES/BENEFITS:

Pension Plan:	ESOP Stock Plan:	Profit Sharing:	Top Exec. Salary: $	Bonus: $
Savings Plan:	Stock Purch. Plan:		Second Exec. Salary: $	Bonus: $

OTHER THOUGHTS:

Apparent Women Officers or Directors: 1
Hot Spot for Advancement for Women/Minorities:

LOCATIONS: ("Y" = Yes)

West:	Southwest:	Midwest:	Southeast:	Northeast:	International:
Y					Y

CANADIAN FOOTBALL LEAGUE

www.cfl.ca

Industry Group Code: 813990 **Ranks within this company's industry group:** Sales: Profits:

Sports:		Services:		Media:		Sales:		Facilities:		Other:	
Leagues/Associations:	Y	Food & Beverage:		TV:		Marketing:		Stadiums:		Gambling:	
Teams:		Agents:		Radio:		Ads:		Fitness Clubs:		Apparel:	
Nonprofits:		Other:		Internet:		Tickets:		Golf Courses:		Equipment:	
Other:				Print:		Retail:		Ski Resorts:		Shoes:	
				Software:		Other:		Other:		Other:	

TYPES OF BUSINESS:

Professional Football League

BRANDS/DIVISIONS/AFFILIATES:

Grey Cup
Hamilton Tiger-Cats
Montreal Alouettes
Toronto Argonauts
British Columbia Lions
Calgary Stampeders
Saskatchewan Roughriders
Winnipeg Blue Bombers

CONTACTS: *Note: Officers with more than one job title may be intentionally listed here more than once.*

Mark Cohon, Commissioner
Michael Copeland, COO
Rob Assimakopoulos, VP-Mktg. & Events
Chris Sonnemann, Mgr.-Tech.
Doug Allison, Dir.-Admin.
Kevin McDonald, Dir.-Football Oper.
Olivier Poulin, Editor-Online (LCF.ca)
Matt Maychak, VP-Comm.
Doug Allison, Dir.-Finance
Gavin Roth, Sr. Dir.-Partnerships
Trevor Hardy, Dir.-Salary & Expenditure Reporting
Tom Higgins, Dir.-Officiating
Chris McCracken, VP-Broadcasting & Media Assets

Phone: 416-322-9650	**Fax:** 416-322-9651
Toll-Free:	
Address: 50 Wellington St. E., 3rd Fl., Toronto, ON M5E 1C8 Canada	

GROWTH PLANS/SPECIAL FEATURES:

The Canadian Football League (CFL) is an eight-team professional league that plays a variation of U.S. football throughout Canada. The major differences between Canadian and American football are that the CFL uses a longer field and a three-down rule. Its teams are divided into two divisions: East (Hamilton Tiger-Cats, Montreal Alouettes and Toronto Argonauts) and West (British Columbia Lions, Calgary Stampeders, Edmonton Eskimos, Saskatchewan Roughriders and Winnipeg Blue Bombers). The organization has a limit on the number of non-Canadian born players on its teams. The league's season, which includes approximately 11 home games and 11 away games per team, runs from June to November and ends with the Grey Cup championship game, which is regularly one of Canada's highest-rated televised sports events. The CFL has boasted several legendary players including Herb Trawick, Granville Liggins, Tommy Joe Coffey, Tobin Rote, Matt Dunigan and Tony Gabriel. During 2008, the CFL averaged 28,914 tickets sold per regular season game, for a regular season total of more than 2 million tickets across the league. On television, the 2008 season averaged roughly 393,000 viewers per game, according to Nielsen ratings. In August 2008, the league announced a five-year agreement with Reebok Canada, making Reebok the exclusive provider of uniforms and sideline apparel for CFL teams. The agreement also includes CFL-branded Reebok merchandise available in retail stores.

FINANCIALS: **Sales and profits are in thousands of dollars—add 000 to get the full amount. 2008 Note: Financial information for 2008 was not available for all companies at press time.**

2008 Sales: $	2008 Profits: $	**U.S. Stock Ticker: Private**
2007 Sales: $	2007 Profits: $	**Int'l Ticker:** Int'l Exchange:
2006 Sales: $	2006 Profits: $	Employees:
2005 Sales: $	2005 Profits: $	Fiscal Year Ends: 6/30
2004 Sales: $	2004 Profits: $	Parent Company:

SALARIES/BENEFITS:

Pension Plan:	ESOP Stock Plan:	Profit Sharing:	Top Exec. Salary: $	Bonus: $
Savings Plan:	Stock Purch. Plan:		Second Exec. Salary: $	Bonus: $

OTHER THOUGHTS:

Apparent Women Officers or Directors: 6
Hot Spot for Advancement for Women/Minorities: Y

LOCATIONS: ("Y" = Yes)

West:	Southwest:	Midwest:	Southeast:	Northeast:	International:
					Y

CANNONDALE BICYCLE CORPORATION

www.cannondale.com

Industry Group Code: 339920 **Ranks within this company's industry group:** Sales: Profits:

Sports:		Services:		Media:		Sales:		Facilities:		Other:	
Leagues/Associations:		Food & Beverage:		TV:		Marketing:		Stadiums:		Gambling:	
Teams:		Agents:		Radio:		Ads:		Fitness Clubs:		Apparel:	Y
Nonprofits:		Other:		Internet:		Tickets:		Golf Courses:		Equipment:	Y
Other:				Print:		Retail:		Ski Resorts:		Shoes:	Y
				Software:		Other:		Other:		Other:	

TYPES OF BUSINESS:

Bicycle Manufacturing
Sports Apparel & Accessories

BRANDS/DIVISIONS/AFFILIATES:

Dorel Industries Inc
Cannondale Sports Group
Taurine
Caffeine
Scalpel
Rush
Moto
SuperSix

CONTACTS:

Note: Officers with more than one job title may be intentionally listed here more than once.

Robert P. (Bob) Baird, Jr., Interim CEO
Scott Struve, Global Dir.-Mktg.
Michael De Leon, Mgr.-Public Rel. & Advocacy
Jeff Frehner, Pres., Cannondale Sports Group

Phone: 203-749-7000	**Fax:** 203-748-4012
Toll-Free:	
Address: 16 Trowbridge Dr., Bethel, CT 06801 US	

GROWTH PLANS/SPECIAL FEATURES:

Cannondale Bicycle Corporation, a subsidiary of Dorel Industries, Inc., is a designer, developer and producer of bicycles. In addition to its locations in Connecticut and Pennsylvania, Cannondale has operations in Canada, Switzerland, Holland, Japan and Australia. The company's bicycles are sold in over 70 countries. The firm's bike varieties include mountain, road, recreation and designs for women. Mountain bikes sold by Cannondale include the Taurine, Caffeine, CO2 and 29'er hardtail models; the Scalpel XC racing model; the Rush marathon model; the Moto and Rize all mountain models; the Chase street model; and the Judge and Perp gravity models. Cannondale's road bikes include the SuperSix, Six and CAAD9 elite road models; the Synapse performance road model; the Slice multisport model; and the Cyclocross model for cyclocross racing. Recreation and fitness models offered by the company include Quick, Adventure, Comfort, Capo, Bad Boy, Street, Touring, Tandem and Law Enforcement models. Models designed for women include mountain, road and recreation bikes. Cannondale additionally sells cycling-related gear, such as bicycle shocks and suspension; men's, women's, team and kid's apparel; road, triathalon, mountain and spinning footwear; bags; bottles and cages; components; bicycle mounted computers; lights; locks; pumps; and tools. The company was acquired from its former parent Pegasus Partners II, LP by Dorel in February 2008 for approximately $200 million. Following its acquisition, Dorel re-organized its recreational/leisure segment to create the Cannondale Sports Group, a division focused exclusively on independent bicycle dealers and containing Cannondale, and Pacific Cycle, a division focused exclusively on the mass merchant channel.

FINANCIALS:

Sales and profits are in thousands of dollars—add 000 to get the full amount. 2008 Note: Financial information for 2008 was not available for all companies at press time.

2008 Sales: $	2008 Profits: $	**U.S. Stock Ticker: Subsidiary**
2007 Sales: $	2007 Profits: $	**Int'l Ticker:** Int'l Exchange:
2006 Sales: $	2006 Profits: $	Employees:
2005 Sales: $	2005 Profits: $	Fiscal Year Ends: 6/30
2004 Sales: $	2004 Profits: $	Parent Company: DOREL INDUSTRIES INC

SALARIES/BENEFITS:

Pension Plan:	ESOP Stock Plan:	Profit Sharing:	Top Exec. Salary: $	Bonus: $
Savings Plan:	Stock Purch. Plan:		Second Exec. Salary: $	Bonus: $

OTHER THOUGHTS:

Apparent Women Officers or Directors:
Hot Spot for Advancement for Women/Minorities:

LOCATIONS: ("Y" = Yes)

West:	Southwest:	Midwest:	Southeast:	Northeast:	International:
				Y	Y

CAROLINA HURRICANES

www.carolinahurricanes.com

Industry Group Code: 711211F **Ranks within this company's industry group:** Sales: 22 Profits: 30

Sports:		Services:		Media:		Sales:		Facilities:		Other:	
Leagues/Associations:		Food & Beverage:		TV:		Marketing:		Stadiums:	Y	Gambling:	
Teams:	Y	Agents:		Radio:		Ads:		Fitness Clubs:		Apparel:	
Nonprofits:		Other:		Internet:		Tickets:	Y	Golf Courses:		Equipment:	
Other:				Print:		Retail:		Ski Resorts:		Shoes:	
				Software:		Other:		Other:		Other:	

TYPES OF BUSINESS:

Professional Hockey Team
Ticket Sales

BRANDS/DIVISIONS/AFFILIATES:

Canes (The)
Hurricanes Hockey, LP
RBC Center
Hartford Whalers
New England Whalers

CONTACTS: *Note: Officers with more than one job title may be intentionally listed here more than once.*

Peter Karmanos, Jr., CEO/Owner/Governor
Jim Rutherford, Pres./Gen. Mgr.
Mike Amendola, CFO
Ben Aycock, Dir.-Mktg. & Brand Dev.
Glenn Johnson, Dir.-IT
Mike Sundheim, Dir.-Media Rel.
Davin Olsen, VP/Gen. Mgr.-RBC Center
Paul Maurice, Head Coach
Ron Francis, Associate Head Coach
Marshall Johnston, Dir.-Pro Scouting

Phone: 919-467-7825 **Fax:** 919-462-0123
Toll-Free:
Address: RBC Center, 1400 Edwards Mill Rd., Raleigh, NC 27607 US

GROWTH PLANS/SPECIAL FEATURES:

The Carolina Hurricanes (also known as the Canes), owned by Hurricanes Hockey, LP, is a National Hockey League (NHL) team based in Raleigh, North Carolina that plays at the RBC Center. The team plays in the Southeast Division of the NHL's Eastern Conference, along with the Atlanta Thrashers, Florida Panthers, Tampa Bay Lightning and Washington Capitals. The franchise was started in 1972 as part of the World Hockey Association (WHA). The first team was known as the New England Whalers, being later changed to the Hartford Whalers. The franchise joined the NHL in 1979 when the WHA ceased operations. Today's team was created when Peter Karmanos, the founder and chairman of Compuware, acquired the Whalers in 1994 and moved the team to its current location in 1997. In 2002, the Hurricanes made it to the Stanley Cup finals for the first time in franchise history, but lost to the Detroit Red Wings. The Hurricanes play in the RBC Center, opened in 1999, also home to N.C. State University's basketball programs. The center resulted from a partnership established by the state called the Centennial Authority who owns the building and surrounding 80 acres. Carolina Hurricanes/Gale Force Sports & Entertainment operates the facility. Notable past players include Ron Francis and Paul Coffey. In the 2008-09 season, the team's average home attendance was approximately 16,600. Forbes recently estimated the team's value to be $168 million.

FINANCIALS: Sales and profits are in thousands of dollars—add 000 to get the full amount. 2008 Note: Financial information for 2008 was not available for all companies at press time.

2008 Sales: $75,000 | 2008 Profits: $-11,500
2007 Sales: $68,000 | 2007 Profits: $-7,500
2006 Sales: $72,000 | 2006 Profits: $ 500
2005 Sales: $ | 2005 Profits: $
2004 Sales: $52,000 | 2004 Profits: $

U.S. Stock Ticker: Subsidiary
Int'l Ticker: Int'l Exchange:
Employees:
Fiscal Year Ends: 6/30
Parent Company: HURRICANES HOCKEY LIMITED PARTNERSHIP

SALARIES/BENEFITS:

Pension Plan: | ESOP Stock Plan: | Profit Sharing: | Top Exec. Salary: $ | Bonus: $
Savings Plan: | Stock Purch. Plan: | | Second Exec. Salary: $ | Bonus: $

OTHER THOUGHTS:

Apparent Women Officers or Directors:
Hot Spot for Advancement for Women/Minorities:

LOCATIONS: ("Y" = Yes)

West:	Southwest:	Midwest:	Southeast:	Northeast:	International:
				Y	

CAROLINA PANTHERS

www.panthers.com

Industry Group Code: 711211C **Ranks within this company's industry group:** Sales: 11 Profits: 17

Sports:		Services:		Media:		Sales:		Facilities:		Other:	
Leagues/Associations:		Food & Beverage:		TV:		Marketing:		Stadiums:		Gambling:	
Teams:	Y	Agents:		Radio:		Ads:		Fitness Clubs:		Apparel:	
Nonprofits:		Other:		Internet:		Tickets:	Y	Golf Courses:		Equipment:	
Other:				Print:		Retail:	Y	Ski Resorts:		Shoes:	
				Software:		Other:		Other:		Other:	

TYPES OF BUSINESS:

Professional Football Team
Ticket Sales
Carolina Panthers Merchandise

BRANDS/DIVISIONS/AFFILIATES:

Carolinas Stadium Corp.
Bank of America Stadium

CONTACTS:

Note: Officers with more than one job title may be intentionally listed here more than once.

Mark Richardson, Pres., Panthers Football, LLC
Dave Olsen, CFO
Phil Youtsey, Dir.-Ticket Sales & Oper.
Jackie Jeffries, Dir.-Human Resources
Jon Credit, Dir.-IT
Rob Rogers, Dir.-Team Admin.
Richard M. Thigpen, General Counsel
Phil Youtsey, Dir.-Oper.
Charlie Dayton, Dir.-Comm.
Jerry Richardson, Owner
Marty Hurney, Gen. Mgr.
John Fox, Head Coach
Brandon Beane, Dir.-Team Oper.

Phone: 704-358-7000 **Fax:** 714-358-7656
Toll-Free:
Address: 800 S. Mint St./Bank of America Stadium, Charlotte, NC 28202 US

GROWTH PLANS/SPECIAL FEATURES:

The Carolina Panthers are a professional football team playing in the National Football League (NFL) and based in Charlotte, North Carolina. The team was formed in 1993 as the first NFL expansion team since 1976, when former Baltimore Colts receiver Jerry Richardson, the second former player to own an NFL team, bought the franchise for $140 million. After winning the NFC conference title in 2003, the team made one Super Bowl appearance, in 2004, but lost to the New England Patriots. In the 2008 season, the team won the NFC South title against the New Orleans Saints. However, the team lost to the Arizona Cardinals in the Divisional Playoffs. The Panthers consistently sell out their home games in the Bank of America Stadium, a 73,504-seat, privately financed, open-air and natural athletic field. The stadium is owned and operated by Carolinas Stadium Corp., a Jerry Richardson company. Notable former team members include Sam Mills and Reggie White. Forbes Magazine recently valued the team at $1.04 billion. The team's average home game attendance in the 2008 season was 73,210.

FINANCIALS:

Sales and profits are in thousands of dollars—add 000 to get the full amount. 2008 Note: Financial information for 2008 was not available for all companies at press time.

2008 Sales: $221,000	2008 Profits: $22,300	**U.S. Stock Ticker: Private**
2007 Sales: $203,000	2007 Profits: $2,500	**Int'l Ticker:** Int'l Exchange:
2006 Sales: $199,000	2006 Profits: $20,700	Employees:
2005 Sales: $195,000	2005 Profits: $	Fiscal Year Ends: 12/31
2004 Sales: $	2004 Profits: $	Parent Company:

SALARIES/BENEFITS:

Pension Plan:	ESOP Stock Plan:	Profit Sharing:	Top Exec. Salary: $	Bonus: $
Savings Plan:	Stock Purch. Plan:		Second Exec. Salary: $	Bonus: $

OTHER THOUGHTS:

Apparent Women Officers or Directors:
Hot Spot for Advancement for Women/Minorities:

LOCATIONS: ("Y" = Yes)

West:	Southwest:	Midwest:	Southeast:	Northeast:	International:
				Y	

CBS CORP

www.cbscorporation.com

Industry Group Code: 513120 **Ranks within this company's industry group:** Sales: 3 Profits: 2

Sports:		Services:		Media:		Sales:		Facilities:		Other:	
Leagues/Associations:		Food & Beverage:		TV:	Y	Marketing:		Stadiums:		Gambling:	
Teams:		Agents:		Radio:		Ads:		Fitness Clubs:		Apparel:	
Nonprofits:		Other:		Internet:	Y	Tickets:		Golf Courses:		Equipment:	
Other:				Print:		Retail:		Ski Resorts:		Shoes:	
				Software:		Other:		Other:		Other:	

TYPES OF BUSINESS:

Broadcast Television
News Organization
Outdoor Advertising
Radio Networks & Programming
Television Production
Cable TV Networks
Book Publishing

BRANDS/DIVISIONS/AFFILIATES:

MP3.Com Inc
CNET Networks Inc
CSTV College Sports Television
CBS Interactive
CBS Paramount Network Television
CBS Television Distribution
Simon & Schuster Inc
CBS Radio

CONTACTS: *Note: Officers with more than one job title may be intentionally listed here more than once.*

Leslie Moonves, CEO
Leslie Moonves, Pres.
Fredric G. Reynolds, CFO
Anthony G. Ambrosio, Exec. VP-Human Resources
David F. Poltrack, Chief Research Officer/Pres., CBS Vision
Amy Berkowitz, CIO/Sr. VP
Anthony G. Ambrosio, Exec. VP-Admin.
Louis J. Briskman, General Counsel/Exec. VP
Martin D. Franks, Exec. VP-Planning, Policy, Gov't Affairs
Gil Schwartz, Chief Comm. Officer/Exec. VP
Martin M. Shea, Exec. VP-Investor Rel.
Susan C. Gordon, Chief Acct. Officer/Controller/Sr. VP
Joseph Ianniello, Deputy CFO
Richard M. Jones, Sr. VP/Gen. Tax Counsel
Angeline Straka, Sr. VP/Deputy General Counsel/Sec.
Sumner M. Redstone, Chmn.

Phone: 212-975-4321 **Fax:** 212-975-4516
Toll-Free:
Address: 51 W. 52nd St., 35th Fl., New York, NY 10019 US

GROWTH PLANS/SPECIAL FEATURES:

CBS Corp. is a leading mass media company in the U.S. operating through five divisions: Television, Radio, Outdoor, Publishing and Interactive. The company's Television division consists of CBS Television, Showtime Networks and CSTV College Sports Television. CBS Television comprises the CBS Network; the company's 30 owned broadcast television stations; and the company's television production and syndication operations, CBS Paramount Network Television and CBS Television Distribution. The CBS Network includes CBS Entertainment, CBS News and CBS Sports. CBS Entertainment provides primetime comedy and drama series; reality-based programming; made-for-television productions; theatrical films; children's programs; daytime dramas; game shows; and late-night programs. CBS News provides such news broadcasts as 60 Minutes, CBS Evening News with Katie Couric and The Early Show. CBS Sports broadcasts include The NFL Today, certain NCAA championships, the U.S. Open Tennis Championships and the AFC championship game. The CBS Radio division owns and operates 140 radio stations in 30 markets. Through CBS Outdoor, the company displays advertising on media, including billboards, transit shelters, buses, mall kiosks and stadium signage. CBS Publishing consists of Simon & Schuster, which publishes and distributes consumer books under imprints such as Simon & Schuster, Pocket Books, Scribner and Free Press. The CBS Interactive division was formed in July 2008 following CBS's acquisition CNET Networks Inc. CBS Interactive combined the firm's existing interactive businesses, which were previously reported in the Television segment, with those of CNET. In January 2008, CBS sold local television stations in four markets to an affiliate of Cerberus Capital Management for $185 million. In April 2008, the company acquired International Outdoor Advertising Group, an advertising company in South America, for $111.4 million. In June 2008, the company sold its 37% investment in Sundance Channel for $168.4 million. That same month, CBS acquired CNET Networks, Inc.

FINANCIALS: **Sales and profits are in thousands of dollars—add 000 to get the full amount. 2008 Note: Financial information for 2008 was not available for all companies at press time.**

2008 Sales: $13,950,400	2008 Profits: $-12,158,700	**U.S. Stock Ticker: CBS**
2007 Sales: $14,072,900	2007 Profits: $2,621,800	**Int'l Ticker:** Int'l Exchange:
2006 Sales: $14,320,200	2006 Profits: $1,660,500	Employees: 23,970
2005 Sales: $14,113,000	2005 Profits: $-7,089,100	Fiscal Year Ends: 12/31
2004 Sales: $14,138,300	2004 Profits: $-17,462,200	Parent Company:

SALARIES/BENEFITS:

Pension Plan:	ESOP Stock Plan:	Profit Sharing:	Top Exec. Salary: $5,323,367	Bonus: $18,500,000
Savings Plan:	Stock Purch. Plan:		Second Exec. Salary: $1,756,731	Bonus: $4,250,000

OTHER THOUGHTS:

Apparent Women Officers or Directors: 4
Hot Spot for Advancement for Women/Minorities: Y

LOCATIONS: ("Y" = Yes)

West:	Southwest:	Midwest:	Southeast:	Northeast:	International:
Y	Y	Y	Y	Y	Y

CENTERPLATE

www.centerplate.com

Industry Group Code: 722310 **Ranks within this company's industry group:** Sales: Profits:

Sports:		Services:		Media:		Sales:		Facilities:		Other:	
Leagues/Associations:		Food & Beverage:	Y	TV:		Marketing:		Stadiums:		Gambling:	
Teams:		Agents:		Radio:		Ads:		Fitness Clubs:		Apparel:	
Nonprofits:		Other:	Y	Internet:		Tickets:		Golf Courses:		Equipment:	
Other:				Print:		Retail:	Y	Ski Resorts:		Shoes:	
				Software:		Other:		Other:		Other:	

TYPES OF BUSINESS:

Food & Beverage Concessions
Catering Services
Merchandise Services
Facility Management

BRANDS/DIVISIONS/AFFILIATES:

Kohlberg & Co. LLC
KKR & Co LP (Kohlberg Kravis Roberts & Co)

CONTACTS:

Note: Officers with more than one job title may be intentionally listed here more than once.

Desmond Hague, CEO
Desmond Hague, Pres.
Kevin F. McNamara, CFO/Exec. VP
William H. Peterson, Exec. VP-Oper.

Phone: 203-975-5900	**Fax:**
Toll-Free:	
Address: 2187 Atlantic St., Stamford, CT 06902 US	

GROWTH PLANS/SPECIAL FEATURES:

Centerplate, Inc. is a leading provider of food and beverage concessions, catering and merchandise services in sports facilities, convention centers and other entertainment facilities. The firm, which operates throughout the U.S. and Canada, is the leading service provider to the National Football League (NFL) and minor league baseball and spring training facilities, and the third largest provider to Major League Baseball (MLB) facilities. The company is also one of the largest providers to major convention centers, such as Jacob Javits Center, San Diego Convention Center and Orange County Convention Center. Centerplate has also provided services for numerous World Series games, Super Bowls, World Cup soccer matches and Presidential Inaugural Balls. Through the operation of food courts in its facilities, Centerplate provides concession services from several different locations that sell a variety of specialty foods and beverages. The company also provides merchandise and program sales services in many of the sports facilities through destination stores, temporary stores, kiosks and customized carts. The company also provides design and consulting services for future locations. Additionally, Centerplate offers full facility management services, including event planning and marketing, logistics, site selection and entertainment engagement. The company generally provides services pursuant to long-term contracts that grant it the exclusive right to provide food and beverage products and services within the facility. Centerplate presently serves more than 130 facilities. In 2008, the company was awarded contracts worth $12 million for three venues in Indianapolis. In January 2009, Centerplate was acquired by Kohlberg and Co. LLC, an affiliate of Kohlberg Kravis Roberts and Co. (KKR). In March 2009, the firm announced that it would no longer provide services for San Jose Convention and Cultural Facilities.

FINANCIALS:

Sales and profits are in thousands of dollars—add 000 to get the full amount. 2008 Note: Financial information for 2008 was not available for all companies at press time.

2008 Sales: $	2008 Profits: $	**U.S. Stock Ticker: Subsidiary**
2007 Sales: $740,700	2007 Profits: $-1,900	**Int'l Ticker:** Int'l Exchange:
2006 Sales: $681,120	2006 Profits: $3,478	Employees: 1,550
2005 Sales: $643,112	2005 Profits: $-4,588	Fiscal Year Ends: 12/31
2004 Sales: $607,154	2004 Profits: $2,320	Parent Company: KKR & CO LP (KOHLBERG KRAVIS ROBERTS & CO)

SALARIES/BENEFITS:

Pension Plan:	ESOP Stock Plan:	Profit Sharing:	Top Exec. Salary: $650,000	Bonus: $222,300
Savings Plan:	Stock Purch. Plan:		Second Exec. Salary: $360,000	Bonus: $273,120

OTHER THOUGHTS:

Apparent Women Officers or Directors:
Hot Spot for Advancement for Women/Minorities:

LOCATIONS: ("Y" = Yes)

West:	Southwest:	Midwest:	Southeast:	Northeast:	International:
Y	Y	Y	Y	Y	Y

CENTRAL HOCKEY LEAGUE

www.centralhockeyleague.com

Industry Group Code: 813990 **Ranks within this company's industry group:** Sales: Profits:

Sports:		Services:		Media:		Sales:		Facilities:		Other:	
Leagues/Associations:	Y	Food & Beverage:		TV:		Marketing:		Stadiums:		Gambling:	
Teams:		Agents:		Radio:		Ads:		Fitness Clubs:		Apparel:	
Nonprofits:		Other:		Internet:		Tickets:		Golf Courses:		Equipment:	
Other:				Print:		Retail:		Ski Resorts:		Shoes:	
				Software:		Other:		Other:		Other:	

TYPES OF BUSINESS:

Hockey League

BRANDS/DIVISIONS/AFFILIATES:

WPHL, Inc.
Global Entertainment Corporation
Western Professional Hockey League
Governors' Cup
Ray Miron President's Cup

CONTACTS: *Note: Officers with more than one job title may be intentionally listed here more than once.*

Duane Lewis, Commissioner
Elizabeth Geeza, Mgr.-Mktg.
Todd Bisson, Mgr.-Hockey Admin.
Jim Wiley, Dir.-Hockey Oper.
Kevin V. Huhn, Dir.-Bus. Dev.
Bob Hoffman, Dir.-Comm.
Aaron Jackson, Dir.-Team Svcs.
Wayne Bonney, Supervisor-Officials
Ray Scapinello, Officiating Supervisor
Don Adam, Officiating Supervisor

Phone: 480-949-8600 **Fax:** 480-949-8616
Toll-Free:
Address: 1600 N. Desert Dr., Ste. 301, Tempe, AZ 85281 US

GROWTH PLANS/SPECIAL FEATURES:

The Central Hockey League (CHL) operates a minor double-A hockey league with 16 teams playing in small- to medium-sized markets, primarily in Texas but also in New Mexico, Arizona, Colorado, Kansas, Oklahoma, Louisiana, Ohio and Mississippi (as part of the Memphis, Tennessee metro area). The league is managed and operated by WPHL, Inc. (also known as Western Professional Hockey League), a subsidiary of Global Entertainment Corporation, which is a diversified sports management, arena development and licensing company. Every year eight CHL teams, the top two teams in each of its four divisions, make it to the playoffs for the Ray Miron President's Cup, while the Governors' Cup is awarded to the regular season champions. The league's teams act as feeders for NHL and AHL teams. For example, the Colorado Eagles, the winner of the 2004-05 Ray Miron President's Cup and the 2004-05 Governors' Cup, is affiliated with the NHL Florida Panthers and the AHL San Antonio Rampage. As with many mid-level sports leagues, the CHL's roster of teams is constantly changing. Recently-added expansion teams have included the Arizona Sundogs, Rocky Mountain Rage and the New Mexico Scorpions, returning to the ice after several years of dormancy. New expansion teams announced for the 2009-10 season include teams based in Independence, Missouri and Allen, Texas.

FINANCIALS: Sales and profits are in thousands of dollars—add 000 to get the full amount. 2008 Note: Financial information for 2008 was not available for all companies at press time.

2008 Sales: $	2008 Profits: $	**U.S. Stock Ticker: Private**
2007 Sales: $	2007 Profits: $	**Int'l Ticker:** Int'l Exchange:
2006 Sales: $	2006 Profits: $	Employees:
2005 Sales: $	2005 Profits: $	Fiscal Year Ends:
2004 Sales: $	2004 Profits: $	Parent Company:

SALARIES/BENEFITS:

Pension Plan:	ESOP Stock Plan:	Profit Sharing:	Top Exec. Salary: $	Bonus: $
Savings Plan:	Stock Purch. Plan:		Second Exec. Salary: $	Bonus: $

OTHER THOUGHTS:

Apparent Women Officers or Directors: 1
Hot Spot for Advancement for Women/Minorities: Y

LOCATIONS: ("Y" = Yes)

West:	Southwest:	Midwest:	Southeast:	Northeast:	International:
	Y				

CHARLOTTE BOBCATS

www.nba.com/bobcats

Industry Group Code: 711211B **Ranks within this company's industry group:** Sales: 26 Profits: 25

Sports:		Services:		Media:		Sales:		Facilities:		Other:	
Leagues/Associations:		Food & Beverage:		TV:		Marketing:		Stadiums:		Gambling:	
Teams:	Y	Agents:		Radio:		Ads:		Fitness Clubs:		Apparel:	
Nonprofits:		Other:		Internet:		Tickets:	Y	Golf Courses:		Equipment:	
Other:				Print:		Retail:	Y	Ski Resorts:		Shoes:	
				Software:		Other:		Other:		Other:	

TYPES OF BUSINESS:

Professional Basketball Team
Ticket Sales
Charlotte Bobcats Merchandise

BRANDS/DIVISIONS/AFFILIATES:

Bobcats Basketball Holdings, LLC
Time Warner Cable Arena
Lady Cats
Rufus Lynx
Rally Cats
Rhythm Cats
Bobcats Charitable Foundation
Charlotte Sting

CONTACTS: *Note: Officers with more than one job title may be intentionally listed here more than once.*

Fred Whitfield, COO
Fred Whitfield, Pres.
Mike Behrman, CFO/Exec. VP
Jim McPhilliamy, Sr. VP-Mktg.
Kay Lowery, VP-Human Resources
Ronnie Bryant, Sr. Mgr.-IT
Andre Walters, Dir.-Legal Affairs
Seth Bennett, VP-Event Oper.
Ed Lewis, VP-Gov't Rel.
Jeffrey Ross, Controller
Robert L. Johnson, Majority Owner
Michael Jordan, Managing Member-Basketball Oper.
Larry Brown, Head Coach

Phone: 704-688-8600 **Fax:** 704-688-8727
Toll-Free:
Address: 333 E. Trade St., Charlotte, NC 28202 US

GROWTH PLANS/SPECIAL FEATURES:

The Charlotte Bobcats, owned and operated by Bobcats Basketball Holdings, LLC, are one of the latest expansion teams within the NBA. The Bobcats were formed in 2003 after its former team, the Charlotte Hornets, relocated to New Orleans for the 2002-03 season. The team is jointly owned by Black Entertainment Television founder, Robert L. Johnson, and former Chicago Bulls guard, Michael Jordan. The Bobcats host all home games in the newly constructed Time Warner Cable Arena (formerly the Charlotte Bobcats Arena), which contains a 19,026 seating capacity for both entertainment and sporting events. Entertainment offered during home games includes the Lady Cats, Rufus Lynx, Rally Cats and Rhythm Cats. The team established the Bobcats Charitable Foundation, which awards grants to area organizations that offers enrichment to children that reside in Charlotte. Other outreach programs include the Jr. Bobcats, Bobcats Wishes and Rollin' Bobcats. Bobcats Basketball Holdings also owns the WNBA team the Charlotte Sting. Since the team's inception, it has never been in the NBA playoffs. In April 2008, the team formed a naming rights deal with Time Warner cable, which allowed the cable provider to change the name of the arena and also ended the agreement that kept the Bobcats' games off of satellite and regional cable television. Forbes recently estimated the team to be worth approximately $284 million. In the 2008-09 season, the team's home attendance average was roughly 14,500 per game.

FINANCIALS: **Sales and profits are in thousands of dollars—add 000 to get the full amount. 2008 Note: Financial information for 2008 was not available for all companies at press time.**

2008 Sales: $95,000
2007 Sales: $93,000
2006 Sales: $89,000
2005 Sales: $73,000
2004 Sales: $

2008 Profits: $-4,900
2007 Profits: $5,300
2006 Profits: $11,900
2005 Profits: $
2004 Profits: $

U.S. Stock Ticker: Private
Int'l Ticker: Int'l Exchange:
Employees:
Fiscal Year Ends: 6/30
Parent Company: BOBCATS BASKETBALL HOLDINGS LLC

SALARIES/BENEFITS:

Pension Plan: ESOP Stock Plan: Profit Sharing: Top Exec. Salary: $ Bonus: $
Savings Plan: Stock Purch. Plan: Second Exec. Salary: $ Bonus: $

OTHER THOUGHTS:

Apparent Women Officers or Directors: 17
Hot Spot for Advancement for Women/Minorities: Y

LOCATIONS: ("Y" = Yes)

West:	Southwest:	Midwest:	Southeast:	Northeast:	International:
				Y	

CHARLTON ATHLETICS

www.cafc.co.uk

Industry Group Code: 711211D **Ranks within this company's industry group:** Sales: Profits:

Sports:		Services:		Media:		Sales:		Facilities:		Other:	
Leagues/Associations:		Food & Beverage:		TV:		Marketing:		Stadiums:	Y	Gambling:	
Teams:	Y	Agents:		Radio:		Ads:		Fitness Clubs:		Apparel:	
Nonprofits:		Other:		Internet:		Tickets:	Y	Golf Courses:		Equipment:	
Other:				Print:		Retail:		Ski Resorts:		Shoes:	
				Software:		Other:		Other:		Other:	

TYPES OF BUSINESS:

Soccer Team

BRANDS/DIVISIONS/AFFILIATES:

Addicks (The)
English Premiership
Valley (The)
Joma Sport
Valley Gold
Red Card
CAFC (Charlton Athletic Football Club)

CONTACTS:

Note: Officers with more than one job title may be intentionally listed here more than once.

Mick Everett, Dir.-Stadium Oper.
Matt Wright, Mgr.-Comm.
Steve Sutherland, Dir.-Commercial
Dave Archer, Mgr.-Commercial Center
Steve Gritt, Mgr.-Youth Academy
Michael Rea, Mgr.-Retail
Richard A. Murray, Chmn.

Phone: 44-20-8333-4000 **Fax:** 44-20-8333-4001
Toll-Free:
Address: The Valley, Floyd Rd., Charlton, London, SE7 8BL UK

GROWTH PLANS/SPECIAL FEATURES:

Charlton Athletic plc, founded in 1905, operates a men's and a women's soccer team playing in the English Premiership. Known as the Addicks, Charlton's teams play at a stadium called the Valley, in east London. Broadcasting rights and game day tickets provide the majority of the company's revenue. Joma Sport provides the team with its uniforms. Charlton's most famous players have included forward Clive Mendonca, mid-fielder Mark Kinsella and defender Richard Rufus. Former manager Alan Curbishley took on the firm's primary team in 1991, when it was on the verge of financial collapse and down in the second division. The team was raised into the Premiership after a division one title in 2000 and has not been relegated back down since then. Phil Parkinson is the current manager of the Addicks. The Charlton Athletic Youth Academy provides daily coaching to boys from the age of nine to 16. The team has two membership services available to fans and accessible through its web site: its Valley Gold scheme is a monthly plan supporting Charlton Athletic's youth academy, while its Red Card scheme is free. The firm's international operations are conducted through CAFC (Charlton Athletic Football Club).

FINANCIALS:

Sales and profits are in thousands of dollars—add 000 to get the full amount. 2008 Note: Financial information for 2008 was not available for all companies at press time.

2008 Sales: $	2008 Profits: $	**U.S. Stock Ticker: Private**
2007 Sales: $	2007 Profits: $	**Int'l Ticker: CLO** Int'l Exchange: London-LSE
2006 Sales: $	2006 Profits: $	Employees: 719
2005 Sales: $73,500	2005 Profits: $2,500	Fiscal Year Ends: 6/30
2004 Sales: $77,000	2004 Profits: $20,100	Parent Company:

SALARIES/BENEFITS:

Pension Plan:	ESOP Stock Plan:	Profit Sharing:	Top Exec. Salary: $	Bonus: $
Savings Plan:	Stock Purch. Plan:		Second Exec. Salary: $	Bonus: $

OTHER THOUGHTS:

Apparent Women Officers or Directors: 2
Hot Spot for Advancement for Women/Minorities:

LOCATIONS: ("Y" = Yes)

West:	Southwest:	Midwest:	Southeast:	Northeast:	International:
					Y

CHELSEA FOOTBALL CLUB

www.chelseafc.com

Industry Group Code: 711211D **Ranks within this company's industry group:** Sales: 2 Profits: 7

Sports:		Services:		Media:		Sales:		Facilities:		Other:	
Leagues/Associations:		Food & Beverage:		TV:	Y	Marketing:	Y	Stadiums:	Y	Gambling:	
Teams:	Y	Agents:		Radio:	Y	Ads:	Y	Fitness Clubs:		Apparel:	
Nonprofits:		Other:		Internet:	Y	Tickets:	Y	Golf Courses:		Equipment:	
Other:				Print:		Retail:		Ski Resorts:		Shoes:	
				Software:		Other:		Other:		Other:	

TYPES OF BUSINESS:

Professional Soccer Team
Tickets
Merchandise
Radio/Online Broadcasting
Travel Agency
TV Sports Broadcasting

BRANDS/DIVISIONS/AFFILIATES:

Chelsea Village
Stamford Bridge Stadium
Chelsea TV
Chelsea TV Online
Chelsea SMS
ChelseaNOW

CONTACTS: *Note: Officers with more than one job title may be intentionally listed here more than once.*

Peter F. Kenyon, CEO
Ray Gourlay, COO
David Barnard, Club Sec.
Simon Greenberg, Dir.-Comm. & Public Affairs
Chris Alexander, Dir.-Finance
Guus Hiddink, Coach-First Team (Temporary)
Ray Wilkins, Asst. Coach-First Team
Michael Emenalo, Head Scout
Christy Fenwick, Match Analyst
Bruce Buck, Chmn.

Phone: 44-207-915-2900	**Fax:** 44-20-7381-4831
Toll-Free:	
Address: Stamford Bridge, Fulham Rd., London, SW6 1HS UK	

GROWTH PLANS/SPECIAL FEATURES:

Chelsea Football Club is an English professional football (soccer) club based in west London. It was founded in 1905, and the team plays in the Premier League. The club is considered one of the best teams in the league, finishing in the top six for more than a decade. A large part of the team's revenue comes from its many media alternatives, such as game broadcasts through Chelsea TV, Chelsea TV Online and the Chelsea SMS service. The team's ChelseaNOW mobile phone service updates fans on team developments, interviews and scores, and is available for a monthly fee. The clubs sponsors include Umbro, Orange, Budweiser, Lucozade, Sky and Tourism Malaysia. The company is currently in the midst of a five-year sponsorship deal with Samsung worth about $100 million. The team is owned and operated by Chelsea Village. In addition to managing the team, Chelsea Village runs the sports complex that includes the team's Stamford Bridge Stadium, along with two hotels, apartment complexes, a sports museum and a fitness center. The company is owned by Russian entrepreneur Roman Abramovich, whose businesses also include a travel agency, merchandising and TV sports production. Chelsea's home is the Stamford Bridge football stadium in Fulham, West London. Stamford Bridge holds 42,055 spectators, and it is owned by Chelsea Pitch Owners plc, a not-for-profit organization. Chelsea has a contract with the Asian Football Confederation, under which it assists Chinese start-up teams in such areas as marketing, media, training, coaching, education and sports medicine. The team made it to the Union of European Football Associations (UEFA) Champions League, also known as the European Cup, for the first time in 2008, eventually losing to Manchester United, in a 1-1 match that had to be decided by a penalty shootout in overtime.

FINANCIALS: **Sales and profits are in thousands of dollars—add 000 to get the full amount. 2008 Note: Financial information for 2008 was not available for all companies at press time.**

2008 Sales: $424,000	2008 Profits: $-13,000	**U.S. Stock Ticker: Private**
2007 Sales: $382,000	2007 Profits: $-5,000	**Int'l Ticker:** Int'l Exchange:
2006 Sales: $283,000	2006 Profits: $-37,000	Employees: 573
2005 Sales: $267,000	2005 Profits: $	Fiscal Year Ends: 6/30
2004 Sales: $264,000	2004 Profits: $	Parent Company:

SALARIES/BENEFITS:

Pension Plan:	ESOP Stock Plan:	Profit Sharing:	Top Exec. Salary: $	Bonus: $
Savings Plan:	Stock Purch. Plan:		Second Exec. Salary: $	Bonus: $

OTHER THOUGHTS:

Apparent Women Officers or Directors: 1
Hot Spot for Advancement for Women/Minorities:

LOCATIONS: ("Y" = Yes)

West:	Southwest:	Midwest:	Southeast:	Northeast:	International:
					Y

CHICAGO BEARS

www.chicagobears.com

Industry Group Code: 711211C **Ranks within this company's industry group:** Sales: 9 Profits: 7

Sports:		Services:		Media:		Sales:		Facilities:		Other:	
Leagues/Associations:		Food & Beverage:		TV:		Marketing:		Stadiums:		Gambling:	
Teams:	Y	Agents:		Radio:		Ads:		Fitness Clubs:		Apparel:	
Nonprofits:		Other:		Internet:		Tickets:	Y	Golf Courses:		Equipment:	
Other:				Print:		Retail:	Y	Ski Resorts:		Shoes:	
				Software:		Other:		Other:		Other:	

TYPES OF BUSINESS:

Professional Football Team

BRANDS/DIVISIONS/AFFILIATES:

Chicago Bears Football Club Inc
Soldier Field

CONTACTS: *Note: Officers with more than one job title may be intentionally listed here more than once.*

Ted Phillips, CEO
Ted Phillips, Pres.
Cliff Stein, General Counsel
Lovie Smith, Head Coach
Jerry Angelo, Gen. Mgr.
Cliff Stein, Sr. Dir.-Football Admin.

Phone: 847-295-6600 **Fax:** 847-295-8986
Toll-Free:
Address: 1000 Football Dr., Lake Forrest, IL 60045 US

GROWTH PLANS/SPECIAL FEATURES:

The Chicago Bears, owned and operated by the Chicago Bears Football Club, Inc., are a team in the National Football League's (NFL) Northern Division of its National Football Conference (NFC). In 1919, the A.E. Staley Company of Decatur, Illinois established a football team called the Decatur Staleys. The next year, Staley gave the reigns to George Halas who relocated the team to Chicago, where it became a charter member of the NFL. Halas purchased the rights of the team for $100. By 1922, the team was known as the Chicago Bears. The team won nine league titles (including Super Bowl XX in 1985), second only to the Green Bay Packers. The Bears have 26 members enshrined in the Pro Football Hall of Fame (an NFL record). Led by Rex Grossman, the Bears reached the Super Bowl in 2006, only to lose to Peyton Manning and the Indianapolis Colts. The team plays its home games at historic Soldier Field in Chicago, Illinois next to Lake Michigan. The stadium was originally completed in 1920, and it was dedicated as a memorial to American soldiers. Renovations to Soldier Field were completed, and the new stadium was hailed as a great accomplishment in architecture and design, seats 61,500 spectators. Among the Bears' legendary Hall of Fame inductees are Dick Butkus, Walter Payton, Mike Singletary, Dan Hampton, Wilber Marhsall and former coach Mike Ditka. Forbes Magazine recently valued the team at $1.06 billion. The team's average home game attendance in the 2008 season was 62,034.

FINANCIALS: **Sales and profits are in thousands of dollars—add 000 to get the full amount. 2008 Note: Financial information for 2008 was not available for all companies at press time.**

2008 Sales: $226,000
2007 Sales: $209,000
2006 Sales: $201,000
2005 Sales: $193,000
2004 Sales: $175,000

2008 Profits: $33,700
2007 Profits: $36,900
2006 Profits: $51,500
2005 Profits: $
2004 Profits: $

U.S. Stock Ticker: Private
Int'l Ticker: Int'l Exchange:
Employees:
Fiscal Year Ends: 2/28
Parent Company: CHICAGO BEARS FOOTBALL CLUB INC

SALARIES/BENEFITS:

Pension Plan: ESOP Stock Plan: Profit Sharing: Top Exec. Salary: $ Bonus: $
Savings Plan: Stock Purch. Plan: Second Exec. Salary: $ Bonus: $

OTHER THOUGHTS:

Apparent Women Officers or Directors:
Hot Spot for Advancement for Women/Minorities:

LOCATIONS: ("Y" = Yes)

West:	Southwest:	Midwest:	Southeast:	Northeast:	International:
		Y			

CHICAGO BLACKHAWKS

www.chicagoblackhawks.com

Industry Group Code: 711211F **Ranks within this company's industry group:** Sales: 20 Profits: 14

Sports:		Services:		Media:		Sales:		Facilities:		Other:	
Leagues/Associations:		Food & Beverage:		TV:		Marketing:		Stadiums:	Y	Gambling:	
Teams:	Y	Agents:		Radio:		Ads:		Fitness Clubs:		Apparel:	
Nonprofits:		Other:		Internet:		Tickets:	Y	Golf Courses:		Equipment:	
Other:				Print:		Retail:	Y	Ski Resorts:		Shoes:	
				Software:		Other:		Other:		Other:	

TYPES OF BUSINESS:

Professional Hockey Team
Ticket Sales
Team Merchandise

BRANDS/DIVISIONS/AFFILIATES:

Chicago Blackhawks Hockey Team, Inc.
Wirtz Corporation
United Center
Norfolk Admirals
Greenville Grrrowl
Hawk Chat
Tommy Hawk

CONTACTS: *Note: Officers with more than one job title may be intentionally listed here more than once.*

John F. McDonough, Pres.
John W. Kerr, Exec. Dir.-Finance
Pete Hassen, Sr. Dir.-Mktg. & Advertising
Marie Sutera, Dir.-Human Resources
Jay Blunk, Sr. VP-Bus. Oper.
Adam Kempenaar, Dir.-New Media & Publications
TJ Skattum, Dir.-Finance
Rocky Wirtz, Owner
Steve Waight, Sr. Dir.-Corp. Sponsorships
Joel Quenneville, Head Coach
Al MacIsaac, Sr. Dir.-Hockey Admin.
W. Rockwell Wirtz, Chmn.

Phone: 312-455-7000	**Fax:** 312-455-7041
Toll-Free:	
Address: 1901 W. Madison St., Chicago, IL 60612 US	

GROWTH PLANS/SPECIAL FEATURES:

The Chicago Blackhawks are one of the six original teams to begin playing in the National Hockey League (NHL) in 1926 and have won three championships in its history, the last in 1961. Despite the team's recent lack of champion status, the Blackhawks have done a good job gathering large crowds at the 20,500-seat United Center. The Blackhawks' parent company, Wirtz Corporation, co-owns the arena with Jerry Reinsdorf, owner of the Chicago Bulls. The team's roster has held the names of such famous players as Stan Mikita, Bobby Hull and the Esposito brothers. Blackhawk affiliations include the Rockford IceHogs, an American Hockey League (AHL) team, and the Pensacola Ice Pilots, an ECHL team, both minor league teams. The team's mascot, Tommy Hawk, makes special visits to fans for $200 per visit during games. Included in the price is a gift bag, a scoreboard announcement, and an 8x10 autographed photo. In addition, the mascot can be hired for parties, school visits and corporate events off-site. The team partners with American Family Insurance to offer Family Nights featuring discounted tickets. Fans can also communicate with each other on Hawk Chat (an online chat) and other message boards on the team's web site. During the 2007-08 season, the Blackhawks introduced more affordable ticket packages and its new Harris Club, luxury suites at a fraction of the cost of ownership. In 2008-09, the team led the NHL in home attendance, averaging over 22,200 fans per game. Forbes recently valued the team at approximately $205 million.

FINANCIALS: **Sales and profits are in thousands of dollars—add 000 to get the full amount. 2008 Note: Financial information for 2008 was not available for all companies at press time.**

2008 Sales: $79,000	2008 Profits: $1,400	**U.S. Stock Ticker: Subsidiary**
2007 Sales: $69,000	2007 Profits: $-3,600	**Int'l Ticker:** Int'l Exchange:
2006 Sales: $67,000	2006 Profits: $3,100	Employees:
2005 Sales: $	2005 Profits: $	Fiscal Year Ends: 6/30
2004 Sales: $71,000	2004 Profits: $	Parent Company: CHICAGO BLACKHAWK HOCKEY TEAM INC

SALARIES/BENEFITS:

Pension Plan:	ESOP Stock Plan:	Profit Sharing:	Top Exec. Salary: $	Bonus: $
Savings Plan:	Stock Purch. Plan:		Second Exec. Salary: $	Bonus: $

OTHER THOUGHTS:

Apparent Women Officers or Directors: 6
Hot Spot for Advancement for Women/Minorities: Y

LOCATIONS: ("Y" = Yes)

West:	Southwest:	Midwest:	Southeast:	Northeast:	International:
		Y			

CHICAGO BULLS

www.nba.com/bulls

Industry Group Code: 711211B **Ranks within this company's industry group:** Sales: 3 Profits: 1

Sports:		Services:		Media:		Sales:		Facilities:		Other:	
Leagues/Associations:		Food & Beverage:		TV:		Marketing:		Stadiums:		Gambling:	
Teams:	Y	Agents:		Radio:		Ads:		Fitness Clubs:		Apparel:	
Nonprofits:		Other:		Internet:		Tickets:	Y	Golf Courses:		Equipment:	
Other:				Print:		Retail:	Y	Ski Resorts:		Shoes:	
				Software:		Other:		Other:		Other:	

TYPES OF BUSINESS:

Professional Basketball Team

BRANDS/DIVISIONS/AFFILIATES:

IncrediBulls
Luvabulls
Bulls Brothers
BullsKidz
CharitaBulls
Bulls/Sox Training Academy
FestaBulls
United Center

CONTACTS: *Note: Officers with more than one job title may be intentionally listed here more than once.*

Irwin Mandel, Sr. VP-Legal
Steve Schanwald, Exec. VP-Bus. Oper.
Tim Hallam, Sr. Dir.-Public & Media Rel.
Irwin Mandel, Sr. VP-Finance
John Paxson, Exec. VP-Basketball Oper.
Scott Sonnenberg, Dir.-Corp. Partnerships
Vinny Del Negro, Head Coach
Jerry Reinsdorf, Chmn./Owner

Phone: 312-455-4000 **Fax:** 312-455-4189
Toll-Free:
Address: United Center, 1901 W. Madison St., Chicago, IL 60612-2459 US

GROWTH PLANS/SPECIAL FEATURES:

The Chicago Bulls is a team playing in the National Basketball Association (NBA). The Bulls joined the NBA during the 1966-67 season. The team struggled for more than two decades until it signed Michael Jordan, who led the Bulls to six championship titles in sets of three back-to-back wins, from 1990 to 1993 and from 1995 to 1998. The team became only the third franchise in history to garner three consecutive titles. Additionally, the Bulls' NBA records include the highest season winning percentage (.87 in 1995 with 72 wins to 10 losses) and the most consecutive home games won (37 in 1995) within one year. Following the retirements of Jordan and Scottie Pippen in 2005 and the losses of Dennis Rodman and coach, Phil Jackson, the Bulls have struggled to return to their former glory. All home games are played in the United Center, which has hosted over twenty million guests since its inception in 1994. The center offers restaurant and amenities such as the Ketel One Club, Bar One, Chicago Stadium Club, the Iron Works Bar and Grill and a theater with multiple capacity configurations. Entertainment offered during games includes the IncrediBulls, the Luvabulls, Bulls Brothers and BullsKidz. The team also sponsors CharitaBulls, which raises funds to benefit children living in the Chicago Area; the Bulls/Sox Training Academy; and FestaBulls, a special dinner and sports memorabilia auction held annually at the Berto Center. In the 2009 NBA Eastern Conference Playoffs, the Bulls won against the Boston Celtics, with player Derrick Rose becoming the second player in history to have a 35-point, 10 assist playoff game. Forbes recently estimated the team to be worth approximately $504 million. In the 2008-09 season, the team's home attendance average was roughly 21,200 per game.

FINANCIALS: **Sales and profits are in thousands of dollars—add 000 to get the full amount. 2008 Note: Financial information for 2008 was not available for all companies at press time.**

2008 Sales: $165,000	2008 Profits: $55,400	**U.S. Stock Ticker: Private**
2007 Sales: $161,000	2007 Profits: $59,300	**Int'l Ticker:** Int'l Exchange:
2006 Sales: $149,000	2006 Profits: $48,500	Employees:
2005 Sales: $136,000	2005 Profits: $	Fiscal Year Ends: 7/31
2004 Sales: $123,000	2004 Profits: $	Parent Company:

SALARIES/BENEFITS:

Pension Plan:	ESOP Stock Plan:	Profit Sharing:	Top Exec. Salary: $	Bonus: $
Savings Plan:	Stock Purch. Plan:		Second Exec. Salary: $	Bonus: $

OTHER THOUGHTS:

Apparent Women Officers or Directors: 1
Hot Spot for Advancement for Women/Minorities:

LOCATIONS: ("Y" = Yes)

West:	Southwest:	Midwest:	Southeast:	Northeast:	International:
		Y			

CHICAGO CUBS

www.cubs.com

Industry Group Code: 711211A **Ranks within this company's industry group:** Sales: 5 Profits: 4

Sports:		Services:		Media:		Sales:		Facilities:		Other:	
Leagues/Associations:		Food & Beverage:		TV:	Y	Marketing:		Stadiums:	Y	Gambling:	
Teams:	Y	Agents:		Radio:	Y	Ads:		Fitness Clubs:		Apparel:	
Nonprofits:		Other:		Internet:		Tickets:		Golf Courses:		Equipment:	
Other:				Print:		Retail:		Ski Resorts:		Shoes:	
				Software:		Other:		Other:		Other:	

TYPES OF BUSINESS:

Professional Baseball Team
Stadium Operation

BRANDS/DIVISIONS/AFFILIATES:

Tribune Co
Wrigley Field
Iowa Cubs
Tennessee Smokies
Daytona Cubs
Peoria Chiefs
Boise Hawks
Mesa Cubs

CONTACTS: *Note: Officers with more than one job title may be intentionally listed here more than once.*

Jodi Reischl, Co-Dir.-Finance
Matthew Wszolek, Dir.-Sales & Promotions
Jenny Surma, Sr. Dir.-Human Resources
Carl Rice, Sr. Dir.-IT & Facility Mgmt.
Michael Lufrano, General Counsel/Sr. VP-Community Affairs
Mark McGuire, Exec. VP-Bus. Oper.
Peter Chase, Dir.-Media Rel.
Terri Lynn Fleischhacker, Co-Dir.-Finance
Jim Hendry, VP/Gen. Mgr.
Lou Piniella, Mgr.
Frank Maloney, Dir.-Ticket Oper.
Lena McDonagh, Dir.-Publications & Creative Svcs.
Crane Kenney, Chmn.

Phone: 773-404-2827	**Fax:** 773-404-4129
Toll-Free:	
Address: Wrigley Field, 1060 W. Addison, Chicago, IL 60613 US	

GROWTH PLANS/SPECIAL FEATURES:

The Chicago Cubs, held by the Chicago National League Ball Club, Inc., is an organization within Major League Baseball (MLB). The team began its history in 1871 as the Chicago White Stockings, one of eight charter members of the National League, and was named the Cubs in 1902 by the Chicago Daily Tribune. The Cubs have played home games at famed Wrigley Field, the second oldest ballpark in the major leagues, for 91 years. Wrigley has hosted many unforgettable baseball moments, including Babe Ruth's called shot in the 1932 World Series. In its heyday, the team won two consecutive World Series, in 1907 and 1908, becoming the first team in baseball history to do so. However, the Cubs have not won a World Series since and have not reached the World Series in nearly 60 years, despite coming close in 2003. The team has, however, won more games historically than any other team except the Giants. The team has included such greats as Rogers Hornsby, Ferguson Jenkins, Hack Wilson, Ernie Banks, Mordecai Brown, Ryne Sandberg and Sammy Sosa. The franchise was sold by the Wrigley family in 1981 to the Tribune Company, makers of the Chicago Tribune newspaper. The Tribune Company was purchased by billionaire Sam Zell, who in 2009, agreed to sell the Cubs to Tom Ricketts, CEO of Incapital LLC, for $900 million. In April 2008, the team had its 10,000th win. Also in 2008, the Cubs went into the postseason in consecutive years for the first time since 1906-1908. Forbes recently estimated the team to be worth approximately $700 million. The team's average home attendance in the 2008 season was over 40,700 fans per game.

FINANCIALS: **Sales and profits are in thousands of dollars—add 000 to get the full amount. 2008 Note: Financial information for 2008 was not available for all companies at press time.**

2008 Sales: $239,000	2008 Profits: $29,700	**U.S. Stock Ticker: Subsidiary**
2007 Sales: $214,000	2007 Profits: $21,400	**Int'l Ticker:** Int'l Exchange:
2006 Sales: $197,000	2006 Profits: $22,200	Employees:
2005 Sales: $179,000	2005 Profits: $	Fiscal Year Ends: 12/31
2004 Sales: $170,000	2004 Profits: $	Parent Company: TRIBUNE CO

SALARIES/BENEFITS:

Pension Plan:	ESOP Stock Plan:	Profit Sharing:	Top Exec. Salary: $	Bonus: $
Savings Plan:	Stock Purch. Plan:		Second Exec. Salary: $	Bonus: $

OTHER THOUGHTS:

Apparent Women Officers or Directors: 4
Hot Spot for Advancement for Women/Minorities: Y

LOCATIONS: ("Y" = Yes)

West:	Southwest:	Midwest:	Southeast:	Northeast:	International:
		Y			

CHICAGO FIRE

chicago.fire.mlsnet.com

Industry Group Code: 711211D **Ranks within this company's industry group:** Sales: Profits:

Sports:		Services:		Media:		Sales:		Facilities:		Other:	
Leagues/Associations:		Food & Beverage:		TV:		Marketing:		Stadiums:	Y	Gambling:	
Teams:	Y	Agents:		Radio:		Ads:		Fitness Clubs:		Apparel:	
Nonprofits:	Y	Other:		Internet:		Tickets:		Golf Courses:		Equipment:	
Other:				Print:		Retail:		Ski Resorts:		Shoes:	
				Software:		Other:		Other:		Other:	

TYPES OF BUSINESS:

Professional Soccer Team

BRANDS/DIVISIONS/AFFILIATES:

Chicago Fire Foundation

CONTACTS:

Note: Officers with more than one job title may be intentionally listed here more than once.

Dave Greeley, Pres.
Mike Humes, Sr. VP-Sales & Mktg.
Deanna Swanson, Mgr.-Human Resources
Eryn Blum, Coordinator-Merch. & Advertising
Joe MacDonell, VP-Bus. Oper.
Eric Smith, VP-Bus. Dev. & Special Projects
Rebecca Carroll, VP-Comm.
Joe MacDonell, VP-Finance
Denis Hamlett, Head Coach
Ryan M. Robbins, Dir.-Ticket Sales
Ron Stern, Dir.-Team Oper.
Dan Parise, Dir.-Mktg.
Andrew Hauptman, Chmn.

Phone: 708-594-7200 **Fax:** 708-496-6050
Toll-Free:
Address: Toyota Park, 7000 S. Harlem Ave., Bridgeview, IL 60455 US

GROWTH PLANS/SPECIAL FEATURES:

The Chicago Fire was added as one of two expansion teams to Major League Soccer (MLS) in 1998. The team is composed of a diverse mixture of European, Hispanic and American soccer players in an attempt to gather interest for the franchise in Chicago, which has one of the largest Polish populations outside of Poland and a growing Hispanic population. In its short career, the Fire has won one MLS Cup Championship, in 1998; four Lamar Hunt U.S. Open Cup Championships, in 1998, 2000, 2003 and 2006; and one MLS Supporters' Shield, in 2003. In two other seasons, the team made it all the way to the MLS Cup, only to be defeated, by the Kansas City Wizards, in 2000, and the San Jose Earthquakes, in 2003. During the 2008 season, the Fire came in second place in the Eastern Division, which also includes teams such as the Columbus Crew, D.C. United, the Kansas City Wizards, Toronto FC, New England Revolution and the New York Red Bulls. The Fire had an average attendance of just over 17,000 spectators for regular season matches in 2008, and an average attendance of 17,300 for the 2008 playoff season. After moving to different Chicago stadiums several times during its early years, the team has played since 2006 in the new $70-million Toyota Park stadium in the Village of Bridgeview, near Chicago's southwest side. Since 2007, the franchise has been owned by Andell Holdings, a private equity firm. In January 2008, Chicago Fire announced a three-year deal making Best Buy the team's official presenting sponsor, as well as the sponsor of its jersey.

FINANCIALS:

Sales and profits are in thousands of dollars—add 000 to get the full amount. 2008 Note: Financial information for 2008 was not available for all companies at press time.

2008 Sales: $	2008 Profits: $	**U.S. Stock Ticker: Private**
2007 Sales: $	2007 Profits: $	**Int'l Ticker:** Int'l Exchange:
2006 Sales: $	2006 Profits: $	Employees:
2005 Sales: $	2005 Profits: $	Fiscal Year Ends:
2004 Sales: $	2004 Profits: $	Parent Company: ANDELL HOLDINGS

SALARIES/BENEFITS:

Pension Plan:	ESOP Stock Plan:	Profit Sharing:	Top Exec. Salary: $	Bonus: $
Savings Plan:	Stock Purch. Plan:		Second Exec. Salary: $	Bonus: $

OTHER THOUGHTS:

Apparent Women Officers or Directors: 22
Hot Spot for Advancement for Women/Minorities: Y

LOCATIONS: ("Y" = Yes)

West:	Southwest:	Midwest:	Southeast:	Northeast:	International:
		Y			

Note: Financial information, benefits and other data can change quickly and may vary from those stated here.

CHICAGO WHITE SOX

chicago.whitesox.mlb.com

Industry Group Code: 711211A **Ranks within this company's industry group:** Sales: 8 Profits: 21

Sports:		Services:		Media:		Sales:		Facilities:		Other:	
Leagues/Associations:		Food & Beverage:		TV:		Marketing:		Stadiums:		Gambling:	
Teams:	Y	Agents:		Radio:		Ads:		Fitness Clubs:		Apparel:	Y
Nonprofits:		Other:		Internet:		Tickets:	Y	Golf Courses:		Equipment:	
Other:				Print:		Retail:	Y	Ski Resorts:		Shoes:	
				Software:		Other:		Other:		Other:	

TYPES OF BUSINESS:

Professional Baseball Team

BRANDS/DIVISIONS/AFFILIATES:

U.S. Cellular Field
Great Falls Voyagers
Birmingham Barons
Winston-Salem Dash
Kannapolis Intimidators
Bristol White Sox
Charlotte Knights

CONTACTS: *Note: Officers with more than one job title may be intentionally listed here more than once.*

Brooks Boyer, Chief Mktg. Officer/VP
Moira Foy, Sr. Dir.-Human Resources
Don Brown, Sr. Dir.-MIS
Don Esposito, Sr. Dir.-Construction & Maintenance
Tim Buzard, Sr. VP-Admin.
John Corvino, General Counsel
Dan Fabian, Dir.-Baseball Oper.
Bob Grim, Sr. Dir.-Bus. Dev. & Broadcasting
Scott Reifert, VP-Comm.
Bill Waters, Sr. Dir.-Finance
Ken Williams, Sr. VP/Gen. Mgr.
Terry Savarise, Sr. VP-Stadium Oper.
Tom Sheridan, Dir.-Ticket Sales
Jim Muno, Sr. Dir.-Corp. Partnerships
Jerry Reinsdorf, Chmn.
Don Esposito, Sr. Dir.-Purchasing

Phone: 312-674-1000 **Fax:** 312-924-3296
Toll-Free: 886-769-4263
Address: 333 W. 35th St., Chicago, IL 60616 US

GROWTH PLANS/SPECIAL FEATURES:

The Chicago White Sox is a Major League Baseball (MLB) franchise. The team plays on the south side of Chicago, Illinois at U.S. Cellular Field, a stadium with a 40,615-seat capacity. As a charter member of the American League, the White Sox organization was strong during the early part of the 20th century. The team won its first World Series in 1906 over their intra-city rival, the Chicago Cubs. The White Sox also won a World Series in 1917 led by baseball legend Shoeless Joe Jackson. Two years later, the outcome of the World Series was allegedly fixed by gamblers, and the White Sox lost to the Cincinnati Reds. The next year, as a result of a different game-fixing event, details of the White Sox scandal came to light. Eventually, eight players, including Jackson, were banned from baseball. In the decades following this indignity, the White Sox were a relatively mediocre team, playing in the World Series only once, in 1959. Finally, in 2005, the White Sox won the World Series, its third in 105 years, defeating the Houston Astros. To its credit, the franchise has three World Championships, five pennants and four division titles. Despite its recent success, the White Sox still has much worse attendance than its cross-town rival the Cubs. Forbes has valued the White Sox at $450 million, 18th among MLB clubs. The team has contributed a number of players to the National Baseball Hall of Fame, including Luis Aparicio, Luke Appling, Eddie Collins, Charles Comiskey, George Davis, Red Faber, Nellie Fox, Ted Lyons, Ray Schalk, Bill Veeck and Ed Walsh. The White Sox ended the 2008 season with 89 wins and 74 losses and total game attendance of over 2.5 million, averaging nearly 30,900 per home game.

FINANCIALS: Sales and profits are in thousands of dollars—add 000 to get the full amount. 2008 Note: Financial information for 2008 was not available for all companies at press time.

2008 Sales: $196,000	2008 Profits: $13,800	**U.S. Stock Ticker: Subsidiary**
2007 Sales: $193,000	2007 Profits: $30,600	**Int'l Ticker:** Int'l Exchange:
2006 Sales: $173,000	2006 Profits: $19,500	Employees:
2005 Sales: $157,000	2005 Profits: $	Fiscal Year Ends: 10/31
2004 Sales: $	2004 Profits: $	Parent Company: CHICAGO WHITE SOX LTD

SALARIES/BENEFITS:

Pension Plan:	ESOP Stock Plan:	Profit Sharing:	Top Exec. Salary: $	Bonus: $
Savings Plan:	Stock Purch. Plan:		Second Exec. Salary: $	Bonus: $

OTHER THOUGHTS:

Apparent Women Officers or Directors: 19
Hot Spot for Advancement for Women/Minorities: Y

LOCATIONS: ("Y" = Yes)

West:	Southwest:	Midwest:	Southeast:	Northeast:	International:
		Y			

CHURCHILL DOWNS INC

www.churchilldownsincorporated.com

Industry Group Code: 713210 **Ranks within this company's industry group:** Sales: 2 Profits: 1

Sports:		Services:		Media:		Sales:		Facilities:		Other:	
Leagues/Associations:		Food & Beverage:		TV:		Marketing:		Stadiums:		Gambling:	
Teams:		Agents:		Radio:		Ads:		Fitness Clubs:		Apparel:	
Nonprofits:		Other:		Internet:		Tickets:		Golf Courses:		Equipment:	
Other:	Y			Print:		Retail:		Ski Resorts:		Shoes:	
				Software:		Other:		Other:		Other:	

TYPES OF BUSINESS:

Horse Racing
Pari-mutuel Wagering
Simulcasting
Video Poker
Computer Graphics & Gambling Software
Online Retail

BRANDS/DIVISIONS/AFFILIATES:

Churchill Downs Investment Company
Kentucky Off-Track Betting, LLC
Arlington Park Racecourse, LLC
Calder Race Course
Fair Grounds Race Course
TwinSpires.com
Video Services, Inc.

CONTACTS: *Note: Officers with more than one job title may be intentionally listed here more than once.*

Robert L. Evans, CEO
Robert L. Evans, Pres.
William E. Mudd, CFO/Exec. VP
Steve Cummins, Sr. Dir.-Human Resources
Rebecca Reed, Sr. VP-Legal Affairs/Corp. Compliance Officer/Sec.
William C. Carstanjen, Exec. VP/Chief Dev. Officer
T. Kevin Flanery, Sr. VP-Comm. & National Public Affairs
Donald R. Richardson, Sr. VP-Racing
Steven P. Sexton, Exec. VP./Pres., Churchill Downs Racetrack
Vernon Niven, Exec. VP-Tech. Initiatives
Roy A. Arnold, Sr. VP-Illinois Oper./Pres., Arlington Park

Phone: 502-636-4400	**Fax:** 502-636-4430
Toll-Free: 800-283-3729	
Address: 700 Central Ave., Louisville, KY 40208 US	

GROWTH PLANS/SPECIAL FEATURES:

Churchill Downs, Inc. (CDI) is a leading multi-jurisdictional owner and operator of pari-mutuel wagering properties and businesses. It also offers gaming products through its slot and video poker operations in Louisiana. The company manages various operations, including Churchill Downs Racetrack in Louisville, Kentucky, an internationally known thoroughbred racing operation and home of the Kentucky Derby; Arlington Park, a thoroughbred racing operation in Arlington Heights along with eleven off-track betting facilities (OTBs) in Illinois; Calder Race Course, a thoroughbred racing operation in Miami Gardens, Florida; Fair Grounds, a thoroughbred racing operation in New Orleans along with nine OTBs and a slot facility in Louisiana; and Video Services, Inc, the owner and operator of more than 600 video poker machines in Louisiana. Churchill Downs Investment Company (CDIC), a wholly-owned subsidiary of Churchill Downs, Inc, oversees its other industry related investments. CDIC holds a 30% interest in NASRIN Services, LLC, a telecommunications service provider for the pari-mutuel and simulcasting industries. CDIC also holds a 5% interest in Kentucky Downs, LLC, a racetrack in Franklin, Kentucky. The firm has a 25% interest in Kentucky Off-Track Betting, LLC, which operates off-track betting facilities in the Kentucky cities of Maysville, Jamestown, Pineville and Corbin. In March 2007, the company completed the sale of its 62% ownership interest in Hoosier Park, L.P. to Centaur Racing, LLC. Also in 2007, Churchill Downs announced the launch of an online advance deposit wagering platform called, TwinSpires.com. In April 2008, the company dissolved Racing World Limited, a joint venture subscription television channel jointly operated with Magna Entertainment Corporation and Racing UK. As a result, Churchill Downs regained all of its in-home video and wagering rights in the U.K.

The company offers its employees medical insurance, life insurance, a 401(k) plan and tuition assistance, among other benefits.

FINANCIALS: **Sales and profits are in thousands of dollars—add 000 to get the full amount. 2008 Note: Financial information for 2008 was not available for all companies at press time.**

2008 Sales: $430,566	2008 Profits: $28,549	**U.S. Stock Ticker: CHDN**
2007 Sales: $410,735	2007 Profits: $15,731	**Int'l Ticker:** Int'l Exchange:
2006 Sales: $376,671	2006 Profits: $29,811	Employees: 2,600
2005 Sales: $356,342	2005 Profits: $78,908	Fiscal Year Ends: 12/31
2004 Sales: $304,888	2004 Profits: $8,915	Parent Company:

SALARIES/BENEFITS:

Pension Plan:	ESOP Stock Plan:	Profit Sharing:	Top Exec. Salary: $450,000	Bonus: $528,725
Savings Plan: Y	Stock Purch. Plan:		Second Exec. Salary: $320,000	Bonus: $245,000

OTHER THOUGHTS:

Apparent Women Officers or Directors: 1
Hot Spot for Advancement for Women/Minorities:

LOCATIONS: ("Y" = Yes)

West:	Southwest:	Midwest:	Southeast:	Northeast:	International:
		Y	Y		

Note: Financial information, benefits and other data can change quickly and may vary from those stated here.

CINCINNATI BENGALS

www.bengals.com

Industry Group Code: 711211C **Ranks within this company's industry group:** Sales: 24 Profits: 18

Sports:		Services:		Media:		Sales:		Facilities:		Other:	
Leagues/Associations:		Food & Beverage:		TV:		Marketing:		Stadiums:		Gambling:	
Teams:	Y	Agents:		Radio:		Ads:		Fitness Clubs:		Apparel:	
Nonprofits:		Other:		Internet:		Tickets:	Y	Golf Courses:		Equipment:	
Other:				Print:		Retail:	Y	Ski Resorts:		Shoes:	
				Software:		Other:		Other:		Other:	

TYPES OF BUSINESS:

Professional Football Team
Tickets
Team Merchandise

BRANDS/DIVISIONS/AFFILIATES:

Paul Brown Stadium
Cincinnati Bengals Inc

CONTACTS:

Note: Officers with more than one job title may be intentionally listed here more than once.

Michael Brown, Pres./Owner
Bill Scanlon, CFO
Vince Cicero, Dir.-Corp. Sales & Mktg.
Andy Ware, Mgr.-Web Site & New Media
Jack Brennan, Dir.-Public Rel.
Johanna Kappner, Controller
Pete Brown, VP-Player Personnel
Marvin Lewis, Head Coach
Bill Connelly, Mgr.-Bus.
Katie Blackburn, Exec. VP

Phone: 513-455-3550	**Fax:** 513-621-3570
Toll-Free:	
Address: 1 Paul Brown Dr., Cincinnati, OH 45202 US	

GROWTH PLANS/SPECIAL FEATURES:

The Cincinnati Bengals are a professional football team playing in the National Football League (NFL) since 1968. The Bengals came out of the 1970s with 74 wins to 70 losses. During the 1980s the team went to the Super Bowl twice and both times lost to the San Francisco 49ers. It set a record in the 1982 Super Bowl by being the first losing team to lead in yardage. For fifteen consecutive years, however, from 1991 to 2005, the team failed to post a winning season. The team held the NFL's worst record throughout the 1990s. From the 2000 to the 2004 season, the team won 28 games and lost 52. This streak of poor play was broken during 2005. Led by NFL superstar quarterback Carson Palmer, the Bengals posted an 11-5 record, winning their division and making a playoff appearance. The team plays its home games at Paul Brown Stadium, constructed in 2000 and named after its late founder and coach. The stadium is owned by Hamilton County, Ohio. Paul Brown's son, Michael, is the current owner of the team. Its training sessions are hosted by Georgetown College in Georgetown, Kentucky. The Bengals' Michael Anthony Munoz, who played offensive tackler from 1980 to 1982, and Charlie Joiner, a wide receiver from 1972 to 1975 were inducted into the Pro Football Hall of Fame in the late 90's. In the 2008 season, the Bengals did not qualify for the playoffs for the third consecutive year. Forbes Magazine recently valued the team at $941 million. The team's average home game attendance in the 2008 season was 64,582.

FINANCIALS:

Sales and profits are in thousands of dollars—add 000 to get the full amount. 2008 Note: Financial information for 2008 was not available for all companies at press time.

2008 Sales: $205,000	2008 Profits: $22,000	**U.S. Stock Ticker: Subsidiary**
2007 Sales: $194,000	2007 Profits: $11,700	**Int'l Ticker:** Int'l Exchange:
2006 Sales: $175,000	2006 Profits: $20,900	Employees:
2005 Sales: $171,000	2005 Profits: $	Fiscal Year Ends: 2/28
2004 Sales: $150,000	2004 Profits: $	Parent Company: CINCINNATI BENGALS INC

SALARIES/BENEFITS:

Pension Plan:	ESOP Stock Plan:	Profit Sharing:	Top Exec. Salary: $	Bonus: $
Savings Plan:	Stock Purch. Plan:		Second Exec. Salary: $	Bonus: $

OTHER THOUGHTS:

Apparent Women Officers or Directors: 2
Hot Spot for Advancement for Women/Minorities: Y

LOCATIONS: ("Y" = Yes)

West:	Southwest:	Midwest:	Southeast:	Northeast:	International:
		Y			

CINCINNATI REDS

cincinnati.reds.mlb.com

Industry Group Code: 711211A **Ranks within this company's industry group:** Sales: 24 Profits: 17

Sports:		Services:		Media:		Sales:		Facilities:		Other:	
Leagues/Associations:		Food & Beverage:		TV:		Marketing:		Stadiums:		Gambling:	
Teams:	Y	Agents:		Radio:		Ads:		Fitness Clubs:		Apparel:	
Nonprofits:		Other:		Internet:		Tickets:	Y	Golf Courses:		Equipment:	
Other:				Print:		Retail:	Y	Ski Resorts:		Shoes:	
				Software:		Other:		Other:		Other:	

TYPES OF BUSINESS:

Professional Baseball Team

BRANDS/DIVISIONS/AFFILIATES:

Great American Ballpark
Louisville Bats
Chattanooga Lookouts
Sarasota Reds
Dayton Dragons
Billings Mustangs
Cincinnati Reds, LLC

CONTACTS: *Note: Officers with more than one job title may be intentionally listed here more than once.*

Robert H. Castellini, CEO
Phillip J. Castellini, COO
Robert H. Castellini, Pres.
Doug Healy, CFO/VP-Finance
Bill Reinberger, VP-Corp. Sales
Barbara Boles, Dir.-Human Resources
Brian Keys, Dir.-IT
Roger Smith, Chief Engineer
James A. Marx, General Counsel/VP
Walt Jocketty, Gen. Mgr./Pres., Baseball Oper.
Brad Blettner, Sr. VP-Bus. Dev.
Rob Butcher, Dir.-Media Rel.
Thomas L. Williams, Treas./Vice Chmn.
Dick Williams, VP-Baseball Oper.
Bob Miller, VP/Asst. Gen. Mgr.
Dusty Baker, Mgr.
Declan Mullin, VP-Ballpark Oper.
W. Joseph Williams, Jr., Chmn.
Jim Stoeckel, Dir.-Int'l Oper.

Phone: 513-765-7000 **Fax:** 513-765-7048
Toll-Free:
Address: 100 Main St., Cincinnati, OH 45202 US

GROWTH PLANS/SPECIAL FEATURES:

The Cincinnati Reds are a Major League Baseball (MLB) team playing in the Central Division of the National League, along with the Chicago Cubs, Houston Astros, Milwaukee Brewers, Pittsburgh Pirates and St. Louis Cardinals. Baseball in Cincinnati goes back to 1866 and the Cincinnati Red Stockings. The first openly all-professional baseball team, the Red Stockings went 57-0 in their first season and won 130 straight games from 1869 to 1870. The current Reds franchise is actually the third Red Stockings incarnation, which began in the American Association in 1882. The Reds later joined the National League and won its first World Series in 1919, though the Chicago White Sox infamously threw the series. In all, the franchise has won five World Series (last in 1990), nine pennants and eight division titles. Famous Reds include Frank Robinson, Johnny Bench, Joe Morgan and Pete Rose, who is MLB's all-time leader in hits. The team has played at the modern, 42,000-seat Great American Ball Park since 2003. In the spring of 2008, the team's general manager Wayne Krivsky was let go by Castellini and replaced by Walt Jocketty. The Reds also recently added several players to their rooster, including outfielder Daniel Perales, right-handed pitcher Josh Fogg and left-handed pitcher Jeremy Affeldt. The club is affiliated with several minor league teams, including the Sarasota Reds, Dayton Dragons, Louisville Bats, Chattanooga Lookouts and the Billings Mustangs.of the Central Division of the National League. In the 2008 season, the team averaged approximately 25,400 fans in attendance per game. A recent Forbes estimate values the team at $342 million.

FINANCIALS: **Sales and profits are in thousands of dollars—add 000 to get the full amount. 2008 Note: Financial information for 2008 was not available for all companies at press time.**

2008 Sales: $171,000	2008 Profits: $17,000	**U.S. Stock Ticker: Subsidiary**
2007 Sales: $161,000	2007 Profits: $19,300	**Int'l Ticker:** Int'l Exchange:
2006 Sales: $146,000	2006 Profits: $22,400	Employees:
2005 Sales: $137,000	2005 Profits: $	Fiscal Year Ends: 10/31
2004 Sales: $	2004 Profits: $	Parent Company: CINCINNATI REDS LLC

SALARIES/BENEFITS:

Pension Plan:	ESOP Stock Plan:	Profit Sharing:	Top Exec. Salary: $	Bonus: $
Savings Plan:	Stock Purch. Plan:		Second Exec. Salary: $	Bonus: $

OTHER THOUGHTS:

Apparent Women Officers or Directors: 6
Hot Spot for Advancement for Women/Minorities: Y

LOCATIONS: ("Y" = Yes)

West:	Southwest:	Midwest:	Southeast:	Northeast:	International:
		Y	Y		Y

CLEAR CHANNEL COMMUNICATIONS INC

www.clearchannel.com

Industry Group Code: 513111 **Ranks within this company's industry group:** Sales: 1 Profits: 1

Sports:		Services:		Media:		Sales:		Facilities:		Other:	
Leagues/Associations:		Food & Beverage:		TV:		Marketing:		Stadiums:		Gambling:	
Teams:		Agents:		Radio:	Y	Ads:	Y	Fitness Clubs:		Apparel:	
Nonprofits:		Other:	Y	Internet:		Tickets:		Golf Courses:		Equipment:	
Other:				Print:		Retail:		Ski Resorts:		Shoes:	
				Software:		Other:		Other:		Other:	

TYPES OF BUSINESS:

Radio Station Owner/Operator
Outdoor Advertising

BRANDS/DIVISIONS/AFFILIATES:

Thomas H Lee Partners LP
Bain Capital LLC
CC Media Holdings
Katz Media
Katz Group of Companies (The)
Providence Equity Partners
Clear Channel Outdoor Holdings Inc

CONTACTS: *Note: Officers with more than one job title may be intentionally listed here more than once.*

Mark Mays, CEO
Randall Mays, Pres.
Randall Mays, CFO/Exec. VP
Bill Hamersly, Sr. VP-Human Resources
David Wilson, CIO/Sr. VP
Joe Shannon, CTO/VP
Andrew W. Levin, Chief Legal Officer/Exec. VP
Lisa Dollinger, Chief Comm. Officer
Randy Palmer, Sr. VP-Investor Rel.
Herb Hill, Chief Acct. Officer/Sr. VP
Jessica Marventano, Sr. VP-Gov't Affairs
Chad Dan, Sr. VP-Real Estate
Julie Hill, Sr. VP-Finance
Kathryn Johnson, Sr. VP-Corp. Rel.
L. Lowry Mays, Chmn.

Phone: 210-822-2828 **Fax:** 210-822-2299
Toll-Free:
Address: 200 E. Basse Rd., San Antonio, TX 78209 US

GROWTH PLANS/SPECIAL FEATURES:

Clear Channel Communications, Inc. is a diversified media company with operations in radio broadcasting, domestic outdoor advertising and international outdoor advertising. The company owns more than 850 core radio stations, and a leading national radio network and holds equity interests in various international radio broadcasting companies. Clear Channel's radio network produces, distributes and represents approximately 70 syndicated radio programs and services for roughly 5,000 radio stations. Some of the company's syndicated programs include Rush Limbaugh, Steve Harvey, Ryan Seacrest and Jeff Foxworthy. Its radio broadcasting segment represents roughly 50% of its revenue. Through ClearChannel Outdoor, the firm owns and operates approximately 200,000 outdoor advertising displays throughout North America and approximately 690,000 international outdoor advertising display faces. Clear Channel's other businesses includes subsidiary Katz Media, which sells national spot advertising time for roughly 3,000 clients in the radio industry and 400 clients in the television industry. In July 2008, the company was acquired by Thomas H. Lee Partners and Bain Capital Partners, LLC , and subsequently became a subsidiary of CC Media Holdings. In January 2009, the company commenced a restructuring program in order to reduce operating costs. As part of the program, the firm eliminated approximately 1,850 full-time positions.

FINANCIALS: **Sales and profits are in thousands of dollars—add 000 to get the full amount. 2008 Note: Financial information for 2008 was not available for all companies at press time.**

2008 Sales: $6,688,683	2008 Profits: $-4,005,473	**U.S. Stock Ticker: Subsidiary**
2007 Sales: $6,921,202	2007 Profits: $938,507	**Int'l Ticker:** Int'l Exchange:
2006 Sales: $6,457,435	2006 Profits: $691,517	Employees: 28,900
2005 Sales: $6,019,029	2005 Profits: $935,662	Fiscal Year Ends: 12/31
2004 Sales: $6,600,954	2004 Profits: $-4,038,169	Parent Company: CC MEDIA HOLDINGS

SALARIES/BENEFITS:

Pension Plan:	ESOP Stock Plan:	Profit Sharing:	Top Exec. Salary: $750,000	Bonus: $4,306,250
Savings Plan: Y	Stock Purch. Plan: Y		Second Exec. Salary: $695,000	Bonus: $4,306,250

OTHER THOUGHTS:

Apparent Women Officers or Directors: 4
Hot Spot for Advancement for Women/Minorities: Y

LOCATIONS: ("Y" = Yes)

West:	Southwest:	Midwest:	Southeast:	Northeast:	International:
Y	Y	Y	Y	Y	Y

CLEVELAND BROWNS

www.clevelandbrowns.com

Industry Group Code: 711211C **Ranks within this company's industry group:** Sales: 12 Profits: 22

Sports:		Services:		Media:		Sales:		Facilities:		Other:	
Leagues/Associations:		Food & Beverage:		TV:		Marketing:		Stadiums:	Y	Gambling:	
Teams:	Y	Agents:		Radio:		Ads:		Fitness Clubs:		Apparel:	
Nonprofits:		Other:		Internet:		Tickets:	Y	Golf Courses:		Equipment:	
Other:				Print:		Retail:	Y	Ski Resorts:		Shoes:	
				Software:		Other:		Other:		Other:	

TYPES OF BUSINESS:

Professional Football Team
Ticket Sales
Team Merchandise

BRANDS/DIVISIONS/AFFILIATES:

Cleveland Browns Stadium
Clevland Browns Football Company LLC

CONTACTS:

Note: Officers with more than one job title may be intentionally listed here more than once.

Michael J. Keenan, Pres.
Brett Reynolds, VP-Mktg. & Sales
Michael Nikolaus, Dir.-Human Resources
Brandon Covert, Dir.-IT
David A. Jenkins, VP-Admin.
Lorne Novick, Legal Counsel
Erin O'Brien, Dir.-Team Oper.
Bill Bonsiewicz, VP-Comm.
David A. Jenkins, VP-Finance
Carl Meyer, VP-Security
George Kokinis, Gen. Mgr.
Eric Mangini, Head Coach
Jim Brown, Exec. Advisor
Bob Kain, Vice Chmn.

Phone: 440-891-5000	**Fax:** 440-891-5009
Toll-Free:	
Address: 76 Lou Groza Blvd., Berea, OH 44017 US	

GROWTH PLANS/SPECIAL FEATURES:

The Cleveland Browns are a professional football team based in Cleveland, Ohio that plays in the National Football League (NFL). The team joined the NFL in 1949, after five years in the short-lived All-American Football Conference. Controversial figure Art Modell purchased the team in 1961 for $4 million. In 1996, Modell announced that he had signed a deal to relocate the Browns to Baltimore for the 1996 season. Over 100 lawsuits were filed by fans, the city of Cleveland and others, and Congress held hearings on the matter. Eventually a settlement was reached that called for Modell's starting a new franchise in Baltimore, and Cleveland retaining the Browns' name, colors, history, awards and archives. The Browns ceased activities from 1996 to 1999, when the team returned to a new, 73,000-seat stadium, Cleveland Browns Stadium, which is owned by the city of Cleveland. In 1998, ownership of the team was sold to Al Lerner for $530 million. When Lerner died in 2002 his 90% stake went to his family. The team has sent 16 players to the Pro Football Hall of Fame, tying with Washington for the fifth-highest total league-wide. These players include Jim Brown, Leroy Kelly, Bobby Mitchell, Ozzie Newsome and Paul Warfield. The Browns have never won the Super Bowl, but has a regular season record of 414-354 and overall record of 425-374 since its NFL inception. Forbes Magazine recently valued the team at $1.03 billion. The team's average home game attendance in the 2008 season was 72,778.

FINANCIALS:

Sales and profits are in thousands of dollars—add 000 to get the full amount. 2008 Note: Financial information for 2008 was not available for all companies at press time.

2008 Sales: $220,000	2008 Profits: $19,300
2007 Sales: $206,000	2007 Profits: $20,600
2006 Sales: $206,000	2006 Profits: $47,100
2005 Sales: $203,000	2005 Profits: $
2004 Sales: $	2004 Profits: $

U.S. Stock Ticker: Subsidiary
Int'l Ticker: Int'l Exchange:
Employees:
Fiscal Year Ends: 12/31
Parent Company: CLEVELAND BROWNS FOOTBALL CO. LLC

SALARIES/BENEFITS:

Pension Plan:	ESOP Stock Plan:	Profit Sharing:	Top Exec. Salary: $	Bonus: $
Savings Plan:	Stock Purch. Plan:		Second Exec. Salary: $	Bonus: $

OTHER THOUGHTS:

Apparent Women Officers or Directors: 6
Hot Spot for Advancement for Women/Minorities: Y

LOCATIONS: ("Y" = Yes)

West:	Southwest:	Midwest:	Southeast:	Northeast:	International:
		Y			

CLEVELAND CAVALIERS

www.nba.com/cavaliers

Industry Group Code: 711211B **Ranks within this company's industry group:** Sales: 5 Profits: 12

Sports:		Services:		Media:		Sales:		Facilities:		Other:	
Leagues/Associations:		Food & Beverage:		TV:		Marketing:		Stadiums:	Y	Gambling:	
Teams:	Y	Agents:		Radio:		Ads:		Fitness Clubs:		Apparel:	
Nonprofits:		Other:		Internet:		Tickets:	Y	Golf Courses:		Equipment:	
Other:				Print:		Retail:	Y	Ski Resorts:		Shoes:	
				Software:		Other:		Other:		Other:	

TYPES OF BUSINESS:

Professional Basketball Team
Ticket Sales
Team Merchandise

BRANDS/DIVISIONS/AFFILIATES:

Quicken Loans Arena
Shoot 4 The Moon Foundation
King for Kids Bike-A-Thon
Cavaliers Youth Hoops Program
Q-TUBE
SMARTVISION
Cavaliers Operating Company, LLC
Cavaliers Youth Fund

CONTACTS: *Note: Officers with more than one job title may be intentionally listed here more than once.*

Len Komoroski, Pres.
David Katzman, Vice Chmn.
Mike Brown, Head Coach
Danny Ferry, Gen. Mgr.
Dan Gilbert, Chmn.

Phone: 216-420-2000	**Fax:**
Toll-Free: 800-332-2287	
Address: 1 Center Court, Cleveland, OH 44115-4001 US	

GROWTH PLANS/SPECIAL FEATURES:

The Cleveland Cavaliers entered the National Basketball Association (NBA) in 1970. Although the team has yet to win a championship, the arrival of Lebron James in 2003 significantly improved franchise records by earning the Cavaliers a seat in the NBA playoffs in both the 2006 and 2007 seasons. In the 2008-09 seasons, the team obtained a record of 66-15. All Cavaliers home games are played in the Quicken Loans Arena, which hosts a 20,500 seating capacity and state-of-the-art technologies such as Q-TUBE, a 28-foot high LED scoreboard; SMARTVISION screens, which display real time statistics and animated graphics; and 562 television monitors throughout the concourse area, which display the game or entertainment in progress for the benefit of those temporarily away from their seats. The arena houses a full-service production facility that includes an on-line production suite, master control, TV and radio studios for video, matrix, lighting, audio services and broadcasting coordination. The Cavaliers have also participated in community outreach programs such as Read To Achieve program, All-Star Kids, Head of the Class, Shoot 4 The Moon Foundation and King for Kids Bike-A-Thon. Camps and programs offered in partnership with the National Basketball Academy include the Cavaliers Youth Hoops Program, which provides clinics, leagues and individualized training. Former Cavaliers Wayne Embry and Lenny Wilkens have both earned spots in the Basketball Hall of Fame. The team's web site offers Cavalier podcasts, archived Call of the Game recordings by Cavaliers radio announcer Joe Tait, and a forum and message board for fans. Forbes recently estimated the team to be worth approximately $477 million. In the 2008-09 season, the team's home attendance average was roughly 20,000 per game.

FINANCIALS: **Sales and profits are in thousands of dollars—add 000 to get the full amount. 2008 Note: Financial information for 2008 was not available for all companies at press time.**

2008 Sales: $159,000	2008 Profits: $13,100
2007 Sales: $152,000	2007 Profits: $31,900
2006 Sales: $115,000	2006 Profits: $23,900
2005 Sales: $102,000	2005 Profits: $
2004 Sales: $93,000	2004 Profits: $

U.S. Stock Ticker: Private
Int'l Ticker: Int'l Exchange:
Employees:
Fiscal Year Ends: 10/31
Parent Company: CAVALIERS OPERATING COMPANY LLC

SALARIES/BENEFITS:

Pension Plan:	ESOP Stock Plan:	Profit Sharing:	Top Exec. Salary: $	Bonus: $
Savings Plan:	Stock Purch. Plan:		Second Exec. Salary: $	Bonus: $

OTHER THOUGHTS:

Apparent Women Officers or Directors:
Hot Spot for Advancement for Women/Minorities:

LOCATIONS: ("Y" = Yes)

West:	Southwest:	Midwest:	Southeast:	Northeast:	International:
		Y			

CLEVELAND INDIANS

www.indians.com

Industry Group Code: 711211A **Ranks within this company's industry group:** Sales: 16 Profits: 14

Sports:		Services:		Media:		Sales:		Facilities:		Other:	
Leagues/Associations:		Food & Beverage:		TV:		Marketing:		Stadiums:	Y	Gambling:	
Teams:	Y	Agents:		Radio:		Ads:		Fitness Clubs:		Apparel:	
Nonprofits:		Other:		Internet:		Tickets:	Y	Golf Courses:		Equipment:	
Other:				Print:		Retail:	Y	Ski Resorts:		Shoes:	
				Software:		Other:		Other:		Other:	

TYPES OF BUSINESS:

Professional Baseball Team
Stadium Operation

BRANDS/DIVISIONS/AFFILIATES:

Cleveland Indians Baseball Company, Inc.
Jacobs Field
Delaware North Companies
Buffalo Bisons
Akron Aeros
Kinston Indians
Mahoning Valley Scrappers
Lake County Captains

CONTACTS:

Note: Officers with more than one job title may be intentionally listed here more than once.

Lawrence J. Dolan, CEO
Paul J. Dolan, Pres.
Ken Stefanov, CFO/Sr. VP-Finance
Victor Gregovits, Sr. VP-Mktg. & Sales
Sara Lehrke, Sr. Dir.-Human Resources & Benefits
Keith Woolner, Mgr.-Baseball Research & Analytics
Dave Powell, Dir.-Info. Systems
Kurt Schloss, Sr. Dir.-Merch.
Jim Folk, VP-Ballpark Oper.
Joe Znidarsic, General Counsel/VP
Chris Antonetti, VP-Baseball Oper.
Dennis Lehman, Exec. VP-Bus.
Bob DiBiasio, VP-Public Rel.
Sarah Taylor, Controller
Mark Shapiro, Exec. VP/Gen. Mgr.
Dan Smith, VP-Food & Beverage
Steve Lubratich, Dir.-Player Personnel
Sanaa Julien, Dir.-Mktg.
Lino Diaz, Dir.-Latin American Oper.

Phone: 216-420-4636	**Fax:** 216-420-4430
Toll-Free:	
Address: Jacobs Field, 2401 Ontario St., Cleveland, OH 44115-4003 US	

GROWTH PLANS/SPECIAL FEATURES:

The Cleveland Indians are a professional baseball franchise playing in the Central Division of the American League in Major League Baseball (MLB), along with the Chicago White Sox, Detroit Tigers, Kansas City Royals and Minnesota Twins. The team began as an American League (AL) franchise in 1901. Cleveland has been home to professional baseball since 1869, when they were the Cleveland Forest Citys. The team has also been called the Spiders (led by pitching legend Cy Young), Blues, Broncos and Naps (named for early star Napoleon Lajoie). The team became the Indians after Lajoie's departure following the 1914 season. The franchise was one of the first to play with an integrated team. Before current owner Lawrence Dolan bought the team in 2000 from Richard Jacobs, the Indians were the first publicly traded team in Major League Baseball. The Indians have made it to postseason play nine times, six times since 1995, including a run of five consecutive appearances from 1995-99. The team has played in five World Series, winning two (1920 and 1948). In the 2001 off-season, John Hart resigned as general manager and his assistant Mark Shapiro took over. Shapiro began a process of rebuilding, characterized by his trade of star pitching ace and fan-favorite Bartolo Colon for Brandon Phillips, Cliff Lee and Grady Sizemore, three players who would be huge factors in later years. The team's first winning season since 2001 was 2005, and they made it to the playoffs in 2007, despite a low-ranking payroll of just $61.7 million. The Indians' home field is Progressive Field in downtown Cleveland. In the 2008 season, the team averaged approximately 27,100 fans in attendance per game. A recent Forbes estimate values the team at $399 million.

FINANCIALS:

Sales and profits are in thousands of dollars—add 000 to get the full amount. 2008 Note: Financial information for 2008 was not available for all companies at press time.

2008 Sales: $181,000	2008 Profits: $19,500	**U.S. Stock Ticker: Subsidiary**
2007 Sales: $181,000	2007 Profits: $29,200	**Int'l Ticker:** Int'l Exchange:
2006 Sales: $158,000	2006 Profits: $24,900	Employees:
2005 Sales: $150,000	2005 Profits: $	Fiscal Year Ends: 12/31
2004 Sales: $	2004 Profits: $	Parent Company: CLEVELAND INDIANS BASEBALL COMPANY INC

SALARIES/BENEFITS:

Pension Plan:	ESOP Stock Plan:	Profit Sharing:	Top Exec. Salary: $	Bonus: $
Savings Plan:	Stock Purch. Plan:		Second Exec. Salary: $	Bonus: $

OTHER THOUGHTS:

Apparent Women Officers or Directors: 4
Hot Spot for Advancement for Women/Minorities: Y

LOCATIONS: ("Y" = Yes)

West:	Southwest:	Midwest:	Southeast:	Northeast:	International:
		Y			Y

Note: Financial information, benefits and other data can change quickly and may vary from those stated here.

CLUB DEPORTIVO CHIVAS USA

chivas.usa.mlsnet.com

Industry Group Code: 711211D **Ranks within this company's industry group:** Sales: Profits:

Sports:		Services:		Media:		Sales:		Facilities:		Other:	
Leagues/Associations:		Food & Beverage:		TV:		Marketing:		Stadiums:		Gambling:	
Teams:	Y	Agents:		Radio:		Ads:		Fitness Clubs:		Apparel:	
Nonprofits:	Y	Other:		Internet:		Tickets:	Y	Golf Courses:		Equipment:	
Other:				Print:		Retail:		Ski Resorts:		Shoes:	
				Software:		Other:		Other:		Other:	

TYPES OF BUSINESS:

Soccer Team

BRANDS/DIVISIONS/AFFILIATES:

Home Depot Center
Club Deportivo Guadalajara
Fundacion Chivas de Corazon

CONTACTS: *Note: Officers with more than one job title may be intentionally listed here more than once.*

Shawn Hunter, CEO/Pres.
Antonio Cue, Pres.
Brandon Raphael, Dir.-Sales
Cynthia Craig, Mgr.-Human Resources
Cedric Foster, Mgr.-Info. Svcs.
Darren McCartney, Dir.-Oper.
Francisco Suinaga, Dir.-Bus. Dev.
Keegan Pierce, Dir.-Comm..
Juan Ceballos, Mgr.-Acct.
Preki Radosavljevic, Head Coach
Veronica Ramirez, Sr. Mgr.-Ticket Oper.
Stephen Hamilton, VP-Soccer Oper.
Alex Gallegos, Dir.-Mktg.

Phone: 310-630-4550	**Fax:** 310-630-4551
Toll-Free: 877-244-8271	
Address: 18400 Avalon Blvd., Ste. 500, Carson, CA 90746 US	

GROWTH PLANS/SPECIAL FEATURES:

Club Deportivo Chivas USA, also known as the CD Chivas USA, is a Major League Soccer (MLS) club founded in 2004 and based in Carson, California. The team takes its origins from a long-standing Guadalajara-based club that plays in the Mexican soccer league named Club Deportivo Guadalajara. The home of CD Chivas USA is the 27,000-seat Home Depot Center in Carson, California. The team's management seeks to build a Hispanic fan base by means of bilingual staffing and media relations, maintaining a sense of the club's Mexican roots and cultivating the image of a team with an authentic Central/South American flavor. The club also manages the Fundacion Chivas de Corazon, a nonprofit organization devoted to creating and supporting programs and events that advance educational and recreational opportunities for southern California's youth. Noteworthy former players include midfielder Ramon Ramirez, forward Ante Razov and defender Claudio Suarez. The team has a multitude of sponsors such as Honda; Marriott Torrance South Bay; Corona Extra; Adidas; Disneyland; and the Home Depot, just to name a few. In 2008, the Chivas finished second in the Western Conference, which qualified the team for the playoffs for the third year in a row. Also in 2008, midfielder Sacha Kljestan was honored by being named MLS Best XI, as well as being named U.S. Soccer Young Male Athlete of the Year. Additionally, in 2008 the team introduced two community initiatives: Kick-it at the Park L.A. with Chivas USA, a series of soccer clinics within the Los Angeles County area; and Practice in the Community, a series of team practices held in various locations throughout the community.

FINANCIALS: **Sales and profits are in thousands of dollars—add 000 to get the full amount. 2008 Note: Financial information for 2008 was not available for all companies at press time.**

2008 Sales: $	2008 Profits: $	**U.S. Stock Ticker: Private**
2007 Sales: $	2007 Profits: $	**Int'l Ticker:** Int'l Exchange:
2006 Sales: $	2006 Profits: $	Employees:
2005 Sales: $	2005 Profits: $	Fiscal Year Ends:
2004 Sales: $	2004 Profits: $	Parent Company:

SALARIES/BENEFITS:

Pension Plan:	ESOP Stock Plan:	Profit Sharing:	Top Exec. Salary: $	Bonus: $
Savings Plan:	Stock Purch. Plan:		Second Exec. Salary: $	Bonus: $

OTHER THOUGHTS:

Apparent Women Officers or Directors: 20
Hot Spot for Advancement for Women/Minorities: Y

LOCATIONS: ("Y" = Yes)

West:	Southwest:	Midwest:	Southeast:	Northeast:	International:
Y					

CLUBCORP INC

www.clubcorp.com

Industry Group Code: 713910 **Ranks within this company's industry group:** Sales: 1 Profits:

Sports:		Services:		Media:		Sales:		Facilities:		Other:	
Leagues/Associations:		Food & Beverage:		TV:		Marketing:		Stadiums:		Gambling:	
Teams:		Agents:		Radio:		Ads:		Fitness Clubs:		Apparel:	
Nonprofits:		Other:		Internet:		Tickets:		Golf Courses:	Y	Equipment:	
Other:				Print:		Retail:		Ski Resorts:		Shoes:	
				Software:		Other:		Other:	Y	Other:	

TYPES OF BUSINESS:

Golf Courses & Country Clubs
Business/Sports Clubs
Resorts

BRANDS/DIVISIONS/AFFILIATES:

KSL Capital LLC
Firestone Country Club
Metropolitan Club
Homestead (The)
Boston College Club
Seville Golf and Country Club
Private Clubs
Tower Club

CONTACTS: *Note: Officers with more than one job title may be intentionally listed here more than once.*

Eric L. Affeldt, CEO
Eric L. Affeldt, Pres.
Curt McClellan, CFO
Jamie Walters, Exec. VP-Sales & Mktg.
Ingrid Keiser, Exec. VP-People Strategy
Daniel T. Tilley, CIO/Exec. VP
Ingrid Keiser, Chief Legal Officer/Corp. Sec.
Mark Murphy, Sr. VP-Strategic Alliances
Mark Burnett, Exec. VP-Golf & Country Club Div.
Mark Murphy, Sr. VP-Global Sales
David B. Woodyard, Exec. VP-New Bus. Dev.
John H. Longstreet, Exec. VP-Oper., ClubCorp USA Inc.
William T. Walden, Sr. VP-Purchasing

Phone: 972-243-6191 **Fax:** 972-406-7856
Toll-Free:
Address: 3030 LBJ Freeway, Ste. 600, Dallas, TX 75234 US

GROWTH PLANS/SPECIAL FEATURES:

ClubCorp, Inc. is an owner and operator of nearly 160 golf courses, country clubs, private clubs, golf resorts and resorts in the U.S., with additional operations in Australia, Europe and Asia. The company has approximately 175,000 memberships and 170 operations in 26 states and the District of Columbia, as well as internationally, including 74 private country clubs, eight semi-private golf clubs, eight public golf facilities, six resorts (including Firestone Country Club, the Homestead and Barton Creek Resort and Spa), four international clubs and more than 60 business/sports clubs (including 35 business clubs, 10 business/sports clubs and three sports clubs). The firm's operations include nationally recognized golf courses and country clubs such as the Firestone Country Club in Akron, Ohio; The Homestead in Hot Springs, Virginia, the oldest resort in America; and the Mission Hills Country Club in Rancho Mirage, California. Additionally, the company's business and sports clubs can be found in major metropolitan areas, including the Boston College Club; City Club on Bunker Hill in Los Angeles; Citrus Club in Orlando, Florida; Columbia Tower Club in Seattle; Metropolitan Club in Chicago; Tower Club in Dallas; and the City Club of Washington, D.C. Some of the company's unique programs include Ace Adventures, a golf tournament vacation package; Club Tournaments 101, a series of complimentary tournament education classes; and Signature Gold, a benefit program offering complimentary golf and dining, discounts and VIP services to members. ClubCorp maintains partnerships with Acura, E-Z-Go/Textron, Titleist and ESPN, among others. The firm is owned by Denver-based KSL Capital, a private-equity investor. In January 2008, ClubCorp acquired Seville Golf and Country Club in Gilbert, Arizona, from Shea Homes. In August 2008, the firm announced the relaunch of Private Clubs, its luxury lifestyle magazine. In January 2009, Tower Club, a ClubCorp property, completed its $3.8 million renovation project.

FINANCIALS: **Sales and profits are in thousands of dollars—add 000 to get the full amount. 2008 Note: Financial information for 2008 was not available for all companies at press time.**

2008 Sales: $1,000,000	2008 Profits: $	**U.S. Stock Ticker: Private**
2007 Sales: $1,000,000	2007 Profits: $	**Int'l Ticker:** Int'l Exchange:
2006 Sales: $1,020,000	2006 Profits: $	Employees: 16,000
2005 Sales: $1,028,088	2005 Profits: $70,754	Fiscal Year Ends: 12/31
2004 Sales: $938,802	2004 Profits: $-6,242	Parent Company:

SALARIES/BENEFITS:

Pension Plan:	ESOP Stock Plan:	Profit Sharing:	Top Exec. Salary: $500,000	Bonus: $281,250
Savings Plan:	Stock Purch. Plan:		Second Exec. Salary: $500,000	Bonus: $235,000

OTHER THOUGHTS:

Apparent Women Officers or Directors: 1
Hot Spot for Advancement for Women/Minorities: Y

LOCATIONS: ("Y" = Yes)

West:	Southwest:	Midwest:	Southeast:	Northeast:	International:
Y	Y	Y	Y	Y	Y

COLEMAN COMPANY INC (THE)

www.coleman.com

Industry Group Code: 339920 **Ranks within this company's industry group:** Sales: Profits:

Sports:		Services:		Media:		Sales:		Facilities:		Other:	
Leagues/Associations:		Food & Beverage:		TV:		Marketing:		Stadiums:		Gambling:	
Teams:		Agents:		Radio:		Ads:		Fitness Clubs:		Apparel:	
Nonprofits:		Other:		Internet:		Tickets:		Golf Courses:		Equipment:	Y
Other:				Print:		Retail:	Y	Ski Resorts:		Shoes:	
				Software:		Other:		Other:		Other:	

TYPES OF BUSINESS:

Camping Equipment
Outdoor Cookware
Lanterns

BRANDS/DIVISIONS/AFFILIATES:

Jarden Corporation
Exponent
Campingaz
Stearns
Sevylor
Sospenders
Hodgman
Get Out More Tour

CONTACTS:

Note: Officers with more than one job title may be intentionally listed here more than once.

Sam A. Solomon, CEO
Sam A. Solomon, Pres.
Daniel J. Hogan, CFO
Jeff Willard, Sr. VP-Mktg.
Jeff Willard, Sr. VP-Prod. Dev.
Scott Henrikson, Sr. VP-Sales
Pat Barnett, Sr. VP-Global Prod. Mgmt.
Bob Fowler, Sr. VP-Supply Chain

Phone: 316-832-2700 **Fax:** 316-832-3060
Toll-Free: 800-835-3278
Address: 3600 N. Hydraulic, Wichita, KS 67219 US

GROWTH PLANS/SPECIAL FEATURES:

The Coleman Company, Inc., a subsidiary of Jarden Corporation, manufactures and markets equipment for outdoor use. Founded in 1900, the firm is based in Wichita, Kansas and operates 13 factory outlet stores in Alabama, Colorado, Georgia, Michigan, Missouri, New Mexico, New York, South Carolina, Tennessee and Texas. Coleman has international operations in Canada, Mexico, Venezuela, Australia, Japan and Europe. The firm's products include lanterns, stoves, coolers, tents, sleeping bags, airbeds, backpacks, outdoor furniture and grills. Its products are sold under the Coleman, Exponent and Campingaz brands. Under the Stearns, Sevylor, Sospenders, Hodgman, Nevin, Helium and Mad Dog Gear brands, Coleman additionally markets flotation devices; towables; rainwear; waders; hunting and fishing gear; and safety and survival equipment. Coleman sells its products online, through its factory outlet stores and through independent retailers such as Wal-Mart, Target and Home Depot. The company offers its clients free advice on topics such as selecting the correct gear for their needs, gear care and repair, packing and preparing for a trip and locating outdoor recreation areas. The firm also sponsors the Get Out More Tour, which features outdoor enthusiasts who tour the country, sharing their love and knowledge of the outdoors.

Coleman offers its employees tuition reimbursement, product discounts, flexible spending accounts and medical, vision, dental, life and disability insurance.

FINANCIALS:

Sales and profits are in thousands of dollars—add 000 to get the full amount. 2008 Note: Financial information for 2008 was not available for all companies at press time.

2008 Sales: $ 2008 Profits: $
2007 Sales: $ 2007 Profits: $
2006 Sales: $ 2006 Profits: $
2005 Sales: $ 2005 Profits: $
2004 Sales: $ 2004 Profits: $

U.S. Stock Ticker: Subsidiary
Int'l Ticker: Int'l Exchange:
Employees: 2,000
Fiscal Year Ends: 12/31
Parent Company: JARDEN CORPORATION

SALARIES/BENEFITS:

Pension Plan: ESOP Stock Plan: Profit Sharing: Top Exec. Salary: $ Bonus: $
Savings Plan: Y Stock Purch. Plan: Y Second Exec. Salary: $ Bonus: $

OTHER THOUGHTS:

Apparent Women Officers or Directors:
Hot Spot for Advancement for Women/Minorities:

LOCATIONS: ("Y" = Yes)

West:	Southwest:	Midwest:	Southeast:	Northeast:	International:
Y	Y	Y	Y	Y	Y

COLORADO AVALANCHE

www.coloradoavalanche.com

Industry Group Code: 711211F **Ranks within this company's industry group:** Sales: 13 Profits: 12

Sports:		Services:		Media:		Sales:		Facilities:		Other:	
Leagues/Associations:		Food & Beverage:		TV:		Marketing:		Stadiums:	Y	Gambling:	
Teams:	Y	Agents:		Radio:		Ads:		Fitness Clubs:		Apparel:	
Nonprofits:		Other:		Internet:		Tickets:	Y	Golf Courses:		Equipment:	
Other:				Print:		Retail:		Ski Resorts:		Shoes:	
				Software:		Other:		Other:		Other:	

TYPES OF BUSINESS:

Professional Hockey Team
Ticket Sales

BRANDS/DIVISIONS/AFFILIATES:

Kroenke Sports Enterprises, LLC
Pepsi Center
Hockey Fights Cancer
Read Team
Av for a Day
Break the Ice
Art of Sport (The)
Team Fit

CONTACTS: *Note: Officers with more than one job title may be intentionally listed here more than once.*

Pierre Lacroix, Pres.
Brad Smith, Dir.-Player Personnel
Jean Martineau, Sr. VP-Bus. Oper.
Jean Martineau, Sr. VP-Comm.
Tony Granato, Head Coach
Craig Billington, Dir.-Player Dev.
E. Stanely Kroenke, Owner
Charlotte Grahame, Exec. Dir.-Hockey Admin.

Phone: 303-405-1100	Fax:
Toll-Free:	
Address: 1000 Chopper Cir., Denver, CO 80204 US	

GROWTH PLANS/SPECIAL FEATURES:

The Colorado Avalanche is a National Hockey League (NHL) hockey team owned by Kroenke Sports Enterprises (KSE) and based in Denver, Colorado. The Avalanche plays in the Northwest Division of the NHL's Western Conference, along with the Calgary Flames, Edmonton Oilers, Minnesota Wild and Vancouver Canucks. The team originally played as the Quebec Nordiques before it was sold and moved to Denver in 1995. The Avalanche is based at the KSE-owned, 670,000-square-foot Pepsi Center in Denver. The stadium seats over 18,000 and features three restaurants, a business center, a retail store, a full-size basketball practice facility and 95 luxury suites. Pepsi Center is also home to three other teams owned by KSE: the National Basketball Association (NBA) Denver Nuggets, the National Lacrosse League (NLL) Colorado Mammoth and the Arena Football League (AFL) Colorado Crush. The Avalanche frequently sells out its home games and has won two Stanley Cup championships, once in 1996 and again in 2001. In 1996, Avalanche was the first Colorado sports franchise to ever win a championship. The team has retired the jersey number of its legendary goalie, Patrick Roy, who played with the team from its inception until 2003. The Avalanche is affiliated with the Lowell Lock Monsters, an American Hockey League (AHL) franchise, and the Johnston Chiefs, an Eastern Collegiate Hockey League (ECHL) team. According to a recent Forbes estimate, the team is worth approximately $231 million. Average home game attendance in the 2008-09 season was 15,429.

FINANCIALS: **Sales and profits are in thousands of dollars—add 000 to get the full amount. 2008 Note: Financial information for 2008 was not available for all companies at press time.**

2008 Sales: $91,000	2008 Profits: $2,300
2007 Sales: $79,000	2007 Profits: $6,600
2006 Sales: $81,000	2006 Profits: $5,900
2005 Sales: $	2005 Profits: $
2004 Sales: $99,000	2004 Profits: $

U.S. Stock Ticker: Subsidiary
Int'l Ticker: Int'l Exchange:
Employees:
Fiscal Year Ends: 6/30
Parent Company: KROENKE SPORTS ENTERPRISES LLC

SALARIES/BENEFITS:

Pension Plan:	ESOP Stock Plan:	Profit Sharing:	Top Exec. Salary: $	Bonus: $
Savings Plan:	Stock Purch. Plan:		Second Exec. Salary: $	Bonus: $

OTHER THOUGHTS:

Apparent Women Officers or Directors: 1
Hot Spot for Advancement for Women/Minorities:

LOCATIONS: ("Y" = Yes)

West:	Southwest:	Midwest:	Southeast:	Northeast:	International:
Y					

Note: Financial information, benefits and other data can change quickly and may vary from those stated here.

COLORADO RAPIDS

www.coloradorapids.com

Industry Group Code: 711211D **Ranks within this company's industry group:** Sales: Profits:

Sports:		Services:		Media:		Sales:		Facilities:		Other:	
Leagues/Associations:		Food & Beverage:		TV:		Marketing:		Stadiums:	Y	Gambling:	
Teams:	Y	Agents:		Radio:		Ads:		Fitness Clubs:		Apparel:	
Nonprofits:		Other:		Internet:		Tickets:	Y	Golf Courses:		Equipment:	
Other:				Print:		Retail:		Ski Resorts:		Shoes:	
				Software:		Other:		Other:		Other:	

TYPES OF BUSINESS:

Major League Soccer Team
Ticket Sales

BRANDS/DIVISIONS/AFFILIATES:

Kroenke Sports Enterprises, LLC
Dick's Sporting Goods Park

CONTACTS:

Note: Officers with more than one job title may be intentionally listed here more than once.

Jeff Plush, Managing Dir.
Kieran Cain, Sr. Dir.-Mktg. & Entertainment
Jeff Mathews, Dir.-Oper.
Michael Benson, Sr. VP-Bus. Affairs/Treas.
Jason Gilham, Dir.-Media Rel.
Charlie Wright, VP-Finance
E. Stanley Kroenke, Owner
Shawn Martinez, Dir.-Game Entertainment
Erik Carlson, Team Admin.
Ken Blasi, Dir.-Corp. Sponsorship

Phone: 303-727-3500	**Fax:** 303-727-3536
Toll-Free:	
Address: Dick's Sporting Goods Park, 6000 Victory Way, Commerce City, CO 80022 US	

GROWTH PLANS/SPECIAL FEATURES:

The Colorado Rapids, incorporated in 1995, are a professional soccer team playing in Major League Soccer (MLS) and based in Denver, Colorado. The team plays at Dick's Sporting Goods Park, a new soccer-specific stadium located in Commerce City, Colorado. The 20,000-seat soccer-specific stadium includes youth soccer fields, retail areas and a new civic center. The stadium is not only the home to the Colorado Rapids but also hosts concerts and other events. E. Stanley Kroenke owns the Rapids through his management team, Kroenke Sports Enterprises, LLC (KSE). He also owns the Colorado Avalanche of the National Hockey League (NHL), the Denver Nuggets of the National Basketball Association (NBA), the Colorado Crush of the Arena Football League, the Colorado Mammoth of the National Lacrosse League and the Pepsi Center arena and entertainment center in Colorado; he is also a partial owner of the St. Louis Rams. In recent years, the average attendance per regular season match was over 13,600, and in the 2006 post season the team averaged attendance of over 4,000. The team plays in the MLS's Western Conference, along with Chivas USA, the Houston Dynamo, FC Dallas, Los Angeles Galaxy, Seattle Sounders FC and Real Salt Lake. Past championship appearances of the club include the 1997 MLS Cup and the 1999 U.S. Open Cup, both times coming in runner-up; and the 2005 and 2006 Rocky Mountain Cup, in which the club placed first. In April 2008, KSE intensified its commercial relationship with popular English Premier League football club, Arsenal. The new agreement includes building the Arsenal Centre of Excellence at Dick's Sporting Goods Park; having KSE's TV sports channel, Altitude Sports & Entertainment, broadcast Arsenal-related content; and having some of Arsenal's coaching resources oversee Rapids' performances. Notable players have included Marcelo Balboa, Paul Bravo and Chris Henderson.

FINANCIALS:

Sales and profits are in thousands of dollars—add 000 to get the full amount. 2008 Note: Financial information for 2008 was not available for all companies at press time.

2008 Sales: $	2008 Profits: $	**U.S. Stock Ticker: Subsidiary**
2007 Sales: $	2007 Profits: $	**Int'l Ticker:** Int'l Exchange:
2006 Sales: $	2006 Profits: $	Employees:
2005 Sales: $	2005 Profits: $	Fiscal Year Ends:
2004 Sales: $	2004 Profits: $	Parent Company: KROENKE SPORTS ENTERPRISES LLC

SALARIES/BENEFITS:

Pension Plan:	ESOP Stock Plan:	Profit Sharing:	Top Exec. Salary: $	Bonus: $
Savings Plan:	Stock Purch. Plan:		Second Exec. Salary: $	Bonus: $

OTHER THOUGHTS:

Apparent Women Officers or Directors: 6
Hot Spot for Advancement for Women/Minorities: Y

LOCATIONS: ("Y" = Yes)

West:	Southwest:	Midwest:	Southeast:	Northeast:	International:
Y					

COLORADO ROCKIES

colorado.rockies.mlb.com

Industry Group Code: 711211A **Ranks within this company's industry group:** Sales: 17 Profits: 10

Sports:		Services:		Media:		Sales:		Facilities:		Other:	
Leagues/Associations:		Food & Beverage:		TV:		Marketing:		Stadiums:	Y	Gambling:	
Teams:	Y	Agents:		Radio:		Ads:		Fitness Clubs:		Apparel:	
Nonprofits:		Other:		Internet:		Tickets:	Y	Golf Courses:		Equipment:	
Other:				Print:		Retail:	Y	Ski Resorts:		Shoes:	
				Software:		Other:		Other:		Other:	

TYPES OF BUSINESS:

Professional Baseball Team
Retail Stores- Rockies Merchandise

BRANDS/DIVISIONS/AFFILIATES:

Colorado Rockies Baseball Club, Ltd.
Coors Field
Colorado Springs Sky Sox
Tulsa Drillers
Modesto Nuts
Asheville Tourists
Tri-City Dust Devils
Casper Ghosts

CONTACTS:

Note: Officers with more than one job title may be intentionally listed here more than once.

Charles K. Monfort, CEO
Keli S. McGregor, Pres.
Harold R. Roth, CFO/Sr. VP
Marcy English Glasser, Sr. Dir.-Corp. Sales
Elizabeth E. Stecklein, VP-Human Resources
Bill Stephani, Dir.-Info. Systems
Aaron Heinrich, Dir.-Retail Oper.
Jim Wiener, Sr. Dir.-Eng. & Facilities
Dave Moore, Dir.-Coors Field Admin. & Dev.
Harold R. Roth, General Counsel
William P. Geivett, Asst. Gen. Mgr./VP-Baseball Oper.
Gregory D. Feasel, Sr. VP-Bus. Oper.
Jay E. Alves, VP-Comm. & Public Rel.
Michael J. Kent, VP-Finance
Daniel J. O'Dowd, Exec. VP/Gen. Mgr.
Kevin H. Kahn, Chief Customer Officer/VP-Ballpark Oper.
James P. Kellogg, VP-Community & Retail Oper.
Sue Ann McClaren, VP-Ticket Sales, Oper. & Svcs.
Charles K. Monfort, Chmn.
Gary Lawrence, Sr. Dir.-Purchasing

Phone: 303-292-0200	**Fax:** 303-312-2116
Toll-Free: 800-388-7625	
Address: 2001 Blake St., Denver, CO 80205-2000 US	

GROWTH PLANS/SPECIAL FEATURES:

The Colorado Rockies are a Major League Baseball (MLB) team that is owned and managed by Colorado Rockies Baseball Club, Ltd., a diverse ownership group. The team plays in the West Division of the National League, alongside the Arizona Diamondbacks, the Los Angeles Dodgers, the San Diego Padres and the San Francisco Giants. Launched in 1993 as an expansion franchise, the team plays at Coors Field in Denver, Colorado, which is the highest altitude stadium in the major leagues. Charles and Richard Monfort have majority ownership of the club; other partial owners include Linda G. Alvarado of Alvarado Construction; Peter Coors of Coors Brewing Co.; Marne Obernauer Sr. of Beverage Distributors Corp.; Clear Channel Communications; Denver Newspaper Agency; and FOX. Throughout the 1990s, the Rockies set attendance records within the National League, with its 1993 season record of 4,483,350 currently remaining the highest in the history of Major League Baseball. Before 2007, the team had only reached the postseason once in its existence, in 1995. Some analysts have speculated that this is due to the disparity of playing in a high-altitude, offense-friendly stadium, where pitches do not break as much, outfielders have more ground to cover, and the ball travels further. Since 2002, the team has stored game baseballs in a humidor; consequently, offense has gone down. The franchise is known for spending a lower proportion of team revenues on player payroll than all but one other organization. The team is worth $373 million, according to a recent Forbes estimate. Average home game attendance in 2008 was approximately 33,100.

FINANCIALS:

Sales and profits are in thousands of dollars—add 000 to get the full amount. 2008 Note: Financial information for 2008 was not available for all companies at press time.

2008 Sales: $178,000	2008 Profits: $24,500	**U.S. Stock Ticker: Subsidiary**
2007 Sales: $169,000	2007 Profits: $26,200	**Int'l Ticker:** Int'l Exchange:
2006 Sales: $151,000	2006 Profits: $23,900	Employees:
2005 Sales: $145,000	2005 Profits: $	Fiscal Year Ends: 12/31
2004 Sales: $	2004 Profits: $	Parent Company: COLORADO ROCKIES BASEBALL CLUB LTD

SALARIES/BENEFITS:

Pension Plan:	ESOP Stock Plan:	Profit Sharing:	Top Exec. Salary: $	Bonus: $
Savings Plan:	Stock Purch. Plan:		Second Exec. Salary: $	Bonus: $

OTHER THOUGHTS:

Apparent Women Officers or Directors: 4
Hot Spot for Advancement for Women/Minorities: Y

LOCATIONS: ("Y" = Yes)

West:	Southwest:	Midwest:	Southeast:	Northeast:	International:
Y					Y

COLUMBIA SPORTSWEAR CO

www.columbia.com

Industry Group Code: 315000A **Ranks within this company's industry group:** Sales: 2 Profits: 2

Sports:		Services:		Media:		Sales:		Facilities:		Other:	
Leagues/Associations:		Food & Beverage:		TV:		Marketing:		Stadiums:		Gambling:	
Teams:		Agents:		Radio:		Ads:		Fitness Clubs:		Apparel:	Y
Nonprofits:		Other:		Internet:		Tickets:		Golf Courses:		Equipment:	Y
Other:				Print:		Retail:	Y	Ski Resorts:		Shoes:	Y
				Software:		Other:		Other:		Other:	

TYPES OF BUSINESS:

Sportswear & Outdoor Apparel
Sports Accessories & Equipment
Footwear
Retail Sales
Bicycles

BRANDS/DIVISIONS/AFFILIATES:

Sorel
Mountain Hardwear, Inc.
Convert
Omni-Dry
Columbia Interchage System
PFG
Radial Sleeve
Montrail, Inc.

CONTACTS: *Note: Officers with more than one job title may be intentionally listed here more than once.*

Timothy Boyle, CEO
Bryan L. Timm, COO
Timothy Boyle, Pres.
Thomas B. Cusick, CFO
Michael W. McCormick, Exec. VP-Global Sales & Mktg.
Susan G. Popp, VP-Human Resources
Mark Nenow, VP-Global Footwear Merch.
Patrick J. Werner, VP-Global Apparel Mfg.
Peter J. Bragdon, General Counsel/Sec./VP
Thomas B. Cusick, VP-Finance
Daniel G. Hanson, VP-Mktg.
Kerry Barnes, VP-Retail
Mark N. Koppes, VP-Apparel
Mark J. Sandquist, VP-Global Apparel & Equipment
Gertrude Boyle, Chmn.
William Tung, VP-Latin America & Asia Pacific Sales

Phone: 503-985-4000	**Fax:** 503-985-5800
Toll-Free:	
Address: 14375 NW Science Park Dr., Portland, OR 97229-5418 US	

GROWTH PLANS/SPECIAL FEATURES:

Columbia Sportswear Co. is a global leader in the design, sourcing, marketing and distribution of active outdoor apparel and footwear, with operations in 90 countries across North America, Europe and Asia. The firm is one of the largest outerwear companies in the world and the leading seller of skiwear in the U.S. Columbia groups its products into four categories. Outerwear, its most established category, includes jackets and other accessories designed to protect the user from weather in everyday use and in outdoor activities including skiing, hiking, hunting and fishing. Sportswear includes fishing and hunting shirts, hiking shorts, fleece and pile products, sweaters, chinos, knit shirts, sweats and jeans. Footwear consists of seasonal outdoor footwear for adults and youth. Related accessories and equipment includes hats, caps, scarves, gloves and headbands, tents and sleeping systems. The firm licenses its brand name for products such as socks, packs and travel bags, leather goods, watches, cutlery and home furnishings. Columbia's brand names include the Columbia Interchange System, Convert, Omni-Dry, PFG, Radial Sleeve, Quadensity, Omni-Grip, Conduit, Montrai, Mountain Hardware, Pacific Trail, Sorel and Quantum. The company's products are sold in approximately 14,000 specialty and department stores throughout the world. In addition, the firm operates a flagship store in Portland, as well as 14 outlet stores located in North America. In June 2008, the company announced plans to open its first branded retail store in Seattle. In August of the same year, the firm partnered with Discovery Channel and will sponsor two Discovery Channel programs, Survivorman and Into the Unknown with Josh Bernstein.

Employees are offered medical, dental and vision insurance; a 401(k) plan; education assistance; life and disability coverage; personal choice spending accounts; an employee assistance plan; product discounts; mass transit subsidies; an on-site fitness center; and a discount stock purchase plan.

FINANCIALS: **Sales and profits are in thousands of dollars—add 000 to get the full amount. 2008 Note: Financial information for 2008 was not available for all companies at press time.**

2008 Sales: $1,317,835	2008 Profits: $95,047	**U.S. Stock Ticker: COLM**
2007 Sales: $1,356,039	2007 Profits: $144,452	**Int'l Ticker:** Int'l Exchange:
2006 Sales: $1,287,672	2006 Profits: $123,018	Employees: 3,163
2005 Sales: $1,155,791	2005 Profits: $130,736	Fiscal Year Ends: 12/31
2004 Sales: $1,095,307	2004 Profits: $138,624	Parent Company:

SALARIES/BENEFITS:

Pension Plan:	ESOP Stock Plan:	Profit Sharing:	Top Exec. Salary: $772,308	Bonus: $916,687
Savings Plan: Y	Stock Purch. Plan: Y		Second Exec. Salary: $759,231	Bonus: $326,930

OTHER THOUGHTS:

Apparent Women Officers or Directors: 3
Hot Spot for Advancement for Women/Minorities: Y

LOCATIONS: ("Y" = Yes)

West:	Southwest:	Midwest:	Southeast:	Northeast:	International:
Y					Y

COLUMBUS BLUE JACKETS

bluejackets.nhl.com

Industry Group Code: 711211F **Ranks within this company's industry group:** Sales: 26 Profits: 24

Sports:		Services:		Media:		Sales:		Facilities:		Other:	
Leagues/Associations:		Food & Beverage:		TV:		Marketing:		Stadiums:	Y	Gambling:	
Teams:	Y	Agents:		Radio:		Ads:		Fitness Clubs:		Apparel:	
Nonprofits:		Other:		Internet:		Tickets:	Y	Golf Courses:		Equipment:	
Other:				Print:		Retail:	Y	Ski Resorts:		Shoes:	
				Software:		Other:		Other:		Other:	

TYPES OF BUSINESS:

Professional Hockey Team

BRANDS/DIVISIONS/AFFILIATES:

JMAC, Inc.
Nationwide Arena
Dispatch Ice Haus
Columbus Blue Jackets Foundation
Championship Partners Club

CONTACTS: *Note: Officers with more than one job title may be intentionally listed here more than once.*

Scott Howson, Gen. Mgr.
Mike Priest, Pres./Alternate Governor
T. J. LaMendola, CFO
Marc Gregory, VP-Mktg.
Kelley Walton, Dir.-Human Resources
Greg Kirstein, General Counsel/Sr. VP
Larry Hoepfner, Sr. VP-Bus. Oper.
Cameron Scholvin, VP-Corp. Dev.
J. Ryan Mulcrone, Mgr.-Multimedia
Todd Shamrock, VP-Public Rel.
Jeremy Manly, Controller
John P. McConnell, Majority Owner/Governor
Ken Hitchcock, Head Coach
Jim Clark, Exec. VP/Assistant Gen. Mgr.
David Paitson, VP-Ticketing

Phone: 614-246-4625 **Fax:** 614-246-4007
Toll-Free:
Address: Nationwide Arena, 200 W. Nationwide Blvd., Columbus, OH 43215 US

GROWTH PLANS/SPECIAL FEATURES:

The Columbus Blue Jackets are a National Hockey League (NHL) team that entered the league as an expansion team in 2000. The Blue Jackets are owned by JMAC, Inc., which also owns Chiller LLC, operator of five Chiller Ice Skating Facilities in the greater Columbus area. The team plays in the Central Division along with Detroit, St. Louis, Nashville and Chicago. Its home arena is the Nationwide Arena, which is also home to Arena Football League's Columbus Destroyers, with seating capacity 18,500 for hockey games, 19,500 for basketball games and 20,000 for concerts. Nationwide boasts two 80-foot party suite towers, a 70-foot glass enclosed atrium and a 135-foot light tower. It is one of the only arenas in the NHL that has the ice rink used for practice, the Dispatch Ice Haus, attached to the arena in which the team plays its games. The Ice Haus also offers ice time for figure skating, youth hockey and public skating. Although the Syracuse Crunch, an American Hockey League (AHL) team playing out of Syracuse, New York, is the team's primary minor league affiliate, the Blue Jackets are also affiliated with ECHL team, the Dayton Bombers based in Dayton, Ohio. The Columbus Blue Jackets Foundation has a commitment to the educational, cultural, health and wellness needs of the people of central Ohio. The team has a Championship Partners Club currently including Anheuser-Busch, Bank One, General Motors, OhioHealth and Pepsi-Cola. The club provides the team with revenue, while the featured companies are given prime advertising visibility on television, radio, print or in-arena exposure. The team is majority-owned by John P. McConnell. In the 2008-09 season, the team averaged approximately 15,500 fans in attendance per game. A recent Forbes estimate values the team at $157 million.

FINANCIALS: **Sales and profits are in thousands of dollars—add 000 to get the full amount. 2008 Note: Financial information for 2008 was not available for all companies at press time.**

2008 Sales: $71,000	2008 Profits: $-7,100	**U.S. Stock Ticker: Private**
2007 Sales: $68,000	2007 Profits: $-7,500	**Int'l Ticker:** Int'l Exchange:
2006 Sales: $66,000	2006 Profits: $-4,000	Employees:
2005 Sales: $	2005 Profits: $	Fiscal Year Ends: 6/30
2004 Sales: $66,000	2004 Profits: $	Parent Company: JMAC INC

SALARIES/BENEFITS:

Pension Plan:	ESOP Stock Plan:	Profit Sharing:	Top Exec. Salary: $	Bonus: $
Savings Plan:	Stock Purch. Plan:		Second Exec. Salary: $	Bonus: $

OTHER THOUGHTS:

Apparent Women Officers or Directors: 5
Hot Spot for Advancement for Women/Minorities: Y

LOCATIONS: ("Y" = Yes)

West:	Southwest:	Midwest:	Southeast:	Northeast:	International:
		Y			

COLUMBUS CREW

columbus.crew.mlsnet.com

Industry Group Code: 711211D **Ranks within this company's industry group:** Sales: Profits:

Sports:		**Services:**		**Media:**		**Sales:**		**Facilities:**		**Other:**	
Leagues/Associations:		Food & Beverage:		TV:		Marketing:		Stadiums:	Y	Gambling:	
Teams:	Y	Agents:		Radio:		Ads:		Fitness Clubs:		Apparel:	
Nonprofits:		Other:		Internet:		Tickets:	Y	Golf Courses:		Equipment:	
Other:				Print:		Retail:		Ski Resorts:		Shoes:	
				Software:		Other:		Other:		Other:	

TYPES OF BUSINESS:

Major League Soccer Team

BRANDS/DIVISIONS/AFFILIATES:

Columbus Crew Stadium

CONTACTS:

Note: Officers with more than one job title may be intentionally listed here more than once.

Chad Schroeder, VP-Corp. Sales & Broadcasting
Tom Patton, VP-Admin.
Scott DeBolt, VP-Oper.
Dave Stephany, Sr. Dir.-Comm. & Community Rel.
Tom Patton, VP-Finance
John Wagner, Pres., Hunt Sports
Tucker Walther, Team Mgr.
Robert Warzycha, Head Coach
Mark McCullers, Gen. Mgr.

Phone: 614-447-2739	**Fax:** 614-447-4109
Toll-Free:	
Address: 1 Black & Gold Blvd., Columbus, OH 43211 US	

GROWTH PLANS/SPECIAL FEATURES:

The Columbus Crew is a Major League Soccer (MLS) team that plays its home games at the 22,555-seat Columbus Crew Stadium in Ohio. The team's player foundation was laid in 1996 when it acquired collegiate All-American Brian McBride, international superstar Doctor Khumalo and Indiana University's Brian Maisonneuve. U.S. National team goalie Brad Friedel gave the team a boost, although he left to play in Europe in the late 90s. The Crew won the U.S. Open Cup Final, the oldest soccer tournament in the U.S., in 2002 with a win over the L.A. Galaxy. The team also won the MLS Supporters' Shield in 2004. In 2008, the team enjoyed average per-game attendance of approximately 14,200 spectators in the regular season. The Glidden Company is the team's shirt sponsor. In 2008, the Crew scored first place in the Eastern Conference and also won the 2008 MLS Cup, beating Red Bull New York by 3-1 and with a spectator count of 27,000.

FINANCIALS:

Sales and profits are in thousands of dollars—add 000 to get the full amount. 2008 Note: Financial information for 2008 was not available for all companies at press time.

2008 Sales: $	2008 Profits: $	**U.S. Stock Ticker: Private**
2007 Sales: $	2007 Profits: $	**Int'l Ticker:** Int'l Exchange:
2006 Sales: $	2006 Profits: $	Employees:
2005 Sales: $	2005 Profits: $	Fiscal Year Ends:
2004 Sales: $	2004 Profits: $	Parent Company:

SALARIES/BENEFITS:

Pension Plan:	ESOP Stock Plan:	Profit Sharing:	Top Exec. Salary: $	Bonus: $
Savings Plan:	Stock Purch. Plan:		Second Exec. Salary: $	Bonus: $

OTHER THOUGHTS:

Apparent Women Officers or Directors:
Hot Spot for Advancement for Women/Minorities:

LOCATIONS: ("Y" = Yes)

West:	Southwest:	Midwest:	Southeast:	Northeast:	International:
		Y			

COMCAST CORP

www.comcast.com

Industry Group Code: 513220 **Ranks within this company's industry group:** Sales: 2 Profits: 2

Sports:		Services:		Media:		Sales:		Facilities:		Other:	
Leagues/Associations:		Food & Beverage:		TV:	Y	Marketing:		Stadiums:		Gambling:	
Teams:	Y	Agents:		Radio:		Ads:	Y	Fitness Clubs:		Apparel:	
Nonprofits:		Other:		Internet:	Y	Tickets:		Golf Courses:		Equipment:	
Other:				Print:		Retail:		Ski Resorts:		Shoes:	
				Software:		Other:		Other:	Y	Other:	Y

TYPES OF BUSINESS:

Cable Television
VoIP Service
Cable Network Programming
High-Speed Internet Service
Video-on-Demand
Advertising Services
Interactive Program Schedules
Wireless Services

BRANDS/DIVISIONS/AFFILIATES:

Fandango Inc
Philadelphia Flyers
Philadelphia 76ers
Fandango Inc
E! Channel
Golf Channel (The)
Comcast Interactive Media
Clearwire Corporation

CONTACTS: *Note: Officers with more than one job title may be intentionally listed here more than once.*

Brian L. Roberts, CEO
Stephen B. Burke, COO
Michael J. Angelakis, CFO
Karen D. Buchholz, VP-Admin.
Arthur R. Block, General Counsel/Sr. VP/Corp. Sec.
Mark A. Coblitz, Sr. VP-Strategic Planning
D'Arcy F. Rudnay, Sr. VP-Corp. Comm.
Marlene S. Dooner, Sr. VP-Investor Rel.
Lawrence J. Salva, Chief Acct. Officer/Controller/Sr. VP
Stephen B. Burke, Pres., Comcast Cable Comm.
David L. Cohen, Exec. VP
Amy L. Banse, Sr. VP/Pres., Comcast Interactive Media
Robert S. Pick, Sr. VP-Corp. Dev.
Brian L. Roberts, Chmn.

Phone: 215-665-1700	**Fax:**
Toll-Free: 800-266-2278	
Address: 1 Comcast Ctr., Philadelphia, PA 19103 US	

GROWTH PLANS/SPECIAL FEATURES:

Comcast Corp. is one of the largest cable operators in the U.S. and offers a variety of entertainment, information and communications services to residential and commercial customers. The firm's cable systems serve roughly 24.2 million video subscribers, 14.9 million high-speed Internet subscribers and 6.5 million telephone subscribers and pass over 50.6 million homes in 39 states and Washington, D.C. The company operates in two segments, cable and programming. The cable segment, which generates approximately 95% of revenue, manages and operates the firm's cable systems, including video, high-speed Internet and phone services, as well as the regional sports networks. The programming segment consists primarily of consolidated national programming networks, including E!, The Golf Channel, VERSUS, G4 and Style. Comcast's other business interests include Comcast Spectacor and Comcast Interactive Media. Comcast Spectacor owns the Philadelphia Flyers, the Philadelphia 76ers and the Philadelphia Phantoms and two large, multipurpose arenas in Philadelphia, in addition to managing other facilities for sporting events, concerts and other events. Comcast Interactive Media develops and operates the company's Internet businesses focused on entertainment, information and communication, including comcast.net, Fancast, thePlatform, Fandango, Plaxo and DailyCandy. Recent acquisitions include cable systems serving Illinois and Indiana due to the dissolution of Insight Midwest, LP. In July 2008, the firm's cable division management structure was reorganized from five divisions to four. In December 2008, the company combined its WiMAX business with that of Sprint Nextel to create a 4G mobile Internet company. The joint venture will operate as Clearwire Corporation. In March 2009, the company and Sony Electronics, Inc. announced the opening of Sony Style Comcast Labs, a co-branded retail store in the Comcast Center.

The company offers its employees health and life insurance; disability benefits; an employee assistance program; adoption assistance; educational assistance; a 401(k) plan; and an employee stock purchase plan.

FINANCIALS: **Sales and profits are in thousands of dollars—add 000 to get the full amount. 2008 Note: Financial information for 2008 was not available for all companies at press time.**

2008 Sales: $34,256,000	2008 Profits: $2,547,000	**U.S. Stock Ticker: CMCSA**
2007 Sales: $30,895,000	2007 Profits: $2,587,000	**Int'l Ticker:** Int'l Exchange:
2006 Sales: $24,966,000	2006 Profits: $2,533,000	Employees: 100,000
2005 Sales: $23,556,000	2005 Profits: $928,000	Fiscal Year Ends: 12/31
2004 Sales: $20,307,000	2004 Profits: $970,000	Parent Company:

SALARIES/BENEFITS:

Pension Plan:	ESOP Stock Plan:	Profit Sharing:	Top Exec. Salary: $2,769,365	Bonus: $881,027
Savings Plan: Y	Stock Purch. Plan: Y		Second Exec. Salary: $2,218,117	Bonus: $5,922,372

OTHER THOUGHTS:

Apparent Women Officers or Directors: 6
Hot Spot for Advancement for Women/Minorities: Y

LOCATIONS: ("Y" = Yes)

West:	Southwest:	Midwest:	Southeast:	Northeast:	International:
Y	Y	Y	Y	Y	Y

CONNECTICUT SUN

www.wnba.com/sun

Industry Group Code: 711211E **Ranks within this company's industry group:** Sales: Profits:

Sports:		Services:		Media:		Sales:		Facilities:		Other:	
Leagues/Associations:		Food & Beverage:		TV:		Marketing:		Stadiums:	Y	Gambling:	Y
Teams:	Y	Agents:		Radio:		Ads:		Fitness Clubs:		Apparel:	
Nonprofits:		Other:		Internet:		Tickets:	Y	Golf Courses:		Equipment:	
Other:				Print:		Retail:		Ski Resorts:		Shoes:	
				Software:		Other:		Other:		Other:	

TYPES OF BUSINESS:

Women's Basketball Team

BRANDS/DIVISIONS/AFFILIATES:

Mohegan Tribal Gaming Authority
Mohegan Sun Casino
Mohegan Sun Arena
Solar Power Dance Team

CONTACTS: *Note: Officers with more than one job title may be intentionally listed here more than once.*

Mitchell Etess, CEO
Jeffrey Hartmann, COO
Paul Munick, Pres.
Gwendolyn Pointer, Dir.-Mktg.
Dave Martinelli, Dir.-Bus. Oper.
Bill Tavares, Mgr.-Media Rel.
Mike Thibault, Head Coach
Chris Sienko, Gen. Mgr.
Jenna Miller-Wassell, VP-Sponsorship Sales

Phone: 860-862-8000	**Fax:** 860-862-7824
Toll-Free: 888-226-7711	
Address: 1 Mohegan Sun Blvd., Uncasville, CT 06382 US	

GROWTH PLANS/SPECIAL FEATURES:

The Connecticut Sun, formerly the Orlando Miracle, is a Women's National Basketball Association (WNBA) team. After joining the WNBA in 2002, the team came to Connecticut from Florida as the result of a 2003 buy-out by the Mohegan Tribal Gaming Authority, well-known for operating one of the world's largest gaming facilities, the Mohegan Sun Casino. The team derives its name from the casino, which also lends its name to the team's home stadium, Mohegan Sun Arena, a 9,518-seat facility located on the casino grounds. The franchise is one of the only WNBA teams that does not share its market with an NBA (National Basketball Association) team and is also one of the only teams not owned by an NBA team owner. The team plays in the WNBA's Eastern Conference, alongside the Chicago Sky, Detroit Shock, Indiana Fever, New York Liberty and Washington Mystics. Sun sponsors include Dunkin' Donuts, Anthem, Contessa, Speedpass, Bank of America, Toyota and Bud Light. The Solar Power Dance Team performs at all Sun home games and participates with Sun players in community initiatives.

The Connecticut Sun offers summer internships for college students interested in the areas of sales, marketing, public relations and community relations.

FINANCIALS: **Sales and profits are in thousands of dollars—add 000 to get the full amount. 2008 Note: Financial information for 2008 was not available for all companies at press time.**

2008 Sales: $	2008 Profits: $	**U.S. Stock Ticker: Subsidiary**
2007 Sales: $	2007 Profits: $	**Int'l Ticker:** Int'l Exchange:
2006 Sales: $	2006 Profits: $	Employees:
2005 Sales: $	2005 Profits: $	Fiscal Year Ends: 9/30
2004 Sales: $	2004 Profits: $	Parent Company: MOHEGAN TRIBAL GAMING AUTHORITY

SALARIES/BENEFITS:

Pension Plan:	ESOP Stock Plan:	Profit Sharing:	Top Exec. Salary: $	Bonus: $
Savings Plan:	Stock Purch. Plan:		Second Exec. Salary: $	Bonus: $

OTHER THOUGHTS:

Apparent Women Officers or Directors: 9
Hot Spot for Advancement for Women/Minorities: Y

LOCATIONS: ("Y" = Yes)

West:	Southwest:	Midwest:	Southeast:	Northeast:	International:
				Y	

CONTINENTAL BASKETBALL ASSOCIATION www.cbahoopsonline.com

Industry Group Code: 813990 **Ranks within this company's industry group:** Sales: Profits:

Sports:		Services:		Media:		Sales:		Facilities:		Other:	
Leagues/Associations:	Y	Food & Beverage:		TV:		Marketing:		Stadiums:		Gambling:	
Teams:		Agents:		Radio:		Ads:		Fitness Clubs:		Apparel:	
Nonprofits:		Other:		Internet:		Tickets:		Golf Courses:		Equipment:	
Other:				Print:		Retail:		Ski Resorts:		Shoes:	
				Software:		Other:		Other:		Other:	

TYPES OF BUSINESS:

Minor League Basketball Association

BRANDS/DIVISIONS/AFFILIATES:

Albany Patroons
Lawton Fort Sill Cavalry
Minot Sky Rockets
Pittsburgh Xplosion
East Kentucky Miners
CBA-ABA Interleague Challenge
CBA

CONTACTS:
Note: Officers with more than one job title may be intentionally listed here more than once.

Ricardo A. Richardson, CEO
Ricardo A. Richardson, Pres.
Dennis Truax, Commissioner
Mark Argenziano, Dir.-Scouting
Jeff Argenziano, Dir.-Player Personnel
Benito R. Fernandez, Chmn.

Phone: 518-694-0100 **Fax:** 518-694-0101
Toll-Free:
Address: 195 Washington Ave., Albany, NY 12210 US

GROWTH PLANS/SPECIAL FEATURES:

The Continental Basketball Association (CBA) is a U.S. men's professional minor league basketball organization. The league currently has four active teams: Albany Patroons in New York; Minot SkyRockets in North Dakota; East Kentucky Miners in Kentucky; and Lawton Fort Sill Cavalry in Oklahoma. The league's fifth team, Pittsburgh Xplosion in Monroeville, Pennsylvania, was unable to operate this year. The league acts as a feeder and talent developer for the NBA; it is also affiliated with USA Basketball, the governing body for basketball in the U.S. The association was founded in 1946 as the Eastern Pennsylvania Basketball League. It managed a substantial amount of success until 1999, when it was bought by an investment group led by former NBA player Isaiah Thomas. By 2001, the CBA was forced into bankruptcy. The league reemerged for the 2001-2002 season. Upon its return, the company negotiated an agreement with the NBA in which CBA players are allowed to sign a 10-day contract with NBA teams, usually to replace an injured player, with the potential of one additional 10-day contract; at the conclusion of this second contract, the player must either be returned to the CBA or be retained by the NBA for the remainder of the season. Between late 2008 and early 2009, the CBA and the American Basketball Association (ABA) competed in the CBA-ABA Interleague Challenge; the CBA won 16 out of 18 interleague games. In February 2009, due to economic conditions, the league was forced to end the playing season six weeks short and hold an impromptu best-of-three games championship series between Albany and Lawton Fort Sill (the teams with the best two CBA records at time of play suspension). Lawton Fort Sill won the series in three games. The CBA is reorganizing operations with hopes to resume play in 2010.

FINANCIALS:
Sales and profits are in thousands of dollars—add 000 to get the full amount. 2008 Note: Financial information for 2008 was not available for all companies at press time.

2008 Sales: $	2008 Profits: $	**U.S. Stock Ticker: Private**
2007 Sales: $	2007 Profits: $	**Int'l Ticker:** Int'l Exchange:
2006 Sales: $	2006 Profits: $	Employees:
2005 Sales: $	2005 Profits: $	Fiscal Year Ends:
2004 Sales: $	2004 Profits: $	Parent Company:

SALARIES/BENEFITS:

Pension Plan:	ESOP Stock Plan:	Profit Sharing:	Top Exec. Salary: $	Bonus: $
Savings Plan:	Stock Purch. Plan:		Second Exec. Salary: $	Bonus: $

OTHER THOUGHTS:

Apparent Women Officers or Directors:
Hot Spot for Advancement for Women/Minorities:

LOCATIONS: ("Y" = Yes)

West:	Southwest:	Midwest:	Southeast:	Northeast:	International:
				Y	

CONVERSE INC

www.converse.com

Industry Group Code: 316219 **Ranks within this company's industry group:** Sales: Profits:

Sports:		Services:		Media:		Sales:		Facilities:		Other:	
Leagues/Associations:		Food & Beverage:		TV:		Marketing:		Stadiums:		Gambling:	
Teams:		Agents:		Radio:		Ads:		Fitness Clubs:		Apparel:	Y
Nonprofits:		Other:		Internet:		Tickets:		Golf Courses:		Equipment:	
Other:				Print:		Retail:		Ski Resorts:		Shoes:	Y
				Software:		Other:		Other:		Other:	

TYPES OF BUSINESS:

Athletic Shoes
Athletic Apparel

BRANDS/DIVISIONS/AFFILIATES:

Nike Inc
Chuck Taylor All Star
Jack Purcell
Converse Sports Lifestyle
Converse Re-Issue
One Star
John Varvatos
Hurley

CONTACTS: *Note: Officers with more than one job title may be intentionally listed here more than once.*

Jack A. Boys, CEO
Geoff Cottrill, Chief Mktg. Officer
Cheryl Calegari, Dir.-Public Rel. & Presence Mktg.
Mark Parker, CEO/Pres., Nike, Inc.
Marsden S. Cason, Chmn.

Phone: 978-983-3300	**Fax:** 978-983-3502
Toll-Free: 888-792-3307	
Address: 1 High St., North Andover, MA 01845-2601 US	

GROWTH PLANS/SPECIAL FEATURES:

Converse, Inc. is a leading designer and producer of athletic shoes and sports apparel. The company, headquartered in Massachusetts, is most famous for its iconic Chuck Taylor All Star canvas basketball shoes. The company has sold over 750 million pairs of this model of shoe alone. The shoe was introduced in 1917 and remained the only high-performance basketball shoe mass-produced for over 50 years after its introduction. The company's products are sold through over 12,000 retailers and licensees in over 100 countries. The Converse collection, built upon its American sports heritage, includes sports performance, sports classics and sports lifestyle athletic footwear for men, women and children, as well as athletic-inspired apparel. The company also designs and sells shoes, apparel and accessories under the All Star, One Star, John Varvatos, Jack Purcell and Hurley brand names. After filing for Chapter 11 bankruptcy in 2001, the firm became a subsidiary of Nike in 2003.

Converse offers its eligible employees tuition reimbursement; medical, dental and disability insurance; and employee assistance programs.

FINANCIALS: **Sales and profits are in thousands of dollars—add 000 to get the full amount. 2008 Note: Financial information for 2008 was not available for all companies at press time.**

2008 Sales: $	2008 Profits: $	**U.S. Stock Ticker: Subsidiary**
2007 Sales: $55,600	2007 Profits: $	**Int'l Ticker:** Int'l Exchange:
2006 Sales: $	2006 Profits: $	Employees: 261
2005 Sales: $	2005 Profits: $	Fiscal Year Ends: 5/31
2004 Sales: $	2004 Profits: $	Parent Company: NIKE INC

SALARIES/BENEFITS:

Pension Plan:	ESOP Stock Plan:	Profit Sharing:	Top Exec. Salary: $	Bonus: $
Savings Plan:	Stock Purch. Plan:		Second Exec. Salary: $	Bonus: $

OTHER THOUGHTS:

Apparent Women Officers or Directors: 1
Hot Spot for Advancement for Women/Minorities:

LOCATIONS: ("Y" = Yes)

West:	Southwest:	Midwest:	Southeast:	Northeast:	International:
				Y	

Note: Financial information, benefits and other data can change quickly and may vary from those stated here.

COX COMMUNICATIONS INC

www.cox.com

Industry Group Code: 513220 **Ranks within this company's industry group:** Sales: 4 Profits:

Sports:		Services:		Media:		Sales:		Facilities:		Other:	
Leagues/Associations:		Food & Beverage:		TV:	Y	Marketing:		Stadiums:		Gambling:	
Teams:		Agents:		Radio:		Ads:		Fitness Clubs:		Apparel:	
Nonprofits:		Other:		Internet:	Y	Tickets:		Golf Courses:		Equipment:	
Other:				Print:		Retail:		Ski Resorts:		Shoes:	
				Software:		Other:		Other:		Other:	

TYPES OF BUSINESS:

Cable TV Service
Digital Cable TV Service
Cable-Based Internet Access
Local & Long-Distance Phone Service
Video-On-Demand
VOIP Service
Commercial Telecommunications Services

BRANDS/DIVISIONS/AFFILIATES:

Cox Enterprises Inc
Cox Cable
Cox Digital Cable
Cox High Speed
Cox Digital Telephone
Cox Business Services
Phone Tools
Cox Radio, Inc.

CONTACTS: *Note: Officers with more than one job title may be intentionally listed here more than once.*

Leo W. Brennan, COO
Patrick J. Esser, Pres.
Mark F. Bowser, CFO/Sr. VP
Joseph J. Rooney, Chief Mktg. Officer/Sr. VP
Mae A. Douglas, Chief People Officer/Sr. VP
Scott A. Hatfield, CIO/Sr. VP
Christopher J. Bowick, CTO/Sr. VP
Christopher J. Bowick, Sr. VP-Eng.
James A. Hatcher, Sr. VP-Legal & Regulatory Affairs
Jill Campbell, Sr. VP-Oper.
Dallas S. Clement, Sr. VP-Strategy & Dev.
Steve M. Gorman, VP-Online Strategy & Interactive Media
James Ashurst, VP-Comm.
William J. Fitzsimmons, Chief Acct. Officer/VP-Acct. & Financial Planning
Andrew I. Albert, VP-Programming
Stephen Bye, VP-Wireless
Susan W. Coker, Treas./VP
Sheila Crosby, VP-Sales & Dist.
James Cox Kennedy, Chmn.

Phone: 404-843-5000	**Fax:**
Toll-Free:	
Address: 1400 Lake Hearn Dr., Atlanta, GA 30319 US	

GROWTH PLANS/SPECIAL FEATURES:

Cox Communications, Inc., owned by Cox Enterprises, Inc., is a cable broadband communications and entertainment company servicing more than 6 million customers throughout the U.S. Cox offers both analog cable television under the Cox Cable brand and advanced digital video service under the Cox Digital Cable brand. The firm provides a range of other communications and entertainment services, including local and long distance telephone under the Cox Digital Telephone brand; and Internet access under the Cox High Speed Internet brand; and commercial voice and data services via Cox Business Services. Additionally, Cox Business Services provides communications solutions for commercial customers, offering Internet, voice and long-distance services, as well as data and video transport services for businesses. Cox Media offers cable advertising in traditional spot and new media formats, along with promotional opportunities and production services. The company also maintains Cox Newspapers; Cox Television; Cox Radio; Manheim; Cox Auto Trader and the Travel Channel. The firm invests in telecommunications companies such as Sprint PCS, as well as programming networks, including the Discovery Channel and TV Works, a provider of software for digital cable systems. Cable television services include basic cable, expanded cable, broadband Internet-supported VoIP service, pay-per-view and entertainment-on-demand packages. Following the dissolution, in late 2008, of a joint venture with Time Warner, Comcast and others aimed at providing mobile phone services through a partnership with Sprint, Cox announced in April 2009 that it was working to build its own cellular network in order to offer its customers bundled packages including cell phone services and wireless broadband access for laptop computers.

Employees are offered medical and dental coverage; life and business travel insurance; health and dependent care spending accounts; tuition reimbursement; an employee assistance program; a pension plan; a 401(k) plan; adoption assistance; discounted Cox services such as cable, telephone and internet where available; and employee discounts with Dell, Sprint, Ford GM to name a few. The firm also operates Cox University, which offers over 150 free online courses.

FINANCIALS: **Sales and profits are in thousands of dollars—add 000 to get the full amount. 2008 Note: Financial information for 2008 was not available for all companies at press time.**

2008 Sales: $8,500,000	2008 Profits: $	**U.S. Stock Ticker: Subsidiary**
2007 Sales: $8,300,000	2007 Profits: $	**Int'l Ticker:** Int'l Exchange:
2006 Sales: $7,300,000	2006 Profits: $	Employees: 22,899
2005 Sales: $7,054,300	2005 Profits: $-230,700	Fiscal Year Ends: 12/31
2004 Sales: $6,106,100	2004 Profits: $-2,375,300	Parent Company: COX ENTERPRISES INC

SALARIES/BENEFITS:

Pension Plan: Y	ESOP Stock Plan:	Profit Sharing:	Top Exec. Salary: $1,322,900	Bonus: $1,166,798
Savings Plan: Y	Stock Purch. Plan:		Second Exec. Salary: $760,000	Bonus: $574,560

OTHER THOUGHTS:

Apparent Women Officers or Directors: 17
Hot Spot for Advancement for Women/Minorities: Y

LOCATIONS: ("Y" = Yes)

West:	Southwest:	Midwest:	Southeast:	Northeast:	International:
Y	Y	Y	Y	Y	

Note: Financial information, benefits and other data can change quickly and may vary from those stated here.

CRESTED BUTTE MOUNTAIN RESORT INC www.crestedbutteresort.com

Industry Group Code: 713920 **Ranks within this company's industry group:** Sales: Profits:

Sports:		Services:		Media:		Sales:		Facilities:		Other:	
Leagues/Associations:		Food & Beverage:	Y	TV:		Marketing:		Stadiums:		Gambling:	
Teams:		Agents:		Radio:		Ads:		Fitness Clubs:		Apparel:	
Nonprofits:		Other:		Internet:		Tickets:		Golf Courses:		Equipment:	
Other:				Print:		Retail:		Ski Resorts:	Y	Shoes:	
				Software:		Other:		Other:	Y	Other:	

TYPES OF BUSINESS:

Ski Resort
Real Estate

BRANDS/DIVISIONS/AFFILIATES:

Grand Lodge Hotel
Lodge at Mountaineer Square (The)
Mountaineering Conference Center
Triple Peaks, LLC
CNL Lifestyle Properties, Inc.

CONTACTS: *Note: Officers with more than one job title may be intentionally listed here more than once.*

Tim Mueller, CEO
Tim Mueller, Pres.
Ken Stone, Chief Mktg. Officer/VP
April Prout, Dir.-Comm.
Gina Prout, Dir.-Public Rel., Mktg. Partnership & Sponsorships

Phone: 970-349-2333	**Fax:** 970-349-2250
Toll-Free: 800-810-7669	
Address: 12 Snowmass Rd., Mt. Crested Butte, CO 81225 US	

GROWTH PLANS/SPECIAL FEATURES:

Crested Butte Mountain Resort, Inc. (CBMR) is part of the Okemo, Vermont and Mount Sunapee, New Hampshire family of resorts. The firm's ski resort is located in the small town of Mt. Crested Butte, which is near the larger town of Crested Butte, Colorado, and is nestled within the Gunnison National Forest in the Elk Mountain Range. In addition to lodging and five restaurants, the 282-acre resort features 121 trails, a super-pipe, a terrain park, a kids' terrain park, a tubing hill, a snowshoe loop and 15 lifts, including three high-speed quad chairs. CBMR operates its lifts in the summer to serve hikers and mountain bikers, and hosts the Wildflower Rush mountain bike race. Other programs include Nordic skiing, snowboarding, dog sledding, snowmobiling and snowshoeing. Recently, the company installed a new fixed-grip quad lift to access its premier ski-in/ski-out Prospect real estate development; and it acquired the commercial units and management of the Grand Lodge Hotel in Mt. Crested Butte, Colorado. The property is in the midst of a five-year, multi-million dollar, resort-wide overhaul. Part of this renovation effort culminated with the opening of The Lodge at Mountaineer Square and the Mountaineering Conference Center. The Lodge is a luxury residential property featuring condominium and hotel accommodations; and the 9,000 square foot Conference Center is reconfigurable to meet the needs of diverse events. In December 2008, the real estate investment trust firm CNL Lifestyle Properties, Inc. acquired the assets of three family owned Triple Peaks, LLC ski and mountain properties including the Crested Butte in Colorado; the Okemo in Vermont; and the Mount Sunapee in New Hampshire. In accordance with the terms of the acquisition, CNL Lifestyles Properties will be leasing the properties back to Triple Peaks under a 40 year lease agreement and they will manage the ski, golf, hospitality and conference operations.

CBMR offers its employees skiing privileges at 11 Colorado resorts, affordable housing opportunities, discounts at its food and beverage operations, rental shops and access to a health club.

FINANCIALS: **Sales and profits are in thousands of dollars—add 000 to get the full amount. 2008 Note: Financial information for 2008 was not available for all companies at press time.**

2008 Sales: $	2008 Profits: $	**U.S. Stock Ticker: Private**
2007 Sales: $	2007 Profits: $	**Int'l Ticker:** Int'l Exchange:
2006 Sales: $	2006 Profits: $	Employees:
2005 Sales: $	2005 Profits: $	Fiscal Year Ends:
2004 Sales: $	2004 Profits: $	Parent Company:

SALARIES/BENEFITS:

Pension Plan:	ESOP Stock Plan:	Profit Sharing:	Top Exec. Salary: $	Bonus: $
Savings Plan:	Stock Purch. Plan:		Second Exec. Salary: $	Bonus: $

OTHER THOUGHTS:

Apparent Women Officers or Directors: 3
Hot Spot for Advancement for Women/Minorities: Y

LOCATIONS: ("Y" = Yes)

West:	Southwest:	Midwest:	Southeast:	Northeast:	International:
Y					

CRYSTAL PALACE FOOTBALL CLUB

www.cpfc.premiumtv.co.uk

Industry Group Code: 711211D **Ranks within this company's industry group:** Sales: Profits:

Sports:		Services:		Media:		Sales:		Facilities:		Other:	
Leagues/Associations:		Food & Beverage:		TV:		Marketing:		Stadiums:	Y	Gambling:	
Teams:	Y	Agents:		Radio:		Ads:		Fitness Clubs:		Apparel:	
Nonprofits:		Other:		Internet:		Tickets:	Y	Golf Courses:		Equipment:	
Other:				Print:		Retail:	Y	Ski Resorts:		Shoes:	
				Software:		Other:		Other:		Other:	

TYPES OF BUSINESS:

Professional Soccer Team
Ticket Sales
Team Merchandise

BRANDS/DIVISIONS/AFFILIATES:

Eagles
Selhurst Park

CONTACTS:

Note: Officers with more than one job title may be intentionally listed here more than once.

Phil Alexander, CEO
Peter Morley, Pres.
Kevin Watts, Dir.-Human Resources & Commerce
Terry Byfield, Mgr.-Comm.
Mark Thickbroom, Dir.-Finance
Ray Shilling, Financial Controller
Peter Taylor, Mgr.-Team
Liz Roake, Mgr.-Retail Oper.
Colin Morris, Mgr.-Projects
Simon Jordan, Chmn.

Phone: 44-20-8768-6000 **Fax:** 44-20-8771-5311
Toll-Free:
Address: Selhurst Park, London, SE25 6PU UK

GROWTH PLANS/SPECIAL FEATURES:

The Crystal Palace Football Club is an English Premiership soccer team formed in 1905. The club, known as the Eagles, is owned by mobile phone retail entrepreneur Simon Jordan. The Eagles' home games are played at the team's Selhurst Park, its base since 1924, which can host up to 51,000 fans. The team has been the home of English international players like Andrew Johnson, Nigel Marytn and John Salako, as well as foreign nationals such as Clinton Morrison, Jovan Kirovski and Alexander Kolinko. The club's most successful season was 1991, when it placed third in the Premiership. Throughout the 1990s and the first years of the new millennium, the team has fluctuated back and forth between the first division and the Premiership. Crystal Palace supports both junior and senior ladies' teams of the same name. Churchill Group and Diadora sponsor the Crystal Palace uniform. Additionally, Crystal Palace has developed several partnerships with respected companies such as Errea; e-On; Gac; Club Savers Account; Thomas Cook; the Football League; and Texaco.

FINANCIALS:

Sales and profits are in thousands of dollars—add 000 to get the full amount. 2008 Note: Financial information for 2008 was not available for all companies at press time.

2008 Sales: $	2008 Profits: $	**U.S. Stock Ticker: Private**
2007 Sales: $	2007 Profits: $	**Int'l Ticker:** Int'l Exchange:
2006 Sales: $	2006 Profits: $	Employees: 620
2005 Sales: $	2005 Profits: $	Fiscal Year Ends: 6/30
2004 Sales: $17,800	2004 Profits: $-16,100	Parent Company:

SALARIES/BENEFITS:

Pension Plan:	ESOP Stock Plan:	Profit Sharing:	Top Exec. Salary: $	Bonus: $
Savings Plan:	Stock Purch. Plan:		Second Exec. Salary: $	Bonus: $

OTHER THOUGHTS:

Apparent Women Officers or Directors: 2
Hot Spot for Advancement for Women/Minorities:

LOCATIONS: ("Y" = Yes)

West:	Southwest:	Midwest:	Southeast:	Northeast:	International:
					Y

CURVES INTERNATIONAL INC

www.curvesinternational.com

Industry Group Code: 713940 **Ranks within this company's industry group:** Sales: Profits:

Sports:		Services:		Media:		Sales:		Facilities:		Other:	
Leagues/Associations:		Food & Beverage:		TV:		Marketing:		Stadiums:		Gambling:	
Teams:		Agents:		Radio:		Ads:		Fitness Clubs:	Y	Apparel:	
Nonprofits:		Other:		Internet:		Tickets:		Golf Courses:		Equipment:	
Other:				Print:		Retail:		Ski Resorts:		Shoes:	
				Software:		Other:		Other:		Other:	

TYPES OF BUSINESS:

Fitness Centers
Magazine Publishing
Health Products
Travel Services
Online Information

BRANDS/DIVISIONS/AFFILIATES:

diane Magazine
CurvesTravel.com
Curves Travel
GlobalFit

CONTACTS:

Note: Officers with more than one job title may be intentionally listed here more than once.

Gary Heavin, CEO/Founder
Michael Raymond, Pres.
Michael Raymond, VP-Mktg.
Becky Frusher, Comm. Specialist
Diane Heavin, Founder/Publisher-diane magazine

Phone: 254-399-9285 **Fax:** 254-399-9731
Toll-Free: 800-848-1096
Address: 100 Ritchie Rd., Waco, TX 76712 US

GROWTH PLANS/SPECIAL FEATURES:

Curves International is one of the largest fitness franchises in the world, with approximately 10,000 franchised locations in 69 countries including the U.S., Canada, Mexico, Central America, the Caribbean, Australia, New Zealand and the U.K. The company provides fitness and weight-loss facilities specifically designed for women. Curves currently provides over 4 million women with exercise and nutritional guidance. Its program provides a 30-minute circuit training workout session where all of the machines are arranged in a circle and clients can talk to each other as they move through the circuit. In addition to 30-minute workout sessions at Curves fitness facilities, the company provides a comprehensive program to educate and train women in healthy eating patterns. This program includes books, meal planners, tracking charts, weekly progress reports and other information geared toward helping women eat healthily. Through its web site, Curves provides links to other sites dedicated to educating women about the dangers of obesity and other serious diseases related to unhealthy living. The web site also features customizable online accounts, where members can access weight loss tips and meal plans. The company is also the creator of diane magazine, a quarterly magazine which features diet success stories, celebrity interviews, fitness tips and healthy recipes. The firm offers Curves Food, with branded versions of cereal, popcorn and granola bars. Curves also offers clothing, vitamins and supplements, and books. Curves recently launched its first franchise in Japan, with 2,000 more planned to open by 2010. Subsidiary Curves Travel operates mainly from CurvesTravel.com and offers deals and free booking and planning services to Curves members. In September 2007, Curves partnered with GlobalFit, a provider of healthy living benefits, to offer millions of American women a chance to enter the Curves program at a discounted rate.

FINANCIALS:

Sales and profits are in thousands of dollars—add 000 to get the full amount. 2008 Note: Financial information for 2008 was not available for all companies at press time.

2008 Sales: $	2008 Profits: $	**U.S. Stock Ticker: Private**
2007 Sales: $	2007 Profits: $	**Int'l Ticker:** Int'l Exchange:
2006 Sales: $	2006 Profits: $	Employees: 138
2005 Sales: $145,999	2005 Profits: $	Fiscal Year Ends: 12/31
2004 Sales: $	2004 Profits: $	Parent Company:

SALARIES/BENEFITS:

Pension Plan:	ESOP Stock Plan:	Profit Sharing:	Top Exec. Salary: $	Bonus: $
Savings Plan:	Stock Purch. Plan:		Second Exec. Salary: $	Bonus: $

OTHER THOUGHTS:

Apparent Women Officers or Directors: 2
Hot Spot for Advancement for Women/Minorities: Y

LOCATIONS: ("Y" = Yes)

West:	Southwest:	Midwest:	Southeast:	Northeast:	International:
Y	Y	Y	Y	Y	Y

DALE EARNHARDT INC

www.daleearnhardtinc.com

Industry Group Code: 711211G **Ranks within this company's industry group:** Sales: 4 Profits: 5

Sports:		Services:		Media:		Sales:		Facilities:		Other:	
Leagues/Associations:		Food & Beverage:		TV:		Marketing:		Stadiums:		Gambling:	
Teams:	Y	Agents:		Radio:		Ads:		Fitness Clubs:		Apparel:	
Nonprofits:		Other:	Y	Internet:		Tickets:		Golf Courses:		Equipment:	
Other:				Print:		Retail:	Y	Ski Resorts:		Shoes:	
				Software:		Other:		Other:	Y	Other:	Y

TYPES OF BUSINESS:

Stock Car Racing
Automotive Assembly
Auto Sales
Conference Services

BRANDS/DIVISIONS/AFFILIATES:

Dale Earnhardt Chevrolet
Dale Earnhardt Foundation
Dale Earnhardt Book Center
Earnhardt Entertainment Division

CONTACTS: *Note: Officers with more than one job title may be intentionally listed here more than once.*

Teresa Earnhardt, CEO
Teresa Earnhardt, Pres.
Max L. Siegel, Pres., Global Oper.

Phone: 704-662-8000 **Fax:** 704-663-7945
Toll-Free: 877-334-9663
Address: 1675 Dale Earnhardt Hwy. 3, Mooresville, NC 28115-8245 US

GROWTH PLANS/SPECIAL FEATURES:

Dale Earnhardt, Inc. (DEI) is a premier organization in NASCAR racing. Originally founded by Dale and Teresa Earnhardt in the early 1980s, the firm is now solely owned by widow Teresa Earnhardt. The company's 240,000-square-foot facility is the base of operations for five Sprint Cup teams and one NASCAR Busch Series team. DEI's headquarters contains complete construction and maintenance facilities for team racecars, including fabrication, body, engine, transmission and engineering shops. The company also maintains several show cars, hosts special events and corporate meetings at its facilities and operates a licensing department to oversee merchandising and promotions. DEI's showroom is open to the public, and an adjacent retail shop sells team promotional items and souvenirs. Retail items include clocks, hats, totes/bags/coolers, shirts, sweatshirts, accessories and holiday merchandise. DEI also owns an auto dealership, Dale Earnhardt Chevrolet, and operates the Dale Earnhardt Foundation, a nonprofit organization dedicated to children's charities and environmental conservation. The Dale Earnhardt Book Center at the Center of Hope is a shelter operated by the Salvation Army in Charlotte, North Carolina. DEI recently created a new division, the Earnhardt Entertainment Division, which will produce and distribute music, film, television and digital content in an effort to reach more fans. In December 2008, the company partnered with Chip Ganassi Racing with Felix Sabates, Inc., to launch a new four-car team.

FINANCIALS: **Sales and profits are in thousands of dollars—add 000 to get the full amount. 2008 Note: Financial information for 2008 was not available for all companies at press time.**

2008 Sales: $86,000	2008 Profits: $5,000	**U.S. Stock Ticker: Private**
2007 Sales: $96,000	2007 Profits: $16,600	**Int'l Ticker:** Int'l Exchange:
2006 Sales: $21,800	2006 Profits: $	Employees:
2005 Sales: $	2005 Profits: $	Fiscal Year Ends:
2004 Sales: $	2004 Profits: $	Parent Company:

SALARIES/BENEFITS:

Pension Plan:	ESOP Stock Plan:	Profit Sharing:	Top Exec. Salary: $	Bonus: $
Savings Plan:	Stock Purch. Plan:		Second Exec. Salary: $	Bonus: $

OTHER THOUGHTS:

Apparent Women Officers or Directors: 1
Hot Spot for Advancement for Women/Minorities:

LOCATIONS: ("Y" = Yes)

West:	Southwest:	Midwest:	Southeast:	Northeast:	International:
				Y	

DALLAS COWBOYS

www.dallascowboys.com

Industry Group Code: 711211C **Ranks within this company's industry group:** Sales: 3 Profits: 10

Sports:		Services:		Media:		Sales:		Facilities:		Other:	
Leagues/Associations:		Food & Beverage:		TV:		Marketing:		Stadiums:	Y	Gambling:	
Teams:	Y	Agents:		Radio:		Ads:		Fitness Clubs:		Apparel:	
Nonprofits:		Other:		Internet:		Tickets:	Y	Golf Courses:		Equipment:	
Other:	Y			Print:		Retail:	Y	Ski Resorts:		Shoes:	
				Software:		Other:		Other:		Other:	

TYPES OF BUSINESS:

Professional Football Team

BRANDS/DIVISIONS/AFFILIATES:

Dallas Cowboys Cheerleaders
Dallas Cowboys
America's Team
Texas Stadium
Dallas Cowboys Football Club, Ltd.

CONTACTS:

Note: Officers with more than one job title may be intentionally listed here more than once.

Stephen Jones, COO/Exec. VP
Jerry Jones, Pres.
Jerry Jones, Jr., Exec. VP/Chief Sales & Mktg. Officer
Jerry Jones, Gen. Mgr./Owner
Wade Phillops, Head Coach
Charlotte Jones Anderson, Exec. VP-Brand Mgmt./Pres., Charities
Jason Garrett, Asst. Head Coach/Offensive Coordinator

Phone: 972-556-9900	**Fax:** 972-556-9304
Toll-Free:	
Address: 1 Cowboys Pkwy., Irving, TX 75063 US	

GROWTH PLANS/SPECIAL FEATURES:

The Dallas Cowboys, owned and operated by Dallas Cowboys Football Club, Ltd., are a professional football team in the National Football League (NFL) based in Dallas, Texas. The franchise was started in 1960. Legendary Cowboys quarterback Roger Staubach, after throwing a desperation touchdown pass in the fourth quarter with only seconds left to wide receiver Drew Pearson in 1975, introduced the term Hail Mary pass, describing the play at a press conference. Along with Staubach, the Cowboys bench has included other Hall of Famers, such as running back Tony Dorsett; quarterback Troy Aikman, one of only three players in NFL history to have led a team to three Super Bowl victories; the team's first head coach Tom Landry, who had the third most wins in NFL history; and the first president and general manager, Tex Schramm, from 1959 to 1989. The Cowboys have gone to eight Super Bowls and won five, including three in four years, back-to-back in 1992 and 1993, and again in 1995, an NFL record, as well as winning six NFC East titles in the last eight seasons. The team is owned by Jerry Jones, and it plays at Texas Stadium, which is owned by the city of Irving. The Cowboys are building a new stadium that will replace Texas Stadium. The $1.1 billion stadium will host its first events during the summer of 2009, with the Cowboys beginning to play there at the open of their 2009 season. The stadium will accommodate approximately 80,000 people, and can also be expanded to fit up to 100,000 for larger events, such as Super Bowl XLV, which is scheduled to be played at the new stadium in 2011. Forbes Magazine recently valued the team at $1.61 billion. The team's average home game attendance in the 2008 season was 63,368.

FINANCIALS:

Sales and profits are in thousands of dollars—add 000 to get the full amount. 2008 Note: Financial information for 2008 was not available for all companies at press time.

2008 Sales: $269,000	2008 Profits: $30,600	**U.S. Stock Ticker: Private**
2007 Sales: $242,000	2007 Profits: $4,300	**Int'l Ticker:** Int'l Exchange:
2006 Sales: $235,000	2006 Profits: $37,100	Employees:
2005 Sales: $231,000	2005 Profits: $	Fiscal Year Ends: 2/28
2004 Sales: $205,000	2004 Profits: $	Parent Company: DALLAS COWBOYS FOOTBALL CLUB LTD

SALARIES/BENEFITS:

Pension Plan:	ESOP Stock Plan:	Profit Sharing:	Top Exec. Salary: $	Bonus: $
Savings Plan:	Stock Purch. Plan:		Second Exec. Salary: $	Bonus: $

OTHER THOUGHTS:

Apparent Women Officers or Directors: 1
Hot Spot for Advancement for Women/Minorities:

LOCATIONS: ("Y" = Yes)

West:	Southwest:	Midwest:	Southeast:	Northeast:	International:
	Y				

Note: Financial information, benefits and other data can change quickly and may vary from those stated here.

DALLAS MAVERICKS

www.nba.com/mavericks

Industry Group Code: 711211B **Ranks within this company's industry group:** Sales: 7 Profits: 29

Sports:		Services:		Media:		Sales:		Facilities:		Other:	
Leagues/Associations:		Food & Beverage:		TV:		Marketing:		Stadiums:		Gambling:	
Teams:	Y	Agents:		Radio:		Ads:		Fitness Clubs:		Apparel:	
Nonprofits:		Other:		Internet:		Tickets:	Y	Golf Courses:		Equipment:	
Other:				Print:		Retail:	Y	Ski Resorts:		Shoes:	
				Software:		Other:	Y	Other:		Other:	

TYPES OF BUSINESS:

Professional Basketball Team
Online Ticket Trading
Ticket Sales

BRANDS/DIVISIONS/AFFILIATES:

American Airlines Center
Mavericks Trading Post
Mavs Foundation
Hoops n Hopes
Mavs Youth League
Mavs Hoop Troop
Mavs Ballkids
Mavs Drumline

CONTACTS: *Note: Officers with more than one job title may be intentionally listed here more than once.*

Terdema Ussery II, CEO
Terdema Ussery II, Pres.
Floyd Jahner, CFO/VP
Paul Monroe, VP-Mktg. & Comm.
Buddy Pittman, Sr. VP-Human Resources
Ken Bonzon, Dir.-Tech. & Info. Systems
Steve Shilts, VP-Merch.
Gina Calvert, Mgr.-Corp. Comm. & Community Rel.
Ronnie Fauss, Controller
George Killebrew, Sr. VP-Corp. Sponsorships
Donnie Nelson, Pres., Basketball Oper./Gen. Mgr.
Mary Jean Gaines, Dir.-Ticket Admin.
Sarah Melton, Dir.-Basketball Comm.

Phone: 214-747-6287 **Fax:** 214-752-3860
Toll-Free:
Address: The Pavilion, 2909 Taylor St., Dallas, TX 75226 US

GROWTH PLANS/SPECIAL FEATURES:

The Dallas Mavericks, a National Basketball Association (NBA) team, was formed in 1980 after the departure of the Dallas Chaparrals to San Antonio, Texas. The Mavericks play in the $420 million American Airlines Center, which has approximately 20,000 seats and 142 luxury suites. On game night, the arena presents entertainment that includes the Mavs Dancers, Mavs Man, Mavs Drumline, Mavs Hoop Troop and Mavs Ballkids. The team also operates the Mavs Foundation, which provides funding for programs designed to assist young people with education, health and community service. Additional outreach services include Hoop Camp, Mavs Youth Leagues and Hoops 'n Hopes, a fundraising activity dedicated specifically to women and children in the Dallas/Fort Worth area. The Mavericks are sponsored by corporations such as American Airlines; Anheuser-Busch; AT&T; Chase; Coca-Cola; DirecTV; Omni Hotels; TXU Energy; and UPS. Star players such as Dirk Nowitzki, Jason Terry and Josh Howard earned the team an 85% winning percentage for the 2006-07 season, and the team has amassed more than 50 wins in every season since 2000-01. The Mavericks are unique in that they are probably as well known for the flamboyant antics of billionaire owner Mark Cuban (co-founder of broadcast.com and HDNet) as for the team's players. Cuban bought the team from Ross Perot, Jr. in 2000 for $280 million and has been a highly visible member of the franchise ever since, sitting in the bleachers with fans and repeatedly racking up enormous fines for fighting with referees, NBA officials and opposing team members (he is also known for matching many of his fines with charitable contributions). Forbes recently estimated the team to be worth approximately $466 million. In the 2008-09 season, the team's home attendance average was roughly 20,000 per game.

FINANCIALS: **Sales and profits are in thousands of dollars—add 000 to get the full amount. 2008 Note: Financial information for 2008 was not available for all companies at press time.**

2008 Sales: $153,000	2008 Profits: $-13,600	**U.S. Stock Ticker: Private**
2007 Sales: $140,000	2007 Profits: $-1,600	**Int'l Ticker:** Int'l Exchange:
2006 Sales: $140,000	2006 Profits: $-24,400	Employees:
2005 Sales: $124,000	2005 Profits: $	Fiscal Year Ends: 6/30
2004 Sales: $117,000	2004 Profits: $	Parent Company:

SALARIES/BENEFITS:

Pension Plan:	ESOP Stock Plan:	Profit Sharing:	Top Exec. Salary: $	Bonus: $
Savings Plan:	Stock Purch. Plan:		Second Exec. Salary: $	Bonus: $

OTHER THOUGHTS:

Apparent Women Officers or Directors: 20
Hot Spot for Advancement for Women/Minorities: Y

LOCATIONS: ("Y" = Yes)

West:	Southwest:	Midwest:	Southeast:	Northeast:	International:
	Y				

Note: Financial information, benefits and other data can change quickly and may vary from those stated here.

DALLAS STARS

www.dallasstars.com

Industry Group Code: 711211F **Ranks within this company's industry group:** Sales: 6 Profits: 5

Sports:		Services:		Media:		Sales:		Facilities:		Other:	
Leagues/Associations:		Food & Beverage:		TV:		Marketing:		Stadiums:		Gambling:	
Teams:	Y	Agents:		Radio:		Ads:		Fitness Clubs:		Apparel:	
Nonprofits:		Other:		Internet:		Tickets:	Y	Golf Courses:		Equipment:	
Other:				Print:		Retail:		Ski Resorts:		Shoes:	
				Software:		Other:		Other:		Other:	

TYPES OF BUSINESS:

Major League Hockey Team

BRANDS/DIVISIONS/AFFILIATES:

Dallas Stars, LP
Southwest Sports Group
North Stars
American Airlines Arena
Iowa Stars

CONTACTS: *Note: Officers with more than one job title may be intentionally listed here more than once.*

Joseph B. Armes, COO
Jeff Cogen, Pres.
Robert Hutson, CFO
Geoff Moore, Exec. VP-Mktg. & Sales
Lesa Moake, Dir.-Hockey Admin.
Randy Locey, Exec. VP-Bus. Oper.
Mark Janko, Dir.-Public Rel.
Robert Hutson, Exec. VP-Finance
Dave Tippet, Head Coach
Brett Hull, Co-Gen. Mgr.
Les Jackson, Co-Gen. Mgr.
Carla Rosenberg, Dir.-Comm. Mktg.
Thomas O. Hicks, Chmn./Owner

Phone: 214-387-5600	**Fax:** 214-387-5610
Toll-Free:	
Address: 2601 Ave. of the Stars, Frisco, TX 75034 US	

GROWTH PLANS/SPECIAL FEATURES:

The Dallas Stars, a National Hockey League (NHL) team, are owned and operated by Dallas Stars, LP, a subsidiary of Southwest Sports Group (SSG). The team, which is based in Dallas, Texas, plays at the American Airlines Arena and is in the Pacific division of the NHL's Western Conference, along with the Anaheim Ducks, Los Angeles Kings, Phoenix Coyotes and San Jose Sharks. In 1967, the franchise was founded in Minnesota as the North Stars. The team became the Dallas Stars in 1993 when then-owner Norm Green moved the Minnesota North Stars to Texas. Current owner Tom Hicks bought the team in 1995 through his holding company, SSG, which also owns the Texas Rangers baseball team. The franchise has made four Stanley Cup appearances, including its 1999 win and most recent 2000 appearance. The team has continued as perennial playoff contenders in subsequent years. The Stars team has also won two President's Trophies, in 1998 and 1999. They also made the playoffs in the spring of 2006 and most recently, 2008. The team also owns the Iowa Stars, Dallas' primary development affiliate in the American Hockey League (AHL) based in Des Moines, Iowa. In the 2008-09 season, the team saw an average home attendance of approximately 17,600 fans. A recent Forbes list valued the team at roughly $273 million.

FINANCIALS: **Sales and profits are in thousands of dollars—add 000 to get the full amount. 2008 Note: Financial information for 2008 was not available for all companies at press time.**

2008 Sales: $105,000	2008 Profits: $14,200	**U.S. Stock Ticker: Subsidiary**
2007 Sales: $91,000	2007 Profits: $10,500	**Int'l Ticker:** Int'l Exchange:
2006 Sales: $89,000	2006 Profits: $10,000	Employees: 85
2005 Sales: $	2005 Profits: $	Fiscal Year Ends: 6/30
2004 Sales: $103,000	2004 Profits: $	Parent Company: SOUTHWEST SPORTS GROUP

SALARIES/BENEFITS:

Pension Plan:	ESOP Stock Plan:	Profit Sharing:	Top Exec. Salary: $	Bonus: $
Savings Plan:	Stock Purch. Plan:		Second Exec. Salary: $	Bonus: $

OTHER THOUGHTS:

Apparent Women Officers or Directors: 1
Hot Spot for Advancement for Women/Minorities:

LOCATIONS: ("Y" = Yes)

West:	Southwest:	Midwest:	Southeast:	Northeast:	International:
	Y				

DC UNITED

dcunited.mlsnet.com

Industry Group Code: 711211D **Ranks within this company's industry group:** Sales: Profits:

Sports:		Services:		Media:		Sales:		Facilities:		Other:	
Leagues/Associations:		Food & Beverage:		TV:		Marketing:		Stadiums:		Gambling:	
Teams:	Y	Agents:		Radio:		Ads:		Fitness Clubs:		Apparel:	
Nonprofits:		Other:		Internet:		Tickets:	Y	Golf Courses:		Equipment:	
Other:				Print:		Retail:		Ski Resorts:		Shoes:	
				Software:		Other:		Other:		Other:	

TYPES OF BUSINESS:

Major League Soccer Team

BRANDS/DIVISIONS/AFFILIATES:

CONTACTS:

Note: Officers with more than one job title may be intentionally listed here more than once.

Kevin J. Payne, CEO
Kevin J. Payne, Pres.
Jamie O'Connor, VP-Mktg.
Ellie Amaguana, Mgr.-Human Resources
Francisco Tobar, Dir.-Team Admin.
Jon Radke, Mgr.-Oper.
Doug Hicks, VP-Comm.
Ellie Amaguana, Mgr.-Finance
Catherine Marquette, Dir.-Comm. & Fan Rel.
Mike Harloff, Dir.-Sales
Fred Matthes, Dir.-Ticket Oper. & Customer Svc.
Tom Soehn, Head Coach

Phone: 202-581-5000 **Fax:** 202-587-5400
Toll-Free:
Address: RFK Stadium, 2400 E. Capitol St. S.E., Washington, DC 20003 US

GROWTH PLANS/SPECIAL FEATURES:

D.C. United is a Major League Soccer (MLS) team based in Washington, D.C. The team is owned and operated by Victor MacFarlane and William H.C. Chang of D.C. United Holdings, which acquired the team for $33 million from Anschutz Entertainment Group, a record price for an MLS team. D.C. United plays out of 56,600-seat Robert F. Kennedy Memorial Stadium in the Eastern Conference of the MLS, which is composed of Chicago Fire, Columbus Crew, Toronto FC, Kansas City Wizards, New England Revolution and New York Red Bulls. Since the MLS's inception in 1996, the team has been a dominant force, winning eight domestic and international championships, as well as four MLS Supporters' Shields. It started this run by winning the 1996 MLS Cup after which the team won the 1996 U.S. Open Cup, the first-ever double in U.S. soccer history. D.C. United then went on to win the 1997 MLS Cup; 1998 CONCACAF Champions Cup, their first international tournament win and the first time an American club team had won a continental championship; the 1998 Interamerican Cup against Brazil, who was the current South American champion; and the 1999 MLS Cup. After its 1999 win, the team struggled through a string of poor seasons during which it changed head coaches and dealt with national team call-ups of key players. In 2002, the team hosted the MLS All-Star Game for the first time and won the inaugural Atlantic Cup trophy against its chief rival, the MetroStars. Average regular season game attendance in 2008 was approximately 19,835. In May 2008, the team announced a five year sponsorship deal with Volkswagen. In early 2009, D.C. United announced its intention to build a new 24,000-seat stadium in neighboring Prince George's County, Maryland.

FINANCIALS:

Sales and profits are in thousands of dollars—add 000 to get the full amount. 2008 Note: Financial information for 2008 was not available for all companies at press time.

2008 Sales: $	2008 Profits: $	**U.S. Stock Ticker: Subsidiary**
2007 Sales: $	2007 Profits: $	**Int'l Ticker:** Int'l Exchange:
2006 Sales: $	2006 Profits: $	Employees:
2005 Sales: $	2005 Profits: $	Fiscal Year Ends:
2004 Sales: $	2004 Profits: $	Parent Company: DC UNITED HOLDINGS

SALARIES/BENEFITS:

Pension Plan:	ESOP Stock Plan:	Profit Sharing:	Top Exec. Salary: $	Bonus: $
Savings Plan:	Stock Purch. Plan:		Second Exec. Salary: $	Bonus: $

OTHER THOUGHTS:

Apparent Women Officers or Directors: 3
Hot Spot for Advancement for Women/Minorities: Y

LOCATIONS: ("Y" = Yes)

West:	Southwest:	Midwest:	Southeast:	Northeast:	International:
				Y	

Note: Financial information, benefits and other data can change quickly and may vary from those stated here.

DELAWARE NORTH COMPANIES INC

www.delawarenorth.com

Industry Group Code: 453220 **Ranks within this company's industry group:** Sales: Profits:

Sports:		Services:		Media:		Sales:		Facilities:		Other:	
Leagues/Associations:		Food & Beverage:	Y	TV:		Marketing:		Stadiums:	Y	Gambling:	Y
Teams:	Y	Agents:		Radio:		Ads:		Fitness Clubs:		Apparel:	
Nonprofits:		Other:	Y	Internet:		Tickets:	Y	Golf Courses:		Equipment:	
Other:				Print:		Retail:	Y	Ski Resorts:		Shoes:	
				Software:		Other:		Other:	Y	Other:	

TYPES OF BUSINESS:

Concession Stands
Catering & Food Services
Park & Resort Visitor Services
Professional Hockey Team
Event Centers
Casinos

BRANDS/DIVISIONS/AFFILIATES:

DNC Sportservice
DNC Travel Hospitality Services
DNC Parks & Resorts
Boston Bruins
DNC Boston
DNC International
DNC Gaming Hospitality Group
TD BankNorth Garden

CONTACTS: *Note: Officers with more than one job title may be intentionally listed here more than once.*

Jeremy M. Jacobs, CEO
Charles E. Moran, COO
Charles E. Moran, Pres.
Wendy A. Watkins, VP-Mktg.
Eileen Morgan, VP-Human Resources
Jamel Perkins, VP-IT
Dennis Szefel, Chief Admin. Officer
Bryan J. Keller, General Counsel/VP/Corp. Sec.
Dan Zimmer, VP-Bus. Oper.
Wendy A. Watkins, VP-Corp. Comm.
Bruce W. Carlson, Controller/VP/Treas.
Jim Houser, VP-Facilities Project Management
Jeffrey Hess, VP-Retail
Steve Nowaczyk, VP-Financial Planning & Analysis
Louis M. Jacobs, Exec. VP
Jeremy M. Jacobs, Chmn.
Jonathan Tribe, Managing Dir.-Delaware North Companies Int'l
Michael Reinert, VP-Supply Mgmt. Svcs.

Phone: 716-858-5000	**Fax:** 716-858-5479
Toll-Free:	
Address: 40 Fountain Plz., Buffalo, NY 14202 US	

GROWTH PLANS/SPECIAL FEATURES:

Delaware North Companies, Inc. (DNC), one of the largest private companies in America, provides food service and hospitality management to over 500 million worldwide customers annually. The firm operates through seven divisions: DNC Gaming and Entertainment; DNC Sportservice; DNC Parks and Resorts; DNC Gaming Hospitality Group; DNC Travel Hospitality Services; DNC Boston; and DNC International. DNC Gaming and Entertainment is one of the largest and most successful managers of pari-mutuel facilities in the U.S., with gaming and racing properties in five states featuring wagering on greyhound and horse racing, video slot gaming and fine dining. DNC Sportservice is one of the largest food service companies in the country, providing food, beverage and retail services at high-profile events and over 50 ballparks, arenas and stadiums in the U.S. and Canada. DNC Parks and Resorts, which utilizes its GreenPath and GuestPath programs, provides recreational visitor services at national attractions including Tenaya Lodge, Grand Canyon, Niagara Falls and Kennedy Space Center. DNC Gaming Hospitality Group offers casinos culinary support and customer service solutions. DNC Travel Hospitality Services operates food service and retail facilities in airports across the world. Through DNC Boston, the firm operates the TD BankNorth Garden, a $160-million facility that houses the Bruins, the Boston Celtics and other entertainment events; DNC's Chairman/Ceo owns the Boston Bruins professional hockey team. DNC International brings the company's food and hospitality services to Australia, Europe, Asia and Africa.

FINANCIALS: **Sales and profits are in thousands of dollars—add 000 to get the full amount. 2008 Note: Financial information for 2008 was not available for all companies at press time.**

2008 Sales: $	2008 Profits: $	**U.S. Stock Ticker: Private**
2007 Sales: $2,000,000	2007 Profits: $	**Int'l Ticker:** Int'l Exchange:
2006 Sales: $2,040,000	2006 Profits: $	Employees: 40,000
2005 Sales: $2,000,000	2005 Profits: $	Fiscal Year Ends: 12/31
2004 Sales: $1,700,000	2004 Profits: $	Parent Company:

SALARIES/BENEFITS:

Pension Plan:	ESOP Stock Plan:	Profit Sharing:	Top Exec. Salary: $	Bonus: $
Savings Plan:	Stock Purch. Plan:		Second Exec. Salary: $	Bonus: $

OTHER THOUGHTS:

Apparent Women Officers or Directors: 4
Hot Spot for Advancement for Women/Minorities: Y

LOCATIONS: ("Y" = Yes)

West:	Southwest:	Midwest:	Southeast:	Northeast:	International:
Y	Y	Y	Y	Y	Y

DELTA APPAREL INC

www.deltaapparel.com

Industry Group Code: 315000A **Ranks within this company's industry group:** Sales: 5 Profits: 5

Sports:		Services:		Media:		Sales:		Facilities:		Other:	
Leagues/Associations:		Food & Beverage:		TV:		Marketing:		Stadiums:		Gambling:	
Teams:		Agents:		Radio:		Ads:		Fitness Clubs:		Apparel:	Y
Nonprofits:		Other:		Internet:		Tickets:		Golf Courses:		Equipment:	
Other:				Print:		Retail:		Ski Resorts:		Shoes:	
				Software:		Other:		Other:		Other:	

TYPES OF BUSINESS:

T-Shirts & Sports Clothing
Knit Apparel

BRANDS/DIVISIONS/AFFILIATES:

Delta Pro-Weight
Delta Magnum Weight
Quail Hollow
Sweet and Sour
Soffe
Junkfood
Intesity Athletics
Junk Mail

CONTACTS: *Note: Officers with more than one job title may be intentionally listed here more than once.*

Robert W. Humphreys, CEO
Robert Humphreys, Pres.
Deborah H. Merrill, CFO
Martha M. Watson, Corp. Sec./VP
Deborah Merrill, Treas./VP
E. Erwin Maddrey, II, Chmn.

Phone: 678-775-6900 **Fax:** 678-775-6992
Toll-Free: 800-285-4456
Address: 2750 Premiere Pkwy., Ste. 100, Duluth, GA 30097 US

GROWTH PLANS/SPECIAL FEATURES:

Delta Apparel, Inc., serving 14,000 customers, manufactures and markets branded and private-label apparel including t-shirts, golf shirts and tank tops. The firm divides its operations in two segments: activewear apparel and retail-ready apparel. The activewear apparel segment consists of the business units primarily focused on garment styles that are characterized by low fashion risk. The division markets, distributes and manufactures unembellished knit apparel under the brand names Delta Pro-Weight, Delta Magnum Weight and Quail Hollow. The products are primarily sold to screen printing companies. In addition, it manufactures products under private labels for retailers, branded sportswear companies, corporate industry programs and sports licensed apparel marketers. The retail-ready apparel segment consists of the business units primarily focused on more specialized apparel garments to meet consumer preferences and fashion trends. The division sells these embellished and unembellished products through specialty and boutique stores, high-end and mid-tier retail stores and sporting goods stores. In addition to these retail channels, it also supplies college bookstores and produces products for the U.S. Military. The products in this segment are marketed under the brands of Soffe, Intensity Athletics, Junkfood, Junk Mail and Sweet and Sour. In an effort to keep a diversified clientele, Delta Apparel maintains the corporate standard that no single customer should account for more than 10% of sales in any given year. The company's manufacturing activity begins with spinning, knitting and finishing operations based in the U.S. and assembly of garments assigned to leased facilities in San Pedro Sula, Honduras and Campeche, Mexico.

FINANCIALS: **Sales and profits are in thousands of dollars—add 000 to get the full amount. 2008 Note: Financial information for 2008 was not available for all companies at press time.**

2008 Sales: $322,034	2008 Profits: $- 508	**U.S. Stock Ticker: DLA**
2007 Sales: $312,438	2007 Profits: $6,343	**Int'l Ticker:** Int'l Exchange:
2006 Sales: $270,108	2006 Profits: $14,844	Employees: 6,400
2005 Sales: $228,065	2005 Profits: $11,243	Fiscal Year Ends: 6/30
2004 Sales: $208,113	2004 Profits: $9,730	Parent Company:

SALARIES/BENEFITS:

Pension Plan:	ESOP Stock Plan:	Profit Sharing:	Top Exec. Salary: $650,000	Bonus: $150,000
Savings Plan:	Stock Purch. Plan:		Second Exec. Salary: $281,538	Bonus: $53,741

OTHER THOUGHTS:

Apparent Women Officers or Directors: 3
Hot Spot for Advancement for Women/Minorities: Y

LOCATIONS: ("Y" = Yes)

West:	Southwest:	Midwest:	Southeast:	Northeast:	International:
Y		Y	Y	Y	Y

DENVER BRONCOS

www.denverbroncos.com

Industry Group Code: 711211C **Ranks within this company's industry group:** Sales: 8 Profits: 25

Sports:		Services:		Media:		Sales:		Facilities:		Other:	
Leagues/Associations:		Food & Beverage:		TV:		Marketing:		Stadiums:	Y	Gambling:	
Teams:	Y	Agents:		Radio:		Ads:		Fitness Clubs:		Apparel:	
Nonprofits:		Other:		Internet:		Tickets:	Y	Golf Courses:		Equipment:	
Other:				Print:		Retail:	Y	Ski Resorts:		Shoes:	
				Software:		Other:		Other:		Other:	

TYPES OF BUSINESS:

Professional Football Team
Ticket Sales
Team Merchandise

BRANDS/DIVISIONS/AFFILIATES:

INVESCO Field at Mile High
Denver Broncos Football Club

CONTACTS:

Note: Officers with more than one job title may be intentionally listed here more than once.

Pat Bowlen, CEO
Joe Ellis, COO
Pat Bowlen, Pres.
Greg Carney, VP-Mktg.
Sheila Thomas, Dir.-Human Resources
Rick Schoenhals, VP-IT
Rich Slivka, Sr. VP-Admin.
Rich Slivka, General Counsel
Chip Conway, VP-Oper.
Jim Saccomano, VP-Public Rel.
Jim Barlow, VP-Finance
Josh McDaniels, Exec. VP-Football Oper./Head Coach
Cindy G. Kellogg, VP-Community Dev.
Jim Goodman, VP-Football Oper./Player Personnel
Brian Xanders, Asst. Gen. Mgr.
Pat Bowlen, Chmn.

Phone: 303-649-9000	**Fax:** 303-649-0562
Toll-Free:	
Address: 13655 Broncos Pkwy., Englewood, CO 80112 US	

GROWTH PLANS/SPECIAL FEATURES:

The Denver Broncos, owned and operated by the Denver Broncos Football Club, are a professional football team playing in the National Football League (NFL) and based in Denver, Colorado. It was founded in 1960 and it is an original franchise of the American Football League. The team won back-to-back Super Bowls in the 1997 and 1998 seasons after four unsuccessful appearances at the championship. The Broncos' success was largely due to Hall of Fame quarterback John Elway and notable running back Terrell Davis. Elway retired in 1999, Davis in 2001. Past great Broncos have included Frank Tripucka and Floyd Little, and current stars include Champ Bailey, Jason Elam, Rod Smith and Trevor Pryce. Some of the team's sponsors include Budweiser, America Online and ViaWest. The Broncos play their games at a $400-million stadium called INVESCO Field at Mile High, which replaced the aging Mile High Stadium in 2001 and has a football capacity of approximately 76,125 fans. Mile High Stadium was famous for sell-outs and home-field advantage for the Broncos, especially in the post-season. INVESCO Field at Mile High is owned by the Denver Metropolitan Football Stadium District. Forbes Magazine recently valued the team at $1.06 billion.

FINANCIALS:

Sales and profits are in thousands of dollars—add 000 to get the full amount. 2008 Note: Financial information for 2008 was not available for all companies at press time.

2008 Sales: $226,000	2008 Profits: $18,800	**U.S. Stock Ticker: Subsidiary**
2007 Sales: $212,000	2007 Profits: $15,900	**Int'l Ticker:** Int'l Exchange:
2006 Sales: $207,000	2006 Profits: $26,900	Employees:
2005 Sales: $202,000	2005 Profits: $	Fiscal Year Ends: 3/31
2004 Sales: $183,000	2004 Profits: $	Parent Company: DENVER BRONCOS FOOTBALL CLUB

SALARIES/BENEFITS:

Pension Plan:	ESOP Stock Plan:	Profit Sharing:	Top Exec. Salary: $	Bonus: $
Savings Plan:	Stock Purch. Plan:		Second Exec. Salary: $	Bonus: $

OTHER THOUGHTS:

Apparent Women Officers or Directors: 2
Hot Spot for Advancement for Women/Minorities: Y

LOCATIONS: ("Y" = Yes)

West:	Southwest:	Midwest:	Southeast:	Northeast:	International:
Y					

DENVER NUGGETS

www.nba.com/nuggets

Industry Group Code: 711211B **Ranks within this company's industry group:** Sales: 18 Profits: 30

Sports:		Services:		Media:		Sales:		Facilities:		Other:	
Leagues/Associations:		Food & Beverage:		TV:		Marketing:		Stadiums:		Gambling:	
Teams:	Y	Agents:		Radio:		Ads:		Fitness Clubs:		Apparel:	
Nonprofits:		Other:		Internet:		Tickets:	Y	Golf Courses:		Equipment:	
Other:				Print:		Retail:		Ski Resorts:		Shoes:	
				Software:		Other:		Other:		Other:	

TYPES OF BUSINESS:

Professional Basketball Team
Ticket Sales

BRANDS/DIVISIONS/AFFILIATES:

Pepsi Center
Kroenke Sports Enterprises, LLC
Nugget for a Day
Team Fit
Junior Nuggets/YMCA Basketball League
Nuggets/Avalanche Prep League
Porter-Billups Leadership Academy (The)
Carmelo Anthony Foundation (The)

CONTACTS: *Note: Officers with more than one job title may be intentionally listed here more than once.*

E. Stanley Kroenke, Owner
Rex Chapman, VP-Player Personnel
Stephen Stieneker, General Counsel/VP
Mark Warkentien, VP-Basketball Oper.
Josh Kroenke, VP-Team Dev.
Eric Sebastian, Dir.-Media Rel.
Tomago Collins, VP-Media & Player Dev.
George Karl, Head Coach
Lisa Johnson, Dir.-Basketball Admin.

Phone: 303-405-1100	**Fax:** 303-575-1920
Toll-Free:	
Address: 1000 Chopper Cir., Denver, CO 80204 US	

GROWTH PLANS/SPECIAL FEATURES:

The Denver Nuggets joined the NBA in 1967 as the Denver Rockets; the team was renamed the Denver Nuggets in 1975. Hall of Fame players include Alex English, David Thompson, Dan Issel and Adrian Dantley. The Nugget's home stadium, the Pepsi Center, located in Platte Valley, occupies 675,000 square feet of space for sports/entertainment events. Both the Pepsi Center and the Nuggets franchise are owned by Kroenke Sports Enterprises, LLC. Entertainment offered during halftime shows includes Nuggets' mascot Rocky the Mountain Lion, the Nuggets Dancers, and the Nuggets Cheer Team. Children are offered membership for the Denver Nuggets Kids Club, which includes a membership ID card and a 10% discount on Altitude Authentics. The team also hosts several community outreach programs for children, including Team Fit, the Junior Nuggets/YMCA Basketball League and Nugget for a Day. In addition, the Nuggets have three player foundations: The Kenyon Martin Foundation and The Carmelo Anthony Foundation both aid underserved children, while The Porter-Billups Leadership Academy helps high school students prepare for college. As part of NBA's western conference, the Nuggets have earned a playoff spot each of the last four seasons. In July 2008, the team traded Marcus Camby to the Los Angeles Clippers in exchange for 2010 NBA Draft second-round rights; signed former New Orleans Hornet Chris Anderson and former Sacramento King Dahntay Jones; and traded Taurean Green, Bobby Jones and a second round 2010 NBA Draft pick to the New York Knicks for Renaldo Balkman and undisclosed cash considerations. Forbes recently estimated the team to be worth approximately $329 million. In the 2008-09 season, the team's home attendance average was roughly 17,200 per game.

FINANCIALS: **Sales and profits are in thousands of dollars—add 000 to get the full amount. 2008 Note: Financial information for 2008 was not available for all companies at press time.**

2008 Sales: $112,000	2008 Profits: $-26,300	**U.S. Stock Ticker: Private**
2007 Sales: $104,000	2007 Profits: $-4,800	**Int'l Ticker:** Int'l Exchange:
2006 Sales: $100,000	2006 Profits: $9,400	Employees:
2005 Sales: $94,000	2005 Profits: $	Fiscal Year Ends: 6/30
2004 Sales: $89,000	2004 Profits: $	Parent Company: KROENKE SPORTS ENTERPRISES LLC

SALARIES/BENEFITS:

Pension Plan:	ESOP Stock Plan:	Profit Sharing:	Top Exec. Salary: $	Bonus: $
Savings Plan:	Stock Purch. Plan:		Second Exec. Salary: $	Bonus: $

OTHER THOUGHTS:

Apparent Women Officers or Directors: 3
Hot Spot for Advancement for Women/Minorities: Y

LOCATIONS: ("Y" = Yes)

West:	Southwest:	Midwest:	Southeast:	Northeast:	International:
Y					

DETROIT LIONS

www.detroitlions.com

Industry Group Code: 711211C **Ranks within this company's industry group:** Sales: 27 Profits: 32

Sports:		Services:		Media:		Sales:		Facilities:		Other:	
Leagues/Associations:		Food & Beverage:		TV:		Marketing:		Stadiums:	Y	Gambling:	
Teams:	Y	Agents:		Radio:		Ads:		Fitness Clubs:		Apparel:	
Nonprofits:	Y	Other:		Internet:		Tickets:	Y	Golf Courses:		Equipment:	
Other:				Print:		Retail:	Y	Ski Resorts:		Shoes:	
				Software:		Other:		Other:		Other:	

TYPES OF BUSINESS:

Professional Football Team
Ticket Sales
Team Merchandise

BRANDS/DIVISIONS/AFFILIATES:

Ford Field
Detroit Lions Charities

CONTACTS: *Note: Officers with more than one job title may be intentionally listed here more than once.*

Tom Lewand, Pres.
Tom Lesnau, CFO
Terri McKay, Dir.-IT
Richard Pinskey, Dir.-Merch.
David Hempstead, Corp. Sec.
Cedric Saunders, VP-Football Oper.
Bill Keenist, Sr. VP-Comm.
Tom Lesnau, Sr. VP-Finance
Jim Schwartz, Head Coach
Martin Mayhew, Gen. Mgr.
Matt Barnhart, Dir.-Media Rel.
Tim Pendell, Sr. Dir.-Community Affairs
William Clay Ford, Chmn./Owner

Phone: 313-216-4000	**Fax:** 313-216-4226
Toll-Free:	
Address: 222 Republic Dr., Allen Park, MI 48101 US	

GROWTH PLANS/SPECIAL FEATURES:

The Detroit Lions are a professional football team playing in the National Football League (NFL) and based in Detroit, Michigan. The team was founded in 1930 as the Portsmouth Spartans (based in Ohio) and moved to Detroit four years later. The team's golden years were in the 1950s, when it reached the NFL championships four times and won three titles (in 1952, 1953 and 1957), led by quarterback Bobby Layne. Later, led by superstar running back Barry Sanders, the Lions made a solid run though the 1990s, making regular post-season appearances and finishing higher in their division on average than in the years prior. The team has failed to make the playoffs since 1999. The Lions' current owner, William Clay Ford (a descendant of Henry Ford), purchased the team in 1964. The Lions play at the indoor, 70,000-seat Ford Field, owned by the city of Detroit and with naming rights claimed by Ford Motor Company until approximately 2022. Ford Motors has further tied the life of the team with its hometown's automobile industry by furnishing the field with a special blend of FieldTurf incorporating recycled Firestone tires. A number of former Lions have been inducted into the Pro Football Hall of Fame over the course of the team's history, including Layne and Sanders, Lem Barney, Jack Christiansen, Earl (Dutch) Clark, Lou Creekmur, Bill Dudley, Dick (Night Train) Lane, Yale Lary, Charlie Sanders, Joe Schmidt, Doak Walker and Alex Wojciechowicz. Forbes Magazine recently valued the team at $917 million. The team's average home game attendance in the 2008 season was 54,497.

FINANCIALS: **Sales and profits are in thousands of dollars—add 000 to get the full amount. 2008 Note: Financial information for 2008 was not available for all companies at press time.**

2008 Sales: $204,000	2008 Profits: $-3,100	**U.S. Stock Ticker: Subsidiary**
2007 Sales: $189,000	2007 Profits: $-1,800	**Int'l Ticker:** Int'l Exchange:
2006 Sales: $178,000	2006 Profits: $16,100	Employees:
2005 Sales: $186,000	2005 Profits: $	Fiscal Year Ends: 2/28
2004 Sales: $168,000	2004 Profits: $	Parent Company: DETROIT LIONS INC

SALARIES/BENEFITS:

Pension Plan:	ESOP Stock Plan:	Profit Sharing:	Top Exec. Salary: $	Bonus: $
Savings Plan:	Stock Purch. Plan:		Second Exec. Salary: $	Bonus: $

OTHER THOUGHTS:

Apparent Women Officers or Directors: 3
Hot Spot for Advancement for Women/Minorities: Y

LOCATIONS: ("Y" = Yes)

West:	Southwest:	Midwest:	Southeast:	Northeast:	International:
		Y			

Note: Financial information, benefits and other data can change quickly and may vary from those stated here.

DETROIT PISTONS

www.nba.com/pistons

Industry Group Code: 711211B **Ranks within this company's industry group:** Sales: 4 Profits: 3

Sports:		Services:		Media:		Sales:		Facilities:		Other:	
Leagues/Associations:		Food & Beverage:		TV:		Marketing:		Stadiums:		Gambling:	
Teams:	Y	Agents:		Radio:		Ads:		Fitness Clubs:		Apparel:	
Nonprofits:		Other:		Internet:		Tickets:	Y	Golf Courses:		Equipment:	
Other:				Print:		Retail:	Y	Ski Resorts:		Shoes:	
				Software:		Other:		Other:		Other:	

TYPES OF BUSINESS:

Professional Basketball Team
Ticket Sales

BRANDS/DIVISIONS/AFFILIATES:

Palace of Auburn Hills (The)
Pistons Drumline
Palace Sports & Entertainment, Inc.
The Flight Crew
Detroit Pistons Youth Training Camp
Pistons Palace Foundation
Bowling for Kids
Black History Month Tour

CONTACTS:

Note: Officers with more than one job title may be intentionally listed here more than once.

Thomas S. Wilson, CEO
Thomas S. Wilson, Pres.
Joe Dumars, Gen. Mgr.
Michael Curry, Head Coach
Karen Davidson, Owner

Phone: 248-377-0100 **Fax:** 248-377-3260
Toll-Free:
Address: 5 Championship Dr., Auburn Hills, MI 48236 US

GROWTH PLANS/SPECIAL FEATURES:

The Detroit Pistons joined the National Basketball Association (NBA) in 1949 as the Fort Wayne Pistons. The franchise officially became known as the Detroit Pistons after it moved to Detroit in 1957. In 1974, founder Fred Zollner sold the team to William Davidson, who owns Palace Sports and Entertainment, the holding company that in turn owns The Palace of Auburn Hills arena, the home stadium of the Pistons. The Palace of Auburn Hills is one of the largest sports arenas in the NBA and hosts a 22,076 seating capacity and 180 luxury suites. Entertainment provided during team games includes the Pistons Drumline, The Flight Crew and the Pistons' horse mascot, Hooper. The franchise also offers Hooper and Zap's Fun zone, an interactive site that allows children to play games and discover upcoming Pistons events; Hooper Bar; and Hooper's Mailbox. Additionally, the team offers the Detroit Pistons Youth Training Camp for children, which features professional-, college- and high-school-level coaches. Community outreach programs include the Pistons Palace Foundation, Bowling for Kids fundraiser and the Black History Month Tour, which is hosted throughout the month of February by former Pistons legend, Rick Mahorn. Since its inception, the Pistons have won two consecutive NBA titles in the 1988-89 and 1989-90 seasons. Forbes Magazine recently estimated the team to be worth approximately $480 million. In the 2008-09 season, the team's home attendance average was roughly 21,900 per game.

FINANCIALS:

Sales and profits are in thousands of dollars—add 000 to get the full amount. 2008 Note: Financial information for 2008 was not available for all companies at press time.

2008 Sales: $160,000	2008 Profits: $40,400	**U.S. Stock Ticker: Private**
2007 Sales: $154,000	2007 Profits: $39,200	**Int'l Ticker:** Int'l Exchange:
2006 Sales: $138,000	2006 Profits: $21,800	Employees:
2005 Sales: $134,000	2005 Profits: $	Fiscal Year Ends: 6/30
2004 Sales: $121,000	2004 Profits: $	Parent Company:

SALARIES/BENEFITS:

Pension Plan:	ESOP Stock Plan:	Profit Sharing:	Top Exec. Salary: $	Bonus: $
Savings Plan:	Stock Purch. Plan:		Second Exec. Salary: $	Bonus: $

OTHER THOUGHTS:

Apparent Women Officers or Directors: 1
Hot Spot for Advancement for Women/Minorities:

LOCATIONS: ("Y" = Yes)

West:	Southwest:	Midwest:	Southeast:	Northeast:	International:
		Y			

DETROIT RED WINGS

www.detroitredwings.com

Industry Group Code: 711211F **Ranks within this company's industry group:** Sales: 4 Profits: 6

Sports:		Services:		Media:		Sales:		Facilities:		Other:	
Leagues/Associations:		Food & Beverage:		TV:		Marketing:		Stadiums:	Y	Gambling:	
Teams:	Y	Agents:		Radio:		Ads:		Fitness Clubs:		Apparel:	
Nonprofits:		Other:		Internet:		Tickets:	Y	Golf Courses:		Equipment:	
Other:				Print:		Retail:	Y	Ski Resorts:		Shoes:	
				Software:		Other:		Other:		Other:	

TYPES OF BUSINESS:

Professional Hockey Team

BRANDS/DIVISIONS/AFFILIATES:

Ilitch Holdings, Inc.
Joe Louis Arena
Inside Hockeytown
ABCs of Detroit Red Wings Hockey (The)

CONTACTS:

Note: Officers with more than one job title may be intentionally listed here more than once.

Mike Ilitch, Governor/Owner
Christopher Ilitch, Pres., Ilitch Holdings, Inc.
Robert E. Carr, General Counsel/Alternate Governor
John Hahn, Sr. Dir.-Comm.
Marian Ilitch, Treas./Corp. Sec.
Christopher Ilitch, CEO-Ilitch Holdings, Inc.
Jim Devellano, Sr. VP/Alternate Governor
Ken Holland, Gen. Mgr./Alternate Governor
Jim Nill, VP/Asst. Gen. Mgr.
Marian Ilitch, Owner

Phone: 313-396-7544 **Fax:** 313-567-0296
Toll-Free:
Address: 600 Civic Center Dr., Detroit, MI 48226 US

GROWTH PLANS/SPECIAL FEATURES:

The Detroit Red Wings are a National Hockey League (NHL) team based in Detroit, Michigan that plays at the Joe Louis Arena. The club plays in the Central Division of the NHL's Western Conference along with Chicago Blackhawks, Columbus Blue Jackets, Nashville Predators and St. Louis Blues. It was founded in 1926 when the roster of the Victoria Cougars, a Pacific Coast Hockey League team and the 1925 Stanley Cup champion, was sold to a group from Detroit that had recently been awarded an NHL franchise. The first team played as the Detroit Cougars until 1930 and then for one year as the Detroit Falcons. In 1932, grain and shipping magnate James Norris, Sr. acquired the team and changed its name to the Detroit Red Wings, after the amateur hockey team he played on in Montreal, the Winged Wheelers. The team won its first Stanley Cup in 1936, a second in 1937 and five more over the next 18 years, the last in 1955. For almost 50 years, the Red Wings went through a sporadic period in which they made it to the playoffs and several finals but never won the Stanley Cup. In 1982, current owners Michael and Marina Ilitch, the founders of Little Caesar's Pizza, acquired the team. Since 1990, the Red Wings have been a perennial playoff contender under the leadership of team captain Steve Yzerman, the longest-serving team captain in NHL history. Beginning in 1997, Yzerman led the team to three Stanley Cup championships after a 42-year hiatus. The team has won 11 Stanley Cup championships. In the 2008-09 season, the team's home attendance average was approximately 19,800 fans per game. Forbes recently valued the team at approximately $303 million.

FINANCIALS:

Sales and profits are in thousands of dollars—add 000 to get the full amount. 2008 Note: Financial information for 2008 was not available for all companies at press time.

2008 Sales: $110,000	2008 Profits: $13,400	**U.S. Stock Ticker: Subsidiary**
2007 Sales: $109,000	2007 Profits: $14,400	**Int'l Ticker:** Int'l Exchange:
2006 Sales: $89,000	2006 Profits: $5,800	Employees:
2005 Sales: $	2005 Profits: $	Fiscal Year Ends: 6/30
2004 Sales: $97,000	2004 Profits: $	Parent Company: ILITCH HOLDINGS INC

SALARIES/BENEFITS:

Pension Plan:	ESOP Stock Plan:	Profit Sharing:	Top Exec. Salary: $	Bonus: $
Savings Plan:	Stock Purch. Plan:		Second Exec. Salary: $	Bonus: $

OTHER THOUGHTS:

Apparent Women Officers or Directors: 5
Hot Spot for Advancement for Women/Minorities: Y

LOCATIONS: ("Y" = Yes)

West:	Southwest:	Midwest:	Southeast:	Northeast:	International:
		Y			

Note: Financial information, benefits and other data can change quickly and may vary from those stated here.

DETROIT SHOCK

www.wnba.com/shock

Industry Group Code: 711211E **Ranks within this company's industry group:** Sales: Profits:

Sports:		Services:		Media:		Sales:		Facilities:		Other:	
Leagues/Associations:		Food & Beverage:		TV:		Marketing:		Stadiums:	Y	Gambling:	
Teams:	Y	Agents:		Radio:		Ads:		Fitness Clubs:		Apparel:	
Nonprofits:		Other:		Internet:		Tickets:	Y	Golf Courses:		Equipment:	
Other:				Print:		Retail:		Ski Resorts:		Shoes:	
				Software:		Other:		Other:		Other:	

TYPES OF BUSINESS:

Women's Professional Basketball Team
Ticket Sales

BRANDS/DIVISIONS/AFFILIATES:

Palace Sports & Entertanment Inc
Palace of Auburn Hills (The)

CONTACTS:

Note: Officers with more than one job title may be intentionally listed here more than once.

Thomas S. Wilson, CEO
Alan Ostfield, COO
Thomas S. Wilson, Pres.
John O'Reilly, CFO/Exec. VP
Ron Melnyk, Sr. VP-Mktg.
Tom Bennett, VP-Human Resources
Susan Greenfield, VP-Legal
Craig Turnbull, VP-Oper.
Peter M. Skorich, Exec. VP-Multimedia
Matt Dobek, VP-Public Rel.
Robert Johnson, VP-Finance
Bill Laimbeer, Head Coach
Alicia Jeffreys, Dir.-Bus. Oper.
Donease Smith, Mgr.-Basketball Oper.
John Ciszewski, Exec. VP

Phone: 246-377-0100	**Fax:** 246-377-2053
Toll-Free:	
Address: The Palace of Auburn Hills, 4 Championship Dr., Auburn Hills, MI 48326 US	

GROWTH PLANS/SPECIAL FEATURES:

The Detroit Shock is a Women's National Basketball Association (WNBA) team. Founded in 1998 as one of the league's first expansion franchises, the Shock plays in the WNBA's Eastern Conference alongside the Chicago Sky, Atlanta Dream, Connecticut Sun, Indiana Fever, New York Liberty and Washington Mystics. Notable former players include Wendy Palmer, Jennifer Azzi and Anna DeForge; the team is coached by former NBA star Bill Laimbeer. The team's home court is The Palace of Auburn Hills, a 22,000-seat stadium located in Auburn Hills, a suburb of Detroit. The team is owned by Palace Sports & Entertainment, Inc. (PS&E), which also owns the Detroit Pistons of the National Basketball Association (NBA) and the Tampa Bay Lightning of the National Hockey League (NHL). It also owns the Palace of Auburn Hills and the DTE Energy Music Theatre, a music venue in Clarkson, Michigan. The Shock made it to but did not win the WNBA playoffs in 1999 and 2004, and won WNBA championship titles in 2003 and 2006, defeating the Los Angeles Sparks and Sacramento Monarchs, respectively. The franchise made it to the championship round again in 2007, but was unable to defend the title against the Phoenix Mercury. In 2008, however, the Shock returned to the finals and beat the San Antonio Stars to win its third WNBA Championship. In June 2008, the team traded LaToya Thomas to the Minnesota Lynx in exchange for Eshaya Murphy. In July 2008, Detroit signed Nancy Lieberman (seven-day contract) and Kelly Schumacher. In August 2008, the team traded Tasha Humphrey, Eshaya Murphy and a 2009 WNBA Draft pick to the Washington Mystics for Taj McWilliams-Franklin; Detroit also signed Ashley Shields to a seven-day contract.

FINANCIALS:

Sales and profits are in thousands of dollars—add 000 to get the full amount. 2008 Note: Financial information for 2008 was not available for all companies at press time.

2008 Sales: $	2008 Profits: $	**U.S. Stock Ticker: Subsidiary**
2007 Sales: $	2007 Profits: $	**Int'l Ticker:** Int'l Exchange:
2006 Sales: $	2006 Profits: $	Employees: 1,400
2005 Sales: $	2005 Profits: $	Fiscal Year Ends: 12/31
2004 Sales: $134,400	2004 Profits: $	Parent Company: PALACE SPORTS & ENTERTAINMENT INC

SALARIES/BENEFITS:

Pension Plan:	ESOP Stock Plan:	Profit Sharing:	Top Exec. Salary: $	Bonus: $
Savings Plan:	Stock Purch. Plan:		Second Exec. Salary: $	Bonus: $

OTHER THOUGHTS:

Apparent Women Officers or Directors: 6
Hot Spot for Advancement for Women/Minorities: Y

LOCATIONS: ("Y" = Yes)

West:	Southwest:	Midwest:	Southeast:	Northeast:	International:
		Y			

DETROIT TIGERS

detroit.tigers.mlb.com

Industry Group Code: 711211A **Ranks within this company's industry group:** Sales: 14 Profits: 30

Sports:		Services:		Media:		Sales:		Facilities:		Other:	
Leagues/Associations:		Food & Beverage:		TV:		Marketing:		Stadiums:	Y	Gambling:	
Teams:	Y	Agents:		Radio:		Ads:		Fitness Clubs:		Apparel:	
Nonprofits:		Other:		Internet:		Tickets:	Y	Golf Courses:		Equipment:	
Other:				Print:		Retail:	Y	Ski Resorts:		Shoes:	
				Software:		Other:		Other:		Other:	

TYPES OF BUSINESS:

Professional Baseball Team
Stadium Operation
Baseball Training Complex

BRANDS/DIVISIONS/AFFILIATES:

Comerica Park
Oneonta Tigers
Toledo Mud Hens
Erie SeaWolves
Lakeland Flying Tigers
West Michigan Whitecaps

CONTACTS: *Note: Officers with more than one job title may be intentionally listed here more than once.*

David Dombrowski, CEO
David Dombrowski, Pres./Gen. Mgr.
Stephen Quinn, CFO/VP-Finance
Ellen Hill Zeringue, VP-Mktg.
Karen Gruca, Dir.-Human Resources
Scott Wruble, Dir.-IT
Stephen Quinn, VP-Admin.
John Westhoff, VP/Baseball Legal Counsel
Duane McLean, Sr. VP-Bus. Oper.
Ron Colangelo, VP-Comm.
Kelli Kollman, Sr. Dir.-Finance
Charles P. Jones, VP-Corp. Suite Sales & Svcs.
Mike Healy, VP-Park Oper.
Al Avila, VP/Assistant Gen. Mgr.
Scott Reid, VP-Player Personnel

Phone: 313-962-4000 **Fax:** 313-471-2138
Toll-Free:
Address: Comerica Park, 2100 Woodward Ave., Detroit, MI 48201 US

GROWTH PLANS/SPECIAL FEATURES:

The Detroit Tigers are a Major League Baseball (MLB) team. The team was an inaugural member of the American League, which started in 1901. In all, the Tigers have won four World Series, 10 pennants and three division titles. Notable Tigers include Al Kaline, Ty Cobb, Hank Greenberg, Lou Whitaker, Charlie Gehringer and Willie Horton. In the past two decades the team has been rather poor, posting 12 consecutive losing seasons from 1994-2005, including 119 losses in 2003, the most since the New York Mets' inaugural 1962 campaign. However, in 2006 the Tigers made the playoffs for the first time in 19 years, converting a Wild Card berth into the American League pennant before losing to the St. Louis Cardinals in the World Series. The team has been owned by Illitch Holdings, Inc., the parent company of the Detroit Red Wings and Little Caesars Pizza, since 1992. In 2000, the team began to play its games in Comerica Park, a $300 million downtown ballpark. The Tigers' performance didn't help attendance, and the new stadium only provided a small spike in numbers. However, the club's recent pennant-winning performance has spurred a rise in attendance, up from 2.02 million and 21st in MLB in 2005 to 3.2 million and 8th in MLB in 2008. Minor league affiliate teams include the Toledo Mud Hens, the Erie SeaWolves, the Lakeland Flying Tigers, the West Michigan Whitecaps and the Oneonta Tigers. The team is worth $371 million, according to a recent Forbes estimate. Average home game attendance in 2008 was approximately 39,500.

FINANCIALS: **Sales and profits are in thousands of dollars—add 000 to get the full amount. 2008 Note: Financial information for 2008 was not available for all companies at press time.**

2008 Sales: $186,000	2008 Profits: $-26,300	**U.S. Stock Ticker: Subsidiary**
2007 Sales: $173,000	2007 Profits: $4,600	**Int'l Ticker:** Int'l Exchange:
2006 Sales: $170,000	2006 Profits: $8,700	Employees:
2005 Sales: $146,000	2005 Profits: $	Fiscal Year Ends: 12/31
2004 Sales: $	2004 Profits: $	Parent Company: ILITCH HOLDINGS INC

SALARIES/BENEFITS:

Pension Plan:	ESOP Stock Plan:	Profit Sharing:	Top Exec. Salary: $	Bonus: $
Savings Plan:	Stock Purch. Plan:		Second Exec. Salary: $	Bonus: $

OTHER THOUGHTS:

Apparent Women Officers or Directors: 4
Hot Spot for Advancement for Women/Minorities: Y

LOCATIONS: ("Y" = Yes)

West:	Southwest:	Midwest:	Southeast:	Northeast:	International:
		Y			

DICK'S SPORTING GOODS INC

www.dickssportinggoods.com

Industry Group Code: 451110 **Ranks within this company's industry group:** Sales: 1 Profits: 1

Sports:		Services:		Media:		Sales:		Facilities:		Other:	
Leagues/Associations:		Food & Beverage:		TV:		Marketing:		Stadiums:		Gambling:	
Teams:		Agents:		Radio:		Ads:		Fitness Clubs:		Apparel:	Y
Nonprofits:		Other:		Internet:		Tickets:		Golf Courses:		Equipment:	Y
Other:				Print:		Retail:	Y	Ski Resorts:		Shoes:	Y
				Software:		Other:		Other:		Other:	

TYPES OF BUSINESS:

Sporting Goods Stores
Outdoor Apparel
Footwear
Hunting & Fishing Supplies
Golf Supplies
Bicycles
Online Sales

BRANDS/DIVISIONS/AFFILIATES:

Golf Galaxy Inc
Chick's Sporting Goods

CONTACTS: *Note: Officers with more than one job title may be intentionally listed here more than once.*

Edward W. Stack, CEO
Joseph H. Schmidt, COO
Joseph H. Schmidt, Pres.
Timothy E. Kullman, CFO
Jeffrey R. Hennion, Chief Mktg. Officer/Exec. VP
Kathy Sutter, Sr. VP-Human Resources
Matthew J. Lynch, CIO/Sr. VP
Gwen Manto, Chief Merch. Officer/Exec. VP
Timothy E. Kullman, Exec. VP-Admin.
Timothy E. Kullman, Exec. VP-Finance
David G. Stanchak, Sr. VP-Real Estate
Edward W. Stack, Chmn.
Lee Belitsky, Sr. VP-Dist. & Transportation

Phone: 724-273-3400 **Fax:**
Toll-Free:
Address: 300 Industry Dr., RIDC Park W., Pittsburgh, PA 15275 US

GROWTH PLANS/SPECIAL FEATURES:

Dick's Sporting Goods, Inc. is a retail sporting goods chain with 483 stores in 41 states, including 384 Dick's Sporting Goods stores, 85 Golf Galaxy stores and 14 Chick's Sporting Goods stores. The firm's stores are primarily in the eastern half of the U.S. The company offers a broad assortment of sporting goods equipment, footwear and apparel under national and private-brand labels, including its own Ativa, Power Bolt, Walter Hagen, Fitness Gear and Acuity brands. Each Dick's Sporting Goods location typically contains five store-within-a-store specialty stores. The company seeks to create a distinct look and feel for each specialty department to heighten the customer's interest in the products offered. A typical facility has the following in-store specialty shops: the Pro Shop, a golf shop with a putting green and hitting area and video monitors featuring golf tournaments and instruction on the Golf Channel or other sources; the Footwear Center, featuring hardwood floors, a track for testing athletic shoes and a bank of video monitors playing sporting events; the Cycle Shop, designed to sell and service bikes, complete with a mechanics' work area and equipment on the sales floor; the Sportsman's Lodge for the hunting and fishing customer, designed to have the look of an authentic bait and tackle shop; and Total Sports, seasonal sports area displaying sports equipment and athletic apparel associated with specific seasonal sports, such as football and baseball. Dick's stores offer a variety of maintenance, repair and support services in all departments, as well as an e-commerce site. Galaxy Golf stores are designed for an interactive shopping environment, which includes an artificial bent grass putting green and golf simulators. Chick's Sporting Goods stores are located in southern California.

FINANCIALS: **Sales and profits are in thousands of dollars—add 000 to get the full amount. 2008 Note: Financial information for 2008 was not available for all companies at press time.**

2008 Sales: $3,888,422
2007 Sales: $3,114,162
2006 Sales: $2,624,987
2005 Sales: $2,109,400
2004 Sales: $1,470,800

2008 Profits: $155,036
2007 Profits: $112,611
2006 Profits: $72,980
2005 Profits: $68,905
2004 Profits: $52,408

U.S. Stock Ticker: DKS
Int'l Ticker: Int'l Exchange:
Employees: 26,400
Fiscal Year Ends: 1/31
Parent Company:

SALARIES/BENEFITS:

Pension Plan: ESOP Stock Plan: Profit Sharing: Top Exec. Salary: $698,077 Bonus: $2,792,308
Savings Plan: Stock Purch. Plan: Second Exec. Salary: $649,038 Bonus: $973,558

OTHER THOUGHTS:

Apparent Women Officers or Directors: 2
Hot Spot for Advancement for Women/Minorities: Y

LOCATIONS: ("Y" = Yes)

West:	Southwest:	Midwest:	Southeast:	Northeast:	International:
Y	Y	Y	Y	Y	

DOVER DOWNS GAMING & ENTERTAINMENT INC

www.doverdowns.com

Industry Group Code: 713210 **Ranks within this company's industry group:** Sales: 3 Profits: 2

Sports:		Services:		Media:		Sales:		Facilities:		Other:	
Leagues/Associations:		Food & Beverage:		TV:		Marketing:		Stadiums:		Gambling:	Y
Teams:		Agents:		Radio:		Ads:		Fitness Clubs:		Apparel:	
Nonprofits:		Other:		Internet:		Tickets:		Golf Courses:		Equipment:	
Other:				Print:		Retail:		Ski Resorts:		Shoes:	
				Software:		Other:		Other:		Other:	

TYPES OF BUSINESS:

Casinos & Gaming Facilities
Slot Machine Casino
Hotel & Conference Center
Horse Racing
Live Events

BRANDS/DIVISIONS/AFFILIATES:

Dover Downs Slots
Dover Downs Hotel & Conference Center
Dover Downs Raceway
Dover Downs, Inc.
Dover Downs Management Corp.
Capital Club

CONTACTS: *Note: Officers with more than one job title may be intentionally listed here more than once.*

Denis McGlynn, CEO
Edward J. Sutor, COO/Exec. VP
Denis McGlynn, Pres.
Timothy R. Horne, CFO
Janie M. Libby, VP-Human Resources
Klaus M. Belohoubek, General Counsel/Corp. Sec./Sr. VP
Timothy R. Horne, Sr. VP-Finance/Treas.
Henry B. Tippie, Chmn.

Phone: 302-674-4600	**Fax:** 302-857-3253
Toll-Free: 800-711-5882	
Address: 1131 N. DuPont Hwy., Dover, DE 19901 US	

GROWTH PLANS/SPECIAL FEATURES:

Dover Downs Gaming & Entertainment, Inc. is a gaming and entertainment company with operations in Delaware, consisting of Dover Downs Casino, a 97,000-square-foot video lottery (slot) machine complex; the Dover Downs Hotel and Conference Center, a 500-room hotel with conference, banquet, fine dining, ballroom, concert hall, swimming pool and spa facilities; and Dover Downs Raceway, a racing track with pari-mutuel wagering on live and simulcast horse races. The casino operates 2,717 slot machines ranging from a penny to $100 to play. In addition, it features various multi-player electronic table games, such as Blackjack and Poker, which accommodate multiple players in an interactive setting featuring a virtual dealer. Through Capital Club, a players club and tracking system, the company identifies and tracks gaming habits, rewarding customer play through various marketing programs. The Capital Club has approximately 147,000 members. In addition to casino activities, the hotel offers entertainment to its guests, such as music concerts and boxing. Dover Downs Raceway, which is adjacent to the hotel and casino, conducts live harness races between October and April, all of which are simulcast to more than 400 tracks and other off-track betting locations across North America on each of the company's more than 130 live race dates. Dover Downs Gaming & Entertainment has two wholly-owned subsidiaries: Dover Downs, Inc. and Dover Downs Management Corp. In October 2008, the company announced the completion of a 70,000-square-foot expansion to the Dover Downs Casino, including a new entrance, 500 additional slot machines and an upscale entertainment lounge with seating for 200 guests, in addition to several new retail spaces and restaurants.

The company offers medical, dental and vision coverage; 401(k) and pension plans; flexible spending accounts; an employee assistance program; educational assistance; and a bonus program.

FINANCIALS: **Sales and profits are in thousands of dollars—add 000 to get the full amount. 2008 Note: Financial information for 2008 was not available for all companies at press time.**

2008 Sales: $239,132	2008 Profits: $19,511	**U.S. Stock Ticker: DDE**
2007 Sales: $242,366	2007 Profits: $26,085	**Int'l Ticker:** Int'l Exchange:
2006 Sales: $236,451	2006 Profits: $25,328	Employees: 898
2005 Sales: $216,852	2005 Profits: $26,040	Fiscal Year Ends: 12/31
2004 Sales: $207,300	2004 Profits: $16,400	Parent Company:

SALARIES/BENEFITS:

Pension Plan: Y	ESOP Stock Plan:	Profit Sharing:	Top Exec. Salary: $250,000	Bonus: $50,000
Savings Plan: Y	Stock Purch. Plan:		Second Exec. Salary: $250,000	Bonus: $50,000

OTHER THOUGHTS:

Apparent Women Officers or Directors: 1
Hot Spot for Advancement for Women/Minorities:

LOCATIONS: ("Y" = Yes)

West:	Southwest:	Midwest:	Southeast:	Northeast:	International:
				Y	

DOVER MOTORSPORTS INC

www.dovermotorsportsinc.com

Industry Group Code: 711212 **Ranks within this company's industry group:** Sales: 3 Profits: 3

Sports:		Services:		Media:		Sales:		Facilities:		Other:	
Leagues/Associations:		Food & Beverage:		TV:	Y	Marketing:		Stadiums:		Gambling:	
Teams:		Agents:		Radio:	Y	Ads:		Fitness Clubs:		Apparel:	
Nonprofits:		Other:		Internet:		Tickets:	Y	Golf Courses:		Equipment:	
Other:				Print:		Retail:		Ski Resorts:		Shoes:	
				Software:		Other:		Other:	Y	Other:	

TYPES OF BUSINESS:

Auto Race Tracks
Race Event Management
Ticket Sales

BRANDS/DIVISIONS/AFFILIATES:

Dover International Speedway
Gateway International Raceway
Memphis Motorsports Park
Nashville Superspeedway
Dover Downs Entertainment
Monster Mile (The)

CONTACTS: *Note: Officers with more than one job title may be intentionally listed here more than once.*

Denis McGlynn, CEO
Denis McGlynn, Pres.
Patrick J. Bagley, CFO/Sr. VP-Finance
Klaus M. Belohoubek, General Counsel/Sr. VP/Sec.
Thomas Wintermantel, Treas.
Michael Tatoian, Exec. VP
Henry B. Tippie, Chmn.

Phone: 302-883-6500	**Fax:** 302-672-0100
Toll-Free:	
Address: 1131 N. DuPont Hwy., Dover, DE 19903 US	

GROWTH PLANS/SPECIAL FEATURES:

Dover Motorsports, Inc. is a public holding company that is a leading marketer and promoter of motorsports entertainment in the United States. Its subsidiaries operate four motorsports tracks in three states and promoted 15 major events during 2008 under the auspices of three of the sanctioning bodies in motorsports: The National Association for Stock Car Auto Racing (NASCAR), the Indy Racing League (IRL) and the National Hot Rod Association (NHRA). The company owns and operates Dover International Speedway in Dover, Delaware, a high-banked, one-mile, concrete superspeedway with permanent seating capacity of approximately 135,000; Gateway International Raceway near St. Louis, Missouri, a 1.25-mile paved oval track with 54,000 permanent seats, a nationally renowned drag strip capable of seating approximately 30,000 people and a road course; Memphis Motorsports Park in Memphis, Tennessee, a 0.75-mile paved tri-oval track with approximately 20,000 permanent seats and a nationally renowned drag strip capable of seating approximately 25,000 people; and Nashville Superspeedway near Nashville, Tennessee, a 1.33-mile concrete superspeedway that has 25,000 permanent grandstand seats with an infrastructure in place to expand to 150,000 seats. In January 2009, the company agreed to sell Memphis Motorsports Park to Gulf Coast Entertainment, L.L.C. for $10 million.

FINANCIALS: Sales and profits are in thousands of dollars—add 000 to get the full amount. 2008 Note: Financial information for 2008 was not available for all companies at press time.

2008 Sales: $84,279	2008 Profits: $-5,679	**U.S. Stock Ticker: DVD**
2007 Sales: $86,052	2007 Profits: $3,744	**Int'l Ticker:** Int'l Exchange:
2006 Sales: $91,274	2006 Profits: $-35,345	Employees: 144
2005 Sales: $90,999	2005 Profits: $4,576	Fiscal Year Ends: 12/31
2004 Sales: $84,188	2004 Profits: $2,440	Parent Company:

SALARIES/BENEFITS:

Pension Plan: Y	ESOP Stock Plan:	Profit Sharing:	Top Exec. Salary: $300,000	Bonus: $
Savings Plan: Y	Stock Purch. Plan:		Second Exec. Salary: $190,000	Bonus: $

OTHER THOUGHTS:

Apparent Women Officers or Directors:
Hot Spot for Advancement for Women/Minorities:

LOCATIONS: ("Y" = Yes)

West:	Southwest:	Midwest:	Southeast:	Northeast:	International:
		Y	Y	Y	

EASTERN MOUNTAIN SPORTS

www.ems.com

Industry Group Code: 451110 **Ranks within this company's industry group:** Sales: Profits:

Sports:		Services:		Media:		Sales:		Facilities:		Other:	
Leagues/Associations:		Food & Beverage:		TV:		Marketing:		Stadiums:		Gambling:	
Teams:		Agents:		Radio:		Ads:		Fitness Clubs:		Apparel:	
Nonprofits:		Other:		Internet:		Tickets:		Golf Courses:		Equipment:	
Other:				Print:		Retail:	Y	Ski Resorts:		Shoes:	
				Software:		Other:		Other:		Other:	

TYPES OF BUSINESS:

Sporting Goods Stores
Outdoor Apparel
Outdoor Gear
Outdoor Sports Instruction

BRANDS/DIVISIONS/AFFILIATES:

EMS Climbing School
EMS Kayak School
EMS Ski School
EMS Adventure Travel

CONTACTS: *Note: Officers with more than one job title may be intentionally listed here more than once.*

William O. Manzer, CEO
Robert Mayerson, COO
William O. Manzer, Pres.
Robert Mayerson, CFO/Exec. VP
Scott Barrett, Chief Mktg. Officer
Mike Corey, Chief Dev. Officer

Phone: 603-924-9571	**Fax:** 603-924-9138
Toll-Free:	
Address: 1 Vose Farm Rd., Peterborough, NH 03458 US	

GROWTH PLANS/SPECIAL FEATURES:

Eastern Mountain Sports (EMS) operates approximately 72 outdoor specialty retail stores in the Northeast. The stores provide an extensive selection of clothing and gear for activities such as rock and ice climbing, mountaineering, kayaking and canoeing, camping, cycling and fitness. EMS stocks most popular brand names in the outdoor industry, including Patagonia, Black Diamond, Sierra Designs, Gregory, Kelty, Thule, The North Face, Marmot and Teva. In addition, EMS designs and offers its own line of outdoor gear and clothing under the EMS name. The company utilizes a large store format that includes comprehensive product offerings and thus lower prices than those offered by local specialty outdoor retailers. EMS has a liberal return policy that allows customers to exchange, return or repair any item with a web invoice or original store receipt, even if the item has been damaged from use. Many of the firm's products are tested and demoed at the firm's various outdoor skills training schools. The EMS Climbing School in New Hampshire offers beginner, intermediate and advanced courses in rock climbing, ice climbing and mountaineering throughout the White Mountains. The EMS Kayak School in Massachusetts provides classes for every level through day and overnight trips throughout the Northeast. The EMS Ski School offers training in a variety of winter sports and winter survival, including avalanche courses and ski mountaineering as well as offering guided tours, overnight programs and hotel packages for skiing trips. Additionally, the firm offers EMS Adventure Travel, which provides trips to locations in Africa, India, Latin America, Tibet, Russia, the U.S. and Canada, including skiing, hiking, mountain climbing and marathons. The company's CEO, William Manzer, recently led a management buyout of the company from its former parent, American Retail Group.

Employees of EMS receive discounts on store merchandise and adventure leave.

FINANCIALS: **Sales and profits are in thousands of dollars—add 000 to get the full amount. 2008 Note: Financial information for 2008 was not available for all companies at press time.**

2008 Sales: $	2008 Profits: $	**U.S. Stock Ticker: Private**
2007 Sales: $	2007 Profits: $	**Int'l Ticker:** Int'l Exchange:
2006 Sales: $	2006 Profits: $	Employees: 1,650
2005 Sales: $200,000	2005 Profits: $	Fiscal Year Ends: 1/31
2004 Sales: $	2004 Profits: $	Parent Company:

SALARIES/BENEFITS:

Pension Plan:	ESOP Stock Plan:	Profit Sharing:	Top Exec. Salary: $	Bonus: $
Savings Plan: Y	Stock Purch. Plan:		Second Exec. Salary: $	Bonus: $

OTHER THOUGHTS:

Apparent Women Officers or Directors:
Hot Spot for Advancement for Women/Minorities:

LOCATIONS: ("Y" = Yes)

West:	Southwest:	Midwest:	Southeast:	Northeast:	International:
				Y	

EASTON-BELL SPORTS INC

www.eastonbellsports.com

Industry Group Code: 339920 **Ranks within this company's industry group:** Sales: 4 Profits: 3

Sports:		Services:		Media:		Sales:		Facilities:		Other:	
Leagues/Associations:		Food & Beverage:		TV:		Marketing:		Stadiums:		Gambling:	
Teams:		Agents:		Radio:		Ads:		Fitness Clubs:		Apparel:	
Nonprofits:		Other:		Internet:		Tickets:		Golf Courses:		Equipment:	Y
Other:				Print:		Retail:		Ski Resorts:		Shoes:	
				Software:		Other:		Other:		Other:	

TYPES OF BUSINESS:

Manufacturing-Sporting Goods
Team Sports Equipment
Action Sports Equipment
Accessories

BRANDS/DIVISIONS/AFFILIATES:

RBG Holdings Corp.
Easton-Bell Sports LLC
Easton
Bell
Riddell
Giro
Blackburn
Savasa

CONTACTS: *Note: Officers with more than one job title may be intentionally listed here more than once.*

Paul E. Harrington, CEO
Donna L. Flood,
Mark A. Tripp, CFO
Jackelyn E. Werblo, Sr. VP-Human Resources
Richard D. Tipton, General Counsel/Sr. VP/Corp. Sec.
Mark A. Tripp, Sr. VP-Finance/Treas.
C. Kwai Kong, Pres., Specialty Bus.
Daniel J. Arment, Pres., Riddell Football
S. Geoffrey Sadowy, Exec VP/Gen. Mgr.-Easton Hockey
Steven T. Bigelow, Exec. VP/Gen. Mgr.-Easton-Bell Sports Mass
James L. Easton, Chmn.
S. Geoffrey Sadowy, Gen. Mgr.-Int'l Sales

Phone: 818-902-5800 **Fax:**
Toll-Free:
Address: 7855 Haskell Ave., Ste. 200, Van Nuys, CA 91406 US

GROWTH PLANS/SPECIAL FEATURES:

Easton-Bell Sports, Inc. was formed in 2006 by the merger of Riddell Sports Group, Easton Sports and Bell Sports. It is a wholly-owned subsidiary of RBG Holdings Corp., which is a wholly-owned subsidiary of EB Sports Corp., which is, in turn, a wholly-owned subsidiary of Easton-Bell Sports, LLC. It is a designer, developer and marketer of sports equipment, protective products and related accessories under authentic brands. The company offers products that are used in baseball, softball, ice hockey, football, lacrosse, cycling, snow sports, powersports and skateboarding. The firm operates in two segments: Team sports and action sports. The team sports segment primarily consists of football, baseball, softball, ice hockey and other team sports products and reconditioning services. The action sports segment primarily consists of helmets, equipment, components and accessories for cycling, snow sports and powersports. Easton-Bell sells its products primarily under four brands: Easton (baseball, softball and ice hockey equipment, apparel and cycling components), Bell (cycling and action sports helmets and accessories), Giro (cycling and snow sports helmets and accessories) and Riddell (football and baseball equipment and reconditioning services). Additionally, the company sells a variety of accessories, including bicycle pumps, headlights, safety lights and reflectors under the Blackburn brand; bicycle trailers and child carrier seats under the Co-Pilot brand; and a line of mats, resistance bands, kits and other fitness accessories designed primarily for strength training, yoga and Pilates under the Bell, Savasa and Bollinger brands.

The firm offers its employees medical and dental insurance; life insurance; an employee assistance program; 401 (k); education assistance; and flexible spending accounts. It also provides training, product discounts, an on-site fitness center, extracurricular programs and holiday celebrations.

FINANCIALS: **Sales and profits are in thousands of dollars—add 000 to get the full amount. 2008 Note: Financial information for 2008 was not available for all companies at press time.**

2008 Sales: $775,539
2007 Sales: $724,639
2006 Sales: $
2005 Sales: $
2004 Sales: $341,600

2008 Profits: $13,413
2007 Profits: $14,469
2006 Profits: $
2005 Profits: $
2004 Profits: $

U.S. Stock Ticker: Subsidiary
Int'l Ticker: Int'l Exchange:
Employees: 2,400
Fiscal Year Ends: 12/31
Parent Company: EASTON-BELL SPORTS LLC

SALARIES/BENEFITS:

Pension Plan: ESOP Stock Plan: Profit Sharing: Top Exec. Salary: $576,923 Bonus: $750,000
Savings Plan: Y Stock Purch. Plan: Second Exec. Salary: $333,269 Bonus: $229,063

OTHER THOUGHTS:

Apparent Women Officers or Directors: 2
Hot Spot for Advancement for Women/Minorities:

LOCATIONS: ("Y" = Yes)

West:	Southwest:	Midwest:	Southeast:	Northeast:	International:
Y					Y

ECHL (EAST COAST HOCKEY LEAGUE)

www.echl.com

Industry Group Code: 813990 **Ranks within this company's industry group:** Sales: Profits:

Sports:		Services:		Media:		Sales:		Facilities:		Other:	
Leagues/Associations:	Y	Food & Beverage:		TV:		Marketing:		Stadiums:		Gambling:	
Teams:		Agents:		Radio:		Ads:		Fitness Clubs:		Apparel:	
Nonprofits:		Other:		Internet:		Tickets:		Golf Courses:		Equipment:	
Other:				Print:		Retail:		Ski Resorts:		Shoes:	
				Software:		Other:		Other:		Other:	

TYPES OF BUSINESS:

Minor Hockey League

BRANDS/DIVISIONS/AFFILIATES:

ECHL
American Conference Championship
National Conference Championship
Kelly Cup
West Coast Hockey League (WCHL)
Florida Everglades (The)
Trenton Devils (The)
Cincinnati Cyclones (The)

CONTACTS:

Note: Officers with more than one job title may be intentionally listed here more than once.

Brian McKenna, Commissioner
Rick Lisk, VP-Mktg.
Lisa Hollenbeck, Mgr.-Hockey Admin.
Ryan Crelin, Mgr.-Bus. Oper.
Rick Lisk, VP-Bus. Dev.
Jack Carnefix, Sr. VP-Comm.
Todd Corliss, Dir.-Finance
Patrick J. Kelly, Commissioner Emeritus
Tara Crane, Dir.-Mktg. & Licensing
John Fierko, Dir.-Team Svcs.
Rod Pasma, Sr. VP-Hockey Oper.

Phone: 609-452-0770	**Fax:** 609-452-7147
Toll-Free:	
Address: 116 Village Blvd., Ste. 304, Princeton, NJ 08540 US	

GROWTH PLANS/SPECIAL FEATURES:

ECHL (formerly the East Coast Hockey League, Inc.), established in 1988, operates a class I-AA minor hockey league of 23 teams playing throughout the U.S. The league operates in two conferences, American and National, which each have two divisions: the American conference contains the South division and the North division, and the National conference contains the West and Pacific divisions. The league manages the American Conference Championship, which is played between the winners of the south and north divisions and the National Conference Championship, which is played between the winners of the Pacific and West divisions. The winners of each conference then play each other in the annual Kelly Cup. ECHL's teams act as feeder teams for a number of American Hockey League (AHL) and National Hockey League (NHL) teams. For example, the Florida Everglades is a feeder team for the AHL's Albany River Rats and Rochester Americans, as well as the NHL's Carolina Hurricanes and Florida Panthers; the Trenton Devils is a feeder team for the AHL's Lowell Devils and the NHL's New Jersey Devils; and the Ontario Reign is a feeder team for the AHL's Manchester Monarchs and the NHL's Los Angeles Kings. Currently, ECHL is affiliated with 25 NHL teams, and has held affiliations with at least 20 AHL teams each of the last eight years. In total, 358 ECHL players have gone on to play in the NHL, including Sean Collins, David Duerden, Zack FitzGerald, Andrew Hutchinson, Alexander Khavanov, Patrick Leahy, Chris Neil, and, most recently, Matt Climie and Jamie Fraser. A new team, the Toledo Walleye, is scheduled to compete in the 2009-10 season. In June 2008, the Cincinnati Cyclones won the Kelly Cup, becoming the city's first pro team to win a major championship in nearly 20 years.

FINANCIALS:

Sales and profits are in thousands of dollars—add 000 to get the full amount. 2008 Note: Financial information for 2008 was not available for all companies at press time.

2008 Sales: $	2008 Profits: $	**U.S. Stock Ticker: Private**
2007 Sales: $	2007 Profits: $	**Int'l Ticker:** Int'l Exchange:
2006 Sales: $	2006 Profits: $	Employees:
2005 Sales: $	2005 Profits: $	Fiscal Year Ends:
2004 Sales: $	2004 Profits: $	Parent Company:

SALARIES/BENEFITS:

Pension Plan:	ESOP Stock Plan:	Profit Sharing:	Top Exec. Salary: $	Bonus: $
Savings Plan:	Stock Purch. Plan:		Second Exec. Salary: $	Bonus: $

OTHER THOUGHTS:

Apparent Women Officers or Directors: 3
Hot Spot for Advancement for Women/Minorities: Y

LOCATIONS: ("Y" = Yes)

West:	Southwest:	Midwest:	Southeast:	Northeast:	International:
				Y	

EDMONTON OILERS HOCKEY CLUB

oilers.nhl.com

Industry Group Code: 711211F **Ranks within this company's industry group:** Sales: 17 Profits: 7

Sports:		Services:		Media:		Sales:		Facilities:		Other:	
Leagues/Associations:		Food & Beverage:		TV:		Marketing:		Stadiums:		Gambling:	
Teams:	Y	Agents:		Radio:		Ads:		Fitness Clubs:		Apparel:	
Nonprofits:		Other:		Internet:		Tickets:	Y	Golf Courses:		Equipment:	
Other:				Print:		Retail:		Ski Resorts:		Shoes:	
				Software:		Other:		Other:		Other:	

TYPES OF BUSINESS:

Major League Hockey Team
Ticket Sales

BRANDS/DIVISIONS/AFFILIATES:

Edmonton Oilers Hockey Club (The)
Rexall Place
Edmonton Investors Group, Ltd.

CONTACTS: *Note: Officers with more than one job title may be intentionally listed here more than once.*

Patrick LaForge, CEO
Patrick LaForge, Pres.
Darryl Boessenkool, CFO
Brad McGregor, VP-Sales
Rick Olczyk, Dir.-Legal Affairs
Kevin Lowe, Pres., Hockey Oper.
Allan Watt, VP-Comm. & Broadcasting
Darryl Boessenkool, VP-Finance
Kevin Prendergast, VP-Hockey Oper.
Daryl Katz, Owner
Steve Tambellini, Gen. Mgr.
Rick Olczyk, Dir.-Hockey Admin.

Phone: 780-414-4000 **Fax:** 780-409-5890
Toll-Free:
Address: 11230 - 110th St., Edmonton, AB T5G 3H7 Canada

GROWTH PLANS/SPECIAL FEATURES:

The Edmonton Oilers Hockey Club is a National Hockey League (NHL) team owned by a group of approximately 40 investors. The team plays in the Northwest division of the NHL's Western Conference, along with the Calgary Flames, Colorado Avalanche, Minnesota Wild and Vancouver Canucks. The Oilers are based in Edmonton, Alberta and play at Rexall Place, a hockey-specific arena built in 1974 that seats close to 17,000 fans. The franchise was started in 1972 as a member of the World Hockey Association (WHA). It joined the NHL in 1979 when the WHA collapsed. The team, led by Wayne Gretzky, dominated the NHL throughout the 1980s, with four Stanley Cup titles in five appearances. The Oilers' first Stanley Cup Final appearance and only loss was in 1983. The franchise won its fifth Stanley Cup in 1990 after trading Gretzky to the Los Angeles Kings. In 1993, the team missed the playoffs for the first time since its inaugural season, and it hasn't returned to the Stanley Cup finals since its 1990 win. Though Wayne Gretzky finished his NHL career with the New York Rangers, he is best known for his achievements while playing with the Oilers. Gretzky is a Hockey Hall of Fame member and one of the sport's most celebrated players, so widely respected that when he retired in 1999, the NHL retired his sweater number (99) across the entire league. He still holds the NHL's All-Time Leading Scorer title. Some of the Oilers' key sponsors are Molson, Coca-Cola, Rexall, Ford and Scotiabank. Forbes recently valued the team at approximately $175 million. The team's average attendance in the 2008-09 season was approximately 16,800 fans per game.

FINANCIALS: **Sales and profits are in thousands of dollars—add 000 to get the full amount. 2008 Note: Financial information for 2008 was not available for all companies at press time.**

2008 Sales: $85,000	2008 Profits: $11,800	**U.S. Stock Ticker: Subsidiary**
2007 Sales: $71,000	2007 Profits: $9,900	**Int'l Ticker:** Int'l Exchange:
2006 Sales: $75,000	2006 Profits: $10,700	Employees:
2005 Sales: $	2005 Profits: $	Fiscal Year Ends: 7/31
2004 Sales: $55,000	2004 Profits: $	Parent Company: EDMONTON INVESTORS GROUP LTD

SALARIES/BENEFITS:

Pension Plan:	ESOP Stock Plan:	Profit Sharing:	Top Exec. Salary: $	Bonus: $
Savings Plan:	Stock Purch. Plan:		Second Exec. Salary: $	Bonus: $

OTHER THOUGHTS:

Apparent Women Officers or Directors:
Hot Spot for Advancement for Women/Minorities:

LOCATIONS: ("Y" = Yes)

West:	Southwest:	Midwest:	Southeast:	Northeast:	International:
					Y

ELECTRONIC ARTS INC

www.ea.com

Industry Group Code: 511208 **Ranks within this company's industry group:** Sales: 1 Profits: 3

Sports:		Services:		Media:		Sales:		Facilities:		Other:	
Leagues/Associations:		Food & Beverage:		TV:		Marketing:		Stadiums:		Gambling:	
Teams:		Agents:		Radio:		Ads:		Fitness Clubs:		Apparel:	
Nonprofits:		Other:		Internet:	Y	Tickets:		Golf Courses:		Equipment:	
Other:				Print:		Retail:		Ski Resorts:		Shoes:	
				Software:		Other:		Other:		Other:	

TYPES OF BUSINESS:

Computer Software-Video Games
Online Interactive Games
E-Commerce Sales
Mobile Games

BRANDS/DIVISIONS/AFFILIATES:

EA Games
EA Sports
EA Casual Entertainment
Bioware Corp
Madden NFL
Pogo.com
ThreeSF Inc
J2MSoft Inc

CONTACTS: *Note: Officers with more than one job title may be intentionally listed here more than once.*

John S. Riccitiello, CEO
John Pleasants, COO/Pres., Global Publishing
Eric Brown, CFO/Exec. VP
Gabrielle Toledano, Exec. VP-Human Resources
Stephen G. Bene, General Counsel/Sec./Sr. VP
Joel Linzner, Exec. VP-Bus. & Legal Affairs
Tammy Schachter, Sr. Dir.-Public Rel.
Ken Barker, Chief Acct. Officer/Sr. VP
Peter Moore, Pres., EA Sports Label
Frank Gibeau, Pres., EA Games Label
Gerhard Florin, Exec. VP-Publishing
Lawrence F. Probst, III, Chmn.

Phone: 650-628-1500 **Fax:** 650-628-1415
Toll-Free:
Address: 209 Redwood Shores Pkwy., Redwood City, CA 94065-1175 US

GROWTH PLANS/SPECIAL FEATURES:

Electronic Arts, Inc. (EA) develops, markets, publishes and distributes video game software. The company designs products for a number of platforms, including video game consoles, such as the Sony PlayStation 3, Microsoft Xbox 360 and Nintendo Wii; handheld game systems, including PlayStation Portable (PSP), Nintendo DS and Apple iPod; personal computers (PCs); and mobile phones. The company operates in four segments, or labels: EA Games, EA Sports, The Sims and EA Casual Entertainment. The EA Games label encompasses the largest percentage of the company's studios and development staff, focused on producing a diverse portfolio of action-adventure, role playing, racing and combat games, as well as massively-multiplayer online role-playing games (MMORPG) such as Warhammer Online. The EA Sports label produces a variety of sports-based video games, including the Madden NFL, FIFA Soccer and Tiger Woods PGA TOUR franchises. EA's The Sims label develops life simulation games and online communities, such as The Sims 2, which offers an online community of over 4 million unique monthly users. The EA Casual Entertainment label develops games that are intended to be quick to learn and play, making them easily accessible for a wide audience. Pogo, an online service with over 1.6 million subscribers, offers a variety of card, puzzle and word games. Through EA Mobile, the firm publishes games and related content for mobile phones. The company distributes games in over 35 countries worldwide. In June 2008, EA acquired ThreeSF, Inc., a gaming-based social network. In December 2008, the company acquired J2MSoft Inc., a Korean-based developer of PC online games. Also in December 2008, Electronic Arts announced plans to cut its worldwide workforce by approximately 10% and to consolidate or close at least nine of its studio and publishing locations.

EA offers its employees discounts on game systems; education reimbursement; medical insurance; a bonus plan; and an employee assistance program.

FINANCIALS: **Sales and profits are in thousands of dollars—add 000 to get the full amount. 2008 Note: Financial information for 2008 was not available for all companies at press time.**

2008 Sales: $3,665,000	2008 Profits: $-454,000	**U.S. Stock Ticker: ERTS**
2007 Sales: $3,091,000	2007 Profits: $76,000	**Int'l Ticker:** Int'l Exchange:
2006 Sales: $2,951,000	2006 Profits: $236,000	Employees: 9,000
2005 Sales: $3,129,000	2005 Profits: $504,000	Fiscal Year Ends: 3/31
2004 Sales: $2,957,141	2004 Profits: $577,292	Parent Company:

SALARIES/BENEFITS:

Pension Plan:	ESOP Stock Plan:	Profit Sharing:	Top Exec. Salary: $752,599	Bonus: $349,358
Savings Plan: Y	Stock Purch. Plan: Y		Second Exec. Salary: $750,000	Bonus: $625,350

OTHER THOUGHTS:

Apparent Women Officers or Directors: 3
Hot Spot for Advancement for Women/Minorities: Y

LOCATIONS: ("Y" = Yes)

West:	Southwest:	Midwest:	Southeast:	Northeast:	International:
Y	Y	Y	Y	Y	Y

ESPN INC

espn.go.com

Industry Group Code: 513210 **Ranks within this company's industry group:** Sales: Profits:

Sports:		Services:		Media:		Sales:		Facilities:		Other:	
Leagues/Associations:		Food & Beverage:		TV:	Y	Marketing:		Stadiums:		Gambling:	
Teams:		Agents:		Radio:	Y	Ads:		Fitness Clubs:		Apparel:	
Nonprofits:		Other:		Internet:	Y	Tickets:		Golf Courses:		Equipment:	
Other:				Print:		Retail:		Ski Resorts:		Shoes:	
				Software:		Other:		Other:		Other:	

TYPES OF BUSINESS:

Sports Television-Cable
Sports Radio Broadcasting
Online Sports Information
Magazine & Book Publishing
Sports Websites

BRANDS/DIVISIONS/AFFILIATES:

ESPN
ESPN2
ESPNEWS
ESPN Deportes
ESPN Regional Television
ESPN Interactive
Walt Disney Company (The)
Hearst Corporation (The)

CONTACTS: *Note: Officers with more than one job title may be intentionally listed here more than once.*

George W. Bodenheimer, Pres.
Christine Driessen, CFO/Exec. VP
Sean H. R. Bratches, Exec. VP-Mktg. & Sales
Paul Richardson, Sr. VP-Human Resources
Paul Cushing, Sr. VP-Mgmt. IT
Chuck Pagano, CTO/Exec. VP
Ed Durso, Exec. VP-Admin.
David Pahl, General Counsel/Sr. VP
Chris LaPlaca, Sr. VP-Comm.
Tony Waggoner, Controller/Sr. VP
George W. Bodenheimer, Pres., ABC Sports
Gary Belsky, Editor in Chief-ESPN The Magazine
Steve Anderson, Exec. VP-News, Talent & Content Oper.
Peter Rosenberger, VP-Special Events Mktg.
George W. Bodenheimer, Chmn.
Tim Bunnell, Sr. VP-Int'l Programming & Mktg.

Phone: 860-766-2000	Fax: 860-766-2213
Toll-Free:	
Address: ESPN Plz., 935 Middle St., Bristol, CT 06010 US	

GROWTH PLANS/SPECIAL FEATURES:

ESPN, Inc. is owned by media giants, the Walt Disney Co. through Disney ABC Cable and by the Hearst Corporation. ESPN is a cable sports broadcaster that airs more than 5,100 live or original hours of sports programming for more than 65 sports yearly. It has seven domestic television networks: ESPN; ESPN2; ESPN Classic; ESPN Deportes; ESPNU ESPN Today; and ESPNEWS. ESPN also operates four high-definition television simulcast services including ESPN HD, ESPN2 HD, ESPNEWS HD and ESPNU HD. ESPN programs the sports schedule on the ABC Television Network, which is branded ESPN on ABC. Additionally, ESPN either owns, has equity interests in or has distribution agreements with 45 international sports networks reaching households in more than 195 countries including a 50% equity interest in ESPN Star Sports, which distributes sports programming throughout most of Asia. ESPN also holds a 30% interest in CTV Specialty Television, Inc., which owns The Sports Network, The Sports Network 2, Le Reseau des Sports, ESPN Classic Canada, the NHL Network and Discovery Canada. The ESPN's Radio Network format is carried on more than 750 stations, of which 355 are full-time, making it the largest sports radio network in the U.S. The company's publishing division includes ESPN The Magazine; Bassmaster Magazine; BASS Times; Fishing Tackle & Retailer; and ESPN Books. Through ESPN Enterprises, the firm has developed new products and businesses using the ESPN brand and assets, including the ESPN Zones sports-themed restaurant chain, a variety of consumer products (Videogames, DVDs, CDs, ESPN25, ESPN Golf Schools and ESPN Russell Racing Schools), the ESPN Sports Poll research polling service and the ESPN Club at Disney World Orlando. ESPN also operates five web sites: ESPN.com; ESPNDeportes.com; ESPNRadio.com; ESPNSoccerNet.com; and EXPN.com.

FINANCIALS: Sales and profits are in thousands of dollars—add 000 to get the full amount. 2008 Note: Financial information for 2008 was not available for all companies at press time.

2008 Sales: $	2008 Profits: $	**U.S. Stock Ticker: Subsidiary**
2007 Sales: $	2007 Profits: $	**Int'l Ticker:** Int'l Exchange:
2006 Sales: $	2006 Profits: $	Employees: 3,400
2005 Sales: $4,031,000	2005 Profits: $	Fiscal Year Ends: 9/30
2004 Sales: $3,223,000	2004 Profits: $	Parent Company: WALT DISNEY COMPANY (THE)

SALARIES/BENEFITS:

Pension Plan:	ESOP Stock Plan:	Profit Sharing:	Top Exec. Salary: $	Bonus: $
Savings Plan:	Stock Purch. Plan:		Second Exec. Salary: $	Bonus: $

OTHER THOUGHTS:

Apparent Women Officers or Directors: 1
Hot Spot for Advancement for Women/Minorities:

LOCATIONS: ("Y" = Yes)

West:	Southwest:	Midwest:	Southeast:	Northeast:	International:
				Y	

EVERLAST WORLDWIDE INC

www.everlast.com

Industry Group Code: 315000A **Ranks within this company's industry group:** Sales: Profits:

Sports:		Services:		Media:		Sales:		Facilities:		Other:	
Leagues/Associations:		Food & Beverage:		TV:		Marketing:		Stadiums:		Gambling:	
Teams:		Agents:		Radio:		Ads:		Fitness Clubs:		Apparel:	Y
Nonprofits:		Other:		Internet:		Tickets:		Golf Courses:		Equipment:	Y
Other:				Print:		Retail:		Ski Resorts:		Shoes:	Y
				Software:		Other:		Other:		Other:	

TYPES OF BUSINESS:

Athletic Apparel
Apparel
Sporting Goods
Boxing Equipment
Work Boots & Safety Footwear

BRANDS/DIVISIONS/AFFILIATES:

Brands Holdings
Sports Direct International
GREATNESS IS WITHIN
USA Boxing
Police Athletic League Boxing
PE4LIFE

CONTACTS:

Note: Officers with more than one job title may be intentionally listed here more than once.

Gary J. Dailey, CFO
Angelo V. Giusti, Sr. VP-Sales
Ronnie Kornblum, Dir.-Human Resources

Phone: 212-239-0990	**Fax:** 212-239-4261
Toll-Free: 888-863-8375	
Address: 1350 Broadway, Ste. 2300, New York, NY 10018 US	

GROWTH PLANS/SPECIAL FEATURES:

Everlast Worldwide, Inc. designs, manufactures, markets and sells active wear, sportswear and outerwear, with a particular focus on boxing related products, such as gloves, heavy bags, speed bags, trunks and other gym equipment. The firm also licenses the Everlast trademark to companies that produce women's and children's apparel, underwear, footwear, eyewear, hats, fragrances, batteries, jewelry and nutritional products, fitness toys, heart rate monitors and other products. The Everlast brand is currently present in approximately 100 countries. Everlast maintains its own marketing and advertising staff, as well a graphic arts department to develop advertising campaigns, provide brand management, packaging solutions, retail advertising and catalogs for all of the company's product lines. The firm has received continued exposure in the print, television and movie media, as well as product placement on the Academy Award winning movie Million Dollar Baby, the reality TV drama The Contender, the movie Cinderella Man and the EA Sports Fight Night videogame. Everlast has partnered with several health and fitness businesses including but not limited to, 24 Fitness, Crunch, Lifetime Fitness, Xtreme Couture MMA, Title Boxing, Gleason's Gym, Five Points Academy and Everlast Sports Nutrition. The company's strategy is to expand its network of retailers carrying Everlast products, focusing on department stores, specialty stores, sporting goods stores, catalog operations and better mass merchandisers.

FINANCIALS:

Sales and profits are in thousands of dollars—add 000 to get the full amount. 2008 Note: Financial information for 2008 was not available for all companies at press time.

2008 Sales: $	2008 Profits: $	**U.S. Stock Ticker: Subsidiary**
2007 Sales: $	2007 Profits: $	**Int'l Ticker:** Int'l Exchange:
2006 Sales: $51,887	2006 Profits: $4,724	Employees: 140
2005 Sales: $43,253	2005 Profits: $- 948	Fiscal Year Ends: 12/31
2004 Sales: $33,497	2004 Profits: $-1,026	Parent Company: BRANDS HOLDINGS

SALARIES/BENEFITS:

Pension Plan:	ESOP Stock Plan:	Profit Sharing:	Top Exec. Salary: $435,000	Bonus: $151,544
Savings Plan:	Stock Purch. Plan:		Second Exec. Salary: $250,079	Bonus: $126,000

OTHER THOUGHTS:

Apparent Women Officers or Directors:
Hot Spot for Advancement for Women/Minorities:

LOCATIONS: ("Y" = Yes)

West:	Southwest:	Midwest:	Southeast:	Northeast:	International:
				Y	

EVERNHAM MOTORSPORTS

www.evernhammotorsports.com

Industry Group Code: 711211G **Ranks within this company's industry group:** Sales: Profits:

Sports:		Services:		Media:		Sales:		Facilities:		Other:	
Leagues/Associations:		Food & Beverage:		TV:		Marketing:	Y	Stadiums:		Gambling:	
Teams:	Y	Agents:		Radio:		Ads:		Fitness Clubs:		Apparel:	
Nonprofits:		Other:		Internet:		Tickets:		Golf Courses:		Equipment:	Y
Other:				Print:		Retail:	Y	Ski Resorts:		Shoes:	
				Software:		Other:		Other:	Y	Other:	Y

TYPES OF BUSINESS:

Racing Teams
Engine Technology
High-Performance Auto Parts
Marketing Services
Merchandise & Apparel

BRANDS/DIVISIONS/AFFILIATES:

Evernham Performance Parts
Evernham Engines
Evernham Motorsports Museum
Dodge R&D Technology Center
Evernham Marketing Services

CONTACTS: *Note: Officers with more than one job title may be intentionally listed here more than once.*

Tom Reddin, CEO
Rick Russell, Pres.
Mark McArdle, VP/Dir.-Competition

Phone: 704-924-9404	**Fax:** 704-924-9495
Toll-Free:	
Address: 320 Aviation Dr., Statesville, NC 28677 US	

GROWTH PLANS/SPECIAL FEATURES:

Evernham Motorsports was founded in 1999 by former racecar driver Ray Evernham, in partnership with the auto manufacturer Dodge. The company manages three Nextel Cup teams and one Busch Series team. Evernham Motorsports is comprised of eight separate businesses, including Evernham Motorsports Race Facilities; Dodge R&D Technology Center; Evernham Motorsports Museum and Gift Shop; Evernham Engines; Evernham Marketing Services; Evernham Performance Parts; Evernham Performance Parts; and Advanced Engine Technology. Evernham's primary hub is a 90,000-square-foot facility in Statesville, North Carolina, where the firm's racecars and pit equipment are all maintained. The facility also houses a state-of-the-art fabrication, body shop, assembly and research and development center, as well as Evernham's administrative and executive offices and the Evernham Motorsports Museum and Gift Shop. At the adjacent Dodge R&D Technology Center, Dodge engineers collect data from the race teams to evaluate and improve their engine, aero and chassis systems. Evernham Engines designs and manufactures high-performance engines for team vehicles in Mooresville, North Carolina. Evernham Performance Parts, also in Mooresville, builds and sells high-performance auto components intended for weekend racers and up-and-coming professionals; this division's products are available to the public. Evernham Marketing Services manages sponsorship programs, licensing agreements, special promotions, speaking engagements and advertising for teams and drivers. The company also retails promotional merchandise, collectible gear and sheet metal used in races. In January 2008, the company and Petty Holdings announced an agreement to form a new NASCAR Sprint Cup team

FINANCIALS: **Sales and profits are in thousands of dollars—add 000 to get the full amount. 2008 Note: Financial information for 2008 was not available for all companies at press time.**

2008 Sales: $	2008 Profits: $	**U.S. Stock Ticker: Private**
2007 Sales: $89,000	2007 Profits: $17,800	**Int'l Ticker:** Int'l Exchange:
2006 Sales: $40,000	2006 Profits: $	Employees: 130
2005 Sales: $46,000	2005 Profits: $	Fiscal Year Ends:
2004 Sales: $	2004 Profits: $	Parent Company:

SALARIES/BENEFITS:

Pension Plan:	ESOP Stock Plan:	Profit Sharing:	Top Exec. Salary: $	Bonus: $
Savings Plan:	Stock Purch. Plan:		Second Exec. Salary: $	Bonus: $

OTHER THOUGHTS:

Apparent Women Officers or Directors:
Hot Spot for Advancement for Women/Minorities:

LOCATIONS: ("Y" = Yes)

West:	Southwest:	Midwest:	Southeast:	Northeast:	International:
				Y	Y

EVERTON FOOTBALL CLUB

www.evertonfc.com

Industry Group Code: 711211D **Ranks within this company's industry group:** Sales: 8 Profits: 5

Sports:		Services:		Media:		Sales:		Facilities:		Other:	
Leagues/Associations:		Food & Beverage:		TV:		Marketing:		Stadiums:	Y	Gambling:	
Teams:	Y	Agents:		Radio:		Ads:		Fitness Clubs:		Apparel:	
Nonprofits:		Other:		Internet:	Y	Tickets:	Y	Golf Courses:		Equipment:	
Other:				Print:		Retail:	Y	Ski Resorts:		Shoes:	
				Software:		Other:	Y	Other:		Other:	

TYPES OF BUSINESS:

English Premiere Soccer Team
Ticket Sales
Team Merchandise

BRANDS/DIVISIONS/AFFILIATES:

eCredits
Goodison Park
Everton Ladies
Academy u18
International Department

CONTACTS:

Note: Officers with more than one job title may be intentionally listed here more than once.

Robert Elstone, CEO
Phillip Carter, Pres.
Tom Shelton, Head-Mktg.
Martin Evans, Company Sec.
David Harrison, Head-Football Oper.
Mark Rowan, Head-Media & Comm.
Martin Evans, Head-Finance
David Moyes, Head Coach
Alan Bowen, Head-Stadium Oper.
Ian Ross, Head-Public Rel. & External Affairs
William Kenwright, Chmn.

Phone: 44-870-442-1878	**Fax:** 44-151-286-9112
Toll-Free:	
Address: Goodison Park, Goodison Rd., Liverpool, L4 4EL UK	

GROWTH PLANS/SPECIAL FEATURES:

Everton Football Club is one of the oldest and most successful soccer teams in the English Premier League. It has remained in the league's top division for over 100 years straight, the only team to boast that distinction. Team revenue is generated largely from payments related to premiership broadcasting rights and home game ticket sales, as well as program sales and concessions. Corporate sponsors include Umbro, Littlewoods, Jjb, Rippleffect and Chang Beer. The club's official web site offers fans an electronic season tickets program as well as an eCredits program, both of which allow exclusive access to e-mails from the coaching staff, contests, promotions, match day commentary and a video lounge, all for a season fee. Everton's stadium, among the first ever to be constructed specifically for soccer, is called Goodison Park and has been a landmark of downtown Liverpool since 1892. David Moyes has been coaching the club since 2002, when the young former player was signed on following the firing of Walter Smith. One of the team's most honored players is William Dixie Dean, with a career legacy of 383 goals he made for the club during the 1920s and 1930s. Everton also has a women's team known as the Everton Ladies and a youth team called Academy u18. The club also manages a newly developed International Department, which works to expand Everton outside of the U.K. by creating long-term and mutually beneficial partnerships with other clubs, sporting organizations, governments and commercial partners in order to form a permanent presence in the world. The club is currently working on projects in the U.S., Australia, China, Japan, India, Malaysia and South Africa.

FINANCIALS:

Sales and profits are in thousands of dollars—add 000 to get the full amount. 2008 Note: Financial information for 2008 was not available for all companies at press time.

2008 Sales: $151,000	2008 Profits: $14,000	**U.S. Stock Ticker: Private**
2007 Sales: $103,000	2007 Profits: $-1,000	**Int'l Ticker:** Int'l Exchange:
2006 Sales: $107,000	2006 Profits: $-15,000	Employees: 999
2005 Sales: $108,000	2005 Profits: $	Fiscal Year Ends: 5/31
2004 Sales: $	2004 Profits: $	Parent Company:

SALARIES/BENEFITS:

Pension Plan:	ESOP Stock Plan:	Profit Sharing:	Top Exec. Salary: $	Bonus: $
Savings Plan:	Stock Purch. Plan:		Second Exec. Salary: $	Bonus: $

OTHER THOUGHTS:

Apparent Women Officers or Directors:
Hot Spot for Advancement for Women/Minorities:

LOCATIONS: ("Y" = Yes)

West:	Southwest:	Midwest:	Southeast:	Northeast:	International:
					Y

EVERYTHING BUT WATER INC

www.everythingbutwater.com

Industry Group Code: 448120 **Ranks within this company's industry group:** Sales: Profits:

Sports:		Services:		Media:		Sales:		Facilities:		Other:	
Leagues/Associations:		Food & Beverage:		TV:		Marketing:		Stadiums:		Gambling:	
Teams:		Agents:		Radio:		Ads:		Fitness Clubs:		Apparel:	Y
Nonprofits:		Other:		Internet:		Tickets:		Golf Courses:		Equipment:	
Other:				Print:		Retail:	Y	Ski Resorts:		Shoes:	
				Software:		Other:		Other:		Other:	

TYPES OF BUSINESS:

Women's Swimwear, Retail
Men's Swimwear
Online Sales

BRANDS/DIVISIONS/AFFILIATES:

Bear Growth Capital Partners
Bear Stearns Merchant Banking
Everythingbutwater.com
Water Water Everywhere
Just Add Water

CONTACTS: *Note: Officers with more than one job title may be intentionally listed here more than once.*

Sheila Arnold, CEO
Sheila Arnold, Pres.
Vikkie Hodgkins, CFO
Abbey Mazzeo, Dir.-Human Resources
Richard D. Sarmiento, Chmn.

Phone: 407-351-4069 **Fax:** 407-363-0967
Toll-Free: 888-796-6661
Address: 7353 Greenbriar Parkway, Orlando, FL 32819 US

GROWTH PLANS/SPECIAL FEATURES:

Everything But Water, Inc. (EBW) is a specialty swimwear retailer in the U.S. with more than 70 stores in 24 U.S. states and Puerto Rico. EBW stores specialize in mix and match separates and offers a selection of designer labels as well as specialty lines for maternity, mastectomy, long torso, D-DD-E cups and plus size. The firm offers swimsuits from over 100 vendors. Swimsuit designs range in size from 2-24 and come in one-piece and two-piece separates. Some styles offered include the classic tank; the empire waist; the surplice; the swim dress; the ballet bra; the triangle top; the halter top; Brazilian bottom; the hipster ; the hot pant; and the sarong pant. EBW carries labels including Michael Kors, Ralph Lauren, Becca, LaBlanca, Lucky, Betsey Johnson, Trina Turk and others, with swimsuit prices ranging from approximately $80 to $250. The firm offers private fittings and fitting parties, which can be arranged during or after store hours at every location by a trained and certified fit consultant. The firm's e-commerce site, Everythingbutwater.com, offers advice from personal shopping experts; a figure solutions chart; and a toll-free number where trained fit specialists can be reached for order placement, product knowledge information and overall customer service. The firm's products have been featured in the following magazines: Sports Illustrated, Fitness, Self, More, Good Housekeeping, Yacht, People, Lucky, Vogue, Teen Vogue, Bazaar, Cosmopolitan, Cosmo Girl, Glamour, Elle, Elle Girl, Marie Claire, O and Oxygen.

FINANCIALS: **Sales and profits are in thousands of dollars—add 000 to get the full amount. 2008 Note: Financial information for 2008 was not available for all companies at press time.**

2008 Sales: $ | 2008 Profits: $
2007 Sales: $ | 2007 Profits: $
2006 Sales: $ | 2006 Profits: $
2005 Sales: $ | 2005 Profits: $
2004 Sales: $ | 2004 Profits: $

U.S. Stock Ticker: Private
Int'l Ticker: Int'l Exchange:
Employees: 500
Fiscal Year Ends: 12/31
Parent Company: BEAR GROWTH CAPITAL PARTNERS

SALARIES/BENEFITS:

Pension Plan: ESOP Stock Plan: Profit Sharing: Top Exec. Salary: $ Bonus: $
Savings Plan: Stock Purch. Plan: Second Exec. Salary: $ Bonus: $

OTHER THOUGHTS:

Apparent Women Officers or Directors: 3
Hot Spot for Advancement for Women/Minorities: Y

LOCATIONS: ("Y" = Yes)

West:	Southwest:	Midwest:	Southeast:	Northeast:	International:
Y	Y	Y	Y	Y	Y

FC DALLAS

fc.dallas.mlsnet.com

Industry Group Code: 711211D **Ranks within this company's industry group:** Sales: Profits:

Sports:		Services:		Media:		Sales:		Facilities:		Other:	
Leagues/Associations:		Food & Beverage:		TV:		Marketing:		Stadiums:	Y	Gambling:	
Teams:	Y	Agents:		Radio:		Ads:		Fitness Clubs:		Apparel:	
Nonprofits:		Other:		Internet:		Tickets:	Y	Golf Courses:		Equipment:	
Other:				Print:		Retail:		Ski Resorts:		Shoes:	
				Software:		Other:		Other:		Other:	

TYPES OF BUSINESS:

Major League Soccer Team

BRANDS/DIVISIONS/AFFILIATES:

Dallas Burn
Frisco Soccer and Entertainment Center
Pizza Hut Park
Hunt Sports Group

CONTACTS:

Note: Officers with more than one job title may be intentionally listed here more than once.

Kelly Weller, VP-Mktg. & Sales
Damon Boettcher, Exec. VP- Bus. Oper.
Tony Nicholson, Mgr.-Media Rel.
Damon Boettcher, Dir.-Finance
Schellas Hyndman, Head Coach
Michael Hitchcock, Gen. Mgr.

Phone: 214-705-6700 **Fax:** 214-705-6799
Toll-Free:
Address: 9200 World Cup Way, Ste. 202, Frisco, TX 75034 US

GROWTH PLANS/SPECIAL FEATURES:

FC Dallas is a Major League Soccer (MLS) team based in Dallas, Texas. The team is the latest incarnation of professional soccer in Dallas, whose soccer history began shortly after the 1966 World Cup. That first team, the Dallas Tornados, played in the North American Soccer League until 1981. Dallas also hosted a professional indoor soccer team, the Dallas Sidekicks, until operations were suspended following the 2004 season. FC Dallas, a charter member of the MLS, began life in 1995 as the Dallas Burn. The team qualified for the playoffs the first seven years of its existence, from 1995 to 2002, and made it to the finals on two occasions. The Burn also won the Lamar Hunt U.S. Open Cup in 1997. In early 2005, the Burn changed their name to FC Dallas when they moved into their new stadium, Pizza Hut Park, a 20,500-seat soccer-specific stadium located in Frisco, Texas. They also changed the color scheme of their uniforms to red, white and blue (the colors of both the U.S. and Texas flag) with a hint of silver. The team is owned and operated by the Hunt Sports Group. FC Dallas saw a 2007 regular season game attendance average of approximately 15,000, with about 12,500 for the postseason. FC Dallas plays in the Western Conference of the MLS, which includes teams such as Chivas USA, the Colorado Rapids, Houston Dynamo, San Jose Earthquakes, Los Angeles Galaxy and Real Salt Lake. Former standout players include forwards Eddie Johnson and Jason Kreis.

FINANCIALS:

Sales and profits are in thousands of dollars—add 000 to get the full amount. 2008 Note: Financial information for 2008 was not available for all companies at press time.

2008 Sales: $	2008 Profits: $	**U.S. Stock Ticker: Subsidiary**
2007 Sales: $	2007 Profits: $	**Int'l Ticker:** Int'l Exchange:
2006 Sales: $	2006 Profits: $	Employees:
2005 Sales: $	2005 Profits: $	Fiscal Year Ends:
2004 Sales: $	2004 Profits: $	Parent Company: HUNT SPORTS GROUP

SALARIES/BENEFITS:

Pension Plan:	ESOP Stock Plan:	Profit Sharing:	Top Exec. Salary: $	Bonus: $
Savings Plan:	Stock Purch. Plan:		Second Exec. Salary: $	Bonus: $

OTHER THOUGHTS:

Apparent Women Officers or Directors: 1
Hot Spot for Advancement for Women/Minorities:

LOCATIONS: ("Y" = Yes)

West:	Southwest:	Midwest:	Southeast:	Northeast:	International:
	Y				

FIFA (FEDERATION INTERNATIONALE DE FOOTBALL ASSOCIATION)

www.fifa.com

Industry Group Code: 813990 **Ranks within this company's industry group:** Sales: 1 Profits: 1

Sports:		Services:		Media:		Sales:		Facilities:		Other:	
Leagues/Associations:	Y	Food & Beverage:		TV:		Marketing:		Stadiums:		Gambling:	
Teams:		Agents:		Radio:		Ads:		Fitness Clubs:		Apparel:	
Nonprofits:	Y	Other:		Internet:		Tickets:		Golf Courses:		Equipment:	
Other:				Print:		Retail:		Ski Resorts:		Shoes:	
				Software:		Other:		Other:		Other:	

TYPES OF BUSINESS:

International Soccer Association
Charities

BRANDS/DIVISIONS/AFFILIATES:

FIFA
International Footbal Association Board
Asian Football Confederation
Confederation Africaine de Football
Confederacion Sudamericana de Futbol
United European Football Association
Oceania Football Confederation
FIFA World Rankings

CONTACTS: *Note: Officers with more than one job title may be intentionally listed here more than once.*

Joseph S. Blatter, Pres.
Urs Linsi, General Sec.
Julio H. Grondona, Sr. VP/Chmn.-Finance Committee

Phone: 41-43-222-77-77	**Fax:** 41-43-222-78-78
Toll-Free:	
Address: Fifa House, Hitzigweg 11, Zurich, 8030 Switzerland	

GROWTH PLANS/SPECIAL FEATURES:

FIFA (Federation Internationale de Football Association) is the international governing body of soccer with over 208 associated countries from Afghanistan to Zimbabwe. It promotes soccer internationally and regulates the transfers of players between its teams. The International Football Association Board (IFAB) maintains the rules and regulations that govern international soccer. It consists of four FIFA representatives and one representative each from the Football Association (the U.K. soccer governing body), the Scottish Football Association, the Football Association of Wales and the Irish Football Association. The organization is composed of six continental confederations: the Asian Football Confederation (AFC) for China, Japan, Saudi Arabia, Uzbekistan and other Middle Eastern and Asian countries; Confederation Africaine de Football (CAF) for Africa; Confederacion Sudamericana de Futbol (CONMEBOL) for South America; Confederation of North, Central American and Caribbean Association Football (CONCACAF); Oceania Football Confederation (OFC) for Australia, New Zealand and other territories in the Pacific Ocean; and United European Football Association (UEFA) for Europe, the most influential of the six. FIFA organizes a wide range of international soccer competitions, including the Football World Cup, Women's World Cup, Olympic Football Tournament, Football World Youth Championship, Football U-17 World Championship, Women's U-19 World Championship, Confederations Cup and the Club World Championship. The organization also awards the FIFA World Player of the Year and publishes the FIFA World Rankings on a monthly basis. Additionally, the organization runs several charities and initiatives aimed at improving the lives of children and stopping child labor. In February 2009, Futsal Republic, the international form of indoor soccer approved by FIFA, opened a 18,000 square foot stadium in Hayward, California.

FINANCIALS: **Sales and profits are in thousands of dollars—add 000 to get the full amount. 2008 Note: Financial information for 2008 was not available for all companies at press time.**

2008 Sales: $902,497	2008 Profits: $183,655	**U.S. Stock Ticker: Private**
2007 Sales: $786,635	2007 Profits: $49,246	**Int'l Ticker:** Int'l Exchange:
2006 Sales: $	2006 Profits: $	Employees: 315
2005 Sales: $	2005 Profits: $	Fiscal Year Ends: 12/31
2004 Sales: $	2004 Profits: $	Parent Company:

SALARIES/BENEFITS:

Pension Plan:	ESOP Stock Plan:	Profit Sharing:	Top Exec. Salary: $	Bonus: $
Savings Plan:	Stock Purch. Plan:		Second Exec. Salary: $	Bonus: $

OTHER THOUGHTS:

Apparent Women Officers or Directors:
Hot Spot for Advancement for Women/Minorities:

LOCATIONS: ("Y" = Yes)

West:	Southwest:	Midwest:	Southeast:	Northeast:	International:
					Y

FILA USA INC

www.fila.com

Industry Group Code: 315000A **Ranks within this company's industry group:** Sales: Profits:

Sports:		Services:		Media:		Sales:		Facilities:		Other:	
Leagues/Associations:		Food & Beverage:		TV:		Marketing:		Stadiums:		Gambling:	
Teams:		Agents:		Radio:		Ads:		Fitness Clubs:		Apparel:	Y
Nonprofits:		Other:		Internet:		Tickets:		Golf Courses:		Equipment:	
Other:				Print:		Retail:		Ski Resorts:		Shoes:	Y
				Software:		Other:		Other:		Other:	

TYPES OF BUSINESS:

Sports Apparel & Accessories
Footwear
Tennis Apparel

BRANDS/DIVISIONS/AFFILIATES:

Fila Korea Ltd
Global Leading Brands House

CONTACTS:

Note: Officers with more than one job title may be intentionally listed here more than once.

Gene Yoon, CEO
Jon Epstein, Pres.
Young-Chan Cho, CFO
Lauren Mallon, Mgr.-Global Mktg.
Young-Chan Cho, Pres., Global Leading Brands House Holdings
Jarita Bridges, Mgr.-Entertainment Mktg.
Gene Yoon, Chmn.

Phone: 410-773-3000 **Fax:** 410-773-4989
Toll-Free: 800-845-3452
Address: 1 Fila Way, Sparks, MD 21152 US

GROWTH PLANS/SPECIAL FEATURES:

Fila USA, Inc., a subsidiary of Fila Korea Ltd., produces footwear, apparel and accessories divided into eight different categories based on intended activities: tennis, running, mountain, golf, fitness, vintage and active wear. These products are tailored to their respective types of athlete and are designed to complement athletes' movements. In addition to athletic wear, Fila offers a line of street clothes designed for a younger, more style conscious shopper. Fila was originally formed in the textiles business before going on to specialize in knitwear production. The company entered the sports industry in 1973, after consolidating its expertise in the Italian textiles industry. Fila established itself in the tennis apparel industry with its innovative tubular manufacturing process that until then was only used for other products. It was also Fila that challenged the white-only tradition on tennis courts by creating a line of colored tennis apparel. The firm is committed to using cutting-edge technology and innovative materials. Fila products are currently available in approximately 50 countries worldwide. In March 2007, Sport Brands International LLC (SBI) completed the sale of Fila USA, Inc. to Fila Korea Ltd. Early in 2008, Fila partnered with Polo Grounds Music in the launch of a joint marketing and public relations program centered on the promotion of up-and-coming music along side current new fashion lifestyle apparel and footwear. In March 2008, the firm sold its subsidiaries, including Fila's European, Middle East, African and Indian businesses.

FINANCIALS:

Sales and profits are in thousands of dollars—add 000 to get the full amount. 2008 Note: Financial information for 2008 was not available for all companies at press time.

2008 Sales: $	2008 Profits: $	**U.S. Stock Ticker: Subsidiary**
2007 Sales: $	2007 Profits: $	**Int'l Ticker:** Int'l Exchange:
2006 Sales: $	2006 Profits: $	Employees:
2005 Sales: $	2005 Profits: $	Fiscal Year Ends: 12/31
2004 Sales: $	2004 Profits: $	Parent Company: FILA KOREA LTD

SALARIES/BENEFITS:

Pension Plan:	ESOP Stock Plan:	Profit Sharing:	Top Exec. Salary: $	Bonus: $
Savings Plan:	Stock Purch. Plan:		Second Exec. Salary: $	Bonus: $

OTHER THOUGHTS:

Apparent Women Officers or Directors:
Hot Spot for Advancement for Women/Minorities:

LOCATIONS: ("Y" = Yes)

West:	Southwest:	Midwest:	Southeast:	Northeast:	International:
				Y	Y

FLORIDA MARLINS

florida.marlins.mlb.com

Industry Group Code: 711211A **Ranks within this company's industry group:** Sales: 30 Profits: 2

Sports:		Services:		Media:		Sales:		Facilities:		Other:	
Leagues/Associations:		Food & Beverage:		TV:		Marketing:		Stadiums:		Gambling:	
Teams:	Y	Agents:		Radio:		Ads:		Fitness Clubs:		Apparel:	
Nonprofits:		Other:		Internet:		Tickets:	Y	Golf Courses:		Equipment:	
Other:				Print:		Retail:	Y	Ski Resorts:		Shoes:	
				Software:		Other:		Other:		Other:	

TYPES OF BUSINESS:

Professional Baseball Team

BRANDS/DIVISIONS/AFFILIATES:

Dolphins Stadium
Jacksonville Suns
New Orleans Zephyrs
Jupiter Hammerheads
Greensboro Grasshoppers
Jamestown Jammers
Gulf Coast Marlins

CONTACTS: *Note: Officers with more than one job title may be intentionally listed here more than once.*

Jeff Loria, Owner
David P. Samson, Pres.
Michael Bussiere, CFO/Exec. VP
Sean Flynn, VP-Mktg.
Ana Hernandez, Dir.-Human Resources
J. David Enriquez, Dir.-IT
Derek Jackson, General Counsel/VP
Larry Beinfest, Pres., Baseball Oper.
Matthew Roebuck, Dir.-Media Rel.
Susan Jaison, Sr. VP-Finance
Stan Meek, Dir.-Scouting
Joel A. Mael, Vice Chmn.
Claude Delorme, Sr. VP-Stadium Dev.
Michael Hill, Gen. Mgr./VP
Jeff Loria, Chmn.
Albert Gonzalez, Dir.-Int'l Oper.

Phone: 305-626-7400 **Fax:** 305-626-7302
Toll-Free:
Address: 2267 Dan Marino Blvd., Miami, FL 33028 US

GROWTH PLANS/SPECIAL FEATURES:

The Florida Marlins, owned and operated by The Florida Marlins, LP, joined Major League Baseball (MLB) as an expansion team in 1993. The Marlins team had only one winning season between its inception in 1993 and its 10-year anniversary in 2003. However, in the team's first two winning seasons, 1997 and 2003, it won the World Series. The club followed both of these victories by gutting the team, either trading away its marquee players (known as a fire sale) or allowing them to leave via free agency. These moves have widely served to alienate a fan base already more committed to other sports. The team has played in Dolphins Stadium (formerly Joe Robbie Stadium and Pro Player Stadium) since its inception. Despite its recent World Series success, the team's most attended year remains its birth year, 1993 (with over 3 million seats filled), while 1997, the Marlins' first winning season, comes in a distant second (2.3 million). Minor league affiliations include the Jupiter Hammerheads, the Jamestown Jammers, the Greensboro Grasshoppers, the New Orleans Zephyrs, the Jacksonville Suns and the Gulf Coast Marlins. After a successful 2006 season in which the Marlins finished with a respectable 78-84, the team struggled in 2007 due mostly to numerous player injuries. The team ended the 2008 season with 84 wins and 77 losses. The outlook for the Marlins' future turned brighter when, in February 2008, after more than a decade of struggle to find a baseball-only stadium for the Marlins, the city of Miami approved the team's plans for a new $515 million, 37,000-seat park on the grounds of the Orange Bowl. The stadium will feature a retractable roof and is slated to be completed by the 2012 baseball season. The team is worth $277 million, according to a recent Forbes estimate. Average home game attendance in 2008 was nearly 16,700.

FINANCIALS: **Sales and profits are in thousands of dollars—add 000 to get the full amount. 2008 Note: Financial information for 2008 was not available for all companies at press time.**

2008 Sales: $139,000 | 2008 Profits: $43,700
2007 Sales: $128,000 | 2007 Profits: $35,600
2006 Sales: $122,000 | 2006 Profits: $43,300
2005 Sales: $119,000 | 2005 Profits: $
2004 Sales: $ | 2004 Profits: $

U.S. Stock Ticker: Subsidiary
Int'l Ticker: Int'l Exchange:
Employees:
Fiscal Year Ends: 10/31
Parent Company: FLORIDA MARLINS LP (THE)

SALARIES/BENEFITS:

Pension Plan: ESOP Stock Plan: Profit Sharing: Top Exec. Salary: $ Bonus: $
Savings Plan: Stock Purch. Plan: Second Exec. Salary: $ Bonus: $

OTHER THOUGHTS:

Apparent Women Officers or Directors: 5
Hot Spot for Advancement for Women/Minorities: Y

LOCATIONS: ("Y" = Yes)

West:	Southwest:	Midwest:	Southeast:	Northeast:	International:
			Y		

FLORIDA PANTHERS

www.floridapanthers.com

Industry Group Code: 711211F **Ranks within this company's industry group:** Sales: 23 Profits: 28

Sports:		Services:		Media:		Sales:		Facilities:		Other:	
Leagues/Associations:		Food & Beverage:		TV:		Marketing:		Stadiums:	Y	Gambling:	
Teams:	Y	Agents:		Radio:		Ads:		Fitness Clubs:		Apparel:	
Nonprofits:		Other:		Internet:		Tickets:	Y	Golf Courses:		Equipment:	
Other:				Print:		Retail:	Y	Ski Resorts:		Shoes:	
				Software:		Other:		Other:		Other:	

TYPES OF BUSINESS:

Professional Hockey Team
Ticket Sales
Team Merchandise

BRANDS/DIVISIONS/AFFILIATES:

BankAtlantic Center
Sunshine Sports & Entertainment

CONTACTS:

Note: Officers with more than one job title may be intentionally listed here more than once.

Alan Cohen, CEO
Michael Yormark, COO
Michael Yormark, Pres.
Evelyn Lopez, CFO/VP-Finance
Chad Johnson, Sr. VP-Mktg. & Sales
Carol Duncanson, VP-Human Resources & Payroll
Kelly Moyer, VP-IT
Jennifer Simmons, Dir.-Merch.
Jacques Martin, Gen. Mgr.-Hockey Oper.
R. J. Martino, VP-Corp. Dev.
Justin Copertino, Mgr.-Comm.
Phillip Reitz, Controller/Sr. Dir.-Acct.
Ryan Bringger, Dir.-Ticket Sales
Jacques Martin, Gen. Mgr.
Peter DeBoer, Head Coach
Ed Wildermuth, VP-Bus. Affairs
Alan Cohen, Chmn.
Laura Barrera, Dir.-Purchasing

Phone: 954-835-7000	**Fax:** 954-835-7600
Toll-Free:	
Address: 1 Panther Pkwy., Sunrise, FL 33323 US	

GROWTH PLANS/SPECIAL FEATURES:

The Florida Panthers, owned by Sunshine Sports & Entertainment, are a professional hockey team playing in the Southeast Division of the Eastern Conference of the National Hockey League (NHL), along with the Atlanta Thrashers, Carolina Hurricanes, Tampa Bay Lightning and Washington Capitals. The franchise entered the NHL in 1993 as an expansion team, and since then it has managed only one Stanley Cup appearance, in 1996. The team earned playoff appearances in 1997 and 2000. Much of its early success is contributed to Hall of Fame manager William Torrey, who stayed with the Panthers for the first few years of its existence. In recent years, the team's record and ticket sales have been somewhat lackluster. The team's minor league affiliates are Eastern Conference team the Florida Everblades and American Hockey League (AHL) team the Rochester Americans. Alan Cohen, Bernie Kosar and a group of investors bought the Panthers from Wayne Huizenga's Boca Resorts in 2001. However, Huizenga, who also owns the Miami Dolphins, still has a minority interest in the Panthers. The team plays at BankAtlantic Center, also managed by Sunshine Sports & Entertainment, which sports roughly 20,000 seats and 70 private suites. The arena is owned by Broward County, Florida. Recently signed players include defensemen Keaton Ellerby, Luke Beaverson, and Jason Garrison; right wing Wade Belak; and center Kamil Kreps. In the 2008-09 season, the team averaged approximately 15,600 fans in attendance per game. A recent Forbes estimate values the team at roughly $163 million.

FINANCIALS:

Sales and profits are in thousands of dollars—add 000 to get the full amount. 2008 Note: Financial information for 2008 was not available for all companies at press time.

2008 Sales: $74,000	2008 Profits: $-9,400	**U.S. Stock Ticker: Subsidiary**
2007 Sales: $67,000	2007 Profits: $-7,100	**Int'l Ticker:** Int'l Exchange:
2006 Sales: $65,000	2006 Profits: $-1,900	Employees:
2005 Sales: $	2005 Profits: $	Fiscal Year Ends: 6/30
2004 Sales: $60,000	2004 Profits: $	Parent Company: SUNSHINE SPORTS & ENTERTAINMENT

SALARIES/BENEFITS:

Pension Plan:	ESOP Stock Plan:	Profit Sharing:	Top Exec. Salary: $	Bonus: $
Savings Plan:	Stock Purch. Plan:		Second Exec. Salary: $	Bonus: $

OTHER THOUGHTS:

Apparent Women Officers or Directors: 5
Hot Spot for Advancement for Women/Minorities: Y

LOCATIONS: ("Y" = Yes)

West:	Southwest:	Midwest:	Southeast:	Northeast:	International:
			Y		

Note: Financial information, benefits and other data can change quickly and may vary from those stated here.

FORTUNE BRANDS INC

www.fortunebrands.com

Industry Group Code: 312140 **Ranks within this company's industry group:** Sales: 1 Profits: 1

Sports:		Services:		Media:		Sales:		Facilities:		Other:	
Leagues/Associations:		Food & Beverage:		TV:		Marketing:		Stadiums:		Gambling:	
Teams:		Agents:		Radio:		Ads:		Fitness Clubs:		Apparel:	Y
Nonprofits:		Other:		Internet:		Tickets:		Golf Courses:		Equipment:	Y
Other:				Print:		Retail:		Ski Resorts:		Shoes:	Y
				Software:		Other:		Other:		Other:	

TYPES OF BUSINESS:

Home & Hardware Products
Spirits & Wine
Golf Products

BRANDS/DIVISIONS/AFFILIATES:

MasterBrand Cabinets, Inc.
Moen, Inc.
Simonton Holdings, Inc.
Beam Global Spirits & Wine, Inc.
Acushnet Co.
Aristokraft
Omega
Cruzan

CONTACTS: *Note: Officers with more than one job title may be intentionally listed here more than once.*

Bruce A. Carbonari, CEO
Bruce A. Carbonari, Pres.
Craig P. Omtvedt, CFO/Sr. VP
Elizabeth R. Lane, VP-Human Resources
Mark A. Roche, General Counsel/Sr. VP/Sec.
Christopher J. Klein, Sr. VP-Strategy & Corp. Dev.
C. Clarkson Hine, VP-Corp. Comm. & Public Affairs
Anthony J. Diaz, VP-Investor Rel.
Mark Hausberg, Sr. VP-Finance/Treas.
Matt Stanton, VP-Public Affairs
Charlie Ryan, VP-Taxes
Allan J. Snape, VP-Bus. Dev.
Edward Wiertel, Controller/VP
Bruce A. Carbonari, Chmn.

Phone: 847-484-4400	**Fax:** 847-478-0073
Toll-Free:	
Address: 520 Lake Cook Rd., Deerfield, IL 60015 US	

GROWTH PLANS/SPECIAL FEATURES:

Fortune Brands, Inc. is a holding company with subsidiaries engaged in the manufacture, production and sale of home and hardware products, premium spirits, and golf products. Home and hardware subsidiaries include MasterBrand Cabinets, Inc., which manufactures custom, semi-custom, stock and ready-to-assemble cabinetry for the kitchen, bath and home sold under brands including Aristokraft, Omega, Kitchen Craft, Schrock, Diamond, Decora and Kemper; Moen, Inc., which manufactures faucets, bath furnishings, accessories, parts and kitchen sinks in North America and China; Therma-Thru Corp., which manufactures fiberglass and steel residential entry door and patio door systems; Simonton Holdings, Inc., whose brands include Simonton Windows, a vinyl-framed windows and patio doors brand; and Fortune Brands Storage and Security, LLC, which manufactures tool storage products and safety and security devices. The premium spirits business operates through holding company Beam Global Spirits & Wine, Inc., whose subsidiaries include Jim Beam Brands Co.; Future Brands, LLC; Jim Brands Australia Pty. Ltd.; Beam Global Espanol S.A.; Beam Global Spirits & Wine (U.K.) Ltd.; Tequila Sauza S.A. de C.F.; Canadian Club Canada, Inc.; Maker's Mark Distillery, Inc.; Courvoisier S.A.S.; and Beam Wine Estates, Inc. The company has significant positions in categories including tequila, cognac, Scotch whisky and Canadian whisky. Brands include Courvosier, Maker's Mark, Cruzan, Sauza, Canadian Club and Laphoaig. It also has significant business in regional and national spirits categories such as German liqueurs and Spanish brandies; and an agency relationship for the importation and marketing of New Zealand and Australian wines of the Lion Nathan Wine Group. The golf business operates through Acushnet Co., a manufacturer and marketer of golf balls, clubs, shoes and gloves. Other products include golf bags, outwear and accessories. Brands include Titleist, Pinnacle, Scotty Cameron, Vokey and FootJoy. In August 2008, the company acquired the Cruzan Rum brand.

FINANCIALS: **Sales and profits are in thousands of dollars—add 000 to get the full amount. 2008 Note: Financial information for 2008 was not available for all companies at press time.**

2008 Sales: $7,608,900	2008 Profits: $317,100	**U.S. Stock Ticker: FO**
2007 Sales: $8,563,100	2007 Profits: $762,600	**Int'l Ticker:** Int'l Exchange:
2006 Sales: $8,769,000	2006 Profits: $830,100	Employees: 30,127
2005 Sales: $7,061,200	2005 Profits: $621,100	Fiscal Year Ends: 12/31
2004 Sales: $7,320,900	2004 Profits: $783,800	Parent Company:

SALARIES/BENEFITS:

Pension Plan:	ESOP Stock Plan:	Profit Sharing:	Top Exec. Salary: $1,250,000	Bonus: $1,243,000
Savings Plan:	Stock Purch. Plan:		Second Exec. Salary: $865,000	Bonus: $1,101,962

OTHER THOUGHTS:

Apparent Women Officers or Directors: 4
Hot Spot for Advancement for Women/Minorities: Y

LOCATIONS: ("Y" = Yes)

West:	Southwest:	Midwest:	Southeast:	Northeast:	International:
		Y			Y

FOX BROADCASTING COMPANY

www.fox.com

Industry Group Code: 513210 **Ranks within this company's industry group:** Sales: Profits:

Sports:		Services:		Media:		Sales:		Facilities:		Other:	
Leagues/Associations:		Food & Beverage:		TV:	Y	Marketing:		Stadiums:		Gambling:	
Teams:		Agents:		Radio:		Ads:		Fitness Clubs:		Apparel:	
Nonprofits:		Other:		Internet:		Tickets:		Golf Courses:		Equipment:	
Other:				Print:		Retail:		Ski Resorts:		Shoes:	
				Software:		Other:		Other:		Other:	

TYPES OF BUSINESS:

Television Broadcasting
Television Stations

BRANDS/DIVISIONS/AFFILIATES:

Fox Entertainment Group Inc
News Corporation Limited (The)
FOX Television Network
Simpsons (The)
American Idol
House
24
COPS

CONTACTS:

Note: Officers with more than one job title may be intentionally listed here more than once.

Kevin Reilly, Pres.
Del Mayberry, CFO
Jon Nesvig, Pres., Sales
Andrew Setos, Pres., Eng.
Del Mayberry, Exec. VP-Admin.
Susan Levison, VP
Peter Liguori, Chmn.

Phone: 310-369-1000	**Fax:** 310-369-1283
Toll-Free:	
Address: 10201 W. Pico Blvd., Los Angeles, CA 90035 US	

GROWTH PLANS/SPECIAL FEATURES:

Fox Broadcasting Company (FOX), a subsidiary of Fox Entertainment Group, Inc., itself a subsidiary of News Corporation, operates the FOX Television Network. The company owns and operates 35 full-power stations located in 9 of the 10 largest designated market areas. Its television broadcast network consists of over 216 affiliated stations, including the full-power television stations that are owned by subsidiaries of FOX, which reach approximately 99% of all U.S. television households. The firm broadcasts approximately 15 hours of primetime, sports events and Sunday morning news television programming created by other Fox Entertainment subsidiaries, including Twentieth Century Fox Television, Fox Television Studios, Fox News Channel, Fox Sports Networks, FX Network and several foreign subsidiaries. The company principally derives its revenues from the sale of advertising time sold to national advertisers. FOX's most prominent primetime programs include The Simpsons; American Idol; House; 24; COPS; and America's Most Wanted. The firm licenses sports programming from organizations such as the NFL, MLB and NASCAR. The median age of the FOX viewer is 43 years.

Employees are offered health benefits; free movie screenings; back up child care; child care discounts; counseling services; credit unions; education reimbursement; employee discounts; and pet insurance.

FINANCIALS:

Sales and profits are in thousands of dollars—add 000 to get the full amount. 2008 Note: Financial information for 2008 was not available for all companies at press time.

2008 Sales: $	2008 Profits: $	**U.S. Stock Ticker: Subsidiary**
2007 Sales: $	2007 Profits: $	**Int'l Ticker:** Int'l Exchange:
2006 Sales: $	2006 Profits: $	Employees: 425
2005 Sales: $2,624,000	2005 Profits: $	Fiscal Year Ends: 6/30
2004 Sales: $4,556,000	2004 Profits: $	Parent Company: NEWS CORP

SALARIES/BENEFITS:

Pension Plan:	ESOP Stock Plan:	Profit Sharing:	Top Exec. Salary: $	Bonus: $
Savings Plan:	Stock Purch. Plan:		Second Exec. Salary: $	Bonus: $

OTHER THOUGHTS:

Apparent Women Officers or Directors: 1
Hot Spot for Advancement for Women/Minorities:

LOCATIONS: ("Y" = Yes)

West:	Southwest:	Midwest:	Southeast:	Northeast:	International:
Y					

FOX SPORTS NET INC

msn.foxsports.com

Industry Group Code: 513210 **Ranks within this company's industry group:** Sales: Profits:

Sports:		Services:		Media:		Sales:		Facilities:		Other:	
Leagues/Associations:		Food & Beverage:		TV:	Y	Marketing:		Stadiums:		Gambling:	
Teams:		Agents:		Radio:		Ads:		Fitness Clubs:		Apparel:	
Nonprofits:		Other:		Internet:		Tickets:		Golf Courses:		Equipment:	
Other:				Print:		Retail:		Ski Resorts:		Shoes:	
				Software:		Other:		Other:		Other:	

TYPES OF BUSINESS:

Sports Broadcasting
Film & TV Production & Distribution
Online Sports Broadcasting
Regional Sports Networks

BRANDS/DIVISIONS/AFFILIATES:

Fox Sports Net
Fox Entertainment Group Inc
News Corporation Limited (The)
National Sports Partners
National Advertising Partners

CONTACTS: *Note: Officers with more than one job title may be intentionally listed here more than once.*

David Hill, CEO
Robert Thompson, Pres.
Robert Gottlieb, Sr. VP-Mktg. & On-Air Promotions
Lou D'Ermilio, Sr. VP-Media Rel.
David Rone, Exec. VP-Rights Acquisitions
Dan Bell, VP-Comm.
George Greenberg, Exec. VP-Programming & Production
David Rone, Exec. VP-Rights Acquisitions
David Hill, Chmn.
Marvin Zepeda, Dir.-Programming, Fox Sports Latin America

Phone: 310-369-6000 **Fax:** 212-354-6902
Toll-Free:
Address: 10201 W. Pico Blvd., Bldg. 103, Los Angeles, CA 90035 US

GROWTH PLANS/SPECIAL FEATURES:

Fox Sports Net (FSN), Inc., owned by Fox Entertainment Group, itself a majority-owned subsidiary of The News Corporation Limited, produces and distributes films and television programs. The company provides professional and collegiate sports programming through interests in 21 regional sports networks (RSNs), as well as through Fox Sports Net, a national sports news program that operates through six additional RSNs. FSN's programming, which is received by approximately 85 million households, combines the content of RSNs with national programming that is consistent throughout all regions. The company has the rights to broadcast the live events of 65 NBA, NHL, MLB teams, as well as several high school and collegiate teams. In addition, the firm hosts the ACC, Big 12 and Pac 10 conferences. Most of the company's revenue is culled through advertising time slots. The company has various partnerships with Rainbow Media Sports, with the result that the two companies have owned different stakes in various regional Fox Sports Net operations.

Fox Sports offers employees medical, dental, and vision plans; life insurance; back up child care and discounts on child care; an employee assistance program; credit union membership; advance movie screenings; educational reimbursement; employee discounts; Hybrid vehicle incentive; fitness and massage services; employee development training; DVD lending library; and salon services.

FINANCIALS: **Sales and profits are in thousands of dollars—add 000 to get the full amount. 2008 Note: Financial information for 2008 was not available for all companies at press time.**

2008 Sales: $ 2008 Profits: $
2007 Sales: $ 2007 Profits: $
2006 Sales: $ 2006 Profits: $
2005 Sales: $ 2005 Profits: $
2004 Sales: $ 2004 Profits: $

U.S. Stock Ticker: Subsidiary
Int'l Ticker: Int'l Exchange:
Employees: 150
Fiscal Year Ends: 6/30
Parent Company: NEWS CORP

SALARIES/BENEFITS:

Pension Plan: Y ESOP Stock Plan: Profit Sharing: Top Exec. Salary: $ Bonus: $
Savings Plan: Y Stock Purch. Plan: Second Exec. Salary: $ Bonus: $

OTHER THOUGHTS:

Apparent Women Officers or Directors:
Hot Spot for Advancement for Women/Minorities:

LOCATIONS: ("Y" = Yes)

West:	Southwest:	Midwest:	Southeast:	Northeast:	International:
Y	Y	Y	Y	Y	

FRANKLIN SPORTS INC

www.franklinsports.com

Industry Group Code: 339920 **Ranks within this company's industry group:** Sales: Profits:

Sports:		Services:		Media:		Sales:		Facilities:		Other:	
Leagues/Associations:		Food & Beverage:		TV:		Marketing:		Stadiums:		Gambling:	
Teams:		Agents:		Radio:		Ads:		Fitness Clubs:		Apparel:	Y
Nonprofits:		Other:		Internet:		Tickets:		Golf Courses:		Equipment:	Y
Other:				Print:		Retail:		Ski Resorts:		Shoes:	
				Software:		Other:		Other:		Other:	Y

TYPES OF BUSINESS:

Sports Equipment
Apparel
Games
Specialty Gloves
Specialty Eyewear

BRANDS/DIVISIONS/AFFILIATES:

UNIFORCE Tactical
Major League Baseball (MLB)

CONTACTS:

Note: Officers with more than one job title may be intentionally listed here more than once.

Irving Franklin, CEO
Larry J. Franklin, Pres.
George Small, CFO/Controller/VP
Charles Quinn, VP-Mktg.
Donald Loiacano, VP-Oper.
Joe Murphy, VP-Sales, U.S.
Irving Franklin, Chmn.

Phone: 781-344-1111 **Fax:** 781-341-3646
Toll-Free: 800-225-8647
Address: 17 Campanelli Pkwy., Stoughton, MA 02072-3703 US

GROWTH PLANS/SPECIAL FEATURES:

Franklin Sports, Inc., founded in 1946, manufactures and markets sports equipment and apparel for baseball, street hockey and soccer, as well as fan products, table games and yard games. The company's products include balls, gloves, protective gear, training aids, hockey sticks, accessories and fan products. Franklin makes equipment for family and yard games such as volleyball, badminton, tetherball, bocce, croquet, horseshoes, table tennis and darts. The firm's youth offerings include table games such as foosball, ping-pong and air hockey; and balls, bats, sticks and rackets made from lighter and softer materials. Franklin's line of fan products includes balls, helmets, jerseys, sports lockers, rubber facemasks and other accessories decorated with team colors and logos. UNIFORCE Tactical, one of the company's operating divisions, produces specialty gloves and eyewear, including tactical police gloves designed to resist laceration, chemicals, pathogens and cold weather. For the last 25 years, UNIFORCE has held the distinction of producing the official batting glove of Major League Baseball. The company's products are sold through various storefront and online retailers, including Sports Authority and Dick's Sporting Goods, as well as through international distributors around the globe.

FINANCIALS:

Sales and profits are in thousands of dollars—add 000 to get the full amount. 2008 Note: Financial information for 2008 was not available for all companies at press time.

2008 Sales: $	2008 Profits: $	**U.S. Stock Ticker: Private**
2007 Sales: $22,400	2007 Profits: $	**Int'l Ticker:** Int'l Exchange:
2006 Sales: $	2006 Profits: $	Employees: 225
2005 Sales: $	2005 Profits: $	Fiscal Year Ends:
2004 Sales: $	2004 Profits: $	Parent Company:

SALARIES/BENEFITS:

Pension Plan:	ESOP Stock Plan:	Profit Sharing:	Top Exec. Salary: $	Bonus: $
Savings Plan:	Stock Purch. Plan:		Second Exec. Salary: $	Bonus: $

OTHER THOUGHTS:

Apparent Women Officers or Directors:
Hot Spot for Advancement for Women/Minorities:

LOCATIONS: ("Y" = Yes)

West:	Southwest:	Midwest:	Southeast:	Northeast:	International:
				Y	

FULHAM FOOTBALL CLUB

www.fulhamfc.com

Industry Group Code: 711211D **Ranks within this company's industry group:** Sales: Profits:

Sports:		Services:		Media:		Sales:		Facilities:		Other:	
Leagues/Associations:		Food & Beverage:		TV:		Marketing:		Stadiums:		Gambling:	
Teams:	Y	Agents:		Radio:		Ads:		Fitness Clubs:		Apparel:	
Nonprofits:		Other:		Internet:		Tickets:	Y	Golf Courses:		Equipment:	
Other:				Print:		Retail:	Y	Ski Resorts:		Shoes:	
				Software:		Other:		Other:		Other:	

TYPES OF BUSINESS:

English Premier Soccer Team
Ticket Sales
Youth & Community Programs

BRANDS/DIVISIONS/AFFILIATES:

Craven Cottage

CONTACTS:

Note: Officers with more than one job title may be intentionally listed here more than once.

Ray Lewington, First Team Coach
Roy Hodgson, Mgr.
Mike Kelly, Asst. Mgr./Goalkeeping Coach
Mohamed Al Fayed, Chmn.

Phone: 44-0870-442-1222 **Fax:** 44-0870-442-0236
Toll-Free:
Address: Motspur Park, New Maiden, Surrey, KT3 6PT UK

GROWTH PLANS/SPECIAL FEATURES:

Fulham Football Club is an English Premiership soccer team based in London. The club plays its home games at Craven Cottage on the banks of the Thames and is owned by Mohamed Al Fayed. It was Al Fayed, a wealthy businessman, who took control of the club in 1997, when it had hit rock bottom and desperately needed a boost to move it up out of division two (the second league below the elite Premiership league). He began by signing well-recognized manager Kevin Keegan and doling out million-pound contracts to obtain Canadian striker Paul Peschisolido and Chris Coleman, who were playing with the competitive Blackburn Rovers. The club facilities were upgraded and, with added media and fan interest, the club won division II, then division I titles to be promoted to the Premiership in 2001. Former Fulham player Chris Coleman made a positive impact during his term as manager from 2003 to early 2007 as a young rookie coach. The club's sponsors include Nike and LG; the club is also partnered with American Airlines, Monster, Buxton, Seatwave and Coral. Various services offered on the club web site include personalized Fulham Football Club license plates and shirts, Fulham TV, matchday programs available online, memorabilia-related auctions and quizzes with prizes, as well as downloadable wallpapers, screensavers and ringtones.

FINANCIALS:

Sales and profits are in thousands of dollars—add 000 to get the full amount. 2008 Note: Financial information for 2008 was not available for all companies at press time.

2008 Sales: $	2008 Profits: $	**U.S. Stock Ticker: Private**
2007 Sales: $	2007 Profits: $	**Int'l Ticker:** Int'l Exchange:
2006 Sales: $	2006 Profits: $	Employees:
2005 Sales: $	2005 Profits: $	Fiscal Year Ends:
2004 Sales: $	2004 Profits: $	Parent Company:

SALARIES/BENEFITS:

Pension Plan:	ESOP Stock Plan:	Profit Sharing:	Top Exec. Salary: $	Bonus: $
Savings Plan:	Stock Purch. Plan:		Second Exec. Salary: $	Bonus: $

OTHER THOUGHTS:

Apparent Women Officers or Directors:
Hot Spot for Advancement for Women/Minorities:

LOCATIONS: ("Y" = Yes)

West:	Southwest:	Midwest:	Southeast:	Northeast:	International:
					Y

GIANT MANUFACTURING CO LTD

www.giant-bicycles.com

Industry Group Code: 339920 **Ranks within this company's industry group:** Sales: Profits:

Sports:		Services:		Media:		Sales:		Facilities:		Other:	
Leagues/Associations:		Food & Beverage:		TV:		Marketing:		Stadiums:		Gambling:	
Teams:		Agents:		Radio:		Ads:		Fitness Clubs:		Apparel:	Y
Nonprofits:		Other:		Internet:		Tickets:		Golf Courses:		Equipment:	Y
Other:				Print:		Retail:		Ski Resorts:		Shoes:	
				Software:		Other:		Other:		Other:	

TYPES OF BUSINESS:

Bicycle Manufacturing
Bicycle Parts & Care Products
Apparel & Accessories
Fitness Equipment

BRANDS/DIVISIONS/AFFILIATES:

Giant Europe BV
Global Giant Mountain Bike Team
ONCE Level 1 Road Team
TCR
Defy
FCR
Anthem
Trance

CONTACTS: *Note: Officers with more than one job title may be intentionally listed here more than once.*

Tony Lo, CEO
Bonnie Tu, CFO/Exec. VP
Jeffrey Sheu, Spokesperson
King Liu, Chmn.

Phone: 886-4-2681-4771	**Fax:** 886-4-2681-0280
Toll-Free:	
Address: 19 Shun-Farn Rd. Tachia, Taichung Hsien, Taiwan	

GROWTH PLANS/SPECIAL FEATURES:

Giant Manufacturing Co., Ltd., based in Taiwan, is a leading global original design and original brand manufacturer of bicycles. The company operates through locations across seven continents and over 50 countries, including four manufacturing facilities in Taiwan, China and Europe that make both Giant-branded bikes and bikes for other popular brands. The company's bikes range in price from $200 to $5,000 and are sold in over 10,000 retail outlets internationally. Giant's manufacturing of bicycles for other bicycle brands accounts for approximately 30% of the company's total manufacturing capacity. Giant began its overseas expansion in 1986 with the establishment of Giant Europe BV in the Netherlands. Giant makes road bikes in the competition-road (TCR model), performance (Defy model), and fitness (FCR model) classes. The firm's mountain bikes include models in the competition (Anthem model), trail (Trance model), all mountain (Reign model), freeride (Glory model), hard tail (XTC model) and sport (Brass model) categories. Models designs specifically for women include road, mountain and lifestyle bikes. Giant's lifestyle models include designs for metro, comfort, cruiser and touring applications, as well as compact models. The company's BMX bikes include dirt (Method Series) and neighborhood (GFR Series) models. Giant also sells kids' bikes, including first bikes and mountain bikes. Beyond bicycles, the firm produces apparel (helmets, team clothing and gloves), frame sets (both road and mountain), bike care products (lube, pumps, tools and locks), carrying items (bags, baby seats and car racks) and lights. As part of its marketing campaign, Giant is the official bicycle sponsor for two international cycling teams, the Global Giant Mountain Bike Team and the ONCE Level 1 Road Team. In July 2008, Giant opened its first location in Vietnam.

FINANCIALS: Sales and profits are in thousands of dollars—add 000 to get the full amount. 2008 Note: Financial information for 2008 was not available for all companies at press time.

2008 Sales: $	2008 Profits: $	**U.S. Stock Ticker: GTMUF.PK**
2007 Sales: $	2007 Profits: $	**Int'l Ticker: 9921** Int'l Exchange: Taipei-TPE
2006 Sales: $	2006 Profits: $	Employees:
2005 Sales: $	2005 Profits: $	Fiscal Year Ends: 12/31
2004 Sales: $	2004 Profits: $	Parent Company:

SALARIES/BENEFITS:

Pension Plan:	ESOP Stock Plan:	Profit Sharing:	Top Exec. Salary: $	Bonus: $
Savings Plan:	Stock Purch. Plan:		Second Exec. Salary: $	Bonus: $

OTHER THOUGHTS:

Apparent Women Officers or Directors: 1
Hot Spot for Advancement for Women/Minorities:

LOCATIONS: ("Y" = Yes)

West:	Southwest:	Midwest:	Southeast:	Northeast:	International:
Y					Y

GLOBAL SPECTRUM LP

www.global-spectrum.com

Industry Group Code: 561210 **Ranks within this company's industry group:** Sales: Profits:

Sports:		Services:		Media:		Sales:		Facilities:		Other:	
Leagues/Associations:		Food & Beverage:	Y	TV:		Marketing:	Y	Stadiums:		Gambling:	
Teams:		Agents:		Radio:		Ads:	Y	Fitness Clubs:		Apparel:	
Nonprofits:		Other:	Y	Internet:		Tickets:		Golf Courses:		Equipment:	
Other:				Print:		Retail:		Ski Resorts:		Shoes:	
				Software:		Other:		Other:	Y	Other:	Y

TYPES OF BUSINESS:

Facilities Management
Consulting Services
Marketing Services
Operations & Engineering Services
Financial Services
Ticketing Services
Food & Beverage Services

BRANDS/DIVISIONS/AFFILIATES:

Comcast-Spectator
Front Row Marketing Services
Global Spectrum Asia, Ltd.
Comcast Corp

CONTACTS: *Note: Officers with more than one job title may be intentionally listed here more than once.*

John Page, COO/Sr. VP
Bob Schwartz, VP-Mktg.
Lane Miller, VP-Human Resources
Bill Savage, Dir.-IT
Phillip Weinberg, General Counsel/Exec. VP
Michael Ahearn, VP-Oper.
Frank E. Russo, Jr., Sr. VP-Bus. Dev. & Client Rel.
Ike Richman, VP-Public Rel.
Jay Halbert, Exec. VP-Finance
Tom M. Mobley, Jr., Sr. VP-Convention Centers
Pat Condon, VP-Internal Audit & Contract Compliance
Michael Hasson, VP-Security & Svcs.
Lewis R. Bostic, VP-Risk Mgmt.
Peter Luukko, Chmn.

Phone: 215-389-9587	**Fax:** 215-952-5651
Toll-Free:	
Address: 3601 S. Broad St., Philadelphia, PA 19148 US	

GROWTH PLANS/SPECIAL FEATURES:

Global Spectrum, L.P. (GS), a subsidiary of Comcast-Spectator, provides full-service management for arenas, stadiums, convention centers, ice rinks, expo centers, auditoriums and theaters. It currently manages over 80 facilities in the U.S and Canada. The company offers services on a turnkey management basis or as a consultant for facility design, construction and ongoing operations. For companies under full or contract management, GS customizes unique management solutions for each client, allowing the owner to retain all the rights and privileges of setting policies while GS establishes procedures to implement the policies. The company's management solutions typically include five key areas: administration and finance, which covers accounting, auditing, human resources administration, information technology, labor negotiations, risk management and other services; sales and marketing, which includes advertising, media relations, market research, event promotions and web site development; operations and engineering, including repairs, maintenance, housekeeping, audio-visual technology, emergency planning and security; ticketing services and box office management; and ancillary services, such as food and beverage, merchandising, parking and guest services. GS also works with clients through all stages in the creation of a new facility, from project conception through grand opening and continuing into day-to-day operations. The firm's portfolio of pre-opening services features feasibility analysis, operational design, financial forecasting, project coordination, booking, scheduling, venue marketing and operational start-up. GS's facility consulting services division assists clients in the design, construction, renovation, repair, expansion and improvement of public assembly venues. Subsidiary Front Row Marketing Services develops, implements and manages sales processes for facilities, teams, colleges, municipalities and sports properties. Front Row targets contractually obligated revenue sources such as premium seating, naming rights, venue advertising, sponsorships and vendor rights. Global Spectrum Asia, Ltd. has offices in 25 cities worldwide and specializes in production and promotion of international trade shows and conventions.

FINANCIALS: Sales and profits are in thousands of dollars—add 000 to get the full amount. 2008 Note: Financial information for 2008 was not available for all companies at press time.

2008 Sales: $	2008 Profits: $	**U.S. Stock Ticker: Subsidiary**
2007 Sales: $	2007 Profits: $	**Int'l Ticker:** Int'l Exchange:
2006 Sales: $	2006 Profits: $	Employees:
2005 Sales: $	2005 Profits: $	Fiscal Year Ends: 12/31
2004 Sales: $	2004 Profits: $	Parent Company: COMCAST CORP

SALARIES/BENEFITS:

Pension Plan:	ESOP Stock Plan:	Profit Sharing:	Top Exec. Salary: $	Bonus: $
Savings Plan:	Stock Purch. Plan:		Second Exec. Salary: $	Bonus: $

OTHER THOUGHTS:

Apparent Women Officers or Directors:
Hot Spot for Advancement for Women/Minorities:

LOCATIONS: ("Y" = Yes)

West:	Southwest:	Midwest:	Southeast:	Northeast:	International:
			Y	Y	Y

GOLDEN STATE WARRIORS

www.nba.com/warriors

Industry Group Code: 711211B **Ranks within this company's industry group:** Sales: 19 Profits: 11

Sports:		Services:		Media:		Sales:		Facilities:		Other:	
Leagues/Associations:		Food & Beverage:		TV:		Marketing:		Stadiums:		Gambling:	
Teams:	Y	Agents:		Radio:		Ads:		Fitness Clubs:		Apparel:	
Nonprofits:		Other:		Internet:		Tickets:	Y	Golf Courses:		Equipment:	
Other:				Print:		Retail:	Y	Ski Resorts:		Shoes:	
				Software:		Other:		Other:		Other:	

TYPES OF BUSINESS:

Professional Basketball Team
Ticket Sales

BRANDS/DIVISIONS/AFFILIATES:

Oracle Arena
Golden State Warriors Foundation
Warrior Basketball Camp
Jr. Warriors Basketball League
Warriors Read To Achieve Program
Get Fit Program

CONTACTS: *Note: Officers with more than one job title may be intentionally listed here more than once.*

Christopher Cohan, Owner
Robert Rowell, Pres.
Neda Kia, Exec. VP-Bus. Dev.
Don Nelson, Head Coach
Mark Grabow, Dir.-Athletic Dev.
Chris Mullin, Gen. Mgr.
Keith Smart, Asst. Coach
Christopher Cohan, Chmn./Majority Owner

Phone: 510-986-2200	**Fax:** 510-452-0132
Toll-Free:	
Address: 1011 Broadway, Oakland, CA 94607 US	

GROWTH PLANS/SPECIAL FEATURES:

The Golden State Warriors joined the American Basketball Association (ABA) as the Philadelphia Warriors in 1946. The team moved to Oakland in 1971 and became known as the Golden State Warriors in the National Basketball Association (NBA). All Warrior home games are played at the Oracle Arena. The arena boasts a 19,596 seating capacity for basketball games and hosted the 1999 WCW SuperBrawl and the 2000 NBA All-Star Game. The team sponsors community outreach programs which include the Warriors Read To Achieve Program, the Get Fit Program, Warriors Basketball Camp and the Jr. Warriors Basketball League for young Northern California basketball players. The Golden State Warriors Foundation was also established during the 1997-98 season to provide opportunities and financial assistance to nonprofit organizations in the greater San Francisco Bay Area. Since its inception, the franchise has obtained one NBA championship in 1975 under its star player, Rick Barry. Other noteworthy Warrior players include Wilt Chamberlain, Nate Thurmond, Tim Hardaway, Mitch Richmond and Chris Mullin, who is currently general manager of the team. Chairman Chris Cohan owns 80% of the team. The Golden State Warriors have endured a 12-year losing streak, but in 2008 made it to the Western Conference Playoffs before being knocked out by the Phoenix Suns. Forbes Magazine recently estimated the team to be worth approximately $335 million. In the 2008-09 season, the team's home attendance average was roughly 18,900 per game.

FINANCIALS: **Sales and profits are in thousands of dollars—add 000 to get the full amount. 2008 Note: Financial information for 2008 was not available for all companies at press time.**

2008 Sales: $112,000	2008 Profits: $14,200	**U.S. Stock Ticker: Private**
2007 Sales: $103,000	2007 Profits: $1,300	**Int'l Ticker:** Int'l Exchange:
2006 Sales: $89,000	2006 Profits: $6,300	Employees:
2005 Sales: $81,000	2005 Profits: $	Fiscal Year Ends: 6/30
2004 Sales: $76,000	2004 Profits: $	Parent Company:

SALARIES/BENEFITS:

Pension Plan:	ESOP Stock Plan:	Profit Sharing:	Top Exec. Salary: $	Bonus: $
Savings Plan:	Stock Purch. Plan:		Second Exec. Salary: $	Bonus: $

OTHER THOUGHTS:

Apparent Women Officers or Directors: 1
Hot Spot for Advancement for Women/Minorities:

LOCATIONS: ("Y" = Yes)

West:	Southwest:	Midwest:	Southeast:	Northeast:	International:
Y					

GOLD'S GYM INTERNATIONAL

www.goldsgym.com

Industry Group Code: 713940 **Ranks within this company's industry group:** Sales: Profits:

Sports:		Services:		Media:		Sales:		Facilities:		Other:	
Leagues/Associations:		Food & Beverage:		TV:		Marketing:		Stadiums:		Gambling:	
Teams:		Agents:		Radio:		Ads:		Fitness Clubs:	Y	Apparel:	
Nonprofits:		Other:		Internet:		Tickets:		Golf Courses:		Equipment:	
Other:				Print:		Retail:		Ski Resorts:		Shoes:	
				Software:		Other:		Other:		Other:	

TYPES OF BUSINESS:

Fitness Centers

BRANDS/DIVISIONS/AFFILIATES:

GoldsGear.com

CONTACTS:

Note: Officers with more than one job title may be intentionally listed here more than once.

James Weaver, CEO
Mike Feinman, COO/Exec. VP
Randy Schultz, CFO
Lisa Zoellner, Chief Mktg. Officer
Bill Wade, CIO
Joel Tallman, VP-Oper.
Joel Tallman, VP-Franchising Oper.

Phone: 214-574-4653	**Fax:** 214-296-5000
Toll-Free: 866-465-3775	
Address: 125 E. John Carpenter Freeway, Ste. 1300, Irving, TX 75062 US	

GROWTH PLANS/SPECIAL FEATURES:

Gold's Gym International, Inc. is one of the largest co-ed gym chains in the world. With nearly 3 million members, Gold's Gym has over 620 franchised gyms in 43 states and in 30 countries, including the U.K., Canada, Australia, Mexico, Peru, the Virgin Islands, Japan, India, Germany and Russia. Members of Gold's not only have access to what are recognized as the industry's leading gyms, but they can also work with personal trainers to devise meal plans and develop weight programs. Gold's Gym works with other companies in the health and fitness industry by offering flexible advertising campaigns, sponsorships and promotional opportunities within its gyms. Each gym offers all of the latest equipment and services, including group exercise classes, cardiovascular equipment, spinning, Pilates and yoga, while maintaining its core weight lifting tradition. In addition to managing its own web site, the firm operates GoldsGear.com, an online store that offers Gold's Gym branded merchandise.

The company offers its employees benefits that include medical, dental and vision insurance; a retirement savings plan; training in a team-oriented work environment; and a free gym membership.

FINANCIALS:

Sales and profits are in thousands of dollars—add 000 to get the full amount. 2008 Note: Financial information for 2008 was not available for all companies at press time.

2008 Sales: $	2008 Profits: $	**U.S. Stock Ticker: Private**
2007 Sales: $48,600	2007 Profits: $	**Int'l Ticker:** Int'l Exchange:
2006 Sales: $	2006 Profits: $	Employees: 2,000
2005 Sales: $	2005 Profits: $	Fiscal Year Ends: 2/28
2004 Sales: $	2004 Profits: $	Parent Company:

SALARIES/BENEFITS:

Pension Plan:	ESOP Stock Plan:	Profit Sharing:	Top Exec. Salary: $	Bonus: $
Savings Plan: Y	Stock Purch. Plan:		Second Exec. Salary: $	Bonus: $

OTHER THOUGHTS:

Apparent Women Officers or Directors:
Hot Spot for Advancement for Women/Minorities:

LOCATIONS: ("Y" = Yes)

West:	Southwest:	Midwest:	Southeast:	Northeast:	International:
Y	Y	Y	Y	Y	Y

Note: Financial information, benefits and other data can change quickly and may vary from those stated here.

GOLF GALAXY INC

www.golfgalaxy.com

Industry Group Code: 451110E **Ranks within this company's industry group:** Sales: Profits:

Sports:		Services:		Media:		Sales:		Facilities:		Other:	
Leagues/Associations:		Food & Beverage:		TV:		Marketing:		Stadiums:		Gambling:	
Teams:		Agents:		Radio:		Ads:		Fitness Clubs:		Apparel:	
Nonprofits:		Other:	Y	Internet:		Tickets:		Golf Courses:		Equipment:	
Other:				Print:		Retail:	Y	Ski Resorts:		Shoes:	
				Software:		Other:		Other:		Other:	

TYPES OF BUSINESS:

Golf Equipment-Retail
Online Sales
Golf Consultation & Instruction
Repair & Maintenance Services

BRANDS/DIVISIONS/AFFILIATES:

Dick's Sporting Goods
Golf Works (The)
Advantage Club
Callaway Golf
TaylorMade
Cobra
Cleveland
PING

CONTACTS:

Note: Officers with more than one job title may be intentionally listed here more than once.

Gregory B. Maanum, COO
Ronald G. Hornbaker, Sr. VP-Sales & Mktg.
Randall K. Zanatta, Chmn.

Phone: 952-941-8848	**Fax:** 952-941-8846
Toll-Free: 800-287-9060	
Address: 7275 Flying Cloud Dr., Eden Prairie, MN 55344 US	

GROWTH PLANS/SPECIAL FEATURES:

Golf Galaxy, Inc., a subsidiary of Dick's Sporting Goods, is a leading golf specialty retailer selling national brand golf merchandise in 31 states. The company operates 90 superstores that range from 16,000 to 18,000 square feet and contain numerous interactive selling features such as artificial putting greens and golf simulators. It also sells merchandise online. Golf Galaxy's product offerings include clubs, bags, balls, gloves, accessories, apparel and footwear, which include such brands as Callaway Golf, TaylorMade, Cobra, Cleveland, PING, Titleist, Ashworth, Greg Norman, Nike Golf, adidas and FootJoy. Service offerings include lessons, ball launch monitor fitting and putter fitting. Golf Galaxy staffs its stores with full-time PGA professionals, who offer customers a consultative selling approach, as well as pro-shop services and golf lessons featuring digital video swing analysis. The firm's store-within-a-store concept, The Golf Works, is present in 27 stores and features golf club components; club making tools and supplies; technical information; and services such as club repair, regripping and club upgrade. The Advantage Club loyalty program offers members, who number over 900,000, in-store events, e-mail bargains and direct mail promotions. Golf Galaxy also purchases pre-owned equipment in exchange for in-store credit. In January 2008, Golf Galaxy opened its first location in the greater Miami, Florida area and opened its third in the greater St. Louis area.

FINANCIALS:

Sales and profits are in thousands of dollars—add 000 to get the full amount. 2008 Note: Financial information for 2008 was not available for all companies at press time.

2008 Sales: $	2008 Profits: $	**U.S. Stock Ticker: Subsidiary**
2007 Sales: $	2007 Profits: $	**Int'l Ticker:** Int'l Exchange:
2006 Sales: $	2006 Profits: $	Employees: 1,460
2005 Sales: $133,080	2005 Profits: $5,266	Fiscal Year Ends: 2/28
2004 Sales: $99,630	2004 Profits: $7,538	Parent Company: DICK'S SPORTING GOODS

SALARIES/BENEFITS:

Pension Plan:	ESOP Stock Plan:	Profit Sharing:	Top Exec. Salary: $256,923	Bonus: $
Savings Plan:	Stock Purch. Plan:		Second Exec. Salary: $236,923	Bonus: $

OTHER THOUGHTS:

Apparent Women Officers or Directors:
Hot Spot for Advancement for Women/Minorities:

LOCATIONS: ("Y" = Yes)

West:	Southwest:	Midwest:	Southeast:	Northeast:	International:
Y	Y	Y	Y	Y	

GOLFSMITH INTERNATIONAL HOLDINGS INC

www.golfsmith.com

Industry Group Code: 451110E **Ranks within this company's industry group:** Sales: 1 Profits: 1

Sports:		Services:		Media:		Sales:		Facilities:		Other:	
Leagues/Associations:		Food & Beverage:		TV:		Marketing:		Stadiums:		Gambling:	
Teams:		Agents:		Radio:		Ads:		Fitness Clubs:		Apparel:	Y
Nonprofits:		Other:		Internet:		Tickets:		Golf Courses:		Equipment:	Y
Other:				Print:		Retail:	Y	Ski Resorts:		Shoes:	Y
				Software:		Other:		Other:		Other:	

TYPES OF BUSINESS:

Golf Equipment Manufacturing
Retail Sales
Catalog Publication
Tennis Equipment
Used Golf and Tennis Equipment

BRANDS/DIVISIONS/AFFILIATES:

Golfsmith International, Inc.
Lynx
Zevo
Snake Eyes
Golfsmith
Killer Bee
Clubmaker Magazine
Don Sherwood Golf & Tennis

CONTACTS: *Note: Officers with more than one job title may be intentionally listed here more than once.*

Martin E. Hanaka, CEO
Sue E. Grove, COO/Exec. VP
Martin E. Hanaka, Pres.
Sue E. Grove, Interim CFO
Matthew Corey, Sr. VP-Mktg. & Brand
Gillian Felix, Sr. VP-Human Resources & Guest Experience
Andrew Spratt, VP-Info. Svcs.
R. Scott Wood, General Counsel/VP/Sec.
Joseph J. Kester, VP-Field Oper.
Matthew Corey, Sr. VP-New Bus. Dev.
David Lowe, VP-Brands & Golf Instruction
Adrian Gonzalez, VP-Store Admin. & Guest Experience
Martin E. Hanaka, Chmn.

Phone: 512-837-8810 **Fax:** 512-821-1245
Toll-Free: 800-813-6897
Address: 11000 North IH-35, Austin, TX 78753 US

GROWTH PLANS/SPECIAL FEATURES:

Golfsmith International Holdings, Inc., operating through Golfsmith International, Inc., a specialty retailer of golf and tennis equipment, apparel and accessories. The company expanded into the tennis category through its acquisition of six Don Sherwood Golf & Tennis stores and the subsequent introduction of tennis equipment, apparel, and accessories in the majority of its stores. The firm is also a catalog retailer, principally publishing Golfsmith Consumer Catalog, which targets the avid golfer, and Golfsmith Clubmaking Catalog, a specialty catalog for people who build their own clubs. Originally founded as a club components and custom club making company, Golfsmith continues to design and manufacture under the various brand names of Lynx, Zevo, Snake Eyes, Golfsmith and Killer Bee. The company founded the Golf Clubmakers Association (GCA), the largest such organization in the golf industry. Golfsmith operates as an integrated multi-channel retailer and has 73 stores across the U.S. In the U.K., the firm sells its equipment through a commissioned sales force directly to retailers. Through most of Europe and parts of Asia, it sells its products through a network of agents, distributors and through its web site. The company has 17 registered domain names that link to golfsmith.com, which itself sells over 50,000 golf and tennis products. In 54 stores, the firm has an activity-based shopping environment, called GolfTEC Learning Centers, where customers can test the performance of golf clubs, obtain precision club-fitting through its SmartFit program and benefit from PGA-certified golf instruction. The company's stores and web site offer a proprietary credit card and product selection that features national brands, Golfsmith's products and pre-owned clubs. The firm's stores generate 79% of the company's revenues.. In December 2008, the company introduced a Live Chat service on its online site.

Employees are offered medical, dental and life insurance; education assistance; and employee discounts.

FINANCIALS: **Sales and profits are in thousands of dollars—add 000 to get the full amount. 2008 Note: Financial information for 2008 was not available for all companies at press time.**

2008 Sales: $378,772	2008 Profits: $- 516	**U.S. Stock Ticker: GOLF**
2007 Sales: $388,157	2007 Profits: $-40,820	**Int'l Ticker:** Int'l Exchange:
2006 Sales: $357,890	2006 Profits: $-8,109	Employees: 1,585
2005 Sales: $323,794	2005 Profits: $2,957	Fiscal Year Ends: 12/31
2004 Sales: $296,202	2004 Profits: $-4,756	Parent Company:

SALARIES/BENEFITS:

Pension Plan:	ESOP Stock Plan:	Profit Sharing:	Top Exec. Salary: $313,846	Bonus: $18,630
Savings Plan: Y	Stock Purch. Plan:		Second Exec. Salary: $207,000	Bonus: $

OTHER THOUGHTS:

Apparent Women Officers or Directors: 3
Hot Spot for Advancement for Women/Minorities: Y

LOCATIONS: ("Y" = Yes)

West:	Southwest:	Midwest:	Southeast:	Northeast:	International:
Y	Y	Y	Y	Y	Y

GREEN BAY PACKERS

www.packers.com

Industry Group Code: 711211C **Ranks within this company's industry group:** Sales: 13 Profits: 19

Sports:		**Services:**		**Media:**		**Sales:**		**Facilities:**		**Other:**	
Leagues/Associations:		Food & Beverage:		TV:		Marketing:		Stadiums:		Gambling:	
Teams:	Y	Agents:		Radio:		Ads:		Fitness Clubs:		Apparel:	
Nonprofits:		Other:		Internet:		Tickets:	Y	Golf Courses:		Equipment:	
Other:				Print:		Retail:	Y	Ski Resorts:		Shoes:	
				Software:		Other:		Other:		Other:	

TYPES OF BUSINESS:

Professional Football Team

BRANDS/DIVISIONS/AFFILIATES:

Green Bay Packers Foundation

CONTACTS:

Note: Officers with more than one job title may be intentionally listed here more than once.

Mark Murphy, CEO
Mark Murphy, Pres.
Craig Benzel, Dir.-Mktg. & Corp. Sales
Nicole Ledvina, Mgr.-Human Resources
Wayne Wichlacz, Dir.-IT
Jason Wied, VP-Admin.
Jason Wied, Corp. Counsel
Mark Wagner, Dir.-Ticket Oper.
Jeff Blumb, Dir.-Public Rel.
Vicki Vannieuwenhoven, VP-Finance
Mark Schiefelbein, Dir.-Admin. Affairs
Duke Copp, Controller
Kate Hogan, Dir.-Retail Oper.
Robert E. Harlan, Chmn. Emeritus

Phone: 920-569-7500	**Fax:** 920-569-7301
Toll-Free:	
Address: 1265 Lombardi Ave., Green Bay, WI 54304 US	

GROWTH PLANS/SPECIAL FEATURES:

The Green Bay Packers are a professional football team playing in the North Division of the National Football Conference in the National Football League (NFL) along with Chicago Bears, Detroit Lions and Minnesota Vikings. The team's ownership structure is notable because its owner, Green Bay Packers Foundation, is a not-for-profit organization. The Packers is the NFL's only community-owned franchise with approximately 112,000 shareholders. The team's shares include voting rights, but do not increase in value or pay dividends and can only be sold back to the team. No individual is allowed to own more than 200,000 shares in order that no one person becomes a majority owner of the club. The franchise was founded in 1919 and became a part of the NFL in 1921. The Packers is the longest-standing team name in NFL history. The franchise counts 20 individuals, both players and coaches, who spent the majority of their careers with the team and are in the Pro Football Hall of Fame. These individuals include Earl L. Lambeau, the franchise's founder, player, head coach and vice president from 1919-49; Bart Starr, a quarterback from 1956-71; Ray Nitschke, a linebacker from 1958-72; and legendary coach Vince Lombardi, the Packer's head coach and general manager from 1959-67. The team's current quarterback, Brett Favre, is the NFL's only three-time MVP (Most Valuable Player). The Packers have won a record 12 championship titles. The Packers play at Lambaeu Field, the longest continually occupied stadium in the NFL. It is owned by the city of Green Bay. In the 2008 season, the team averaged approximately 70,700 fans in attendance per game. A recent Forbes estimate values the team at roughly $1 billion.

FINANCIALS:

Sales and profits are in thousands of dollars—add 000 to get the full amount. 2008 Note: Financial information for 2008 was not available for all companies at press time.

2008 Sales: $218,000	2008 Profits: $21,900	**U.S. Stock Ticker: Private**
2007 Sales: $197,000	2007 Profits: $20,300	**Int'l Ticker:** Int'l Exchange:
2006 Sales: $208,400	2006 Profits: $18,000	Employees: 150
2005 Sales: $189,000	2005 Profits: $	Fiscal Year Ends: 3/31
2004 Sales: $179,200	2004 Profits: $29,100	Parent Company: GREEN BAY PACKERS FOUNDATION

SALARIES/BENEFITS:

Pension Plan:	ESOP Stock Plan:	Profit Sharing:	Top Exec. Salary: $	Bonus: $
Savings Plan:	Stock Purch. Plan:		Second Exec. Salary: $	Bonus: $

OTHER THOUGHTS:

Apparent Women Officers or Directors: 6
Hot Spot for Advancement for Women/Minorities: Y

LOCATIONS: ("Y" = Yes)

West:	Southwest:	Midwest:	Southeast:	Northeast:	International:
		Y			

HEAD NV

www.head.com

Industry Group Code: 339920 **Ranks within this company's industry group:** Sales: 5 Profits: 5

Sports:		Services:		Media:		Sales:		Facilities:		Other:	
Leagues/Associations:		Food & Beverage:		TV:		Marketing:		Stadiums:		Gambling:	
Teams:		Agents:		Radio:		Ads:		Fitness Clubs:		Apparel:	Y
Nonprofits:		Other:		Internet:		Tickets:		Golf Courses:		Equipment:	Y
Other:				Print:		Retail:		Ski Resorts:		Shoes:	Y
				Software:		Other:		Other:		Other:	

TYPES OF BUSINESS:

Sporting Goods
Racquet Sports Equipment
Ski & Snowboard Equipment
Diving Equipment & Accessories
Licensing

BRANDS/DIVISIONS/AFFILIATES:

Penn
Tyrolia
Mares
Mojo
Worldcup
HeatFit
Liquidmetal
Mares

CONTACTS:

Note: Officers with more than one job title may be intentionally listed here more than once.

Johan Eliasch, CEO
Ralf Bernhart, CFO
Jeremy Sherwood, Exec. Dir.-Global Sales
Clare Vincent, Dir.-Investor Rel.
Gunter Hagspiel, VP-Finance & Controlling
Gerald Skrobanek, Exec. VP-Diving Div.
Klaus Hotter, Exec. VP-Ski Div.
Robert Marte, Exec. VP-Racquet Sports Div.
Georg Kroell, Exec. VP-Licensing Div.
Johan Eliasch, Chmn.

Phone: 31-20-6251291 **Fax:** 31-20-6250956
Toll-Free:
Address: Rokin 55, Amsterdam, 1012 KK The Netherlands

GROWTH PLANS/SPECIAL FEATURES:

Head NV is a global manufacturer and marketer of branded sports equipment. Founded in 1950 by Howard Head, an engineer and the inventor credited with developing the first laminated metal skis, the company later expanded into other sporting goods through the acquisition of the Tyrolia bindings and Mares diving brands in the 1970s. In the 1990s, the firm acquired the Penn balls and Dacor diving brands. The company's products are now sold by nearly 30,000 dealers in 85 countries worldwide, including specialty retailers, mass merchants and pro shops. Head NV's operations are organized under four divisions: winter sports, racquet sports, diving and licensing. Under its winter sports division, Head NV designs and manufactures such ski lines as its Mojo, Monster, Worldcup and i.XRC. The company also manufactures ski boots including EDGE, EZ-on and HeatFit. Head NV offers a snowboard line including the i.Con, FORCE, DEFIANCE and MATRIX boards. Additionally, the firm manufactures accessories such as helmets, goggles, bags and poles. Head NV's racquet sports division manufactures equipment for tennis, squash and racquetball. Some of its racquets include the Flexpoint, Liquidmetal, Ti.Agassi (endorsed by tennis legend Andre Agassi) and Radical lines. The company's diving division is consolidated under the Mares' name. Mares' wares include regulators, computers, instruments, vests, diving suits, masks, snorkels, water shoes and other diving accessories. Head NV's final division, licensing, grants rights to the Head brand for product categories such as apparel, footwear, luggage, eyewear, watches, bikes, toiletries, skates, bags and golf clubs. In January 2009, the company announced that it would close its tennis ball factory in Phoenix, Arizona, shifting volume to plants in China.

Head offers its employees discounts on company products.

FINANCIALS:

Sales and profits are in thousands of dollars—add 000 to get the full amount. 2008 Note: Financial information for 2008 was not available for all companies at press time.

2008 Sales: $474,830	2008 Profits: $-13,720
2007 Sales: $466,060	2007 Profits: $-15,840
2006 Sales: $564,800	2006 Profits: $6,800
2005 Sales: $553,700	2005 Profits: $10,400
2004 Sales: $467,000	2004 Profits: $-36,900

U.S. Stock Ticker: HED
Int'l Ticker: HEAD Int'l Exchange: Vienna-VSX
Employees: 2,366
Fiscal Year Ends: 12/31
Parent Company:

SALARIES/BENEFITS:

Pension Plan: Y	ESOP Stock Plan:	Profit Sharing:	Top Exec. Salary: $762,000	Bonus: $
Savings Plan:	Stock Purch. Plan:		Second Exec. Salary: $738,000	Bonus: $

OTHER THOUGHTS:

Apparent Women Officers or Directors: 1
Hot Spot for Advancement for Women/Minorities:

LOCATIONS: ("Y" = Yes)

West:	Southwest:	Midwest:	Southeast:	Northeast:	International:
	Y			Y	Y

HEALTH FITNESS CORP

www.hfit.com

Industry Group Code: 713940 **Ranks within this company's industry group:** Sales: 3 Profits: 2

Sports:		Services:		Media:		Sales:		Facilities:		Other:	
Leagues/Associations:		Food & Beverage:		TV:		Marketing:		Stadiums:		Gambling:	
Teams:		Agents:		Radio:		Ads:		Fitness Clubs:	Y	Apparel:	
Nonprofits:		Other:	Y	Internet:		Tickets:		Golf Courses:		Equipment:	Y
Other:				Print:		Retail:		Ski Resorts:		Shoes:	
				Software:		Other:		Other:	Y	Other:	Y

TYPES OF BUSINESS:

Fitness Center Management
Consulting Services
Corporate & Hospital-Based Fitness Centers
Fitness Center Design
Wellness Programs
Health & Fitness Assessment
On-Site Physical Therapy Services

BRANDS/DIVISIONS/AFFILIATES:

INSIGHT Health Risk Assessment
HFC Wellness Programs
HFC Fitness Programs
JumpStart
Science Advisory Board
INSIGHT Health Risk Assessment
EMPOWERED Health Coaching
Partner Program

CONTACTS: *Note: Officers with more than one job title may be intentionally listed here more than once.*

Greg Lehman, CEO
John Griffin, COO
Greg Lehman, Pres.
Wesley Winnekins, CFO
Debra Marshall, VP-Mktg.
Jeanne Crawford, Chief Human Resources Officer
Jim Reynolds, Chief Medical Officer
John Ellis, CIO
J.Mark McConnell, Sr. VP-Bus. & Corp. Dev.
David Hurt, VP-Fitness Mgmt. Account Svcs.
Katherine Meacham, VP-Health Mgmt. Account Svcs.
Brian Gagne, Sr. VP-Account Management
Mark W. Sheffert, Chmn.

Phone: 952-831-6830 **Fax:** 952-897-5173
Toll-Free: 800-639-7913
Address: 1650 W. 82nd St., Ste. 1100, Minneapolis, MN 55431 US

GROWTH PLANS/SPECIAL FEATURES:

HealthFitness Corp. (HFC) and its subsidiaries provide fitness and wellness management services and programs to corporations, hospitals, communities and universities in the U.S. and Canada. The firm also provides injury prevention programs and on-site physical therapy services. Currently, HFC is under contract to manage approximately 400 sites, including 215 corporate, hospital, community and university fitness centers; 166 corporate health management sites; and 99 unstaffed health management locations. Through its two business segments, Fitness Management Services and Health Management Services, the company provides a full range of development, management, marketing and consulting services, including demographic analysis; interior/floor plan and fitness program design; and occupational health consulting services. HFC programs include INSIGHT Health Risk Assessment, a full range of tools to assess the health and well-being of individuals; JumpStart, a six-week weight loss program; HFC Wellness Programs, a menu of lifestyle programs addressing the specific needs of a company's workforce, including weight loss and stress management; and HFC Fitness Programs, customized exercise-based programs including personal training and specialty group classes. In recent years, HFC formed a Science Advisory Board to review HFC's research programs and the quality of HFC's products and services. In April 2008, the company agreed to partner with Pfizer Health Solutions to develop Senior Risk Reduction Demonstration, a project aimed at helping senior citizens prevent chronic diseases/conditions. In November 2008, HFC launched Partner Program, which offers small employers a health package that combines eHealth portal, INSIGHT Health Risk Assessment and EMPOWERED Health Coaching solutions. In April 2009, the firm agreed to partner with Nebraska to develop and implement an inclusive health management program for over 17,000 of the state's employees.

HFC offers employees medical, dental, long-term disability and vision insurance; flexible spending accounts; life and AD&D insurance; employee assistance; a 401(k) plan; and an employee stock purchase plan.

FINANCIALS: **Sales and profits are in thousands of dollars—add 000 to get the full amount. 2008 Note: Financial information for 2008 was not available for all companies at press time.**

2008 Sales: $77,676	2008 Profits: $2,722	**U.S. Stock Ticker: HFIT**
2007 Sales: $69,958	2007 Profits: $ 910	**Int'l Ticker:** Int'l Exchange:
2006 Sales: $63,578	2006 Profits: $1,352	Employees: 3,472
2005 Sales: $54,942	2005 Profits: $1,204	Fiscal Year Ends: 12/31
2004 Sales: $52,455	2004 Profits: $1,588	Parent Company:

SALARIES/BENEFITS:

Pension Plan:	ESOP Stock Plan:	Profit Sharing:	Top Exec. Salary: $275,000	Bonus: $15,000
Savings Plan: Y	Stock Purch. Plan: Y		Second Exec. Salary: $264,423	Bonus: $66,000

OTHER THOUGHTS:

Apparent Women Officers or Directors: 4
Hot Spot for Advancement for Women/Minorities: Y

LOCATIONS: ("Y" = Yes)

West:	Southwest:	Midwest:	Southeast:	Northeast:	International:
Y	Y	Y	Y	Y	Y

HENDRICK MOTORSPORTS

www.hendrickmotorsports.com

Industry Group Code: 711211G **Ranks within this company's industry group:** Sales: 1 Profits: 1

Sports:		Services:		Media:		Sales:		Facilities:		Other:	
Leagues/Associations:		Food & Beverage:		TV:		Marketing:		Stadiums:		Gambling:	
Teams:	Y	Agents:		Radio:		Ads:		Fitness Clubs:		Apparel:	
Nonprofits:		Other:	Y	Internet:		Tickets:		Golf Courses:		Equipment:	Y
Other:				Print:		Retail:	Y	Ski Resorts:		Shoes:	
				Software:		Other:		Other:	Y	Other:	Y

TYPES OF BUSINESS:

Stock Car Racing Teams
Automotive Engineering
Racing Merchandise

BRANDS/DIVISIONS/AFFILIATES:

Hendrick Engine Program
General Motors Corp (GM)
Hendrick Motorsports Museum
HMSteamStore.com

CONTACTS: *Note: Officers with more than one job title may be intentionally listed here more than once.*

J. Richard (Rick) Hendrick, III, CEO
Scott Lampe, CFO/VP
Patrick (Pat) Perkins, VP-Mktg.
Doug Duchardt, VP-Dev.
Marshall Carlson, Gen. Mgr./Exec. VP
Ken Howes, VP-Competition
J. Richard (Rick) Hendrick, III, Chmn.

Phone: 704-455-3400 **Fax:** 704-455-0346
Toll-Free: 877-467-4890
Address: 4400 Papa Joe Hendrick Blvd., Charlotte, NC 28262 US

GROWTH PLANS/SPECIAL FEATURES:

Hendrick Motorsports (HMS) is a stock car racing organization that owns four full-time Sprint Cup teams. Sprint Cup Series cars and drivers include Mark Martin in the No. 5 Kellogg's/CARQUEST Chevrolets; four-time champion Jeff Gordon in the No. 24 DuPont Chevrolets; three-time defending Sprint Cup champion Jimmie Johnson in the No. 48 Lowe's Chevrolets and Dale Earnhardt, Jr. in the No. 88 AMP Energy/National Guard Chevrolets. The organization's sponsor partners include Adidas, AMP Energy Drink, Army National Guard, Bosch, CARQUEST, Chevrolet, Club Car, Delphi, DuPont, Freightliner, Gatorade, Georgia-Pacific, GoDaddy.com, Goodyear, HAAS, Kellogg's, LORD Corporation, Lowe's, Mac Tools, MAHLE Clevite, Mechanix Wear, Nicorette, Panasonic Toughbook, Pepsi, Quaker State, Siemens, Stanley Tools, Time Warner Cable, Wix Filters and Wrangler. The company constructs all its racecars at its 100-acre complex and builds or rebuilds more than 550 engines yearly. The Hendrick Engine Program employs over 82 specialists. In addition to exploring cutting-edge engine technologies, the engine department conducts developmental work for General Motors. HMS builds engines for various Sprint Cup programs, both for its own teams and for external lease programs. The Hendrick chassis department, one of the first in-house chassis-engineering departments, has built over 300 Chevrolet Monte Carlos and Luminas in the past decade and can construct a rolling chassis with completed body in less than one week. The chassis department supplies cars for superspeedways, intermediate tracks, short tracks and road courses. The company operates a pit crew training program. HMS also operates the 15,000-square-foot Hendrick Motorsports Museum and sells merchandise online through HMSteamStore.com. Other company activities include marketing, public relations, sponsor services and licensing show cars. The firm has won eight NASCAR Sprint Cup Series championships, three NASCAR Camping World Truck Series titles and one NASCAR Nationwide Series crown (formerly Busch Series).

FINANCIALS: **Sales and profits are in thousands of dollars—add 000 to get the full amount. 2008 Note: Financial information for 2008 was not available for all companies at press time.**

2008 Sales: $179,000	2008 Profits: $21,300	**U.S. Stock Ticker: Private**
2007 Sales: $163,000	2007 Profits: $38,900	**Int'l Ticker:** Int'l Exchange:
2006 Sales: $	2006 Profits: $	Employees:
2005 Sales: $77,000	2005 Profits: $	Fiscal Year Ends:
2004 Sales: $	2004 Profits: $	Parent Company:

SALARIES/BENEFITS:

Pension Plan:	ESOP Stock Plan:	Profit Sharing:	Top Exec. Salary: $	Bonus: $
Savings Plan:	Stock Purch. Plan:		Second Exec. Salary: $	Bonus: $

OTHER THOUGHTS:

Apparent Women Officers or Directors:
Hot Spot for Advancement for Women/Minorities:

LOCATIONS: ("Y" = Yes)

West:	Southwest:	Midwest:	Southeast:	Northeast:	International:
				Y	

HIBBETT SPORTS INC

www.hibbett.com

Industry Group Code: 451110 **Ranks within this company's industry group:** Sales: 6 Profits: 3

Sports:		Services:		Media:		Sales:		Facilities:		Other:	
Leagues/Associations:		Food & Beverage:		TV:		Marketing:		Stadiums:		Gambling:	
Teams:		Agents:		Radio:		Ads:		Fitness Clubs:		Apparel:	Y
Nonprofits:		Other:		Internet:		Tickets:		Golf Courses:		Equipment:	Y
Other:				Print:		Retail:	Y	Ski Resorts:		Shoes:	Y
				Software:		Other:		Other:		Other:	

TYPES OF BUSINESS:

Sporting Goods Stores
Sports Apparel
Athletic Shoes
Training Equipment

BRANDS/DIVISIONS/AFFILIATES:

Hibbett Sports
Sports & Co.
Sports Additions
Hibbett Team Sales, Inc.

CONTACTS:

Note: Officers with more than one job title may be intentionally listed here more than once.

Michael J. Newsome, CEO
Jeffry O. Rosenthal, COO
Jeffry O. Rosenthal, Pres.
Gary A. Smith, CFO/VP
David Benck, General Counsel/VP
Cathy E. Pryor, VP-Store Oper.
Jeff Gray, VP-Real Estate
Michael J. Newsome, Chmn.

Phone: 205-942-4292 **Fax:** 205-912-7290
Toll-Free:
Address: 451 Industrial Ln., Birmingham, AL 35211 US

GROWTH PLANS/SPECIAL FEATURES:

Hibbett Sports, Inc. is an operator of sporting goods stores in small to mid-sized markets predominantly in the Sunbelt, Mid-Atlantic and Midwest. Its stores offer a broad assortment of athletic equipment, footwear and apparel. The company's merchandise assortment features a broad selection of brand name merchandise emphasizing team sports complemented by localized apparel and accessories designed to appeal to a wide range of customers. The firm's primary retail format is Hibbett Sports, a 5,000 square foot store located in enclosed malls or in strip centers that are generally the center of commerce within an area and that are usually anchored by a Wal-Mart store. The Hibbett Sports stores strive to respond quickly to major sporting events of local interests. The Sports Additions stores are small, mall-based stores averaging 2,500 square feet with roughly 90% of merchandise consisting of athletic footwear and the remainder consisting of caps and a limited assortment of apparel. Sports Additions stores offer a broader assortment of athletic footwear, with a greater emphasis on fashion than the athletic footwear assortment offered by Hibbett Sports stores. The Sports & Co. superstores average 25,000 square feet and offer a broader assortment of athletic footwear, apparel and equipment than the Hibbett Sports stores. Hibbett Sports operates over 650 stores in 23 states. Subsidiary Hibbett Team Sales, Inc. supplies customized athletic apparel, equipment and footwear to school, athletic and youth programs primarily in Alabama. It sells its merchandise directly to educational institutions and youth associations.

Employees are offered medical and dental insurance; life insurance; short-and long-term disability coverage; a vision care plan; a stock purchase plan; a 401(k) plan; employee discounts; and a 529 college savings plan.

FINANCIALS:

Sales and profits are in thousands of dollars—add 000 to get the full amount. 2008 Note: Financial information for 2008 was not available for all companies at press time.

2008 Sales: $520,720 | 2008 Profits: $30,329
2007 Sales: $512,094 | 2007 Profits: $38,073
2006 Sales: $440,269 | 2006 Profits: $33,624
2005 Sales: $377,534 | 2005 Profits: $25,147
2004 Sales: $320,964 | 2004 Profits: $20,348

U.S. Stock Ticker: HIBB
Int'l Ticker: Int'l Exchange:
Employees: 5,400
Fiscal Year Ends: 1/31
Parent Company:

SALARIES/BENEFITS:

Pension Plan: ESOP Stock Plan: Profit Sharing: Top Exec. Salary: $465,000 Bonus: $12,730
Savings Plan: Y Stock Purch. Plan: Y Second Exec. Salary: $265,000 Bonus: $6,100

OTHER THOUGHTS:

Apparent Women Officers or Directors: 1
Hot Spot for Advancement for Women/Minorities:

LOCATIONS: ("Y" = Yes)

West:	Southwest:	Midwest:	Southeast:	Northeast:	International:
	Y	Y	Y	Y	

HICKS SPORTS GROUP HOLDINGS

www.hickssportsgroup.com

Industry Group Code: 551110 **Ranks within this company's industry group:** Sales: Profits:

Sports:		Services:		Media:		Sales:		Facilities:		Other:	
Leagues/Associations:		Food & Beverage:		TV:		Marketing:	Y	Stadiums:	Y	Gambling:	
Teams:	Y	Agents:		Radio:		Ads:	Y	Fitness Clubs:		Apparel:	
Nonprofits:		Other:		Internet:		Tickets:		Golf Courses:		Equipment:	
Other:				Print:		Retail:		Ski Resorts:		Shoes:	
				Software:		Other:		Other:	Y	Other:	Y

TYPES OF BUSINESS:

Holding Company
Advertising
Sponsorship

BRANDS/DIVISIONS/AFFILIATES:

Texas Rangers
American Airlines Center
Dallas Stars
National Hockey League (NHL)
Mesquite Championship Rodeo
Frisco Rough Riders
Hicks Sports Marketing Group
Liverpool Football Club

CONTACTS:
Note: Officers with more than one job title may be intentionally listed here more than once.

Thomas O. Hicks, CEO
Casey Coffman, COO
Nolan Ryan, Pres., Texas Rangers
Robert Hutson, CFO
Geoff Moore, Exec. VP-Mktg., Dallas Stars
Kellie Fischer, Exec. VP/CFO-Texas Rangers
Jeff Cogen, Pres., Dallas Stars
Mack H. Hicks, VP-Hicks Holdings LLC
Thomas O. Hicks, Jr., VP-Hicks Holdings LLC
Thomas O. Hicks, Chmn.

Phone: 817-273-5222 **Fax:** 817-273-5174
Toll-Free:
Address: 1000 Ballpark Way, Ste. 400, Arlington, TX 76011 US

GROWTH PLANS/SPECIAL FEATURES:

Hicks Sports Group Holdings, LLC. (HSG), formerly known as Southwest Sports Group, Inc., is owned by Hicks Holdings, LLC., a Texas-based firm created to manage billionaire Thomas Hicks' and his family's various assets. HSG controls the Hicks' sports assets, and is thereby the holding company for the Texas Rangers Major League Baseball (MLB) team; the Dallas Stars National Hockey League (NHL) hockey team; the Mesquite Championship Rodeo in Dallas, Texas; a 50% interest in the Frisco Rough Riders minor league baseball team; and a 50% interest in Liverpool Football Club, a soccer team in the English Premier League. In addition, HSG owns various ice-skating rinks and real estate properties in the Dallas, Texas area; and a 50% interest in the American Airlines Center (also in Dallas). The Hicks Sports Marketing Group is a division of HSG that sells sponsorship and advertising for the company's sports teams, and represents many other real estate and sports properties throughout the U.S. and Europe. In April 2009, the firm's creditors found the company to be in default on i$525 million in loans. Hicks Sports has stated it is willing to sell a controlling interest in the Texas Rangers.

FINANCIALS:
Sales and profits are in thousands of dollars—add 000 to get the full amount. 2008 Note: Financial information for 2008 was not available for all companies at press time.

2008 Sales: $ | 2008 Profits: $
2007 Sales: $ | 2007 Profits: $
2006 Sales: $ | 2006 Profits: $
2005 Sales: $ | 2005 Profits: $
2004 Sales: $ | 2004 Profits: $

U.S. Stock Ticker: Private
Int'l Ticker: Int'l Exchange:
Employees:
Fiscal Year Ends: 12/31
Parent Company: HICKS HOLDINGS LLC

SALARIES/BENEFITS:

Pension Plan: ESOP Stock Plan: Profit Sharing: Top Exec. Salary: $ Bonus: $
Savings Plan: Stock Purch. Plan: Second Exec. Salary: $ Bonus: $

OTHER THOUGHTS:

Apparent Women Officers or Directors: 2
Hot Spot for Advancement for Women/Minorities:

LOCATIONS: ("Y" = Yes)

West:	Southwest:	Midwest:	Southeast:	Northeast:	International:
	Y				

HILLERICH & BRADSBY CO

www.slugger.com

Industry Group Code: 339920 **Ranks within this company's industry group:** Sales: Profits:

Sports:		Services:		Media:		Sales:		Facilities:		Other:	
Leagues/Associations:		Food & Beverage:		TV:		Marketing:		Stadiums:		Gambling:	
Teams:		Agents:		Radio:		Ads:		Fitness Clubs:		Apparel:	Y
Nonprofits:		Other:		Internet:		Tickets:		Golf Courses:		Equipment:	Y
Other:				Print:		Retail:		Ski Resorts:		Shoes:	
				Software:		Other:		Other:		Other:	

TYPES OF BUSINESS:

Baseball Equipment
Golf Equipment
Hockey Equipment
Apparel
Orthopedic Gloves

BRANDS/DIVISIONS/AFFILIATES:

Louisville Slugger
Major League Baseball (MLB)
PowerBilt Golf
TPS Hockey
Bionic Gloves
Louisville Slugger Museum and Factory
Louisville Slugger Japan
Silver Slugger Award

CONTACTS:

Note: Officers with more than one job title may be intentionally listed here more than once.

John A. Hillerich, IV, CEO
John A. Hillerich, IV, Pres.
Rick Redman, VP-Corp. Comm.
Brian Hillerich, Mgr.-Professional Bat Production
Jack Hillerich, Chmn.

Phone: 502-585-5226 **Fax:** 502-585-1179
Toll-Free:
Address: 800 W. Main St., Louisville, KY 40202 US

GROWTH PLANS/SPECIAL FEATURES:

Hillerich & Bradsby Co. (HBC), founded in 1884, is a manufacturer of equipment for baseball and other sports. The company's best-known product is the Louisville Slugger baseball bat, the official bat of Major League Baseball, which is used by over 60% of all major league players. HBC offers a full line of wooden, metal, composite and customized bats, as well as baseball gloves, helmets, protective gear and practice equipment. The firm produces approximately 1 million bats per year. It owns approximately 8,500 acres of timberland in Pennsylvania and New York and also purchases lumber for its bats from other sources. Other HBC divisions are PowerBilt Golf, which makes golf clubs and accessories; TPS Hockey, which offers hockey sticks, protective gear, equipment bags and apparel; and Bionic Gloves, a maker of high-quality orthopedic gloves designed to protect hands and joints in activities such as gardening, golf, hockey and baseball. HBC also operates the Louisville Slugger Museum and Factory in Louisville, Kentucky where visitors can take guided factory tours, experience hands-on demonstrations and see historic baseball memorabilia. The company operates internationally through Louisville Slugger Japan. HBC sponsors two yearly awards for Major League Baseball, the Silver Slugger Award and the Silver Bat Award. The Silver Bat Award, a silver plated bat, goes to the batting champions in the American League and the National League. The Silver Slugger Award goes to the best offensive players for each position in both leagues.

FINANCIALS:

Sales and profits are in thousands of dollars—add 000 to get the full amount. 2008 Note: Financial information for 2008 was not available for all companies at press time.

2008 Sales: $
2007 Sales: $
2006 Sales: $
2005 Sales: $
2004 Sales: $

2008 Profits: $
2007 Profits: $
2006 Profits: $
2005 Profits: $
2004 Profits: $

U.S. Stock Ticker: Private
Int'l Ticker: Int'l Exchange:
Employees: 470
Fiscal Year Ends: 6/30
Parent Company:

SALARIES/BENEFITS:

Pension Plan: ESOP Stock Plan: Profit Sharing: Top Exec. Salary: $ Bonus: $
Savings Plan: Stock Purch. Plan: Second Exec. Salary: $ Bonus: $

OTHER THOUGHTS:

Apparent Women Officers or Directors:
Hot Spot for Advancement for Women/Minorities:

LOCATIONS: ("Y" = Yes)

West:	Southwest:	Midwest:	Southeast:	Northeast:	International:
		Y			Y

HOUSTON ASTROS

www.astros.com

Industry Group Code: 711211A **Ranks within this company's industry group:** Sales: 11 Profits: 16

Sports:		Services:		Media:		Sales:		Facilities:		Other:	
Leagues/Associations:		Food & Beverage:		TV:		Marketing:		Stadiums:	Y	Gambling:	
Teams:	Y	Agents:		Radio:		Ads:		Fitness Clubs:		Apparel:	
Nonprofits:		Other:		Internet:		Tickets:	Y	Golf Courses:		Equipment:	
Other:				Print:		Retail:		Ski Resorts:		Shoes:	
				Software:		Other:		Other:		Other:	

TYPES OF BUSINESS:

Professional Baseball Team
Stadium Operation
International Baseball Academies

BRANDS/DIVISIONS/AFFILIATES:

Minute Maid Park
Round Rock Express
Corpus Christi Hooks
Salem Avalanche
Lexington Legends
Tri-City Valley Cats
Greeneville Astros

CONTACTS: *Note: Officers with more than one job title may be intentionally listed here more than once.*

Drayton McLane, CEO
Ed Wade, Gen. Mgr.
Pam Gardner, Pres., Bus. Oper.
Jennifer Germer, VP-Mktg.
Larry Stokes, VP-Human Resources
Steve Reese, Dir.-IT
Austin Malone, Asst. Dir.-Eng.
Jackie Traywick, Sr. VP-Admin.
Tal Smith, Pres., Baseball Oper.
Rosi Hernandez, VP-Market Dev.
Jay Lucas, Sr. VP-Comm.
Jackie Traywick, Sr. VP-Finance
Bobby Forrest, VP-Facilities Oper.
Jonathan Germer, Controller
Kala Sorenson, VP-Conference Center & Special Events
Jaime Hildreth, Sr. VP-Premium Sponsorships
Drayton McLane, Chmn.
Seth Courtney, Dir.-Purchasing

Phone: 713-259-8000 **Fax:** 713-259-8025
Toll-Free:
Address: 501 Crawford St., Ste. 400, Houston, TX 77002 US

GROWTH PLANS/SPECIAL FEATURES:

The Houston Astros is an organization within Major League Baseball (MLB). Originally called the Colt .45s and founded in 1962, the club was renamed the Astros in 1965 and played for many years in the Astrodome, the world's first domed ballpark. The Astros have a history of making it to the National League playoffs, but always falling short of the World Series. In 2005, the team capitalized on its Wild Card playoff berth to win the League Championship, but lost the World Series. Since 1993, the Astros have been owned by Texas businessman Drayton McLane, who vowed to keep the team in Houston after the previous ownership attempted to move to Washington, D.C. McLane's tenure has coincided with continual team success, as a group of hitting stars known as the Killer Bs came to prominence. Craig Biggio, Jeff Bagwell, Derek Bell and Sean Berry were the initial group; it later included Lance Berkman. During this period the team reinvented itself several times, changing its logos and team colors in 1993 and again in 2000, coinciding with the opening of the new stadium, Enron Field. Today the stadium is called Minute Maid Park, a $250-million stadium with a retractable roof situated in downtown Houston. The venue is known for a dramatically short left field fence and a hill in deep center field with a padded flagpole in fair territory. The organization has international baseball academies in Venezuela, Columbia and the Dominican Republic. The Astros have contributed a number of players to the National Baseball Hall of Fame, including Nelly Fox, Joe Morgan and Nolan Ryan. In 2009, Forbes valued the franchise at $445 million, 12th highest in baseball. Average home game attendance in 2008 was 34,741.

FINANCIALS: **Sales and profits are in thousands of dollars—add 000 to get the full amount. 2008 Note: Financial information for 2008 was not available for all companies at press time.**

2008 Sales: $194,000	2008 Profits: $17,000	**U.S. Stock Ticker: Private**
2007 Sales: $193,000	2007 Profits: $20,400	**Int'l Ticker:** Int'l Exchange:
2006 Sales: $184,000	2006 Profits: $18,400	Employees:
2005 Sales: $173,000	2005 Profits: $	Fiscal Year Ends: 12/31
2004 Sales: $	2004 Profits: $	Parent Company:

SALARIES/BENEFITS:

Pension Plan:	ESOP Stock Plan:	Profit Sharing:	Top Exec. Salary: $	Bonus: $
Savings Plan:	Stock Purch. Plan:		Second Exec. Salary: $	Bonus: $

OTHER THOUGHTS:

Apparent Women Officers or Directors: 6
Hot Spot for Advancement for Women/Minorities: Y

LOCATIONS: ("Y" = Yes)

West:	Southwest:	Midwest:	Southeast:	Northeast:	International:
	Y				Y

HOUSTON DYNAMO

houston.mlsnet.com

Industry Group Code: 711211D **Ranks within this company's industry group:** Sales: Profits:

Sports:		Services:		Media:		Sales:		Facilities:		Other:	
Leagues/Associations:		Food & Beverage:		TV:		Marketing:		Stadiums:		Gambling:	
Teams:	Y	Agents:		Radio:		Ads:		Fitness Clubs:		Apparel:	
Nonprofits:		Other:		Internet:		Tickets:	Y	Golf Courses:		Equipment:	
Other:				Print:		Retail:		Ski Resorts:		Shoes:	
				Software:		Other:		Other:		Other:	

TYPES OF BUSINESS:

Major League Soccer Team

BRANDS/DIVISIONS/AFFILIATES:

Anschutz Entertainment Group
Anschutz Company
AEG
Brener International Group
Golden Boy Promotions

CONTACTS:

Note: Officers with more than one job title may be intentionally listed here more than once.

Chris Canetti, COO
Oliver Luck, Pres.
Lindsay Daywalt, Dir.-Mktg.
Paul Byrne, Sr. Dir.-Oper.
Steven N. Powell, Sr. VP-Bus. Dev.
Lester Gretsch, Dir.-Comm.
Dominic Kinnear, Head Coach
Oliver Luck, Gen. Mgr.
Bryan Kraham, Sr. Dir.-Sponsorship

Phone: 713-276-7500 **Fax:** 713-276-7580
Toll-Free:
Address: 1415 Louisiana, Ste. 3400, Houston, TX 77002 US

GROWTH PLANS/SPECIAL FEATURES:

The Houston Dynamo, formerly playing in the Major League Soccer (MLS) circuit as the San Jose Earthquakes, is a soccer franchise owned and operated by Anschutz Entertainment Group (AEG), Brener International Group and Golden Boy Promotions. The team changed name and location in December 2005 in time for the 2006 season. Houston's name and colors (orange and black) were announced in early March 2006. The team's moniker, Dynamo, hearkens back to an earlier time in Houston sports, when the city fielded a team called the Dynamos in the short-lived United Soccer League. Most of the team's members in the inaugural season were players from the former Earthquakes team, with the addition of players from the 2006 and 2007 MLS draft. The team currently plays in the 30,000-seat Robertson Stadium on the University of Houston campus until plans for a soccer-specific stadium are finalized. The team plays in MLS' Western Conference, along with Chivas USA, the Colorado Rapids, FC Dallas, Los Angeles Galaxy, Real Salt Lake, the Seattle Sounders FC and the new San Jose Earthquakes. In 2008, the average attendance per regular season match was nearly 17,000, and the 2008 post-season the team averaged attendance of over 30,500. The Houston team is one of the few clubs to win back-to-back league championships, including its inaugural 2006 season and its 2007 season. In 2008, following a ruling by the MLS governing body dictating that no ownership group can own more than one team, it was announced that AEG, which also owns the Los Angeles Galaxy, sold a stake to a partnership of Brener International Group and Golden Boy Promotions, owned by the famed boxer Oscar de la Hoya. Notable players have included Brian Ching, Dwayne de Rosario and Ryan Cochrane.

FINANCIALS:

Sales and profits are in thousands of dollars—add 000 to get the full amount. 2008 Note: Financial information for 2008 was not available for all companies at press time.

2008 Sales: $	2008 Profits: $	**U.S. Stock Ticker: Subsidiary**
2007 Sales: $	2007 Profits: $	**Int'l Ticker:** Int'l Exchange:
2006 Sales: $	2006 Profits: $	Employees:
2005 Sales: $	2005 Profits: $	Fiscal Year Ends:
2004 Sales: $	2004 Profits: $	Parent Company: ANSCHUTZ ENTERTAINMENT GROUP

SALARIES/BENEFITS:

Pension Plan:	ESOP Stock Plan:	Profit Sharing:	Top Exec. Salary: $	Bonus: $
Savings Plan:	Stock Purch. Plan:		Second Exec. Salary: $	Bonus: $

OTHER THOUGHTS:

Apparent Women Officers or Directors: 14
Hot Spot for Advancement for Women/Minorities: Y

LOCATIONS: ("Y" = Yes)

West:	Southwest:	Midwest:	Southeast:	Northeast:	International:
	Y				

HOUSTON ROCKETS

www.nba.com/rockets

Industry Group Code: 711211B **Ranks within this company's industry group:** Sales: 6 Profits: 4

Sports:		Services:		Media:		Sales:		Facilities:		Other:	
Leagues/Associations:		Food & Beverage:		TV:		Marketing:		Stadiums:		Gambling:	
Teams:	Y	Agents:		Radio:		Ads:		Fitness Clubs:		Apparel:	
Nonprofits:		Other:		Internet:		Tickets:	Y	Golf Courses:		Equipment:	
Other:				Print:		Retail:	Y	Ski Resorts:		Shoes:	
				Software:		Other:		Other:		Other:	

TYPES OF BUSINESS:

Professional Basketball Team

BRANDS/DIVISIONS/AFFILIATES:

Toyota Center
San Diego Rockets
Rockets Power Dancers
Little Dippers
Launch Crew
Red Rowdies
Clutch City Foundation

CONTACTS:

Note: Officers with more than one job title may be intentionally listed here more than once.

Thaddeus B. Brown, CEO
Marcus Jolibois, CFO
Ken Sheirr, Dir.-Mktg. Oper.
Olga Piskor, Dir.-Human Resources
Victor Tan, Dir.-IT & Telecom
Rafael Stone, General Counsel
Keith Jones, Sr. VP-Basketball Oper.
Chris Dacey, Chief Strategy Officer/VP
Paul Suarez, Mgr.-e-commerce
Seliece C. Fulweber, VP-Bus. Comm. & Ticket Sales
Larry Kaiser, Controller
Leslie Alexander, Owner
Rick Adelman, Head Coach
Doug Hall, VP/Gen. Mgr.-Toyota Center
Sarah Joseph, Dir.-Community Rel.

Phone: 713-758-7200 **Fax:** 713-758-7315
Toll-Free:
Address: 1510 Polk St., Houston, TX 77002 US

GROWTH PLANS/SPECIAL FEATURES:

The Houston Rockets originally entered the National Basketball Association (NBA) as the San Diego Rockets in 1967. The team was later renamed as the Houston Rockets after its move to Houston in 1971. All home games are played at the Toyota Center, which opened in October 2003. The Toyota Center occupies 750,000 square feet of downtown Houston and features an 18,300 seating capacity for basketball fans. The team's fan zone includes the Red Rowdies, the Rockets Power Dancers, the G-Force step team, Little Dippers, the Launch Crew and the Rockets' official mascot, Clutch. Community outreach programs include the Clutch City Foundation, which raises money for local charities with emphasis on education, grassroots basketball and grassroots outreach for children. The Rockets have also partnered with Direct Energy and AIG Retirement to award exemplary Houston-area students with game tickets. Programs designed specifically for children include the All Stars Reader Challenge, the Read to Achieve initiative and the T-MAC Basketball Camp. The Rockets won consecutive NBA championships in 1994 and 1995 under center Hakeem Olajuwon and coach Rudy Tomjanovich. The team also earned playoffs seats in the 2003-04, 2004-05, 2006-07 and 2007-08 seasons. Other notable former players include Elvin Hayes, Robert Reid, Moses Malone, Ralph Sampson, Clyde Drexler, Charles Barkley and Rodney McCray. The arrival of center Yao Ming from Shanghai, China, in 2002 drew a huge fan following from surrounding Houston Chinese communities, as well as international interest in the team. The Rocket's corporate partners include Toyota, Comcast, Bud Light, T Mobile, Southwest Airlines, HP, Hooters and Papa John's Pizza, among others. Forbes Magazine recently estimated the team to be worth approximately $469 million. In the 2008-09 season, the team's home attendance average was roughly 17,500 per game.

FINANCIALS:

Sales and profits are in thousands of dollars—add 000 to get the full amount. 2008 Note: Financial information for 2008 was not available for all companies at press time.

2008 Sales: $156,000	2008 Profits: $31,200	**U.S. Stock Ticker: Private**
2007 Sales: $149,000	2007 Profits: $29,700	**Int'l Ticker:** Int'l Exchange:
2006 Sales: $142,000	2006 Profits: $21,400	Employees:
2005 Sales: $141,000	2005 Profits: $	Fiscal Year Ends: 6/30
2004 Sales: $125,000	2004 Profits: $	Parent Company:

SALARIES/BENEFITS:

Pension Plan:	ESOP Stock Plan:	Profit Sharing:	Top Exec. Salary: $	Bonus: $
Savings Plan:	Stock Purch. Plan:		Second Exec. Salary: $	Bonus: $

OTHER THOUGHTS:

Apparent Women Officers or Directors: 3
Hot Spot for Advancement for Women/Minorities: Y

LOCATIONS: ("Y" = Yes)

West:	Southwest:	Midwest:	Southeast:	Northeast:	International:
	Y				

HOUSTON TEXANS

www.houstontexans.com

Industry Group Code: 711211C **Ranks within this company's industry group:** Sales: 4 Profits: 2

Sports:		Services:		Media:		Sales:		Facilities:		Other:	
Leagues/Associations:		Food & Beverage:		TV:		Marketing:		Stadiums:		Gambling:	
Teams:	Y	Agents:		Radio:		Ads:		Fitness Clubs:		Apparel:	
Nonprofits:		Other:		Internet:		Tickets:	Y	Golf Courses:		Equipment:	
Other:				Print:		Retail:	Y	Ski Resorts:		Shoes:	
				Software:		Other:		Other:		Other:	

TYPES OF BUSINESS:

Professional Football Team

BRANDS/DIVISIONS/AFFILIATES:

CONTACTS:

Note: Officers with more than one job title may be intentionally listed here more than once.

Robert C. McNair, CEO
Jamey Rootes, Pres.
Scott E. Schwinger, CFO
John Vidalin, VP-Mktg. & Sales
Glenda Morrison, Dir.-Human Resources
Jeff Schmitz, Dir.-IT
Suzie Thomas, Chief Admin. Officer
Suzie Thomas, General Counsel/Sr. VP
Greg Grissom, Dir.-Corp. Dev.
Tony Wyllie, VP-Comm.
Kristina Humiston, Investor Rel.
Scott E. Schwinger, Treas./Sr. VP
Missy Rentz, Dir.-Advertising & Branding
Gary Kubiak, Head Coach
Rick Smith, Gen. Mgr.
Kevin Cooper, Dir.-Public Rel.
Robert C. McNair, Chmn.

Phone: 832-667-2000	**Fax:** 832-667-2188
Toll-Free:	
Address: 2 Reliant Park, Houston, TX 77054 US	

GROWTH PLANS/SPECIAL FEATURES:

The Houston Texans, owned by Houston NFL Holdings, L.P., are a professional football team in the National Football League (NFL) based in Houston, Texas. The franchise was founded as an expansion team in 1999 and played its first game in 2002. Even though the Texans were only the NFL's second expansion team to win its first game, its performance on the field since then has been decidedly mixed. The team's overall record from its first season up to 2008 has been 40-72, and it has failed to finish above third place in its division. In 2005, the team made its most controversial move to date by drafting defensive end Mario Williams over a number of higher-profile prospects, including superstar college running back Reggie Bush and hometown hero Vince Young. The team is owned by Robert McNair, who is founder of Cogen Technologies and responsible for bringing the Texans to Houston. The team's home, Reliant Stadium, is owned by Harris County, Texas, and seats up to 71,500 fans. It was the first NFL stadium to feature a retractable roof. Toro, a blue longhorn bull dressed in a Texan football uniform, is the team's mascot. In the spring of 2008, the Texans signed seven undrafted free agents: Auburn tight end Cole Bennett; Hawaii wide receiver Ryan Grice-Mullen; Miami, Florida wide receiver Darnell Jenkins; Utah defensive tackle Gabe Long; South Florida linebacker Ben Moffitt; Colorado State defensive end Jesse Nading; and Troy linebacker Marcus Richardson. The team's playing has become more consistent in recent years, with the 2007 and 2008 seasons yielding their best results so far. Despite the Texans' struggles on the field, the franchise is currently considered one of the most valuable in the NFL, ranked sixth (at approximately $1.13 billion) by Forbes in 2008. The team's average home game attendance in the 2008 season was 70,682.

FINANCIALS:

Sales and profits are in thousands of dollars—add 000 to get the full amount. 2008 Note: Financial information for 2008 was not available for all companies at press time.

2008 Sales: $239,000	2008 Profits: $43,900	**U.S. Stock Ticker: Private**
2007 Sales: $225,000	2007 Profits: $25,900	**Int'l Ticker:** Int'l Exchange:
2006 Sales: $222,000	2006 Profits: $57,600	Employees:
2005 Sales: $215,000	2005 Profits: $	Fiscal Year Ends:
2004 Sales: $201,000	2004 Profits: $	Parent Company: HOUSTON NFL HOLDINGS LP

SALARIES/BENEFITS:

Pension Plan:	ESOP Stock Plan:	Profit Sharing:	Top Exec. Salary: $	Bonus: $
Savings Plan:	Stock Purch. Plan:		Second Exec. Salary: $	Bonus: $

OTHER THOUGHTS:

Apparent Women Officers or Directors: 6
Hot Spot for Advancement for Women/Minorities: Y

LOCATIONS: ("Y" = Yes)

West:	Southwest:	Midwest:	Southeast:	Northeast:	International:
	Y				

Note: Financial information, benefits and other data can change quickly and may vary from those stated here.

HUFFY BICYCLE CO

www.huffybikes.com

Industry Group Code: 339920 **Ranks within this company's industry group:** Sales: Profits:

Sports:		Services:		Media:		Sales:		Facilities:		Other:	
Leagues/Associations:		Food & Beverage:		TV:		Marketing:		Stadiums:		Gambling:	
Teams:		Agents:		Radio:		Ads:		Fitness Clubs:		Apparel:	
Nonprofits:		Other:		Internet:		Tickets:		Golf Courses:		Equipment:	Y
Other:				Print:		Retail:		Ski Resorts:		Shoes:	
				Software:		Other:		Other:		Other:	

TYPES OF BUSINESS:

Manufacturing-Bicycles & Scooters

BRANDS/DIVISIONS/AFFILIATES:

Green Machine

CONTACTS: *Note: Officers with more than one job title may be intentionally listed here more than once.*

Michael Buenzow, CEO
Michael Buenzow, Pres.
Robert L. Diekman, Sr. VP-Oper.
Robert L. Diekman, Sr. VP-Logistics

Phone: 937-865-2800 **Fax:** 937-865-5470
Toll-Free: 800-872-2453
Address: 6551 Centerville Business Pkwy, Centerville, OH 45459 US

GROWTH PLANS/SPECIAL FEATURES:

Huffy Bicycle Company, founded in 1892, designs and sells Huffy brand products, mainly bicycles and scooters. The wheeled products are imported from Southeast Asian locations including Taiwan and China and are sold in over 10,000 retailers nationwide, including Wal-Mart, The Sports Authority; Ace; Target; TrueValue; Toys R Us; Meijer; Academy Sports + Outdoors; Dunham's Sports; Hardware Hank; Bigg's; Amazon.com; and Kmart. It offers several categories of wheeled products, including tricycles for children 4 years and younger, scooters and kids bikes for those 10 and up. Popular children's products available include the Green Machine and branded bicycle's with cartoon characters, such as Dora the Explorer and Disney Fairies. The firm also offers mountain bikes and what it calls comfort bikes, which are designed more for teens and adults. In recent years, the firm has extended its product offerings to include swing sets/play centers.

FINANCIALS: **Sales and profits are in thousands of dollars—add 000 to get the full amount. 2008 Note: Financial information for 2008 was not available for all companies at press time.**

2008 Sales: $	2008 Profits: $	**U.S. Stock Ticker: Private**
2007 Sales: $	2007 Profits: $	**Int'l Ticker:** Int'l Exchange:
2006 Sales: $	2006 Profits: $	Employees: 1,068
2005 Sales: $	2005 Profits: $	Fiscal Year Ends: 12/31
2004 Sales: $	2004 Profits: $	Parent Company:

SALARIES/BENEFITS:

Pension Plan:	ESOP Stock Plan:	Profit Sharing:	Top Exec. Salary: $620,000	Bonus: $
Savings Plan:	Stock Purch. Plan:		Second Exec. Salary: $316,346	Bonus: $

OTHER THOUGHTS:

Apparent Women Officers or Directors:
Hot Spot for Advancement for Women/Minorities:

LOCATIONS: ("Y" = Yes)

West:	Southwest:	Midwest:	Southeast:	Northeast:	International:
		Y			

ILITCH HOLDINGS INC

www.ilitchholdings.com

Industry Group Code: 551110 **Ranks within this company's industry group:** Sales: 1 Profits:

Sports:		Services:		Media:		Sales:		Facilities:		Other:	
Leagues/Associations:	Y	Food & Beverage:	Y	TV:		Marketing:		Stadiums:		Gambling:	
Teams:	Y	Agents:		Radio:		Ads:		Fitness Clubs:		Apparel:	
Nonprofits:		Other:	Y	Internet:		Tickets:		Golf Courses:		Equipment:	
Other:				Print:		Retail:	Y	Ski Resorts:		Shoes:	
				Software:		Other:	Y	Other:	Y	Other:	Y

TYPES OF BUSINESS:

Holding Company

BRANDS/DIVISIONS/AFFILIATES:

Little Ceasars Pizza
Detroit Red Wings
Detroit Tigers
Olympia Entertainment
Hockeytown Café
Little Caesars Amateur Hockey League
Little Caesars AAA Hockey
Fox Theatre

CONTACTS: *Note: Officers with more than one job title may be intentionally listed here more than once.*

Christopher Ilitch, CEO
Christopher Ilitch, Pres.
Scott Fisher, CFO
Joni C. Nelson, VP-Human Resources
Todd Seroka, CIO
Karen Cullen, VP-Corp. Comm.
Marian Ilitch, Vice Chmn.
Dave Scrivano, Pres., Little Caesars Enterprises, Inc.
Sharon Arend, Dir-Archives & Historical Documents
C. Michael Healy, Dir.-Risk Management
Michael Ilitch, Chmn.

Phone: 313-983-6600	**Fax:** 313-983-6094
Toll-Free:	
Address: 2211 Woodward Ave., Detroit, MI 48201 US	

GROWTH PLANS/SPECIAL FEATURES:

Ilitch Holdings, Inc. is a sports holding company based in Detroit, Michigan. It was created in 1999 to provide professional and technical services to all the various companies owned by Michael and/or Marian Ilitch. These companies include Little Caesars Pizza; the Detroit Red Wings, a hockey league; the Detroit Tigers, a Major League Baseball team; Olympia Entertainment; Olympia Development; Blue Line Foodservice Distribution; Champion Foods; Uptown Entertainment; Little Caesars Pizza Kit Fundraising Program; and a variety of venues within these entities. Little Caesars Pizza, founded by Michael and Marian Ilitch in 1959, is estimated to be the fourth largest pizza restaurant chain in the U.S., thanks in part to its tremendous brand-recognition based on successful ad-campaigns, including the famous Pizza! Pizza! phrase, introduced in 1979. Based on the success of this initial business undertaking, the Ilitches purchased the Red Wings in 1982 and the Tigers in 1992. In recent years, Ilitch Holdings announced downtown Detroit development projects, including the restoration of the company-owned historic Fox Theatre and Office Centre, which is currently the company's corporate headquarters. The Fox tower signage will be restored, following a two-year, $2 million restoration of the 75 year-old theatre's exterior terra-cotta facade. Other projects, including the restoration of the historic Detroit Life Building, are under the purview of Ilitch's real estate unit, Olympia Development.

FINANCIALS: **Sales and profits are in thousands of dollars—add 000 to get the full amount. 2008 Note: Financial information for 2008 was not available for all companies at press time.**

2008 Sales: $2,000,000	2008 Profits: $	**U.S. Stock Ticker: Private**
2007 Sales: $1,520,000	2007 Profits: $	**Int'l Ticker:** Int'l Exchange:
2006 Sales: $1,480,000	2006 Profits: $	Employees: 17,000
2005 Sales: $1,500,000	2005 Profits: $	Fiscal Year Ends: 12/31
2004 Sales: $	2004 Profits: $	Parent Company:

SALARIES/BENEFITS:

Pension Plan:	ESOP Stock Plan:	Profit Sharing:	Top Exec. Salary: $	Bonus: $
Savings Plan:	Stock Purch. Plan:		Second Exec. Salary: $	Bonus: $

OTHER THOUGHTS:

Apparent Women Officers or Directors: 4
Hot Spot for Advancement for Women/Minorities: Y

LOCATIONS: ("Y" = Yes)

West:	Southwest:	Midwest:	Southeast:	Northeast:	International:
		Y			

IMG WORLDWIDE INC

www.imgworld.com

Industry Group Code: 711410 **Ranks within this company's industry group:** Sales: Profits:

Sports:		Services:		Media:		Sales:		Facilities:		Other:	
Leagues/Associations:		Food & Beverage:		TV:	Y	Marketing:	Y	Stadiums:		Gambling:	
Teams:		Agents:	Y	Radio:		Ads:		Fitness Clubs:		Apparel:	
Nonprofits:		Other:		Internet:		Tickets:		Golf Courses:		Equipment:	
Other:				Print:		Retail:		Ski Resorts:		Shoes:	
				Software:		Other:		Other:		Other:	

TYPES OF BUSINESS:

Agents-Athletes
Agents-Models
Agents-Writers, Artists & Musicians
Event Marketing
Corporate Marketing Consulting Services
Sports Television Programming
Sports Schools & Training

BRANDS/DIVISIONS/AFFILIATES:

IMG Coaches
IMG Models
IMG Artists
IMG Consulting
Darlow Smithson Productions
Tiger Aspect Productions
Forstmann Little & Co.
Tennis Week Magazine

CONTACTS: *Note: Officers with more than one job title may be intentionally listed here more than once.*

Theodore J. Forstmann, CEO
Jim Tucker, VP-U.S. Bus. Dev.
Chris Albrecht, Pres., IMG Global Media
Michel Masquelier, Exec. VP/Head-Acquisition & Sales Worldwide
George Pyne, Pres., IMG Sports & Entertainment
Lee Rosenbaum, VP-Publishing
Theodore J. Forstmann, Chmn.
Ian Todd, Pres., IMG Int'l

Phone: 216-522-1200 **Fax:** 216-522-1145
Toll-Free:
Address: 1360 E. 9th St., Ste. 100, Cleveland, OH 44114 US

GROWTH PLANS/SPECIAL FEATURES:

IMG Worldwide, Inc. is one of largest sports and lifestyle marketing and management agencies in the world. The company represents some of the world's top athletes, broadcasters, models, classical musicians, authors and newsmakers throughout more than 60 offices in 30 countries. The agency operates three divisions: Sports, Entertainment and Media. The Sports division handles everything from events and sponsorships to client representation and training. The company owns, produces and manages several prestigious sporting events including events at Wimbledon and Nobel Prize functions. Sports clients include golfers Tiger Woods; tennis player Venus Williams; baseball player Derek Jeter; basketball player Charles Barkley; and hockey player Jaromir Jagr. The Entertainment division handles a multitude of fashion related events and personalities. This segment represents a variety of models such as Gisele and Cindy Crawford. The Media department creates, distributes, sells and represents content across every medium. IMG's Media division, along with the firm's subsidiaries TWI, Darlow Smithson Productions, CSI Sports, Tiger Aspect Productions, Tigress Productions Limited and Nunet AG, is one of the world's largest independent producers and distributors of televised sports programming. It annually produces and distributes 11,000 hours of original programming to over 220 countries. IMG is held by private equity firm Forstmann Little & Co. Recent acquisitions include Tennis Week Magazine, tennisweek.com, CSI Sports, Nunet AG, BSI Speedway, Quintus, Collegiate Licensing Company and Partners International. In 2008, the company signed a deal with Chinese national TV broadcaster CCTV to launch a joint venture aimed at increasing commercialization of sports in China.

FINANCIALS: **Sales and profits are in thousands of dollars—add 000 to get the full amount. 2008 Note: Financial information for 2008 was not available for all companies at press time.**

2008 Sales: $ 2008 Profits: $
2007 Sales: $ 2007 Profits: $
2006 Sales: $ 2006 Profits: $
2005 Sales: $ 2005 Profits: $
2004 Sales: $ 2004 Profits: $

U.S. Stock Ticker: Private
Int'l Ticker: Int'l Exchange:
Employees: 2,300
Fiscal Year Ends: 12/31
Parent Company: FORSTMANN LITTLE & CO

SALARIES/BENEFITS:

Pension Plan: ESOP Stock Plan: Profit Sharing: Top Exec. Salary: $ Bonus: $
Savings Plan: Stock Purch. Plan: Second Exec. Salary: $ Bonus: $

OTHER THOUGHTS:

Apparent Women Officers or Directors:
Hot Spot for Advancement for Women/Minorities:

LOCATIONS: ("Y" = Yes)

West:	Southwest:	Midwest:	Southeast:	Northeast:	International:
Y		Y	Y	Y	Y

INDIANA FEVER

www.wnba.com/fever

Industry Group Code: 711211E **Ranks within this company's industry group:** Sales: Profits:

Sports:		Services:		Media:		Sales:		Facilities:		Other:	
Leagues/Associations:		Food & Beverage:		TV:		Marketing:		Stadiums:	Y	Gambling:	
Teams:	Y	Agents:		Radio:		Ads:		Fitness Clubs:		Apparel:	
Nonprofits:	Y	Other:		Internet:		Tickets:		Golf Courses:		Equipment:	
Other:				Print:		Retail:		Ski Resorts:		Shoes:	
				Software:		Other:		Other:		Other:	

TYPES OF BUSINESS:

Women's National Basketball Association Team

BRANDS/DIVISIONS/AFFILIATES:

Conseco Fieldhouse
Pacers Sports & Entertainment

CONTACTS: *Note: Officers with more than one job title may be intentionally listed here more than once.*

Kelly Krauskopf, COO/Gen. Mgr.
Kevin Bower, CFO
Larry Mago, Sr. VP-Mktg.
Donna Wilkinson, VP-Human Resources
Kevin Naylor, VP-MIS
Tom Rutledge, VP-Facilities Oper.
Kelli Towles, Mgr.-Community Rel. & Special Projects
Kevin Bower, Sr. VP-Finance
Melvin Simon, Co-Owner
Herbert Simon, Co-Owner
Larry Bird, Pres., Basketball Oper.
Harry James, VP-Facilities Admin.

Phone: 317-917-2500	**Fax:** 317-917-2599
Toll-Free:	
Address: 1 Conseco Ct., 125 S. Pennsylvania St., Indianapolis, IN 46204 US	

GROWTH PLANS/SPECIAL FEATURES:

The Indiana Fever is a Women's National Basketball Association (WNBA) team that gained league entry in 2000. It plays in the Eastern Conference against teams including the Chicago Sky, Atlanta Dream, Connecticut Sun, Detroit Shock, New York Liberty and Washington Mystics. The Fever plays its home games in the Conseco Fieldhouse, which also hosts the Fever's brother team, the Indianapolis Pacers. All three entities, the two teams and the arena, are owned by Herbert and Melvin Simon through their company, Pacers Sports & Entertainment. In February 2008, the team re-signed Tamika Catchings, a 5-time WNBA All-Star and an Olympic gold medalist, securing her in with a four-year contract. An unrestricted free agent until now, Tamika has played every season with the Fever since she joined the WNBA in 2001. She is generally considered one of the most skilled athletes in the WNBA, having set numerous defensive and offensive records. In February 2008, the Fever completed one of the biggest trades in WNBA history. It acquired Katie Douglas of the Connecticut Sun, in exchange for Tamika Whitmore, the rights to shooting guard Jessica Foley and the Fever's first round pick in the 2008 draft. In March 2008, the Fever signed three free agents, Erin Lawless, Angelina Williams and LaToya Bond.

FINANCIALS: Sales and profits are in thousands of dollars—add 000 to get the full amount. 2008 Note: Financial information for 2008 was not available for all companies at press time.

2008 Sales: $	2008 Profits: $	**U.S. Stock Ticker: Subsidiary**
2007 Sales: $	2007 Profits: $	**Int'l Ticker:** Int'l Exchange:
2006 Sales: $	2006 Profits: $	Employees:
2005 Sales: $	2005 Profits: $	Fiscal Year Ends: 6/30
2004 Sales: $	2004 Profits: $	Parent Company: PACERS SPORTS & ENTERTAINMENT

SALARIES/BENEFITS:

Pension Plan:	ESOP Stock Plan:	Profit Sharing:	Top Exec. Salary: $	Bonus: $
Savings Plan:	Stock Purch. Plan:		Second Exec. Salary: $	Bonus: $

OTHER THOUGHTS:

Apparent Women Officers or Directors: 15
Hot Spot for Advancement for Women/Minorities: Y

LOCATIONS: ("Y" = Yes)

West:	Southwest:	Midwest:	Southeast:	Northeast:	International:
		Y			

INDIANA PACERS

www.nba.com/pacers

Industry Group Code: 711211B **Ranks within this company's industry group:** Sales: 21 Profits: 27

Sports:		Services:		Media:		Sales:		Facilities:		Other:	
Leagues/Associations:		Food & Beverage:		TV:		Marketing:		Stadiums:	Y	Gambling:	
Teams:	Y	Agents:		Radio:		Ads:		Fitness Clubs:		Apparel:	
Nonprofits:		Other:		Internet:		Tickets:	Y	Golf Courses:		Equipment:	
Other:				Print:		Retail:	Y	Ski Resorts:		Shoes:	
				Software:		Other:		Other:		Other:	

TYPES OF BUSINESS:

Professional Basketball Team

BRANDS/DIVISIONS/AFFILIATES:

Pacers Sports & Entertainment
Conseco Fieldhouse Arena
Indiana Pacemates
Pacers Foundation, Inc.
Pacers Care
Indiana Jr. NBA
Jermaine O'Neal Super Shootout

CONTACTS: *Note: Officers with more than one job title may be intentionally listed here more than once.*

Donnie Walsh, CEO
Donnie Walsh, Pres.
Kevin Bower, CFO
Larry Mago, Sr. VP-Mktg.
Donna Wilkinson, VP-Human Resources
Larry Taylor, VP-MIS
David Morway, Sr. VP-Basketball Admin.
Quinn Buckner, VP-Comm.
Kevin Bower, Sr. VP-Finance
Rick Carlisle, Head Coach
Larry Bird, Pres., Basketball Oper.
Herbert Simon, Owner/CEO/Chmn.-Pacers Sports & Entertainment
Melvin Simon, Owner

Phone: 317-917-2500 **Fax:** 317-917-2599
Toll-Free:
Address: 125 S. Pennsylvania St., Indianapolis, IN 46204 US

GROWTH PLANS/SPECIAL FEATURES:

The Indiana Pacers entered the American Basketball Association (ABA) in the 1967-68 season and entered the National Basketball Association (NBA) when the ABA and NBA merged. The Pacers are owned by Pacers Sports & Entertainment, which is based in Indianapolis, Indiana. The team arena is located in the Conseco Fieldhouse, which has an 18,345 seating capacity. Entertainment offered during game nights includes the Indiana Pacemates; team mascots, Boomer and Bowser; and contest promotions and giveaways. The team has established the Pacers Foundation, Inc. in order to provide support to children through community activities and education. Additional community outreach programs include the Pacers Care ticket program, which provides underprivileged children opportunities to attend Pacers games; the Indiana Jr. NBA; and the Jermaine O'Neal Super Shootout for central Indiana's finest high school basketball players. Notable former players of the Pacers include George McGinnis, Mel Daniels and Roger Brown. Since the retirement of one of the Pacers' best players, Reggie Miller, in the 2004-05 season, the Pacers have struggled as a team. One incident that particularly impaired the Pacers was the infamous fight with the Detroit Pistons in November 2004, which resulted in the suspension of several keys Pacers, including Ron Arteset, Stephen Jackson and Jermaine O'Neal. In January 2008, player David Harrison was suspended by the NBA for five games for violating the terms of the NBA anti-drug program. A recent estimate from Forbes Magazine valued the team at approximately $303 million. In the 2008-09 season, the team's home attendance average was roughly 14,200 per game.

FINANCIALS: Sales and profits are in thousands of dollars—add 000 to get the full amount. 2008 Note: Financial information for 2008 was not available for all companies at press time.

2008 Sales: $101,000	2008 Profits: $-6,500	**U.S. Stock Ticker: Private**
2007 Sales: $107,000	2007 Profits: $-1,300	**Int'l Ticker:** Int'l Exchange:
2006 Sales: $110,000	2006 Profits: $-12,500	Employees:
2005 Sales: $108,000	2005 Profits: $	Fiscal Year Ends: 6/30
2004 Sales: $104,000	2004 Profits: $	Parent Company: PACERS SPORTS & ENTERTAINMENT

SALARIES/BENEFITS:

Pension Plan:	ESOP Stock Plan:	Profit Sharing:	Top Exec. Salary: $	Bonus: $
Savings Plan:	Stock Purch. Plan:		Second Exec. Salary: $	Bonus: $

OTHER THOUGHTS:

Apparent Women Officers or Directors: 1
Hot Spot for Advancement for Women/Minorities:

LOCATIONS: ("Y" = Yes)

West:	Southwest:	Midwest:	Southeast:	Northeast:	International:
		Y			

INDIANAPOLIS COLTS

www.colts.com

Industry Group Code: 711211C **Ranks within this company's industry group:** Sales: 28 Profits: 26

Sports:		Services:		Media:		Sales:		Facilities:		Other:	
Leagues/Associations:		Food & Beverage:	Y	TV:		Marketing:		Stadiums:	Y	Gambling:	
Teams:	Y	Agents:		Radio:		Ads:		Fitness Clubs:		Apparel:	Y
Nonprofits:		Other:		Internet:		Tickets:	Y	Golf Courses:		Equipment:	
Other:				Print:		Retail:	Y	Ski Resorts:		Shoes:	
				Software:		Other:		Other:		Other:	

TYPES OF BUSINESS:

Professional Football Team

BRANDS/DIVISIONS/AFFILIATES:

Baltimore Colts
Lucas Oil Stadium

CONTACTS:

Note: Officers with more than one job title may be intentionally listed here more than once.

James Irsay, CEO/Owner
Bill Polian, Pres.
Tom Zupancic, Sr. VP-Sales & Mktg.
Dan Emerson, General Counsel
Chris Polian, VP-Football Oper.
Craig Kelley, VP-Public Rel.
Kurt Humphrey, VP-Finance
Jim Caldwell, Head Coach
Pete Ward, Sr. Exec. VP
Bob Terpening, Exec. VP
Larry Hall, VP-Ticket Oper. & Guest Svcs.

Phone: 317-297-2658 **Fax:** 317-297-8971
Toll-Free:
Address: 7001 W. 56th St., Indianapolis, IN 46254 US

GROWTH PLANS/SPECIAL FEATURES:

The Indianapolis Colts are a professional football team in the National Football League's (NFL) Southern Division of the American Football Conference (AFC). The team plays at the 63,000 seat Lucas Oil Stadium in downtown Indianapolis, Indiana. The franchise was founded in 1953 when Carroll Rosenbloom won the rights to a new team in Baltimore; thus, the Baltimore Colts was founded. In 1972, Rosenbloom traded the Colts to Robert Isray for the Los Angeles Rams. The two teams, however, stayed in their respected cities. The Baltimore Colts won four NFL league championships (1958, 1959, 1968 and 1970), the first two coached by Hall of Famer Weeb Ewbank. The team's head coach, Tony Dungy, became the first African American head coach to win the Super Bowl. In March 1984, Isray controversially moved the Baltimore Colts to Indianapolis over a dispute with the city of Baltimore. Football legend Johnny Unitas, a Baltimore Colt, asked the NFL Hall of Fame to remove his museum display unless it made clear reference to his being a Baltimore Colt. The Colts, led by franchise quarterback Peyton Manning, won the 2006 Super Bowl. In March 2006, the Colts announced that Lucas Oil Products, a California-based motor sports company, won the naming rights for their new stadium in downtown Indianapolis. The 2008 season marked the first time the team played in the Lucas Oil Stadium. Forbes has recently estimated the team to be worth approximately $1.07 billion. The team's average home game attendance in the 2008 season was 66,378.

FINANCIALS:

Sales and profits are in thousands of dollars—add 000 to get the full amount. 2008 Note: Financial information for 2008 was not available for all companies at press time.

2008 Sales: $203,000	2008 Profits: $16,100	**U.S. Stock Ticker: Private**
2007 Sales: $184,000	2007 Profits: $-17,300	**Int'l Ticker:** Int'l Exchange:
2006 Sales: $167,000	2006 Profits: $25,000	Employees:
2005 Sales: $166,000	2005 Profits: $	Fiscal Year Ends: 1/31
2004 Sales: $145,000	2004 Profits: $	Parent Company:

SALARIES/BENEFITS:

Pension Plan:	ESOP Stock Plan:	Profit Sharing:	Top Exec. Salary: $	Bonus: $
Savings Plan:	Stock Purch. Plan:		Second Exec. Salary: $	Bonus: $

OTHER THOUGHTS:

Apparent Women Officers or Directors: 1
Hot Spot for Advancement for Women/Minorities:

LOCATIONS: ("Y" = Yes)

West:	Southwest:	Midwest:	Southeast:	Northeast:	International:
		Y			

INDY RACING LEAGUE LLC

www.indycar.com

Industry Group Code: 711212 **Ranks within this company's industry group:** Sales: Profits:

Sports:		Services:		Media:		Sales:		Facilities:		Other:	
Leagues/Associations:	Y	Food & Beverage:		TV:		Marketing:		Stadiums:		Gambling:	
Teams:		Agents:		Radio:		Ads:		Fitness Clubs:		Apparel:	
Nonprofits:		Other:		Internet:		Tickets:		Golf Courses:		Equipment:	
Other:				Print:		Retail:		Ski Resorts:		Shoes:	
				Software:		Other:		Other:	Y	Other:	

TYPES OF BUSINESS:

Automobile Racing League

BRANDS/DIVISIONS/AFFILIATES:

Indianapolis Motor Speedway Radio Network
Indianapolis Motor Speedway
Indianapolis 500
IndyCar Series
Indy Pro Series
Hulman and Co.
Champ Car World Series LLC

CONTACTS: *Note: Officers with more than one job title may be intentionally listed here more than once.*

Anton H. George, CEO
Brian Barnhart, COO
John Lewis, VP-Mktg.
Les MacTaggart, Sr. Dir.-Tech.
Tiffany Hemmer, Dir.-Admin.
Brian Barnhart, Pres., Oper. & Competition
John Lewis, VP-League Dev.
Fred J. Nation, Exec. VP-Corp. Comm. & Public Rel.
Michael Olinger, Sr. Dir.-Medical Svcs.
John Griffin, VP-Public Rel.
Ruthie Forbes, Dir.-Special Events
Gerald Raines, Dir.-National Service Sales

Phone: 317-492-6526 **Fax:**
Toll-Free:
Address: 4565 W. 16th St., Indianapolis, IN 46222 US

GROWTH PLANS/SPECIAL FEATURES:

Indy Racing League, LLC (IRL), founded in 1994, manages the Indy class of racecars and operates racing circuits. The league is owned by Hulman and Co., which also owns the Indianapolis Motor Speedway. The IRL was masterminded by Anton George in 1994. George created a lower-cost alternative to CART, a racing association which broke away from the United States Automobile Club (USAC) in 1979. Though the IRL initially attracted smaller teams, the league now hosts a few of the wealthy teams that previously belonged to the CART series. The IRL maintains a mix of oval and road/street courses. The League's flagship race, the Indianapolis 500, is held annually at the Indianapolis Motor Speedway in Speedway, Indiana. IRL's Indy-class racing cars are open-wheel with an open-cockpit and a single seat, featuring front and rear wings with airboxes. Chassis and engine manufacturers apply to the league to supply cars for three-year cycles. Currently, Dallara provides the chassis, while Honda provides the engines and Firestone provides the tires. IRL also uses 100% fuel-grade ethanol. IRL is the governing body for two racing tours, the IndyCar Series and the Indy Pro Series. The IndyCar Series, its primary circuit tour, was first held at the Walt Disney World speedway in 1996. The tour features approximately 20 drivers competing in 16 races across the U.S. and one race in Japan. The league includes some well-known names, such as Marco Andretti, Ed Carpenter and Danica Patrick. The Pro Series, held in Japan, is the developmental series for IndyCar. The organization's races are broadcast on ABC, ESPN and ESPN2, as well as on radio through affiliates of the Indianapolis Motor Speedway Radio Network, including XM Satellite Radio. In 2008, IRL merged with former competitor Champ Car World Series LLC, organizer of the Champ Car circuit.

FINANCIALS: **Sales and profits are in thousands of dollars—add 000 to get the full amount. 2008 Note: Financial information for 2008 was not available for all companies at press time.**

2008 Sales: $ | 2008 Profits: $
2007 Sales: $ | 2007 Profits: $
2006 Sales: $ | 2006 Profits: $
2005 Sales: $ | 2005 Profits: $
2004 Sales: $ | 2004 Profits: $

U.S. Stock Ticker: Subsidiary
Int'l Ticker: Int'l Exchange:
Employees:
Fiscal Year Ends:
Parent Company: HULMAN AND CO

SALARIES/BENEFITS:

Pension Plan: ESOP Stock Plan: Profit Sharing: Top Exec. Salary: $ Bonus: $
Savings Plan: Stock Purch. Plan: Second Exec. Salary: $ Bonus: $

OTHER THOUGHTS:

Apparent Women Officers or Directors: 3
Hot Spot for Advancement for Women/Minorities: Y

LOCATIONS: ("Y" = Yes)

West:	Southwest:	Midwest:	Southeast:	Northeast:	International:
		Y			

INTERNATIONAL BOXING FEDERATION

www.ibf-usba-boxing.com

Industry Group Code: 813990 **Ranks within this company's industry group:** Sales: Profits:

Sports:		Services:		Media:		Sales:		Facilities:		Other:	
Leagues/Associations:	Y	Food & Beverage:		TV:		Marketing:		Stadiums:		Gambling:	
Teams:		Agents:		Radio:		Ads:		Fitness Clubs:		Apparel:	
Nonprofits:		Other:		Internet:		Tickets:		Golf Courses:		Equipment:	
Other:				Print:		Retail:		Ski Resorts:		Shoes:	
				Software:		Other:		Other:		Other:	

TYPES OF BUSINESS:

Boxing Association

BRANDS/DIVISIONS/AFFILIATES:

United States Boxing Association (USBA)
USBA-International
International Boxing Hall of Fame (IBHOF)
World Boxing Association
World Boxing Council (WBC)
World Boxing Organization (WBO)
IBF USBA Reporter

CONTACTS:

Note: Officers with more than one job title may be intentionally listed here more than once.

Marian Muhammad, Pres.
Lindsey Tucker, Chmn.-Championship
Daryl Peoples, Chmn.-Ratings

Phone: 973-414-0300	**Fax:** 973-414-0307
Toll-Free:	
Address: 516 Main St., 2nd Fl., East Orange, NJ 07018 US	

GROWTH PLANS/SPECIAL FEATURES:

The International Boxing Federation (IBF) is a major sponsor sanctioning championship boxing matches. The federation is affiliated with the United States Boxing Association (USBA), a regional championships organization, having been founded by a former president of the USBA as the USBA-International. The IBF operates as one of the four organizations recognized by the International Boxing Hall of Fame (IBHOF) to sanction world championship boxing bouts, alongside the World Boxing Association (WBA), the World Boxing Council (WBC) and the World Boxing Organization (WBO). Notable IBF champions include Wladimir Klitschko, Clinton Woods, Arthur Abraham, Cory Spinks, Ricky Hatton, Julio Diaz, Steve Molitor and Rafael Marquez. The federation's web site provides access to the IBF USBA Reporter, its official newsletter; contest, bout and championship rules; ratings; a bout schedule; and links to the WBA, WBC and WBO web sites.

FINANCIALS:

Sales and profits are in thousands of dollars—add 000 to get the full amount. 2008 Note: Financial information for 2008 was not available for all companies at press time.

2008 Sales: $	2008 Profits: $	**U.S. Stock Ticker: Private**
2007 Sales: $	2007 Profits: $	**Int'l Ticker:** Int'l Exchange:
2006 Sales: $	2006 Profits: $	Employees:
2005 Sales: $	2005 Profits: $	Fiscal Year Ends:
2004 Sales: $	2004 Profits: $	Parent Company:

SALARIES/BENEFITS:

Pension Plan:	ESOP Stock Plan:	Profit Sharing:	Top Exec. Salary: $	Bonus: $
Savings Plan:	Stock Purch. Plan:		Second Exec. Salary: $	Bonus: $

OTHER THOUGHTS:

Apparent Women Officers or Directors: 1
Hot Spot for Advancement for Women/Minorities:

LOCATIONS: ("Y" = Yes)

West:	Southwest:	Midwest:	Southeast:	Northeast:	International:
				Y	

INTERNATIONAL OLYMPIC COMMITTEE (IOC)

www.olympic.org

Industry Group Code: 813990 **Ranks within this company's industry group:** Sales: Profits:

Sports:		Services:		Media:		Sales:		Facilities:		Other:	
Leagues/Associations:	Y	Food & Beverage:		TV:		Marketing:		Stadiums:		Gambling:	
Teams:		Agents:		Radio:		Ads:	Y	Fitness Clubs:		Apparel:	
Nonprofits:	Y	Other:		Internet:		Tickets:	Y	Golf Courses:		Equipment:	
Other:				Print:		Retail:		Ski Resorts:		Shoes:	
				Software:		Other:		Other:		Other:	

TYPES OF BUSINESS:

Sports Association
Ticket Sales
Licensing & Broadcast Rights

BRANDS/DIVISIONS/AFFILIATES:

Olympic Games
Paralympic Games
National Olympic Committee
International Olympic Sports Federations
Organizing Committees of the Olympic Games
IOC
SPORTFIVE International Sàrl

CONTACTS: *Note: Officers with more than one job title may be intentionally listed here more than once.*

Urs Lacotte, Dir. Gen.
Jacques Rogge, Pres.
Jean-Benoit Gauthier, Dir.-Tech.
Thomas Bach, VP
Lambis V. Nikolaou, VP
Chiharu Igaya, VP
Zaiqing Yu, VP

Phone: 41-21-621-61-11	**Fax:** 41-21-621-62-16
Toll-Free:	
Address: Chateau de Vidy, Lausanne, 1007 Switzerland	

GROWTH PLANS/SPECIAL FEATURES:

International Olympic Committee (IOC) organizes the Olympic Games, in which approximately 200 countries participate, and the Paralympics Games, for disabled athletes. The summer and winter Olympics alternate on a two-year schedule, with the most recent event being the 2008 Beijing Summer Olympics. The next events will be the 2010 Vancouver Winter Olympics, 2012 London Summer Olympics and 2014 Sochi Winter Olympics (in Russia). To qualify as an Olympic sport, a game must have an international governing organization, 50 countries on three continents with men participating in the sport and/or 35 countries on three continents with women participating in the sport. IOC officially recognizes a sport for a three-year examination period after which it becomes an official Olympic sport or is no longer recognized. IOC's revenue comes from selling broadcast rights for the Olympics, corporate sponsorship, ticketing and licensing the Olympic symbol. About 92% of its revenue is distributed to National Olympic Committees, International Sports Federations and the host city's Organizing Committees of the Olympic Games, while IOC retains 8%. NBC paid $5.7 billion for the television rights in the U.S. until 2012. In February 2008, Singapore was chosen to host the first Youth Olympic Summer Games in 2010, which is expected to gather 3,200 athletes and 800 officials. In April 2008, the IOC awarded the Japan Broadcasting Corporation (NHK) and The National Association of Commercial Broadcasters in Japan (NAB) Japanese broadcasting rights for the 2010 and 2012 Olympic Games. In February 2009, IOC announced that SPORTFIVE International Sarl (SPORTFIVE) had acquired the Olympic broadcast rights across 40 countries in Europe (excluding France, Germany, Italy, Spain, Turkey and the U.K.) for the 2014 Sochi Winter Olympics and 2016 Summer Olympics. These rights cover distribution across all media platforms, including free-to-air television, subscription television, Internet and mobile phone.

FINANCIALS: Sales and profits are in thousands of dollars—add 000 to get the full amount. 2008 Note: Financial information for 2008 was not available for all companies at press time.

2008 Sales: $	2008 Profits: $	**U.S. Stock Ticker: Private**
2007 Sales: $	2007 Profits: $	**Int'l Ticker:** Int'l Exchange:
2006 Sales: $	2006 Profits: $	Employees: 307
2005 Sales: $	2005 Profits: $	Fiscal Year Ends: 12/31
2004 Sales: $1,845,600	2004 Profits: $	Parent Company:

SALARIES/BENEFITS:

Pension Plan:	ESOP Stock Plan:	Profit Sharing:	Top Exec. Salary: $	Bonus: $
Savings Plan:	Stock Purch. Plan:		Second Exec. Salary: $	Bonus: $

OTHER THOUGHTS:

Apparent Women Officers or Directors:
Hot Spot for Advancement for Women/Minorities:

LOCATIONS: ("Y" = Yes)

West:	Southwest:	Midwest:	Southeast:	Northeast:	International:
					Y

INTERNATIONAL SPEEDWAY CORP

www.iscmotorsports.com

Industry Group Code: 711212 **Ranks within this company's industry group:** Sales: 1 Profits: 1

Sports:		Services:		Media:		Sales:		Facilities:		Other:	
Leagues/Associations:		Food & Beverage:	Y	TV:		Marketing:		Stadiums:		Gambling:	
Teams:		Agents:		Radio:	Y	Ads:		Fitness Clubs:		Apparel:	
Nonprofits:		Other:		Internet:		Tickets:		Golf Courses:		Equipment:	
Other:				Print:		Retail:	Y	Ski Resorts:		Shoes:	
				Software:		Other:		Other:	Y	Other:	

TYPES OF BUSINESS:

Motorsports Racing & Facilities
Theme Park
Sports Radio Network
Concession Operations
Motorsports Merchandising

BRANDS/DIVISIONS/AFFILIATES:

Daytona International Speedway
California Speedway
Talladega Superspeedway
DAYTONA 500 Experience
Americrown Service Corporation
Motorsports Authentics
Raceway Associates, LLC
Motor Racing Network, Inc.

CONTACTS:

Note: Officers with more than one job title may be intentionally listed here more than once.

James C. France, CEO
John Saunders, COO/Exec. VP
Lesa France Kennedy, Pres.
Daniel W. Houser, CFO/VP
Daryl Wolfe, VP/Chief Mktg. Officer
W. Gary Crotty, General Counsel/Sr. VP/Corp. Sec.
W. Grant Lynch, Jr., Sr. VP-Bus. Oper.
Brian K. Wilson, VP-Corp. Dev.
Daniel W. Houser, Treas.
Roger VanDerSnick, Sr. VP-Mktg. & Bus. Oper.
Glenn Padgett, VP/Chief Counsel-Oper./Chief Compliance Officer
Tracie K. Winters, VP-Bus. Dev.
James C. France, Chmn.

Phone: 386-254-2700 **Fax:** 386-947-6816
Toll-Free:
Address: 1801 W. International Speedway Blvd., Daytona Beach, FL 32114 US

GROWTH PLANS/SPECIAL FEATURES:

International Speedway Corporation (ISC) is a leading promoter of motorsports entertainment in the U.S. The company owns and operates 12 major motorsports facilities, including Daytona International Speedway in Florida, home of the Daytona 500; Talladega Superspeedway in Alabama, the fastest stock car track in the U.S.; and the Auto Club Speedway of Southern California. The company also owns Raceway Associates, LLC, which owns and operates two nationally recognized motorsports facilities, Chicagoland Speedway and Route 66 Raceway, in Illinois. In addition, the firm owns and operates Motor Racing Network, Inc. (MRN Radio), which produces and syndicates motorsports-related programming for syndication to both terrestrial and satellite radio stations. MRN Radio covers events held at ISC facilities and other venues, and also produces and syndicates daily and weekly NASCAR racing themed programs. Moreover, the firm owns and operates the DAYTONA 500 EXperience, a motorsports-themed entertainment complex that includes interactive media, theaters, historical memorabilia and exhibits. The DAYTONA 500 EXperience is the official attraction of NASCAR. ISC's Americrown Service Corporation subsidiary conducts the food, beverage and souvenir concession operations at the firm's facilities and provides catering services to customers in suites and chalets at speedways. Another subsidiary, Motorsports Authentics, produces and markets motorsports licensed merchandise. ISC promotes over 100 stock car, open wheel, sports car, truck, motorcycle and other racing events annually, including NASCAR Sprint Cup Series events; NASCAR Nationwide Series events; Indy Racing League IndyCar Series events; National Hot Rod Association POWERade drag racing events; and a number of other auto and motorcycle races. Chairman James C. France and President Lesa France Kennedy, along with other members of the France family, collectively own 38% of the company, as well as a controlling interest in NASCAR. In June 2008, the firm sold Pikes Peak International Raceway, in Colorado, to a private company.

FINANCIALS:

Sales and profits are in thousands of dollars—add 000 to get the full amount. 2008 Note: Financial information for 2008 was not available for all companies at press time.

2008 Sales: $787,254
2007 Sales: $814,228
2006 Sales: $796,165
2005 Sales: $740,129
2004 Sales: $647,848

2008 Profits: $134,595
2007 Profits: $86,201
2006 Profits: $116,804
2005 Profits: $159,361
2004 Profits: $156,318

U.S. Stock Ticker: ISCA
Int'l Ticker: Int'l Exchange:
Employees: 1,000
Fiscal Year Ends: 11/30
Parent Company:

SALARIES/BENEFITS:

Pension Plan: ESOP Stock Plan: Profit Sharing: Top Exec. Salary: $590,801 Bonus: $82,892
Savings Plan: Y Stock Purch. Plan: Second Exec. Salary: $491,885 Bonus: $63,128

OTHER THOUGHTS:

Apparent Women Officers or Directors: 2
Hot Spot for Advancement for Women/Minorities: Y

LOCATIONS: ("Y" = Yes)

West:	Southwest:	Midwest:	Southeast:	Northeast:	International:
Y	Y	Y	Y	Y	

INTRAWEST CORPORATION

www.intrawest.com

Industry Group Code: 713920 **Ranks within this company's industry group:** Sales: Profits:

Sports:		Services:		Media:		Sales:		Facilities:		Other:	
Leagues/Associations:		Food & Beverage:	Y	TV:		Marketing:		Stadiums:		Gambling:	
Teams:		Agents:		Radio:		Ads:		Fitness Clubs:		Apparel:	
Nonprofits:		Other:	Y	Internet:		Tickets:		Golf Courses:	Y	Equipment:	
Other:				Print:		Retail:		Ski Resorts:	Y	Shoes:	
				Software:		Other:		Other:	Y	Other:	

TYPES OF BUSINESS:

Ski Resorts
Golf Courses
Beach Resorts
Meeting & Conference Planning
Vacation Ownership Club
Luxury Adventure Travel
Helicopter Skiing & Hiking

BRANDS/DIVISIONS/AFFILIATES:

Fortress Investment Group LLC
Blue Mountain Resort
Copper Mountain Resort
Winter Park Resort
Mountain Creek Resort
Whistler Blackcomb Ski Resort
Mont Tremblant Ski Resort
Abercrombie & Kent Group

CONTACTS: *Note: Officers with more than one job title may be intentionally listed here more than once.*

Bill Jensen, CEO
Brian Collins, Pres.
Michael Forsayeth, CFO
Andy Wirth, Chief Mktg. Officer
Mara Pagotto, Chief People Officer
Doug Feely, CIO
Stephen Richards, Chief Legal Officer
Kevin Smith, CFO-Intrawest Resort Operations
David Barry, CEO-Alpine Helicopters/Canadian Mountain Holidays
James J. Gibbons, Pres., Intrawest Resort Club Group
Steve Sammut, CFO-Intrawest Real Estate

Phone: 604-669-9777 **Fax:** 604-669-0605
Toll-Free:
Address: 200 Burrand St., Ste. 800, Vancouver, BC V6C 3L6 Canada

GROWTH PLANS/SPECIAL FEATURES:

Intrawest Corporation, an affiliate of Fortress Investment Group LLC, is one of North America's largest developers and operators of destination resorts. It recently went private after being acquired by private equity firm Fortress Investment Group LLC for about $2.8 billion. The firm operates 11 ski resorts including Blue Mountain Resort in Ontario; Mountain Creek Resort in New Jersey; Panorama Mountain Village in British Columbia; Sandestin Golf and Beach Resort in Florida; Snowshoe Mountain Resort in West Virginia; Copper Mountain Resort, Steamboat Ski & Resort and Winter Park Resort in Colorado; Stratton Mountain Ski Resort in Vermont; Mont Tremblant Ski Resort in Quebec; and Whistler Blackcomb Resort, which will host the 2010 Winter Olympics. Intrawest owns 100% of most of these resorts with the exception of the 50%-owned Blue Mountain; the 77%-owned Whistler Blackcomb and Winter Park, which it leases from the City and County of Denver; and a 15% interest in Mammoth Mountain in California. Together its resorts have over 8 million annual visitors. Other Intrawest properties include its 14 managed resort villages, hotels and time-share properties in France, the U.S. and Canada. The firm runs Club Intrawest, a flexible vacation ownership concept offering over 40,000 member's worldwide access to eight Intrawest properties. Additionally, it has an equity interest in the Abercrombie & Kent Group, one of the world's leading luxury adventure travel companies. In January 2009, the firm opened the first phase of its newest resort in Hawaii, Honua Kai Resort & Spa. The second phase of the resort is expected to open in 2010 and will offer full ownership opportunities to potential buyers.

Employees of Intrawest receive tuition reimbursement, referral bonuses and resort discounts, which include discounted or free stays at lodges and discounts on food and equipment.

FINANCIALS: **Sales and profits are in thousands of dollars—add 000 to get the full amount. 2008 Note: Financial information for 2008 was not available for all companies at press time.**

2008 Sales: $
2007 Sales: $1,315,700
2006 Sales: $1,601,800
2005 Sales: $1,669,900
2004 Sales: $1,543,900

2008 Profits: $
2007 Profits: $
2006 Profits: $72,600
2005 Profits: $32,600
2004 Profits: $59,900

U.S. Stock Ticker: Private
Int'l Ticker: ITW Int'l Exchange: Toronto-TSX
Employees: 24,000
Fiscal Year Ends: 6/30
Parent Company: FORTRESS INVESTMENT GROUP LLC

SALARIES/BENEFITS:

Pension Plan: ESOP Stock Plan: Profit Sharing: Top Exec. Salary: $ Bonus: $
Savings Plan: Y Stock Purch. Plan: Second Exec. Salary: $ Bonus: $

OTHER THOUGHTS:

Apparent Women Officers or Directors: 1
Hot Spot for Advancement for Women/Minorities:

LOCATIONS: ("Y" = Yes)

West:	Southwest:	Midwest:	Southeast:	Northeast:	International:
Y	Y		Y	Y	Y

JACKSONVILLE JAGUARS

www.jaguars.com

Industry Group Code: 711211C **Ranks within this company's industry group:** Sales: 26 Profits: 11

Sports:		Services:		Media:		Sales:		Facilities:		Other:	
Leagues/Associations:		Food & Beverage:		TV:		Marketing:		Stadiums:		Gambling:	
Teams:	Y	Agents:		Radio:		Ads:		Fitness Clubs:		Apparel:	
Nonprofits:		Other:		Internet:		Tickets:	Y	Golf Courses:		Equipment:	
Other:				Print:		Retail:	Y	Ski Resorts:		Shoes:	
				Software:		Other:		Other:		Other:	

TYPES OF BUSINESS:

Professional Football Team

BRANDS/DIVISIONS/AFFILIATES:

Jacksonville Jaguars, Ltd.
Jacksonville Municipal Stadium

CONTACTS:

Note: Officers with more than one job title may be intentionally listed here more than once.

Wayne Weaver, CEO
Bill Prescott, CFO/Sr. VP-Stadium Oper.
Bruce Swindell, Exec. Dir.-IT
Paul Vance, General Counsel/Sr. VP-Football Oper.
Skip Richardson, Dir.-Football Oper. & Facilities
Tim Connolly, Sr. VP-Bus. Dev.
Dan Edwards, VP-Comm. & Media
Tim Bishko, Dir.-Ticket Oper.
Macky Weaver, Exec. Dir.-Corp. Sponsorship
Jack Del Rio, Head Coach
Wayne Weaver, Chmn.

Phone: 904-633-6000	**Fax:** 904-633-6050
Toll-Free:	
Address: 1 ALLTEL Stadium Pl., Jacksonville, FL 32202 US	

GROWTH PLANS/SPECIAL FEATURES:

The Jacksonville Jaguars are a professional football team in the National Football League (NFL) based in Jacksonville, Florida. The franchise began in 1995 as the NFL's 30th expansion team. In 1997, the team not only made it to the playoffs but also reached the American Football Conference (AFC) Championship in 1997, its second year playing. The team, however, lost the championship game to the New England Patriots. In 1998, the team won the AFC Central Division title and became the first NFL expansion team to make the playoffs three times in its first four seasons of play. In 1999, the Jaguars finished the regular season with the best record for that year in the NFL, 14-2. The franchise hosted its first Super Bowl, Super Bowl XXXIX in February 2005. In the 2008 season, the Jaguars obtained a 5-11 finish, the team's worst record since 2003. The team is owned and operated by Jacksonville Jaguars, Ltd., which, in turn, is owned by Wayne Weaver, a businessman who also owns Carnival Shoes and Nine West. The team plays its home games at Jacksonville Municipal Stadium, which is owned by the city of Jacksonville and holds up to 76,877 spectators. Forbes has recently estimated the team to be worth approximately $876 million. The team's average home game attendance in the 2008 season was 65,167.

FINANCIALS:

Sales and profits are in thousands of dollars—add 000 to get the full amount. 2008 Note: Financial information for 2008 was not available for all companies at press time.

2008 Sales: $204,000	2008 Profits: $27,600	**U.S. Stock Ticker: Subsidiary**
2007 Sales: $189,000	2007 Profits: $22,100	**Int'l Ticker:** Int'l Exchange:
2006 Sales: $173,000	2006 Profits: $22,500	Employees:
2005 Sales: $169,000	2005 Profits: $	Fiscal Year Ends: 3/31
2004 Sales: $153,000	2004 Profits: $	Parent Company: JACKSONVILLE JAGUARS LTD

SALARIES/BENEFITS:

Pension Plan:	ESOP Stock Plan:	Profit Sharing:	Top Exec. Salary: $	Bonus: $
Savings Plan:	Stock Purch. Plan:		Second Exec. Salary: $	Bonus: $

OTHER THOUGHTS:

Apparent Women Officers or Directors:
Hot Spot for Advancement for Women/Minorities:

LOCATIONS: ("Y" = Yes)

West:	Southwest:	Midwest:	Southeast:	Northeast:	International:
			Y		

JARDEN CORP

www.jarden.com

Industry Group Code: 315000 **Ranks within this company's industry group:** Sales: 2 Profits: 2

Sports:		Services:		Media:		Sales:		Facilities:		Other:	
Leagues/Associations:		Food & Beverage:		TV:		Marketing:		Stadiums:		Gambling:	
Teams:		Agents:		Radio:		Ads:		Fitness Clubs:		Apparel:	Y
Nonprofits:		Other:		Internet:		Tickets:		Golf Courses:		Equipment:	Y
Other:				Print:		Retail:		Ski Resorts:		Shoes:	
				Software:		Other:		Other:		Other:	Y

TYPES OF BUSINESS:

Manufacturing - Consumer Products
Manufacturing - Outdoor Products
Manufacturing - Sports Equipment
Manufacturing - Consumables

BRANDS/DIVISIONS/AFFILIATES:

Pure Fishing, Inc.
K2 Inc
Coleman
Marmot
Crock-Pot
Bee
Coleman Company Inc (The)
Rawlings Sporting Goods Company Inc

CONTACTS: *Note: Officers with more than one job title may be intentionally listed here more than once.*

Martin E. Franklin, CEO
James E. Lillie, COO
James E. Lillie, Pres.
Ian G. H. Ashken, CFO/Vice Chmn.
J. David Tolbert, Sr. VP-Human Resources & Corp. Risk
John E. Capps, General Counsel/Corp. Sec./Sr. VP
Richard T. Sansone, Chief Acct. Officer/Sr. VP
Patricia A. Mount, Chief Transition Officer/Sr. VP
Martin E. Franklin, Chmn.
Patricia J. Gaglione, Sr. VP-Supply Chain

Phone: 914-967-9400 **Fax:** 914-967-9405
Toll-Free:
Address: 555 Theodore Fremd Ave., Ste. B-302, Rye, NY 10580 US

GROWTH PLANS/SPECIAL FEATURES:

Jarden Corp. is a leading global manufacturer, marketer and distributor of niche consumer products in four categories: Outdoor solutions, consumer solutions, process solutions and branded consumables. In its outdoor solutions segment, Jarden provides camping, backpacking, tailgating and outdoor cooking products under its Campinaz and Coleman brands; water sports equipment and all-terrain vehicle equipment under its Stearns, Sevylor, and Mad Dog Gear brands; fishing equipment under its Abu Garcia, Berkley, Fenwick, Gulp!, Penn, Stren, Trilene, Pure Fishing and Ugly Stik brands; baseball, softball, football, basketball and lacrosse products under its deBeer, Rawlings and Worth brands; skiing, snowboarding, snowshoeing and in-line skating products under its K2, Marker and Volkl brands; and technical outdoor apparel and equipment under its Adio, Marmot and Planet Earth brands. In its consumer solutions segment, the company provides coffeemakers, bedding, home vacuum packaging machines, heating pads, slow cookers, air cleaning products, fans, heaters, pet care products and personal grooming products. Its kitchen products are sold under such brands as Crock-Pot, FoodSaver, Mr. Coffee, Oster, Rival, Seal-a-Meal, Sunbeam and VillaWare. Personal care products include such brands as Health o meter, Oster and Sunbeam. Jarden's air conditioning brands include Bionaire, Holmes and Patton. In its branded consumables segment, the company provides such products as arts and crafts items; collectible tins; playing cards; clothespins; toothpicks; plastic cutlery; home canning supplies; rope, cord and twine; firelogs and firestarters; kitchen matches; and home safety equipment. Brand names in this segment include Ball, Bee, Bicycle, Crawford, Diamond, Dicon, First Alert, Forster, Hoyle, Java-Log, Kerr, Lehigh, Leslie-Lock, Loew-Cornell and Pine Mountain. The process solutions segment includes the company's plastic, monofilament and zinc businesses and includes the Shakespeare brand.

FINANCIALS: **Sales and profits are in thousands of dollars—add 000 to get the full amount. 2008 Note: Financial information for 2008 was not available for all companies at press time.**

2008 Sales: $5,383,300	2008 Profits: $-58,900	**U.S. Stock Ticker: JAH**
2007 Sales: $4,660,100	2007 Profits: $28,100	**Int'l Ticker:** Int'l Exchange:
2006 Sales: $3,846,300	2006 Profits: $106,000	Employees: 20,000
2005 Sales: $3,189,100	2005 Profits: $60,700	Fiscal Year Ends: 12/31
2004 Sales: $	2004 Profits: $	Parent Company:

SALARIES/BENEFITS:

Pension Plan:	ESOP Stock Plan:	Profit Sharing:	Top Exec. Salary: $1,998,750	Bonus: $1,499,688
Savings Plan:	Stock Purch. Plan:		Second Exec. Salary: $922,500	Bonus: $792,519

OTHER THOUGHTS:

Apparent Women Officers or Directors: 2
Hot Spot for Advancement for Women/Minorities:

LOCATIONS: ("Y" = Yes)

West:	Southwest:	Midwest:	Southeast:	Northeast:	International:
				Y	Y

JOE GIBBS RACING

www.joegibbsracing.com

Industry Group Code: 711211G **Ranks within this company's industry group:** Sales: 3 Profits: 3

Sports:		Services:		Media:		Sales:		Facilities:		Other:	
Leagues/Associations:		Food & Beverage:		TV:		Marketing:		Stadiums:		Gambling:	
Teams:	Y	Agents:		Radio:		Ads:		Fitness Clubs:		Apparel:	
Nonprofits:		Other:		Internet:		Tickets:		Golf Courses:		Equipment:	Y
Other:				Print:		Retail:	Y	Ski Resorts:		Shoes:	
				Software:		Other:		Other:	Y	Other:	Y

TYPES OF BUSINESS:

Racing Team
Retail Merchandise
Motor Oil

BRANDS/DIVISIONS/AFFILIATES:

Joe Gibbs Performance MicroZol XP1
JGR Souvenir Store
Joe Gibbs Racing/Reggie White Drive for Diversity

CONTACTS:

Note: Officers with more than one job title may be intentionally listed here more than once.

J. D. Gibbs, Pres.
Amy Wilson, Admin.-Mktg.
Gwen Roberts, Mgr.-Human Resources
Joe Gibbs, Owner
Jimmy Makar, Sr. VP
Brooks Busby, Dir.-Licensing

Phone: 704-944-5000	**Fax:** 704-944-5059
Toll-Free:	
Address: 13415 Reese Blvd. W., Huntersville, NC 28078 US	

GROWTH PLANS/SPECIAL FEATURES:

Joe Gibbs Racing (JGR) is a NASCAR racing company, which fields three cars in the NEXTEL Cup Series and three cars in the Busch Series. The company is headquartered in a 225,000-square-foot, state-of-the-art race shop in Huntersville, North Carolina. JGR drivers have won three series titles, one Daytona 500, one Brickyard 400 and more than 40 NEXTEL Cup races. Major sponsors of the company's cars include FedEx, Home Depot, Interstate Batteries and Rockwell Automation. The JGR race shop is open to public viewing, and the adjacent JGR Souvenir Store retails NASCAR and Joe Gibbs team merchandise. The primary drivers for the company include Kyle Busch, Denny Hamlin, Marc Davis, Brad Coleman, Kevin Conway and Joey Logano. Two show cars are available for hire at special events. In addition to the company's racing efforts, JGR sells Joe Gibbs Performance MicroZol XP1 synthetic racing oil. The company has launched the Joe Gibbs Racing/Reggie White Drive for Diversity program, which aims to expand participation and interest in stock car racing among minorities. Company owner Joe Gibbs also served as the head coach of the NFL's Washington Redskins.

FINANCIALS:

Sales and profits are in thousands of dollars—add 000 to get the full amount. 2008 Note: Financial information for 2008 was not available for all companies at press time.

2008 Sales: $116,000	2008 Profits: $11,700	**U.S. Stock Ticker: Private**
2007 Sales: $110,000	2007 Profits: $23,600	**Int'l Ticker:** Int'l Exchange:
2006 Sales: $	2006 Profits: $	Employees:
2005 Sales: $57,000	2005 Profits: $	Fiscal Year Ends:
2004 Sales: $	2004 Profits: $	Parent Company:

SALARIES/BENEFITS:

Pension Plan:	ESOP Stock Plan:	Profit Sharing:	Top Exec. Salary: $	Bonus: $
Savings Plan:	Stock Purch. Plan:		Second Exec. Salary: $	Bonus: $

OTHER THOUGHTS:

Apparent Women Officers or Directors: 2
Hot Spot for Advancement for Women/Minorities: Y

LOCATIONS: ("Y" = Yes)

West:	Southwest:	Midwest:	Southeast:	Northeast:	International:
				Y	

JOHNSON OUTDOORS INC

www.johnsonoutdoors.com

Industry Group Code: 339920 **Ranks within this company's industry group:** Sales: 6 Profits: 6

Sports:		Services:		Media:		Sales:		Facilities:		Other:	
Leagues/Associations:		Food & Beverage:		TV:		Marketing:		Stadiums:		Gambling:	
Teams:		Agents:		Radio:		Ads:		Fitness Clubs:		Apparel:	
Nonprofits:		Other:		Internet:		Tickets:		Golf Courses:		Equipment:	Y
Other:				Print:		Retail:		Ski Resorts:		Shoes:	
				Software:		Other:		Other:		Other:	Y

TYPES OF BUSINESS:

Outdoor Recreation Products
Tents & Backpacks
Marine Electronics
Watercraft
Diving Equipment
Field Compasses

BRANDS/DIVISIONS/AFFILIATES:

Minn Kota
Humminbird
Eureka!
Silva
Tech40
Ocean Kayak
SCUBAPRO
UWATEC

CONTACTS: *Note: Officers with more than one job title may be intentionally listed here more than once.*

Helen Johnson-Leipold, CEO
David W. Johnson, CFO/VP
Sara Vidian, VP-Human Resources
John C. Moon, CIO/VP
Alisa D. Swire, Corp. Sec/VP-Legal Affairs
Alisa D. Swire, VP-Bus. Dev.
Cynthia A. Georgeson, VP-Worldwide Corp. Comm.
Joseph B. Stella, VP-Diving
Kelly T. Grindle, VP-Marine Electronics
William S. Kelly, VP-Outdoor Equipment
Mark E. Leopold, VP-Watercraft
Helen Johnson-Leipold, Chmn.

Phone: 262-631-6600	**Fax:** 262-631-6601
Toll-Free:	
Address: 555 Main St., Racine, WI 53403 US	

GROWTH PLANS/SPECIAL FEATURES:

Johnson Outdoors, Inc. designs, manufactures and markets outdoor recreation products in four categories: marine electronics, outdoor equipment, diving and watercraft. Johnson's marine electronics division manufactures Minn Kota brand battery-powered electric motors used on fishing boats and other boats for quiet trolling power or primary propulsion; Humminbird brand underwater sonar and GPS technology equipment; Geonav chartplotters for navigation; and Cannon brand downriggering fishing equipment. The company's marine electronics brands are sold in the U.S., Canada, Europe, South America and the Pacific Basin through large outdoor specialty store chains such as Bass Pro Shops and Cabelas; large retail store chains; marine distributors; international distributors; and original equipment manufacturers. Johnson's outdoor equipment division manufactures Eureka! brand military, commercial and consumer tents, sleeping bags and backpacks; Silva brand field compasses and digital instruments; and Tech40 performance measurement instruments. Eureka! brand consumer tents, sleeping bags and backpacks compete primarily in the mid- to high-price range and are sold in the U.S. and Canada primarily to sporting goods stores; catalog and mail order houses; and camping and backpacking specialty stores. The company's watercraft division manufactures and markets kayaks, canoes, paddles, oars, specialty watercraft, personal floatation devices and small thermoformed recreational boats under the Old Town, Carlisle Paddles, Ocean Kayak, Pacific Kayak, Canoe Sports, Necky, Escape, Extrasport, Lendal Paddle and Dimension brands. Johnson's diving division manufactures and markets underwater diving products for technical and recreational divers under the SCUBAPRO, UWATEC and Seemann brand names. Underwater diving and snorkeling equipment sold by the company includes regulators, stabilizing jackets, dive computers, dive gauges, wetsuits, masks, fins, snorkels and accessories.

FINANCIALS: **Sales and profits are in thousands of dollars—add 000 to get the full amount. 2008 Note: Financial information for 2008 was not available for all companies at press time.**

2008 Sales: $420,789	2008 Profits: $-71,034	**U.S. Stock Ticker: JOUT**
2007 Sales: $430,604	2007 Profits: $9,234	**Int'l Ticker:** Int'l Exchange:
2006 Sales: $393,950	2006 Profits: $8,715	Employees: 1,400
2005 Sales: $380,690	2005 Profits: $7,101	Fiscal Year Ends: 9/30
2004 Sales: $355,274	2004 Profits: $8,689	Parent Company:

SALARIES/BENEFITS:

Pension Plan:	ESOP Stock Plan:	Profit Sharing:	Top Exec. Salary: $555,000	Bonus: $
Savings Plan:	Stock Purch. Plan:		Second Exec. Salary: $250,273	Bonus: $

OTHER THOUGHTS:

Apparent Women Officers or Directors: 4
Hot Spot for Advancement for Women/Minorities: Y

LOCATIONS: ("Y" = Yes)

West:	Southwest:	Midwest:	Southeast:	Northeast:	International:
Y		Y	Y	Y	Y

KANSAS CITY CHIEFS

www.kcchiefs.com

Industry Group Code: 711211C **Ranks within this company's industry group:** Sales: 17 Profits: 29

Sports:		Services:		Media:		Sales:		Facilities:		Other:	
Leagues/Associations:		Food & Beverage:		TV:		Marketing:		Stadiums:		Gambling:	
Teams:	Y	Agents:		Radio:		Ads:		Fitness Clubs:		Apparel:	
Nonprofits:		Other:		Internet:		Tickets:	Y	Golf Courses:		Equipment:	
Other:				Print:		Retail:	Y	Ski Resorts:		Shoes:	
				Software:		Other:		Other:		Other:	

TYPES OF BUSINESS:

Professional Football Team

BRANDS/DIVISIONS/AFFILIATES:

Kansas City Chiefs Football Club, Inc.
Arrowhead Stadium

CONTACTS:

Note: Officers with more than one job title may be intentionally listed here more than once.

Scott Pioli, Gen. Mgr.
Denny Thum, Pres.
Bill Kuharich, VP-Player Personnel
Bill Newman, Sr. VP-Admin.
Woodie Dixon, General Counsel
Lynn Stiles, VP-Football Oper.
Todd Haley, Head Coach
Jim Siegfried, Sec.
Clark Hunt, Chmn.

Phone: 816-920-9300	**Fax:** 816-923-4719
Toll-Free:	
Address: 1 Arrowhead Dr., Kansas City, MO 64129 US	

GROWTH PLANS/SPECIAL FEATURES:

The Kansas City Chiefs are a professional football team playing in the Western Division of the American Football Conference of the National Football League (NFL). Oilman Lamar Hunt, one of the founding members and the key originator of the American Football League (AFL), as well as its first president, founded the franchise in 1959. The team, a member of the AFL, was known as the Dallas Texans. As part of the AFL, the franchise won three AFL League Championships (1962, 1966 and 1969). In 1963, the team moved to Kansas City, Missouri and became the Kansas City Chiefs. In 1964, the Chiefs played in the first game between AFL and NFL teams, beating the Chicago Bears 66-24. In 1967, the team played in but lost the first title match between the AFL and the NFL, which would later be called Super Bowl I. In 1970, the franchise joined the NFL when the AFL and NFL merged. The team also won Super Bowl IV that year. Since then, the franchise has won five AFC West Championships (1971, 1993, 1995, 1997 and 2003) but no AFC Championships and has yet to return to the Super Bowl. The team is owned and operated by the Hunt family and is run by Clark Hunt, son of founder Lamar Hunt and founding investor-owner in Major League Soccer. The team plays at the Arrowhead Stadium, which is owned by Jackson County and accommodates up to 79,451 spectators. In the 2008 season, the team averaged approximately 74,000 fans in attendance per game. A recent Forbes estimate values the team at roughly $1 billion.

FINANCIALS:

Sales and profits are in thousands of dollars—add 000 to get the full amount. 2008 Note: Financial information for 2008 was not available for all companies at press time.

2008 Sales: $214,000	2008 Profits: $11,900	**U.S. Stock Ticker: Subsidiary**
2007 Sales: $196,000	2007 Profits: $35,200	**Int'l Ticker:** Int'l Exchange:
2006 Sales: $186,000	2006 Profits: $28,200	Employees:
2005 Sales: $181,000	2005 Profits: $	Fiscal Year Ends: 1/31
2004 Sales: $159,000	2004 Profits: $	Parent Company: KANSAS CITY CHIEFS FOOTBALL CLUB INC

SALARIES/BENEFITS:

Pension Plan:	ESOP Stock Plan:	Profit Sharing:	Top Exec. Salary: $	Bonus: $
Savings Plan:	Stock Purch. Plan:		Second Exec. Salary: $	Bonus: $

OTHER THOUGHTS:

Apparent Women Officers or Directors: 1
Hot Spot for Advancement for Women/Minorities:

LOCATIONS: ("Y" = Yes)

West:	Southwest:	Midwest:	Southeast:	Northeast:	International:
		Y			

KANSAS CITY ROYALS

www.royals.com

Industry Group Code: 711211A **Ranks within this company's industry group:** Sales: 29 Profits: 24

Sports:		Services:		Media:		Sales:		Facilities:		Other:	
Leagues/Associations:		Food & Beverage:	Y	TV:		Marketing:		Stadiums:		Gambling:	
Teams:	Y	Agents:		Radio:		Ads:		Fitness Clubs:		Apparel:	
Nonprofits:		Other:		Internet:		Tickets:	Y	Golf Courses:		Equipment:	
Other:				Print:		Retail:	Y	Ski Resorts:		Shoes:	
				Software:		Other:		Other:		Other:	

TYPES OF BUSINESS:

Professional Baseball Team

BRANDS/DIVISIONS/AFFILIATES:

Kauffman Stadium
Omaha Royals
Northwest Arkansas Naturals
Wilmington Blue Rocks
Burlington Bees
Surprise Royals
Idaho Falls Chukars
Kansas City Royals Baseball Corporation

CONTACTS: *Note: Officers with more than one job title may be intentionally listed here more than once.*

David Glass, CEO
Dan Glass, Pres.
David Laverentz, VP-Sales & Mktg.
Tom Pfannenstiel, Sr. Dir.-Payroll, Benefits & Human Resources
Jim Edwards, Sr. Dir.-Info. Systems
Don Costante, Sr. Dir.-Entertainment & Prod.
Dale Rohr, VP-Admin.
Dick Nixon, General Counsel
Kevin Uhlich, Sr. VP-Bus. Oper.
Erin Koncak, Mgr.-Online & Target Mktg.
Michael Swanson, VP-Comm. & Broadcasting
Dale Rohr, VP-Finance
Dayton Moore, Sr. VP-Baseball Oper./Gen. Mgr.
Dean Taylor, VP-Baseball Oper./Asst. Gen. Mgr.
Toby Cook, VP-Comm. Affairs & Publicity
Neil Harwell, VP-Corp. Alliance
David Glass, Chmn.

Phone: 816-921-8000 **Fax:** 816-921-1366
Toll-Free:
Address: 1 Royal Way, Kansas City, MO 64129 US

GROWTH PLANS/SPECIAL FEATURES:

The Kansas City Royals is a Major League Baseball (MLB) team playing in the Central Division of the American League along with the Chicago White Sox, Cleveland Indians, Detroit Tigers and Minnesota Twins. The team was born in 1969 after the Kansas City Athletics moved to Oakland. An expansion team, the Royals got off to a fast start. Its early roster included 1969 Rookie of the Year Lou Piniella. The team won three straight division championships from 1976 to 1978, and made its first World Series appearance in 1980. The Royals developed young talent throughout the 80s and early 90s including George Brett, Bret Saberhagen and Bo Jackson. The team won the World Series in 1985, defeating their intra-state rivals, the St. Louis Cardinals. Since 2000, the team has been owned by David Glass, former president and CEO of Wal-Mart Stores, Inc. The franchise has played at Kauffman Stadium since 1973, which seats approximately 40,700. A recently approved renovation that began in 2008 includes a 360-degree concourse; additional video boards around the stadium; 1,500 new seats in left field; new ticket offices; renovated press boxes and luxury suites; additional fan amenities; and other structural modifications and improvements. In the 2008 season, the team averaged approximately 20,000 fans in attendance per game. A recent Forbes estimate values the team at $314 million.

FINANCIALS: **Sales and profits are in thousands of dollars—add 000 to get the full amount. 2008 Note: Financial information for 2008 was not available for all companies at press time.**

2008 Sales: $143,000 — 2008 Profits: $9,000
2007 Sales: $131,000 — 2007 Profits: $7,400
2006 Sales: $123,000 — 2006 Profits: $8,400
2005 Sales: $117,000 — 2005 Profits: $
2004 Sales: $ — 2004 Profits: $

U.S. Stock Ticker: Subsidiary
Int'l Ticker: Int'l Exchange:
Employees:
Fiscal Year Ends:
Parent Company: KANSAS CITY ROYALS BASEBALL CORPORATION

SALARIES/BENEFITS:

Pension Plan: ESOP Stock Plan: Profit Sharing: Top Exec. Salary: $ Bonus: $
Savings Plan: Stock Purch. Plan: Second Exec. Salary: $ Bonus: $

OTHER THOUGHTS:

Apparent Women Officers or Directors: 3
Hot Spot for Advancement for Women/Minorities: Y

LOCATIONS: ("Y" = Yes)

West:	Southwest:	Midwest:	Southeast:	Northeast:	International:
		Y			Y

KANSAS CITY WIZARDS

kc.wizards.mlsnet.com

Industry Group Code: 711211D **Ranks within this company's industry group:** Sales: Profits:

Sports:		Services:		Media:		Sales:		Facilities:		Other:	
Leagues/Associations:		Food & Beverage:		TV:		Marketing:		Stadiums:		Gambling:	
Teams:	Y	Agents:		Radio:		Ads:		Fitness Clubs:		Apparel:	
Nonprofits:		Other:		Internet:		Tickets:	Y	Golf Courses:		Equipment:	
Other:				Print:		Retail:	Y	Ski Resorts:		Shoes:	
				Software:		Other:		Other:		Other:	

TYPES OF BUSINESS:

Major League Soccer Team
Soccer Camps

BRANDS/DIVISIONS/AFFILIATES:

Kicks for Kids
Arrowhead Stadium
Dynamo the Dragon
OnGoal LLC

CONTACTS:

Note: Officers with more than one job title may be intentionally listed here more than once.

Robb Heineman, Pres.
Rob Thomson, VP-Mktg.
Jacques Tournoy, VP-Merch.
Greg Cotton, General Counsel/Exec. VP
Chris Wyche, VP-Oper.
David Ficklin, VP-Dev.
Rob Thomson, VP-Comm.
Shawn Quesnell, VP-Finance
Curt Onalfo, Head Coach
Shayne Donohue, VP-Ticket Sales
Todd Adams, VP-Sponsorship Sales

Phone: 913-387-3400	**Fax:** 913-387-3401
Toll-Free:	
Address: 8900 State Line Rd., 5th Fl., Leawood, KS 66206 US	

GROWTH PLANS/SPECIAL FEATURES:

The Kansas City Wizards, owned and operated by OnGoal LLC are a Major League Soccer (MLS) club, playing in the Eastern Conference. Chairman Alan Rothenberg introduced the team into the MLS as the Kansas City Wiz, one of the league's 10 charter members. After the 1996 season the team officially extended its name to the Kansas City Wizards. Over the course of the club's history, the Wizards have acquired key players such as Preki, Diego Guitierrez, Josh Wolff and Diego Walsh, adding to a line-up that has included national team players Chris Klein, Nick Garcia and Kerry Zavagnin. The team's head coach is Curt Onalfo. The Wizards play their home games at Arrowhead Stadium, which is also the home of the Kansas City Chiefs football team. It is connected to the Harry Truman Sports Complex, which includes a 42,000-seat baseball stadium. Between 1999 and 2003, the Wizards went five consecutive seasons with continual attendance growth, an MLS record. In 2008, the Wizards had an average regular season attendance of approximately 10,700 and an average playoff attendance of approximately 10,400. A recent Forbes estimate valued the team at approximately $22 million.

FINANCIALS:

Sales and profits are in thousands of dollars—add 000 to get the full amount. 2008 Note: Financial information for 2008 was not available for all companies at press time.

2008 Sales: $	2008 Profits: $	**U.S. Stock Ticker: Subsidiary**
2007 Sales: $	2007 Profits: $	**Int'l Ticker:** Int'l Exchange:
2006 Sales: $	2006 Profits: $	Employees:
2005 Sales: $	2005 Profits: $	Fiscal Year Ends:
2004 Sales: $	2004 Profits: $	Parent Company: ONGOAL LLC

SALARIES/BENEFITS:

Pension Plan:	ESOP Stock Plan:	Profit Sharing:	Top Exec. Salary: $	Bonus: $
Savings Plan:	Stock Purch. Plan:		Second Exec. Salary: $	Bonus: $

OTHER THOUGHTS:

Apparent Women Officers or Directors:
Hot Spot for Advancement for Women/Minorities:

LOCATIONS: ("Y" = Yes)

West:	Southwest:	Midwest:	Southeast:	Northeast:	International:
		Y			

KELLWOOD CO

www.kellwood.com

Industry Group Code: 315000 **Ranks within this company's industry group:** Sales: Profits:

Sports:		Services:		Media:		Sales:		Facilities:		Other:	
Leagues/Associations:		Food & Beverage:		TV:		Marketing:		Stadiums:		Gambling:	
Teams:		Agents:		Radio:		Ads:		Fitness Clubs:		Apparel:	Y
Nonprofits:		Other:		Internet:		Tickets:		Golf Courses:		Equipment:	Y
Other:				Print:		Retail:		Ski Resorts:		Shoes:	
				Software:		Other:		Other:		Other:	

TYPES OF BUSINESS:

Apparel Design
Women's Sportswear
Intimate Apparel
Infant Apparel
Children's Apparel

BRANDS/DIVISIONS/AFFILIATES:

Cardinal Integrated, LLC
Jolt
Sag Harbor
Jax
Briggs New York
Vince
Phat
Phat Fashions LLC

CONTACTS: *Note: Officers with more than one job title may be intentionally listed here more than once.*

Michael W. Kramer, CEO
W. Lee Capps III, COO
Michael W. Kramer, Pres.
Gregory W. Kleffner, CFO
George Sokolowski, Chief Mktg. Officer
J. David LaRocca, Jr., VP-Human Resources
Michael M. Saunders, CIO/VP
Thomas H. Pollihan, General Counsel/Corp. Sec./Exec. VP
George Sokolowski, VP-Strategy
Donna B. Weaver, VP-Corp. Comm.
Samuel W. Duggan, II, VP-Investor Rel.
Samuel W. Duggan, II, Treas.
Bob Rose, VP-Retail
Kimora Lee Simmons, Pres., Phat Fashions LLC
Suzanne Desiderio, Pres., XOXO
Caren Belair, Pres., My Michelle
Robert C. Skinner, Jr., Chmn.

Phone: 314-576-3100	**Fax:** 314-576-3460
Toll-Free:	
Address: 600 Kellwood Pkwy., Chesterfield, MO 63017 US	

GROWTH PLANS/SPECIAL FEATURES:

Kellwood Co., a subsidiary of Cardinal Integrated, LLC, is a marketer of apparel and soft goods primarily for women, offering branded as well as private-label products to all channels of distribution. The company was acquired in February 2008 by Cardinal Integrated, a jointly owned subsidiary of Sun Capital Partners, LLC, for $767 million. The apparel maker designs, merchandises and sells designer and lifestyle sportswear for women. Its products (including blazers, dresses, sweaters, blouses, vests, skirts, jeans and pants) consists of branded goods sold at popular to moderate price points, as well as some upper-price-point lines, sold to specialty stores, department stores and catalog houses. Brands in this division include Koret, Sag Harbor, Jax, David Dart, Dorby, My Michelle, Briggs New York, Phat Fashions and David Brooks. The firm's Vince label designs clothing and accessories for men and women. Its children's segment consists of brands such as Jolt and Rewind. Late in 2008, the company sold two children's business units, Gerber Childrenswear LLC and Hanna Andersson LLC, to Childrenswear, LLC, part of Sun Capital Partners, Inc., for $179 million. Going forward, the firm plans to focus its business efforts primarily on its women's apparel business, more specifically, its juniors, contemporary and mainstream women's sportswear brands.

FINANCIALS: **Sales and profits are in thousands of dollars—add 000 to get the full amount. 2008 Note: Financial information for 2008 was not available for all companies at press time.**

2008 Sales: $	2008 Profits: $	**U.S. Stock Ticker: Private**
2007 Sales: $	2007 Profits: $	**Int'l Ticker:** Int'l Exchange:
2006 Sales: $2,062,144	2006 Profits: $-38,413	Employees: 32,000
2005 Sales: $2,199,976	2005 Profits: $66,336	Fiscal Year Ends: 1/31
2004 Sales: $2,346,481	2004 Profits: $71,085	Parent Company: CARDINAL INTEGRATED LLC

SALARIES/BENEFITS:

Pension Plan:	ESOP Stock Plan:	Profit Sharing:	Top Exec. Salary: $1,250,000	Bonus: $312,500
Savings Plan:	Stock Purch. Plan:		Second Exec. Salary: $850,000	Bonus: $225,000

OTHER THOUGHTS:

Apparent Women Officers or Directors: 6
Hot Spot for Advancement for Women/Minorities: Y

LOCATIONS: ("Y" = Yes)

West:	Southwest:	Midwest:	Southeast:	Northeast:	International:
Y		Y	Y	Y	Y

KING PAR CORPORATION

www.kingpar.com

Industry Group Code: 339920 **Ranks within this company's industry group:** Sales: Profits:

Sports:		Services:		Media:		Sales:		Facilities:		Other:	
Leagues/Associations:		Food & Beverage:		TV:		Marketing:		Stadiums:		Gambling:	
Teams:		Agents:		Radio:		Ads:		Fitness Clubs:		Apparel:	Y
Nonprofits:		Other:		Internet:		Tickets:		Golf Courses:		Equipment:	Y
Other:				Print:		Retail:	Y	Ski Resorts:		Shoes:	
				Software:		Other:		Other:		Other:	

TYPES OF BUSINESS:

Golf Equipment
Golf Apparel
Retail Operations

BRANDS/DIVISIONS/AFFILIATES:

Orlimar Golf Company
King Par Superstore
Affinity
Fortune
Knight
Strategy
Intech
Ti-Tech

CONTACTS:

Note: Officers with more than one job title may be intentionally listed here more than once.

Bill Baird, CEO
Doug Hinton, Mgr.-Sales
Ryan Coffell, Controller

Phone: 810-732-2470 **Fax:** 810-732-6662
Toll-Free: 888-502-4653
Address: G-5140 Flushing Rd., Flushing, MI 48433 US

GROWTH PLANS/SPECIAL FEATURES:

King Par Corporation is one of the largest specialty golf equipment stores in the Mid-West. The company carries a wide array of products from respected vendors including Affinity; Fortune; Knight; Strategy; Back Nine; Ben Hogan; Bette and Court; Tommy Hilfiger; Knight La Jolla Club; Max Fli Mizuno; Nike; Never Compromise; Greg Norman Oakley; TaylorMade Tehama; TopFlite; U.S. Kids Golf; Intech; and more. In addition to its 22,000-square-foot superstore in Flushing, Michigan, the company also operates a driving range located just behind the store. The range includes 32 covered and heated tees, an open tee area with 10 natural grass tees, a practice bunker and putting green; and a par-three golf course. King Par also offers private-label products such as the Ti-Tech line for Wal-Mart, the Golf Master line for JJB Sports and the Stellar line for the National Golf Buyers Association. King Par's new house-brand products are designed and tested at its superstore facility, allowing the company to interact with customers and catch early market trends. The store features a comprehensive array of equipment and supplies for golfers, as well as a repair center. Also within its retail facility the company operates the King Par Golf Academy, which offers group and individual lessons and access to extensive custom fitting, swing analysis and game improvement technology. Subsidiary Orlimar Golf Company manufactures the TriMetal and HipTi series clubs.

FINANCIALS:

Sales and profits are in thousands of dollars—add 000 to get the full amount. 2008 Note: Financial information for 2008 was not available for all companies at press time.

2008 Sales: $	2008 Profits: $	**U.S. Stock Ticker: Private**
2007 Sales: $	2007 Profits: $	**Int'l Ticker:** Int'l Exchange:
2006 Sales: $	2006 Profits: $	Employees: 100
2005 Sales: $	2005 Profits: $	Fiscal Year Ends: 12/31
2004 Sales: $65,700	2004 Profits: $	Parent Company:

SALARIES/BENEFITS:

Pension Plan:	ESOP Stock Plan:	Profit Sharing:	Top Exec. Salary: $	Bonus: $
Savings Plan:	Stock Purch. Plan:		Second Exec. Salary: $	Bonus: $

OTHER THOUGHTS:

Apparent Women Officers or Directors:
Hot Spot for Advancement for Women/Minorities:

LOCATIONS: ("Y" = Yes)

West:	Southwest:	Midwest:	Southeast:	Northeast:	International:
		Y			

KROENKE SPORTS ENTERPRISES LLC

www.pepsicenter.com

Industry Group Code: 551110 **Ranks within this company's industry group:** Sales: Profits:

Sports:		Services:		Media:		Sales:		Facilities:		Other:	
Leagues/Associations:		Food & Beverage:	Y	TV:		Marketing:		Stadiums:	Y	Gambling:	
Teams:	Y	Agents:		Radio:		Ads:		Fitness Clubs:		Apparel:	Y
Nonprofits:		Other:	Y	Internet:		Tickets:	Y	Golf Courses:		Equipment:	
Other:				Print:		Retail:	Y	Ski Resorts:		Shoes:	
				Software:		Other:		Other:	Y	Other:	

TYPES OF BUSINESS:

Holding Company

BRANDS/DIVISIONS/AFFILIATES:

Denver Nuggets
Colorado Crush
Coloardo Avalanche
Colorado Mammoth
Pepsi Center
Denver Post Newsroom
Qwest Business Center
Blue Sky Grill

CONTACTS: *Note: Officers with more than one job title may be intentionally listed here more than once.*

E. Stanley Kroenke, Owner/Governor
Mike Kurowski, VP-Corp. Sales & Partnership Mktg.
Charles R. Wright, VP-New Bus. Oper.
Mark Waggoner, Sr. VP-Finance
Michael Benson, Sr. VP-Bus. Affairs/Treas.
Deb Dowling-Canino, VP-Community Rel.
Shawn Stokes, VP-Venue Projects

Phone: 303-405-1100 **Fax:** 303-575-1920
Toll-Free:
Address: 1000 Chopper Circle, Denver, CO 80204 US

GROWTH PLANS/SPECIAL FEATURES:

Kroenke Sports Enterprises (KSE) is the holding company of Wal-Mart heir Stan Kroenke. KSE owns and operates the Pepsi Center, which opened in 1999 and has hosted a wide variety of events since, including hockey and basketball games, musical acts, ice extravaganzas and circuses. The approximately 675,000-square-foot facility is home to KSE's four owned and operated sports franchises, the National Basketball Association's (NBA) Denver Nuggets, the National Hockey League's (NHL) Colorado Avalanche, the Arena Football League's (AFL) Colorado Crush and the National Lacrosse League's (NLL) Colorado Mammoth. The Pepsi Center seats over 19,000 for basketball games and over 18,000 for hockey, arena football and lacrosse games. Contingent upon stage configuration, the venue can seat up to 20,000 for concerts and other events. The Pepsi Center boasts 95 luxury suites and 1,900 club seats; The Lexus Club, a fine dining restaurant seating up to 350; The Denver Post Newsroom, a granite-countertop and stuffed-leather-chair lounge with views of the Rocky Mountains; Blue Sky Grill, which offers western cuisine in a mountain lodge setting; the Qwest Business Center, located on the Club Level concourse, which features five state-of-the-art conference rooms, each with a balcony overlooking the Rocky Mountains; and Altitude Authentics, specializing in merchandise for the teams who call the Pepsi Center home. The Pepsi Center also features a cutting-edge sound and lighting system and a massive center-hung scoreboard, with an eight-sided matrix/game-in-progress board and a four-sided Sony LED JumboTron.

FINANCIALS: Sales and profits are in thousands of dollars—add 000 to get the full amount. 2008 Note: Financial information for 2008 was not available for all companies at press time.

2008 Sales: $ 2008 Profits: $
2007 Sales: $ 2007 Profits: $
2006 Sales: $ 2006 Profits: $
2005 Sales: $ 2005 Profits: $
2004 Sales: $ 2004 Profits: $

U.S. Stock Ticker: Private
Int'l Ticker: Int'l Exchange:
Employees:
Fiscal Year Ends: 6/30
Parent Company:

SALARIES/BENEFITS:

Pension Plan: ESOP Stock Plan: Profit Sharing: Top Exec. Salary: $ Bonus: $
Savings Plan: Stock Purch. Plan: Second Exec. Salary: $ Bonus: $

OTHER THOUGHTS:

Apparent Women Officers or Directors: 1
Hot Spot for Advancement for Women/Minorities:

LOCATIONS: ("Y" = Yes)

West:	Southwest:	Midwest:	Southeast:	Northeast:	International:
Y					

Note: Financial information, benefits and other data can change quickly and may vary from those stated here.

K-SWISS INC

www.kswiss.com

Industry Group Code: 316219 **Ranks within this company's industry group:** Sales: 6 Profits: 5

Sports:		Services:		Media:		Sales:		Facilities:		Other:	
Leagues/Associations:		Food & Beverage:		TV:		Marketing:		Stadiums:		Gambling:	
Teams:		Agents:		Radio:		Ads:		Fitness Clubs:		Apparel:	Y
Nonprofits:		Other:		Internet:		Tickets:		Golf Courses:		Equipment:	
Other:				Print:		Retail:		Ski Resorts:		Shoes:	Y
				Software:		Other:		Other:		Other:	Y

TYPES OF BUSINESS:

Footwear Manufacturing
Athletic Footwear & Apparel
Slip-On Footwear
Online Sales

BRANDS/DIVISIONS/AFFILIATES:

K-Swiss Classic
Royal Elastics

CONTACTS: *Note: Officers with more than one job title may be intentionally listed here more than once.*

Steven Nichols, CEO
George Powlick, COO
Steven Nichols, Pres.
George Powlick, CFO/VP-Finance/Sec.
Yvette Conen, Dir.-Payroll & Benefits
Yvette Conen, Dir.-Admin.
Lee Green, Corp. Counsel
Edward Flora, VP-Oper.
Kimberly Scully, Corp. Controller
Brian Sullivan, VP-National Accounts
David Nichols, Exec. VP
Steven Nichols, Chmn.

Phone: 818-706-5100	**Fax:** 818-706-5390
Toll-Free: 800-938-8000	
Address: 31248 Oak Crest Dr., Westlake Village, CA 91361 US	

GROWTH PLANS/SPECIAL FEATURES:

K-Swiss, Inc. designs, develops and markets an array of athletic footwear for high-performance sports use and fitness activities and casual wear under the K-Swiss brand. The company also designs and manufactures footwear under the Royal Elastics brand. Royal Elastics is a wholly-owned subsidiary and a creator of slip-on, laceless footwear. K-Swiss also markets a line of branded apparel and accessories, as well as a line of high-tech tennis apparel including skirts, shorts, tops, polos, dresses and warm-ups. The firm's apparel is aimed at upscale buyers of athletic gear and suburban casual wear. The company's products are manufactured by independent suppliers, primarily in China, and sold in department and specialty retail stores, as well as directly through the firm's web site. The company works internationally through nine subsidiaries and 16 distributors. K-Swiss is known for the K-Swiss Classic shoe, an all-white, all-weather, all-leather tennis shoe that was the firm's first shoe. As a marketing strategy, the company endeavors to use classic styling instead of fashion-oriented footwear in order to reduce the impact of changes in consumer preferences and prolong the life cycle of its products. K-Swiss market its products in about 98 countries.

FINANCIALS: **Sales and profits are in thousands of dollars—add 000 to get the full amount. 2008 Note: Financial information for 2008 was not available for all companies at press time.**

2008 Sales: $340,160	2008 Profits: $20,885	**U.S. Stock Ticker: KSWS**
2007 Sales: $410,432	2007 Profits: $39,073	**Int'l Ticker:** Int'l Exchange:
2006 Sales: $501,148	2006 Profits: $76,864	Employees: 584
2005 Sales: $508,574	2005 Profits: $75,248	Fiscal Year Ends: 12/31
2004 Sales: $484,079	2004 Profits: $71,251	Parent Company:

SALARIES/BENEFITS:

Pension Plan:	ESOP Stock Plan:	Profit Sharing:	Top Exec. Salary: $942,450	Bonus: $55,649
Savings Plan:	Stock Purch. Plan:		Second Exec. Salary: $306,567	Bonus: $25,376

OTHER THOUGHTS:

Apparent Women Officers or Directors: 1
Hot Spot for Advancement for Women/Minorities: Y

LOCATIONS: ("Y" = Yes)

West:	Southwest:	Midwest:	Southeast:	Northeast:	International:
Y					Y

LA FITNESS INTERNATIONAL LLC

www.lafitness.com

Industry Group Code: 713940 **Ranks within this company's industry group:** Sales: Profits:

Sports:		Services:		Media:		Sales:		Facilities:		Other:	
Leagues/Associations:		Food & Beverage:		TV:		Marketing:		Stadiums:		Gambling:	
Teams:		Agents:		Radio:		Ads:		Fitness Clubs:	Y	Apparel:	
Nonprofits:		Other:		Internet:		Tickets:		Golf Courses:		Equipment:	
Other:				Print:		Retail:		Ski Resorts:		Shoes:	
				Software:		Other:		Other:		Other:	

TYPES OF BUSINESS:

Fitness Clubs

BRANDS/DIVISIONS/AFFILIATES:

Seidler Equity Partners
CIVC Partners
Madison Dearborn Partners LLC

CONTACTS:

Note: Officers with more than one job title may be intentionally listed here more than once.

Louis Welch, Pres.
Jill Greuling, Special Counsel
William B. Horner, Chief Real Estate Officer/Sr. VP

Phone: 949-255-7333 **Fax:** 949-255-7489
Toll-Free:
Address: 8105 Irvine Center D., Ste. 200, Irvine, CA 92618 US

GROWTH PLANS/SPECIAL FEATURES:

LA Fitness International LLC is a company that owns and operates a chain of gymnasiums and fitness clubs across the U.S. and Canada. The company's gyms are equipped with facilities for basketball, free weights, racquetball, swimming, indoor cycling, cardio training and personal training. In addition, LA Fitness offers a number of classes for its members, including cardio kickboxing, aerobics, pilates, yoga and belly dancing, among many others. Most of the company's properties offer league play and tournaments for sports such as basketball and racquetball, and many offer private lessons. At its Warner Center, California location, LA Fitness operates a 13 court tennis facility that hosts leagues and tournaments, as well as tennis camps and private lessons. The firm's web site offers customers an online account access page, where they can pay bills, view workout and class schedules and sign up for personal training. In addition to sports and training facilities, many of the company's gyms feature juice bars. These juice bars, doing business under the Nrgize Lifestyle Cafe brand, are owned and operated independently by franchisees of Kahala Corp. The firm has over 200 locations in 22 U.S. states, as well as Ontario, Canada. Major investors in LA Fitness include Seidler Equity Partners, CIVC Partners and Madison Dearborn Partners.

FINANCIALS:

Sales and profits are in thousands of dollars—add 000 to get the full amount. 2008 Note: Financial information for 2008 was not available for all companies at press time.

2008 Sales: $	2008 Profits: $	**U.S. Stock Ticker: Private**
2007 Sales: $	2007 Profits: $	**Int'l Ticker:** Int'l Exchange:
2006 Sales: $	2006 Profits: $	Employees:
2005 Sales: $	2005 Profits: $	Fiscal Year Ends:
2004 Sales: $	2004 Profits: $	Parent Company:

SALARIES/BENEFITS:

Pension Plan:	ESOP Stock Plan:	Profit Sharing:	Top Exec. Salary: $	Bonus: $
Savings Plan:	Stock Purch. Plan:		Second Exec. Salary: $	Bonus: $

OTHER THOUGHTS:

Apparent Women Officers or Directors:
Hot Spot for Advancement for Women/Minorities:

LOCATIONS: ("Y" = Yes)

West:	Southwest:	Midwest:	Southeast:	Northeast:	International:
Y	Y	Y	Y	Y	Y

LADIES PROFESSIONAL GOLF ASSOCIATION (LPGA)

www.lpga.com

Industry Group Code: 813990 **Ranks within this company's industry group:** Sales: Profits:

Sports:		Services:		Media:		Sales:		Facilities:		Other:	
Leagues/Associations:	Y	Food & Beverage:		TV:		Marketing:		Stadiums:		Gambling:	
Teams:		Agents:		Radio:		Ads:		Fitness Clubs:		Apparel:	
Nonprofits:	Y	Other:		Internet:		Tickets:		Golf Courses:		Equipment:	
Other:				Print:		Retail:		Ski Resorts:		Shoes:	
				Software:		Other:		Other:		Other:	

TYPES OF BUSINESS:

Golf Association
Charitable Activities
Scholarships
Golf Tour

BRANDS/DIVISIONS/AFFILIATES:

LPGA
LPGA Teaching & Club Professional Division
LPGA Tour
LPGA Tour Junior Golf Clinics
LPGA-USGA Girls Golf
LPGA Urban Youth Golf Program
LPGA Foundation
FUTURES Golf Tour

CONTACTS: *Note: Officers with more than one job title may be intentionally listed here more than once.*

Carolyn Bivens, Commissioner
Christopher Higgs, COO/Sr. VP
Dawn E. Hudson, Chmn.

Phone: 386-274-6200	**Fax:** 386-274-1099
Toll-Free:	
Address: 100 International Golf Dr., Daytona Beach, FL 32124 US	

GROWTH PLANS/SPECIAL FEATURES:

The Ladies Professional Golf Association (LPGA) is the longest-running women's sports association in the world and celebrated its 58th anniversary in 2008. Though the firm initially operated as a playing tour, the LPGA has evolved into a nonprofit organization involved in every facet of golf. The LPGA is organized into two segments, the LPGA Tour and the LPGA Teaching & Club Professional Division. The LPGA Tour hosts approximately 30 events each year with prize money totaling over $50 million. The LPGA Teaching & Club Professional Division, founded in 1959, has the largest membership of women golf professionals in the country, with more than 1,200 members. Member programs include teaching and business training programs; tournaments; sponsor and licensee benefits; employment services; golf clinics; and junior golf programs. The LPGA Foundation, established in 1991, maintains a strong focus on charity through tournaments, junior programs, women's programs and its affiliation with the Susan G. Komen Breast Cancer Foundation. Charitable programs include the Ronald McDonald House Charities, LPGA Tour Junior Golf Clinics, LPGA-USGA Girls Golf and the LPGA Urban Youth Golf Program. The LPGA is based in Daytona Beach, Florida. The firm's headquarters, known as the LPGA International, feature two 18-hole golf courses called the Champions and the Legends. The LPGA additionally sponsors an official developmental tour called the Duramed FUTURES Golf Tour, which runs from March through October with more than 300 players from around the world. The organization maintains a 22-member LPGA Tour Hall of Fame, honoring current and former players such as Annika Sorenstam, Louise Suggs, Patty Berg, Betsy Rawls, Kathy Whitworth and Mildred (Babe) Didrikson Zaharias. The 2009 LPGA Tour features 31 events in 10 countries with official prize monies of nearly $55 million, or approximately $1.767 million per event on average.

FINANCIALS: **Sales and profits are in thousands of dollars—add 000 to get the full amount. 2008 Note: Financial information for 2008 was not available for all companies at press time.**

2008 Sales: $	2008 Profits: $	**U.S. Stock Ticker: Private**
2007 Sales: $	2007 Profits: $	**Int'l Ticker:** Int'l Exchange:
2006 Sales: $	2006 Profits: $	Employees:
2005 Sales: $	2005 Profits: $	Fiscal Year Ends:
2004 Sales: $	2004 Profits: $	Parent Company:

SALARIES/BENEFITS:

Pension Plan:	ESOP Stock Plan:	Profit Sharing:	Top Exec. Salary: $	Bonus: $
Savings Plan:	Stock Purch. Plan:		Second Exec. Salary: $	Bonus: $

OTHER THOUGHTS:

Apparent Women Officers or Directors: 2
Hot Spot for Advancement for Women/Minorities: Y

LOCATIONS: ("Y" = Yes)

West:	Southwest:	Midwest:	Southeast:	Northeast:	International:
			Y		

LEVY RESTAURANTS

www.levyrestaurants.com

Industry Group Code: 722110 **Ranks within this company's industry group:** Sales: Profits:

Sports:		Services:		Media:		Sales:		Facilities:		Other:	
Leagues/Associations:		Food & Beverage:	Y	TV:		Marketing:		Stadiums:		Gambling:	
Teams:		Agents:		Radio:		Ads:		Fitness Clubs:		Apparel:	
Nonprofits:		Other:	Y	Internet:		Tickets:		Golf Courses:		Equipment:	
Other:				Print:		Retail:		Ski Resorts:		Shoes:	
				Software:		Other:		Other:		Other:	

TYPES OF BUSINESS:

Restaurants
Sporting & Entertainment Concessions
Catering & Event Planning
Consulting

BRANDS/DIVISIONS/AFFILIATES:

Chicago White Sox
Spiaggia
Bistro 100
Fulton's Crab House
Wolfgang Puck Cafe
STAPLES Center
Dodger Stadium
Wrigley Field

CONTACTS: *Note: Officers with more than one job title may be intentionally listed here more than once.*

Andrew J. Lansing, CEO
Andrew J. Lansing, Pres.
Bob Seiffert, CFO
Katie Kirby, Dir.-Comm.
Bob Seiffert, Exec. VP-Financial Services
Lawrence F. (Larry) Levy, Chmn.

Phone: 312-664-8200 **Fax:**
Toll-Free:
Address: 980 N. Michigan Ave., Chicago, IL 60611 US

GROWTH PLANS/SPECIAL FEATURES:

Levy Restaurants owns, manages and operates 99 locations, comprised of 24 restaurants and 75 sports and entertainment venues, throughout the U.S., Puerto Rico, the U.K. and Canada. Levy pioneered the concept of offering fine dining at sporting venues in 1982 in Comisky Park, home of the Chicago White Sox. The company's restaurants include Spiaggia and Bistro 100 in Chicago; and Fulton's Crab House and Wolfgang Puck Cafe in Walt Disney World Resort. Spiaggia, Levy's flagship upscale restaurant, is an award-winning Italian food restaurant. Through its sports and entertainment division, the firm manages convention facilities; music and performance venues; and stadiums and arenas for all major sports leagues. Levy's stadiums and arenas include STAPLES Center and Dodger Stadium in Los Angeles; American Airlines Arena in Miami; Wrigley Field in Chicago; and Lambeau Field in Green Bay. The company also owns and operates the Hershey's retail locations in Chicago, Wrigley Field and Arlington Park. Levy's portfolio of serviced events includes the Super Bowl, the Grammy Awards, the World Series, NBA games, NHL All-Star games and the Kentucky Derby. Levy additionally operates a consulting and advisory division which offers full-service catering for corporate and private gatherings in select U.S. cities, as well as Canada, the U.K. and Puerto Rico. Levy maintains a strategic partnership with Compass Group North America, a subsidiary of U.K.-based Compass Group PLC, one of the largest foodservice companies in the world. In 2009, the firm formed partnerships with Washington D.C.'s Nationals Park; Aces Ballpark in Reno; and LaGrave field in Fort Worth.

FINANCIALS: **Sales and profits are in thousands of dollars—add 000 to get the full amount. 2008 Note: Financial information for 2008 was not available for all companies at press time.**

2008 Sales: $	2008 Profits: $	**U.S. Stock Ticker: Private**
2007 Sales: $	2007 Profits: $	**Int'l Ticker:** Int'l Exchange:
2006 Sales: $735,000	2006 Profits: $	Employees: 15,000
2005 Sales: $610,000	2005 Profits: $	Fiscal Year Ends: 12/31
2004 Sales: $470,000	2004 Profits: $	Parent Company:

SALARIES/BENEFITS:

Pension Plan:	ESOP Stock Plan:	Profit Sharing:	Top Exec. Salary: $	Bonus: $
Savings Plan:	Stock Purch. Plan:		Second Exec. Salary: $	Bonus: $

OTHER THOUGHTS:

Apparent Women Officers or Directors: 1
Hot Spot for Advancement for Women/Minorities: Y

LOCATIONS: ("Y" = Yes)

West:	Southwest:	Midwest:	Southeast:	Northeast:	International:
Y	Y	Y	Y	Y	Y

LIFE TIME FITNESS INC

www.lifetimefitness.com

Industry Group Code: 713940 **Ranks within this company's industry group:** Sales: 1 Profits: 1

Sports:		Services:		Media:		Sales:		Facilities:		Other:	
Leagues/Associations:		Food & Beverage:	Y	TV:		Marketing:		Stadiums:		Gambling:	
Teams:		Agents:		Radio:		Ads:		Fitness Clubs:	Y	Apparel:	
Nonprofits:		Other:	Y	Internet:		Tickets:		Golf Courses:		Equipment:	
Other:				Print:		Retail:		Ski Resorts:		Shoes:	
				Software:		Other:		Other:	Y	Other:	

TYPES OF BUSINESS:

Fitness Center
Cardiovascular Equipment
Free Weights
Individual Training
Fitness Classes
Magazine
Nutrition

BRANDS/DIVISIONS/AFFILIATES:

LIFE TIME FITNESS
Pilates
LifeSpa
LifeCafe
TEAM Weight Loss
Experience Life
FCA Construction

CONTACTS:

Note: Officers with more than one job title may be intentionally listed here more than once.

Bahram Akradi, CEO
Michael J. Gerend, COO
Michael J. Gerend, Pres.
Michael R. Robinson, CFO/Exec. VP
Scott C. Lutz, Chief Mktg. Officer/Exec. VP
Eric J. Buss, General Counsel/Corp. Sec./Exec. VP
Jeffrey G. Zwiefel, Exec. VP-Oper.
Mark L. Zaebst, Exec. VP-Real Estate Dev.
Bahram Akradi, Chmn.

Phone: 952-947-0000	**Fax:** 952-947-9137
Toll-Free:	
Address: 2902 Corporate Pl., Chanhassen, MN 55317 US	

GROWTH PLANS/SPECIAL FEATURES:

Life Time Fitness, Inc. (LTF) operates 83 multi-use sports, athletic, professional fitness, family recreation, resort and spa centers located across 18 states under the LIFE TIME FITNESS brand. LTF additionally operates a satellite center. The company's month-to-month membership plans typically include 24-hour access to over 400 pieces of cardio, resistance and free-weight training equipment; locker and towel service; a range of educational programs; and other amenities. The company operates 74 large format design centers, of which it considers 50 to be its current model design, which target roughly 8,500 to 11,500 memberships and average 113,000 square feet in size. Its centers provide group fitness studios; personal certified trainers; educational seminars; rock climbing walls; basketball courts; squash and racquetball courts; Pilates and yoga studios; dry saunas; whirlpools; indoor and outdoor aquatic centers featuring two-story waterslides, zero-depth recreation pools and a lap pool; a pool-side bistro; a child center featuring a play maze; a computer center; separate infant playrooms; a separate family locker room; LifeSpa, providing hair, nail, skin and therapeutic massage services; and LifeCafe, providing nutritional food and beverage services. In addition, 12 of LTF's current model and large format centers and its satellite center have tennis courts. In the fitness area, the company's centers are equipped with a comprehensive system of large screen televisions. LTF's small group activities include its TEAM (Training Education Accountability Motivation) Weight Loss program, which focuses on exercise, education and nutrition. In addition to offering regular and add-on package memberships, the firm also offers corporate memberships that can be customized according to company needs. LTF also publishes Experience Life, a magazine which offers health, fitness and quality-of-life topics. Subsidiary FCA Construction oversees the design and construction of each of the company's centers through opening and all remodels. In November 2008, the company opened a location in Westminster, Colorado.

FINANCIALS:

Sales and profits are in thousands of dollars—add 000 to get the full amount. 2008 Note: Financial information for 2008 was not available for all companies at press time.

2008 Sales: $769,621	2008 Profits: $71,821	**U.S. Stock Ticker: LTM**
2007 Sales: $655,786	2007 Profits: $68,019	**Int'l Ticker:** Int'l Exchange:
2006 Sales: $511,897	2006 Profits: $50,565	Employees: 250
2005 Sales: $390,116	2005 Profits: $41,213	Fiscal Year Ends: 12/31
2004 Sales: $312,033	2004 Profits: $25,338	Parent Company:

SALARIES/BENEFITS:

Pension Plan:	ESOP Stock Plan:	Profit Sharing:	Top Exec. Salary: $335,000	Bonus: $93,500
Savings Plan:	Stock Purch. Plan:		Second Exec. Salary: $335,000	Bonus: $93,500

OTHER THOUGHTS:

Apparent Women Officers or Directors: 1
Hot Spot for Advancement for Women/Minorities:

LOCATIONS: ("Y" = Yes)

West:	Southwest:	Midwest:	Southeast:	Northeast:	International:
Y	Y	Y	Y	Y	

Note: Financial information, benefits and other data can change quickly and may vary from those stated here.

LITTLE GYM INTERNATIONAL INC (THE)

www.thelittlegym.com

Industry Group Code: 713940 **Ranks within this company's industry group:** Sales: Profits:

Sports:		**Services:**		**Media:**		**Sales:**		**Facilities:**		**Other:**	
Leagues/Associations:		Food & Beverage:		TV:		Marketing:		Stadiums:		Gambling:	
Teams:		Agents:		Radio:		Ads:		Fitness Clubs:	Y	Apparel:	
Nonprofits:		Other:		Internet:		Tickets:		Golf Courses:		Equipment:	
Other:				Print:		Retail:		Ski Resorts:		Shoes:	
				Software:		Other:		Other:		Other:	

TYPES OF BUSINESS:

Children's Gymnasiums
Birthday Parties
Summer & Holiday Camps

BRANDS/DIVISIONS/AFFILIATES:

CONTACTS:

Note: Officers with more than one job title may be intentionally listed here more than once.

Robert Bingham, CEO
Robert Bingham, Pres.
Michael Gragg, CFO/Sr. VP
Gerald Moore, VP-Real Estate Dev.

Phone: 480-948-2878	**Fax:** 480-948-2765
Toll-Free:	
Address: 7001 N. Scottsdale Rd., Ste. 1050, Scottsdale, AZ 85253 US	

GROWTH PLANS/SPECIAL FEATURES:

The Little Gym International, Inc. provides various exercise programs for children between the ages of four months to 12 years old. Programs are offered through approximately 300 franchised locations throughout 35 U.S. states and 20 countries around the world. The programs focus on developing motor skills, as well as striving to foster social, emotional and intellectual skills. Additionally, the firm's programs are structured in a manner that fosters a non-competitive, warm, nurturing environment. The children participate in several activities such as gymnastics, sports skills development, dance, cheerleading, karate, as well as several parent/child classes. The company offers two gymnastics programs: pre-school/kindergarten gymnastics and grade school gymnastics. Pre-school/kindergarten gymnastics classes caters to children between the ages of three to six; while the grade school gymnastics program works with children between the ages of six and 12 years old. The programs focus on strength and flexibility training; improving skill proficiency; and group participation. The sports skills classes, for children ages 3-6, offer basic training in throwing, kicking, catching and striking, taught while playing soccer, baseball, basketball and football. The Little Gym's dance program, for children ages 3-12, teaches children tap, ballet, creative movement, and basic gymnastics to improve balance, posture and grace. These classes are designed to help the children build strength and coordination as well as basic motor skills. Cheerleading classes, for children ages 3-12, focus primarily on teambuilding exercises, in addition to chants; cheering; jumps; gymnastics; stunts; and tumbling. Karate classes, for children ages 4-12, combine music with other activities to teach the basics of karate. The Little Gym also offers summer and holiday camps, for children ages 2-8. Additionally, facilities may be rented to host birthday parties for children ages 1-10, with the firm handling everything from invitations to clean-up, including providing music, activities and games designed specifically for each child.

FINANCIALS:

Sales and profits are in thousands of dollars—add 000 to get the full amount. 2008 Note: Financial information for 2008 was not available for all companies at press time.

2008 Sales: $	2008 Profits: $	**U.S. Stock Ticker: Private**
2007 Sales: $	2007 Profits: $	**Int'l Ticker:** Int'l Exchange:
2006 Sales: $87,600	2006 Profits: $	Employees: 45
2005 Sales: $	2005 Profits: $	Fiscal Year Ends:
2004 Sales: $	2004 Profits: $	Parent Company:

SALARIES/BENEFITS:

Pension Plan:	ESOP Stock Plan:	Profit Sharing:	Top Exec. Salary: $	Bonus: $
Savings Plan:	Stock Purch. Plan:		Second Exec. Salary: $	Bonus: $

OTHER THOUGHTS:

Apparent Women Officers or Directors:
Hot Spot for Advancement for Women/Minorities:

LOCATIONS: ("Y" = Yes)

West:	Southwest:	Midwest:	Southeast:	Northeast:	International:
Y	Y	Y	Y	Y	Y

LIVERPOOL FOOTBALL CLUB

www.liverpoolfc.tv

Industry Group Code: 711211D **Ranks within this company's industry group:** Sales: 3 Profits: 4

Sports:		Services:		Media:		Sales:		Facilities:		Other:	
Leagues/Associations:		Food & Beverage:		TV:		Marketing:	Y	Stadiums:	Y	Gambling:	
Teams:	Y	Agents:		Radio:		Ads:	Y	Fitness Clubs:		Apparel:	
Nonprofits:		Other:		Internet:		Tickets:	Y	Golf Courses:		Equipment:	
Other:				Print:		Retail:	Y	Ski Resorts:		Shoes:	
				Software:		Other:		Other:		Other:	

TYPES OF BUSINESS:

Professional Soccer Team
Ticket Sales
Merchandise
Advertising
Youth Programs
Women's Soccer

GROWTH PLANS/SPECIAL FEATURES:

The Liverpool Football Club is a professional English football club based in Liverpool. The club plays in the English Premier League, and it has historically enjoyed tremendous winning success. Liverpool FC was founded in 1892 by John Houlding. In its long history, the club has won 18 First Division titles, seven League Cups, seven FA Cups and five European Cups. The team's most recent big success was in 2001 when they took the FA Cup, England's elite, club soccer tournament, in a win over the London-based team Arsenal. The team has an Official Liverpool Supporters Club now in its sixth year. The Supporters Club provides fans with discounts on club merchandise, team magazine subscriptions and a historical highlights DVD, among other things, for a seasonal fee of around $60. Reebok supplies the club with uniforms and Carlsburg sponsors the team. The broadcasting rights and ticket sales with concessions supply the majority of club's revenue. Liverpool FC plays at Anfield, a football stadium in the district of Anfield in Liverpool. The team has played at Anfield since its inception in 1892. The stadium holds 45,362 and it is owned by Liverpool FC. The team regularly sells out home games, and in its most recent season had an average attendance of 45,362. In June 2008, the franchise started construction on a new 60,000-seat stadium next to its current stadium. The new facility is expected to be completed by 2011.

BRANDS/DIVISIONS/AFFILIATES:

Official Liverpool Supporters Club

CONTACTS: *Note: Officers with more than one job title may be intentionally listed here more than once.*

Rick N. Parry, CEO
Rafael Benitez, Head Coach
Tom Hicks, Co-Chmn.
George Gillett, Jr., Co-Chmn.

Phone: 44-151-263-2361 **Fax:** 44-151-260-8813
Toll-Free:
Address: Anfield Rd., Liverpool, L4 OTH UK

FINANCIALS: **Sales and profits are in thousands of dollars—add 000 to get the full amount. 2008 Note: Financial information for 2008 was not available for all companies at press time.**

2008 Sales: $332,000
2007 Sales: $269,000
2006 Sales: $225,000
2005 Sales: $219,000
2004 Sales: $170,000

2008 Profits: $50,000
2007 Profits: $60,000
2006 Profits: $37,000
2005 Profits: $13,200
2004 Profits: $-33,200

U.S. Stock Ticker: Private
Int'l Ticker: Int'l Exchange:
Employees: 1,025
Fiscal Year Ends: 7/31
Parent Company:

SALARIES/BENEFITS:

Pension Plan: ESOP Stock Plan: Profit Sharing: Top Exec. Salary: $ Bonus: $
Savings Plan: Stock Purch. Plan: Second Exec. Salary: $ Bonus: $

OTHER THOUGHTS:

Apparent Women Officers or Directors:
Hot Spot for Advancement for Women/Minorities:

LOCATIONS: ("Y" = Yes)

West:	Southwest:	Midwest:	Southeast:	Northeast:	International:
					Y

LOS ANGELES ANGELS OF ANAHEIM

angels.mlb.com

Industry Group Code: 711211A **Ranks within this company's industry group:** Sales: 7 Profits: 23

Sports:		Services:		Media:		Sales:		Facilities:		Other:	
Leagues/Associations:		Food & Beverage:		TV:		Marketing:		Stadiums:	Y	Gambling:	
Teams:	Y	Agents:		Radio:		Ads:		Fitness Clubs:		Apparel:	
Nonprofits:		Other:		Internet:		Tickets:	Y	Golf Courses:		Equipment:	
Other:				Print:		Retail:	Y	Ski Resorts:		Shoes:	
				Software:		Other:		Other:		Other:	

TYPES OF BUSINESS:

Professional Baseball Team
Stadium Operation

BRANDS/DIVISIONS/AFFILIATES:

Angels Baseball, L.P.
Angel Stadium of Anaheim
Salt Lake Bees
Arkansas Travelers
Rancho Cucamonga Quakes
Cedar Rapids Kernels
Tempe Angels
Orem Owlz

CONTACTS: *Note: Officers with more than one job title may be intentionally listed here more than once.*

Dennis Kuhl, Pres.
Bill Beverage, CFO
John Carpino, Sr. VP-Sales & Mktg.
Jenny Price, Dir.-Human Resources
Al Castro, Mgr.-Info. Svcs.
Sam Maida, Dir.-Ballpark Oper.
David Cohen, Dir.-Legal Affairs & Risk Mgmt.
Tory Hernandez, Mgr.-Baseball Oper.
Tim Mead, VP-Comm.
Molly Taylor, VP-Finance
Tony Reagins, Gen. Mgr.
Bill Stoneman, Sr. Advisor
Robert Alvarado, VP-Mktg. & Ticket Sales
Richard McClemmy, VP-Corp. Sales
Arturo Moreno, Owner
Ron Sparks, Mgr.-Purchasing

Phone: 714-940-2000	**Fax:** 714-940-2001
Toll-Free:	
Address: 2000 Gene Autrey Way, Anaheim, CA 92806 US	

GROWTH PLANS/SPECIAL FEATURES:

The Los Angeles Angels of Anaheim, owned and operated by Angels Baseball LP, are a Major League Baseball (MLB) franchise. Originally owned by singer and actor Gene Autry, the team began playing in the American League in 1961. In 1966, the Angels moved into a new ballpark in Anaheim, and became the California Angels. The 1970s were kind to the Angels, as they acquired legendary pitcher Nolan Ryan from the New York Mets in 1972. In California, Ryan pitched four no-hitters, and in 1973, he struck out 383 batters to set a new single season strikeout record. In 1979, though, general manager Buzzie Bavasi ignominiously let Ryan become a free agent. Throughout the 1970s and 1980s, the Angels would come quite close to playing in the World Series, yet would continually fall just short. In 1996, the team was acquired by the Disney Corporation and the California Angels became the Anaheim Angels. In 2002, the Angels at last won a World Series, defeating intra-state rivals in San Francisco. In 2003, the Angels were sold to Angels Baseball, L.P., a group headed by advertising entrepreneur Arturo Moreno; Moreno thereby became the first Hispanic baseball team owner. In 2005, the Angels changed their name yet again, this time to their current moniker, the Los Angeles Angels of Anaheim. The team, which plays at Angel Stadium of Anaheim, still plays a secondary role to the Dodgers in L.A., though they have finished no worse than fifth the last four years in overall attendance. The organization has a baseball complex at San Pedro de Macoris in the Dominican Republic. Forbes recently valued the Angels franchise at $509 million. In the 2008 season, the team averaged approximately 41,200 fans in attendance per game.

FINANCIALS: **Sales and profits are in thousands of dollars—add 000 to get the full amount. 2008 Note: Financial information for 2008 was not available for all companies at press time.**

2008 Sales: $212,000	2008 Profits: $10,300	**U.S. Stock Ticker: Private**
2007 Sales: $200,000	2007 Profits: $15,200	**Int'l Ticker:** Int'l Exchange:
2006 Sales: $187,000	2006 Profits: $11,500	Employees:
2005 Sales: $167,000	2005 Profits: $	Fiscal Year Ends: 12/31
2004 Sales: $	2004 Profits: $	Parent Company: ANGELS BASEBALL LP

SALARIES/BENEFITS:

Pension Plan:	ESOP Stock Plan:	Profit Sharing:	Top Exec. Salary: $	Bonus: $
Savings Plan:	Stock Purch. Plan:		Second Exec. Salary: $	Bonus: $

OTHER THOUGHTS:

Apparent Women Officers or Directors: 2
Hot Spot for Advancement for Women/Minorities: Y

LOCATIONS: ("Y" = Yes)

West:	Southwest:	Midwest:	Southeast:	Northeast:	International:
Y					Y

LOS ANGELES CLIPPERS

www.nba.com/clippers

Industry Group Code: 711211B **Ranks within this company's industry group:** Sales: 24 Profits: 13

Sports:		Services:		Media:		Sales:		Facilities:		Other:	
Leagues/Associations:		Food & Beverage:		TV:		Marketing:		Stadiums:		Gambling:	
Teams:	Y	Agents:		Radio:		Ads:		Fitness Clubs:		Apparel:	
Nonprofits:		Other:		Internet:		Tickets:	Y	Golf Courses:		Equipment:	
Other:				Print:		Retail:	Y	Ski Resorts:		Shoes:	
				Software:		Other:		Other:		Other:	

TYPES OF BUSINESS:

Professional Basketball Team
Sports Merchandise
Ticket Sales

BRANDS/DIVISIONS/AFFILIATES:

Staples Center
Spirit Dance Team
Carl's Jr. Fan Patrol
Jr. Jam Squad
Los Angeles Clippers Fastbreak to Fitness
Los Angeles Clippers Foundation
Clippers Charity Golf Classic

CONTACTS: *Note: Officers with more than one job title may be intentionally listed here more than once.*

Donald T. Sterling, Owner
Carl Lahr, Sr. VP-Mktg. & Sales
Lori Balsamo, Human Resources Admin.
Bob Platt, General Counsel
Elgin Baylor, VP-Basketball Oper.
Joe Safety, VP-Corp. Comm.
Donna Johnson, VP-Finance
Mike Dunleavy, Head Coach
Christian Howard, VP-Mktg. & Broadcasting
Donald T. Sterling, Chmn.

Phone: 213-742-7500 **Fax:** 213-742-7570
Toll-Free:
Address: Staples Center, 1111 S. Figueroa St., Ste. 1100, Los Angeles, CA 90015 US

GROWTH PLANS/SPECIAL FEATURES:

The Los Angeles Clippers originally joined the National Basketball Association (NBA) in 1970 as the Buffalo Braves and changed its name to the San Diego Clippers in 1978 after its subsequent relocation to California. In 1984, the Clippers moved to Los Angeles and officially become known as the Los Angeles Clippers. The Clippers play all home games at the Staples Center, which is situated in downtown Los Angeles. The $375 million arena was opened in 1999 and is home to an additional four sports franchises: The Los Angeles Lakers, Los Angeles Sparks, Los Angeles Kings and the Los Angeles Avengers. There are 1,200 television monitors, 23 refreshment stands and an 18,997 seating capacity. Game night entertainment includes the Spirit Dance Team, the Carl's Jr. Fan Patrol and the Jr. Jam Squad. Community outreach programs include the Los Angeles Clippers Fastbreak to Fitness and the Los Angeles Clippers Foundation, which offers the Clippers Charity Golf Classic and various scholarships to college bound students. Although the Clippers have had few successes in advancing to the playoffs in the past, the Clippers finally participated in the playoffs in the 2005-06 season. However, the Clippers were unable to win a spot in the 2006-07 or 2007-08 NBA playoffs. Forbes Magazine recently estimated the team to be worth approximately $297 million. In the 2008-09 season, the team's home attendance average was roughly 16,200 per game.

FINANCIALS: **Sales and profits are in thousands of dollars—add 000 to get the full amount. 2008 Note: Financial information for 2008 was not available for all companies at press time.**

2008 Sales: $99,000	2008 Profits: $10,700	**U.S. Stock Ticker: Private**
2007 Sales: $98,000	2007 Profits: $9,800	**Int'l Ticker:** Int'l Exchange:
2006 Sales: $95,000	2006 Profits: $15,700	Employees:
2005 Sales: $83,000	2005 Profits: $	Fiscal Year Ends: 7/31
2004 Sales: $77,000	2004 Profits: $	Parent Company:

SALARIES/BENEFITS:

Pension Plan:	ESOP Stock Plan:	Profit Sharing:	Top Exec. Salary: $	Bonus: $
Savings Plan:	Stock Purch. Plan:		Second Exec. Salary: $	Bonus: $

OTHER THOUGHTS:

Apparent Women Officers or Directors: 2
Hot Spot for Advancement for Women/Minorities: Y

LOCATIONS: ("Y" = Yes)

West:	Southwest:	Midwest:	Southeast:	Northeast:	International:
Y					

LOS ANGELES DODGERS

losangeles.dodgers.mlb.com

Industry Group Code: 711211A **Ranks within this company's industry group:** Sales: 4 Profits: 18

Sports:		Services:		Media:		Sales:		Facilities:		Other:	
Leagues/Associations:		Food & Beverage:		TV:		Marketing:		Stadiums:	Y	Gambling:	
Teams:	Y	Agents:		Radio:		Ads:		Fitness Clubs:		Apparel:	
Nonprofits:		Other:		Internet:		Tickets:	Y	Golf Courses:		Equipment:	
Other:				Print:		Retail:	Y	Ski Resorts:		Shoes:	
				Software:		Other:		Other:		Other:	

TYPES OF BUSINESS:

Professional Baseball Team
Stadium Operation
Baseball Academy

BRANDS/DIVISIONS/AFFILIATES:

Dodgers Stadium
Albuquerque Isotopes
Chattanooga Lookouts
Great Lakes Loons
Ogden Raptors
Arizona League Dodgers
Santo Domingo Dodgers
Inland Empire 66ers

CONTACTS: *Note: Officers with more than one job title may be intentionally listed here more than once.*

Jamie McCourt, CEO
Dennis Mannion, COO
Dennis Mannion, Pres.
Peter Wilhelm, CFO
Joe Walsh, VP-Human Resources
Marco White, VP-IT
Vanessa Leyvas, Dir.-Admin., Creative & Comm.
Sam Fernandez, General Counsel/Sr. VP
Ellen Harrigan, Dir.-Baseball Oper.
Josh Rawitch, VP-Comm.
Marlo Vandemore, VP-Finance
Ned Colletti, Gen. Mgr.
David Siegel, Dir.-Ticket Sales
Kim Ng, VP/Assistant Gen. Mgr.
Charles Steinberg, Exec. VP-Creative & Comm.
Frank McCourt, Chmn./Owner
Joseph Reaves, Dir.-Int'l Oper.

Phone: 323-224-1500	**Fax:** 323-224-1269
Toll-Free:	
Address: 1000 Elysian Park Ave., Los Angeles, CA 90012-1199 US	

GROWTH PLANS/SPECIAL FEATURES:

The Los Angeles Dodgers are an organization within Major League Baseball (MLB). The team was founded in 1884 in Brooklyn and had several other names before settling on Dodgers in 1932. The team moved west in 1957, becoming the Los Angeles Dodgers. The franchise made baseball history while still in Brooklyn, becoming the first MLB team to allow a black player, Jackie Robinson, to join its roster. Other famous Dodgers include Roy Campanella, Pee Wee Reese, Don Drysdale, Sandy Koufax, Orel Hershiser, Ralph Branca and manager Tommy Lasorda, who led the team to its 1981 and 1988 World Series wins and is now special advisor to the chairman in the team's front office. The Dodgers play home games for up to 56,000 spectators at Dodgers Stadium, built for roughly $23 million in 1962. One of baseball's most venerable franchises, the Dodgers have won six World Series titles, 21 pennants and 10 division titles and made 30 post-season appearances. The team hasn't been back to the World Series since 1988, despite making it to postseason play in 1995, 1996, 2004, 2006 and 2008. The Dodgers, who have been owned by Boston real estate developer Frank McCourt since 2004, went in a different direction with their management after an injury-riddled and disappointing 2005. General manager Paul DePodesta, known for his reliance on statistical analysis and the science of sabermetrics, was replaced by the more traditionally-minded Ned Colletti. The team surged to 88 wins and a Wild Card playoff berth in 2006. The 2008 season ended with 84 wins, 78 losses and another division title for the team. The Dodgers have been in the top three MLB teams in attendance every year since 2003, and were recently valued by Forbes at $722 million, 4th in baseball. Average home attendance in 2008 was 46,000.

FINANCIALS: **Sales and profits are in thousands of dollars—add 000 to get the full amount. 2008 Note: Financial information for 2008 was not available for all companies at press time.**

2008 Sales: $241,000	2008 Profits: $16,500	**U.S. Stock Ticker: Subsidiary**
2007 Sales: $224,000	2007 Profits: $20,000	**Int'l Ticker:** Int'l Exchange:
2006 Sales: $211,000	2006 Profits: $27,500	Employees:
2005 Sales: $189,000	2005 Profits: $	Fiscal Year Ends: 10/31
2004 Sales: $	2004 Profits: $	Parent Company: LOS ANGELES DODGERS INC

SALARIES/BENEFITS:

Pension Plan:	ESOP Stock Plan:	Profit Sharing:	Top Exec. Salary: $	Bonus: $
Savings Plan:	Stock Purch. Plan:		Second Exec. Salary: $	Bonus: $

OTHER THOUGHTS:

Apparent Women Officers or Directors: 14
Hot Spot for Advancement for Women/Minorities: Y

LOCATIONS: ("Y" = Yes)

West:	Southwest:	Midwest:	Southeast:	Northeast:	International:
Y					Y

LOS ANGELES GALAXY

la.galaxy.mlsnet.com

Industry Group Code: 711211D **Ranks within this company's industry group:** Sales: Profits:

Sports:		Services:		Media:		Sales:		Facilities:		Other:	
Leagues/Associations:		Food & Beverage:		TV:		Marketing:		Stadiums:		Gambling:	
Teams:	Y	Agents:		Radio:		Ads:		Fitness Clubs:		Apparel:	
Nonprofits:		Other:		Internet:		Tickets:	Y	Golf Courses:		Equipment:	
Other:				Print:		Retail:	Y	Ski Resorts:		Shoes:	
				Software:		Other:		Other:		Other:	

TYPES OF BUSINESS:

Major League Soccer Team

BRANDS/DIVISIONS/AFFILIATES:

Anschutz Entertainment Group
Home Depot Center
Cozmo

CONTACTS:

Note: Officers with more than one job title may be intentionally listed here more than once.

Alexi Lalas, Pres./Gen. Mgr.
Veronica Avila, Dir.-Mktg.
Martha Romero, Dir.-Admin.
James Shilkret, Dir.-Oper.
Patrick Donnelly, Dir.-Comm.
Tim Martin, Sr. Dir.-Sales
Blane Shepard, Dir.-Special Projects
Maria Vega, Mgr.-Ticket Oper.
Bruce Arena, Head Coach/Gen. Mgr.

Phone: 310-630-2200 **Fax:** 310-630-2250

Toll-Free: 877-342-5299

Address: Home Depot Center. 18400 Avalon Blvd., Ste. 200, Carson, CA 90746 US

GROWTH PLANS/SPECIAL FEATURES:

The Los Angeles Galaxy, one of the 10 founding members of Major League Soccer (MLS), is a team owned by Anschutz Entertainment Group, a leading sports and entertainment presenter. The Galaxy plays in MLS's Western Division, alongside teams such as Chivas USA, the Colorado Rapids, FC Dallas, Houston Dynamo, San Jose Earthquakes and Real Salt Lake. The team continues to expand its corporate sponsorship. It is actively involved in community outreach programs and soccer organizations. The team's mascot is an extraterrestrial frog named Cozmo. The Galaxy plays its home games at the Home Depot Center, which has a capacity of 27,000. The team doubled up on its MLS Cup Championships with a 2005 victory over the New England Revolution in the finals, adding to the title the club won in 2002. The 2005 season also saw the team with a win at the U.S. Open Cup Championship. The team has hosted a number of MLS's star players, including forward Landon Donovan, defender Alexi Lalas and midfielder Paul Caligiuri. In 2007, the club recruited international superstar David Beckham from Real Madrid in a deal reportedly worth $50 million. The Galaxy are the first team in the MLS to take advantage of the so-called Designated Player Rule, which permits a team to sign one player considered to be outside of the teams' salary cap. In May 2008, the team obtained their first winning record in two years and won first place in the Western Division by beating the Kansas City Wizards 3-1. However, in August, after a 3-2 loss to the San Jose Earthquakes, the Galaxy had a seven-game losing streak and fell outside of playoff contention.

FINANCIALS:

Sales and profits are in thousands of dollars—add 000 to get the full amount. 2008 Note: Financial information for 2008 was not available for all companies at press time.

2008 Sales: $	2008 Profits: $	**U.S. Stock Ticker: Subsidiary**
2007 Sales: $	2007 Profits: $	**Int'l Ticker:** Int'l Exchange:
2006 Sales: $	2006 Profits: $	Employees:
2005 Sales: $	2005 Profits: $	Fiscal Year Ends:
2004 Sales: $	2004 Profits: $	Parent Company: ANSCHUTZ ENTERTAINMENT GROUP

SALARIES/BENEFITS:

Pension Plan:	ESOP Stock Plan:	Profit Sharing:	Top Exec. Salary: $	Bonus: $
Savings Plan:	Stock Purch. Plan:		Second Exec. Salary: $	Bonus: $

OTHER THOUGHTS:

Apparent Women Officers or Directors: 5
Hot Spot for Advancement for Women/Minorities: Y

LOCATIONS: ("Y" = Yes)

West:	Southwest:	Midwest:	Southeast:	Northeast:	International:
Y					

LOS ANGELES KINGS

kings.nhl.com

Industry Group Code: 711211F **Ranks within this company's industry group:** Sales: 14 Profits: 15

Sports:		Services:		Media:		Sales:		Facilities:		Other:	
Leagues/Associations:		Food & Beverage:		TV:		Marketing:		Stadiums:	Y	Gambling:	
Teams:	Y	Agents:		Radio:		Ads:		Fitness Clubs:		Apparel:	
Nonprofits:	Y	Other:		Internet:		Tickets:	Y	Golf Courses:		Equipment:	
Other:				Print:		Retail:	Y	Ski Resorts:		Shoes:	
				Software:		Other:		Other:		Other:	

TYPES OF BUSINESS:

National Hockey League Team

BRANDS/DIVISIONS/AFFILIATES:

Staples Center
Manchester Monarchs

CONTACTS:

Note: Officers with more than one job title may be intentionally listed here more than once.

Timothy J. (Tim) Leiweke, Governor
Dan Beckerman, COO/Exec. VP
Dean Lombardi, Pres./Gen. Mgr.
Dan Beckerman, CFO/Exec. VP
Chris McGowan, Sr. VP/Chief Mktg. Officer
LaShawnda Mikhael, Mgr.-Human Resources
Sean Ryan, VP-Merch.
Jeff Solomon, VP-Legal Affairs
Luc Robitaille, Pres., Bus. Oper.
Ben Robert, VP-Bus. Dev.
Mario Herrera, Coordinator-New Media
Michael Altieri, VP-Comm. & Broadcasting
Philip F. Anschutz, Co-Owner
Edward P. Roski, Jr., Co-Owner
Ron Hextall, VP/Assistant Gen. Mgr.
Terry Murray, Head Coach

Phone: 213-742-7100 **Fax:** 213-742-7296
Toll-Free:
Address: 1111 S. Figueroa St., Ste. 3100, Los Angeles, CA 90015 US

GROWTH PLANS/SPECIAL FEATURES:

The Los Angeles Kings Hockey Club LP is a professional hockey team playing for the National Hockey League (NHL). The most famous King in club history is Wayne Gretzky, who led the team to a 1993 Championship game. Unfortunately, the Kings lost that game to the Montreal Canadians and have yet to win a Stanley Cup. However, the showing did lead to spreading enthusiasm for hockey across Southern California. Other team heroes have included Marcel Dionne and Luc Robitaille. The Kings play home games at the Staples Center, a $375 million facility that is also home to five other professional sports franchises. The team is owned by Denver billionaire Philip Anschutz and his Anschutz Entertainment Group (AEG), which also owns the Staples Center, along with Los Angeles developer Edward Roski. The team's minor league affiliates include the Manchester Monarchs of the American Hockey League (AHL). During the 2008-09 season, the Kings ranked 21 in NHL average attendance ratings, with an average home game attendance of 16,488. The Kings opened the 2007-08 NHL regular season at the new O2 Arena in London, owned by the team's parent AEG. The games were the team's first ever to be played outside of North America and the first ever NHL regular season games to be played in Europe. Forbes recently estimated the team to be worth approximately $210 million.

FINANCIALS:

Sales and profits are in thousands of dollars—add 000 to get the full amount. 2008 Note: Financial information for 2008 was not available for all companies at press time.

2008 Sales: $91,000	2008 Profits: $1,200	**U.S. Stock Ticker: Subsidiary**
2007 Sales: $84,000	2007 Profits: $2,000	**Int'l Ticker:** Int'l Exchange:
2006 Sales: $82,000	2006 Profits: $7,100	Employees:
2005 Sales: $	2005 Profits: $	Fiscal Year Ends: 7/31
2004 Sales: $80,000	2004 Profits: $	Parent Company: ANSCHUTZ ENTERTAINMENT GROUP

SALARIES/BENEFITS:

Pension Plan:	ESOP Stock Plan:	Profit Sharing:	Top Exec. Salary: $	Bonus: $
Savings Plan:	Stock Purch. Plan:		Second Exec. Salary: $	Bonus: $

OTHER THOUGHTS:

Apparent Women Officers or Directors: 23
Hot Spot for Advancement for Women/Minorities: Y

LOCATIONS: ("Y" = Yes)

West:	Southwest:	Midwest:	Southeast:	Northeast:	International:
Y					

Note: Financial information, benefits and other data can change quickly and may vary from those stated here.

LOS ANGELES LAKERS

www.nba.com/lakers

Industry Group Code: 711211B **Ranks within this company's industry group:** Sales: 2 Profits: 2

Sports:		Services:		Media:		Sales:		Facilities:		Other:	
Leagues/Associations:		Food & Beverage:		TV:		Marketing:		Stadiums:		Gambling:	
Teams:	Y	Agents:		Radio:		Ads:		Fitness Clubs:		Apparel:	
Nonprofits:		Other:		Internet:		Tickets:	Y	Golf Courses:		Equipment:	
Other:				Print:		Retail:	Y	Ski Resorts:		Shoes:	
				Software:		Other:		Other:		Other:	

TYPES OF BUSINESS:

Professional Basketball Team

BRANDS/DIVISIONS/AFFILIATES:

Los Angeles Lakers, Inc.
Los Angeles Sparks

CONTACTS:

Note: Officers with more than one job title may be intentionally listed here more than once.

Jerry Buss, Pres.
Jeanie Buss, Exec. VP-Bus. Oper.
Ronnie Lester, Asst. Gen. Mgr.
Phil Jackson, Head Coach
Kareem Abdul-Jabbar, Assistant Coach
Gary Vitti, Athletic Trainer
Jerry Buss, Chmn.

Phone: 310-426-6000	**Fax:**
Toll-Free:	
Address: 555 N. Nash St., El Segundo, CA 90245 US	

GROWTH PLANS/SPECIAL FEATURES:

The Los Angeles Lakers basketball team, founded in 1946, has made significant contributions within the National Basketball Association (NBA), setting records that include the highest winning percentage (60%), highest number of finals appearances (30), second highest number of championships (15) and the most consecutive wins within a season (33). The team is owned and operated by The Los Angeles Lakers, Inc. The Lakers originally joined the NBL as the Minneapolis Lakers, and was later renamed the Los Angeles Lakers after the team moved to California in 1960. The Lakers have had a long history of Hall of Fame players, including Wilt 'The Stilt' Chamberlain, Earvin 'Magic' Johnson, Kareem Abdul-Jabbar and Jerry West. Other notable members of the team include legendary coach Phil Jackson, Kobe Bryant and (formerly) Shaquille O'Neal. In the 2008-2009 season, the Lakers overcame the Orlando Magic to win the NBA World Championship. The Lakers play at the Staples Center, a $375 million facility in downtown Los Angeles with an 18,997 seating capacity. Forbes Magazine recently estimated the team to be worth approximately $584 million. In the 2008-09 season, the team's home attendance average was roughly 19,000 per game. The franchise hosts a variety of community outreach programs such as CourtStars Clinics, Zoom Kobe 1 and the Los Angeles Lakers Youth foundation, which assists nonprofit communities in the use of athletics to promote education.

FINANCIALS:

Sales and profits are in thousands of dollars—add 000 to get the full amount. 2008 Note: Financial information for 2008 was not available for all companies at press time.

2008 Sales: $191,000	2008 Profits: $47,900	**U.S. Stock Ticker: Subsidiary**
2007 Sales: $170,000	2007 Profits: $31,800	**Int'l Ticker:** Int'l Exchange:
2006 Sales: $167,000	2006 Profits: $33,300	Employees:
2005 Sales: $156,000	2005 Profits: $	Fiscal Year Ends: 7/31
2004 Sales: $170,000	2004 Profits: $	Parent Company: LOS ANGELES LAKERS INC

SALARIES/BENEFITS:

Pension Plan:	ESOP Stock Plan:	Profit Sharing:	Top Exec. Salary: $	Bonus: $
Savings Plan:	Stock Purch. Plan:		Second Exec. Salary: $	Bonus: $

OTHER THOUGHTS:

Apparent Women Officers or Directors: 1
Hot Spot for Advancement for Women/Minorities:

LOCATIONS: ("Y" = Yes)

West:	Southwest:	Midwest:	Southeast:	Northeast:	International:
Y					

LOS ANGELES SPARKS

www.wnba.com/sparks

Industry Group Code: 711211E **Ranks within this company's industry group:** Sales: Profits:

Sports:		**Services:**		**Media:**		**Sales:**		**Facilities:**		**Other:**	
Leagues/Associations:		Food & Beverage:		TV:		Marketing:		Stadiums:		Gambling:	
Teams:	Y	Agents:		Radio:		Ads:		Fitness Clubs:		Apparel:	
Nonprofits:		Other:		Internet:		Tickets:	Y	Golf Courses:		Equipment:	
Other:				Print:		Retail:	Y	Ski Resorts:		Shoes:	
				Software:		Other:		Other:		Other:	

TYPES OF BUSINESS:

Women's National Basketball Association Team

BRANDS/DIVISIONS/AFFILIATES:

Staples Center
Cooper's Coaches Clinic
Read to Achieve
SparKids
Ole Skool Crew

CONTACTS: *Note: Officers with more than one job title may be intentionally listed here more than once.*

Kristin Bernert, Pres.
Libby Berlacher, Dir.-Mktg. & Event Prod.
Alayne Ingram, Dir.-Public Rel.
Aaron McLennan, Dir.-Finance
Carla Christofferson, Co-Owner
Katherine Goodman, Co-Owner
Michael Cooper, Head Coach
Penny Toler, Gen. Mgr./VP

Phone: 213-929-1300 **Fax:** 213-929-1325
Toll-Free:
Address: 888 S. Figueroa St., Ste. 2010, Los Angeles, CA 90017 US

GROWTH PLANS/SPECIAL FEATURES:

The Los Angeles Sparks are one of the eight original Women's National Basketball Association (WNBA) teams founded in 1997, and played in the WNBA's inaugural game against the New York Liberty. It lost that game, 57-67. The team made the playoffs eight years in a row, from 1999-2006, and won the WNBA Championship in 2001 and 2002. It is the sister team of the LA Lakers National Basketball Association (NBA) team. Long-time Sparks captain and WNBA icon Lisa Leslie has helped the U.S. women's basketball team take the gold metal in the 1996, 2000 and 2004 Olympics. Leslie has won virtually every WNBA award for exceptional play, and in 2002, she was the first women to dunk the ball in a game. The sparks head coach, Michael Cooper, is a former WNBA Coach of the Year. The team plays its home games at the Staples Center, an 18,977-seat arena that also plays host to the Lakers and LA Kings, a National Hockey League (NHL) team. Club community initiatives include Cooper's Coaches Clinic and Read to Achieve. The Sparks also sponsor the SparKids, a WNBA youth dance team for kids ages 8-13, and the Ole Skool Crew, a dance troop for women over 40 that have performed at Staples Center, Madison Square Garden, on TV and at various fitness, sports and dance exhibitions. The team plays in the Western Conference of the WBNA, with teams such as the Minnesota Lynx, Phoenix Mercury, Sacramento Monarchs, San Antonio Silver Stars and Seattle Storm. In the 2008 playoffs, the Sparks made it to the Western Finals, but lost game three to the San Antonio Silver Stars, stopping the Sparks from moving on to the WNBA finals.

FINANCIALS: **Sales and profits are in thousands of dollars—add 000 to get the full amount. 2008 Note: Financial information for 2008 was not available for all companies at press time.**

2008 Sales: $	2008 Profits: $	**U.S. Stock Ticker: Private**
2007 Sales: $	2007 Profits: $	**Int'l Ticker:** Int'l Exchange:
2006 Sales: $	2006 Profits: $	Employees:
2005 Sales: $	2005 Profits: $	Fiscal Year Ends:
2004 Sales: $	2004 Profits: $	Parent Company:

SALARIES/BENEFITS:

Pension Plan:	ESOP Stock Plan:	Profit Sharing:	Top Exec. Salary: $	Bonus: $
Savings Plan:	Stock Purch. Plan:		Second Exec. Salary: $	Bonus: $

OTHER THOUGHTS:

Apparent Women Officers or Directors: 6
Hot Spot for Advancement for Women/Minorities: Y

LOCATIONS: ("Y" = Yes)

West:	Southwest:	Midwest:	Southeast:	Northeast:	International:
Y					

LULULEMON ATHLETICA INC

www.lululemon.com

Industry Group Code: 315000A **Ranks within this company's industry group:** Sales: 7 Profits: 4

Sports:		Services:		Media:		Sales:		Facilities:		Other:	
Leagues/Associations:		Food & Beverage:		TV:		Marketing:		Stadiums:		Gambling:	
Teams:		Agents:		Radio:		Ads:		Fitness Clubs:		Apparel:	Y
Nonprofits:		Other:		Internet:		Tickets:		Golf Courses:		Equipment:	
Other:				Print:		Retail:		Ski Resorts:		Shoes:	
				Software:		Other:		Other:		Other:	

TYPES OF BUSINESS:

Athletic Apparel
Organic Products
Accessories

BRANDS/DIVISIONS/AFFILIATES:

lululemon athletica
oqoqo

CONTACTS:

Note: Officers with more than one job title may be intentionally listed here more than once.

Christine Day, CEO
John E. Currie, CFO
Sheree Waterson, Exec. VP-General Merch. Mgmt.
Dennis J. Wilson, Chief Prod. Designer
Dennis J. Wilson, Chmn.
Sheree Waterson, Exec. VP-Sourcing

Phone: 604-732-6124	**Fax:**
Toll-Free: 877-263-9300	
Address: 2285 Clark Dr., Vancouver, BC V5N 3G9 Canada	

GROWTH PLANS/SPECIAL FEATURES:

Lululemon Athletica, Inc. is a designer and retailer of technical athletic apparel in North America. Its yoga-inspired apparel is marketed under the lululemon athletica brand name. The company offers a comprehensive line of performance apparel and accessories for both women and men. The apparel assortment, including items such as fitness pants, shorts, tops and jackets, is designed for healthy lifestyle activities such as yoga, dance, running and general fitness. The firm's fitness-related accessories include an array of items such as bags, socks, hats, underwear, balance balls, yoga mats, yoga bricks, towels, water bottles and headbands. Lululemon currently incorporates the following fabrics in its products: luon, made of nylon and lycra, wicks away moisture, moves with the body and is designed to eliminate irritation; silverescent, which incorporates silver directly into the fabric to reduce odors as a result of antibacterial properties of the silver; vitasea, derived from a seaweed compound, which releases amino acids, minerals and vitamins directly into the skin; and Stretch French Terry, a fabric made from cotton, polyester and lyrca that holds shape well and allows for easy movement. The company also offers a line of casual, organic products made from at least 75% natural, organic or sustainable recyclable materials, such as soy, bamboo and vitasea. These products are typically sold under the oqoqo brand name. The firm sells its products through nearly 100 stores in Canada and the U.S. Most recently, the firm has opened stores in Maryland, Texas, New Jersey, Massachusetts, Washington State, Connecticut, New York, California and Washington, D.C. During 2008, the company closed its stores in Japan.

FINANCIALS:

Sales and profits are in thousands of dollars—add 000 to get the full amount. 2008 Note: Financial information for 2008 was not available for all companies at press time.

2008 Sales: $269,942	2008 Profits: $30,843	**U.S. Stock Ticker: LULU**
2007 Sales: $147,964	2007 Profits: $7,666	**Int'l Ticker:** Int'l Exchange:
2006 Sales: $84,129	2006 Profits: $1,394	Employees: 2,861
2005 Sales: $	2005 Profits: $	Fiscal Year Ends: 12/31
2004 Sales: $	2004 Profits: $	Parent Company:

SALARIES/BENEFITS:

Pension Plan:	ESOP Stock Plan:	Profit Sharing:	Top Exec. Salary: $568,200	Bonus: $477,288
Savings Plan:	Stock Purch. Plan:		Second Exec. Salary: $371,224	Bonus: $227,189

OTHER THOUGHTS:

Apparent Women Officers or Directors: 5
Hot Spot for Advancement for Women/Minorities: Y

LOCATIONS: ("Y" = Yes)

West:	Southwest:	Midwest:	Southeast:	Northeast:	International:
Y	Y	Y	Y	Y	Y

MAGNA ENTERTAINMENT CORP

www.magnaent.com

Industry Group Code: 713210 **Ranks within this company's industry group:** Sales: Profits:

Sports:		Services:		Media:		Sales:		Facilities:		Other:	
Leagues/Associations:		Food & Beverage:		TV:		Marketing:		Stadiums:		Gambling:	
Teams:		Agents:		Radio:		Ads:		Fitness Clubs:		Apparel:	
Nonprofits:		Other:		Internet:		Tickets:		Golf Courses:		Equipment:	
Other:				Print:		Retail:		Ski Resorts:		Shoes:	
				Software:		Other:		Other:	Y	Other:	

TYPES OF BUSINESS:

Racetracks-Horse Racing
Cable Television Network
Simulcasting
Account Wagering
Horse Bedding Products
Pari-Mutuel Gambling Information Technology

BRANDS/DIVISIONS/AFFILIATES:

StreuFex
Gulfstream Park
XpressBet
HorseRacing TV
Racetrack Television Network
Magnabet
TrackNet Media Group LLC
AmTote International Inc

CONTACTS: *Note: Officers with more than one job title may be intentionally listed here more than once.*

Frank Stronach, Interim CEO
Ron Charles, COO
Blake S. Tohana, CFO/Exec. VP
William G. Ford, Sec.
Mary L. Seymour, VP/Controller
Frank DeMarco, Jr., VP-Regulatory Affairs
Frank Stronach, Chmn.

Phone: 905-726-2462 **Fax:**
Toll-Free:
Address: 337 Magna Dr., Aurora, ON L4G 7K1 Canada

GROWTH PLANS/SPECIAL FEATURES:

Magna Entertainment Corp. (MEC) is a leading North American owner and operator of horse racetracks and one of the world's leading simulcast broadcasters of live racing content to inter-track, off-track and account wagering markets. The company currently operates or manages seven thoroughbred racetracks, including Santa Anita Park, Gulfstream Park, Pimlico Race Course, Laurel Park, Golden Gate Fields, Thistledown and Portland Meadows; one standardbred harness racing track, The Meadows; and two racetracks running both thoroughbred and standardbred meets, Lone Star Park at Grand Prairie and Remington Park. Three of the company's racetracks include casino operations. MEC operates off-track betting facilities and a national account wagering business named XpressBet, which permits customers to place wagers by telephone and over the Internet on horse races at over 100 North American racetracks and internationally on races in Australia, South Africa and Dubai. MEC also owns a European-based account wagering business known as Magnabet. MEC owns a 50% share in HorseRacingTV and a minority interest in the Racetrack Television Network. Churchill Downs Inc. (CDI) and MEC recently formed a joint venture called TrackNet Media Group LLC, through which the companies' respective horse racing content will be available to each company's various distribution platforms and to third parties. In addition, MEC, CDI and Racing UK Limited agreed to partner in a venture called Racing World that serves as a distribution vehicle for account wagering rights and audio-visual signals in the U.K. AmTote International, Inc., a provider of totalisator services to the pari-mutuel industry, is a wholly-owned subsidiary of MEC. The company also owns and operates several thoroughbred training centers: San Luis Rey Downs, in California; Palm Meadows Training Center in Florida; and Bowie Training Center in Maryland. The company also owns and operates production facilities in Austria and North Carolina for StreuFex, a straw-based horse bedding product. The firm filed for bankruptcy in March 2009.

FINANCIALS: **Sales and profits are in thousands of dollars—add 000 to get the full amount. 2008 Note: Financial information for 2008 was not available for all companies at press time.**

2008 Sales: $
2007 Sales: $625,715
2006 Sales: $574,198
2005 Sales: $526,663
2004 Sales: $683,393

2008 Profits: $
2007 Profits: $-113,759
2006 Profits: $-87,351
2005 Profits: $-105,293
2004 Profits: $-95,636

U.S. Stock Ticker: MECA
Int'l Ticker: MEC Int'l Exchange: Toronto-TSX
Employees: 5,300
Fiscal Year Ends: 12/31
Parent Company:

SALARIES/BENEFITS:

Pension Plan: ESOP Stock Plan: Profit Sharing: Top Exec. Salary: $508,558 Bonus: $
Savings Plan: Y Stock Purch. Plan: Second Exec. Salary: $280,740 Bonus: $117,703

OTHER THOUGHTS:

Apparent Women Officers or Directors: 1
Hot Spot for Advancement for Women/Minorities:

LOCATIONS: ("Y" = Yes)

West:	Southwest:	Midwest:	Southeast:	Northeast:	International:
Y	Y	Y	Y	Y	Y

MAJESTIC ATHLETIC

www.majesticathletic.com

Industry Group Code: 339920 **Ranks within this company's industry group:** Sales: Profits:

Sports:		Services:		Media:		Sales:		Facilities:		Other:	
Leagues/Associations:		Food & Beverage:		TV:		Marketing:		Stadiums:		Gambling:	
Teams:		Agents:		Radio:		Ads:		Fitness Clubs:		Apparel:	Y
Nonprofits:		Other:		Internet:		Tickets:		Golf Courses:		Equipment:	
Other:				Print:		Retail:		Ski Resorts:		Shoes:	
				Software:		Other:		Other:		Other:	

TYPES OF BUSINESS:

Professional Sports Uniforms
Apparel & Outerwear

BRANDS/DIVISIONS/AFFILIATES:

VF Imagewear, Inc.
VF Corp
Major League Baseball (MLB)
National Basketball Association (NBA)
Arena Football League LLC
National Pro Fastpitch Softball
MLB Authentic Collection
Majestic Clubhouse Store

CONTACTS: *Note: Officers with more than one job title may be intentionally listed here more than once.*

Faust Capobianco, III, CEO
Faust Capobianco, IV, Pres.
Matthew S. Hoffman, VP-Merch. & Brand Mgmt.
Faust Capobianco, III, Chmn.

Phone: 610-746-6800	**Fax:** 610-746-7728
Toll-Free:	
Address: 2320 Newlins Mill Rd., Easton, PA 18045 US	

GROWTH PLANS/SPECIAL FEATURES:

Majestic Athletic, a subsidiary of VF Imagewear, Inc., is one of the largest designers, marketers and manufacturers of athletic team uniforms, performance apparel and outerwear in the U.S. Majestic was acquired by VF Imageware, itself a subsidiary of VF Corp., in 2007. The company is the official, and exclusive, provider of apparel for Major League Baseball (MLB), the National Basketball Association (NBA), the Arena Football League (AFL), National Pro Fastpitch Softball and numerous college and university sports teams. Majestic provides all the teams of these leagues with uniforms, which include jackets, jerseys, MLB Authentic Collection outerwear, turtlenecks, t-shirts and fleece. All decorations and embroidery on Majestic products are done by hand. Majestic sporting gear can be found in retail stores such as Foot Locker, Champs, Sears, JC Penney and The Sports Authority, as well as at concession stands and sporting events. Subsidiary Majestic Athletic Europe markets clothing that combines MLB team logos with European urban street fashion influences, using licenses from the New York Yankees, LA Dodgers and Chicago White Sox. The firm's web site, majesticathletic.com, features apparel available for purchase online. It also offers Team Outfitter, a search feature geared toward coaches and league administrators that allows them to search for Majestic products and to find local authorized Majestic team dealers; and uniform news, a blog chronicling uniform events. In April 2009, the company opened its first retail store, the Majestic Clubhouse Store at Fenway Park in Boston.

FINANCIALS: **Sales and profits are in thousands of dollars—add 000 to get the full amount. 2008 Note: Financial information for 2008 was not available for all companies at press time.**

2008 Sales: $	2008 Profits: $	**U.S. Stock Ticker: Subsidiary**
2007 Sales: $29,800	2007 Profits: $	**Int'l Ticker:** Int'l Exchange:
2006 Sales: $	2006 Profits: $	Employees: 650
2005 Sales: $	2005 Profits: $	Fiscal Year Ends: 6/30
2004 Sales: $	2004 Profits: $	Parent Company: VF CORP

SALARIES/BENEFITS:

Pension Plan:	ESOP Stock Plan:	Profit Sharing:	Top Exec. Salary: $	Bonus: $
Savings Plan:	Stock Purch. Plan:		Second Exec. Salary: $	Bonus: $

OTHER THOUGHTS:

Apparent Women Officers or Directors:
Hot Spot for Advancement for Women/Minorities:

LOCATIONS: ("Y" = Yes)

West:	Southwest:	Midwest:	Southeast:	Northeast:	International:
				Y	Y

MAJOR LEAGUE BASEBALL (MLB)

mlb.mlb.com

Industry Group Code: 813990 **Ranks within this company's industry group:** Sales: Profits:

Sports:		Services:		Media:		Sales:		Facilities:		Other:	
Leagues/Associations:	Y	Food & Beverage:		TV:	Y	Marketing:	Y	Stadiums:		Gambling:	
Teams:		Agents:		Radio:		Ads:		Fitness Clubs:		Apparel:	
Nonprofits:		Other:	Y	Internet:	Y	Tickets:		Golf Courses:		Equipment:	
Other:				Print:		Retail:		Ski Resorts:		Shoes:	
				Software:		Other:		Other:		Other:	

TYPES OF BUSINESS:

Professional Baseball League

BRANDS/DIVISIONS/AFFILIATES:

National League
American League
All-Star Game
World Series
MLB Advanced Media LP
MLB Productions
MLB.TV
MLB Network

CONTACTS: *Note: Officers with more than one job title may be intentionally listed here more than once.*

Allan H. (Bud) Selig, Commissioner-Baseball
Robert A. DuPuy, COO
Robert A. DuPuy, Pres.
Rob Manfred, Exec. VP-Human Resources & Labor Rel.
John McHale, Jr., CIO
John McHale, Jr., Exec. VP-Admin.
Jimmie Lee Solomon, Exec. VP-Baseball Oper.
Jonathan Mariner, Exec. VP-Finance
Timothy J. Brosnan, Exec. VP-Bus.

Phone: 212-931-7800 **Fax:** 212-949-8636
Toll-Free:
Address: 245 Park Ave., 31st Fl., New York, NY 10167 US

GROWTH PLANS/SPECIAL FEATURES:

Major League Baseball (MLB), created through the mergers of the National League (NL) and the American League (AL), is the men's professional baseball league in the U.S., with 30 franchises in 28 cities. Both the NL and AL teams are divided into three regional divisions: Central, West and East. Each league team operates as a separate business, while the league sets official rules; regulates team ownership; collects licensing fees for merchandise; hires and maintains umpiring crews; and negotiates marketing and labor contracts. It also sells national broadcasting rights and distributes broadcasting fees to the teams. Regional broadcasting rights are held by each franchise. MLB's regular season consists of 162 games per team, running from April through the beginning of October. The post-season consists of two elimination rounds in the AL and NL, culminating in the World Series, a series played between the league champions. The organization also holds the All-Star Game, an exhibition game in early July. MLB players are represented by the powerful Major League Baseball Players Association (MLBPA), which called work stoppages in 1981 and 1994. Unlike the other major U.S. professional sports leagues, MLB does not have a cap on player salaries. However, the league does impose a luxury tax on team salaries that is redistributed amongst smaller clubs; since its inception in 2003, the New York Yankees, the Boston Red Sox, the Los Angeles Angels and the Detroit Tigers are the only teams to have paid the tax. The league's production and multimedia subsidiary is MLB Advanced Media, which maintains mlb.com and all 30 of the individual team web sites. MLB Productions is a video and broadcast subsidiary. In January 2009, MLB launched the MLB Network, a cable channel dedicated to coverage of baseball. MLB holds approximately two-thirds of the venture, with the remainder divided between Comcast, DirecTV, Time Warner and Cox Communications.

FINANCIALS: **Sales and profits are in thousands of dollars—add 000 to get the full amount. 2008 Note: Financial information for 2008 was not available for all companies at press time.**

2008 Sales: $	2008 Profits: $	**U.S. Stock Ticker: Private**
2007 Sales: $6,100,000	2007 Profits: $	**Int'l Ticker:** Int'l Exchange:
2006 Sales: $	2006 Profits: $	Employees:
2005 Sales: $	2005 Profits: $	Fiscal Year Ends: 10/31
2004 Sales: $4,100,000	2004 Profits: $	Parent Company:

SALARIES/BENEFITS:

Pension Plan:	ESOP Stock Plan:	Profit Sharing:	Top Exec. Salary: $	Bonus: $
Savings Plan:	Stock Purch. Plan:		Second Exec. Salary: $	Bonus: $

OTHER THOUGHTS:

Apparent Women Officers or Directors:
Hot Spot for Advancement for Women/Minorities:

LOCATIONS: ("Y" = Yes)

West:	Southwest:	Midwest:	Southeast:	Northeast:	International:
				Y	Y

MAJOR LEAGUE SOCCER (MLS)

www.mlsnet.com

Industry Group Code: 813990 **Ranks within this company's industry group:** Sales: Profits:

Sports:		Services:		Media:		Sales:		Facilities:		Other:	
Leagues/Associations:	Y	Food & Beverage:		TV:		Marketing:		Stadiums:		Gambling:	
Teams:		Agents:		Radio:		Ads:		Fitness Clubs:		Apparel:	
Nonprofits:		Other:		Internet:		Tickets:		Golf Courses:		Equipment:	
Other:				Print:		Retail:		Ski Resorts:		Shoes:	
				Software:		Other:		Other:		Other:	

TYPES OF BUSINESS:

Professional Soccer League

BRANDS/DIVISIONS/AFFILIATES:

MLS Cup
SuperDraft
Red Bull New York
Toronto FC
FC Dallas
Houston Dynamo
DC United
Los Angeles Galaxy

CONTACTS: *Note: Officers with more than one job title may be intentionally listed here more than once.*

Mark Abbott, Pres.
Sean Prendergast, CFO
Stu Crystal, VP-Mktg.
Susie Goldsmith, Dir.-Human Resources
William Z. Ordower, VP-Bus. & Legal Affairs
Evan Dabby, Sr. Dir.-Oper.
Nelson Rodriguez, Sr. VP-Bus. Dev.
, Mgr.-Online Sales
Ivan Gazidis, Deputy Commissioner
Don Garber, Commissioner
Douglas Quinn, Pres., Soccer United Mktg.
Will Wilson, Exec. VP-Int'l Bus.

Phone: 212-450-1200	**Fax:** 212-450-1302
Toll-Free:	
Address: 420 5th Ave., New York, NY 10018 US	

GROWTH PLANS/SPECIAL FEATURES:

Major League Soccer, LLC (MLS) is the U.S.'s 15-team men's professional soccer league. League teams compete from April to November with 30 regular season games per team, 15 at home and 15 away, and its championship game, the MLS Cup. The playoffs for the cup start in mid-October until the final championship match in mid-November. The league is organized into a two-conference format. The Eastern Conference includes the Chicago Fire, the Columbus Crew, D.C. United, Toronto FC, Kansas City Wizards, New York Red Bulls and New England Revolution. The Western Conference includes Club Deportivo Chivas, Colorado Rapids, FC Dallas, Los Angeles Galaxy, Real Salt Lake, San Jose Earthquakes, Seattle Sounders FC and Houston Dynamo. Each MLS team player roster is composed of up to 28 players: 18 players on the senior roster and no more than 10 players, but a minimum of six players, on the developmental roster. The senior roster can include up to four players designated as senior internationals (non-domestic players who turn 25 years or older during the season in question) and up to three youth international players (non-domestic and 24 years old or younger). Developmental roster players can be either domestic or international and must be 24 years of age or younger during the season. Unlike most established professional sports leagues, MLS contracts directly with the players in an effort to control spending and labor costs and share revenue. The league has instituted a Designated Player Rule, which allows each team one player exempted from the salary cap. Designated Players have included superstars such as David Beckham, Cuauhtemoc Blanco and Claudio Reyna. Nearly 95% of all league games can be viewed on live television. The league is on track to add at least three more teams in coming years, including Philidelphia (2010), Portland (2011) and Vancouver (2011).

FINANCIALS: **Sales and profits are in thousands of dollars—add 000 to get the full amount. 2008 Note: Financial information for 2008 was not available for all companies at press time.**

2008 Sales: $	2008 Profits: $	**U.S. Stock Ticker: Private**
2007 Sales: $11,300	2007 Profits: $	**Int'l Ticker:** Int'l Exchange:
2006 Sales: $	2006 Profits: $	Employees: 90
2005 Sales: $	2005 Profits: $	Fiscal Year Ends:
2004 Sales: $	2004 Profits: $	Parent Company:

SALARIES/BENEFITS:

Pension Plan:	ESOP Stock Plan:	Profit Sharing:	Top Exec. Salary: $	Bonus: $
Savings Plan:	Stock Purch. Plan:		Second Exec. Salary: $	Bonus: $

OTHER THOUGHTS:

Apparent Women Officers or Directors:
Hot Spot for Advancement for Women/Minorities:

LOCATIONS: ("Y" = Yes)

West:	Southwest:	Midwest:	Southeast:	Northeast:	International:
				Y	

MANCHESTER CITY FOOTBALL CLUB

www.mcfc.co.uk

Industry Group Code: 711211D **Ranks within this company's industry group:** Sales: 7 Profits: 9

Sports:		Services:		Media:		Sales:		Facilities:		Other:	
Leagues/Associations:		Food & Beverage:		TV:		Marketing:		Stadiums:		Gambling:	
Teams:	Y	Agents:		Radio:		Ads:		Fitness Clubs:		Apparel:	
Nonprofits:		Other:		Internet:		Tickets:	Y	Golf Courses:		Equipment:	
Other:				Print:		Retail:	Y	Ski Resorts:		Shoes:	
				Software:		Other:		Other:		Other:	

TYPES OF BUSINESS:

Professional Soccer Team
Merchandise
Tickets

BRANDS/DIVISIONS/AFFILIATES:

CONTACTS:

Note: Officers with more than one job title may be intentionally listed here more than once.

Alistair Mackintosh, CEO
David Pullan, Mktg. Officer
Derak Fazaxkerley, Head Coach
Eric Steele, Goalkeeping Coach
Steffano Marrone, Fitness Coach
David Pullan, Brand Officer
John Wardle, Chmn.

Phone: 44-870-062-1894	**Fax:** 44-161-438-7999
Toll-Free:	
Address: City of Manchester Stadium, SportCity, Manchester, M11 3FF UK	

GROWTH PLANS/SPECIAL FEATURES:

Manchester City Football Club is an English Premiership Soccer team based in Manchester, England. The team plays its home games at the 48,000-seat City of Manchester Stadium, which is situated next to Reebok City, a complex that includes a mall, museum, cafe and sports bar. A Manchester City ladies team plays its matches at the Abbey Stadium in Gorton. The men's club experienced winning success in the late 1960s and early 1970s, but since then it has never finished higher than ninth in the Premiership standings. The club continues to exist in the shadow of neighboring soccer powerhouse Manchester United. On a high note, in 2003 the team signed arguably the best midfielder born in the U.S., Claudio Reyna, who previously had short stints with the Scottish team, Rangers, and the Premier League Sunderland. Manchester City sponsors include Thomas Cook, a travel company featured on Manchester City jerseys, and Singha Beer. Other revenue comes from ticket sales, both individual and season, and Manchester City team merchandise. The club contributes to a number of charities, including Genesis, a British charity dedicated to breast cancer prevention; Youth Charter for Sports and Arts; 42nd Street, a mental health support service for Manchester youth; and City in the Community, a charity designed to promote sport, health and education to Manchester communities through soccer-related activities.

FINANCIALS:

Sales and profits are in thousands of dollars—add 000 to get the full amount. 2008 Note: Financial information for 2008 was not available for all companies at press time.

2008 Sales: $164,000	2008 Profits: $-16,000	**U.S. Stock Ticker: Private**
2007 Sales: $114,000	2007 Profits: $27,000	**Int'l Ticker:** Int'l Exchange:
2006 Sales: $114,000	2006 Profits: $9,000	Employees: 204
2005 Sales: $109,000	2005 Profits: $	Fiscal Year Ends: 5/31
2004 Sales: $114,000	2004 Profits: $	Parent Company:

SALARIES/BENEFITS:

Pension Plan:	ESOP Stock Plan:	Profit Sharing:	Top Exec. Salary: $	Bonus: $
Savings Plan:	Stock Purch. Plan:		Second Exec. Salary: $	Bonus: $

OTHER THOUGHTS:

Apparent Women Officers or Directors:
Hot Spot for Advancement for Women/Minorities:

LOCATIONS: ("Y" = Yes)

West:	Southwest:	Midwest:	Southeast:	Northeast:	International:
					Y

Note: Financial information, benefits and other data can change quickly and may vary from those stated here.

MANCHESTER UNITED FOOTBALL CLUB

www.manutd.com

Industry Group Code: 711211D **Ranks within this company's industry group:** Sales: 1 Profits: 1

Sports:		Services:		Media:		Sales:		Facilities:		Other:	
Leagues/Associations:		Food & Beverage:	Y	TV:	Y	Marketing:	Y	Stadiums:	Y	Gambling:	
Teams:	Y	Agents:		Radio:	Y	Ads:	Y	Fitness Clubs:		Apparel:	Y
Nonprofits:		Other:		Internet:	Y	Tickets:	Y	Golf Courses:		Equipment:	
Other:				Print:		Retail:	Y	Ski Resorts:		Shoes:	
				Software:		Other:		Other:		Other:	

TYPES OF BUSINESS:

English Premiership Soccer Club
Online Services
Ticket Sales
Youth Programs
Charity Programs
Merchandise
Financial Services
Media Services

BRANDS/DIVISIONS/AFFILIATES:

United Magazine
Academy (The)
MU Finance
MU Media
MU TV
Old Trafford

CONTACTS: *Note: Officers with more than one job title may be intentionally listed here more than once.*

David Gill, CEO
Michael Bolingbroke, COO
Malcolm Glazer, Owner
Alex Ferguson, Team Mgr.
Mick Phelan, Coach

Phone: 44-161-868-8000 **Fax:** 44-161-868-8804
Toll-Free:
Address: Sir Matt Busby Way, Old Trafford, Manchester, M16 0RA UK

GROWTH PLANS/SPECIAL FEATURES:

Manchester United Football Club (MU) is an elite English Premier League football (soccer) club. The team plays its home games at the legendary Old Trafford stadium, which holds up to 76,000 people. The stadium complex also includes the Red Cafe, the East Stand Megastore, the Golden Tulip Hotel and a selection of suites for conferences and exhibitions. Ticket sales amount to roughly a third of total club sales. For the 2007-08 season, the team raised general ticket prices and slightly lowered junior and senior tickets prices. The team won Europe's Champions League Cup twice, once in 1968 and again in 1999, and has won Britain's FA Challenge Cup a record 11 times. George Best, one of the game's legendary players and a national hero in England, served his career on Manchester United. The club has a competitive youth program known as The Academy, which serves as an elite minor league for the first squad. Through the web site, users can also gain access to the club's financial segment, MU Finance, which deals in home, car and travel insurance, as well as savings, mortgages and loans; and a variety of multimedia, including MU TV, the United Magazine and a newsletter. MU TV, available for around $7 per month, includes access to club news, interviews, audio and video clips and manager commentary, as well as delayed screenings of club games. American International Group, Inc. (AIG) sponsors MU uniforms in a $98.9 million four-year deal, with MU shirts bearing the AIG logo until 2010. This deal was one of the largest of its kind in the U.K. Other official sponsors of the club include Nike, Hublot Watches, Smirnoff and Budweiser. Manchester United is among the most valuable sports teams in the world, valued at approximately $1.8 billion as of early 2009.

FINANCIALS: **Sales and profits are in thousands of dollars—add 000 to get the full amount. 2008 Note: Financial information for 2008 was not available for all companies at press time.**

2008 Sales: $512,000	2008 Profits: $160,000	**U.S. Stock Ticker: Private**
2007 Sales: $394,000	2007 Profits: $111,000	**Int'l Ticker:** Int'l Exchange:
2006 Sales: $310,000	2006 Profits: $92,000	Employees:
2005 Sales: $298,000	2005 Profits: $	Fiscal Year Ends: 7/31
2004 Sales: $315,000	2004 Profits: $	Parent Company:

SALARIES/BENEFITS:

Pension Plan:	ESOP Stock Plan:	Profit Sharing:	Top Exec. Salary: $	Bonus: $
Savings Plan:	Stock Purch. Plan:		Second Exec. Salary: $	Bonus: $

OTHER THOUGHTS:

Apparent Women Officers or Directors:
Hot Spot for Advancement for Women/Minorities:

LOCATIONS: ("Y" = Yes)

West:	Southwest:	Midwest:	Southeast:	Northeast:	International:
					Y

Note: Financial information, benefits and other data can change quickly and may vary from those stated here.

MAPLE LEAF SPORTS & ENTERTAINMENT LTD

www.theaircanadacentre.com

Industry Group Code: 551110 **Ranks within this company's industry group:** Sales: Profits:

Sports:		Services:		Media:		Sales:		Facilities:		Other:	
Leagues/Associations:		Food & Beverage:		TV:	Y	Marketing:		Stadiums:	Y	Gambling:	
Teams:	Y	Agents:		Radio:		Ads:		Fitness Clubs:		Apparel:	
Nonprofits:		Other:		Internet:	Y	Tickets:	Y	Golf Courses:		Equipment:	
Other:				Print:		Retail:	Y	Ski Resorts:		Shoes:	
				Software:		Other:		Other:		Other:	

TYPES OF BUSINESS:

Holding Company

BRANDS/DIVISIONS/AFFILIATES:

Toronto Maple Leafs
Toronto Raptors
Leafs TV
Raptors NBA TV
Air Canada Centre
Toronto FC

CONTACTS:

Note: Officers with more than one job title may be intentionally listed here more than once.

Richard A. Peddie, CEO
Tom Anselmi, COO/Exec. VP
Richard A. Peddie, Pres.
Michael Doyle, Dir.-Food & Beverage
Lawrence M. (Larry) Tanenbaum, Chmn.

Phone: 416-815-5500	**Fax:** 416-359-9332
Toll-Free:	
Address: 40 Bay St., Ste. 400, Toronto, ON M5J 2X2 Canada	

GROWTH PLANS/SPECIAL FEATURES:

Maple Leaf Sports & Entertainment Ltd. (MLSEL) owns the Toronto Maple Leafs, the Toronto Raptors, Air Canada Centre (ACC), Leafs TV and Raptors NBA TV. MLSEL is controlled by Ontario Teachers' Pension Plan, which owns a 58% interest. MLSEL is one of the largest sports and entertainment companies in North America. Located in downtown Toronto, the 665,000-square-foot ACC has hosted more than 26.8 million fans at approximately 2,000 events. Along with sporting events, the ACC is home to various concerts and events. The venue features 1,020 club seats, 40 platinum lounges, 65 executive suites, 32 theatre suites, 16 loge suites (second and third level loges) and three group sales areas. The ACC is home to the NHL's Toronto Maple Leafs and the NBA's Toronto Raptors. Together the teams have approximately 50 blue chip corporate partners, who represent the leaders in their respective industries. A few ACC partners include Coca Cola; IBM; Air Canada; TD Waterhouse; McDonald's Restaurants of Canada; Paramount; Canon; Sony of Canada; Re/Max; Sirius Satellite Radio; Master Card; Adidas; and Under Armour. The Toronto Maple Leafs is a leading global hockey brand, averaging approximately 20,000 fans per game. Leafs TV is the only television channel in North America devoted strictly to one sports team. The Raptors' season ticket renewal rate is one of the best in the NBA.

FINANCIALS:

Sales and profits are in thousands of dollars—add 000 to get the full amount. 2008 Note: Financial information for 2008 was not available for all companies at press time.

2008 Sales: $	2008 Profits: $	**U.S. Stock Ticker: Private**
2007 Sales: $	2007 Profits: $	**Int'l Ticker:** Int'l Exchange:
2006 Sales: $	2006 Profits: $	Employees:
2005 Sales: $	2005 Profits: $	Fiscal Year Ends: 6/30
2004 Sales: $	2004 Profits: $	Parent Company:

SALARIES/BENEFITS:

Pension Plan:	ESOP Stock Plan:	Profit Sharing:	Top Exec. Salary: $	Bonus: $
Savings Plan:	Stock Purch. Plan:		Second Exec. Salary: $	Bonus: $

OTHER THOUGHTS:

Apparent Women Officers or Directors:
Hot Spot for Advancement for Women/Minorities:

LOCATIONS: ("Y" = Yes)

West:	Southwest:	Midwest:	Southeast:	Northeast:	International:
					Y

MARINEMAX INC

www.marinemax.com

Industry Group Code: 441222 **Ranks within this company's industry group:** Sales: 1 Profits: 2

Sports:		Services:		Media:		Sales:		Facilities:		Other:	
Leagues/Associations:		Food & Beverage:		TV:		Marketing:		Stadiums:		Gambling:	
Teams:		Agents:		Radio:		Ads:		Fitness Clubs:		Apparel:	
Nonprofits:		Other:		Internet:		Tickets:		Golf Courses:		Equipment:	
Other:				Print:		Retail:	Y	Ski Resorts:		Shoes:	
				Software:		Other:		Other:		Other:	

TYPES OF BUSINESS:

Recreational Boats, Retail
Boat Parts & Accessories
Boat Repair & Maintenance
Boat Financing & Insurance
Slip & Storage Accommodations

BRANDS/DIVISIONS/AFFILIATES:

Imperial Marine
Port Jacksonville Marine
VT Inc

CONTACTS: *Note: Officers with more than one job title may be intentionally listed here more than once.*

William H. McGill, CEO
William H. McGill, Pres.
Michael H. McLamb, CFO/Exec. VP
T. Glenn Sandridge, VP-Mktg.
Jay J. Avelino, VP-Human Resources & Team Dev.
Michael H. McLamb, Corp. Sec.
Edward A. Russell, Exec. VP-Oper. & Sales
Jack P. Ezzell, Chief Acct. Officer/VP
Kurt M. Frahn, VP-Finance
William H. McGill, Chmn.

Phone: 727-531-1700	**Fax:** 727-531-0123
Toll-Free: 800-732-7297	
Address: 18167 US 19 N., Ste. 499, Clearwater, FL 33764 US	

GROWTH PLANS/SPECIAL FEATURES:

MarineMax, Inc. is the largest recreational boat dealer in the U.S., operating through 90 retail locations in 22 states. The company's product offerings feature Brunswick recreational and fishing boat lines and Ferretti yachts. Most boats sold are new, but used boats account for about 18.8% of the company's revenue. Sales of Brunswick products account for approximately 57% of the company's revenue. MarineMax also sells marine parts and accessories, including engines, propellers, oils, lubricants, steering and controlling systems, corrosion control products and engine service products. In addition, the company offers its customers novelty items, including shirts, caps and floor mats bearing manufacturers' or dealers' logos. The firm offers maintenance and repair services at most of its retail locations, as well as arrangements for financing. In many of its markets, MarineMax provides mobile maintenance and repair services at the location of the customer's boat. The majority of the company's stores are located on waterfront properties, including the Sacramento River Delta Basin in California and the St. Croix River in Minnesota. The waterfront retail locations are easily accessible to the boating populace, serve as in-water showrooms and enable the sales force to give the customer immediate in-water boat demonstrations. Many facilities offer storage services, both at in-water slips and on land. MarineMax's average selling price for a new boat in 2007 was approximately $115,000. In 2008, the company began offering the Meridian Yachts brand to Arizona, Nevada, Utah, Colorado and South Carolina; the CABO, Hatteras and Azimut brands to Florida; and Hatteras to Texas.

MarineMax offers its employees medical insurance; life insurance; a 401(k) savings plan; an Employee Stock Purchase Plan; and boating supply discounts.

FINANCIALS: **Sales and profits are in thousands of dollars—add 000 to get the full amount. 2008 Note: Financial information for 2008 was not available for all companies at press time.**

2008 Sales: $885,407	2008 Profits: $-134,277	**U.S. Stock Ticker: HZO**
2007 Sales: $1,255,985	2007 Profits: $20,069	**Int'l Ticker:** Int'l Exchange:
2006 Sales: $1,213,541	2006 Profits: $39,382	Employees: 1,759
2005 Sales: $947,300	2005 Profits: $33,800	Fiscal Year Ends: 9/30
2004 Sales: $762,000	2004 Profits: $26,300	Parent Company:

SALARIES/BENEFITS:

Pension Plan:	ESOP Stock Plan:	Profit Sharing:	Top Exec. Salary: $500,000	Bonus: $848,667
Savings Plan: Y	Stock Purch. Plan: Y		Second Exec. Salary: $325,000	Bonus: $280,924

OTHER THOUGHTS:

Apparent Women Officers or Directors:
Hot Spot for Advancement for Women/Minorities:

LOCATIONS: ("Y" = Yes)

West:	Southwest:	Midwest:	Southeast:	Northeast:	International:
Y	Y	Y	Y	Y	

MEMPHIS GRIZZLIES

www.nba.com/grizzlies

Industry Group Code: 711211B **Ranks within this company's industry group:** Sales: 27 Profits: 24

Sports:		Services:		Media:		Sales:		Facilities:		Other:	
Leagues/Associations:		Food & Beverage:		TV:		Marketing:		Stadiums:		Gambling:	
Teams:	Y	Agents:		Radio:		Ads:		Fitness Clubs:		Apparel:	
Nonprofits:		Other:		Internet:		Tickets:	Y	Golf Courses:		Equipment:	
Other:				Print:		Retail:	Y	Ski Resorts:		Shoes:	
				Software:		Other:		Other:		Other:	

TYPES OF BUSINESS:

Professional Basketball Team
Ticket Sales
Sports Merchandise

BRANDS/DIVISIONS/AFFILIATES:

FedExForum

GROWTH PLANS/SPECIAL FEATURES:

The Memphis Grizzlies started as a 1995 National Basketball Association (NBA) expansion team in 1995 in Vancouver, Canada. In 2001, the franchise moved to Memphis and began playing home games in the FedExForum. The $250 million arena is located in downtown Memphis and has a 19,000 seating capacity with 27 courtside suites, 32 club suites, four party suites and 80 club boxes. Community programs of the team include fundraisers, tickets for kids and wish granting, which is conducted in partnership with Make-a-Wish Foundation and St. Jude's Children's Research Hospital. The team has alliances and corporate partnerships with brands such as Anheuser-Busch, FedEx, ServiceMaster and Toyota. While the Grizzlies have yet to achieve any championship success, they have shown steady improvement and have made the playoffs in the 2003-04, 2004-05 and 2005-06 seasons. In the 2008-09 season, the team's home attendance average was roughly 12,700 per game. Forbes Magazine recently estimated the team to be worth approximately $294 million.

CONTACTS: *Note: Officers with more than one job title may be intentionally listed here more than once.*

Michael Heisley, Owner
John Pugliese, Sr. Dir.-Mktg. Comm.
Andy Dolich, Pres., Bus. Oper.
Greg Campbell, VP-Finance
Jerry West, Gen. Mgr./Pres., Basketball Oper.
Mike Fratello, Head Coach
Mike Redlick, Sr. VP-Corp. Partnership
Randy Stephens, Sr. VP-Broadcasting

Phone: 901-888-4667 **Fax:** 901-205-1235
Toll-Free:
Address: 191 Beale St., Memphis, TN 38103 US

FINANCIALS: Sales and profits are in thousands of dollars—add 000 to get the full amount. 2008 Note: Financial information for 2008 was not available for all companies at press time.

2008 Sales: $95,000	2008 Profits: $-3,200	**U.S. Stock Ticker: Private**
2007 Sales: $98,000	2007 Profits: $-10,900	**Int'l Ticker:** Int'l Exchange:
2006 Sales: $101,000	2006 Profits: $-18,500	Employees:
2005 Sales: $98,000	2005 Profits: $	Fiscal Year Ends: 6/30
2004 Sales: $75,000	2004 Profits: $	Parent Company:

SALARIES/BENEFITS:

Pension Plan:	ESOP Stock Plan:	Profit Sharing:	Top Exec. Salary: $	Bonus: $
Savings Plan:	Stock Purch. Plan:		Second Exec. Salary: $	Bonus: $

OTHER THOUGHTS:

Apparent Women Officers or Directors:
Hot Spot for Advancement for Women/Minorities:

LOCATIONS: ("Y" = Yes)

West:	Southwest:	Midwest:	Southeast:	Northeast:	International:
			Y		

MIAMI DOLPHINS

www.miamidolphins.com

Industry Group Code: 711211C **Ranks within this company's industry group:** Sales: 6 Profits: 6

Sports:		Services:		Media:		Sales:		Facilities:		Other:	
Leagues/Associations:		Food & Beverage:		TV:		Marketing:		Stadiums:	Y	Gambling:	
Teams:	Y	Agents:		Radio:		Ads:		Fitness Clubs:		Apparel:	
Nonprofits:		Other:		Internet:		Tickets:	Y	Golf Courses:		Equipment:	
Other:				Print:		Retail:	Y	Ski Resorts:		Shoes:	
				Software:		Other:		Other:		Other:	

TYPES OF BUSINESS:

Professional Football Team

BRANDS/DIVISIONS/AFFILIATES:

Dolphins Stadium

CONTACTS:

Note: Officers with more than one job title may be intentionally listed here more than once.

Joseph A. Bailey, III, CEO
Bryan Wiedmeier, COO
Bryan Wiedmeier, Pres.
George Torres, Sr. Dir.-Mktg. & Comm.
Yolanda Barreto, Sr. Dir.-Human Resources, Dolphin Stadium
Tery Howard, VP-IT
Bill Pierce, Exec. VP-Bus. & Admin.
Matt Thomas, General Counsel
Bill Galante, Sr. VP-Oper.
Scott Stone, Sr. Dir.-Internet & Publications
Jill R. Strafaci, Sr. VP-Finance & Admin.
Tony Sparano, Head Coach
Bill Parcells, Exec. VP-Football Oper.
Harvey Greene, Sr. VP-Media Rel.
M. Bruce Schulze, Pres., Dolphin Stadium
Stephen M. Ross, Chmn.

Phone: 954-452-7000	**Fax:** 954-452-7027
Toll-Free:	
Address: 7500 S.W. 30th St., Davie, FL 33314 US	

GROWTH PLANS/SPECIAL FEATURES:

The Miami Dolphins are a professional football team in the National Football League (NFL) that plays in the Eastern Division of the American Football Conference (AFC). The Dolphins began play as a 1966 expansion team in the AFL, and joined the NFL as part of the league merger. In 1972, the Dolphins completed a perfect season, winning every regular season game, all its playoff appearances and Super Bowl VII. It is the only NFL team to have ever been undefeated throughout an entire season. The Dolphins won Super Bowl VIII the next year, making it the first NFL team to appear in three consecutive Super Bowls. Throughout these years of success, the team was coached by Don Shula, the head coach with the most wins in NFL history, and led by quarterback Bob Griese. During the 1980s and 1990s, the Dolphins continued their winning ways led by quarterback Dan Marino. He led the team to multiple playoff appearances and Super Bowl XIX, which it lost to the San Francisco 49ers. H. Wayne Huizenga, who had owned the team since 1994, sold a 50% share in both the Dolphins and Dolphin Stadium to real estate developer Stephen M. Ross in February 2008 for approximately $550 million. In January 2009, for an additional $1 billion, Ross purchased another 45%, giving him a 95% ownership of the team and its stadium, with Huizenga retaining the other 5%. After a number of mediocre seasons, including a dismal 1-15 record in 2007, the Dolphins came back in 2008, under the direction of new head of football operations Bill Parcells, to finish the season 11-5 and make the playoffs for the first time since 2001. In the 2008 season, the team averaged approximately 65,489 fans in attendance per game. A recent Forbes estimate values the team at roughly $1.04 billion.

FINANCIALS:

Sales and profits are in thousands of dollars—add 000 to get the full amount. 2008 Note: Financial information for 2008 was not available for all companies at press time.

2008 Sales: $232,000	2008 Profits: $36,100	**U.S. Stock Ticker: Subsidiary**
2007 Sales: $215,000	2007 Profits: $11,200	**Int'l Ticker:** Int'l Exchange:
2006 Sales: $194,000	2006 Profits: $33,400	Employees:
2005 Sales: $190,000	2005 Profits: $	Fiscal Year Ends: 12/31
2004 Sales: $	2004 Profits: $	Parent Company: DOLPHINS ENTERPRISES LLC

SALARIES/BENEFITS:

Pension Plan:	ESOP Stock Plan:	Profit Sharing:	Top Exec. Salary: $	Bonus: $
Savings Plan:	Stock Purch. Plan:		Second Exec. Salary: $	Bonus: $

OTHER THOUGHTS:

Apparent Women Officers or Directors: 22
Hot Spot for Advancement for Women/Minorities: Y

LOCATIONS: ("Y" = Yes)

West:	Southwest:	Midwest:	Southeast:	Northeast:	International:
			Y		

MIAMI HEAT

www.nba.com/heat

Industry Group Code: 711211B **Ranks within this company's industry group:** Sales: 12 Profits: 23

Sports:		Services:		Media:		Sales:		Facilities:		Other:	
Leagues/Associations:		Food & Beverage:		TV:		Marketing:		Stadiums:		Gambling:	
Teams:	Y	Agents:		Radio:		Ads:		Fitness Clubs:		Apparel:	
Nonprofits:		Other:		Internet:		Tickets:	Y	Golf Courses:		Equipment:	
Other:				Print:		Retail:	Y	Ski Resorts:		Shoes:	
				Software:		Other:		Other:		Other:	

TYPES OF BUSINESS:

Professional Basketball Team
HEAT Merchandise
Ticket Sales

BRANDS/DIVISIONS/AFFILIATES:

Heat Group (The)
American Airlines Arena
Miami HEAT Dancers
HEAT Golden Oldies
WhiteHotHeat.com
HEAT Academy
Miami HEAT FUN-raiser
HEAT & SOL Pep Rally For Education

CONTACTS: *Note: Officers with more than one job title may be intentionally listed here more than once.*

Micky Arison, Managing Gen. Partner
Pat Riley, Pres.
Sammy Schulman, CFO/Sr. VP
Michael McCullough, Chief Mktg. Officer/Exec. VP
Sonia Harty, VP-Human Resources
Tony Cuba, CIO/Sr. VP
Raquel Libman, General Counsel/Exec. VP
Jim Spencer, VP-Oper.
Eric Woolworth, Pres., Bus. Oper.
Tim Donovan, VP-Sports Media Rel.
Jeff Morris, VP-Finance
Stephen Weber, Exec. VP-Sales
Kim Stone, Exec. VP/Gen. Mgr.
Mike Walker, Exec. VP-Heat Group Enterprises
Erik Spoelstra, Head Coach

Phone: 786-777-1000	**Fax:** 786-777-1615
Toll-Free:	
Address: American Airlines Arena, 601 Biscayne Blvd., Miami, FL 33132 US	

GROWTH PLANS/SPECIAL FEATURES:

The Miami HEAT franchise is operated by the Heat Group, which is owned by Carnival CEO, Micky Arison. The HEAT's home stadium is the AmericanAirlines Arena, which is a $213 million building with a 16,000 to 19,600 seating capacity. The arena also contains the Waterfront Theater, which is currently one of Florida's largest theaters. Live entertainment offered during game nights includes the Miami HEAT Dancers and the HEAT Golden Oldies. The team has also initiated a special playoff web site called WhiteHotHeat.com, which offers team news, promotional information and White Hot photo galleries. The HEAT provides educational services such as HEAT Academy, HEAT and SOL Pep Rally For Education, the Miami HEAT FUN-raiser, Shoot For the Stars Summer Clinics and the Nike/HEAT Youth Basketball League. The HEAT entered the NBA in 1988 and recently won their first NBA champion in the 2005-06 season by defeating the Dallas Mavericks in the finals. Despite making several roster changes during the 2007-08 season, including sending Shaquille O'Neal to the Phoenix Suns in exchange for four-time All-Star Shawn Marion and Marcus Banks, the Miami HEAT ended a disappointing season with the worst record in the NBA, 15-67. In the 2008-09 season, the team's home attendance average was roughly 18,200 per game. Forbes Magazine recently estimated the team to be worth approximately $393 million.

FINANCIALS: **Sales and profits are in thousands of dollars—add 000 to get the full amount. 2008 Note: Financial information for 2008 was not available for all companies at press time.**

2008 Sales: $131,000	2008 Profits: $-1,100	**U.S. Stock Ticker: Subsidiary**
2007 Sales: $131,000	2007 Profits: $17,900	**Int'l Ticker:** Int'l Exchange:
2006 Sales: $132,000	2006 Profits: $20,500	Employees:
2005 Sales: $119,000	2005 Profits: $	Fiscal Year Ends: 6/30
2004 Sales: $93,000	2004 Profits: $	Parent Company: HEAT GROUP (THE)

SALARIES/BENEFITS:

Pension Plan:	ESOP Stock Plan:	Profit Sharing:	Top Exec. Salary: $	Bonus: $
Savings Plan:	Stock Purch. Plan:		Second Exec. Salary: $	Bonus: $

OTHER THOUGHTS:

Apparent Women Officers or Directors: 5
Hot Spot for Advancement for Women/Minorities: Y

LOCATIONS: ("Y" = Yes)

West:	Southwest:	Midwest:	Southeast:	Northeast:	International:
			Y		

MIDDLESBROUGH FOOTBALL CLUB

www.mfc.premiumtv.co.uk

Industry Group Code: 711211D **Ranks within this company's industry group:** Sales: Profits:

Sports:		Services:		Media:		Sales:		Facilities:		Other:	
Leagues/Associations:		Food & Beverage:		TV:		Marketing:		Stadiums:		Gambling:	
Teams:	Y	Agents:		Radio:		Ads:		Fitness Clubs:		Apparel:	
Nonprofits:		Other:		Internet:		Tickets:	Y	Golf Courses:		Equipment:	
Other:				Print:		Retail:	Y	Ski Resorts:		Shoes:	
				Software:		Other:		Other:		Other:	

TYPES OF BUSINESS:

Soccer Team
Ticket Sales
Conference Center

BRANDS/DIVISIONS/AFFILIATES:

Riverside Stadium
Middlesbrough Football Community Project
Enterprise Academy

CONTACTS:

Note: Officers with more than one job title may be intentionally listed here more than once.

Keith Lamb, CEO
Neil Bausor, COO
Alan Bage, Head-Admin.
Alan Bage, Head-Finance
Gareth Southgate, Mgr.
Malcolm Crosby, Assistant Mgr.
Ccolin Cooper, First Team Coach
Stephen Pears, Goalkeeping Coach
Steve Gibson, Chmn.

Phone: 44-1642-757-656	**Fax:** 44-1642-757-690
Toll-Free:	
Address: The Riverside Stadium, Middlesbrough, TS3 6RS UK	

GROWTH PLANS/SPECIAL FEATURES:

Middlesbrough Football Club was founded by members of the Middlesbrough Cricket Club in 1876. Throughout the 1970s and 1980s, the soccer club was promoted and relegated up and down the English Football League System's three divisions. Middlesbrough was an inaugural team in the English Premiership League, and was the most lucrative and prestigious football league in England. Middlesbrough FC hit bottom in 1986 when it was both relegated to the Third Division and facing bankruptcy. That year, Steve Gibson, founder and chairman of Bulkhaul Limited, purchased the team. Throughout the mid-1990s and into the 2000s, the team's star has been rising. In 1994, under player-manager Bryan Robson, Middlesbrough FC solidified its place in the Premiership League; it also signed star players Nick Barmby and Juninho. The team won the Football League First Division in the 1994-95 season and won the League Cup in the 2003-04 season. During the 2005-06 season, the Middlesbrough FC was a finalist in the UEFA Cup. The club plays at Riverside Stadium in Middlesbrough, which seats 35,100 spectators.

FINANCIALS:

Sales and profits are in thousands of dollars—add 000 to get the full amount. 2008 Note: Financial information for 2008 was not available for all companies at press time.

2008 Sales: $	2008 Profits: $	**U.S. Stock Ticker: Private**
2007 Sales: $	2007 Profits: $	**Int'l Ticker:** Int'l Exchange:
2006 Sales: $	2006 Profits: $	Employees: 177
2005 Sales: $	2005 Profits: $	Fiscal Year Ends: 7/31
2004 Sales: $	2004 Profits: $	Parent Company:

SALARIES/BENEFITS:

Pension Plan:	ESOP Stock Plan:	Profit Sharing:	Top Exec. Salary: $	Bonus: $
Savings Plan:	Stock Purch. Plan:		Second Exec. Salary: $	Bonus: $

OTHER THOUGHTS:

Apparent Women Officers or Directors:
Hot Spot for Advancement for Women/Minorities:

LOCATIONS: ("Y" = Yes)

West:	Southwest:	Midwest:	Southeast:	Northeast:	International:
					Y

MIDWAY GAMES INC

www.midway.com

Industry Group Code: 511208 **Ranks within this company's industry group:** Sales: 2 Profits: 2

Sports:		Services:		Media:		Sales:		Facilities:		Other:	
Leagues/Associations:		Food & Beverage:		TV:		Marketing:		Stadiums:		Gambling:	
Teams:		Agents:		Radio:		Ads:		Fitness Clubs:		Apparel:	
Nonprofits:		Other:		Internet:		Tickets:		Golf Courses:		Equipment:	
Other:				Print:		Retail:		Ski Resorts:		Shoes:	
				Software:		Other:		Other:		Other:	

TYPES OF BUSINESS:

Computer Software, Games & Entertainment

BRANDS/DIVISIONS/AFFILIATES:

Pong
Spy Hunter
Mortal Kombat
High Voltage Software, Inc.
Artificial Mind and Movement Inc.
Midway Games SAS
Midway Games GmbH
Midway Games Ltd.

CONTACTS: *Note: Officers with more than one job title may be intentionally listed here more than once.*

Matthew V. Booty, CEO
Matthew V. Booty, Pres.
Ryan G. O'Desky, Interim CFO
Deborah K. Fulton, General Counsel/Sr. VP/Corp. Sec.
Ryan G. O'Desky, VP-Finance/Controller
Miguel Iribarren, Sr. VP-Publishing
Peter C. Brown, Chmn.
Martin Spiess, Exec. VP-Int'l, Midway Games Limited

Phone: 773-961-2222	**Fax:**
Toll-Free:	
Address: 2704 W. Roscoe St., Chicago, IL 60618 US	

GROWTH PLANS/SPECIAL FEATURES:

Midway Games, Inc. is a leading developer and publisher of gaming software for all major videogame systems, including Playstation 3 from Sony; Xbox 360 from Microsoft; Nintendo's Wii and Game Boy Advance systems; and personal computers. The company focuses its product development efforts on the creation of a diverse portfolio of titles across many popular video game genres such as action, adventure, driving, fighting, shooting and sports. The firm generally favors internally-developed products due to the favorable profit margin contribution and the ability to leverage these products into sequels and derivative products. Additionally, Midway has licensed certain intellectual properties from leading entertainment companies in an effort to diversify its portfolio. To date, the company has published over 400 titles. The firm's early games in the 1980s included Pong, Asteroids, Gauntlet, Defender and Spy Hunter, while its current offerings include Blitz, Rampage, Happy Feet, The Grim Adventures of Billy & Mandy, The Ant Bully, Unreal Anthology and the Mortal Kombat series. Mortal Kombat has been the company's most successful game, selling in excess of 20 million copies across eight major home consoles, as well as being licensed into other areas such as film and television. The largest purchasers of Midway games are retailers Wal-Mart and Gamestop. Midway Games GmbH in Germany, Midway Games SAS in France and Midway Games Ltd. in the U.K. are responsible for the company's European sales, marketing and distribution operations. As of 2008, the firm maintained nine internal product development teams staffed with approximately 700 developers, and held game development agreements with third-party development groups, such as Artificial Mind and Movement Inc. and High Voltage Software, Inc. In July 2008, Midway announced that it was combining the operations of Midway Studios in Los Angeles with those of Midway Home Entertainment in San Diego, where the newly-combined operations will be located. In February 2009, the firm and its U.S. subsidiaries filed for bankruptcy protection. The bankruptcy did not include its non-U.S. operations.

FINANCIALS: **Sales and profits are in thousands of dollars—add 000 to get the full amount. 2008 Note: Financial information for 2008 was not available for all companies at press time.**

2008 Sales: $219,556	2008 Profits: $-190,974	**U.S. Stock Ticker: MWY**
2007 Sales: $157,195	2007 Profits: $-99,592	**Int'l Ticker:** Int'l Exchange:
2006 Sales: $165,574	2006 Profits: $-77,783	Employees: 540
2005 Sales: $150,078	2005 Profits: $-112,487	Fiscal Year Ends: 12/31
2004 Sales: $161,600	2004 Profits: $-19,945	Parent Company:

SALARIES/BENEFITS:

Pension Plan:	ESOP Stock Plan:	Profit Sharing:	Top Exec. Salary: $600,630	Bonus: $
Savings Plan:	Stock Purch. Plan:		Second Exec. Salary: $360,326	Bonus: $73,900

OTHER THOUGHTS:

Apparent Women Officers or Directors: 1
Hot Spot for Advancement for Women/Minorities:

LOCATIONS: ("Y" = Yes)

West:	Southwest:	Midwest:	Southeast:	Northeast:	International:
Y	Y	Y			Y

MILWAUKEE BREWERS

www.brewers.com

Industry Group Code: 711211A **Ranks within this company's industry group:** Sales: 22 Profits: 22

Sports:		Services:		Media:		Sales:		Facilities:		Other:	
Leagues/Associations:		Food & Beverage:		TV:		Marketing:		Stadiums:		Gambling:	
Teams:	Y	Agents:		Radio:		Ads:		Fitness Clubs:		Apparel:	
Nonprofits:		Other:		Internet:		Tickets:	Y	Golf Courses:		Equipment:	
Other:				Print:		Retail:	Y	Ski Resorts:		Shoes:	
				Software:		Other:		Other:		Other:	

TYPES OF BUSINESS:

Professional Baseball Team
Ticket Sales
Milwaukee Brewers Merchandise

BRANDS/DIVISIONS/AFFILIATES:

Miller Park
Nashville Sounds
Huntsville Stars
Brevard County Manatees
West Virginia Power
Helena Brewers
Arizona Brewers
Brewers Charities, Inc.

CONTACTS:

Note: Officers with more than one job title may be intentionally listed here more than once.

Todd Taylor, VP-Consumer Mktg.
Sally Andrist, VP-Human Resources & Office Mgmt.
John Winborn, VP-Info. Systems
John Winborn, VP-Tech.
Bob Quinn, Exec. VP-Admin.
Marti Wronski, General Counsel
Rick Schlesinger, Exec. VP-Bus. Oper.
Tyler Barnes, VP-Comm.
Nichole Kinateder, Coordinator-Investor Rel.
Joe Zidanic, Controller/VP
Doug Melvin, Exec. VP/Gen. Mgr.
Bob Stark, Sr. Administrator-Baseball Oper.
Gord Ash, VP/Asst. Gen. Mgr.
Tom Hecht, VP-Corp. Mktg.
Mark Attanasio, Chmn./Principal Owner

Phone: 414-902-4400 **Fax:** 414-902-4053
Toll-Free:
Address: 1 Brewers Way, Milwaukee, WI 53214-3652 US

GROWTH PLANS/SPECIAL FEATURES:

The Milwaukee Brewers are an organization within Major League Baseball (MLB). The third professional baseball team to play for Milwaukee and the second to carry the Brewers name, this incarnation came about in 1970 when the Seattle Pilots, an expansion franchise started in 1969, moved to Milwaukee. The team's most successful years were 1981 and 1982, when they featured such players as Robin Yount, Rollie Fingers and Paul Molitor, making the playoffs both years only to fall one game short of winning the World Series in 1982. In the years following, the Brewers were mostly a mediocre team, with relatively strong showings in 1987, 1988 and 1992. In 1994, when MLB adopted an expanded playoff system, the team transferred from the American League to the National League. In 2001, the Brewers moved to newly-constructed Miller Park, which features a retractable roof, manual scoreboards and seating for 42,000. In late 2004, the team was sold to Los Angeles investment banker Mark Attanasio, ending over three decades of ownership by current MLB commissioner Bud Selig and his family. In 2005, after 13 years of losing records, the team finished with an even 81 wins and 81 losses. Since 2002, the club's general manager has been Doug Melvin. Hailing from the statistical analysis-based school of baseball management, Melvin has kept the Brewers in rebuilding mode for the past several seasons, not signing any large contracts, often trading away overrated veterans and snatching underrated commodities off of waivers. The team made it to the playoffs in 2008 for the first time in 26 years, as the wildcard selection. The Brewers changed its coaching staff after the 2008 season. In 2008, the team averaged approximately 37,882 fans in attendance per home game. A recent Forbes estimate values the team at $235 million.

FINANCIALS:

Sales and profits are in thousands of dollars—add 000 to get the full amount. 2008 Note: Financial information for 2008 was not available for all companies at press time.

2008 Sales: $173,000	2008 Profits: $11,800	**U.S. Stock Ticker: Private**
2007 Sales: $158,000	2007 Profits: $19,200	**Int'l Ticker:** Int'l Exchange:
2006 Sales: $144,000	2006 Profits: $20,800	Employees:
2005 Sales: $131,000	2005 Profits: $	Fiscal Year Ends: 10/31
2004 Sales: $	2004 Profits: $	Parent Company:

SALARIES/BENEFITS:

Pension Plan:	ESOP Stock Plan:	Profit Sharing:	Top Exec. Salary: $	Bonus: $
Savings Plan:	Stock Purch. Plan:		Second Exec. Salary: $	Bonus: $

OTHER THOUGHTS:

Apparent Women Officers or Directors: 4
Hot Spot for Advancement for Women/Minorities: Y

LOCATIONS: ("Y" = Yes)

West:	Southwest:	Midwest:	Southeast:	Northeast:	International:
		Y			Y

MILWAUKEE BUCKS

www.nba.com/bucks

Industry Group Code: 711211B **Ranks within this company's industry group:** Sales: 29 Profits: 18

Sports:		Services:		Media:		Sales:		Facilities:		Other:	
Leagues/Associations:		Food & Beverage:		TV:		Marketing:		Stadiums:	Y	Gambling:	
Teams:	Y	Agents:		Radio:		Ads:		Fitness Clubs:		Apparel:	
Nonprofits:		Other:		Internet:		Tickets:	Y	Golf Courses:		Equipment:	
Other:				Print:		Retail:	Y	Ski Resorts:		Shoes:	
				Software:		Other:		Other:		Other:	

TYPES OF BUSINESS:

Professional Basketball Team
Ticket Sales
Milwaukee Bucks Merchandise

BRANDS/DIVISIONS/AFFILIATES:

Bradley Center

CONTACTS:

Note: Officers with more than one job title may be intentionally listed here more than once.

Herb Kohl, Pres./Owner
Mike Burr, CFO
Jim Grayson, Dir.-Sales
Ron Kiepert, Mgr.-IT
John Steinmiller, VP-Bus. Oper.
Konni Hibicke, Group Sales Mgr.-New Bus. Dev.
Michael Grahl, Mgr.-Website Mktg.
Cheri Hanson, Dir.-Public Rel.
Jim Woloszyk, Dir.-Finance
John Hammond, Gen. Mgr.
Ron Walter, VP/Alternate Governor
Scott Skiles, Head Coach
Steve Tarachow, Mgr.-Group Ticket Sales

Phone: 414-227-0500	**Fax:** 414-227-0543
Toll-Free:	
Address: Bradley Center, 1001 N. 4th St., Milwaukee, WI 53203 US	

GROWTH PLANS/SPECIAL FEATURES:

The Milwaukee Bucks is a team playing in the National Basketball Association (NBA). The franchise began its run in the NBA in 1968 when the franchise was awarded to a group of Milwaukee investors named Milwaukee Professional Sports and Services. By 1971, the team won its first (and only) championship under the leadership of the legendary Kareem Abdul-Jabbar. Other notable players on the Bucks include Oscar Robertson, who played for them in the late 1970s, and Sidney Moncrief, who played throughout the 1980s. Despite numerous playoff appearances, however, the team has not been able to match its past success. They failed to reach the post-season in the 2004-05 season, but they made it in 2005-06. Wisconsin senator Herb Kohl, whose family founded the popular Kohl's department stores, owns the Bucks, who play in the Bradley Center. The team entered its 41st season in 2008-09 as the ninth winningest franchise in NBA history (sixth winningest among current franchises). In the 2008-09 season, the team's home attendance average was roughly 15,400 per game. Forbes Magazine recently estimated the team to be worth approximately $278 million.

FINANCIALS:

Sales and profits are in thousands of dollars—add 000 to get the full amount. 2008 Note: Financial information for 2008 was not available for all companies at press time.

2008 Sales: $94,000	2008 Profits: $5,400	**U.S. Stock Ticker: Private**
2007 Sales: $88,000	2007 Profits: $1,700	**Int'l Ticker:** Int'l Exchange:
2006 Sales: $87,000	2006 Profits: $1,500	Employees:
2005 Sales: $78,000	2005 Profits: $	Fiscal Year Ends: 6/30
2004 Sales: $77,000	2004 Profits: $	Parent Company:

SALARIES/BENEFITS:

Pension Plan:	ESOP Stock Plan:	Profit Sharing:	Top Exec. Salary: $	Bonus: $
Savings Plan:	Stock Purch. Plan:		Second Exec. Salary: $	Bonus: $

OTHER THOUGHTS:

Apparent Women Officers or Directors: 6
Hot Spot for Advancement for Women/Minorities: Y

LOCATIONS: ("Y" = Yes)

West:	Southwest:	Midwest:	Southeast:	Northeast:	International:
		Y			

Note: Financial information, benefits and other data can change quickly and may vary from those stated here.

MINNESOTA LYNX

www.wnba.com/lynx

Industry Group Code: 711211E **Ranks within this company's industry group:** Sales: Profits:

Sports:		Services:		Media:		Sales:		Facilities:		Other:	
Leagues/Associations:		Food & Beverage:		TV:		Marketing:		Stadiums:		Gambling:	
Teams:	Y	Agents:		Radio:		Ads:		Fitness Clubs:		Apparel:	
Nonprofits:		Other:		Internet:		Tickets:	Y	Golf Courses:		Equipment:	
Other:				Print:		Retail:	Y	Ski Resorts:		Shoes:	
				Software:		Other:		Other:		Other:	

TYPES OF BUSINESS:

Women's Basketball Team

BRANDS/DIVISIONS/AFFILIATES:

Minnesota Timberwolves
Target Center

CONTACTS:

Note: Officers with more than one job title may be intentionally listed here more than once.

Rob Moor, CEO
Conrad Smith, COO
Chris Wright, Pres.
Nicole Smith, Mgr.-Bus. Oper. & Fan Rel.
Angela Taylor, VP-Bus. Dev.
Aaron Seehusen, Coordinator-Public Rel.
Glen Taylor, Owner
Don Zierden, Head Coach
Ed Prohofsky, Assistant Coach
Anna Mercado, Mgr.-Mktg.

Phone: 612-673-1600 **Fax:** 612-673-8367
Toll-Free:
Address: 600 First Ave. N., Minneapolis, MN 55403 US

GROWTH PLANS/SPECIAL FEATURES:

The Minnesota Lynx is a Women's National Basketball Association (WNBA) team that came into existence in 1999, two years after the WNBA's inception. The team plays in the Western Conference of the WNBA, along with the Los Angeles Sparks, Phoenix Mercury, Sacramento Monarchs, San Antonio Silver Stars and Seattle Storm. The Lynx are owned by Glen Taylor, a businessman and former state senator who also owns the Lynx's brother NBA (National Basketball Association) team, the Minnesota Timberwolves. The team's home attendance at the Target Center averages 7,500 fans per game. Part of the Lynx's community outreach efforts include donating tickets to schools, shelters and non-profit programs through Lynx Tickets for Kids; sending players out to visit hospitals, schools, basketball camps and other local events; and raising money for breast cancer research through the U.S. Bank Minnesota Lynx Great Basketball Dribble. The Lynx also host youth basketball clinics and a youth game that allows younger players to taste the WNBA experience, including playing in the Target Center and having the players announced as they enter the arena. Youth game participants also receive gifts such as basketballs and other items. Throughout the season, the Lynx hold special youth games held at half time, allowing the young players to perform before a crowd of 10,000.

FINANCIALS:

Sales and profits are in thousands of dollars—add 000 to get the full amount. 2008 Note: Financial information for 2008 was not available for all companies at press time.

2008 Sales: $ 2008 Profits: $
2007 Sales: $ 2007 Profits: $
2006 Sales: $ 2006 Profits: $
2005 Sales: $ 2005 Profits: $
2004 Sales: $ 2004 Profits: $

U.S. Stock Ticker: Private
Int'l Ticker: Int'l Exchange:
Employees:
Fiscal Year Ends:
Parent Company:

SALARIES/BENEFITS:

Pension Plan: ESOP Stock Plan: Profit Sharing: Top Exec. Salary: $ Bonus: $
Savings Plan: Stock Purch. Plan: Second Exec. Salary: $ Bonus: $

OTHER THOUGHTS:

Apparent Women Officers or Directors: 6
Hot Spot for Advancement for Women/Minorities: Y

LOCATIONS: ("Y" = Yes)

West:	Southwest:	Midwest:	Southeast:	Northeast:	International:
		Y			

MINNESOTA TIMBERWOLVES

www.nba.com/timberwolves

Industry Group Code: 711211B **Ranks within this company's industry group:** Sales: 22 Profits: 26

Sports:		Services:		Media:		Sales:		Facilities:		Other:	
Leagues/Associations:		Food & Beverage:		TV:		Marketing:		Stadiums:		Gambling:	
Teams:	Y	Agents:		Radio:		Ads:		Fitness Clubs:		Apparel:	
Nonprofits:		Other:		Internet:		Tickets:	Y	Golf Courses:		Equipment:	
Other:				Print:		Retail:	Y	Ski Resorts:		Shoes:	
				Software:		Other:		Other:		Other:	

TYPES OF BUSINESS:

Professional Basketball Team

BRANDS/DIVISIONS/AFFILIATES:

Target Center

CONTACTS:

Note: Officers with more than one job title may be intentionally listed here more than once.

Rob Moor, CEO
Chris Wright, Pres.
Kevin McHale, VP-Basketball Oper.
Glen A. Taylor, Owner
Jim Stack, Gen. Mgr.
Randy Wittman, Head Coach
Zarko Durisic, Dir.-Player Personnel

Phone: 612-673-1600 **Fax:** 612-673-1699
Toll-Free:
Address: 600 First Ave. N., Minneapolis, MN 55403 US

GROWTH PLANS/SPECIAL FEATURES:

The Minnesota Timberwolves, founded in 1988, are a team playing in the National Basketball Association (NBA). The team is majority-owned by Glen Taylor, a former Minnesota senator and chairman of a huge printing company, the Taylor Corporation. The Timberwolves' vice president of basketball operations is former Boston Celtics' great Kevin McHale, and the team is coached by Randy Wittman. The team had a very promising 2003-04 season, making it to the Western Conference finals, but failing to make the playoffs in either the 2005-06 season or the 2006-07 season. The team resides in the Target Center, a 20,500-seat arena in downtown Minneapolis that also serves the Timberwolves' sister team, the Minnesota Lynx. The Timberwolves' star players include Latrell Sprewell, Sam Cassell, and Kevin Garnett, a dynamic trio that led the team's strong but thwarted efforts in the 2003-04 playoff season. The team plays in the Northwest Division of the NBA's Western Conference, alongside the Denver Nuggets, Portland Trail Blazers, Seattle SuperSonics and Utah Jazz. In the 2008-09 season, the team's home attendance average was roughly 14,500 per game. Forbes Magazine recently estimated the team to be worth approximately $301 million.

FINANCIALS:

Sales and profits are in thousands of dollars—add 000 to get the full amount. 2008 Note: Financial information for 2008 was not available for all companies at press time.

2008 Sales: $100,000	2008 Profits: $-5,700	**U.S. Stock Ticker: Private**
2007 Sales: $103,000	2007 Profits: $-1,900	**Int'l Ticker:** Int'l Exchange:
2006 Sales: $103,000	2006 Profits: $4,600	Employees:
2005 Sales: $101,000	2005 Profits: $	Fiscal Year Ends: 6/30
2004 Sales: $97,000	2004 Profits: $	Parent Company:

SALARIES/BENEFITS:

Pension Plan:	ESOP Stock Plan:	Profit Sharing:	Top Exec. Salary: $	Bonus: $
Savings Plan:	Stock Purch. Plan:		Second Exec. Salary: $	Bonus: $

OTHER THOUGHTS:

Apparent Women Officers or Directors:
Hot Spot for Advancement for Women/Minorities:

LOCATIONS: ("Y" = Yes)

West:	Southwest:	Midwest:	Southeast:	Northeast:	International:
		Y			

MINNESOTA TWINS

minnesota.twins.mlb.com

Industry Group Code: 711211A **Ranks within this company's industry group:** Sales: 27 Profits: 7

Sports:		Services:		Media:		Sales:		Facilities:		Other:	
Leagues/Associations:		Food & Beverage:	Y	TV:		Marketing:		Stadiums:		Gambling:	
Teams:	Y	Agents:		Radio:		Ads:		Fitness Clubs:		Apparel:	Y
Nonprofits:	Y	Other:		Internet:		Tickets:	Y	Golf Courses:		Equipment:	
Other:				Print:		Retail:	Y	Ski Resorts:		Shoes:	
				Software:		Other:		Other:		Other:	

TYPES OF BUSINESS:

Professional Baseball Team

BRANDS/DIVISIONS/AFFILIATES:

Twins Sports, Inc.
Hubert H. Humphrey Metrodome
Rochester Red Wings
New Britain Rock Cats
Fort Myers Miracle
Beloit Snappers
Elizabethtown Twins
Gulf Coast League Twins

CONTACTS:

Note: Officers with more than one job title may be intentionally listed here more than once.

Dave St. Peter, Pres.
Patrick Klinger, VP-Mktg.
Raenell Dorn, VP-Human Resources & Diversity
Wade Navratil, Dir.-Info. Systems
John Avenson, VP-Tech.
Kip Elliott, Sr. VP-Bus. Admin.
Matt Hoy, VP-Oper.
Laura Day, Sr. VP-Bus. Dev.
Kevin Smith, Exec. Dir.-Public Affairs & Twins Comm. Fund
Andy Weinstein, Dir.-Finance
Brad Steil, Dir.-Baseball Oper.
Bill Smith, Sr. VP/Gen. Mgr.
Rob Gardenhire, Mgr.
Jim Pohlad, Owner
Howard Fox, Chmn.
Bud Hanley, Dir.-Purchasing

Phone: 612-375-1366	**Fax:** 612-375-7473
Toll-Free:	
Address: 34 Kirby Puckett Pl., Minneapolis, MN 55415 US	

GROWTH PLANS/SPECIAL FEATURES:

The Minnesota Twins are a Major League Baseball (MLB) team. The club started in 1901 as the Washington Senators. Declining fan attendance and field performance moved the organization to Minneapolis for the 1961 season. In 1987 and 1991 the Twins were World Champions, but went on to eight straight losing seasons from 1993-2000. However, 2006 was the Twin's sixth straight winning season. In all, the franchise has won three World Series, six pennants and eight division titles. In 2002, the team was nearly disbanded, as MLB voted to contract two teams, including the Twins. However, the team avoided contraction as they were forced to play out their lease in the Hubert H. Humphrey Metrodome, which they shared with the Minnesota Vikings. In 2005, the Twins won a court decision that allowed them to escape their lease, and a stadium financing deal was approved in May 2006. In August 2007, construction began on Target Field, a new 40,000-seat baseball-only stadium, expected to be completed for the 2010 home opener. Valued at only $356 million by Forbes Magazine, the Twins have continued to win despite a small payroll. The team's minor league affiliates include the Rochester Red Wings, the New Britain Rock Cats, the Ft. Myers Miracle, the Beloit Snappers, the Elizabethton Twins and the Gulf Coast League Twins. In the 2008 season, the team averaged approximately 28,400 fans in attendance per game.

FINANCIALS:

Sales and profits are in thousands of dollars—add 000 to get the full amount. 2008 Note: Financial information for 2008 was not available for all companies at press time.

2008 Sales: $158,000	2008 Profits: $26,800	**U.S. Stock Ticker: Private**
2007 Sales: $149,000	2007 Profits: $23,800	**Int'l Ticker:** Int'l Exchange:
2006 Sales: $131,000	2006 Profits: $14,800	Employees:
2005 Sales: $114,000	2005 Profits: $	Fiscal Year Ends: 12/31
2004 Sales: $	2004 Profits: $	Parent Company:

SALARIES/BENEFITS:

Pension Plan:	ESOP Stock Plan:	Profit Sharing:	Top Exec. Salary: $	Bonus: $
Savings Plan:	Stock Purch. Plan:		Second Exec. Salary: $	Bonus: $

OTHER THOUGHTS:

Apparent Women Officers or Directors: 10
Hot Spot for Advancement for Women/Minorities: Y

LOCATIONS: ("Y" = Yes)

West:	Southwest:	Midwest:	Southeast:	Northeast:	International:
		Y			Y

MINNESOTA VIKINGS

www.vikings.com

Industry Group Code: 711211C **Ranks within this company's industry group:** Sales: 32 Profits: 24

Sports:		Services:		Media:		Sales:		Facilities:		Other:	
Leagues/Associations:		Food & Beverage:		TV:		Marketing:		Stadiums:		Gambling:	
Teams:	Y	Agents:		Radio:		Ads:		Fitness Clubs:		Apparel:	
Nonprofits:		Other:		Internet:		Tickets:	Y	Golf Courses:		Equipment:	
Other:				Print:		Retail:	Y	Ski Resorts:		Shoes:	
				Software:		Other:		Other:		Other:	

TYPES OF BUSINESS:

Professional Football Team

BRANDS/DIVISIONS/AFFILIATES:

Metrodome (The)
Minnesota Vikings Football Club, Inc.
Vikings Children's Fund

CONTACTS: *Note: Officers with more than one job title may be intentionally listed here more than once.*

Mark Wilf, Pres./Owner
Steve Poppen, CFO
Steve LaCroix, Chief Mktg. Officer/VP-Sales
Lisa Larson, Mgr.-Human Resources
Kevin Warren, Chief Admin. Officer
Kevin Warren, VP-Legal Affairs
Lester Bagley, VP-Public Affairs & Stadium Dev.
Steve Poppen, VP-Finance
Rob Brzezinski, VP-Football Oper.
Dave Blando, Dir.-Football Admin.
Rick Spielman, Gen. Mgr.
Brad Childress, Head Coach
Zygi Wilf, Chmn./Owner

Phone: 952-828-6500	**Fax:** 952-828-6540
Toll-Free:	
Address: 9520 Viking Dr., Eden Prairie, MN 55344 US	

GROWTH PLANS/SPECIAL FEATURES:

The Minnesota Vikings, owned by the Minnesota Vikings Football Club, Inc., are a professional football team in the National Football League (NFL) based in Minneapolis, Minnesota. The team entered the NFL in 1961, and made it to the Super Bowl on four occasions, all unsuccessful. The also appeared in the playoffs 25 times, the last in 2008. Well known players such as Fran Tarkenton and Warren Moon have played for the team. The team is owned principally by lawyer and businessman Zygi Wilf, who headed the financial group that purchased the team in 2005 from Red McCombs for $600 million. The Vikings play in the Metrodome for the time being; however, plans are in the works to construct a new retractable roof stadium with supporting facilities, including retail shops, restaurants, residential housing, space for small businesses, corporate offices, a hotel, a medical facility and 260 acres of preserved wetlands and trails. Zygi Wilf has offered to invest $1 billion of private capital for the venture. To this end, in June 2007, the Wilf ownership group acquired four city blocks near the Metrodome, with the goal of redevelopment to support the Vikings' new stadium. The team hosts a number of community football programs for youth, high school and college-level participants. The Viking's Children's Fund, which supports pediatric research and child-related wellness programs, has given over $7.65 million in grants to date. In the 2008-09 season, the Vikings won the NFC North Championship against the New York Giants 20-19. In January 2009, the team hosted the Philadelphia Eagles for the Wild Card round but were defeated 26-14. In the 2008 season, the team averaged approximately 63,267 fans in attendance per game. A recent Forbes estimate values the team at roughly $839 million.

FINANCIALS: **Sales and profits are in thousands of dollars—add 000 to get the full amount. 2008 Note: Financial information for 2008 was not available for all companies at press time.**

2008 Sales: $195,000
2007 Sales: $182,000
2006 Sales: $167,000
2005 Sales: $164,000
2004 Sales: $145,000

2008 Profits: $18,900
2007 Profits: $-19,100
2006 Profits: $16,300
2005 Profits: $
2004 Profits: $

U.S. Stock Ticker: Subsidiary
Int'l Ticker: Int'l Exchange:
Employees:
Fiscal Year Ends: 1/31
Parent Company: MINNESOTA VIKINGS FOOTBALL CLUB INC

SALARIES/BENEFITS:

Pension Plan:	ESOP Stock Plan:	Profit Sharing:	Top Exec. Salary: $	Bonus: $
Savings Plan:	Stock Purch. Plan:		Second Exec. Salary: $	Bonus: $

OTHER THOUGHTS:

Apparent Women Officers or Directors:
Hot Spot for Advancement for Women/Minorities:

LOCATIONS: ("Y" = Yes)

West:	Southwest:	Midwest:	Southeast:	Northeast:	International:
		Y			

MINNESOTA WILD

wild.nhl.com

Industry Group Code: 711211F **Ranks within this company's industry group:** Sales: 12 Profits: 18

Sports:		Services:		Media:		Sales:		Facilities:		Other:	
Leagues/Associations:		Food & Beverage:		TV:		Marketing:		Stadiums:		Gambling:	
Teams:	Y	Agents:		Radio:		Ads:		Fitness Clubs:		Apparel:	
Nonprofits:		Other:		Internet:		Tickets:	Y	Golf Courses:		Equipment:	
Other:				Print:		Retail:	Y	Ski Resorts:		Shoes:	
				Software:		Other:		Other:		Other:	

TYPES OF BUSINESS:

National Hockey League Team

BRANDS/DIVISIONS/AFFILIATES:

Minnesota Sports & Entertainment
Xcel Energy Center

CONTACTS: *Note: Officers with more than one job title may be intentionally listed here more than once.*

Matt Majka, COO
Doug Risebrough, Pres./Gen. Mgr.
Jeff Pellegrom, CFO/Exec. VP
Jamie Spencer, VP-Sales & Service
Jim Ibister, VP-Facilities Admin.
Bill Robertson, VP-Comm. & Broadcasting
Jac Sperling, Vice Chmn.
Craig Leipold, Owner/Governor
John Maher, VP-Brand Mktg.
Robert O. Naegele Jr., Chmn.

Phone: 651-602-6000	**Fax:** 651-222-1055
Toll-Free:	
Address: 317 Washington St., St. Paul, MN 55102 US	

GROWTH PLANS/SPECIAL FEATURES:

The Minnesota Wild is a National Hockey League (NHL) team that entered the league as an expansion team in 2000 along with the Columbus Blue Jackets. The team plays in the Northwest Division of the NHL's Western Conference, along with the Calgary Flames, Colorado Avalanche, Edmonton Oilers and Vancouver Canucks. When the Minnesota North Stars moved south to Texas in 1993, the void left a host of hockey fans without a team. The creation of the new team set NHL records for ticket sales by an expansion team. Minnesota Sports & Entertainment owns and operates the club and manages the team's arena. The team plays its home games at the multipurpose sports and entertainment facility known as the Xcel Energy Center. The arena seats 18,568 fans and includes executive suites, dining facilities and a state-of-the-art sound system and video display. Games are broadcast through WCCO Radio, the station with exclusive rights to pre-season, regular season and Stanley Cup playoff games. A recent Forbes list valued the team at roughly $217 million. In the 2008-09 season, the team saw an average home attendance of approximately 18,568 fans, selling every seat in the house plus standing room for every home game.

FINANCIALS: **Sales and profits are in thousands of dollars—add 000 to get the full amount. 2008 Note: Financial information for 2008 was not available for all companies at press time.**

2008 Sales: $94,000	2008 Profits: $ 700	**U.S. Stock Ticker: Subsidiary**
2007 Sales: $78,000	2007 Profits: $-1,700	**Int'l Ticker:** Int'l Exchange:
2006 Sales: $71,000	2006 Profits: $4,700	Employees:
2005 Sales: $	2005 Profits: $	Fiscal Year Ends: 6/30
2004 Sales: $71,000	2004 Profits: $	Parent Company: MINNESOTA SPORTS & ENTERTAINMENT

SALARIES/BENEFITS:

Pension Plan:	ESOP Stock Plan:	Profit Sharing:	Top Exec. Salary: $	Bonus: $
Savings Plan:	Stock Purch. Plan:		Second Exec. Salary: $	Bonus: $

OTHER THOUGHTS:

Apparent Women Officers or Directors:
Hot Spot for Advancement for Women/Minorities:

LOCATIONS: ("Y" = Yes)

West:	Southwest:	Midwest:	Southeast:	Northeast:	International:
		Y			

MINOR LEAGUE BASEBALL

www.minorleaguebaseball.com

Industry Group Code: 813990 **Ranks within this company's industry group:** Sales: Profits:

Sports:		Services:		Media:		Sales:		Facilities:		Other:	
Leagues/Associations:	Y	Food & Beverage:		TV:		Marketing:		Stadiums:		Gambling:	
Teams:		Agents:		Radio:		Ads:		Fitness Clubs:		Apparel:	
Nonprofits:		Other:		Internet:		Tickets:		Golf Courses:		Equipment:	
Other:				Print:		Retail:		Ski Resorts:		Shoes:	
				Software:		Other:		Other:		Other:	

TYPES OF BUSINESS:

Minor League Baseball Association

BRANDS/DIVISIONS/AFFILIATES:

Eastern League
Southern League
Texas League
International League
Mexican League
Pacific Coast League
New York-Penn League
South Atlantic League

CONTACTS:

Note: Officers with more than one job title may be intentionally listed here more than once.

Pat O'Conner, CEO
Tim Purpura, COO/Exec. VP
Pat O'Conner, Pres.
Rod Meadows, Exec. Dir.-Mktg. & Sales
Rob Colamarino, Dir.-IT
Scott Poley, General Counsel
John Cook, Sr. VP-Bus. Oper.
Jeff Carrier, Mgr.-Acct.
Stan Brand, VP
Plinio Escalante, Pres., Mexican League
Tim Brunswick, Exec. Dir.-Baseball Oper.
Branch Rickey, Pres., Pacific Coast League
Randy Mobley, Pres., Int'l League

Phone: 727-822-6937 **Fax:** 727-821-5819
Toll-Free: 866-644-2687
Address: 201 Bayshore Dr. SE, St. Petersburg, FL 33731 US

GROWTH PLANS/SPECIAL FEATURES:

Minor League Baseball (MiLB), formerly The National Association of Professional Baseball Leagues, Inc., is the governing body for 19 leagues and approximately 250 teams in the U.S. and internationally. Each league is classified in ascending order as either Rookie, Class A, Class Double-A or Class Triple-A. Rookie leagues include the Appalachian League; Arizona League; Dominican Summer League; and Venezuelan Summer League. Class A leagues are divided into three categories labeled Class A Short Season, Class A and Class A Advanced. Some of the organization's Class A leagues are the New York-Penn League; South Atlantic League; California League; Carolina League; and Florida State League. MiLB's three Double-A leagues are the Eastern League, Southern League and Texas League; its three Class Triple-A leagues are the International League, Mexican League and Pacific Coast League. Each minor league team is also affiliated with a major league team. For example, the Boston Red Sox, the 2004 World Series champion, has seven feeder teams: GCL Red Sox and DSL Red Sox, both Rookie teams; Lowell Spinners, a Class A short-season team; Greenville Drive, a Class A team; Wilmington Blue Rocks, a Class A advanced team; Portland Sea dogs, a Double-A team; and Pawtucket Red Sox, a Triple-A team. The company's new program, Minor League Baseball Green Team, was formed to take steps to make MiLB operations more environmentally friendly.

FINANCIALS:

Sales and profits are in thousands of dollars—add 000 to get the full amount. 2008 Note: Financial information for 2008 was not available for all companies at press time.

2008 Sales: $	2008 Profits: $	**U.S. Stock Ticker: Private**
2007 Sales: $	2007 Profits: $	**Int'l Ticker:** Int'l Exchange:
2006 Sales: $	2006 Profits: $	Employees:
2005 Sales: $	2005 Profits: $	Fiscal Year Ends: 12/31
2004 Sales: $	2004 Profits: $	Parent Company:

SALARIES/BENEFITS:

Pension Plan:	ESOP Stock Plan:	Profit Sharing:	Top Exec. Salary: $	Bonus: $
Savings Plan:	Stock Purch. Plan:		Second Exec. Salary: $	Bonus: $

OTHER THOUGHTS:

Apparent Women Officers or Directors:
Hot Spot for Advancement for Women/Minorities:

LOCATIONS: ("Y" = Yes)

West:	Southwest:	Midwest:	Southeast:	Northeast:	International:
			Y		Y

MONTREAL CANADIENS

www.canadiens.com

Industry Group Code: 711211F **Ranks within this company's industry group:** Sales: 2 Profits: 2

Sports:		Services:		Media:		Sales:		Facilities:		Other:	
Leagues/Associations:		Food & Beverage:		TV:		Marketing:		Stadiums:	Y	Gambling:	
Teams:	Y	Agents:		Radio:		Ads:		Fitness Clubs:		Apparel:	
Nonprofits:		Other:		Internet:		Tickets:	Y	Golf Courses:		Equipment:	
Other:				Print:		Retail:	Y	Ski Resorts:		Shoes:	
				Software:		Other:		Other:		Other:	

TYPES OF BUSINESS:

Major League Hockey Team

BRANDS/DIVISIONS/AFFILIATES:

Montreal Canadiens
National Hockey League (NHL)
Stanley Cup
Hockey Hall of Fame
Heritage Classic
Bell Centre
Molson Centre
Booth Creek Ski Holdings, Inc.

CONTACTS: *Note: Officers with more than one job title may be intentionally listed here more than once.*

Pierre Boivin, Pres.
Fred Steer, CFO
Ray Lalonde, VP-Mktg. & Sales
Donald Beauchamp, VP-Comm. & Community Rel.
George N. Gillet, Jr., Owner
Foster Gillett, Managing Partner
Bob Gainey, Exec. VP/Gen. Mgr.
Guy Carbonneau, Head Coach
Jeff Joyce, Vice Chairman

Phone: 514-932-2582	**Fax:** 514-932-8736
Toll-Free:	
Address: 1275 Saint Antoine St. W., Montreal, QC H3C 5L2 Canada	

GROWTH PLANS/SPECIAL FEATURES:

The Montreal Canadiens, in French known as Le Club de Hockey Canadien, is a professional ice hockey team and Quebec's only National Hockey League (NHL) team. Founded in 1909, the Canadiens are the oldest team in the NHL and have won a record 24 Stanley Cups (11 more than any other team), the first of which was in 1916, before the NHL existed, and the most recent of which was in 1993. Approximately 50 former Canadiens players have been inducted into the Hockey Hall of Fame. In 1995, the team began a general decline when it missed the playoffs for the first time in 25 years. The team then missed the playoffs for three straight seasons between 1999 and 2001. The Canadiens went back to the playoffs in 2002 and 2004 but missed the interim playoffs in 2003. The team participated in the Heritage Classic, the first outdoor hockey game in the history of the NHL, during 2003. The Canadiens play their home games at the Bell Centre (formerly the Molson Centre), one of the largest arenas in the NHL, with an arena capacity of up to 21,500. Since its opening in 1996, the arena has consistently been listed as one of the busiest in the world, with an average attendance during the 2008/9 season of 21,273. George N. Gillett, Jr., chairman of Booth Creek Ski Holding (a U.S.-based ski resort developer), owns both the team and the Bell Centre. The team will host the 2009 NHL All-Star Game and is bidding to host an outdoor game in Montreal three days before the All-Star Game as part of its centennial year celebrations. Forbes recently estimated the team is worth roughly $334 million.

FINANCIALS: **Sales and profits are in thousands of dollars—add 000 to get the full amount. 2008 Note: Financial information for 2008 was not available for all companies at press time.**

2008 Sales: $139,000	2008 Profits: $39,600	**U.S. Stock Ticker: Private**
2007 Sales: $109,000	2007 Profits: $25,200	**Int'l Ticker:** Int'l Exchange:
2006 Sales: $90,000	2006 Profits: $17,500	Employees:
2005 Sales: $	2005 Profits: $	Fiscal Year Ends: 8/31
2004 Sales: $90,000	2004 Profits: $	Parent Company:

SALARIES/BENEFITS:

Pension Plan:	ESOP Stock Plan:	Profit Sharing:	Top Exec. Salary: $	Bonus: $
Savings Plan:	Stock Purch. Plan:		Second Exec. Salary: $	Bonus: $

OTHER THOUGHTS:

Apparent Women Officers or Directors: 1
Hot Spot for Advancement for Women/Minorities:

LOCATIONS: ("Y" = Yes)

West:	Southwest:	Midwest:	Southeast:	Northeast:	International:
					Y

MOTORSPORTS AUTHENTICS INC

www.action-performance.com

Industry Group Code: 451120 **Ranks within this company's industry group:** Sales: Profits:

Sports:		Services:		Media:		Sales:		Facilities:		Other:	
Leagues/Associations:		Food & Beverage:		TV:		Marketing:		Stadiums:		Gambling:	
Teams:		Agents:		Radio:		Ads:		Fitness Clubs:		Apparel:	Y
Nonprofits:		Other:		Internet:		Tickets:		Golf Courses:		Equipment:	
Other:				Print:		Retail:		Ski Resorts:		Shoes:	
				Software:		Other:		Other:		Other:	Y

TYPES OF BUSINESS:

Toys & Collectibles
Auto Racing Collectibles & Memorabilia
Motorsports Apparel & Merchandise

BRANDS/DIVISIONS/AFFILIATES:

International Speedway
Speedway Motorsports, Inc.
Action Racing Collectibles
Brookfield Collector's Guild
Winner's Circle
Revell
Chase Authentics
Minichamps

CONTACTS:

Note: Officers with more than one job title may be intentionally listed here more than once.

Mark Dyer, CEO
Mark Dyer, Pres.
Pat Harvey, CFO
Scott Warfield, Dir.-Mktg.
Scott Warfield, Dir.-Public Rel.

Phone: 704-454-4000 **Fax:** 704-454-4006
Toll-Free: 888-332-4000
Address: 6301 Performance Dr., Concord, NC 28027 US

GROWTH PLANS/SPECIAL FEATURES:

Motorsports Authentics, Inc., an International Speedway and Speedway Motorsports joint-venture, is a leading designer of licensed NASCAR, NHRA, Formula One, IRL and World of Outlaws die-cast scaled replicas of vehicles, apparel and memorabilia. The company manages a total of 51 brands. The firm's business plan is focused on harboring long-term licensing agreements with motorsports drivers and team owners, providing the company with the exclusive rights to design and develop products bearing the team and driver's name, likeness and image. The company has agreements with NASCAR drivers such as Dale Earnhardt Jr., Jeff Gordon, Jimmie Johnson, Tony Stewart, Kevin Harvick, Carl Edwards and Kasey Kahne. In addition to its die cast memorabilia, the firm produces and markets a line of officially licensed NASCAR apparel under the Chase Authentics brand name, which bills itself as the authentic trackside apparel of NASCAR. This apparel includes a line of jackets, hats, t-shirts and jerseys featuring the names, likenesses and color schemes of popular NASCAR drivers. The Action Racing Collectibles, AP, Revell and Brookfield Collector's Guild brands are sold in 45 countries through some 10,000 retailers, 30 trackside stores, and the firm's goracing.com web site. The Winner's Circle brand of die-cast products and Racing Collectibles Club of America brands are managed by QVC. Additionally, the company has agreements with wholesale distributors throughout Germany, where Motorsports Authentics markets its Minichamps collectibles die-cast brand. Motorsports designs every die-cast collectible that it manufactures.

FINANCIALS:

Sales and profits are in thousands of dollars—add 000 to get the full amount. 2008 Note: Financial information for 2008 was not available for all companies at press time.

2008 Sales: $	2008 Profits: $	**U.S. Stock Ticker: Joint Venture**
2007 Sales: $	2007 Profits: $	**Int'l Ticker:** Int'l Exchange:
2006 Sales: $	2006 Profits: $	Employees: 590
2005 Sales: $	2005 Profits: $	Fiscal Year Ends: 9/30
2004 Sales: $344,300	2004 Profits: $ 500	Parent Company:

SALARIES/BENEFITS:

Pension Plan:	ESOP Stock Plan:	Profit Sharing:	Top Exec. Salary: $798,250	Bonus: $
Savings Plan:	Stock Purch. Plan:		Second Exec. Salary: $401,700	Bonus: $

OTHER THOUGHTS:

Apparent Women Officers or Directors:
Hot Spot for Advancement for Women/Minorities:

LOCATIONS: ("Y" = Yes)

West:	Southwest:	Midwest:	Southeast:	Northeast:	International:
Y	Y	Y	Y	Y	Y

NASCAR

www.nascar.com

Industry Group Code: 711212 **Ranks within this company's industry group:** Sales: Profits:

Sports:		Services:		Media:		Sales:		Facilities:		Other:	
Leagues/Associations:	Y	Food & Beverage:		TV:	Y	Marketing:	Y	Stadiums:		Gambling:	
Teams:		Agents:		Radio:	Y	Ads:	Y	Fitness Clubs:		Apparel:	Y
Nonprofits:		Other:		Internet:	Y	Tickets:		Golf Courses:		Equipment:	
Other:				Print:		Retail:		Ski Resorts:		Shoes:	
				Software:		Other:		Other:		Other:	

TYPES OF BUSINESS:

Professional Stock Car Racing Association

BRANDS/DIVISIONS/AFFILIATES:

National Association for Stock Car Auto Racing
NASCAR Sprint Cup Series
Nationwide Series
Craftsman Truck Series
Whelen Modified Tour
Camping World Series
Canada Tire Series
Mexico Series

CONTACTS:

Note: Officers with more than one job title may be intentionally listed here more than once.

Brian France, CEO
Mike Helton, Pres.
R. Todd Wilson, CFO
Steven Phelps, Chief Mktg. Officer
Gary Crotty, General Counsel/Sec.
Leslie Maxie, Public Rel.
Bill France, Jr., Vice Chmn.
Jay Abraham, COO-NASCAR Media Group
Lisa Kennedy, Exec. VP
Brian France, Chmn.

Phone: 386-253-0611	**Fax:** 386-681-4041
Toll-Free:	
Address: 1801 W. International Speedway Blvd., Daytona Beach, FL 32114 US	

GROWTH PLANS/SPECIAL FEATURES:

National Association for Stock Car Auto Racing, Inc. (NASCAR) is the largest sanctioning body of motorsports in the U.S. and one of the country's fastest-growing spectator sports. The organization runs more than 100 stock car races each year throughout the U.S. through three racing circuits: the NASCAR Sprint Cup Series, Nationwide Series and Craftsman Truck Series. The NASCAR Sprint Cup Series is the sport's highest level of professional competition, and consequently it is the most popular and most profitable NASCAR series. The Sprint Cup circuit consists of 36 races each season, with well over $4 million in total prize money at stake in each race. The Nationwide Series is NASCAR's second-tier stock car racing series, featuring a mix of young talent, series veterans and high-profile drivers in the 35-race season, which includes races in Canada and Mexico. The Craftsman Truck Series is a racing series for modified pick-up trucks, composed of 25 races a year. In addition to its three main race series, NASCAR operates four regional series, one grassroots series and two international series. Regional series include the Camping World Series, racing in both the eastern and western regions of the U.S.; the Whelen Modified Tour, which takes place in New Hampshire, Pennsylvania, Massachusetts, Connecticut and New York; the Whelen Southern Modified Tour, a similar race for the southeastern states; and the Whelen All-American Series, utilizing more than 60 tracks across North America. NASCAR's two international series are the Canadian Tire Series and the Mexico Series. NASCAR races are broadcasted in more than 150 countries and 30 languages.

FINANCIALS:

Sales and profits are in thousands of dollars—add 000 to get the full amount. 2008 Note: Financial information for 2008 was not available for all companies at press time.

2008 Sales: $	2008 Profits: $	**U.S. Stock Ticker: Private**
2007 Sales: $	2007 Profits: $	**Int'l Ticker:** Int'l Exchange:
2006 Sales: $	2006 Profits: $	Employees:
2005 Sales: $	2005 Profits: $	Fiscal Year Ends: 12/31
2004 Sales: $	2004 Profits: $	Parent Company:

SALARIES/BENEFITS:

Pension Plan:	ESOP Stock Plan:	Profit Sharing:	Top Exec. Salary: $	Bonus: $
Savings Plan:	Stock Purch. Plan:		Second Exec. Salary: $	Bonus: $

OTHER THOUGHTS:

Apparent Women Officers or Directors: 2
Hot Spot for Advancement for Women/Minorities:

LOCATIONS: ("Y" = Yes)

West:	Southwest:	Midwest:	Southeast:	Northeast:	International:
Y	Y	Y	Y	Y	Y

NASHVILLE PREDATORS

www.nashvillepredators.com

Industry Group Code: 711211F **Ranks within this company's industry group:** Sales: 28 Profits: 19

Sports:		Services:		Media:		Sales:		Facilities:		Other:	
Leagues/Associations:		Food & Beverage:		TV:		Marketing:		Stadiums:	Y	Gambling:	
Teams:	Y	Agents:		Radio:		Ads:		Fitness Clubs:		Apparel:	Y
Nonprofits:		Other:		Internet:		Tickets:	Y	Golf Courses:		Equipment:	
Other:				Print:		Retail:	Y	Ski Resorts:		Shoes:	
				Software:		Other:		Other:		Other:	

TYPES OF BUSINESS:

Professional Hockey Team
Predators Merchandise & Apparel

BRANDS/DIVISIONS/AFFILIATES:

Predators Holdings LLC
Preds (The)
Sommet Center
Powers Management

CONTACTS: *Note: Officers with more than one job title may be intentionally listed here more than once.*

David Poile, Gen. Mgr./Alternate Governor
Randy Campbell, VP-Mktg.
Allison Winters, Dir.-Human Resources
Blake Grant, Dir.-Technical Oper.
Mark Floyd, Exec. VP-Admin.
David Poile, Pres., Hockey Oper.
Chris Parker, Sr. VP-Corp. Dev.
Jay Levin, Mgr.-Internet Dev.
Gerry Helper, Sr. VP-Comm. & Dev.
Mark Floyd, Exec. VP-Finance
Barry Trotz, Head Coach
Ed Lang, Pres., Bus. Oper./Alternate Governor
Paul Fenton, Assistant Gen. Mgr.
Nat Harden, VP-Ticket Sales
David Freeman, Chmn./Governor

Phone: 615-770-2300 **Fax:** 615-770-2309
Toll-Free:
Address: Sommet Ctr., 501 Broadway, Nashville, TN 37203 US

GROWTH PLANS/SPECIAL FEATURES:

The Nashville Predators are a National Hockey League (NHL) team started in 1998 as an expansion team. The Preds, as they are popularly known, play in the Central Division of the NHL's Western Conference, along with the Chicago Blackhawks, Columbus Blue Jackets, Detroit Red Wings and St. Louis Blues. Although the franchise struggled through its first few years, it finally won a place in the Western Conference finals, the quarterfinals for the Stanley Cup, for the first time in the 2003-04 season, but lost to the Detroit Red Wings. The team's home stadium is Sommet Center, built in 1996. The stadium was known as Gaylord Entertainment Center from 1999-2007 and as Nashville Arena from March-May 2007. Sommet Center seats over 17,100 for hockey games, 20,000 for basketball games and 10,000-20,000 for concerts, depending on where the musicians perform. It has occasionally been used to host Broadway and other theater performances, and can seat around 5,100 for those shows. The stadium is owned by the Sports Authority of Nashville and Davidson County; and is operated by Powers Management, a subsidiary of the Predators franchise. The team is currently owned by a consortium of local businessmen operating under the Predators Holdings LLC banner. The group acquired the team and Powers Management from majority owner and former Chairman Craig Leipold for $193 million after Mr. Leipold contemplated moving the team to a different city. In February 2009, the team's owners entered into discussions with Canadian billionaire Brett Wilson regarding the potential purchase of a stake in the team by Mr. Wilson. Forbes recently estimated the team to be worth $164 million. The team's average home attendance in the 2008-09 season was approximately 15,000 fans per game.

Employees of the franchise receive life, health, dental and medical insurance; paid vacations and holidays; and flexible spending accounts.

FINANCIALS: **Sales and profits are in thousands of dollars—add 000 to get the full amount. 2008 Note: Financial information for 2008 was not available for all companies at press time.**

2008 Sales: $70,000	2008 Profits: $-1,300	**U.S. Stock Ticker: Subsidiary**
2007 Sales: $65,000	2007 Profits: $-9,400	**Int'l Ticker:** Int'l Exchange:
2006 Sales: $61,000	2006 Profits: $-1,100	Employees:
2005 Sales: $	2005 Profits: $	Fiscal Year Ends:
2004 Sales: $42,000	2004 Profits: $	Parent Company: PREDATORS HOLDINGS LLC

SALARIES/BENEFITS:

Pension Plan:	ESOP Stock Plan:	Profit Sharing:	Top Exec. Salary: $	Bonus: $
Savings Plan: Y	Stock Purch. Plan:		Second Exec. Salary: $	Bonus: $

OTHER THOUGHTS:

Apparent Women Officers or Directors: 23
Hot Spot for Advancement for Women/Minorities: Y

LOCATIONS: ("Y" = Yes)

West:	Southwest:	Midwest:	Southeast:	Northeast:	International:
			Y		

Note: Financial information, benefits and other data can change quickly and may vary from those stated here.

NATIONAL BASKETBALL ASSOCIATION (NBA)

www.nba.com

Industry Group Code: 813990 **Ranks within this company's industry group:** Sales: Profits:

Sports:		Services:		Media:		Sales:		Facilities:		Other:	
Leagues/Associations:	Y	Food & Beverage:		TV:	Y	Marketing:	Y	Stadiums:		Gambling:	
Teams:		Agents:		Radio:	Y	Ads:	Y	Fitness Clubs:		Apparel:	Y
Nonprofits:		Other:		Internet:	Y	Tickets:		Golf Courses:		Equipment:	Y
Other:				Print:		Retail:	Y	Ski Resorts:		Shoes:	Y
				Software:		Other:		Other:		Other:	

TYPES OF BUSINESS:

Professional Basketball League
Cable Television Channel

BRANDS/DIVISIONS/AFFILIATES:

NBA
National Basketball Development League
Euroleague Basketball
USA Basketball
NBA TV
DirecTV
Anschutz Entertainment Group

CONTACTS:

Note: Officers with more than one job title may be intentionally listed here more than once.

David Stern, Commissioner
Adam Silver, COO/Deputy Commissioner
Heidi Ueberroth, Pres., Mktg. Partnerships & Int'l Bus. Oper.
Michael Gliedman, CIO/Sr. VP
Richard Buchanan, General Counsel/Exec. VP
Renee Brown, Chief Basketball Oper. & Player Rel.
Kenneth I. Adelson, Sr. VP-Planning & Prod. Oper.
Robert Criqui, Exec. VP-Finance
Stu Jackson, Exec. VP-Basketball Oper.
Ski Austin, Exec. VP-Events & Attractions
Joel M. Litvin, Pres., League & Basketball Oper.
Michael Bass, Sr. VP-Mktg. Comm.
Mark Fischer, Sr. VP-NBA China

Phone: 212-826-7000 **Fax:** 212-754-6414
Toll-Free:
Address: Olympic Tower, 645 5th Ave., New York, NY 10022 US

GROWTH PLANS/SPECIAL FEATURES:

The National Basketball Association (NBA) is one of the world's largest professional basketball leagues. Formed in 1946 as the Basketball Association of America, it adopted its current name in 1949 after merging with its rival, the National Basketball League. David Stern, the league's commissioner since 1984, has overseen the creation of the now-independent WNBA, created the NBA Cares social programs, introduced a strict dress code for players and introduced a new microfiber ball, which he promptly recalled after mounting player concerns. The league currently includes 30 teams, 29 in the U.S. and one in Toronto, Canada, as well as 17 teams in the NBA Development League (D-League), with the newest D-League team, announced in March 2009, to play out of Springfield, Massachusetts. The NBA's regular season begins in the last week of October and ends in April. In a regular season, each team plays 82 games, 41 home and 41 away games. The league owns and operates a television network called NBA TV, which is dedicated to showing live and classic basketball games and promoting the sport. The NBA has a partnership deal with DirecTV to broadcast the channel 24-hours-a-day. The channel also occasionally broadcasts Euroleague Basketball, Europe's professional basketball association, and other international games. NBA TV is available in the U.S. and 79 other countries and territories. The NBA is an active member of USA Basketball, the national governing body for basketball in the U.S. In October 2008, the NBA announced a joint venture with Anschutz Entertainment Group (AEG) to design and develop 12 multi-purpose sports and entertainment arenas in major cities throughout China.

The NBA offers employees medical, dental and life insurance; health club and educational reimbursement; flexible spending accounts; a college savings plan; pre-paid legal services; employee discounts; and a 401(k) and pension plan.

FINANCIALS:

Sales and profits are in thousands of dollars—add 000 to get the full amount. 2008 Note: Financial information for 2008 was not available for all companies at press time.

2008 Sales: $	2008 Profits: $	**U.S. Stock Ticker: Private**
2007 Sales: $	2007 Profits: $	**Int'l Ticker:** Int'l Exchange:
2006 Sales: $	2006 Profits: $	Employees:
2005 Sales: $3,200,000	2005 Profits: $	Fiscal Year Ends: 8/31
2004 Sales: $3,000,000	2004 Profits: $	Parent Company:

SALARIES/BENEFITS:

Pension Plan: Y	ESOP Stock Plan:	Profit Sharing:	Top Exec. Salary: $	Bonus: $
Savings Plan: Y	Stock Purch. Plan:		Second Exec. Salary: $	Bonus: $

OTHER THOUGHTS:

Apparent Women Officers or Directors: 6
Hot Spot for Advancement for Women/Minorities: Y

LOCATIONS: ("Y" = Yes)

West:	Southwest:	Midwest:	Southeast:	Northeast:	International:
Y			Y	Y	Y

NATIONAL FOOTBALL LEAGUE (NFL)

www.nfl.com

Industry Group Code: 813990 **Ranks within this company's industry group:** Sales: Profits:

Sports:		Services:		Media:		Sales:		Facilities:		Other:	
Leagues/Associations:	Y	Food & Beverage:		TV:	Y	Marketing:		Stadiums:		Gambling:	
Teams:		Agents:		Radio:		Ads:		Fitness Clubs:		Apparel:	
Nonprofits:		Other:	Y	Internet:	Y	Tickets:		Golf Courses:		Equipment:	
Other:				Print:		Retail:		Ski Resorts:		Shoes:	
				Software:		Other:		Other:		Other:	

TYPES OF BUSINESS:

Professional Football League
Television Network

BRANDS/DIVISIONS/AFFILIATES:

NFL
American Football Conference
National Football Conference
Super Bowl
NFL Network

CONTACTS:

Note: Officers with more than one job title may be intentionally listed here more than once.

Roger Goodell, Commissioner
Anthony Noto, CFO
Mark Waller, Sr. VP-Sales & Mktg.
Nancy Gill, Sr. VP-Human Resources
Adolpho Birch, VP-Law & Labor Policy
Ray Anderson, Exec. VP-Football Oper.
Neil Glat, Sr. VP-Corp. Dev.
Brian Rolapp, Sr. VP-Digital Media
Joe Browne, Exec. VP-Comm. & Public Affairs
Steven M. Bornstein, Pres./CEO-NFL Network
Brian McCarthy, VP-Corp. Comm.
Jim Steeg, VP-Special Events
Frank Supovicz, Sr. VP-Events
Gordon Smeaton, VP-Int'l

Phone: 212-450-2000 **Fax:** 212-681-7599
Toll-Free:
Address: 280 Park Ave., New York, NY 10017 US

GROWTH PLANS/SPECIAL FEATURES:

The National Football League (NFL), an unincorporated organization controlled by its members, is one of the largest and most popular professional sports leagues in the U.S. Founded in 1920, the modern NFL was born when the league merged with the American Football League (AFL) in 1966. An echo of the two leagues still exists in the NFL's two conferences, the American Football Conference (AFC) and the National Football Conference (NFC). The NFL's 32 franchised teams are equally divided between the two conferences, which are each subdivided into four divisions. NFL matches draw an average of more than 67,000 spectators per game. The NFL season begins on the Thursday after Labor Day, and runs until late December or early January. About half of the 16 games each team plays in a regular season are against its division rivals, with the remainder consisting of inter-division and inter-conference games. Every year at the end of the season, there are 12 inner-conference playoff games played by the top six teams in each conference, consisting of the four division champions and the top two remaining non-division champion teams with the best record. The resulting AFC champion then plays the NFC champion in the Super Bowl, one of the most-watched television events in the U.S. The 2009 Super Bowl XLIII (43) was one of the most-watched television events of all time and had the biggest audience of any Super Bowl in history, drawing an estimated 98.7 million television viewers to watch the Pittsburg Steelers beat the Arizona Cardinals 27-23. The league owns the NFL Network, a television network that operates 24-hours-a-day, seven-days-a-week, 365-days-a-year and is dedicated solely to the NFL and the sport of football. Although individual league teams act as separate businesses, the NFL maintains a revenue-sharing plan aimed at promoting greater parity between various franchises.

FINANCIALS:

Sales and profits are in thousands of dollars—add 000 to get the full amount. 2008 Note: Financial information for 2008 was not available for all companies at press time.

2008 Sales: $	2008 Profits: $	**U.S. Stock Ticker: Private**
2007 Sales: $	2007 Profits: $	**Int'l Ticker:** Int'l Exchange:
2006 Sales: $	2006 Profits: $	Employees: 450
2005 Sales: $	2005 Profits: $	Fiscal Year Ends: 3/31
2004 Sales: $6,000,000	2004 Profits: $	Parent Company:

SALARIES/BENEFITS:

Pension Plan:	ESOP Stock Plan:	Profit Sharing:	Top Exec. Salary: $	Bonus: $
Savings Plan:	Stock Purch. Plan:		Second Exec. Salary: $	Bonus: $

OTHER THOUGHTS:

Apparent Women Officers or Directors:
Hot Spot for Advancement for Women/Minorities:

LOCATIONS: ("Y" = Yes)

West:	Southwest:	Midwest:	Southeast:	Northeast:	International:
				Y	

Note: Financial information, benefits and other data can change quickly and may vary from those stated here.

NATIONAL HOCKEY LEAGUE (NHL)

www.nhl.com

Industry Group Code: 813990 **Ranks within this company's industry group:** Sales: Profits:

Sports:		Services:		Media:		Sales:		Facilities:		Other:	
Leagues/Associations:	Y	Food & Beverage:		TV:		Marketing:	Y	Stadiums:		Gambling:	
Teams:		Agents:		Radio:		Ads:		Fitness Clubs:		Apparel:	
Nonprofits:		Other:		Internet:		Tickets:		Golf Courses:		Equipment:	
Other:				Print:		Retail:		Ski Resorts:		Shoes:	
				Software:		Other:		Other:		Other:	

TYPES OF BUSINESS:

Professional Ice Hockey League

BRANDS/DIVISIONS/AFFILIATES:

Stanley Cup
NHL CenterIce
NHL Network
XM Home Ice
Detroit Redwings
Pittsburgh Penguins
Eastern Conference
Western Conference

CONTACTS: *Note: Officers with more than one job title may be intentionally listed here more than once.*

Gary B. Bettman, Commissioner
John Collins, COO
Craig Harnett, CFO/Exec. VP
David Zimmerman, General Counsel/Exec. VP
Colin Campbell, Exec. VP-Hockey Oper.
William Daly, Deputy Commissioner
Stephen Walkom, Dir.-Officiating

Phone: 212-789-2000	**Fax:** 212-789-2020
Toll-Free:	
Address: 1185 Ave. of the Americas, 12th Fl., New York, NY 10020 US	

GROWTH PLANS/SPECIAL FEATURES:

The National Hockey League (NHL) is the largest professional ice hockey league in the U.S., and currently includes 30 member teams throughout the U.S. and Canada. The firm's teams are divided into two conferences, the Eastern Conference (EC) and the Western Conference (WC), each of which has three divisions that are composed of five teams. EC's three divisions are Atlantic (New Jersey Devils, New York Islanders, New York Rangers, Philadelphia Flyers and Pittsburg Penguins), Northeast (Boston Bruins, Buffalo Sabers, Montreal Canadians, Ottawa Senators and Toronto Maple Leafs) and Southeast (Atlanta Thrashers, Carolina Hurricanes, Florida Panthers, Tampa Bay Lighting and Washington Capitals). WC's three divisions are Central (Chicago Blackhawks, Columbus Blue Jackets, Detroit Red Wings, Nashville Predators and St. Louis Blues), Northwest (Calgary Flames, Colorado Avalanche, Edmonton Oilers, Minnesota Wild and the Vancouver Canucks) and Pacific (Anaheim Ducks, Dallas Stars, Los Angeles Kings, Phoenix Coyotes and San Jose Sharks). Each season, the teams within a division will play elimination games against each other to produce a division champion. The division champions in each conference then play each other until one remains. The victors go on to play each other for the Stanley Cup. Every year the NHL awards the Stanley Cup to the champion of its playoff tournament. The company sets the rules, regulates team ownerships, governs the game and collects licensing fees for merchandise, as well as negotiating fees for national broadcasting rights. In the 2008 NHL All-Star game, played between the Eastern and Western Conferences, the Eastern All-Stars emerged victorious, with player Eric Staal taking the honor of most valuable player (MVP); the Eastern Conference also won the 2009 All-Star game in a 12-11 shootout, with Alexei Kovalev receiving MVP honors. The Detroit Redwings beat the Pittsburgh Penguins to become the 2008 Stanley Cup Champions.

FINANCIALS: **Sales and profits are in thousands of dollars—add 000 to get the full amount. 2008 Note: Financial information for 2008 was not available for all companies at press time.**

2008 Sales: $	2008 Profits: $	**U.S. Stock Ticker: Private**
2007 Sales: $	2007 Profits: $	**Int'l Ticker:** Int'l Exchange:
2006 Sales: $	2006 Profits: $	Employees:
2005 Sales: $	2005 Profits: $	Fiscal Year Ends: 6/30
2004 Sales: $2,100,000	2004 Profits: $	Parent Company:

SALARIES/BENEFITS:

Pension Plan:	ESOP Stock Plan:	Profit Sharing:	Top Exec. Salary: $	Bonus: $
Savings Plan:	Stock Purch. Plan:		Second Exec. Salary: $	Bonus: $

OTHER THOUGHTS:

Apparent Women Officers or Directors:
Hot Spot for Advancement for Women/Minorities:

LOCATIONS: ("Y" = Yes)

West:	Southwest:	Midwest:	Southeast:	Northeast:	International:
Y	Y	Y	Y	Y	Y

NATIONAL THOROUGHBRED RACING ASSOCIATION www.ntra.com

Industry Group Code: 813990 **Ranks within this company's industry group:** Sales: Profits:

Sports:		Services:		Media:		Sales:		Facilities:		Other:	
Leagues/Associations:	Y	Food & Beverage:		TV:	Y	Marketing:		Stadiums:		Gambling:	
Teams:		Agents:		Radio:		Ads:		Fitness Clubs:		Apparel:	
Nonprofits:	Y	Other:		Internet:		Tickets:		Golf Courses:		Equipment:	
Other:				Print:		Retail:		Ski Resorts:		Shoes:	
				Software:		Other:		Other:		Other:	

TYPES OF BUSINESS:

Thoroughbred Racing Association

BRANDS/DIVISIONS/AFFILIATES:

Triple Crown
Breeders' Cup Limited
NTRA Charities
NTRA Advantage LLC
NTRA Investments LLC
NTRA Productions
American Horse Council
Unwanted Horse Coalition

CONTACTS: *Note: Officers with more than one job title may be intentionally listed here more than once.*

Alex Waldrop, CEO
Alex Waldrop, Pres.
Vicki Baumgardner, CFO
Keith Chamblin, Sr. VP-Mktg.
Peggy Hendershot, Sr. VP-Legislative Affairs
Keith Chamblin, Sr. VP-Industry Rel.
Robert Elliston, Chmn.
Terry McElfresh, Sr. VP-Purchasing

Phone: 859-245-6872 **Fax:**
Toll-Free: 800-792-6872
Address: 2525 Harrodsburg Rd., Ste. 400, Lexington, KY 40504 US

GROWTH PLANS/SPECIAL FEATURES:

The National Thoroughbred Racing Association (NTRA), a not-for-profit organization, is the trade organization and convening authority for the U.S. thoroughbred horse industry, charged with strengthening the thoroughbred racing industry by increasing public awareness, creating a centralized national structure, implementing comprehensive marketing strategies and enhancing the industry's economic condition. The organization's lobbying efforts focus on legislation relating to equine drug testing, animal welfare, wagering technology and sales integrity. The NTRA organizes races throughout the U.S., including all three Triple Crown races. In addition, the NTRA and Breeders' Cup Limited administer the Breeder's Cup Stakes Program, the qualifying races for the Breeder's Cup World Thoroughbred Championships. NTRA's network includes approximately 110 member tracks. Subsidiary NTRA Charities is a not-for-profit organization focused on promoting and supporting charities in or related to the thoroughbred industry. NTRA Charities' national partner is Ronald McDonald House Charities, Inc.; its industry partners include the Jockey Club Foundation, Race for Education, Thoroughbred Charities of America, Thoroughbred Retirement Foundation and Tranquility Farm. Other subsidiaries include NTRA Advantage LLC, focused on delivering cost savings and value-added services to NTRA members through group purchasing; a 75% interest in NTRA Investments LLC, a for-profit company that makes strategic acquisitions to benefit NTRA members; and its subsidiary NTRA Productions, a producer of horse racing programming and controller of the world's largest archive of horse racing videos. NTRA Productions also holds all NTRA programming contracts. Together with the American Horse Council, the organization participates in various committees relating to horse health and safety, such as the Unwanted Horse Coalition, whose mission is the reduction of the number of unwanted horses in the U.S. In July 2008, Pinnacle Race Course in Huron Township, Michigan became an NTRA member track.

FINANCIALS: **Sales and profits are in thousands of dollars—add 000 to get the full amount. 2008 Note: Financial information for 2008 was not available for all companies at press time.**

2008 Sales: $	2008 Profits: $	**U.S. Stock Ticker: Private**
2007 Sales: $	2007 Profits: $	**Int'l Ticker:** Int'l Exchange:
2006 Sales: $	2006 Profits: $	Employees: 30
2005 Sales: $77,700	2005 Profits: $4,100	Fiscal Year Ends: 12/31
2004 Sales: $66,200	2004 Profits: $	Parent Company:

SALARIES/BENEFITS:

Pension Plan:	ESOP Stock Plan:	Profit Sharing:	Top Exec. Salary: $	Bonus: $
Savings Plan:	Stock Purch. Plan:		Second Exec. Salary: $	Bonus: $

OTHER THOUGHTS:

Apparent Women Officers or Directors: 3
Hot Spot for Advancement for Women/Minorities: Y

LOCATIONS: ("Y" = Yes)

West:	Southwest:	Midwest:	Southeast:	Northeast:	International:
		Y		Y	

Note: Financial information, benefits and other data can change quickly and may vary from those stated here.

NBA DEVELOPMENT LEAGUE

www.nba.com/dleague

Industry Group Code: 813990 **Ranks within this company's industry group:** Sales: Profits:

Sports:		Services:		Media:		Sales:		Facilities:		Other:	
Leagues/Associations:	Y	Food & Beverage:		TV:		Marketing:		Stadiums:		Gambling:	
Teams:		Agents:		Radio:		Ads:		Fitness Clubs:		Apparel:	
Nonprofits:		Other:		Internet:		Tickets:		Golf Courses:		Equipment:	
Other:				Print:		Retail:		Ski Resorts:		Shoes:	
				Software:		Other:		Other:		Other:	

TYPES OF BUSINESS:

Minor League Basketball

BRANDS/DIVISIONS/AFFILIATES:

NBA
NBDL
NBA FutureCast
Idaho Stampede (The)
Austin Toros (The)
Maine Red Claws (The)

CONTACTS:

Note: Officers with more than one job title may be intentionally listed here more than once.

Dan Reed, Pres.
Bobby Sharma, General Counsel
Chris Alpert, VP-Basketball Oper.
Kris Kolehmain, Coordinator-Bus. Dev.
Kent Patridge, VP-Comm.

Phone: 212-407-8700	**Fax:** 212-759-1412
Toll-Free:	
Address: 477 Madison Ave., 3rd Fl., New York, NY 10022 US	

GROWTH PLANS/SPECIAL FEATURES:

The National Basketball Development League (NBDL or D-League), a division of the National Basketball Association (NBA), was created by the NBA in 2002 to act as its in-house minor league. The league currently has 16 teams: the L.A. D-fenders; Iowa Energy; Idaho Stampede; Fort Wayne Mad Ants; Erie BayHawks; Dakota Wizards; Colorado 14ers; Bakersfield Jam; Anaheim Arsenal; Reno Bighorns; Rio Grande Valley Vipers; Sioux Falls Skyforce; Tulsa 66ers; Utah Flash; Austin Toros; and the Albuquerque Thunderbirds. Each of the NBDL teams is affiliated with one to three NBA teams, and NBA teams may assign players in their first two seasons to the NBDL. Players are eligible for the league if they are over the age of 20 and have passed the tryout, as well as those players who were drafted into the NBA. The NBDL season lasts 20 weeks and teams play a 48-game schedule. NBDL offers NBA FutureCast, an online link on its web site which offers fans the chance to watch live and archived games for free. In April 2008, the Idaho Stampede beat the Austin Toros to become the league's champions. In March and April 2009, the league announced the creation of two new teams: Springfield (team name not yet decided) and the Maine Red Claws; both teams are scheduled to compete in the 2009-10 season.

FINANCIALS:

Sales and profits are in thousands of dollars—add 000 to get the full amount. 2008 Note: Financial information for 2008 was not available for all companies at press time.

2008 Sales: $	2008 Profits: $	**U.S. Stock Ticker: Private**
2007 Sales: $	2007 Profits: $	**Int'l Ticker:** Int'l Exchange:
2006 Sales: $	2006 Profits: $	Employees:
2005 Sales: $	2005 Profits: $	Fiscal Year Ends: 8/31
2004 Sales: $	2004 Profits: $	Parent Company:

SALARIES/BENEFITS:

Pension Plan:	ESOP Stock Plan:	Profit Sharing:	Top Exec. Salary: $	Bonus: $
Savings Plan:	Stock Purch. Plan:		Second Exec. Salary: $	Bonus: $

OTHER THOUGHTS:

Apparent Women Officers or Directors:
Hot Spot for Advancement for Women/Minorities:

LOCATIONS: ("Y" = Yes)

West:	Southwest:	Midwest:	Southeast:	Northeast:	International:
				Y	

NBC UNIVERSAL

www.nbcuni.com

Industry Group Code: 513120 **Ranks within this company's industry group:** Sales: 1 Profits: 1

Sports:		Services:		Media:		Sales:		Facilities:		Other:	
Leagues/Associations:		Food & Beverage:		TV:	Y	Marketing:	Y	Stadiums:		Gambling:	
Teams:		Agents:		Radio:	Y	Ads:	Y	Fitness Clubs:		Apparel:	
Nonprofits:		Other:		Internet:	Y	Tickets:		Golf Courses:		Equipment:	
Other:				Print:		Retail:		Ski Resorts:		Shoes:	
				Software:		Other:		Other:	Y	Other:	

TYPES OF BUSINESS:

Television Broadcasting
Online News & Information
TV & Movie Production
Radio Broadcasting
Interactive Online Content
Cable Television Programming
Theme Parks
Film, TV & Home Video Distribution

BRANDS/DIVISIONS/AFFILIATES:

General Electric Co (GE)
Vivendi Universal Entertainment
Hulu LLC
Universal Pictures
Universal Studios
MSNBC
Universal Parks & Resorts
Ivillage Inc

CONTACTS: *Note: Officers with more than one job title may be intentionally listed here more than once.*

Jeff Zucker, CEO
Jeff Zucker, Pres.
Lynn Calpeter, CFO/Exec. VP
Michael Pilot, Pres., Sales & Mktg.
Marc Chini, Exec. VP-Human Resources
John Eck, CIO/Pres., Media Works
Richard Cotton, General Counsel/Exec. VP
Salil Mehta, Pres., Bus. Oper., Strategy & Dev.
Cory Shields, Exec. VP-Comm.
Steve Capus, Pres., NBC News
Jeff Gaspin, Pres., Universal Television Group
Mark Hoffman, Pres., CNBC
Michael Bass, Sr. VP-Strategic Initiatives
Peter Smith, Pres., NBC Universal Int'l

Phone: 212-664-4444	**Fax:** 212-664-4085
Toll-Free:	
Address: 30 Rockefeller Plz., New York, NY 10112 US	

GROWTH PLANS/SPECIAL FEATURES:

NBC Universal, Inc. is one of the world's largest media and entertainment companies in the development, production and marketing of entertainment, news and information to a global audience. The company is a subsidiary of General Electric Co. (GE) and the product of a 2004 merger of Vivendi Universal Entertainment with NBC (National Broadcasting Company). The company is 20%-owned by Vivendi Universal and 80%-owned by GE. Assets merged into the new organization include Universal Pictures, Universal Television and the Universal Studios theme parks. In addition, the company oversees the NBC Television Network. NBC Universal TV Stations operates 10 NBC affiliate stations and 16 Telemundo stations in major U.S. markets, offering original programming, news, movies, sports and more. The firm operates cable channels including Bravo, CNBC, MSNBC and USA Networks and holds a partial interest in A&E. NBC Internet, Inc., a wholly-owned subsidiary of NBC, operates a network of web sites centered around nbci.com and msnbc.com, integrating access across all of its major media platforms, including Internet, broadcast and cable television and radio. The division also owns 50% of Hulu.com, an online video service jointly-owned by NBC Universal and News Corp. International assets include sales and distribution positions for video and DVD titles, television programming and feature films in more than 200 countries around the world. Universal Recreation Group brings together the operations of Universal Parks and Resorts, including wholly-owned Universal Studios Hollywood and Universal CityWalk Hollywood, and major interests in both Universal Orlando properties (including Islands of Adventure, CityWalk Orlando and Universal Studios Florida) and international locations including Universal Studios Japan and Universal Mediterranean in Spain.

FINANCIALS: **Sales and profits are in thousands of dollars—add 000 to get the full amount. 2008 Note: Financial information for 2008 was not available for all companies at press time.**

2008 Sales: $16,969,000	2008 Profits: $3,131,000	**U.S. Stock Ticker: Subsidiary**
2007 Sales: $15,416,000	2007 Profits: $3,107,000	**Int'l Ticker:** Int'l Exchange:
2006 Sales: $16,188,000	2006 Profits: $2,919,000	Employees: 15,500
2005 Sales: $14,689,000	2005 Profits: $3,092,000	Fiscal Year Ends: 12/31
2004 Sales: $12,886,000	2004 Profits: $2,558,000	Parent Company: GENERAL ELECTRIC CO (GE)

SALARIES/BENEFITS:

Pension Plan:	ESOP Stock Plan:	Profit Sharing:	Top Exec. Salary: $	Bonus: $450,000
Savings Plan: Y	Stock Purch. Plan:		Second Exec. Salary: $336,549	Bonus: $336,549

OTHER THOUGHTS:

Apparent Women Officers or Directors: 2
Hot Spot for Advancement for Women/Minorities: Y

LOCATIONS: ("Y" = Yes)

West:	Southwest:	Midwest:	Southeast:	Northeast:	International:
Y		Y		Y	Y

Note: Financial information, benefits and other data can change quickly and may vary from those stated here.

NEW BALANCE ATHLETIC SHOE INC

www.newbalance.com

Industry Group Code: 316219 **Ranks within this company's industry group:** Sales: 5 Profits:

Sports:		Services:		Media:		Sales:		Facilities:		Other:	
Leagues/Associations:		Food & Beverage:		TV:		Marketing:		Stadiums:		Gambling:	
Teams:		Agents:		Radio:		Ads:		Fitness Clubs:		Apparel:	Y
Nonprofits:		Other:		Internet:		Tickets:		Golf Courses:		Equipment:	Y
Other:				Print:		Retail:		Ski Resorts:		Shoes:	Y
				Software:		Other:		Other:		Other:	

TYPES OF BUSINESS:

Athletic Footwear & Apparel
Sports Equipment
Leather Boots
Lacrosse Equipment

BRANDS/DIVISIONS/AFFILIATES:

Warrior
Dunham
PF Flyers
Abzorb
Aravon
Brine

CONTACTS:

Note: Officers with more than one job title may be intentionally listed here more than once.

Robert DeMartini, CEO
Jim Tompkins, COO
Jim Tompkins, Pres.
John Withee, CFO/Exec. VP
Chris Quinn, Exec. VP- North American Sales
Carol O'Donnell, VP-Corp. Human Resources
John Wilson, Exec. VP-Mfg.
Anne Davis, Exec. VP-Admin.
Jim Conners, VP-Global Dev. & Design
Bill Hayden, VP-Finance
Kerry Kligerman, Exec. VP-Apparel
Joe Preston, Exec. VP-Global Footwear, Product & Mktg.
Edith Harmon, VP-Advanced Concepts
Edward Haddad, VP-Intellectual Property & Licensed Products
James S. Davis, Chmn.
Alan Hed, VP-Int'l
Jim Sciabarrasi, VP-Sourcing & Procurement

Phone: 617-783-4000	**Fax:** 617-787-9355
Toll-Free: 800-253-7463	
Address: Brighton Landing, 20 Guest St., Boston, MA 02135-2088 US	

GROWTH PLANS/SPECIAL FEATURES:

New Balance Athletic Shoe, Inc. is an athletic footwear and apparel company, which began as an arch-support company in the early 1900s. The firm manufactures men's and women's shoes for running, cross-training, basketball, tennis, baseball, cheerleading, hiking and golf. The company also offers fitness apparel and kids' shoes. In addition, New Balance owns Warrior, a cutting-edge global manufacturer of lacrosse equipment; men's footwear maker Dunham; PF-Flyers, a line of active comfort shoes; Aravon, a women's casual footwear line; and Brine, a line of performance products for lacrosse, soccer, hockey and volleyball. New Balance makes use of advanced technology in the production of its shoes, using products like Abzorb foam, which is a complex blend of rubber and proprietary materials which provide extra cushioning and compression properties. The company is also known for its wide selection of shoe widths. It is the only major maker of athletic shoes that still has plants in the U.S., while its major competitors get most or all of their shoes from Asia. New Balance sells its products in over 120 countries around the world. The firm also maintains numerous licensees, joint ventures and distributors in the U.K., France, Germany, Sweden, Hong Kong, Singapore, Australia, New Zealand, Mexico, Canada, Japan, Brazil and South Africa. New Balance is an active sponsor of athletic and community organizations, including Sesame Street, the La Salle Bank Chicago Marathon and the Susan G. Komen Breast Cancer Foundation. In June 2008, the firm announced plans to restructure its lifestyle strategic business unit.

Employees are offered medical and dental coverage; a 401(k) plan; flexible spending accounts; flextime work schedule, tuition reimbursement; employee purchase program; college saving plan; corporate gift matching; employee discounts; and an on-site wellness program.

FINANCIALS:

Sales and profits are in thousands of dollars—add 000 to get the full amount. 2008 Note: Financial information for 2008 was not available for all companies at press time.

2008 Sales: $1,500,000	2008 Profits: $	**U.S. Stock Ticker: Private**
2007 Sales: $1,500,000	2007 Profits: $	**Int'l Ticker:** Int'l Exchange:
2006 Sales: $1,550,000	2006 Profits: $	Employees: 2,800
2005 Sales: $1,540,000	2005 Profits: $	Fiscal Year Ends: 12/31
2004 Sales: $	2004 Profits: $	Parent Company:

SALARIES/BENEFITS:

Pension Plan:	ESOP Stock Plan:	Profit Sharing:	Top Exec. Salary: $	Bonus: $
Savings Plan:	Stock Purch. Plan:		Second Exec. Salary: $	Bonus: $

OTHER THOUGHTS:

Apparent Women Officers or Directors: 4
Hot Spot for Advancement for Women/Minorities: Y

LOCATIONS: ("Y" = Yes)

West:	Southwest:	Midwest:	Southeast:	Northeast:	International:
				Y	Y

NEW ENGLAND PATRIOTS

www.patriots.com

Industry Group Code: 711211C **Ranks within this company's industry group:** Sales: 2 Profits: 5

Sports:		Services:		Media:		Sales:		Facilities:		Other:	
Leagues/Associations:		Food & Beverage:	Y	TV:		Marketing:		Stadiums:	Y	Gambling:	
Teams:	Y	Agents:		Radio:		Ads:		Fitness Clubs:		Apparel:	Y
Nonprofits:		Other:		Internet:		Tickets:	Y	Golf Courses:		Equipment:	
Other:				Print:		Retail:	Y	Ski Resorts:		Shoes:	
				Software:		Other:		Other:		Other:	

TYPES OF BUSINESS:

Professional Football Team

BRANDS/DIVISIONS/AFFILIATES:

Gillette Stadium

CONTACTS:

Note: Officers with more than one job title may be intentionally listed here more than once.

Robert Kraft, CEO/Owner
Jonathan Kraft, Pres.
Nick Caserio, Dir.-Player Personnel
Bill Belichick, Head Coach
Jon Robinson, Dir.-College Scouting
Jason Licht, Dir.-Pro Personnel
Ernie Adams, Dir.-Football Research
Robert Kraft, Chmn.

Phone: 508-543-8200 **Fax:** 508-543-0285
Toll-Free: 800-543-1776
Address: 1 Patriot Pl., Foxborough, MA 02035-1388 US

GROWTH PLANS/SPECIAL FEATURES:

The New England Patriots are a professional football team playing in the Eastern Division of the American Football Conference (AFC) of the National Football League (NFL) along with the Buffalo Bills, Miami Dolphins and New York Jets. The team formed in 1960 as an original member of the American Football League under the name of the Boston Patriots. In 1970, the Patriots joined the NFL in the league merger, and the next year, in 1971, the Patriots moved to their current home in Foxborough, Massachusetts, a suburb of Boston. From its inception in 1960 through the early 1990s, the team underwent many changes of ownership, coaching turnovers and poor seasons. In 1994, Robert Kraft obtained full ownership of the Patriots, beginning a move toward stability and positive play on the field. In 1996, the team reached Super Bowl XXXI, but it lost to the Green Bay Packers. In 2001, the Patriots completed an amazing turnaround that resulted in three Super Bowl titles in four years (2001, 2003 and 2004), a new stadium (Gillette Stadium, privately funded, owned and operated by Robert Kraft) and a revitalized fan base. The Patriots were undefeated through much of the 2007-08 football season, losing in the Super Bowl to the New York Giants; however, in the 2008-09 season, the team failed to make the playoffs despite an 11-5 record. Notable players have included Tom Brady, Andre Tippett and Mike Haynes. Forbes recently valued the team at approximately $1.32 billion. In the 2008 season, the team averaged approximately 63,267 fans in attendance per game.

FINANCIALS:

Sales and profits are in thousands of dollars—add 000 to get the full amount. 2008 Note: Financial information for 2008 was not available for all companies at press time.

2008 Sales: $282,000
2007 Sales: $255,000
2006 Sales: $250,000
2005 Sales: $236,000
2004 Sales: $

2008 Profits: $39,200
2007 Profits: $34,900
2006 Profits: $43,600
2005 Profits: $
2004 Profits: $

U.S. Stock Ticker: Private
Int'l Ticker: Int'l Exchange:
Employees:
Fiscal Year Ends: 12/31
Parent Company:

SALARIES/BENEFITS:

Pension Plan: ESOP Stock Plan: Profit Sharing: Top Exec. Salary: $ Bonus: $
Savings Plan: Stock Purch. Plan: Second Exec. Salary: $ Bonus: $

OTHER THOUGHTS:

Apparent Women Officers or Directors: 1
Hot Spot for Advancement for Women/Minorities:

LOCATIONS: ("Y" = Yes)

West:	Southwest:	Midwest:	Southeast:	Northeast:	International:
				Y	

NEW ENGLAND REVOLUTION

www.revolutionsoccer.net

Industry Group Code: 711211D **Ranks within this company's industry group:** Sales: Profits:

Sports:		Services:		Media:		Sales:		Facilities:		Other:	
Leagues/Associations:		Food & Beverage:		TV:		Marketing:		Stadiums:		Gambling:	
Teams:	Y	Agents:		Radio:		Ads:		Fitness Clubs:		Apparel:	
Nonprofits:	Y	Other:		Internet:		Tickets:	Y	Golf Courses:		Equipment:	
Other:				Print:		Retail:	Y	Ski Resorts:		Shoes:	
				Software:		Other:		Other:		Other:	

TYPES OF BUSINESS:

Major League Soccer Team
Soccer Camps

BRANDS/DIVISIONS/AFFILIATES:

Kraft Soccer
Mass Youth Soccer

CONTACTS:

Note: Officers with more than one job title may be intentionally listed here more than once.

Brian Bilello, COO/VP
Craig Tornberg, Gen. Mgr.
Jennifer Ferron, VP-Mktg.
Robert Kraft, Owner
Jonathan Kraft, Operator
Mike Burns, Dir.-Soccer
Steve Nicol, Head Coach

Phone: 508-543-1776	**Fax:**
Toll-Free:	
Address: Gillette Stadium, 1 Patriot Pl., Foxborough, MA 02035-1388 US	

GROWTH PLANS/SPECIAL FEATURES:

The New England Revolution, owned by holding company Kraft Soccer, is a Major League Soccer (MLS) team based in Massachusetts and playing at the Gillette Stadium. It was one of the 10 founding teams of the MLS, and has fielded star players such as defender Alexi Lalas, midfielder Clint Dempsey, defender Mike Burns and forward Joe-Max Moore. The team plays in the Eastern Conference of the MLS along with the Chicago Fire, Columbus Crew, D.C. United, Toronto FC, Kansas City Wizards and New York Red Bulls. In the team's 11-year history, it has made the playoffs three times but has never won the championship. The New England Revolution is actively devoted to the development of youth soccer, and it runs various training camps and programs tailored to specific age groups and skill sets. The team runs Mass Youth Soccer, a non-profit that aims to develop and educate both coaches and players, as well as increase standards of sportsmanship. In 2007, regular season game attendance averaged 16,700 and post season attendance averaged 10,200, an increase of approximately 5,000 and 800 over the previous year, respectively. The team currently plays home games at Gillette Stadium, but is actively looking at sites around New England for the development of a soccer-specific stadium and training facility. The club has held preliminary discussions with the city of Somerville about building a 20,000- to 25,000-seat stadium on a 100-acre site near Interstate 93, with a potential cost anywhere between $50 and $200 million. The design would be based on other similar soccer-specific stadiums built by MLS teams.

FINANCIALS:

Sales and profits are in thousands of dollars—add 000 to get the full amount. 2008 Note: Financial information for 2008 was not available for all companies at press time.

2008 Sales: $	2008 Profits: $	**U.S. Stock Ticker: Subsidiary**
2007 Sales: $	2007 Profits: $	**Int'l Ticker:** Int'l Exchange:
2006 Sales: $	2006 Profits: $	Employees:
2005 Sales: $	2005 Profits: $	Fiscal Year Ends:
2004 Sales: $	2004 Profits: $	Parent Company: KRAFT SOCCER

SALARIES/BENEFITS:

Pension Plan:	ESOP Stock Plan:	Profit Sharing:	Top Exec. Salary: $	Bonus: $
Savings Plan:	Stock Purch. Plan:		Second Exec. Salary: $	Bonus: $

OTHER THOUGHTS:

Apparent Women Officers or Directors: 1
Hot Spot for Advancement for Women/Minorities:

LOCATIONS: ("Y" = Yes)

West:	Southwest:	Midwest:	Southeast:	Northeast:	International:
				Y	

NEW JERSEY DEVILS

www.newjerseydevils.com

Industry Group Code: 711211F **Ranks within this company's industry group:** Sales: 8 Profits: 13

Sports:		Services:		Media:		Sales:		Facilities:		Other:	
Leagues/Associations:		Food & Beverage:		TV:		Marketing:		Stadiums:		Gambling:	
Teams:	Y	Agents:		Radio:		Ads:		Fitness Clubs:		Apparel:	
Nonprofits:		Other:		Internet:		Tickets:	Y	Golf Courses:		Equipment:	
Other:				Print:		Retail:	Y	Ski Resorts:		Shoes:	
				Software:		Other:		Other:		Other:	

TYPES OF BUSINESS:

Major League Hockey Team

BRANDS/DIVISIONS/AFFILIATES:

National Hockey League (NHL)
Kansas City Scouts
Colorado Rockies
Stanley Cup
Prudential Center
Rock (The)
Continental Airlines Arena
Izod Center

CONTACTS: *Note: Officers with more than one job title may be intentionally listed here more than once.*

Louis A. (Lou) Lamoriello, CEO
Chris Modrzynski, COO/Sr. Exec. VP
Louis A. (Lou) Lamoriello, Pres./Gen. Mgr.
Scott Struble, CFO/Exec. VP
Sandra Van Meek, VP-Mktg. & Community Dev.
Gordon Lavalette, Exec. VP-Admin.
Joseph C. Benedetti, General Counsel/Sr. VP
David Conte, Exec. VP-Hockey Oper./Dir.-Scouting
Mike Levine, Sr. VP-Info. & Publications
Brent Sutter, Head Coach
Chris Lamoriello, Sr. VP-Hockey Oper.
Peter S. McMullen, Exec. VP
Terry Farmer, Sr. VP-Ticket Oper.
Jeffrey (Jeff) Vanderbeek, Chmn./Owner/Managing Partner

Phone: 201-935-6050	**Fax:** 201-935-2127
Toll-Free:	
Address: 50 Rte. 120 N., East Rutherford, NJ 07073 US	

GROWTH PLANS/SPECIAL FEATURES:

The New Jersey Devils franchise is a professional ice hockey team playing in the National Hockey League (NHL) based in East Rutherford, New Jersey. The franchise plays in the Atlantic Division of the Eastern Conference along with New York Rangers, New York Islanders, Philadelphia Flyers and Pittsburgh Penguins. The team was founded in 1974 in Kansas City, Missouri as the Kansas City Scouts, which it remained until 1976. The franchise then moved to Denver, Colorado and changed its name to the Colorado Rockies. The team finally became the New Jersey Devils when it moved to East Rutherford, New Jersey in 1982. The Devils had a general losing streak until 1990. Between 1990 and 1993, the team made the playoffs each year, only to lose in the first round. In 1995, the franchise won its first Stanley Cup title. The team went on to make four more consecutive Stanley Cup finals appearances, winning the first in 2000 and the last in 2003 for a total of three Stanley Cups. The Devils have made the playoffs in 18 out of the last 20 seasons, including all of the last 11. The Devils are owned by Jeffrey Vanderbeek, who led an investment group takeover in early 2005. The team's home arena is the Prudential Center, locally known as The Rock. The new arena, with a seating capacity of 17,625, replaced the team's former home arena, the Continental Airlines Arena (now the Izod Center) in 2007. In the 2008-09 season, the team averaged approximately 15,800 fans in attendance per game. A recent Forbes estimate values the team at $222 million.

FINANCIALS: **Sales and profits are in thousands of dollars—add 000 to get the full amount. 2008 Note: Financial information for 2008 was not available for all companies at press time.**

2008 Sales: $97,000	2008 Profits: $1,900	**U.S. Stock Ticker: Private**
2007 Sales: $65,000	2007 Profits: $-15,300	**Int'l Ticker:** Int'l Exchange:
2006 Sales: $62,000	2006 Profits: $-6,700	Employees:
2005 Sales: $	2005 Profits: $	Fiscal Year Ends: 6/30
2004 Sales: $61,000	2004 Profits: $	Parent Company:

SALARIES/BENEFITS:

Pension Plan:	ESOP Stock Plan:	Profit Sharing:	Top Exec. Salary: $	Bonus: $
Savings Plan:	Stock Purch. Plan:		Second Exec. Salary: $	Bonus: $

OTHER THOUGHTS:

Apparent Women Officers or Directors: 2
Hot Spot for Advancement for Women/Minorities:

LOCATIONS: ("Y" = Yes)

West:	Southwest:	Midwest:	Southeast:	Northeast:	International:
				Y	

NEW JERSEY NETS

www.nba.com/nets

Industry Group Code: 711211B **Ranks within this company's industry group:** Sales: 25 Profits: 22

Sports:		Services:		Media:		Sales:		Facilities:		Other:	
Leagues/Associations:		Food & Beverage:		TV:		Marketing:		Stadiums:		Gambling:	
Teams:	Y	Agents:		Radio:		Ads:		Fitness Clubs:		Apparel:	
Nonprofits:		Other:		Internet:		Tickets:	Y	Golf Courses:		Equipment:	
Other:				Print:		Retail:	Y	Ski Resorts:		Shoes:	
				Software:		Other:		Other:		Other:	

TYPES OF BUSINESS:

Professional Basketball Team
Sports Merchandise
Ticket Sales

BRANDS/DIVISIONS/AFFILIATES:

Nets Sports & Entertainment, LLC
New Jersey Americans
New York Nets
Nets Dancers
Nets Kids
Nets Drumline
Nets Athlete Assist Program
Team Hype

CONTACTS:

Note: Officers with more than one job title may be intentionally listed here more than once.

Rod Thorn, Pres.
Charlie Mierswa, CFO/Sr. VP
Fred Mangione, Sr. VP-Mktg. &Ticket Sales
Kimberly Blanco, Exec. Dir.-Human Resources
Mimi Viau, Sr. Dir.-IT
Jeff Gewirtz, General Counsel/Sr. VP
Bobby Marks, VP-Basketball Oper.
Gary Sussman, VP-Public Rel.
Paul Koehler, Controller
Brett Yormark, CEO/Pres., Nets Sports & Entertainment
Lawrence Frank, Head Coach
Bruce Ratner, Principal Owner
Kiki Vandeweghe, Gen. Mgr.

Phone: 201-935-8888 **Fax:** 201-939-1088
Toll-Free: 800-765-6387
Address: 390 Murray Hill Pkwy., East Rutherford, NJ 07073 US

GROWTH PLANS/SPECIAL FEATURES:

The New Jersey Nets, currently owned and managed by Nets Sports & Entertainment, LLC, joined the American Basketball Association (ABA) in 1967 as the New Jersey Americans. The team was renamed the New York Nets after its move to Long Island. After the merger of the ABA with the National Basketball Association (NBA), the Nets officially joined the NBA and were later renamed the New Jersey Nets for the 1977-78 season. The team's home games are played at the Continental Airlines Arena, which is located in the IZOD Center in East Rutherford, New Jersey. The arena boasts a 20,049 seating capacity and attracts resident from both the New York metropolitan and New Jersey areas. Featured entertainment during game nights include the Nets Dancers, Net Kids, Team Hype and Nets Drumline. The team has sponsored community outreach programs such as the Student Rewards Program and the Nets Athlete Assist Program. With the assistance of former player Jason Kidd, the Nets appeared in the NBA Finals in the 2002-03 and 2004-05 seasons, but were defeated every time before advancement to the finals. In the 2007-08 season, the Nets finished with a 41.5% record, failing to make the NBA playoffs. Following the season, the team's owner, Bruce Ratner, announced plans to move the team to Brooklyn, New York. In the 2008-09 season, the team's home attendance average was roughly 15,100 per game. Forbes Magazine recently estimated the team to be worth approximately $295 million.

FINANCIALS:

Sales and profits are in thousands of dollars—add 000 to get the full amount. 2008 Note: Financial information for 2008 was not available for all companies at press time.

2008 Sales: $98,000	2008 Profits: $- 900
2007 Sales: $102,000	2007 Profits: $-1,300
2006 Sales: $93,000	2006 Profits: $-8,000
2005 Sales: $87,000	2005 Profits: $
2004 Sales: $93,000	2004 Profits: $

U.S. Stock Ticker: Subsidiary
Int'l Ticker: Int'l Exchange:
Employees:
Fiscal Year Ends: 6/30
Parent Company: NETS SPORTS & ENTERTAINMENT LLC

SALARIES/BENEFITS:

Pension Plan:	ESOP Stock Plan:	Profit Sharing:	Top Exec. Salary: $	Bonus: $
Savings Plan:	Stock Purch. Plan:		Second Exec. Salary: $	Bonus: $

OTHER THOUGHTS:

Apparent Women Officers or Directors: 7
Hot Spot for Advancement for Women/Minorities: Y

LOCATIONS: ("Y" = Yes)

West:	Southwest:	Midwest:	Southeast:	Northeast:	International:
				Y	

NEW ORLEANS HORNETS

www.nba.com/hornets

Industry Group Code: 711211B **Ranks within this company's industry group:** Sales: 28 Profits: 19

Sports:		Services:		Media:		Sales:		Facilities:		Other:	
Leagues/Associations:		Food & Beverage:		TV:		Marketing:		Stadiums:		Gambling:	
Teams:	Y	Agents:		Radio:		Ads:		Fitness Clubs:		Apparel:	
Nonprofits:		Other:		Internet:		Tickets:	Y	Golf Courses:		Equipment:	
Other:				Print:		Retail:	Y	Ski Resorts:		Shoes:	
				Software:		Other:		Other:		Other:	

TYPES OF BUSINESS:

Professional Basketball Team
Sports Merchandise
Ticket Sales

BRANDS/DIVISIONS/AFFILIATES:

New Orleans Arena
Honeybees
Stingers
Loud City Patrol
Academy Sports Krewe
Oklahoma City Hornets

CONTACTS: *Note: Officers with more than one job title may be intentionally listed here more than once.*

Hugh Weber, Pres.
Matt Biggers, VP-Mktg.
Donna Rochon, Dir.-Human Resources
Stephen Clark, CTO
Richard House, General Counsel/VP
Sam Russo, Sr. VP-Oper.
Bill Bailey, Sr. VP-Corp. Strategic Dev.
Jim Eichenhofer, Mgr.-Publications & New Media
Michael Thompson, Dir.-Corp. Comm.
Dan Crumb, VP-Finance
Jeff Bower, Gen. Mgr.
Byron Scott, Head Coach
Darrell Walker, Assistant Coach
Nathan Hubbell, Dir.-Bus. Dev.
George Shinn, Owner

Phone: 504-593-4700 **Fax:** 504-593-4701
Toll-Free:
Address: 1250 Poydras St., Fl. 19, New Orleans, LA 70113 US

GROWTH PLANS/SPECIAL FEATURES:

The New Orleans Hornets began as an NBA expansion team in Charlotte, North Carolina in 1988. Due to poor attendance, the team relocated to New Orleans in 2002. The team stadium is located in the $84 million New Orleans Arena, which is situated next to the New Orleans Superdome and has an 18,000 seating capacity. Promotional entertainment groups of the team include the Honeybees, the Stingers, Loud City Patrol and Academy Sports Krewe. Noteworthy players of the Hornets have included include Larry Johnson, Muggsy Bogues, Alonzo Mourning and Glen Rice. After the 2005 Hurricane Katrina disaster, the team was temporarily relocated to Oklahoma City for the 2005-06 and 2006-07 seasons. Although the Hornets have made the finals sporadically throughout the 1990's, the team has failed to gain a playoff seat for the past two seasons. In the beginning of 2007, the Hornets declined a relocation offer by Oklahoma City, which would have Oklahoma the permanent home of the Hornets. In October 2007, the team opened the 2007-08 regular season at home in New Orleans for the first time since the 2004-05 season, beating the Sacramento Kings 104-90. After a successful 2007-08 season, the Hornets lost to the Spurs 3-4 in the Western Conference Semi-finals. Forbes Magazine recently estimated the team to be worth approximately $285 million. In the 2008-09 season, the team's home attendance average was roughly 17,000 per game.

FINANCIALS: **Sales and profits are in thousands of dollars—add 000 to get the full amount. 2008 Note: Financial information for 2008 was not available for all companies at press time.**

2008 Sales: $95,000 | 2008 Profits: $3,200
2007 Sales: $91,000 | 2007 Profits: $10,200
2006 Sales: $83,000 | 2006 Profits: $12,900
2005 Sales: $78,000 | 2005 Profits: $
2004 Sales: $80,000 | 2004 Profits: $

U.S. Stock Ticker: Private
Int'l Ticker: Int'l Exchange:
Employees:
Fiscal Year Ends: 6/30
Parent Company:

SALARIES/BENEFITS:

Pension Plan: ESOP Stock Plan: Profit Sharing: Top Exec. Salary: $ Bonus: $
Savings Plan: Stock Purch. Plan: Second Exec. Salary: $ Bonus: $

OTHER THOUGHTS:

Apparent Women Officers or Directors: 7
Hot Spot for Advancement for Women/Minorities: Y

LOCATIONS: ("Y" = Yes)

West:	Southwest:	Midwest:	Southeast:	Northeast:	International:
			Y		

NEW ORLEANS SAINTS

www.neworleanssaints.com

Industry Group Code: 711211C **Ranks within this company's industry group:** Sales: 20 Profits: 20

Sports:		Services:		Media:		Sales:		Facilities:		Other:	
Leagues/Associations:		Food & Beverage:		TV:		Marketing:		Stadiums:		Gambling:	
Teams:	Y	Agents:		Radio:		Ads:		Fitness Clubs:		Apparel:	
Nonprofits:		Other:		Internet:		Tickets:	Y	Golf Courses:		Equipment:	
Other:				Print:		Retail:	Y	Ski Resorts:		Shoes:	
				Software:		Other:		Other:		Other:	

TYPES OF BUSINESS:

Professional Football Team

BRANDS/DIVISIONS/AFFILIATES:

Gumbo
Saintsations

CONTACTS:

Note: Officers with more than one job title may be intentionally listed here more than once.

Tom Benson, Co-Owner
Dennis Lauscha, CFO/Sr. VP
Ben Hales, VP-Mktg.
Laura Russett, Coordinator-Human Resources
Jeff Huffman, Mgr.-IT & Network
Vicky Neumeyer, General Counsel/VP
James Nagaoka, Dir.-Oper.
Ben Hales, VP-Bus. Dev.
Doug Miller, Sr. Dir.-New Media
Greg Bensel, VP-Comm.
Charleen Sharpe, Comptroller
Mickey Loomis, Exec. VP/Gen. Mgr.
Rita Benson LeBlanc, Co-Owner/Exec. VP
Sean Payton, Head Coach
Justin Macione, Dir.-Media & Public Rel.

Phone: 504-733-0255	**Fax:** 504-731-1700
Toll-Free:	
Address: 5800 Airline Dr., Metairie, LA 70003 US	

GROWTH PLANS/SPECIAL FEATURES:

The New Orleans Saints, owned and operated by New Orleans Saints, L.P., are a professional football team playing in the National football League (NFL) based in New Orleans, Louisiana. The team was founded as an expansion team on All Saints' Day in 1966. Led by coach Jim Haslett, the team won its first playoff game at the end of the 2000 season. Haslett took over in 2000 from Mike Ditka, former coach of the Chicago Bears. In 2006, Sean Payton took over as the Saints head coach, leading the team to its best record, the league's top-ranked offense and an appearance in the NFC Championship game. Costumed mascot Gumbo the Saint Bernard and the Saintsations cheering squad add to the esprit de corps of the Saints. Team owner Tom Benson, the owner of an automobile dealership empire, bought the team in 1985 to prevent it being sold to outside interests and moved from New Orleans. Benson also owns the New Orleans VooDoo, an Arena Football League team based in New Orleans. The Saints play their home games in the Louisiana Superdome, the largest fixed domed structure in the world. Damaged by Hurricane Katrina in 2005, New Orleans spent $186 million to repair and refurbish the stadium. It seats approximately 71,000 spectators, and it is owned by the Louisiana Stadium/Expo District. The Saints have contributed a number of former players to the Pro Football Hall of Fame, including Doug Atkins, Earl Campbell, Jim Finks and Jim Taylor, as well as former coach Hank Stram. Forbes recently valued the team at approximately $937 million. In the 2008 season, the team averaged approximately 68,756 fans in attendance per game.

FINANCIALS:

Sales and profits are in thousands of dollars—add 000 to get the full amount. 2008 Note: Financial information for 2008 was not available for all companies at press time.

2008 Sales: $213,000	2008 Profits: $21,500	**U.S. Stock Ticker: Subsidiary**
2007 Sales: $194,000	2007 Profits: $25,200	**Int'l Ticker:** Int'l Exchange:
2006 Sales: $160,000	2006 Profits: $-4,100	Employees:
2005 Sales: $175,000	2005 Profits: $	Fiscal Year Ends: 3/31
2004 Sales: $157,000	2004 Profits: $	Parent Company: NEW ORLEANS SAINTS LP

SALARIES/BENEFITS:

Pension Plan:	ESOP Stock Plan:	Profit Sharing:	Top Exec. Salary: $	Bonus: $
Savings Plan:	Stock Purch. Plan:		Second Exec. Salary: $	Bonus: $

OTHER THOUGHTS:

Apparent Women Officers or Directors: 5
Hot Spot for Advancement for Women/Minorities: Y

LOCATIONS: ("Y" = Yes)

West:	Southwest:	Midwest:	Southeast:	Northeast:	International:
			Y		

NEW YORK GIANTS

www.giants.com

Industry Group Code: 711211C **Ranks within this company's industry group:** Sales: 18 Profits: 3

Sports:		Services:		Media:		Sales:		Facilities:		Other:	
Leagues/Associations:		Food & Beverage:		TV:		Marketing:	Y	Stadiums:	Y	Gambling:	
Teams:	Y	Agents:		Radio:		Ads:		Fitness Clubs:		Apparel:	Y
Nonprofits:		Other:		Internet:		Tickets:	Y	Golf Courses:		Equipment:	
Other:				Print:		Retail:	Y	Ski Resorts:		Shoes:	
				Software:		Other:		Other:		Other:	

TYPES OF BUSINESS:

Professional Football Team

BRANDS/DIVISIONS/AFFILIATES:

New York Football Giants
Giants Stadium

CONTACTS:

Note: Officers with more than one job title may be intentionally listed here more than once.

John K. Mara, CEO
John K. Mara, Pres./Co-Owner
Christine Procops, CFO/VP
Mike Stevens, Chief Mktg. Officer/Sr. VP
Raymond J. Walsh, Jr., Dir.-R&D
Justin Warren, Dir.-IT, Network & Systems
Jim Phelan, Dir.-Admin.
Pat Hanlon, VP-Comm.
Jonathan Tisch, Treas.
Jerry Reese, Sr. VP/Gen. Mgr.
Tom Coughlin, Head Coach
Steve Tisch, Co-Owner
Steve Hamrahi, Controller
Steve Tisch, Chmn./Exec. VP

Phone: 201-935-8111	**Fax:** 201-935-8493
Toll-Free:	
Address: Giants Stadium, East Rutherford, NJ 07073 US	

GROWTH PLANS/SPECIAL FEATURES:

The New York Giants are a professional football team in the National Football League (NFL). The franchise plays in the Eastern Division of the National Football Conference (NFC). The team joined the NFL in 1925 along with four other teams, and it is the only remaining team from that year. The Giants won its first title in 1927. Since then, the team has won six more NFL Championships, three being Super Bowls (1986, 1990 and 2007). Notable Giants of the past include Lawrence Taylor, Jim Thorpe, Vince Lombardi, Larry Csonka, Frank Gifford and Tom Landry. In 1991, 50% of the ownership of the team passed from the Mara family, who had owned the team since its 1925 inception, to Preston Robert Tisch, a successful businessman whose operations included the Loews Corporation and Diamond Offshore Drilling. The Tisch and Mara families continue to co-own the New York Giants. The team plays at Giants Stadium, which is located in the Meadowlands Sports Complex in East Rutherford, New Jersey. The stadium, which also hosts New York Jets home games, holds 80,064 spectators. However, a new 2.1 million square foot, $1.6 billion stadium is being built for the teams near the old Giants Stadium. The new stadium, which is scheduled to open in 2010, will have a seating capacity of 82,500. Forbes recently valued the team at approximately $1.18 million. In the 2008 season, the team averaged approximately 79,069 fans in attendance per game.

FINANCIALS:

Sales and profits are in thousands of dollars—add 000 to get the full amount. 2008 Note: Financial information for 2008 was not available for all companies at press time.

2008 Sales: $214,000	2008 Profits: $41,200	**U.S. Stock Ticker: Private**
2007 Sales: $195,000	2007 Profits: $10,700	**Int'l Ticker:** Int'l Exchange:
2006 Sales: $182,000	2006 Profits: $26,900	Employees:
2005 Sales: $175,000	2005 Profits: $	Fiscal Year Ends: 2/28
2004 Sales: $154,000	2004 Profits: $	Parent Company: NEW YORK FOOTBALL GIANTS, INC.

SALARIES/BENEFITS:

Pension Plan:	ESOP Stock Plan:	Profit Sharing:	Top Exec. Salary: $	Bonus: $
Savings Plan:	Stock Purch. Plan:		Second Exec. Salary: $	Bonus: $

OTHER THOUGHTS:

Apparent Women Officers or Directors: 12
Hot Spot for Advancement for Women/Minorities: Y

LOCATIONS: ("Y" = Yes)

West:	Southwest:	Midwest:	Southeast:	Northeast:	International:
				Y	

NEW YORK ISLANDERS

www.newyorkislanders.com

Industry Group Code: 711211F **Ranks within this company's industry group:** Sales: 30 Profits: 26

Sports:		Services:		Media:		Sales:		Facilities:		Other:	
Leagues/Associations:		Food & Beverage:		TV:		Marketing:		Stadiums:		Gambling:	
Teams:	Y	Agents:		Radio:		Ads:		Fitness Clubs:		Apparel:	
Nonprofits:		Other:		Internet:		Tickets:	Y	Golf Courses:		Equipment:	
Other:				Print:		Retail:		Ski Resorts:		Shoes:	
				Software:		Other:		Other:		Other:	

TYPES OF BUSINESS:

Professional Hockey Team

BRANDS/DIVISIONS/AFFILIATES:

National Hockey League (NHL)
New York Mets
Stanley Cup
Nassau Veterans Memorial Coliseum

CONTACTS:

Note: Officers with more than one job title may be intentionally listed here more than once.

Charles B. Wang, Governor/Owner
Chris Dey, Pres./Alternate Governor
John Lyons, Mgr.-Human Resources
Pawel Tauter, Mgr.-IT
Seth Sylvan, Dir.-Comm.
Ralph Sellitti, Controller
Scott Gordon, Head Coach
Garth Snow, Gen. Mgr./Alternate Governor
Bryan Trottier, Dir.-Player Dev.
Ken Morrow, Dir.-Pro Scouting
Vellu-Pekka Kautonen, Chief European Scout

Phone: 516-501-6700	**Fax:** 516-501-6762
Toll-Free:	
Address: 1535 Old Country Rd., Plainview, NY 11803 US	

GROWTH PLANS/SPECIAL FEATURES:

The New York Islanders franchise, owned and operated by New York Islanders Hockey Club, L.P., is a professional hockey team playing in the NHL based in New York City. The team was founded in 1972 by William Shea, the originator of the New York Mets professional baseball team. It started out with one of the worst records in professional hockey history, but by the late 1970s, the Islanders began to improve. The team won four Stanley Cup Championships back to back between 1980 and 1983. The Islanders are owned by Charles Wang, who originally became a co-owner in 2000 and acquired majority ownership in 2004. The Islanders play home games at the Nassau Veterans Memorial Coliseum, which has a 16,297-person capacity. The Coliseum is owned by Nassau County, New York. The Islanders had a 2008-09 average home attendance of approximately13,770 fans. Forbes recently valued the team at approximately $154 million.

FINANCIALS:

Sales and profits are in thousands of dollars—add 000 to get the full amount. 2008 Note: Financial information for 2008 was not available for all companies at press time.

2008 Sales: $64,000	2008 Profits: $-8,800	**U.S. Stock Ticker: Private**
2007 Sales: $60,000	2007 Profits: $-11,600	**Int'l Ticker:** Int'l Exchange:
2006 Sales: $56,000	2006 Profits: $-9,200	Employees:
2005 Sales: $	2005 Profits: $	Fiscal Year Ends: 8/31
2004 Sales: $64,000	2004 Profits: $	Parent Company:

SALARIES/BENEFITS:

Pension Plan:	ESOP Stock Plan:	Profit Sharing:	Top Exec. Salary: $	Bonus: $
Savings Plan:	Stock Purch. Plan:		Second Exec. Salary: $	Bonus: $

OTHER THOUGHTS:

Apparent Women Officers or Directors: 12
Hot Spot for Advancement for Women/Minorities: Y

LOCATIONS: ("Y" = Yes)

West:	Southwest:	Midwest:	Southeast:	Northeast:	International:
				Y	

Note: Financial information, benefits and other data can change quickly and may vary from those stated here.

NEW YORK JETS

www.newyorkjets.com

Industry Group Code: 711211C **Ranks within this company's industry group:** Sales: 19 Profits: 14

Sports:		Services:		Media:		Sales:		Facilities:		Other:	
Leagues/Associations:		Food & Beverage:		TV:		Marketing:		Stadiums:		Gambling:	
Teams:	Y	Agents:		Radio:		Ads:		Fitness Clubs:		Apparel:	
Nonprofits:		Other:		Internet:		Tickets:	Y	Golf Courses:		Equipment:	
Other:				Print:		Retail:	Y	Ski Resorts:		Shoes:	
				Software:		Other:		Other:		Other:	

TYPES OF BUSINESS:

Professional Football Team

BRANDS/DIVISIONS/AFFILIATES:

New York Jets Football Club, Inc.

CONTACTS:

Note: Officers with more than one job title may be intentionally listed here more than once.

Robert W. Johnson, IV, CEO
Michael Gerstle, CFO
Lee Stacey, Sr. VP-Mktg. & Sales
Terry Bradway, Sr. Exec.-Personnel
Michael Gerstle, VP-Finance
Rex Ryan, Head Coach
Mike Tannenbaum, Exec. VP/Gen. Mgr.
Joey Clinkscales, VP-College Scouting
Elliot Pellman, Dir.-Medical Svcs.
Robert W. Johnson, IV, Chmn.

Phone: 973-549-4800	**Fax:**
Toll-Free: 800-469-5387	
Address: 1 Jets Drive, Florham Park, NJ 07932 US	

GROWTH PLANS/SPECIAL FEATURES:

The New York Jets, owned by Robert Woody Johnson IV, are a professional football team in the National Football League (NFL). The team plays in the Eastern Division of the NFL's American Football Conference (AFC). The Jets originated as the New York Titans, a charter member of the American Football League, in 1960. After a few poor seasons, the team was bought out by a group headed by Sonny Werblin, head of MCA. In 1963, the team's name changed to the Jets due to its new stadium's proximity to LaGuardia Airport. In 1965, the Jets signed Joe Namath, their foremost franchise player and one of the most celebrated quarterbacks of all time. Namath simultaneously propelled the Jets onto the national scene and made them the most beloved football team in New York. Besides this, the star power of Namath was a deciding factor in the success of the AFL-NFL merger in 1970. Unfortunately, the 1970s saw the Jets plagued by injuries and coaching changes. Beginning in 1984, the Jets play all home games at Giants Stadium located in East Rutherford, New Jersey. The team shares this stadium with the New York Giants football team. In 2000, Robert Woody Johnson IV purchased the team for $635 million. Currently, the team is in the process of building a new Jets stadium. The new stadium is expected to be complete by 2010. Forbes recently valued the team at approximately $1.17 billion. In the 2008 season, the team averaged approximately 78,482 fans in attendance per game.

FINANCIALS:

Sales and profits are in thousands of dollars—add 000 to get the full amount. 2008 Note: Financial information for 2008 was not available for all companies at press time.

2008 Sales: $213,000	2008 Profits: $25,900	**U.S. Stock Ticker: Subsidiary**
2007 Sales: $193,000	2007 Profits: $26,400	**Int'l Ticker:** Int'l Exchange:
2006 Sales: $179,000	2006 Profits: $33,100	Employees:
2005 Sales: $172,000	2005 Profits: $	Fiscal Year Ends: 2/28
2004 Sales: $152,000	2004 Profits: $	Parent Company: NEW YORK JETS FOOTBALL CLUB INC

SALARIES/BENEFITS:

Pension Plan:	ESOP Stock Plan:	Profit Sharing:	Top Exec. Salary: $	Bonus: $
Savings Plan:	Stock Purch. Plan:		Second Exec. Salary: $	Bonus: $

OTHER THOUGHTS:

Apparent Women Officers or Directors:
Hot Spot for Advancement for Women/Minorities:

LOCATIONS: ("Y" = Yes)

West:	Southwest:	Midwest:	Southeast:	Northeast:	International:
				Y	

NEW YORK KNICKERBOCKERS

www.nba.com/knicks

Industry Group Code: 711211B **Ranks within this company's industry group:** Sales: 1 Profits: 5

Sports:		Services:		Media:		Sales:		Facilities:		Other:	
Leagues/Associations:		Food & Beverage:		TV:		Marketing:		Stadiums:	Y	Gambling:	
Teams:	Y	Agents:		Radio:		Ads:		Fitness Clubs:		Apparel:	
Nonprofits:		Other:		Internet:		Tickets:	Y	Golf Courses:		Equipment:	
Other:				Print:		Retail:	Y	Ski Resorts:		Shoes:	
				Software:		Other:		Other:		Other:	

TYPES OF BUSINESS:

Professional Basketball Team

BRANDS/DIVISIONS/AFFILIATES:

Madison Square Garden, L.P.

CONTACTS:

Note: Officers with more than one job title may be intentionally listed here more than once.

James L. Dolan, CEO
Steve Mills, COO
James L. Dolan, Pres.
Hunter Lochmann, VP-Mktg.
Dwight Tierney, Sr. VP-Human Resources
Dwight Tierney, Sr. VP-Admin.
Marc Schoenfeld, Sr. VP-Legal Affairs, MSG
Donnie Walsh, Pres., Basketball Oper.
Karin Buchholz, VP-Comm. Rel. & Fan Dev.
John Cudmore, Sr. VP-Finance/Controller
Glen Grunwald, Sr. VP-Basketball Oper.
Mark Piazza, Sr. VP-Sports Team Oper.
Jonathan Supranowitz, VP-Public Rel.
Mike D'Antoni, Head Coach
James L. Dolan, Chmn.-MSG
Kevin Wilson, Dir.-Int'l Scouting

Phone: 212-465-6471 **Fax:** 212-465-6498
Toll-Free: 877-695-3865
Address: Madison Square Garden, 2 Pennsylvania Plz., New York, NY 10121-0091 US

GROWTH PLANS/SPECIAL FEATURES:

The New York Knickerbockers (known as the Knicks) are one of only two charter members of the National Basketball Association (NBA) still playing in their original city (the other being the Boston Celtics). The Knicks franchise was founded in 1946 by Madison Square Garden (MSG) president Ned Irish. The team is still owned by MSG, which remains the site of the Knicks' home games. MSG, which is a subsidiary of Cablevision Systems Corporation, also owns the New York Rangers hockey club and the New York Liberty WNBA team. The Knicks have risen to NBA prominence in three different decades: the early 50s, when they played for the NBA title three times; the 70s, when the team won two NBA championships with a roster including Willis Reed, Walt Frazier, Dave DeBusschere, Earl Monroe and Bill Bradley; and the 90s, with center Patrick Ewing leading a team which included Jon Starks (currently a member of the Knicks' front office), advancing the team to the NBA finals in 1994 and 1999. The team has struggled in recent years and has not had a winning record since the 2000-01 season. Forbes Magazine recently estimated the team to be worth approximately $613 million. In the 2008-09 season, the team's home attendance average was roughly 19,300 per game.

FINANCIALS:

Sales and profits are in thousands of dollars—add 000 to get the full amount. 2008 Note: Financial information for 2008 was not available for all companies at press time.

2008 Sales: $208,000 | 2008 Profits: $29,600
2007 Sales: $196,000 | 2007 Profits: $-42,200
2006 Sales: $185,000 | 2006 Profits: $-39,000
2005 Sales: $181,000 | 2005 Profits: $
2004 Sales: $170,000 | 2004 Profits: $

U.S. Stock Ticker: Subsidiary
Int'l Ticker: Int'l Exchange:
Employees:
Fiscal Year Ends: 12/31
Parent Company: CABLEVISION SYSTEMS CORP

SALARIES/BENEFITS:

Pension Plan: | ESOP Stock Plan: | Profit Sharing: | Top Exec. Salary: $ | Bonus: $
Savings Plan: | Stock Purch. Plan: | | Second Exec. Salary: $ | Bonus: $

OTHER THOUGHTS:

Apparent Women Officers or Directors: 4
Hot Spot for Advancement for Women/Minorities: Y

LOCATIONS: ("Y" = Yes)

West:	Southwest:	Midwest:	Southeast:	Northeast:	International:
				Y	

NEW YORK LIBERTY

www.wnba.com/liberty

Industry Group Code: 711211E **Ranks within this company's industry group:** Sales: Profits:

Sports:		Services:		Media:		Sales:		Facilities:		Other:	
Leagues/Associations:		Food & Beverage:		TV:		Marketing:		Stadiums:	Y	Gambling:	
Teams:	Y	Agents:		Radio:		Ads:		Fitness Clubs:		Apparel:	
Nonprofits:		Other:		Internet:		Tickets:	Y	Golf Courses:		Equipment:	
Other:				Print:		Retail:		Ski Resorts:		Shoes:	
				Software:		Other:		Other:		Other:	

TYPES OF BUSINESS:

Women's Professional Basketball Team

BRANDS/DIVISIONS/AFFILIATES:

Cablevision Systems Corporation
Madison Square Garden LP
Maddie
Liberty Outdoor Classic
Liberty Summer Camp

CONTACTS: *Note: Officers with more than one job title may be intentionally listed here more than once.*

Carol Blazejowski, Gen. Mgr.
Carol Blazejowski, Pres.
Howard Jacobs, Sr. VP-Mktg.
Marc Schoenfeld, Sr. VP-Legal Affairs
Jason Vogel, VP-Sports Team Oper.
Heather Pariseau, VP-MSG Interactive
Amy Scheer, VP-Comm. & Mktg.
Patrick McDonough, VP-Finance
James L. Dolan, Owner
Pat Coyle, Head Coach
Catherine Proto, Mgr.-Scouting & Video Oper.
Rob Scolaro, VP-Team Sponsorships

Phone: 212-564-9622 **Fax:** 212-465-6250
Toll-Free:
Address: Madison Square Garden, 2 Pennsylvania Plz., New York, NY 10121-0091 US

GROWTH PLANS/SPECIAL FEATURES:

The New York Liberty is a Women's National Basketball Association (WNBA) team, as well as one of the eight original Women's National Basketball Association (WNBA) teams founded in 1997. The team has made the WNBA playoffs almost every season and has appeared in the Finals several times but has yet to win a championship. The Liberty, the New York Knickerbockers (Knicks) and the New York Rangers are all owned by Cablevision Systems Corporation through its subsidiary Madison Square Garden, LP (MSG). MSG owns Madison Square Garden arena, which serves as the home court of the three teams. The arena seats 18,649 for basketball games and is available for rent for various special occasions including religious festivals and ceremonies; corporate outings; conferences and trade shows; receptions; graduations; and meetings. The Liberty's canine mascot, Maddie, is named after Madison Square Garden. The team's games have been broadcast by the MSG Network cable channel since the team's inaugural season. The Liberty sponsors a basketball camp, Liberty Summer Camp, for girls ages 8-17, teaching the campers basketball skills and offering them a chance to meet a current Liberty player. In 2008, the team drafted shooting guard Essence Carson, forward Erlana Larkins, as well as signing point guard Leilani Mitchell during preseason. The 2008 season also featured the first professional regular season basketball game to be played in the outdoors, the Liberty Outdoor Classic. The game was played at the Arthur Ashe Stadium.

FINANCIALS: **Sales and profits are in thousands of dollars—add 000 to get the full amount. 2008 Note: Financial information for 2008 was not available for all companies at press time.**

2008 Sales: $	2008 Profits: $	**U.S. Stock Ticker: Subsidiary**
2007 Sales: $	2007 Profits: $	**Int'l Ticker:** Int'l Exchange:
2006 Sales: $	2006 Profits: $	Employees:
2005 Sales: $	2005 Profits: $	Fiscal Year Ends: 12/31
2004 Sales: $	2004 Profits: $	Parent Company: MADISON SQUARE GARDEN LP

SALARIES/BENEFITS:

Pension Plan:	ESOP Stock Plan:	Profit Sharing:	Top Exec. Salary: $	Bonus: $
Savings Plan:	Stock Purch. Plan:		Second Exec. Salary: $	Bonus: $

OTHER THOUGHTS:

Apparent Women Officers or Directors: 12
Hot Spot for Advancement for Women/Minorities: Y

LOCATIONS: ("Y" = Yes)

West:	Southwest:	Midwest:	Southeast:	Northeast:	International:
				Y	

Note: Financial information, benefits and other data can change quickly and may vary from those stated here.

NEW YORK METS

newyork.mets.mlb.com

Industry Group Code: 711211A **Ranks within this company's industry group:** Sales: 3 Profits: 11

Sports:		Services:		Media:		Sales:		Facilities:		Other:	
Leagues/Associations:		Food & Beverage:		TV:	Y	Marketing:		Stadiums:	Y	Gambling:	
Teams:	Y	Agents:		Radio:		Ads:		Fitness Clubs:		Apparel:	
Nonprofits:		Other:		Internet:		Tickets:	Y	Golf Courses:		Equipment:	
Other:				Print:		Retail:	Y	Ski Resorts:		Shoes:	
				Software:		Other:		Other:		Other:	

TYPES OF BUSINESS:

Professional Baseball Team
Cable Television Network

BRANDS/DIVISIONS/AFFILIATES:

New York Mets
SportsNet New York
Sterling Mets LP
Binghamton Mets
St. Lucie Mets
Savannah Sand Gnats
Brooklyn Cyclones
Citi Field

CONTACTS:

Note: Officers with more than one job title may be intentionally listed here more than once.

Fred Wilpon, CEO
Jeff Wilpon, COO
Saul Katz, Pres.
Mark Peskin, CFO
Tom Murphy, Sr. VP-Corp. Sales & Svcs.
David Cohen, General Counsel/Exec. VP
Dave Howard, Exec. VP-Bus. Oper.
David Newman, Sr. VP-Mktg. & Comm.
Leonard Labita, Controller/VP
Omar Minaya, Exec. VP-Baseball Oper./Gen. Mgr.
Karl Smolarz, VP-Facilities
Jay Horwitz, VP-Media Rel.
Jerry Manuel, Mgr.
Fred Wilpon, Chmn.

Phone: 718-507-6387 **Fax:** 718-507-6395
Toll-Free:
Address: Citi Field, 126th St. & Roosevelt Ave., Flushing, NY 11368 US

GROWTH PLANS/SPECIAL FEATURES:

The New York Mets, owned and operated by Sterling Mets LP, entered Major League Baseball as an expansion team in 1962. The Mets play at Citi Field, a new ball park adjacent to their former playing place, Shea Stadium. Despite 120 defeats in their first season, the Mets went on to win their first World Series in 1969, after only seven years as a franchise. The team won its second World Series in 1986 and have made it to the World Series four times, including the all-New York Subway Series in 2000, in which the Mets lost to the Yankees. Former Mets stars include Gil Hodges, Tug McGraw, Tom Seaver, Daryl Strawberry, Howard Johnson, Dwight Gooden, Mookie Wilson, Casey Stengel, Ed Kranepool, Yogi Berra and Mike Piazza. After years of mediocre performance, in 2005 Sterling Doubleday Enterprises sold the team to Fred Wilpon, who promised to upgrade the team on the field. He made significant changes in the team's management strategy, including the establishment of their own cable network, SportsNet New York, to broadcast the team's games. He then hired Omar Minaya as general manager, the first Hispanic general manager in Major League Baseball. The team is known for bringing in Hispanic players, and in 2007, the Mets had more minorities on its roster than any other major league team. The 2008 season marked the last season that the Mets would play at Shea Stadium. In 2009, Citi Field opened with the first exhibition match versus Boston Red Sox. The first regular season home game at the new stadium was played against the San Diego Padres. Forbes recently estimated the team to be worth approximately $912 million. In the 2008 season, the team's average home game attendance was 51,165.

FINANCIALS:

Sales and profits are in thousands of dollars—add 000 to get the full amount. 2008 Note: Financial information for 2008 was not available for all companies at press time.

2008 Sales: $261,000
2007 Sales: $235,000
2006 Sales: $217,000
2005 Sales: $195,000
2004 Sales: $

2008 Profits: $23,500
2007 Profits: $32,900
2006 Profits: $24,400
2005 Profits: $
2004 Profits: $

U.S. Stock Ticker: Subsidiary
Int'l Ticker: Int'l Exchange:
Employees:
Fiscal Year Ends: 9/30
Parent Company: STERLING METS LP

SALARIES/BENEFITS:

Pension Plan: ESOP Stock Plan: Profit Sharing: Top Exec. Salary: $ Bonus: $
Savings Plan: Stock Purch. Plan: Second Exec. Salary: $ Bonus: $

OTHER THOUGHTS:

Apparent Women Officers or Directors:
Hot Spot for Advancement for Women/Minorities:

LOCATIONS: ("Y" = Yes)

West:	Southwest:	Midwest:	Southeast:	Northeast:	International:
				Y	

NEW YORK RANGERS

rangers.nhl.com

Industry Group Code: 711211F **Ranks within this company's industry group:** Sales: 3 Profits: 3

Sports:		Services:		Media:		Sales:		Facilities:		Other:	
Leagues/Associations:		Food & Beverage:		TV:		Marketing:		Stadiums:		Gambling:	
Teams:	Y	Agents:		Radio:		Ads:		Fitness Clubs:		Apparel:	
Nonprofits:		Other:		Internet:		Tickets:	Y	Golf Courses:		Equipment:	
Other:				Print:		Retail:	Y	Ski Resorts:		Shoes:	
				Software:		Other:		Other:		Other:	

TYPES OF BUSINESS:

Professional Hockey Team

BRANDS/DIVISIONS/AFFILIATES:

Madison Square Garden
Cablevision Systems Corp

CONTACTS: *Note: Officers with more than one job title may be intentionally listed here more than once.*

Glen Sather, Gen. Mgr.
Glen Sather, Pres.
Jeanie Baumgartner, VP-Mktg.
John Rosasco, VP-Public Rel.
John Cudmore, Sr. VP-Finance/Controller
Sean Barror, Sr. VP-Sales
John Tortorella, Head Coach

Phone: 212-465-6000	**Fax:** 212-465-6494
Toll-Free:	
Address: 2 Pennsylvania Plz., New York, NY 10121 US	

GROWTH PLANS/SPECIAL FEATURES:

The New York Rangers is a professional hockey team playing in the National Hockey League (NHL) based in New York City. The franchise plays in the Atlantic Division of the Eastern Conference along with New Jersey Devils, New York Islanders, Philadelphia Flyers and Pittsburgh Penguins. The team, though originally incorporated as the New York Giants Hockey Club in 1926, soon became known as Tex's Rangers after initial owner Tex Rickard. In 1928, only its second year, the team won the Stanley Cup. The early Rangers team also won the Stanley Cup in 1933 and 1940, but for the most part, the team played mediocre hockey until the late 1960s. In 1968, the team moved into Madison Square Garden, marking an era of rejuvenation. The Rangers made the playoffs consistently throughout the modern era, but the team faced post-season setbacks nonetheless, failing to win a Stanley Cup for over 50 years. Finally, in the 1993-94 season, the Rangers put together a team whose roster featured Mark Messier, Adam Graves, Brian Leetch and Sergei Zubov. The team won the President's Trophy, Leetch became the first American to win the Conn Smythe Trophy and the Rangers again won the Stanley Cup. The Rangers team, along with The New York Knicks and New York Liberty, is owned by Cablevision Systems Corp., which also owns the Madison Square Garden. Cablevision's sports holdings also include the television rights for the Knicks, Rangers, Liberty, New York Islands, New Jersey Devils and Red Bull New York. In the 2008-09 season, the team averaged approximately 18,100 fans in attendance per game. A recent Forbes estimate values the team at $411 million.

FINANCIALS: **Sales and profits are in thousands of dollars—add 000 to get the full amount. 2008 Note: Financial information for 2008 was not available for all companies at press time.**

2008 Sales: $137,000	2008 Profits: $30,700	**U.S. Stock Ticker: Subsidiary**
2007 Sales: $122,000	2007 Profits: $25,400	**Int'l Ticker:** Int'l Exchange:
2006 Sales: $109,000	2006 Profits: $17,700	Employees:
2005 Sales: $	2005 Profits: $	Fiscal Year Ends: 12/31
2004 Sales: $118,000	2004 Profits: $	Parent Company: CABLEVISION SYSTEMS CORP

SALARIES/BENEFITS:

Pension Plan:	ESOP Stock Plan:	Profit Sharing:	Top Exec. Salary: $	Bonus: $
Savings Plan:	Stock Purch. Plan:		Second Exec. Salary: $	Bonus: $

OTHER THOUGHTS:

Apparent Women Officers or Directors:
Hot Spot for Advancement for Women/Minorities:

LOCATIONS: ("Y" = Yes)

West:	Southwest:	Midwest:	Southeast:	Northeast:	International:
				Y	

Note: Financial information, benefits and other data can change quickly and may vary from those stated here.

NEW YORK RED BULLS

redbull.newyork.mlsnet.com

Industry Group Code: 711211D **Ranks within this company's industry group:** Sales: Profits:

Sports:		Services:		Media:		Sales:		Facilities:		Other:	
Leagues/Associations:		Food & Beverage:		TV:		Marketing:		Stadiums:		Gambling:	
Teams:	Y	Agents:		Radio:		Ads:		Fitness Clubs:		Apparel:	
Nonprofits:		Other:		Internet:		Tickets:		Golf Courses:		Equipment:	
Other:				Print:		Retail:		Ski Resorts:		Shoes:	
				Software:		Other:		Other:		Other:	

TYPES OF BUSINESS:

Major League Soccer Team

BRANDS/DIVISIONS/AFFILIATES:

Red Bull GmBH
MetroStars
Red Bull New York

CONTACTS:

Note: Officers with more than one job title may be intentionally listed here more than once.

Erik Stover, Managing Dir.
Andrew Lafiosca, VP-Mktg. & Sales
Jackie Jacobson, Dir.-Human Resources
Peter Katic, Mgr.-IT
Shaun Oliver, Dir.-Oper.
Andy McGowan, VP-Comm. & Community Rel.
Greg Domico, VP-Finance
Juan Carlos Osorio, Head Coach

Phone: 201-583-7000	**Fax:** 201-583-7055
Toll-Free:	
Address: 1 Harmon Plz., 3rd Fl., Secaucus, NJ 07094 US	

GROWTH PLANS/SPECIAL FEATURES:

The New York Red Bulls, formerly the MetroStars, is one of the oldest teams in Major League Soccer (MLS), formed at the league's inception in 1996. The club competes in the Eastern Conference of the MLS alongside teams such as Toronto FC, Chicago Fire, Columbus Crew, D.C. United, Kansas City Wizards and New England Revolution. The Red Bulls are owned and operated by Austrian beverage company Red Bull GmBH, which purchased the company in March 2006 from Anschutz Entertainment Group. As part of the agreement, the two companies have partnered in the development of a planned outdoor stadium complex to be located in Harrison, New Jersey. The new Harrison soccer stadium (estimated completion date in 2009) will see Red Bull GmBH overseeing all aspects of construction and stadium management. The stadium will be known as Red Bull Arena and will have an estimated seating capacity of approximately 25,000. Currently, the team plays out of Giants Stadium, which has a seating capacity of approximately 80,242. Average attendance in 2007 was approximately 16,500 for regular season matches and 14,100 for post season matches, although the team has seen single-game match attendance totaling upwards of 79,000 fans. The team made it to the 2008 MLS cup final but lost 3-1 against the Columbus Crew. The Red Bulls have a sister team located in Salzburg, Austria. The club recently announced plans to build a permanent training center in Hanover, New Jersey, which will include six soccer fields, a 50,000 square-foot two-story building and a one-story fieldhouse.

FINANCIALS:

Sales and profits are in thousands of dollars—add 000 to get the full amount. 2008 Note: Financial information for 2008 was not available for all companies at press time.

2008 Sales: $	2008 Profits: $	**U.S. Stock Ticker: Subsidiary**
2007 Sales: $	2007 Profits: $	**Int'l Ticker:** Int'l Exchange:
2006 Sales: $	2006 Profits: $	Employees:
2005 Sales: $	2005 Profits: $	Fiscal Year Ends:
2004 Sales: $	2004 Profits: $	Parent Company: RED BULL GMBH

SALARIES/BENEFITS:

Pension Plan:	ESOP Stock Plan:	Profit Sharing:	Top Exec. Salary: $	Bonus: $
Savings Plan:	Stock Purch. Plan:		Second Exec. Salary: $	Bonus: $

OTHER THOUGHTS:

Apparent Women Officers or Directors: 1
Hot Spot for Advancement for Women/Minorities:

LOCATIONS: ("Y" = Yes)

West:	Southwest:	Midwest:	Southeast:	Northeast:	International:
				Y	

NEW YORK YANKEES

newyork.yankees.mlb.com

Industry Group Code: 711211A **Ranks within this company's industry group:** Sales: 1 Profits: 29

Sports:		Services:		Media:		Sales:		Facilities:		Other:	
Leagues/Associations:		Food & Beverage:		TV:	Y	Marketing:	Y	Stadiums:	Y	Gambling:	
Teams:	Y	Agents:		Radio:		Ads:	Y	Fitness Clubs:		Apparel:	Y
Nonprofits:		Other:		Internet:		Tickets:	Y	Golf Courses:		Equipment:	
Other:				Print:		Retail:	Y	Ski Resorts:		Shoes:	
				Software:		Other:		Other:		Other:	

TYPES OF BUSINESS:

Professional Baseball Team

BRANDS/DIVISIONS/AFFILIATES:

Yankee Stadium
Yankees Entertainment & Sports Network (YES)
Yankee Global Enterprises
Scranton/Wilkes-Barre Yankees
Trenton Thunder
Tampa Yankees
Charleston RiverDogs
Staten Island Yankees

CONTACTS: *Note: Officers with more than one job title may be intentionally listed here more than once.*

George Steinbrenner, Owner
Lonn A. Trost, COO
Randy Levine, Pres.
Robert Brown, CFO/VP-Acct.
Deborah A. Tymon, Sr. VP-Mktg.
Betsy Peluso, Dir.-Human Resources
Mike Lane, Sr. Dir.-Tech.
Alan Chang, Deputy General Counsel/VP-Legal Affairs
Mark Newman, Sr. VP-Baseball Oper.
Jim Ross, Sr. VP-Bus. Dev.
Brian Smith, VP-Corp. & Comm. Rel.
Scott Krug, VP/CFO-Financial Oper.
Brian Cashman, Sr. VP/Gen. Mgr.
Derrick Baio, Controller
Sonny Hight, Chief Security Officer/VP
Michael J. Tusiani, Sr. VP-Corp. Sales & Sponsorships
George M. Steinbrenner, III, Chmn.
Anthony Bruno, VP/CFO-Yankee Global Enterprises

Phone: 718-293-4300	**Fax:** 718-293-8431
Toll-Free:	
Address: Yankee Stadium, E. 161st St. & River Ave., Bronx, NY 10451 US	

GROWTH PLANS/SPECIAL FEATURES:

The New York Yankees is a baseball team playing in Major League Baseball's Eastern Division of the American League. The team is one of the most successful franchises in the history of professional sports. The venerable club has won 26 World Series titles, 39 league pennants and 15 division titles. The Yankees have also made 47 post-season appearances since 1921 and posted 39 consecutive winning seasons from 1926 to 1964. The team has fielded a number of legendary players, including Mickey Mantle, Reggie Jackson, Derek Jeter, Whitey Ford, Joe DiMaggio, Lou Gehrig and Babe Ruth. Opened in 1923, the team's famed Yankee Stadium was the first triple-decked structure built for baseball. In addition to housing the Yankees, the venue has hosted football, soccer, political assemblies, concerts and papal visits. The Yankees have led the league in attendance every year from 2003 to 2008, despite not winning the World Series since 2000. Since 1973 the Yankees have been owned by George Steinbrenner, who purchased the team from CBS for $10 million. His reign has been known for an excessive interest in the team, the constant hiring and rehiring of managers, meddling micromanagement, enormous payrolls, and great success. Recently, he has ceded much of the control of the team to his son, Hank Steinbrenner, who has proved similarly outspoken. The team's games are broadcast on The Yankees Entertainment and Sports Network (YES), a partnership of the Yankees and the New Jersey Nets, a pro basketball team. In 2009 Forbes valued the team at $1.5 billion, the highest in baseball. A new $1.6 billion Yankee Stadium, located across the street from the original Yankee Stadium, opened in April 2009.

FINANCIALS: **Sales and profits are in thousands of dollars—add 000 to get the full amount. 2008 Note: Financial information for 2008 was not available for all companies at press time.**

2008 Sales: $375,000	2008 Profits: $-3,700	**U.S. Stock Ticker: Private**
2007 Sales: $327,000	2007 Profits: $-47,300	**Int'l Ticker:** Int'l Exchange:
2006 Sales: $302,000	2006 Profits: $-25,200	Employees:
2005 Sales: $277,000	2005 Profits: $	Fiscal Year Ends: 12/31
2004 Sales: $315,000	2004 Profits: $	Parent Company: NEW YORK YANKEES PARTNERSHIP

SALARIES/BENEFITS:

Pension Plan:	ESOP Stock Plan:	Profit Sharing:	Top Exec. Salary: $	Bonus: $
Savings Plan:	Stock Purch. Plan:		Second Exec. Salary: $	Bonus: $

OTHER THOUGHTS:

Apparent Women Officers or Directors: 10
Hot Spot for Advancement for Women/Minorities: Y

LOCATIONS: ("Y" = Yes)

West:	Southwest:	Midwest:	Southeast:	Northeast:	International:
				Y	Y

Note: Financial information, benefits and other data can change quickly and may vary from those stated here.

NEWCASTLE UNITED FOOTBALL CLUB

www.nufc.premiumtv.co.uk

Industry Group Code: 711211D **Ranks within this company's industry group:** Sales: 6 Profits: 8

Sports:		Services:		Media:		Sales:		Facilities:		Other:	
Leagues/Associations:		Food & Beverage:		TV:		Marketing:		Stadiums:	Y	Gambling:	
Teams:	Y	Agents:		Radio:		Ads:		Fitness Clubs:		Apparel:	
Nonprofits:		Other:		Internet:		Tickets:	Y	Golf Courses:		Equipment:	
Other:				Print:		Retail:		Ski Resorts:		Shoes:	
				Software:		Other:		Other:		Other:	

TYPES OF BUSINESS:

Soccer Team
Ticket Sales
Team Merchandise
TV Broadcasting
Web Promotions

BRANDS/DIVISIONS/AFFILIATES:

English Premier League
Newcastle East End
Newcastle West End
St. James' Park
Freemen of Newcastle upon Tyne

CONTACTS: *Note: Officers with more than one job title may be intentionally listed here more than once.*

Sharon Fletcher, Head-Corp. Sales
David Williamson, Exec. Dir.-Oper.
Dennis Wise, Exec. Dir.-Football
Tony Jimenez, VP-Player Recruitment
Mike Ashley, Owner
Kate Bradley, Mgr.-Charitable Foundation
Derek Llambias, Chmn.

Phone: 44-191-201-8400 **Fax:** 44-191-201-8600
Toll-Free:
Address: St. James' Park, Newcastle, NE1 4ST UK

GROWTH PLANS/SPECIAL FEATURES:

Newcastle United Football Club is a professional English football (soccer) team that plays in the English Premier League. Founded in 1891 through the merger of the Newcastle East End and the Newcastle West End, the team did well throughout the pre-Premiership era, winning four First Division championships, six FA Cups, an Inter-Cities Fairs Cup, two Texaco Cups and an Anglo-Italian Cup. However, by 1992 the club was facing relegation into Division Three. Kevin Keegan, a one-time Newcastle player late in his career, returned as a manager that year kicking off the team's marvelous recovery. By the 1993-94 season, Newcastle was promoted to the FA Premier League, where it resides today. The club invested heavily in international talent, and gained intermittent access to the lucrative Champions' League. Keegan left the team in 1997 only to return again for a short stint during 2008. During Keegan's departure from Newcastle, the team went through eight different managers and its play was inconsistent. Newcastle plays its home games at St. James' Park in Newcastle upon Tyne. The stadium has been the team's home since its founding in 1891 and, following various expansions, boasts the third highest capacity of stadiums in England, with 52,387 seats. St. James' Park is owned by the Freemen of Newcastle upon Tyne. During the 2007-08 season, the team had the third highest average attendance in the English Premier League, after Manchester United and Arsenal, at 51,320. Since 2007, the club has been owned by English sporting goods billionaire Mike Ashley and his St. James Holdings Ltd.

FINANCIALS: **Sales and profits are in thousands of dollars—add 000 to get the full amount. 2008 Note: Financial information for 2008 was not available for all companies at press time.**

2008 Sales: $198,000
2007 Sales: $175,000
2006 Sales: $159,000
2005 Sales: $156,000
2004 Sales: $166,000

2008 Profits: $-13,000
2007 Profits: $12,000
2006 Profits: $11,000
2005 Profits: $
2004 Profits: $7,600

U.S. Stock Ticker: Subsidiary
Int'l Ticker: Int'l Exchange:
Employees: 1,376
Fiscal Year Ends: 7/31
Parent Company: ST JAMES HOLDINGS LTD

SALARIES/BENEFITS:

Pension Plan: ESOP Stock Plan: Profit Sharing: Top Exec. Salary: $ Bonus: $
Savings Plan: Stock Purch. Plan: Second Exec. Salary: $ Bonus: $

OTHER THOUGHTS:

Apparent Women Officers or Directors: 3
Hot Spot for Advancement for Women/Minorities: Y

LOCATIONS: ("Y" = Yes)

West:	Southwest:	Midwest:	Southeast:	Northeast:	International:
					Y

NEWPORT SPORTS MANAGEMENT

www.thehockeyagency.com

Industry Group Code: 711410 **Ranks within this company's industry group:** Sales: Profits:

Sports:		Services:		Media:		Sales:		Facilities:		Other:	
Leagues/Associations:		Food & Beverage:		TV:		Marketing:	Y	Stadiums:		Gambling:	
Teams:		Agents:	Y	Radio:		Ads:		Fitness Clubs:		Apparel:	
Nonprofits:		Other:	Y	Internet:		Tickets:		Golf Courses:		Equipment:	
Other:				Print:		Retail:		Ski Resorts:		Shoes:	
				Software:		Other:		Other:		Other:	

TYPES OF BUSINESS:

Athlete Management Agency
Professional Hockey Representation
Athlete & Corporate Marketing Services
Contract Negotiations & Draft Preparation Services
Financial Management Services
Athlete Training & Development Services

BRANDS/DIVISIONS/AFFILIATES:

National Hockey League (NHL)

CONTACTS:
Note: Officers with more than one job title may be intentionally listed here more than once.

Donald E. Meehan, Pres.
Jamie Rolph, Mgr.-New Mktg. Initiatives & Properties
Patrick Morris, Mgr.-Player Recruitment
Rand Simon, Mgr.-Finance
Mark Guy, VP-Recruiting, Player Dev. & Contract Negotiations
Patrick J. Morris, Mgr.-Recruiting & Contract Negotiations
Rand L. Simon, Mgr.-Client Finance & Investment Mgmt.
Susanna Goruvan, Mgr.-Russian Client Care Needs

Phone: 905-275-2800 **Fax:** 905-275-4025
Toll-Free:
Address: 201 City Centre Dr., Ste. 400, Mississauga, ON L5B 2T4 Canada

GROWTH PLANS/SPECIAL FEATURES:

Newport Sports Management (NSM), based in Canada, is an athlete management and representation agency for professional hockey players. It is one of the largest agencies in professional hockey, with more than 100 National Hockey League (NHL) clients. Some of NSM's most well-known players include Al MacInnis, Pat LaFontaine, Vladislav Tretiak and retired players Wendel Clark, Brent Sutter and Dave Manson. NSM is headquartered in Mississauga, Ontario and has regional offices in Alberta, Quebec, the U.S., Russia, the Czech Republic, Finland and Sweden. The firm provides its services through three divisions: Athlete services, athlete marketing and corporate marketing. Its athlete services division provides contract negotiations; financial management; tax and estate planning; insurance; training and development; and draft preparation. NSM's athlete marketing division provides clients with additional revenue opportunities such as promotional assignments, endorsements and spokesperson roles. The division specializes in sponsorship sales, corporate sponsorship programs and the evaluation of hockey properties to meet the needs and goals of corporate sponsors. NSM's corporate marketing division provides property representation, corporate consultation, sales promotion, information technology and event management services. This division specializes in sponsorship sales, development of corporate sponsorship packages, media exposure, on-site recognition, pre- and post-event publicity, corporate hospitality, logo usage rights, licensing rights, merchandising rights and cross promotions.

FINANCIALS:
Sales and profits are in thousands of dollars—add 000 to get the full amount. 2008 Note: Financial information for 2008 was not available for all companies at press time.

2008 Sales: $
2007 Sales: $
2006 Sales: $
2005 Sales: $
2004 Sales: $

2008 Profits: $
2007 Profits: $
2006 Profits: $
2005 Profits: $
2004 Profits: $

U.S. Stock Ticker: Private
Int'l Ticker: Int'l Exchange:
Employees:
Fiscal Year Ends:
Parent Company:

SALARIES/BENEFITS:

Pension Plan: ESOP Stock Plan: Profit Sharing: Top Exec. Salary: $ Bonus: $
Savings Plan: Stock Purch. Plan: Second Exec. Salary: $ Bonus: $

OTHER THOUGHTS:

Apparent Women Officers or Directors: 2
Hot Spot for Advancement for Women/Minorities:

LOCATIONS: ("Y" = Yes)

West:	Southwest:	Midwest:	Southeast:	Northeast:	International:
		Y			Y

Note: Financial information, benefits and other data can change quickly and may vary from those stated here.

NIKE INC

www.nike.com

Industry Group Code: 316219 **Ranks within this company's industry group:** Sales: 1 Profits: 1

Sports:		Services:		Media:		Sales:		Facilities:		Other:	
Leagues/Associations:		Food & Beverage:		TV:		Marketing:		Stadiums:		Gambling:	
Teams:		Agents:		Radio:		Ads:		Fitness Clubs:		Apparel:	Y
Nonprofits:		Other:		Internet:		Tickets:		Golf Courses:		Equipment:	Y
Other:				Print:		Retail:	Y	Ski Resorts:		Shoes:	Y
				Software:		Other:		Other:		Other:	

TYPES OF BUSINESS:

Athletic Shoes/Apparel Manufacturing
Athletic Equipment
Sports Accessories
Retail Stores
Sports Apparel
Plastic Products
Hockey Products
Swimwear

BRANDS/DIVISIONS/AFFILIATES:

Cole Haan Holdings, Inc.
Nike Bayer Hockey Corp.
Nike Bauer Hockey U.S.A., Inc
Converse Inc
Hurley International, LLC
Chuck Taylor
Bragano
All Star

CONTACTS: *Note: Officers with more than one job title may be intentionally listed here more than once.*

Mark G. Parker, CEO
Mark G. Parker, Pres.
Donald Blair, CFO/VP
John F. Slusher, VP-Global Sports Mktg.
Ronald D. McCray, Chief Admin. Officer/VP
Gary M. DeStefano, VP/Pres., Global Oper.
Bernard F. Pliska, VP/Corp. Controller
Charlie Denson, Pres., Nike Brand
Trevor A. Edwards, VP-Global Brand & Category Mgmt.
Eric D. Sprunk, VP-Global Footwear
Peter Hudson, VP-Footwear Design
Philip H. Knight, Chmn.
Nick Athanasakos, VP-Global Supply Chain

Phone: 503-671-2500	Fax:
Toll-Free: 800-344-6453	
Address: 1 Bowerman Dr., Beaverton, OR 97005 US	

GROWTH PLANS/SPECIAL FEATURES:

Nike, Inc. designs, develops and markets footwear, apparel, equipment and accessories. It is one of the largest sellers of athletic footwear and athletic apparel in the world. The company's athletic footwear products are designed primarily for specific athletic use, although a large percentage of the products are worn for casual or leisure purposes. Running, training, basketball, soccer, sport-inspired urban shoes and children's shoes are the firm's top-selling product categories. Nike also markets shoes designed for tennis, golf, baseball, football, lacrosse, walking, outdoor activities, skateboarding, bicycling, volleyball, wrestling, cheerleading, aquatic activities and other athletic and recreational uses. The firm maintains several wholly-owned subsidiaries including Cole Haan, a line of casual footwear, apparel and accessories for men and women; Converse, Inc., a line of footwear, apparel and accessories; Hurley International LLC, a collection of action sports apparel; and Umbro Ltd., a line of athletic and casual footwear, apparel and equipment, primarily for soccer. Nike sells its products to retail accounts, through Nike-owned retail stores and through a mix of independent distributors and licensees, in more than 180 countries. Within the U.S., the firm operates 296 Nike Brand and subsidiary retail stores. U.S. sales generate approximately 43% of the firm's total revenues. In the international market, which includes several countries within Europe, Asia, South America, and Africa, the firm maintains 260 retail stores. The international market accounts for 57% of total revenues. In March 2008, the firm acquired Umbro Ltd., a line that designs, distributes, and licenses athletic and casual footwear, apparel and equipment.

The company offers employees medical coverage; life insurance; a profit sharing retirement program; fitness center memberships; a 401(k) plan; employee stock purchase plan; an annual performance sharing plan; scholarships for children of employees; adoption assistance; tuition assistance; employee discounts; and an employee assistance plan.

FINANCIALS: **Sales and profits are in thousands of dollars—add 000 to get the full amount. 2008 Note: Financial information for 2008 was not available for all companies at press time.**

2008 Sales: $18,627,000	2008 Profits: $1,883,400	**U.S. Stock Ticker: NKE**
2007 Sales: $16,325,900	2007 Profits: $1,491,500	**Int'l Ticker:** Int'l Exchange:
2006 Sales: $14,954,900	2006 Profits: $1,392,000	Employees: 32,500
2005 Sales: $13,739,700	2005 Profits: $1,211,600	Fiscal Year Ends: 5/31
2004 Sales: $12,253,100	2004 Profits: $945,600	Parent Company:

SALARIES/BENEFITS:

Pension Plan:	ESOP Stock Plan:	Profit Sharing: Y	Top Exec. Salary: $1,376,923	Bonus: $2,682,684
Savings Plan: Y	Stock Purch. Plan: Y		Second Exec. Salary: $1,192,308	Bonus: $2,222,727

OTHER THOUGHTS:

Apparent Women Officers or Directors: 14
Hot Spot for Advancement for Women/Minorities: Y

LOCATIONS: ("Y" = Yes)

West:	Southwest:	Midwest:	Southeast:	Northeast:	International:
Y	Y	Y	Y	Y	Y

NINTENDO CO LTD

www.nintendo.com

Industry Group Code: 334111 **Ranks within this company's industry group:** Sales: 1 Profits: 1

Sports:		Services:		Media:		Sales:		Facilities:		Other:	
Leagues/Associations:		Food & Beverage:		TV:		Marketing:		Stadiums:		Gambling:	
Teams:		Agents:		Radio:		Ads:		Fitness Clubs:		Apparel:	
Nonprofits:		Other:		Internet:		Tickets:		Golf Courses:		Equipment:	
Other:				Print:		Retail:		Ski Resorts:		Shoes:	
				Software:		Other:		Other:		Other:	

TYPES OF BUSINESS:

Video Games
Video Game Hardware & Software

BRANDS/DIVISIONS/AFFILIATES:

GameCube
Nintendo DS
Game Boy Advance
Wii
Mario Brothers
Legend of Zelda (The)
Donkey Kong
Pokemon

CONTACTS: *Note: Officers with more than one job title may be intentionally listed here more than once.*

Satoru Iwata, CEO
Satoru Iwata, Pres.
Genyo Takeda, Gen. Mgr.-Integrated R&D Div./Sr. Managing Dir.
Yoshihiro Mori, Sr. Managing Dir.
Shinji Hatano, Sr. Managing Dir.
Shigeru Miyamoto, Sr. Managing Dir.
Nobuo Nagai, Sr. Managing Dir.
Reginald Fils-Aime, COO/Pres., Nintendo of America, Inc.

Phone: 81-75-662-9600	**Fax:** 81-75-662-9620
Toll-Free:	
Address: 11-1 Kamitoba, Hokotate-cho, Minami-ku, Kyoto, 601-8116 Japan	

GROWTH PLANS/SPECIAL FEATURES:

Nintendo Co., Ltd. makes video game hardware and software, including the well-known video game titles Mario Brothers, Donkey Kong, Pokemon and The Legend of Zelda. Based in Kyoto, Japan, Nintendo owns subsidiaries in the U.S., Canada, Korea, Australia and several European countries, with overseas sales accounting for 48.2% of 2008 sales. Its main products are the video game systems and related software and merchandise for the Nintendo DS and DS Lite, which by the end of 2008 had sold approximately 70.6 million units cumulatively since it was introduced; Game Boy Advance, 81.1 million; GameCube, 21.7 million; and Wii, 24.5 million. Nintendo has recently increased focus on selling the DS and the Game Boy Advance, its portable devices. While the Game Boy Advance is essentially a portable version of home-based video consoles, the DS sports a dual-screen format, an LCD touch screen, wireless connectivity and voice recognition capabilities. Nintendo's newest console and successor to the GameCube, the Wii, features a unique motion-sensitive controller, resembling a TV remote, which allows for point-and-click-style game play. The company's latest products include the Wii system and the new Touch! Generations software line, which includes Nintendo DS titles such as Nintendogs, a virtual pet program, and Brain Age. In December 2007, Nintendo launched the Wii Fit in Japan; in April 2008, Wii Fit launched in Europe; and in May 2008 it launched in Australia and North America. Wii Fit features a unique floor board controller that used in balance related games and activities, including skiing, yoga, meditation and boxing.

FINANCIALS: **Sales and profits are in thousands of dollars—add 000 to get the full amount. 2008 Note: Financial information for 2008 was not available for all companies at press time.**

2008 Sales: $16,724,230	2008 Profits: $2,573,426	**U.S. Stock Ticker: NTDOY**
2007 Sales: $8,183,173	2007 Profits: $1,477,038	**Int'l Ticker: 7974** Int'l Exchange: Tokyo-TSE
2006 Sales: $4,327,100	2006 Profits: $836,600	Employees: 2,977
2005 Sales: $4,788,400	2005 Profits: $812,800	Fiscal Year Ends: 3/31
2004 Sales: $4,869,400	2004 Profits: $314,200	Parent Company:

SALARIES/BENEFITS:

Pension Plan:	ESOP Stock Plan:	Profit Sharing:	Top Exec. Salary: $	Bonus: $
Savings Plan:	Stock Purch. Plan:		Second Exec. Salary: $	Bonus: $

OTHER THOUGHTS:

Apparent Women Officers or Directors:
Hot Spot for Advancement for Women/Minorities:

LOCATIONS: ("Y" = Yes)

West:	Southwest:	Midwest:	Southeast:	Northeast:	International:
Y					Y

Note: Financial information, benefits and other data can change quickly and may vary from those stated here.

NORTH FACE INC (THE)

www.thenorthface.com

Industry Group Code: 339920 **Ranks within this company's industry group:** Sales: Profits:

Sports:		Services:		Media:		Sales:		Facilities:		Other:	
Leagues/Associations:		Food & Beverage:		TV:		Marketing:		Stadiums:		Gambling:	
Teams:		Agents:		Radio:		Ads:		Fitness Clubs:		Apparel:	Y
Nonprofits:		Other:		Internet:		Tickets:		Golf Courses:		Equipment:	Y
Other:				Print:		Retail:	Y	Ski Resorts:		Shoes:	Y
				Software:		Other:		Other:		Other:	

TYPES OF BUSINESS:

Outdoor Apparel & Equipment
Footwear
Eyewear
Tents
Sleeping Bags
Backpacks

BRANDS/DIVISIONS/AFFILIATES:

VF Corp.

CONTACTS:

Note: Officers with more than one job title may be intentionally listed here more than once.

Steve Rendle, Pres.
Jim Gerson, VP-Research, Design & Dev.
Pamela Bennett, Public Rel. Officer
J.P. Borod, Dir.-Footwear Prod. Mgmt.
Barry McGeough, VP-Hardgoods
Patrick Frisk, VP/Gen. Mgr.-EMEA

Phone: **Fax:**
Toll-Free: 866-715-3223
Address: 14450 Doolittle Dr., San Leandro, CA 94577 US

GROWTH PLANS/SPECIAL FEATURES:

The North Face, Inc., a subsidiary of VF Corp., is a leading designer, distributor and marketer of technically sophisticated outdoor apparel and equipment, with a 40-year history as a provider of equipment to many of the world's most challenging high-altitude and polar expeditions. The company offers a broad range of outerwear, sportswear, footwear, eyewear, snow sports gear, bicycles tents, sleeping bags and backpacks. Many of the company's products are designed for extreme applications such as mountaineering; rock and ice climbing; endurance running; and backcountry skiing and snowboarding. The North Face puts extensive effort into the research and development of new products. The company works in conjunction with leading materials engineering companies, including Gore (makers of GORE-TEX fabrics), Polartec and Primaloft, as well as professional athletes to create technically advanced fabrics, and it employs or sponsors numerous world-class mountaineers and athletes to test its gear in the field. In the fields of alpine and rock climbing, skiing, snowboarding and endurance sports, the company has sponsorships arranged with over 50 athletes. The North Face's products are distributed to thousands of wholesale customers worldwide, and it operates 20 retail locations in the U.S. The North Face's authorized retailers include Sports Authority, EMS, Moosejaw Mountaineering, Urban Outfitters, Hudson Trail Outfitters, Great Outdoor Provision, Mountain Gear and REI.

The North Face offers its employees a benefits package that includes educational assistance, dependent care spending accounts, a scholarship program, vacation and ski resort discounts and outdoor adventure training programs.

FINANCIALS:

Sales and profits are in thousands of dollars—add 000 to get the full amount. 2008 Note: Financial information for 2008 was not available for all companies at press time.

2008 Sales: $	2008 Profits: $	**U.S. Stock Ticker: Subsidiary**
2007 Sales: $	2007 Profits: $	**Int'l Ticker:** Int'l Exchange:
2006 Sales: $	2006 Profits: $	Employees:
2005 Sales: $	2005 Profits: $	Fiscal Year Ends: 12/31
2004 Sales: $	2004 Profits: $	Parent Company: VF CORP

SALARIES/BENEFITS:

Pension Plan:	ESOP Stock Plan:	Profit Sharing:	Top Exec. Salary: $	Bonus: $
Savings Plan:	Stock Purch. Plan:		Second Exec. Salary: $	Bonus: $

OTHER THOUGHTS:

Apparent Women Officers or Directors: 1
Hot Spot for Advancement for Women/Minorities:

LOCATIONS: ("Y" = Yes)

West:	Southwest:	Midwest:	Southeast:	Northeast:	International:
Y		Y		Y	Y

NORWICH CITY FOOTBALL CLUB

www.canaries.co.uk

Industry Group Code: 711211D **Ranks within this company's industry group:** Sales: Profits:

Sports:		Services:		Media:		Sales:		Facilities:		Other:	
Leagues/Associations:		Food & Beverage:		TV:		Marketing:	Y	Stadiums:	Y	Gambling:	Y
Teams:	Y	Agents:		Radio:		Ads:	Y	Fitness Clubs:		Apparel:	Y
Nonprofits:		Other:	Y	Internet:		Tickets:	Y	Golf Courses:		Equipment:	
Other:				Print:		Retail:	Y	Ski Resorts:		Shoes:	
				Software:		Other:	Y	Other:		Other:	Y

TYPES OF BUSINESS:

Soccer Team
Insurance Policy & Financial Product Sales
Branded Credit Cards
Security Services
Lotteries
Online Merchandise Sales

BRANDS/DIVISIONS/AFFILIATES:

Canaries (The)
Canary Direct Insurance
Norwich City Canary Card (Mastercard)
Norwich City Holiday Club (The)
Canary Financial Services
Canary Corporate Insurance
Boswell Group
Canary Telecom

CONTACTS: *Note: Officers with more than one job title may be intentionally listed here more than once.*

Neil Doncaster, CEO
Will Hoy, Head-Mktg.
Kevan Platt, Club Sec.
Sam Gordon, Dir.-Oper.
Joe Ferrari, Head-Media
Sam Gordon, Dir.-Finance
Bryan Gunn, Team Mgr.
Ian Cook, First Team Coach
Andy Batley, Mgr.-Safety
Richard Gough, Mgr.-Customer Svc.
Roger Munby, Chmn.

Phone: 44-805-6593-17 **Fax:**
Toll-Free:
Address: Carrow Rd., Norwich, Norfolk NR1 1JE UK

GROWTH PLANS/SPECIAL FEATURES:

Norwich City Football Club, known as the Canaries, is an English Premiership soccer team. The team, established in 1902, has played home games at Carrow Road stadium since 1935. Carrow Road has held, at its highest, nearly 44,000 fans. The team was an FA Cup semifinalist in 1989 and 1992 and experienced its best Premier League finish ever (third) in 1992-93. The 2001-02 season was crucial for the team under the new managerial stewardship of Nigel Worthington. The team acquired Clint Easton, Mark Rivers, Paul Crichton, Neil Emblen and Marc Libbra and was a contender for league promotion for the first time in years. The club continued to improve, culminating in a 2003-04 Premiership promotion and a first division title. The club partners with local insurance brokers to offer Canary Direct home and motor insurance. For every policy sold, brokers donate approximately $22 to the club. The club has also partnered with the Boswell Group, a financial company, which allows the group to sell financial products and services under the names Canary Financial Services and Canary Corporate Insurance. A portion of these proceeds are donated to the football club. The club offers the Norwich City Canary Card, a credit card from MasterCard. Additional partnerships have formed The Canary Account, The Norwich City Holiday Club, Canary Telecom and other services that help fund the team's operations. EventGuard, the security subsidiary of the Canaries, provides private customers as well as the club with a range of security services. The club runs three local lotteries for fundraising, and offers hospitality/catering services as well. In March 2009, the team sold 75.1% interest in EventGuard to Norfolk County Services.

FINANCIALS: **Sales and profits are in thousands of dollars—add 000 to get the full amount. 2008 Note: Financial information for 2008 was not available for all companies at press time.**

2008 Sales: $
2007 Sales: $
2006 Sales: $
2005 Sales: $
2004 Sales: $

2008 Profits: $
2007 Profits: $
2006 Profits: $
2005 Profits: $
2004 Profits: $

U.S. Stock Ticker: Private
Int'l Ticker: Int'l Exchange:
Employees:
Fiscal Year Ends: 12/31
Parent Company:

SALARIES/BENEFITS:

Pension Plan: ESOP Stock Plan: Profit Sharing: Top Exec. Salary: $ Bonus: $
Savings Plan: Stock Purch. Plan: Second Exec. Salary: $ Bonus: $

OTHER THOUGHTS:

Apparent Women Officers or Directors: 3
Hot Spot for Advancement for Women/Minorities: Y

LOCATIONS: ("Y" = Yes)

West:	Southwest:	Midwest:	Southeast:	Northeast:	International:
					Y

Note: Financial information, benefits and other data can change quickly and may vary from those stated here.

NTN BUZZTIME INC

www.ntn.com

Industry Group Code: 511208 **Ranks within this company's industry group:** Sales: 3 Profits: 1

Sports:		Services:		Media:		Sales:		Facilities:		Other:	
Leagues/Associations:		Food & Beverage:		TV:		Marketing:		Stadiums:		Gambling:	
Teams:		Agents:		Radio:		Ads:		Fitness Clubs:		Apparel:	
Nonprofits:		Other:		Internet:		Tickets:		Golf Courses:		Equipment:	
Other:				Print:		Retail:		Ski Resorts:		Shoes:	
				Software:		Other:		Other:		Other:	

TYPES OF BUSINESS:

Interactive Sports & Trivia Games
On-Site Wireless Communications Products
Restaurant & Hospitality Software

BRANDS/DIVISIONS/AFFILIATES:

NTN Communications
Buzztime Play-Along TV
Buzztime Interactive Television Network
iTV Network
Buzztime Distribution
Buzztime Entertainment
iTV2
Playmaker

CONTACTS: *Note: Officers with more than one job title may be intentionally listed here more than once.*

Kendra Berger, CFO
Peter Boylan, Exec. VP-Sales
Kendra Berger, Corp. Sec.
Jeffrey A. Berg, Chmn.

Phone: 760-438-7400	**Fax:** 760-438-3505
Toll-Free:	
Address: 5966 La Place Ct., Ste. 100, Carlsbad, CA 92008 US	

GROWTH PLANS/SPECIAL FEATURES:

NTN Buzztime, Inc., formerly NTN Communications, develops and distributes multiplayer interactive television entertainment through the Buzztime Play-Along TV brand. The company's entertainment division is comprised of the Buzztime Interactive Television Network (iTV Network) and Buzztime Distribution, formerly known as Buzztime Entertainment. The iTV Network distributes an interactive promotional television game network to approximately 3,900 restaurants, sports bars, taverns and pubs primarily in North America and the U.K. The iTV Network includes approximately 3,490 U.S. subscribers, 322 Canadian subscribers and 65 U.K. subscribers. Approximately 28% of its subscribers come from leading national chains in the casual dining restaurant segment such as Buffalo Wild Wings, TGIFriday's, Applebee's and Damon's Grill. The company also has a technology platform, iTV2, which allows two channels of Buzztime entertainment programming to be electronically delivered to each location, allowing channel one to remain as a primarily trivia-based offering to its long-time loyal players, while channel two is devoted to new content such as Texas Hold'em, Buzztime Billiards and Crazy Golf. The iTV2 system uses the Playmaker, a hand-held 900 MHz radio frequency device with a monochrome LCD display and sealed keypad. The company has also developed a more advanced 2.4 GHz Playmaker. Buzztime Distribution distributes the company's content and technology to other third-party consumer platforms, including cable television; satellite television; mobile phones; online; retail games and toys; airlines; and books. In March 2007, NTN Buzztime sold NTN Wireless Communications to HM Electronics, and in October 2007 the company sold its NTN Software Solutions intellectual property assets for approximately $215,000.

The company offers its employees medical and dental benefits, stock options, flexible schedules and a wellness program.

FINANCIALS: **Sales and profits are in thousands of dollars—add 000 to get the full amount. 2008 Note: Financial information for 2008 was not available for all companies at press time.**

2008 Sales: $27,496	2008 Profits: $-6,466	**U.S. Stock Ticker: NTN**
2007 Sales: $30,542	2007 Profits: $-5,026	**Int'l Ticker:** Int'l Exchange:
2006 Sales: $32,985	2006 Profits: $-4,773	Employees: 134
2005 Sales: $30,749	2005 Profits: $-2,019	Fiscal Year Ends: 12/31
2004 Sales: $26,284	2004 Profits: $-4,979	Parent Company:

SALARIES/BENEFITS:

Pension Plan:	ESOP Stock Plan:	Profit Sharing:	Top Exec. Salary: $400,000	Bonus: $
Savings Plan:	Stock Purch. Plan:		Second Exec. Salary: $250,000	Bonus: $

OTHER THOUGHTS:

Apparent Women Officers or Directors: 1
Hot Spot for Advancement for Women/Minorities:

LOCATIONS: ("Y" = Yes)

West:	Southwest:	Midwest:	Southeast:	Northeast:	International:
Y	Y		Y		Y

OAKLAND ATHLETICS

athletics.mlb.com

Industry Group Code: 711211A **Ranks within this company's industry group:** Sales: 25 Profits: 8

Sports:		Services:		Media:		Sales:		Facilities:		Other:	
Leagues/Associations:		Food & Beverage:		TV:		Marketing:		Stadiums:	Y	Gambling:	
Teams:	Y	Agents:		Radio:		Ads:		Fitness Clubs:		Apparel:	
Nonprofits:		Other:		Internet:		Tickets:	Y	Golf Courses:		Equipment:	
Other:				Print:		Retail:	Y	Ski Resorts:		Shoes:	
				Software:		Other:		Other:		Other:	

TYPES OF BUSINESS:

Professional Baseball Team
Stadium Operation

BRANDS/DIVISIONS/AFFILIATES:

A's
Oakland Stadium
Athletics Investment Group LLC (The)

CONTACTS:

Note: Officers with more than one job title may be intentionally listed here more than once.

Lew Wolff, Managing Partner/Owner
Michael Crowley, Pres.
Jim Leahey, VP-Mktg. & Sales
Kim Kubo, Mgr.-Human Resources
Nathan Hayes, Mgr.-Info. Systems
Steve Johnston, General Counsel
Billy Beane, VP-Oper./Gen. Mgr.
Ken Pries, VP-Comm. & Broadcasting
Paul Wong, VP-Finance
Heather Rajeski, Mgr.-Special Events & Promotions
Eric Kubota, Dir.-Scouting
Kieth Lieppman, Dir.-Player Dev.
Mike Ono, Mgr.-Creative Svcs.

Phone: 510-638-4900 **Fax:**
Toll-Free:
Address: 7000 Coliseum Way, Oakland, CA 94621 US

GROWTH PLANS/SPECIAL FEATURES:

The Oakland Athletics is a Major League Baseball (MLB) team who are better known as the A's. The A's are owned by The Athletics Investment Group, LLC. The team became part of the American League in 1901. For its first fifty years, the team was managed by Hall of Famer Connie Mack. The A's moved from Philadelphia to Kansas City in 1955 and to Oakland in 1968. The team plays its home games in Oakland Coliseum, which was built in 1968 and seats about 50,000. The A's are one of three baseball teams who still share a stadium with an NFL team. The club experienced success in the early 70s, and again in 1988-90, when it played in three straight World Series, winning in 1989. This A's line-up was well stocked with stars like Rickey Henderson, Jose Canseco, Mark McGwire, Dennis Eckersley and Dave Stewart. A new era for the A's dawned in 1997 when Billy Beane became the general manager. Beane brought consistent success to the team through the application of sabermetrics, the analysis of baseball through objective statistical evidence. Sabermetrics allows small market teams such as the A's to compete with large-market teams like the Yankees by identifying undervalued and overvalued commodities in the baseball market. After the A's won an American League best 103 games in 2002 despite having the sixth lowest payroll in baseball, Beane and his approach to baseball business was the subject of a book called Moneyball, which has created a lot of both positive and negative stir. The team has finished first or second in its division every year since 1999, making the playoffs five times; however, they have failed to reach the World Series. In 2008, average home game attendance was 20,558. Forbes recently estimated the team's value to be $319 million.

FINANCIALS:

Sales and profits are in thousands of dollars—add 000 to get the full amount. 2008 Note: Financial information for 2008 was not available for all companies at press time.

2008 Sales: $160,000
2007 Sales: $154,000
2006 Sales: $146,000
2005 Sales: $134,000
2004 Sales: $

2008 Profits: $26,200
2007 Profits: $15,400
2006 Profits: $14,500
2005 Profits: $
2004 Profits: $

U.S. Stock Ticker: Subsidiary
Int'l Ticker: Int'l Exchange:
Employees: 135
Fiscal Year Ends: 10/31
Parent Company: ATHLETICS INVESTMENT GROUP LLC (THE)

SALARIES/BENEFITS:

Pension Plan: ESOP Stock Plan: Profit Sharing: Top Exec. Salary: $ Bonus: $
Savings Plan: Stock Purch. Plan: Second Exec. Salary: $ Bonus: $

OTHER THOUGHTS:

Apparent Women Officers or Directors: 22
Hot Spot for Advancement for Women/Minorities: Y

LOCATIONS: ("Y" = Yes)

West:	Southwest:	Midwest:	Southeast:	Northeast:	International:
Y					Y

OAKLAND RAIDERS

www.raiders.com

Industry Group Code: 711211C **Ranks within this company's industry group:** Sales: 25 Profits: 12

Sports:		Services:		Media:		Sales:		Facilities:		Other:	
Leagues/Associations:		Food & Beverage:		TV:		Marketing:		Stadiums:		Gambling:	
Teams:	Y	Agents:		Radio:		Ads:		Fitness Clubs:		Apparel:	
Nonprofits:		Other:		Internet:		Tickets:	Y	Golf Courses:		Equipment:	
Other:				Print:		Retail:	Y	Ski Resorts:		Shoes:	
				Software:		Other:		Other:		Other:	

TYPES OF BUSINESS:

Professional Football Team

BRANDS/DIVISIONS/AFFILIATES:

Oakland-Alameda County Coliseum

CONTACTS:

Note: Officers with more than one job title may be intentionally listed here more than once.

Amy Trask, CEO
Marc Badain, CFO
Mark Jackson, Dir.-Football Dev.
Al Davis, Owner
Tom Cable, Head Coach

Phone: 510-864-5000	**Fax:** 510-864-5160
Toll-Free:	
Address: 1220 Harbor Bay Pkwy., Alameda, CA 94502 US	

GROWTH PLANS/SPECIAL FEATURES:

The Oakland Raiders are a National Football League (NFL) team. The team was founded in 1960 as part of the American Football League (AFL), and joined the NFL in 1970. The franchise resided in Los Angeles between 1982 and 1994. The Raiders have won the Super Bowl three times, in 1977, 1980 and 1983. Most recently the team advanced to the Super Bowl in the 2002-03 season, but lost to the Tampa Bay Buccaneers. Former coach John Madden helped make the Raiders one of the most successful franchises in NFL history. The team has been home to many Hall of Fame members and other star players, including Marcus Allen, Jim Otto, Art Shell, Billy Cannon, multi-sport star Bo Jackson and Ken Stabler. The Raiders are owned and managed by Al Davis, who has been involved in the league since 1960. Davis became the head coach and general manager of the Raiders in 1963 and was able to gain enough shares to assume total control of the franchise by 1976. He was the first owner to appoint a Latino head coach (1979) and an African American head coach (1989). Additionally, in hiring CEO Amy Trask, he helped place a woman in a one of the highest positions of power in any NFL team. The Raiders currently play at the Oakland-Alameda County Coliseum, which holds 63,026 spectators and is owned jointly by the City of Oakland and Alameda County. Forbes recently valued the team at approximately $861 million. In the 2008 season, the team averaged approximately 57,850 fans in attendance per game.

FINANCIALS:

Sales and profits are in thousands of dollars—add 000 to get the full amount. 2008 Note: Financial information for 2008 was not available for all companies at press time.

2008 Sales: $205,000	2008 Profits: $27,000	**U.S. Stock Ticker: Private**
2007 Sales: $189,000	2007 Profits: $46,200	**Int'l Ticker:** Int'l Exchange:
2006 Sales: $171,000	2006 Profits: $9,100	Employees:
2005 Sales: $169,000	2005 Profits: $	Fiscal Year Ends: 6/30
2004 Sales: $149,000	2004 Profits: $	Parent Company:

SALARIES/BENEFITS:

Pension Plan:	ESOP Stock Plan:	Profit Sharing:	Top Exec. Salary: $	Bonus: $
Savings Plan:	Stock Purch. Plan:		Second Exec. Salary: $	Bonus: $

OTHER THOUGHTS:

Apparent Women Officers or Directors: 1
Hot Spot for Advancement for Women/Minorities:

LOCATIONS: ("Y" = Yes)

West:	Southwest:	Midwest:	Southeast:	Northeast:	International:
Y					

OCTAGON WORLDWIDE

www.octagon.com

Industry Group Code: 711410 **Ranks within this company's industry group:** Sales: Profits:

Sports:		Services:		Media:		Sales:		Facilities:		Other:	
Leagues/Associations:		Food & Beverage:		TV:	Y	Marketing:	Y	Stadiums:		Gambling:	
Teams:		Agents:	Y	Radio:		Ads:	Y	Fitness Clubs:		Apparel:	
Nonprofits:		Other:	Y	Internet:		Tickets:		Golf Courses:		Equipment:	
Other:				Print:		Retail:		Ski Resorts:		Shoes:	
				Software:		Other:		Other:		Other:	

TYPES OF BUSINESS:

Sports Marketing
Athlete Representation
Consulting Services
Event Management
Media Services
Licensing & Merchandising

BRANDS/DIVISIONS/AFFILIATES:

Interpublic Group of Companies, Inc.
First Call
Passion Drivers

CONTACTS: *Note: Officers with more than one job title may be intentionally listed here more than once.*

Rick Dudley, CEO
Rick Dudley, Pres.
Lisa Murray, Chief Mktg. Officer/Exec. VP
Jeff Shifrin, Pres., Octagon Mktg. North America
Phil de Picciotto, Pres., Athletes & Personalities

Phone: 203-354-7400 **Fax:** 203-354-7401
Toll-Free:
Address: 800 Connecticut Ave., 2nd Fl., Norwalk, CT 06854 US

GROWTH PLANS/SPECIAL FEATURES:

Octagon Worldwide, a unit of the Interpublic Group, is a global provider of sports and entertainment marketing services. With locations in 18 countries throughout Australia, Africa, Asia, Europe and North America, the firm offers such services as consulting, events, promotions, public relations and property representation for engagement marketing; representation, management and talent procurement for athletes and personalities; and consulting, management and production for music and entertainment. Octagon's clients include over 500 organizations and 800 athletes and personalities, with over 3,200 events managed by the firm. Through subsidiary First Call, Octagon provides celebrity advisory services for advertising campaigns, public relations programs, corporate speeches, meet-and-greets and hospitality, as well as customized research. The company's Passion Drivers research is designed to provide information regarding the consumer/sports relationship for the development of sponsorship activation strategies and programs. Noteworthy clients have included John Elway, Anna Kournikova, Mia Hamm and Michael Phelps. Corporate clients include Altadis, BMW, Coca-Cola, IBM, Kraft, MasterCard, MTV, Red Bull, Samsung and Vodafone. In October 2008, the company acquired the baseball operations of CSMG Sports, adding players such as Randy Johnson and Chien-Ming Wang to the firm's roster of represented athletes.

FINANCIALS: **Sales and profits are in thousands of dollars—add 000 to get the full amount. 2008 Note: Financial information for 2008 was not available for all companies at press time.**

2008 Sales: $ | 2008 Profits: $
2007 Sales: $ | 2007 Profits: $
2006 Sales: $ | 2006 Profits: $
2005 Sales: $ | 2005 Profits: $
2004 Sales: $ | 2004 Profits: $

U.S. Stock Ticker: Private
Int'l Ticker: Int'l Exchange:
Employees: 1,000
Fiscal Year Ends: 12/31
Parent Company: INTERPUBLIC GROUP OF COMPANIES INC

SALARIES/BENEFITS:

Pension Plan: ESOP Stock Plan: Profit Sharing: Top Exec. Salary: $ Bonus: $
Savings Plan: Stock Purch. Plan: Second Exec. Salary: $ Bonus: $

OTHER THOUGHTS:

Apparent Women Officers or Directors: 1
Hot Spot for Advancement for Women/Minorities:

LOCATIONS: ("Y" = Yes)

West:	Southwest:	Midwest:	Southeast:	Northeast:	International:
Y			Y	Y	Y

Note: Financial information, benefits and other data can change quickly and may vary from those stated here.

OKLAHOMA CITY THUNDER

www.nba.com/thunder

Industry Group Code: 711211B **Ranks within this company's industry group:** Sales: 30 Profits: 28

Sports:		Services:		Media:		Sales:		Facilities:		Other:	
Leagues/Associations:		Food & Beverage:	Y	TV:		Marketing:		Stadiums:		Gambling:	
Teams:	Y	Agents:		Radio:		Ads:		Fitness Clubs:		Apparel:	Y
Nonprofits:		Other:		Internet:		Tickets:	Y	Golf Courses:		Equipment:	
Other:				Print:		Retail:	Y	Ski Resorts:		Shoes:	
				Software:		Other:		Other:		Other:	

TYPES OF BUSINESS:

Professional Basketball Team
Ticket Sales
Sports Merchandise

BRANDS/DIVISIONS/AFFILIATES:

Professional Basketball Club LLC
Tulsa 66ers (The)
INTEGRIS Health
Seattle Supersonics
Ford Center (The)

CONTACTS: *Note: Officers with more than one job title may be intentionally listed here more than once.*

Katy Semtner, VP-Human Resources
Matt Keller, Coordinator-IT
Jeremy Owen, Dir.-Merch.
Danny Barth, Chief Admin. Officer/Exec. VP
John R. Croley, VP-Bus. Dev.
Dan Mahoney, VP-Corp. Comm.
Staci Johnson, Controller
Scott Brooks, Head Coach
Sam Presti, Gen. Mgr./Exec. VP
Ken Adelson, Sr. VP/Exec. Producer
Brian Byrnes, Sr. VP-Ticket Sales & Svcs.
Clayton I. Bennett, Chmn./Owner

Phone: 405-208-4800	**Fax:** 405-429-7900
Toll-Free:	
Address: 211 N. Robinson Ave., Ste. 300, Oklahoma City, OK 73102 US	

GROWTH PLANS/SPECIAL FEATURES:

The Oklahoma City Thunder, formerly the Seattle SuperSonics, are a National Basketball Association (NBA) team created in 1967 as Seattle's first professional sports team. It plays in the Northwest Division along with the Utah Jazz, Denver Nuggets, Portland Trail Blazers and Minnesota Timberwolves. As the Sonics, the team made many appearances in the NBA finals, but only succeeded in winning one championship in the 1978-79 season. The team's home court is the Ford Center in Oklahoma City, which can seat over 18,000 fans for basketball games. The NBA D-league team, the Tulsa 66ers, acts as a feeder for the Thunder. Professional Basketball Club, LLC, a private Oklahoma City-based group led by businessman Clayton (Clay) Bennett, recently acquired the Thunder from the franchises' previous owner, the Basketball Club of Seattle, LLC, for $350 million; as part of the deal, the city of Seattle maintains rights to the SuperSonics name, history and colors. In April 2008, the NBA Board of Governors voted to allow Bennett to move the team from Seattle to Oklahoma City. In January 2009, the franchise partnered with INTEGRIS Health, making INTEGRIS the Thunder's official health care provider. Forbes Magazine recently estimated the team to be worth approximately $300 million. In the 2008-09 season, the team's home attendance average was roughly 18,700 per game.

FINANCIALS: **Sales and profits are in thousands of dollars—add 000 to get the full amount. 2008 Note: Financial information for 2008 was not available for all companies at press time.**

2008 Sales: $82,000	2008 Profits: $-9,400
2007 Sales: $81,000	2007 Profits: $-5,700
2006 Sales: $81,000	2006 Profits: $3,600
2005 Sales: $81,000	2005 Profits: $
2004 Sales: $	2004 Profits: $

U.S. Stock Ticker: Subsidiary
Int'l Ticker: Int'l Exchange:
Employees:
Fiscal Year Ends: 12/31
Parent Company: PROFESSIONAL BASKETBALL CLUB LLC

SALARIES/BENEFITS:

Pension Plan:	ESOP Stock Plan:	Profit Sharing:	Top Exec. Salary: $	Bonus: $
Savings Plan:	Stock Purch. Plan:		Second Exec. Salary: $	Bonus: $

OTHER THOUGHTS:

Apparent Women Officers or Directors: 2
Hot Spot for Advancement for Women/Minorities: Y

LOCATIONS: ("Y" = Yes)

West:	Southwest:	Midwest:	Southeast:	Northeast:	International:
Y					

ORLANDO MAGIC

www.nba.com/magic

Industry Group Code: 711211B **Ranks within this company's industry group:** Sales: 23 Profits: 17

Sports:		Services:		Media:		Sales:		Facilities:		Other:	
Leagues/Associations:		Food & Beverage:		TV:		Marketing:		Stadiums:		Gambling:	
Teams:	Y	Agents:		Radio:		Ads:		Fitness Clubs:		Apparel:	
Nonprofits:		Other:		Internet:		Tickets:	Y	Golf Courses:		Equipment:	
Other:				Print:		Retail:	Y	Ski Resorts:		Shoes:	
				Software:		Other:		Other:		Other:	

TYPES OF BUSINESS:

Professional Basketball Team
Ticket Sales
Sports Merchandise

BRANDS/DIVISIONS/AFFILIATES:

RDV Sportsplex
Orlando Magic Arena
Orlando Magic Basketball Camp
Orlando Magic Kids Club
Magic Dancers
Dunking Dancers

CONTACTS: *Note: Officers with more than one job title may be intentionally listed here more than once.*

Bob Vander Weide, CEO
Alex Martins, COO
Bob Vander Weide, Pres.
Jim Fritz, CFO
Steve Griggs, Exec. VP-Mktg. & Sales
Audra Hollifield, VP-Human Resources
Jason Coleman, VP-IT
Audra Hollifield, VP-Admin.
Jim Fritz, Exec. VP-Oper.
Charles Freeman, VP-Bus. Strategy
Jack Swope, Sr. VP-Corp. Comm.
Jeff Bissey, Controller
Otis Smith, Gen. Mgr.
Pat Williams, Sr. VP
Scott Bowman, VP-Season Ticket Svcs.
Stan Van Gundy, Head Coach
Rich DeVos, Chmn.

Phone: 407-916-2400	**Fax:** 407-916-2830
Toll-Free:	
Address: 8701 Maitland Summit Blvd., Orlando, FL 32801-5915 US	

GROWTH PLANS/SPECIAL FEATURES:

The Orlando Magic joined the National Basketball Association (NBA) in 1989 and has won two Atlantic division championships and one Eastern Conference title. The team plays in the Amway Arena, which will be their temporary home until the opening of the new Orlando Magic Arena in downtown Orlando. The franchise hosts the Orlando Magic Basketball Camp, the Orlando Magic Kids Club and ticket programs. Game night entertainment includes the Magic Dancers, Stuff the Magic Mascot and the Dunking Dancers. In 1992, the Magic drafted one of its most noted players, Shaquille O'Neal, who played for the team for four years and left for the Los Angeles Lakers in 1996. In franchise history, the team has only made the NBA finals once in the 1994-95 season, but were swept by the Houston Rockets after four games. The team managed to make the NBA playoffs in the 2006-07 season as the eighth seed in the Eastern Conference. The team emerged as the Southeast Division champions in the 2007-08 season. In March 2008, the team won the Southeast Division title against the Washington Wizards, its third division title. Forbes Magazine recently estimated the team to be worth approximately $349 million. In the 2008-09 season, the team's home attendance average was roughly 17,000 per game.

FINANCIALS: Sales and profits are in thousands of dollars—add 000 to get the full amount. 2008 Note: Financial information for 2008 was not available for all companies at press time.

2008 Sales: $100,000	2008 Profits: $6,200	**U.S. Stock Ticker: Private**
2007 Sales: $92,000	2007 Profits: $4,600	**Int'l Ticker:** Int'l Exchange:
2006 Sales: $89,000	2006 Profits: $-20,400	Employees:
2005 Sales: $82,000	2005 Profits: $	Fiscal Year Ends: 6/30
2004 Sales: $78,000	2004 Profits: $	Parent Company:

SALARIES/BENEFITS:

Pension Plan:	ESOP Stock Plan:	Profit Sharing:	Top Exec. Salary: $	Bonus: $
Savings Plan:	Stock Purch. Plan:		Second Exec. Salary: $	Bonus: $

OTHER THOUGHTS:

Apparent Women Officers or Directors: 4
Hot Spot for Advancement for Women/Minorities: Y

LOCATIONS: ("Y" = Yes)

West:	Southwest:	Midwest:	Southeast:	Northeast:	International:
			Y		

Note: Financial information, benefits and other data can change quickly and may vary from those stated here.

ORVIS COMPANY (THE)

www.orvis.com

Industry Group Code: 451110 **Ranks within this company's industry group:** Sales: Profits:

Sports:		Services:		Media:		Sales:		Facilities:		Other:	
Leagues/Associations:		Food & Beverage:		TV:		Marketing:		Stadiums:		Gambling:	
Teams:		Agents:		Radio:		Ads:		Fitness Clubs:		Apparel:	
Nonprofits:		Other:		Internet:		Tickets:		Golf Courses:		Equipment:	
Other:				Print:		Retail:	Y	Ski Resorts:		Shoes:	
				Software:		Other:		Other:		Other:	

TYPES OF BUSINESS:

Outdoor Apparel, Retail
Fly-Fishing & Hunting Equipment
Home Furnishings
Catalog & Online Sales
Luggage & Accessories
Guided Trips & Travel Services
Firearms
Log Home Design & Construction

BRANDS/DIVISIONS/AFFILIATES:

Orvis Travel
Orvis Destinations
Orvis Distinctive Country Lifestyle
Rocky Mountain Log Homes Co.

CONTACTS: *Note: Officers with more than one job title may be intentionally listed here more than once.*

Leigh Perkins, Jr., CEO
Brian Gowan, COO
Leigh Perkins, Jr., Pres.
Brian Gowan, CFO
Leigh Perkins, Sr., Chmn.

Phone: 802-362-1300 **Fax:** 802-362-0141
Toll-Free: 888-235-9763
Address: 178 Conservation Way, Sunderland, VT 05250-4465 US

GROWTH PLANS/SPECIAL FEATURES:

The Orvis Company, Inc., retails fly fishing equipment, outdoor apparel and home products through retailers, outlets and authorized dealers in the U.S. and U.K. The company's outdoor apparel includes men's and women's clothing, outerwear, footwear and accessories such insect-repellent clothing, hats, luggage and wallets. Its fly-fishing products include waders and boots, lines and leaders, rods, reels, vests and packs, and fly-fishing apparel. The firm's hunting products include shotguns, shotgun accessories and hunting apparel. In addition, Orvis runs fly-fishing and shooting schools and seminars; guided fishing and hunting trips through its series of lodges; and Orvis Travel helps customers plan international vacations with a focus on outdoor activities, including everything from Alaskan cruises to African safaris. The company's home furnishings include bedding, lighting, dining and kitchen furniture, bedroom furniture, tables and chairs, desks, tableware, outdoor furniture and fireplace accessories. It also offers dog and cat products including apparel, beds, crates and toys. The firm operates through nearly 500 authorized dealers, 39 retail stores and 11 outlet stores in the U.S. Orvis additionally operates 24 separate retail stores in the U.K. Products sold through authorized Orvis dealers focus are primarily fly-fishing products and apparel, although there are over 100 full line dealers worldwide. In addition to its retail locations, Orvis sells through catalogs and an e-commerce web site. The company also operates Orvis Log Homes, a division which includes six log home designs and complete construction options through Rocky Mountain Log Homes Co. In October 2007, Orvis began seeking permits to rebuild its fly-fishing school, one of the oldest schools of its kind in the world. Orvis opened five new retail locations and one new outlet location in 2008.

Orvis donates 5% of pre-tax profits annually to organizations that protect fish and wildlife habitat.

FINANCIALS: **Sales and profits are in thousands of dollars—add 000 to get the full amount. 2008 Note: Financial information for 2008 was not available for all companies at press time.**

2008 Sales: $	2008 Profits: $	**U.S. Stock Ticker: Private**
2007 Sales: $	2007 Profits: $	**Int'l Ticker:** Int'l Exchange:
2006 Sales: $	2006 Profits: $	Employees: 3,000
2005 Sales: $	2005 Profits: $	Fiscal Year Ends: 9/30
2004 Sales: $	2004 Profits: $	Parent Company:

SALARIES/BENEFITS:

Pension Plan:	ESOP Stock Plan:	Profit Sharing:	Top Exec. Salary: $	Bonus: $
Savings Plan:	Stock Purch. Plan:		Second Exec. Salary: $	Bonus: $

OTHER THOUGHTS:

Apparent Women Officers or Directors:
Hot Spot for Advancement for Women/Minorities:

LOCATIONS: ("Y" = Yes)

West:	Southwest:	Midwest:	Southeast:	Northeast:	International:
Y	Y	Y	Y	Y	Y

OTTAWA SENATORS

senators.nhl.com

Industry Group Code: 711211F **Ranks within this company's industry group:** Sales: 11 Profits: 10

Sports:		Services:		Media:		Sales:		Facilities:		Other:	
Leagues/Associations:		Food & Beverage:		TV:		Marketing:		Stadiums:	Y	Gambling:	
Teams:	Y	Agents:		Radio:		Ads:		Fitness Clubs:		Apparel:	
Nonprofits:		Other:		Internet:		Tickets:	Y	Golf Courses:		Equipment:	
Other:				Print:		Retail:	Y	Ski Resorts:		Shoes:	
				Software:		Other:		Other:		Other:	

TYPES OF BUSINESS:

Major League Hockey Team
Ticket Sales
Ottawa Senators Merchandise

BRANDS/DIVISIONS/AFFILIATES:

Scotiabank Place
Ottawa Silver Seven
Binghamton Senators
Elmira Jackals

GROWTH PLANS/SPECIAL FEATURES:

The Ottawa Senators Hockey Club, based in Ottawa, Ontario, is a professional hockey team playing in the National Hockey League (NHL). The original Ottawa Senators franchise, first named the Ottawa Silver Seven, was founded in 1883. The team competed in the National Hockey Association and the NHL, winning nine Stanley Cups between 1903 and 1927 before moving to St. Louis, Missouri and changing its name to the St. Louis Eagles in 1934. The team folded a year later in bankruptcy. The modern-day Senators franchise entered the NHL as an expansion team in 1992. The Senators play at Scotiabank Place, formerly known as Corel Centre. The arena has a seating capacity of 19,153 and a total capacity, including standing room, of 20,500. The Team's current owner, Toronto pharmaceutical billionaire Eugene Melnyk, bought Scotiabank Place and the Senators after they declared bankruptcy in 2003. The Binghamton Senators and the Elmira Jackals are the team's minor league affiliates. During the 2008-09 season, the Senators averaged 19,821 fans per games. Forbes recently estimated the team to be worth approximately $207 million.

CONTACTS: *Note: Officers with more than one job title may be intentionally listed here more than once.*

Roy Mlakar, CEO
Cyril M. Leeder, COO
Roy Mlakar, Pres.
Erin Crowe, CFO
Jeff Kyle, VP-Mktg.
Brent Flahr, Dir.-Hockey Oper.
Phil Legault, VP-Comm.
Bryan Murray, Gen. Mgr.
Tim Murray, Assistant Gen. Mgr.
Danielle Robinson, Pres., Ottawa Senators Foundation
Mark Bonneau, Sr. VP-Corp. Sales
Eugene N. Melnyk, Chmn./Governor/Owner

Phone: 613-599-0250 **Fax:** 613-599-0358
Toll-Free:
Address: 1000 Palladium Dr., Ottawa, ON K2V 1A5 Canada

FINANCIALS: Sales and profits are in thousands of dollars—add 000 to get the full amount. 2008 Note: Financial information for 2008 was not available for all companies at press time.

2008 Sales: $96,000	2008 Profits: $4,700	**U.S. Stock Ticker: Private**
2007 Sales: $93,000	2007 Profits: $10,400	**Int'l Ticker:** Int'l Exchange:
2006 Sales: $76,000	2006 Profits: $4,200	Employees:
2005 Sales: $	2005 Profits: $	Fiscal Year Ends: 6/30
2004 Sales: $70,000	2004 Profits: $	Parent Company:

SALARIES/BENEFITS:

Pension Plan:	ESOP Stock Plan:	Profit Sharing:	Top Exec. Salary: $	Bonus: $
Savings Plan:	Stock Purch. Plan:		Second Exec. Salary: $	Bonus: $

OTHER THOUGHTS:

Apparent Women Officers or Directors: 2
Hot Spot for Advancement for Women/Minorities:

LOCATIONS: ("Y" = Yes)

West:	Southwest:	Midwest:	Southeast:	Northeast:	International:
					Y

PACIFIC CYCLE LLC

www.pacific-cycle.com

Industry Group Code: 339920 **Ranks within this company's industry group:** Sales: Profits:

Sports:		Services:		Media:		Sales:		Facilities:		Other:	
Leagues/Associations:		Food & Beverage:		TV:		Marketing:		Stadiums:		Gambling:	
Teams:		Agents:		Radio:		Ads:		Fitness Clubs:		Apparel:	
Nonprofits:		Other:		Internet:		Tickets:		Golf Courses:		Equipment:	Y
Other:				Print:		Retail:		Ski Resorts:		Shoes:	
				Software:		Other:		Other:		Other:	

TYPES OF BUSINESS:

Bicycles & Scooters
Electric Toys
Juvenile Recreation Equipment

BRANDS/DIVISIONS/AFFILIATES:

Schwinn
Mongoose
GT
Schwinn Motor Scooters
Kustom Kruiser
Roadmaster
Pacific
Dyno

CONTACTS:

Note: Officers with more than one job title may be intentionally listed here more than once.

Alice Tillett, Pres.
Bob Kmoch, CFO
Bruno Maier, Exec. VP-Mktg.
Bruno Maier, Exec. VP-New Bus. Dev.

Phone: 608-268-2468	**Fax:**
Toll-Free: 800-666-8813	
Address: 4902 Hammersley Rd., Madison, WI 53711 US	

GROWTH PLANS/SPECIAL FEATURES:

Pacific Cycle, LLC, a subsidiary of Dorel Industries, Inc., designs, markets and distributes a variety of branded bicycles and scooters, as well as other recreational products. The firm's brands include Schwinn, Mongoose, Schwinn Motorsports, Kid Trax, Playsafe, Powerlite, Roadmaster, Pacific, Dyno, Powerlite, InSTEP and Pacific Outdoors. The firm also produces Eddie Bauer-branded bicycles, which include adult comfort and mountain models designed for a broad range of terrain and riders. The company's bikes are sold throughout the U.S. through discount and mass merchandisers such as Wal-Mart, Toys R Us and Target; sporting goods chains such as Dick's, and Academy Sports; and independent bicycle dealers that serve the local market. The firm sells its bicycles in over 60 countries through the operations of over 50 international vendors. Pacific Cycle's bikes include designs for BMX race, dirt, vert, street, stunt, downhill, freeride and cross-country riders. The firm also maintains a professional rider program which many celebrated athletes have participated in.

Pacific Cycle offers employees medical, dental and vision coverage; life insurance; a 401(k) plan; a flexible spending account plan; profit sharing; a bonus program.

FINANCIALS:

Sales and profits are in thousands of dollars—add 000 to get the full amount. 2008 Note: Financial information for 2008 was not available for all companies at press time.

2008 Sales: $	2008 Profits: $	**U.S. Stock Ticker: Subsidiary**
2007 Sales: $80,700	2007 Profits: $	**Int'l Ticker:** Int'l Exchange:
2006 Sales: $	2006 Profits: $	Employees: 360
2005 Sales: $	2005 Profits: $	Fiscal Year Ends: 12/31
2004 Sales: $	2004 Profits: $	Parent Company: DOREL INDUSTRIES INC

SALARIES/BENEFITS:

Pension Plan:	ESOP Stock Plan:	Profit Sharing: Y	Top Exec. Salary: $	Bonus: $
Savings Plan: Y	Stock Purch. Plan:		Second Exec. Salary: $	Bonus: $

OTHER THOUGHTS:

Apparent Women Officers or Directors:
Hot Spot for Advancement for Women/Minorities:

LOCATIONS: ("Y" = Yes)

West:	Southwest:	Midwest:	Southeast:	Northeast:	International:
		Y			

PALACE SPORTS & ENTERTAINMENT INC

www.palacenet.com

Industry Group Code: 551110 **Ranks within this company's industry group:** Sales: Profits:

Sports:		Services:		Media:		Sales:		Facilities:		Other:	
Leagues/Associations:		Food & Beverage:	Y	TV:		Marketing:	Y	Stadiums:	Y	Gambling:	
Teams:	Y	Agents:		Radio:		Ads:		Fitness Clubs:		Apparel:	
Nonprofits:		Other:	Y	Internet:		Tickets:	Y	Golf Courses:		Equipment:	
Other:				Print:		Retail:		Ski Resorts:		Shoes:	
				Software:		Other:		Other:	Y	Other:	

TYPES OF BUSINESS:

Holding Company
Professional Basketball Team Ownership
Music & Events Venues

BRANDS/DIVISIONS/AFFILIATES:

Palace of Auburn Hills (The)
DTE Energy Music Theatre
Meadow Brook Music Festival
Detroit Pistons
Detroit Shock
Tampa Bay Lightning

CONTACTS:

Note: Officers with more than one job title may be intentionally listed here more than once.

Thomas S. (Tom) Wilson, CEO
Alan Otsfield, COO
Thomas S. (Tom) Wilson, Pres.
Marilyn Hauser, Exec. VP-Mktg. & Booking

Phone: 248-377-0100 **Fax:**
Toll-Free:
Address: 5 Championship Dr., Auburn Hills, MI 48326 US

GROWTH PLANS/SPECIAL FEATURES:

Palace Sports & Entertainment, Inc. (PS&E) is a sports holding company that owns and operates two professional basketball teams and three entertainment venues. Its teams are the WNBA's Detroit Shock and the NBA's Detroit Pistons, and its entertainment venues are The Palace of Auburn Hills (PAH), DTE Energy Music Theatre (DTE) and the Meadow Brook Music Festival. PAH, besides being the company's corporate headquarters, is also the home court where the Pistons and Shock play. Additionally, it hosts music events, with several big name performers scheduled for 2009, including Billy Joel, Elton John, Keith Urban, Jonas Brothers, AC/DC and No Doubt. Private suites and several on-site restaurants complement the venues' other offerings. Restaurants include upscale eateries such as The Palace Grille, Chairman's Club, Caesars Windsor Club and Club 53; and other establishments such as Red Bull, a cocktail lounge. As the name implies, DTE mainly hosts concerts, with several older and more contemporary bands scheduled for 2009. Examples of older groups include Chicago, Judas Priest, Bad Company, Def Leppard and Jimmy Buffett. More contemporary performers include Korn, Nickelback, Brad Paisley, Coldplay, The Fray and Incubus. The Meadow Brook Music Festival was first hosted in 1964, with its management functions transferred to PS&E in 1994, namely event booking, group sales, marketing, security, parking and maintenance. Many new additions have been made to the facility since PS&E took it over, including new signage, a new concessions building and newly expanded seating areas. Music performers scheduled for the 2009 Festival include the All-American Rejects, Crosby, Stills & Nash, Abba and the Detroit Symphony Orchestra (DSO). DSO's events this year will include All Gershwin, Tchaikovsky Spectacular, Big Band Bash, All Beethoven and Musical Magic. PS&E was formed by billionaire William Davidson.

FINANCIALS:

Sales and profits are in thousands of dollars—add 000 to get the full amount. 2008 Note: Financial information for 2008 was not available for all companies at press time.

2008 Sales: $	2008 Profits: $	**U.S. Stock Ticker: Private**
2007 Sales: $	2007 Profits: $	**Int'l Ticker:** Int'l Exchange:
2006 Sales: $	2006 Profits: $	Employees:
2005 Sales: $	2005 Profits: $	Fiscal Year Ends: 12/31
2004 Sales: $	2004 Profits: $	Parent Company:

SALARIES/BENEFITS:

Pension Plan:	ESOP Stock Plan:	Profit Sharing:	Top Exec. Salary: $	Bonus: $
Savings Plan:	Stock Purch. Plan:		Second Exec. Salary: $	Bonus: $

OTHER THOUGHTS:

Apparent Women Officers or Directors:
Hot Spot for Advancement for Women/Minorities:

LOCATIONS: ("Y" = Yes)

West:	Southwest:	Midwest:	Southeast:	Northeast:	International:
		Y			

Note: Financial information, benefits and other data can change quickly and may vary from those stated here.

PATAGONIA

www.patagonia.com

Industry Group Code: 315000A **Ranks within this company's industry group:** Sales: 6 Profits:

Sports:		Services:		Media:		Sales:		Facilities:		Other:	
Leagues/Associations:		Food & Beverage:		TV:		Marketing:		Stadiums:		Gambling:	
Teams:		Agents:		Radio:		Ads:		Fitness Clubs:		Apparel:	Y
Nonprofits:		Other:		Internet:		Tickets:		Golf Courses:		Equipment:	Y
Other:				Print:		Retail:	Y	Ski Resorts:		Shoes:	
				Software:		Other:		Other:		Other:	

TYPES OF BUSINESS:

Outdoor Apparel, Manufacturing
Outdoor Equipment
Catalog Sales
Surfing Apparel
Surfing Equipment

BRANDS/DIVISIONS/AFFILIATES:

Lost Arrow Corporation
Capilene
Synchilla
Regulator System (The)
1% for the Planet
Lotus Designs
Point Blanks Surfboards
Water Girl USA

CONTACTS: *Note: Officers with more than one job title may be intentionally listed here more than once.*

Casey Sheahan, CEO
Casey Sheahan, Pres.
Martha Groszewski, CFO
Rob BonDurant, VP-Mktg. & Comm.
Martha Groszewski, VP-Finance

Phone: 805-643-8616	**Fax:** 800-543-5522
Toll-Free: 800-638-6464	
Address: 259 W. Santa Clara St., Ventura, CA 93001 US	

GROWTH PLANS/SPECIAL FEATURES:

Patagonia, Inc., the primary subsidiary and brand name of the Lost Arrow Corporation, markets and sells outdoor clothing and equipment developed and designed for a broad range of extreme sports, such as rock climbing, mountaineering, white-water kayaking, mountain biking, surfing and skiing. Patagonia sells its products through 26 Patagonia specific retail outlets throughout the U.S. and 22 abroad, including stores in France, Italy, Germany, Ireland, Japan, Korea, Hong Kong, Argentina and Chile, as well as through hundreds of other outdoor gear and clothing stores. Patagonia has pioneered many materials now considered essential for outdoor enthusiasts, such as polypropylene, Capilene and Synchilla, which are designed to retain warmth even when the material becomes moist from precipitation or sweat. The Regulator System combines soft shells, insulation and moisture transition layers into jackets and pants to create an integrated clothing system designed to keep people warm and dry even in the most adverse weather conditions. The company has also introduced Beneficial T's, made from organically grown cotton, and PCR Clothing, a fleece product line made from recycled plastic soda bottles. Patagonia also markets gear specifically for whitewater paddling under the Lotus Designs brand name and gear for surfing under the Point Blanks name. Water Girl USA, Inc. is the company's subsidiary dedicated to making surfing, paddling, swimming and kayaking clothing for women. The company is currently expanding its surfing line, which includes wet suits and surfboards. Surfing products currently account for approximately 10% of Patagonia sales. Patagonia recently opened a new retail store in Austin, Texas.

Employees at the company's headquarters have access to an on-site child care facility, as well as four months leave for both mothers and fathers after a birth or adoption, two of which are paid.

FINANCIALS: **Sales and profits are in thousands of dollars—add 000 to get the full amount. 2008 Note: Financial information for 2008 was not available for all companies at press time.**

2008 Sales: $300,000	2008 Profits: $	**U.S. Stock Ticker: Subsidiary**
2007 Sales: $290,000	2007 Profits: $	**Int'l Ticker:** Int'l Exchange:
2006 Sales: $270,000	2006 Profits: $	Employees:
2005 Sales: $250,000	2005 Profits: $	Fiscal Year Ends: 4/30
2004 Sales: $	2004 Profits: $	Parent Company: LOST ARROW CORPORATION

SALARIES/BENEFITS:

Pension Plan:	ESOP Stock Plan:	Profit Sharing:	Top Exec. Salary: $	Bonus: $
Savings Plan:	Stock Purch. Plan:		Second Exec. Salary: $	Bonus: $

OTHER THOUGHTS:

Apparent Women Officers or Directors:
Hot Spot for Advancement for Women/Minorities:

LOCATIONS: ("Y" = Yes)

West:	Southwest:	Midwest:	Southeast:	Northeast:	International:
Y	Y	Y	Y	Y	Y

PENN NATIONAL GAMING INC

www.pngaming.com

Industry Group Code: 713210 **Ranks within this company's industry group:** Sales: 1 Profits: 3

Sports:		Services:		Media:		Sales:		Facilities:		Other:	
Leagues/Associations:		Food & Beverage:		TV:		Marketing:		Stadiums:		Gambling:	Y
Teams:		Agents:		Radio:		Ads:		Fitness Clubs:		Apparel:	
Nonprofits:		Other:		Internet:		Tickets:		Golf Courses:		Equipment:	
Other:				Print:		Retail:		Ski Resorts:		Shoes:	
				Software:		Other:		Other:	Y	Other:	Y

TYPES OF BUSINESS:

Horse Racetracks
Casinos
Online Wagering

BRANDS/DIVISIONS/AFFILIATES:

Penn National Race Course
Telebet
eBetUSA.com, Inc.
eBet Limited
Freehold Racetrack

CONTACTS: *Note: Officers with more than one job title may be intentionally listed here more than once.*

Peter M. Carlino, CEO
Timothy Wilmott, COO
Timothy Wilmott, Pres.
William J. Clifford, CFO
Gaye Gullo, VP-Mktg.
Gene Clark, Sr. VP-Human Resources
Jordan B. Savitch, General Counsel/Sr. VP
John Finamore, Sr. VP-Regional Oper.
Steven T. Snyder, Sr. VP-Corp. Dev.
James Baum, Sr. VP-Project Dev.
Peter M. Carlino, Chmn.

Phone: 610-373-2400 **Fax:** 610-373-4966
Toll-Free:
Address: 825 Berkshire Blvd., Ste. 200, Wyomissing, PA 19610 US

GROWTH PLANS/SPECIAL FEATURES:

Penn National Gaming, Inc. owns and operates gaming properties and horse racetracks. It owns 19 facilities in New Mexico, Colorado, Iowa, Illinois, Indiana, Ohio, Missouri, Mississippi, Louisiana, Florida, West Virginia, New Jersey, Pennsylvania and Maine, and operates an additional facility in Ontario, Canada. These facilities, which are focused on serving customers within driving distance, include three thoroughbred racetracks, three harness racetracks, one greyhound racetrack, seven land-based casinos and nine dockside casinos. Penn National also runs four off-track wagering facilities throughout Pennsylvania. Penn National Race Course operates Telebet, which offers account wagering for 80 U.S. racetracks. The firm accepts online horseracing bets from residents in 14 U.S. states and the U.S. Virgin Islands through subsidiary eBetUSA.com, Inc., operated under license from Australian-based eBet Limited. The firm's casinos total 903,335 square feet of gaming space, and contain a combined 25,438 gaming machines, 409 table games and 1,884 hotel rooms. The Freehold Racetrack, located in Monmouth, NJ, is a 50%-owned joint venture with Greenwood Limited Jersey, Inc.

Employees are offered medical, dental and vision insurance; an employee assistance program; life insurance; short-and long-term disability coverage; a 401(k) savings plan; and flexible spending accounts.

FINANCIALS: **Sales and profits are in thousands of dollars—add 000 to get the full amount. 2008 Note: Financial information for 2008 was not available for all companies at press time.**

2008 Sales: $2,423,053	2008 Profits: $-153,323	**U.S. Stock Ticker: PENN**
2007 Sales: $2,436,793	2007 Profits: $160,053	**Int'l Ticker:** Int'l Exchange:
2006 Sales: $2,244,547	2006 Profits: $327,088	Employees: 14,693
2005 Sales: $1,369,105	2005 Profits: $120,930	Fiscal Year Ends: 12/31
2004 Sales: $1,105,290	2004 Profits: $71,484	Parent Company:

SALARIES/BENEFITS:

Pension Plan:	ESOP Stock Plan:	Profit Sharing:	Top Exec. Salary: $1,500,000	Bonus: $3,690,000
Savings Plan: Y	Stock Purch. Plan:		Second Exec. Salary: $750,000	Bonus: $1,383,750

OTHER THOUGHTS:

Apparent Women Officers or Directors: 2
Hot Spot for Advancement for Women/Minorities:

LOCATIONS: ("Y" = Yes)

West:	Southwest:	Midwest:	Southeast:	Northeast:	International:
Y	Y	Y	Y	Y	Y

PENSKE RACING

www.penskeracing.com

Industry Group Code: 711211G **Ranks within this company's industry group:** Sales: 5 Profits: 4

Sports:		Services:		Media:		Sales:		Facilities:		Other:	
Leagues/Associations:		Food & Beverage:		TV:		Marketing:		Stadiums:		Gambling:	
Teams:	Y	Agents:		Radio:		Ads:		Fitness Clubs:		Apparel:	
Nonprofits:		Other:		Internet:		Tickets:		Golf Courses:		Equipment:	
Other:				Print:		Retail:		Ski Resorts:		Shoes:	
				Software:		Other:		Other:		Other:	

TYPES OF BUSINESS:

Racing Teams

BRANDS/DIVISIONS/AFFILIATES:

Penske Corporation

CONTACTS:

Note: Officers with more than one job title may be intentionally listed here more than once.

Roger Penske, CEO
Tim Cindric, Pres.
Ron Ruzewski, Race Engineer
Rick Mears, Team Advisor
Clive Howell, General Mgr.
Tom Wurtz, Team Mgr.
Jerry Breon, Facilities Mgr.
Roger Penske, Chmn.

Phone: 704-664-2300	**Fax:**
Toll-Free:	
Address: 200 Penske Way, Mooresville, NC 28115 US	

GROWTH PLANS/SPECIAL FEATURES:

Penske Racing, Inc., the racing unit of Penske Corporation, manages four racing teams, which compete in two premier North American racing series, IndyCar and NASCAR. Cars owned and prepared by the firm have more than 250 major race wins, including 14 Indianapolis 500 wins, over 290 pole positions and 18 national championships. The company's top six sponsors are ALLTEL; Dodge; Exxonmobile Oil Corporation; Kodak; Miller Brewing Company; and Philip Morris USA. Penske Racing has two drivers in the Indy Car Series, Helio Castroneves and Ryan Briscoe. The company's three NASCAR series drivers are Ryan Newman, Kurt Busch and Sam Hornish Jr. The company also competes in the American Le Mans Series, a set of long-distance endurance races, with drivers including Sascha Maassen, Timo Bernhard, Romain Dumas and Patrick Long. The firm races the LMP2 Porsche RS Spyder in the American Le Mans series under the sponsorship of DHL Global Mail; Hugo Boss; Mobil 1; Michelin; Hyatt; and ZF Sachs. The RS Spyder, a relatively new car design, boasts a Porsche MR6 water-cooled V8 550-600 hp engine and a GR6-engineered sequential six-speed constant mesh transmission.

FINANCIALS:

Sales and profits are in thousands of dollars—add 000 to get the full amount. 2008 Note: Financial information for 2008 was not available for all companies at press time.

2008 Sales: $85,000	2008 Profits: $8,600	**U.S. Stock Ticker: Private**
2007 Sales: $65,000	2007 Profits: $9,700	**Int'l Ticker:** Int'l Exchange:
2006 Sales: $	2006 Profits: $	Employees:
2005 Sales: $	2005 Profits: $	Fiscal Year Ends:
2004 Sales: $	2004 Profits: $	Parent Company:

SALARIES/BENEFITS:

Pension Plan:	ESOP Stock Plan:	Profit Sharing:	Top Exec. Salary: $	Bonus: $
Savings Plan:	Stock Purch. Plan:		Second Exec. Salary: $	Bonus: $

OTHER THOUGHTS:

Apparent Women Officers or Directors:
Hot Spot for Advancement for Women/Minorities:

LOCATIONS: ("Y" = Yes)

West:	Southwest:	Midwest:	Southeast:	Northeast:	International:
				Y	

Note: Financial information, benefits and other data can change quickly and may vary from those stated here.

PETTY ENTERPRISES

www.pettyracing.com

Industry Group Code: 711211G **Ranks within this company's industry group:** Sales: 6 Profits: 6

Sports:		Services:		Media:		Sales:		Facilities:		Other:	
Leagues/Associations:		Food & Beverage:		TV:		Marketing:		Stadiums:		Gambling:	
Teams:	Y	Agents:		Radio:		Ads:		Fitness Clubs:		Apparel:	
Nonprofits:		Other:		Internet:		Tickets:		Golf Courses:		Equipment:	
Other:	Y			Print:		Retail:	Y	Ski Resorts:		Shoes:	
				Software:		Other:		Other:		Other:	

TYPES OF BUSINESS:

Racing Teams
Racing Apparel & Merchandise
Training Programs

BRANDS/DIVISIONS/AFFILIATES:

Gillett Evernham Motorsports
NASCAR
Boston Ventures
Dodge
Richard Petty Driving Experience
Victory Junction Gang Camp
Petty Holdings

CONTACTS: *Note: Officers with more than one job title may be intentionally listed here more than once.*

Tom Reddin, CEO
Rick Russell, Pres.
Robbie Loomis, Dir.-Race Oper.
Ray Evernham, Crew Chief
Mark McArdle, VP/Managing Dir.-Competition

Phone: 704-924-9404 **Fax:**
Toll-Free:
Address: 320 Aviation Dr, Statesville, NC 28677 US

GROWTH PLANS/SPECIAL FEATURES:

Richard Petty Motorsports, formerly known as Petty Enterprises, is a leading American motorsports organization, having won 282 races and and seven championships. The company currently fields two teams in the NASCAR Winston Cup series and uses Dodge-manufactured cars. The firm also owns Richard Petty Driving Experience, which offers recreational racecar ride-alongs, driving opportunities, training programs and sells company apparel and merchandise. The Pettys are co-founders of the Victory Junction Gang Camp, an independent not-for-profit organization that offers recreational camping experiences to children with chronic or life-threatening illnesses. The company's partners include 3M; Allstate; Bank of America; Bosch; Budweiser; Charter communications; Coca Cola; Dodge Dealers; Freightliner Trucks; Gillette; McDonald's; Mechanix Wear; Puma; Miller Welders; Siemens; Super 8; U.S. Air Force; Valvoline; and more. In the 2009 season, the newly formed team plans to run a Dodge vehicle in eight races including the Budweiser Shootout. In January 2009, the Petty Enterprises merged with Gillett Evernham Motorsports and was renamed Richard Petty Motorsports. Currently, the team is co-owned by Richard Petty, Petty Holdings, Boston Ventures and Gillett Evernham Motorsports.

FINANCIALS: **Sales and profits are in thousands of dollars—add 000 to get the full amount. 2008 Note: Financial information for 2008 was not available for all companies at press time.**

2008 Sales: $37,000
2007 Sales: $41,000
2006 Sales: $
2005 Sales: $
2004 Sales: $

2008 Profits: $2,900
2007 Profits: $6,600
2006 Profits: $
2005 Profits: $
2004 Profits: $

U.S. Stock Ticker: Private
Int'l Ticker: Int'l Exchange:
Employees:
Fiscal Year Ends:
Parent Company:

SALARIES/BENEFITS:

Pension Plan: ESOP Stock Plan: Profit Sharing: Top Exec. Salary: $ Bonus: $
Savings Plan: Stock Purch. Plan: Second Exec. Salary: $ Bonus: $

OTHER THOUGHTS:

Apparent Women Officers or Directors:
Hot Spot for Advancement for Women/Minorities:

LOCATIONS: ("Y" = Yes)

West:	Southwest:	Midwest:	Southeast:	Northeast:	International:
				Y	

PHILADELPHIA 76ERS

www.nba.com/sixers

Industry Group Code: 711211B **Ranks within this company's industry group:** Sales: 16 Profits: 20

Sports:		Services:		Media:		Sales:		Facilities:		Other:	
Leagues/Associations:		Food & Beverage:		TV:		Marketing:		Stadiums:	Y	Gambling:	
Teams:	Y	Agents:		Radio:		Ads:		Fitness Clubs:		Apparel:	
Nonprofits:		Other:		Internet:		Tickets:	Y	Golf Courses:		Equipment:	
Other:				Print:		Retail:	Y	Ski Resorts:		Shoes:	
				Software:		Other:		Other:		Other:	

TYPES OF BUSINESS:

Professional Basketball Team

BRANDS/DIVISIONS/AFFILIATES:

Comcast-Spectacor
Wachovia Center
Comcast Corp.
Philly Live
76ers Drive for Kids
76ers Hometown Heroes

CONTACTS:

Note: Officers with more than one job title may be intentionally listed here more than once.

Ed Stefanski, Pres./Gen. Mgr.
Eric Blankenship, VP-Mktg.
Lara Price, Sr. VP-Bus. Oper.
Michael Preston, Dir.-Public Rel.
Andy Speiser, Sr. VP-Finance
Tony DiLeo, Head Coach
Peter Luukko, Pres./COO-Comcast-Spectator
Tina Szwak, Controller
Shawn Anderson, VP-Ticket Sales
Ed Snider, Chmn.

Phone: 215-339-7676	**Fax:** 215-339-7632
Toll-Free:	
Address: 3601 S. Broad St., Philadelphia, PA 19148 US	

GROWTH PLANS/SPECIAL FEATURES:

The Philadelphia 76ers, a professional basketball team playing in the National Basketball Association (NBA), is based in Philadelphia, Pennsylvania. The team began as the Syracuse Nationals and relocated to Pennsylvania in 1963. The 76ers have won two championships: one under the lead of the legendary Wilt Chamberlain in 1967 and the second in 1983 due to Julius Erving. While the franchise has not had championship success in recent years, it has maintained winning records and made it to the finals in the 2000-01 season. The 76ers are owned by Comcast-Spectator, a sports and entertainment company. Comcast-Spectator also owns the National Hockey League's Philadelphia Flyers and the American Hockey League's Philadelphia Phantoms. In addition to these sports franchises, Comcast-Spectator owns and manages the Wachovia Center, where the 76ers play home games. The Wachovia Center seats 21,600 spectators. The team's community programs include the 76ers Drive for Kids, Sixers Charities, Read to Achieve and 76ers Hometown Heroes. The 76ers are also part of the Summer Hoops Tour. In January 2008, the team's parent company, Comcast-Spectator, formed a partnership with The Cordish Company to develop Philly Live!, a retail, dining and entertainment district adjacent to the Wachovia Center. Forbes Magazine recently estimated the team to be worth approximately $360 million. In the 2008-09 season, the team's home attendance average was roughly 15,800 per game.

FINANCIALS:

Sales and profits are in thousands of dollars—add 000 to get the full amount. 2008 Note: Financial information for 2008 was not available for all companies at press time.

2008 Sales: $116,000	2008 Profits: $ 300	**U.S. Stock Ticker: Subsidiary**
2007 Sales: $112,000	2007 Profits: $-2,800	**Int'l Ticker:** Int'l Exchange:
2006 Sales: $110,000	2006 Profits: $-6,200	Employees:
2005 Sales: $110,000	2005 Profits: $	Fiscal Year Ends: 12/31
2004 Sales: $107,000	2004 Profits: $	Parent Company: COMCAST CORP

SALARIES/BENEFITS:

Pension Plan:	ESOP Stock Plan:	Profit Sharing:	Top Exec. Salary: $	Bonus: $
Savings Plan:	Stock Purch. Plan:		Second Exec. Salary: $	Bonus: $

OTHER THOUGHTS:

Apparent Women Officers or Directors: 4
Hot Spot for Advancement for Women/Minorities: Y

LOCATIONS: ("Y" = Yes)

West:	Southwest:	Midwest:	Southeast:	Northeast:	International:
				Y	

PHILADELPHIA EAGLES

www.philadelphiaeagles.com

Industry Group Code: 711211C **Ranks within this company's industry group:** Sales: 5 Profits: 8

Sports:		Services:		Media:		Sales:		Facilities:		Other:	
Leagues/Associations:		Food & Beverage:		TV:		Marketing:		Stadiums:		Gambling:	
Teams:	Y	Agents:		Radio:		Ads:		Fitness Clubs:		Apparel:	
Nonprofits:		Other:		Internet:		Tickets:	Y	Golf Courses:		Equipment:	
Other:				Print:		Retail:	Y	Ski Resorts:		Shoes:	
				Software:		Other:		Other:		Other:	

TYPES OF BUSINESS:

Professional Football Team

BRANDS/DIVISIONS/AFFILIATES:

CONTACTS:

Note: Officers with more than one job title may be intentionally listed here more than once.

Jeffrey Lurie, CEO
Joe Banner, COO
Joe Banner, Pres.
Don Smolenski, CFO/Sr. VP
Howie Roseman, VP-Player Resources
Andy Reid, Exec. VP-Football Oper.
Mark Donovan, Sr. VP-Bus. Dev.
Andy Reid, Head Coach
Tom Heckert, Gen. Mgr.
Pamela Crawley, Sr. VP-Public Affairs & Gov't Rel.
Jeffrey Lurie, Chmn.

Phone: 215-463-2500	**Fax:** 215-339-5464
Toll-Free:	
Address: 1 NovaCare Way, Philadelphia, PA 19145 US	

GROWTH PLANS/SPECIAL FEATURES:

The Philadelphia Eagles are a professional football team in the Eastern Division of the National Football League's (NFL) National Football Conference (NFC) along with the New York Giants, the Dallas Cowboys and Washington Redskins. The team is based in Philadelphia, Pennsylvania. The franchise has won three NFL titles and gained two Super Bowl appearances since its inception in 1933. Struggling at first, the Eagles appeared in three consecutive NFL championship games during the 1940s, winning two of them in 1948 and 1949. The team won its third NFL championship in 1960. However, since then the Eagles' performance on the field has been plagued by difficulties. Between 1988 and 1996 the team qualified for the playoffs six times. In 1999, the Eagles hired head coach Andy Reid, who drafted quarterback superstar Donovan McNabb. This new era of Eagles football achieved four consecutive trips to the NFC conference championship between 2001 and 2004, but the team only reached the Super Bowl once, which was lost to the New England Patriots. The Eagles are owned by Jeffrey Lurie, a former Hollywood producer, who bought the team for $195 million in 1994. The Eagles play at Lincoln Financial Field, which holds 68,532 spectators. The stadium is owned by the city of Philadelphia. In the 2008 season, the team averaged 69,144 fans in attendance per game. A recent Forbes estimate values the team at $1.1 billion.

FINANCIALS:

Sales and profits are in thousands of dollars—add 000 to get the full amount. 2008 Note: Financial information for 2008 was not available for all companies at press time.

2008 Sales: $237,000	2008 Profits: $33,500	**U.S. Stock Ticker: Private**
2007 Sales: $224,000	2007 Profits: $25,700	**Int'l Ticker:** Int'l Exchange:
2006 Sales: $218,000	2006 Profits: $54,200	Employees:
2005 Sales: $216,000	2005 Profits: $	Fiscal Year Ends: 12/31
2004 Sales: $	2004 Profits: $	Parent Company:

SALARIES/BENEFITS:

Pension Plan:	ESOP Stock Plan:	Profit Sharing:	Top Exec. Salary: $	Bonus: $
Savings Plan:	Stock Purch. Plan:		Second Exec. Salary: $	Bonus: $

OTHER THOUGHTS:

Apparent Women Officers or Directors:
Hot Spot for Advancement for Women/Minorities:

LOCATIONS: ("Y" = Yes)

West:	Southwest:	Midwest:	Southeast:	Northeast:	International:
				Y	

PHILADELPHIA FLYERS

www.flyers.nhl.com

Industry Group Code: 711211F **Ranks within this company's industry group:** Sales: 7 Profits: 20

Sports:		Services:		Media:		Sales:		Facilities:		Other:	
Leagues/Associations:		Food & Beverage:		TV:		Marketing:		Stadiums:		Gambling:	
Teams:	Y	Agents:		Radio:		Ads:		Fitness Clubs:		Apparel:	
Nonprofits:		Other:		Internet:		Tickets:	Y	Golf Courses:		Equipment:	
Other:				Print:		Retail:	Y	Ski Resorts:		Shoes:	
				Software:		Other:		Other:		Other:	

TYPES OF BUSINESS:

Professional Hockey Team

BRANDS/DIVISIONS/AFFILIATES:

Comcast-Spectacor
Comcast Cable
Flyers Wives (The)
Pucks & Kisses
Wachovia Center
Comcast Corp.

CONTACTS:

Note: Officers with more than one job title may be intentionally listed here more than once.

Paul Holmgren, Gen. Mgr.
Peter Luukko, COO
Peter Luukko, Pres.
Joe Croce, Sr. VP-Sales
Shawn Tilger, Sr. VP-Bus. Oper.
Zack Hill, Sr. Dir.-Comm.
Dave Jablonski, VP-Finance
Lisa Cataldo, Controller
John Stevens, Head Coach
Bryan Hardenberg, Dir.-Team Svcs.
Ed Snider, Chmn.

Phone: 215-465-4500	**Fax:** 215-389-9403
Toll-Free:	
Address: 3601 S. Broad St., Philadelphia, PA 19148 US	

GROWTH PLANS/SPECIAL FEATURES:

The Philadelphia Flyers are a National Hockey League (NHL) team playing in the Atlantic Division of the Eastern Conference New Jersey Devils, New York Islanders, New York Rangers and Pittsburgh Penguins. The team is owned by Comcast-Spectacor, headed by team chairman Ed Snider and Comcast. The Flyers were founded in 1967 during NHL's first expansion in 40 years. The team was hampered early on by league restrictions that kept major talent with the original six NHL teams. The Flyers play at the 19,519-seat Wachovia Center, which it shares with the Philadelphia 76ers. The team has made seven Stanley Cup final appearances. It won the 1974 and 1975 championships and played in but lost the 1976, 1980, 1985, 1987 and 1997 championships. The Flyers have some of the highest attendance records in the NHL. In a March 2004 game, the Flyers became the first NHL expansion team to score 10,000 total goals. During that same game, the Flyers and the Ottawa Senators got into several brawls and set an NHL record for the most penalty minutes in a game with 419. The team's NHL Hall of Famers includes Bobby Clarke, Pelle Lindbergh, Bernie Parent, Bill Barber and Paul Coffey. In the 2008-09 season, the team averaged approximately 19,545 fans in attendance per game. A recent Forbes estimate values the team at $275 million.

FINANCIALS:

Sales and profits are in thousands of dollars—add 000 to get the full amount. 2008 Note: Financial information for 2008 was not available for all companies at press time.

2008 Sales: $102,000
2007 Sales: $87,000
2006 Sales: $88,000
2005 Sales: $
2004 Sales: $106,000

2008 Profits: $-1,800
2007 Profits: $5,700
2006 Profits: $ 900
2005 Profits: $
2004 Profits: $

U.S. Stock Ticker: Subsidiary
Int'l Ticker: Int'l Exchange:
Employees:
Fiscal Year Ends: 6/30
Parent Company: COMCAST CORP

SALARIES/BENEFITS:

Pension Plan:	ESOP Stock Plan:	Profit Sharing:	Top Exec. Salary: $	Bonus: $
Savings Plan:	Stock Purch. Plan:		Second Exec. Salary: $	Bonus: $

OTHER THOUGHTS:

Apparent Women Officers or Directors: 2
Hot Spot for Advancement for Women/Minorities: Y

LOCATIONS: ("Y" = Yes)

West:	Southwest:	Midwest:	Southeast:	Northeast:	International:
				Y	

PHILADELPHIA PHILLIES

philadelphia.phillies.mlb.com

Industry Group Code: 711211A **Ranks within this company's industry group:** Sales: 6 Profits: 19

Sports:		Services:		Media:		Sales:		Facilities:		Other:	
Leagues/Associations:		Food & Beverage:		TV:		Marketing:		Stadiums:		Gambling:	
Teams:	Y	Agents:		Radio:		Ads:		Fitness Clubs:		Apparel:	
Nonprofits:		Other:		Internet:		Tickets:	Y	Golf Courses:		Equipment:	
Other:				Print:		Retail:	Y	Ski Resorts:		Shoes:	
				Software:		Other:		Other:		Other:	

TYPES OF BUSINESS:

Professional Baseball Team

BRANDS/DIVISIONS/AFFILIATES:

Citizens Bank Park
Tri-Play Associates
Double Play, Inc.
Giles Limited Partnership
Ottawa Lynx
Reading Phillies
Clearwater Threshers
Lakewood BlueClaws

CONTACTS: *Note: Officers with more than one job title may be intentionally listed here more than once.*

David Montgomery, CEO/Gen. Partner
David Montgomery, Pres.
John Nickolas, CFO/VP
David Buck, Sr. VP-Mktg. & Advertising Sales
JoAnn Marano, Dir.-Employee Benefits & Svcs.
Brian Lamoreaux, Dir.-Info. Systems
Scott Brandreth, Mgr.-Merch.
Michael Stiles, Sr. VP-Admin.
Bill Webb, General Counsel/Sr. VP
Michael Stiles, Sr. VP-Oper.
Bonnie Cark, VP-Comm.
Jerry Clothier, VP-Finance & Bus.
Pat Gillick, Sr. VP/Gen. Mgr.
Richard Deats, VP-Phillies Enterprises
John Weber, VP-Ticket Sales & Oper.
Charlie Manuel, Mgr.
Bill Giles, Chmn.

GROWTH PLANS/SPECIAL FEATURES:

The Philadelphia Phillies are a baseball team playing in the Major League Baseball (MLB). The franchise is owned by six partners, with controlling interest held by chairman Bill Giles. The team, which plays at the Citizens Bank Park, a baseball-only field built in 2004 and located adjacent to the team's former location, was founded as the Philadelphia Quakers in 1882, but was soon renamed the Phillies. The organization is the oldest continuous one-name, one-city franchise in all of American professional sports The team won two World Series titles, five National League Pennants and six Division titles but has a reputation for futility and failure, especially in crucial moments, and is the all-time leader in team losses with more than 10,000. The Phillies enjoyed surprising playoff contention in 2006, when, after trading away many players near the trading deadline in an effort to rebuild for future years, the team surged only to fall short as they had done many times before. Since late 2005 the team's general manager has been Pat Gillick, who previously led the Toronto Blue Jays, Baltimore Orioles and Seattle Mariners into the playoffs. The team's World Series wins were in 1980 against the Kansas City Royals and in 2008 against the Tampa Bay Rays. Notable former players include Jackie Robinson, Jim Bunning, Mike Schmidt, Steve Carlton and Grover C. Alexander. In 2008, average home game attendance was 42,254. Forbes recently estimated the team's value to be $496 million.

Phone: 215-463-6000 **Fax:** 215-389-3050
Toll-Free:
Address: 1 Citizens Bank Way, Philadelphia, PA 19148 US

FINANCIALS: Sales and profits are in thousands of dollars—add 000 to get the full amount. 2008 Note: Financial information for 2008 was not available for all companies at press time.

2008 Sales: $216,000	2008 Profits: $16,300	**U.S. Stock Ticker: Private**
2007 Sales: $192,000	2007 Profits: $14,300	**Int'l Ticker:** Int'l Exchange:
2006 Sales: $183,000	2006 Profits: $11,300	Employees:
2005 Sales: $176,000	2005 Profits: $	Fiscal Year Ends: 10/31
2004 Sales: $	2004 Profits: $	Parent Company:

SALARIES/BENEFITS:

Pension Plan:	ESOP Stock Plan:	Profit Sharing:	Top Exec. Salary: $	Bonus: $
Savings Plan:	Stock Purch. Plan:		Second Exec. Salary: $	Bonus: $

OTHER THOUGHTS:

Apparent Women Officers or Directors: 9
Hot Spot for Advancement for Women/Minorities: Y

LOCATIONS: ("Y" = Yes)

West:	Southwest:	Midwest:	Southeast:	Northeast:	International:
				Y	

Note: Financial information, benefits and other data can change quickly and may vary from those stated here.

PHOENIX COYOTES

www.phoenixcoyotes.com

Industry Group Code: 711211F **Ranks within this company's industry group:** Sales: 29 Profits: 29

Sports:		Services:		Media:		Sales:		Facilities:		Other:	
Leagues/Associations:		Food & Beverage:		TV:		Marketing:		Stadiums:		Gambling:	
Teams:	Y	Agents:		Radio:		Ads:		Fitness Clubs:		Apparel:	
Nonprofits:		Other:		Internet:		Tickets:	Y	Golf Courses:		Equipment:	
Other:	Y			Print:		Retail:	Y	Ski Resorts:		Shoes:	
				Software:		Other:		Other:		Other:	

TYPES OF BUSINESS:

Professional Hockey Team

BRANDS/DIVISIONS/AFFILIATES:

Coyotes Hockey, LLC
Cool School Assembly
Phoenix Polar Bears Hockey Association
Peoria Coyotes Junior Hockey Club
Coyotes Amateur Hockey Association
Arizona Sting
Arizona Icecats
Arizona Icers

CONTACTS:

Note: Officers with more than one job title may be intentionally listed here more than once.

Jeff A. Shumway, CEO
Douglas Moss, COO
Douglas Moss, Pres.
Mike Nealy, CFO/Exec. VP
Michael Bucek, Chief Mktg. Officer/Exec. VP
Julie Atherton, Exec. Dir.-Human Resources
Jay Gaskin, Sr. Dir.-IT
Davis Leckie, Chief Engineer
Steve Weinreich, General Counsel/VP
Douglas Vanderheyden, Dir.-Ticket Oper.
Scott Storkan, Mgr.-Hockey Dev.
Jeff Holbrook, Chief Comm. Officer/Exec. VP
Joe Leibried, Controller/VP
Wayne Gretzky, Head Coach/Managing Partner
Don Maloney, Gen. Mgr.
Judd Norris, VP-Corp. Partnerships
Keith Gretzky, Dir.-Amateur Scouting
Jeff A. Shumway, Chmn.

Phone: 623-772-3200	**Fax:** 623-872-2000
Toll-Free:	
Address: 6751 N. Sunset Blvd., Ste. 200, Glendale, AZ 85305 US	

GROWTH PLANS/SPECIAL FEATURES:

The Phoenix Coyotes are members of the Pacific Division of the Western Conference of the National Hockey League (NHL). The team is owned and operated by Coyotes Hockey, LLC, a group of investors whose members include hockey legend Wayne Gretzky and majority owner Jerry Moyes, the founder and CEO of Swift Transportation, a trucking company based in Phoenix. The team entered into the NHL in 1979, playing originally as the Jets, for the city of Winnipeg in Manitoba, Canada. In 1996, the team moved to its current home in Arizona. The team's home stadium is the Jobing.com Arena (formerly the Glendale Arena) a facility that was constructed in late 2003 that seats more than 17,600 and also serves as home to the Arizona Sting lacrosse team. The Coyotes run the Cool School Assembly program, designed to teach school children the importance of safety while playing sports, riding bicycles and skateboards, and provides teachers with grade-specific teaching tools. In addition, the team offers a free street hockey program called Street Coyotes, as well as running and sponsoring numerous amateur hockey associations for all ages include the Coyotes Amateur Hockey Association, Peoria Coyotes Junior Hockey Club, Desert Youth Hockey Association, Peoria Roadrunners Travel Hockey Association, Phoenix Polar Bears Hockey Association, Storm and the University of Arizona's Arizona Icecats and Icers. In 2009, the team signed Justin Bernhardt and acquired Scottie Upshall, Matthew Lombardi and Brandon Prust. A recent Forbes list valued the team at roughly $142 million, the lowest in the league. In the 2008-09 season, the team saw an average home attendance of approximately 14,875 fans. In May 2009, facing mounting financial losses, the team's ownership filed for Chapter 11 bankruptcy protection.

FINANCIALS:

Sales and profits are in thousands of dollars—add 000 to get the full amount. 2008 Note: Financial information for 2008 was not available for all companies at press time.

2008 Sales: $68,000	2008 Profits: $-9,700	**U.S. Stock Ticker: Subsidiary**
2007 Sales: $67,000	2007 Profits: $8,100	**Int'l Ticker:** Int'l Exchange:
2006 Sales: $63,000	2006 Profits: $-6,000	Employees:
2005 Sales: $	2005 Profits: $	Fiscal Year Ends: 6/30
2004 Sales: $57,000	2004 Profits: $	Parent Company: COYOTES HOCKEY LLC

SALARIES/BENEFITS:

Pension Plan:	ESOP Stock Plan:	Profit Sharing:	Top Exec. Salary: $	Bonus: $
Savings Plan:	Stock Purch. Plan:		Second Exec. Salary: $	Bonus: $

OTHER THOUGHTS:

Apparent Women Officers or Directors: 7
Hot Spot for Advancement for Women/Minorities: Y

LOCATIONS: ("Y" = Yes)

West:	Southwest:	Midwest:	Southeast:	Northeast:	International:
	Y				

PHOENIX MERCURY

www.wnba.com/mercury

Industry Group Code: 711211E **Ranks within this company's industry group:** Sales: Profits:

Sports:		Services:		Media:		Sales:		Facilities:		Other:	
Leagues/Associations:		Food & Beverage:		TV:		Marketing:		Stadiums:		Gambling:	
Teams:	Y	Agents:		Radio:		Ads:		Fitness Clubs:		Apparel:	
Nonprofits:		Other:		Internet:		Tickets:	Y	Golf Courses:		Equipment:	
Other:				Print:		Retail:		Ski Resorts:		Shoes:	
				Software:		Other:		Other:		Other:	

TYPES OF BUSINESS:

Women's Professional Basketball Team
Ticket Sales

BRANDS/DIVISIONS/AFFILIATES:

US Airways Center

CONTACTS:

Note: Officers with more than one job title may be intentionally listed here more than once.

Jay L. Parry, COO/Co-Pres.
Rick Welts, Co-Pres.
Lynn Agnello, Sr. VP-Mktg. Partnerships
Jim Pitman, Exec. VP-Admin.
Kip Helt, VP-Game Oper.
Steven J. Koek, Mgr.-Web & Multimedia
Lesley Factor, Public & Community Rel. Mgr.
Jim Pitman, Exec. VP-Finance
Ann Meyers-Drysdale, Gen. Mgr.
Robert Sarver, Managing Partner/Majority Owner
Corey Gaines, Head Coach
Drew Cloud, VP-Sales & Svcs.
Jerry Colangelo, Chmn.

Phone: 602-514-8333	**Fax:** 602-514-8303
Toll-Free:	
Address: US Airways Ctr., 201 E. Jefferson St., Phoenix, AZ 85004 US	

GROWTH PLANS/SPECIAL FEATURES:

The Phoenix Mercury was one of the eight original teams to join the Women's National Basketball Association (WNBA), founded in 1997. It is the sister team to the Phoenix Suns, a National Basketball Association (NBA) team. Both teams play out of US Airways Center. The stadium, which was built through the efforts of Mercury chairman Jerry Colangelo, is now owned by the City of Phoenix. Arizona businessman Robert G. Sarver is the majority owner of both the Mercury and the Suns, having acquired them from Colangelo. After Sarver, two of the team's largest investors include Phoenix businesswomen Anne Mariucci and Kathy Munro, who own a combined 25% interest in the Mercury. Although the team made it to the playoffs three times, in 1997, 1998 and 2000, they didn't win their first WNBA Championship until 2007. The Mercury beat Detroit Shock, the defending champion, in the Shock's home stadium, making the Mercury the first WNBA team to win a championship on the road. Mercury hall-of-famer members have included player Nancy Lieberman, general manager Ann Meyers Drysdale and former coach Cheryl Miller. The franchise has retired one number, 7, which was worn by retired player Michele Timms and is one of only three numbers retired in the WNBA.

FINANCIALS:

Sales and profits are in thousands of dollars—add 000 to get the full amount. 2008 Note: Financial information for 2008 was not available for all companies at press time.

2008 Sales: $	2008 Profits: $	**U.S. Stock Ticker: Private**
2007 Sales: $	2007 Profits: $	**Int'l Ticker:** Int'l Exchange:
2006 Sales: $	2006 Profits: $	Employees:
2005 Sales: $	2005 Profits: $	Fiscal Year Ends:
2004 Sales: $	2004 Profits: $	Parent Company:

SALARIES/BENEFITS:

Pension Plan:	ESOP Stock Plan:	Profit Sharing:	Top Exec. Salary: $	Bonus: $
Savings Plan:	Stock Purch. Plan:		Second Exec. Salary: $	Bonus: $

OTHER THOUGHTS:

Apparent Women Officers or Directors: 8
Hot Spot for Advancement for Women/Minorities: Y

LOCATIONS: ("Y" = Yes)

West:	Southwest:	Midwest:	Southeast:	Northeast:	International:
	Y				

PHOENIX SUNS

www.nba.com/suns

Industry Group Code: 711211B **Ranks within this company's industry group:** Sales: 9 Profits: 6

Sports:		Services:		Media:		Sales:		Facilities:		Other:	
Leagues/Associations:		Food & Beverage:		TV:		Marketing:		Stadiums:		Gambling:	
Teams:	Y	Agents:		Radio:		Ads:		Fitness Clubs:		Apparel:	
Nonprofits:		Other:		Internet:		Tickets:	Y	Golf Courses:		Equipment:	
Other:				Print:		Retail:	Y	Ski Resorts:		Shoes:	
				Software:		Other:		Other:		Other:	

TYPES OF BUSINESS:

Professional Basketball Team
Ticket Sales
Team Merchandise

BRANDS/DIVISIONS/AFFILIATES:

US Airways Center
Phoenix Suns Limited Partnership

CONTACTS:

Note: Officers with more than one job title may be intentionally listed here more than once.

Jerry Colangelo, CEO
Rick Welts, COO
Rick Welts, Pres.
Harvey Shank, Sr. VP-Corp. Sales
Peter Wong, VP-Human Resources
Jim Pitman, Exec. VP-Admin.
Tom O'Malley, General Counsel/Sr. VP
Alvan Adams, Sr. VP-Oper.
John Walker, Sr. VP-Bus. Dev.
Julie Fie, VP-Basketball Comm.
Jim Pitman, Exec. VP-Finance
Robert Sarver, Managing Partner
Steve Kerr, Gen. Mgr.
Ray Artigue, Sr. VP-Mktg. Comm.
Al McCoy, Sr. VP-Broadcasting
Jerry Colangelo, Chmn.

Phone: 602-379-7900	Fax: 602-379-7990
Toll-Free:	
Address: 201 E. Jefferson St., Phoenix, AZ 85004 US	

GROWTH PLANS/SPECIAL FEATURES:

The Phoenix Suns, owned and operated by Phoenix Suns Limited Partnership, are a professional basketball team based in Phoenix, Arizona. The Suns play in the National Basketball Association (NBA). The team was founded in 1968 by a group of investors in Tucson, Arizona. The team played well throughout the 1970s, reaching the NBA Finals in 1976 only to lose to the Boston Celtics. In the mid-1980s, problems on and off the court dirtied the reputation of the team, which in 1987 led to the team's being sold for $44 million to an investor group led by Colangelo. That season, the Suns began their streak of 13 consecutive playoff appearances, which ended only at the end of the 2002 season. During that span, the Suns featured several NBA superstars, including Jeff Hornacek, Dan Majerle, Charles Barkley and Jason Kidd. The 2004-05 season was particularly successful for the Suns, finishing with the best record in the NBA (62-20). In 2005-06, another strong record gave the team a Pacific Division title and a firm entrance into the 2006 playoffs. Former majority owner Jerry Colangelo, still CEO, sold the team to an investment group headed by Robert Sarver, a real estate executive, for $401 million in 2004. Colangelo currently owns the Women's National Basketball Association (WNBA) team Phoenix Mercury and Arena Football's Arizona Rattlers. The Suns play at US Airways Center (formerly America West Arena), which it shares with Mercury, the Rattlers, and the ECHL's Phoenix Roadrunners. Forbes Magazine recently estimated the team to be worth approximately $452 million. In the 2008-09 season, the team's home attendance average was roughly 18,400 per game.

FINANCIALS:

Sales and profits are in thousands of dollars—add 000 to get the full amount. 2008 Note: Financial information for 2008 was not available for all companies at press time.

2008 Sales: $148,000	2008 Profits: $28,900	**U.S. Stock Ticker: Private**
2007 Sales: $145,000	2007 Profits: $37,300	**Int'l Ticker:** Int'l Exchange:
2006 Sales: $132,000	2006 Profits: $34,500	Employees:
2005 Sales: $132,000	2005 Profits: $	Fiscal Year Ends: 6/30
2004 Sales: $111,000	2004 Profits: $	Parent Company: PHOENIX SUNS LIMITED PARTNERSHIP

SALARIES/BENEFITS:

Pension Plan:	ESOP Stock Plan:	Profit Sharing:	Top Exec. Salary: $	Bonus: $
Savings Plan:	Stock Purch. Plan:		Second Exec. Salary: $	Bonus: $

OTHER THOUGHTS:

Apparent Women Officers or Directors: 1
Hot Spot for Advancement for Women/Minorities:

LOCATIONS: ("Y" = Yes)

West:	Southwest:	Midwest:	Southeast:	Northeast:	International:
	Y				

PINNACLE ENTERTAINMENT INC

www.pnkinc.com

Industry Group Code: 721120 **Ranks within this company's industry group:** Sales: 1 Profits: 1

Sports:		Services:		Media:		Sales:		Facilities:		Other:	
Leagues/Associations:		Food & Beverage:		TV:		Marketing:		Stadiums:		Gambling:	Y
Teams:		Agents:		Radio:		Ads:		Fitness Clubs:		Apparel:	
Nonprofits:		Other:		Internet:		Tickets:		Golf Courses:		Equipment:	
Other:				Print:		Retail:		Ski Resorts:		Shoes:	
				Software:		Other:		Other:	Y	Other:	

TYPES OF BUSINESS:

Casinos
Hospitality & Entertainment Facilities

BRANDS/DIVISIONS/AFFILIATES:

L'Auberge du Lac
Belterra Casino Resort
Boomtown Bossier
Boomtown Reno
Lumiere Place
Admiral Riverboad Casino
Casino Magic Argentina

CONTACTS:

Note: Officers with more than one job title may be intentionally listed here more than once.

Daniel R. Lee, CEO
Alain Uboldi, COO
Stephen H. Capp, CFO/Exec. VP
Arthur Schleifer, Chief Mktg. Officer/VP
Guido Bologna, VP-IT
John A. Godfrey, General Counsel/Exec. VP/Sec.
Carlos Ruisanchez, Exec. VP-Strategic Planning & Dev.
Lewis Fanger, VP-Investor Rel.
Russell Stokes, Sr. Dir.-IT Oper. & Applications
Keith Hensen, VP-Casino Oper.
Win Person, VP-Food & Beverage
Alex Stolyar, VP-Corp. Dev.
Daniel R. Lee, Chmn.

Phone: 702-784-7777 **Fax:** 702-784-7778
Toll-Free:
Address: 3800 Howard Hughes Pkwy., Ste. 1800, Las Vegas, NV 89169 US

GROWTH PLANS/SPECIAL FEATURES:

Pinnacle Entertainment, Inc. is a developer, owner and operator of casinos and related hospitality and entertainment facilities. The company currently operates six domestic casinos, three of which are being expanded and enhanced. The firm has two additional casino facilities under construction. The company's casino resort, L'Auberge du Lac in Louisiana, offers roughly 1,000 guestrooms and suites; 1,600 slot machines; 60 table games; an 18-hole championship golf course; retail shops; and a full-service spa. Pinnacle's Indiana property, Belterra Casino Resort, features a 608-guestroom hotel; seven restaurants; a large casino with 1,650 slot machines and 55 table games; a 1,500-seat entertainment showroom; a spa; and an 18-hole championship golf course. The Boomtown Bossier property in Louisiana features a regional hotel built around a dockside riverboat casino and includes a 188-guestroom hotel, four restaurants, 1,200 slot machines and 30 table games. The firm also has a Boomtown New Orleans casino with 1,600 slot machines and 50 tables. The Boomtown Reno Nevada-based property offers 318 guestrooms; three restaurants; an 80-seat lounge; a 30,000-square-foot amusement center; and roughly 1,000 slot machines. In addition, the property also has a full-service truck stop with a satellite casino; a gas station and mini-mart; and a 203-space recreational vehicle park. Pinnacle's most recent property is the 495-suite Lumiere Place hotel and casino in St. Louis, which has 2,000 slot machines; the Admiral Riverboat Casino, with 696 slot machines. It also owns the Casino Magic Argentina, with 1,014 slot machines. Currently Pinnacle has four properties under development in Louisiana, Missouri and New Jersey. In January 2009, the company closed The Casino at Emerald Bay in the Bahamas.

Employees are offered health, vision and dental insurance; life insurance; short-and long-term disability coverage; and tuition reimbursement.

FINANCIALS:

Sales and profits are in thousands of dollars—add 000 to get the full amount. 2008 Note: Financial information for 2008 was not available for all companies at press time.

2008 Sales: $1,044,684	2008 Profits: $-322,597
2007 Sales: $921,814	2007 Profits: $-1,406
2006 Sales: $911,460	2006 Profits: $76,886
2005 Sales: $668,463	2005 Profits: $6,125
2004 Sales: $466,543	2004 Profits: $9,161

U.S. Stock Ticker: PNK
Int'l Ticker: Int'l Exchange:
Employees: 7,825
Fiscal Year Ends: 12/31
Parent Company:

SALARIES/BENEFITS:

Pension Plan:	ESOP Stock Plan:	Profit Sharing:	Top Exec. Salary: $1,000,000	Bonus: $733,275
Savings Plan: Y	Stock Purch. Plan:		Second Exec. Salary: $550,000	Bonus: $500,000

OTHER THOUGHTS:

Apparent Women Officers or Directors: 2
Hot Spot for Advancement for Women/Minorities: Y

LOCATIONS: ("Y" = Yes)

West:	Southwest:	Midwest:	Southeast:	Northeast:	International:
Y		Y	Y	Y	Y

PITTSBURGH PENGUINS

www.pittsburghpenguins.com

Industry Group Code: 711211F **Ranks within this company's industry group:** Sales: 16 Profits: 9

Sports:		Services:		Media:		Sales:		Facilities:		Other:	
Leagues/Associations:		Food & Beverage:		TV:		Marketing:		Stadiums:	Y	Gambling:	
Teams:	Y	Agents:		Radio:		Ads:		Fitness Clubs:		Apparel:	
Nonprofits:		Other:		Internet:		Tickets:	Y	Golf Courses:		Equipment:	
Other:				Print:		Retail:	Y	Ski Resorts:		Shoes:	
				Software:		Other:		Other:		Other:	

TYPES OF BUSINESS:

Hockey Team

BRANDS/DIVISIONS/AFFILIATES:

Lemieux Group
Mellon Arena
Civic Arena
Igloo (The)
National Hockey League (NHL)
New Pittsburgh Arena
Pittsburgh Technology Council

CONTACTS:

Note: Officers with more than one job title may be intentionally listed here more than once.

Ken Sawyer, CEO
David Morehouse, Pres.
Ron Porter, Sr. Consultant
Ray Shero, Gen. Mgr.
Ron Burkle, Co-Owner
Dan Bylsma, Head Coach
Mario Lemieux, Chmn./Co-Owner

Phone: 412-642-1300 **Fax:** 412-642-1859
Toll-Free:
Address: 1 Chatham Center, Ste. 400, Pittsburgh, PA 15219-3447 US

GROWTH PLANS/SPECIAL FEATURES:

The Pittsburgh Penguins franchise is a professional hockey team playing in the NHL since 1967. In its early years, the team met with mixed results on the ice due to a strong offense and weak defense. In 1984, the team drafted Mario Lemieux, who would go on to become one of the greatest players in the NHL and an integral part of the Penguins franchise. Along with Jaromir Jagr, Lemieux led the team to two Stanley Cups in 1990 and 1991. After being diagnosed with Hodgkin's disease, Lemieux came back to the ice after only two months. He retired in 1997. However, with the team facing bankruptcy, and by virtue of his being owed millions of dollars by the team in deferred salary, Lemieux became owner of the Penguins through the Lemieux Group. Lemieux began playing for the team again in 2000, and led it to the playoffs in 2001. However, the team has experienced financial difficulties since then which have forced it to trade away most of its talent. The Penguins play at the Mellon Arena (a.k.a., Civic Arena and The Igloo), which seats 16,958 hockey spectators and is the oldest NHL arena. The team signed an agreement to stay in Pittsburgh for the next 20 years following an agreement with the city of Pittsburgh for the construction of a new facility. The $290 million arena is expected to open in time for the 2010-11 NHL season and have a capacity of 18,500. The team sold out its season for the first time in its history during 2007-08. In the 2008-09 season, the team saw an average home attendance of approximately 17,000 fans. A recent Forbes list valued the team at roughly $203 million.

FINANCIALS:

Sales and profits are in thousands of dollars—add 000 to get the full amount. 2008 Note: Financial information for 2008 was not available for all companies at press time.

2008 Sales: $87,000
2007 Sales: $67,000
2006 Sales: $63,000
2005 Sales: $
2004 Sales: $52,000

2008 Profits: $5,100
2007 Profits: $8,100
2006 Profits: $4,800
2005 Profits: $
2004 Profits: $

U.S. Stock Ticker: Private
Int'l Ticker: Int'l Exchange:
Employees:
Fiscal Year Ends: 6/30
Parent Company: LEMIEUX GROUP

SALARIES/BENEFITS:

Pension Plan:	ESOP Stock Plan:	Profit Sharing:	Top Exec. Salary: $	Bonus: $
Savings Plan:	Stock Purch. Plan:		Second Exec. Salary: $	Bonus: $

OTHER THOUGHTS:

Apparent Women Officers or Directors:
Hot Spot for Advancement for Women/Minorities:

LOCATIONS: ("Y" = Yes)

West:	Southwest:	Midwest:	Southeast:	Northeast:	International:
				Y	

PITTSBURGH PIRATES

pittsburgh.pirates.mlb.com

Industry Group Code: 711211A **Ranks within this company's industry group:** Sales: 28 Profits: 20

Sports:		Services:		Media:		Sales:		Facilities:		Other:	
Leagues/Associations:		Food & Beverage:		TV:		Marketing:		Stadiums:		Gambling:	
Teams:	Y	Agents:		Radio:		Ads:		Fitness Clubs:		Apparel:	
Nonprofits:		Other:		Internet:		Tickets:	Y	Golf Courses:		Equipment:	
Other:				Print:		Retail:	Y	Ski Resorts:		Shoes:	
				Software:		Other:		Other:		Other:	

TYPES OF BUSINESS:

Professional Baseball Team

BRANDS/DIVISIONS/AFFILIATES:

PNC Park
Pittsburgh Baseball Club
Altoona Curve
Hickory Crawdads
State College Spikes
State College Spikes
Bradenton Pirates
San Joaquin Pirates

CONTACTS: *Note: Officers with more than one job title may be intentionally listed here more than once.*

Frank Coonelly, Pres.
Jim Plake, CFO/Exec. VP
Brian Chiera, Sr. Dir.-Consumer Mktg. & Ticket Sales
Pam Nelson Minteer, Sr. Dir.-Human Resources
Terry Zeigler, Sr. Dir.-IT
Larry Silverman, General Counsel/VP
Bryan Minniti, Dir.-Baseball Oper.
Jim Alexander, Sr. Dir.-Bus. Dev.
Patty Paytas, VP-Community & Pub. Affairs
David Bowman, Controller
Neal Huntington, Gen. Mgr.
John Russell, Mgr.
Kyle Stark, Sr. Dir.-Player Dev.
Dennis DaPra, Sr. VP/Gen. Mgr.-PNC Park
Bob Nutting, Chmn.
Rene Gayo, Dir.-Latin American Scouting

Phone: 412-323-5000	**Fax:** 412-325-4410
Toll-Free:	
Address: 115 Federal St., Pittsburgh, PA 15212 US	

GROWTH PLANS/SPECIAL FEATURES:

The Pittsburgh Pirates are a Major League Baseball (MLB) team. Playing its first season with the National League as the Pittsburgh Alleghenies in 1887, the team became the Pirates in 1891. The team's most famous players include Honus Wagner, Pie Traynor, Roberto Clemente, Willie Stargell and Barry Bonds. In 1970, the Pirates fielded what is believed to be the first all-minority lineup in MLB. The Pirates have won five World Series (last in 1979) and nine pennants. Since its last postseason appearance in 1992, the team has not posted a winning record. The Pirates were majority-owned by Kevin McClatchy from 1996 to 2006, when he was replaced by current majority owner, Robert Nutting. The 2001 season saw the opening of PNC Park, a new 38,500-seat stadium. Another in the trend of classic-style ballparks, the stadium provided only a momentary spike in attendance, as the team filled 2.4 million seats that year and fell to 28th in MLB by 2004 with less than 1.6 million tickets sold on the season. Attendance was up to 1.86 million in 2006, the year the Pirates hosted the Major League All-Star Game. Most recently, average home game attendance stood at 20,113. Forbes Magazine recently valued the Pirates at $288 million.

Employees are offered medical, dental and vision insurance; flexible spending accounts; life insurance; short-and long-term disability coverage; a 401(k) plan; a pension plan; an onsite fitness center; free baseball tickets; and an employee assistance program.

FINANCIALS: Sales and profits are in thousands of dollars—add 000 to get the full amount. 2008 Note: Financial information for 2008 was not available for all companies at press time.

2008 Sales: $144,000	2008 Profits: $15,900	**U.S. Stock Ticker: Subsidiary**
2007 Sales: $139,000	2007 Profits: $17,600	**Int'l Ticker:** Int'l Exchange:
2006 Sales: $137,000	2006 Profits: $25,300	Employees:
2005 Sales: $125,000	2005 Profits: $	Fiscal Year Ends: 10/31
2004 Sales: $	2004 Profits: $	Parent Company: PITTSBURGH BASEBALL CLUB

SALARIES/BENEFITS:

Pension Plan: Y	ESOP Stock Plan:	Profit Sharing:	Top Exec. Salary: $	Bonus: $
Savings Plan: Y	Stock Purch. Plan:		Second Exec. Salary: $	Bonus: $

OTHER THOUGHTS:

Apparent Women Officers or Directors: 2
Hot Spot for Advancement for Women/Minorities: Y

LOCATIONS: ("Y" = Yes)

West:	Southwest:	Midwest:	Southeast:	Northeast:	International:
				Y	

Note: Financial information, benefits and other data can change quickly and may vary from those stated here.

PITTSBURGH STEELERS

www.steelers.com

Industry Group Code: 711211C **Ranks within this company's industry group:** Sales: 14 Profits: 27

Sports:		Services:		Media:		Sales:		Facilities:		Other:	
Leagues/Associations:		Food & Beverage:		TV:		Marketing:		Stadiums:		Gambling:	
Teams:	Y	Agents:		Radio:		Ads:		Fitness Clubs:		Apparel:	
Nonprofits:		Other:		Internet:		Tickets:	Y	Golf Courses:		Equipment:	
Other:				Print:		Retail:	Y	Ski Resorts:		Shoes:	
				Software:		Other:		Other:		Other:	

TYPES OF BUSINESS:

Professional Football Team

BRANDS/DIVISIONS/AFFILIATES:

Pittsburgh Steelers Sports, Inc.
Art Rooney Memorial Scholarship
Best of the Batch Foundation
Max Starks Fund

CONTACTS:

Note: Officers with more than one job title may be intentionally listed here more than once.

Arthur J. Rooney, II, Pres.
Tony Quatrini, Dir.-Mktg.
Geraldine Glenn, VP-Human Rel.
Scott Phelps, Mgr.-IT
Tim Carey, Exec. Officer-Merch.
Kevin Colbert, Dir.-Football Oper.
Mark Hart, Dir.-Bus.
David Lockett, Comm. Coordinator
Bob Tyler, Controller
Ron Hughes, College Scouting Coordinator
Burt Lauten, Mgr.-Public Rel. & Media
Mike Tomlin, Head Coach
Kathy Wallace, Mgr.-Corp. Sales & Mktg.
Daniel M. Rooney, Chmn.

Phone: 412-432-7800 **Fax:** 412-432-7878
Toll-Free:
Address: 3400 S. Water St., Pittsburgh, PA 15203-2349 US

GROWTH PLANS/SPECIAL FEATURES:

The Pittsburgh Steelers, owned and operated by Pittsburgh Steelers Sports, Inc., are a professional football team in the National Football League (NFL). The team plays in the Northern Division of the NFL's American Football Conference (AFC). The Steelers franchise was founded in 1933 as the Pittsburgh Pirates, and its name changed to its current form in 1941. The team reached the playoffs only once before 1972. The Steelers' fortunes turned in 1969 with the hiring of legendary head coach Chuck Noll. Noll possessed an uncanny ability to select premium players in the NFL draft. Between 1969 and 1974, he drafted eight Hall of Fame superstar players. The Steelers made the playoffs every year between 1972 and 1979, and they won the Super Bowl four times in this span. The team most recently won the Super Bowl in the 2005-2006 season. The team plays at Heinz Field, which overlooks the Ohio River in downtown Pittsburgh and seats 65,050 spectators. In July 2008, the owners of the Steelers (Dan Rooney and his five sons: Art Rooney II, Art Jr., Timothy, Patrick and John) agreed to a restructuring of ownership in order to comply with NFL ownership regulations. Under the terms of the agreement, Dan and Art Rooney II maintain a 30% stake while each of the other brothers sold the majority or total of their shares. In March 2009, the team added three additional investors, most noteworthy, Hall of Famer John Stallworth. In the 2008 season, the team averaged 62,890 fans in attendance per game. A recent Forbes estimate values the team at $1.01 billion.

FINANCIALS:

Sales and profits are in thousands of dollars—add 000 to get the full amount. 2008 Note: Financial information for 2008 was not available for all companies at press time.

2008 Sales: $216,000	2008 Profits: $14,400
2007 Sales: $198,000	2007 Profits: $20,000
2006 Sales: $187,000	2006 Profits: $25,500
2005 Sales: $182,000	2005 Profits: $
2004 Sales: $159,000	2004 Profits: $

U.S. Stock Ticker: Subsidiary
Int'l Ticker: Int'l Exchange:
Employees:
Fiscal Year Ends: 3/31
Parent Company: PITTSBURGH STEELERS SPORTS INC

SALARIES/BENEFITS:

Pension Plan:	ESOP Stock Plan:	Profit Sharing:	Top Exec. Salary: $	Bonus: $
Savings Plan:	Stock Purch. Plan:		Second Exec. Salary: $	Bonus: $

OTHER THOUGHTS:

Apparent Women Officers or Directors: 6
Hot Spot for Advancement for Women/Minorities: Y

LOCATIONS: ("Y" = Yes)

West:	Southwest:	Midwest:	Southeast:	Northeast:	International:
				Y	

PORTLAND TRAILBLAZERS

www.nba.com/blazers

Industry Group Code: 711211B **Ranks within this company's industry group:** Sales: 17 Profits: 21

Sports:		Services:		Media:		Sales:		Facilities:		Other:	
Leagues/Associations:		Food & Beverage:		TV:		Marketing:		Stadiums:		Gambling:	
Teams:	Y	Agents:		Radio:		Ads:		Fitness Clubs:		Apparel:	
Nonprofits:		Other:		Internet:		Tickets:	Y	Golf Courses:		Equipment:	
Other:				Print:		Retail:	Y	Ski Resorts:		Shoes:	
				Software:		Other:		Other:		Other:	

TYPES OF BUSINESS:

Professional Basketball Team

BRANDS/DIVISIONS/AFFILIATES:

Rose Garden Arena
Vulcan, Inc.

CONTACTS: *Note: Officers with more than one job title may be intentionally listed here more than once.*

Larry Miller, Pres.
Gregg Olson, CFO/Sr. VP
Sarah Mensah, Chief Mktg. Officer
Traci Reandeau, Dir.-Human Resources
Chris Dill, CIO/VP
Mike Janes, Dir.-Eng. & Tech. Oper.
Mike Fennell, General Counsel/Sr. VP
Brad Weinrich, Dir.-Basketball Oper.
J. E. Isaac, Sr. VP-Bus. Affairs
Cheri Hanson, VP-Comm.
Linda Glasser, Controller
Paul G. Allen, Owner
Kevin Pritchard, Gen. Mgr.
Nate McMillan, Head Coach
Dick Vardanega, VP-Broadcasting & Prod.

Phone: 503-234-9291 **Fax:** 503-736-2187
Toll-Free:
Address: 1 Centre Ct., Ste. 200, Portland, OR 97227 US

GROWTH PLANS/SPECIAL FEATURES:

The Portland Trail Blazers are a National Basketball Association (NBA) team. The team entered the league in 1970 as an expansion team and won its first and only NBA championship in 1977. The Trailblazers have historically been a strong contender in the league, and appear frequently in the playoffs. However, the team's best times have been shared with the surge of some unusually strong teams. Both the Detroit Pistons in the late 1980s and the Chicago Bulls of the early 1990s prevented the Trail Blazers from recapturing a title. Among the Trail Blazer's many great players are Hall-of-Fame inductees Clyde Drexler, Dr. Jack Ramsey (a coach), Bill Walton and Lenny Wilkens. The Trail Blazers averaged 19,550 visitors per home game for the 2007-08 season, or 97.8% of stadium capacity. Paul G. Allen, co-founder of Microsoft purchased the team from Larry Weinberg in 1988 for $70 million. The team is currently owned and operated by Vulcan, Inc., Allen's private asset management company, which also owns the Seattle Seahawks National Football League (NFL) franchise and the Seattle Sounders Major League Soccer team. Paul was instrumental in developing and funding the Trailblazers' home court, Rose Garden Arena, which seats 20,630 for basketball games. Forbes Magazine recently estimated the team to be worth approximately $452 million. In the 2008-09 season, the team's home attendance average was roughly 18,400 per game.

FINANCIALS: **Sales and profits are in thousands of dollars—add 000 to get the full amount. 2008 Note: Financial information for 2008 was not available for all companies at press time.**

2008 Sales: $114,000
2007 Sales: $82,000
2006 Sales: $77,000
2005 Sales: $78,000
2004 Sales: $88,000

2008 Profits: $- 900
2007 Profits: $-25,100
2006 Profits: $-15,200
2005 Profits: $
2004 Profits: $

U.S. Stock Ticker: Subsidiary
Int'l Ticker: Int'l Exchange:
Employees:
Fiscal Year Ends: 6/30
Parent Company: VULCAN INC

SALARIES/BENEFITS:

Pension Plan: ESOP Stock Plan: Profit Sharing: Top Exec. Salary: $ Bonus: $
Savings Plan: Stock Purch. Plan: Second Exec. Salary: $ Bonus: $

OTHER THOUGHTS:

Apparent Women Officers or Directors: 4
Hot Spot for Advancement for Women/Minorities: Y

LOCATIONS: ("Y" = Yes)

West:	Southwest:	Midwest:	Southeast:	Northeast:	International:
Y					

PORTSMOUTH FOOTBALL CLUB

www.portsmouthfc.co.uk

Industry Group Code: 711211D **Ranks within this company's industry group:** Sales: Profits:

Sports:		Services:		Media:		Sales:		Facilities:		Other:	
Leagues/Associations:		Food & Beverage:	Y	TV:		Marketing:		Stadiums:	Y	Gambling:	
Teams:	Y	Agents:		Radio:		Ads:		Fitness Clubs:		Apparel:	
Nonprofits:		Other:		Internet:		Tickets:	Y	Golf Courses:		Equipment:	
Other:				Print:		Retail:		Ski Resorts:		Shoes:	
				Software:		Other:		Other:		Other:	Y

TYPES OF BUSINESS:

Soccer Team
Hospitality

BRANDS/DIVISIONS/AFFILIATES:

Pompey
Fratton Park Stadium
Portsmouth FC
Pompey Ladies (The)
Seatwave

CONTACTS:

Note: Officers with more than one job title may be intentionally listed here more than once.

Pete Storrie, CEO
Carolyn Anderson, Head-Mktg.
Sheldon Davis, Head-IT
Paul Weld, Corp. Sec.
Lucius Peart, Head-Oper.
Paul Bell, Dir.-Bus. Dev.
Gary Double, Dir.-Comm.
Karen Whitren, Head-Finance
Gary Owers, Head-Community
Elaine Giles, Mgr.-Ticket Office
Philippa Atkinson, Head-Commercial Sales
Paul Hart, Acting First Team Mgr.
Pete Storrie, Chmn.

Phone: 44-23-9273-1204 **Fax:** 44-23-9273-4129
Toll-Free:
Address: Rodney Rd., Portsmouth, PO4 8SX UK

GROWTH PLANS/SPECIAL FEATURES:

Portsmouth Football Club (Portsmouth FC) is an English Premiership soccer team often known as Pompey. Established in 1898, the team plays its games at Fratton Park in Portsmouth. The team's goal, which had been simply to stay in the Premiership, is now to land a finish in the league top 10. Portsmouth Football Club has a uniform sponsorship contract with OKI Printing Solutions. Former Pompey greats include defenders Andy Awford and Jimmy Allen; winger Darren Anderton; forward Paul Walsh; goalkeeper Alan Knight; half back Harry Harris; and full back Kenny Swain. The club also has a women's soccer team, the Pompey Ladies. In addition to soccer, the company offers hospitality services for various events, including Christmas parties and weddings. Portsmouth FC is owned by Russian businessman Alexandre Gaydamak. In recent years, the club announced plans to renovate its Fratton Park Stadium. Originally, Pompey planned to leave the stadium and build a new 36,000-seat stadium in three stages by Barr, Ltd. near the city's naval dockyards; however, economic conditions have forced the team to abandon such plans. In September 2008, Portsmouth FC announced that Seatwave would be its new ticket exchange partner.

FINANCIALS:

Sales and profits are in thousands of dollars—add 000 to get the full amount. 2008 Note: Financial information for 2008 was not available for all companies at press time.

2008 Sales: $	2008 Profits: $	**U.S. Stock Ticker: Private**
2007 Sales: $	2007 Profits: $	**Int'l Ticker:** Int'l Exchange:
2006 Sales: $	2006 Profits: $	Employees:
2005 Sales: $	2005 Profits: $	Fiscal Year Ends:
2004 Sales: $	2004 Profits: $	Parent Company:

SALARIES/BENEFITS:

Pension Plan:	ESOP Stock Plan:	Profit Sharing:	Top Exec. Salary: $	Bonus: $
Savings Plan:	Stock Purch. Plan:		Second Exec. Salary: $	Bonus: $

OTHER THOUGHTS:

Apparent Women Officers or Directors: 7
Hot Spot for Advancement for Women/Minorities: Y

LOCATIONS: ("Y" = Yes)

West:	Southwest:	Midwest:	Southeast:	Northeast:	International:
					Y

PRINCE SPORTS INC

www.princetennis.com

Industry Group Code: 339920 **Ranks within this company's industry group:** Sales: Profits:

Sports:		Services:		Media:		Sales:		Facilities:		Other:	
Leagues/Associations:		Food & Beverage:		TV:		Marketing:		Stadiums:		Gambling:	
Teams:		Agents:		Radio:		Ads:		Fitness Clubs:		Apparel:	Y
Nonprofits:		Other:		Internet:		Tickets:		Golf Courses:		Equipment:	Y
Other:				Print:		Retail:		Ski Resorts:		Shoes:	Y
				Software:		Other:		Other:		Other:	

TYPES OF BUSINESS:

Manufacturing-Tennis Equipment
Tennis, Squash & Badminton Racquets
Sports Apparel & Accessories
Footwear
Tennis Racquet Strings & Grips
Stringing & Ball Machines

BRANDS/DIVISIONS/AFFILIATES:

Shark
Excel
Lite
Hot Shot
Spectator
On Court
Agility
O3 Speedport

CONTACTS: *Note: Officers with more than one job title may be intentionally listed here more than once.*

George Napier, CEO
Charles Osborn, VP/Mgr.-US National Sales
Linda Glassel, VP-Sports Mktg. & Comm., Prince Sports USA
George Napier, Chmn.

Phone: 609-291-5800	**Fax:** 609-291-5900
Toll-Free:	
Address: 1 Advantage Ct., Bordentown, NJ 08505 US	

GROWTH PLANS/SPECIAL FEATURES:

Prince Sports, Inc. is a sports equipment manufacturer that produces racquets, shoes, tennis balls, apparel, sports bags and tennis court machines. Its racquets, which are its most famous items, come in three categories: Performance, including O3, Shark, AIR, Diablo and Classic brands); recreational, such as Rebel, Lob, Pro and Synergy brands; and graduated length, including Shark, Diablo, Hot Shot and Cool Shot brands. Its women's apparel is sold under the Atmosphere, Bluette, OnCourt, TidePool and Serve collections, while its men's apparel is sold under the On Court, Grandstand, Radius and Quarry collections. The firm's footwear products include men's, women's and junior footwear, and its accessories include hats visors, sweatbands and socks. Prince's other products include strings from the Playability, All-Around and Durability series; replacement grips and OverGrips; sports bags from the Elements, Premier, Courtside, Team and O3 collections; and machines and court items such as electronic stringing machines, stringing tools and ball machines. Prince currently sponsors several professional tennis players on the ATP and WTA tour. Its ATP players include Matt Behrmann and Alex Bogomolov from the U.S., Evgeny Korolev from Russia, Xavier Malisse from Belgium, Alessio Di Mauro from Italy and David Ferrer from Spain. Its WTA players include Maria Sharapova from Russia, Shahar Peer from Israel, Ai Sugiyama from Japan, Lisa Raymond from the U.S. and Yuliana Fedak from Ukraine. Prince recently launched the O3 Speedport racquet, which is designed to deliver a significant boost in a player's swing speed. In January 2009, the company launched the EXO3, a four model high performance racquet line.

FINANCIALS: **Sales and profits are in thousands of dollars—add 000 to get the full amount. 2008 Note: Financial information for 2008 was not available for all companies at press time.**

2008 Sales: $	2008 Profits: $	**U.S. Stock Ticker: Private**
2007 Sales: $	2007 Profits: $	**Int'l Ticker:** Int'l Exchange:
2006 Sales: $	2006 Profits: $	Employees: 112
2005 Sales: $	2005 Profits: $	Fiscal Year Ends: 9/30
2004 Sales: $12,200	2004 Profits: $	Parent Company:

SALARIES/BENEFITS:

Pension Plan:	ESOP Stock Plan:	Profit Sharing:	Top Exec. Salary: $	Bonus: $
Savings Plan:	Stock Purch. Plan:		Second Exec. Salary: $	Bonus: $

OTHER THOUGHTS:

Apparent Women Officers or Directors: 1
Hot Spot for Advancement for Women/Minorities:

LOCATIONS: ("Y" = Yes)

West:	Southwest:	Midwest:	Southeast:	Northeast:	International:
				Y	

PROFESSIONAL BOWLERS ASSOCIATION

www.pba.com

Industry Group Code: 813990 **Ranks within this company's industry group:** Sales: Profits:

Sports:		Services:		Media:		Sales:		Facilities:		Other:	
Leagues/Associations:	Y	Food & Beverage:		TV:		Marketing:		Stadiums:		Gambling:	
Teams:		Agents:		Radio:		Ads:		Fitness Clubs:		Apparel:	Y
Nonprofits:		Other:		Internet:	Y	Tickets:		Golf Courses:		Equipment:	
Other:				Print:		Retail:		Ski Resorts:		Shoes:	
				Software:		Other:		Other:		Other:	

TYPES OF BUSINESS:

Bowling Association

BRANDS/DIVISIONS/AFFILIATES:

United States Bowling Congress Masters
PBA World Championship
PBA Tournament of Champions
Lumber Liquidators U.S. Open
PBA Regional Tour
PBA Senior Tour
PBA Women's Series

CONTACTS: *Note: Officers with more than one job title may be intentionally listed here more than once.*

Fred Schreyer, CEO
Tom Clark, COO/VP
Fred Schreyer, Pres.
Chris Peters, Chmn.

Phone: 206-332-9688	**Fax:** 206-654-6030
Toll-Free:	
Address: 719 2nd Ave., Ste. 701, Seattle, WA 98104 US	

GROWTH PLANS/SPECIAL FEATURES:

The Professional Bowlers Association (PBA) is the worldwide governing body for the sport of major league professional bowling. Founded in 1958 with 33 charter members, the PBA currently has nearly 4,300 members in 13 countries: Australia, Bermuda, Canada, China, the U.K., Finland, France, Germany, Japan, Korea, Sweden, the U.S. and Venezuela. The organization usually hosts 21 regular season tournaments annually in 15 U.S. states, as well as one pre-season charity tournament held in September during the 2008-09 season. Major tournaments include the PBA World Championship, PBA Tournament of Champions, United States Bowling Congress (USBC) Masters and the 66th Lumber Liquidators U.S. Open. Corporate sponsors include Brunswick, GEICO, Bayer, Pepsi-Cola, Denny's, H&R Block, Etonic, Motel 6, Lumber Liquidators and the USBC. Televised PBA games are broadcast on ESPN. Three former Microsoft executives purchased the PBA in 2000 with aspirations to transform it into the next emerging global sport. The association has enacted several rules changes since the new ownership came aboard, including setting a defined season, October through April; relaxing the existing dress code, so that players can customize their look; featuring a 64-bowler exempt format; changing the tournament format in an effort to make the sport more entertaining; banning sideline coaching; and increasing the overall prize fund to around $9 million for the Lumber Liquidators PBA Tour, PBA Regional Tour, PBA Senior Tour and PBA Women's Series. The PBA and Go Play Network have combined forces to create the Lumber Liquidators PBA Tour Fantasy Bowling game. The pba.com web site features Xtra Frame, an archive of videos ranging from player interviews to bowling tips. In 2008, the PBA signed a three-year deal with Lumber Liquidators to serve as the tour's title sponsor.

FINANCIALS: **Sales and profits are in thousands of dollars—add 000 to get the full amount. 2008 Note: Financial information for 2008 was not available for all companies at press time.**

2008 Sales: $	2008 Profits: $	**U.S. Stock Ticker: Private**
2007 Sales: $3,000	2007 Profits: $	**Int'l Ticker:** Int'l Exchange:
2006 Sales: $	2006 Profits: $	Employees: 35
2005 Sales: $	2005 Profits: $	Fiscal Year Ends:
2004 Sales: $	2004 Profits: $	Parent Company:

SALARIES/BENEFITS:

Pension Plan:	ESOP Stock Plan:	Profit Sharing:	Top Exec. Salary: $	Bonus: $
Savings Plan:	Stock Purch. Plan:		Second Exec. Salary: $	Bonus: $

OTHER THOUGHTS:

Apparent Women Officers or Directors:
Hot Spot for Advancement for Women/Minorities:

LOCATIONS: ("Y" = Yes)

West:	Southwest:	Midwest:	Southeast:	Northeast:	International:
Y					

PROFESSIONAL BULL RIDERS INC

www.pbrnow.com

Industry Group Code: 813990 **Ranks within this company's industry group:** Sales: Profits:

Sports:		Services:		Media:		Sales:		Facilities:		Other:	
Leagues/Associations:	Y	Food & Beverage:		TV:		Marketing:		Stadiums:		Gambling:	
Teams:		Agents:		Radio:		Ads:		Fitness Clubs:		Apparel:	
Nonprofits:		Other:		Internet:		Tickets:		Golf Courses:		Equipment:	
Other:				Print:		Retail:		Ski Resorts:		Shoes:	
				Software:		Other:	Y	Other:		Other:	

TYPES OF BUSINESS:

Professional Bull Riding Association

BRANDS/DIVISIONS/AFFILIATES:

Built Ford Tough Series
US Smokeless Tobacco Company Challenger Tour
Enterprise-Rent-A-Car Tour
Discovery Tour
PBR World Cup
Pro Bull Rider Magazine
Spire Capital Partners, L.P.

CONTACTS: *Note: Officers with more than one job title may be intentionally listed here more than once.*

Randy Bernard, CEO
Sean Gleason, COO
Rodd Granger, CFO
Lynn Wittenburg, VP-Mktg.
Alicia Sandoval, Mgr.-Human Resources
Matthew A. Rivela, General Counsel
Dennis Gach, Sr. VP-Oper.
Katharine Sherrer, Mgr.-Public Rel.
Jean Ryan, VP-Partnership Mktg.
Andy Thwaite, VP-Digital Media
Jeff Kent, Regional Representative-Pacific Northwest
Rhonda Truett, VP-Licensing
Dave Cordovano, Sr. VP-Int'l Bus.

Phone: 719-242-2800	**Fax:** 719-242-2855
Toll-Free:	
Address: 101 W. Riverwalk, Pueblo, CO 81003 US	

GROWTH PLANS/SPECIAL FEATURES:

Professional Bull Riders, Inc. (PBR), founded in 1992 by 20 celebrated bull riders, is jointly owned by its members and private equity organization Spire Capital Partners, L.P. The organization has more than 1,200 bull-riding members who compete in over 300 PBR competitions throughout the U.S., Australia, Brazil, Canada and Mexico. The company organizes and manages four primary touring competitions: The Built Ford Tough Series (BFT), its elite and largest tour covering more than 30 cities; the U.S. Smokeless Tobacco Company Challenger Tour; the Enterprise Rent-A-Car Tour; and Discovery Tour. Bull riders compete to qualify for the PBR Finals in Las Vegas where the PBR World Champion is decided. Total annual prize money has grown to over $10 million. In addition to the four primary competitions, PBR also hosts a PBR World Cup, which is slated to be held in Brazil in 2009. Fans of PBR can become members by following links on the web site or by calling PBR's phone number. Most members receive a subscription to the Pro Bull Rider magazine, which PBR sends out bi-monthly to individuals with a gold or platinum level membership. PBR's current corporate sponsors include Ford, Wrangler, Jack Daniel's, U.S. Smokeless Tobacco Company, Dickies, Bass Pro Shops, The Home Depot and the city of Las Vegas. The company's events attract over 1.5 million attendees annually and are broadcast through outlets such as the VERSUS cable network, NBC and FOX Sports. In addition to its Colorado headquarters, the firm maintains international offices in Australia, Brazil, Canada and Mexico.

FINANCIALS: **Sales and profits are in thousands of dollars—add 000 to get the full amount. 2008 Note: Financial information for 2008 was not available for all companies at press time.**

2008 Sales: $	2008 Profits: $	**U.S. Stock Ticker: Private**
2007 Sales: $	2007 Profits: $	**Int'l Ticker:** Int'l Exchange:
2006 Sales: $	2006 Profits: $	Employees:
2005 Sales: $	2005 Profits: $	Fiscal Year Ends:
2004 Sales: $	2004 Profits: $	Parent Company: SPIRE CAPITAL PARTNERS LP

SALARIES/BENEFITS:

Pension Plan:	ESOP Stock Plan:	Profit Sharing:	Top Exec. Salary: $	Bonus: $
Savings Plan:	Stock Purch. Plan:		Second Exec. Salary: $	Bonus: $

OTHER THOUGHTS:

Apparent Women Officers or Directors: 5
Hot Spot for Advancement for Women/Minorities: Y

LOCATIONS: ("Y" = Yes)

West:	Southwest:	Midwest:	Southeast:	Northeast:	International:
Y					Y

PROFESSIONAL GOLFERS ASSOCIATION OF AMERICA (PGA)

www.pga.com

Industry Group Code: 813990 **Ranks within this company's industry group:** Sales: Profits:

Sports:		Services:		Media:		Sales:		Facilities:		Other:	
Leagues/Associations:	Y	Food & Beverage:		TV:		Marketing:	Y	Stadiums:		Gambling:	
Teams:		Agents:		Radio:		Ads:	Y	Fitness Clubs:		Apparel:	Y
Nonprofits:		Other:		Internet:		Tickets:	Y	Golf Courses:	Y	Equipment:	Y
Other:				Print:		Retail:	Y	Ski Resorts:		Shoes:	Y
				Software:		Other:		Other:		Other:	

TYPES OF BUSINESS:

Professional Golf Association
Event Sponsorship
Junior Tournaments
Golf Instruction

BRANDS/DIVISIONS/AFFILIATES:

PGA Championship
PGA Grand Slam of Golf
Senior PGA Championship
PGA Tour
PGA Village
Ryder Cup
PGA Center for Golf Learning & Performance

CONTACTS: *Note: Officers with more than one job title may be intentionally listed here more than once.*

Joe Steranka, CEO
Jim Remy, Pres.
Ted Bishop, Corp. Sec.
Allen Wronowski, VP
Brian Whitcomb, Honorary Pres.

Phone: 561-624-8400	**Fax:** 561-624-8448
Toll-Free:	
Address: 100 Ave. of the Champions, Palm Beach Gardens, FL 33410 US	

GROWTH PLANS/SPECIAL FEATURES:

The Professional Golfers Association of America (PGA) is an organization comprised of approximately 28,000 PGA Professionals. These professionals, mainly instructors but also businesspeople and community leaders, have been promoting and teaching the game of golf since the association's founding in 1916. The PGA's function is to conduct the PGA Tour's PGA Championship, one of U.S. golf's four major tournaments, as well as to conduct the Ryder Cup, the Senior PGA Championship, the PGA Grand Slam of Golf and approximately 40 other large tournaments. The PGA runs a golf instruction school and resort, known as the PGA Village, in Port St. Lucie, Florida. This resort, featuring 54 holes and a short course, was named one of GolfWorld Reader's Choice Awards Top 50 Public Golf Courses. Additionally, the PGA Learning Center is a 35-acre practice facility providing over 11,000 square feet of classroom space and provides cost-efficient education programs to serve both PGA members and apprentice professionals. The PGA also sponsors youth programs and tournaments around the country. Great former/current players include Tiger Woods, Jack Nicklaus, Don Essig III, Claude Harmon Sr. and Phil Mickelson. From the association's web site, golfers can access information concerning golf equipment, PGA Tour news, golf travel, rulebooks and golf etiquette. The PGA.com store is also available on the association's web site, featuring apparel, caps, club headcovers, golf bags and other items with logos from the PGA and its major tournaments. PGA of America sponsors include American Express, GolfDigest, Golf Channel and Rolex. In January 2009, Mercedes-Benz USA became an Official Patron of the organization. In March 2009, the PGA Learning Center was renamed the PGA Center for Golf Learning and Performance.

FINANCIALS: **Sales and profits are in thousands of dollars—add 000 to get the full amount. 2008 Note: Financial information for 2008 was not available for all companies at press time.**

2008 Sales: $	2008 Profits: $	**U.S. Stock Ticker: Private**
2007 Sales: $16,700	2007 Profits: $	**Int'l Ticker:** Int'l Exchange:
2006 Sales: $	2006 Profits: $	Employees: 178
2005 Sales: $	2005 Profits: $	Fiscal Year Ends: 6/30
2004 Sales: $	2004 Profits: $	Parent Company:

SALARIES/BENEFITS:

Pension Plan:	ESOP Stock Plan:	Profit Sharing:	Top Exec. Salary: $	Bonus: $
Savings Plan:	Stock Purch. Plan:		Second Exec. Salary: $	Bonus: $

OTHER THOUGHTS:

Apparent Women Officers or Directors:
Hot Spot for Advancement for Women/Minorities:

LOCATIONS: ("Y" = Yes)

West:	Southwest:	Midwest:	Southeast:	Northeast:	International:
Y	Y	Y	Y	Y	

PUMA AG RUDOLF DASSLER SPORT

www.puma.com

Industry Group Code: 316219 **Ranks within this company's industry group:** Sales: 3 Profits: 3

Sports:		Services:		Media:		Sales:		Facilities:		Other:	
Leagues/Associations:		Food & Beverage:		TV:		Marketing:		Stadiums:		Gambling:	
Teams:		Agents:		Radio:		Ads:		Fitness Clubs:		Apparel:	Y
Nonprofits:		Other:		Internet:		Tickets:		Golf Courses:		Equipment:	Y
Other:				Print:		Retail:	Y	Ski Resorts:		Shoes:	Y
				Software:		Other:		Other:		Other:	

TYPES OF BUSINESS:

Athletic Shoes Manufacturing
Athletic Apparel
Sports Equipment
Retail Stores

BRANDS/DIVISIONS/AFFILIATES:

PUMA
Tretorn
Mayfair
PumaMoto

CONTACTS: *Note: Officers with more than one job title may be intentionally listed here more than once.*

Jochen Zeitz, CEO
Dieter Bock, CFO
Antonio Bertone, Chief Mktg. Officer
Dieter Bock, Dir.-Investor Rel.
Dieter Bock, Dir.-Finance
Antonio Bertone, Dir.-Brand Mgmt.
Melody Harris-Jensbach, Deputy CEO
Stefano Caroti, Chief Commercial Officer
Hussein Chalayan, Dir.-Creative
Jochen Zeitz, Chmn.
Reiner Seiz, Chief Supply Chain

Phone: 49-9132-81-0	**Fax:** 49-9132-81-2246
Toll-Free:	
Address: Puma-Way 1, Herzogenaurach, 91074 Germany	

GROWTH PLANS/SPECIAL FEATURES:

PUMA AG Rudolph Dassler Sport (PUMA) is an international athletic apparel, casual apparel and accessories company based in Germany. It develops and markets footwear, t-shirts, shorts, pants, jackets, caps, swimwear, socks and head- and wristbands as well as a variety of athletic equipment. Products are distributed in more than 80 countries through sporting goods stores, department stores and 80 PUMA sports boutiques located around the world. The firm designs products for multiple sports, including running, soccer, football, tennis, baseball, cricket and motocross. The company's corporate development currently focuses on heavy investment in research and development, marketing and retail operations. In addition, the company is implementing a web-based supply chain management system to increase efficiency. The company structure consists of two divisions: vertical focus and horizontal focus. The vertical focus segment, consisting of its German headquarters as well as core offices in the U.S. and Hong Kong, concentrates on product supply, branding, growth, structure, and culture. The horizontal focus segment, based out of various PUMA locations around the world, oversees PUMA distributors, licensees and several subsidiaries. The firm relies on celebrity endorsement as well as high-profile advertising campaigns to fulfill its marketing strategies. The company provides apparel to the national soccer team of Cameroon, Belgium's Club Brugge, tennis star Serena Williams, baseball player Johnny Damon, motocross medalist Travis Pastrana and a variety of teams playing in the World Athletics Championships for the Jamaican Federation. PUMA brands include PUMA + Alexander McQueen, Mihara, Rudolf Dassler Schuhfabrik, PUMA – The Black Label and Tretorn. In January 2009, the firm announced it has signed an agreement to acquired Brandon Company AB, a corporate merchandising firm. In December 2008, PUMA announced plans to acquire the majority holding of Dobotex. In February 2008, the firm acquired the majority share of Hussein Chalayan, a fashion line based in London.

FINANCIALS: **Sales and profits are in thousands of dollars—add 000 to get the full amount. 2008 Note: Financial information for 2008 was not available for all companies at press time.**

2008 Sales: $3,333,260	2008 Profits: $317,420	**U.S. Stock Ticker:**
2007 Sales: $3,134,250	2007 Profits: $355,220	**Int'l Ticker: PUM** Int'l Exchange: Frankfurt-Euronext
2006 Sales: $3,150,325	2006 Profits: $349,980	Employees: 6,381
2005 Sales: $2,105,100	2005 Profits: $338,500	Fiscal Year Ends: 12/31
2004 Sales: $2,087,300	2004 Profits: $351,000	Parent Company:

SALARIES/BENEFITS:

Pension Plan:	ESOP Stock Plan:	Profit Sharing:	Top Exec. Salary: $	Bonus: $
Savings Plan:	Stock Purch. Plan:		Second Exec. Salary: $	Bonus: $

OTHER THOUGHTS:

Apparent Women Officers or Directors: 1
Hot Spot for Advancement for Women/Minorities:

LOCATIONS: ("Y" = Yes)

West:	Southwest:	Midwest:	Southeast:	Northeast:	International:
				Y	Y

QUIKSILVER INC

www.quiksilverinc.com

Industry Group Code: 315000A **Ranks within this company's industry group:** Sales: 1 Profits: 6

Sports:		Services:		Media:		Sales:		Facilities:		Other:	
Leagues/Associations:		Food & Beverage:		TV:		Marketing:		Stadiums:		Gambling:	
Teams:		Agents:		Radio:		Ads:		Fitness Clubs:		Apparel:	Y
Nonprofits:		Other:		Internet:		Tickets:		Golf Courses:		Equipment:	Y
Other:				Print:		Retail:	Y	Ski Resorts:		Shoes:	
				Software:		Other:		Other:		Other:	

TYPES OF BUSINESS:

Sports Apparel & Equipment
Snow & Surf Apparel & Equipment
Accessories
Swimwear
Retail Stores

BRANDS/DIVISIONS/AFFILIATES:

Boardriders Club
Roxy
Look
DC
Roxy Girl
Dynastar
Lange
Kerma

CONTACTS: *Note: Officers with more than one job title may be intentionally listed here more than once.*

Robert B. McKnight, Jr., CEO
Robert B. McKnight, Jr., Pres.
Joseph Scirocco, CFO/Exec. VP
Charles S. Exon, Chief Admin. Officer
Charles S. Exon, General Counsel/Corp. Sec.
Craig Stevenson, Pres., Quiksilver America
Robert B. McKnight, Jr., Chmn.
Pierre Agnes, Pres., Quicksilver Europe

Phone: 714-889-2200	**Fax:** 714-889-3700
Toll-Free:	
Address: 15202 Graham St., Huntington Beach, CA 92649 US	

GROWTH PLANS/SPECIAL FEATURES:

Quiksilver, Inc. is a globally diversified company that designs, produces, retails and distributes branded apparel, wintersports equipment, footwear, accessories and related products. It operates in three segments: the Americas, which includes the U.S. and Canada; Europe, which includes primarily countries located in Western Europe; and Asia/Pacific, which includes Australia, Japan, New Zealand and Indonesia. The company's brands are focused on different sports within the outdoor market. Quiksilver and Roxy are rooted in the sport of surfing and are leading brands representing the boardriding lifestyle, which includes not only surfing, but also skateboarding and snowboarding. Quiksilver has grown to include shirts, walkshorts, t-shirts, pants, jackets, fleece, pants, snowboardwear, footwear, hats, backpacks, wetsuits, watches, eyewear and other accessories. In addition, the brand has expanded its target market to include boys, toddlers and infants. The Roxy brand includes sportswear, footwear, backpacks, snowboardwear, swimwear, backpacks, snowboard boots, skis, fragrance, beauty care, bedroom furnishings and other accessories for young women. The brand now contains the Teenie Wahine and Roxy Girl brands for girls and infants. DC's reputation is based on its technical shoes made for skateboarding. The firm also developed a portfolio of other brands also inspired by surfing, skateboarding and snowboarding. The wintersports brands include Dynastar, Look, Lange and Kerma, which are focused on equipment for alpine skiing but have extended into areas of wintersports, including snowboarding, freestyle skiing, Nordic skiing and technical outwear. Quiksilver's products are sold in over 90 countries in a wide range of distribution channels, including surf shops, ski shops, snowboard shops, the proprietary Boardriders Club shops, other specialty stores and select department stores. In November 2008, the company sold its Rossignol brand to Chartreuse & Mont Blanc.

FINANCIALS: **Sales and profits are in thousands of dollars—add 000 to get the full amount. 2008 Note: Financial information for 2008 was not available for all companies at press time.**

2008 Sales: $2,264,636	2008 Profits: $-226,265	**U.S. Stock Ticker: ZQK**
2007 Sales: $2,047,072	2007 Profits: $-121,119	**Int'l Ticker:** Int'l Exchange:
2006 Sales: $1,722,150	2006 Profits: $93,016	Employees: 8,400
2005 Sales: $1,780,869	2005 Profits: $107,120	Fiscal Year Ends: 10/31
2004 Sales: $1,266,939	2004 Profits: $81,369	Parent Company:

SALARIES/BENEFITS:

Pension Plan:	ESOP Stock Plan:	Profit Sharing:	Top Exec. Salary: $981,300	Bonus: $660,000
Savings Plan: Y	Stock Purch. Plan:		Second Exec. Salary: $562,500	Bonus: $585,000

OTHER THOUGHTS:

Apparent Women Officers or Directors:
Hot Spot for Advancement for Women/Minorities:

LOCATIONS: ("Y" = Yes)

West:	Southwest:	Midwest:	Southeast:	Northeast:	International:
Y					Y

RAWLINGS SPORTING GOODS COMPANY INC

www.rawlings.com

Industry Group Code: 339920 **Ranks within this company's industry group:** Sales: Profits:

Sports:		Services:		Media:		Sales:		Facilities:		Other:	
Leagues/Associations:		Food & Beverage:		TV:		Marketing:		Stadiums:		Gambling:	
Teams:		Agents:		Radio:		Ads:		Fitness Clubs:		Apparel:	Y
Nonprofits:		Other:		Internet:		Tickets:		Golf Courses:		Equipment:	Y
Other:				Print:		Retail:		Ski Resorts:		Shoes:	
				Software:		Other:		Other:		Other:	

TYPES OF BUSINESS:

Sporting Goods & Equipment
Baseballs, Softballs & Helmets
Footballs
Basketballs
Protective Gear

BRANDS/DIVISIONS/AFFILIATES:

Jarden Corp.
Minor League Baseball
Major League Baseball (MLB)
NJCAA
NAIA Men & Woman's League Championships

CONTACTS:

Note: Officers with more than one job title may be intentionally listed here more than once.

Robert M. Parish, Pres.
J. Michael Thompson, Sr. VP-Sales & Mktg.
Mark Malone, VP-Finance

Phone: 314-819-2800 **Fax:** 314-819-2988
Toll-Free: 800-729-5464
Address: 510 Maryville University Dr., Ste. 110, St. Louis, MO 63141 US

GROWTH PLANS/SPECIAL FEATURES:

Rawlings Sporting Goods Company, Inc., a subsidiary of Jarden Corporation, is a leading manufacturer, marketer and distributor of equipment and protective gear for baseball, softball, football, basketball and other sports throughout the U.S. Rawlings is the official supplier of baseballs and helmets to Major League Baseball, and the official supplier of baseballs to Minor League Baseball, NAIA Men & Woman's League Championships and the NCAA baseball championships. Rawlings primary offerings are geared toward baseball, football and baseball but the company also offers a more limited selection of merchandise for volleyball and soccer. The firms baseball products include gloves; composite and aluminum bats; wood bats; helmets; batting gloves; balls; bags; apparel; and protective gear such as chest protectors. Basketball products offered by Rawlings include approximately 13 different balls; various types of apparel; and accessories such as ball bags, pumps, team equipment bags and advisory staff briefcases. Rawlings is the official basketball supplier for the NAIA and NJCAA championships. The company's football products include a variety of footballs; gloves; apparel; protective gear such as advanced impact management systems, neck rolls and various protective pads; and accessories including kicking tees; briefcases, needles and pumps. The company also sells stock and custom uniforms for baseball, basketball and football. The company's products are manufactured primarily in Asia and Costa Rica and are sold through mass merchandisers, sporting goods retailers and online. Rawlings licenses its name for a wide range of merchandise, including sports apparel, shoes, sporting equipment, eyewear, books and toys.

Employees of Rawlings Sporting Goods are offered medical, dental and vision coverage; health and dependent care accounts; a fitness center membership; life insurance; adoption assistance; a 401(k) plan); an employee stock purchase plan at a 15% discount; training and development programs; and an employee discount purchase program.

FINANCIALS:

Sales and profits are in thousands of dollars—add 000 to get the full amount. 2008 Note: Financial information for 2008 was not available for all companies at press time.

2008 Sales: $
2007 Sales: $156,100
2006 Sales: $
2005 Sales: $
2004 Sales: $

2008 Profits: $
2007 Profits: $
2006 Profits: $
2005 Profits: $
2004 Profits: $

U.S. Stock Ticker: Subsidiary
Int'l Ticker: Int'l Exchange:
Employees: 1,500
Fiscal Year Ends: 12/31
Parent Company: JARDEN CORPORATION

SALARIES/BENEFITS:

Pension Plan: ESOP Stock Plan: Profit Sharing: Top Exec. Salary: $ Bonus: $
Savings Plan: Y Stock Purch. Plan: Second Exec. Salary: $ Bonus: $

OTHER THOUGHTS:

Apparent Women Officers or Directors:
Hot Spot for Advancement for Women/Minorities:

LOCATIONS: ("Y" = Yes)

West:	Southwest:	Midwest:	Southeast:	Northeast:	International:
Y		Y	Y	Y	

REAL SALT LAKE

real.saltlake.mlsnet.com

Industry Group Code: 711211D **Ranks within this company's industry group:** Sales: Profits:

Sports:		Services:		Media:		Sales:		Facilities:		Other:	
Leagues/Associations:		Food & Beverage:		TV:		Marketing:		Stadiums:	Y	Gambling:	
Teams:	Y	Agents:		Radio:		Ads:		Fitness Clubs:		Apparel:	
Nonprofits:		Other:		Internet:		Tickets:		Golf Courses:		Equipment:	
Other:				Print:		Retail:		Ski Resorts:		Shoes:	
				Software:		Other:		Other:		Other:	

TYPES OF BUSINESS:

Major League Soccer Team

BRANDS/DIVISIONS/AFFILIATES:

Major League Soccer (MLS)
MLS Western Conference
University of Utah
Rice-Eccles Stadium
Real Salt Lake Stadium
Real Madrid

CONTACTS: *Note: Officers with more than one job title may be intentionally listed here more than once.*

Dean L. Howes, CEO
Bill Manning, Pres.
Gary Reimer, CFO/Sr. VP
Davy Ratchford, Dir.-Mktg. & Comm.
Lynne Heygster, Dir.-Human Resources & Acct.
Brett Fischer, Dir.-Merch.
John Kimball, VP-Bus. Oper.
Trey Fitz-Gerald, Sr. Dir.-Public Rel. & Broadcasting
Nikki Reimer, Controller
Garth Lagerwey, Gen. Mgr./VP
David W. Checketts, Owner
Jason Kreis, Head Coach
Kai Murray, Sr. Mgr.-Fan Rel.

Phone: 801-924-8585	**Fax:** 801-933-4713
Toll-Free: 866-976-2237	
Address: 515 S. 700 E., Ste. 2R, Salt Lake City, UT 84102 US	

GROWTH PLANS/SPECIAL FEATURES:

Real Salt Lake (RSL) is one of Major League Soccer's (MLS) newest expansion teams, playing in the MLS Western Conference. The team was formed in 2004 and commenced playing in April 2005. RLS is Utah's second professional sports organization. MLS chose Salt Lake City, Utah as a base for an expansion team because of the city's demographics, including its strong international connections, rapidly growing Hispanic population and sizeable Eastern European communities. Another factor in MLS' choice of Salt Lake City was its role in hosting the 2002 Olympic Games, which established the city as a world-class center for sports and athletic events. The club has fielded former greats including midfielder/forward Clint Mathis and forward Jason Kreis, now its head coach. RLS has an agreement with Real Madrid that includes a biennial friendly match between the teams in Salt Lake City; annual training for RSL at the Real Madrid practice facility in Spain; and the creation of a $25-million elite youth academy in Salt Lake City for which the teams will split the cost, which will train up to 200 players ages 12-18 and will include academic facilities and dormitory housing. In October 2008, RSL completed construction of its $115 million Rio Tinto Stadium, located in Sandy, a suburban city in the Salt Lake Valley.

FINANCIALS: **Sales and profits are in thousands of dollars—add 000 to get the full amount. 2008 Note: Financial information for 2008 was not available for all companies at press time.**

2008 Sales: $	2008 Profits: $	**U.S. Stock Ticker: Private**
2007 Sales: $	2007 Profits: $	**Int'l Ticker:** Int'l Exchange:
2006 Sales: $	2006 Profits: $	Employees:
2005 Sales: $	2005 Profits: $	Fiscal Year Ends:
2004 Sales: $	2004 Profits: $	Parent Company:

SALARIES/BENEFITS:

Pension Plan:	ESOP Stock Plan:	Profit Sharing:	Top Exec. Salary: $	Bonus: $
Savings Plan:	Stock Purch. Plan:		Second Exec. Salary: $	Bonus: $

OTHER THOUGHTS:

Apparent Women Officers or Directors: 17
Hot Spot for Advancement for Women/Minorities: Y

LOCATIONS: ("Y" = Yes)

West:	Southwest:	Midwest:	Southeast:	Northeast:	International:
Y					

RECREATIONAL EQUIPMENT INC (REI)

www.rei.com

Industry Group Code: 451110 **Ranks within this company's industry group:** Sales: 4 Profits: 4

Sports:		Services:		Media:		Sales:		Facilities:		Other:	
Leagues/Associations:		Food & Beverage:		TV:		Marketing:		Stadiums:		Gambling:	
Teams:		Agents:		Radio:		Ads:		Fitness Clubs:		Apparel:	Y
Nonprofits:		Other:	Y	Internet:		Tickets:		Golf Courses:		Equipment:	Y
Other:				Print:		Retail:	Y	Ski Resorts:		Shoes:	Y
				Software:		Other:		Other:		Other:	

TYPES OF BUSINESS:

Outdoor Gear & Clothing, Retail
Sporting Equipment Retail & Rental
Adventure Travel Services
Catalog & Online Sales

BRANDS/DIVISIONS/AFFILIATES:

REI
REI Adventures
REI-Outlet.com
REI.com

CONTACTS: *Note: Officers with more than one job title may be intentionally listed here more than once.*

Sally Jewell, CEO
Sally Jewel, Pres.
Brad Johnson, CFO/Sr. VP
Matt Hyde, Exec. VP-Mktg.
Michelle Clements, VP-Human Resources
Bill Baumann, VP-IT
Matt Hyde, Exec. VP-Merch.
Brad Johnson, Chief Admin. Officer
Catherine Walker, General Counsel/Corp. Sec./Sr. VP-Legal
Brian Umacht, Sr. VP-Sales, Svc., Store Dev. & Logistics
Brad Brown, VP-Web Strategy & E-commerce
Michael Collins, VP-Public Affairs
Tim Spangler, Regional VP-Retail Stores-Western Region
Lee Fromson, VP-REI Gear & Apparel
Janet Hopkins, Regional VP-Retail Stores, Midwest & East Region
Doug Walker, Chmn.
David Presley, VP-Logistics & Dist.

Phone: 253-395-3780 **Fax:** 253-891-2523
Toll-Free: 800-426-4840
Address: 6750 S. 228th St., Kent, WA 98032 US

GROWTH PLANS/SPECIAL FEATURES:

Recreational Equipment, Inc. (REI) is one of the largest consumer cooperatives in the U.S. The firm offers quality gear, clothing and footwear selected for performance and durability in outdoor recreation, including hiking, climbing, camping, bicycling, paddling and winter sports. Today, REI has more than 3 million active members served by over 100 retail stores in 27 states. Stores include a variety of facilities for testing equipment, including bike test trails, climbing pinnacles and camp stove demonstration tables. The firm also operates several Internet sites: REI.com and REI-Outlet.com; it also operates an adventure travel company, REI Adventures. While anyone may shop at the stores, customers who pay a small fee to become members receive special discounts and a share in the company's profits through an annual patronage refund based on their purchases. REI's e-commerce site is one of the biggest outdoor online stores, offering a comprehensive library of product information, expert gear advice and outdoor recreation information. REI-Outlet.com offers brand-name closeouts, overstocks and seconds at discounts of 30% to 60%. REI Adventures has been operating small group tours throughout the world for more than 20 years, avoiding standard tourist routes and emphasizing outdoor activities. Each year, REI Adventures plans more than 90 domestic and international bicycling, trekking, kayaking, hiking, camping and mountaineering adventures. The firm invests millions of dollars on an annual basis to build trails, clean up the environment and teach children outdoor ethics. In 2008, new REI locations opened in Michigan, Colorado, Illinois, California, Nevada and Texas.

REI has been selected as one of the 100 best companies to work for by Fortune Magazine for 12 years in a row. REI offers employees health, life and disability plans, tuition reimbursement, adoption and relocation assistance, an employee discount program and a public transit subsidy.

FINANCIALS: Sales and profits are in thousands of dollars—add 000 to get the full amount. 2008 Note: Financial information for 2008 was not available for all companies at press time.

2008 Sales: $1,434,569	2008 Profits: $14,465	**U.S. Stock Ticker: Private**
2007 Sales: $1,342,024	2007 Profits: $41,427	**Int'l Ticker:** Int'l Exchange:
2006 Sales: $1,181,531	2006 Profits: $40,273	Employees: 9,780
2005 Sales: $1,022,326	2005 Profits: $32,726	Fiscal Year Ends: 12/31
2004 Sales: $887,809	2004 Profits: $25,315	Parent Company:

SALARIES/BENEFITS:

Pension Plan: Y	ESOP Stock Plan:	Profit Sharing: Y	Top Exec. Salary: $	Bonus: $
Savings Plan:	Stock Purch. Plan:		Second Exec. Salary: $	Bonus: $

OTHER THOUGHTS:

Apparent Women Officers or Directors: 10
Hot Spot for Advancement for Women/Minorities: Y

LOCATIONS: ("Y" = Yes)

West:	Southwest:	Midwest:	Southeast:	Northeast:	International:
Y	Y	Y	Y	Y	

REEBOK CCM HOCKEY

www.thehockeycompany.com

Industry Group Code: 339920 **Ranks within this company's industry group:** Sales: Profits:

Sports:		Services:		Media:		Sales:		Facilities:		Other:	
Leagues/Associations:		Food & Beverage:		TV:		Marketing:		Stadiums:		Gambling:	
Teams:		Agents:		Radio:		Ads:		Fitness Clubs:		Apparel:	Y
Nonprofits:		Other:		Internet:		Tickets:		Golf Courses:		Equipment:	Y
Other:				Print:		Retail:		Ski Resorts:		Shoes:	
				Software:		Other:		Other:		Other:	

TYPES OF BUSINESS:

Hockey Equipment & Apparel
NHL Replica Jerseys

BRANDS/DIVISIONS/AFFILIATES:

Adidas AG
Reebok International Ltd.
JOFA
CCM
Reebok
KOHO

CONTACTS:

Note: Officers with more than one job title may be intentionally listed here more than once.

Robert A. Desrosiers, CFO
Michel Benoit, VP-Global Mktg.
Dany Paradis, VP-Human Resources
Robert A. Desrosiers, VP-Admin.
Robert A. Desrosiers, VP-Finance
Len Rhodes, Gen. Mgr.

Phone: 514-461-8000 **Fax:**
Toll-Free: 800-451-4600
Address: 3400 Raymond Lasnier, Saint-Laurent, QC H4R 3L3 Canada

GROWTH PLANS/SPECIAL FEATURES:

Reebok-CCM Hockey is a division of Reebok International Ltd., which is itself a subsidiary of Adidas AG. It is headquartered in Montreal, Canada with operations in Europe and North America. The company is one of the world's largest designer, manufacturer and marketer of hockey equipment such as skates, sticks, helmets, protective equipment products and related apparel. Reebok-CCM Hockey brings together four global hockey brand names (Reebok, CCM, JOFA and KOHO), and it holds the exclusive license to produce and sell replica jerseys for the National Hockey League. Reebok-CCM also serves as the sole supplier of on-ice game jerseys to NHL teams. In addition to its NHL license, the firm maintains exclusive agreements with the Canadian Hockey League, the American Hockey League and several NCAA and national teams. JOFA protective equipment is used by approximately 99% of NHL professional hockey players. Reebok-CCM Hockey distributes its products in 45 countries through diverse retail channels, including specialty shops and sporting goods retailers.

FINANCIALS:

Sales and profits are in thousands of dollars—add 000 to get the full amount. 2008 Note: Financial information for 2008 was not available for all companies at press time.

2008 Sales: $	2008 Profits: $	**U.S. Stock Ticker: Subsidiary**
2007 Sales: $190,500	2007 Profits: $	**Int'l Ticker:** Int'l Exchange:
2006 Sales: $	2006 Profits: $	Employees: 1,250
2005 Sales: $	2005 Profits: $	Fiscal Year Ends: 12/31
2004 Sales: $	2004 Profits: $	Parent Company: ADIDAS AG

SALARIES/BENEFITS:

Pension Plan:	ESOP Stock Plan:	Profit Sharing:	Top Exec. Salary: $	Bonus: $
Savings Plan:	Stock Purch. Plan:		Second Exec. Salary: $	Bonus: $

OTHER THOUGHTS:

Apparent Women Officers or Directors:
Hot Spot for Advancement for Women/Minorities:

LOCATIONS: ("Y" = Yes)

West:	Southwest:	Midwest:	Southeast:	Northeast:	International:
				Y	Y

REEBOK INTERNATIONAL LTD

www.reebok.com

Industry Group Code: 316219 **Ranks within this company's industry group:** Sales: Profits:

Sports:		Services:		Media:		Sales:		Facilities:		Other:	
Leagues/Associations:		Food & Beverage:		TV:		Marketing:		Stadiums:		Gambling:	
Teams:		Agents:		Radio:		Ads:		Fitness Clubs:		Apparel:	Y
Nonprofits:		Other:		Internet:		Tickets:		Golf Courses:		Equipment:	
Other:				Print:		Retail:	Y	Ski Resorts:		Shoes:	Y
				Software:		Other:		Other:		Other:	

TYPES OF BUSINESS:

Athletic Shoes
Apparel
Accessories
Athletic Equipment
Online Sales
Retail Stores

BRANDS/DIVISIONS/AFFILIATES:

Adidas AG
CCM
Jofa
Koho
Reebok CCM Hockey

CONTACTS:

Note: Officers with more than one job title may be intentionally listed here more than once.

Herbert Hainer, CEO
Uli Becker, Pres.
Glenn Bennett, Dir.-Global Oper.
Robin J. Stalker, Dir.-Finance
Erich Stamminger, Pres./CEO-Adidas Brand
Hans Friderichs, Chmn.

Phone: 781-401-5000 **Fax:** 781-401-7402
Toll-Free:
Address: 1895 J.W. Foster Blvd., Canton, MA 02021 US

GROWTH PLANS/SPECIAL FEATURES:

Reebok International, Ltd., a subsidiary of Adidas AG, operates under the brand names Reebok, CCM, Jofa and Koho Brands. The company operates approximately 200 stores across the U.S. and an online store. Reebok has regional offices in Amsterdam, Montreal, Hong Kong and Mexico City. The firm's online store features a shopping guide, which offers sizing and product information, as well as a comprehensive portfolio of products available for direct consumer purchase. The firm offers apparel, footwear and special collections for men, women and children, as well as accessories such as socks and caps. Reebok also markets and distributes athletic equipment, including treadmills, heart rate monitors, recumbent bikes, upright bikes and elliptical machines. The company has a number of licensing agreements with several professional sporting groups and teams, including the National Football League (NFL), National Hockey League (NHL) and the Women's National Basketball Association (WNBA). Through these partnerships, the firm provides specialty equipment to professional teams and also distributes jerseys and sporting gear with professional logos directly to consumers. Reebok continues to endorse many professional athletes and celebrities, including Vince Young of the Tennessee Titans and actress Scarlett Johansson.

FINANCIALS:

Sales and profits are in thousands of dollars—add 000 to get the full amount. 2008 Note: Financial information for 2008 was not available for all companies at press time.

2008 Sales: $
2007 Sales: $310,800
2006 Sales: $300,000
2005 Sales: $300,000
2004 Sales: $

2008 Profits: $
2007 Profits: $
2006 Profits: $
2005 Profits: $
2004 Profits: $

U.S. Stock Ticker: Subsidiary
Int'l Ticker: Int'l Exchange:
Employees: 9,102
Fiscal Year Ends: 12/31
Parent Company: ADIDAS AG

SALARIES/BENEFITS:

Pension Plan: ESOP Stock Plan: Profit Sharing: Top Exec. Salary: $1,271,154 Bonus: $1,683,898
Savings Plan: Stock Purch. Plan: Second Exec. Salary: $1,210,000 Bonus: $

OTHER THOUGHTS:

Apparent Women Officers or Directors:
Hot Spot for Advancement for Women/Minorities:

LOCATIONS: ("Y" = Yes)

West:	Southwest:	Midwest:	Southeast:	Northeast:	International:
Y	Y	Y	Y	Y	Y

ROGERS COMMUNICATIONS INC

www.rogers.com

Industry Group Code: 513220 **Ranks within this company's industry group:** Sales: 3 Profits: 1

Sports:		Services:		Media:		Sales:		Facilities:		Other:	
Leagues/Associations:		Food & Beverage:		TV:	Y	Marketing:		Stadiums:	Y	Gambling:	
Teams:	Y	Agents:		Radio:	Y	Ads:		Fitness Clubs:		Apparel:	
Nonprofits:		Other:		Internet:	Y	Tickets:		Golf Courses:		Equipment:	
Other:				Print:		Retail:		Ski Resorts:		Shoes:	
				Software:		Other:		Other:		Other:	

TYPES OF BUSINESS:

Cable TV Service
Internet Service Provider
Cellular Phone Service
Video Stores
Television Broadcasting
Magazine Publishing
Radio Stations
Telephone Service

BRANDS/DIVISIONS/AFFILIATES:

Rogers Telecom Holdings Inc
Rogers Wireless Communications Inc
Rogers Cable Inc
Toronto Blue Jays
Rogers Centre
Rogers Video
Aurora Cable TV Limited
Outdoor Life Network

CONTACTS: *Note: Officers with more than one job title may be intentionally listed here more than once.*

Nadir Mohamed, CEO
Nadir Mohamed, Pres.
William W. Linton, CFO/Sr. VP-Finance
Kevin P. Pennington, Chief Human Resources Officer/Sr. VP
Jerry Brace, Sr. VP-IT
Robert F. Berner, CTO/VP
David P. Miller, General Counsel/Sr. VP/Sec.
Melinda M. Rogers, Sr. VP-Strategy & Dev.
Alan D. Horn, Pres./CEO-Rogers Telecommunications, Ltd.
Anthony P. Viner, Sr. VP-Media/Pres., Rogers Media, Inc.
Robert Bruce, Sr. VP-Comm. Group/Pres., Rogers Wireless, Inc.
Alan D. Horn, Chmn.

Phone: 416-935-3525 **Fax:** 416-935-3597
Toll-Free:
Address: 333 Bloor St. E., 10th Fl., Toronto, ON M4W 1G9 Canada

GROWTH PLANS/SPECIAL FEATURES:

Rogers Communications, Inc. is a Canadian company engaged in a wide variety of television, broadband, cellular telephone and publishing businesses. Rogers conducts business via three subsidiaries: Rogers Wireless, Inc.; Rogers Cable Communications, Inc.; and Rogers Media, Inc. Rogers Wireless is one of Canada's largest wireless voice and data communications service providers, serving nearly 8 million customers. The company provides coverage to approximately 94% of Canada's population. Rogers Cable is one of Canada's largest cable television service providers, with a territory covering approximately 3.5 million homes in Ontario, New Brunswick, Newfoundland and Labrador. Its services include cable television, digital cable, high-definition television, video-on-demand and high-speed Internet. The cable division also operates approximately 450 retail stores, some selling wireless products and some operating under the Rogers Video brand, Canada's second largest chain of video stores. Rogers Media is composed of Rogers Broadcasting and Rogers Publishing. Rogers Broadcasting operates 52 radio stations throughout Canada, as well as multiple television stations, including The Shopping Channel and The Biography Channel Canada. In addition, the firm owns the Toronto Blue Jays baseball team, the Rogers Centre stadium (home to the Blue Jays and the Toronto Argonauts football team) and a 50% stake in Dome Productions, a mobile production and distribution joint venture. Rogers Publishing is one of Canada's largest magazine publishers, producing approximately 70 consumer magazines and trade publications. In April 2008, Rogers acquired Vancouver-area multicultural television station channel m from Multivan Broadcast Corporation. In June 2008, the firm acquired Aurora Cable TV Limited, and in July 2008 it acquired the remaining two-thirds of Outdoor Life Network (OLN) which it did not already own.

Rogers offers its employees a pension plan; medical and dental coverage; education assistance; service recognition awards; family assistance programs; and product discounts.

FINANCIALS: **Sales and profits are in thousands of dollars—add 000 to get the full amount. 2008 Note: Financial information for 2008 was not available for all companies at press time.**

2008 Sales: $10,330,500	2008 Profits: $3,700,210	**U.S. Stock Ticker: RCI**
2007 Sales: $10,200,000	2007 Profits: $640,000	**Int'l Ticker: RCI.B** Int'l Exchange: Toronto-TSX
2006 Sales: $7,583,888	2006 Profits: $669,318	Employees: 22,500
2005 Sales: $6,419,688	2005 Profits: $-268,207	Fiscal Year Ends: 12/31
2004 Sales: $4,656,529	2004 Profits: $-224,700	Parent Company:

SALARIES/BENEFITS:

Pension Plan: Y	ESOP Stock Plan:	Profit Sharing:	Top Exec. Salary: $1,313,152	Bonus: $1,969,729
Savings Plan:	Stock Purch. Plan:		Second Exec. Salary: $704,308	Bonus: $882,797

OTHER THOUGHTS:

Apparent Women Officers or Directors: 4
Hot Spot for Advancement for Women/Minorities: Y

LOCATIONS: ("Y" = Yes)

West:	Southwest:	Midwest:	Southeast:	Northeast:	International:
					Y

Note: Financial information, benefits and other data can change quickly and may vary from those stated here.

ROUSH FENWAY RACING

www.roushfenway.com

Industry Group Code: 711211G **Ranks within this company's industry group:** Sales: 2 Profits: 2

Sports:		Services:		Media:		Sales:		Facilities:		Other:	
Leagues/Associations:		Food & Beverage:		TV:		Marketing:		Stadiums:		Gambling:	
Teams:	Y	Agents:		Radio:		Ads:		Fitness Clubs:		Apparel:	
Nonprofits:		Other:		Internet:		Tickets:		Golf Courses:		Equipment:	
Other:				Print:		Retail:		Ski Resorts:		Shoes:	
				Software:		Other:		Other:		Other:	

TYPES OF BUSINESS:

NASCAR Racing Teams

BRANDS/DIVISIONS/AFFILIATES:

Roush Industries Inc
Fenway Sports Group
Team Caliber

CONTACTS:

Note: Officers with more than one job title may be intentionally listed here more than once.

Jack Roush, CEO
Geoff Smith, Pres.
Robin Johnson, Exec. VP-Bus. Dev.
Sam Belnavis, Chief Diversity Officer
Jon Sands, Sr. VP-Bus. Dev.
Anne Ewing, Dir.-Bus. Dev.

Phone: 704-720-4600 **Fax:** 704-720-4605
Toll-Free:
Address: 4600 Roush Place, Concord, NC 28027 US

GROWTH PLANS/SPECIAL FEATURES:

Roush Fenway Racing (RFR), formerly Roush Racing, a subsidiary of Roush Industries, Inc., is a racing team that competes in NASCAR racing. In recent years, RFR sold a 50% interest in the company to the Fenway Sports Group (FSG), a subsidiary of New England Sports Ventures. The teams are managed by racing legend Jack Roush, who also founded Roush Industries, which primarily provides engineering, management and prototype services to the transportation industry. The company currently has eight drivers and manages five Sprint Cup Series (formerly Nextel Cup) teams, seven Nationwide Series (formerly Busch Series) teams, three Craftsman Truck Series teams and one ARCA RE/MAX Series team. The Sprint Cup team drivers include Carl Edwards, who claimed the 2007 Nationwide Series Championship; Greg Biffle; Matt Kenseth; Jamie McMurray; and David Ragan. All of these drivers also race in the Nationwide Series. Additional racers in the Nationwide Series include Colin Braun and Erik Darnell, who race in the Craftsman Truck Series. The team races exclusively with Ford automobiles, using the Ford Fusion in the Sprint Cup and Nationwide Series and the Ford F-150 in the Craftsman Truck Series. Headquartered in Concord, North Carolina, the race shops, where team members prepare for their races, are located in Concord and Mooreseville, NC. RFR also operates two Roush Fenway Racing Museums, one in the Charlotte, North Carolina area and one in Livonia, Michigan. The firm manages roushfenway.com, which includes news, race previews and recaps, photos and in-depth corporate information. Some of the teams' key sponsors include AAA; Coca Cola; Citi; DeWalt Racing; and Crown Royal.

FINANCIALS:

Sales and profits are in thousands of dollars—add 000 to get the full amount. 2008 Note: Financial information for 2008 was not available for all companies at press time.

2008 Sales: $173,000	2008 Profits: $21,300	**U.S. Stock Ticker: Subsidiary**
2007 Sales: $189,000	2007 Profits: $39,100	**Int'l Ticker:** Int'l Exchange:
2006 Sales: $	2006 Profits: $	Employees:
2005 Sales: $108,000	2005 Profits: $	Fiscal Year Ends:
2004 Sales: $	2004 Profits: $	Parent Company: ROUSH INDUSTRIES INC

SALARIES/BENEFITS:

Pension Plan:	ESOP Stock Plan:	Profit Sharing:	Top Exec. Salary: $	Bonus: $
Savings Plan:	Stock Purch. Plan:		Second Exec. Salary: $	Bonus: $

OTHER THOUGHTS:

Apparent Women Officers or Directors: 1
Hot Spot for Advancement for Women/Minorities:

LOCATIONS: ("Y" = Yes)

West:	Southwest:	Midwest:	Southeast:	Northeast:	International:
		Y		Y	

RUSSELL CORP

www.russellcorp.com

Industry Group Code: 315000A **Ranks within this company's industry group:** Sales: Profits:

Sports:		Services:		Media:		Sales:		Facilities:		Other:	
Leagues/Associations:		Food & Beverage:		TV:		Marketing:		Stadiums:		Gambling:	
Teams:		Agents:		Radio:		Ads:		Fitness Clubs:		Apparel:	Y
Nonprofits:		Other:		Internet:		Tickets:		Golf Courses:		Equipment:	Y
Other:				Print:		Retail:		Ski Resorts:		Shoes:	Y
				Software:		Other:		Other:		Other:	

TYPES OF BUSINESS:

Athletic Apparel & Equipment
Athletic Uniforms

BRANDS/DIVISIONS/AFFILIATES:

Spalding
Russell Athletic
Mossy Oak Apparel
JERZEES
Moving Comfort
Russell Artwear
Brooks Sports
Berkshire Hathaway, Inc.

CONTACTS: *Note: Officers with more than one job title may be intentionally listed here more than once.*

John B. Holland, CEO
Robert D. Koney, Jr., CFO/Sr. VP
Edsel W. Flowers, Sr. VP-Human Resources
Robert P. Keefe, CIO/Sr. VP
Floyd G. Hoffman, General Counsel/Corp. Sec.
Floyd G. Hoffman, Sr. VP-Corp. Dev.
Nancy N. Young, VP-Comm.
Victoria W. Beck, Corp. Controller/VP
Scott H. Creelman, VP/CEO-Spalding
James Weber, VP/CEO-Brooks Sports
John B. Holland, Chmn.

Phone: 678-742-8000 **Fax:** 678-742-8300
Toll-Free:
Address: 3330 Cumberland Blvd., Ste. 800, Atlanta, GA 30339 US

GROWTH PLANS/SPECIAL FEATURES:

Russell Corp., a Berkshire Hathaway company, is a leading branded athletic, active wear and outdoor gear company that markets athletic uniforms, apparel, footwear, sporting goods, athletic equipment and accessories for a wide variety of sports, outdoor and fitness activities. The firm's well-known brands include Russell Athletic, JERZEES, Brooks Sports, Mossy Oak, Cross Creek, Moving Comfort, Discus, Bike, Spalding, Dudley, Huffy and Sherrin. The company markets and manufactures a variety of apparel products, including fleece, t-shirts, casual shirts, jackets, athletic shorts, socks and camouflage attire for men, women, boys and girls. Russell is also a leading supplier of uniforms and related apparel to college, high school and other organized sports teams. The company is the largest provider of basketball equipment in the world, due in part to its eight-year global partnership with the National Basketball Association. Russell markets its products in the U.S., Canada and approximately 100 additional countries through mass merchandisers, sporting goods dealers, department and sports specialty stores, college stores, online retailers, mail-order houses, art wear distributors, screen printers and embroiderers. The company's largest customer is Wal-Mart, making up approximately 20% of annual sales. In January 2009, the company closed its fabric operations in Alexander City, Alabama. Also in January 2009, the company announced it will relocate to Bowling Green, Kentucky by the end of 2009.

FINANCIALS: **Sales and profits are in thousands of dollars—add 000 to get the full amount. 2008 Note: Financial information for 2008 was not available for all companies at press time.**

2008 Sales: $	2008 Profits: $	**U.S. Stock Ticker: Subsidiary**
2007 Sales: $	2007 Profits: $	**Int'l Ticker:** Int'l Exchange:
2006 Sales: $	2006 Profits: $	Employees: 14,400
2005 Sales: $1,434,605	2005 Profits: $34,430	Fiscal Year Ends: 12/31
2004 Sales: $1,298,252	2004 Profits: $47,936	Parent Company: BERKSHIRE HATHAWAY INC

SALARIES/BENEFITS:

Pension Plan:	ESOP Stock Plan:	Profit Sharing:	Top Exec. Salary: $845,600	Bonus: $
Savings Plan:	Stock Purch. Plan:		Second Exec. Salary: $343,834	Bonus: $71,099

OTHER THOUGHTS:

Apparent Women Officers or Directors: 2
Hot Spot for Advancement for Women/Minorities:

LOCATIONS: ("Y" = Yes)

West:	Southwest:	Midwest:	Southeast:	Northeast:	International:
Y		Y	Y	Y	Y

Note: Financial information, benefits and other data can change quickly and may vary from those stated here.

SACRAMENTO KINGS

www.nba.com/kings

Industry Group Code: 711211B **Ranks within this company's industry group:** Sales: 15 Profits: 15

Sports:		Services:		Media:		Sales:		Facilities:		Other:	
Leagues/Associations:		Food & Beverage:		TV:		Marketing:		Stadiums:	Y	Gambling:	
Teams:	Y	Agents:		Radio:		Ads:		Fitness Clubs:		Apparel:	
Nonprofits:		Other:		Internet:		Tickets:	Y	Golf Courses:		Equipment:	
Other:				Print:		Retail:	Y	Ski Resorts:		Shoes:	
				Software:		Other:		Other:		Other:	

TYPES OF BUSINESS:

Professional Basketball Team
Ticket Sales
Team Merchandise

BRANDS/DIVISIONS/AFFILIATES:

Maloof Sports and Entertainment
Arco Arena
Maloofs and You Foundation
Adrienne Maloof's Camp Kindness
Kings Women's Organization
Sacramento Monarchs

CONTACTS:

Note: Officers with more than one job title may be intentionally listed here more than once.

John Thomas, Pres.
Danette Leighton, VP-Mktg. & Brand Dev.
Donna Ruiz, VP-Human Resources
John Rinehart, Sr. VP- Bus. Oper.
Mitch Germann, VP-Bus. Comm.
Darrin May, Exec. Dir.-Media Rel.
Ruth Hill, Dir.-Finance
Geoff Petrie, Pres., Basketball Oper.
Kenny Natt, Head Coach
Ben Milsom, VP-Ticket Sales
Mark Stone, Sr. VP-Arena Svcs.

Phone: 916-928-0000 **Fax:** 916-928-8109
Toll-Free:
Address: Arco Arena, 1 Sports Pkwy., Sacramento, CA 95834 US

GROWTH PLANS/SPECIAL FEATURES:

The Sacramento Kings franchise is a professional basketball team playing in the National Basketball Association (NBA) and based in Sacramento, California. The team was founded in 1945 in Rochester, New York. The Kings moved to Sacramento in 1985. The team did very poorly in the NBA until the 1998-99 season, when it acquired Jason Williams, Vlade Divac, Chris Webber and Peja Stojakovic. These moves were attributed to general manager Geoff Petrie, a several time-winner of the NBA Executive of the Year award. This improvement of performance coincided with team's acquisition by the Maloof family. The team is now owned and operated by Maloof Sports and Entertainment. The Maloof family also owns and operates The Palms hotel and casino in Las Vegas, Nevada, and the King's sister Women's National Basketball Association (WNBA) team, the Sacramento Monarchs. The Kings and the Monarchs play in ARCO Arena, which seats 17,317 spectators and is also owned by Maloof Sports and Entertainment. Forbes Magazine recently estimated the team to be worth approximately $350 million. In the 2008-09 season, the team's home attendance average was roughly 12,571 per game.

FINANCIALS:

Sales and profits are in thousands of dollars—add 000 to get the full amount. 2008 Note: Financial information for 2008 was not available for all companies at press time.

2008 Sales: $117,000
2007 Sales: $128,000
2006 Sales: $126,000
2005 Sales: $119,000
2004 Sales: $118,000

2008 Profits: $7,000
2007 Profits: $20,500
2006 Profits: $16,400
2005 Profits: $
2004 Profits: $

U.S. Stock Ticker: Subsidiary
Int'l Ticker: Int'l Exchange:
Employees:
Fiscal Year Ends: 6/30
Parent Company: MALOOF SPORTS AND ENTERTAINMENT

SALARIES/BENEFITS:

Pension Plan: ESOP Stock Plan: Profit Sharing: Top Exec. Salary: $ Bonus: $
Savings Plan: Stock Purch. Plan: Second Exec. Salary: $ Bonus: $

OTHER THOUGHTS:

Apparent Women Officers or Directors: 11
Hot Spot for Advancement for Women/Minorities: Y

LOCATIONS: ("Y" = Yes)

West:	Southwest:	Midwest:	Southeast:	Northeast:	International:
Y					

SACRAMENTO MONARCHS

www.wnba.com/monarchs

Industry Group Code: 711211E **Ranks within this company's industry group:** Sales: Profits:

Sports:		Services:		Media:		Sales:		Facilities:		Other:	
Leagues/Associations:		Food & Beverage:		TV:		Marketing:		Stadiums:	Y	Gambling:	
Teams:	Y	Agents:		Radio:		Ads:		Fitness Clubs:		Apparel:	
Nonprofits:		Other:		Internet:		Tickets:	Y	Golf Courses:		Equipment:	
Other:				Print:		Retail:		Ski Resorts:		Shoes:	
				Software:		Other:		Other:	Y	Other:	

TYPES OF BUSINESS:

Women's Professional Basketball Team

BRANDS/DIVISIONS/AFFILIATES:

ARCO Arena

CONTACTS:

Note: Officers with more than one job title may be intentionally listed here more than once.

John Thomas, Pres.
Danette Leighton, VP-Mktg. & Brand Dev./Bus. Oper.
Donna Ruiz, VP-Human Resources
John Rinehart, Sr. VP-Bus. Oper.
Tom Hunt, Sr. VP-Strategic Alliances
Mitch Germann, VP-Bus. Comm.
Ruth Hill, VP-Finance
Jenny Boucek, Head Coach
Mark Stone, Sr. VP-Arena Svcs.
Craig Amazeen, VP-Broadcasting Oper. & Prod.
Ben Milsom, VP-Ticket Sales

Phone: 916-928-0000	**Fax:** 916-928-0727
Toll-Free:	
Address: ARCO Arena, 1 Sports Pkwy., Sacramento, CA 95834 US	

GROWTH PLANS/SPECIAL FEATURES:

The Sacramento Monarchs were one of the eight original Women's National Basketball Association (WNBA) teams founded in 1997. The Monarchs play in the Western Conference of the WNBA along with the Los Angeles Sparks, Minnesota Lynx, Phoenix Mercury, Seattle Storm and San Antonio Silver Stars. The franchise is the sister team to the Sacramento Kings, a National Basketball Association (NBA) team. The name Monarch implies both a type of ruler, signaling the team's affiliation with the Kings, and a type of butterfly, which is reflected in the team's logo, a crowned butterfly. The team has made the playoffs every year since 1999, and won the WNBA Championship in 2005 with a victory over the Connecticut Suns, marking the first professional championship title brought to the city of Sacramento. The Monarchs have been coached by Jenny Boucek since 2006. Boucek previously played with the Cleveland Rockers during the WNBA's inaugural 1997 season. Prior to joining the Monarchs, she served as an assistant coach and scout for the Seattle Storm. Joe and Gavin Maloof own the team through their company, Maloof Sports & Entertainment, which also owns the Kings and the 17,000-seat ARCO Arena, the home court of both teams. Other Maloof companies own the Palms Casino Resort in Las Vegas, as well as other investments in the hotel, food service and transportation businesses. The ARCO Arena draws in over 2 million visitors who come to see the venue's 200 annual events, including concerts by artists including Paul McCartney, Prince and the Jonas Brothers; National Hockey League (NHL) and Arena Football sporting events; and the Ringling Bros. and Barnum & Bailey Circus. The Monarchs finished the 2008 season with 18 wins and 16 losses, entering the playoffs but losing in the first round to the San Antonio Silver Stars.

FINANCIALS:

Sales and profits are in thousands of dollars—add 000 to get the full amount. 2008 Note: Financial information for 2008 was not available for all companies at press time.

2008 Sales: $	2008 Profits: $	**U.S. Stock Ticker: Private**
2007 Sales: $	2007 Profits: $	**Int'l Ticker:** Int'l Exchange:
2006 Sales: $	2006 Profits: $	Employees:
2005 Sales: $	2005 Profits: $	Fiscal Year Ends: 6/30
2004 Sales: $	2004 Profits: $	Parent Company: MALOOF SPORTS & ENTERTAINMENT

SALARIES/BENEFITS:

Pension Plan:	ESOP Stock Plan:	Profit Sharing:	Top Exec. Salary: $	Bonus: $
Savings Plan:	Stock Purch. Plan:		Second Exec. Salary: $	Bonus: $

OTHER THOUGHTS:

Apparent Women Officers or Directors: 4
Hot Spot for Advancement for Women/Minorities: Y

LOCATIONS: ("Y" = Yes)

West:	Southwest:	Midwest:	Southeast:	Northeast:	International:
Y					

SAN ANTONIO SILVER STARS

www.wnba.com/silverstars

Industry Group Code: 711211E **Ranks within this company's industry group:** Sales: Profits:

Sports:		Services:		Media:		Sales:		Facilities:		Other:	
Leagues/Associations:		Food & Beverage:		TV:		Marketing:	Y	Stadiums:	Y	Gambling:	
Teams:	Y	Agents:		Radio:		Ads:	Y	Fitness Clubs:		Apparel:	
Nonprofits:		Other:		Internet:		Tickets:	Y	Golf Courses:		Equipment:	
Other:				Print:		Retail:	Y	Ski Resorts:		Shoes:	
				Software:		Other:		Other:		Other:	

TYPES OF BUSINESS:

Women's Professional Basketball Team

BRANDS/DIVISIONS/AFFILIATES:

AT&T Center
Spurs Sports & Entertainment
San Antonio Spurs
San Antonio Rampage

CONTACTS: *Note: Officers with more than one job title may be intentionally listed here more than once.*

Peter M. Holt, CEO
Dan Hughes, Gen. Mgr./Head Coach
Sandy Brondello, Assistant Coach
Olaf Lange, Assistant Coach
Jeanne Garza, Dir.-Corp. Partnerships
Peter M. Holt, Chmn./Owner

Phone: 210-444-5050 **Fax:**
Toll-Free:
Address: 1 AT&T Ctr., San Antonio, TX 78219 US

GROWTH PLANS/SPECIAL FEATURES:

The San Antonio Silver Stars were one of the eight original Women's National Basketball Association (WNBA) teams founded in 1997. The franchise moved to Texas in 2003, prior to which the Silver Stars were the Utah Starzz based in Salt Lake City. The Silver Stars play in the WNBA's Western Conference, alongside the Los Angeles Sparks, Minnesota Lynx, Phoenix Mercury, Sacramento Monarchs and Seattle Storm. The franchise is the sister team of the San Antonio Spurs of the National Basketball Association (NBA), and both teams are owned and operated by Spurs Sports & Entertainment, owned by Peter M. Holt. Both the Spurs and Silver Stars play at the AT&T Center, formerly the SCB Center, a $175-million, 18,700-seat entertainment center. The AT&T Center also hosts the San Antonio Rampage, a minor league hockey team owned by Spurs Sports & Entertainment; and the San Antonio Stock Show & Rodeo, as well as concerts and other entertainment events. The AT&T Center is owned by Bexar County, which encompasses San Antonio, and is operated by Spurs Sports & Entertainment. Shannon Johnson and Vickie Johnson, two of the Silver Stars' best players, have been nominated for the WNBA's All-Decade Team. Members of the All-Decade team are selected based on their over-all contribution to the WNBA's ten years of existence. Recently, the team has partnered with several charitable organizations, OwnUp SA, the American Heart Association, the Boys & Girls Club of San Antonio and CHRISTUS Santa Rosa. San Antonio made it to the WNBA Finals for the first time in its history, but lost to the Detroit Shock.

FINANCIALS: **Sales and profits are in thousands of dollars—add 000 to get the full amount. 2008 Note: Financial information for 2008 was not available for all companies at press time.**

2008 Sales: $	2008 Profits: $	**U.S. Stock Ticker: Subsidiary**
2007 Sales: $	2007 Profits: $	**Int'l Ticker:** Int'l Exchange:
2006 Sales: $	2006 Profits: $	Employees:
2005 Sales: $	2005 Profits: $	Fiscal Year Ends:
2004 Sales: $	2004 Profits: $	Parent Company: SPURS SPORTS & ENTERTAINMENT

SALARIES/BENEFITS:

Pension Plan:	ESOP Stock Plan:	Profit Sharing:	Top Exec. Salary: $	Bonus: $
Savings Plan:	Stock Purch. Plan:		Second Exec. Salary: $	Bonus: $

OTHER THOUGHTS:

Apparent Women Officers or Directors: 3
Hot Spot for Advancement for Women/Minorities: Y

LOCATIONS: ("Y" = Yes)

West:	Southwest:	Midwest:	Southeast:	Northeast:	International:
	Y				

Note: Financial information, benefits and other data can change quickly and may vary from those stated here.

SAN ANTONIO SPURS

www.nba.com/spurs

Industry Group Code: 711211B **Ranks within this company's industry group:** Sales: 10 Profits: 9

Sports:		Services:		Media:		Sales:		Facilities:		Other:	
Leagues/Associations:		Food & Beverage:		TV:		Marketing:		Stadiums:		Gambling:	
Teams:	Y	Agents:		Radio:		Ads:		Fitness Clubs:		Apparel:	
Nonprofits:		Other:		Internet:		Tickets:	Y	Golf Courses:		Equipment:	
Other:				Print:		Retail:	Y	Ski Resorts:		Shoes:	
				Software:		Other:		Other:		Other:	

TYPES OF BUSINESS:

Professional Basketball Team
Ticket Sales

BRANDS/DIVISIONS/AFFILIATES:

SBC Center
Silver Dancers
AT&T Coyote Crew
Coyote's Den
Spurs Foundation
El Loco Lobo
San Antonio Spurs LLC

CONTACTS: *Note: Officers with more than one job title may be intentionally listed here more than once.*

Peter M. Holt, CEO
Bruce Guthrie, VP-Mktg.
Paula Winslow, VP-Human Resources
Leo Gomez, VP-Corp. Admin.
Russ Bookbinder, Exec. VP-Bus. Oper.
Rick Pych, Exec. VP-Corp. Dev.
Leo Gomez, VP-Public Affairs
Rick Pych, Exec. VP-Finance
R. C. Buford, Gen. Mgr./Sr. VP
Gregg Popovich, Head Coach/Exec. VP-Basketball Oper.
Dell Demps, Dir.-Player Personnel
Peter M. Holt, Chmn.

Phone: 210-444-5000	**Fax:** 210-444-5100
Toll-Free:	
Address: 1 AT&T Center Pkwy., San Antonio, TX 78219 US	

GROWTH PLANS/SPECIAL FEATURES:

The San Antonio Spurs have historically been one of the top teams in the National Basketball Association's (NBA) Western Conference. The Spurs have won three championships in the past seven years, with victories in 1999, 2003 and 2005. The Spurs began in 1967 as the Dallas Chaparrals in the ABA, and have since moved to San Antonio in 1973 as the San Antonio Spurs. The Spurs arena is located in the AT&T center, which was completed during the 2002-03 NBA season. The stadium has an 18,500-seat capacity and contains 50 luxury suites. During game nights, the arena hosts the Silver Dancers, the AT&T Coyote Crew and the Coyote's Den for its mascot, El Loco Lobo. The Spurs offer basketball training camps for children and the Spurs Foundation, which supports more than 1,800 area organizations with over $10 million in cash contributions with tickets and autographed memorabilia donations. The Spurs team was led to its championships by the legendary duo of David Robinson and Tim Duncan, a long time power forward/center for the team who has won three Finals MVP awards. Prior to Duncan, San Antonio's most famed player was George Gervin, or Iceman, who led the Spurs to five division titles in the 1970s and 80s. The Spurs finished the 2007-08 regular season with a 68.3 winning percentage and has entered the NBA finals as the third seed in the West. Forbes Magazine recently estimated the team to be worth approximately $415 million. In the 2008-09 season, the team's home attendance average was roughly 18,300 per game.

FINANCIALS: **Sales and profits are in thousands of dollars—add 000 to get the full amount. 2008 Note: Financial information for 2008 was not available for all companies at press time.**

2008 Sales: $138,000	2008 Profits: $19,000	**U.S. Stock Ticker: Private**
2007 Sales: $131,000	2007 Profits: $15,500	**Int'l Ticker:** Int'l Exchange:
2006 Sales: $122,000	2006 Profits: $11,700	Employees:
2005 Sales: $121,000	2005 Profits: $	Fiscal Year Ends: 6/30
2004 Sales: $108,000	2004 Profits: $	Parent Company: SAN ANTONIO SPURS LLC

SALARIES/BENEFITS:

Pension Plan:	ESOP Stock Plan:	Profit Sharing:	Top Exec. Salary: $	Bonus: $
Savings Plan:	Stock Purch. Plan:		Second Exec. Salary: $	Bonus: $

OTHER THOUGHTS:

Apparent Women Officers or Directors:
Hot Spot for Advancement for Women/Minorities:

LOCATIONS: ("Y" = Yes)

West:	Southwest:	Midwest:	Southeast:	Northeast:	International:
	Y				

SAN DIEGO CHARGERS

www.chargers.com

Industry Group Code: 711211C **Ranks within this company's industry group:** Sales: 21 Profits: 23

Sports:		Services:		Media:		Sales:		Facilities:		Other:	
Leagues/Associations:		Food & Beverage:		TV:		Marketing:		Stadiums:		Gambling:	
Teams:	Y	Agents:		Radio:		Ads:		Fitness Clubs:		Apparel:	
Nonprofits:		Other:		Internet:		Tickets:	Y	Golf Courses:		Equipment:	
Other:				Print:		Retail:	Y	Ski Resorts:		Shoes:	
				Software:		Other:		Other:		Other:	

TYPES OF BUSINESS:

Professional Football Team

BRANDS/DIVISIONS/AFFILIATES:

San Diego Chargers Football Co.
Qualcomm Stadium
Alex Spanos All-Star Classic
Chargers Community Foundation
Community Quarterback Awards Program

CONTACTS: *Note: Officers with more than one job title may be intentionally listed here more than once.*

Dean Spanos, CEO
Jim Steeg, COO/Exec. VP
Dean Spanos, Pres.
Jeanne M. Bonk, CFO/Exec. VP
Ken Derrett, Chief Mktg. Officer/VP
Starlene Gangitano, Human Resources/Payroll
Ed McGuire, Exec. VP-Football Oper./Assistant Gen. Mgr.
A.G. Spanos, Dir.-Bus. Dev. & Mktg. Programs
Joel Price, Mgr.-Internet Svcs./Webmaster
Bill Johnston, Dir.-Public Rel.
Marsha Wells, Controller
Norv Turner, Head Coach
Jimmy Raye, Dir.-Player Personnel
Sean O'Connor, Dir.-Stadium, Game Oper. & Special Events
Kimberley Layton, Dir.-Public Affairs, Corp. & Community Rel.

Phone: 858-874-4500 **Fax:** 878-292-2760
Toll-Free:
Address: 4020 Murphy Canyon Rd., San Diego, CA 92123 US

GROWTH PLANS/SPECIAL FEATURES:

The San Diego Chargers, a National Football League (NFL) team playing in the Western Division of the American Football Conference (AFC), are owned and operated by San Diego Chargers Football Co. The club was originally known as the Los Angeles Chargers when it began play in 1960 as a charter member of the American Football League (AFL). The Chargers only spent one season in Los Angeles before moving to San Diego. In 1963, the Chargers won the AFL title. After the league merger in 1970, the Chargers enjoyed some small successes, but they failed to advance very far during the post season. In 1995, the Chargers made their first and only Super Bowl appearance, but they lost to the San Francisco 49ers. The team is owned by Alex Spanos, founder and chairman of A.G. Spanos Companies. The Chargers play their home games at Qualcomm Stadium, formerly known as San Diego Stadium and Jack Murphy Stadium. Its seating capacity is 71,500 spectators. The Chargers Community Foundation, started in 1995, provides financial assistance to community groups involved with youth sports programs; grants scholarships and computers to students, schools and educators through the Chargers Champions program; and honors outstanding volunteers across the country through the annual Community Quarterback Awards Program. Also, Alex Spanos sponsors the annual Alex Spanos All-Star Classic, a premier match-up between the country's top high school senior players, divided into teams by region. Other Chargers community programs include blood drives, food drives, a teddy bear drive, Toys for Tots and support for the Susan G. Komen Breast Cancer Foundation. In the 2008 season, the team averaged 68,138 fans in attendance per game. A recent Forbes estimate values the team at $888 million.

FINANCIALS: **Sales and profits are in thousands of dollars—add 000 to get the full amount. 2008 Note: Financial information for 2008 was not available for all companies at press time.**

2008 Sales: $207,000
2007 Sales: $192,000
2006 Sales: $170,000
2005 Sales: $165,000
2004 Sales: $

2008 Profits: $19,000
2007 Profits: $19,200
2006 Profits: $24,800
2005 Profits: $
2004 Profits: $

U.S. Stock Ticker: Private
Int'l Ticker: Int'l Exchange:
Employees:
Fiscal Year Ends: 12/31
Parent Company: SAN DIEGO CHARGERS FOOTBALL CO

SALARIES/BENEFITS:

Pension Plan:	ESOP Stock Plan:	Profit Sharing:	Top Exec. Salary: $	Bonus: $
Savings Plan:	Stock Purch. Plan:		Second Exec. Salary: $	Bonus: $

OTHER THOUGHTS:

Apparent Women Officers or Directors: 2
Hot Spot for Advancement for Women/Minorities: Y

LOCATIONS: ("Y" = Yes)

West:	Southwest:	Midwest:	Southeast:	Northeast:	International:
Y					

Note: Financial information, benefits and other data can change quickly and may vary from those stated here.

SAN DIEGO PADRES

padres.mlb.com

Industry Group Code: 711211A **Ranks within this company's industry group:** Sales: 21 Profits: 12

Sports:		Services:		Media:		Sales:		Facilities:		Other:	
Leagues/Associations:		Food & Beverage:		TV:		Marketing:		Stadiums:		Gambling:	
Teams:	Y	Agents:		Radio:		Ads:		Fitness Clubs:		Apparel:	
Nonprofits:		Other:		Internet:		Tickets:	Y	Golf Courses:		Equipment:	
Other:				Print:		Retail:	Y	Ski Resorts:		Shoes:	
				Software:		Other:		Other:		Other:	

TYPES OF BUSINESS:

Professional Baseball Team

BRANDS/DIVISIONS/AFFILIATES:

San Diego Padres Baseball Club, LP
PETCO Park
Padres Foundation
Portland Beavers
San Antonio Missions
Lake Elsinore Storm
Fort Wayne Wizards
Peoria Sports Complex

CONTACTS: *Note: Officers with more than one job title may be intentionally listed here more than once.*

Jeff Moorad, CEO/Vice Chmn.
Tom Garfinkle, COO
Tom Garfinkle, Pres.
Fred Gerson, CFO/Exec. VP
Jim Ballweg, VP-Sales
Tamara Furman, Exec. Dir.-Human Resources
Lucy Freeman, Exec. Dir.-Admin.
Katie Pothier, General Counsel/Exec. VP
Jeff Overton, Exec. VP-Bus. Oper.
Michele Anderson, VP-Comm. Rel.
Jordana Ryan, Controller
Bud Black, Mgr.
Kevin Towers, Exec. VP/Gen. Mgr.
Mark Guglielmo, Ballpark Oper.
Grady Fuson, VP-Scouting & Player Dev.
John Moores, Chmn.

Phone: 619-881-5000 **Fax:** 619-497-5339
Toll-Free:
Address: 9449 Friars Rd., San Diego, CA 92108 US

GROWTH PLANS/SPECIAL FEATURES:

The San Diego Padres, owned and operated by San Diego Padres Baseball Club, LP, are a Major League Baseball (MLB) team playing in MLB's Western Division. Founded in 1969, the Padres struggled as a young team, beginning with nine straight losing seasons. In 1984, the team appeared in the first of its two World Series, losing to the Tigers. The Padres made it to the postseason three more times, losing another World Series in 1998. The Padres' most famous players include Tony Gwynn, who won eight batting titles with the team and was inducted to the Hall of Fame in 2007; and Dave Winfield, who is now a vice president and a special advisor in the team's front office. In 2004, the Padres changed playing facilities from Qualcomm Stadium, which they shared with the San Diego Chargers, to their own $450-million stadium, PETCO Park, which seats 42,445. With this change of address and the team's first winning season since 1998, came the franchise's highest attendance numbers, topping 3 million tickets sold. Even though the team won its division that year and the next, attendance at PETCO was down to 2.66 million in 2006, 12th in MLB. In 2008, the team averaged attendance of almost 30,000 per home game. Since 1995, the Padres have been owned by software millionaire John Moores, who bought the team for $94 million. Forbes Magazine recently valued the franchise at $401 million. The team plays spring training games at the Peoria Sports Complex in Arizona, sharing the stadium with the Seattle Mariners.

FINANCIALS: Sales and profits are in thousands of dollars—add 000 to get the full amount. 2008 Note: Financial information for 2008 was not available for all companies at press time.

2008 Sales: $174,000 | 2008 Profits: $22,900
2007 Sales: $167,000 | 2007 Profits: $23,600
2006 Sales: $160,000 | 2006 Profits: $5,200
2005 Sales: $158,000 | 2005 Profits: $
2004 Sales: $ | 2004 Profits: $

U.S. Stock Ticker: Subsidiary
Int'l Ticker: Int'l Exchange:
Employees:
Fiscal Year Ends: 10/31
Parent Company: SAN DIEGO PADRES BASEBALL CLUB LP

SALARIES/BENEFITS:

Pension Plan: ESOP Stock Plan: Profit Sharing: Top Exec. Salary: $ Bonus: $
Savings Plan: Stock Purch. Plan: Second Exec. Salary: $ Bonus: $

OTHER THOUGHTS:

Apparent Women Officers or Directors: 8
Hot Spot for Advancement for Women/Minorities: Y

LOCATIONS: ("Y" = Yes)

West:	Southwest:	Midwest:	Southeast:	Northeast:	International:
Y					

SAN FRANCISCO 49ERS

www.sf49ers.com

Industry Group Code: 711211C **Ranks within this company's industry group:** Sales: 31 Profits: 31

Sports:		Services:		Media:		Sales:		Facilities:		Other:	
Leagues/Associations:		Food & Beverage:		TV:		Marketing:	Y	Stadiums:		Gambling:	
Teams:	Y	Agents:		Radio:		Ads:		Fitness Clubs:		Apparel:	Y
Nonprofits:		Other:		Internet:		Tickets:	Y	Golf Courses:		Equipment:	
Other:				Print:		Retail:	Y	Ski Resorts:		Shoes:	
				Software:		Other:		Other:		Other:	

TYPES OF BUSINESS:

Professional Football Team

BRANDS/DIVISIONS/AFFILIATES:

DeBartolo Corporation
San Francisco Forty Niners, Ltd.

CONTACTS:

Note: Officers with more than one job title may be intentionally listed here more than once.

Andy Dolich, COO
Jed York, Pres./Owner
Larry MacNeil, CFO/VP
Michael P. Williams, VP-Mktg.
Tina De Vora Rojas, Sr. Mgr.-Human Resources
Alexander Ignacio, Dir.-IT
Paraag Marathe, VP-Football Oper.
Jed York, VP-Strategic Planning
Lisa Lang, VP-Comm.
Debye Whelchel, Controller
Scot McCloughan, Gen. Mgr.
Mike Singletary, Head Coach
Jim Mercurio, VP-Stadium Oper. & Security
John York, Co-Chmn.
Denise DeBartolo York, Co-Chmn.

Phone: 408-562-4949 **Fax:** 408-727-4937
Toll-Free:
Address: 4949 Centennial Blvd., Santa Clara, CA 95054 US

GROWTH PLANS/SPECIAL FEATURES:

The San Francisco 49ers are a National Football League (NFL) team in the National Football Conference (NFC). The team was the first major league professional sports franchise on the West Coast. Brothers Anthony and Victor Morabito founded the franchise in 1946 as part of the All American Football Conference (AAFC). The team joined the NFL in 1950 when the AAFC collapsed. In 1977, the brothers sold the franchise to Edward DeBartolo, who revamped the franchise. Since 1981, the 49ers have won 13 division titles and five conference championships, and it was the first franchise in NFL history to win five Super Bowl titles, most recently in 1994. The 49ers dominated the 1980s when they won four of their five Super Bowl Championships (1981, 1984, 1988 and 1989). San Francisco is the only NFL team to produce 10 or more wins for 16 consecutive seasons, from 1983 to 1998. After Edward DeBartolo's death in 1994, his children contended for control of DeBartolo Corporation. They finally split the company's assets in 1999, when daughter Denise DeBartolo York gained full control of the 49ers. The team is now owned and operated by the San Francisco Forty Niners, Ltd., a subsidiary of DeBartolo Corporation. Thirteen former 49ers are in the Pro Football Hall of Fame, including head coach Bill Walsh, who led the 49ers to three Super Bowl titles; quarterback Joe Montana, who retired with the highest quarterback rating in NFL history; and Steve Young, who won six NFL passing titles. The team currently plays in Candlestick Park in San Francisco, but plans to move to a new stadium by the start of the 2012 season. A recent Forbes estimate values the team at $865 million.

FINANCIALS:

Sales and profits are in thousands of dollars—add 000 to get the full amount. 2008 Note: Financial information for 2008 was not available for all companies at press time.

2008 Sales: $201,000	2008 Profits: $4,100	**U.S. Stock Ticker: Subsidiary**
2007 Sales: $186,000	2007 Profits: $9,900	**Int'l Ticker:** Int'l Exchange:
2006 Sales: $171,000	2006 Profits: $11,800	Employees:
2005 Sales: $171,000	2005 Profits: $	Fiscal Year Ends: 12/31
2004 Sales: $	2004 Profits: $	Parent Company: DEBARTOLO CORPORATION

SALARIES/BENEFITS:

Pension Plan:	ESOP Stock Plan:	Profit Sharing:	Top Exec. Salary: $	Bonus: $
Savings Plan:	Stock Purch. Plan:		Second Exec. Salary: $	Bonus: $

OTHER THOUGHTS:

Apparent Women Officers or Directors: 3
Hot Spot for Advancement for Women/Minorities: Y

LOCATIONS: ("Y" = Yes)

West:	Southwest:	Midwest:	Southeast:	Northeast:	International:
Y					

SAN FRANCISCO GIANTS

sanfrancisco.giants.mlb.com

Industry Group Code: 711211A **Ranks within this company's industry group:** Sales: 9 Profits: 13

Sports:		Services:		Media:		Sales:		Facilities:		Other:	
Leagues/Associations:		Food & Beverage:		TV:		Marketing:	Y	Stadiums:	Y	Gambling:	
Teams:	Y	Agents:		Radio:		Ads:		Fitness Clubs:		Apparel:	
Nonprofits:	Y	Other:		Internet:		Tickets:	Y	Golf Courses:		Equipment:	
Other:				Print:		Retail:		Ski Resorts:		Shoes:	
				Software:		Other:		Other:		Other:	

TYPES OF BUSINESS:

Professional Baseball Team
Stadium Operation

BRANDS/DIVISIONS/AFFILIATES:

AT&T Park
National League West Division
Junior Giants

CONTACTS:

Note: Officers with more than one job title may be intentionally listed here more than once.

William H. Neukom, CEO
Lawrence M. Baer, COO/Exec. VP
Lawrence M. Baer, Pres.
John F. Yee, CFO/Sr. VP
Tom McDonald, Sr. VP-Consumer Mktg.
Joyce Thomas, VP-Human Resources
Bill Schlough, CIO/Sr. VP
Alfonso G. Felder, VP-Admin.
Jack F. Bair, General Counsel/Sr. VP
Bobby Evans, VP-Baseball Oper.
Staci Slaughter, Sr. VP-Comm.
Lisa Pantages, VP-Finance
Brian R. Sabean, Sr. VP/Gen. Mgr.
Jeff Tucker, VP-Sales
Shana Daum, Dir.-Community Affairs & Community Rel.
Dick Tidrow, VP-Player Personnel
Shun Kakazu, Coordinator-Japan Oper.

Phone: 415-972-2000 **Fax:** 415-947-2800
Toll-Free:
Address: AT&T Park, 24 Willie Mays Plz., San Francisco, CA 94107 US

GROWTH PLANS/SPECIAL FEATURES:

The San Francisco Giants are a professional baseball team playing in the National League West Division within Major League Baseball (MLB). The team began in New York as the Gothams in 1883 and became the New York Giants in 1885 before moving west in 1958. The team began its history playing at the famed Polo Grounds, which witnessed the Shot Heard Round the World homerun by Bobby Thomson on October 3, 1951 that won the pennant against the Brooklyn Dodgers. The Giants now play their home games at AT&T Park, completed in 2000 and seating 41,500 fans. The stadium was privately financed by Giants owner Peter McGowan, replacing the much-maligned Candlestick Park. Famous Giants players have included Willie Mays, Willie McCovey, Juan Marichal, Will Clark and Barry Bonds, who broke the single-season home run record in 2001 and the all-time home run record in 2007. The Giants have won five World Series titles, its last in 1954, in addition to 20 pennants and six division titles. The team also operates the Junior Giants program, a free baseball program for boys and girls between the ages of 5 to 18 years olds that that seeks to offer alternatives to drugs, gangs and crime for at risk youth. As of 2008, the team had more wins than any other team in history and trailed only the Yankees in winning percentage. In 2008, the team saw an average home game attendance 35,356. Forbes Magazine recently valued the Giants at $471 million.

FINANCIALS:

Sales and profits are in thousands of dollars—add 000 to get the full amount. 2008 Note: Financial information for 2008 was not available for all companies at press time.

2008 Sales: $196,000
2007 Sales: $197,000
2006 Sales: $184,000
2005 Sales: $171,000
2004 Sales: $

2008 Profits: $22,400
2007 Profits: $19,900
2006 Profits: $18,500
2005 Profits: $
2004 Profits: $

U.S. Stock Ticker: Subsidiary
Int'l Ticker: Int'l Exchange:
Employees:
Fiscal Year Ends: 12/31
Parent Company: SAN FRANCISCO BASEBALL ASSOCIATES LP

SALARIES/BENEFITS:

Pension Plan:	ESOP Stock Plan:	Profit Sharing:	Top Exec. Salary: $	Bonus: $
Savings Plan:	Stock Purch. Plan:		Second Exec. Salary: $	Bonus: $

OTHER THOUGHTS:

Apparent Women Officers or Directors: 8
Hot Spot for Advancement for Women/Minorities: Y

LOCATIONS: ("Y" = Yes)

West:	Southwest:	Midwest:	Southeast:	Northeast:	International:
Y					

Note: Financial information, benefits and other data can change quickly and may vary from those stated here.

SAN JOSE EARTHQUAKES

web.mlsnet.com/t110/

Industry Group Code: 711211D **Ranks within this company's industry group:** Sales: Profits:

Sports:		Services:		Media:		Sales:		Facilities:		Other:	
Leagues/Associations:		Food & Beverage:		TV:		Marketing:		Stadiums:		Gambling:	
Teams:	Y	Agents:		Radio:		Ads:		Fitness Clubs:		Apparel:	
Nonprofits:		Other:		Internet:		Tickets:		Golf Courses:		Equipment:	
Other:				Print:		Retail:		Ski Resorts:		Shoes:	
				Software:		Other:		Other:		Other:	

TYPES OF BUSINESS:

Soccer Team

BRANDS/DIVISIONS/AFFILIATES:

Earthquakes Soccer, LLC

CONTACTS: *Note: Officers with more than one job title may be intentionally listed here more than once.*

Mike Crowley, Pres.
Ann Rodriguez, VP-Mktg. & Sales
Steve Johnston, General Counsel
Billy Beane, Exec. VP-Sports Oper.
David Alioto, Exec. VP-Bus. Oper.
Flor Rivera, Mgr.-Comm.
Ashmi Shah, Dir.-Finance
John Doyle, Gen. Mgr.-Soccer Oper.
Frank Yallop, Head Coach
Lew Wolff, Owner
Jed Mettee, Sr. Dir.-Broadcasting & Comm.

Phone: 408-556-7700	**Fax:**
Toll-Free:	
Address: 451 El Camino Real, Ste 220, Santa Clara, CA 95050 US	

GROWTH PLANS/SPECIAL FEATURES:

The San Jose Earthquakes are a Major League Soccer (MLS) team playing in the Western Conference alongside teams such as Club Deportivo Chivas USA, Colorado Rapids, FC Dallas, Houston Dynamo, Los Angeles Galaxy and Real Salt Lake. The organization, which was one of the inaugural MLS clubs, has recently returned from a two-year hiatus that saw the team's entire operations moved to Houston, Texas to form the Houston Dynamo. The team returned to the field in 2008 as an expansion team owned by Lewis Wolff, who also owns Major League Baseball's Oakland Athletics. Because the Earthquakes have retained the former team's records, colors and logos, the team bears the odd distinction of being both an MLS founding member and one of the league's most recent expansion teams. The club plays most home games at Buck Shaw Stadium in Santa Clara, California, although when in need of extra capacity the team currently turns to McAfee Coliseum. Prior to the hiatus, the team had an average all-time attendance of approximately 13,000 in the regular season and 13,500 in the post season. A new soccer-specific stadium, known as Earthquake Stadium, is in the works. The new stadium is planed to have 22,000 permanent seats but be expandable to 30,000 seats. Earthquake Stadium is expected to be completed by 2010 or 2011.

FINANCIALS: **Sales and profits are in thousands of dollars—add 000 to get the full amount. 2008 Note: Financial information for 2008 was not available for all companies at press time.**

2008 Sales: $	2008 Profits: $	**U.S. Stock Ticker: Private**
2007 Sales: $	2007 Profits: $	**Int'l Ticker:** Int'l Exchange:
2006 Sales: $	2006 Profits: $	Employees:
2005 Sales: $	2005 Profits: $	Fiscal Year Ends:
2004 Sales: $	2004 Profits: $	Parent Company: EARTHQUAKE SOCCER LLC

SALARIES/BENEFITS:

Pension Plan:	ESOP Stock Plan:	Profit Sharing:	Top Exec. Salary: $	Bonus: $
Savings Plan:	Stock Purch. Plan:		Second Exec. Salary: $	Bonus: $

OTHER THOUGHTS:

Apparent Women Officers or Directors: 8
Hot Spot for Advancement for Women/Minorities: Y

LOCATIONS: ("Y" = Yes)

West:	Southwest:	Midwest:	Southeast:	Northeast:	International:
Y					

SAN JOSE SHARKS

sharks.nhl.com

Industry Group Code: 711211F **Ranks within this company's industry group:** Sales: 18 Profits: 11

Sports:		Services:		Media:		Sales:		Facilities:		Other:	
Leagues/Associations:		Food & Beverage:		TV:		Marketing:		Stadiums:	Y	Gambling:	
Teams:	Y	Agents:		Radio:		Ads:		Fitness Clubs:		Apparel:	
Nonprofits:		Other:		Internet:		Tickets:	Y	Golf Courses:		Equipment:	
Other:				Print:		Retail:		Ski Resorts:		Shoes:	
				Software:		Other:		Other:		Other:	

TYPES OF BUSINESS:

Professional Hockey Team

BRANDS/DIVISIONS/AFFILIATES:

HP Pavilion
San Jose Arena
Shark Tank (The)

CONTACTS:

Note: Officers with more than one job title may be intentionally listed here more than once.

Greg Jamison, CEO
Greg Jamison, Pres.
Charlie Faas, CFO/Exec. VP
Kent Russell, VP-Mktg. & Sales
Cathy Chandler, Dir.-Human Resources
Uy Ut, Dir.-IT
Don Gralnek, General Counsel/Exec. VP
Malcolm Bordelon, Exec. VP- Bus. Oper.
Scott Emmert, VP-Media Rel.
Ken Caveney, VP-Finance
Jim Goddard, Exec. VP/Gen. Mgr.-HP Pavilion
Doug Wilson, Exec. VP/Gen. Mgr.-Sharks
Rich Sotelo, VP-Building Oper.
Todd McLellan, Head Coach

Phone: 408-287-7070	**Fax:** 408-999-5797
Toll-Free:	
Address: 525 W. Santa Clara St., San Jose, CA 95113 US	

GROWTH PLANS/SPECIAL FEATURES:

The San Jose Sharks are a professional ice hockey team playing in the National Hockey League (NHL) and based in San Jose, California. The team was founded in 1991 by Cleveland businessmen George and Gordon Gund. In its early years, the franchise was a relatively poor team on the ice. At the beginning of its third season, the Sharks moved to their current home, the HP Pavilion (also known as the San Jose Arena and The Shark Tank). This move marked a turnaround in the team's performance. That year the Sharks not only made the playoffs, but also upset the heavily favored Detroit Red Wings in the first round. After years of mixed results, a local group of investors headed by team president Greg Jamison bought out the team in 2002. San Jose Sports & Entertainment Enterprises currently owns and manages the Sharks. George Gund, who also owns the Cleveland Cavaliers, still has a significant interest in the team. The HP Pavilion seats 16,000 hockey spectators, and in the 2008-09 season, the team saw an average home attendance of approximately 14,875 fans. The Sharks ended the 2008-09 season with 53 wins, 18 losses and 117 points, earning the team a shot at the Stanley Cup as well as their first Presidents' Trophy, awarded by the NHL each year to the team finishing the regular season with the most points. A recent Forbes list valued the team at roughly $179 million.

FINANCIALS:

Sales and profits are in thousands of dollars—add 000 to get the full amount. 2008 Note: Financial information for 2008 was not available for all companies at press time.

2008 Sales: $85,000	2008 Profits: $2,400
2007 Sales: $72,000	2007 Profits: $-5,100
2006 Sales: $69,000	2006 Profits: $1,800
2005 Sales: $	2005 Profits: $
2004 Sales: $74,000	2004 Profits: $

U.S. Stock Ticker: Subsidiary
Int'l Ticker: Int'l Exchange:
Employees:
Fiscal Year Ends: 7/31
Parent Company: SAN JOSE SPORTS & ENTERTAINMENT ENTERPRISES

SALARIES/BENEFITS:

Pension Plan:	ESOP Stock Plan:	Profit Sharing:	Top Exec. Salary: $	Bonus: $
Savings Plan:	Stock Purch. Plan:		Second Exec. Salary: $	Bonus: $

OTHER THOUGHTS:

Apparent Women Officers or Directors: 2
Hot Spot for Advancement for Women/Minorities:

LOCATIONS: ("Y" = Yes)

West:	Southwest:	Midwest:	Southeast:	Northeast:	International:
Y					

SEATTLE MARINERS

seattle.mariners.mlb.com

Industry Group Code: 711211A **Ranks within this company's industry group:** Sales: 12 Profits: 27

Sports:		Services:		Media:		Sales:		Facilities:		Other:	
Leagues/Associations:		Food & Beverage:		TV:		Marketing:		Stadiums:	Y	Gambling:	
Teams:	Y	Agents:		Radio:		Ads:		Fitness Clubs:		Apparel:	
Nonprofits:		Other:		Internet:		Tickets:	Y	Golf Courses:		Equipment:	
Other:				Print:		Retail:	Y	Ski Resorts:		Shoes:	
				Software:		Other:		Other:		Other:	

TYPES OF BUSINESS:

Professional Baseball Team
Stadium Operation

BRANDS/DIVISIONS/AFFILIATES:

Baseball Club of Seattle, LP (The)
Nintendo
Safeco Field
Tacoma Rainiers
West Tenn Diamond Jaxx
High Desert Mavericks
Wisconsin Timber Rattlers
Everett AquaSox

CONTACTS: *Note: Officers with more than one job title may be intentionally listed here more than once.*

Howard Lincoln, CEO
Chuck Armstrong, Pres.
Kevin Martinez, VP-Mktg.
Marianne Short, VP-Human Resources
Dave Curry, Dir.-Info. Svcs.
Jim LaShell, Sr. Dir.-Retail Oper.
Bart Waldman, General Counsel/Exec. VP
Bob Aylward, Exec. VP-Bus. Oper.
Randy Adamack, VP-Comm. & Broadcasting
Kevin Mather, Exec. VP-Finance & Ballpark Oper.
Bill Bavasi, Exec. VP-Baseball Oper./Gen. Mgr.
Lee Pelekoudas, VP/Associate Gen. Mgr.
Howard Lincoln, Chmn.
Sandy Fielder, Dir.-Procurement

Phone: 206-346-4001	**Fax:** 206-346-4100
Toll-Free:	
Address: 1250 First Ave. S., Seattle, WA 98134 US	

GROWTH PLANS/SPECIAL FEATURES:

The Seattle Mariners, owned and operated by The Baseball Club of Seattle, LP, are an organization founded in 1977 within Major League Baseball (MLB). The team struggled in its early years, with a string of 14 straight losing seasons from 1977 to 1990. The Mariners have made it to the postseason four times but have been unable to advance to the World Series, including the 2001 season in which the team won an impressive 116 games. The team has featured superstars such as Randy Johnson, Ken Griffey, Jr. and Alex Rodriguez, as well as Japanese import Ichiro Suzuki. Nintendo is the majority owner of the Mariners. Other investors include Howard Lincoln, the team's chairman and CEO, who formerly worked with Nintendo's U.S. operations. The team's general manager is Bill Bavasi, who came aboard in late 2003. Bavasi has been widely criticized for toeing the line between assembling a contending team and rebuilding for future years. Despite the team's high payroll, which was an average of $85.7 million during Bavasi's years as general manager, the Mariners have only posted one winning season (2007) since Bavasi came aboard. The Mariners play at Safeco Field, which opened in 1999 with a seating capacity of 47,116 and featured a fully retractable roof. Attendance had been on the decline since its peak in 2002, falling to 15th overall in 2006 but rising in 2007 to nearly 2.7 million visitors (still well shy of 2002's mark of over 3.5 million). Home game attendance in 2008 averaged 28,761. The team was recently ranked the 13th most valuable in MLB by Forbes Magazine, which estimated the team's worth at $426 million.

FINANCIALS: **Sales and profits are in thousands of dollars—add 000 to get the full amount. 2008 Note: Financial information for 2008 was not available for all companies at press time.**

2008 Sales: $189,000	2008 Profits: $3,800	**U.S. Stock Ticker: Subsidiary**
2007 Sales: $194,000	2007 Profits: $10,100	**Int'l Ticker:** Int'l Exchange:
2006 Sales: $182,000	2006 Profits: $21,500	Employees:
2005 Sales: $179,000	2005 Profits: $	Fiscal Year Ends: 10/31
2004 Sales: $	2004 Profits: $	Parent Company: BASEBALL CLUB OF SEATTLE LP (THE)

SALARIES/BENEFITS:

Pension Plan:	ESOP Stock Plan:	Profit Sharing:	Top Exec. Salary: $	Bonus: $
Savings Plan:	Stock Purch. Plan:		Second Exec. Salary: $	Bonus: $

OTHER THOUGHTS:

Apparent Women Officers or Directors: 5
Hot Spot for Advancement for Women/Minorities: Y

LOCATIONS: ("Y" = Yes)

West:	Southwest:	Midwest:	Southeast:	Northeast:	International:
Y					

SEATTLE SEAHAWKS

www.seahawks.com

Industry Group Code: 711211C **Ranks within this company's industry group:** Sales: 16 Profits: 30

Sports:		Services:		Media:		Sales:		Facilities:		Other:	
Leagues/Associations:		Food & Beverage:		TV:		Marketing:		Stadiums:		Gambling:	
Teams:	Y	Agents:		Radio:		Ads:		Fitness Clubs:		Apparel:	Y
Nonprofits:		Other:		Internet:		Tickets:	Y	Golf Courses:		Equipment:	
Other:				Print:		Retail:	Y	Ski Resorts:		Shoes:	
				Software:		Other:		Other:		Other:	

TYPES OF BUSINESS:

Professional Football Team

BRANDS/DIVISIONS/AFFILIATES:

Sea Gals (The)
Qwest Field
Seattle Seahawks Inc
Paul G. Allen

CONTACTS:

Note: Officers with more than one job title may be intentionally listed here more than once.

Tod Leiweke, CEO
John Rizzardini, COO
Martha Fuller, CFO
Bill Chapin, Dir.-Mktg.
Cindy Kelley, Dir.-Human Resources
Lance Lopes, General Counsel/VP
Tim Ruskell, Pres., Football Oper.
Suzanne Lavender, Dir.-Corp. Comm.
Karen Harrison, Dir.-Finance
Tim Ruskell, Gen. Mgr.
Dave Pearson, VP-Comm. & Broadcasting
Susan Darrington, VP-Facility Oper. & Svcs.
Jim Mora, Head Coach
Paul G. Allen, Chmn.

Phone: 425-203-8000	**Fax:**
Toll-Free: 888-635-4295	
Address: 12 Seahawks Way, Renton, WA 98056 US	

GROWTH PLANS/SPECIAL FEATURES:

The Seattle Seahawks are a National Football League (NFL) football team playing in the Western Division of the National Football Conference. The team entered the league in 1976 in an NFL expansion along with the Tampa Bay Buccaneers. During its early years, the Seahawks played mediocre football with highlights provided by Hall of Fame receiver Steve Largent. The team made its first playoff appearance in 1983 when they reached the conference championship game. In 2005, the team reached the Super Bowl, though they lost to the Pittsburgh Steelers. The Seattle Seahawks team is owned by Microsoft co-founder Paul G. Allen. The team moved its home playing field in 2002 and now plays in Qwest Field, which was built for $430 million and is owned by the city of Seattle through the Washington State Public Stadium Authority; another company owned by Paul Allen, First & Goal, operates the stadium. Qwest Field seats approximately 67,000 spectators. The Sea Gals, a cheerleading troop comprised of 26 women, accompany the Seahawks on away games and perform halftime shows for games at home. A recent Forbes estimate values the team at $1.01 billion. In the 2008 season, the team averaged 67,995 fans in attendance per game.

FINANCIALS:

Sales and profits are in thousands of dollars—add 000 to get the full amount. 2008 Note: Financial information for 2008 was not available for all companies at press time.

2008 Sales: $215,000	2008 Profits: $8,900	**U.S. Stock Ticker: Subsidiary**
2007 Sales: $196,000	2007 Profits: $-2,600	**Int'l Ticker:** Int'l Exchange:
2006 Sales: $189,000	2006 Profits: $5,000	Employees:
2005 Sales: $183,000	2005 Profits: $	Fiscal Year Ends: 1/31
2004 Sales: $158,000	2004 Profits: $	Parent Company: SEATTLE SEAHAWKS INC

SALARIES/BENEFITS:

Pension Plan:	ESOP Stock Plan:	Profit Sharing:	Top Exec. Salary: $	Bonus: $
Savings Plan:	Stock Purch. Plan:		Second Exec. Salary: $	Bonus: $

OTHER THOUGHTS:

Apparent Women Officers or Directors: 3
Hot Spot for Advancement for Women/Minorities: Y

LOCATIONS: ("Y" = Yes)

West:	Southwest:	Midwest:	Southeast:	Northeast:	International:
Y					

SEATTLE SOUNDERS FC

www.soundersfc.com

Industry Group Code: 711211D **Ranks within this company's industry group:** Sales: Profits:

Sports:		Services:		Media:		Sales:		Facilities:		Other:	
Leagues/Associations:		Food & Beverage:		TV:		Marketing:		Stadiums:		Gambling:	
Teams:	Y	Agents:		Radio:		Ads:		Fitness Clubs:		Apparel:	
Nonprofits:		Other:		Internet:		Tickets:		Golf Courses:		Equipment:	
Other:				Print:		Retail:		Ski Resorts:		Shoes:	
				Software:		Other:		Other:		Other:	

TYPES OF BUSINESS:

Soccer Team

BRANDS/DIVISIONS/AFFILIATES:

CONTACTS:

Note: Officers with more than one job title may be intentionally listed here more than once.

Adrian Hanauer, Gen. Mgr.
John Rizzardini, COO
Lance Lopes, General Counsel/VP
Gary Wright, Sr. VP-Bus. Oper.
Bart Wiley, Dir.-Bus. Dev.
Dave Pearson, VP-Comm. & Broadcasting
Sigi Schmid, Head Coach
Susan Darrington, VP-Facility Oper. & Svcs.
Ron Jenkins, VP-Corp. Partnerships
Mike Flood, VP-Community Rel.

Phone:	Fax:
Toll-Free: 877-657-4625	
Address: 12 Seahawks Way, Renton, WA 98056 US	

GROWTH PLANS/SPECIAL FEATURES:

Seattle Sounders FC is a Major League Soccer (MLS) soccer franchise based out of Seattle, Washington. The team is the latest iteration of soccer in Seattle, celebrating its inaugural season in 2009, and the third to bear the Sounders name. The original Sounders played from 1974-83 in the North American Soccer League; the second team under the Sounders banner played from 1994-2008 in the United Soccer Leagues First Division. The franchise plays in MLS' Western Conference, along with Chivas USA, the Colorado Rapids, FC Dallas, Los Angeles Galaxy, Real Salt Lake and the Houston Dynamo. The Sounders currently have matches in Qwest Field, a multipurpose stadium with a soccer capacity of 27,000. The team is owned by a consortium of businessmen and entertainers, including Joe Roth, a Hollywood producer; Adrian Hanauer, owner of the former Seattle Sounders soccer team; Paul Allen, Microsoft cofounder and owner of the Seattle Supersonics and Drew Carey. The team is the only professional soccer team in North America to feature a marching band. In 2009, the Sounders signed a five-year sponsorship deal with Microsoft and Xbox 360 in 2009 in a deal worth roughly $20 million.

FINANCIALS:

Sales and profits are in thousands of dollars—add 000 to get the full amount. 2008 Note: Financial information for 2008 was not available for all companies at press time.

2008 Sales: $	2008 Profits: $	**U.S. Stock Ticker: Private**
2007 Sales: $	2007 Profits: $	**Int'l Ticker:** Int'l Exchange:
2006 Sales: $	2006 Profits: $	Employees:
2005 Sales: $	2005 Profits: $	Fiscal Year Ends:
2004 Sales: $	2004 Profits: $	Parent Company:

SALARIES/BENEFITS:

Pension Plan:	ESOP Stock Plan:	Profit Sharing:	Top Exec. Salary: $	Bonus: $
Savings Plan:	Stock Purch. Plan:		Second Exec. Salary: $	Bonus: $

OTHER THOUGHTS:

Apparent Women Officers or Directors: 2
Hot Spot for Advancement for Women/Minorities:

LOCATIONS: ("Y" = Yes)

West:	Southwest:	Midwest:	Southeast:	Northeast:	International:
Y					

Note: Financial information, benefits and other data can change quickly and may vary from those stated here.

SEATTLE STORM

www.wnba.com/storm

Industry Group Code: 711211E **Ranks within this company's industry group:** Sales: Profits:

Sports:		Services:		Media:		Sales:		Facilities:		Other:	
Leagues/Associations:		Food & Beverage:		TV:		Marketing:		Stadiums:		Gambling:	
Teams:	Y	Agents:		Radio:		Ads:		Fitness Clubs:		Apparel:	
Nonprofits:		Other:		Internet:		Tickets:	Y	Golf Courses:		Equipment:	
Other:				Print:		Retail:	Y	Ski Resorts:		Shoes:	
				Software:		Other:		Other:		Other:	

TYPES OF BUSINESS:

Women's Basketball Team

BRANDS/DIVISIONS/AFFILIATES:

Force 10 Hoops LLC
KeyArena
Professional Basketball Club LLC

CONTACTS:

Note: Officers with more than one job title may be intentionally listed here more than once.

Karen Bryant, CEO
Brian Byrnes, Sr. VP-Mktg. & Sales
Katy Semtner, Dir.-Human Resources
Allan Hoffman, Administrator-Network & Comm.
Jeremy Owen, Dir.-Merch.
Missy Bequette, Dir.-Basketball Oper.
Chip Bowers, VP-Bus. Dev.
Tom Savage, Dir.-Public Rel.
Madeleine O'Rourke, Controller
Brian Agler, Head Coach/Dir.-Player Personnel
Shelley Patterson, Assistant Coach
Pete Winemiller, VP-Guest Rel.
John Croley, VP-Facility Sales & Svcs.
Anne Levinson, Chmn.

Phone: 206-217-9622	**Fax:**
Toll-Free:	
Address: 1201 3rd Ave., Ste. 1000, 10th Fl., Seattle, WA 98101 US	

GROWTH PLANS/SPECIAL FEATURES:

The Seattle Storm is a Women's National Basketball Association (WNBA) team. It plays in the Western Conference of the WNBA along with the Los Angeles Sparks, Minnesota Lynx, Phoenix Mercury, Sacramento Monarchs and San Antonio Silver Stars. The team's home court, KeyArena in the Seattle Center, is owned and operated by the city of Seattle. Head coach Anne Donovan was the first female coach to win a WNBA title when the Storm won the 2004 WNBA championship. The Storm Dance Troupe is an all-kid squad assembled to help the team develop a family friendly image. The Storm and brother National Basketball Association (NBA) team the Seattle SuperSonics were acquired in 2006 for $350 million by Professional Basketball Club, LLC, an investment group from Oklahoma led by Clay Bennett. The SuperSonics were subsequently moved to Oklahoma to begin playing as the Oklahoma City Thunder; the Storm stayed in Seattle after current franchise owner Force 10 Hoops, LLC acquired the Storm from Professional Basketball Club in February 2008. The Force 10 acquisition makes the Storm the seventh WNBA team to be owned independent of an NBA team. Force 10 Hoops is led by four prominent women who have been active in Seattle, mainly serving as executives and politicians.

FINANCIALS:

Sales and profits are in thousands of dollars—add 000 to get the full amount. 2008 Note: Financial information for 2008 was not available for all companies at press time.

2008 Sales: $	2008 Profits: $	**U.S. Stock Ticker: Subsidiary**
2007 Sales: $	2007 Profits: $	**Int'l Ticker:** Int'l Exchange:
2006 Sales: $	2006 Profits: $	Employees:
2005 Sales: $	2005 Profits: $	Fiscal Year Ends:
2004 Sales: $	2004 Profits: $	Parent Company: FORCE 10 HOOPS LLC

SALARIES/BENEFITS:

Pension Plan:	ESOP Stock Plan:	Profit Sharing:	Top Exec. Salary: $	Bonus: $
Savings Plan:	Stock Purch. Plan:		Second Exec. Salary: $	Bonus: $

OTHER THOUGHTS:

Apparent Women Officers or Directors: 36
Hot Spot for Advancement for Women/Minorities: Y

LOCATIONS: ("Y" = Yes)

West:	Southwest:	Midwest:	Southeast:	Northeast:	International:
Y					

Note: Financial information, benefits and other data can change quickly and may vary from those stated here.

SIRIUS XM RADIO INC

www.sirius.com

Industry Group Code: 513111A **Ranks within this company's industry group:** Sales: 1 Profits: 1

Sports:		Services:		Media:		Sales:		Facilities:		Other:	
Leagues/Associations:		Food & Beverage:		TV:		Marketing:		Stadiums:		Gambling:	
Teams:		Agents:		Radio:	Y	Ads:		Fitness Clubs:		Apparel:	
Nonprofits:		Other:		Internet:		Tickets:		Golf Courses:		Equipment:	
Other:				Print:		Retail:		Ski Resorts:		Shoes:	
				Software:		Other:		Other:		Other:	

TYPES OF BUSINESS:

Satellite Radio Broadcasting

BRANDS/DIVISIONS/AFFILIATES:

Sirius
Liberty Media Corp.
XM Radio

CONTACTS: *Note: Officers with more than one job title may be intentionally listed here more than once.*

Mel Karmazin, CEO
Scott Greenstein, Pres.
David J. Frear, CFO/Exec. VP
James Meyer, Pres., Sales
Dara Altman, Chief Admin. Officer/Exec. VP
Patrick L. Donnelly, General Counsel/Exec. VP/Sec.
James Meyer, Pres., Oper.
Scott Greenstein, Chief Content Officer
Gary M. Parsons, Chmn.

Phone: 212-899-5100 **Fax:** 212-899-5050
Toll-Free:
Address: 1221 Ave. of the Americas, 36th Fl., New York, NY 10020 US

GROWTH PLANS/SPECIAL FEATURES:

Sirius XM Radio, Inc. is a satellite radio provider in the U.S. It offers over 130 channels to its subscribers, 63 channels of 100% commercial-free music and 54 channels of sports, news, talk, entertainment, traffic and weather. The company's primary source of revenue is subscription fees, with most of its customers subscribing to Sirius on an annual, semi-annual, quarterly or monthly basis. The firm has over 19 million subscribers. Most subscribers receive service through Sirius radios, which are sold through its web site and by automakers, consumer electronics retailers and mobile audio dealers. Sirius radios for the car, truck, home, RV and boat are available in more than 19,000 retail locations, including Best Buy, Crutchfield, Costco, Target, Wal-Mart, Sam's Club and RadioShack. Sirius has agreements with every major automaker to offer its radios as factory or dealer-installed options in their vehicles. The company offers programming over multiple platforms in addition to its satellite and terrestrial repeater network. Sirius Internet Radio is an Internet-only version of the firm's service, which delivers a simulcast of select music and non-music channels. Sirius' music channels are also available to certain DISH satellite television subscribers. The company also offers service in Canada. In July 2008, Sirius and XM Radio completed their merger. The $11.4 billion merger created the second largest radio company (based on revenue). In early 2009, Sirius XM, after years of massive losses, agreed to a new alliance with Liberty Media, which also owns a major stake in satellite TV firm DirecTV. In total, Liberty will provide loans totaling $530 million in exchange for a large equity stake.

The company offers its employees medical, dental and vision insurance; domestic partner benefits; an employee assistance program; life and AD&D insurance; healthcare spending accounts; short- and long-term disability insurance; and a 401(k) plan.

FINANCIALS: **Sales and profits are in thousands of dollars—add 000 to get the full amount. 2008 Note: Financial information for 2008 was not available for all companies at press time.**

2008 Sales: $1,663,992 — 2008 Profits: $-5,313,288
2007 Sales: $922,066 — 2007 Profits: $-565,252
2006 Sales: $637,235 — 2006 Profits: $-1,104,867
2005 Sales: $242,245 — 2005 Profits: $-862,997
2004 Sales: $66,854 — 2004 Profits: $-712,162

U.S. Stock Ticker: SIRI
Int'l Ticker: Int'l Exchange:
Employees: 1,640
Fiscal Year Ends: 12/31
Parent Company:

SALARIES/BENEFITS:

Pension Plan: — ESOP Stock Plan: — Profit Sharing: — Top Exec. Salary: $1,250,000 — Bonus: $4,000,000
Savings Plan: Y — Stock Purch. Plan: — Second Exec. Salary: $891,667 — Bonus: $512,500

OTHER THOUGHTS:

Apparent Women Officers or Directors:
Hot Spot for Advancement for Women/Minorities:

LOCATIONS: ("Y" = Yes)

West:	Southwest:	Midwest:	Southeast:	Northeast:	International:
				Y	

SKIS ROSSIGNOL SA

www.rossignol.com

Industry Group Code: 339920 **Ranks within this company's industry group:** Sales: Profits:

Sports:		Services:		Media:		Sales:		Facilities:		Other:	
Leagues/Associations:		Food & Beverage:		TV:		Marketing:		Stadiums:		Gambling:	
Teams:		Agents:		Radio:		Ads:		Fitness Clubs:		Apparel:	Y
Nonprofits:		Other:		Internet:		Tickets:		Golf Courses:		Equipment:	Y
Other:				Print:		Retail:		Ski Resorts:		Shoes:	Y
				Software:		Other:		Other:		Other:	

TYPES OF BUSINESS:

Ski Equipment
Winter Sports Accessories
Outerwear & Apparel

BRANDS/DIVISIONS/AFFILIATES:

Quicksilver, Inc.
Dynastar
Lange
Hammer Snowboards

CONTACTS: *Note: Officers with more than one job title may be intentionally listed here more than once.*

Jean-Francois Gautier, CEO
Jean-Francois Gautier, Pres.
Jean-Francois Gautier, Chmn.

Phone: 33-4-38-03-80-38	**Fax:** 33-4-38-03-80-00
Toll-Free:	
Address: 220 rue Pommarin, Moirans, 38430 France	

GROWTH PLANS/SPECIAL FEATURES:

Skis Rossignol S.A. is a leading manufacturer of winter sports goods, as well as products designed for year-round mountain sports and the lifestyle associated with such sports. The company is a wholly-owned subsidiary of Quiksilver, Inc., a leading outdoor apparel and equipment manufacturer, which acquired Rossignol in August 2005 for $320 million. Rossignol offers a full range of ski and snowboard products, including alpine and Nordic skis, telemark skis, boots, bindings, poles, snowboards, snowboard boots, ice skates, backpacks and accessories. The company also sells a number of soft goods, including outerwear designed for backcountry, travel and casual use; jackets and windbreakers; hats; belts; and luggage products, including a variety of technical backpacks, wallets, rolling bags and miscellaneous bags. The company's brand names include Rossignol, Dynastar, Lange and Hammer. Western Europe and North America account for the majority of the company's sales, though it also has significant distribution in Eastern Europe, Asia and Oceania. Rossignol's primary production facilities for ski equipment are located in France, Spain and Italy; its clothing lines, accessories, in-line skates and many product components are outsourced to Eastern Europe and Asia. The company provides equipment to many top competitors in alpine, Nordic and freestyle racing. The firm operates a North American headquarters in Utah. In late 2008, the company was acquired by Macquarie Group Ltd. firm Chartreuse & Mont. Blanc for $50.9 million. In March 2009, the company announced it will cut its global work force be 30% as an attempt to return to profitability.

FINANCIALS: **Sales and profits are in thousands of dollars—add 000 to get the full amount. 2008 Note: Financial information for 2008 was not available for all companies at press time.**

2008 Sales: $	2008 Profits: $	**U.S. Stock Ticker: Subsidiary**
2007 Sales: $	2007 Profits: $	**Int'l Ticker:** Int'l Exchange:
2006 Sales: $	2006 Profits: $	Employees: 2,902
2005 Sales: $	2005 Profits: $	Fiscal Year Ends: 3/31
2004 Sales: $602,700	2004 Profits: $8,800	Parent Company: CHARTREUSE & MONT BLANC

SALARIES/BENEFITS:

Pension Plan:	ESOP Stock Plan:	Profit Sharing:	Top Exec. Salary: $	Bonus: $
Savings Plan:	Stock Purch. Plan:		Second Exec. Salary: $	Bonus: $

OTHER THOUGHTS:

Apparent Women Officers or Directors:
Hot Spot for Advancement for Women/Minorities:

LOCATIONS: ("Y" = Yes)

West:	Southwest:	Midwest:	Southeast:	Northeast:	International:
Y					Y

SMG MANAGEMENT

www.smgworld.com

Industry Group Code: 561210 **Ranks within this company's industry group:** Sales: Profits:

Sports:		Services:		Media:		Sales:		Facilities:		Other:	
Leagues/Associations:		Food & Beverage:	Y	TV:		Marketing:		Stadiums:	Y	Gambling:	
Teams:		Agents:		Radio:		Ads:		Fitness Clubs:		Apparel:	
Nonprofits:		Other:	Y	Internet:		Tickets:	Y	Golf Courses:		Equipment:	
Other:				Print:		Retail:		Ski Resorts:		Shoes:	
				Software:		Other:		Other:	Y	Other:	

TYPES OF BUSINESS:

Facilities Management Services
Food & Beverage Services
Event Booking & Management
Construction & Expansion Services

BRANDS/DIVISIONS/AFFILIATES:

ARAMARK Corporation
Hyatt Hotel Company
SMG Europe
SMGBooking.com

CONTACTS: *Note: Officers with more than one job title may be intentionally listed here more than once.*

Wes Westly, CEO
Wes Westly, Pres.
John Burns, CFO/Exec. VP
Maureen Ginty, Exec. VP-Mktg. Svcs.
Maureen Ginty, Exec. VP-Human Resources
Gregg Caren, Sr. VP-Strategic Bus. Dev.
Michael R. Evans, Sr. VP-Sports & Entertainment
Bob Cavalieri, Sr. VP-Sales & Dev.
Bob McClintock, Sr. VP-SMG Convention Centers
Hank Abate, Sr. VP-SMG Arenas
Thomas L. Connors, Sr. Regional VP-SMG Latin America

Phone: 610-792-7900 **Fax:** 610-792-1590
Toll-Free:
Address: 300 Conshohocken State Rd. Ste. 770, W. Conshohocken, PA 19428 US

GROWTH PLANS/SPECIAL FEATURES:

SMG Management, Inc., a joint venture between ARAMARK Corp. and Hyatt Hotel Company, is one of the world's largest entertainment facility management companies. The firm manages over 250 facilities throughout North America and Europe. These facilities annually host more than 9,000 events attended by 50 million people and gross over $1 billion. The company provides facilities management services through four location-specific divisions: Stadiums, arenas, convention centers and collegiate. It currently manages nine stadiums with a total of 422,000 seats; 76 arenas, including collegiate venues; 63 convention centers; 47 performing arts centers; and 40 other recreational facilities, including ice and roller-skating rinks, equestrian centers, aquariums, airfields and visitors/tourism bureaus. SMG Europe, a company subsidiary, is the largest operator of sports and entertainment venues in the U.K. and Europe, controlling 75,000 seats in eight facilities, including the Manchester Evening News Arena, the largest indoor facility in Europe. SMG provides its services through three divisions: Event booking and management; convention center services; and operations development. The event booking and management division provides services for over 1.5 million entertainment seats worldwide. The convention center services segment offers clients sales and marketing programs, lead generation, telemarketing programs, contract to facilitate bookings and tradeshow exposure. The operations development division provides new construction and expansion services, including operating budget preparation, audit and pre-opening public relations services. It works directly with project architects, consultants, contractors and other vendors on behalf of its clients. SMG runs a proprietary web-based booking system, SMGBooking.com.

FINANCIALS: **Sales and profits are in thousands of dollars—add 000 to get the full amount. 2008 Note: Financial information for 2008 was not available for all companies at press time.**

2008 Sales: $	2008 Profits: $	**U.S. Stock Ticker: Joint Venture**
2007 Sales: $	2007 Profits: $	**Int'l Ticker:** Int'l Exchange:
2006 Sales: $	2006 Profits: $	Employees:
2005 Sales: $	2005 Profits: $	Fiscal Year Ends:
2004 Sales: $	2004 Profits: $	Parent Company:

SALARIES/BENEFITS:

Pension Plan:	ESOP Stock Plan:	Profit Sharing:	Top Exec. Salary: $	Bonus: $
Savings Plan:	Stock Purch. Plan:		Second Exec. Salary: $	Bonus: $

OTHER THOUGHTS:

Apparent Women Officers or Directors: 1
Hot Spot for Advancement for Women/Minorities:

LOCATIONS: ("Y" = Yes)

West:	Southwest:	Midwest:	Southeast:	Northeast:	International:
Y	Y	Y	Y	Y	Y

Note: Financial information, benefits and other data can change quickly and may vary from those stated here.

SNAP FITNESS

www.snapfitness.com

Industry Group Code: 713940 **Ranks within this company's industry group:** Sales: Profits:

Sports:		Services:		Media:		Sales:		Facilities:		Other:	
Leagues/Associations:		Food & Beverage:		TV:		Marketing:		Stadiums:		Gambling:	
Teams:		Agents:		Radio:		Ads:		Fitness Clubs:	Y	Apparel:	
Nonprofits:		Other:		Internet:		Tickets:		Golf Courses:		Equipment:	
Other:				Print:		Retail:		Ski Resorts:		Shoes:	
				Software:		Other:		Other:		Other:	

TYPES OF BUSINESS:

Fitness Clubs
Franchising
Nutrition Supplement Plans

BRANDS/DIVISIONS/AFFILIATES:

mysnapfitness.com

CONTACTS:

Note: Officers with more than one job title may be intentionally listed here more than once.

Peter Taunton, CEO
Bill Rodriguez, VP-Mktg.
Steve Lundquist, VP/Controller
Gary Findley, Sr. VP-Franchise Sales
John Motschenbacher, VP-Systems Integration
Bob Powers, VP-Franchise Compliance

Phone: 952-474-5422	**Fax:** 952-474-5416
Toll-Free:	
Address: 2025 Coulter Blvd., Chanhassen, MN 55317 US	

GROWTH PLANS/SPECIAL FEATURES:

Snap Fitness is a franchisor of 24/7 fitness centers featuring cardio and strength-training equipment. The company has 910 clubs in 46 states and 400,000 members. International locations include Mexico, Canada, India, Australia and New Zealand. Membership fees are approximately $35 monthly and members have the ability to freeze memberships for up to three months. Membership benefits consist of free personal wellness plans; free fast-start equipment orientation; free online training center access and online nutrition and meal planning at mysnapfitness.com; and 30-day nutritional supplement plans. Because centers are staffed about 40 hours weekly, members use magnetic cards to gain access, with U.S. members having access to any center in the country. In addition, members are offered a Refer-a-Friend Rewards program that awards a $35 gift card for ever referral that joins. Cards are also redeemable for fitness gear, equipment and cruises. The company distinguishes its fitness centers from larger competitor centers by emphasizing its smaller size (at 2,500 square feet each) and safe, less populous atmosphere. Snap Fitness cost franchises about $175,000 to open a club and 60% of franchisees are absentee owners.

FINANCIALS:

Sales and profits are in thousands of dollars—add 000 to get the full amount. 2008 Note: Financial information for 2008 was not available for all companies at press time.

2008 Sales: $	2008 Profits: $	**U.S. Stock Ticker: Private**
2007 Sales: $	2007 Profits: $	**Int'l Ticker:** Int'l Exchange:
2006 Sales: $	2006 Profits: $	Employees:
2005 Sales: $	2005 Profits: $	Fiscal Year Ends:
2004 Sales: $	2004 Profits: $	Parent Company:

SALARIES/BENEFITS:

Pension Plan:	ESOP Stock Plan:	Profit Sharing:	Top Exec. Salary: $	Bonus: $
Savings Plan:	Stock Purch. Plan:		Second Exec. Salary: $	Bonus: $

OTHER THOUGHTS:

Apparent Women Officers or Directors:
Hot Spot for Advancement for Women/Minorities:

LOCATIONS: ("Y" = Yes)

West:	Southwest:	Midwest:	Southeast:	Northeast:	International:
Y	Y	Y	Y	Y	Y

SNOWDANCE INC

www.ascutney.com

Industry Group Code: 713920 **Ranks within this company's industry group:** Sales: Profits:

Sports:		Services:		Media:		Sales:		Facilities:		Other:	
Leagues/Associations:		Food & Beverage:	Y	TV:		Marketing:		Stadiums:		Gambling:	
Teams:		Agents:		Radio:		Ads:		Fitness Clubs:	Y	Apparel:	
Nonprofits:		Other:	Y	Internet:		Tickets:		Golf Courses:		Equipment:	
Other:				Print:		Retail:		Ski Resorts:	Y	Shoes:	
				Software:		Other:		Other:	Y	Other:	

TYPES OF BUSINESS:

Ski Resort
Time Shares & Condominiums
Spa Services
Summer Activities

BRANDS/DIVISIONS/AFFILIATES:

Ascutney Mountain Resort
Interval International
Snowdance Vacation Club

CONTACTS: *Note: Officers with more than one job title may be intentionally listed here more than once.*

John Plausteiner, Gen. Mgr.
Steven Plausteiner, Pres.
Susan Plausteiner, CFO
Bill Henne, Dir.-Mktg.
Susan Plausteiner, Corp. Sec.

Phone: 802-484-7000 **Fax:** 802-484-3925
Toll-Free: 800-243-0011
Address: P.O. Box 699, Rte. 44, Brownsville, VT 05037 US

GROWTH PLANS/SPECIAL FEATURES:

Snowdance, Inc. owns the Snowdance Vacation Club and Ascutney Mountain Resort, a ski resort located in Brownsville, Vermont, approximately four hours from New York City. Ascutney is a four-season resort with 57 trails, six chairlifts and diverse terrain. Ascutney's 95% overall snowmaking coverage is the highest figure in Vermont. The area receives approximately 200 inches of snow per year. The summit's elevation is 2,520 feet, and the mountain has significant amounts of runs for the novice, intermediate and advanced skier. The resort features a 215-room full-service hotel that includes a fully equipped sports/fitness center as well as a deluxe spa. Other amenities include cross-country and snowshoe trails, a terrain park with sound system, a teens-only club and a theater showing new release family films. Ascutney offers summer activities including mountain biking, tennis and miniature golf, with horseback riding, canoeing, antiquing and many additional restaurants nearby. The resort also accommodates events such as conferences and weddings. Through its Snowdance Vacation Club, the company sells weekly vacation ownership intervals in the resort's two- and three-bedroom condominiums. Through this exchange system, access is provided to more than 1,500 worldwide resorts. Ascutney Resort members are also offered discounts on ski lift tickets, restaurants and hotel accommodations and are offered complimentary use of the fitness club facilities. Lastly, the resort offers live music in various locales on the property.

Full-time employee benefits at the Ascutney Resort include skiing and snowboarding for employees and their immediate families, free rentals and lessons and discounts for mountain restaurants, pubs, hotels and child care. The company has a wide selection of seasonal job opportunities.

FINANCIALS: **Sales and profits are in thousands of dollars—add 000 to get the full amount. 2008 Note: Financial information for 2008 was not available for all companies at press time.**

2008 Sales: $
2007 Sales: $3,700
2006 Sales: $
2005 Sales: $
2004 Sales: $3,700

2008 Profits: $
2007 Profits: $
2006 Profits: $
2005 Profits: $
2004 Profits: $

U.S. Stock Ticker: Private
Int'l Ticker: Int'l Exchange:
Employees: 100
Fiscal Year Ends: 12/31
Parent Company:

SALARIES/BENEFITS:

Pension Plan: ESOP Stock Plan: Profit Sharing: Top Exec. Salary: $ Bonus: $
Savings Plan: Stock Purch. Plan: Second Exec. Salary: $ Bonus: $

OTHER THOUGHTS:

Apparent Women Officers or Directors: 2
Hot Spot for Advancement for Women/Minorities: Y

LOCATIONS: ("Y" = Yes)

West:	Southwest:	Midwest:	Southeast:	Northeast:	International:
				Y	

SOCCER UNITED MARKETING

www.sumworld.com

Industry Group Code: 541800 **Ranks within this company's industry group:** Sales: Profits:

Sports:		Services:		Media:		Sales:		Facilities:		Other:	
Leagues/Associations:	Y	Food & Beverage:		TV:	Y	Marketing:	Y	Stadiums:		Gambling:	
Teams:		Agents:		Radio:		Ads:		Fitness Clubs:		Apparel:	
Nonprofits:		Other:		Internet:		Tickets:		Golf Courses:		Equipment:	
Other:				Print:		Retail:		Ski Resorts:		Shoes:	
				Software:		Other:		Other:		Other:	

TYPES OF BUSINESS:

Soccer Marketing

BRANDS/DIVISIONS/AFFILIATES:

Major League Soccer (MLS)
United States Soccer Federation
InterLiga
SuperLiga
CONCACAF Gold Cup

CONTACTS:

Note: Officers with more than one job title may be intentionally listed here more than once.

Don Garber, CEO
Douglas Quinn, Pres.
Michael Gandler, Dir.-Bus. Dev.
Chris Schlosser, Dir.-Digital Strategy
Marisabel Munoz, Dir.-Public Rel.
Kathryn Carter, Exec. VP
Orlando Conguta, Dir.-Int'l Matches
Will Wilson, Exec. VP-Int'l Bus. & Special Events

Phone: 212-450-1200 **Fax:** 212-450-1302
Toll-Free:
Address: 420 5th Ave., New York, NY 10018 US

GROWTH PLANS/SPECIAL FEATURES:

Soccer United Marketing (SUM), founded in 2002, acts as the marketing branch of the Major League Soccer organization. The company is virtually the only major player in the U.S. in the soccer marketing field. SUM holds exclusive rights to all broadcast rights to Major League Soccer; the United States Soccer Federation; promotional and marketing rights to all Mexican National Team games played in the U.S.; the promotions and marketing of the CONCACAF (Confederation of North, Central American and Caribbean Association Football) Gold Cup; and the promotional, marketing and broadcast rights to the InterLiga, an eight team Mexican club qualifier tournament. Additionally, SUM, within the U.S., manages the promotional and marketing rights for two teams: Club Deportivo Guadalajara (Chivas) of Mexico and FCBarcelona of Spain. The form also created two international club competitions: SuperLiga, a tournament held annually between MLS and Mexico's First Division; and the Pan-Pacific, which is a special event that crowns the top Pan-Pacific region club. The company recently signed a deal with Fox Soccer Channel in which the station has an exclusive five-year programming deal with Soccer United Marketing including live and exclusive English-language rights to a selection of Major League Soccer, international friendly and U.S. Men and Women's National Team matches through 2010.

FINANCIALS:

Sales and profits are in thousands of dollars—add 000 to get the full amount. 2008 Note: Financial information for 2008 was not available for all companies at press time.

2008 Sales: $
2007 Sales: $
2006 Sales: $
2005 Sales: $
2004 Sales: $

2008 Profits: $
2007 Profits: $
2006 Profits: $
2005 Profits: $
2004 Profits: $

U.S. Stock Ticker: Private
Int'l Ticker: Int'l Exchange:
Employees:
Fiscal Year Ends:
Parent Company:

SALARIES/BENEFITS:

Pension Plan: ESOP Stock Plan: Profit Sharing: Top Exec. Salary: $ Bonus: $
Savings Plan: Stock Purch. Plan: Second Exec. Salary: $ Bonus: $

OTHER THOUGHTS:

Apparent Women Officers or Directors: 1
Hot Spot for Advancement for Women/Minorities:

LOCATIONS: ("Y" = Yes)

West:	Southwest:	Midwest:	Southeast:	Northeast:	International:
				Y	

SOUTHAMPTON FOOTBALL CLUB

www.saintsfc.co.uk

Industry Group Code: 711211D **Ranks within this company's industry group:** Sales: Profits:

Sports:		Services:		Media:		Sales:		Facilities:		Other:	
Leagues/Associations:		Food & Beverage:		TV:		Marketing:		Stadiums:	Y	Gambling:	
Teams:	Y	Agents:		Radio:	Y	Ads:		Fitness Clubs:		Apparel:	
Nonprofits:		Other:	Y	Internet:		Tickets:	Y	Golf Courses:		Equipment:	
Other:				Print:		Retail:	Y	Ski Resorts:		Shoes:	
				Software:		Other:	Y	Other:		Other:	Y

TYPES OF BUSINESS:

Professional Soccer Teams
Radio Station
Insurance & Financial Services

BRANDS/DIVISIONS/AFFILIATES:

Saints
Southampton Leisure Holdings plc
Women's Southampton Football Club
St. Mary's Stadium
107.8 The Saint

CONTACTS: *Note: Officers with more than one job title may be intentionally listed here more than once.*

David Jones, Exec. Dir.-Finance
Rupert Lowe, Exec. Chmn.

Phone: 08-45-688-9448 **Fax:** 08-45-688-9445
Toll-Free:
Address: St. Mary's Stadium, Britannia Rd., Southampton, SO14 5FP UK

GROWTH PLANS/SPECIAL FEATURES:

The Southampton Football Club, also called the Saints, is a soccer team owned by Southampton Leisure Holdings plc, which also owns and manages the Women's Southampton Football Club, all located in the U.K. The Southampton Football Club lost its place in the English Premier League in 2005 and now plays in the English Championship League. Current team sponsors include Carlsberg; Coca-Cola; Cedar Group; Draper; Flybe; Breeze Southampton Volkswagen; and paddypower.com sponsor the club. Both teams play at the Friends Provident St. Mary's Stadium. Fans may purchase paving stones or bricks with personalized engraved messages to be a part of the Friends Provident St. Mary's Stadium. The Saints team is Britain's only soccer team to own its own local FM radio station (107.8 The Saint), which provides live commentary on every game. Great former Saints players include fullback Micky Adams, fullback Reuben Agboola, Derek Allan and Paul Allen. To support its community, the club provides bi-weekly coaching sessions for its disability football program. The Saints also sell insurance and financial products, including financial advisory services; household insurance; motor vehicle insurance including motorcycle, commercial vehicle and yacht; travel, public and employer liability; professional indemnity and special event insurance policies; as well as employee benefit plans. Despite management turnover, the team managed to secure sixth place, the last playoff place during the 2007-08 season. In April 2009, Southampton Leisure Holdings plc put the firm up for sale, the 30,000-seat St. Mary's stadium and its training ground are not included in the offer.

FINANCIALS: **Sales and profits are in thousands of dollars—add 000 to get the full amount. 2008 Note: Financial information for 2008 was not available for all companies at press time.**

2008 Sales: $
2007 Sales: $20,500
2006 Sales: $
2005 Sales: $
2004 Sales: $91,400

2008 Profits: $
2007 Profits: $
2006 Profits: $
2005 Profits: $
2004 Profits: $2,900

U.S. Stock Ticker: Subsidiary
Int'l Ticker: Int'l Exchange:
Employees: 206
Fiscal Year Ends: 5/31
Parent Company: SOUTHAMPTON LEISURE HOLDINGS PLC

SALARIES/BENEFITS:

Pension Plan: ESOP Stock Plan: Profit Sharing: Top Exec. Salary: $ Bonus: $
Savings Plan: Stock Purch. Plan: Second Exec. Salary: $ Bonus: $

OTHER THOUGHTS:

Apparent Women Officers or Directors:
Hot Spot for Advancement for Women/Minorities:

LOCATIONS: ("Y" = Yes)

West:	Southwest:	Midwest:	Southeast:	Northeast:	International:
					Y

SPECIALIZED BICYCLE COMPONENTS INC

www.specialized.com

Industry Group Code: 339920 **Ranks within this company's industry group:** Sales: Profits:

Sports:		Services:		Media:		Sales:		Facilities:		Other:	
Leagues/Associations:		Food & Beverage:		TV:		Marketing:		Stadiums:		Gambling:	
Teams:	Y	Agents:		Radio:		Ads:		Fitness Clubs:		Apparel:	Y
Nonprofits:		Other:		Internet:		Tickets:		Golf Courses:		Equipment:	Y
Other:				Print:		Retail:		Ski Resorts:		Shoes:	Y
				Software:		Other:		Other:		Other:	

TYPES OF BUSINESS:

Bicycles
Biking Accessories

BRANDS/DIVISIONS/AFFILIATES:

Stumpjumper
Enduro
Epic
S-Works
Enduro SL
Rockhopper
Fatboy
Crosstrail

CONTACTS:

Note: Officers with more than one job title may be intentionally listed here more than once.

Michael Haynes, COO
Mike Sinyard, Pres.
Ron Pollard, CIO

Phone: 408-779-6229	**Fax:** 408-779-1631
Toll-Free:	
Address: 15130 Concord Cir., Morgan Hill, CA 95037 US	

GROWTH PLANS/SPECIAL FEATURES:

Specialized Bicycle Components, Inc., based in California, is a leading manufacturer of bicycles, accessories and apparel. The firm's original Stumpjumper, introduced in 1981, was displayed in the Smithsonian and was one of the first mass-produced mountain bikes, establishing the company as a top-seller. Now Specialized markets a full line of men's and women's mountain bikes under the brands S-Works, Stumpjumper, Enduro SL, Epic, Rockhopper, Fatboy and Hardrock; and road bikes under the brands Tricross and Crosstrail. Specialized also makes BMX bikes, commuter/city bikes, children's bikes and accessories such as bags, team gear, component parts, computers, grips and shoes. The firm sponsors a range of professional teams as well as local teams organized through Specialized retailers. Specialized has several concept stores in operation and under construction. Additionally, Specialized maintains a tech lab that develops gear and equipment specifically for riding. Its bicycle saddles use proprietary Body Geometry Technology, which features an ergonomic design to reduce soreness and numbness related to bicycling. Mike Sinyard, the firm's president and founder, owns a majority stake in the company. New apparel in 2008 includes the women's Body Geometry Pro shorts, transition shorts, Mira jersey, Trail Top, Atlas Top, Calypso Top and print jersey; the men's bib shorts, transition shorts, SL jersey, Pro jersey, Avilan jersey, Offset jersey, Avilan sleeveless top, Trail Top and Apollo Top; and team jerseys.

FINANCIALS:

Sales and profits are in thousands of dollars—add 000 to get the full amount. 2008 Note: Financial information for 2008 was not available for all companies at press time.

2008 Sales: $	2008 Profits: $	**U.S. Stock Ticker: Private**
2007 Sales: $20,200	2007 Profits: $	**Int'l Ticker:** Int'l Exchange:
2006 Sales: $	2006 Profits: $	Employees: 348
2005 Sales: $	2005 Profits: $	Fiscal Year Ends: 12/31
2004 Sales: $	2004 Profits: $	Parent Company:

SALARIES/BENEFITS:

Pension Plan:	ESOP Stock Plan:	Profit Sharing:	Top Exec. Salary: $	Bonus: $
Savings Plan:	Stock Purch. Plan:		Second Exec. Salary: $	Bonus: $

OTHER THOUGHTS:

Apparent Women Officers or Directors:
Hot Spot for Advancement for Women/Minorities:

LOCATIONS: ("Y" = Yes)

West:	Southwest:	Midwest:	Southeast:	Northeast:	International:
Y		Y		Y	

SPEEDWAY MOTORSPORTS INC

www.speedwaymotorsports.com

Industry Group Code: 711212 **Ranks within this company's industry group:** Sales: 2 Profits: 2

Sports:		Services:		Media:		Sales:		Facilities:		Other:	
Leagues/Associations:		Food & Beverage:	Y	TV:		Marketing:	Y	Stadiums:		Gambling:	
Teams:		Agents:		Radio:		Ads:		Fitness Clubs:		Apparel:	
Nonprofits:		Other:		Internet:		Tickets:		Golf Courses:		Equipment:	
Other:				Print:		Retail:	Y	Ski Resorts:		Shoes:	
				Software:		Other:		Other:	Y	Other:	Y

TYPES OF BUSINESS:

Automobile Race Tracks
Motorsports Entertainment
Concession Operations
Licensing-Broadcast Rights
Radio Programming
Merchandising

BRANDS/DIVISIONS/AFFILIATES:

Atlanta Motor Speedway
Bristol Motor Speedway
Infineon Raceway
Las Vegas Motor Speedway
Lowe's Motor Speedway
New Hampshire Motor Speedway
Kentucky Speedway
600 Racing

CONTACTS: *Note: Officers with more than one job title may be intentionally listed here more than once.*

O. Bruton Smith, CEO
Marcus G. Smith, COO
Marcus G. Smith, Pres.
William R. Brooks, CFO
Janet Kirkley, Media Rel.
William R. Brooks, Treas.
M. Jeffrey Byrd, VP/Gen. Mgr.-BMS
Edwin R. Clark, VP/Gen. Mgr.-AMS
William E. Gossage, VP/Gen. Mgr.-TMS
Steve Page, Pres., IR
O. Bruton Smith, Chmn.

Phone: 704-455-3239 **Fax:** 704-455-2547
Toll-Free:
Address: 5555 Concord Pkwy. S., Concord, NC 28027 US

GROWTH PLANS/SPECIAL FEATURES:

Speedway Motorsports, Inc. is a promoter, marketer and sponsor of motorsports activities in the U.S. Through its subsidiaries, the firm owns and operates Atlanta Motor Speedway; New Hampshire Motor Speedway; Bristol Motor Speedway; Infineon Raceway; Las Vegas Motor Speedway; Lowe's Motor Speedway; and Texas Motor Speedway. Its racing facilities are located in ten top U.S. markets, including three of the top ten television broadcasting markets, and collectively have a seating capacity of 900,000. Speedway offers many additional services through its subsidiaries, such as: event food and beverage hospitality, catering and souvenir merchandising services through its SMI Properties subsidiaries and Motorsports Authentics joint venture; radio programming, production and distribution through Performance Racing Network; wholesale and retail racing and other sports souvenir merchandise through The Source International; and the manufacture and distribution of smaller-scale, modified racing cars and parts through its 600 Racing subsidiary. Speedway derives revenue principally from the sale of tickets to automobile races and other events held at its speedways; food and beverage concessions; souvenir sales; the sale of sponsorships to companies that wish to advertise or sell products or services; and the licensing of television, cable network and radio rights to broadcast events. Approximately 82% of the company's total revenues are from NASCAR-sanctioned events. In December 2008, Speedway Motorsports purchased Kentucky Speedway from Kentucky Speedway LLC.

FINANCIALS: Sales and profits are in thousands of dollars—add 000 to get the full amount. 2008 Note: Financial information for 2008 was not available for all companies at press time.

2008 Sales: $610,993 — 2008 Profits: $80,040
2007 Sales: $561,646 — 2007 Profits: $38,394
2006 Sales: $567,365 — 2006 Profits: $111,222
2005 Sales: $544,068 — 2005 Profits: $108,135
2004 Sales: $446,519 — 2004 Profits: $73,654

U.S. Stock Ticker: TRK
Int'l Ticker: Int'l Exchange:
Employees: 1,114
Fiscal Year Ends: 12/31
Parent Company:

SALARIES/BENEFITS:

Pension Plan: — ESOP Stock Plan: — Profit Sharing: — Top Exec. Salary: $600,000 — Bonus: $1,300,000
Savings Plan: Y — Stock Purch. Plan: — Second Exec. Salary: $500,000 — Bonus: $700,000

OTHER THOUGHTS:

Apparent Women Officers or Directors:
Hot Spot for Advancement for Women/Minorities:

LOCATIONS: ("Y" = Yes)

West:	Southwest:	Midwest:	Southeast:	Northeast:	International:
Y	Y		Y	Y	

SPORT CHALET INC

www.sportchalet.com

Industry Group Code: 451110 **Ranks within this company's industry group:** Sales: 7 Profits: 6

Sports:		Services:		Media:		Sales:		Facilities:		Other:	
Leagues/Associations:		Food & Beverage:		TV:		Marketing:		Stadiums:		Gambling:	
Teams:		Agents:		Radio:		Ads:		Fitness Clubs:		Apparel:	
Nonprofits:		Other:		Internet:		Tickets:		Golf Courses:		Equipment:	
Other:				Print:		Retail:	Y	Ski Resorts:		Shoes:	
				Software:		Other:		Other:		Other:	

TYPES OF BUSINESS:

Sporting Goods Stores
Equipment Repair
Scuba Training
Equipment Rental
Sports-Related Services
Online Sales

BRANDS/DIVISIONS/AFFILIATES:

GSI Commerce, Inc.

CONTACTS:

Note: Officers with more than one job title may be intentionally listed here more than once.

Craig L. Levra, CEO
Craig L. Levra, Pres.
Howard K. Kaminsky, CFO/Exec. VP-Finance
David Hacker, Dir.-Advertising & Mktg.
Cynthia Stein, Dir.-Human Resources & Training
Theodore F. Jackson, CIO/VP-IT
Tom Tennyson, Chief Merch. Officer/Exec. VP
Howard K. Kaminsky, Sec.
Tim A. Anderson, Sr. VP-Store Oper.
Dennis D. Trausch, Exec. VP-Growth & Dev.
Laura Hensley, Dir.-Acct./Controller
Jason Gautereaux, VP-Planning & Inventory Mgmt.
Kenneth Brackett, Div. Merch. Mgr.-Hardlines
John Davidson, Dir.-Facilities & Store Construction
Brad Morton, Dir.-Team Sales
Craig L. Levra, Chmn.
Steve Belardi, VP-Logistics

Phone: 818-949-5300 **Fax:**
Toll-Free:
Address: 1 Sport Chalet Dr., La Canada, CA 91011 US

GROWTH PLANS/SPECIAL FEATURES:

Sport Chalet, Inc. is a leading operator of full-service sporting goods superstores in California, Arizona, Utah and Nevada. The company's 52 stores feature a number of specialty sporting goods divisions, offering a large assortment of brand-name merchandise at competitive prices. The stores offer traditional sporting goods merchandise, including footwear, apparel and equipment, as well as specialty products, such as snowboarding, skateboarding, mountaineering and SCUBA. A typical Sport Chalet store features multiple specialty shops for beginners to experts in multiple sports, including traditional and nontraditional sports equipment and athletic footwear for a variety of sports. Additionally, the stores feature custom fitting services, including custom wet suits, scuba masks and boot mountings. Sport Chalet stores also generally offer more than 50 services for customers, such as backpacking, canyoneering, and kayaking instruction; custom golf club fitting and repair; snowboard and ski rental and repair; SCUBA training and certification; SCUBA boat charters; team sales; racquet stringing; and bicycle tune-up and repair. A typical store features a natural and outdoor-feel color scheme, 30-foot clear ceilings, a pool for SCUBA and water sports instruction and demonstrations, and a 100 foot shoe wall. To keep its stores stocked, the firm operates a 326,000 square foot distribution center in Ontario, California. In addition, the company has a retail e-commerce store operated by GSI Commerce, Inc. at sportchalet.com. Sport Chalet recently entered the Utah market with the opening of a store in West Jordan, Utah, as well as opening additional stores in Arizona, California and Nevada. In May 2008, Sport Chalet announced that it had entered into a joint training and operations agreement with Ocean Enterprises, a specialty dive center, through which the companies will cooperate to conduct employee and dive instructor training and certification, as well as joint merchandising and marketing initiatives.

FINANCIALS:

Sales and profits are in thousands of dollars—add 000 to get the full amount. 2008 Note: Financial information for 2008 was not available for all companies at press time.

2008 Sales: $402,534	2008 Profits: $-3,362	**U.S. Stock Ticker: SPCHB**
2007 Sales: $388,209	2007 Profits: $7,099	**Int'l Ticker:** Int'l Exchange:
2006 Sales: $343,204	2006 Profits: $- 87	Employees: 4,300
2005 Sales: $309,090	2005 Profits: $6,171	Fiscal Year Ends: 3/31
2004 Sales: $264,237	2004 Profits: $4,644	Parent Company:

SALARIES/BENEFITS:

Pension Plan:	ESOP Stock Plan:	Profit Sharing:	Top Exec. Salary: $380,000	Bonus: $
Savings Plan: Y	Stock Purch. Plan:		Second Exec. Salary: $228,000	Bonus: $

OTHER THOUGHTS:

Apparent Women Officers or Directors: 2
Hot Spot for Advancement for Women/Minorities:

LOCATIONS: ("Y" = Yes)

West:	Southwest:	Midwest:	Southeast:	Northeast:	International:
Y	Y				

SPORT SUPPLY GROUP INC

www.sportsupplygroup.com

Industry Group Code: 454110A **Ranks within this company's industry group:** Sales: 2 Profits: 1

Sports:		Services:		Media:		Sales:		Facilities:		Other:	
Leagues/Associations:		Food & Beverage:		TV:		Marketing:		Stadiums:		Gambling:	
Teams:		Agents:		Radio:		Ads:		Fitness Clubs:		Apparel:	Y
Nonprofits:		Other:		Internet:		Tickets:		Golf Courses:		Equipment:	
Other:				Print:		Retail:		Ski Resorts:		Shoes:	
				Software:		Other:		Other:		Other:	Y

TYPES OF BUSINESS:

Sporting Goods, Direct Sales
Online Sales
Catalogs
Telemarketing
Physical Education Products

BRANDS/DIVISIONS/AFFILIATES:

Collegiate Pacific, Inc.
Sport Supply Group Asia, Ltd.
MacGregor Team Sports
New England Camp
BSN Sports
Tomark Sports
Voit
Triple Threat

CONTACTS:

Note: Officers with more than one job title may be intentionally listed here more than once.

Adam Blumenfeld, CEO
Terrence M. Babilla, COO
Terrence M. Babilla, Pres.
John E. Pitts, CFO
Kurt Hagen, Exec. VP-Sales & Mktg.
Terrence M. Babilla, General Counsel/Sec.
Trevis Martin, Exec. VP-U.S. Oper.
Peggy Rozelle, Dir.-Investor Rel.
Adam Blumenfeld, Chmn.

Phone: 972-484-9484	**Fax:**
Toll-Free:	
Address: 1901 Diplomat Dr., Farmers Branch, TX 75234 US	

GROWTH PLANS/SPECIAL FEATURES:

Sport Supply Group, Inc. (formerly Collegiate Pacific, Inc.) is a leading direct-mail marketer of sporting goods, physical education products, recreational items and leisure equipment. The firm primarily sells its products through three million direct catalogs, e-commerce sites, telemarketers and an outside sales force of 197 people. Sport Supply Group offers brand name and private-label products, including Voit, MacGregor, Triple Threat, Alumagoal, Pro Down and Bulldog. The firm also has resale contracts with major brands such as Adidas, Rawlings and Nike Team. Catalogs include BSN Sports, Tomark Sports, MacGregor Team Sports and New England Camp. The firm's web sites, each of which is targeted to a specific customer group or product line, enable consumers to place orders, access account information, track orders and perform routine customer service inquiries. In addition, the company has licenses and marketing alliances with national organizations such as YMCA, YWCA, Little League Baseball and American Youth Football. The company markets its 18,500 products to the U.S. institutional market, which comprises schools, colleges, universities, government agencies, military facilities, athletic clubs, athletic teams and dealers, youth sports leagues and recreational organizations. A customer database of over 400,000 names, a call center, combined distribution centers, worldwide sourcing and domestic manufacturing facilities all support Sports Supply Group's marketing efforts.

Employees are offered health benefits, as well as a 401(k) plan.

FINANCIALS:

Sales and profits are in thousands of dollars—add 000 to get the full amount. 2008 Note: Financial information for 2008 was not available for all companies at press time.

2008 Sales: $251,394	2008 Profits: $9,733	**U.S. Stock Ticker: RBI**
2007 Sales: $236,855	2007 Profits: $3,860	**Int'l Ticker:** Int'l Exchange:
2006 Sales: $224,238	2006 Profits: $1,896	Employees: 762
2005 Sales: $106,339	2005 Profits: $3,601	Fiscal Year Ends: 3/31
2004 Sales: $83,867	2004 Profits: $-1,688	Parent Company:

SALARIES/BENEFITS:

Pension Plan:	ESOP Stock Plan:	Profit Sharing:	Top Exec. Salary: $400,000	Bonus: $250,000
Savings Plan: Y	Stock Purch. Plan:		Second Exec. Salary: $375,000	Bonus: $187,500

OTHER THOUGHTS:

Apparent Women Officers or Directors: 1
Hot Spot for Advancement for Women/Minorities:

LOCATIONS: ("Y" = Yes)

West:	Southwest:	Midwest:	Southeast:	Northeast:	International:
	Y		Y		

SPORTS AUTHORITY INC (THE)

www.sportsauthority.com

Industry Group Code: 451110 **Ranks within this company's industry group:** Sales: Profits:

Sports:		Services:		Media:		Sales:		Facilities:		Other:	
Leagues/Associations:		Food & Beverage:		TV:		Marketing:		Stadiums:		Gambling:	
Teams:		Agents:		Radio:		Ads:		Fitness Clubs:		Apparel:	
Nonprofits:		Other:		Internet:		Tickets:		Golf Courses:		Equipment:	
Other:				Print:		Retail:	Y	Ski Resorts:		Shoes:	
				Software:		Other:		Other:		Other:	

TYPES OF BUSINESS:

Sporting Goods Stores
Athletic Apparel & Footwear
Team Sports Equipment

BRANDS/DIVISIONS/AFFILIATES:

CONTACTS:

Note: Officers with more than one job title may be intentionally listed here more than once.

John D. Morton, CEO
David Campisi, Pres.
Thomas Hendrickson, CFO
Thomas Hendrickson, Chief Admin. Officer
Thomas Hendrickson, Treas.
John D. Morton, Chmn.

Phone: 303-200-5050	**Fax:** 303-863-2240
Toll-Free:	
Address: 1050 W. Hampden Ave., Englewood, CO 80110 US	

GROWTH PLANS/SPECIAL FEATURES:

The Sports Authority, Inc. is a full-line sporting goods dealer based in the U.S., with about 422 stores in 45 states. Stores offer an extensive product selection for sports and leisure activities including golf, tennis, skiing, cycling, hunting, fishing and bowling. Merchandise includes men's, women's and children's athletic apparel; athletic footwear; and team sports equipment. Sports Authority stores are located primarily in regional strip or power centers, although some stores are located in malls and stand-alone locations. Sports Authority emphasizes features such as specialty stores within stores, interactive kiosks, in-store customer clinics, demonstrations, small batting cages or basketball courts and a wide array of audiovisual entertainment. The firm's merchandise assortment includes over 700 brand names, such as Adidas, Champion, Mongoose, Nike, Reebok, Shakespeare and Wilson. Additionally, the company tailors merchandise to reflect customer preferences at each store location, which may mean the elimination of items such as stationary bicycles or swimming goods at certain stores. Sports Authority operates a joint venture with AEON Co., Ltd., which runs about 40 Sports Authority stores in Japan; and an e-commerce site, SportsAuthority.com, operated by GSI Commerce. The company recently went private. In October 2008, the firm opened 13 new stores in 10 states.

FINANCIALS:

Sales and profits are in thousands of dollars—add 000 to get the full amount. 2008 Note: Financial information for 2008 was not available for all companies at press time.

2008 Sales: $	2008 Profits: $	**U.S. Stock Ticker: Private**
2007 Sales: $2,980,000	2007 Profits: $	**Int'l Ticker:** Int'l Exchange:
2006 Sales: $2,509,300	2006 Profits: $55,400	Employees: 15,825
2005 Sales: $2,435,863	2005 Profits: $33,467	Fiscal Year Ends: 1/31
2004 Sales: $1,760,450	2004 Profits: $16,262	Parent Company:

SALARIES/BENEFITS:

Pension Plan:	ESOP Stock Plan:	Profit Sharing:	Top Exec. Salary: $934,999	Bonus: $
Savings Plan:	Stock Purch. Plan:		Second Exec. Salary: $582,692	Bonus: $

OTHER THOUGHTS:

Apparent Women Officers or Directors:
Hot Spot for Advancement for Women/Minorities:

LOCATIONS: ("Y" = Yes)

West:	Southwest:	Midwest:	Southeast:	Northeast:	International:
Y	Y	Y	Y	Y	Y

SPORTS ILLUSTRATED

sportsillustrated.cnn.com

Industry Group Code: 511120 **Ranks within this company's industry group:** Sales: Profits:

Sports:		Services:		Media:		Sales:		Facilities:		Other:	
Leagues/Associations:		Food & Beverage:		TV:		Marketing:		Stadiums:		Gambling:	
Teams:		Agents:		Radio:		Ads:	Y	Fitness Clubs:		Apparel:	
Nonprofits:		Other:		Internet:	Y	Tickets:		Golf Courses:		Equipment:	
Other:				Print:		Retail:		Ski Resorts:		Shoes:	
				Software:		Other:		Other:		Other:	

TYPES OF BUSINESS:

Sports Magazine
Merchandising

BRANDS/DIVISIONS/AFFILIATES:

Sports Illustrated KIDS
Sports Illustrated Almanac
Sports Illustrated Swimsuit Issue
SI China
FanNation.com
Golf.com

CONTACTS: *Note: Officers with more than one job title may be intentionally listed here more than once.*

Ann S. Moore, CEO
Mark Ford, Pres./Publisher
Andrew R. Judelson, Chief Mktg. Officer
Liz Mattila, Dir.-Human Resources
Judith R. Margolin, Dir.-Legal
Robert Kanell, Dir.-Oper.
Jeff Price, Pres., SI Digital
Scott Novak, VP-Comm.
Susan Roberson, VP-Finance
John Huey, Editor-in-Chief
Paul Fichtenbaum, Managing Editor-SI.com
Terry McDonell, Editor-Sports Illustrated Group
Bob Der, Managing Editor-SI Kids
Ann S. Moore, Chmn.

Phone: 212-522-1212 **Fax:** 212-522-0475
Toll-Free: 800-528-5000
Address: 1271 Ave. of the Americas, 32nd Fl., New York, NY 10020-1339 US

GROWTH PLANS/SPECIAL FEATURES:

Sports Illustrated (SI), a subsidiary of Time Warner, Inc., is a leading sports publication. Published weekly, SI has a total readership of approximately 21 million adults. The magazine has over 3 million subscribers, one of the highest subscription circulations in the country. In print since 1954, SI offers comprehensive news coverage of the sports industry, including the National Football League (NFL), National Baseball Association (NBA), Major League Baseball (MLB), college football, college basketball, golf, NASCAR racing, tennis, hockey, soccer, boxing, cycling, horse racing, track and field, cricket, rugby, mixed martial arts (MMA), Olympic events, winter sports and international sporting events. SI's reporting includes stories on games, scores, players, team management, leagues and sports trends. The company also publishes an annual swimsuit issue, a very popular offering that generates its own related television shows, videos and calendars. The swimsuit issue is read by roughly 32% of all U.S. adults ages 18 and up and serves as an important component in SI's annual revenue, both through increased magazine sales and premium advertising prices charged for the issue. Other publications include Sports Illustrated KIDS, with coverage aimed at children and young teens, as well as the annual Sports Illustrated Almanac. SI also publishes a sports magazine in China called SI China, carrying mostly original content produced by a China-based team with some translated stories from the American version of the magazine. Additionally, SI offers a variety of online content, including its main web site, which is affiliated with CNN news and features more than 150 original stories weekly; FanNation.com, with approximately 4 million unique visitors monthly; and Golf.com, with approximately 1.2 million unique users and 16 million page views monthly. In November 2008, the company announced that it would suspend publication of SI Latino, a free Spanish-language sports magazine that was published six times per year.

FINANCIALS: **Sales and profits are in thousands of dollars—add 000 to get the full amount. 2008 Note: Financial information for 2008 was not available for all companies at press time.**

2008 Sales: $ | 2008 Profits: $
2007 Sales: $ | 2007 Profits: $
2006 Sales: $ | 2006 Profits: $
2005 Sales: $ | 2005 Profits: $
2004 Sales: $ | 2004 Profits: $

U.S. Stock Ticker: Subsidiary
Int'l Ticker: Int'l Exchange:
Employees:
Fiscal Year Ends: 12/31
Parent Company: TIME WARNER INC

SALARIES/BENEFITS:

Pension Plan: ESOP Stock Plan: Profit Sharing: Top Exec. Salary: $ Bonus: $
Savings Plan: Stock Purch. Plan: Second Exec. Salary: $ Bonus: $

OTHER THOUGHTS:

Apparent Women Officers or Directors: 5
Hot Spot for Advancement for Women/Minorities: Y

LOCATIONS: ("Y" = Yes)

West:	Southwest:	Midwest:	Southeast:	Northeast:	International:
Y	Y	Y	Y	Y	Y

SPORTSMAN'S GUIDE INC (THE)

www.sportsmansguide.com

Industry Group Code: 451110 **Ranks within this company's industry group:** Sales: Profits:

Sports:		**Services:**		**Media:**		**Sales:**		**Facilities:**		**Other:**	
Leagues/Associations:		Food & Beverage:		TV:		Marketing:		Stadiums:		Gambling:	
Teams:		Agents:		Radio:		Ads:		Fitness Clubs:		Apparel:	Y
Nonprofits:		Other:		Internet:	Y	Tickets:		Golf Courses:		Equipment:	Y
Other:				Print:		Retail:	Y	Ski Resorts:		Shoes:	Y
				Software:		Other:		Other:		Other:	

TYPES OF BUSINESS:

Outdoor & Hunting Products
Online & Catalog Sales
Outdoor Apparel & Footwear
Golf Equipment

BRANDS/DIVISIONS/AFFILIATES:

Redcats USA
sportsmansguide.com
tgw.com
BargainOutfitters.com
boatingsavings.com
Buyer's Club

CONTACTS: *Note: Officers with more than one job title may be intentionally listed here more than once.*

Gregory R. Binkley, CEO
Gregory R. Binkley, Pres.
John M. Casler, Exec. VP-Mktg. & Creative Svcs.
Dale D. Monson, CIO/Sr. VP
John M. Casler, Exec. VP-Merch.
Dale D. Monson, Sr. VP-Oper.
Charles B. Lingen, Exec. VP-Finance/Treas.

Phone: 651-451-3030	**Fax:** 651-450-6130
Toll-Free: 888-844-0667	
Address: 411 Farwell Ave. S., St. Paul, MN 55075 US	

GROWTH PLANS/SPECIAL FEATURES:

The Sportsman's Guide, Inc., a subsidiary of Redcats USA (which is owned by Redcats Group), is a multi-channel direct marketer of value-priced outdoor gear and clothing, golf equipment and general merchandise. The company sells its products through main and specialty catalogs and several e-commerce sites, including sportsmansguide.com; tgw.com, which focuses on golf products; and bargainoutfitters.com, a liquidation outlet. The firm's main catalog is mailed monthly, and offers merchandise across a broad range of categories. Additional specialized catalogs are also offered during the course of each year and focus on individual categories such as camping, government surplus, ammunition and shooting supplies, gifts and hunting. The Buyer's Club, which customers can join for an annual fee, offers 10% discounts on most merchandise (5% on ammunition), a monthly Buyer's Advantage Catalog and exclusive special offers. The Sportsman's Guide e-commerce site offers a selection similar to its print catalog in addition to certain specialty catalogs available exclusively online, such as Truck/SUV and ATV. More than 60% of the company's sales come through its web site. An online resource center features a variety of articles, advice columns and information about outdoor lifestyles and pursuits, including a section specifically aimed at women outdoor enthusiasts. In addition, customers can find maps, fish and game forecasts, local guide and outfitter listings, ballistics charts, useful links and other information on the web site. Orders can be placed 24-hours-a-day by phone or online, and the company ships all orders directly from its 330,000-square-foot warehouse. In 2008, Sportsmen's Guide launched the boatingsavings.com e-commerce site, which aims to be a one-stop shop for fishing and boating enthusiasts.

FINANCIALS: **Sales and profits are in thousands of dollars—add 000 to get the full amount. 2008 Note: Financial information for 2008 was not available for all companies at press time.**

2008 Sales: $	2008 Profits: $	**U.S. Stock Ticker: Subsidiary**
2007 Sales: $	2007 Profits: $	**Int'l Ticker:** Int'l Exchange:
2006 Sales: $	2006 Profits: $	Employees: 754
2005 Sales: $285,120	2005 Profits: $11,453	Fiscal Year Ends: 12/31
2004 Sales: $232,465	2004 Profits: $7,593	Parent Company: REDCATS GROUP

SALARIES/BENEFITS:

Pension Plan:	ESOP Stock Plan:	Profit Sharing:	Top Exec. Salary: $296,923	Bonus: $655,000
Savings Plan:	Stock Purch. Plan:		Second Exec. Salary: $234,615	Bonus: $330,000

OTHER THOUGHTS:

Apparent Women Officers or Directors:
Hot Spot for Advancement for Women/Minorities:

LOCATIONS: ("Y" = Yes)

West:	Southwest:	Midwest:	Southeast:	Northeast:	International:
		Y			

ST LOUIS BLUES

www.stlouisblues.com

Industry Group Code: 711211F **Ranks within this company's industry group:** Sales: 25 Profits: 25

Sports:		Services:		Media:		Sales:		Facilities:		Other:	
Leagues/Associations:		Food & Beverage:		TV:		Marketing:		Stadiums:	Y	Gambling:	
Teams:	Y	Agents:		Radio:		Ads:		Fitness Clubs:		Apparel:	
Nonprofits:		Other:		Internet:		Tickets:	Y	Golf Courses:		Equipment:	
Other:				Print:		Retail:	Y	Ski Resorts:		Shoes:	
				Software:		Other:		Other:		Other:	

TYPES OF BUSINESS:

Professional Hockey Team
Ticket Sales
Team Merchandise

BRANDS/DIVISIONS/AFFILIATES:

National Hockey League (NHL)
Scottrade Center
Sports Capital Partners Worldwide
Peoria Rivermen
American Hockey League (AHL)
Alaska Aces
ECHL

CONTACTS: *Note: Officers with more than one job title may be intentionally listed here more than once.*

Peter McLoughlin, CEO
Brent P. Karasiuk, COO
John Davidson, Pres.
Mark Toffolo, Sr. VP-Corp. & Sponsorship Sales
Val Brinker, Dir.-Human Resources
Tony Kostansek, Mgr.-IT
Phil Siddle, VP-Admin. & Finance
Brent P. Karasiuk, General Counsel
John Davidson, Pres., Hockey Oper./Alternate Governor
Eric Stisser, Sr. VP-Bus. Dev.
Michael Caruso, Dir.-Media Rel. & Team Svcs.
Craig Bryant, Mgr.-Acct.
Michael McCarthy, Partner/Alternate Governor/Vice Chmn.
Kenneth W. Munoz, Partner/Alternate Governor
Andy Murray, Head Coach
Larry Pleau, Gen. Mgr./Sr. VP
David W. (Dave) Checketts, Chmn./Governor

Phone: 314-622-2500	**Fax:** 314-622-2582
Toll-Free:	
Address: 1401 Clark Ave., St. Louis, MO 63103 US	

GROWTH PLANS/SPECIAL FEATURES:

The St. Louis Blues franchise, owned and operated by St. Louis Blues Hockey Club L.L.C. and based in St. Louis, Missouri, is a professional ice hockey team playing in the Central Division of the Western Conference of the National Hockey League (NHL), along with the Chicago Blackhawks, Columbus Blue Jackets, Detroit Red Wings and Nashville Predators. Though the Blues have never won the Stanley Cup, the team reached the playoffs in 25 consecutive seasons from 1979 to 2003. Five players from the team's history have been elevated to Hall of Fame status. While the Blues had traditionally received enthusiastic fan support, ranked in the top five for NHL average attendance ratings from 2001 to 2004, in 2005 its fan support began to fade and it ranked 30th in NHL average attendance ratings for the 2005-06 season. This was in part due to the team finishing its 2005-06 season with its worst record in 27 years, missing the playoffs for the fourth time in its history. The team plays its home games at the 19,150 capacity Scottrade Center arena. The team is owned by Dave Checketts, who acquired it in 2006 through his sports consulting and investment services firm Sports Capital Partners Worldwide. The team is currently undergoing a rebuilding effort and is looking to build a strong American base of players. The Blues team is affiliated with the Peoria Rivermen of the AHL and the Alaska Aces of the ECHL. In the 2008-09 season, the team averaged approximately 18,554 fans in attendance per game. A recent Forbes estimate values the team at $162 million.

FINANCIALS: **Sales and profits are in thousands of dollars—add 000 to get the full amount. 2008 Note: Financial information for 2008 was not available for all companies at press time.**

2008 Sales: $73,000	2008 Profits: $-8,600	**U.S. Stock Ticker: Private**
2007 Sales: $66,000	2007 Profits: $-5,500	**Int'l Ticker:** Int'l Exchange:
2006 Sales: $66,000	2006 Profits: $1,000	Employees:
2005 Sales: $	2005 Profits: $	Fiscal Year Ends: 6/30
2004 Sales: $66,000	2004 Profits: $	Parent Company: SPORTS CAPITAL PARTNERS WORLDWIDE

SALARIES/BENEFITS:

Pension Plan:	ESOP Stock Plan:	Profit Sharing:	Top Exec. Salary: $	Bonus: $
Savings Plan:	Stock Purch. Plan:		Second Exec. Salary: $	Bonus: $

OTHER THOUGHTS:

Apparent Women Officers or Directors: 10
Hot Spot for Advancement for Women/Minorities: Y

LOCATIONS: ("Y" = Yes)

West:	Southwest:	Midwest:	Southeast:	Northeast:	International:
		Y			

ST LOUIS CARDINALS

stlouis.cardinals.mlb.com

Industry Group Code: 711211A **Ranks within this company's industry group:** Sales: 10 Profits: 1

Sports:		Services:		Media:		Sales:		Facilities:		Other:	
Leagues/Associations:		Food & Beverage:		TV:		Marketing:		Stadiums:	Y	Gambling:	
Teams:	Y	Agents:		Radio:		Ads:		Fitness Clubs:		Apparel:	
Nonprofits:		Other:		Internet:		Tickets:	Y	Golf Courses:		Equipment:	
Other:				Print:		Retail:	Y	Ski Resorts:		Shoes:	
				Software:		Other:		Other:		Other:	

TYPES OF BUSINESS:

Professional Baseball Team
Ticket Sales
St. Louis Cardinals Merchandise

BRANDS/DIVISIONS/AFFILIATES:

Busch Stadium
Memphis Redbirds
Springfield Cardinals
Palm Beach Cardinals
St. Louis Cardinals LP
St. Louis Brown Stockings
Busch Stadium

CONTACTS: *Note: Officers with more than one job title may be intentionally listed here more than once.*

William O. DeWitt Jr., Gen. Partner
Bill DeWitt III, Pres.
Dan Farrell, Sr. VP-Sales & Mktg.
Christine Nelson, Dir.-Human Resources
Vicki Bryant, VP-Event Svcs. & Merch.
Joe Abernathy, VP-Stadium Oper.
Bill DeWitt III, Sr. VP-Bus. Dev.
Brian Bartow, Dir.-Media Rel.
Brad Wood, Sr. VP/Controller
John Mozeliak, Sr. VP/Gen. Mgr.
Jeff Luhnow, VP-Player Dev./Amateur Scouting
Andrew N. Baur, Treas./Sec.
Tony La Russa, Mgr.-Field
William O. DeWitt, Jr., Chmn.

Phone: 314-345-9600	**Fax:** 314-345-9523
Toll-Free:	
Address: 700 Clark St., St. Louis, MO 63102 US	

GROWTH PLANS/SPECIAL FEATURES:

The St. Louis Cardinals, one of the oldest teams in Major League Baseball (MLB), began as the St. Louis Brown Stockings of the American Association in 1882 and has played under its current name since 1900. A long-time rival of the Chicago Cubs, the Cardinals have been far more successful, with a total of 10 World Series victories, 20 pennants and eight division titles. Led by player/manager Rogers Hornsby, the team shocked the world in 1926 by beating the New York Yankees in the World Series. The team was a contender for many years to come, and in the 1930s had a group of players known as the Gashouse Gang, which featured such legends as Dizzy Dean, Joe Medwick, Pepper Martin and Leo Durocher. The 1940s were its best decade by far, as the team won three World Series and featured star player Stan Musial. The team won three more pennants in the 1960s and three in the 1980s. In the latter decade the team was noted for its speedy runners and sparkling defense, and featured Vince Coleman, Ozzie Smith, Wille McGee, Jack Clark, Bruce Sutter and others. In 2004, the Cardinals achieved its best season record since the 1940s at 105 wins, but in 2006, with merely 83 wins, the team outlasted all others to become World Series Champions. That year, the Cardinals played in a new $400 million facility, the third to be named Busch Stadium. The new venue features a hand-operated scoreboard, a natural grass playing surface and seating for over 50,000. The team was purchased by William DeWitt, Jr. in 1996 for $150 million. Home game attendance in 2008 averaged 42,353. The team was recently ranked the 8th most valuable in MLB by Forbes Magazine, which estimated the team's worth at $486 million.

FINANCIALS: **Sales and profits are in thousands of dollars—add 000 to get the full amount. 2008 Note: Financial information for 2008 was not available for all companies at press time.**

2008 Sales: $195,000	2008 Profits: $66,000	**U.S. Stock Ticker: Subsidiary**
2007 Sales: $194,000	2007 Profits: $21,500	**Int'l Ticker:** Int'l Exchange:
2006 Sales: $184,000	2006 Profits: $14,000	Employees:
2005 Sales: $165,000	2005 Profits: $	Fiscal Year Ends: 10/31
2004 Sales: $	2004 Profits: $	Parent Company: ST LOUIS CARDINALS LP

SALARIES/BENEFITS:

Pension Plan:	ESOP Stock Plan:	Profit Sharing:	Top Exec. Salary: $	Bonus: $
Savings Plan:	Stock Purch. Plan:		Second Exec. Salary: $	Bonus: $

OTHER THOUGHTS:

Apparent Women Officers or Directors: 2
Hot Spot for Advancement for Women/Minorities:

LOCATIONS: ("Y" = Yes)

West:	Southwest:	Midwest:	Southeast:	Northeast:	International:
		Y			

ST LOUIS RAMS

www.stlouisrams.com

Industry Group Code: 711211C **Ranks within this company's industry group:** Sales: 23 Profits: 13

Sports:		Services:		Media:		Sales:		Facilities:		Other:	
Leagues/Associations:		Food & Beverage:		TV:		Marketing:	Y	Stadiums:		Gambling:	
Teams:	Y	Agents:		Radio:		Ads:		Fitness Clubs:		Apparel:	Y
Nonprofits:		Other:		Internet:		Tickets:	Y	Golf Courses:		Equipment:	
Other:				Print:		Retail:	Y	Ski Resorts:		Shoes:	
				Software:		Other:		Other:		Other:	

TYPES OF BUSINESS:

Professional Football Team

BRANDS/DIVISIONS/AFFILIATES:

Edward Jones Dome
Rams Football Company, Inc. (The)

CONTACTS: *Note: Officers with more than one job title may be intentionally listed here more than once.*

Kevin Demoff, COO
John Shaw, Pres.
Mike O'Keefe, VP-Sales
Tony Softli, VP-Player Personnel
Robert E. Wallace, Jr., General Counsel/Exec. VP
John Oswald, VP-Oper.
Rick Smith, VP-Public Rel.
Michael T. Naughton, VP-Finance
Steve Spagnuolo, Head Coach
Billy Devaney, Gen. Mgr.
Kevin Demoff, Exec. VP-Football Oper.
Jeff Brewer, Treas.
Chip Rosenbloom, Chmn.

Phone: 314-982-7267 **Fax:** 314-770-9261
Toll-Free:
Address: 1 Rams Way, St. Louis, MO 63045 US

GROWTH PLANS/SPECIAL FEATURES:

The St. Louis Rams are a professional football team playing in the National Football League (NFL) based in St. Louis, Missouri. The team began its history in 1937, playing in Cleveland, Ohio as a second version of the previous Cleveland Rams team, a charter member of the American Football League. The franchise then became known as the Los Angeles Rams after the club moved to Los Angeles, California, in 1946. In 1995, the team moved to its current home in St. Louis. The Rams have won one Super Bowl championship (1999-2000), two NFL Championships (1945, 1951) three National Football Conference (NFC) Championships and eight NFC West Division titles. Notable former players include Kurt Warner and Marshall Faulk. Wal-Mart heir Stan Kroenke, who also owns the Colorado Avalanche, the Denver Nuggets and the Pepsi Center in Denver, Colorado, is part-owner of the team. Lucia Rodriguez and Chip Rosenbloom, son of previous team owners Georgia Frontiere and Carroll Rosenbloom, are the franchise's other two owners. The Rams organization was recently named as part of NFL commissioner Paul Tagliabue's committee to determine how a new revenue-sharing plan will work under the league's labor deal. The Rams play at the Edward Jones Dome, which opened in November 1995 and has a seating capacity of 66,000. The stadium is owned by the St. Louis Regional Sports Authority. A recent Forbes estimate values the team at $929 million. In the 2008 season, the team averaged 59,980 fans in attendance per home game.

FINANCIALS: **Sales and profits are in thousands of dollars—add 000 to get the full amount. 2008 Note: Financial information for 2008 was not available for all companies at press time.**

2008 Sales: $206,000	2008 Profits: $26,400	**U.S. Stock Ticker: Subsidiary**
2007 Sales: $193,000	2007 Profits: $17,900	**Int'l Ticker:** Int'l Exchange:
2006 Sales: $179,000	2006 Profits: $33,200	Employees:
2005 Sales: $176,000	2005 Profits: $	Fiscal Year Ends: 12/31
2004 Sales: $	2004 Profits: $	Parent Company: THE RAMS FOOTBALL COMPANY, INC.

SALARIES/BENEFITS:

Pension Plan:	ESOP Stock Plan:	Profit Sharing:	Top Exec. Salary: $	Bonus: $
Savings Plan:	Stock Purch. Plan:		Second Exec. Salary: $	Bonus: $

OTHER THOUGHTS:

Apparent Women Officers or Directors: 1
Hot Spot for Advancement for Women/Minorities:

LOCATIONS: ("Y" = Yes)

West:	Southwest:	Midwest:	Southeast:	Northeast:	International:
		Y			

TAMPA BAY BUCCANEERS

www.buccaneers.com

Industry Group Code: 711211C **Ranks within this company's industry group:** Sales: 10 Profits: 4

Sports:		Services:		Media:		Sales:		Facilities:		Other:	
Leagues/Associations:		Food & Beverage:		TV:		Marketing:		Stadiums:	Y	Gambling:	
Teams:	Y	Agents:		Radio:		Ads:		Fitness Clubs:		Apparel:	Y
Nonprofits:		Other:		Internet:		Tickets:	Y	Golf Courses:		Equipment:	
Other:				Print:		Retail:	Y	Ski Resorts:		Shoes:	
				Software:		Other:		Other:		Other:	

TYPES OF BUSINESS:

Professional Football Team

BRANDS/DIVISIONS/AFFILIATES:

Raymond James Stadium
Malcolm Glazer
Bucs

CONTACTS:

Note: Officers with more than one job title may be intentionally listed here more than once.

Malcolm I. Glazer, Pres.
Nick Reader, CFO
Raheem Morris, Head Coach
Edward Glazer, Co-Chmn.
Joel Glazer, Co-Chmn.
Mark Dominik, Gen. Mgr.
Bryan Glazer, Co-Chmn.

Phone: 813-870-2700	**Fax:** 813-878-0813
Toll-Free:	
Address: 1 Buccaneer Pl., Tampa, FL 33607 US	

GROWTH PLANS/SPECIAL FEATURES:

The Tampa Bay Buccaneers franchise is a professional football team playing in the National Football League (NFL), as part of the Southern Division of the National Football Conference (NFC). Professional football came to Tampa as part of the 1976 NFL expansion. Nicknamed the Bucs by fans, the team had a bumpy start, losing every game its first season and all but two the next. The team was able to turn these poor records around quickly in its fourth season in the NFL the team made the playoffs. The Buccaneers' success didn't last long, as the team only managed two winning seasons between 1980 and 1996. The Bucs rosters have included many football greats, such as Vinny Testaverde, Warrick Dunn, Steve Young, Keyshawn Johnson and Warren Sapp. In 1996, Malcolm Glazer, owner of Manchester United (a top club in England's FA Premier League) bought the team for $192 million, the highest sum paid for a professional sports franchise at that time. Under the ownership of the Glazer family, the Bucs reached the playoffs five times between 1998 and 2003 and won the franchise's first Super Bowl in 2003. The team plays in the 65,647-seat Raymond James Stadium, which opened in 1998. The Buccaneers share the stadium with the University of South Florida football team. A recent Forbes estimate values the team at $1.05 billion. In the 2008 season, the team averaged 64,511 fans in attendance per home game.

FINANCIALS:

Sales and profits are in thousands of dollars—add 000 to get the full amount. 2008 Note: Financial information for 2008 was not available for all companies at press time.

2008 Sales: $224,000	2008 Profits: $39,300	**U.S. Stock Ticker: Private**
2007 Sales: $205,000	2007 Profits: $39,500	**Int'l Ticker:** Int'l Exchange:
2006 Sales: $203,000	2006 Profits: $56,900	Employees:
2005 Sales: $195,000	2005 Profits: $	Fiscal Year Ends: 12/31
2004 Sales: $	2004 Profits: $	Parent Company:

SALARIES/BENEFITS:

Pension Plan:	ESOP Stock Plan:	Profit Sharing:	Top Exec. Salary: $	Bonus: $
Savings Plan:	Stock Purch. Plan:		Second Exec. Salary: $	Bonus: $

OTHER THOUGHTS:

Apparent Women Officers or Directors:
Hot Spot for Advancement for Women/Minorities:

LOCATIONS: ("Y" = Yes)

West:	Southwest:	Midwest:	Southeast:	Northeast:	International:
			Y		

TAMPA BAY LIGHTNING

www.tampabaylightning.com

Industry Group Code: 711211F **Ranks within this company's industry group:** Sales: 19 Profits: 16

Sports:		Services:		Media:		Sales:		Facilities:		Other:	
Leagues/Associations:		Food & Beverage:		TV:		Marketing:		Stadiums:	Y	Gambling:	
Teams:	Y	Agents:		Radio:		Ads:		Fitness Clubs:		Apparel:	
Nonprofits:		Other:		Internet:		Tickets:	Y	Golf Courses:		Equipment:	
Other:				Print:		Retail:	Y	Ski Resorts:		Shoes:	
				Software:		Other:		Other:		Other:	

TYPES OF BUSINESS:

Professional Hockey Team

BRANDS/DIVISIONS/AFFILIATES:

National Hockey League (NHL)
Kokusai Green
St. Pete Times Forum
Norfolk Admirals
American Hockey League
Mississippi Sea Wolves
Palace Sports & Entertainment Inc
OK Hockey LLC

CONTACTS:

Note: Officers with more than one job title may be intentionally listed here more than once.

Thomas S. (Tom) Wilson, CEO/Governor
Sean Henry, COO/Exec. VP
Ronald J. (Ron) Campbell, Pres./Alternate Governor
Joe Fada, CFO/Exec. VP-Finance
Harry Hutt, Exec. VP-Corp. Sales & Mktg.
Debbie Nye, Mgr.-Human Resources
Rosie Chhuor, Assistant Mgr.-Information Svcs.
David Everett, Sr. VP-Admin.
Paul Davis, VP-Legal Affairs/Legal Counsel
Jamie Williams, Web Admin.
Ron Pierce, VP-Comm. Affairs & Gov't Rel.
Doug Riefler, Dir.-Acct.
Jay H. Feaster, Exec. VP/Gen. Mgr./Alternate Governor
John Tortorella, Head Coach

Phone: 813-301-6600	**Fax:** 813-301-1487
Toll-Free:	
Address: 401 Channellside Dr., Tampa, FL 33602 US	

GROWTH PLANS/SPECIAL FEATURES:

The Tampa Bay Lightning hockey club is a National Hockey League (NHL) team based in Tampa, Florida. The team was founded in 1992 by former NHL player Phil Esposito as an expansion franchise. Although the Lightning met with success in its early years, it floundered in the years that followed due to mismanagement and financial troubles from its backing by a consortium of Japanese businesses headed by Kokusai Green, a Japanese golf course and resort operator. When Kokusai Green decided to sell the Lightning in 1997, the team had debt equaling 236% of its value. The team's ownership has changed hands several times since and it continued to struggle for several years with the debt and management problems that remained from Kokusai Green's former management. While the Lightning has only managed five winning seasons since its inception, it has been to the playoffs and in 2004, it won the Stanley Cup Championships. The Lightning plays in the St. Pete Times Forum arena, which has a hockey seating capacity of 19,500. The team's minor league affiliates include the Norfolk Admirals of the American Hockey League and the Mississippi Sea Wolves of the ECHL (formerly the East Coast Hockey League). Palace Sports & Entertainment currently owns the Lightning, although in February 2008, the firm agreed to sell the team to OK Hockey LLC, a group headed by Hollywood movie producer Oren Kroules. For the 2009-09 season, the Lightning's average home attendance was approximately 16,500. Forbes recently estimated the team's value at roughly $200 million.

FINANCIALS:

Sales and profits are in thousands of dollars—add 000 to get the full amount. 2008 Note: Financial information for 2008 was not available for all companies at press time.

2008 Sales: $84,000	2008 Profits: $1,200	**U.S. Stock Ticker: Subsidiary**
2007 Sales: $85,000	2007 Profits: $ 600	**Int'l Ticker:** Int'l Exchange:
2006 Sales: $82,000	2006 Profits: $5,000	Employees:
2005 Sales: $	2005 Profits: $	Fiscal Year Ends: 6/30
2004 Sales: $88,000	2004 Profits: $	Parent Company: PALACE SPORTS & ENTERTAINMENT INC

SALARIES/BENEFITS:

Pension Plan:	ESOP Stock Plan:	Profit Sharing:	Top Exec. Salary: $	Bonus: $
Savings Plan:	Stock Purch. Plan:		Second Exec. Salary: $	Bonus: $

OTHER THOUGHTS:

Apparent Women Officers or Directors: 29
Hot Spot for Advancement for Women/Minorities: Y

LOCATIONS: ("Y" = Yes)

West:	Southwest:	Midwest:	Southeast:	Northeast:	International:
			Y		

Note: Financial information, benefits and other data can change quickly and may vary from those stated here.

TAMPA BAY RAYS

tampabay.devilrays.mlb.com

Industry Group Code: 711211A **Ranks within this company's industry group:** Sales: 26 Profits: 5

Sports:		Services:		Media:		Sales:		Facilities:		Other:	
Leagues/Associations:		Food & Beverage:		TV:		Marketing:		Stadiums:		Gambling:	
Teams:	Y	Agents:		Radio:		Ads:		Fitness Clubs:		Apparel:	
Nonprofits:		Other:		Internet:		Tickets:	Y	Golf Courses:		Equipment:	
Other:				Print:		Retail:	Y	Ski Resorts:		Shoes:	
				Software:		Other:		Other:		Other:	

TYPES OF BUSINESS:

Professional Baseball Team

BRANDS/DIVISIONS/AFFILIATES:

Tropicana Field
Tampa Bay Rays Ltd.

CONTACTS:

Note: Officers with more than one job title may be intentionally listed here more than once.

Matthew Silverman, Pres.
Stuart Sternberg, Principal Owner

Phone: 727-825-3137	**Fax:** 727-825-3111
Toll-Free:	
Address: 1 Tropicana Dr., St. Petersburg, FL 33705 US	

GROWTH PLANS/SPECIAL FEATURES:

The Tampa Bay Rays, formerly the Tampa Bay Devil Rays, are a team within Major League Baseball (MLB) that was formed as part of the 1998 league expansion. The genesis of the Rays was difficult, with many bids to place a team in St. Petersburg, Florida (the team's home) but none panning out until a group led by Vince Naimoli gained approval in the 1998 expansion. Once the team was off the ground, it finished in last place in its division every season from 1998 to 2003. The Rays signed legendary manager Lou Piniella during the 2003 off season, and in 2004, it finished with a 70-91 record. The team plays at Tropicana Field, an artificial turf stadium with a 43,500-spectator capacity. In 2005, Stuart Sternberg led a group that purchased a controlling interest of the team from Naimoli. In 2008, the team earned the American League Pennant for the first time in club history and advanced to the World Series, where the team was defeated by the Philadelphia Phillies. Also in 2008, the team acquired a minor league baseball team in Vero Beach, Florida (the team will be relocated to Charlotte County); and announced plans to construct a baseball training facility in Brazil. The academy will consist of two full playing fields and two diamonds for youth teams, as well as dormitories to accommodate up to 40 players The Rays are currently awaiting approval by the Tampa Bay City Council on a new $450 million, waterfront ballpark featuring a retractable roof with a seat capacity of approximately 34,000 that would be ready for the 2012 season. In 2008, average home game attendance was 22,259. Forbes recently estimated the team to be worth $320 million.

FINANCIALS:

Sales and profits are in thousands of dollars—add 000 to get the full amount. 2008 Note: Financial information for 2008 was not available for all companies at press time.

2008 Sales: $160,000	2008 Profits: $29,400	**U.S. Stock Ticker: Subsidiary**
2007 Sales: $138,000	2007 Profits: $29,700	**Int'l Ticker:** Int'l Exchange:
2006 Sales: $134,000	2006 Profits: $20,200	Employees:
2005 Sales: $116,000	2005 Profits: $	Fiscal Year Ends: 10/31
2004 Sales: $	2004 Profits: $	Parent Company: TAMPA BAY RAYS LTD

SALARIES/BENEFITS:

Pension Plan:	ESOP Stock Plan:	Profit Sharing:	Top Exec. Salary: $	Bonus: $
Savings Plan:	Stock Purch. Plan:		Second Exec. Salary: $	Bonus: $

OTHER THOUGHTS:

Apparent Women Officers or Directors:
Hot Spot for Advancement for Women/Minorities:

LOCATIONS: ("Y" = Yes)

West:	Southwest:	Midwest:	Southeast:	Northeast:	International:
			Y		

TECNICA SPA

www.tecnica.it

Industry Group Code: 339920 **Ranks within this company's industry group:** Sales: Profits:

Sports:		Services:		Media:		Sales:		Facilities:		Other:	
Leagues/Associations:		Food & Beverage:		TV:		Marketing:		Stadiums:		Gambling:	
Teams:		Agents:		Radio:		Ads:		Fitness Clubs:		Apparel:	Y
Nonprofits:		Other:		Internet:		Tickets:		Golf Courses:		Equipment:	Y
Other:				Print:		Retail:		Ski Resorts:		Shoes:	Y
				Software:		Other:		Other:		Other:	

TYPES OF BUSINESS:

Sports Equipment
Ski & Snowboard Equipment
Technical Clothing
In-Line Skates
Performance Footwear
Outdoor Sports Accessories

BRANDS/DIVISIONS/AFFILIATES:

Nordica
Rollerblade
Dolomite
Moon Boot
elan
Lowa
Nitro Snowboards
Think Pink

CONTACTS: *Note: Officers with more than one job title may be intentionally listed here more than once.*

Giancarlo Zanatta, CEO
Maurizio Di Trani, Dir.-Mktg.
Maurizio Di Trani, Dir.-Comm.
Karl Hofstatter, CEO-Sports Blizzard Gmbh
Giancarlo Zanatta, Chmn.

Phone: 39-0422-8841 **Fax:** 39-0422-775-178
Toll-Free:
Address: Via Fante D'ltalia 56, Giavera del Montello, 31040 Italy

GROWTH PLANS/SPECIAL FEATURES:

Tecnica S.p.A. is an Italian-based manufacturer and marketer of action sports equipment, primarily footwear. The firm's array of products includes equipment for winter sports activities such as skis, ski boots, ski bindings and snowboards. Additionally, the company sells in-line skates, performance footwear, goggles, helmets, technical outerwear and sportswear. Tecnica sells its products primarily within three different headings: Skiboots, Outdoor and Footwear. The Skiboots section is divided into different groups based on various brand names that are best known for competitions, sports, women and youths. The Outdoor section is subdivided into footwear for mountaineering and backpacking; hiking and fastpacking; amphibian activities; beachwear; sandals and sport; and women's footwear. The Footwear section contains lines of shoes designed for everyday wear either in summer or winter conditions. The company's offerings include numerous leading brand names in their respective markets. Tecnica's brand names include Magneto, Nordica, Diablo, Dolomite, Rollerblade, Blizzard, Think Pink, Volkl, Moon Boot and Marker. The company has distribution agreements with a number of companies worldwide, including Comercial Valle Amarillo S.A., Marker Volkl and Tecnica USA Skiboot Corp. in North America; Bentley Sports PTY, Ltd. and Gravity Sports Imports in Australia and New Zealand; Fidia SA in South America; as well as eight other companies in Asia and approximately 55 in Europe. Tecnica sponsors many professional ski racers and free skiing athletes worldwide, including Alex Busca, Elena Spalenza, Deville Christian, Herbst Reinfried, Holaus Maria and Hosp Nicole.

FINANCIALS: **Sales and profits are in thousands of dollars—add 000 to get the full amount. 2008 Note: Financial information for 2008 was not available for all companies at press time.**

2008 Sales: $
2007 Sales: $
2006 Sales: $
2005 Sales: $
2004 Sales: $682,000

2008 Profits: $
2007 Profits: $
2006 Profits: $
2005 Profits: $
2004 Profits: $

U.S. Stock Ticker: Private
Int'l Ticker: Int'l Exchange:
Employees:
Fiscal Year Ends: 12/31
Parent Company:

SALARIES/BENEFITS:

Pension Plan: ESOP Stock Plan: Profit Sharing: Top Exec. Salary: $ Bonus: $
Savings Plan: Stock Purch. Plan: Second Exec. Salary: $ Bonus: $

OTHER THOUGHTS:

Apparent Women Officers or Directors:
Hot Spot for Advancement for Women/Minorities:

LOCATIONS: ("Y" = Yes)

West:	Southwest:	Midwest:	Southeast:	Northeast:	International:
				Y	Y

Note: Financial information, benefits and other data can change quickly and may vary from those stated here.

TENNESSEE TITANS

www.titansonline.com

Industry Group Code: 711211C **Ranks within this company's industry group:** Sales: 15 Profits: 15

Sports:		Services:		Media:		Sales:		Facilities:		Other:	
Leagues/Associations:		Food & Beverage:		TV:		Marketing:		Stadiums:	Y	Gambling:	
Teams:	Y	Agents:		Radio:		Ads:		Fitness Clubs:		Apparel:	
Nonprofits:		Other:		Internet:		Tickets:	Y	Golf Courses:		Equipment:	
Other:				Print:		Retail:	Y	Ski Resorts:		Shoes:	
				Software:		Other:		Other:		Other:	

TYPES OF BUSINESS:

Professional Football Team

BRANDS/DIVISIONS/AFFILIATES:

Tennessee Football, Inc.
Titans Caravan
Tennessee Titans Foundation

CONTACTS:

Note: Officers with more than one job title may be intentionally listed here more than once.

K. S. (Bud) Adams, Jr., CEO
K. S. (Bud) Adams, Jr., Pres.
Robert McBurnett, CFO
Ralph Ockenfels, VP-Mktg.
Don MacLachlan, VP-Admin. & Facilities
Steve Underwood, General Counsel/Sr. Exec. VP
Stuart Spears, Sr. Dir.-Oper.
Bob Hyde, VP-Comm. Rel.
Robert McBurnett, VP-Finance
Mike Reinfeldt, Exec. VP/Gen. Mgr.
Jeff Fisher, Head Coach/Exec. VP
Jenneen Kaufman, Controller
Stuart Spears, Sr. Dir.-Sales
K. S. (Bud) Adams, Jr., Chmn.

Phone: 615-565-4300	**Fax:**
Toll-Free:	
Address: 1 Titans Way, Nashville, TN 37213 US	

GROWTH PLANS/SPECIAL FEATURES:

The Tennessee Titans are a National Football League (NFL) team owned by K.S. (Bud) Adams, Jr. and Nancy N. Adams through Tennessee Football, Inc. The Titans, formerly the Oilers, moved from Houston and its dilapidated Astrodome to Nashville in 1996, after local voters overwhelmingly approved the use of public funding to construct a new stadium downtown. The team was able to move into the new stadium in 1999, which was called the Adelphia Coliseum until 2002 when team sponsor Adelphia filed for bankruptcy. LP Field, as it is now known, hosts a variety of events, including Tennessee State University football games. The stadium is owned by the city of Nashville and Davidson County. The Titans boast a solid and devoted fan base, with ticket prices commanding the fifth-highest sum in the NFL and regular sell-outs of the team's stadium. The Titans also regularly have the second-highest sales of team and NFL-branded merchandise. The team has made periodic appearances in divisional playoffs but has yet to repeat its ill-fated trip to Super Bowl XXXIV in 2000. One of the team's traditions is Titan Tuesdays, when players make special appearances throughout the community in hospitals and Nashville middle schools. The team plays in the AFC South conference, alongside the Jacksonville Jaguars, Indianapolis Colts and Houston Texans. Notable players have included Steve McNair, Eddie George, Frank Wycheck, Drew Bennett and Samari Rolle. A recent Forbes estimate values the team at $994 million. In the 2008 season, the team averaged 69,143 fans in attendance per home game.

FINANCIALS:

Sales and profits are in thousands of dollars—add 000 to get the full amount. 2008 Note: Financial information for 2008 was not available for all companies at press time.

2008 Sales: $216,000	2008 Profits: $24,500
2007 Sales: $196,000	2007 Profits: $24,200
2006 Sales: $189,000	2006 Profits: $48,300
2005 Sales: $186,000	2005 Profits: $
2004 Sales: $164,000	2004 Profits: $

U.S. Stock Ticker: Private
Int'l Ticker: Int'l Exchange:
Employees:
Fiscal Year Ends: 3/31
Parent Company: TENNESSEE FOOTBALL INC

SALARIES/BENEFITS:

Pension Plan:	ESOP Stock Plan:	Profit Sharing:	Top Exec. Salary: $	Bonus: $
Savings Plan:	Stock Purch. Plan:		Second Exec. Salary: $	Bonus: $

OTHER THOUGHTS:

Apparent Women Officers or Directors: 1
Hot Spot for Advancement for Women/Minorities:

LOCATIONS: ("Y" = Yes)

West:	Southwest:	Midwest:	Southeast:	Northeast:	International:
			Y		

TEXAS RANGERS

texas.rangers.mlb.com

Industry Group Code: 711211A **Ranks within this company's industry group:** Sales: 19 Profits: 15

Sports:		Services:		Media:		Sales:		Facilities:		Other:	
Leagues/Associations:		Food & Beverage:		TV:		Marketing:		Stadiums:	Y	Gambling:	
Teams:	Y	Agents:		Radio:		Ads:		Fitness Clubs:		Apparel:	
Nonprofits:		Other:		Internet:		Tickets:	Y	Golf Courses:		Equipment:	
Other:				Print:		Retail:	Y	Ski Resorts:		Shoes:	
				Software:		Other:		Other:		Other:	

TYPES OF BUSINESS:

Professional Baseball Team

BRANDS/DIVISIONS/AFFILIATES:

Hicks Holdings LLC
Hicks Sports Group Holdings LLC
Rangers Ballpark
Dr Pepper Youth Ballpark
Texas Rangers Baseball Foundation
Washington Senators

CONTACTS:

Note: Officers with more than one job title may be intentionally listed here more than once.

Nolan Ryan, Pres.
Kellie Fischer, CFO
Andrew Silverman, Exec. VP-Sales
Terry Turner, VP-Human Resources
Mike Bullock, Asst. VP-IT
Diane Atkinson, Asst. VP-Merch.
Kate Jett, Associate Counsel
Rob Matwick, Exec. VP-Ballpark Oper.
Jim Sundberg, Sr. Exec. VP-Corp. Comm. & Public Rel.
Kellie Fischer, Exec. VP-Finance
Jon Daniels, Gen. Mgr.
John Blake, Exec. VP-Comm.
Casey Coffman, COO-Hicks Sports Group
Dale Petroskey, VP-Mtkg. & Comm. Dev.
Thomas O. Hicks, Chmn./Owner

Phone: 817-273-5222 **Fax:** 817-273-5174
Toll-Free:
Address: 1000 Ballpark Way, Ste. 400, Arlington, TX 76011 US

GROWTH PLANS/SPECIAL FEATURES:

The Texas Rangers are a Major League Baseball (MLB) team based in Arlington, Texas. The team began as the third incarnation of the Washington Senators in 1961, but moved to Texas and became the Rangers in 1972. The team has never appeared in a World Series or won a pennant, only managing to make it to the postseason three times in its history, in 1996, 1998 and 1999. The Rangers are a business segment of Hicks Sports Group Holdings LLC (HSG), which is owned by billionaire Thomas O. Hicks' Hicks Holdings LLC. HSG also owns the Texas-based hockey team the Dallas Stars. Popular ex-players include shortstop Alex Rodriguez and Hall-of-Fame pitcher Nolan Ryan (now the Rangers' President). The team plays at the Rangers Park in Arlington, a 49,115-seat open-air ballpark. The team sponsors the Texas Rangers Baseball Foundation, a nonprofit organization that supports the construction of youth baseball parks and the operation of youth incentive programs, as well as awarding college scholarships to local students. In May 2008, the Rangers announced that renovations to the Dr Pepper Youth Ballpark, a state-of-the-art youth league baseball facility, had been completed. These renovations largely included expansion and upgraded features, such as a 20-foot high retaining wall and see-through screening in the left field wall for additional viewing. In 2008, average home game attendance was 24,320. Forbes recently estimated the team to be worth $405 million.

FINANCIALS:

Sales and profits are in thousands of dollars—add 000 to get the full amount. 2008 Note: Financial information for 2008 was not available for all companies at press time.

2008 Sales: $176,000
2007 Sales: $172,000
2006 Sales: $155,000
2005 Sales: $153,000
2004 Sales: $

2008 Profits: $17,400
2007 Profits: $17,200
2006 Profits: $11,200
2005 Profits: $
2004 Profits: $

U.S. Stock Ticker: Subsidiary
Int'l Ticker: Int'l Exchange:
Employees:
Fiscal Year Ends: 12/31
Parent Company: HICKS SPORTS GROUP HOLDINGS LLC

SALARIES/BENEFITS:

Pension Plan:	ESOP Stock Plan:	Profit Sharing:	Top Exec. Salary: $	Bonus: $
Savings Plan:	Stock Purch. Plan:		Second Exec. Salary: $	Bonus: $

OTHER THOUGHTS:

Apparent Women Officers or Directors: 20
Hot Spot for Advancement for Women/Minorities: Y

LOCATIONS: ("Y" = Yes)

West:	Southwest:	Midwest:	Southeast:	Northeast:	International:
	Y				

TICKETMASTER ENTERTAINMENT INC

www.ticketmaster.com

Industry Group Code: 454110A **Ranks within this company's industry group:** Sales: 1 Profits: 2

Sports:		Services:		Media:		Sales:		Facilities:		Other:	
Leagues/Associations:		Food & Beverage:		TV:		Marketing:		Stadiums:		Gambling:	
Teams:		Agents:		Radio:		Ads:		Fitness Clubs:		Apparel:	
Nonprofits:		Other:		Internet:		Tickets:	Y	Golf Courses:		Equipment:	
Other:				Print:		Retail:		Ski Resorts:		Shoes:	
				Software:		Other:		Other:		Other:	

TYPES OF BUSINESS:

Event Ticket Sales
Campsite Reservation
Web-Based Ticketing Software
Network Ticketing Services
Artist Management
Talent Agents and Representatives

BRANDS/DIVISIONS/AFFILIATES:

Emma Entertainment Holdings HK Limited
Front Line Management Group
Admission.com
LiveDaily
Cottonblend
TicketWeb
TicketsNow.com
Getmein.com

CONTACTS: *Note: Officers with more than one job title may be intentionally listed here more than once.*

Irving Azoff, CEO
Brian Regan, CFO/Exec. VP
Beverly K. Carmichael, Chief People Officer/Sr. VP-Human Resources
Brian Pike, CTO
Edward J. Weiss, General Counsel/Exec. VP
Mike McGee, Exec. VP-North American Bus. Oper.
Wendy Markus Webb, Chief Comm. Officer
Wendy Markus Webb, Chief Investor Rel. Officer
Eric Korman, Pres.
Barry Diller, Chmn.
Tommy Higgins, Exec. VP-Ticketmaster Europe

Phone: 310-360-3300 **Fax:**
Toll-Free:
Address: 8800 W. Sunset Blvd, West Hollywood, CA 90069 US

GROWTH PLANS/SPECIAL FEATURES:

Ticketmaster is a provider of ticketing and marketing services for live entertainment offering a variety of events such as live music, sports, arts and family entertainment events. Ticketmaster operates internationally in 20 global markets, providing ticket sales, ticket resale services, marketing and distribution through Ticketmaster.com, one of the largest e-commerce sites on the Internet; approximately 7,100 retail outlets; and 17 worldwide call centers. The company serves its clients worldwide, providing exclusive ticketing services for leading arenas, stadiums, professional sports franchises and leagues, college sports teams, performing arts venues, museums, and theaters. The company sold more than 141 million tickets in 2008. Additionally, the firm has several e-commerce businesses that generate revenue including Tickeweb.com; Slotix.com; Billettservice.no; Livedaily.com; Admission.com; and Ticktacticket.com, to name a few. Ticketmaster also offers regional web sites such as ReserveAmerica, a provider of campsite reservation services and campsite reservation software in North America, serving more than 100,000 campsites in approximately 48 states. It mainly works with U.S. state and federal agencies. TicketWeb is a provider of Internet-based box-office ticketing software and services, offering TicketWeb 2.0 Software that allows clients to perform box office functions, such as ticket and seating reservation, through a standard web browser. In 2008, the firm was spun off by former parent firm IAC/InterActiveCorp. In January 2008, Ticketmaster acquired Getmein.com, a web site marketplace for live entertainment in Europe. In February 2008, the company acquired TicketsNow.com, a web site that sells music, sports and other live entertainment events tickets. In October 2008, the firm acquired a controlling interest in Front Line Management, a leading artist management company. In early 2009, Ticketmaster and Live Nation announced plans to merge, which would create a giant entertainment firm with Barry Diller as Chairman and Michael Rapino as CEO.

Employees of Ticketmaster are offered medical, dental, vision coverage; three weeks paid vacation per year; tuition reimbursement; a 401(k) plan; a flexible spending plan; an employee assistance program; discounts with various retailer such as Apple and Verizon; discounts on tickets for select events and health cub discounts.

FINANCIALS: Sales and profits are in thousands of dollars—add 000 to get the full amount. 2008 Note: Financial information for 2008 was not available for all companies at press time.

2008 Sales: $1,454,525	2008 Profits: $-1,005,499	**U.S. Stock Ticker: TKTM**
2007 Sales: $1,240,477	2007 Profits: $169,351	**Int'l Ticker:** Int'l Exchange:
2006 Sales: $1,062,672	2006 Profits: $176,701	Employees: 5,800
2005 Sales: $950,200	2005 Profits: $218,700	Fiscal Year Ends: 12/31
2004 Sales: $	2004 Profits: $	Parent Company:

SALARIES/BENEFITS:

Pension Plan:	ESOP Stock Plan:	Profit Sharing:	Top Exec. Salary: $	Bonus: $250,000
Savings Plan: Y	Stock Purch. Plan:		Second Exec. Salary: $387,500	Bonus: $387,500

OTHER THOUGHTS:

Apparent Women Officers or Directors: 2
Hot Spot for Advancement for Women/Minorities:

LOCATIONS: ("Y" = Yes)

West:	Southwest:	Midwest:	Southeast:	Northeast:	International:
Y	Y	Y	Y	Y	Y

TIME WARNER INC

www.timewarner.com

Industry Group Code: 513220 **Ranks within this company's industry group:** Sales: 1 Profits: 5

Sports:		Services:		Media:		Sales:		Facilities:		Other:	
Leagues/Associations:		Food & Beverage:		TV:	Y	Marketing:		Stadiums:		Gambling:	
Teams:		Agents:		Radio:		Ads:		Fitness Clubs:		Apparel:	
Nonprofits:		Other:		Internet:	Y	Tickets:		Golf Courses:		Equipment:	
Other:				Print:		Retail:		Ski Resorts:		Shoes:	
				Software:		Other:		Other:		Other:	

TYPES OF BUSINESS:

Cable TV Networks
Television Production
Cable TV Service
Magazine Publishing
Entertainment Investments
Film Production

BRANDS/DIVISIONS/AFFILIATES:

Home Box Office, Inc.
Time Warner Cable Inc
Warner Bros Entertainment Inc
Time Inc
New Line Cinema
Turner Broadcasting System, Inc.
Central European Media Company
AOL LLC

CONTACTS: *Note: Officers with more than one job title may be intentionally listed here more than once.*

Jeffrey L. Bewkes, CEO
Jeffrey L. Bewkes, Pres.
John K. Martin, CFO/Exec. VP
Patricia Fili-Krushel, Exec. VP-Admin.
Paul T. Cappuccio, General Counsel/Exec. VP
Edward I. Adler, Exec. VP-Corp. Comm.
James Burtson, Sr. VP-Investor Rel.
Carol Melton, Exec. VP-Global Public Policy
Olaf Olafsson, Exec. VP
Richard Parsons, Chmn.

Phone: 212-484-8000	Fax:
Toll-Free:	
Address: 1 Time Warner Ctr., New York, NY 10019 US	

GROWTH PLANS/SPECIAL FEATURES:

Time Warner, Inc. is a global media and entertainment company. The firm operates in four segments: networks, filmed entertainment, publishing and AOL LLC. The networks segment consists principally of domestic and international basic cable networks and pay television programming services. This division includes basic cable networks owned by subsidiary Turner Broadcasting System, Inc. (TBS) and pay television programming, such as the HBO and Cinemax channels, operated by Home Box Office, Inc. The segment also produces original programming such as Sex and the City, The Sopranos, Entourage, Rome and True Blood. The filmed entertainment segment, operated principally through subsidiary Warner Bros. Entertainment Group, produces and distributes theatrical motion pictures, television shows, animation and other programming, distributes home video product, and licenses rights to the company's feature films, television programming and characters. Time Warner's publishing business consists principally of magazine publishing and related web sites as well as a number of direct-marketing and direct-selling businesses. Time, Inc. publishes 23 magazines in the U.S., including People, Sports Illustrated, Time, InStyle, Real Simple, Southern Living and Fortune, and over 90 magazines outside the U.S., primarily through IPC Media in the U.K. and Grupo Editorial Expansion in Mexico. AOL LLC is a digital content and Internet access provider that offers publishing, advertising and social media products. In March 2009, Time Warner completed the spin-off of cable television provider Time Warner Cable, Inc. In May 2009, the company acquired a 31% interest in Central European Media Company. That same month, the company announced plans to spin off AOL, making it an independent, publicly traded company.

Employees of the firm are offered healthcare packages for families and domestic partners; disability, life and long-term care benefits; an employee assistance program; reimbursement for wellness activities; onsite fitness center and health services; onsite child care options; and career development programs.

FINANCIALS: **Sales and profits are in thousands of dollars—add 000 to get the full amount. 2008 Note: Financial information for 2008 was not available for all companies at press time.**

2008 Sales: $46,984,000	2008 Profits: $-13,402,000	**U.S. Stock Ticker: TWX**
2007 Sales: $46,482,000	2007 Profits: $4,387,000	**Int'l Ticker:** Int'l Exchange:
2006 Sales: $43,690,000	2006 Profits: $6,552,000	Employees: 86,400
2005 Sales: $42,401,000	2005 Profits: $2,671,000	Fiscal Year Ends: 12/31
2004 Sales: $40,993,000	2004 Profits: $3,108,000	Parent Company:

SALARIES/BENEFITS:

Pension Plan:	ESOP Stock Plan:	Profit Sharing:	Top Exec. Salary: $1,500,000	Bonus: $8,500,000
Savings Plan:	Stock Purch. Plan:		Second Exec. Salary: $1,250,000	Bonus: $7,500,000

OTHER THOUGHTS:

Apparent Women Officers or Directors: 4
Hot Spot for Advancement for Women/Minorities: Y

LOCATIONS: ("Y" = Yes)

West:	Southwest:	Midwest:	Southeast:	Northeast:	International:
Y	Y	Y	Y	Y	Y

Note: Financial information, benefits and other data can change quickly and may vary from those stated here.

TOPPS COMPANY INC (THE)

www.topps.com

Industry Group Code: 311330 **Ranks within this company's industry group:** Sales: Profits:

Sports:		Services:		Media:		Sales:		Facilities:		Other:	
Leagues/Associations:		Food & Beverage:		TV:		Marketing:		Stadiums:		Gambling:	
Teams:		Agents:		Radio:		Ads:		Fitness Clubs:		Apparel:	
Nonprofits:		Other:		Internet:		Tickets:		Golf Courses:		Equipment:	
Other:				Print:		Retail:		Ski Resorts:		Shoes:	
				Software:		Other:		Other:		Other:	Y

TYPES OF BUSINESS:

Candy & Gum Manufacturing
Collectibles
Trading Cards
Collectible Strategy Games

BRANDS/DIVISIONS/AFFILIATES:

Bazooka
Ring Pop
Push Pop
Football Flix
Topps Heritage
WizKids

CONTACTS: *Note: Officers with more than one job title may be intentionally listed here more than once.*

Scott Silverstein, CEO
Scott Silverstein, Pres.
Joseph Del Toro, CFO/VP
John S. Budd, VP-Mktg., Confectionary
Ira Friedman, VP-New Product Dev. & Publishing
Warren Friss, VP/Gen. Mgr.-Entertainment
John C. Buscaglia, VP-Sales, Entertainment
Christopher Rodman, VP-Topps Europe
Sherry L. Schultz, VP/Gen. Mgr.-Confectionery
Michael P. Clancy, VP-Int'l

Phone: 212-376-0300	**Fax:** 212-376-0573
Toll-Free:	
Address: 1 Whitehall St., New York, NY 10004 US	

GROWTH PLANS/SPECIAL FEATURES:

The Topps Company, Inc. is a marketer of premium-branded confectionery products and collectible entertainment products. The firm markets a variety of products such as lollipops, including the Ring Pop, Push Pop and Baby Bottle Pop; Bazooka-brand bubble gum; and certain licensed candy items. In addition to candies and gum, the company markets products such as comic books; trading cards; sticker album collections featuring professional athletes, popular television shows, movies and other licensed characters; and collectible strategy games. The firm has subsidiaries in the U.K., Canada, Italy and Argentina, as well as its U.S. headquarters located in New York City and operations center located in Duryea, Pennsylvania. The firm also operates an extensive web site that offers feature stories on various athletes and national sports teams; the Card Connect Message board for card trading; the Topps Spokesmen link; and the Topps Direct link, which allows access to the Topps Online Store (to purchase candy), eTopps (an interactive trading card site), and the Topps Vault (a link that allows customers to bid on rare and limited items). The firms corporate partners includes Alex Rodriquez; Barry Bonds; Beckett Magazine; Major League Baseball; Major League Baseball Association; National Basketball Association; National Basketball Players Association; National Football League; Sporting News; National Football League Players Association; Take 2 Interactive; and Mickey Mantle.

FINANCIALS: **Sales and profits are in thousands of dollars—add 000 to get the full amount. 2008 Note: Financial information for 2008 was not available for all companies at press time.**

2008 Sales: $	2008 Profits: $	**U.S. Stock Ticker: Private**
2007 Sales: $326,700	2007 Profits: $	**Int'l Ticker:** Int'l Exchange:
2006 Sales: $293,838	2006 Profits: $1,239	Employees: 422
2005 Sales: $294,231	2005 Profits: $10,915	Fiscal Year Ends: 2/28
2004 Sales: $294,917	2004 Profits: $12,884	Parent Company:

SALARIES/BENEFITS:

Pension Plan:	ESOP Stock Plan:	Profit Sharing:	Top Exec. Salary: $985,000	Bonus: $197,000
Savings Plan: Y	Stock Purch. Plan:		Second Exec. Salary: $376,654	Bonus: $90,850

OTHER THOUGHTS:

Apparent Women Officers or Directors: 1
Hot Spot for Advancement for Women/Minorities:

LOCATIONS: ("Y" = Yes)

West:	Southwest:	Midwest:	Southeast:	Northeast:	International:
Y				Y	Y

TORONTO BLUE JAYS

www.bluejays.com

Industry Group Code: 711211A **Ranks within this company's industry group:** Sales: 23 Profits: 28

Sports:		Services:		Media:		Sales:		Facilities:		Other:	
Leagues/Associations:		Food & Beverage:		TV:		Marketing:	Y	Stadiums:	Y	Gambling:	
Teams:	Y	Agents:		Radio:		Ads:		Fitness Clubs:		Apparel:	
Nonprofits:		Other:		Internet:		Tickets:	Y	Golf Courses:		Equipment:	
Other:				Print:		Retail:	Y	Ski Resorts:		Shoes:	
				Software:		Other:		Other:		Other:	

TYPES OF BUSINESS:

Baseball Team
Retail Merchandise

BRANDS/DIVISIONS/AFFILIATES:

Blue Jays Holdco, Inc.
Rogers Communications, Inc.
Rogers Centre
Syracuse SkyChiefs
New Hampshire Fisher Cats
Dunedin Blue Jays
Lansing Lugnuts
Auburn Doubledays

CONTACTS: *Note: Officers with more than one job title may be intentionally listed here more than once.*

Paul V. Godfrey, CEO
Paul V. Godfrey, Pres.
Laurel Lindsay, VP-Mktg.
Michelle Carter, Mgr.-Human Resources
Jacques Farand, Dir.-IT
Anthony Partipilo, Managing Dir.-TBJ Merch.
John Boots, VP-Admin.
Richard Wong, Sr. VP-Stadium Oper.
Mark Lemmon, VP-Corp. Partnerships & Bus. Dev.
John Matthew IV, Mktg. Producer-BlueJays.com
Jay Stenhouse, VP-Comm.
John Boots, VP-Finance
Alex Anthopoulos, VP-Baseball Oper./Asst. Gen. Mgr.
Bart Given, VP-Baseball Oper./Asst. Gen. Mgr.
J. P. Ricciardi, Sr. VP-Baseball Oper./Gen. Mgr.
Wilna Behr, VP-Stadium Initiatives

Phone: 416-341-1000 **Fax:** 416-341-1250
Toll-Free: 888-654-6529
Address: 1 Blue Jays Way, Ste. 3200, Toronto, ON M5V 1J1 Canada

GROWTH PLANS/SPECIAL FEATURES:

The Toronto Blue Jays were founded in 1976 as an American League expansion team by a group consisting of Imperial Trust Ltd., Labatt's Breweries and the Canadian Imperial Bank of Commerce. Today, the team is owned by Rogers Communications, the leading cable television and wireless phone service provider in Canada. The Blue Jays had a strong run of postseason play in the late eighties and early nineties, including consecutive World Series victories in 1992 and 1993. The Jays' home stadium is the Rogers Centre, situated next to the CN Tower in Toronto, and boasts a 348-room hotel in center field, the largest Jumbotron scoreboard in the world and a recently added VIP seating section with amenities including a gourmet restaurant, in-seat food service, a wine lounge and a high-end bar. Since its World Series trips in the early nineties, the team has struggled, with only four winning seasons since 1994. Attendance has also flagged since the early nineties, when the seasonal average was approximately 4 million, even though the Jays are now the only major league team in Canada. However, in recent years attendance has improved; in 2008, the team ranked 18 out of 30 with a home game average attendance of 29,626. The Blue Jays' general manager since late 2001 has been J.P. Ricciardi, who was director of player development under Athletics' GM Billy Beane, known for his statistically-based low-payroll, high value management. Arriving in Toronto, Ricciardi immediately began to slash the budget; however, he has increased the payroll significantly in each of the last few years in an effort to compete. It is unlikely, however, that the team will be able to surpass their large market divisional rivals in Boston and New York. Forbes recently valued the Blue Jays at $353 million, 23rd among major league teams.

FINANCIALS: **Sales and profits are in thousands of dollars—add 000 to get the full amount. 2008 Note: Financial information for 2008 was not available for all companies at press time.**

2008 Sales: $172,000 | 2008 Profits: $3,000
2007 Sales: $160,000 | 2007 Profits: $-1,800
2006 Sales: $157,000 | 2006 Profits: $11,000
2005 Sales: $136,000 | 2005 Profits: $
2004 Sales: $107,000 | 2004 Profits: $

U.S. Stock Ticker: Subsidiary
Int'l Ticker: Int'l Exchange:
Employees:
Fiscal Year Ends: 12/31
Parent Company: ROGERS COMMUNICATIONS INC

SALARIES/BENEFITS:

Pension Plan: ESOP Stock Plan: Profit Sharing: Top Exec. Salary: $ Bonus: $
Savings Plan: Stock Purch. Plan: Second Exec. Salary: $ Bonus: $

OTHER THOUGHTS:

Apparent Women Officers or Directors: 3
Hot Spot for Advancement for Women/Minorities: Y

LOCATIONS: ("Y" = Yes)

West:	Southwest:	Midwest:	Southeast:	Northeast:	International:
					Y

TORONTO FC

toronto.fc.mlsnet.com

Industry Group Code: 711211F **Ranks within this company's industry group:** Sales: Profits:

Sports:		Services:		Media:		Sales:		Facilities:		Other:	
Leagues/Associations:		Food & Beverage:		TV:		Marketing:		Stadiums:		Gambling:	
Teams:	Y	Agents:		Radio:		Ads:		Fitness Clubs:		Apparel:	
Nonprofits:		Other:		Internet:		Tickets:	Y	Golf Courses:		Equipment:	
Other:				Print:		Retail:	Y	Ski Resorts:		Shoes:	
				Software:		Other:		Other:		Other:	

TYPES OF BUSINESS:

Major League Soccer Team

BRANDS/DIVISIONS/AFFILIATES:

Maple Leaf Sports & Entertainment Ltd
BMO Field

CONTACTS:

Note: Officers with more than one job title may be intentionally listed here more than once.

Richard Peddie, CEO-Maple Leaf Sports & Entertainment
Richard Peddie, Pres., Maple Leaf Sports & Entertainment
Cesar Velasco, Mgr.-Mktg.
Paul Beirne, Dir.-Bus. Oper.
Cesar Velasco, Mgr.-Comm.
Mo Johnston, Gen. Mgr./Dir.-Soccer
Kevin Matchett, Mgr.-Sales & Service
Sharolyn Kenworthy, Coordinator-Mktg. & Promotions
Stephanie Cambell, Coordinator-Community Rel.

Phone: 416-815-5500	**Fax:** 416-359-9332
Toll-Free:	
Address: 40 Bay Street , Ste. 400, Toronto, ON M5J 2X2 Canada	

GROWTH PLANS/SPECIAL FEATURES:

Toronto FC is a Canadian soccer franchise playing U.S.'s Major League Soccer (MLS) organization. The team is owned and operated by Maple Leaf Sports & Entertainment Ltd., who also owns the Toronto Maple Leafs, the Toronto Raptors and the Toronto Marlies. Toronto's name and colors (red and grey) were announced in May 2006. The team's moniker, Toronto FC, is a throwback to the European tradition of calling city football clubs by the initials FC (football club). Coach Mo Johnston heads the Toronto team. The club plays at BMO Field, a soccer-specific stadium that seats approximately 20,500 people. BMO is the largest soccer-specific stadium in Canada. Attendance in the 2008 regular season was at or near capacity all season, averaging around 20,100 per game. Toronto FC plays in MLS' Eastern Conference, along with Chicago Fire, Columbus Crew, D.C. United, Kansas City Wizards, New England Revolution and New York Red Bulls.

FINANCIALS:

Sales and profits are in thousands of dollars—add 000 to get the full amount. 2008 Note: Financial information for 2008 was not available for all companies at press time.

2008 Sales: $	2008 Profits: $	**U.S. Stock Ticker: Subsidiary**
2007 Sales: $	2007 Profits: $	**Int'l Ticker:** Int'l Exchange:
2006 Sales: $	2006 Profits: $	Employees:
2005 Sales: $	2005 Profits: $	Fiscal Year Ends: 6/30
2004 Sales: $	2004 Profits: $	Parent Company: MAPLE LEAF SPORTS & ENTERTAINMENT LTD

SALARIES/BENEFITS:

Pension Plan:	ESOP Stock Plan:	Profit Sharing:	Top Exec. Salary: $	Bonus: $
Savings Plan:	Stock Purch. Plan:		Second Exec. Salary: $	Bonus: $

OTHER THOUGHTS:

Apparent Women Officers or Directors: 7
Hot Spot for Advancement for Women/Minorities: Y

LOCATIONS: ("Y" = Yes)

West:	Southwest:	Midwest:	Southeast:	Northeast:	International:
					Y

TORONTO MAPLE LEAFS

www.mapleleafs.com

Industry Group Code: 711211F **Ranks within this company's industry group:** Sales: 1 Profits: 1

Sports:		Services:		Media:		Sales:		Facilities:		Other:	
Leagues/Associations:		Food & Beverage:		TV:		Marketing:		Stadiums:	Y	Gambling:	
Teams:	Y	Agents:		Radio:		Ads:		Fitness Clubs:		Apparel:	
Nonprofits:		Other:		Internet:		Tickets:	Y	Golf Courses:		Equipment:	
Other:				Print:		Retail:	Y	Ski Resorts:		Shoes:	
				Software:		Other:		Other:		Other:	

TYPES OF BUSINESS:

Hockey Team

BRANDS/DIVISIONS/AFFILIATES:

National Hockey League (NHL)
Toronto Arenas
Toronto St. Patricks
Air Canada Centre
Maple Leaf Sports & Entertainment Ltd
Toronto Raptors
Ontario Teachers' Pension Plan
Toronto-Dominion Bank (TD Bank)

CONTACTS:

Note: Officers with more than one job title may be intentionally listed here more than once.

Brian Burke, Gen. Mgr.
Brian Burke, Pres.
Dave Nonis, Sr. VP-Hockey Oper.
Ron Wilson, Head Coach
Dallas Eakins, Dir.-Player Dev.
Reid Mitchell, Dir.-Hockey Scouting & Admin.
Dave Griffiths, Mgr.-Team Svcs.
Lawrence M. (Larry) Tanenbaum, Chmn.

Phone: 416-815-5700 **Fax:** 416-359-9205
Toll-Free:
Address: Air Canada Centre, 40 Bay St., Ste. 400, Toronto, ON M5J 2X2 Canada

GROWTH PLANS/SPECIAL FEATURES:

The Toronto Maple Leaf Hockey Club is an ice hockey team playing in the NHL. The team was founded in 1917 as one of the original six NHL clubs. The Maple Leafs started out as the Toronto Arenas, but due to financial difficulties, the Arenas withdrew from the NHL shortly after their first season. The team reemerged in the 1919-20 season, this time as the Toronto St. Patricks. In 1927, Conn Smythe purchased the team and re-christened them the Maple Leafs, and in 1931, he gave the team a new stadium, Maple Leaf Gardens. The franchise, while still the Arenas, won the Stanley Cup in its first season, as well as its first season as the St. Pats, and in numerous others, appearing 13 times between 1918 and 1967. During the 1970s and 80s, the team wallowed in relative obscurity and failure, but in the 90s, the Maple Leafs looked primed to bounce back into contention. With such players as Doug Gilmour and Mats Sundin, the team made several runs at the Stanley Cup, but failed to win the championship. The club is the only original-six team to fail to appear in the Stanley Cup finals since the league expansion in 1967. In 1999, the team moved to the Air Canada Centre. Maple Leaf Sports & Entertainment, Inc. owns the franchise, as well as the NBA's Toronto Raptors and the stadium in which both teams play. Maple Leaf Sports & Entertainment is 58%-owned by the Ontario Teachers' Pension Plan. Other investors include the firm's chairman, Larry Tanenbaum, and TD Capital, a unit of Toronto-Dominion Bank. Forbes recently valued the team at $448 million, listing it as the NHL's most valuable team. In the 2008-09 season, the team averaged roughly 19,300 fans in attendance per game.

FINANCIALS:

Sales and profits are in thousands of dollars—add 000 to get the full amount. 2008 Note: Financial information for 2008 was not available for all companies at press time.

2008 Sales: $160,000	2008 Profits: $66,400	**U.S. Stock Ticker: Subsidiary**
2007 Sales: $138,000	2007 Profits: $52,700	**Int'l Ticker:** Int'l Exchange:
2006 Sales: $119,000	2006 Profits: $41,500	Employees:
2005 Sales: $	2005 Profits: $	Fiscal Year Ends: 6/30
2004 Sales: $117,000	2004 Profits: $	Parent Company: MAPLE LEAF SPORTS & ENTERTAINMENT LTD

SALARIES/BENEFITS:

Pension Plan:	ESOP Stock Plan:	Profit Sharing:	Top Exec. Salary: $	Bonus: $
Savings Plan:	Stock Purch. Plan:		Second Exec. Salary: $	Bonus: $

OTHER THOUGHTS:

Apparent Women Officers or Directors: 2
Hot Spot for Advancement for Women/Minorities:

LOCATIONS: ("Y" = Yes)

West:	Southwest:	Midwest:	Southeast:	Northeast:	International:
					Y

TORONTO RAPTORS

www.nba.com/raptors

Industry Group Code: 711211B **Ranks within this company's industry group:** Sales: 11 Profits: 7

Sports:		Services:		Media:		Sales:		Facilities:		Other:	
Leagues/Associations:		Food & Beverage:		TV:		Marketing:		Stadiums:	Y	Gambling:	
Teams:	Y	Agents:		Radio:		Ads:		Fitness Clubs:		Apparel:	
Nonprofits:		Other:		Internet:		Tickets:	Y	Golf Courses:		Equipment:	
Other:				Print:		Retail:	Y	Ski Resorts:		Shoes:	
				Software:		Other:		Other:		Other:	

TYPES OF BUSINESS:

Basketball Team

BRANDS/DIVISIONS/AFFILIATES:

Maple Leaf Sports & Entertainment
Raptors NBA TV
Ford Raptors High School All-Stars Recognition

CONTACTS:

Note: Officers with more than one job title may be intentionally listed here more than once.

Richard A. Peddie, CEO
Tom Anselmi, COO/Exec. VP
Richard A. Peddie, Pres.
Ian Clarke, CFO
Robin Brudner, General Counsel/Corp. Sec./Sr. VP
Ian Clarke, Exec. VP-Bus. Dev.
Kevin Nonomura, VP-Finance
Bryan Colangelo, Pres./Gen. Mgr.
Jay Triano, Interim Head Coach
Larry Tannenbaum, Chmn.

Phone: 416-815-5600 **Fax:** 416-359-9213
Toll-Free:
Address: Air Canada Centre, 40 Bay St., Ste. 400, Toronto, ON M5J 2X2 Canada

GROWTH PLANS/SPECIAL FEATURES:

The Toronto Raptors are a professional basketball team playing in the National Basketball Association (NBA) and based in Toronto, Ontario. The team was established in 1995. It has gone to the postseason three times, in the 2000-01 season; 2001-02 season; and the 2006-07 season. The Raptors advanced to the conference semi-finals in 2001. Raptors' stars have included Damon Stoudamire; Vince Carter, who led the team from his 1998-99 rookie season until being traded in 2004; and Alonzo Mourning. While playing with the team, Carter was named Rookie of the Year in 1999 and an NBA All-Star five times. The team has only posted three winning seasons in its history. In 2004, along with trading Carter, the team signed new head coach Sam Mitchell. The reorganization of the team's management has continued, with the recent release of general manager Rob Babcock, replaced by Bryan Colangelo. The Raptors are owned by Maple Leaf Sports & Entertainment, which also owns the Toronto Maple Leafs hockey team. The Raptors play at the Air Canada Centre, which they share with the Maple Leafs. The Air Canada Centre holds approximately 19,800 fans and is owned by Maple Leaf Sports & Entertainment. In June 2008, the team announced that it will be affiliated with the Idaho Stampede, an NBA development league team, for the 2008-09 season. Forbes Magazine recently estimated the team to be worth approximately $400 million. In the 2008-09 season, the team's home attendance average was roughly 18,800 per game.

FINANCIALS:

Sales and profits are in thousands of dollars—add 000 to get the full amount. 2008 Note: Financial information for 2008 was not available for all companies at press time.

2008 Sales: $138,000 | 2008 Profits: $27,700
2007 Sales: $124,000 | 2007 Profits: $28,800
2006 Sales: $105,000 | 2006 Profits: $8,400
2005 Sales: $94,000 | 2005 Profits: $
2004 Sales: $100,000 | 2004 Profits: $

U.S. Stock Ticker: Subsidiary
Int'l Ticker: Int'l Exchange:
Employees:
Fiscal Year Ends: 6/30
Parent Company: MAPLE LEAF SPORTS & ENTERTAINMENT

SALARIES/BENEFITS:

Pension Plan: ESOP Stock Plan: Profit Sharing: Top Exec. Salary: $ Bonus: $
Savings Plan: Stock Purch. Plan: Second Exec. Salary: $ Bonus: $

OTHER THOUGHTS:

Apparent Women Officers or Directors:
Hot Spot for Advancement for Women/Minorities:

LOCATIONS: ("Y" = Yes)

West:	Southwest:	Midwest:	Southeast:	Northeast:	International:
					Y

TOTTENHAM HOTSPUR FOOTBALL CLUB

www.spurs.co.uk

Industry Group Code: 711211D **Ranks within this company's industry group:** Sales: 5 Profits: 2

Sports:		Services:		Media:		Sales:		Facilities:		Other:	
Leagues/Associations:		Food & Beverage:		TV:		Marketing:		Stadiums:	Y	Gambling:	
Teams:	Y	Agents:		Radio:		Ads:		Fitness Clubs:		Apparel:	
Nonprofits:		Other:		Internet:		Tickets:	Y	Golf Courses:		Equipment:	
Other:				Print:		Retail:	Y	Ski Resorts:		Shoes:	
				Software:		Other:		Other:		Other:	Y

TYPES OF BUSINESS:

Soccer Team

BRANDS/DIVISIONS/AFFILIATES:

Tottenham Hotspur plc
White Hart Lane
Tottenham Hotspur Ladies Football Club
Spurs Ladies

CONTACTS:

Note: Officers with more than one job title may be intentionally listed here more than once.

William Nicholson, Pres.
Matthew J. Collecott, Company Sec./Exec. Dir.
Harry Redknapp, Mgr.
Daniel P. Levy, Exec. Chmn.

Phone: 844-499-5000 **Fax:**
Toll-Free:
Address: Bill Nicholson Way, 748 High Rd., Tottenham, London, N17 OAP UK

GROWTH PLANS/SPECIAL FEATURES:

Tottenham Hotspur Football Club, founded in 1882, is an English Premier League soccer team owned and operated by Tottenham Hotspur plc. The name Hotspur is thought to come from Sir Henry Percy, immortalized as Harry Hotspur in Shakespeare's King Henry IV, Part I. Also known as The Spurs, the team has played at White Hart Lane in North London since the 36,310-seat stadium opened in 1899, and average nearly 36,000 spectators per game. During the 1960-61 season, The Spurs became the first team in the 20th century to win the both the Football League Cup and Football Association (FA) Cup, sometimes called a Double. The franchise has consistently been one of London's top soccer teams and has enjoyed a long-standing rivalry with nearby competitors Arsenal. It has won two league championships, eight FA Cups and four Football League Cups, most recently in 2008. Beyond the men's professional soccer team, the franchise sponsors the Hotspur's youth feeder teams (ages 8-18) and the Tottenham Hotspur Ladies Football Club (THL), which manages a semi-professional women's team, the Spurs Ladies, a reserve women's team and six girls teams (ages 10-15). Other subsidiaries of the parent include White Hart Lane Stadium Limited, which owns and operates the stadium; Stardare Limited and Paxton Road Limited, which each hold certain properties; and Tottenham Hotspur Finance Company Limited, a loan issuer. In April 2008, The club announced its intent to build a new stadium or expand White Hart Lane.

FINANCIALS:

Sales and profits are in thousands of dollars—add 000 to get the full amount. 2008 Note: Financial information for 2008 was not available for all companies at press time.

2008 Sales: $228,000
2007 Sales: $207,000
2006 Sales: $137,000
2005 Sales: $127,000
2004 Sales: $122,000

2008 Profits: $70,000
2007 Profits: $64,000
2006 Profits: $9,000
2005 Profits: $
2004 Profits: $-4,800

U.S. Stock Ticker: Subsidiary
Int'l Ticker: Int'l Exchange:
Employees: 226
Fiscal Year Ends: 6/30
Parent Company: TOTTENHAM HOTSPUR PLC

SALARIES/BENEFITS:

Pension Plan: ESOP Stock Plan: Profit Sharing: Top Exec. Salary: $ Bonus: $
Savings Plan: Stock Purch. Plan: Second Exec. Salary: $ Bonus: $

OTHER THOUGHTS:

Apparent Women Officers or Directors:
Hot Spot for Advancement for Women/Minorities:

LOCATIONS: ("Y" = Yes)

West:	Southwest:	Midwest:	Southeast:	Northeast:	International:
					Y

TOWN SPORTS INTERNATIONAL HOLDINGS INC

www.mysportsclubs.com

Industry Group Code: 713940 **Ranks within this company's industry group:** Sales: 2 Profits: 3

Sports:		Services:		Media:		Sales:		Facilities:		Other:	
Leagues/Associations:		Food & Beverage:		TV:		Marketing:		Stadiums:		Gambling:	
Teams:		Agents:		Radio:		Ads:		Fitness Clubs:	Y	Apparel:	
Nonprofits:		Other:		Internet:		Tickets:		Golf Courses:		Equipment:	
Other:				Print:		Retail:		Ski Resorts:		Shoes:	
				Software:		Other:		Other:		Other:	

TYPES OF BUSINESS:

Fitness Centers/Health Clubs

BRANDS/DIVISIONS/AFFILIATES:

New York Sports Clubs
Boston Sports Clubs
Washington Sports Clubs
Philadelphia Sports Clubs
Sports Clubs for Kids

CONTACTS: *Note: Officers with more than one job title may be intentionally listed here more than once.*

Alexander Alimanestianu, CEO
Martin Annese, COO
Alexander Alimanestianu, Pres.
Daniel Gallagher, CFO
Chris Stabile, VP-Corp. Sales
James Rizzo, Sr. VP-Human Resources
Jennifer Prue, CIO
Ed Trainor, VP-Prod. Dev., Fitness & Svcs.
David Kastin, General Counsel/Sr. VP/Sec.
Raymond Dewhirst, VP-Dev. & Real Estate
Lisa Hufcut, Media Contact
David Mercado, VP-Finance
Karl Derleth, VP-Facilities
Cheryl Mueller Jones, VP-Programs & Svcs.
Timothy Keightley, VP-Fitness
Rich Destasio, VP-Regional Fitness
Paul Arnold, Chmn.

Phone: 212-246-6700	**Fax:** 212-246-8422
Toll-Free:	
Address: 5 Penn Plz., 4th Fl., New York, NY 10001 US	

GROWTH PLANS/SPECIAL FEATURES:

Town Sports International Holdings, Inc. (TSI) is an owner and operator of 166 sports and fitness clubs in the Northeast and Mid-Atlantic areas of the U.S. with approximately 510,000 total members. TSI operates under the brand names of New York Sports Clubs, with 112 locations; Boston Sports Clubs, with 25 locations; Washington Sports Clubs, with 19 locations; and Philadelphia Sports Clubs, with seven locations. The firm has 40 locations in Manhattan alone. In addition, the company owns three facilities in Switzerland. Targeted members are between the ages of 21 and 60 with income levels between $50,000 and $150,000 per year. Sales are handled by approximately 420 in-club membership consultants who sell three types of membership: Passport, Regional Passport and Gold. Passport Membership ($96 to $106 per month) entitles members to use any club at any time. Passport members comprise about 36% of total membership. A Passport Premium Membership at two select clubs includes a greater array of member services and facilities, at prices ranging from $105 to $116 per month. The Regional Passport Membership ($72 to $96 per month) entitles members to use any club within one region at a time. These members account for 2% of total membership. Gold Membership ($39 to $89 per month) enables members to use a specific club at any time and other clubs at off-peak times. Gold members comprise about 62% of total membership. In addition to memberships, TSI generates non-membership revenue through personal training services, small group training programs and the Sports Clubs for Kids program at selected clubs. In 2008, the firm opened nine new clubs.

Employees are offered company paid medical benefits; membership to company clubs; and a 401(k).

FINANCIALS: Sales and profits are in thousands of dollars—add 000 to get the full amount. 2008 Note: Financial information for 2008 was not available for all companies at press time.

2008 Sales: $506,709	2008 Profits: $2,337	**U.S. Stock Ticker: CLUB**
2007 Sales: $472,915	2007 Profits: $13,646	**Int'l Ticker:** Int'l Exchange:
2006 Sales: $433,080	2006 Profits: $4,647	Employees: 9,300
2005 Sales: $388,556	2005 Profits: $1,769	Fiscal Year Ends: 12/31
2004 Sales: $353,031	2004 Profits: $-3,905	Parent Company:

SALARIES/BENEFITS:

Pension Plan:	ESOP Stock Plan:	Profit Sharing:	Top Exec. Salary: $505,870	Bonus: $200,000
Savings Plan: Y	Stock Purch. Plan:		Second Exec. Salary: $283,250	Bonus: $120,000

OTHER THOUGHTS:

Apparent Women Officers or Directors: 4
Hot Spot for Advancement for Women/Minorities: Y

LOCATIONS: ("Y" = Yes)

West:	Southwest:	Midwest:	Southeast:	Northeast:	International:
				Y	Y

TREK BICYCLE CORPORATION

www.trekbikes.com

Industry Group Code: 339920 **Ranks within this company's industry group:** Sales: Profits:

Sports:		Services:		Media:		Sales:		Facilities:		Other:	
Leagues/Associations:		Food & Beverage:		TV:		Marketing:		Stadiums:		Gambling:	
Teams:	Y	Agents:		Radio:		Ads:		Fitness Clubs:		Apparel:	Y
Nonprofits:		Other:	Y	Internet:		Tickets:		Golf Courses:		Equipment:	Y
Other:				Print:		Retail:		Ski Resorts:		Shoes:	
				Software:		Other:		Other:		Other:	

TYPES OF BUSINESS:

Bicycles
Cycling Accessories and Apparel
Guided Cycling Tours

BRANDS/DIVISIONS/AFFILIATES:

Tour de France
Project One
Madone
Equinox
Astana
Session
Trek Travel
One World, Two Wheels

CONTACTS:
Note: Officers with more than one job title may be intentionally listed here more than once.

John Burke, CEO
John Burke, Pres.
Joe Siefkes, CFO

Phone: 920-478-2191 **Fax:**
Toll-Free:
Address: 801 W. Madison St., Waterloo, WI 53594 US

GROWTH PLANS/SPECIAL FEATURES:

Trek Bicycle Corporation is a designer and manufacturer of bicycles. Trek was the exclusive supplier of bicycles for Lance Armstrong during his seven consecutive wins of the Tour de France. The company manufactures a variety of bicycles intended for road, triathlon, mountain, urban and children's activities, as well as specialty bicycles. The company's WSD line offers bicycles and accessories created specifically for women, and Project One allows customers to design and order bicycles to custom specifications. Some of Trek's best-known models are the Madone, Astana, Equinox, Allant, Session and the new Top Fuel. Accessories manufactured by Trek include apparel, helmets, Bontranger cycling shoes, bicycle computers, lights, locks, racks, water bottles and maintenance supplies. The company has operations in the U.S. and Canada as well as nine European countries, Australia, Japan and China. The firm also operates an international bicycle touring division under the name Trek Travel, which offers more than 50 guided cycling tours through Europe, North America, Latin America and the Asia Pacific region. Trek's One World, Two Wheels program is focused on increasing the number of trips taken in the U.S. by bicycle from the current 1% to 5% by 2017.

FINANCIALS:
Sales and profits are in thousands of dollars—add 000 to get the full amount. 2008 Note: Financial information for 2008 was not available for all companies at press time.

2008 Sales: $	2008 Profits: $	**U.S. Stock Ticker: Private**
2007 Sales: $69,100	2007 Profits: $	**Int'l Ticker:** Int'l Exchange:
2006 Sales: $	2006 Profits: $	Employees: 1,189
2005 Sales: $	2005 Profits: $	Fiscal Year Ends: 9/30
2004 Sales: $	2004 Profits: $	Parent Company:

SALARIES/BENEFITS:

Pension Plan:	ESOP Stock Plan:	Profit Sharing:	Top Exec. Salary: $	Bonus: $
Savings Plan:	Stock Purch. Plan:		Second Exec. Salary: $	Bonus: $

OTHER THOUGHTS:

Apparent Women Officers or Directors:
Hot Spot for Advancement for Women/Minorities:

LOCATIONS: ("Y" = Yes)

West:	Southwest:	Midwest:	Southeast:	Northeast:	International:
		Y			Y

TURNER BROADCASTING SYSTEM

www.turner.com

Industry Group Code: 513210 **Ranks within this company's industry group:** Sales: Profits:

Sports:		Services:		Media:		Sales:		Facilities:		Other:	
Leagues/Associations:		Food & Beverage:		TV:	Y	Marketing:		Stadiums:		Gambling:	
Teams:	Y	Agents:		Radio:		Ads:		Fitness Clubs:		Apparel:	
Nonprofits:		Other:		Internet:		Tickets:	Y	Golf Courses:		Equipment:	
Other:				Print:		Retail:	Y	Ski Resorts:		Shoes:	
				Software:		Other:		Other:		Other:	

TYPES OF BUSINESS:

Cable Programming
News Programs
Sports Teams
Internet Sites
Interactive Media

BRANDS/DIVISIONS/AFFILIATES:

Cable News Network LP LLLP
TBS
TNT
CourtTV
Cartoon Network
Boomerang
TCM Latin America
Time Warner, Inc.

CONTACTS: *Note: Officers with more than one job title may be intentionally listed here more than once.*

Philip I. Kent, CEO
Greg D'Alba, COO
Steve Koonin, Pres.
John E. Kampfe, CFO/Exec. VP
Louis Gutierrez, Sr. VP-Human Resources
Scott Teissler, CTO/Exec. VP-Tech.
Louise Sams, General Counsel/Exec. VP
Jim McCaffrey, Exec. VP-Oper.
Jim McCaffrey, Exec. VP-Strategy/Chief Strategy Officer
Kelly Regal, Exec. VP-Corp. Comm.
Andrew T. Heller, Pres., Domestic Distribution
Steve Koonin, Pres., Turner Entertainment Networks
Jim Walton, Pres., CNN Worldwide
Philip I. Kent, Chmn.
Louise Sams, Pres., TBS Int'l

Phone: 404-827-1700 **Fax:** 404-827-2437
Toll-Free: 866-463-6899
Address: 1 CNN Center, 100 International Blvd., Atlanta, GA 30303 US

GROWTH PLANS/SPECIAL FEATURES:

Turner Broadcasting System (TBS), a Time Warner subsidiary, produces news and entertainment programming internationally, as well as basic cable programming. The company's domestic program subsidiaries include news stations CNN, CNN Headline News and CNNfn (financial news); cable broadcasting networks TBS, TNT, TCM, TNT HD and truTV; and animation networks Cartoon Network, Game Tap and Boomerang. Internationally, the firm owns CNN International and CNN Espanol, as well as seven regional CNN stations in news; TNT Latin America TNT Asia Pacific, TCM Europe and TCM Classic Hollywood in Latin America in entertainment; and versions of the Cartoon Network in Latin America, Asia Pacific, Europe, Japan and Korea, as well as Pogo, Boomerang U.K. and Toonami U.K. in animation. TBS also owns the Atlanta Braves baseball team and the pga.com and nascar.com sports web sites. In October 2007, the company acquired seven of Latin American firm Claxson Interactive's pay television networks, including Fashion TV, HTV, Infinito, I.Sat, MuchMusic, Retro and Space. Turner's websites, particularly CNN, are among the most visited sites on the Internet.

TBS offers its employees domestic partner and dependent insurance, transportation reimbursement, a credit union, an on-site athletic facility, tuition reimbursement, company-wide advancement training and an employee assistance program. In addition, employees are entitled to infertility treatment benefits, adoption assistance, back-up child care reimbursement, veterinary pet insurance, free sports tickets, free admission to studio series performances, as well as discounts at the Turner Store and on Time Warner merchandise.

FINANCIALS: Sales and profits are in thousands of dollars—add 000 to get the full amount. 2008 Note: Financial information for 2008 was not available for all companies at press time.

2008 Sales: $	2008 Profits: $	**U.S. Stock Ticker: Subsidiary**
2007 Sales: $	2007 Profits: $	**Int'l Ticker:** Int'l Exchange:
2006 Sales: $	2006 Profits: $	Employees:
2005 Sales: $9,611,000	2005 Profits: $	Fiscal Year Ends: 12/31
2004 Sales: $9,054,000	2004 Profits: $	Parent Company: TIME WARNER INC

SALARIES/BENEFITS:

Pension Plan:	ESOP Stock Plan:	Profit Sharing:	Top Exec. Salary: $	Bonus: $
Savings Plan:	Stock Purch. Plan:		Second Exec. Salary: $	Bonus: $

OTHER THOUGHTS:

Apparent Women Officers or Directors: 3
Hot Spot for Advancement for Women/Minorities: Y

LOCATIONS: ("Y" = Yes)

West:	Southwest:	Midwest:	Southeast:	Northeast:	International:
			Y	Y	

UNDER ARMOUR INC

www.underarmour.com

Industry Group Code: 315000A **Ranks within this company's industry group:** Sales: 4 Profits: 3

Sports:		Services:		Media:		Sales:		Facilities:		Other:	
Leagues/Associations:		Food & Beverage:		TV:		Marketing:		Stadiums:		Gambling:	
Teams:		Agents:		Radio:		Ads:		Fitness Clubs:		Apparel:	Y
Nonprofits:		Other:		Internet:		Tickets:		Golf Courses:		Equipment:	
Other:				Print:		Retail:	Y	Ski Resorts:		Shoes:	
				Software:		Other:		Other:		Other:	

TYPES OF BUSINESS:

Compression Performance Apparel
Outdoor and Sports Apparel
Shirts

BRANDS/DIVISIONS/AFFILIATES:

HeatGear
ColdGear
AllSeasonGear

CONTACTS:

Note: Officers with more than one job title may be intentionally listed here more than once.

Kevin Plank, CEO
Wayne Marino, COO
David W. McCreight, Pres.
Brad Dickerson, CFO
William J. Kraus, Sr. VP-Mktg.
Melissa A. Wallace, VP-Human Resources
Kip J. Fulks, Sr. VP-Prod. Dev., Sourcing & Quality Assurance
Kevin M. Haley, House Counsel/Sec./VP
Matthew C. Mirchin, VP-North American Sales
Suzanne Karkus, Sr. VP-Apparel
J. Scott Plank, Sr. VP-Retail
Stephen J. Battista, Sr. VP-Brand
Kevin Plank, Chmn.
Peter Mahrer, Pres./Managing Dir.-Under Armour Europe, B.V.
James E. Calo, Chief Supply Chain Officer

GROWTH PLANS/SPECIAL FEATURES:

Under Armour, Inc. (UA) designs, developments, markets and distributes technologically advanced, branded performance products for men, women and youth. It offers several lines of apparel and accessories that utilize a variety of synthetic microfiber fabrications engineered to replace cotton in the world of athletics and fitness with performance alternatives. UA's active wear and sports apparel accessories are designed to wick perspiration away from the skin; help regulate body temperature; enhance comfort and mobility; and improve performance regardless of weather condition. Its products are designed and merchandised along three gearlines: HEATGEAR, for when it is hot; COLDGEAR, for cold weather; and ALLSEASONGEAR, for times between the extremes. Within each gearline, Under Armour's garments come in three fit types: compression (tight fitting), fitted (athletic cut) and loose (relaxed). Products primarily consist of t-shirts designed to be worn under uniforms, ski vests or protective gear; athletic shoes; and batting, football, golf and running gloves. UA markets its products at multiple price levels to compete with cotton and other traditional products.The firm's products are offered worldwide in over 15,000 retail stores and can currently be purchased across the U.S., Canada, Japan and Western Europe through large national and regional chains of retailers, as well as smaller, independent and specialty retailers. Unaffiliated manufacturers operating in 19 countries manufacture virtually all of the company's products. International professional football, baseball, basketball, hockey, rugby and soccer players, as well as athletes in major collegiate and Olympic sports, wear its products. The company is the official supplier of footwear to the NFL (National Football League).

Phone: 410-454-6428 **Fax:** 410-468-2516
Toll-Free:
Address: 1020 Hull St., 3rd Fl., Baltimore, MD 21230 US

FINANCIALS:

Sales and profits are in thousands of dollars—add 000 to get the full amount. 2008 Note: Financial information for 2008 was not available for all companies at press time.

2008 Sales: $725,244	2008 Profits: $38,229	**U.S. Stock Ticker: UA**
2007 Sales: $606,561	2007 Profits: $52,558	**Int'l Ticker:** Int'l Exchange:
2006 Sales: $430,689	2006 Profits: $38,979	Employees: 1,400
2005 Sales: $281,053	2005 Profits: $19,719	Fiscal Year Ends: 12/31
2004 Sales: $205,181	2004 Profits: $16,322	Parent Company:

SALARIES/BENEFITS:

Pension Plan:	ESOP Stock Plan:	Profit Sharing:	Top Exec. Salary: $500,000	Bonus: $1,000,000
Savings Plan: Y	Stock Purch. Plan:		Second Exec. Salary: $300,000	Bonus: $225,000

OTHER THOUGHTS:

Apparent Women Officers or Directors: 2
Hot Spot for Advancement for Women/Minorities: Y

LOCATIONS: ("Y" = Yes)

West:	Southwest:	Midwest:	Southeast:	Northeast:	International:
Y				Y	Y

Note: Financial information, benefits and other data can change quickly and may vary from those stated here.

UNION OF EUROPEAN FOOTBALL ASSOCIATIONS www.uefa.com

Industry Group Code: 813990 **Ranks within this company's industry group:** Sales: Profits:

Sports:		Services:		Media:		Sales:		Facilities:		Other:	
Leagues/Associations:	Y	Food & Beverage:		TV:		Marketing:		Stadiums:		Gambling:	
Teams:		Agents:		Radio:		Ads:		Fitness Clubs:		Apparel:	
Nonprofits:		Other:		Internet:		Tickets:		Golf Courses:		Equipment:	
Other:	Y			Print:		Retail:		Ski Resorts:		Shoes:	
				Software:		Other:		Other:		Other:	

TYPES OF BUSINESS:

Professional Soccer Association

BRANDS/DIVISIONS/AFFILIATES:

UEFA
UEFA Champions League
UEFA Cup
UEFA Super Cup
UEFA Intertoto Cup
UEFA Women's Cup
Federation Internationale de Football Association
FIFA

CONTACTS: *Note: Officers with more than one job title may be intentionally listed here more than once.*

Michel Platini, Pres.
Philippe Le Floc'h, Dir.-Mktg. & Media Rights
Jean-Paul Turrian, Dir.-Svcs., Human Resources
Alexandre Fourtoy, CEO-UEFA Media Technologies S.A.
Gianni Infantino, Dir.-Legal Affairs & Club Licensing
Jean-Paul Turrian, Dir.-Svcs., Oper. & Dev.
Giorgio Marchetti, Dir.-Professional Football
William Gaillard, Dir.-Comm. & Public Affairs
Hanspeter Jenni, Dir.-Finance Div.
Martin Kallen, CEO-UEFA Events, S.A./Euro 2008, S.A.
Philippe Margraff, Dir.-UEFA Mktg. & Media Mgmt.
Theodore Theodoridis, Dir.-Nat'l Associations Div.
Jean-Paul Turrian, Dir.-Svcs., Logistical Support

Phone: 41-848-00-2727 **Fax:** 41-848-01-2727
Toll-Free:
Address: Route de Geneve 46, Case Postale, Nyon 2, CH-1260 Switzerland

GROWTH PLANS/SPECIAL FEATURES:

The Union of European Football Associations (UEFA) is the administrative and controlling body of European soccer. It represents 53 national football associations in Europe, running three national, three youth/amateur, four women's, four club and two Futsal competitions. Futsal is the type of indoor five-a-side soccer officially sanctioned by the Federation Internationale de Football Association (FIFA), the international governing body of soccer. Five-a-side is so named because each team fields five players instead of the normal 11. The organization's main competitions include the UEFA Champions League, for national league champions, one of the most prestigious club trophies; the UEFA Cup, an invitational for top positioned national teams in most leagues and in select leagues up to the fifth place in the standings; and the UEFA Super Cup (or European Super Cup), a game between the winners of the Championships League and the UEFA Cup. Other competitions include the UEFA Intertoto Cup, a summer qualifying competition for European clubs that have not qualified for the UEFA Champions League or the UEFA Cup; the UEFA Women's Cup, for women's club teams; and the UEFA Regions Cup, for semi-professional teams. The association controls the prize money, regulations and media rights for the competitions it manages. Its member associations include some of the wealthiest football clubs in the world, particularly in the U.K., Italy, Spain and Germany. Due to this financial power and influence, UEFA is one of the strongest members of the six continental confederations that comprise FIFA. Almost all of the world's top soccer players play in UEFA leagues.

FINANCIALS: Sales and profits are in thousands of dollars—add 000 to get the full amount. 2008 Note: Financial information for 2008 was not available for all companies at press time.

2008 Sales: $	2008 Profits: $	**U.S. Stock Ticker: Private**
2007 Sales: $	2007 Profits: $	**Int'l Ticker:** Int'l Exchange:
2006 Sales: $	2006 Profits: $	Employees:
2005 Sales: $	2005 Profits: $	Fiscal Year Ends:
2004 Sales: $	2004 Profits: $	Parent Company:

SALARIES/BENEFITS:

Pension Plan:	ESOP Stock Plan:	Profit Sharing:	Top Exec. Salary: $	Bonus: $
Savings Plan:	Stock Purch. Plan:		Second Exec. Salary: $	Bonus: $

OTHER THOUGHTS:

Apparent Women Officers or Directors:
Hot Spot for Advancement for Women/Minorities:

LOCATIONS: ("Y" = Yes)

West:	Southwest:	Midwest:	Southeast:	Northeast:	International:
					Y

Note: Financial information, benefits and other data can change quickly and may vary from those stated here.

UNITED SOCCER LEAGUES

www.uslsoccer.com

Industry Group Code: 813990 **Ranks within this company's industry group:** Sales: Profits:

Sports:		Services:		Media:		Sales:		Facilities:		Other:	
Leagues/Associations:	Y	Food & Beverage:		TV:		Marketing:		Stadiums:		Gambling:	
Teams:		Agents:		Radio:		Ads:		Fitness Clubs:		Apparel:	
Nonprofits:		Other:		Internet:		Tickets:		Golf Courses:		Equipment:	
Other:				Print:		Retail:		Ski Resorts:		Shoes:	
				Software:		Other:		Other:		Other:	

TYPES OF BUSINESS:

Soccer League

BRANDS/DIVISIONS/AFFILIATES:

USL First Division
USL Second Division
Premier Development League
W-League
Super Y-League
USL Super-20 League
Demoshere International, Inc.
USL

CONTACTS: *Note: Officers with more than one job title may be intentionally listed here more than once.*

Tim Holt, COO/Exec. VP
Francisco Marcos, Pres.
Seth Witkowicz, Mgr.-Mktg.
Lee Cohen, Dir.-PDL Oper.
James Ward, Sr. Dir.-Commercial Dev.
Gerald Barnhart, Dir.-Public Rel.
Neels Van Wyk, Dir.-Financial Svcs.
Matt Weibe, Sr. Dir.-Franchise Dev.
Jeff McRaney, Sr. Dir.-Youth League Dev.

Phone: 813-963-3909	**Fax:** 813-963-3807
Toll-Free:	
Address: 14497 N. Dale Mabry Highway, Ste. 201, Tampa, FL 33618 US	

GROWTH PLANS/SPECIAL FEATURES:

United Soccer Leagues (USL) is one of the largest organizations of soccer leagues in North America with more than 100 teams throughout the U.S., Canada and the Caribbean. Established in 1986, the company has two divisions of professional men's soccer teams: USL First Division, which has teams in 11 markets, and USL Second Division, which has nine teams. The firm also manages four amateur soccer leagues: Premier Development League (PDL) for men's soccer; W-League for women's soccer; USL Super-20 League for under-20 men and women's soccer; and Super Y-League, a youth soccer league. The USL First Division teams play 30 regular season matches and participate in the Lamar Hunt U.S. Open Cup, CONCACAF Champions League and other American/International tournaments. The USL Second Division plays 20 regular season matches, and also competes in the Lamar Hunt U.S. Open Cup. The PDL is the top amateur league for men under the age of 23. The league has 68 teams divided into four conferences and each team plays a total of 16 games. The W-League has 37 teams divided into four conferences, with each team playing either 12 or 14 games. The Super-20 league is the top amateur league for men and women under the age of 20. The league features four conferences with teams playing anywhere from eight to ten games per season. The Super-Y, which was established to further the development of potential professional players, maintains hundreds of teams. Past USL players include Giovanni Savarese, Marcelo Balboa, Julie Foudy and Rob Ukrop. USL holds various partnerships with several organizations, including Demoshere International, Inc.; FOX Soccer Channel; the Canadian Soccer Association; and the U.S. Soccer Federation. In December 2008, USL partnered with U.S. Specialty Sports Association, making the fellow U.S. Soccer Federation member USL's registration/insurance administrator for the Super-20 and Super-Y leagues.

FINANCIALS: **Sales and profits are in thousands of dollars—add 000 to get the full amount. 2008 Note: Financial information for 2008 was not available for all companies at press time.**

2008 Sales: $	2008 Profits: $	**U.S. Stock Ticker: Private**
2007 Sales: $	2007 Profits: $	**Int'l Ticker:** Int'l Exchange:
2006 Sales: $	2006 Profits: $	Employees:
2005 Sales: $	2005 Profits: $	Fiscal Year Ends:
2004 Sales: $	2004 Profits: $	Parent Company:

SALARIES/BENEFITS:

Pension Plan:	ESOP Stock Plan:	Profit Sharing:	Top Exec. Salary: $	Bonus: $
Savings Plan:	Stock Purch. Plan:		Second Exec. Salary: $	Bonus: $

OTHER THOUGHTS:

Apparent Women Officers or Directors: 5
Hot Spot for Advancement for Women/Minorities: Y

LOCATIONS: ("Y" = Yes)

West:	Southwest:	Midwest:	Southeast:	Northeast:	International:
			Y		

UNITED STATES CYCLING FEDERATION (USCF) www.usacycling.org

Industry Group Code: 813990 **Ranks within this company's industry group:** Sales: Profits:

Sports:		Services:		Media:		Sales:		Facilities:		Other:	
Leagues/Associations:	Y	Food & Beverage:		TV:		Marketing:		Stadiums:		Gambling:	
Teams:		Agents:		Radio:		Ads:		Fitness Clubs:		Apparel:	
Nonprofits:	Y	Other:		Internet:		Tickets:		Golf Courses:		Equipment:	
Other:				Print:		Retail:		Ski Resorts:		Shoes:	
				Software:		Other:		Other:		Other:	

TYPES OF BUSINESS:

Cycling Organization

BRANDS/DIVISIONS/AFFILIATES:

USCF
National Off Road Bicycle Association
United States Professional Racing Organization
USPRO
Cyclocross National Championships
Lance Armstrong Junior Olympic Road Series
Alison Dulap Junior Olympic Mountain Bike Series

CONTACTS: *Note: Officers with more than one job title may be intentionally listed here more than once.*

Steve Johnson, CEO
Sean Petty, COO
Mark Abramson, Pres.
Todd Sowl, CFO
Debbie Francis, Dir.-Human Resources
Bill Griffin, Dir.-IT
Gregory Cross, Dir.-Oper.
Jess Schwartzkopf, Dir.-Sponsorship & Bus. Dev.
Andy Lee, Dir.-Comm.
Bob Plutt, Mgr.-Acct.
Jim Miller, Dir.-Athletics
Justin Rogers, Dir.-Nat'l Events
Theresa Johnson, VP-Member Svcs.
Daniel Matheny, Mgr.-Collegiate & High School Cycling
Gregory Cross, Dir.-Logistics

Phone: 719-434-4200	**Fax:** 719-866-4300
Toll-Free:	
Address: 210 USA Cycling Point, Colorado Springs, CO 80919 US	

GROWTH PLANS/SPECIAL FEATURES:

United States Cycling Federation (USCF), a non-profit organization, is the only official cycling organization in the U.S. recognized by the U.S. Olympic Committee. USCF is responsible for identifying, training and selecting cyclists to represent the U.S. in international road, track and mountain biking competitions. The company, which operates as USCF, National Off Road Bicycle Association (NORBA) and United States Professional Racing Organization (USPRO), controls nearly 24 major events per year and issues permits for up to 3,000 more. Its major track events include the Track World Cup Qualifiers, Junior Track National Championships and Masters Track National Championships, while its mountain bike events include the National Mountain Bike Race Series, NORBA 24-hour National Championship, American Mountain Bike Challenge Series, U.S. Mountain Bike National Championships and Collegiate Mountain Bike National Championships. USCF's road events include the Collegiate Road Nationals, Elite Road Nationals & Selection Race and Cyclocross National Championships. The company also organizes and runs track, road and mountain bike state championships. In addition, the organization has two junior events series: the Lance Armstrong Junior Olympic Road Series (a.k.a. LAJORS) and the Alison Dunlap Junior Olympic Mountain Bike Series. Both series include races for riders from 10-22 years of age.

FINANCIALS: **Sales and profits are in thousands of dollars—add 000 to get the full amount. 2008 Note: Financial information for 2008 was not available for all companies at press time.**

2008 Sales: $	2008 Profits: $	**U.S. Stock Ticker: Private**
2007 Sales: $	2007 Profits: $	**Int'l Ticker:** Int'l Exchange:
2006 Sales: $	2006 Profits: $	Employees:
2005 Sales: $	2005 Profits: $	Fiscal Year Ends:
2004 Sales: $	2004 Profits: $	Parent Company:

SALARIES/BENEFITS:

Pension Plan:	ESOP Stock Plan:	Profit Sharing:	Top Exec. Salary: $	Bonus: $
Savings Plan:	Stock Purch. Plan:		Second Exec. Salary: $	Bonus: $

OTHER THOUGHTS:

Apparent Women Officers or Directors: 13
Hot Spot for Advancement for Women/Minorities: Y

LOCATIONS: ("Y" = Yes)

West:	Southwest:	Midwest:	Southeast:	Northeast:	International:
Y					

UNITED STATES GOLF ASSOCIATION (USGA)

www.usga.org

Industry Group Code: 813990 **Ranks within this company's industry group:** Sales: 2 Profits:

Sports:		Services:		Media:		Sales:		Facilities:		Other:	
Leagues/Associations:	Y	Food & Beverage:		TV:		Marketing:		Stadiums:		Gambling:	
Teams:		Agents:		Radio:		Ads:		Fitness Clubs:		Apparel:	
Nonprofits:	Y	Other:	Y	Internet:		Tickets:		Golf Courses:	Y	Equipment:	
Other:				Print:		Retail:		Ski Resorts:		Shoes:	
				Software:		Other:		Other:	Y	Other:	Y

TYPES OF BUSINESS:

Golf Association
Golf Tournaments
Youth Programs
Turf Grass Research
Golf Museum

BRANDS/DIVISIONS/AFFILIATES:

U.S. Open
U.S. Amateur Championship
U.S. Junior Championship
USGA Museum
Rules of Golf
Walker Cup Match
Curtis Cup Match
USGA Handicap System

CONTACTS: *Note: Officers with more than one job title may be intentionally listed here more than once.*

James F. Vernon, Pres.
Joseph Anthony, General Counsel
Irving Fish, Treas.
James B. Hyler Jr., VP
Cameron Jay Rains, VP
James T. Bunch, Sec.
Reed K. Mackenzie, Chmn.

Phone: 908-234-2300	**Fax:** 908-234-9687
Toll-Free:	
Address: Golf House, Liberty Corner Rd., Far Hills, NJ 07931 US	

GROWTH PLANS/SPECIAL FEATURES:

The United States Golf Association (USGA) is a nonprofit national governing body for the game of golf. The association was founded in 1894 to write formal rules, conduct national championships and establish a national system of handicapping; it continues to perform these duties and also supports course maintenance practices, funds grassroots programs and historicizes the game of golf in its Museum and Archives in Far Hills, New Jersey. The USGA is supported significantly by its members. The USGA is perhaps best known for the professional and amateur tournaments it conducts in the U.S. and internationally. In addition to conducting 10 national amateur championships and the State Team Championships, the USGA manages the U.S. Open, the U.S. Women's Open and the U.S. Senior Open. The association also runs three international competitions: The Walker Cup Match, the Curtis Cup Match and the Men's/Women's World Amateur Team Championships. The USGA Handicap System, which is nationally recognized, was established in 1912. The handicap program allows golfers of differing abilities to enjoy fair competition. Both professionals and amateurs look to the USGA as the authority for official golfing rules, and in keeping with this role, the association continually tests golf equipment to ensure that new technology does not overrun the core elements of the game. Research is also conducted on turfgrass management to help course officials improve golf course maintenance. In February 2009, USGA partnered with the Oregon Golf Association (OGA) and the Golf Association of Michigan (GAM) to offer members of these organizations the benefits of USGA at no additional cost. In April 2009, the organization agreed to partner with the Professional Golfers Association of America (PGA) to launch a new Junior Golf Program with the purpose of boosting young persons' interest in the game.

FINANCIALS: **Sales and profits are in thousands of dollars—add 000 to get the full amount. 2008 Note: Financial information for 2008 was not available for all companies at press time.**

2008 Sales: $155,814	2008 Profits: $	**U.S. Stock Ticker: Private**
2007 Sales: $136,772	2007 Profits: $	**Int'l Ticker:** Int'l Exchange:
2006 Sales: $126,672	2006 Profits: $	Employees: 340
2005 Sales: $99,561	2005 Profits: $	Fiscal Year Ends: 11/30
2004 Sales: $122,239	2004 Profits: $	Parent Company:

SALARIES/BENEFITS:

Pension Plan:	ESOP Stock Plan:	Profit Sharing:	Top Exec. Salary: $	Bonus: $
Savings Plan:	Stock Purch. Plan:		Second Exec. Salary: $	Bonus: $

OTHER THOUGHTS:

Apparent Women Officers or Directors: 2
Hot Spot for Advancement for Women/Minorities:

LOCATIONS: ("Y" = Yes)

West:	Southwest:	Midwest:	Southeast:	Northeast:	International:
				Y	

UNITED STATES OLYMPIC COMMITTEE (USOC)

www.usoc.org

Industry Group Code: 813990 **Ranks within this company's industry group:** Sales: Profits:

Sports:		Services:		Media:		Sales:		Facilities:		Other:	
Leagues/Associations:	Y	Food & Beverage:		TV:		Marketing:		Stadiums:	Y	Gambling:	
Teams:		Agents:		Radio:		Ads:		Fitness Clubs:		Apparel:	
Nonprofits:	Y	Other:	Y	Internet:		Tickets:		Golf Courses:		Equipment:	
Other:				Print:		Retail:		Ski Resorts:		Shoes:	
				Software:		Other:		Other:	Y	Other:	

TYPES OF BUSINESS:

Olympic Association
Athletic Training

BRANDS/DIVISIONS/AFFILIATES:

International Olympic Committee
US Olympic Education Center
Lakeshore Foundation
Home Depot Olympic Training Center
US Olympic Fan Club
Olympic Bridging Program

CONTACTS: *Note: Officers with more than one job title may be intentionally listed here more than once.*

Stephanie Streeter, Acting CEO
Norman Bellingham, COO
Walter Glover, CFO
Lisa Baird, Chief Mktg. Officer
Pam Sawyer, Dir.-Human Resources
Trevor Miller, Managing Dir.-IT
Rana Dershowitz, General Counsel/Chief-Legal & Gov't Affairs
Rebecca Crawford, Dir.-Games Oper.
Dragomir Cioroslan, Dir.-Int'l Strategies & Dev.
Darryl Seibel, Chief Comm. Officer
Morane Kerek, Controller
Chester Wheeler, Dir.-Sponsorship Sales & Svcs.
Charlie Huebner, Chief-U.S. Paralympics
Mike English, Interim Chief-Sport Performance
John Ruger, Athlete Ombudsman
Larry Probst, Chmn.
Robert Fasulo, Chief-Int'l Rel.

Phone: 719-632-5551 **Fax:** 719-866-4654
Toll-Free: 888-659-8687
Address: 1 Olympic Plz., Colorado Springs, CO 80909 US

GROWTH PLANS/SPECIAL FEATURES:

United States Olympic Committee (USOC) is a nonprofit group that operates training centers to help prepare athletes for the Olympics, Paralympics and Pan-American games. The group receives funding from the International Olympic Committee, which organizes the Olympic Games. Additional funding is provided by the sales of USOC apparel from participating retail stores and the organization's web site, as well as corporate sponsorships and private contributions. USOC provides amateur athletes with an Athlete Ombudsman, who provides free independent advice and dispute mediation assistance to athletes and national governing bodies on subjects relating to an athlete's ability to participate in the Olympic or Pan-American Games. It also operates the U.S. Olympic Fan Club, in which members receive access to exclusive Olympic videos, podcasts and publications, as well as discounts on USOC merchandise. Available to everyone, the USCO web site has biographic information about the athletes, downloadable photos and other information, including travel tips for Americans wishing to attend international Olympics competitions, such as Beijing in 2008. USOC runs three training centers, one each in California, Colorado and New York; and partners with Northern Michigan University to operate the U.S. Olympic Education Center (USOEC), a school located on the university's campus. The USOEC provides athletes with an Olympic-level training program combined with a high school or college education, in which a minimum GPA is required. The committee has also designated additional official Olympic training sites that are run by third parties, such as the Lakeshore Foundation, a 45 acre campus in Birmingham, Alabama primarily designed to help disabled athletes train for the Paralympics; and the Home Depot Olympic Training Center, a 125 acre facility in Carson, California run by Anshutz Entertainment Group (AEG). In March 2009, the USOC announced staff cuts affecting 54 employees, or roughly 13% of its workforce, as well as related budget cuts and cost-saving measures.

FINANCIALS: **Sales and profits are in thousands of dollars—add 000 to get the full amount. 2008 Note: Financial information for 2008 was not available for all companies at press time.**

2008 Sales: $	2008 Profits: $	**U.S. Stock Ticker: Private**
2007 Sales: $221,300	2007 Profits: $	**Int'l Ticker:** Int'l Exchange:
2006 Sales: $	2006 Profits: $	Employees: 400
2005 Sales: $116,707	2005 Profits: $	Fiscal Year Ends: 12/31
2004 Sales: $229,218	2004 Profits: $	Parent Company:

SALARIES/BENEFITS:

Pension Plan:	ESOP Stock Plan:	Profit Sharing:	Top Exec. Salary: $	Bonus: $
Savings Plan:	Stock Purch. Plan:		Second Exec. Salary: $	Bonus: $

OTHER THOUGHTS:

Apparent Women Officers or Directors: 24
Hot Spot for Advancement for Women/Minorities: Y

LOCATIONS: ("Y" = Yes)

West:	Southwest:	Midwest:	Southeast:	Northeast:	International:
Y		Y	Y	Y	

UNITED STATES TENNIS ASSOCIATION (USTA)

www.usta.com

Industry Group Code: 813990 **Ranks within this company's industry group:** Sales: Profits:

Sports:		Services:		Media:		Sales:		Facilities:		Other:	
Leagues/Associations:	Y	Food & Beverage:		TV:	Y	Marketing:	Y	Stadiums:	Y	Gambling:	
Teams:		Agents:		Radio:		Ads:		Fitness Clubs:		Apparel:	
Nonprofits:	Y	Other:		Internet:		Tickets:	Y	Golf Courses:		Equipment:	
Other:				Print:		Retail:	Y	Ski Resorts:		Shoes:	
				Software:		Other:		Other:	Y	Other:	

TYPES OF BUSINESS:

Tennis Association
Tennis Facilities
Sports Marketing
Ticket Sales
Merchandising

BRANDS/DIVISIONS/AFFILIATES:

U.S. Open
U.S. Open Series
USA Tennis High Performance
USTA National Tennis Center
Davis Cup
Fed Cup

CONTACTS: *Note: Officers with more than one job title may be intentionally listed here more than once.*

Jane Brown Grimes, Pres.
Harry Beeth, CFO
Harlan Stone, Chief Mktg. Officer
Lawrence Bonfante, CIO
Andrea Hirsch, General Counsel/Chief Legal Officer
Joseph Healy, Controller
Karlyn Lothery, Chief Diversity Officer
Kurt Kamperman, CEO-Community Tennis Dev.
Paul Roetert, Managing Dir.-Player Dev.
Jane Brown Grimes, Chmn.
Ed Brandt, Dir.-Purchasing

Phone: 914-696-7000	**Fax:** 914-696-7019
Toll-Free:	
Address: 70 W. Red Oak Ln., White Plains, NY 10604 US	

GROWTH PLANS/SPECIAL FEATURES:

The United States Tennis Association (USTA), a nonprofit organization, is the U.S. governing body for the sport of tennis and one of the largest tennis organizations in the world. It currently has more than 700,000 individual members of all age and skill levels and 7,000 organizational members. The organization sets the rules of play and develops and promotes the sport at the local and professional levels. At the community level, it supports a wide range of programs designed to help people learn and play tennis. At the professional level, the organization operates as a sports marketing, entertainment and media group that generates revenue through television, sponsorship, ticket sales, merchandising, membership and advanced media. The revenue it generates is used to support its community initiatives and promote the sport of tennis. USTA owns the U.S. Open, the annual Grand Slam event in the U.S. held at the Arthur Ashe Stadium in Flushing Meadows, New York. It also recently launched the U.S. Open Series, which links 10 summer tournaments to the U.S. Open. In addition, the organization oversees three professional tour events, 96 Pro Circuit events nationwide, all operations of the USTA National Tennis Center (one of the world's largest public tennis facilities and home of the U.S. Open), and it manages and selects the U.S. tennis teams for the Davis Cup, Fed Cup, the Olympics and the Paralympic Games. Through USA Tennis High Performance, UTSA provides promising American tennis players with access to some of the best training, coaching and competitions.

FINANCIALS: Sales and profits are in thousands of dollars—add 000 to get the full amount. 2008 Note: Financial information for 2008 was not available for all companies at press time.

2008 Sales: $	2008 Profits: $	**U.S. Stock Ticker: Private**
2007 Sales: $222,900	2007 Profits: $	**Int'l Ticker:** Int'l Exchange:
2006 Sales: $	2006 Profits: $	Employees: 100
2005 Sales: $	2005 Profits: $	Fiscal Year Ends: 12/31
2004 Sales: $205,900	2004 Profits: $	Parent Company:

SALARIES/BENEFITS:

Pension Plan:	ESOP Stock Plan:	Profit Sharing:	Top Exec. Salary: $	Bonus: $
Savings Plan:	Stock Purch. Plan:		Second Exec. Salary: $	Bonus: $

OTHER THOUGHTS:

Apparent Women Officers or Directors: 20
Hot Spot for Advancement for Women/Minorities: Y

LOCATIONS: ("Y" = Yes)

West:	Southwest:	Midwest:	Southeast:	Northeast:	International:
Y	Y	Y	Y	Y	Y

US FIGURE SKATING

www.usfigureskating.org

Industry Group Code: 813990 **Ranks within this company's industry group:** Sales: Profits:

Sports:		Services:		Media:		Sales:		Facilities:		Other:	
Leagues/Associations:	Y	Food & Beverage:		TV:		Marketing:		Stadiums:		Gambling:	
Teams:		Agents:		Radio:		Ads:		Fitness Clubs:		Apparel:	
Nonprofits:		Other:	Y	Internet:		Tickets:		Golf Courses:		Equipment:	
Other:				Print:		Retail:		Ski Resorts:		Shoes:	
				Software:		Other:		Other:		Other:	

TYPES OF BUSINESS:

Figure Skating Association
Rink Management Resources
Magazine Publication
Training Events
Competitions

BRANDS/DIVISIONS/AFFILIATES:

STAR
SKATING Magazine
NBC Sports
U.S. International Theater On Ice Competition

CONTACTS:

Note: Officers with more than one job title may be intentionally listed here more than once.

David Raith, Exec. Dir.
Ramsey Baker, Sr. Dir.-Mktg. & Comm.
Mark Vogtner, Sr. Dir.-IT
Juliet Newcomer, Dir.-Tech. Svcs.
Kevin Burns, Sr. Dir.-Dev.
Mickey Brown, Mgr.-Interactive Media
Scottie Bibb, Dir.-Media & Public Rel.
Mario Rede, Sr. Dir.-Finance
Susi Wehrli-McLaughlin, Sr. Dir.-Membership
Troy Schwindt, Dir.-Publications
Bob Dunlop, Sr. Dir.-Events
Kelly Hodge, Dir.-Synchronized Skating & Collegiate Programs
Teresa McDonald, Purchasing Agent

Phone: 719-635-5200	**Fax:** 719-635-9548
Toll-Free:	
Address: 20 First St., Colorado Springs, CO 80906 US	

GROWTH PLANS/SPECIAL FEATURES:

U.S. Figure Skating is recognized by the U.S. Olympic Committee and International Skating Union as the official governing body for figure skating in the U.S. Established in 1921, the firm's primary aim has been to encourage participation and achievement in figure skating, and it sanctions approximately 1,300 performances, exhibitions and competitions each year. U.S. Figure Skating creates rules for the holding of tests, competitions and other activities, and organizes and sponsors competitions, mainly through eight programs. The Synchronized Skating, Collegiate and Adults programs offer information and training events for skaters interested in competition. For beginners, the organization offers the Basic Skills program. U.S. Figure Skating has organized a Theater on Ice program for teams of 8-30, with all ages and skill levels welcome to participate in its annual U.S. International Theater On Ice Competition. School Programs are mainly designed to help high school team members balance competition and academics. The Competitive Test Track program is an event that redesigns certain elements of a non-qualifying skating competition in order to help assess competitors on an even playing field. Lastly, the National Showcase program is a competition for single skaters, duets, small ensembles of three to seven and production numbers of eight to thirty skaters, who incorporate theatrical elements into their performances. The organization also publishes SKATING Magazine, which provides in-depth factual coverage of recent programs, competitions and special events. U.S. Figure Skating and USA Hockey have formed a joint venture, STAR (Serving The American Rinks), a membership association that provides technical and management training, quality programming, expense reduction and insurance coverage to professionals and vendors in the rink and arena industry. U.S. Figure Skating's sponsors include AT&T, Smuckers, United, NBC Sports, US Bank, IceNetwork.com and, after an agreement in October 2008, State Farm Insurance Companies.

FINANCIALS:

Sales and profits are in thousands of dollars—add 000 to get the full amount. 2008 Note: Financial information for 2008 was not available for all companies at press time.

2008 Sales: $	2008 Profits: $	**U.S. Stock Ticker: Private**
2007 Sales: $18,100	2007 Profits: $	**Int'l Ticker:** Int'l Exchange:
2006 Sales: $	2006 Profits: $	Employees: 40
2005 Sales: $	2005 Profits: $	Fiscal Year Ends:
2004 Sales: $	2004 Profits: $	Parent Company:

SALARIES/BENEFITS:

Pension Plan:	ESOP Stock Plan:	Profit Sharing:	Top Exec. Salary: $	Bonus: $
Savings Plan:	Stock Purch. Plan:		Second Exec. Salary: $	Bonus: $

OTHER THOUGHTS:

Apparent Women Officers or Directors: 28
Hot Spot for Advancement for Women/Minorities: Y

LOCATIONS: ("Y" = Yes)

West:	Southwest:	Midwest:	Southeast:	Northeast:	International:
Y					

US SOCCER FEDERATION

www.ussoccer.com

Industry Group Code: 813990 **Ranks within this company's industry group:** Sales: Profits:

Sports:		Services:		Media:		Sales:		Facilities:		Other:	
Leagues/Associations:	Y	Food & Beverage:		TV:		Marketing:		Stadiums:		Gambling:	
Teams:		Agents:		Radio:		Ads:		Fitness Clubs:		Apparel:	
Nonprofits:	Y	Other:		Internet:		Tickets:		Golf Courses:		Equipment:	
Other:	Y			Print:		Retail:	Y	Ski Resorts:		Shoes:	
				Software:		Other:		Other:		Other:	

TYPES OF BUSINESS:

Soccer Organization
Youth Programs
Men's & Women's U.S. National Teams
International Soccer Tournaments

BRANDS/DIVISIONS/AFFILIATES:

Major League Soccer
United Soccer Leagues
National Premier Soccer League
Major Indoor Soccer League
U.S. Adult Soccer Association
U.S. National Soccer Team Players Association
U.S. Club Soccer
U.S. Youth Soccer

CONTACTS: *Note: Officers with more than one job title may be intentionally listed here more than once.*

Dan Flynn, CEO
Sunil Gulati, Pres.
Bill Goaziou, Treas.
Mike Edwards, Exec. VP
Dan Flynn, Sec. Gen.
Paul Marstaller, Dir.-Events

Phone: 312-808-1300 **Fax:** 312-808-1301
Toll-Free:
Address: 1801 S. Prairie Ave., Chicago, IL 60616 US

GROWTH PLANS/SPECIAL FEATURES:

The U.S. Soccer Federation (USCF) is the governing body of soccer in the U.S., designed to promote soccer on both the competitive and recreational levels. The federation has overseen the operation of several international tournaments. In addition to the 2003 FIFA Women's World Cup, U.S. Soccer was the host federation for World Cup USA in 1995, as well as the host National Governing Body for two recent U.S. Olympic soccer tournaments, 1984 in Los Angeles and 1996 in Atlanta. The organization is a nonprofit, largely volunteer organization administered through a national council of elected officials. This council represents the organization's four administrative branches: youth players, adult players, the professional division and athletes. The federation's men's national team, recently a major player in the competitive global arena, was advanced through the coaching of Bora Milutinovic in the early 1990s, Steve Sampson in the mid-1990s and Bruce Arena in the late 1990s and early 2000s. The team is currently coached by 2006 MLS coach of the year Bob Bradley. Priorities of the organization also include promoting youth soccer organizations, funding facilities and camps; initiating Major League Soccer in the U.S. as a training ground for the country's best players; and promoting the U.S. Women's National Team. Teams that are affiliated with the USCF include U.S. men's national soccer team, U.S. women's national soccer team, U.S. U-21 women's national soccer team, U.S. U-23 men's national soccer team, U.S. U-20 men's national soccer team, U.S. U-17 men's national soccer team and East Lansing U-13 Boys Blue. Affiliated leagues and organizations include Major League Soccer, United Soccer Leagues, National Premier Soccer League, Major Indoor Soccer League, U.S. Adult Soccer Association, US National Soccer Team Players Association, U.S. Club Soccer, U.S. Youth Soccer, Capital Area Soccer League and Grand Valley Elite League.

FINANCIALS: **Sales and profits are in thousands of dollars—add 000 to get the full amount. 2008 Note: Financial information for 2008 was not available for all companies at press time.**

2008 Sales: $ | 2008 Profits: $
2007 Sales: $ | 2007 Profits: $
2006 Sales: $ | 2006 Profits: $
2005 Sales: $ | 2005 Profits: $
2004 Sales: $16,900 | 2004 Profits: $

U.S. Stock Ticker: Private
Int'l Ticker: Int'l Exchange:
Employees: 78
Fiscal Year Ends: 8/31
Parent Company:

SALARIES/BENEFITS:

Pension Plan: ESOP Stock Plan: Profit Sharing: Top Exec. Salary: $ Bonus: $
Savings Plan: Stock Purch. Plan: Second Exec. Salary: $ Bonus: $

OTHER THOUGHTS:

Apparent Women Officers or Directors:
Hot Spot for Advancement for Women/Minorities:

LOCATIONS: ("Y" = Yes)

West:	Southwest:	Midwest:	Southeast:	Northeast:	International:
Y	Y	Y	Y	Y	

USA BASKETBALL

www.usabasketball.com

Industry Group Code: 813990 **Ranks within this company's industry group:** Sales: Profits:

Sports:		Services:		Media:		Sales:		Facilities:		Other:	
Leagues/Associations:	Y	Food & Beverage:		TV:		Marketing:		Stadiums:		Gambling:	
Teams:		Agents:		Radio:		Ads:		Fitness Clubs:		Apparel:	
Nonprofits:	Y	Other:		Internet:		Tickets:		Golf Courses:		Equipment:	
Other:				Print:		Retail:		Ski Resorts:		Shoes:	
				Software:		Other:		Other:		Other:	

TYPES OF BUSINESS:

Basketball Association

BRANDS/DIVISIONS/AFFILIATES:

Amateur Athletic Union
Continental Basketball Association
National Association of Basketball Coaches
National Association of Intercollegiate Athletics
National Basketball Association
National Basketball Association Development League
National Collegiate Athletic Association
National Wheelchair Basketball Association

CONTACTS: *Note: Officers with more than one job title may be intentionally listed here more than once.*

Jim Tooley, Exec. Dir.
Brent Baumberger, CFO
Heather Mosher Awtrey, Dir.-Admin.
Craig Miller, Chief Comm. & Media Officer
Heather Mosher Awtrey, Dir.-Finance
Carol Callan, Dir.-Women's National Team
Sean Ford, Dir.-Men's National Team
Caroline Williams, Dir.-Comm.

Phone: 719-590-4800 **Fax:** 719-590-4811
Toll-Free:
Address: 5465 Mark Dabling Blvd., Colorado Springs, CO 80918-3842 US

GROWTH PLANS/SPECIAL FEATURES:

USA Basketball, based in Colorado Springs, Colorado, is a nonprofit organization and the national governing body for men's and women's basketball in the U.S. The organization is the recognized governing body for basketball in the U.S. by the International Basketball Federation (FIBA) and the United States Olympic Committee (USOC), and is responsible for the selection, training and fielding of U.S. teams that compete in FIBA-sponsored international basketball competitions, as well as some national competitions. The organization is composed of five member categories. The professional category consists of the Continental Basketball Association, National Basketball Association, National Basketball Association Development League and Women's National Basketball Association. The collegiate category includes the National Association of Intercollegiate Athletics, National Collegiate Athletic Association and National Junior College Athletic Association. The scholastic category consists of sports organizations that operate basketball programs through educational institutions under the collegiate level and is made up of the National Federation of High Schools. The youth category includes the Amateur Athletic Union and is open to community-based sports organizations not affiliated with educational institutions and is for players under the age of 19. The associate category is for organizations that conduct basketball programs or are affiliated with basketball but do not fit qualify for the above mentioned categories. Associates consist of the Harlem Globetrotters, International Sports Exchange, Latin America League of Los Angeles, National Amateur Basketball Association, National Basketball Players Association, National Wheelchair Basketball Association, Sports Tours International, USA Deaf Sports Federation, United States Armed Forces, Women's Basketball Coaches Association, Athletes in Action, Basketball Travelers and College Commissioners Association. The competitions in which USA Basketball teams regularly compete include the Olympics, FIBA World Championships, Pan American Games, World University Games, Junior National/U19 World Championships, Hoop Summit and USA Basketball Youth Development Festivals.

FINANCIALS: **Sales and profits are in thousands of dollars—add 000 to get the full amount. 2008 Note: Financial information for 2008 was not available for all companies at press time.**

2008 Sales: $ | 2008 Profits: $
2007 Sales: $ | 2007 Profits: $
2006 Sales: $ | 2006 Profits: $
2005 Sales: $ | 2005 Profits: $
2004 Sales: $ | 2004 Profits: $

U.S. Stock Ticker: Private
Int'l Ticker: Int'l Exchange:
Employees:
Fiscal Year Ends:
Parent Company:

SALARIES/BENEFITS:

Pension Plan: ESOP Stock Plan: Profit Sharing: Top Exec. Salary: $ Bonus: $
Savings Plan: Stock Purch. Plan: Second Exec. Salary: $ Bonus: $

OTHER THOUGHTS:

Apparent Women Officers or Directors: 7
Hot Spot for Advancement for Women/Minorities: Y

LOCATIONS: ("Y" = Yes)

West:	Southwest:	Midwest:	Southeast:	Northeast:	International:
Y					

Note: Financial information, benefits and other data can change quickly and may vary from those stated here.

USA GYMNASTICS

www.usa-gymnastics.org

Industry Group Code: 813990 **Ranks within this company's industry group:** Sales: Profits:

Sports:		Services:		Media:		Sales:		Facilities:		Other:	
Leagues/Associations:	Y	Food & Beverage:		TV:	Y	Marketing:		Stadiums:		Gambling:	
Teams:		Agents:		Radio:		Ads:		Fitness Clubs:		Apparel:	
Nonprofits:	Y	Other:		Internet:		Tickets:		Golf Courses:		Equipment:	
Other:				Print:		Retail:		Ski Resorts:		Shoes:	
				Software:		Other:		Other:		Other:	

TYPES OF BUSINESS:

Gymnastics Association
Television Production
Magazine Publishing

BRANDS/DIVISIONS/AFFILIATES:

USA Gymnastics
Technique

CONTACTS:

Note: Officers with more than one job title may be intentionally listed here more than once.

Steve Penny, Pres.
Kelly Feilke, Sr. Dir.-Mktg.
Mike Bowman, Mgr.-Computer Systems
Matt Steinke, Mgr.-Web Content
Leslie King, Sr. Dir.-Comm.
John Hewett, Controller
Kathy Kelly, VP-Women's Program
Ron Galimore, VP-Events, Olympic Rel. & Men's Program
Kathy Feldmann, VP-Member Svcs.
Carisa Laughon, Dir.-Educational Svcs.
Peter Vidmar, Chmn.

Phone: 317-237-5050	**Fax:** 317-237-5069
Toll-Free: 800-345-4719	
Address: 132 E. Washington St., Ste. 700, Indianapolis, IN 46204 US	

GROWTH PLANS/SPECIAL FEATURES:

USA Gymnastics is a non-profit organization that serves as the national governing body for gymnastics within the U.S. It is designated by the U.S. Olympic Committee, and the International Gymnastics Federation (FIG). The organization sets the rules and policies that govern men's and women's gymnastics, rhythmic gymnastics, trampoline and tumbling, group gymnastics and sport acrobatics. It also trains and selects the U.S. gymnastics teams for the Olympics and World Championships. Currently, USA Gymnastics has over 110,000 members, including more than 20,000 club members, professionals and instructors; and over 90,000 athletes. It is composed of 21 member organizations, including the YMCA, Amateur Athletic Union and National High School Gymnastics Association. The organization annually sanctions approximately 3,500 competitions and events throughout the U.S. USA Gymnastics itself conducts and produces 5-6 nationally televised annual events for national championships and international invitational competitions, including U.S. Olympic Team Trials. It produces two magazines: USA Gymnastics, a bi-monthly publication geared towards athletes, coaches and gymnastics enthusiasts; and Technique, a black and white technical publication designed for professional members of gymnastics. USA Gymnastics also maintains an online store that sells training videos and books.

FINANCIALS:

Sales and profits are in thousands of dollars—add 000 to get the full amount. 2008 Note: Financial information for 2008 was not available for all companies at press time.

2008 Sales: $	2008 Profits: $	**U.S. Stock Ticker: Private**
2007 Sales: $	2007 Profits: $	**Int'l Ticker:** Int'l Exchange:
2006 Sales: $	2006 Profits: $	Employees:
2005 Sales: $	2005 Profits: $	Fiscal Year Ends:
2004 Sales: $	2004 Profits: $	Parent Company:

SALARIES/BENEFITS:

Pension Plan:	ESOP Stock Plan:	Profit Sharing:	Top Exec. Salary: $	Bonus: $
Savings Plan:	Stock Purch. Plan:		Second Exec. Salary: $	Bonus: $

OTHER THOUGHTS:

Apparent Women Officers or Directors: 18
Hot Spot for Advancement for Women/Minorities: Y

LOCATIONS: ("Y" = Yes)

West:	Southwest:	Midwest:	Southeast:	Northeast:	International:
		Y			

USA HOCKEY

www.usahockey.com

Industry Group Code: 813990 **Ranks within this company's industry group:** Sales: 3 Profits:

Sports:		Services:		Media:		Sales:		Facilities:		Other:	
Leagues/Associations:	Y	Food & Beverage:		TV:		Marketing:		Stadiums:		Gambling:	
Teams:		Agents:		Radio:		Ads:		Fitness Clubs:		Apparel:	
Nonprofits:		Other:		Internet:		Tickets:		Golf Courses:		Equipment:	
Other:				Print:		Retail:		Ski Resorts:		Shoes:	
				Software:		Other:		Other:		Other:	Y

TYPES OF BUSINESS:

Amateur Hockey Association
Tournaments
Insurance

BRANDS/DIVISIONS/AFFILIATES:

USAH
USA Hockey Foundation
USA Hockey InLine
Total Hockey

CONTACTS:

Note: Officers with more than one job title may be intentionally listed here more than once.

Dave Ogrean, Exec. Dir.
Lee Meyer, Sr. Dir.-Mktg.
Ralph Heffter, Mgr.-Database Applications & Programming
Gretchen Hursh, Mgr.-Mktg. & Consumer Prod.
Robert Weldon, Assistant Exec. Dir.-Admin.
Jim Johannson, Assistant Exec. Dir.-Hockey Oper.
Keith Gizzi, Chief Dev. Officer
Cameron Eickmeyer, Managing Editor-Internet Comm.
Dave Fischer, Dir.-Media & Public Rel.
Robert Weldon, Assistant Exec. Dir.-Finance
Mike Bertsch, Assistant Exec. Dir.-Mktg. & Comm.
Pat Kellehar, Assistant Exec. Dir.-Membership Dev.
Ashley Bevan, Dir.-Adult Ice Hockey
Lou Vairo, Dir.-Special Projects
Kim Folsom, Coordinator-Int'l Admin. & Event Oper.

Phone: 719-576-8724 **Fax:** 719-538-1160
Toll-Free:
Address: 1775 Bob Johnson Dr., Colorado Springs, CO 80906-4090 US

GROWTH PLANS/SPECIAL FEATURES:

USA Hockey, Inc. (USAH) is the national governing body for ice hockey in the U.S., as well as an official representative to the United States Olympic Committee (USOC) and the International Ice Hockey Federation. USA Hockey is responsible for organizing and training men's and women's teams for international tournaments, including the IIHF World Championships and the Olympic and Paralympic Winter Games. It is a membership service organization with over 585,000 members including players, coaches, officials, volunteers and other non-participants involved in ice and inline hockey. USAH's member services include standardizing playing rules, streamlining league and tournament sanctioning procedures, providing comprehensive insurance coverage benefits, offering resource materials for all participants and organizing special events and tournaments. The company incorporated the USA Hockey Foundation (USAHF), a non-profit organization dedicated to promoting the sport, as well as providing financial support for USA Hockey. The organization also promotes the sport of ice hockey and its development through its affiliation with amateur leagues throughout the U.S. The organization holds a number of adult classic tournaments every year, adult ice hockey national championships for amateur men's hockey in the elite checking, U.S. checking, 30+, 40+ and 50+ age brackets; and women's hockey in the senior A, B and C classes and 30+ age bracket. It also holds youth ice hockey national championships for Tier I and II boys' hockey in the 12 and under (12U), 14U, 16U and 18U age brackets; girls' hockey in the 12U, 14U, 16U and 19U age brackets; and Junior Tier I, II and III hockey. USA Hockey InLine, a subsidiary of USAH, sanctions local and travel inline hockey leagues and provides member services. In 2008, USAH announced the creation of a membership development department, and an agreement with Total Hockey to be USAH's Official Ice Hockey Equipment Retailer through 2012.

FINANCIALS:

Sales and profits are in thousands of dollars—add 000 to get the full amount. 2008 Note: Financial information for 2008 was not available for all companies at press time.

2008 Sales: $26,806
2007 Sales: $25,010
2006 Sales: $
2005 Sales: $
2004 Sales: $22,300

2008 Profits: $
2007 Profits: $
2006 Profits: $
2005 Profits: $
2004 Profits: $

U.S. Stock Ticker: Private
Int'l Ticker: Int'l Exchange:
Employees: 38
Fiscal Year Ends: 8/31
Parent Company:

SALARIES/BENEFITS:

Pension Plan: ESOP Stock Plan: Profit Sharing: Top Exec. Salary: $ Bonus: $
Savings Plan: Stock Purch. Plan: Second Exec. Salary: $ Bonus: $

OTHER THOUGHTS:

Apparent Women Officers or Directors: 22
Hot Spot for Advancement for Women/Minorities: Y

LOCATIONS: ("Y" = Yes)

West:	Southwest:	Midwest:	Southeast:	Northeast:	International:
Y					

USA SWIMMING

www.usaswimming.org

Industry Group Code: 813990 **Ranks within this company's industry group:** Sales: Profits:

Sports:		Services:		Media:		Sales:		Facilities:		Other:	
Leagues/Associations:	Y	Food & Beverage:		TV:		Marketing:		Stadiums:		Gambling:	
Teams:		Agents:		Radio:		Ads:		Fitness Clubs:		Apparel:	Y
Nonprofits:	Y	Other:	Y	Internet:		Tickets:		Golf Courses:		Equipment:	
Other:				Print:		Retail:		Ski Resorts:		Shoes:	
				Software:		Other:		Other:	Y	Other:	Y

TYPES OF BUSINESS:

Swimming Association
Publications

BRANDS/DIVISIONS/AFFILIATES:

USA Swimming Foundation
XP Apparel
Club Excellence Program
Virtual Club Championships
I.M. Xtreme Challenge

CONTACTS:

Note: Officers with more than one job title may be intentionally listed here more than once.

Chuck Wielgus, Exec. Dir.
Mike Unger, Asst. Exec. Dir.
Manny Banks, Dir.-Consumer Mktg.
John Burbidge, Dir.-IT
George Heidinger, Coordinator-Tech. Svcs.
Kathy Parker, Exec. Coordinator
Matt Farrell, Managing Dir.-Bus. Dev.
Jamie Fabos Olsen, Dir.-Comm.
Jim Harvey, Managing Dir.-Financial Affairs
Lindsay Goodson, Dir.-Corp. Mktg.
Mark Schubert, General Mgr./Head Coach-National Team
Pat Hogan, Managing Dir.-Club Dev.
Chris LaBianco, Chief Dev. Officer
Mike Wilkinson, Supervisor-Shipping & Receiving

Phone: 719-866-4578	Fax: 719-866-4669
Toll-Free:	
Address: 1 Olympic Plz., Colorado Springs, CO 80909 US	

GROWTH PLANS/SPECIAL FEATURES:

USA Swimming is the national governing body for the sport of amateur swimming, administering competitive swimming in accordance with the Amateur Sports Act. It has over 300,000 members scattered throughout all 50 states. The organization is responsible for selecting and training teams for international competitions such as the Olympic Games, and asks its members to promote the sport as much as possible, participating in organizing and competitive efforts on the local, regional and national level. In addition, the group organizes and promotes national swim camps and clinics throughout the country. While the majority of these camps are private, USA Swimming also organizes scholarship-funded camps to encourage swimmers from ethnically under-represented populations. The organization provides programs and services for members, supporters, affiliates and the interested public. In addition, members can apply to train at the group's headquarters at the Olympic Training Center in Colorado Springs, Colorado. Acceptance is based on facilities availability and the athlete's skill level. USA Swimming provides member swim clubs with an array of programs and services, such as field services and consultations; governance education; fundraising assistance; and recognition and incentive programs such as the Club Excellence Program, the Virtual Club Championships and the I.M. Xtreme Challenge, in which swimmers are ranked nationally based on their performance in five or six events. The National Team Division of the organization works with qualifying athletes and coaches to prepare them for high-level international competition. This division also provides numerous resources for high-level competitive athletes, including information on nutrition, race psychology, physiology and anti-doping policies. The USA Swimming Foundation is responsible for the organization's fundraising activities. The organization's web site links to various swimwear merchandisers, including the official USA Swimming online store, managed by partner XP Apparel. The organization's corporate sponsors include Conoco-Phillips, Mutual of Omaha, AT&T, Speedo and Hilton.

FINANCIALS:

Sales and profits are in thousands of dollars—add 000 to get the full amount. 2008 Note: Financial information for 2008 was not available for all companies at press time.

2008 Sales: $	2008 Profits: $	**U.S. Stock Ticker: Private**
2007 Sales: $	2007 Profits: $	**Int'l Ticker:** Int'l Exchange:
2006 Sales: $	2006 Profits: $	Employees:
2005 Sales: $	2005 Profits: $	Fiscal Year Ends:
2004 Sales: $	2004 Profits: $	Parent Company:

SALARIES/BENEFITS:

Pension Plan:	ESOP Stock Plan:	Profit Sharing:	Top Exec. Salary: $	Bonus: $
Savings Plan:	Stock Purch. Plan:		Second Exec. Salary: $	Bonus: $

OTHER THOUGHTS:

Apparent Women Officers or Directors: 34
Hot Spot for Advancement for Women/Minorities: Y

LOCATIONS: ("Y" = Yes)

West:	Southwest:	Midwest:	Southeast:	Northeast:	International:
Y					

USA TRACK & FIELD INC

www.usatf.org

Industry Group Code: 813990 **Ranks within this company's industry group:** Sales: Profits:

Sports:		Services:		Media:		Sales:		Facilities:		Other:	
Leagues/Associations:	Y	Food & Beverage:		TV:		Marketing:		Stadiums:		Gambling:	
Teams:		Agents:		Radio:		Ads:		Fitness Clubs:		Apparel:	
Nonprofits:	Y	Other:		Internet:		Tickets:		Golf Courses:		Equipment:	
Other:				Print:		Retail:		Ski Resorts:		Shoes:	
				Software:		Other:		Other:		Other:	Y

TYPES OF BUSINESS:

Track & Field Organization

BRANDS/DIVISIONS/AFFILIATES:

USATF
Visa Championship Series
Team USA

CONTACTS:

Note: Officers with more than one job title may be intentionally listed here more than once.

Doug Logan, CEO
Michael A. McNees, COO
Stephanie Hightower, Pres.
Jim Elias, CFO
Jill Geer, Dir.-Comm.
Jack Wickens, Vice Chmn.
Stephanie Hightower, Chmn.

Phone: 317-261-0500 **Fax:** 317-261-0481
Toll-Free:
Address: 132 E. Washington St., Ste. 800, Indianapolis, IN 46204 US

GROWTH PLANS/SPECIAL FEATURES:

USA Track & Field, Inc. (USATF), a non-profit organization, is the U.S. national governing body (NGB) for the sports of track and field, race walking and long-distance running. It sets and enforces rules and regulations; selects the U.S. track and field teams for the Olympics, World Championships and over 12 other international events each year; and promotes the sport through programs of training and competition for people of all ages. More than 14,000 coaches have been educated at USATF instructional programs designed to elevate and standardize the level of coaching across the country. Additionally, athlete clinics are held nationwide, covering a wide range of disciplines, from race walking to pole vault. The organization also sanctions more than 4,000 events annually throughout the U.S., certifies courses for accuracy, validates records and provides insurance to sanctioned events, members clubs and member-athletes. For professional athletes, the organization holds the Visa Championship Series, a series of indoor and outdoor track and field events throughout the year. Athletes compete for prize money at each meet, and the top athletes share in a bonus pool of $100,000. The organization currently has nearly 100,000 members and approximately 700 athletes wear a Team USA uniform in any given year. Its member organizations include the U.S. Olympic Committee, NCAA, NAIA, Road Runners Club of America, Running USA and the National Federation of State High School Associations. USATF also has 57 member associations that oversee the sport at its 2,500 clubs at the local level. In April 2008, the four NGBs already located in Indiana, USATF, U.S. Synchronized Swimming, USA Gymnastics and USA Diving, consolidated their separate office locations into a single 32,000 square foot office space. The move was prompted, in part, by the demolition of USATF's former headquarters, the RCA Dome, which was carried out in December.

FINANCIALS:

Sales and profits are in thousands of dollars—add 000 to get the full amount. 2008 Note: Financial information for 2008 was not available for all companies at press time.

2008 Sales: $	2008 Profits: $	**U.S. Stock Ticker: Private**
2007 Sales: $13,700	2007 Profits: $	**Int'l Ticker:** Int'l Exchange:
2006 Sales: $	2006 Profits: $	Employees: 40
2005 Sales: $	2005 Profits: $	Fiscal Year Ends: 12/31
2004 Sales: $11,300	2004 Profits: $	Parent Company:

SALARIES/BENEFITS:

Pension Plan:	ESOP Stock Plan:	Profit Sharing:	Top Exec. Salary: $	Bonus: $
Savings Plan:	Stock Purch. Plan:		Second Exec. Salary: $	Bonus: $

OTHER THOUGHTS:

Apparent Women Officers or Directors: 2
Hot Spot for Advancement for Women/Minorities: Y

LOCATIONS: ("Y" = Yes)

West:	Southwest:	Midwest:	Southeast:	Northeast:	International:
Y		Y			

UTAH JAZZ

www.nba.com/jazz

Industry Group Code: 711211B **Ranks within this company's industry group:** Sales: 13 Profits: 14

Sports:		Services:		Media:		Sales:		Facilities:		Other:	
Leagues/Associations:		Food & Beverage:		TV:		Marketing:		Stadiums:	Y	Gambling:	
Teams:	Y	Agents:		Radio:		Ads:		Fitness Clubs:		Apparel:	Y
Nonprofits:		Other:		Internet:		Tickets:	Y	Golf Courses:		Equipment:	
Other:				Print:		Retail:	Y	Ski Resorts:		Shoes:	
				Software:		Other:		Other:		Other:	

TYPES OF BUSINESS:

Professional Basketball Team
Ticket Sales

BRANDS/DIVISIONS/AFFILIATES:

Larry H. Miller Group
EnergySolutions Arena
Junior Jazz
myJazz Mobile
Larry H. Miller Charities
Jazzbots

CONTACTS: *Note: Officers with more than one job title may be intentionally listed here more than once.*

Greg Miller, CEO
Randy Rigby, Pres.
Robert Hyde, CFO/Exec. VP
Jim Olson, Sr. VP-Mktg. & Sales
Paul Welsh, Dir.-Human Resources
Shawn Waters, Dir.-Info Systems.
Robert Tingey, General Counsel
Dan Knight, Dir.-Oper.
Patti Balli, Dir.-Community Rel.
John Larson, VP-Finance
Kevin O'Connor, Gen. Mgr./Exec.. VP-Basketball Oper.
Jerry Sloan, Head Coach
Walt Perrin, VP-Player Personnel
Chris Baum, Sr. VP-Broadcasting

Phone: 801-325-2500	**Fax:** 801-325-2578
Toll-Free:	
Address: Energy Solutions Arena. 301 W. S. Temple, Salt Lake City, UT 84101 US	

GROWTH PLANS/SPECIAL FEATURES:

The Utah Jazz is a professional basketball team in the National Basketball Association (NBA) based in Salt Lake City, Utah. The franchise originated in the NBA as the New Orleans Jazz in 1974, relocating to Salt Lake City in 1979 to play in the EnergySolutions Arena. While the team has never won a championship, the Jazz has had many excellent playoff-caliber teams with legendary players such as Pete Maravich, Jon Stockton, Karl Malone and Jeff Hornacek. The Jazz ended the 2005-06 season with a victory over the Golden State Warriors, although it was not enough to place them in the Championship brackets. In the 2007-08 season, the team won first place in the Northwest division. In the 2008-09 season the team won third place. Community programs the Jazz is affiliated with include the Junior Jazz youth sports program, NBA Cares, Read to Achieve, Kirilenko's Kids and the Larry H. Miller Charities. The Larry H. Miller Group, an auto dealership company, owns the team. The firm became co-owner of the Jazz in 1985 for $8 million, and the group then purchased the remainder in 1986 for $14 million. The Larry H. Miller Group owns and operates the Jazz's home arena and the Salt Lake Bees, a Triple-A baseball team, and the Salt Lake Golden Eagles, an ice hockey team. The Jazz web site includes features such as myJazz Mobile text alerts, the Jazzbots team blog, myJazz Connection membership, wallpapers and desktop applications. Forbes Magazine recently estimated the team to be worth approximately $358 million. In the 2008-09 season, the team's home attendance average was roughly 19,900 per game.

FINANCIALS: **Sales and profits are in thousands of dollars—add 000 to get the full amount. 2008 Note: Financial information for 2008 was not available for all companies at press time.**

2008 Sales: $119,000	2008 Profits: $8,800	**U.S. Stock Ticker: Subsidiary**
2007 Sales: $114,000	2007 Profits: $5,700	**Int'l Ticker:** Int'l Exchange:
2006 Sales: $96,000	2006 Profits: $1,400	Employees:
2005 Sales: $91,000	2005 Profits: $	Fiscal Year Ends: 6/30
2004 Sales: $88,000	2004 Profits: $	Parent Company: LARRY H MILLER GROUP

SALARIES/BENEFITS:

Pension Plan:	ESOP Stock Plan:	Profit Sharing:	Top Exec. Salary: $	Bonus: $
Savings Plan:	Stock Purch. Plan:		Second Exec. Salary: $	Bonus: $

OTHER THOUGHTS:

Apparent Women Officers or Directors: 10
Hot Spot for Advancement for Women/Minorities: Y

LOCATIONS: ("Y" = Yes)

West:	Southwest:	Midwest:	Southeast:	Northeast:	International:
Y					

VAIL RESORTS INC

www.vailresorts.com

Industry Group Code: 713920 **Ranks within this company's industry group:** Sales: 1 Profits: 1

Sports:		Services:		Media:		Sales:		Facilities:		Other:	
Leagues/Associations:		Food & Beverage:		TV:		Marketing:		Stadiums:		Gambling:	
Teams:		Agents:		Radio:		Ads:		Fitness Clubs:		Apparel:	
Nonprofits:		Other:		Internet:		Tickets:		Golf Courses:		Equipment:	
Other:				Print:		Retail:	Y	Ski Resorts:	Y	Shoes:	
				Software:		Other:		Other:	Y	Other:	Y

TYPES OF BUSINESS:

Ski Resorts
Luxury Hotels & Lodging
Real Estate Development

BRANDS/DIVISIONS/AFFILIATES:

RockResorts
Grand Teton Lodge Company
Vail Resorts Development Company
Vail Resorts Management Company
Vail Resorts Lodging Company

CONTACTS: *Note: Officers with more than one job title may be intentionally listed here more than once.*

Robert A. Katz, CEO
Jeffrey W. Jones, CFO/Sr. Exec. VP
Derek C. Koenig, Chief Mktg. Officer/Sr. VP
Mark R. Gasta, Chief Human Resources Officer/Sr. VP
Robert N. Urwiler, CIO/Sr. VP
Fiona E. Arnold, General Counsel/Sr. VP
Keith A. Fernandez, Pres., Vail Resorts Dev. Company
Mark L. Schoppet, Chief Acct. Officer/Sr. VP/Controller
Christopher E. Jarnot, COO/Sr. VP-Vail
John McD. Garnsey, COO/Exec. VP-Beaver Creek
Blaise T. Carrig, COO/Exec. VP-Heavenly
Robert A. Katz, Chmn.

Phone: 303-404-1800 **Fax:**
Toll-Free:
Address: 390 Interlocken Crescent, Ste. 1000, Broomfield, CO 80021 US

GROWTH PLANS/SPECIAL FEATURES:

Vail Resorts, Inc. (VRI), one of the leading resort operators in North America, is organized as a holding company, operating through various subsidiaries. VRI currently operates in three business segments: mountain, lodging and real estate. In the mountain segment, which represents 59% of total revenue, the company owns and operates five ski resorts and related ancillary businesses at Vail, Breckenridge, Keystone and Beaver Creek mountains in Colorado and the Heavenly Ski Resort in the Lake Tahoe area of California and Nevada. These resorts use federal land under the terms of Special Use Permits granted by the USDA Forest Service. The company also holds a roughly 69.3% interest in SSI Venture, LLC, a retail and rental company. In the lodging segment, VRI owns and operates various hotels, as well as RockResorts International, LLC, a luxury hotel management company, and Grand Teton Lodge Company, (GTLC) which operates three resorts within Grand Teton National Park (under a National Park Service concessionaire contract), and the Jackson Hole Golf & Tennis Club in Wyoming. Vail Resorts Development Company, a wholly-owned subsidiary, conducts the operations of the company's real estate segment. VRI's mountain business and its lodging properties at or around the company's ski resorts are seasonal in nature, with peak operating seasons from mid-November through mid-April. The company's operations at GTLC generally run from mid-May through mid-October. The firm also has non-majority owned investments in various other entities. In June 2008, the company agreed to acquire Colorado Mountain Express, a resort ground transportation business, from East West Resort Transportation Holdings, LLC. In March 2009, the firm implemented a companywide wage reduction plan, affecting employees on a sliding scale from 2.5% to 10%.

Employees are offered medical, dental, and vision insurance; flexible spending accounts; life insurance; short-and long-term disability benefits; an employee assistance program; and ski passes.

FINANCIALS: **Sales and profits are in thousands of dollars—add 000 to get the full amount. 2008 Note: Financial information for 2008 was not available for all companies at press time.**

2008 Sales: $1,152,156	2008 Profits: $102,927	**U.S. Stock Ticker: MTN**
2007 Sales: $940,536	2007 Profits: $61,397	**Int'l Ticker:** Int'l Exchange:
2006 Sales: $838,852	2006 Profits: $45,756	Employees: 15,100
2005 Sales: $809,987	2005 Profits: $23,138	Fiscal Year Ends: 7/31
2004 Sales: $726,643	2004 Profits: $-5,959	Parent Company:

SALARIES/BENEFITS:

Pension Plan:	ESOP Stock Plan:	Profit Sharing:	Top Exec. Salary: $835,414	Bonus: $210,881
Savings Plan: Y	Stock Purch. Plan:		Second Exec. Salary: $447,933	Bonus: $147,661

OTHER THOUGHTS:

Apparent Women Officers or Directors: 3
Hot Spot for Advancement for Women/Minorities: Y

LOCATIONS: ("Y" = Yes)

West:	Southwest:	Midwest:	Southeast:	Northeast:	International:
Y	Y			Y	

VANCOUVER CANUCKS

canucks.nhl.com

Industry Group Code: 711211F **Ranks within this company's industry group:** Sales: 5 Profits: 4

Sports:		Services:		Media:		Sales:		Facilities:		Other:	
Leagues/Associations:		Food & Beverage:		TV:		Marketing:		Stadiums:	Y	Gambling:	
Teams:	Y	Agents:		Radio:		Ads:		Fitness Clubs:		Apparel:	
Nonprofits:		Other:		Internet:		Tickets:	Y	Golf Courses:		Equipment:	
Other:				Print:		Retail:	Y	Ski Resorts:		Shoes:	
				Software:		Other:		Other:		Other:	

TYPES OF BUSINESS:

Hockey Team

BRANDS/DIVISIONS/AFFILIATES:

Canucks Sports and Entertainment
Aquilini Investment Group
General Motors Place
Manitoba Moose

CONTACTS:

Note: Officers with more than one job title may be intentionally listed here more than once.

Chris Zimmerman, CEO
Victor de Bonis, COO
Chris Zimmerman, Pres.
Todd Kobus, CFO
Janeil Mackay, Dir.-Retail & Consumer Prod. Mktg.
Susanne Haine, VP-People Dev.
Al Hutchings, Dir.-Eng.
Jon Festinger, General Counsel/Exec. VP-Bus.
Harvey Jones, VP/Gen. Mgr.-Arena Oper.
Gord Forbes, VP-Bus. Dev.
T. C. Carling, Dir.-Media Rel.
Todd Kobus, VP-Finance
Michael D. Gillis, Gen. Mgr.
Alain Vigneault, Head Coach
Laurence Gilman, VP-Hockey Oper.
Lorne Henning, VP-Player Personnel
Francesco Aquilini, Chmn.

Phone: 604-899-7400 **Fax:** 604-899-7401
Toll-Free: 888-672-7522
Address: 800 Griffiths Way, Vancouver, BC V6B 6G1 Canada

GROWTH PLANS/SPECIAL FEATURES:

The Vancouver Canucks have been a National Hockey League (NHL) team since 1970. The Canucks play in the Northwest Division of the NHL's Western Conference, along with the Calgary Flames, Colorado Avalanche, Edmonton Oilers and Minnesota Wild. Although named the Canucks, the team's logo and mascot consist of a killer whale. Its home stadium is the General Motors Place in Vancouver, which seats 18,630 for hockey games and hosts approximately 170 events each year including Vancouver Canucks games. The stadium will play host to both the men's and women's ice hockey portion of the 2010 Vancouver Winter Olympics. Both the Canucks and General Motors Place are owned and operated by Canucks Sports and Entertainment, formerly Orca Bay Sports & Entertainment, which is run by Aquilini Investment Group, a Vancouver-based company led by Francesco Aquilini. One of the Canucks' most memorable players was Stan Smyl, nicknamed the Steamer, who joined the team in 1978 and played for it throughout his entire 13 season professional career until he retired in 1991. Immediately following his retirement as a player, the Canucks hired him as an assistant coach, a position he held until 1999, when he became the head coach of Canucks' top American Hockey League (AHL) affiliate, the Syracuse Crunch. Syml recently took over as director of player development. His jersey, number 12, was retired in 1991. Other members whose jerseys have been retired include Trevor Linden, number 16 and Wayne Gretzky, number 99. The team has claimed two conference championships, in 1981-82 (under Smyl's captaincy) and 1993-94; and five division championships, in 1974-75, 1991-92, 1992-93, 2003-04 and 2006-07. According to a recent Forbes estimate, the team is worth approximately $236 million. Average home game attendance in the 2008-09 season was 18,630.

FINANCIALS:

Sales and profits are in thousands of dollars—add 000 to get the full amount. 2008 Note: Financial information for 2008 was not available for all companies at press time.

2008 Sales: $107,000
2007 Sales: $96,000
2006 Sales: $80,000
2005 Sales: $
2004 Sales: $74,000

2008 Profits: $19,200
2007 Profits: $12,800
2006 Profits: $1,100
2005 Profits: $
2004 Profits: $

U.S. Stock Ticker: Subsidiary
Int'l Ticker: Int'l Exchange:
Employees:
Fiscal Year Ends: 6/30
Parent Company: CANUCKS SPORTS AND ENTERTAINMENT

SALARIES/BENEFITS:

Pension Plan: ESOP Stock Plan: Profit Sharing: Top Exec. Salary: $ Bonus: $
Savings Plan: Stock Purch. Plan: Second Exec. Salary: $ Bonus: $

OTHER THOUGHTS:

Apparent Women Officers or Directors: 8
Hot Spot for Advancement for Women/Minorities: Y

LOCATIONS: ("Y" = Yes)

West:	Southwest:	Midwest:	Southeast:	Northeast:	International:
					Y

VARSITY BRANDS INC

www.varsity.com

Industry Group Code: 315000A **Ranks within this company's industry group:** Sales: Profits:

Sports:		Services:		Media:		Sales:		Facilities:		Other:	
Leagues/Associations:		Food & Beverage:		TV:		Marketing:		Stadiums:		Gambling:	
Teams:		Agents:		Radio:		Ads:		Fitness Clubs:		Apparel:	Y
Nonprofits:		Other:	Y	Internet:		Tickets:		Golf Courses:		Equipment:	
Other:				Print:		Retail:		Ski Resorts:		Shoes:	
				Software:		Other:		Other:		Other:	

TYPES OF BUSINESS:

Cheerleader & Dance Team Uniforms
Camps, Events & Competitions
Travel Services
Direct Sales

BRANDS/DIVISIONS/AFFILIATES:

Leonard Green & Partners, L.P.
Company Dance
Starlight
Varsity Spirit Fashions
Universal Cheerleaders Association
Intropa

CONTACTS:

Note: Officers with more than one job title may be intentionally listed here more than once.

Jeffrey G. (Jeff) Webb, CEO
Jeffrey G. (Jeff) Webb, Pres.
Ronald Pilcher, CIO
Nicole Lauchaire, Dir.-Varsity.com
Kris Shepherd, Exec. VP
Marci Neumeister, VP-Sales, Apparel Div.
Jeffrey G. (Jeff) Webb, Chmn.

Phone: 901-387-4300	**Fax:** 800-792-4337
Toll-Free:	
Address: 6745 Lenox Center Ct., Ste. 300, Memphis, TN 38115 US	

GROWTH PLANS/SPECIAL FEATURES:

Varsity Brands, Inc. is a top designer, marketer and supplier of cheerleader and dance team uniforms and accessories. Over 100,000 catalogs featuring the company's uniforms and accessories are mailed annually to schools, school spirit advisors and coaches. The firm supplements its direct sales force and catalog sales with a telemarketing sales force. The company web site allows customers to design their own uniforms with numerous colors and styles and search for events based on location, type and dates. Varsity promotes its products through active association with championships and specials including the National High School Cheerleading Championship, the National Dance Team Championship, the National All Star Cheerleading Championship and the Company Dance Championship. With an annual attendance of over 350,000 participants, Varsity is also a leading operator of cheerleading and dance team training camps, conventions, competitions and clinics. Joint venture Company Dance, formed in partnership with Paula Abdul, hosts conventions and competitions held in approximately 30 cities. Besides its training camps, the firm also offers various educational materials through its web site, such as downloadable PDF documents, featuring information on topics including becoming a cheerleader, being a male cheerleader, being the parent of a cheerleader, coaching cheerleaders, transitioning from high school to college cheerleading squads, practical tips on developing cheerleading skills and other issues. Additionally, tour company subsidiary Intropa specializes in organizing trips for cheerleaders, bands, choirs and orchestras, dance and theater groups and other school-affiliated groups. Varsity is owned by investment firm Leonard Green & Partners, L.P.

FINANCIALS:

Sales and profits are in thousands of dollars—add 000 to get the full amount. 2008 Note: Financial information for 2008 was not available for all companies at press time.

2008 Sales: $	2008 Profits: $	**U.S. Stock Ticker: Private**
2007 Sales: $156,400	2007 Profits: $	**Int'l Ticker:** Int'l Exchange:
2006 Sales: $	2006 Profits: $	Employees: 700
2005 Sales: $	2005 Profits: $	Fiscal Year Ends: 12/31
2004 Sales: $	2004 Profits: $	Parent Company:

SALARIES/BENEFITS:

Pension Plan:	ESOP Stock Plan:	Profit Sharing:	Top Exec. Salary: $	Bonus: $
Savings Plan:	Stock Purch. Plan:		Second Exec. Salary: $	Bonus: $

OTHER THOUGHTS:

Apparent Women Officers or Directors:
Hot Spot for Advancement for Women/Minorities:

LOCATIONS: ("Y" = Yes)

West:	Southwest:	Midwest:	Southeast:	Northeast:	International:
			Y		

VF CORP

www.vfc.com

Industry Group Code: 315000 **Ranks within this company's industry group:** Sales: 1 Profits: 1

Sports:		Services:		Media:		Sales:		Facilities:		Other:	
Leagues/Associations:		Food & Beverage:		TV:		Marketing:		Stadiums:		Gambling:	
Teams:		Agents:		Radio:		Ads:		Fitness Clubs:		Apparel:	Y
Nonprofits:		Other:		Internet:		Tickets:		Golf Courses:		Equipment:	
Other:				Print:		Retail:	Y	Ski Resorts:		Shoes:	Y
				Software:		Other:		Other:		Other:	Y

TYPES OF BUSINESS:

Jeans-Manufacturing
Swimsuits
Outdoor Gear & Apparel
Image Wear
Outlet Stores
Footwear

BRANDS/DIVISIONS/AFFILIATES:

Van Inc
Majestic Athlete
North Face Inc (The)
lucy activewear, inc.
Seven For All Mankind, LLC
Napapijri
Lee
Nautica Enterprises Inc

CONTACTS: *Note: Officers with more than one job title may be intentionally listed here more than once.*

Eric C. Wiseman, CEO
Eric C. Wiseman, Pres.
Robert K. Shearer, CFO/Sr. VP
Susan Larson Williams, VP-Human Resources
Martin S. Schneider, CIO/VP
Candace S. Cummings, VP-Admin.
Candace S. Cummings, General Counsel/Corp. Sec.
Stephen F. Dull, VP-Strategy
Cindy Knoebel, VP-Financial & Corp. Comm.
Frank C. Pickard, III, Treas./VP
Michael T. Gannaway, VP-Customer Teams, VF Direct
Franklin L. Terkelsen, VP-Mergers & Acquisitions
Bradley Batten, Chief Acct. Officer/VP/Controller
Karen Murray, VP-Sportswear
Eric C. Wiseman, Chmn.
Boyd Rogers, VP/Pres., Supply Chain

Phone: 336-424-6000	**Fax:**
Toll-Free:	
Address: 105 Corporate Ctr. Blvd., Greensboro, NC 27408 US	

GROWTH PLANS/SPECIAL FEATURES:

VF Corp., organized in 1899, is one of the world's largest brand-name apparel manufacturers and a leading producer of jeans, outdoor products, image apparel and sportswear. The company's top brands include Lee, Wrangler, Rustler, Maverick and Riders jeans; The North Face, Vans, JanSport, Eastpak, Kipling, Napapijri, Reef and Eagle Creek outdoor products; Red Kap, Bulwark, Majestic, Chef and The Force imagewear; Nautica and John Varvatos sportswear; and lucy activewear and Seven For All Mankind contemporary brand apparel. VF sells its products through 689 specialty stores, upscale and traditional department stores, national chains and mass merchants nationwide and abroad in over 150 countries. It also operates a chain of 76 VF Outlet stores, half carrying only one brand and half carrying many VF brands. Over the past several years, the company has moved production from its U.S. plants to lower-cost offshore facilities in Mexico, the Caribbean and Asia. Approximately 26% of the company's domestic sales in 2007 were manufactured in VF-owned facilities, primarily in Mexico and Central America, and 74% were obtained from contractors, primarily in Asia. Acquisitions in 2007 included Eagle Creek, Inc.; Majestic Athlete, Inc.; The North Face branded business in China; lucy activewear, inc.; and Seven For All Mankind LLC. In April 2007, VF sold its intimate apparel business to Fruit of the Loom. In August 2007, the company formed a joint venture with Mitsui & Co., Ltd. for the marketing and distribution of Napapijri brand products in Japan. In June 2008, VF acquired 33% of Mo Industries, owner of the Splendid and Ella Moss women's contemporary sportswear brands. The company has been expanding its own retail operations in recent years, opening 89 new stores over the course of 2008; in March 2009, VF announced plans to add at least 70 more stores in the coming year.

VF Corporation offers its employees medical, dental and vision coverage; tuition assistance; employee assistance programs; flexible spending accounts; scholarships for employees' children; wellness programs; and training and development programs.

FINANCIALS: **Sales and profits are in thousands of dollars—add 000 to get the full amount. 2008 Note: Financial information for 2008 was not available for all companies at press time.**

2008 Sales: $7,642,600	2008 Profits: $602,748	**U.S. Stock Ticker: VFC**
2007 Sales: $7,219,359	2007 Profits: $591,621	**Int'l Ticker:** Int'l Exchange:
2006 Sales: $6,215,794	2006 Profits: $533,516	Employees: 46,600
2005 Sales: $5,654,155	2005 Profits: $506,702	Fiscal Year Ends: 12/31
2004 Sales: $5,218,066	2004 Profits: $474,702	Parent Company:

SALARIES/BENEFITS:

Pension Plan:	ESOP Stock Plan:	Profit Sharing:	Top Exec. Salary: $1,180,000	Bonus: $2,088,600
Savings Plan: Y	Stock Purch. Plan:		Second Exec. Salary: $775,000	Bonus: $1,239,000

OTHER THOUGHTS:

Apparent Women Officers or Directors: 4
Hot Spot for Advancement for Women/Minorities: Y

LOCATIONS: ("Y" = Yes)

West:	Southwest:	Midwest:	Southeast:	Northeast:	International:
Y	Y	Y	Y	Y	Y

Note: Financial information, benefits and other data can change quickly and may vary from those stated here.

VIACOM INC

www.viacom.com

Industry Group Code: 513210 **Ranks within this company's industry group:** Sales: 2 Profits: 2

Sports:		Services:		Media:		Sales:		Facilities:		Other:	
Leagues/Associations:		Food & Beverage:		TV:	Y	Marketing:		Stadiums:		Gambling:	
Teams:		Agents:		Radio:		Ads:		Fitness Clubs:		Apparel:	
Nonprofits:		Other:		Internet:		Tickets:		Golf Courses:		Equipment:	
Other:				Print:		Retail:		Ski Resorts:		Shoes:	
				Software:		Other:		Other:		Other:	

TYPES OF BUSINESS:

Cable TV Networks
Television Production/Syndication
Film Production
Online Media
Video Distribution
Video Games

BRANDS/DIVISIONS/AFFILIATES:

National Amusement, Inc.
MTV Networks
Nickelodeon
Comedy Central
CMT: Country Music Television
Paramount Pictures Corp
United Paramount Network (UPN)
DreamWorks SKG

CONTACTS:

Note: Officers with more than one job title may be intentionally listed here more than once.

Philippe Dauman, CEO
Philippe P. Dauman, Pres.
Thomas E. Dooley, CFO
Denise White, Exec. VP-Human Resources & Admin.
Thomas E. Dooley, Chief Admin. Officer/Sr. Exec. VP
Michael D. Fricklas, General Counsel/Sec./Exec. VP
Wade Davis, Sr. VP-Strategy, Mergers & Acquisitions
Carl D. Folta, Exec. VP-Corp. Comm.
James Bombassei, Sr. VP-Investor Rel.
Jacques Tortoroli, Chief Acct. Officer/Corp. Controller/Sr. VP
Brad Grey, Chmn./CEO-Paramount Motion Picture Group
Debra Lee, CEO/Pres., BET Networks
Judy McGrath, Chmn./CEO-MTV Networks
DeDe Lea, Exec. VP-Gov't Affairs
Sumner M. Redstone, Exec. Chmn.

Phone: 212-258-6000	**Fax:** 212-258-6464
Toll-Free: 800-516-4399	
Address: 1515 Broadway, New York, NY 10036 US	

GROWTH PLANS/SPECIAL FEATURES:

Viacom, Inc., spun off from now CBS Corp. (formerly Viacom, Inc.), is an international media conglomerate. National Amusement, Inc., owned by the Redstone family, owns 73% of Viacom. Viacom is composed of two segments: Media Networks, which includes MTV Networks and BET Networks, and Filmed Entertainment. Through a combination of original and acquired programming and other entertainment content, the Media Networks brands are focused on providing content that appeals to key demographics attractive to advertisers across multiple distribution platforms, including cable television, satellite, mobile and digital media assets. Media Networks operates more than 135 television networks and accounted for 60% of the firm's 2007 revenues. The Filmed Entertainment segment produces, finances and distributes motion pictures and other entertainment content through its well-known group of brands including Paramount Pictures Corp. Revenues from the Filmed Entertainment segment are generated primarily from feature film production and distribution, including exhibition of motion pictures in theatrical release, sale of home entertainment product, and distribution to pay and basic cable television, broadcast television, syndicated television and digital media. This division accounted for 40% of 2007 revenues. The company's online gaming communication and community platform include Xfire, Inc.; Atom Entertainment, Inc., an online game, short film and animation destination; and Harmonix Music Systems, Inc., popular videogame title Guitar Hero developer. Viacom also owns DreamWorks, which produces movies and television programming and markets these properties for home entertainment. Other Paramount companies include Paramount Vantage, Paramount Classics, MTV Films and Nickelodeon Movies.

FINANCIALS:

Sales and profits are in thousands of dollars—add 000 to get the full amount. 2008 Note: Financial information for 2008 was not available for all companies at press time.

2008 Sales: $14,625,000	2008 Profits: $1,251,000	**U.S. Stock Ticker: VIA**
2007 Sales: $13,423,100	2007 Profits: $1,838,100	**Int'l Ticker:** Int'l Exchange:
2006 Sales: $11,361,100	2006 Profits: $1,592,100	Employees: 11,500
2005 Sales: $9,609,600	2005 Profits: $1,256,900	Fiscal Year Ends: 12/31
2004 Sales: $8,132,200	2004 Profits: $293,700	Parent Company:

SALARIES/BENEFITS:

Pension Plan: Y	ESOP Stock Plan:	Profit Sharing:	Top Exec. Salary: $2,000,000	Bonus: $
Savings Plan: Y	Stock Purch. Plan:		Second Exec. Salary: $1,000,000	Bonus: $

OTHER THOUGHTS:

Apparent Women Officers or Directors: 6
Hot Spot for Advancement for Women/Minorities: Y

LOCATIONS: ("Y" = Yes)

West:	Southwest:	Midwest:	Southeast:	Northeast:	International:
Y		Y		Y	Y

VULCAN INC

www.vulcan.com

Industry Group Code: 551110 **Ranks within this company's industry group:** Sales: Profits:

Sports:		Services:		Media:		Sales:		Facilities:		Other:	
Leagues/Associations:		Food & Beverage:		TV:		Marketing:		Stadiums:		Gambling:	
Teams:	Y	Agents:		Radio:		Ads:		Fitness Clubs:		Apparel:	
Nonprofits:		Other:		Internet:		Tickets:		Golf Courses:		Equipment:	
Other:				Print:		Retail:		Ski Resorts:		Shoes:	
				Software:		Other:		Other:		Other:	

TYPES OF BUSINESS:

Company & Enterprise Management
Film Production
Entertainment Investments
Telecommunications Investments
Sports Teams
Real Estate
Museums

BRANDS/DIVISIONS/AFFILIATES:

Vulcan Productions
Science Fiction Museum & Hall of Fame
Hospital (The)
Seattle Seahawks
Portland Trailblazers
SpaceShipOne
Wired-World
DreamWorks SKG

CONTACTS: *Note: Officers with more than one job title may be intentionally listed here more than once.*

Jody Patton, CEO
Jody Patton, Pres.
Chris Purcell, VP-Tech.
Bill McGrath, General Counsel/Exec. VP
Denise Wolf, VP-Oper.
Denise Wolf, VP-Corp. Dev.
Steven C. Crosby, VP-Corp. Comm.
Lance Conn, VP-Investment Mgmt.
Ada M. Healey, VP-Real Estate Dev.
Richard E. Hutton, VP-Media Dev.
Bruce Lowry, VP-Tax
Paul G. Allen, Chmn.

Phone: 206-342-2000	**Fax:** 206-342-3000
Toll-Free:	
Address: 505 Fifth Ave. S, Ste. 900, Seattle, WA 98104 US	

GROWTH PLANS/SPECIAL FEATURES:

Vulcan, Inc. was founded by Paul Allen, Microsoft's co-founder, to research and implement his investments, and does everything from building museums and making original motion pictures to launching businesses and developing new technologies. It invests heavily in the Pacific Northwest and primarily focuses on projects involving education, preserving history and the arts. Though the company believes that technology can enhance these projects and deliver them to a broader audience, achieving high levels of creativity is its main objective. Its creative projects include Vulcan Productions, several museums and The Hospital. Vulcan Productions is an independent film studio whose recent productions include Hard Candy and several documentaries, including The Blues, executive produced by Martin Scorsese. Vulcan's museums include the Science Fiction Museum and Hall of Fame, the Microcomputer Gallery and the Flying Heritage Collection of rare WWII airplanes. The Hospital is a multi-use venue for international music and film professionals created from the derelict St. Paul's Hospital in the London borough of Camden. The firm owns two major league sports teams, the Seattle Seahawks and Portland Trail Blazers, as well as various real estate properties, including 505 Union Station in Seattle, a 291,860 square foot office building where the company headquarters are located. Vulcan won the $10 million X Prize with SpaceShipOne, the first privately built spacecraft to successfully enter outer space. Vulcan invests in companies that fit Allen's Wired-World strategy to contribute to or benefit from the technology of other companies within Vulcan's extensive investment portfolio. Other investments in telecommunications, media, retail, software, hardware and biotechnology, include companies such as DreamWorks SKG, Oxygen Media and RCN Corporation.

Vulcan offers its employees apartment assistance, an employee assistance plan, insurance benefits for domestic partners, tuition reimbursement, up to $100 a month for transportation, an on-premises athletic facility and health club membership.

FINANCIALS: **Sales and profits are in thousands of dollars—add 000 to get the full amount. 2008 Note: Financial information for 2008 was not available for all companies at press time.**

2008 Sales: $	2008 Profits: $	**U.S. Stock Ticker: Private**
2007 Sales: $	2007 Profits: $	**Int'l Ticker:** Int'l Exchange:
2006 Sales: $	2006 Profits: $	Employees:
2005 Sales: $	2005 Profits: $	Fiscal Year Ends: 12/31
2004 Sales: $	2004 Profits: $	Parent Company:

SALARIES/BENEFITS:

Pension Plan:	ESOP Stock Plan:	Profit Sharing:	Top Exec. Salary: $	Bonus: $
Savings Plan: Y	Stock Purch. Plan:		Second Exec. Salary: $	Bonus: $

OTHER THOUGHTS:

Apparent Women Officers or Directors: 4
Hot Spot for Advancement for Women/Minorities: Y

LOCATIONS: ("Y" = Yes)

West:	Southwest:	Midwest:	Southeast:	Northeast:	International:
Y					

Note: Financial information, benefits and other data can change quickly and may vary from those stated here.

WALT DISNEY COMPANY (THE)

disney.go.com/index

Industry Group Code: 513210 **Ranks within this company's industry group:** Sales: 1 Profits: 1

Sports:		Services:		Media:		Sales:		Facilities:		Other:	
Leagues/Associations:		Food & Beverage:		TV:	Y	Marketing:	Y	Stadiums:		Gambling:	
Teams:		Agents:		Radio:	Y	Ads:	Y	Fitness Clubs:		Apparel:	Y
Nonprofits:		Other:		Internet:	Y	Tickets:	Y	Golf Courses:	Y	Equipment:	
Other:				Print:		Retail:	Y	Ski Resorts:		Shoes:	Y
				Software:		Other:	Y	Other:	Y	Other:	

TYPES OF BUSINESS:

Cable TV Networks, Broadcasting & Entertainment
Filmed Entertainment
Merchandising
Television Networks
Music & Book Publishing
Online Entertainment Programs
Theme Parks, Resorts & Cruise Lines

BRANDS/DIVISIONS/AFFILIATES:

Walt Disney Parks & Resorts
ESPN Inc
ABC Inc
Walt Disney Studios (The)
Walt Disney World Resort
Miramax Film Corp
Walt Disney Pictures
ABC Entertainment Group

CONTACTS: *Note: Officers with more than one job title may be intentionally listed here more than once.*

Robert A. Iger, CEO
Robert A. Iger, Pres.
Thomas O. Staggs, CFO/Sr. Exec. VP
Dennis W. Shuler, Chief Human Resources Officer/Exec. VP
Kevin Mayer, Exec. VP-Tech. Group
Alan Braverman, General Counsel/Sr. Exec. VP/Corp. Sec.
Kevin Mayer, Exec. VP-Corp. Strategy & Bus. Dev.
Zenia Mucha, Exec. VP-Corp. Comm.
Christine M. McCarthy, Exec. VP-Corp. Finance & Real Estate/Treas.
Ronald L. Iden, Sr. VP-Security
Preston Padden, Exec. VP-Worldwide Gov't Rel.
Brent Woodford, Sr. VP-Planning & Control
Richard Cook, Chmn.-The Walt Disney Studios
John E. Pepper, Jr., Chmn.
Diego Lerner, Pres., EMEA

Phone: 818-560-1000	**Fax:** 818-560-1930
Toll-Free:	
Address: 500 S. Buena Vista St., Burbank, CA 91521 US	

GROWTH PLANS/SPECIAL FEATURES:

The Walt Disney Company is an international entertainment company operating in four major business segments: media networks; studio entertainment; consumer products; and parks and resorts. The media networks segment, which operates ABC Television Network, is involved in domestic broadcast television networks and stations; cable/satellite networks; international broadcast operations; television production and distribution; domestic broadcast radio networks and stations; and Internet and mobile operations. The company also owns interest in and/or operates many cable networks, including ESPN, ABC Family, the History Channel and A&E. The studio entertainment segment produces and acquires live action and animated motion pictures, direct-to-video programming, musical recordings and live stage plays. The consumer products segment designs, promotes and sells merchandise based on the firm's intellectual property. The parks and resorts segment owns/operates Florida's Walt Disney World Resort and the Disney Cruise Line; the Disneyland resort in California; ESPN Zone facilities in several states; and the Disney Vacation Club. It also holds interest in the Disneyland Resort Paris and Hong Kong Disneyland, and licenses the Tokyo Disney Resort in Japan. The Walt Disney World Resort includes Magic Kingdom, Epcot, Disney's Hollywood Studios and Disney's Animal Kingdom. It also owns/operates hotels, the Wide World of Sports complex and more. The firm operates eight ESPN Zones, located in California, Georgia, Maryland, Illinois, Colorado, Nevada, New York and Washington, D.C. In December 2008, the company signed a joint venture agreement with Russian firm Media-One Holdings Limited to launch a Disney-branded television channel in Russia. That same month, Disney acquired all outstanding shares of Jetix Europe. In January 2009, the company combined the operations of its ABC Entertainment and ABC Studios subsidiaries, which now operate as ABC Entertainment Group. In March 2009, Disney's media networks division and YouTube agreed to launch ad-supported channels which will show clips from the Disney/ABC Television Group and ESPN.

FINANCIALS: **Sales and profits are in thousands of dollars—add 000 to get the full amount. 2008 Note: Financial information for 2008 was not available for all companies at press time.**

2008 Sales: $37,843,000	2008 Profits: $4,427,000	**U.S. Stock Ticker: DIS**
2007 Sales: $35,510,000	2007 Profits: $4,687,000	**Int'l Ticker:** Int'l Exchange:
2006 Sales: $33,747,000	2006 Profits: $3,374,000	Employees: 150,000
2005 Sales: $31,374,000	2005 Profits: $2,533,000	Fiscal Year Ends: 9/30
2004 Sales: $30,752,000	2004 Profits: $2,345,000	Parent Company:

SALARIES/BENEFITS:

Pension Plan: Y	ESOP Stock Plan:	Profit Sharing:	Top Exec. Salary: $2,000,000	Bonus: $13,945,493
Savings Plan: Y	Stock Purch. Plan:		Second Exec. Salary: $1,187,019	Bonus: $4,100,000

OTHER THOUGHTS:

Apparent Women Officers or Directors: 6
Hot Spot for Advancement for Women/Minorities: Y

LOCATIONS: ("Y" = Yes)

West:	Southwest:	Midwest:	Southeast:	Northeast:	International:
Y	Y	Y	Y	Y	Y

Note: Financial information, benefits and other data can change quickly and may vary from those stated here.

WARNACO SWIMWEAR INC

www.speedousa.com

Industry Group Code: 315000A **Ranks within this company's industry group:** Sales: Profits:

Sports:		Services:		Media:		Sales:		Facilities:		Other:	
Leagues/Associations:		Food & Beverage:		TV:		Marketing:		Stadiums:		Gambling:	
Teams:		Agents:		Radio:		Ads:		Fitness Clubs:		Apparel:	Y
Nonprofits:		Other:		Internet:		Tickets:		Golf Courses:		Equipment:	Y
Other:				Print:		Retail:	Y	Ski Resorts:		Shoes:	
				Software:		Other:		Other:		Other:	

TYPES OF BUSINESS:

Swimwear Apparel
Online Sales
Fitness Apparel
Swim Accessories

BRANDS/DIVISIONS/AFFILIATES:

Warnaco Group, Inc. (The)
Speedo
SpeedoUSA.com
FastSkin FS-Pro
FastSkin LZR Racer
Aqualab
Michael Kors
Nautica

CONTACTS: *Note: Officers with more than one job title may be intentionally listed here more than once.*

Larry Burak, COO
Paula Schneider, Pres.
Stu Isaac, VP-Team Sales & Mktg.

Phone: 323-726-1262	**Fax:** 323-721-3613
Toll-Free: 888-477-3336	
Address: 6040 Bandini Blvd., Los Angeles, CA 90040 US	

GROWTH PLANS/SPECIAL FEATURES:

Warnaco Swimwear, Inc., the swimwear marketing arm of its parent company, The Warnaco Group, Inc., designs, manufactures and markets swimwear, swim accessories and active fitness apparel. Its products are primarily sold under the Speedo brand name, which the firm has licensed, in North America and the Caribbean, from British firm the Pentland Group, whose Speedo International affiliate provides the company with various apparel accessories. Throughout the U.S., Mexico, Canada and the Caribbean, Warnaco distributes Speedo fitness and fashion swimwear; Speedo swimwear for kids; and Speedo active apparel. Distribution channels include Federated Department Stores, independent retailers such as Nordstrom, chain stores such as J.C. Penny and Kohl's, sporting goods stores, team dealers, membership clubs such as Costco, Target, the military, and other retailers, including the Victoria's Secret Catalog, The Sports Authority, and the company's SpeedoUSA.com web site. The swimwear accessories line includes a diverse range of products such as swim goggles, swimming caps, nose clips, masks, snorkels, ear plugs, kickboards, flotation devices and aquatic exercise gear. The firm also develops garments for use in a wide variety of fitness activities, ranging from aerobics and running to triathlons and cycling. The company often forms long-term promotional contracts with Olympic medalists and world-champion swimmers to better market its products. Warnaco Swimwear recently introduced FastSkin FS-Pro, a line of high-quality skin-like bodysuits for swim racing; and in July 2008 released FastSkin LZR Racer, which was co-developed by Speedo's research and development facility, Aqualab, and NASA.

FINANCIALS: **Sales and profits are in thousands of dollars—add 000 to get the full amount. 2008 Note: Financial information for 2008 was not available for all companies at press time.**

2008 Sales: $	2008 Profits: $	**U.S. Stock Ticker: Subsidiary**
2007 Sales: $	2007 Profits: $	**Int'l Ticker:** Int'l Exchange:
2006 Sales: $	2006 Profits: $	Employees: 400
2005 Sales: $	2005 Profits: $	Fiscal Year Ends: 12/31
2004 Sales: $	2004 Profits: $	Parent Company: WARNACO GROUP INC (THE)

SALARIES/BENEFITS:

Pension Plan:	ESOP Stock Plan:	Profit Sharing:	Top Exec. Salary: $	Bonus: $
Savings Plan:	Stock Purch. Plan:		Second Exec. Salary: $	Bonus: $

OTHER THOUGHTS:

Apparent Women Officers or Directors: 1
Hot Spot for Advancement for Women/Minorities:

LOCATIONS: ("Y" = Yes)

West:	Southwest:	Midwest:	Southeast:	Northeast:	International:
Y					

WASHINGTON CAPITALS

capitals.nhl.com

Industry Group Code: 711211F **Ranks within this company's industry group:** Sales: 24 Profits: 23

Sports:		Services:		Media:		Sales:		Facilities:		Other:	
Leagues/Associations:		Food & Beverage:		TV:		Marketing:	Y	Stadiums:		Gambling:	
Teams:	Y	Agents:		Radio:		Ads:		Fitness Clubs:		Apparel:	
Nonprofits:		Other:		Internet:		Tickets:	Y	Golf Courses:		Equipment:	
Other:				Print:		Retail:	Y	Ski Resorts:		Shoes:	
				Software:		Other:		Other:		Other:	

TYPES OF BUSINESS:

Hockey Team

BRANDS/DIVISIONS/AFFILIATES:

Lincoln Holdings LLC
Hershey Bears (The)
Lincoln Hockey LLC
Verizon Center (The)
South Carolina Stingrays (The)

CONTACTS: *Note: Officers with more than one job title may be intentionally listed here more than once.*

Dick Patrick, Pres.
Ellen Folts, CFO-Lincoln Holdings LLC
Tim McDermott, Chief Mktg. Officer/Sr. VP
Brian McPartland, Mgr.-IT
Kurt Kehl, VP-Comm.
Keith Burrows, VP-Finance
Nate Ewell, Dir.-Media Rel.
Bruce Boudreau, Head Coach
George McPhee, VP/Gen. Mgr.
Ted Leonsis, Chmn.

Phone: 202-266-2200 **Fax:** 202-266-2360
Toll-Free:
Address: 627 N. Glebe Rd., Ste. 850, Arlington, VA 22203 US

GROWTH PLANS/SPECIAL FEATURES:

The Washington Capitals are a hockey team and member of the National Hockey League (NHL). The Capitals play in the Southeast Division of the NHL's Eastern Conference, along with the Atlanta Thrashers, Carolina Hurricanes, Florida Panthers and Tampa Bay Lightning. The team, which played its first season in 1974, is majority-owned and operated by Lincoln Holdings LLC, through subsidiary Lincoln Hockey LLC. The Capitals franchise has won one conference championship (1997-98) and three division championships (1988-89, 1999-00 and 2000-01). The Capitals play in the Verizon Center, which is owned by Washington Sports and Entertainment and Lincoln Holdings LLC; the arena also hosts the home games of the Washington Wizards, a National Basketball Association (NBA) team; the Washington Mystics, a Women's National Basketball Association (WNBA) team; and multiple sports events for the Georgetown University Hoyas. Notable Washington Capital players of the past include Denis Dupere, Bengt Gustafsson, Mike Gartner, Dennis Maruk and Calle Johansson. Washington is affiliated with two minor league teams: the Hershey Bears of the American Hockey League (AHL) and the South Carolina Stingrays of the ECHL league. In 2008-09, the team averaged over 18,000 fans per game. Forbes recently valued the franchise at approximately $160 million.

FINANCIALS: **Sales and profits are in thousands of dollars—add 000 to get the full amount. 2008 Note: Financial information for 2008 was not available for all companies at press time.**

2008 Sales: $73,000	2008 Profits: $-6,900	**U.S. Stock Ticker: Subsidiary**
2007 Sales: $66,000	2007 Profits: $1,000	**Int'l Ticker:** Int'l Exchange:
2006 Sales: $63,000	2006 Profits: $4,600	Employees:
2005 Sales: $	2005 Profits: $	Fiscal Year Ends: 7/31
2004 Sales: $61,000	2004 Profits: $	Parent Company: LINCOLN HOLDINGS LLC

SALARIES/BENEFITS:

Pension Plan:	ESOP Stock Plan:	Profit Sharing:	Top Exec. Salary: $	Bonus: $
Savings Plan:	Stock Purch. Plan:		Second Exec. Salary: $	Bonus: $

OTHER THOUGHTS:

Apparent Women Officers or Directors: 3
Hot Spot for Advancement for Women/Minorities: Y

LOCATIONS: ("Y" = Yes)

West:	Southwest:	Midwest:	Southeast:	Northeast:	International:
				Y	

WASHINGTON MYSTICS

www.wnba.com/mystics

Industry Group Code: 711211E **Ranks within this company's industry group:** Sales: Profits:

Sports:		Services:		Media:		Sales:		Facilities:		Other:	
Leagues/Associations:		Food & Beverage:		TV:		Marketing:		Stadiums:		Gambling:	
Teams:	Y	Agents:		Radio:		Ads:		Fitness Clubs:		Apparel:	
Nonprofits:		Other:		Internet:		Tickets:	Y	Golf Courses:		Equipment:	
Other:				Print:		Retail:	Y	Ski Resorts:		Shoes:	
				Software:		Other:		Other:		Other:	

TYPES OF BUSINESS:

Women's Basketball Team

BRANDS/DIVISIONS/AFFILIATES:

Lincoln Holdings LLC
Verizon Center
Mystics in Training
Mayhem
Mystics Foundation

CONTACTS:

Note: Officers with more than one job title may be intentionally listed here more than once.

Greg Bibb, COO
Sheila Johnson, Pres./Managing Partner
Michael Ragan, Sr. Dir.-Ticket Sales & Guest Svcs.
Crystal Hudson, Mgr.-Game Oper. & New Media
Ketsia Colimon, VP-Comm.
Julie Plank, Head Coach
Dana Simonelli, Dir.-Ticket Mktg. & Promotions
Mikhail Ovechkin, Mgr.-Team Oper.
Marty Lerner, Dir.-Corp. Partnerships
Ted Leonsis, Chmn.

Phone: 202-527-7540 **Fax:** 202-527-7539
Toll-Free:
Address: Verizon Ctr., 3rd Fl., 601 F St., N.W., Washington, DC 20004 US

GROWTH PLANS/SPECIAL FEATURES:

The Washington Mystics are a Women's National Basketball Association (WNBA) team. The Mystics, sister team to National Basketball Association's (NBA) Washington Wizards, play in the Eastern Conference along with the Chicago Sky, Connecticut Sun, Detroit Shock, Indiana Fever and New York Liberty. Lincoln Holdings LLC, led by the Mystics current Chairman Ted Leonsis, purchased the Mystics and the National Hockey League's (NHL) Washington Capitals, as well as 44% of the Wizards, from Washington Sports & Entertainment LP (WSELP) for approximately $10 million. The Verizon Center, the Mystics' home court, also plays host to the Wizards, the Capitals and other sporting events, including games for the Georgetown University Hoyas. Aside from Verizon Wireless, the teams other corporate sponsors include AARP; Adidas; American Express; Chevy Chase Bank; D.C. Lottery; Discover Card; Pitney Bowes; Washington Business Journal; The Washington Post; and others. The franchise's non-profit organization, the Washington Mystics foundation, focuses on youth health and well-being programs, with a special focus on childhood obesity. It promotes Mystics in Training (MIT) a year-long exercise program targeting 3rd and 4th graders in the areas surrounding D.C., including Virginia and Maryland. It includes elements such as the Mystics Mile, which encourages students to walk at least a mile with their teachers. The MIT program also offers lessons in nutrition, and every month a special guest, sometimes Mystics players and staff, visits the children to walk with them. The Mystics' official dance team, called the Mayhem, performs at all the team's home games. The dance team consists of local boys and girls between the ages of 7-17.

FINANCIALS:

Sales and profits are in thousands of dollars—add 000 to get the full amount. 2008 Note: Financial information for 2008 was not available for all companies at press time.

2008 Sales: $ | 2008 Profits: $
2007 Sales: $ | 2007 Profits: $
2006 Sales: $ | 2006 Profits: $
2005 Sales: $ | 2005 Profits: $
2004 Sales: $ | 2004 Profits: $

U.S. Stock Ticker: Subsidiary
Int'l Ticker: Int'l Exchange:
Employees:
Fiscal Year Ends: 1/31
Parent Company: LINCOLN HOLDINGS LLC

SALARIES/BENEFITS:

Pension Plan: ESOP Stock Plan: Profit Sharing: Top Exec. Salary: $ Bonus: $
Savings Plan: Stock Purch. Plan: Second Exec. Salary: $ Bonus: $

OTHER THOUGHTS:

Apparent Women Officers or Directors: 25
Hot Spot for Advancement for Women/Minorities: Y

LOCATIONS: ("Y" = Yes)

West:	Southwest:	Midwest:	Southeast:	Northeast:	International:
				Y	

WASHINGTON NATIONALS

washington.nationals.mlb.com

Industry Group Code: 711211A **Ranks within this company's industry group:** Sales: 15 Profits: 3

Sports:		Services:		Media:		Sales:		Facilities:		Other:	
Leagues/Associations:		Food & Beverage:	Y	TV:		Marketing:		Stadiums:		Gambling:	
Teams:	Y	Agents:		Radio:		Ads:		Fitness Clubs:		Apparel:	Y
Nonprofits:	Y	Other:		Internet:		Tickets:	Y	Golf Courses:		Equipment:	
Other:				Print:		Retail:	Y	Ski Resorts:		Shoes:	
				Software:		Other:		Other:		Other:	

TYPES OF BUSINESS:

Professional Baseball Team

BRANDS/DIVISIONS/AFFILIATES:

Montreal Expos
Washington Nationals Dream Foundation
Nationals Park
Syracuse Chiefs
Harrisburg Senators
Potomac Nationals
Hagerstown Suns
Vermont Lake Monsters

CONTACTS:

Note: Officers with more than one job title may be intentionally listed here more than once.

Theodore N. Lerner, Managing Principal Owner
Stan Kasten, Pres.
Lori Creasy, CFO
Chris Gargani, VP/Managing Dir.-Sales & Mktg.
Bettina Deynes, VP-Human Resources
Jason Zachariah, Dir.-IT
Elise Holman, VP-Admin.
Damon T. Jones, VP/Club Counsel
Mike Rizzo, VP-Baseball Oper./Assistant Gen. Mgr.
Catherine Silver, Sr. Dir.-Bus. Dev. & Ballpark Enterprises
Chartese Burnett, VP-Comm. & Community Rel.
Ted Towne, Controller
Gregory McCarthy, VP-Gov't & Municipal Affairs
Bob Boone, VP-Player Dev./Assistant Gen. Mgr.
Bob Wolfe, Exec. VP
Squire Galbreath, Assistant Gen. Mgr.-Baseball Admin.

Phone: 202-675-6287 **Fax:** 202-640-7999
Toll-Free:
Address: 1500 S. Capitol St., SE, Washington, DC 20003-1507 US

GROWTH PLANS/SPECIAL FEATURES:

The Washington Nationals, formerly the Montreal Expos, are an organization within Major League Baseball (MLB). The Expos team was an expansion franchise in 1969 and experienced success in only two seasons, the strike-shortened years of 1981 and 1994. In 2002, Expos owner Jeffrey Loria sold the team to the other 29 MLB owners after years of disappointing league performances and dismal home attendance records. It was expected that the team would be contracted along with the Minnesota Twins, but legal issues protected the Twins and Expos from this fate. Loria, expecting contraction, had taken most of his personnel and equipment with him to the Florida Marlins, where he was the new owner. Consequently, a severely gutted Expos organization played under common ownership in Montreal for two years before moving, returning baseball to Washington D.C. in 2005, 34 years after the previous Senators left D.C. to become the Texas Rangers. In May 2006, MLB sold the team for $450 million to the highest acceptable bidder, a large ownership group headed by Theodore Lerner. Upon moving, the Nationals originally played in the 56,000-seat RFK Stadium, former home of the Washington Redskins. Before the sale of the team was completed, plans for a new, publicly-financed ballpark were approved by the D.C. Council and MLB. The new stadium, Nationals Park, opened in March 2008. The stadium seats approximately 41,888. The franchise has contributed a few former players and managers to the Baseball Hall of Fame, including Tony Perez, Gary Carter and Frank Robinson. In April 2009, Forbes Magazine valued the Nationals at $406 million. The team's average home game attendance in 2008 was roughly 29,000.

FINANCIALS:

Sales and profits are in thousands of dollars—add 000 to get the full amount. 2008 Note: Financial information for 2008 was not available for all companies at press time.

2008 Sales: $184,000
2007 Sales: $153,000
2006 Sales: $144,000
2005 Sales: $145,000
2004 Sales: $

2008 Profits: $42,600
2007 Profits: $43,700
2006 Profits: $19,500
2005 Profits: $
2004 Profits: $

U.S. Stock Ticker: Private
Int'l Ticker: Int'l Exchange:
Employees:
Fiscal Year Ends: 10/31
Parent Company:

SALARIES/BENEFITS:

Pension Plan: ESOP Stock Plan: Profit Sharing: Top Exec. Salary: $ Bonus: $
Savings Plan: Stock Purch. Plan: Second Exec. Salary: $ Bonus: $

OTHER THOUGHTS:

Apparent Women Officers or Directors: 11
Hot Spot for Advancement for Women/Minorities: Y

LOCATIONS: ("Y" = Yes)

West:	Southwest:	Midwest:	Southeast:	Northeast:	International:
				Y	

WASHINGTON REDSKINS

www.redskins.com

Industry Group Code: 711211C **Ranks within this company's industry group:** Sales: 1 Profits: 1

Sports:		Services:		Media:		Sales:		Facilities:		Other:	
Leagues/Associations:		Food & Beverage:		TV:		Marketing:		Stadiums:	Y	Gambling:	
Teams:	Y	Agents:		Radio:		Ads:		Fitness Clubs:		Apparel:	
Nonprofits:		Other:		Internet:		Tickets:	Y	Golf Courses:		Equipment:	
Other:				Print:		Retail:	Y	Ski Resorts:		Shoes:	
				Software:		Other:		Other:		Other:	

TYPES OF BUSINESS:

Professional Football Team

BRANDS/DIVISIONS/AFFILIATES:

Washington Football, Inc.
FedEx Field

CONTACTS:

Note: Officers with more than one job title may be intentionally listed here more than once.

Daniel M. Snyder, CEO
Jay Sloan, CFO
Janice Schmidt, Sr. VP-Mktg.
Vinny Cerrato, Exec. VP-Football Oper.
Karl Swanson, Sr. VP-Public Rel.
Jim Zorn, Head Coach
Scott Campbell, Dir.-Player Personnel
Eric Schaffer, VP-Football Admin.
Joel Patten, Scout-National

Phone: 703-726-7000 **Fax:** 703-726-7086
Toll-Free:
Address: 21300 Redskins Park Dr., Ashburn, VA 20147 US

GROWTH PLANS/SPECIAL FEATURES:

The Washington Redskins, owned and operated by Washington Football, Inc., are a professional football team based in Washington, D.C. playing in the NFL. The team has been in the league since 1932, tracing its origins to Boston, Massachusetts, where it played for a time in Fenway Park (home of the Boston Red Sox). Due to poor attendance in the Boston area, the team was moved in 1937 to Washington, D.C. Over the course of the team's history, the Redskins have won five NFL Championships, including three of the five Super Bowls in which they have played. In 1999, the Redskins club was sold to Daniel Snyder, chairman of Six Flags, Inc. and founder of Snyder Communications, Inc. Under terms of the deal, Snyder purchased the team and their then two-year-old stadium, FedEx Field, for $800 million following the death of previous owner, Jack Kent Cooke. Under Snyder's ownership, team revenues have increased to over $300 million per year, and Forbes Magazine has cited the Redskins as among the most valuable sports teams in the world, valued at approximately $1.5 billion in 2008. Despite the team's lucrative financial run under Snyder, however, its on-field performance has been disappointing to fans. Under Snyder's tenure, the team has reached the playoffs just twice, in large part due to the rehiring of legendary coach Joe Gibbs, who had previously led the team to all three of its Super Bowl victories. The Redskins have contributed approximately 25 former players and coaching staff to the Pro Football Hall of Fame, including George Allen, Cliff Battles, Sammy Baugh, Turk Edwards, Darrell Green, Sonny Jurgensen and Art Monk. A recent Forbes estimate values the team at $1.53 billion. In the 2008 season, the team averaged 88,604 fans in attendance per home game.

FINANCIALS:

Sales and profits are in thousands of dollars—add 000 to get the full amount. 2008 Note: Financial information for 2008 was not available for all companies at press time.

2008 Sales: $327,000	2008 Profits: $58,100	**U.S. Stock Ticker: Subsidiary**
2007 Sales: $312,000	2007 Profits: $66,000	**Int'l Ticker:** Int'l Exchange:
2006 Sales: $303,000	2006 Profits: $108,400	Employees:
2005 Sales: $287,000	2005 Profits: $	Fiscal Year Ends: 1/31
2004 Sales: $245,000	2004 Profits: $	Parent Company: WASHINGTON FOOTBALL INC

SALARIES/BENEFITS:

Pension Plan:	ESOP Stock Plan:	Profit Sharing:	Top Exec. Salary: $	Bonus: $
Savings Plan:	Stock Purch. Plan:		Second Exec. Salary: $	Bonus: $

OTHER THOUGHTS:

Apparent Women Officers or Directors: 1
Hot Spot for Advancement for Women/Minorities:

LOCATIONS: ("Y" = Yes)

West:	Southwest:	Midwest:	Southeast:	Northeast:	International:
				Y	

WASHINGTON WIZARDS

www.nba.com/wizards

Industry Group Code: 711211B **Ranks within this company's industry group:** Sales: 14 Profits: 10

Sports:		Services:		Media:		Sales:		Facilities:		Other:	
Leagues/Associations:		Food & Beverage:		TV:		Marketing:		Stadiums:	Y	Gambling:	
Teams:	Y	Agents:		Radio:		Ads:		Fitness Clubs:		Apparel:	
Nonprofits:		Other:		Internet:		Tickets:	Y	Golf Courses:		Equipment:	
Other:				Print:		Retail:	Y	Ski Resorts:		Shoes:	
				Software:		Other:		Other:		Other:	

TYPES OF BUSINESS:

NBA Basketball Team
Sports Merchandise
Ticket Sales

BRANDS/DIVISIONS/AFFILIATES:

Washington Sports & Entertainment LP
Verizon Center
Wizards Dancers
G-Wiz
Gilbert Scores for Schools
Pollin Award

CONTACTS: *Note: Officers with more than one job title may be intentionally listed here more than once.*

Ernie Grunfeld, Pres.
Irene Pollin, Co-Owner
Abe Pollin, Co-Chmn.
Flip Saunders, Head Coach
Tommy Sheppard, VP-Basketball Admin.

Phone: 202-661-5000	**Fax:** 202-661-5101
Toll-Free:	
Address: 601 F St. NW, Washington, DC 20004 US	

GROWTH PLANS/SPECIAL FEATURES:

The Washington Wizards are a National Basketball Association (NBA) team managed by Washington Sports & Entertainment, L.P. Co-Chairmen Irene and Abe Pollin have owned the franchise since 1964, making them some of the longest tenured team owners in NBA history. Since its creation in 1961, the team has undergone numerous name changes, starting with the Chicago Packers, followed by the Chicago Zephyrs, Baltimore Bullets, Capital Bullets and Washington Bullets before becoming, in 1996, the Washington Wizards. In franchise history, the Wizards won only one championship, in 1978, under the leadership of Wes Unseld and Phil Chenier. Although the Wizards are still in a rebuilding phase after a decline in the late 1990's, many new talents, including guard Gilbert Arenas and forward Caron Butler, have earned the team playoff seats for the last three playing seasons. The Wizards received major publicity coverage when former Chicago Bulls star, Michael Jordan, returned from retirement and played on the team for the 2001-02 and 2002-03 seasons. All home games are played at the Verizon Center, which is also owned by Washington Sports & Entertainment, and has seating capacity for over 20,173 fans. Game night entertainment includes the Wizards Dancers, the Dunking Dancers, Capital Kids and mascots G-Wiz and G-Man. Forbes Magazine recently estimated the team to be worth approximately $353 million. In the 2008-09 season, the team's home attendance average was roughly 16,600 per game.

FINANCIALS: **Sales and profits are in thousands of dollars—add 000 to get the full amount. 2008 Note: Financial information for 2008 was not available for all companies at press time.**

2008 Sales: $118,000
2007 Sales: $112,000
2006 Sales: $108,000
2005 Sales: $106,000
2004 Sales: $94,000

2008 Profits: $14,900
2007 Profits: $11,600
2006 Profits: $14,800
2005 Profits: $
2004 Profits: $

U.S. Stock Ticker: Subsidiary
Int'l Ticker: Int'l Exchange:
Employees:
Fiscal Year Ends: 6/30
Parent Company: WASHINGTON SPORTS & ENTERTAINMENT LP

SALARIES/BENEFITS:

Pension Plan:	ESOP Stock Plan:	Profit Sharing:	Top Exec. Salary: $	Bonus: $
Savings Plan:	Stock Purch. Plan:		Second Exec. Salary: $	Bonus: $

OTHER THOUGHTS:

Apparent Women Officers or Directors: 1
Hot Spot for Advancement for Women/Minorities:

LOCATIONS: ("Y" = Yes)

West:	Southwest:	Midwest:	Southeast:	Northeast:	International:
				Y	

WASSERMAN MEDIA GROUP LLC

www.wmgllc.com

Industry Group Code: 541800 **Ranks within this company's industry group:** Sales: Profits:

Sports:		Services:		Media:		Sales:		Facilities:		Other:	
Leagues/Associations:		Food & Beverage:		TV:		Marketing:	Y	Stadiums:		Gambling:	
Teams:		Agents:	Y	Radio:		Ads:		Fitness Clubs:		Apparel:	
Nonprofits:		Other:	Y	Internet:		Tickets:		Golf Courses:		Equipment:	
Other:				Print:		Retail:		Ski Resorts:		Shoes:	
				Software:		Other:	Y	Other:		Other:	

TYPES OF BUSINESS:

Sports Management Agency
Marketing and Branding Services

BRANDS/DIVISIONS/AFFILIATES:

Takkle
RAM Sports & Entertainment

CONTACTS: *Note: Officers with more than one job title may be intentionally listed here more than once.*

Casey Wasserman, CEO
Josh Swartz, COO
Michael Watts, CFO
Jeff Knapple, Principal-Sales
Arn Tellem, Principal-Mgmt.
Steven Astephen, Principal-Action Sports
Gary Stevenson, Principal-Consulting
Casey Wasserman, Chmn.

Phone: 310-407-0200 **Fax:**
Toll-Free:
Address: 12100 W. Olympic Blvd., Ste. 200, Los Angeles, CA 90064 US

GROWTH PLANS/SPECIAL FEATURES:

Wasserman Media Group LLC (WMG) is a leading global sports marketing agency involved in athlete management, property representation, consulting and digital content services. The company operates through three segments: sports management, sales and consulting. In its sports management segment, WMG represents athletes in baseball, basketball, BMX, golf, motocross, rugby, skateboarding, snowboarding, soccer, surfing, boxing, triathlon, racing and cricket. The firm's sales segment represents a variety of properties and has closed over $2 billion in sponsorship revenue. Sales capabilities include naming rights, sponsorship sales and entitlements. Another division of the sales segment represents teams and properties in their premium and hospitality products. Its consulting group works with companies to assist with marketing strategies, strategic alliance development and brand promotion. Within this segment, WMG's properties and media division negotiates television rights, creates economic models, packages assets and develops investment strategies for sports and entertainment properties. Consulting capabilities include corporate consulting, with such services as deal constructs, rights negotiation, sponsorship portfolio management, evaluation of new marketing opportunities, creation of customer entertainment programs, event management, strategic alliances, program development and public relations; and properties and media, with such services as media rights development, property acquisition and sponsorship development. The company's investment portfolio includes Takkle, an online social network for high school sports. In September 2008, WMG acquired RAM Sports and Entertainment in the U.K.

FINANCIALS: Sales and profits are in thousands of dollars—add 000 to get the full amount. 2008 Note: Financial information for 2008 was not available for all companies at press time.

2008 Sales: $
2007 Sales: $41,100
2006 Sales: $
2005 Sales: $
2004 Sales: $

2008 Profits: $
2007 Profits: $
2006 Profits: $
2005 Profits: $
2004 Profits: $

U.S. Stock Ticker: Private
Int'l Ticker: Int'l Exchange:
Employees: 90
Fiscal Year Ends:
Parent Company:

SALARIES/BENEFITS:

Pension Plan: ESOP Stock Plan: Profit Sharing: Top Exec. Salary: $ Bonus: $
Savings Plan: Stock Purch. Plan: Second Exec. Salary: $ Bonus: $

OTHER THOUGHTS:

Apparent Women Officers or Directors:
Hot Spot for Advancement for Women/Minorities:

LOCATIONS: ("Y" = Yes)

West:	Southwest:	Midwest:	Southeast:	Northeast:	International:
Y				Y	Y

WEST BROMWICH ALBION FOOTBALL CLUB

www.wba.co.uk

Industry Group Code: 711211D **Ranks within this company's industry group:** Sales: Profits:

Sports:		Services:		Media:		Sales:		Facilities:		Other:	
Leagues/Associations:		Food & Beverage:		TV:		Marketing:		Stadiums:	Y	Gambling:	
Teams:	Y	Agents:		Radio:		Ads:		Fitness Clubs:		Apparel:	
Nonprofits:		Other:		Internet:		Tickets:		Golf Courses:		Equipment:	
Other:				Print:		Retail:		Ski Resorts:		Shoes:	
				Software:		Other:		Other:		Other:	Y

TYPES OF BUSINESS:

Soccer Team
Event Venue

BRANDS/DIVISIONS/AFFILIATES:

Baggies
Hawthorns (The)
T-Mobile Football Centre

CONTACTS:

Note: Officers with more than one job title may be intentionally listed here more than once.

John G. Silk, Pres.
Phil Everitt, Head-Tech.
Darren Eales, Dir.-Legal/Sec.
Michelle Davies, Dir.-Oper.
John Simpson, Press Officer
Mark Jenkins, Dir.-Finance
Tony Mowbray, Team Mgr.
Mark Venus, Assistant Mgr.
Mark Miles, Dir.-Facilities
Mark Firth, Head-Venue Sales & Hospitality
Jeremy Peace, Chmn.

Phone: 44-0870-066-8888	**Fax:** 44-0870-066-2861
Toll-Free:	
Address: The Hawthorns, West Bromwich, West Midlands, B71 4LF UK	

GROWTH PLANS/SPECIAL FEATURES:

West Bromwich Albion Football Club, doing business as West Bromwich Albion (Albion), is a football (soccer) team based in the U.K., which currently plays in the Premier League. Formed in 1878, Albion has played at its current home stadium, The Hawthorns, since the stadium's completion in 1900. The stadium seats nearly 28,000 and was one of the first to feature big screens in widescreen format, which were added at the beginning of the 2002-03 season. The Hawthorns is available to rent for special events such as business meetings, exhibitions, trade events, conferences, banquets, dinners, social occasions and wedding receptions. The stadium has a dedicated conference and events department and offers rooms of various sizes to suit gatherings ranging from small business meetings to conferences of 300 attendees. Albion was the first professional team to win in Soviet Russia, in 1957, as well as the first British team to play in China, in 1978. The team was originally nicknamed the Throstles after the thrush on their jerseys, but in 1905 earned the nickname the Baggies, the origin of which is uncertain. The team runs a community program that recently became a full-fledged charity, sponsoring various after-school clubs for children and other sports education programs. Albion recently completed the $3.3 million T-Mobile Football Center, an indoor training facility with a full-size pitch, located on Halfords Lane, near The Hawthorns. Albion has earned a number of honors over the course of the club's history, including several FA Cups and division championships, most recently winning the Football League Championship in the 2007-08 season.

FINANCIALS:

Sales and profits are in thousands of dollars—add 000 to get the full amount. 2008 Note: Financial information for 2008 was not available for all companies at press time.

2008 Sales: $	2008 Profits: $	**U.S. Stock Ticker: Private**
2007 Sales: $	2007 Profits: $	**Int'l Ticker:** Int'l Exchange:
2006 Sales: $	2006 Profits: $	Employees:
2005 Sales: $	2005 Profits: $	Fiscal Year Ends: 6/30
2004 Sales: $	2004 Profits: $	Parent Company:

SALARIES/BENEFITS:

Pension Plan:	ESOP Stock Plan:	Profit Sharing:	Top Exec. Salary: $	Bonus: $
Savings Plan:	Stock Purch. Plan:		Second Exec. Salary: $	Bonus: $

OTHER THOUGHTS:

Apparent Women Officers or Directors: 3
Hot Spot for Advancement for Women/Minorities: Y

LOCATIONS: ("Y" = Yes)

West:	Southwest:	Midwest:	Southeast:	Northeast:	International:
					Y

WEST MARINE INC

www.westmarine.com

Industry Group Code: 441222 **Ranks within this company's industry group:** Sales: 2 Profits: 1

Sports:		Services:		Media:		Sales:		Facilities:		Other:	
Leagues/Associations:		Food & Beverage:		TV:		Marketing:		Stadiums:		Gambling:	
Teams:		Agents:		Radio:		Ads:		Fitness Clubs:		Apparel:	
Nonprofits:		Other:	Y	Internet:		Tickets:		Golf Courses:		Equipment:	Y
Other:				Print:		Retail:	Y	Ski Resorts:		Shoes:	
				Software:		Other:	Y	Other:		Other:	

TYPES OF BUSINESS:

Boating Supplies, Retail
Catalog & Online Sales
Wholesale Operations
Marine Insurance
Financing
Boating Services

BRANDS/DIVISIONS/AFFILIATES:

West Advantage
West Marine Express
Port Supply
West Marine Boat Services
Seafit
West Marine Rigging Shop

CONTACTS: *Note: Officers with more than one job title may be intentionally listed here more than once.*

Geoff Eisenberg, CEO
Geoff Eisenberg, Pres.
Tom Moran, CFO/Sr. VP
Ron Japinga, Exec. VP-Mktg.
Ashlee Aldridge, CIO/Sr. VP
Ron Japinga, Exec. VP-Merch.
Christopher Bolling, Sr. VP-Bus. Dev.
Bruce Edwards, Exec. VP-Stores & Port Supply
Ashlee Aldridge, Sr. VP-Direct Sales
Larry Smith, Sr. VP-Planning & Replenishment
Randy Repass, Chmn.
Pat Murphy, Sr. VP-Dist. & Logistics

Phone: 831-728-2700	**Fax:** 831-728-2736
Toll-Free:	
Address: 500 Westridge Dr., Watsonville, CA 95076-4100 US	

GROWTH PLANS/SPECIAL FEATURES:

West Marine, Inc. is a specialty retailer of recreational and commercial boating supplies in North America. The company operates approximately 344 stores in 38 states, Puerto Rico and Canada under the brand name West Marine. The firm offers a selection of over 50,000 marine products ranging from boats and engines to clothing, safety products, deck hardware, navigational equipment and electronics. West Marine sells directly through its catalogs, an e-commerce web site and through its virtual call center, allowing customers access to technical product advice through trained sales representatives. The firm maintains two distribution centers located in Rock Hill, South Carolina and Hollister, California. West Marine's wholesale division, Port Supply, offers marine equipment at wholesale prices to more than 43,000 boat manufacturers, commercial vessel operators and government agencies. Additionally, the firm sells private label products under the brand names West Marine and Seafit. West Marine offers a wide variety of services to boaters, including marine insurance, boat financing, custom rigging services, towing services and a company credit card. The firm also operates the West Advantage Rewards program, a New Boat Owner Program and offers the Mariner's Product Protection program, a 2-year extended warranty available on most products. The company maintains two in-house service centers that provide customers with access to factory authorized repairs and provides professional installation and maintenance services through subsidiary West Marine Boat Services. West Marine's web site features several resources for boaters, including weather and hurricane information, boating safety tips, product assistance, pertinent boating articles and a community forum. Over the course of 2008, West Marine opened four new stores, including its first franchised store, in Istanbul, Turkey.

West Marine provides its employees with medical insurance, long-term disability, paid life and accident insurance, tuition reimbursement, flexible spending accounts, a 401(k) program and merchandise discounts.

FINANCIALS: **Sales and profits are in thousands of dollars—add 000 to get the full amount. 2008 Note: Financial information for 2008 was not available for all companies at press time.**

2008 Sales: $631,258	2008 Profits: $-38,800	**U.S. Stock Ticker: WMAR**
2007 Sales: $679,561	2007 Profits: $-49,976	**Int'l Ticker:** Int'l Exchange:
2006 Sales: $716,644	2006 Profits: $-7,624	Employees: 4,897
2005 Sales: $692,137	2005 Profits: $-3,022	Fiscal Year Ends: 12/31
2004 Sales: $682,996	2004 Profits: $22,178	Parent Company:

SALARIES/BENEFITS:

Pension Plan:	ESOP Stock Plan:	Profit Sharing:	Top Exec. Salary: $518,192	Bonus: $
Savings Plan: Y	Stock Purch. Plan: Y		Second Exec. Salary: $375,231	Bonus: $

OTHER THOUGHTS:

Apparent Women Officers or Directors: 2
Hot Spot for Advancement for Women/Minorities:

LOCATIONS: ("Y" = Yes)

West:	Southwest:	Midwest:	Southeast:	Northeast:	International:
Y	Y	Y	Y	Y	Y

WILLIAM MORRIS ENDEAVOR ENTERTAINMENT LLC

www.wma.com

Industry Group Code: 711410 **Ranks within this company's industry group:** Sales: Profits:

Sports:		Services:		Media:		Sales:		Facilities:		Other:	
Leagues/Associations:		Food & Beverage:		TV:		Marketing:	Y	Stadiums:		Gambling:	
Teams:		Agents:	Y	Radio:		Ads:		Fitness Clubs:		Apparel:	
Nonprofits:		Other:	Y	Internet:		Tickets:		Golf Courses:		Equipment:	
Other:				Print:		Retail:		Ski Resorts:		Shoes:	
				Software:		Other:		Other:		Other:	

TYPES OF BUSINESS:

Talent Agency
Literary Agency
Sports Marketing & Agents
Media Consulting
Book Publishing

BRANDS/DIVISIONS/AFFILIATES:

William Morris Agency Inc
Endeavor Agency (The)

CONTACTS: *Note: Officers with more than one job title may be intentionally listed here more than once.*

Ariel Zev Emanuel, Co-CEO
Irv Weintraub, COO
David Wirtschafter, Co-CEO
Irv Weintraub, CFO
Patrick Whitesell, Co-CEO

Phone: 310-285-9000	**Fax:** 310-859-4462
Toll-Free:	
Address: 1 William Morris Pl., Beverly Hills, CA 90212 US	

GROWTH PLANS/SPECIAL FEATURES:

William Morris Endeavor Entertainment LLC, formed in April 2009 by the merger of the former William Morris Agency and the Endeavor Agency, is one of the largest talent and literary agencies in the world. The firm operates in departments including books, commercials, lectures, motion pictures, music, sports and entertainment, television, voice-overs and theatre. The books department represents a multitude of fiction and non-fiction authors. The department works closely with the motion picture and television departments to bring books to both large and small screens. The commercials department creates special interest home videos, infomercials, home shopping and industrial programming, as well as overseeing sponsorships and promotional events. The lectures division represents a roster of speakers across a broad spectrum of issues and topics. The motion picture department represents both established and up-and-coming directors and actors. The music group represents clients across a range of musical genres. The sports and entertainment department represents athletes and sports properties and seeks to secure endorsements, sponsorships and other opportunities on behalf of its clients. The television group represents television programming and creative talent. The voice-over division represents a range of voice-over talent including Spanish language voice-over. The theatre group represents writers, composers, lyricists, directors, choreographers, actors and producers. The company also represents Broadway and theatrical tours; books agency clients into fairs and special events; and coordinates public, corporate and private speaking engagements. William Morris was originally founded in 1898 and has long been a part of entertainment history, with former clients including the Marx Brothers, Frank Capra, Marilyn Monroe and Elvis Presley. Endeavor, meanwhile, brought strong film and television assets, as well as a talent roster that includes actors such as Robert de Niro and Matt Damon and directors such as Martin Scorsese and Danny Boyle, whose Slumdog Millionaire won both the best picture and best director prizes at the February 2009 Academy Awards. Subsequent to the merger, the William Morris Agency eliminated roughly 10% of its workforce.

FINANCIALS: **Sales and profits are in thousands of dollars—add 000 to get the full amount. 2008 Note: Financial information for 2008 was not available for all companies at press time.**

2008 Sales: $	2008 Profits: $	**U.S. Stock Ticker: Private**
2007 Sales: $	2007 Profits: $	**Int'l Ticker:** Int'l Exchange:
2006 Sales: $	2006 Profits: $	Employees:
2005 Sales: $	2005 Profits: $	Fiscal Year Ends: 12/31
2004 Sales: $	2004 Profits: $	Parent Company:

SALARIES/BENEFITS:

Pension Plan:	ESOP Stock Plan:	Profit Sharing:	Top Exec. Salary: $	Bonus: $
Savings Plan:	Stock Purch. Plan:		Second Exec. Salary: $	Bonus: $

OTHER THOUGHTS:

Apparent Women Officers or Directors:
Hot Spot for Advancement for Women/Minorities:

LOCATIONS: ("Y" = Yes)

West:	Southwest:	Midwest:	Southeast:	Northeast:	International:
Y			Y	Y	Y

Note: Financial information, benefits and other data can change quickly and may vary from those stated here.

WILSON SPORTING GOODS CO

www.wilson.com

Industry Group Code: 339920 **Ranks within this company's industry group:** Sales: Profits:

Sports:		Services:		Media:		Sales:		Facilities:		Other:	
Leagues/Associations:		Food & Beverage:		TV:		Marketing:		Stadiums:		Gambling:	
Teams:		Agents:		Radio:		Ads:		Fitness Clubs:		Apparel:	Y
Nonprofits:		Other:		Internet:		Tickets:		Golf Courses:		Equipment:	Y
Other:				Print:		Retail:	Y	Ski Resorts:		Shoes:	Y
				Software:		Other:		Other:		Other:	

TYPES OF BUSINESS:

Sporting Goods
Apparel
Sports Accessories
Pitching Machines
Golf Equipment
Balls

BRANDS/DIVISIONS/AFFILIATES:

Amer Sports Corporation
Century Sports, Inc.
Wilson Sport Socks
Duke (The)
NXTGEN
Apple Sports, Inc.
Every Pass Counts: Ultimate Assist

CONTACTS: *Note: Officers with more than one job title may be intentionally listed here more than once.*

Chris Considine, Pres.
Ed Matthews, Dir.-IT
Jim Sanderson, Dir.-Bus. Dev.
Molly Wallace, Dir.-Corp. Comm.
Joe Dudy, VP-Finance
Mike Kuehne, Gen. Mgr.-Basketball

Phone: 773-714-6400	**Fax:** 773-714-4565
Toll-Free: 800-333-8326	
Address: 8750 W. Bryn Mawr Ave., Chicago, IL 60631 US	

GROWTH PLANS/SPECIAL FEATURES:

Wilson Sporting Goods Co., a subsidiary of Finland-based Amer Sports Corporation, is one of the world's leading manufacturers and marketers of ball sports equipment. The company serves customers in over 100 countries. Wilson is structured into three business areas: team sports, which specializes in baseball, fast pitch/slow pitch softball, basketball, volleyball, football, soccer and training equipment; racquet sports, such as tennis, racquetball, badminton and squash; and golf, which is sold through the Wilson Staff brand. Wilson also sells socks through Wilson Sport Socks, additional golf accessories through Apple Sports, Inc., and tennis court equipment through Century Sports, Inc. The company also sells apparel, athletic footwear and other sport accessories. Products are sold globally through an extensive sales network with specialty stores and chain sporting goods stores. Wilson's web site features a section that helps customers choose the right gear by age, position and type of play. The company is a primary official corporate sponsor of Little League baseball. Wilson and the NFL recently announced the re-branding of the NFL's official football, the first since 1969. The official ball became The Duke, in honor of football legend Wellington Duke Mara. Recently, the company released the NXTGEN batting helmet, which is fitted with specialized neck padding for increased spinal cord protection and has a high-impact ABS shell. In January 2009, Wilson became the official ball sponsor of NCAA Soccer. In March 2009, the firm partnered with NCAA Basketball to launch Every Pass Counts: Ultimate Assist. The program works through Facebook, and donates ten cents every time a person clicks on the pass button; Wilson and the NCAA hope to raise $50,000 for cancer research through the online drive.

FINANCIALS: **Sales and profits are in thousands of dollars—add 000 to get the full amount. 2008 Note: Financial information for 2008 was not available for all companies at press time.**

2008 Sales: $	2008 Profits: $	**U.S. Stock Ticker: Subsidiary**
2007 Sales: $556,800	2007 Profits: $	**Int'l Ticker:** Int'l Exchange:
2006 Sales: $	2006 Profits: $	Employees: 2,440
2005 Sales: $	2005 Profits: $	Fiscal Year Ends: 12/31
2004 Sales: $	2004 Profits: $	Parent Company: AMER SPORTS CORPORATION

SALARIES/BENEFITS:

Pension Plan:	ESOP Stock Plan:	Profit Sharing:	Top Exec. Salary: $	Bonus: $
Savings Plan:	Stock Purch. Plan:		Second Exec. Salary: $	Bonus: $

OTHER THOUGHTS:

Apparent Women Officers or Directors: 1
Hot Spot for Advancement for Women/Minorities:

LOCATIONS: ("Y" = Yes)

West:	Southwest:	Midwest:	Southeast:	Northeast:	International:
		Y			Y

WINTER SPORTS INC

www.bigmtn.com

Industry Group Code: 713920 **Ranks within this company's industry group:** Sales: Profits:

Sports:		Services:		Media:		Sales:		Facilities:		Other:	
Leagues/Associations:		Food & Beverage:		TV:		Marketing:		Stadiums:		Gambling:	
Teams:		Agents:		Radio:		Ads:		Fitness Clubs:		Apparel:	
Nonprofits:		Other:		Internet:		Tickets:		Golf Courses:		Equipment:	
Other:				Print:		Retail:		Ski Resorts:	Y	Shoes:	
				Software:		Other:		Other:	Y	Other:	

TYPES OF BUSINESS:

Ski Resorts
Property Management

BRANDS/DIVISIONS/AFFILIATES:

Big Mountain Ski & Summer Resort
Hibernation House
Big Mountain Sports
Big Mountain Development Corp.
Big Mountain Club, LLC
Big Mountain Water Co.
Morning Eagle
Walk in the Treetops

CONTACTS: *Note: Officers with more than one job title may be intentionally listed here more than once.*

Daniel Graves, CEO
Daniel Graves, Pres.
Nick Polumbus, Dir.-Mktg.

Phone: 406-862-1900	**Fax:** 406-862-2955
Toll-Free:	
Address: 3910 Big Mountain Rd., Whitefish, MT 59937 US	

GROWTH PLANS/SPECIAL FEATURES:

Winter Sports, Inc. (WSI) operates the Big Mountain Ski and Summer Resort, located on 4,000 acres in the Rocky Mountains of Montana. Big Mountain's ski facilities include 13 chairlifts (including two high-speed quad lifts) and two T-bar lifts, which serve approximately 85 runs and over 3,000 skiable acres. WSI also operates the Hibernation House (hotel facilities), Big Mountain Sports (a ski rental, retail and repair shop), a ski school, the Summit House (a retail store at the mountain's peak) and the Outpost (a ski shop and services operation). Associated recreational opportunities include snowshoeing, Nordic skiing, tubing, snowmobiling, dog sledding, ice-skating, snowcat-served off-piste skiing and winter tours of nearby Glacier National Park. In addition, the company operates a property management business and owns over 700 acres at the base of the mountain. Approximately 47% of company revenues come from lease arrangements with other companies who use this land. The firm also operates on a limited basis between June and October, hosting a chairlift and gondola ride to the summit for sightseeing, hiking, mountain biking and other recreational activities, such as Walk in the Treetops, an elevated boardwalk in the treetop canopy. WSI has two wholly-owned subsidiaries: Big Mountain Water Co., which supplies the resort and adjacent properties with domestic water; and Big Mountain Development Corp., which oversees and coordinates the planning of land owned by WSI.

Employees at WSI receive free season passes for themselves and discounted passes for their immediate families; free group ski and snowboard lessons; discounts on equipment rentals, food and beverage purchases; free transportation from Whitefish; and supplemental health benefits.

FINANCIALS: **Sales and profits are in thousands of dollars—add 000 to get the full amount. 2008 Note: Financial information for 2008 was not available for all companies at press time.**

2008 Sales: $	2008 Profits: $	**U.S. Stock Ticker: Private**
2007 Sales: $13,400	2007 Profits: $	**Int'l Ticker:** Int'l Exchange:
2006 Sales: $	2006 Profits: $	Employees: 200
2005 Sales: $	2005 Profits: $	Fiscal Year Ends: 5/31
2004 Sales: $	2004 Profits: $	Parent Company:

SALARIES/BENEFITS:

Pension Plan:	ESOP Stock Plan:	Profit Sharing:	Top Exec. Salary: $115,895	Bonus: $
Savings Plan:	Stock Purch. Plan:		Second Exec. Salary: $	Bonus: $

OTHER THOUGHTS:

Apparent Women Officers or Directors:
Hot Spot for Advancement for Women/Minorities:

LOCATIONS: ("Y" = Yes)

West:	Southwest:	Midwest:	Southeast:	Northeast:	International:
Y					

WOMENS NATIONAL BASKETBALL ASSOCIATION (WNBA)

www.wnba.com

Industry Group Code: 813990 **Ranks within this company's industry group:** Sales: Profits:

Sports:		Services:		Media:		Sales:		Facilities:		Other:	
Leagues/Associations:	Y	Food & Beverage:		TV:		Marketing:		Stadiums:		Gambling:	
Teams:		Agents:		Radio:		Ads:		Fitness Clubs:		Apparel:	
Nonprofits:		Other:		Internet:		Tickets:		Golf Courses:		Equipment:	
Other:				Print:		Retail:		Ski Resorts:		Shoes:	
				Software:		Other:		Other:		Other:	

TYPES OF BUSINESS:

Women's Basketball League

BRANDS/DIVISIONS/AFFILIATES:

WNBA Enterprises LLC
National Basketball Association (NBA)

CONTACTS: *Note: Officers with more than one job title may be intentionally listed here more than once.*

Donna Orender, Pres.
Carol Albert, Sr. VP-Mktg.
Jamin S. Dershowitz, General Counsel
Renee Brown, Chief-Basketball Oper. & Player Rel.
Rachel Jacobson, VP-Bus. Dev.
Brian McIntyre, Sr. VP-Basketball Comm.
Steve Richard, Sr. VP-Finance
Bonnie Thurston, Mgr.-Player Programs
Donna Daniels, VP-Team Mktg. & Strategic Planning
Christopher Heck, Sr. VP-Team Mktg. & Bus. Oper.
Ski Austin, Exec. VP-Events & Attractions

Phone: 212-688-9622 **Fax:** 212-750-9622
Toll-Free:
Address: Olympic Tower, 645 5th Ave., New York, NY 10022 US

GROWTH PLANS/SPECIAL FEATURES:

The Women's National Basketball Association (WNBA) operates the first women's professional basketball league fully supported by the National Basketball Association (NBA), which owned the WNBA until 2002. The WNBA name and logo, as well as those of wnba.com, are owned by WNBA Enterprises LLC. The league plays from May to September, after the NBA regular season, leaving many WNBA players able to use the off-season to play for teams overseas. League games are broadcast through partnerships with NBC, ESPN and Lifetime Television. Marketing partners of the league include Nike; Gatorade; Adidas; Southwest Airlines; T-Mobile; IHOP; EA Sports; General Mills; Pitney Bowes; Hewlett Packard; Sanofi Pasteur; and Toyota. The WNBA began with just eight teams, five of which still survive, including the Phoenix Mercury, Sacramento Monarchs, Utah Starzz (now San Antonio Silver Stars), New York Liberty and Los Angeles Sparks. Three original teams, including the Charlotte Sting and the Cleveland Rockers, have since folded, with the most recent team to fold being the Houston Comets in December 2008. The very first WNBA game was played between the New York Liberty and Los Angeles Sparks in 1997. Two teams joined the WNBA in 1998, the Detroit Shock and the Washington Mystics; two more in 1999, the Minnesota Lynx and the Orlando Miracle (now the Connecticut Sun); and four more in 2000, the Indiana Fever, the Seattle Storm, the Miami Sol and the Portland Fire. Both the Sol and Fire folded in 2002. The Chicago Sky joined in 2006. The Atlanta Dream is the newest addition to the WNBA, having joined the league in 2008. The WNBA's short history has included superstars Cynthia Cooper, Rebecca Lobo and Lisa Leslie. The Detroit Shock won the 2008 WNBA Championship against the San Antonio Silver Stars.

FINANCIALS: Sales and profits are in thousands of dollars—add 000 to get the full amount. 2008 Note: Financial information for 2008 was not available for all companies at press time.

2008 Sales: $	2008 Profits: $	**U.S. Stock Ticker: Subsidiary**
2007 Sales: $2,600	2007 Profits: $	**Int'l Ticker:** Int'l Exchange:
2006 Sales: $	2006 Profits: $	Employees: 20
2005 Sales: $	2005 Profits: $	Fiscal Year Ends: 6/30
2004 Sales: $	2004 Profits: $	Parent Company: WNBA ENTERPRISES LLC

SALARIES/BENEFITS:

Pension Plan: Y	ESOP Stock Plan:	Profit Sharing:	Top Exec. Salary: $	Bonus: $
Savings Plan: Y	Stock Purch. Plan:		Second Exec. Salary: $	Bonus: $

OTHER THOUGHTS:

Apparent Women Officers or Directors: 39
Hot Spot for Advancement for Women/Minorities: Y

LOCATIONS: ("Y" = Yes)

West:	Southwest:	Midwest:	Southeast:	Northeast:	International:
				Y	

WOMENS TENNIS ASSOCIATION (WTA) www.sonyericssonwtatour.com

Industry Group Code: 813990 **Ranks within this company's industry group:** Sales: Profits:

Sports:		Services:		Media:		Sales:		Facilities:		Other:	
Leagues/Associations:	Y	Food & Beverage:		TV:		Marketing:		Stadiums:		Gambling:	
Teams:		Agents:		Radio:		Ads:		Fitness Clubs:		Apparel:	
Nonprofits:		Other:		Internet:		Tickets:		Golf Courses:		Equipment:	
Other:				Print:		Retail:		Ski Resorts:		Shoes:	
				Software:		Other:		Other:		Other:	

TYPES OF BUSINESS:

Tennis Association

BRANDS/DIVISIONS/AFFILIATES:

Sony Ericsson WTA Tour
Commonwealth Bank Tournament
Sony Ericsson Championships
Championships at Wimbledon
U.S. Open
Grand Slam Events
Australian Open

CONTACTS: *Note: Officers with more than one job title may be intentionally listed here more than once.*

Larry Scott, CEO
David Shoemaker, COO
Stacey Allastar, Pres.
Kirsten Fisher, VP-Mktg. & Sales, Asia-Pacific
David Shoemaker, General Counsel
Peachy Kellmeyer, Sr. VP-Tour Oper.
Scott MacLeod, Sr. VP-Bus. Dev.
Michael Rowe, VP-Television & Digital Media
Andrew Walker, VP-Comm. & Global Mktg.
Ron McQuate, VP-Finance
Peter Johnston, Sr. VP-Competition & Member Rel.
Kathleen Stroia, VP-Sport Sciences & Medicine and PRO U
Larry Scott, Chmn.
David Shoemaker, Head-Asia Pacific

Phone: 727-895-5000 **Fax:** 727-894-1982
Toll-Free:
Address: 1 Progress Plz., Ste. 1500, St. Petersburg, FL 33701 US

GROWTH PLANS/SPECIAL FEATURES:

The Women's Tennis Association (WTA) manages the Sony Ericsson WTA Tour, an international professional tennis organization with more than 2,200 female athletes representing 96 countries. The association was founded in 1970 with only nine players who were inspired to build a future for women's tennis. Currently, WTA's players compete for more than $86 million in prize money at the Tour's 51 events in 31 countries. The tour currently has 24 tournaments in Europe; 14 in North/Central America; 10 in Asia; five in Australia/New Zealand; 1 in South America and 1 in Africa. The tour consists of the season-ending, Sony Ericsson Championships (SEC), the Commonwealth Bank Tournament of Champions, four Grand Slam events, as well as 49 Tier events. The SEC is held in November in Qatar and features the top eight singles players and the top four doubles players. This tournament offers players a chance at $4,550,000 in prize money. The Commonwealth Bank Tournament is held in Bali, Indonesia and offers players up to $600,000 in prize money. The Tournament features 12 singles player in the International-Level tournaments. The Grand Slam events include the official championships of Australia (the Australian Open), France (Roland Garros), Great Britain (the Championships at Wimbledon) and the U.S. (U.S. Open). Tiered events are divided into two categories: premier and international. The premier segment offers tournaments having prize money between $600,000 and $4,500,000. Premier holds 19 events in addition to the season ending match. The international division is comprised of 30 events plus the Commonwealth Bank Tournament of Champions. The international segment offers a minimum of $220,000 in prize money. In September 2008, the WTA and ATP Media launched a digital streaming partnership. The partnership will create a web site that streams live tennis matches.

FINANCIALS: **Sales and profits are in thousands of dollars—add 000 to get the full amount. 2008 Note: Financial information for 2008 was not available for all companies at press time.**

2008 Sales: $	2008 Profits: $	**U.S. Stock Ticker: Private**
2007 Sales: $	2007 Profits: $	**Int'l Ticker:** Int'l Exchange:
2006 Sales: $	2006 Profits: $	Employees:
2005 Sales: $	2005 Profits: $	Fiscal Year Ends: 8/31
2004 Sales: $	2004 Profits: $	Parent Company:

SALARIES/BENEFITS:

Pension Plan:	ESOP Stock Plan:	Profit Sharing:	Top Exec. Salary: $	Bonus: $
Savings Plan:	Stock Purch. Plan:		Second Exec. Salary: $	Bonus: $

OTHER THOUGHTS:

Apparent Women Officers or Directors: 5
Hot Spot for Advancement for Women/Minorities: Y

LOCATIONS: ("Y" = Yes)

West:	Southwest:	Midwest:	Southeast:	Northeast:	International:
			Y		Y

WORLD BOXING ASSOCIATION

www.wbaonline.com

Industry Group Code: 813990 **Ranks within this company's industry group:** Sales: Profits:

Sports:		Services:		Media:		Sales:		Facilities:		Other:	
Leagues/Associations:	Y	Food & Beverage:		TV:		Marketing:		Stadiums:		Gambling:	
Teams:		Agents:		Radio:		Ads:		Fitness Clubs:		Apparel:	
Nonprofits:		Other:		Internet:		Tickets:		Golf Courses:		Equipment:	
Other:				Print:		Retail:		Ski Resorts:		Shoes:	
				Software:		Other:		Other:		Other:	

TYPES OF BUSINESS:

Boxing Association

BRANDS/DIVISIONS/AFFILIATES:

CONTACTS:
Note: Officers with more than one job title may be intentionally listed here more than once.

Gilberto Mendoza, Pres.
Robert Mack, Dir.-Legal
Julio Thyme, Dir.-Oper.
Alberto Sarmiento, Dir.-Treasury
Gilberto Jesus Mendoza, Exec. VP
Yang Sup Shim, 1st VP
Shigeru Kojima, 2nd VP
Renzo Bagnariol, Int'l Coordinator
York Van Nixon, Coordinator-Int'l

Phone: 507-340-6425	**Fax:**
Toll-Free:	
Address: Av. Aquilino de la Guardia, Ocean Bus. Ctr., Fl 14, Panama, Panama	

GROWTH PLANS/SPECIAL FEATURES:

The World Boxing Association (WBA) is devoted to the governing and control of boxing matches, with limited jurisdiction in the U.S. It sets rules and recognizes champions under its jurisdiction, which includes about 50 agencies in the U.S. as well as organizations in Canada, South America, Europe and Asia. The firm is the original sanctioning body of professional boxing, tracing its origins back to the National Boxing Association of the U.S., organized in 1921 for the heavyweight title bout of Jack Dempsey and Georges Carpentier in New Jersey. It changed its name to the WBA in 1962. The WBA currently maintains a central office in Venezuela and an executive office in Panama. The company is affiliated with four regional associations: the Pan Asian Boxing Association (PABA), covering 31 countries including Russia, Australia, China, Mongolia, Thailand, India, Indonesia and Kazakhstan; Federacion Latinamericana de Comisiones de Boxeo Professional (FEDELATIN), covering Latin America; the European Boxing Association (EBA), covering Europe and some surrounding nations; and the North American Boxing Association, which mainly covers Canadian fighters but also conducts sub-regional title fights in the U.S. and Mexico. The WBA also organizes and oversees women's boxing. Current champions include Ruslan Chagaev, Nicolay Valuev, Guillermo Jones, Hugo Garay, Mikkel Kessler, Felix Strum, Daniel Santos, Shane Mosley, Vyacheslav Senchenko, Andreas Kotelnik, Juan Manuel Marquez, Paulus Moses, Jorge Linares, Chris John, Celestino Caballero, Bernard Dunne, Anselmo Moreno, Neomar Cermeno, Vic Darchinyan, Nobuo Nashiro, Denkaosan Kaovichit, Brahim Asloum, Giovanni Segura and Roman Gonzalez.

FINANCIALS:
Sales and profits are in thousands of dollars—add 000 to get the full amount. 2008 Note: Financial information for 2008 was not available for all companies at press time.

2008 Sales: $	2008 Profits: $	**U.S. Stock Ticker: Private**
2007 Sales: $	2007 Profits: $	**Int'l Ticker:** Int'l Exchange:
2006 Sales: $	2006 Profits: $	Employees:
2005 Sales: $	2005 Profits: $	Fiscal Year Ends:
2004 Sales: $	2004 Profits: $	Parent Company:

SALARIES/BENEFITS:

Pension Plan:	ESOP Stock Plan:	Profit Sharing:	Top Exec. Salary: $	Bonus: $
Savings Plan:	Stock Purch. Plan:		Second Exec. Salary: $	Bonus: $

OTHER THOUGHTS:

Apparent Women Officers or Directors:
Hot Spot for Advancement for Women/Minorities:

LOCATIONS: ("Y" = Yes)

West:	Southwest:	Midwest:	Southeast:	Northeast:	International:
					Y

WORLD BOXING COUNCIL

www.wbcboxing.com

Industry Group Code: 813990 **Ranks within this company's industry group:** Sales: Profits:

Sports:		Services:		Media:		Sales:		Facilities:		Other:	
Leagues/Associations:	Y	Food & Beverage:		TV:		Marketing:		Stadiums:		Gambling:	
Teams:		Agents:		Radio:		Ads:		Fitness Clubs:		Apparel:	
Nonprofits:		Other:		Internet:		Tickets:		Golf Courses:		Equipment:	
Other:				Print:		Retail:		Ski Resorts:		Shoes:	
				Software:		Other:		Other:		Other:	

TYPES OF BUSINESS:

Boxing Association

BRANDS/DIVISIONS/AFFILIATES:

African Boxing Union (ABU)
European Boxing Union (EBU)
Asian Boxing Council (ABCO)
Caribbean Boxing Federation (CABOFE)
Central American Boxing Federation (FECARBOX)
CIS and Slovenian Boxing Bureau (CISBB)
North American Boxing Federation (NABF)
Oriental and Pacific Boxing Federation (OPBF)

CONTACTS: *Note: Officers with more than one job title may be intentionally listed here more than once.*

Jose Sulaiman Chagnon, Pres.
Avel Gonzalez, General Counsel
Juan J. Sanchez, Treas.
Houcine Houichi, VP-Tunisia
Edmund Lipinski, VP-Russia
Chul Kee Kim, VP-Korea
Kovid Bhakdibhumi, VP-Thailand
Jose Sulaiman, Chmn.
Charles Giles, VP-Great Britain

Phone: 52-55-5119-5273 **Fax:** 52-55-5119-5293
Toll-Free:
Address: Cuzco 872, Colonia Lindavista, 07300 Mexico

GROWTH PLANS/SPECIAL FEATURES:

The World Boxing Council (WBC) hosts and officiates boxing matches around the world. The council was created in 1963 by founders from eleven countries (the U.S., Argentina, the U.K., France, Mexico, the Philippines, Panama, Chile, Peru, Venezuela and Brazil) who sought to create an international boxing organization and control the expansion of the sport. The council currently works in 161 affiliated countries with nine continental boxing federations, including the African Boxing Union (ABU); European Boxing Union (EBU); Asian Boxing Council (ABCO); Caribbean Boxing Federation (CABOFE); Central American Boxing Federation (FECARBOX); Commonwealth of Independent States and Slovenian Boxing Bureau (CISBB); North American Boxing Federation (NABF); Oriental and Pacific Boxing Federation (OPBF); and the South American Boxing Federation (FESUBOX). The organization is also affiliated with the British Boxing Board of Control (BBBofC). The council is responsible for the organization and operation of the annual WBC International Championship, which is one of the world's largest boxing tournaments. Since its inception, the council has established guidelines for judges, instated a point deduction system for fouls, required the use of a mouthpiece, regulated the size of the boxing ring, introduced the thumb-attached glove and developed an official constitution of rules and regulations. The council also maintains a WBC Female division and WBC Female Championship Committee. WBC world champions include Vitaly Klitschko, Adrian Diaconu, Giacobbe Fragomeni, Carl Froch, Kelly Pavlik, Andre Berto, Vernon Forrest, Edwin Valero, Timothy Bradley, Humberto Soto, Takahiro Aoh, Daisuke Naito, Toshiaki Nishioka, Vic Darchinyan, Edgar Sosa and Oleydong Sithsanerchai. Female champions have included Christy Martin and Laila Ali.

FINANCIALS: **Sales and profits are in thousands of dollars—add 000 to get the full amount. 2008 Note: Financial information for 2008 was not available for all companies at press time.**

2008 Sales: $ 2008 Profits: $
2007 Sales: $ 2007 Profits: $
2006 Sales: $ 2006 Profits: $
2005 Sales: $ 2005 Profits: $
2004 Sales: $ 2004 Profits: $

U.S. Stock Ticker: Private
Int'l Ticker: Int'l Exchange:
Employees:
Fiscal Year Ends:
Parent Company:

SALARIES/BENEFITS:

Pension Plan: ESOP Stock Plan: Profit Sharing: Top Exec. Salary: $ Bonus: $
Savings Plan: Stock Purch. Plan: Second Exec. Salary: $ Bonus: $

OTHER THOUGHTS:

Apparent Women Officers or Directors:
Hot Spot for Advancement for Women/Minorities:

LOCATIONS: ("Y" = Yes)

West:	Southwest:	Midwest:	Southeast:	Northeast:	International:
					Y

ADDITIONAL INDEXES

Contents:

INDEX OF FIRMS NOTED AS HOT SPOTS FOR ADVANCEMENT FOR WOMEN & MINORITIES

NEW YORK YANKEES
NEWCASTLE UNITED FOOTBALL CLUB
NIKE INC
NORWICH CITY FOOTBALL CLUB
OAKLAND ATHLETICS
OKLAHOMA CITY THUNDER
ORLANDO MAGIC
PHILADELPHIA 76ERS
PHILADELPHIA FLYERS
PHILADELPHIA PHILLIES
PHOENIX COYOTES
PHOENIX MERCURY
PINNACLE ENTERTAINMENT INC
PITTSBURGH PIRATES
PITTSBURGH STEELERS
PORTLAND TRAILBLAZERS
PORTSMOUTH FOOTBALL CLUB
PROFESSIONAL BULL RIDERS INC
REAL SALT LAKE
RECREATIONAL EQUIPMENT INC (REI)
ROGERS COMMUNICATIONS INC
SACRAMENTO KINGS
SACRAMENTO MONARCHS
SAN ANTONIO SILVER STARS
SAN DIEGO CHARGERS
SAN DIEGO PADRES
SAN FRANCISCO 49ERS
SAN FRANCISCO GIANTS
SAN JOSE EARTHQUAKES
SEATTLE MARINERS
SEATTLE SEAHAWKS
SEATTLE STORM
SNOWDANCE INC
SPORTS ILLUSTRATED
ST LOUIS BLUES
TAMPA BAY LIGHTNING
TEXAS RANGERS
TIME WARNER INC
TORONTO BLUE JAYS
TORONTO FC
TOWN SPORTS INTERNATIONAL HOLDINGS INC
TURNER BROADCASTING SYSTEM
UNDER ARMOUR INC
UNITED SOCCER LEAGUES
UNITED STATES CYCLING FEDERATION (USCF)
UNITED STATES OLYMPIC COMMITTEE (USOC)
UNITED STATES TENNIS ASSOCIATION (USTA)
US FIGURE SKATING
USA BASKETBALL
USA GYMNASTICS
USA HOCKEY
USA SWIMMING
USA TRACK & FIELD INC
UTAH JAZZ
VAIL RESORTS INC
VANCOUVER CANUCKS
VF CORP
VIACOM INC
VULCAN INC
WALT DISNEY COMPANY (THE)
WASHINGTON CAPITALS
WASHINGTON MYSTICS
WASHINGTON NATIONALS
WEST BROMWICH ALBION FOOTBALL CLUB
WOMENS NATIONAL BASKETBALL ASSOCIATION (WNBA)
WOMENS TENNIS ASSOCIATION (WTA)

INDEX OF SUBSIDIARIES, BRAND NAMES AND AFFILIATIONS

Brand or subsidiary, followed by the name of the related corporation

INDEX OF SUBSIDIARIES, BRAND NAMES AND AFFILIATIONS, CONT.

INDEX OF SUBSIDIARIES, BRAND NAMES AND AFFILIATIONS, CONT.

INDEX OF SUBSIDIARIES, BRAND NAMES AND AFFILIATIONS, CONT.

INDEX OF SUBSIDIARIES, BRAND NAMES AND AFFILIATIONS, CONT.

INDEX OF SUBSIDIARIES, BRAND NAMES AND AFFILIATIONS, CONT.

INDEX OF SUBSIDIARIES, BRAND NAMES AND AFFILIATIONS, CONT.

INDEX OF SUBSIDIARIES, BRAND NAMES AND AFFILIATIONS, CONT.

INDEX OF SUBSIDIARIES, BRAND NAMES AND AFFILIATIONS, CONT.

INDEX OF SUBSIDIARIES, BRAND NAMES AND AFFILIATIONS, CONT.

INDEX OF SUBSIDIARIES, BRAND NAMES AND AFFILIATIONS, CONT.

INDEX OF SUBSIDIARIES, BRAND NAMES AND AFFILIATIONS, CONT.

INDEX OF SUBSIDIARIES, BRAND NAMES AND AFFILIATIONS, CONT.

INDEX OF SUBSIDIARIES, BRAND NAMES AND AFFILIATIONS, CONT.

INDEX OF SUBSIDIARIES, BRAND NAMES AND AFFILIATIONS, CONT.

INDEX OF SUBSIDIARIES, BRAND NAMES AND AFFILIATIONS, CONT.

INDEX OF SUBSIDIARIES, BRAND NAMES AND AFFILIATIONS, CONT.

INDEX OF SUBSIDIARIES, BRAND NAMES AND AFFILIATIONS, CONT.

INDEX OF SUBSIDIARIES, BRAND NAMES AND AFFILIATIONS, CONT.

INDEX OF SUBSIDIARIES, BRAND NAMES AND AFFILIATIONS, CONT.

INDEX OF SUBSIDIARIES, BRAND NAMES AND AFFILIATIONS, CONT.

INDEX OF SUBSIDIARIES, BRAND NAMES AND AFFILIATIONS, CONT.

INDEX OF SUBSIDIARIES, BRAND NAMES AND AFFILIATIONS, CONT.

INDEX OF SUBSIDIARIES, BRAND NAMES AND AFFILIATIONS, CONT.